LOCAL BUSINESS VOICE

Local Business Voice

The History of Chambers of
Commerce in Britain, Ireland,
and Revolutionary America
1760–2011

ROBERT J. BENNETT

OXFORD
UNIVERSITY PRESS

OXFORD

UNIVERSITY PRESS

Great Clarendon Street, Oxford OX2 6DP

Oxford University Press is a department of the University of Oxford.
It furthers the University's objective of excellence in research, scholarship,
and education by publishing worldwide in

Oxford New York

Auckland Cape Town Dar es Salaam Hong Kong Karachi
Kuala Lumpur Madrid Melbourne Mexico City Nairobi
New Delhi Shanghai Taipei Toronto

With offices in

Argentina Austria Brazil Chile Czech Republic France Greece
Guatemala Hungary Italy Japan Poland Portugal Singapore
South Korea Switzerland Thailand Turkey Ukraine Vietnam

Oxford is a registered trade mark of Oxford University Press
in the UK and in certain other countries

Published in the United States
by Oxford University Press Inc., New York

British Library Cataloguing in Publication Data

Data available

Library of Congress Cataloging in Publication Data

Data available

Typeset by SPI Publisher Services, Pondicherry, India
Printed and bound by
CPI Group (UK) Ltd
Croydon, CR0 4YY

ISBN 978-0-19-958473-4

1 3 5 7 9 10 8 6 4 2

Preface

This book seeks to provide the first systematic scholarly study of chambers of commerce and related organizations. It seeks to be definitive and exhaustive in order to provide to other researchers, and to the chamber system itself, a proper understanding of both local variations and broad trends and dynamics. The book also constructs a resource of long-term aligned local data that can be used for future benchmarking and long-term comparative research, which has been deposited at the UK Data Archive.

The preparation of the book has depended chiefly on a wide range of sources held in Local Record and Archive Offices, Libraries, Universities, and Local Studies Centres, and in local chambers themselves. National sources have also been heavily used: chiefly the London Guildhall Library and London Metropolitan Archives, British Library, Newspaper Library (Colindale), The National Archives at Kew, Public Record Office Northern Ireland, Irish National Archives, National Library of Scotland, British Library, Oxford Bodleian Library, London School of Economics, Cambridge University Library, University College London, Society of Genealogists, Sheffield Archives (Wentworth-Woodhouse Muniments), US Library of Congress, and the two national organizations (the British Chambers of Commerce, and Chambers Ireland). In addition, for incorporated chambers, the Companies Registers have been extensively used at Cardiff (and TNA), Belfast, and Dublin. A full trawl has also been made of the major electronic archive sources for material from the 18th century onwards. Particularly valuable is *Eighteenth Century On-line*, *Making of the Modern World* (the Goldsmiths Kress papers); the *Parliamentary Papers* Archive, and *Irish Parliamentary Papers*; and searches of The National Archives, A2A, and related websites; but many other e-sources have also been used, as cited. Although meeting with only limited success, efforts to track down records in Exeter and Macclesfield (which are the least well preserved of the significant chambers) have benefited from the help of local historians Todd Gray (Exeter) and Rod Thorn (Macclesfield Silk Museum). In other areas, Joan Hanford (Liverpool Athenaeum library), the Library Company of Philadelphia, and the Pennsylvania Historical Association gave invaluable help with sources; in York, Jill Redford provided information and help with the archives of the York Merchant Adventurers. To the staff in each of these archives I very gratefully record my thanks.

To help the process of consulting local records, 23 Cambridge University students were trained and visited 60 Record Offices and Libraries over the summer of 2005. This provided about 20% of the total numerical data collected, and greatly helped with initial scoping of the local sources by gathering paper-based catalogue entries (which still characterizes many sources). Their work was quality-checked against other sources, and the work of three students redone by the author, with other areas expanded. I am pleased to record my thanks to the students involved: Alex Capewell, Matthew Cullen, Karen Eyre, Andrew Farquhar, Melanie Jones,

Nikolai Koval, Charlotte Lambie, Andy Liggins, Kim MacDonald, Steven Martin, Claire McCarroll, Esther Morgan, Laura Osbaldeston, Caroline Pay, Kirsten Purcell, Sarah Quartermain, Jenny Reid, Chris Rimmer, Sian Scaife, Marc Thompson, Helen Walton, Charlotte Wood, and Samuel Wring. At Cambridge, Jan Parsons provided invaluable support and keyed some of the early versions of the chapters; and the figures were drawn by Philip Stickler.

Ron Taylor's book in 2007 has contributed greatly to our understanding of chambers, and it contains some unique information and insights unavailable elsewhere. As ABCC director general he was responsible for commissioning my original involvement with chambers, to contribute to their *Development Strategy* in 1990–1. It is a source of great regret that his premature death on 28 September 2009 (obituary: *The Times*, 5 November 2009) prevented him commenting on the final text. He was most generous in comments on the original specification of the research in which he hoped to be involved, and was able to comment on various aspects of the early text, which is cited where it arises. His successor at BCC over 2002–11, David Frost, has been equally generous in supporting this study, has given very helpful comments on the text, and allowed access to much BCC information, including *Benchmarking* data and back-store materials. The book itself remains independent and does not represent BCC opinion. Other BCC staff have also been invaluable, particularly Sue Deans and Ronan Quigley, and in earlier periods Alan Bartlett, Andrew Lansley, Sally Low, Ian Peters, David Lennan, and Chris Humphries. Without Lansley, who ferreted out the early chamber *Censuses* of the period 1979–83 and passed copies to the author many years ago, it is doubtful that this information would have survived since no trace of the originals can now be found. In Ireland, Ian Talbot, chief executive of Chambers Ireland was also most helpful and has commented on relevant sections of the text. Many local chambers have also provided very extensive help with accessing their private archives. I would particularly like to thank the following chambers for providing access to their records: Barnstaple, Cambridge, Chesterfield, Cork, Coventry, Croydon, Derby, Dover, Hereford and Worcester, Ipswich and Suffolk, Isle of Wight, Jersey, Lancaster, Limerick, London, Luton, Portsmouth, Preston, St Helens, York, and Waterford. Others have given valuable comments, particularly Ian Kelly (Hull); and Liverpool chamber laid on magnificent support for the publication of its 18th-century history.

Significant support for modern analysis, intellectual development, and discussions has also been derived from four PhD students who have worked with the author at the LSE and Cambridge: William Bratton, Danijel Mekic, Susan Priest, and John Sellgren. The first three were supported by the ESRC as collaborative CASE students with BCC; I am most grateful to them and ESRC and BCC for their support and insights. My co-authors and researchers on other studies have also provided critical insights into the agencies that work with chambers: particularly Andrew McCoshan, Peter Wicks, Gunter Krebs, Diane Payne, Mark Ramsden, Crispian Fuller, and Paul Robson. Their contributions are fully cited in the text where they arise. Financial support has chiefly come from two British Academy small grants (SG39253 and SG44870), but significant benefits have also been derived from several studies financed by the Leverhulme Trust and Anglo-German Foundation, which have employed the researchers noted above.

Thanks are also due to Chris Law (Salford University) and Brian Robson (Manchester University) for making available the original data used in their studies of British population for the 19th century. The original data, stored on record cards in a shoebox, have been re-keyed for this study by Su Yin Tan. Corrections to these data for the early years have been made available by Jack Langton (Oxford University). Population data for the 20th century were provided by Tony Champion (Newcastle University). These sources have been supplemented where necessary (e.g. for Ireland). Other academic advice has been invaluable in helping locate sources, interpret the evidence, or comment on some of the text. I would like to thank Martin Daunton, Richard Smith, and John Thompson at Cambridge; Paul Langford at Oxford; Alison Olson at University of Maryland; as well as all others who have provided suggestions. The publishers have proved magnificently supportive. Last and not least, my wife, Elizabeth, deserves special thanks for forbearance, and for reading and improving the text. The errors and omissions of course remain my own.

Robert Bennett

Contents

x   *Contents*

List of Abbreviations

ABCC	Association of British Chambers of Commerce, 1919–96
ACC	Association of Chambers of Commerce (sometimes referred to as Associated Chambers of Commerce), 1860–1919
ACCI	Advisory Committee on Commercial Intelligence, within BoT, 1900–14
BCC	British Chambers of Commerce, 1996–
BCU	British Commonwealth Union
BEC	British Employers Confederation
BETC	British Electrical Traction Company
BIS	Department of Business Innovation and Skills 2009–
BiTC	Business in the Community
BoT	Board of Trade (also used to refer to the Committee of Trade and Plantations in early years); became DTI in 1970, and BIS in 2009
BL	British Library
BPC	British Productivity Council (later NPACI)
BRC	British Retail Consortium
BRE	Better Regulation Executive
BSETC	Boston Society for Encouraging Trade and Commerce
BTC	British Trade Corporation
CBB	Confederation of British Business
CBI	Confederation of British Industry, 1965–
CCI	Chamber of commerce and industry
CCJ	*Chamber of Commerce Journal*, published by London chamber
CCTE	Chamber of commerce training and enterprise
Chamber	Refers to chamber of commerce, chamber of commerce and industry, or CCTE (and *not* chamber of trade or other body), unless otherwise stated
CI	Chambers Ireland, the national association
CIB	Commercial Intelligence Branch (of BoT after 1899)
CIC	Community Interest Company
City	'The City' refers to the City of London throughout
CoT	Chamber of Trade
DAB	Dictionary of American Biography
DBERR	Department for Business, Enterprise and Regulatory Reform
DNB	Dictionary of National Biography
DOT	Department of Overseas Trade

DTI	Department of Trade and Industry from 1970 (split 1974–83); renamed Department of Business Innovation and Skills (BIS) 2009
EBP	Education Business Partnership
EEF	Engineering Employers Federation, 1896–
EIC	East India Company
EPC	Employers' Parliamentary Council, 1898
ERDF	European Regional Development Fund
ET	Employment Training; adult unemployment programme
EU	European Union; used to embrace all former titles such as EEC
FBI	Federation of British Industry, 1916–65
FCO	Foreign and Commonwealth Office
FE	Further Education
FO	Foreign Office
FPB	Forum of Private Business
FSB	Federation of Small Business
GATT	General Agreement on Tariffs and Trade
GPC	General Purposes Committee
GTA	Group Training Association
ICC	International chamber of commerce
IDAC	Import Duties Advisory Committee
IGI	International Genealogical Index (Mormon Church database)
IoD	Institute of Directors
ISG	Implementation Strategy Group
ITB	Industry Training Board
LBP	Local Business Partnership
LCC	London County Council
LCIA	London Court of International Arbitration
LEA	Local Education Authority
LEC	Local Enterprise Company, 1990–2001
LEN	Local Employer Network
LEntA	London Enterprise Agency
LEP	Local Enterprise Partnership, 2010–
LMA	London Metropolitan Archives
LPDL	Liberty and Property Defence League
LSC	Learning and Skills Council, 2001–10
LSE	London School of Economics
LSP	Local Strategic Partnership
MFN	Most Favoured Nation

MP	Member of Parliament
MSC	Manpower Services Commission
NAFE	Non-Advanced Further Education
NAO	National Audit Office
NATPS	National Association of Trade Protection Societies
NCT	National Chamber of Trade
NEDC	National Economic Development Council
NEDO	National Economic Development Office
NFU	National Farmers Union
NOSJC	National Organization Standing Joint Committee
NPACI	National Productivity Advisory Council for Industry
NSTO	Non-Statutory Training Organization
NUM	National Union of Manufacturers; later termed National Association of British Manufacturers, NABM
PRONI	Public Record Office of Northern Ireland
RDA	Regional Development Agency
REPC	Regional Economic Planning Council
RO	Record Office
RSA	Royal Society for Encouragement of Arts and Manufactures and Commerce (Society of Arts)
SBS	Small Business Service
SFLGS	Small Firm Loan Guarantee Scheme
SFS	Small Firms Service
SME	Small and medium sized enterprise
SMV	Society of Merchant Venturers, Bristol
SRB	Single Regeneration Budget
TEC	Training and Enterprise Council, 1990–2001
TNA	The UK National Archives (Kew)
TPS	Trade Protection Society
TUC	Trade Union Congress
TVEI	Technical and Vocational Education Initiative
UCL	University College London
UDC	Urban Development Corporation
UKTI	UK Trade International
UN	United Nations
USP	Unique selling point
YT	Youth Training programme

PART 1
OVERVIEW

1

Local Business Voice and the Chambers of Commerce

1.1 CHAMBERS AS STRUCTURED VOICE

This book is the first scholarly and systematic history of chambers of commerce, but it also aims to engage modern chamber managers and members, and better inform contemporary policy makers. Whilst history is never repeated, we can all learn from the past and for chambers the resonances across their 250-year history are remarkable. Indeed, many of the experiences are repeated over time, and modern readers may find some closer modern resemblances to the 18th century than any of the intervening years.

The book gives an overview, but combines this with local detail. It is written mainly from the bottom up using local archives and modern local sources: it is a story of local leaders and local communities combining their efforts nationally. Since chambers are about voice, readers will be able to recognize the role of personalities, since voluntary bodies are all about people. Chamber voice involves lobbying, representing, informing, and making the concerns of business known to government and other agents. As quintessentially local bodies, this voice articulates the voice of local communities of businesses. The book emphasizes intertextuality, taking the reader to the mindset and context of those giving voice, and how they reflected the society and concepts of their time. Chambers had their origins in the 1760s when the voice of the business community took new form and shape, driven by new local demands to represent, and by the perceived inattentiveness of government. Modern chambers will recognize the same core issues today, though the vocabulary has evolved.

The chambers investigated are those in the UK, Ireland, and early America, because this grouping has common origins and the unifying characteristic of being formed under common law as voluntary bodies. These chambers differ fundamentally from the European systems under public law. The analysis of the American chambers becomes brief after the 1840s, due to lack of space, but its developments are included where relevant. The Irish chambers are given thorough treatment until 1923, and then included as fully as possible within the space available; but there is certainly scope for further Irish research, for which this book should provide an important starting point.

Because chambers are voluntary, definitions can be difficult. This book takes as the five defining characteristics of the bodies investigated that they seek to act as *voices* of the local business community; are *voluntary* (hence expressing independent, grass-roots local needs/desires); represent *general* interests (not individual interests of a firm or sectors); are *locally rooted* in a specific business community or an area; and their voice is derived from and legitimized by a *deliberated* process in an open and transparent way (such as consultation required by a memorandum and articles of association).

The chambers of commerce are the main focus of the book. These are the longest established and historically the most significant agents of local business voice anywhere in the English-speaking world. Their foundation in the 1760s far pre-dates any other surviving business organization in the UK, Ireland, or America: the forerunner of the CBI, for example, was established only in 1916; and the national US Chamber of Commerce in 1912. Local chambers of commerce continue to be the main agents representing the interests of businesses in their areas, play a role as partners with local and national government and other organizations in promoting and supporting their local economies, and also provide direct services and advice to their members (and often to non-members). But there are also other current and former organizations. The book looks more briefly at other bodies to understand how they interplay across different geographies, missions, and rival repertoires of voice that compete with chambers of commerce. This includes chambers of trade, chambers of agriculture, and the trade protection societies that formed rival or complementary networks from the 1850s, many still surviving today. In modern times there are also bodies representing small firms, national bodies, and sector bodies that may have regional or local structures.

1.2 OVERVIEW

It is surprising that there has been no previous systematic study of chambers and related local bodies. There have been two valuable 'official' histories covering the whole chamber system in Britain, but nothing for Ireland or early America.[1] There are local 'official' and other histories for many of the major chambers, published at various dates.[2] However, these previous histories do not give a full coverage of the system in an inclusive way. There have also been a number of significant errors and misinterpretations that this book seeks to redress, particularly concerning origins and early history.[3] In addition, there are many important places for which there are

---

[1] Ilersic and Liddle (1960) and Taylor (2007). Note that whilst Ilersic and Liddle was indeed a commissioned official history, Taylor's is a far more objective and wide-ranging study, written as a former director general of the national chambers association when in retirement, and adopted for induction training of senior staff. It is a valuable study, particularly for the commentary on his years as director general, 1984–98.

[2] See the Bibliography of Local Chamber Histories, below.

[3] There has also been copying of errors between sources; and many chamber histories draw on a booklet by Dunwoody (1935), secretary of the ABCC, which contains misleading dates and statements about the early period.

no fully developed local chamber histories. One major gap, the first Liverpool chamber of 1774–96, has been published as a separate book by the author, which is drawn on where relevant.[4] For related bodies there is only brief coverage.[5]

This book offers the systematic framework previously lacking. It seeks to be definitive and (within reason) exhaustive in order to provide to other researchers, and those in the chamber system itself, a firm foundation of detailed assessment, and a resource of long-term aligned local data and definitions. It particularly seeks to combine statistical generalities with local stories, using an aligned database of statistical materials. The result should be a context for future local studies and a guide to sources. All significant local and national archive, library, and other sources have been consulted. The result is a focus on the bottom-up views of the locality, allowing local voices to speak within the evolution of larger national and international events. The book also looks at those who received chamber materials in government and administrative departments; it is concerned with reception as well as delivery of local voice. This has generally been lacking in previous studies, although in two areas (the Corn Laws and the debate over free trade) there have been historical studies of the politics that have drawn on chamber activities.

This book is innovative substantively, since much of the early history of chambers has been either unresearched or misunderstood. The book also seeks to be innovative theoretically, in combining primary historical, economic, and political analysis to give statistical overviews, but highlighting local contingency, personality, and the geography of place—to explain why chambers are, and were, *where* they are. It also combines analysis of management decisions and member choices to understand how chambers have been *used, managed, and valued*.

For such a long period of study, from the 1760s up to 2011, it is not possible to treat all material in equal depth. Instead, detail is provided on the major critical events and activities. In many cases these are the first detailed studies ever made for either the national or local picture. They thus seek to provide a new primary source of analysis. This is matched by a full coverage of the wider developments in lesser depth, including statistical analyses, which are again the first ever undertaken for the earlier chambers. In summary the book is heavy on the 18th century, because this has been previously little covered; it follows subsequent evolution through a series of detailed studies of critical developments; the book becomes heavy again in systematic cover from the late 1970s, since this is the period when the most significant changes to the historical development of chambers occurred, and of course this period is most relevant to understanding the modern chambers.

The book follows a thematic rather than a purely narrative historical structure, chiefly because developments are complex and locally very diverse, with the result that the evolution is not strictly chronological across what is a geographically distributed system. A thematic approach also allows specific trends and changes

---

[4] Bennett (2010).
[5] For chambers of trade, see NCT (1957); for chambers of agriculture, Matthews (1915), and Jeffcock (1937), though these are brief; there has been no attempt to give a history of trade protection societies, though a recent PhD thesis covers some of the ground for the Leicester TPS (Wood, 1999).

in the system to be examined more thoroughly. Also two previous national studies, by Ilersic and Liddle, and by Taylor, provide a narrative coverage that does not need to be repeated. However, to allow the themes to be put in context, Chapter 2 provides a historical overview of the different rival organizations of local voice.

Forces, origins, and diffusion

Part 2 of the book introduces the first group of themes: the forces underlying the origin, diffusion, and governance of chambers. Chapter 3 introduces the multiple theoretical frameworks utilized in the book. It assesses how unity of local voice has been achieved and changed over time and observes the balances that usually have to be struck between individual and collective action, and between voice and services offered to members, resulting in the development of 'bundled' products. However, services are insufficient alone to explain resolute action that led to foundation and subsequent development. Chapter 4 shows that local protest and anger provided the spark for many early foundations. But chambers were rarely protest or party political entities; instead they tended to draw inspiration from political movements of the day, and then adapt and shape ideas into 'respectable' opinion, generally based, legitimized by cautious local deliberation. From the outset, most chamber members sought to work to 'reform' rather than to challenge the existing political system: chambers offered a rather special reinterpretation of the concept of 'contention'.

Local context was critical. As shown in Chapter 5, the first chambers in America and Ireland were all in large ports; in Britain the great majority (70–80%) were in the ports. Mostly they had major hinterlands and were focused on international trade, especially the Atlantic economy. Some early British chambers, however, were in the 'new' inland manufacturing centres, such as Birmingham, Manchester, and Leeds, and it is these that have been the subject of most previous academic analysis.[6] However, this chapter challenges the 'model' that early chambers were a response by the 'new manufacturers' searching for voice.[7] It argues instead that chambers originated chiefly from an environment of protest against disruptions to international trade resulting from government actions, efforts to reform local government and other institutions, and industrial diversification into complex corporate organizations of proto-global trading companies that were challenging the customary social and political structures. This all offered the opportunity for, or even required, a new model for local business voice that was chiefly focused in the ports and was not mainly attributable to the 'new manufacturers'. By the 1860s it was clear that 'every town should have one': for 'place status' and respectability.

---

[6] See chamber histories: respectively, Wright (1913); Redford (1934); Redford and Clapp (1956); Beresford (1951).
[7] Bowden (1919–20, 1965); Checkland (1952, 1958); Norris (1957); Money (1977); who have been largely followed by Rose (2000) and others.

Structural tensions

Part 3 of the book examines three fields of tension: governance, status, and degree of centralization. The resources and governance structures of chambers became more complex over time, which introduced new challenges, assessed in Chapter 6: to align councils, members, and staff. Chapter 7 discusses how chambers sought to gain greater attention. In France, official local chambers of commerce in the major centres were formed in the 1700s, termed the Conseils du Commerce; abolished by the Revolution, they were reconstituted by Napoleon. Similar *public law systems* came to dominate much of mainland Europe from the 18th and 19th centuries: in Austria-Hungary, Germany, Greece, Italy, Luxembourg, and Spain. Public law status seemed to offer advantages over voluntary systems that stimulated a debate in Britain about chamber recognition, 'locus standi', and possible public law foundation. This overlapped with pressures for chambers to have formal legal adjudicatory powers, as court 'tribunals of commerce'. The current position in Britain and Ireland is control of the *chamber title*.

Successful articulation of local voice requires it to reach the centre of government decision making. This needs some form of national mechanism. This can be ad hoc, through frequent local deputations, or through agents; but national associations became the favoured method. In-built into these associations are tensions about who acts as national advocate, the centre or the localities, and how diverse local opinions are managed. Balancing national voice with local diversity therefore became a major political and managerial challenge, investigated in Chapter 8.

Activities

Since voice is the defining characteristic of chambers, considerable attention is given to it in Chapters 9 and 10. A systematic overview of lobbies and thematic case studies are used to illustrate how the process of deploying voice developed. Despite the reluctance of chambers to campaign through party politics, they nevertheless were at critical times to contribute changes to the frames and repertoires of discussion by party and government, particularly during 'great events'. A critical aspect of voice is the deliberation process. Chapter 11 is devoted to how deliberation interrelated with providing milieus for discourse, social exchange, and economic understanding. Early chambers strongly overlapped with coffee houses, hotels, and other offerings, but evolved into distinctive milieus for forming views, with many maintaining their own coffee house facilities. In modern chambers changes in communication technologies and the age of the Internet have offered new opportunities for deliberation.

No chamber remained solely a body for voice; all also developed other services. Chapter 12 examines these services and how the bundle of different services interacted. Service support to firms naturally led to chambers becoming enmeshed in government's agendas for various public service developments, assessed in Chapter 13. The earliest examples of this were local partnerships and initiatives directed at improvement of city infrastructure. After WW1 this extended to national collaboration with government for delivering commercial information and foreign missions. Wider national partnerships developed from the 1960s, particularly concerning provision of work-based training and apprenticeships. In the 1980s this extended to business *leadership* of local economies and other initiatives. From these emerged, in the UK in the 1990s, an awkward relationship of many chambers, with the government-financed Training and Enterprise Councils, and since 2010 with Local Enterprise Partnerships. Similar trends in Ireland have seen extensive involvement of local chambers and the national association in economic development and employee training, with significant support from European programmes.

The members

Business voice necessarily requires a level of 'interest'. Chapter 14 examines how far this was, and is, based on local, individual, general, or sector demands; the role of religious and gender structures; how far it was affected by trends in corporate organization; what level of market penetration was and is achieved; and how far this is affected by the service activities provided and pricing decisions made (especially about subscriptions). Analysis of the role of 'leadership' and networking among businesses casts new light on the evolution of networks, which helps to better understand the modern context of 'clusters' that has become a key focus of policy debate. Chapter 15 reviews in detail the motives for membership; joining; remaining a member; lapsing; and the evolution of associational commitment (exit, voice, and loyalty). Chapter 16 places motives in the context of membership dynamics: the extent of stability or 'churn' through joining and lapsing; the influences of subscription structures and costs; and the role of chamber activities and the external 'environment' on membership dynamics.

Then, now, and the future

The chambers are not just historical; they are also current and very active entities. The conclusion of the book looks at their present challenges and the likely unfolding of future developments in the light of their history. Grass-roots provision to meet needs remains a critical ingredient of the bundled offer; and tailored services will remain a critical part of this. But voice is the unique selling point (USP) of the chamber brand. The position of the chambers became confused by close interrelation with government from the 1980s. However, acting as a major contractor with government to provide services remains an important part of the portfolio of the local chamber system, and of the national body in both Britain and Ireland. Hence, there will continue to be an important challenge of balancing government involvement with the voluntarism and independence of voice. The conclusion of the book in Chapter 17 suggests means to balance and better manage the inevitable tensions in the light of the dynamics of the emerging economy of the 21st century.

1.3 A GUIDE TO READING THE BOOK

This book combines local and national archive sources, current chamber records, and a wide range of other information. The full sources of information on each chamber are listed in Appendix 1, which also records their dates of foundation, changing names, and geographical coverage. The book covers the period up to the start of 2011.

Some systematic statistical presentations are given throughout, where an attempt has been made to align historical materials with modern definitions. These are based on current benchmarking data for the chambers, with earlier sources and alignment of data discussed in Appendix 2. These data are developed for 16 cross-sections in time, every 10–20 years from 1790. To facilitate the research of others, and to provide a permanent resource to the chamber system, the actual data have been deposited at the UK Data Archive, with a guide given in Appendix 2. Many graphs show the distribution of chamber characteristics using the mean as the overall descriptor, but because of the variability of the system, the range (minimum and maximum) is also usually given, as well as 20% and 80% box plots. These show the values for the smallest 20% or largest 80% of the chambers; the box between these two points contains the majority (60%) of the individual chambers. It should be noted that the records of many of the smallest chambers of commerce and chambers of trade do not survive, so that those included in the database and discussion are biased towards the larger of the small chambers; whilst all chambers of commerce are covered, as far as records allow. Generally at least 90% coverage has been achieved. The periods of WW1 and WW2 are excluded from the data cross-sections as the aim is to focus on general patterns; but the war years are treated in more detail in separate discussion.

All references to 'chamber' or 'chambers' as a single word refer to chambers of commerce; other types of chamber and other bodies are referred to by their full name. Abbreviations and acronyms have been kept to a minimum, listed separately. Financial data are quoted in the contemporary currency: £ s. d. in Britain, Ireland, and early America (or dollars where relevant); £ and pence after decimalization in the UK in 1970; IR£ in Ireland after independence in 1923; and Euros in Ireland after 1 January 1999. For clarity, all quotations have been rendered into modern spelling, and capitalizations of words have been reduced to a minimum, but all original punctuation and vocabulary has been retained. The single form, Board of Trade (BoT), is used to cover the earlier Committee of Trade and later terminology. Newcastle refers to Newcastle-upon-Tyne, unless otherwise stated.

Sources of local archives are listed fully in Appendix 1. In the text, reference is generally made solely to the documentary source; e.g. minutes, report, etc.; but where there might be ambiguity, the source is fully noted in the text footnotes. All of the more individual sources, such as stray records of individual chambers, and sources from national archives and libraries are given fully. There is a separate bibliography of histories of local chambers and related bodies, which provide important sources. To save space these are usually cited in the footnotes as 'specific chamber: history'.

The approach of this book is to use an inclusive definition of 'chamber' as those bodies with the five characteristics of: exerting voice, voluntary independent associations, expressing general interests, locally rooted, with deliberated transparent governance. There are, however, many problems with the use of the 'chamber' title. Each body using this title does not necessarily have the same characteristics and some may not be representative bodies at all: some may be no more than one-man operations, others may be government bodies. There is scope for misuse of title and fraud. Particular confusion arises after the emergence of chambers of trade in 1897. Also other bodies, not called chambers initially, grew into or merged with them, e.g. the Devonport Mercantile Association or the Norwich Marine Insurance Association. Some traditional bodies, such as the US Boston Society for Encouraging Trade and Commerce, and the Bristol, York, and Newcastle Merchant Adventurers, acted like chambers at some points. Other entities, particularly those formed by local government, have taken on the title of chamber to seek a broader legitimacy and improved brand; but they are not self-governing chambers. For example, the 'Parliament and Commerce Committee of the Town Council of Darlington' was a member of the Association of Chambers of Commerce in the 1913 period; yet is was essentially a local government body.[8] More recently, several local chambers have been formed by district and county councils, being used essentially as promotional bodies. These bodies are not strictly relevant to this study because they are not voluntary and independent, but their existence has been taken into account where relevant.

Checks on the group of bodies included in this book have been made by investigating local record offices and libraries, by inspecting chamber national association records, by contacting the modern chambers themselves and inspecting their archives, by checks on all other major library catalogues, and web searches. An important cross-check has also been made by investigating the archives of the main recipients of local voice: chiefly the Board of Trade, Foreign Office, Ministers, and Prime Ministers of the time. These checks have focused on the early foundations and have revealed activity and bodies that were not previously recognized to have existed or been active. Whilst it will never be possible to conclude that this has led to all bodies and their archival materials being discovered, it is believed that all major chambers that have any current or historically recognized local significance have been included. It is hoped that this book is as systematic, inclusive, and definitive as possible.

The national associations of local chambers and related bodies are also included. In the UK this was called the Association of Chambers of Commerce, or Associated Chambers of Commerce (ACC) over 1860–1919; then the Association of British Chambers of Commerce (ABCC) from 1919 until 1994; and after 1994 the British Chambers of Commerce (BCC). In Ireland an Association of Chambers of Commerce of the Irish Free State was formed in 1923, in modern times referred to as Chambers of Commerce of Ireland (CCI), and after 2005 as Chambers

---

[8] Wolfe (1915a), p. 15.

Ireland (CI). The contemporary names are used in the text for each period. In America a US federation of chambers was formed in 1912, termed the Chamber of Commerce of the USA.

Some chamber bodies are not included: (i) the British chambers of commerce abroad (15 in 1913, over 50 in 2010, including seven in China); (ii) foreign chambers based in the UK (12 in 1913, plus the Federation of Foreign Chambers of Commerce in the UK); (iii) international bodies such as the International Chamber of Commerce and Eurochambres; (iv) national 'chambers' in the UK, e.g. the chamber of shipping; and (v) the junior chambers of commerce. The first three are excluded from detailed analysis because the primary focus here is on national representation. However, some were members of the national association of chambers (ACC) until 1919, and the counts of membership of this body have been adjusted to remove them for comparative purposes (not always done in other analyses). National 'chambers' are excluded since they are de facto sector trade associations. However, one national chamber, the General Chamber of Manufacturers, which existed 1785–7, is included because it involved delegates from local chambers and has crucial historical significance. The junior chambers are not included systematically, but comment is made on them where they are significant (primarily as seedbeds for recruitment).

2

Historical Overview

2.1 COMPETITION FOR SPACE

This book takes a thematic approach. Nevertheless, it is important to have a historical overview to put the themes of the rest of the book into context, and this chapter seeks to give that coverage. Most attention is devoted to chambers of commerce, chambers of trade, trade protection societies, and then chambers of agriculture. The chapter also gives a brief overview of sector trade associations and the national structure of representation of voice, particularly how these bodies affected the opportunity for chambers.

The general evolution of the four main locally based bodies exercising voice is shown in Figure 2.1. In this figure the chambers in the Irish Republic are shown separately, even though they were part of the same system for the majority of the period. The Irish chambers include both chambers of commerce and the smaller chambers of trade, as they would be termed in Britain. The figure shows that the development of chambers of commerce was slow, in Britain taking 200 years to reach a peak in numbers during the 1960s and 1970s, after which numbers stabilized, but then declined sharply after 1995 as mergers took place as a result of a *Development Strategy* to consolidate towards larger areas with greater resources. The peak of chamber numbers in Ireland was in the 1990s after which minor consolidation has also occurred. Although the first trade protection societies were as early as the chambers (in 1776), it was not until the 1840s they began to emerge in numbers; this occurred in both Britain and Ireland, with a rapid growth after 1900. The most numerous and widely diffused bodies were the chambers of trade, reaching a peak of about 800 in the 1960s and 1970s; the chambers of agriculture peaked in 1913. As a result, in the 1930–70 period there were about 1200 local bodies of different types seeking voice across Britain and Ireland. They covered the large cities, most of the small towns, and many rural areas. This was paralleled by the rise of sector-based associations, which grew from small numbers to a few hundred in 1900, probably reaching a peak of about 3000 in the 1980s.

This expansion of numbers is paralleled in North America, which also has an entirely voluntary system of associations. Again chamber numbers were modest until the 1850s, but grew rapidly during the late 19th century, probably peaking in the 1980s with about 8000 State-local 'chamber' bodies, and a further *c.*3000 sector bodies. Like Britain and Ireland, these local bodies represent only part of the population of business associations, about 60%. In total, all associations numbered about 2000 in 1890, 2944 in 1898, and 3356 in 1913, staying roughly constant over

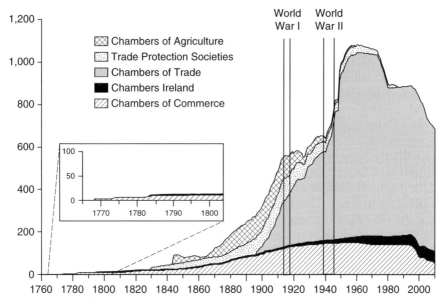

Fig. 2.1. Numbers of chambers and other organizations offering local voice, 1768–2010. Numbers have to be treated as approximate; not all bodies were members of their national associations at any point in time.

WW1, then increasing to 5800 in 1920, and over 11,000 by 1923.[1] Of these, 1500 were national, 2000 State, and 7700 local bodies. Many areas had and still have several bodies: for example, in the 1890s Boston had 48 local business associations, Baltimore 21, Philadelphia 20, Buffalo 16, and most major cities at least ten.[2]

For non-commercial societies, Langford and Clark have shown that the 18th century was a period of rapid development of voluntary societies and associations; they call it an 'associational world'.[3] But for the commercial bodies that are the focus of this book, it is the 20th century that seems to deserve this sobriquet. This is a previously unremarked phenomenon, though it has been implicit in some previous studies.[4]

2.2 CHAMBERS OF COMMERCE

The first organizations with the formal title of 'chamber of commerce' in the English-speaking world were in Jersey in 1767–8,[5] and New York in 1768, with

---

[1] From Sabine (1859); Orr (1895); Sturges (1915); US Department of Commerce (1923), and earlier volumes.

[2] Orr (1895), p. 54.

[3] Langford (1989, 1991); Clark (2000a).

[4] e.g. Grant (1987, 1993, 2000).

[5] Jersey chamber's foundation is stated as 1768 in most sources, but its minutes show its first AGM on 9 May 1768, re-electing a committee that had 'served for a year'; similarly on 14 May 1770 the chamber was re-established 'for three more years'; hence the chamber existed from *c.*14 May 1767.

a North Staffordshire potters chamber beginning about 1767.[6] There was also a probable foundation in Guernsey in 1769. Other early chambers were Manchester and Liverpool in 1774, Jamaica in 1778, and a proposal in Quebec in 1776–8. A second phase of development occurred in Dublin, Glasgow, and Belfast in 1783, Edinburgh and Leeds in 1785, Waterford in 1787, the General Chamber of Manufacturers of 1785–7, and a specialist arbitration chamber in London 1782–1800. Londonderry began a chamber in 1790.

In addition there were other committees of the period with similar objectives, that sometimes used the title of chamber and liaised with the other formal chambers. These included the North Staffordshire potters chamber (1767), Blackburn, Lancaster, and Whitehaven. Several other committees were stimulated by the activities of the General Chamber of Manufacturers (1785–7), often calling themselves 'chambers': Exeter, Halifax, Hull, London, Norwich, Nottingham, Sheffield, and probably other towns. Some of these formed a 'union' of chambers in 1793 that existed at least until 1805. By 1800 there was also some presence at Portsmouth. Other chambers were established in the period up to 1819 in Limerick (1807), Guernsey (refounded 1808), Plymouth and Greenock (1813), Newcastle (1815), Cork (1814 and 1819), Dundee (1819), and the special case of the American chamber at Liverpool (1802).

By 1819, therefore, there were about 19 formal chambers operating, or that had operated in Britain and Ireland, and a further 10–12 areas that had 'delegates' or 'deputies' that represented their area at national meetings. These are listed in Table 2.1, together with the early chambers in America and the Caribbean that were developing at the same time. Of those in the British Isles, perhaps about 14 were genuinely active in 1819. But the number in formal existence steadily grew to 24 by 1850, reaching a stable number of 90–105 chambers from 1900 until 1990; after 1990 mergers and reorganization reduced their numbers to 54 in 2010.[7]

Early development

The emergence of the chambers from the 1760s seems to derive from two thrusts. First, there was a mêlée of ideas about evolving institutions. This was a period in which there was much writing and discourse about commercial difficulties, settling debts and disputes, and finding reliable insurance. There had been several debt crises, and wars had been disruptive to trade and credit. The underlying institutions were under question, or were evolving. The old 'law merchant', as an international code, was receding under the advance of independent national codes; the relationship with the colonies was recognized as needing adjustment; the insurance industry was evolving from informal and 'club' based institutions to a more formal market (such as Lloyds); the banking system was evolving from dispersed individuals and scriveners towards 'country banks' and then larger-scale and farther-reaching institutions. A number of writers had improved the understanding of these issues, and had taken up the need for

---

[6] Most lists of chamber foundations derive from Ilersic and Liddle (1960), which contains a number of inaccuracies and omissions; the dates used here come from the sources outlined in Appendix 1.
[7] All numbers approximate (see Appendix 1).

Table 2.1. The first chambers of commerce in the English-speaking world up to 1819

British and Irish chambers	UK chamber committees: local 'delegates' and 'deputies'	North American and Caribbean chambers
		[Halifax, Nova Scotia 1750–90]
1. Jersey 1767– (formally from 1768)	North Staffordshire potters chamber *c*.1767–90	[Boston Society (BSETC), *c*.1760–76]
2. Guernsey *c*.1769–90; 1808–		1. New York 1768–75; 1775–83; 1787–1802; 1817–
3. Manchester 1774–81; 1781–7; 1793–1802; 1820–		2. Charleston 1773–80; 1784–
4. Liverpool 1774–96; 1849–		
	[Blackburn 1779; Lancaster 1781]	[Quebec 1776–8 proposal, with continued activity to *c*.1789]
5. London 1782–1800; 1882–		Jamaica 1778–85; 1839–
6. Glasgow 1783–		
7. Birmingham 1783–1812; 1813–31; 1842–	[Whitehaven 1783]	
8. Dublin 1783–91; 1805–12; 1820–	*Delegates 1784–c.1805* N. Staffordshire (potters	
9. Belfast 1783–96; 1802– [General Chamber of Manufacturers 1785–7]	committee of commerce) 1784–90 London Hull Norwich Exeter Halifax Sheffield	[Philadelphia 1784—proposal]
10. Edinburgh 1785–	Wolverhampton	3. Boston 1785–90; 1794; board of trade 1805–12; 1815–
11. Leeds 1785–92; 1851–	Nottingham *c*.1785–90	
12. Waterford 1787–97; 1804–		
13. Londonderry 1790–*c*.1830; 1890–		4. New Haven 1794
	Portsmouth *c*.1798	5. Philadelphia 1801
		6. Norfolk 1803
[American chamber of commerce at Liverpool 1802–1908]	Rochdale *c*.1804	Halifax, Nova Scotia 1803–22; 1822–33; 1865–[Baltimore Manufacturers Committee 1805]
14. Limerick 1807–		7. Savannah 1806
15. Plymouth 1813–		Quebec 1809–
16. Greenock 1813–		
17. Newcastle and Gateshead 1815–		

(continued)

Table 2.1. (*Continued*)

British and Irish chambers	UK chamber committees: local 'delegates' and 'deputies'	North American and Caribbean chambers
18. Cork 1814–19 informally; 1819– formally		
19. Forfarshire (Dundee) 1819–34; Dundee 1836–		

Notes: In order of date of establishment, and, where applicable, their date of demise and re-establishment. Column two shows 'chambers' that may have had no more than 'delegates' representing their areas at national meetings. Other committees and organizations are listed in Chapter 5.

rationalization and reform. Malachy Postlethwayt in the 1750s had widely publicized the benefits of the French central Council of Commerce and its local chambers; Thomas Mortimer by 1772, and John Weskett in 1781 and 1782, advocated the development of locally based chambers of assurance and chambers of commerce. These books were widely disseminated, would have been known by all the leading merchants of the time, and probably led to the general adoption of the title 'chamber'.

The second thrust primarily came from events. The Seven Years War with France (1756–63), and then the disastrous American war of 1775–81, were very disruptive. Apart from the immediate effect of fracturing the critically important trade with the colonies, the processes of interest representation and voice with government were challenged, which stimulated protests, and rebellion in the American colonies. These wars also led to a step change in government taxation, particularly Excise levies on items of manufacturing and commerce. A ratchet of government intervention was begun, and the evolution of commercial interests having to work more intensively with government, or respond to its threats, was set on a course that has continued up to the present.

However, the chamber system did not establish as a single template. Rather it evolved through a series of experiments: what could be termed 'collective organizational learning'. There were several start-ups of organizations some of which became quiescent, latent or failed, followed by phases of restarts. Nevertheless, the early chambers had all the key ingredients that shaped subsequent development:

- Means to organize collective action, meeting a general local demand different from traditional sector combinations, and a means to underpin legitimacy through discourse, deliberation, and governance structures.
- Level of activity very much influenced by the level of government activity: the main threat emerging was government itself: government 'bads' as well as 'goods'.
- A search for status, acceptance, and brand.

These themes became ever more forceful in the next periods of development.

Nineteenth-century developments

The early 19th century saw chambers begin to diffuse more widely and develop some services. Major successes were achieved, most prominently the repeal of the Corn Laws in 1846. The publicity surrounding this, for the leading players of Manchester and Glasgow, had important impacts on spreading the brand, positioning the chambers locally and nationally, and encouraging recruitment, retention, and loyalty of members. From the mid to late 19th century important changes occurred:[8]

- The development of closer joint working between areas from the 1820s, with the foundation of the national association in the UK, the ACC, in 1860.

- Engagement with government policies on a larger scale and a very much wider range of agendas.

- The association of the chamber brand with the dominant economic policy frame of 'free trade' after Corn Law abolition in 1846.

- A strong focus on stimulating improvements in education and training: pressure to establish the Royal Commission Technical Education (1881), leading chambers to establish new examination systems, and school, college, and university scholarships, prizes, and lectureships.

- The more widespread development of 'business support services', chiefly from the 1880s: statistics and enquiry services; more widespread arbitration services; labour conciliation boards (though mostly short-lived); document certification; more extensive library and reading rooms; international exhibitions, and missions.

- Significant improvements in professionalization of proceedings, minutes, reports, financial accounts, publications and dissemination, and a widening of specialist committees to improve member involvement and to better form lobby cases.

The establishment of the ACC was an important step, but it was relatively slow to evolve. The critically important chambers of Liverpool, Glasgow, and Manchester were not members for most of the first 40–50 years.[9] Many other significant chambers, like Edinburgh, Leicester, and Worcester, also continued to pass over invitations to join the ACC. Only by 1910 did the network of chambers become a truly national system with all the chambers becoming members of the ACC: Liverpool (in 1899), Edinburgh (1893), Manchester (1898), and Glasgow (1910).

The early 20th century

The period after 1900 saw rapid change. First, from 1905 there was a Liberal government concerned to enact various welfare reforms; the state now initiated more commercial legislation, not merely responding to initiatives from business

---

[8] Taylor (2007), chapters 3 and 4; Ilersic and Liddle (1960); and later chapters below.
[9] The national–local tensions are discussed further in Chapter 8.

itself; the 'free trade' paradigm was challenged; tariff protection and national government regulation was increasingly pressed, finally becoming inevitable during the 1930s slump. Second, the size of chambers also expanded. From predominantly small organizations until about 1900, many chambers became bodies of many thousands of members, as shown in Figure 2.2. Whilst the world wars had a significant short-term effect on a few chambers (such as London, Sheffield, and Newcastle), the dominant pattern was one of expanding size of the major city chambers from the 1920s, converging towards chambers with a size of 1000 members or more.

Third was the influence of WW1, the slump, and WW2. Each radically increased the platform for state control, planning, leadership of industrial strategy, and taxation. The chambers gained resources and a fillip from WW1 activities that lifted many; WW2 had similar effects. But government was now moving to centre stage as a consumer of national resources and as a regulator. For the first time systematically, government started to look at the effectiveness of business bodies as partners in policy development and for delivery of government services. This model, 'co-production' of economic support, later developed as 'corporatism', meant that the chambers came under scrutiny, began to be directly influenced by government policy, but were eclipsed by other bodies, particularly the FBI, founded in 1916, the predecessor of the CBI. As a delegate remark at the ABCC's 1920 conference noted: 'the FBI were prepared to get work done and unfortunately up to the present time the Association [of chambers] had not been prepared to do that. If the members of the Association did not look out they would find the Association snuffed out by that new organisation.'[10] Taylor concludes that the FBI 'had the undoubted result of weakening the chamber position and reducing its influence on government',[11] which was exacerbated by the growth of other large-scale sector trade and professional associations.

One interpretation of this period for Britain is the eclipse of the local by the national, and by the emergence of 'peak' and sector organizations that sought roles in the emerging corporatist state.[12] However, this takes no account of the rise of the chambers of trade, in the 1900–20 period, and their rapid development up to the 1980s. More local, in both small towns and cities, and even smaller and more poorly resourced than the chambers of commerce, they blossomed in this period of growing state dominance, and began to compete with the chambers of commerce for members and attention, taking on the retailer and small trader largely eschewed by the earlier chambers, as well as some manufacturers and professional services and businesses. As a result, the chamber system became an increasingly confused brand, and characterized by differences between the 'large' and 'small' chambers, which had different goals and capacities.

---

[10] Craig-Brown, South of Scotland chamber; in Ilersic and Liddle (1960), p. 185.
[11] Taylor (2007), p. 64.
[12] See e.g. Webb and Webb (1920); Grant (1993, 2000); Grant and Marsh (1977); Jordan and Richardson (1987); Wootton (1975).

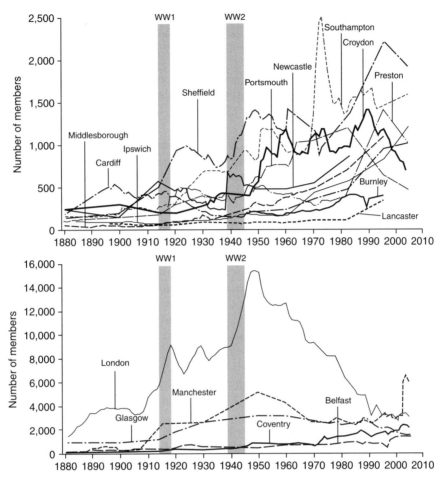

Fig. 2.2. Trends in membership of selected chambers of commerce, 1880–2009; the data vary by locality from annual to decade slices. Because of amalgamations, comparable series cannot be shown for Newcastle, Burnley, Lancaster, and Middlesbrough for later years.

There was also an important challenge from the emergence of junior chambers in Britain after 1925. By 1935 there were 23, and 75 by 1962; by 1964 there were 81 (about the same number as ABCC chambers), with 6000 members; by 1968 there were 100.[13] Whilst these became the seedbeds for future chamber presidents and council members, Taylor concludes that they had a 'downside... [that] contributed yet again to the diffusion of the chamber of commerce brand and to confusion

---

[13] The Junior Chambers movement was founded in St Louis, USA, in 1915; it spread to the UK in 1925 (Lincoln), Birmingham and Sheffield (1927), Nottingham (1928); see Dunwoody (1935), pp. 19–21; Knowles (1952), p. 5; ABCC, *Annual Reports*; Taylor (2007) pp. 66–7.

over the chamber title'. The junior chambers were considered by the ABCC in 1925, but the decision was made not to incorporate them into the national structure: the ABCC 'speaks with an authoritative voice on behalf of the commercial community and the attachment of such bodies might do harm to the chamber of commerce movement'.[14] Any action was to be decided at local level, with much variability and in some cases rivalry with the established chambers. Nationally the junior chambers had their own body. This created mission confusion and was a lost opportunity.

In Ireland after independence in 1923 the major chambers continued to play a major role in national developments, but there was also expansion of smaller chambers. An Irish chambers association was formed in 1923, was slow to develop, but later became a major force in Irish political negotiations.

The late 20th century

In the immediate aftermath of WW2 businesses in Britain were confronted by a Labour government with a mandate to develop a large-scale welfare state, extensive state nationalization of industry, a stringent regime of planning and regulatory controls (particularly town planning), and later a governmental system of economic planning through sectoral boards and committees which subsequently became the NEDC. The ABCC was largely excluded and had increasing difficulty in making its voice heard. Similarly the 1964 Industrial Training Act established sectoral industrial training boards, with a tripartite structure of the CBI and trade associations representing business, the TUC representing labour, and the government. An abortive effort to merge with the CBI following the 1972 Devlin Report also weakened the status of ABCC.

But the late 1970s saw a major shift of fortunes. This occurred at two levels: reform of internal organization; and an increasing relationship with government to act as partner or contractor for service delivery. Internally, stronger ABCC central resources and manpower were developed after 1967. For the first time, in 1973, systematic comparative financial data was collected from each chamber to allow monitoring, and inspections were begun, which laid the foundations for the modern benchmarking and accreditation process.[15] In addition, although a fruitless debate about public law status and compulsory business registration occurred, in 1999 an Act restricting the use of the chamber title was finally achieved.[16] A major step also occurred in 1992 through merger with the NCT, the national body for the chambers of trade. This removed one long-running competitor from the scene.[17]

More formal relationships with government had been presaged by earlier developments, but in 1981 the government launched the New Training Initiative, the centrepiece of which was the Youth Training Scheme, which desperately needed

---

[14] ABCC, *Monthly Proceedings*, 14 September (1925).
[15] By the Association of Chamber Secretaries, a body within ABCC; see Chapter 8.
[16] The Company and Business Names (Chamber of Commerce etc.) Act, 1999.
[17] See later in this chapter.

business placements for unemployed young people. Many chambers, as well as many other bodies, became managing agents for this training. After various other partnerships, in 1990 the Training and Enterprise Councils (TECs) were launched. Whilst encouraging presence from local business leaders, these did not explicitly include chambers, and the two organizations had mutually suspicious relationships in their early years. But a rapprochement in 1995 allowed mergers to create CCTEs.[18] Between 1995 and 1997, 16 new CCTE chamber bodies were created. The chambers proved amenable to seduction by this and other initiatives: the largest received over £25m from government. This made them large and more important organizations, but very vulnerable to the pendulum of government policy change. The expansions of government contracting to chambers were mainly Conservative government initiatives of the 1979–97 Thatcher–Major years.

In Ireland major changes in chamber funding and partnering with government occurred after Irish membership of the EU. But unlike the UK, the Irish Chambers Association also became a major partner and contractor. This role expanded rapidly mainly after 1985, focusing chiefly on training, small firm supports, networking events, and local development activities.

The 21st century

In Britain the pendulum swung in 1997 to a new Labour government. Initially, there was no dramatic change, but in 2001 the TECs were abolished, and with them the funding for the 16 merged CCTE chambers. For many chambers their world collapsed. Of the 16 CCTEs, five disappeared and all the rest had major recovery challenges. The total income of the chamber system experienced major decline. The contracts for training became more difficult to obtain; colleges were in a better position to cover high administrative cost overheads and now carried greater political favour. The world collapsed for another group of chambers after 2007 as contracts for business support were reallocated. However, the tectonic plates shifted again with the 2010 election. The Coalition government announced the abolition of Labour's regional bodies from 2012, replaced by Local Enterprise Partnerships (LEPs), and an austerity package for public finance that cut many spending budgets. This brought new challenges to chambers, but most became involved in the LEPs in a substantial way.

In Ireland the evolving partnership of chambers with government has also been challenged. The major EU funding programmes to the Irish Chambers Association were withdrawn in 2005 after a financial and management crisis at the Association. Local chambers continued to participate in many government and EU pro-grammes, but after 2007 the transformation of Ireland from a 'Celtic tiger' economy to one wrestling with severe deficit and banking crises has reduced the government largesse available even more than in the UK. Hence the paths for the

---

[18] Chambers of Commerce, Training, and Enterprise.

future of chambers of commerce offer many new challenges as the government interfaces evolve.

2.3 CHAMBERS OF TRADE

The main local bodies that challenged chambers of commerce were the chambers of trade. These were, and are, essentially the same as chambers of commerce in structure and objectives, but at a more local level and with a different membership mix. The title 'chamber of trade' (CoT) came to be used during the early 20th century as a generic description for smaller chambers predominantly in the towns rather than cities, and primarily with membership of retailers, distributors, and small traders. But the origin of these chambers in many cases was far earlier, in local sector associations, with titles that were very varied.[19] The earliest were probably the licensed victuallers (in the 18th century). Then during the 19th century came pawnbrokers, chemists, bakers, and butchers, and then tailors, drapers, grocers, and other associations where there were issues of managing customer credit.

A short-lived National Chamber of Trade (NCT) was formed in 1871. In 1879–80 this sought a licence from BoT to incorporate under the Companies Act. At this time it had 24 branches, with 1636 total membership, mainly in the south of England (except Cardiff, Hereford, and Wolverhampton).[20] The application to BoT was withdrawn, and nothing further is preserved until the establishment of the modern NCT in 1897. This had 15 local member associations and 40 individual traders as founding members, with a stronger national spread. These bodies were not initially for the most part called CoTs, but held other titles. Analysis of the first NCT membership book gives the titles in c.1905 of the first 60 local members: one half were Tradesmen's Associations, and only 23% chambers of trade. The others held names from specific sectors, such as Credit Drapers Association, Drapers Association, Shopkeepers Union, Coal Merchants Association, or Mercantile Association. One was a Tradesmen's Protection Association.[21]

The chambers of trade began, therefore, as a very varied group, and were not mutually exclusive with single sector traders' associations;[22] the two overlapped in title and location. The concept and brand of a generic retail and traders chamber was thus slow to emerge. By 1918, of the 234 NCT members, only 76 (32%) were titled CoT.[23] Moreover, brand confusion was already emerging: 38 (13%) held the title of 'chamber of commerce', of which one (Merthyr) called itself a chamber of trade and commerce. By 1919, there were 45 'chambers of commerce' among the CoTs.[24] Some of these 'chambers of commerce' are recognizable ACC chambers (about

---

[19] Crossick (1984), pp. 240–1.
[20] Application for licence, and *Second Annual Report* of NCT (1873): in BT 58/5/COS/750A.
[21] NCT Membership Book; MS29342; this is similar to the 1870s NCT, where Tradesmen's Associations were most frequent, with only one CoT (*Second Annual Report* of NCT, 1873).
[22] As claimed by Crossick (1984), p. 241.
[23] Report of NCT 1919 Annual Meeting, List of Affiliated Associations MS29343/1.
[24] NCT Membership Book; MS29342.

half), and three were retail sections of ACC chambers, but the others were merely assuming the title. From an early date, therefore, brand confusion developed.

The new CoTs and other smaller local bodies had a choice of national affiliations, the ACC or the NCT. For the ACC this represented competition, though it initially welcomed the body, and even seemed relieved that it could now encourage retailers to look elsewhere. For individual ACC chambers the NCT was also usually welcomed, since it provided support for their retail sectors. Birmingham, Reading, and Wolverhampton were the first to join (by 1919); the other major ACC chambers to join the NCT before 1925 (chiefly through their retail sections) were Newcastle, Coventry, Portsmouth, Plymouth, Southampton, Winchester, Hereford, Walsall, and Lincoln.

Diffusion and development

The development of the NCT was strong and steady. As shown in Figure 2.1, there appear to have been no major setbacks in the continued growth of numbers from 1897 until the 1970s, by which time it claimed 867 member chambers. Of those about 70 were also ACC chambers, representing about 85–90% of all ACC chambers. The overlap, complexity, and brand confusion of the two systems thus continued to grow.

In addition to its local association members, NCT differed from the ABCC in having direct membership by individuals.[25] These grew to about 1000 in 1920, dropping in the 1920s, but reached 1100–1200 in the 1945–55 period, declining to about 200 in the 1980s. The NCT saw its individual members as key assets giving direct grass-roots information to supplement the views of member associations: direct members could fill in for the associations when 'business commitments and financial considerations may make it difficult on occasion for a local association to achieve full strength of representation at conferences'.[26] But they were also seen as a key source of information: 'it is on the individual, whether he be a direct member or a member of a local association, that the chamber must in the main depend for reports of instances of . . . unfair trading or issues that need to be addressed'.[27] Individual members also had voting rights, provided that their local association was also an NCT member. There was something about the NCT that attracted individuals as well as local associations. It also had members from national and regional trade associations: 16 by 1929, increasing to 33 between 1945 and 1955.[28] The NCT incorporated in 1925.

The character of the CoTs and the NCT was very different from that of the ACC and its chambers. They generally covered smaller geographical areas, commonly a town or suburb. Some had large memberships, but the resources were usually very

[25] ABCC also had a small number of direct members 1914–58, but they were never significant financially or for governance. The maximum number was 272 in 1930, dropping back to reaching 206 in 1949. An attempt to revive individual ABCC membership in 1961–4 was even less successful, having only 25–30 members over the four years; ABCC Annual Accounts and minutes.

[26] NCT (1957), p. 20.

[27] NCT (1957), p. 46.

[28] Note that all numbers quoted are approximate since records give only fragmentary information.

small because the subscription that could be raised was less. Where the ACC chambers generally charged a guinea, the CoTs charged 2s. 6d. or 5s. By 1960 many still charged only 10s. Nevertheless, some had greater resources and a few employed part-time staff, in the same way as some ACC chambers, by using the input of a local trader, solicitor, or accountant in return for an honorarium. A few (less than 3% in 1956) had a full-time secretary.[29]

Their smallness, and their generally narrower field of interest, focusing on the local market and local trades, seems to have made them more willing to cooperate with each other. The NCT did not experience the problems of having its constituent local bodies wanting to speak nationally for themselves. This is not to say that the same tensions did not exist, but the much greater number and smaller scale of their local bodies gave the NCT a more natural and less challenged leadership role. In Ireland after 1923 the CoTs became indistinguishable from chambers of commerce and no NCT body was formed; all affiliated to CI, or remained on their own.

The primacy of voice

The prime purpose of NCT and local chambers was from the start, and continued to be, campaigning and lobbying; they had few other services.[30] They also, unlike most chambers of commerce, often took a very active role in local and national elections. They ran campaigns for particular candidates and programmes from about 1905, and particularly in the 1920s.[31] Lobbying was also the founding and main objective of the NCT, and in only its second year, 1898, it mounted a high-profile campaign to withdraw the government monopoly from the National Telephone Company.[32] By the time of the parliamentary debate on this topic, nearly half of MPs had received letters from local NCT chambers pressing for an inquiry and reform. The case was reasoned and drew on material the NCT had gathered from British consuls throughout the world on the telephone systems of other countries. A Committee of Inquiry was won, and a successful reform of the telephone system was achieved (albeit to pass it to the Post Office) in 1900. According to the NCT Jubilee History this was largely a result of its pressure, which it claimed was resisted by the ACC, because some of the larger chamber members were mainly users of trunk lines or shareholders in the company. The NCT claim that they had successfully raised public opinion and made an important contribution to 'really popularise the telephone'.[33]

This early success, whether it was due to NCT or not, gave a strong platform for marketing the NCT and was, perhaps, their Anti-Corn Law moment. Subsequent campaigns concerned: prevention of municipal and government trading; rating valuation; reform of the Co-operative movement tax status; public contracts;

[29] NCT (1956), *Select Committee Report*, p. 11; MS29343/5.
[30] See *Local Trade Organisation* (1921); *NCT Handbook* (1960); *NCT: What it is and what it does* (1979) leaflets: MS29343/1; 29346; 29343/12.
[31] See Chapter 3.
[32] This account is based on the summary in the history of NCT (1957), pp. 11–13.
[33] NCT (1957), p. 13; there is no comment on this issue by Ilersic and Liddle (1960).

government income and taxation levels; railway charges; bankruptcy law; County Court reform (to cheapen and streamline procedures); half-day shop closing; shop working hours; holidays with pay; school curriculum and truancy. With the development of government regulation in WW1, the NCT became firm advocates of abolishing local Trade Boards, 'socialistic regimes', and 'socialism'.[34] After WW2 they were strong opponents of nationalization. In addition to earlier concerns the main new lobbies were: local government planning; layout of shopping centres following post-war reconstruction; municipal contracts; equality of rating; local government taxation; income policy and price controls.

Services

Whilst lobbying was the key role of the NCT, the local CoTs had some service development. This is difficult to assess fully because, of the 1000 or more chambers that ever existed, only a very few have surviving records (about 5%) and it appears that these are chiefly for the larger local organizations. The evidence suggests that most held member meetings, some had newsletters, but most relied for publications on NCT leaflets and its *Journal*, established in 1936 and running in various formats until the late 1980s.[35] Hence, the public face of the main CoTs was highly uniform. Of the more significant chambers in 1955, a NCT survey showed that 290 (70%) took the NCT *Journal* and 172 (41%) issued some form of their own publication.[36]

An important service for a significant minority of CoTs was debt collection. Pure debt collection associations were not welcome members of NCT;[37] however many joined. Local plate glass insurance to protect shop windows also became important. This started on a small scale in the 19th century, but by the early 1900s many CoTs were acting as local agents for the Plate Glass Insurance Society. For example Trowbridge chamber had such a society with 117 policies issued by 1910 (membership of the chamber only 52), which achieved a rebate of 62.5% of the costs, and generated an annual surplus of about £10 for the chamber (about 50% of its income).[38]

In addition, for most of the more significant CoTs, a key role was the organization of local shopping hours, as well as opening hours at Christmas and holiday periods. From the 1930s this expanded to involvement in regulation of car parking, street furniture, street signage, window boxes, and flower competitions, Christmas lighting, summer tourist promotions, and other town centre issues. From the 1980s and 1990s CoTs became important contributors to town centre management, CCTV and crime reduction, and similar shopping improvement schemes.

---

[34] NCT Council minutes; e.g. 16 February 1927; MS29340/3; NCT papers 1921, 1922, 1923; MS29343/1.

[35] *The NCT: The Chamber's Services*, leaflet, 25 October 1960; MS29343/7.

[36] NCT, *Report of Select Committee* (1956); MS29343/5.

[37] e.g. in 1909 the Birmingham Tradesmen's Association was described as 'really a debt collection association'. Though its membership was considered at length, it was allowed to join. NCT, minutes, 3 June 1909; MS29340.

[38] Trowbridge chamber, *Annual Report* (1910), p. 8 and accounts, p. 11.

Variety

Some measure of the varied character of the local CoTs can be gauged from the survey of its members undertaken by NCT in 1955.[39] This is probably not a representative survey, since only 416 out of 860 affiliated CoTs replied (48%), which were probably the larger and more effective bodies. However, even for these respondents, 13% held no meetings, and 31% held only one or two meetings per year; 70% took the NCT *Journal*; 32% had representatives that had regularly attended an NCT area meeting; and a further 12% had attended only one. Thus most chambers were not very active or effective bodies and many (including perhaps all those that did not reply) may have been no more than a title with a few officers who liaised informally.

Moreover, instability of the local organizations, particularly in the earlier years, was high. Analysis of the membership book for 1905–19 shows 167 (46%) of the 366 chambers that had existed over this period to be out of membership by 1918; 21% were defunct, and 71% had lapsed or been struck off for not paying NCT subscriptions; 7% resigned and 1% had merged with other bodies.[40] As a result, NCT tried to help improve the smaller and more inadequate local CoTs.[41] One outcome was a helpful *Handbook* of 1960 for local chambers,[42] which briefed them on establishment, development, and administration. It gave specimen letters, model rules, subscription guidance, suggestions for speakers and meetings, defined the role of the secretary, briefed on membership campaigns, guided on engaging the local press, and offered NCT help. In the following decades the NCT council continued attempts to stimulate improvements, but there were few, if any, benchmarks of success set, or achieved.

The contribution of the NCT and its demise

There were four key aspects of NCT that shaped its development. First and foremost, CoTs were lobby organizations and the establishment of the NCT was the result of a sense of need for a national coordination of lobbying for the small trader. It was one of the first small firms' lobbies. Second, the organization was always narrow and focused in its objectives: 'those who sit in high authority have no ear for fugitive and inexperienced opinion. To achieve attention requires a strenuous application, effective unity, [and] action along well ordered lines.'[43] It was focused on being what we would now call a 'peak' organization.

Third, there was an ideological stance of defending private enterprise. For example, in 1904 NCT was protesting to the Church that some ministers were preaching sermons in favour of Co-operative societies and against the 'legitimate

---

[39] NCT (1956), *Report of Select Committee*; MS29343/5, p. 11.
[40] Analysis of scribbled comments in Membership Book; MS29342.
[41] NCT (1956), *Report of Select Committee*; MS29343/5.
[42] NCT (1960), *Handbook*; MS29346.
[43] NCT leaflet (1921), *Local Trade Organisation*; MS29343/1, p. 1.

retail trader'.[44] The concerns became more urgent and strident in the immediate aftermath of WW1. The NCT vigorously opposed the government's Trade Boards of the 1920s. While the war was recognized as requiring a level of government action and coordination, the NCT wanted these mechanisms to be abolished quickly. Its 1921 position is clearly stated:

> in some quarters there may be an opinion that ... the public will be ready and willing to give support to schemes designed to eliminate the retailer from the field of opera- tions ... the primary purpose of the local and national trade organisation is to demon- strate the principle that a well founded and healthy system of competitive trading, activated by the impulse of private enterprise, is far far better for the community as a whole than schemes of a socialist or nationalised character resting upon the heavy hand of bureaucracy.[45]

The *Drapers Record* of 1924 applauded this approach: 'think of the direction in which certain powerful tendencies operate today. Industrial interests of great magnitude are united together. Trade unionism has brought under one flag all or nearly all the great labour forces. An equal case exists for the proper recognition of distributive trading.'[46] No wonder that the NCT welcomed Mrs Thatcher's election as leader of the Conservative Party in 1975 as 'one of us! ... —No politician could have wished for a warmer welcome.' The press commented: 'The shopkeepers of the nation rose in revolt yesterday against spiralling rates and discriminatory taxes—and found a champion.'[47]

Fourth, the NCT and CoTs represented a very real feeling by an underdog. Reflecting on its first 60 years, the official NCT history observes, 'though it is not recorded in any minute-book or report, perhaps one of the chamber's greatest achievements ... is to be found in the present-day status of the shopkeeper'. By the 1950s the appointment of local traders to be magistrates or candidates for local or parliamentary elections, or honours 'occasions no surprise'.[48] Thus the NCT was seen as an important means for the retailer to be recognized.

The NCT had an outstandingly successful life up to about 1980. Ironically just when Mrs Thatcher came to power as prime minister, the membership began to plummet and the finances became progressively more dire. By the mid-1980s it was living on its assets. Its current account deficit increased from £20,476 in 1985, to £71,232 in 1990, and £82,800 in 1992.[49] It was saved from bankruptcy by merger with the ABCC in 1992. Many former NCT chambers became 'affiliated' with their larger local ABCC chambers. It seemed at that point, at last, the competition for voice between the local chambers, and the confusion of the brand of 'chamber',

---

[44] NCT minutes, 14 October 1904, reporting on Annual Meeting of Co-operative Societies at Stratford; the NCT had written to a number of clergy protesting against this; MS29340/1.
[45] NCT leaflet (1921), *Local Trade Organisation*, pp. 2–3; MS29343/1.
[46] NCT, *The Drapers Record*, 20 September (1924), pp. 649–50.
[47] NCT newsletter, *Intercom*, March (1975), p. 2; MS29343/11; *Daily Express*, 23 March 1975.
[48] NCT (1957), pp. 13 and 15.
[49] NCT *Accounts*; Companies House, and LMA.

was a thing of the past and the chambers could look forward to a more aligned presence with government.

An interpretation of this merger is given in Chapter 8. But despite its occurrence, most small chambers remained alive. As always with voluntary systems there is no certainty about numbers, but an extensive search of directories, websites, and other sources in 2006–7 yielded a total of 591 non-BCC chambers in Britain and Northern Ireland, only a minority of which were affiliated members of their local BCC chambers. Whatever the actual numbers, the NCT-ABCC merger itself was not the main cause of change, since, by the time of the merger the NCT membership had already declined to only 188 CoTs. It would seem that the merger helped the national voice of chambers by aligning the representation at Westminster around one central organization with a single brand. But at local level, voice is as varied as ever, with many other bodies and MPs unable to distinguish recognized and non-recognized BCC chambers. The small local chamber is thus still alive and often well.

2.4 TRADE PROTECTION SOCIETIES

The trade protection societies (TPS) overlapped with both CoTs and chambers of commerce and provided a significant service to both as credit check and debt collection bodies. They originated from the 1770s though, like the early chambers of trade, the history of the earliest bodies is obscure. No scholarly study of them appears to have been made.[50] The earliest TPS found is the Guardians or Society for the Protection of Trade against Swindlers and Sharpers, initiated in London on 25 March 1776. The second was Liverpool in 1823, then Manchester in 1826.[51] They became more widespread from the 1840s, in both large cities and small towns. However, they were more similar in number to chambers of commerce than to CoTs, reaching a maximum of about 120 across Britain and Ireland in the 1920s. The national association of TPS covered the UK, Channel Islands, and Ireland, even after Irish independence.[52]

They probably owed much to the evolution of local courts and other local initiatives of the 1750s–1780s to enlarge the range of legal action to recover small debts and other financial claims. The local courts were expanded by local initiatives to obtain parliamentary Acts over this period, with most of the main cities covered by 1790.[53] However, unremarked in previous studies was the

---

[50] But there is one study of the Leicester TPS 1850–1900 (Wood, 1999). This is generally reliable on the Leicester TPS, but contains some misinterpretations of the NATPS and relations with chambers.

[51] *A List of Members of Guardians or Society for the Protection of Trade against Swindlers and Sharpers*, London, together with by-laws and report for 1799, pp. 30 ff; BL 8246.a.15; Liverpool Society of Guardians for the Protection of Trade against Swindlers and Sharpers, 26 February 1823; BL Mic. A.7191.(11); Manchester Guardian Society for Protection of Trade, September (1826), *History 1826–1926*; BL 08244.h.39. The Manchester history incorrectly states that it was the second society after Liverpool; it was the third after London.

[52] Jersey joined in 1869, although it remained as a member for only a few years; DE3512/25.

[53] Langford (1991), pp. 158–64.

considerable flowering of local societies to prosecute felons and swindlers.[54] These were important in providing an 'insurance' for businesses that the costs of a legal action could be shared with others. The TPSs developed from these, generally represented all sectors, covering inter-business debt more strongly than retail debt, and usually contained the more major businesses and local bankers as well as smaller firms.

The societies were generally run by a 'manager' and clerks, and became quite large before most chambers. By the 1860s Manchester, Liverpool, and Leicester had at least three staff, and there were 11 in Leicester by 1900. The London APT in 1861 had a manager, eight clerks, and two or three officers who circulated enquiries, plus staff in its three regional branches.[55] Their scale of activities was also considerable. In 1838 Manchester received 95,000 written and 30,000 verbal enquiries of credit status. Debts recovered increased from £44,500 in 1888 to £320,000 by 1949. In addition, cases were entered at County Courts, as well as in Courts in other areas. The Leicester society represented creditors in the area and elsewhere and its secretary (manager) was appointed as receiver or trustee for deeds of assignment or bankruptcy.[56] An analysis of the Leicester County Court records shows that of 325,000 cases over 1870–1900, 44% were brought by the Leicester TPS and rates of debt recovery were high, at relatively low cost.[57]

Coordination and the National Association

There were about five TPSs by 1835, and probably about 25–30 in 1850, across the whole British Isles (i.e. including Ireland). Many came together to form the Association of Trade Protection Societies of the UK in 1850, which began as a relatively informal meeting of the secretaries of each society.[58] It was reconstructed in 1866 and changed its name to the National Association of Trade Protection Societies (NATPS) in 1933. The initial 12 society members in 1850 were:

Liverpool	Birmingham	Preston
Manchester (Brazenose St.)	Hull	Bristol
Manchester (King St.)	Leeds and W. Riding	Manchester & Salford
London metropolitan	Glasgow	Dublin

To this initial group were added another 15 members over the period up to 1862:

Newcastle-upon-Tyne	Blackburn	Chelmsford
Leicester	Hastings	Aberdeen

---

[54] A full trawl has not been undertaken, but the following foundations should be noted: Liverpool (Ormskirk and Aughton) (*Williamsons Advertiser*, 3 July 1783); Grantham and Newark 1785; Nottingham 1786; and many smaller parishes (*Nottingham Journal*, 5 February 1785; 1 July 1786; 8 December 1787).

[55] Quoted in letter from Henry Whitworth, 1 August 1861, *Union of Trade Protection Societies*, attached to NATPS Special Meeting minutes, 4 August 1861; DE3848/52.

[56] All statistics from *Annual Reports* and minutes of Leicester TPS; DE3848/4-9; also see Chapter 12.

[57] Wood (1999), pp. 31, 62–5, 105–6.

[58] NATPS minutes, 21 March 1850; DE3848/52.

Wolverhampton	Nottingham	Edinburgh
London (Regent St.)	Chorley	Penrith
Worthing	Macclesfield	London (Old Bond St.)

Other societies mentioned, but not in early membership were Wigan, Preston, and Margate.[59] The largest societies by 1960, in descending rank order of membership, were London, Manchester, Liverpool, Dublin, Leicester, Leeds, Birmingham, Glasgow, and Halifax.

The major TPSs were a *formal* network of information exchange locally, and through their association also across the British Isles, with increasing attempts to expand exchanges with other organizations internationally. The coordination needed was a high transaction cost activity, with very large volumes of transactions, for which highly specific technical skills were needed, with considerable collection and exchange of information, involving high coordination costs: referred to in 1867 as 'a vast machinery tending to give confidence to the manufacturer and merchant in the extension of sound, legitimate trading'.[60] As a result, the main service activities of the TPSs remained the preserve of the local societies, but the coordination process became the chief role of the national association.

The information that was generally most important was an agent in other areas, so that a local society could check credit status or pursue a debt recovery in another part of the country. The NATPS gathered from each society, and from its own enquiries, a list of these agents, which it published periodically (every 5–10 years), with annual or half-yearly updates. This list contained about 3000 names 'in 2500 towns and places' by 1868, referred to as 'solicitors, agents or correspondents' that would answer status enquires or initiate proceedings for claims.[61] By 1894–5 the list contained about 5000 agents,[62] and 7000 by the 1930s.[63] The local societies were the main contributors to the lists (56%) in 1929, but this had switched to 67% from the NATPS itself by 1938.[64] This was complemented by publication of lists of county court decisions, bankruptcy orders, etc. By 1895 there were 355 semi-weekly, 2727 weekly, 1550 fortnightly, and 5970 monthly *Circulars* sent out by NATPS, with an additional 2655 copies of locally headed monthlies (of which Leicester was the main user), and a further 2122 lists of creditors in England and Wales, 1410 lists in Scotland, and 678 in Ireland.[65] This was a formidable undertaking, maintained from 1866 into the 1990s (latterly by the local societies).

A major role of the national association was also lobbying. The Association's first resolution in 1850 was promotion of an Absconding Debtors Arrest Act, a big part of which was 'legislation for summarily arresting (those) absconding or

---

[59] NATPS minutes; DE3842/52.

[60] NATPS minutes, 7 May 1867; *Annual Report*, p. 10; DE 3512/25.

[61] NATPS minutes, 18 June 1868; DE3512/25.

[62] NATPS minutes, containing lists, 1894, 1895; DE3512/27.

[63] NATPS minutes, referring to lists 8 March 1910; DE3512/30, and subsequent minutes; DE3512/31–5.

[64] *Statistics*, in NATPS *Annual Report* (1939), Table 4; DE3512/42.

[65] *Particulars as to Lists*, NATPS minutes, 10 April 1895; DE3512/27, p. 122.

contemplating absconding from the country owing to any debt due', with power to issue warrants extended to judges of County Courts, commissioners in bankruptcy, mayors of corporations, and stipendiary magistrates. This lobby was successful in an 1857 Act, using Mr Baines MP as their advocate. Other critical lobbies in 1850–6 were:[66] for a national Register of Assignments or transfer of personal property as security for debts; Improvement Act on Bills of Sale; uniformity of legislation between Britain and Ireland with court judgements having force in both countries; reduction in County Court fees 'by not less than one third' and extension of their jurisdiction to sums of £50; extension of law on goods obtained under false pretences; amendment of bankruptcy law; all partner names to be registered in partnerships. Similar fields were continued in later lobbies. There was a modern and progressive agenda, including lobbying for independent debts of husbands and separated wives, and women's property rights.[67]

Relations with the chambers

As a voice the NATPS was generally aligned with chambers of commerce and other trade lobbies, but was more vigorous in seeking to maintain imprisonment for debt for 'wilful defaulting' in the 1874–80 period; and it also took a different line with the Juridicature Committee deliberations in 1870–1, favouring improvement in the County Courts over the ACC's lobby for tribunals of commerce.[68] Unlike the ACC and NCT, however, it had very few lobbies on wider government policies. The exceptions were in 1897, over government budgets and expenditure levels; and in 1899–1900 support for wider national concerns against the extension of munic-ipal trading activities, particularly conditions on subcontractors that 'raise cost to ratepayers'; it took a stand 'that Parliament should exercise limiting powers over municipal enterprise'.[69] A further exception, which ran for some years from 1904, was lobbying against the income tax treatment of Co-operative societies. Its only party political campaigning appears to have been the 1905 general election where the NATPS issued a *Manifesto of the Association*, and prepared a pamphlet with 21 questions for parliamentary candidates that all derived from specific TPS campaigns.[70]

The chambers of commerce seem to have developed a loose liaison with TPS. The NATPS stated in 1894 that it 'has always worked in consort with the Associated Chambers of Commerce, and has repeatedly cooperated in the intro-duction and progress of Bills'.[71] This is repeated in subsequent publicity leaflets for the TPS from 1901. This accommodation seems to have worked in most

[66] NATPS minutes; DE3848/52.

[67] NATPS minutes; DE 3512/25–35.

[68] See Chapter 7; London's chamber of commerce initiative to set up a Court of Arbitration in 1892 is merely noted in the NATPS minutes, with no further reference to chamber arbitration activities.

[69] NATPS minutes, Annual Meeting of 1899, and agreed motion to 1900 meeting from Leicester TPS.

[70] NATPS minutes (1905), *Manifesto*; DE3512/29.

[71] NATPS minutes: Jubilee Banquet Statement of 11 May 1898; and Leaflets, e.g. in 1901; DE3512/28–9.

cases.[72] The cross-membership of the TPS with chambers of commerce was quite limited. In the early years, Aberdeen was the only chamber member of NATPS, from 1857. A few other chambers were members in ensuing years. In the first listing by society full name in the NATPS members book for 1917, of 98 TPS only five recognizable chambers of commerce are listed: Aberdeen, Colchester (which called itself a chamber of commerce and TPS), Dover, Dublin, and Tunbridge Wells, though only two of these were ACC chambers at this time. In addition, there were 11 others calling themselves chambers of trade or commerce, though most were not ACC or NCT members.[73] By 1930 the NATPS membership was down to 56, of which the same five chambers of commerce are listed. By 1960 only six of 38 (16%) TPS are listed as chambers of commerce or trade.[74]

Local underpinnings of commercial trust

This brief overview of the TPS shows them to be an important part of the evolving structure of local business voice from 1850 until the 1980s. They also provided a large-scale debt recovery and credit status service. The huge scale of their services undermines arguments that trust-based relational exchange alone is enough to ensure stable commercial relations; mechanisms are also needed to check trust and collect debts!

The NATPS appears to have suffered from its overlap with the CoTs after WW1, but after loss of mostly its smaller members to NCT, it remained an important body for its 40–60 member societies. After 1963 the NATPS was wound up, with its main coordination activities taken over by the larger member societies (a reversion to the pre-1866 situation). But the local societies were also under pressure, probably as a result of the expanded national markets of many trading firms (particularly the multiples), and increasing availability of other credit rating structures. However, some of the major local societies continued for a long period, in Leicester up to 1992, when it merged with the local chamber of commerce.

2.5 CHAMBERS OF AGRICULTURE

The chambers of agriculture are included in this study because they are localized, geographically defined, deliberated bodies providing voice and service activities. But in one crucial respect they differ from the other chambers: they were sector based, representing the single activity of agriculture. However, they have three features of interest for this book. First, for many years they were the only rurally based entities seeking voice; they were thus an important counterpart of the other chambers.

[72] A comment for Leicester TPS seems exceptional, that it was set up in opposition to the exclusiveness of the local chamber of commerce; quoted in Leicester TPS, *Centenary History* (1950), pp. 7–9, from *Leicester Mercury*. See also Wood (1999), p. 210.
[73] NATPS Membership Book; DE3848/51.
[74] *Table of Annual Statistics* (1960), p. 3 footnote; DE3512/35. The chambers were Canterbury, Colchester, Eastbourne, Penrith, Weston-super-Mare, and Wimbledon. All were CoTs at that time.

Second, some of the earliest agricultural societies that evolved to become chambers of agriculture were strongly interlinked with early chambers, most significantly in Manchester in 1772–4. Third, the foundation of many chambers of agriculture, as a general movement, was initially specifically to oppose the chambers of commerce, as a competitive voice, during the Anti-Corn Law campaign. It is important to understand them, therefore, as part of the wider span of interlinked and competing organizations. There are two official histories of these chambers, and some scholarly attention in relation to the Corn Laws and later policies.[75]

Origins

The chambers of agriculture had origins in a diverse range of agricultural improvement societies and farming clubs, many of which date from the 18th century. For example the Manchester Agricultural Society founded in 1772 was closely associated with early improvement initiatives in Salford hundred, and this was interlinked with the needs of the towns for food, and especially the feed for the main means of commercial transport: the horse. The members of the society were heavily cross-linked with the early chamber of commerce members and other industrial associations in Manchester. Other early societies were in Glamorgan and Breconshire.[76] The main strength of these bodies was at the local level, where they offered bounties, prizes, practical advice, and also developed insurance schemes, exhibitions, and shows.

Some of these early agricultural improvement societies came together to form a short-lived central organization to promote farmers' clubs in the 1830s. There had also been a proposal for a chamber of agriculture in 1802, as a 'voice' and 'jury' under the Board of Agriculture.[77] The first formal foundation was the Central Agricultural Association in about 1838; but there was no major attempt to act as voice until the 1840s. As noted by Matthews, it was taken for granted that the landed interest in parliament would safeguard agricultural interests. Indeed, 'the idea that some machinery was required to spur their Member [MP] into his duty . . . would have been looked upon as little less than profane'.[78]

Response to the Anti-Corn Law League

The complacent political position of agriculture was shaken in the 1840s by the Anti-Corn Law League, with which the chambers of commerce were closely associated. The first local society to resist the League was founded in Uxbridge in March 1843, there were three by July (two in London and one in Essex).[79] A Central Committee for Protection of Agriculture of the UK was founded in

---

[75] Official histories are by their former secretaries (Matthews, 1915; Jeffcock, 1937); other studies are Ernle (1936); Mosse (1947); Self and Storing (1962); Evans (1996).
[76] References to other societies in *Manchester Mercury*, 1 and 22 March 1774.
[77] *Farmers Magazine* (1802), p. 48.
[78] Matthews (1915), pp. 2–3.
[79] Maydwell (1845).

December 1843, following a meeting at the Smithfield Show, explicitly as an 'Anti-League'. By that time the League was a formidable and well-organized force for which the Anti-League was a poor match. Its president and prime mover was the Duke of Richmond, with vice-president the Duke of Buckingham, both prominent in earlier governments, and Buckingham had resigned from Peel's government of the time. It drew heavily on backbench MPs from the landed interest 'squires', of which Charles Newdegate and William Miles were most prominent. The movement was slow to organize and many of its leaders had disdain for the tactics required. Although claiming to be an association of the tenantry, its leaders and prime concern was for the large farmer and the landed interest.[80] There was also tension over strategies; Isaac Maydwell, who claimed to have alerted agriculturalists to the threat from the League with a pamphlet in 1840, criticized Richmond in 1845 in an aptly named pamphlet, *Is it a plot or is it not?*[81]

There was a brief period in which the Anti-League held a possibly significant leverage, and this was after a meeting on 12 January 1846 when electioneering was initiated. A by-election was won by Anti-Leaguers in Nottinghamshire, and a group of 60–70 MPs formed a Protectionist Party.[82] But this was late in the day. Peel had discounted the scope for an opposition victory and was able to win repeal with the support of the Whigs, though there were more fundamental consequences for the unity of the Tory party.[83] Some pamphlets attacking free trade as 'an intellectual delusion' were published, but these were unconvincing.[84] The Anti-League effectively relied on its presence in parliament, and it failed to develop a coherent central organization with a convincing repertoire. It collapsed in 1847 once the abolition of the Corn Laws was clearly irreversible, though a few local societies continued.

The Central Chamber of Agriculture

The establishment of the Central Chamber of Agriculture in 1865 was a more grass-roots development, the result of later concerns for a dedicated lobby, voiced by some local organizations, and led by circular letters from Charles Clay in the West Riding. It was the outcome of the efforts of 'the most far sighted and most intelligent of the landed classes'.[85] Clay's blueprint was for a 'peak' national organization to which each local farmers' club and society paid a fee of five guineas. The chief activity was to be 'measures in the Houses of Parliament and before the government, calculated to benefit agriculture, as well as to oppose or modify any movement detrimental to that important interest'. The 'chamber' brand name was adopted, and Clay sought to copy the ACC:

---

[80] Mosse (1947); Wootton (1975), pp. 73–5.
[81] Maydwell (1845).
[82] Lawson-Tancred (1960), pp. 179–82.
[83] Lawson-Tancred (1960), pp. 162–9; Evans (1996), pp. 281–4.
[84] e.g. Beaumont (1844); Everard (1850).
[85] Matthews (1915), p. 3.

the prominence with which . . . 'the manufacturer' has continued to push forward his own measures seems to be obliterating the fact that there is such an interest as agriculture—which equally requires and fully deserves the application of those free trade and progressive principles which have been of so much benefit to commercial enterprise.[86]

This view demonstrates not only that the chambers of commerce were seen as competitors, but also that agriculture could only gain attention by reframing its case within the paradigm of 'free trade'.

Societies in membership of the central chamber grew to about 75 in 1904, and probably peaked at 108 in 1913. By the 1920s there were 50–60 members, dropping to 36 by 1928, and averaging 44–8 over the 1930s. These had a quoted total membership through the individual societies of 32,538 in 1930. There were also 300–400 individual direct members, which included 101 MPs in 1904, and some of the most prominent of the large aristocratic landowners. It gradually lost local member societies after WW1,[87] was eclipsed by the National Farmers Union (NFU) from the 1920s, and was finally wound up in 1959, with its assets transferred to the NFU and Country Landowners Association.[88]

One of its most important campaigns was 50% de-rating of agricultural land. Led by Lord Lowther, it also achieved considerable success with the Agriculture Rating Act (1896) against vigorous opposition. Although supposedly a temporary measure, this relief became a central part of the rates system. The local shortfall in rates was made up by central government; hence transferring general taxation to help farmers. In the 1920s further pressure was exerted for reductions in income tax on earnings from agriculture and forestry. Chaired by Sir Trustram Eve, and working with the Country Landowners Association, the chamber's local taxation committee, achieved eventual passage of compensating rate reliefs in the Agricultural Rates Act (1923). Further attacks on rating valuation and tithes continued into the 1930s.[89]

The Corn Law issues resurfaced in 1903. The chamber opposed revision of the corn duty and sent a deputation to the prime minister, Balfour. They received a polite but firm refusal to do anything, Balfour stating that he found 'considerable exaggeration as to the protective effect' that increased corn duties would offer the miller.[90] Later in 1903, however, the chamber was deploying its support for Chamberlain 'to consolidate and advance the Empire at large' through general tariffs which would include agriculture.[91] As in the 1840s, agriculturalists opposed free trade and sought protection; and the tide was now running more in their direction.[92] As with NCT and the NATPS, the 1905 general election was a watershed, and the central chamber organized lobbying of MPs, listing their voting

[86] Charles Clay letter, 5 December 1865; quoted in Matthews (1915), p. 393.
[87] Central chamber, *Annual Reports* (1913–32); BL: Ac 3486.
[88] See *The British Farmer*, 22 August (1959), p. 27; quoted in Self and Storing (1962), pp. 38–9.
[89] Jeffcock (1937), pp. 30–50.
[90] *Proceedings of the Central Chamber* (1903), p. 159.
[91] *Proceedings*, 3 November (1903), p. 224.
[92] See Chapter 10.

in divisions for and against Agricultural Bills and deploying local societies to exert pressure.[93]

One successful campaign managed by the chamber was for the appointment of a Minister of Agriculture, with a Ministry or Board. This was part of Clay's original objectives, which he hoped 'might *eventually lead to the appointment of a Minister or Board of Agriculture*'.[94] This campaign succeeded in 1888 with a Minister of Agriculture and Department, though this was more due to the agricultural interests in parliament than to the chamber. This was in marked contrast to the long-running and unsuccessful campaign by the ABCC for a Minister of Commerce.[95]

Assessment

The chambers of agriculture represent another system of geographically distributed local voices, organized with affiliation to a national association, focused on a single sector, but diffusing the chamber concept into rural areas and small towns.[96] The chambers of agriculture were therefore another significant voice using the chamber brand, with attendant confusion, competition, and overlaps at the local level. The supplanting of the chambers of agriculture by the NFU mirrors the pressure on the chambers of commerce from the FBI/CBI, sector associations, and the trade unions over the same period. The small business and tenant farmer were far more numerous than the large landowner; the trade union model was more relevant than the business association model, and the FBI came to cover the industrial aspects of agriculture.[97] As noted by Self and Storing: the year 1915 'was perhaps the last time the landed interest could speak with such supreme confidence in its own leadership'.[98]

2.6 OTHER LOCAL, SECTOR, AND NATIONAL BODIES

Local business associations such as chambers are only part of a large scene. Other industrial associations numbered 1222 in 1913. There was then rapid growth over WW1, with association numbers rising to 1528 in 1914, 1824 in 1917, and 2849 in 1919, of which about one-half were in manufacturing.[99] From the mid-1990s there have been about 3000 trade and professional associations in Britain, of which about 56% are sector trade bodies, still about one-half in manufacturing, in addition to the chambers of commerce and trade. The aggregate membership of these bodies in 1998 exceeded 4.5 million, which was greater than the total business population; hence, many businesses belonged to more than one

---

[93] *Proceedings* (1904) ff.
[94] Charles Clay letter, 5 December 1865; quoted in Matthews (1915), p. 393; emphasis in original.
[95] Ilersic and Liddle (1960); also see Chapter 7.
[96] Clarke (2000a), chapter 22.
[97] CCA/ECU (1931).
[98] Self and Storing (1962), p. 39.
[99] Turner (1978), pp. 530–1; Turner (1984, 1988); Hilton (1917); PEP (1952, 1957).

organization, although some belonged to none. The mean membership was about 1.7 associations per business; sole traders joined an average of about 0.9 associations, but larger companies joined an average of 7.2 associations (for companies of over 200 employees);[100] companies like ICI and Lever Bros. in the 1950s were members of 50–80 associations.[101]

Most of these associations were, and still are, small, but many are *very* small. For trade associations about 14% have ten members or less, although these might be major international companies; 52% have 50 members or less, whilst only 4% have over 1000 members. Efforts at reform have occurred at various times, most recently following a 1994 government initiative to improve association governance and capacity.[102] One of the most significant outcomes of the number, small size, and complexity of these bodies has been the evolution of 'peak' bodies, which are federations or groupings of the smaller associations.

Sector bodies before WW1

There were few major rivals to the chambers as a business voice until the late 19th century. Specific industrial lobbies for some sectors and trading markets existed, as with the American Merchants in London, and the West India Association. An early national body resisted the Factory Acts in the 1840s, which had no direct chamber involvement. But the first more systematic rivals to chambers emerged in the late 19th century when the increasing size and complexity of the economy, combined with improved transport infrastructure, saw evolution towards national markets and integrated production in the manufacturing sector, which encouraged the formation and rapid growth of sector bodies for whole industries, or specialized subsectors of an industry, a process markedly accelerated by WW1. Wootton sees these trade and professional associations as predominantly protective, wanting to set minimum prices, restrict market entry, and control markets. Their density of membership as a proportion of their sectors grew rapidly in the period up to WW1, which allowed them to exercise greater control.[103] The market itself was becoming more concentrated within large firms and combines. This played directly to the emerging trade unions that also wanted to maintain wages and employment, and the extension of their power, as embodied in the Trade Disputes Act 1906, and Trade Union Act 1913. In 1902 there were 853 employer associations concerned primarily with labour negotiations, and about 1000 by 1914.[104]

---

[100] Bennett (1998a, 1998b).
[101] PEP (1957), p. 240.
[102] DTI (1996), *A Best Practice Guide for the Model Trade Association*; Bennett (1997); Greaves (2008); see Chapter 13.
[103] Wootton (1975), pp. 76–7, 85–6.
[104] BoT, *Directory of Industrial Associations* (1902–19); Turner (1984); Wootton (1975); PEP (1957).

The new policy frame after 1918

WW1 crystallized a fundamental change in the relation of business associations with government. As noted by Grant and Marsh, although there were some earlier examples, WW1 created a systematic intervention by government in the organization of industry.[105] Or as noted by Wootton: associations felt a 'pull towards, or propelled themselves into close relations with government by means of consultation, traceable to the 1880s, but systematized during the course of the World War.... Existing trade associations were drawn into a close embrace. Where trade associations did not exist the government saw to it that they were invented.'[106]

By the end of the war, it was possible to discern two main elements of government priorities, both of which were to continue. First, there was an interest in improving association capacity. Various BoT targets and criteria were laid down as 'standards' of what associations should offer, which usually focused on incorporation. From this pressure, the chambers of commerce, chambers of trade, and the TPSs began a period of 'reconstruction' through to the 1920s. For the sector trade associations, the first incorporation is claimed to be in 1881, and there were only 30 by 1913. By 1919 incorporation had increased to 62; to 115 by 1939, and 192 by 1955.[107]

A second government concern was to encourage associations to help 'plan' their sectors. This was a direct challenge to the chambers. There was little attempt by government at a geographical structure, as there was perceived to be little need for it, though some chambers became strongly involved where there was a large local concentration of a particular sector, e.g. Manchester chamber and the cotton industry.[108] But for the trade associations, government progressively accepted the sectors' own agendas to control competition, markets, output, and prices. This had been necessary during WW1, but a Committee on Trusts of 1919 urged continuation of government-sanctioned price and output cartels, either through associations, by combinations (such as price rings), or by amalgamation into larger companies. This policy also played to a period in which tariffs, 'safeguarding', and protection began to replace 'free trade': they became 'strategic industries'. As stated by the Committee on Trusts: 'considerable advantages were recognized [by government] in dealing with combinations and associations for war purposes. It was found that the larger-minded and more moderate men had a beneficial effect upon the attitude of the trades as a whole, that the best technical advice was more easily available.'[109] This formed the dominant frame up to and immediately after WW2: 'The modern trade association is the result of the realisation that unrestricted competition is unnatural and fallacious.'[110]

From this period ensues an increasingly close, but often uneasy, relationship of associations with government. As Nettl puts it, this was the point where the

---

[105] Grant and Marsh (1977), p. 19; see also Turner (1988); Grant (1987, 1993).
[106] Wootton (1975), p. 92 and 91.
[107] PEP (1957), pp. 3–4.
[108] See Chapters 6 and 13.
[109] Committee on Trusts (1918).
[110] Davies (1946), p. 32.

influence from government became greater than that from industry on government.[111] The local chambers were largely excluded; 1918 marks the growing eclipse of local by national voices of sectors and federations of sectors. It is claimed that the chambers became perceived as too divided, too localized, or too frustratingly time consuming to retain the commitment of the emerging 'captains of industry' who increasingly sought to act directly on the national stage.[112]

The emergence of 'peak' organizations

The period from WW1 also saw the emergence of significant 'peak' organizations representing the interests of many member associations. The ABCC, NCT, NATPS, and Central Chamber of Agriculture were 'peak' federations of *local* bodies. However, government wanted a national consultation and negotiating machinery for sector wages and working conditions.[113] The major outcome of this pressure was the foundation of the Federation of British Industries (FBI) in 1916. Dudley Docker, who had formed the British Manufacturers Association (BMA) in 1905 and a Business League in 1911, was a leading spirit behind this. The FBI grew out of a meeting between the British Electrical and Allied Manufacturers Association (BEAMA), which had been formed in 1911 as a peak organization for the electrical manufacturing associations, and the Employers' Parliamentary Association (EPA) founded in 1898.[114] They agreed to launch a Central Association of Employers Organizations in December 1915. A speech by Dudley Docker was important in shaping an agenda to gain more influence in government, to develop it as a 'Business Parliament'.

By July 1916 this had become the FBI, with 124 companies and associations subscribing £1000 each to join, which elected a Grand Council. The Council grew to 450, divided into 24 groups for each leading sector. An Executive Council formed in September 1916 was mainly drawn from companies closely linked to Docker or to his views; he became the first president.[115] By 1917 FBI represented over £2500 million of invested capital and could claim that its membership 'is as complete as it is going to be'.[116] It grew to 4072 firms and 280 association members by 1964.[117] The three initial senior executives of the FBI were secondees from the Foreign Office (Roland Nugent who became FBI director, and Ernest Fitzjohn Oldham who became assistant director) and Colonial Office (Charles Tennyson, another assistant director), none of whom had business experience. This alarmed the ABCC as the Foreign Office support seemed to tread on their dominant concern with trade.

---

[111] Nettl (1965).
[112] Ilersic and Liddle (1960), pp. 168–70.
[113] McDonald (1973), p. 32.
[114] It received a charter in 1923. This discussion draws on PEP (1957); Blank (1973); Grant and Marsh (1973, 1977); Wootton (1975); Davenport-Hines (1984).
[115] Davenport-Hines (1984), pp. 105–13; see also PEP (1957); Devlin (1972), p. 20.
[116] Evidence to *Commercial and Industrial Policy Committee*, p. 572: TNA BT 55/10.
[117] Grant and Marsh (1977).

The FBI had a muddled beginning. Blank argues that it was never a powerful and influential body and tended to follow government's agendas, lacking the resources (or leadership) to act as an independent force. Turner concludes that it remained emasculated by internal divisions over the tariff issue until 1932, and was lacklustre and subservient to government.[118] The rapid expansion of the FBI membership also diluted the founders' objectives, frustrating Docker's plans for it to be a manufacturers' political party.

There was also competition with rival national peak bodies, especially the Engineering Employers Federation (EEF), the National Confederation of Employers Organization (NCEO) (later called the British Employers Confederation: BEC, and linked to the EEF), which were employer organizations concerned with labour negotiations, and the Imperial Association of Commerce established in July 1918 specifically to oppose Docker. The last had Lord Inchcape as president, and was a powerful force that sought to 'act as a medium of communication between all bona fide British traders and government' to oppose 'any form of restriction or control of trade'.[119] These organizations were the ones that were increasingly used by government, and chambers were challenged. WW2 consolidated the FBI position, but the major challenge resulted from the merger of the BEC with the FBI in 1965 to create the Confederation of British Industry (CBI). The CBI, together with the EEF, TUC, and others, was used by the Labour government after 1964 to take a stronger lead on prices and wages through a tripartite structure involving a 'Statement of Intent' by industry, the unions, and government.[120] The CBI became an 'insider' body until 1979, with all the tensions that entailed. It was also the business lead body on a strengthened National Economic Development Council (NEDC) of which sector committees ('little neddies') were critical components feeding specialized information. After a 200-year history, the chambers were demoted to a second tier role, advising CBI appointees to the NEDC.[121]

The small firms lobby

The development of small firm interests squeezed chambers from the other end. The neglect of small businesses went back to the reorientation of government policy during and after WW1. With government encouragement to combines and trusts,[122] there was little space for the smaller firm in the policy agenda. The Macmillan Committee in 1930,[123] and the development of Keynesian thinking during and after WW2, saw small businesses deliberately excluded; Keynes saw

[118] Blank (1973); Turner (1988), p. 8.
[119] Nugent papers, memorandum 15 May 1918; *North China Herald*, 3 August 1918; quoted in Davenport-Hines (1984), p. 119.
[120] Grant (1991); also Fraser (1967); Blank (1973); Wootton (1975); Devlin (1972); Grant and Marsh (1977); Middlemas (1979).
[121] See Chapter 10; Ilersic and Liddle (1960); Taylor (2007). In Middlemas (1983), for example, there is only one reference to the ABCC, at the setting up of NEDC.
[122] Macgregor (1934), pp. 120–30.
[123] Macmillan Committee: *Report of Committee on Finance and Banking* (1930), Cmd. 3897.

small firms as 'unmanageable uncertainty' and 'animal behaviour' in conflict with the dominant view of government planning through corporatist 'manageable' risk using large corporations.[124]

A significant readjustment of these assumptions was caused by the Bolton Report on small firms in 1971, which introduced a new 'frame' of policy. The Devlin Report in 1972 also responded to this, calling for coordination through a CBI Small Business Council.[125] The CBI had recognized small firms by establishing a Regional and Small Firms Directorate in 1971; and the ABCC and local chambers claimed to represent small business. But the reality, recognized by Bolton, was that there was 'not a coherent or powerful representation of small businesses and no national organisation claiming to speak for the whole of small business so that small firms cannot bring effective pressure to bear on government'.[126]

The Bolton Report stimulated a number of bodies to be established or reformed. The first explicit small business body had been set up in 1965, called the Society of Independent Manufacturers, subsequently renamed the Smaller Business Association, and then the Association of Independent Businesses. This originated in concerns about the CBI becoming 'a tool of government policy'; it had about 1000 direct members in 1976.[127] It was reconstituted in its modern form as the Forum of Private Business (FPB) in 1977. The DTI established a Small Firms Division in 1971, which began to respond to small firm concerns and tried to act as a force within government, probably most useful in commissioning the collection of statistics on firm size for the first time. Perhaps most important, however, was the National Federation of Self Employed (NFSE), established in 1974, subsequently incorporated as the National Federation of Self Employed and Small Business Ltd in 1977, and branded as the Federation of Small Businesses (FSB). In addition, there was the Institute of Directors (IoD), which had been established in 1903, and which began to play a more significant policy role. Many other organizations also began to develop a small business voice along with their other concerns; e.g. the NCT, EEF, some trade unions that covered independent craft traders, the NFU, and many sector associations. The approximate scale of the main small firm bodies is compared in Table 2.2. The rapid growth of specific small business associations is clear after Bolton. Since 1970, over 220,000 small business members have been added to the system of business voice.

The FSB has become the major modern challenge for chambers, as it is large and locally based. It was an activist protest movement from the outset, founded in 1974 largely as a reaction against a series of government decisions that fed a grass-roots feeling by smaller firm owners and entrepreneurs that their interests were being neglected by tripartism. By 1974 wage inflation in the economy was running at over 20% and the 'social contract' concept of tripartism was demonstrably a failure. The introduction of VAT in 1973 as a result of alignment of taxes in the run-up to

---

[124] Quoted in Dannreuther (2005).
[125] Devlin Report (1972), pp. 79–80.
[126] Bolton Report (1971).
[127] *The Times*, 3 March 1965; quoted in Grant and Marsh (1977), pp. 26 and 96.

Table 2.2. Membership of small business associations in 1975 and 2006

	1975	2006
CBI (small business members only)	c.700	870 (but 200,000 indirectly through trade associations)
ABCC/BCC (small business members only)	42,000	74,000
NCT (and non-BCC chambers)	50,000	c.45,000
Smaller Business Association/FPB	1,000	10,000–15,000
FSB	30,000	185,000
IoD	26,000	55,000
Total	149,7000	370,870

Note: All numbers are approximate, but represent real members, not claimed sizes. Small businesses are defined as those with less than 200 employees.
Sources: Grant and Marsh (1977); Bettsworth (1999); Bolton Report (1971); Devlin Report (1972); Mekic (2007); NCT archives; IoD.

entry to the European Community was very unpopular; but the breaking point was a government budget proposal in 1974 to raise Class 4 National Insurance Contributions (NIC) for the self-employed in proportion to their earnings.[128]

The NFSE/FSB was founded by one of these angered entrepreneurs, Norman Small, who was rapidly joined by others to confront the government. After a September 1974 launch, 1000 members had joined. Through the skilful use of advertisements and newspaper letters there were 30,000 members by August 1975, and in September 1975 a 250,000-signature petition was delivered to Downing St. A direct action (or 'extra-legal') campaign saw 1000 members pay their NIC bills to the FSB (£57,000) instead of paying the Inland Revenue.[129] When the NIC proposal was withdrawn a major victory was claimed which provided the launch of the organization's brand: this was the FSB's 'Corn Law moment'. The FSB strap-line 'to fight for your rights' was very attractive. The activism of the FSB contrasted with the NCT that voted against militant actions in May 1975.[130] Perhaps it was from this point that the chambers of trade began to be eclipsed.

Membership of FSB reached 40,000 by 1976, and 45,000 by 1985, where it remained until another period of rapid growth after a 1992 reorganization of recruitment to use canvassers and modified policy committees to involve more members. Membership then grew to 185,000 by 2003, where it has tended to remain.[131] The FSB works on different principles from the chambers and other bodies: activist volunteers are the main lifeblood. By 2001 there were about 790 individuals holding 1153 committee positions, with many staff positions held full time or part time by members. The 1992 restructuring of the FSB also introduced a bundled service package that covered legal, insurance, and helpline services. It also introduced branches, numbering over 300 in 32 regions in 2006, based on counties

[128] Bettsworth (1999); see also King and Nugent (1979); McHugh (1979).
[129] Bettsworth (1999); McHugh (1979).
[130] Jordan and Halpin (2003), p. 317.
[131] See McHugh (1979); Bettsworth (1999); Jordan and Halpin (2003, 2004); Mekic (2007).

or groups of counties not dissimilar to chamber areas.[132] This challenge to chambers is replicated in a different way by the IoD. Again a large body, with 47 regional branches in 2010 mainly based on counties, it is an important rival to chambers for meetings, drop-in milieu, service helplines, and national policy voice.

2.7 CONCLUSION

This chapter has sought to give a historical overview of development of the chambers of commerce, chambers of trade, trade protection societies, and chambers of agriculture. It has shown how local voice developed and became progressively challenged by how government developed its mechanisms for exchanging information and developing its policies through and with associations. Periods of paradigmatic change in frames of policy occurred. These are the focuses for later chapters, so-called periods of 'transgressive contention'. These all fundamentally shifted the frames of policy debate, and the mechanisms, or repertoires, by which business organizations engaged with government and on what terms. There have been three key dimensions of these shifts.

First, the chambers of commerce, through a deliberate internal policy of mergers, have recently concentrated their voice into larger bodies and expanded their territories and resources in the hope of increasing effectiveness and sustainability. Second, the more grass-roots structure of smaller community voices has survived through small chambers of trade, often affiliated with the large chambers of commerce, but in many cases also independent of them. Third, there has been growing competition for national voice, especially since the foundation of FBI in 1916, CBI in 1965, and small firm bodies from the 1970s.

This chapter has set out to show the evolution of each major body, leading up to the present. The associational world of business–government relations of the 20th century needed a lot of resources to maintain it, through financial and voluntary inputs, and through attention from the relevant parts of government. This had begun to look increasingly difficult to sustain, but in the 21st century costs have been turned on their head by changes in electronic communications. This may offer local voice new opportunities in the future, or it may lead to further consolidation. The following chapters assess each theme in more detail.

[132] Mekic (2007), pp. 15-315 to 15-324.

PART 2

FORCES, ORIGINS, AND DIFFUSION

3

Forces of Local Association

3.1 INTRODUCTION

What brings people to associate and join bodies like chambers? Are the stimuli for initiating this process different from those that are necessary to maintain it? What makes it more economically viable to organize some activities collectively rather than purchasing services through normal business practices? What are the specifically local aspects of this process? How does government influence these choices? Were the forces that encouraged the formation of the new local voice in the 18th century similar to, or different from, those that continue today? This chapter seeks to engage with these questions by examining the forces that lay behind the earliest chambers, and how they have developed and continue to operate. This provides a framework for interpretation used in the following chapters.

The definition of a 'unity' of interest forms the starting point, but a critical aspect of the discussion is that individual business motivation and association development is rarely dependent on a single factor. Rather, chambers and related bodies relied in the past, and continue to rely now, on a 'bundle' of activities, which in turn seeks to meet a bundle of demands, and result in a mix of incentives and opportunities to members and to association managers. Hence, although chambers have as their core function, and 'unique selling point' (USP), to act as a unified local voice, this has always been intrinsically interrelated with other economic, social, and political functions.

3.2 'UNITY' OF LOCAL VOICE

The central purpose and USP of the chambers was, and is, voice. But behind that simple statement lies considerable challenge to how that voice is developed so that it reflects a common position acceptable to members, and is coherent, persuasive, and convincing to government. In the early period, this was often referred to as forming a 'unity' of interests. In this, the local context was critical. The unity had to be one that allowed a group of businesses to cohere. The geographical context was a milieu that allowed ready communication, but was also a place where other networks and connections existed, and where there was a strong commonality of interests. Hence, geographical context and the search for unity of voice were interlocked.

This is clear in many chamber statements of objectives. The earliest in the British Isles, Jersey in 1768, was founded for the 'well-being of trade and to support and keep the merchants upon a respectable footing, in unity'.[1] Manchester, in April 1774, states its aims 'to consider proper means for the security and encouragement, of trade of that town and its neighbourhood'.[2] Liverpool, founded in June 1774, had a convoluted statement tied up with trying to take over the Corporation's town dues and local representation; it can be summarized: 'common utility, mutual wants, and the necessity of mutual services . . . The amazing extension of commerce . . . affords a most convincing proof of the wisdom . . . [of] an increase of attention, and an increase of public expense [by] . . . raising a fund for the public support of commercial interests of this port'.[3] Glasgow had similar lengthy, but broader, aims in 1783 which can be summarized as: protection and improvement of trade and manufactures; establishing rules of foreign trade; discussion of memorials to government; aiding members applying to the Board of Trade etc.; and procuring relief of grievances affecting trade and manufactures.[4]

These concepts were transferred between chambers. Liverpool's subscription structure was probably copied from Jersey.[5] Glasgow's charter was copied and adapted by the next group of chambers, Dublin and Belfast later in 1783, and Edinburgh in 1785. When Dublin was relaunched in 1820 it obtained the constitutions of Glasgow, Cork, Waterford, Birmingham, and the former Dublin chamber. It stated its purpose as 'promotion of the interests of the trade and commerce of the city of Dublin [and] to increasing and take cognisance of such matters, laws and regulations affecting the commerce and manufactures of Ireland generally'.[6] Belfast's foundation statement was 'to attend to the interests of commerce, to have a watchful attention to the proceedings of parliament respecting trade in both Kingdoms';[7] this was restated in 1823: 'to ensure a general cooperation, both among its members, and with other communities, for the general good. Without this, the wants of the public, and their complaints, would be unheard, or not directed to the proper channel'.[8] Manchester's refoundation in 1794 stated objectives 'to adopt such regulations as may tend to the benefit of their trade, add to its safety, and promote more regular payments [i.e. business credit]' and 'to watch over the interests of their trade at large, and co-operate jointly in all applications to government, or in any measure which may from time to time, be thought necessary for the good of the whole'. Londonderry in 1790 aimed 'to promote the interests of trade . . . by the union of commercial knowledge'.[9] Limerick in 1807 stated its purpose as 'the promotion, regulation, and protection of trade . . . [forming] such plans and regulations for the trade in general as they shall deem advantageous

---

[1] Article 13 of founding *Deed*, Jersey chamber minutes, 1768; also see Syvret and Stevens (1998), p. 192.
[2] Report of the first public meeting of the Manchester chamber, *Williamsons Liverpool Advertiser*, 15 April 1774; also quoted in *The London Magazine or Gentleman's Monthly Intelligencer*, 43 (1774), p. 502.
[3] *Draft of an Article, for settling a chamber of commerce in Liverpool*, 21 April 1774; in Heywood papers, Liverpool Athenaeum, Gladstone MSS no. 52; see also Bennett (2010).
[4] Glasgow chamber rules, abbreviated; Glasgow chamber history etc.
[5] Bennett (2010), pp. 16–17.
[6] Dublin chamber, General Meeting minutes, 17 October 1820 and 7 November 1820.
[7] Belfast chamber minutes, 27 May 1783.
[8] Belfast, Report to Council, 19 November 1823; D1857/1/G/3.
[9] Londonderry chamber, 1793, statement of founding purpose, p. 10 in *Translation of the Charter Granted by King Charles II . . .* ; ESTC microfilm T193966 (original in Bodleian).

and likely to extend it'.[10] Guernsey was refounded in 1832 restating its 1808 aims 'to watch over the commercial interest of the Island and to deliberate on and to adopt all such means and measures' necessary.[11] These statements all sought to interlock local geography, local needs, and unity of purpose for voice, across a wide range of *general* local business interests; as stated by London's proposal of 1823: 'an institution comprising in itself an union of every description of mercantile interest'.[12]

The early American chambers had similar objectives. For New York in early 1768, its purpose was 'promoting and encouraging commerce, supporting industry, adjusting disputes relative to trade and navigation, and procuring such laws and regulations as may be found necessary for the benefit of trade in general'.[13] In Charleston in 1774 its object, in addition to immediate responses to revolutionary pressures, was 'to dispatch such business as may be brought before them, and establish such further regulation . . . as may be necessary'; i.e. to resolve local disputes.[14] In Boston, a 1763 refoundation of its earlier commercial society as a de facto chamber was a 'society for the emerging trade and commerce within the preserve of Massachusetts Bay'.[15]

General unity of interests has remained the core chamber concept up to the present. Thus Manchester's later refoundation gives its key objective, summarized in its Code of Laws for the 1870s, as 'the promotion of measures calculated to benefit and protect the trading interests of its members, and the general trade of the city and neighbourhood of Manchester'.[16] Bradford chamber in 1900 notes that whilst 'its operations have literally extended "from China to Peru" . . . the chamber has never lost sight of what is after all the primary duty of a chamber of commerce, viz., the safeguarding of local interests'.[17] Nottingham in 1949 stated its view that the chamber 'has a unique standing as a voluntary association of civic-minded citizens engaged in collective efforts to promote the welfare of the community'.[18] Swindon stated its purpose in 1958: 'to foster and stimulate good business relationships in the town . . . [and] to promote and maintain a spirit of goodwill and unity among all connected with trade and commerce'.[19] Warrington in 1961 stated the chambers as 'the only body which represents . . . the views of local industry as a whole'.[20] A typical modern view is that of Southampton in 2006: 'Our main role . . . is to be the local and independent voice of business.'[21]

---

[10] Limerick chamber minutes, initial pages, May 1807, founding articles and role of committee.
[11] Guernsey chamber minutes, 21 January 1832: 'Fundamental Principles'.
[12] Report of committee to form a London chamber; *Morning Chronicle*, 19 March 1824.
[13] Quoted in Stevens (1867); see also Bishop (1918).
[14] *Rules of Charleston Chamber of Commerce*, Rule 1; Library Company of Philadelphia 13194; also Rogers (1974), p. 161.
[15] Andrews (1916), pp. 3–7.
[16] Manchester chamber, *Annual Report* (1871), p. 39.
[17] Bradford chamber, *Annual Report* (1900), p. 14.
[18] Nottingham chamber minutes, Report of Council, 1948–9, p. 7.
[19] Swindon chamber, *Rules* (1958).
[20] Warrington chamber, *Yearbook* (1961), p. 22.
[21] Southampton and Fareham chamber, *Directory* (2006), p. 7.

The ABCC view was that chambers were 'a centre for . . . utterance of commercial opinion . . . the "eyes and ears" of commerce'.[22] An ABCC statement published in many local chamber journals in the 1920s was that chambers contributed 'to the common welfare', offering 'an important and, in some localities, the only agency whereby men are afforded the opportunity to assist in this way. . . . Organised to secure not petty business advantage for individuals but to furnish organised aid to individuals and firms to enable them to build up the highest type of commercial development for the benefit of every inhabitant.'[23]

Voluntary and independent

These statements are important not only for crystallizing the purpose as the local community of business interests, but also the intertextuality of voluntary basis: voice had to be *independent* and free of external influence. Voice was developed democratically by a group of elected officers of the chamber, whose legitimacy came not from the state, but from the support of their peers and their position as business representatives of the local economy. They believed they had a separate and superior knowledge of economic issues, because they were dealing with these issues daily, directly, and recurrently, whilst government had wider roles and different objectives, and could not be expected to be expert nor always sympathetic to business interests. The context of Britain, Ireland, and early America has also to be borne in mind: all associations are voluntary: associations are private law bodies, with no compulsory membership. This is different from many European systems.

The central importance of voluntary leadership is echoed again and again in chamber papers.[24] One of the earliest statements is that by Patrick Colquhoun in his 1788 plan for a national chamber agency: the 'information which is *only* to be obtained by the voluntary communications of commercial people';[25] i.e. the information to be derived through public appointments like the 18th-century French chambers of commerce was likely to be tainted. Bradford restated the principles in 1951: the chamber 'must equip itself so that it could tackle the problems which now beset the business world. Its status must be such that it could call upon first class voluntary service from men who were willing to serve the interests of the community and business as a whole'.[26] The strength of voluntarism is therefore not only superior information but also independence. In the ABCC view of 1949, this made chambers an alternative democratic force: 'in this country, all the separate chambers are voluntary organisations, autonomous and independent of government or any outside influence. . . . Their constitution is democratic, being governed by its members through honorary officers and a Council, acting

---

[22] Algernon Firth, president of ACC; quoted in ACC *Monthly Proceedings*, 4 October (1917), p. 9.

[23] Written by Dunwoody Secretary of ABCC, quoted e.g. in Belfast chamber, *Journal*, July (1924), pp. 51–2.

[24] Though there is an important exception to this in the debate about public 'status'; see Chapter 7.

[25] *Plan of a Public Agency in London*: Glasgow chamber, TD 1670/4/52, October 1788, p. 1; emphasis added.

[26] Bradford chamber, *Journal* (December 1951), p. 16.

according to the provisions of its own constitution, and depending for its revenue on the subscriptions of its members.'[27] Indeed chambers had begun to call themselves 'parliaments of commerce' from the 1880s.

Deliberated governance

Local cohesion, independence, democratic decision making, and processes of transparent governance were thus the clear underpinnings of the system. But how was this to allow the formation of a coherent voice? The challenge was, and is, that opinion is often divided, and a strong policy position is difficult to present. As a result, voice may be restricted to the lowest common denominator of all interests, which ends up saying nothing of value for the chamber or government. Analysis of the internal discussions of chamber lobby campaigns, considered in detail in Chapters 9 and 10, shows how they overcame this challenge in major campaigns; but also how on some occasions there was no scope for agreement so that the chamber, or some members, remained 'neutral'. The general process was by deliberation.

Deliberation was the process that delivered two key strengths. First, it helped to manage diverse views: open debate allowed the talking out of a problem, which could lead to a strong case that achieved agreement and could be convincingly advocated. Deliberation was thus a way to form a common view: to align interests. In early chambers which had a strong dissenter membership, the Quaker tenet may have been influential: that votes should never be held, but instead decisions should rest on a 'sense of the meeting'. This required long discussions in order for all to develop a common and consensual view. Deliberation was thus a key part of a process; almost a devotional act of membership.

Second, deliberation was a means to increase the strength of the lobby arguments and to evidence the problem: it moved beyond a collective opinion and assertion to a reasoned case and credible statement of a lobby position. This of course is not the equivalent of modern evidenced-based research, but was a process of convincing each other and testing it against the opinions of leaders who understood how it might be presented to government; and success often depended on careful husbandry of opinion—leadership. For the 1914 London chamber, Musgrave notes that it offered to 'correctly interpret commercial opinion'. Deliberation was not an end in itself, but a means to help inform and shape opinion. The chamber 'is not an academic debating society, but a practical deliberative body . . . a "clearing house for commercial ideas" [that] involve at least an intelligent appreciation of the views and opinions of experts'.[28] Government would gain from a chamber's deliberations: 'Ministers would themselves derive a sort of security for the consideration that every subject had undergone the investigation of such a body before it was propounded to government'.[29]

[27] ABCC Report, *Financial Times*, 9 March 1949; reprinted in Westminster chamber *Yearbook* (1949), p. 40.
[28] Musgrave (1914), pp. 6 and 61; see also Olson (1971), p. 61.
[29] R. Shaw, quoted in report on establishment of a London chamber of commerce, *Morning Chronicle*, 29 August 1823.

Third, deliberation brought expertise to bear. A chamber 'would be ready to furnish to His Majesty's ministers accurate and practical information on all points connected with the commerce . . . [and] contribute to improve regulations, and the municipal and fiscal laws affecting the trade, manufactures and navigation'. A chamber had experts among the members

> who, from their habits and experience, would be qualified to afford the best infor-
> mation, and which by being furnished by an associated body, embracing in itself
> so many interests, would not be exposed to the suspicion of interested or partial
> motives; but entitle their opinions to respect, and aid most powerfully in resisting
> importunities which have for their object undue protection in favour of particular
> classes . . . conveying to the councils of the nation the *deliberate opinion* of the great
> mercantile body upon any public commercial question . . . [and] in many cases remove
> misconceptions.[30]

That is, business people usually know better than government what the effects of policies will be, and with proper marshalling can provide the best evidence base. Or, as put by the small Bath chamber in 1902, 'the chamber forms a convenient and reliable defence', where government 'may threaten to act in a manner calculated to check the cause of commercial prosperity'.[31]

In the earliest bodies, deliberation was in meetings of the whole membership. Some had massive attendance and involvement. Others had meagre support. As time progressed, specialist committees, the chamber's executive committee or council, or the leading members, took more responsibility for the lobby positions adopted. As described by Musgrave, secretary of the London chamber in 1914, the committees of the chamber acted as its 'practical deliberative body, composed of 137 selected representatives . . . willing to agree to differ without friction on any one controversial point when there are ninety-nine others where agreement is possible. On these lines business can always be done.'[32] This in turn demonstrates the critical role of the chamber's senior staff (secretary or chief executive) and the elected voluntary officers, and the chemistry of working relationships between them, who became the key facilitators of the deliberation process.[33] The use of committees aided this process, but ultimately leadership and facilitation was required, and the statement of voice had to be signed off by the council of the chamber and defended to the members.

Today deliberation is supplemented by consultation over a wider range of views, and more evidence is collected. Electronic communications can facilitate the process and involve more people at lower cost. Committees are more significant in shaping responses. But the processes remain essentially the same. As recognized in a 1965 comment: 'it is absolutely useless to "protest", "deplore" or "regret" . . .

---

[30] Report of committee to form a London chamber, *Morning Chronicle*, 19 March 1824; emphasis added.

[31] Bath chamber, *First Annual Report* (1902), p. 4.

[32] Musgrave (1914), p. 61; the 137 representatives refers to members of section committees and Council.

[33] Discussed further in Chapter 6.

without the possession of indisputable fact and evidence'.[34] Modern lobbying is no different in requiring cases to be very well developed to have any hope of influence.

Marketing voice to members: self-esteem

Positions stated as lobbies had to carry the whole membership, or at least win acquiescence. In early chambers this was often done through the press or leaflets that informed everyone: the members not able to be present at the discussion, and the wider public. It was thus a very transparent process. As committees and more formal structures developed more effort had to be made to justify and to sell policy positions to members. Inevitably some of this is self-congratulatory and self-promotional. For example, statements such as Worcester 1839: 'a body of individuals, associated for one common object, is far more likely to succeed than one individual by his single exertions'.[35] Or Isle of Wight, 1910: 'they had two courses open to them, to sit still and grumble, or to combine and bring pressure to bear for remedying matters in a way which no isolated action would secure (hear, hear). Union was strength, and with a chamber of commerce they would secure some benefits without even fighting for them, so effective was the force of cooperation'.[36]

Numerous annual reports also summarize and applaud the chambers' actions on particular national or local issues. For example, Liverpool's *Abstract* covering its first three years, 1774–7, gives a self-assessment of success claiming that on the 32 issues with a definite resolution, 12 (37.5%) were judged by the chamber as successful, a further three were probably successful, and five had some influence even if not entirely positive. Thus 62.5% had some positive outcome.[37] Or in Bradford in 1900: 'in numerous instances action has been taken with a view to removing or ameliorating taxes and restraints on trade, improving and extending railway, postal and telegraphic facilities, promoting or (when necessary) preventing commercial legislation, fostering the growth and improving the quality of wool, mohair, etc., settling commercial disputes, giving information and advice on commercial matters, and generally furthering the trading interests of the city and district'.[38]

Statements by senior government members in support of chamber representational inputs were also important, and frequently quoted. For example, Rt. Hon. G. J. Goschen spoke strongly in favour of the London chamber's establishment: 'chambers of commerce will be so infinitely valuable [because] they will bring to bear, if their meetings are properly attended, the intelligence and actual views of the members of the various trades and manufacturers', which was greatly preferable to

---

[34] ABCC, Association of Chamber Secretaries: *Report on the Role of Chambers of Commerce in the Changing Economy;* paper SA. 20-65, September 1965.

[35] Worcester chamber, *Report of a Provisional Committee Appointed to Promote the Formation of a Chamber*, 7 May 1939, p. 4.

[36] Speech by Mr A. Millward JP (of Ryde), inaugural meeting of Isle of Wight chamber; *Isle of Wight County Press*, 4 March 1910.

[37] Analysis of *Abstract* of activities, Bennett (2010), table 2.

[38] Bradford chamber, *Annual Report* (1900), p. 14.

the process of petitioning.[39] The accepted value of chamber voice was consideration and deliberation. Similar comments give grounds for believing at least some of the chambers' self-congratulatory comments. The relatively slow development of other rival bodies, up to about 1916, also suggests that the chambers were filling most of the potential market for local voice up to that time.

3.3 INSTABILITY AND LATENCY?

The chamber of commerce system evolved relatively slowly through a series of experiments, and not all early chambers were continuously successful. Early chambers sometimes required revival. The causes of instability have often been misinterpreted. For example, in his history of the Leeds chamber, Beresford states that 'dissolution and reformation occur regularly', due to 'sectional troubles ... [that] plagued the eighteenth century chambers'; and 'the union of chambers in the eighteenth century had floundered because of divergent interests'.[40] Similarly, Redford, commenting on Manchester, claims that the decline of commercial societies at the end of the 18th century was due to fundamental divergence of opinion over tariff policy as well as general 'dissatisfaction with the financial results of collective action'.[41] Unfortunately Ilersic and Liddle, and Taylor reproduce these views. Rose states that 'the majority of early associations were a localised response to a specific set of circumstances, [hence] it is not surprising that they were generally short-lived and ineffective'; whilst Daunton asserts that 'the main concern of many employers was their own town ... with attempts to move to national coverage ... short lived'.[42]

The assessment here is different. Early chambers were part of a more general and continuous thrust of development, with national and international focus, and the general momentum of the new concept of chamber was certainly sustained. Even in local cases where there at first appears to have been a dissolution, there was often a succession structure to a new body. For many early chambers the constitutional structure is also confusing. Jersey's founding Article 14 states that 'each subscription is to be for three years certain'. This led to a process by which the chamber had to be dissolved by revoking the previous agreement (allowing members to retrieve their capital), and reconstituted at the end of each three-year period, with the new subscribers then forming a new shareholding membership, with the capital reinvested. The whole model was more akin to a debenture than the annual subscriptions that are familiar today. Jersey retained this structure until 1837.[43] Gaps in its *formal* records occurred, but the chamber continued to operate. This model was also used in Liverpool over 1774–7, and was probably used in Manchester for two

[39] Quoted in Musgrave (1914), London chamber history, p. 6.
[40] Beresford (1951), Leeds chamber history, pp. 13, 62, and 103.
[41] Redford (1934), p. 45; see also p. 60.
[42] Rose (2000), p. 135; Daunton (1995), p. 281; see also Langton (1984).
[43] Jersey chamber minutes 1768–1837; it became an annual subscription of £1 and £2; 2 March 1837.

periods over 1774–80; but both chambers continued to operate over these re-establishments. Gaps in record survival and failure to understand these structures has confused some commentators.

There is also a failure to recognize that the very effectiveness of the chambers, particularly the General Chamber in its 1785–7 campaigns, caused some local chambers to seek a lower profile, to lobby quietly, and avoid 'noise'.[44] It is also important to recognize that there were difficulties of holding formal meetings by any associations after 1796 as a result of anti-sedition laws; minutes could be used as evidence of treason. As a result, instead of dying, some of these early chambers became invisible. This is different from a political agitation where media coverage is often seen as an end itself, to stimulate recruitment and raise financial support.[45] This makes their history more difficult to trace.

Many chambers also had complex and very burdensome rules for attendance and quorums. This meant that they might easily hold meetings where the conditions were not met and thus formal minutes could not be recorded. In any case the minutes were usually kept by volunteers who might sometimes be dilatory, and preservation of records can be haphazard. Thus lack of formal minutes alone cannot be taken as evidence of non-existence. In other cases there may have been no activities, or merely a 'watching brief' kept. For example in Belfast over 21 April to 20 October 1784 there were many meetings, but 'no business'; for the period May 1787 to May 1791 there were no recorded minutes, but minutes resume continuously after the gap.[46] Waterford has no minutes between 1797 and 1804, but when the minutes restarted the secretary was thanked for his work and there is reference to adjusting fees agreed in 1797 and continuing subscriptions, so some form of chamber continued.[47] Similarly, in Birmingham over 1787–93 there is an on-off evolution of the early chamber, but most of the same people were involved at each stage.[48] In Leeds, the continuous minutes of 1785–90 have a gap from 1790 until 1793, when the result of dye tests initiated in 1790 is recorded; there is then no further minute, though newspapers record the committee in 1800 and it participated in the Union of chambers until at least 1805.[49] North Staffordshire had an early existence and a potters chamber in the 1770s, was re-established over 1831–51 as a potters' association for wages and prices, existed in 1860 and became a member of ACC, but was refounded in 1874 as a wider body becoming a true chamber (though even then over 70% of its members were potters), but some form of meetings was clearly continuous.[50]

There were also succession structures that are not always obvious. For example in Dundee the formal minutes of the Forfarshire chamber finish in December 1830,

[44] See Chapter 9.
[45] See summaries in Tarrow (1994).
[46] Belfast chamber, minutes and Council papers.
[47] Waterford chamber minutes, 7 February 1804, 3 April 1805.
[48] Note the continuity of business leaders shown in the listings given in Wright (1913).
[49] Leeds chamber minutes; see Chapter 9. Beresford (1951) incorrectly suggests the chamber was invoked in 1800 only to dignify 'formality and continuity'.
[50] North Staffordshire chamber *Yearbook* (1920).

with an AGM in June 1831; but letterbooks refer to decisions at meetings and show it was active until 1834. Moreover, when reconstituted as Dundee chamber in 1836, over 60% of the committee were the same people.[51] Dover chamber was established in 1850; became inactive by the late 1860s; was re-established in 1870 chiefly to raise substantial donations for a new technical college; needed re-establishing again in 1879; was reconstituted as a chamber of trade in 1885, reverted to a chamber of commerce in 1890; but continued in some form continuously throughout.[52] In Salisbury no accounts were produced over 1916–18, and there were no meetings over late 1917 to early 1918 but the chamber clearly continued in existence.[53] In Limerick it was complained that there was often little business in formal chamber meetings in the 1930s, but the chamber building was full of other groups holding meetings mostly attended by chamber members.[54]

Thus there was an actual or 'latent' existence of many bodies that at first sight seem unstable. Formal revival with new minutes and re-established formality often depended on circumstances, degree of threat, and need, especially the need to be able to claim a representational base or legitimacy which required resolutions and minutes. At other times a few leaders could act through informal liaison, using their informal networks, without the tedium of minutes and the problems of managing open meetings; and they could call special open meetings when necessary; businesses tend to organize only when they need to. This is clearly evident in early Birmingham, where Samuel Garbett only undertook the burdensome task of holding meetings if there was something to discuss.[55] The early history of chambers, largely dismissed by Beresford, and suggested as ineffective by Redford, needs careful revisiting.

3.4 SERVICE DEVELOPMENT: INDIVIDUAL OR COLLECTIVE?

From the earliest stages, the chambers were seeking not only voice, but also some limited service provision to members. Some of this was for individual businesses: for example, commercial dispute arbitration or provision of advice and answering enquiries. Some was broader based: for example, the provision of meeting rooms, coffee rooms and hotels, libraries and publications. Some were major collective regulatory services, as in several early Irish chambers and industrial chambers in England, which ran butter quality marks, weigh-houses and control schemes, managed harbours, or operated other market activities and local taxes. This spread of objectives to include services led to some significant challenges and tensions.

---

[51] Terrell (2006), chamber history, p. 11. Terrell also believes that the chamber narrowed to exclude Angus: letter to author, 3 March 2006.

[52] Dover chamber, minutes. The minute of the 1870 re-establishment begins with the technical school subscription without any discussion, indicating that the matter had been under consideration for some time; the minutes continued because of the need for the formality to levy subscriptions.

[53] Salisbury chamber history, p. 6.

[54] Limerick chamber minutes, 22 February 1938.

[55] Wright (1913), Birmingham chamber history.

Later statements in memoranda and articles of incorporation began to include slightly wider service functions. For example, Middlesbrough's memorandum and articles of 1873 stated the objectives as 'the advancement of the commerce and manufacturers of Middlesbrough and its neighbourhood; . . . The collection and dissemination of statistical and other information relating to the said commerce and manufacturers, and the promotion of all public measures having their object the environment thereof; and arbitration.' Similarly, Southampton's incorporation in 1875 states its objectives as 'the promotion of trade and commerce, the shipping and manufactures of the town and port; . . . The collection and dissemination of statistical and other information relating to trade, commerce, shipping and manufactures; the promotion, supporting, or opposing legislative and other measures affecting the aforesaid interests; arbitration; . . . all other things as may be conducive to the extension of trade, commerce, or manufactures'. Information provision, statistical information gathering, and local promotion became widespread 19th-century service functions.

Nevertheless, during the 19th and early 20th centuries, there was no question that voice remained the key activity. This is summed up by a report on the re-establishment of the Leeds chamber in 1857, 'nothing could justify a chamber interfering in the details of practical business or with individual [firms]. There are sufficient public questions in which we are all interested.'[56]

Dual functions: voice and services

By WW1, and in a few chambers much earlier, services were being developed on a major scale. Some of these services were collective goods, such as meetings, and publication of statistical information. Others were specific services available to individual members when required, such as arbitration, debt collection, coffee rooms and libraries, enquiry and advisory services, and certification. This was a natural evolution. General statements such as that by Nottingham in 1932 that the chamber 'exists to assist and benefit the trading community in general'[57] easily evolved progressively from representation of voice, to collective services, and then to specific help. Some of this activity naturally evolved from data collection related to lobbying: 'one of the most useful functions a chamber of commerce can perform is to circulate all the information possible on economic questions and thus help to form a healthy public opinion which can resist quack remedies and keep our trade and commerce on sound principles'.[58] Following WW2 the balanced concern for collective representational *and* individual services was well established: the evolution of the bundled service package had emerged.

A good summary of the position is that in Derby in 1916:

---

[56] *Leeds Mercury,* 1851, quoted in Beresford (1951), Leeds chamber history, p. 59.
[57] Nottingham chamber, *Journal* (1932).
[58] Thomas Cook, retired president, Burnley chamber, in *Handbook of Burnley* (1927), p. 13.

the functions of chambers of commerce may be roughly divided under two heads—deliberate and administrative. The discussions that arise cover a wide range of subjects, which are viewed naturally from a commercial standpoint and judged by their relation to the interests of manufacturers, merchants and employers generally.... As an administrative body the chamber is now indispensable to many of its members, especially those who are interested directly or indirectly in foreign or colonial trade. Statistics and information concerning the trade and industry of every part of the world are collected, indexed, filed, and where necessary disseminated, and details of any subject of commercial importance can be obtained through its influence.[59]

Similarly in Swindon, in 1920, there is a clear statement of its multiple objectives:

To promote a spirit of friendliness and unity amongst traders by means of meetings ...; to obtain and impart to members information which may be useful in the prevention of bad debts; to assist members by means of advice, arbitration or legal assistance...in cases of difficulty or disputes that may arise between them and wholesale houses, railway companies, or others; to assist in the defence of any action against a member which shall be considered unjust, frivolous or vexatious; and generally, to advance the interest of all members as circumstances arise and funds permit.[60]

The dual emphasis, collective/representational, and individual/services, was national policy of the chambers by 1949. An article in the *Financial Times* of that date stated the chamber role as based on two broad functions:[61]

on the one hand a part of their organisation considers and takes action upon matters of interest to the business community or a substantial part of it. It may examine a Bill before Parliament and make representations to the Government; or it may press for modifications to render existing legislation more practicable;...or it may tender advice, either on its own initiative or by invitation, on the outstanding industrial, economic and financial problems of the day. On the other hand, a part of a Chamber's organisation concentrates on helping individual members in their specific problems. ...Although it is the former class of work which brings a Chamber of Commerce into the public eye, yet, *in the last analysis*, it is the supply of information, guidance and help to individual members on an innumerable selection of separate items,...by which its services are ultimately judged.

The ABCC view (the sponsors of the 1949 *Financial Times* article) had, therefore, now evolved strongly to a position where services were what kept a chamber alive—it was believed that it was the prime motive for membership. This is a vivid statement of potential sidelining of voice as a by-product. The 1949 statement goes beyond agreed ABCC policy of the time and may reflect chamber activities in the aftermath of WW2. The statement also goes beyond any considered analysis of the state of chamber management capacity at the time. In 1950 the staff of

[59] Derby chamber, *Commercial Yearbook* (1916), p. 41.
[60] Swindon chamber, *Annual Report* (1920), inside front cover.
[61] *Financial Times,* 9 March 1949; in Westminster chamber *Yearbook* (1949), pp. 39–43, emphasis added.

chambers still consisted chiefly of just a single secretary with limited clerical assistance (median staff numbers 1.75, mode 2.0), and median non-subscription income was only about 12% of total income. Thus significant service capacity did not generally exist, though it was certainly available in the larger chambers.

Modern statements embody this bundled structure into the terminology of *voice* and *business support*. Hull's balance of its aims is stated in 2005 as: 'A strong, vibrant business voice and private sector business support organisation'.[62] Or Southampton in 2006: 'some of our schemes will save you money; others will keep you out of jail. All could help you get more out of your business.... Our main role, however, is to be the local and independent voice of business'.[63]

3.5 MANAGING THE 'OFFER' TO MEMBERS: 'BUNDLING'

Allegiance to a cause, and support for voice to lobby for their area, was the key founding force behind the early chambers. But it is important to remember that we are dealing in this book with bodies that had economic intent: their members were businesses, or their owners, directors, and leading managers. They had economic reasons to found and join a chamber. In terms of the 'theory of the firm' an association, such as a local chamber, can provide support to the decision making and competitive position of a business, and it can add to the resource composition of the firm.[64] This is why the bundled product is so important.

A classification of chamber services

Bundled services combine two dimensions of chamber interactions with members: first, whether the service is only available to the member; second, whether individually tailored or for all businesses, as shown in Table 3.1.

Individual excludable services (the top left of Table 3.1) are delivered to an individual firm and are available only through membership; tailored and targeted on the strategic needs of the business. Although they are membership services, they may carry a fee, which may or may not be at a discount to the market. For example, liability insurance and legal advice services are usually provided at a discount, but other services, such as room hire, are often at similar rates to that available elsewhere, offering a benefit of location or brand. Many chambers also provide in-house consultancy services that are at similar cost to commercial consultancies but have the advantage of the trust, technical knowledge, or independence that are associated with the chamber brand. Information provision, however, is often free to members, at least at a basic level. A modern example of certification services is ChamberSign, which is a form of pre-assured member certification.[65] Badging of

---

[62] Hull chamber, *Report and Accounts* (2004–5), p. 4.
[63] Southampton and Fareham chamber, *Directory* (2006), p. 7.
[64] Based on the resource theory of the firm: see e.g. Priem and Butler (2001); Edwards et al. (2002).
[65] See Chapter 8.

Table 3.1. A classification of chamber of commerce activities

	Individual	Collective
Excludable	■ Information, helpline ■ Advice and consultancy ■ Specific services (training, recruitment, translation) ■ Member discounts ■ Certification, badge, and kudos ■ Some government contracts to deliver services	■ Coffee rooms, hotels ■ Meeting rooms, libraries ■ Meetings and groups ■ Bulk purchasing, group insurance schemes ■ Some social events ■ Self-regulation
Non-excludable	■ Exhibitions and events ■ Trade missions ■ Sale of services ■ Arbitration ■ Some social events ■ Some government contracts to deliver services	■ Lobbying, representation ■ Promotion of locality ■ Economic and other surveys ■ Newsletters and journals ■ Websites, directories ■ Collective bargaining

Source: Developed from Bennett and Ramsden (2007).

membership can indicate a form of kudos or status, which was important to NCT, who frequently displayed membership in shop windows, and is still used by FSB. However, chambers of commerce have usually sought to prevent use of the chamber's name other than on their own communications.

Collective excludable services are provided equally to all members, usually as a benefit of the subscription, but are not accessible by non-members. Examples are group insurance, group debt collection, bulk purchasing, member-only social events and forums, libraries, and member meeting rooms. A special group of collective services from which others are excluded is self-regulation, where membership is subject to test of standards, conduct, or qualifications; this has been used by many trade associations, but rarely by chambers.

Collective services that are not non-excludable. Some aspects of collective provision that are the *raison d'être* are not excludable, particularly acting as a voice 'to represent the interests of their members', which usually cannot exclude non-members from the benefits, locally or nationally. All relevant firms benefit from a change in new government regulations that an association may win, such as reducing taxes or bureaucracy. Similarly the many surveys of the economy or their area provide information benefits to all, irrespective of whether they are members. This also tends to apply to newsletters and journals (and more recently to email newsletters and website news pages). They may appear to be excludable services, but frequently they are widely disseminated to both members and non-members, and indeed are often used as part of their membership marketing. Non-excludable collective services potentially create a large pool of free riders, who benefit but do not pay.

Individual non-excludable services often overlap with those that are excludable. Many services offered to members as individual benefits involve free provision or discounts, and they are often also offered to non-members, but at a higher cost; such as exhibitions and events where members usually receive a discount, but there is also widespread general marketing since members and the chamber are often anxious to get maximum attendance. Services available in the market may be offered to members through discount schemes, such as health insurance, book discounts, etc. Services provided on behalf of government also tend to fall into this category. For example, over 1993–2010 the government's Business Link, which was managed by chambers and some other agents as partners or franchisees, offered individual services to firms. These services were usually available to all, although membership discounts might apply.

A special class of services are social events, which may offer excludable or non-excludable benefits, depending on the criteria for attendance used. Member-only activity can confer exclusivity and shape the character of the networking and improve solidarity. Networking events are often one of the most important motives for chamber membership, especially for small firms.[66]

Tensions of 'bundling'

Because of the scope to manage exclusiveness for services, there has been considerable theoretical discussion of how members' demands and the managerial priorities of an association interact. In a seminal study, Olson highlighted the impediments to collective action: businesses have to agree a means to work together (e.g. through a constitution) and they have to find a way to finance, monitor, and maintain that mechanism. Because of the costs, some potential collective activity may have no efficient way to deliver it.[67] The overall transaction costs can be analysed and this has provided one means to understand what associations can provide efficiently, at realistic cost-benefit ratios, and compared to alternative means of provision.[68]

Detailed assessment of chambers suggests that their transaction cost advantages in supply of services lie with high frequency, medium cost, medium intensity, and high personnel and transaction specificity, as shown in Table 3.2. Cost and quality benefits are particularly important from the 'soft' supports of advice and information (which are major association activities), but also cover some 'hard' impacts (on profit and turnover), with chambers offering more benefit from the combination of 'hard' as well as 'soft' supports than most other associations. Their position as independent voices may also offer chamber services a brand advantage of trust as a 'friend', scope for close tailoring because of understanding of needs, and/or confidentiality of transactions,[69] as shown in the final row of Table 3.2.

[66] See e.g. Huggins (2000); Mekic (2007); also see Chapter 15.
[67] Olson (1971; first edition 1965).
[68] See e.g. Lindberg, Campbell, and Hollingsworth (1991); Schneiberg and Hollingsworth (1991); Taylor and Singleton (1993); Bennett (1996a, 1996b). For historical discussions see North (1985); Casson and Cox (1993); Casson and Rose (1997); Casson (1997); see also Weisbrod (1988, 1998).
[69] See e.g. Bennett and Robson (1999a, 2004b).

Table 3.2. Transaction cost characteristics of chamber-member activities in modern chambers of commerce

	Lobbying	Information provision	Export-import support	Business training, seminars	Business counselling, consultancy	Meeting rooms, libraries
Coordination costs	High	Low	Low	Moderate	Low	Moderate
Frequency	Low	Moderate	Moderate	Moderate	Low	High
Duration	Moderate	Low	Low	Low	Low	Low
Complexity	High	Mixed	Mixed	Moderate	Mixed	Low
Asset specificity: human	High	High	High	High	High	Low
plant and documents	—	High	—	—	—	High
premises	—	—	—	Moderate	—	Low
Connectedness to: similar transactions	High	High	High	High	High	High
other transactions	High	High	High	High	High	High
Trust	High	Moderate	High	Moderate	High	Low

Source: Extended from Bennett (1996b), table 4.

The costs of developing collective solutions tend to favour the incumbency of an existing body. Although market entry is easy and cheap—anyone can set up an association—successful large associations are extremely costly to develop. New services are often very costly to develop, and the larger the membership often the more costly this will be.[70] Hence, established brand recognition and visibility are very valuable assets, usually painstakingly slow to take hold. As a result, new demands tend to be directed to existing bodies like chambers because it is expected that they may have the appropriate staff to find a solution. This provides incumbent benefits, but their effectiveness may be questionable and their expertise may not stretch to new problems. This is reinforced, in general, by chambers often operating as a *bureau*: member loyalty is high (which reduces adaptability); zero-based budgeting is rare; and, because of the complexity of governance and management through collective committees, change is slow, inertia considerable. Thus 'path dependency', and slowness to change from the past, are major characteristics,[71] which increases vulnerability to changed frames and repertoires.

Collective action may also be difficult to sustain because of *free riders*. Solidarity alone may not be a sufficient incentive to join or remain as members, since firms and individuals can obtain some of the benefits anyway. As noted by Exeter chamber in 1930, lack of membership is 'evidence of a lack of public spirit and a mean desire to profit from the labours of others'.[72] This tends to result in smaller memberships than the market potential would suggest, and the services that are provided may be under-resourced and hence of lower quality than desirable. There are two potential strategies used by association managers to mitigate this problem.

One strategy is to appeal to altruism and solidarity: every firm should join because it is 'the thing to do'. This can work well in a small or focused constituency because the free rider will be known, visible, and hence open to embarrassment and social leverage.[73] This clearly worked to a significant extent in the early chambers, probably because their membership was small and their localities were very 'tight'—everyone knew each other. But smallness has the difficulty that the bodies may be too weak to have influence or to provide services. Also large size is not necessarily an impediment, if commitment is strong. This is the approach used by the Dublin chamber, which in 1989 neatly stated how it saw by-product effects being overcome: 'our members join not just out of self-interest. Many join from a sense of responsibility in relation to their community and their city and the opportunity the chamber offers to fulfil this duty. Backed by the resources our members provide, the chamber sets out to identify the real needs of our city and the opportunities for economic growth.'[74]

Because of the limitations, a second strategy to reduce free riding uses bundling. Individual benefits provide specific, tailored incentives to join and maintain

[70] Hansen (1985), pp. 93–4.
[71] Olson (1971); North (1990); Bennett (1998a).
[72] Exeter chamber, *Annual Report* (1930), p. 20.
[73] Olson (1971); Buchanan (1975); Chamberlain (1974).
[74] Dublin Chamber of Commerce, *Annual Report* (1989), p. 2.

membership, which help to finance the collective services that suffer from free-rider behaviour.[75] For chambers the mix combines the mutual and collective aspects of being a 'non-profit' (obligation, donor commitment), with the commercial characteristics of entrepreneurial services.[76] However, this can lead to a different tension: that the collective services become a *by-product* of individual services:[77] peripheralized, or starved of resources, which undermines their quality and impact. This results in managers having to maintain a delicate balance.

Nevertheless, bundling offers economies of scale and scope across and within service categories, chiefly by maximizing the benefits of specialist staff skills and marketing opportunities. This provides transaction cost advantages for chambers through interconnectedness, as shown in Table 3.2. It also raises entry barriers for competitors, and reduces search costs for the members by allowing cross-shopping.

Bundling also provides chambers with an 'insurance' offer: services can be marketed to businesses as a range that is available as a result of membership, 'just in case', and that they can use at different times or stages of their development. This can be particularly useful to start-up and smaller businesses that expect to use different types of services at different times.[78] Even if services are not used, there is reassurance that help is immediately available, at low cost, when needed.[79] The benefits of bundling also interact with brand, by creating a reality, or impression, of quality services; venerability offers potential to be trusted; and is one of the main components underpinning images of quality.[80] Impressions may also be a key element in stimulating solidarity, holding members of a chamber together.

Networks and search

A further aspect of chamber activities is the scope they offer for members to benefit from a ready-made network for marketing and meeting other business people and potential advisers. In modern times, as in the past, there is enthusiasm for marketing opportunities, networking events, and social activities that allow development of peer-to-peer exchange. As stated by Bath chamber in 1902, as well as lobbying, the 'additional advantage has been the interchange of views'.[81] An association can offer a network of connections beyond those that are narrowly economic, allowing trust to develop between firms: this draws on and contributes to 'un-traded interdependencies'.[82] The intensity and extent of such networks is probably fairly

---

[75] Often called the combining of the 'logic of services' and the 'logic of influence': Olson (1971); Streeck and Schmitter (1985); Van Waarden (1991); Dunleavy (1991).
[76] Hansmann (1980), p. 842; Ben-Ner and Van Hoomisson (1991).
[77] Olson (1971), chapter 6.
[78] Curran and Blackburn (1994), p. 93.
[79] See Bennett (1996a, 1996b); Bennett and Robson (2001); consistent with Curran and Blackburn (1994, p. 105) that many memberships are nominal (only 20% claimed to be active); for many, a 'just in case' decision.
[80] Clark (1995); Bennett and Ramsden (2007).
[81] Bath chamber, *First Annual Report* (1902), p. 4.
[82] See e.g. Lyons and Mehta (1997); Huggins (2000); Pearson and Richardson (2001); Wilson and Popp (2003a, 2003b).

constrained in practice,[83] but they nonetheless offer important potential membership benefits, and may be a mechanism of social motivation that encourages commitment. Indeed, historically, social activity itself was an important motive for joining chambers, both for the activity enjoyed, and also for any status of exclusiveness offered. For business people, social networking events continue as an important part of business life as they are of personal life.

Networking is likely to be strongest in a local or regional setting where any sense of community, clustering, and group solidarity is easier to develop: propinquity is a key facilitator of collective motivation, particularly in earlier economies where transport was more difficult. North has argued that reciprocity and 'gift exchange' was important historically, because it reduced the costs of agreement, monitoring, and enforcement.[84] Boswell suggests that communities of beliefs tend to be strongest within rather than between sectors, and where there is a conformity of firm size, similarity of needs/views about politics leading to a more ready consensus on lobbying activities, and similar industrial history or market structure. Thus homogeneity of business often facilitates associability.[85] Checkland argues that historically this was inter-bedded with other stimuli to network, such as social and religious affiliation, particularly in the new centres such as Birmingham, Glasgow, Liverpool, and Manchester.[86] Religion was a means for social mixing and possible upward progress, with its own norms and opportunities. The historical importance of such networks is critical to some early chamber formation, as shown in Chapters 4, 5, and 14.

Networks and trust

Underlying networking is the concept of trust; it is claimed that associations have a USP in providing 'trust goods'.[87] Trust is a major component of most chamber services, as indicated in Table 3.2. The trust structure of networks is controversial, with some authors arguing that 'calculative' or 'self-interested' trust is merely a special form of brand/repute.[88] Trust is certainly usually underpinned by 'hard' criteria of reliability, on-time delivery, and standards.[89] Indeed, hard evidence that trust was well placed was a key activity of trade protection societies, through a massive service of credit assessment and personal status enquiries.[90] Most key historical networks, like modern ones, required 'hard' content, whilst also drawing on 'soft' information. Thus, analysis of business relations in the early Atlantic trade shows that few trading arrangements existed without a written statement; 'informal

---

[83] As in Curran and Blackburn (1994); Huggins (2000); for historical evolution see Wilson and Popp (2003a).

[84] North (1985); see also Casson and Cox (1993); Casson and Rose (1997); Rose (2000).

[85] Boswell (1980); see also Lane (1997); Bennett (1998a); see also Ouchi (1980).

[86] Checkland (1952, 1958), for Liverpool; see also Bradley (1990); Hall (1998), pp. 19–20.

[87] e.g. Hansmann (1980); Ben-Ner and Van Hoomissen (1991); Chang and Tuckmann (1991).

[88] See e.g. Coleman (1988); Coleman (1990); Kreps (1999).

[89] Moellering (2003); Bennett and Robson (2004b); Ramsden and Bennett (2005).

[90] As summarized in Chapter 2.

partnerships' were underpinned by formal agreements, normally for two years or seven years, with specification of how capital, commissions, and profits would be shared.[91] As a balance to the overemphasis on personal trust in the academic literature, it is important to recognize that 'soft' trust (personal, affective, and relational) is most important in the search process for markets and trading partners, and for some capital assembly; it usually cannot (and has not historically) existed without 'hard' trust (reliability, written agreements, and evidence of economic results): trust has to deliver.

Networks are also an instrumental force, since developing 'unity' relies on sounding out member views, forming opinion, managing alignments, and deploying the support of key network members as critical ingredients of lobbying.[92] Networks underpin the all-important 'deliberation' function. Lobby statements are not merely opinion, but argued and balanced judgements based on weighing different interests, advocated and represented by those who are technical experts and acknowledged 'leaders'. Thus strong networks can be both cause and effect of successful collective voice.

Networks draw from and contribute to the institutional environment, locally and nationally. They offer and draw from social capital. This can be influenced by the level of government support (or resistance) to development of associations like chambers.[93] Government-backed supply of services by associations usually provides higher levels of trust and greater levels of satisfaction than government agencies; it is also usually more highly regarded than pure self-regulation, though this in turn depends on the form of government backing and the extent of government intrusiveness.[94] Chambers have benefited from some significant government backing, particularly export services, as discussed in Chapter 12; but they have also suffered from intrusion from mis-designed government programmes and perverse incentives, as discussed in Chapter 13.

Interaction with government: contracting and co-option

As well as experiencing support or intrusion from government, chambers can also provide services for government. There is an active modern debate about the boundaries of the state and how far government should provide directly or contract others to do so. This has taken on a new life in the UK and Ireland following the financial collapse of 2007–9 and the need for greater government thrift. In brief from this enormous literature, there are argued to be potential efficiency gains, cost reductions, quality increases, and better targeting to needs from contracting out public services. The extent of benefits depends on the services, type of demand, and type of alternative supplier. For business associations we are concerned primarily with economic services and supports. The argument for government provision at all

[91] Price (1980); Jensen (1963); Haggerty (2006).
[92] Galaskiewicz (1979); Knoke (1983); Lauman and Pappi (1976); Mizruchi (1982); Mizruchi and Galaskiewicz (1994); Lauman and Knoke (1987); Coleman (1988); Coleman (1990); DiMaggio and Powell (1990).
[93] Lamoreaux (1985); Tilly (2005).
[94] Bennett (2000); Lane (1997); Bennett and Robson (1999a, 2004b); Moellering (2003).

in this case is much weaker than for social welfare needs. An active debate has identified gaps in market provision ('market failures') for some business services, arising from lack of information, insufficient advice, access to finance, unwillingness to train staff, and other fields. But the extent of these supposed gaps is contentious, with enthusiasts for government involvement having to draw more on general welfare arguments rather than genuine market failures.[95] Most assessments concentrate on the narrowness and specificity of the gaps that exist, which need similarly constrained and focused government action.[96] In any case market failures are often balanced by government failures that limit the ability of the state to provide effective alternatives.[97]

Supply of government's business services through chambers, and other business associations, offers an intermediate means of provision: between state and market.[98] Where there is some aspect of a market failure, government can help to fill this gap. This can be through a direct contract; through co-opting involvement of individual business people or associations to help oversee/manage public provision; or through subsidy/support to the associations themselves. This has led to a very active debate about how 'mutuals' and 'non-profits' can best work with government.

Government and 'non-preferred' services

An outcome of working with government is that chambers widen their service bundle. As well as their USP activities and broader services, chambers can also take on *non-preferred services*.[99] These services can be either private (such as working with large companies to deliver a sub-contracted programme, or support for corporate social responsibility activities, as with Irish chambers in the 2000s) or government schemes where the chamber acts to deliver programmes to raise income, to improve outcomes, or to fend off rivals.

Services that support the collective mission and USP of chambers are unchallenging for the membership.[100] But when we move to *non-preferred services* major tensions arise. For commercial non-preferred services the risks are usually low and exit is easy if demand or supply prove unsatisfactory; though it might produce brand damage where the chamber is perceived as 'just another vendor', and might undermine donor and altruistic commitments of the membership or leadership. But the highest-risk category has been contracting for government services. The risk level depends on the nature of the service. A pure contract to deliver a delegated training or information service, for example, should be no more risky than other services. But a programme that comes with extensive ties and government managerial or political targets may undermine brand and service quality. If the programme

---

[95] e.g. Storey (1994, 2003).
[96] e.g. Bolton Report (1971); Bannock (1981, 1989); Bennett (2006).
[97] e.g. Wolf (1988); Le Grand (1991).
[98] Streeck and Schmitter (1985); Grant (1993, 2000); Bennett (1998a, 1998b).
[99] Weisbrod (1998), pp. 48–50.
[100] The following draws from and adapts Ben-Ner and Van Hoomisson (1991); James (1998); Weisbrod (1988, 1998); Wolf (1988); Le Grand (1991).

draws on the mutual obligations of members and the leadership, then the risks are even higher. This is a special form of crowding out by the public sector, under-mining donor and obligational commitment.[101] It challenges independence, mis-sion focus, and management efficiency, by encouraging over-bureaucratization, and distorts recruitment of personnel or existing managerial behaviour: so-called man-agement 'sorting'.[102] The worst result is that the staff and leadership of the chamber is so distorted that they are no longer fit for the core mission. This is a form of the 'Samaritan's dilemma': those who might support the chamber hold back because government is now seen to be taking the financial load, or their altruism is displaced by others (chamber staff or volunteers) seeking profit or aggrandizement with government rather than serving members.[103]

The survivors in this situation are those with strongest underlying assets, most diverse revenues, highest operating margins,[104] or who are politically strong enough to bend government towards more economically sustainable options. This has been one of the key challenges facing the UK chambers after the development, then withdrawal, of TEC, Business Link, and other government schemes over 1990–2010. Chambers Ireland has been similarly challenged through involvement with EU social and other programmes with low operating margins and high administrative overheads, as discussed in Chapter 13.

3.6 CONTENTION AND CHANGE

Associations may exist purely because they provide lower transaction costs as a result of their unique market position as collective bodies, but economic benefits alone, even for business associations, are not usually enough to sustain them. Bundling for chambers is distinct from market bundling, because it involves a degree of linking social or political commitment to economic services; there are thus 'soft' incentives as well as 'hard' ones.[105]

Campaigning and 'a cause'

For chambers of commerce, their self-identification as a 'movement' that was 'campaigning' was explicit and clear from the outset, and was maintained in the terminology used in their literature, especially that of their national association. This changed in the 1970s to a more service-focused concept of 'network' or 'system'. For the chambers of trade and agriculture, founded on a more specific principle of gaining attention for specific interests, the terminology of 'campaign' and 'movement' tended to continue.

---

[101] Feldstein (1980); Rose-Ackerman (1987); Steinberg (1991).
[102] Weisbrod (1988).
[103] Buchanan (1975); Bennett and Krebs (1991, Chapter 3); Bennett, Krebs, and Zimmermann (1993), pp. 155–6.
[104] Chang and Tuckman (1991).
[105] Opp (1986).

The early chambers were essentially campaigning for specific 'causes', within a broader attack on reforming the structures of government, trade, and business involvement, at a time when these were subjects of vigorous contention and presented significant external threats. As noted by Hansen, a threat offers the potential for losses, and it was this that was as much a stimulus for chamber membership as benefits:[106] 'bads' can be more important than benefits as a stimulus, particularly if potential threats are large. Threats of 'bads' are still usually the main motives for chamber campaigns today.

The motives for campaigns have been analysed in many studies, but with little research on business bodies. It is generally concluded that the effectiveness and sustenance of campaigns depend on: the extent of external threat or opportunity; the degree to which the status quo of public policy is satisfactory or can be accommodated (or can be avoided by non-compliance!); the structure of agents and networks that already exist (and their effectiveness); the extent of shared ideas and agendas that motivate common causes (*frames*); and the accessibility and effectiveness of mechanisms for exchange (*repertoires*).[107] More specifically, Meister has suggested that campaign bodies are most intensely developed by those most affected, those with greatest aspiration, and where there is the greatest heterogeneity of the milieu so that different voices have greater need for separate representation. There will also be age and gender effects, as people respond differently.[108]

With chambers we are not dealing with the broad population, but instead with businesses, often the largest among them, which have an inbuilt focus on economic objectives—primarily on maintaining or expanding markets, income, and profitability. Their potential for losses from campaigns is much larger than individuals, and their attitude to risk is also different; generally much more risk averse at low-level threats, but more willing to engage in campaigning against major threats. A question for this book, therefore, is how such focused interests, and their elites, or those that aspire to be among them, deal with contention and campaigns: does this differ from social movements, and how do business elites handle social and broader contention?

At one level, business campaigns are no different from any other. They require a sustained economic base: like other activities, they have transaction costs and require entrepreneurism, organization, finance, and leadership.[109] But this is more challenging for businesses because they additionally depend on mobilization and collective activity that is not as natural as it is for individuals.[110] Campaigns also set loose new and unpredictable forces, which challenge existing mechanisms, which may be economically dangerous: this explains muted responses by business to low threat levels.

---

[106] Hansen (1985), pp. 80–1; see also Kahnemann and Tversky (1979).
[107] See McAdam, Tarrow, and Tilley (2001), extended here; also Tilly (1978); Tarrow (1994).
[108] Meister (1984), chapter 4.
[109] See discussions in Zald and McCarthy (1987); Tarrow (1994).
[110] Tilly (1978), chapter 3; Grant (1993, 2000).

Success of popular campaigns is their main marketing tool. But this is beset by potentials for tension. First, campaigns for a cause are more likely than any other activity to lead to division and discord that can tear members apart. This is a major challenge for leadership, and involves a lot of demanding time and energy. Clearly exhibiting this challenge is the view of Henry Cruger, MP for Bristol in 1775 and nephew of the New York chamber chair:

> Notwithstanding it always gives me pains as a man to impair or injure the private interests of individuals. Yet, as a member of the community (who prefers greater to an inferior good) I must have promoted the public interest, though it might unfortunately have interfered with that of a few private persons: having been long since convinced that no human scheme can exactly coincide with the interests of all parties.[111]

A second tension is that campaigning is another playing field on which free-rider problems have to be overcome, which often leaves the effort to be found from a narrow group of volunteers and leaders, and stretches the resources of the organization, which can sap morale and commitment of staff and volunteers, or leave it struggling to make ends meet.[112] Alternatively, the campaign enlarges by-product risks, takes over the organization, and identifies it with a specific and narrow group of interests and pleaders.

A third tension is that chambers cannot be sustained by commitment alone. Shared values and beliefs that create a group identity for social movements can equally sustain rational or irrational and hysterical lobbies, as long as people are willing to support them. Businesses are no less subject to hysteria, but to convince other business leaders and government they have to resort primarily to rationality. This throws strong emphasis on the critical importance of deliberation, or its modern counterpart of detailed evidence-based research. Campaigns usually come at high cost and high risk.

A fourth tension arises over the possible use of *extra-legal activity*. Social and political movements are rife with examples of civil disobedience, riots, and boycotts; these are the stuff of academic studies that try to identify how new political frames are forced onto government from revolutions with class-based origins.[113] But less attention has been given to how elite movements, and business organizations, respond to pressure for extra-legal activity. Civil disobedience is a high-cost and high-risk strategy for any organization. Business people are far less likely to engage in it because they have more to lose. E. P. Thompson would see this as their 'class interest', but it also expresses concerns with practical issues about how a society will function during and after civil disturbances. Businesses, which provide the mechanisms for trade and wealth creation, perhaps understand better than

---

[111] Henry Cruger to Bristol Venturers, 7 April 1775, re Stourbridge Canal Bill; Bristol RO; SMV/ 2/4/2/19 (11).

[112] See e.g. Mackenzie (1955); Stewart (1958); Grove (1962); Beer (1965); Eckstein (1960); Finer (1966). Recent commentary summarized in Grant (2000).

[113] See e.g. Thompson (1963), Morris (1986, 1992); and the modern efforts to generalize the origins and mechanics of revolutions and disturbances by Tilly (1978, 1994, 2004); Tarrow (1994); McAdam, Tarrow, and Tilley (2001); see also Godwin (1988); Dunleavy (1991).

rioters the constraints and risks of extra-legal activity as opposed to alternative ways of trying to gain influence and change agendas. It is natural therefore that chambers have generally been bodies advocating reform rather than revolution; which became a critical aspect of their proximate origins, as explored in Chapter 4. It was with reluctance that most business leaders in this period broke with established routes of protected consultation and sometimes flirted with extra-legal activity.

One way of handling these tensions is to set up or work with separate campaigning bodies, as occurred for chambers with the Anti-Corn Law League in 1839–46, and over the arguments for free trade or tariffs in 1900–32. This takes the potential for discord into another organization, but may lead to the incumbent being challenged. This occurred for chambers in the 1970s when faced with the rise of the Federation of Small Business, which initially used quasi-extra legal antics: 'the mushrooming of organisations dedicated to militancy... [has] demonstrated that they are able to collect considerable sums of money from their supporters,... [which] undoubtedly have an unsettling effect on the more frustrated members of the chambers of commerce'. But the chambers believed that 'these bodies tend to have a very short lifespan'[114] and hence could be ignored. The subsequent competition to chambers from the FSB shows that this was misplaced. For the NCT it was part of their death knell. For BCC chambers the FSB remains a challenge. In 2006 a long-term member of the Croydon chamber felt that 'the FSB gained from speaking up for business against government, their competition is very strong; you never hear anything from chambers or BCC'.[115]

Frames and repertoires: great events and opportunities

The scope for, and success of, campaigns depends on the government of the day. Campaign effectiveness depends on the government's capacity to manage the problems of the moment using existing avenues of consultation. *Constrained contention* is possible where established agents and the existing consultation machinery can resolve the issues of concern. *Transgressive contention* arises when new agents, new structures, and new strategies emerge because the incumbents cannot resolve the new challenges.[116] The proximate origin of chambers derives from the transgressive contention of the 1760s–1780s. For business associations Castles has classified the extent and form of business mobilization into categories based on the extent of need or 'strain' and the degree of legitimacy of the government. In periods of severe strain and low government legitimacy, businesses are more likely to press their cause through public campaigning and alliances with political parties (particularly the opposition); where government has higher perceived legitimacy then there is a stronger tendency to work through existing government machinery and to compromise.[117]

---

[114] Comments by ABCC director general, Tony Newsome, ABCC *Annual Report* (1975), p. 4.
[115] Interview with Bryan Treherne, 6 October 2006; member of Croydon chamber for 25 years.
[116] Tilly (1978, 2004); McAdam, Tarrow, and Tilley (2001).
[117] Castles (1969), p. 164.

Thus business campaigning depends not just on ability to mobilize, but also the character, legitimacy, and accessibility of the government recipients of the campaign: what Tilly calls the avenues of protected consultation. Nettl extends this to argue that business groups and campaigns take different shapes depending on the scope and form of the state, with the common law system of Britain presenting more challenges for associations than the formal public law systems of Europe, in which chambers and some other bodies have direct access and a protected public status.[118] This also influences the overall 'policy culture' of each country.[119] Without formal status, British business associations depend on the receptiveness of the government, and are thus more subject to recruitment and inclusion by the state into its own agendas, potentially diverting them towards non-preferred services, and away from the independent interests of their members: this is perhaps their most severe dilemma in modern times.

One of the most valuable aspects of studies of campaign movements is the insight they offer into episodes of transgressive contention: periods when the existing mechanisms and agents are challenged, where new 'discourse coalitions' emerge, leading to new *repertoires*, where new *frames* of individual and group identification emerge as the dominant focus of the media and policy discussions.[120] Frames are the dominant paradigm that define the current narratives and shape the behaviour of agents. Developing new narratives is itself a critical element of a campaign: success in opening opportunities for changing frames and getting a new narrative taken up can yield dividends for years as these push other policies to the margins and open scope for new alliances of supporters.

As a result lobbyists work at two levels: routine campaigns on specific policies, often in response to proposals from government; and longer-term efforts to proactively change the frames and agendas. For this, 'great events' that introduce new threats that challenge existing agents may provide the greatest opportunities to reshape agendas: historically, the end of wars, major economic downturns, and unpopular government decisions provide the focus for such opportunities, and often encourage large-scale participation.[121] The history of chambers demonstrates both of these types of activity.

3.7 VOICE, LOBBYING, AND GOVERNMENT

Campaigning and voice are focused on agents that it is sought to influence. Whilst these can be various, in practice the pressure is almost always focused on the institution of government (local, national, and international) and its agencies. Over time, the scale of state activities has increased massively however it is measured (extent of legal regulation, level of expenditure or tax burden). During the two world wars of the 20th century, and the American, Napoleonic, and Boer

---

[118] Nettl (1965, 1968).   [119] See e.g. Eckstein (1960); Beer (1965).
[120] Tilly (1978, 1994); Hardin (1981); Tarrow (1994); Hajer and Wagenaar (2003).
[121] Tarrow (1994).

Wars there were step changes in public expenditure/taxation and government regulatory involvement.[122] Financial crises such as the 1930s slump, and the 2007–9 banking crisis, have had similar effects. These have tended to lead to permanently higher levels of expenditure from which it was difficult to retreat: the so-called 'ratchet effect'. In addition, *Wagner's law* suggests that, with progressive increases in economic well-being, the pressures for political goods supplied by government increases inexorably with the financial ability to provide them.[123] Hence, over time it is to be expected that the scale of association activity to lobby and represent businesses' interests will have expanded as the state expanded; and more rapid periods of expansion will coincide with periods of rapid state expansion, or periods where the state's policies are perceived as particularly threatening.

Countervailing power

An effect of the government's growth has been the expansion of other interest groups. Business associations are only one of the many interests that influence the state's institutions. There are many others which have become countervailing powers to the business interest. It is the strengths of these countervailing interests, as well as chance events and the political process, that has a major effect on what is on the political agenda.[124] Previous analyses of these trends suggest that whilst other interest groups emerged for short campaigns, they began to become significantly more permanent and highly organized in the late 1700s, particularly after the American rebellion, and became very significant from the mid-19th century onwards.[125] For chambers the countervailing powers in early years were the state chartered monopolies (East India, African Company, etc.), and dispersed smaller artisan concerns (such as the 'mechanics', weavers, and framework knitters); from the late 19th century local municipalism, trade unions, and socialist developments became countervailing threats; from the mid-20th century onwards it was consumer, environmental, and special interest groups.[126]

Pluralism and corporatism

A wide range of theories and concepts has developed to explain how different interest groups and government interact. In one of the main traditional interpretations, *pluralism*, different interest groups lobby on their different agendas and promote democracy through articulating their interests and competing with other interests. This offers a means by which society rationalizes power and meets

---

[122] See e.g. Grant (1987); van Waarden (1991).
[123] Wagner (1890); see Pigou (1947); Peacock and Wiseman (1961); Kay and King (2006).
[124] Grant (1993), pp. 40, 66–83; Grant (1987, 1993); Jordan and Maloney (1997).
[125] Wootton (1975); Norris (1957); Finer (1955); Clapham (1926); see also Chapters 9 and 10.
[126] Rose (1989); Grant (1993, 2000).

different needs—a process of '*concertation*'.[127] An idealist view is that of Becker: 'political equilibrium [is produced that] has the property that all groups maximise their incomes by spending their optimal amount on political pressure, given the productivity of their expenditures, and the behaviour of other groups'.[128] Once formed, the group's goals stimulate joining by new members who identify with similar political and other goals. Lapsing occurs when the group's goals change, or when individuals no longer share the same goals, or the group fails to be effective.[129] The pluralist model is a counsel of perfection since it assumes that the state's role in the process is neutral; that individuals are perfectly informed about the group's goals; that each has power in proportion to the relative value of their views; and that the group's managers and leaders perfectly reflect their members' views.

An alternative explanation of how interest groups operate comes from *corporatism*. This asserts an active role for the state as a dominant agent that can intervene, recruit, co-opt, and coerce: to bend chambers and others to offer 'non-preferred goods'. Much public–private partnership activity has this characteristic, and is sometimes referred to as the emergence of a 'governance' regime rather than separate public and private interests operating in different spheres,[130] or entering into 'deliberative policy making'.[131] This leads to co-option of the leaders; recruitment into key agencies; 'leverage' of their funds; recognition, kudos, and other rewards to personnel, leaders, or organizations; and potential for greater control of members.[132] This can improve efficiencies in government services and help them better meet policy objectives.[133] Or as stated by Middlemas, 'interest groups cross . . . the political threshold and become part of the state'.[134] The price of partnership is the loss of autonomy, and acceptance of the state's policy frames,[135] as investigated in Chapter 13.

'Privileged' interest?

Because businesses not only organize voice, but also exercise power through their investment and managerial/employment decisions, it has been argued by some that they are 'privileged interests'—more powerful than others, particularly labour unions.[136] Similarly it is argued that business has a 'single' economic purpose and so should be easier to align into a common interest.[137] Businesses may also share with

---

[127] In the most idealist statement of Jean Monnet of 'economie concertée', generalized group exchange leads to the most appropriate policy solutions: Schmitter and Lehmbruch (1979).
[128] Becker (1983), pp. 376 and 396.
[129] Dahl (1956); Jordan and Richardson (1987); Jordan and Maloney (1997); Tilly (1978); Tarrow (1994).
[130] Jordan and Richardson (1987); Grant (1993, 2000); Schmitter and Lehmbruch (1979).
[131] Hajer and Wagenaar (2003); Fischer (2003).
[132] See Selznick (1949); Pfeffer and Salancik (1978); Burt (1980); Crouch (1983).
[133] Williamson (1985, 1993); Aldrich (1976); Lindberg, Campbell, and Hollingsworth (1991).
[134] Middlemas (1979), p. 373; Middlemas (1983, 1990).
[135] Grant (1993), p. 28.
[136] e.g. Thompson (1963); see also Miliband (1969); Morris (1986); Offee and Wissenthal (1985); Gamble (2002).
[137] Offee and Wiesenthal (1985).

other elites a concern to limit change in the political system, as this would be disruptive to the economy.[138] There are various limitations to these arguments.

First and foremost, privilege can apply only to large businesses in concentrated and often protected markets. There is no scope for privilege for small firms in an open and dispersed economy subject to high levels of local and global competition. Indeed, the small firm interest was systematically ignored by governments until the 1970s. Hence, the view of business as a privileged interest applies essentially to the corporatist state-sanctioned monopolies and nationalized industries of the 20th century. Second, the view of business as a single interest demonstrates ignorance of its typical dispersion and fragmentation. Businesses rarely find themselves capable of lobbying with a uniform voice. A few industries manage this, but usually only when concentrated in a few large firms. Normally, the converse is the norm, of endemic fragmentation, under-resourcing, and division of power between individual businesses, sectors, localities, and trading interests.[139] This makes representation and negotiations with government difficult; as evidenced by government often seeking to 'organize' business interests,[140] introducing various distortions. Third, whilst businesses may in certain circumstances have a privileged position, in terms of government decisions it is ultimately government that decides, not business. As we shall see, at many times it is the (economically) 'perverse' politics of government decision making on the economy that causes business such concern.

Until the Reform Acts of the 1830s (and effectively until further reforms in the 1870s) it was not business but the aristocracy that had a privileged interest; and this explains the anger that stimulated many early chamber foundations. Moreover, during much of the 1920s–1970s in Britain and Ireland, business was on the defensive, and had little effective influence against the forces favouring nationalization, municipalism, and socialism.[141] There is indeed a strong counter-argument, that those in a privileged position with the British government in this period were the trade unions, since they had created the Labour Party for that purpose, and held strong financial and ideological sway over its leadership and policies, even exerting major influence over the Labour government of 1997–2010, and in opposition after 2010. Hence, there is rarely a guarantee of any privileged outcome for business, or any other interest, at any particular time. Everything is contingent and has to be fought for on every occasion. Or as put by Cain and Hopkins, what is important is how business pressures actually operate and the extent of human agency.[142]

Political and economic efficiency

This situation leads to viewing government as a battleground of contention and vying interests. As a result, from a business point of view there is seldom a desirable

---

[138] Miliband (1969).
[139] e.g. Finer (1955); Grant (1993, 2000); Jordan and Richardson (1987).
[140] See Olson (1971); Streeck and Schmitter (1985); Sadowski and Jacobi (1991); Lanzalaco (1992).
[141] See also Chapter 10.
[142] Cain and Hopkins (2002), p. 9.

outcome; there is government failure as much as market failure.[143] First, the most powerful groups in the political process at the outset of bargaining normally achieve the bias of decisions and regulations in their favour. They form a policy community[144] that manages the repertoire, which tends to exclude other interests. There is no reason to believe that the outcome of a 'political-efficient' bargaining process will be 'economically efficient'. As stated by North, 'democracy is not to be equated with competitive markets'.[145]

Second, an economically efficient decision along the lines of pluralist *'concertation'* requires *full arbitrage*, whereby all trade-offs and outcomes are evaluated and resolved to achieve an economically efficient outcome. This is never likely to be achieved in a political and administrative negotiation because of imperfect and asymmetric information, unequal power and resources, slowness of political and administrative decision making compared to economic change, and most important of all, the influence of other political or administrative objectives.

Indeed government is often trapped into a third set of interrelated problems: of *adverse selection* (supporting the weakest businesses and interests) that often distorts decision making. Government encourages people, places, and businesses to play an 'eligibility game' as clients—to maximize the aspects that qualify them for benefits and aid; targeting results in a 'dependency culture' where government, in effect, acts like an insurance company whose customers are selected as the most risky. This in turn leads to *moral hazard*, where business behaviour is changed to become less careful and efficient, and 'chases the funding'. This has particularly influenced chambers since the 1980s.

Fourth, there is significant *information asymmetry* between government and business (and other interests), which means that all lobbies are met to some extent by a wall of ignorance and/or neglect. Mortimer referred to this in 1772 as the 'imbecility of entire administrations'.[146] Warrington chamber illustrates the general chamber viewpoint in 1876: 'trade does not pass from a state of prosperity to a state of decay without errors and mistakes. . . . If our chambers of commerce could collect the facts . . . [to] demonstrate how they have led to the present state of things, they would do the state some service.'[147] Modern business views of government and civil servants are scarcely more flattering. However, even when government is properly informed, it often does not know how to use and manage the information, or has other priorities than business interests. This means that the strength of the case may be less important than how persistently it is argued, and how politically sensitive it is. To influence government requires the 'necessity of a long and tedious attendance personally in London to the injury of their affairs at home'.[148]

---

[143] See Wolf (1988); Le Grand (1991); also summary in Bennett (1995, 2008); Bennett and Payne (2000), pp. 45–8.

[144] See Richardson and Jordan (1979); Blank (1973); Rhodes (1992).

[145] North (1990), p. 57; see also Bennett (1995).

[146] For full discussion of Mortimer see Chapters 4 and 7.

[147] H. Bleckly JP, Warrington chamber, First General Meeting, 31 July 1876, p. 9 (Warrington Library, WP1849).

[148] Patrick Colquhoun, *Plan of a Public Agency in London for Commercial Affairs*: Glasgow chamber papers, TD 1670/4/52, October 1788, p. 6.

Hence policy outcomes will depend on the policy position of each agent and government; the importance or salience attached to each issue; the power or capability of each agent; the constraints of commitment, resources, and time (the budget constraint) that act on each agent; and the extent to which agents can command a stable solidarity of support.[149] As a result, an exchange, or political 'log-rolling', occurs whereby agents bargain and form alliances. There may be game-like behaviour in this structure with Nash and other sub-optimal outcomes.[150] Also, from Adam Smith onwards, it has been observed that more success may be accorded to discrete lobbying than noisy and public activity that can make it more difficult for ministers and government to shift positions.[151] This makes it difficult to know what has happened: a critical problem for untangling early chamber history.

3.8 VOICE AND POLITICS

Different interest groups have a varied range of opportunities to become directly involved in politics by aligning their cause with a particular party. For political movements in general, political alignment may be critical to their success, albeit by seeking to modify the frame and agenda of party objectives.[152] But business interests have usually been much more reluctant to align with a particular party. The BCC's modern position is that chambers are 'non-political'. This arises for five key reasons.[153]

First, most economic interests that concern politics are long term. Businesses have to work with governments of all parties. There is considerable danger in achieving a concession from one government that is not going to be maintained by subsequent governments. This indeed is a further stimulus for business interests to work hard to maintain a supportive repertoire and frame that covers a wide range of issues. Second, chambers do not want to be frozen out by a subsequent government, as reputedly occurred when the CBI called for a 'bare knuckle' fight with the Wilson government in 1974.[154] Third, chambers have members that usually have a diversity of political allegiances, or no strong allegiance at all. If chambers are perceived to be too closely aligned with one political party this will undermine their credibility with others.

Fourth, an interest that works too closely with a particular government, or indeed with governments in general, on a long-term basis is subject to 'capture' by public policy interests rather than member interests: the problem of 'non-preferred

---

[149] Eckstein (1960); Finer (1966); Rose (1989).
[150] Coleman (1988); Stokman and Stokman (1995); Bueno de Mesquita (1994); Bennett and Payne (2000).
[151] Adam Smith (1776), p. 200; see also Mackenzie (1955); Finer (1955, 1966); Grant (2000).
[152] Tilly (1978, 1994); Zald and McCarthy (1987); Hardin (1991); Tarrow (1994).
[153] See Finer (1966); Rose (1989); Grant (2000); and later Chapters.
[154] See Grant and Marsh (1977), pp. 88–9 for CBI director general's remarks against the government in 1974.

goods', which may alienate members. Fifth, as observed by Rose, becoming insiders also affects how voice is delivered: 'not-for-profit groups that depend upon the cooperation of Whitehall departments for funds, for access to information, or for status can criticise government policies. But if they do so, this must be done in the discreet language of Whitehall without aligning with the opposition party.'[155]

Avoiding party politics

As a result of these features chambers have generally sought to draw a line between their lobbying, and party political involvement. The closest most modern British and Irish chambers come to politics is to issue 'business manifestos', of objectives sought from candidates or future governments, as the UK chambers did for all candidates in the 2009 EU elections, and in 2010 for the general election. This is a contrast to the US Chamber of Commerce which is usually strongly politically aligned.

There are many examples that illustrate the favoured chamber approach of adopting a *general* economic interest, above party. Thus London asserted in 1885 that 'it has always been affirmed that English chambers should not deal with political questions'.[156] Limerick in 1902 stated that 'no political or religious discussion be allowed at any meeting'.[157] In Warrington in 1876, 'we have given evidence of our good-will by nominating the mayor of the borough for the time being as an honorary member . . . we are not aggressive in that direction neither do we meddle with political conflicts. Trade is of no party.'[158] Or in Camborne in 1908, 'the chamber being instituted for commercial and general purposes and comprising members of various political persuasions, questions of party politics general, or local, are excluded'.[159] For Derby in 1916, 'questions of party politics rigidly excluded'.[160] A more modern comment is Swindon chamber that, 'as a body we are apolitical and needs must remain so to be an effective voice in a community of multi-political influence'.[161] Fearing politics, the Worcester proposal for its chamber in 1839 states firmly that 'it should be borne in mind that the views and designs of the promoters of this association are strictly and exclusively *commercial*; and upon the rigid exclusion of every topic and feeling opposed or irrelevant to this its avowed object, its very existence will depend'.[162] When the Manchester chamber started its journal (*Monthly Record*) in 1890, it stated firmly that it wanted to encourage correspondence from members, but 'on matters non-political

---

[155] Rose (1989), p. 231; see also Maloney, Jordan, and McLaughlin (1994).
[156] London, *CCJ*, 5 September (1885), p. 227.
[157] Limerick chamber, *Bye-laws* (1902); P1/58.
[158] H. Bleckly Esq., JP, Warrington chamber, First General Meeting, 31 July 1876, p. 4 (Warrington Library, WP1849).
[159] Cambourne chamber, *Rules* (1908), quoted in chamber history, p. 13.
[160] Derby chamber, *Commercial Yearbook* (1916), p. 1.
[161] Swindon chamber, AGM minutes, 10 March 1987, p. 1.
[162] Worcester chamber, 7 May 1839; *Report of a Provisional Committee to Promote the Formation of the Chamber*; emphasis in original.

affecting the interests and prosperity of the various branches of trade'.[163] Politics above all was seen as divisive and hence threatening to the chamber as a whole.

An exception was briefly aired in the 1880s, when the London chamber mooted the creation of a political, but non-aligned independent party in the House of Commons. 'The presence of a body of thirty to fifty gentlemen in parliament whose interests were wholly commercial, and who were pledged neither to political nor to party servitude, would completely alter the now degenerated tone of proceedings at Westminster.' This would also overcome the problem that, 'once within the walls of the legislative assembly, our business men appear to drop their connection with commercial questions, and devote their time to anything except trade'.[164] Again in 1891, Birmingham chamber noted that 'if a distinct commercial party was formed . . . many long-delayed commercial reforms might be carried out'.[165] Some of these ideas fed into seeking business people to become MPs; e.g. in 1911 the ACC Executive was considering seeking enfranchisement of mercantile companies and corporations so that they could vote in municipal elections, though this was not pursued.[166] However, generally these pressures were not supported by ACC and did not take off.

The tensions are nicely summarized in a minute in the Cardiff chamber in 1931, which had sought advice from the ABCC and the two leading chambers of London and Birmingham:

> The president reported that the Secretary had communicated with the ABCC, the London chamber and the Birmingham chamber in reference to the manner in which they overcame any provisions . . . prohibiting the discussion of matters of general or local party politics when they desired to discuss questions relating to tariffs, safeguarding, etc.

The secretary read replies received from these organizations. The ABCC stated that 'their Articles did not preclude the discussion of questions of party politics; in their opinion matters of national importance, such as safeguarding and protection, transcended questions of general or local party politics, and even if such a condition existed, chambers of commerce would not be precluded from discussing such questions.' The London and Birmingham chambers replied to the effect that, whilst 'their articles did contain provision excluding from discussion questions of a political character, they no longer regarded questions relating to tariffs and safeguarding as political'.[167] The modern position is summed up by a 1976 ABCC comment that chambers 'should seek to cooperate with and work with the government of the day. This stance in no way inhibits chambers from opposing government measures . . . But it is seen to be no part of the chamber of commerce role to campaign for change of the party in government.'[168]

[163] Manchester *Monthly Record*, 20 January (1890), p. 1.
[164] London *CCJ*, 5 September (1885), pp. 227–8.
[165] Birmingham chamber, quoted in London *CCJ*, 10 April (1891).
[166] ACC Executive minutes, 12 November 1911.
[167] Cardiff chamber, Council minutes, 9 November 1931.
[168] ABCC *Annual Report* (1976), p. 4.

The influence of dissension

When a switch of ground occurred to engage in an issue previously deemed 'political', or a leading member of a chamber was seen as assisting a lobby because of their political allegiance, considerable tension could result. This might lead individual members to exit, or the body to break up. Indeed, the 'apathy' of some early chambers appears to have been to some extent the result of internal dissension on political lines which rendered them impotent to give voice; e.g. this appears to have affected Birmingham 1790–1820; Manchester 1790–1800; and Dublin 1790–1820. This had advantages of maintaining solidarity, but could undermine the weight of the chamber. Guernsey decided to stand back from comments on electoral reform in 1898, even after pressure at a special general meeting to take a position.[169] Grimsby chamber in 1923 could not decide whether a Humber tunnel would be good or bad for Grimsby, and 'left the matter in abeyance'.[170] Similarly the Goole chamber alternated between resistance and support for a bridge across the Humber between 1882 and 1930 because of disagreement between the shippers (who resisted it because it would be a barrier to shipping) and the other traders (who wanted it).[171]

But dissension could also lead to reinvigoration of a chamber. The most celebrated case is the throwing out of the 'old guard' from the Manchester chamber in 1839 when the chamber's directors were reluctant to support a vigorous Anti-Corn Law campaign, and the president was perceived to have been captured by the government's patronage.[172] The directors were forced to resign and seek re-election. Another case occurred in 1878 when the 21 members of Liverpool chamber's Council were forced to resign for perceived political bias. In the words of one of the council members, P. H. Rathbone, there was a lot of apathy and 'not widespread confidence' as the chamber was perceived to have 'too much of one tone of thought'. The keeping of minutes had become irregular, and activities minimal. Attendances had fallen and, as put by Christopher Bushell, a founding member of the chamber of 1849: 'gentlemen who were present at the meeting nominated their friends, and, in consequence of this and other causes, the council came to be of one colour and called a clique.' It seems that the chamber had become part of the Liberal corporation clan, but with a Conservative national government, was now an opposition body. In the diagnosis of another council member William. B. Forwood (who was leader of the Liberal clan), this was because Conservatives had not come forward. But in the views of Capt. Hatfield the problem stemmed from a chamber resolution, proposed by Forwood, intended as a snub to the Prime Minister (Disraeli).[173] A reconstruction

---

[169] Guernsey chamber, minutes 23 May 1898; Special General Meeting, 8 June 1898.

[170] Grimsby chamber history, p. 6.

[171] Goole chamber, Memorial 12 December 1882, opposing bridge as 'affecting the port of Goole and the rates of carriage'; *Annual Report* (1910), p. 7 in favour of bridge; chamber meeting in favour of bridge but criticism that 'shipping might be strangled and the town wiped out', *Goole Times*, 3 October 1930.

[172] See Chapter 10.

[173] Liverpool chamber, Report of Adjourned AGM, 30 January 1878.

committee was established and recommended various reforms, the most critical being to set up trade sections to better balance different interests, and to allow press reporters to attend meetings in order to increase interest. This was to overcome the perception of irrelevance, as 'The Chamber of Chat', according to Rathbone. In future all political comments and resolutions were banned. As commented by Col. Paris, 'a chamber of commerce should have plenty to do without mixing itself up with party politics; and if it had not plenty to do, it should not be in existence.'[174]

Political campaigning

There are a few examples where chambers have broken the general rule of remaining outside party politics. Celebrated examples discussed in Chapters 9 and 10 were during the American rebellion in 1775, trade negotiations in 1783–7, the Corn Law campaign 1839–46, and over tariffs. These politicized campaigns were rare, but there were some notable local examples in Ireland, and over the vexed British election of 1905.

Campaigning tensions in Ireland

Given the difficult political situation of Ireland it is not surprising that tensions arose. Cork had the most prominent tensions. The chamber had a large Liberal and Catholic presence from its outset, but also included others, so that the explicit association of the chamber with politics was divisive. Its meeting room, as a local focal point, threw the chamber into early difficulties. The founding rule 3 of 1819 had allowed petitions to be freely introduced into the room, so that it was permitted as a potential political milieu for hustings from the outset. There was a strong nationalist vein running through the chamber's council; and in 1832 the chamber was able to claim to its members that it had helped 'overthrow of an intolerant oligarchy which has long reigned dominant . . . [and] the return of the four proper candidates pledged upon all points to support the cause of the people [which] form subjects of pure and unalloyed congratulation to the chamber'. In 1834, referring to the Commission on Municipal Corporations that reported in 1835, it noted that 'the abuses of a monopolising party were so fully and so ably exposed by some independent members of your body'.[175]

The role of the Cork chamber as a venue for political meetings became more explicit by 1852: 'it is essential to the future interest of the Liberal Party of this city that the chamber of commerce should *as of old* be the rallying place for the burgesses of the different wards'. However, the expansion of the chamber had drawn in a wide membership, and from this point disputes about politics rose to prominence. Under pressure from some members, the chamber drew up rules for the use of the room by politicians, and it was proposed that 'town councillors of the Liberal Party

[174] Liverpool chamber, Report of Special General Meeting, 10 April 1878; Martin (1950), Liverpool chamber history, p. 8.
[175] Cork chamber minutes, 2 and 5 January 1832.

should become subscribers to the room and thus place themselves in a position to obtain the sanction of the majority for the holding of ward meetings whenever required'.[176]

The particular storm of 1852 passed. But the chamber's room became a larger battleground when Charles Stuart Parnell was elected president in 1881. As president of the Land League and a vigorous MP, he identified the chamber very explicitly with Irish independence, used it as part of his political campaign on Irish land reform, and addressed huge crowds from the first floor windows of the chamber's reading room, prominently at the centre of Patrick St. Although he remained President until 1890, many members of the chamber 'felt that the interests of the chamber were being substituted to political interest' and founded a second chamber called the Incorporated Cork Chamber of Commerce and Shipping. The membership of the two bodies was similar in terms of business type, but differed in politics, with the 'Incorporated' being a 'loyalist' body that affiliated with ABCC, and the old chamber being much more nationalist, though both had mixed religious adherents, and many businesses were members of both. The two bodies continued separate existence until merged in December 1951.[177]

The Dublin chamber was also continually under pressure to take a stand, primarily from Protestant loyalists. The chamber suffered an un-healable division between those favouring Irish independence and loyal unionists in 1791, when it appears to have died. Efforts to revive the chamber in 1805–12 were short-lived and it was accused of being dominated by Catholics. The relaunched chamber of 1820 had similar tensions with repeated calls to stay out of politics, which were only partly adhered to. In 1826 there was a resolution for a new MP for the city 'who shall advocate efficiently its commercial and general interests without regard to party'. But it was agreed to leave this to individuals acting alone outside the chamber, 'confining ourselves to those commercial objects in which we have all a common interest'.[178] Again in 1827 it is reported that the chamber sought 'to maintain that strict neutrality, on all extraneous topics, so suitable to the character, and so indispensable to the usefulness of a commercial institution'. The tensions continued in the run-up to independence, with all the main chambers attempting to stay outside the politics of the election for the first Free State candidates; e.g. the Dublin chamber, then loyalist, refused to have the election subscription list to the 'Treaty Fund' in its buildings.[179]

The Irish chambers continued to be more politically engaged up to the 1980s, behaving more like some UK chambers of trade, by supporting a slate of 'commercial candidates' which were committed to holding down local rates or national taxes, as discussed in Chapter 10.

---

[176] Cork chamber minutes, 6 January 1852, emphases added.
[177] Based on comparison of membership lists of both chambers; see also *Chamber of Commerce Journal* (Dublin), 3(2), February (1952), p. 10.
[178] Dublin chamber, General Meeting minutes, 4 April 1826.
[179] Dublin chamber, Report of Council (1827), p. 35; (1922), p. 10.

Campaign activism by small chambers

For the NCT and many small chambers, vigorous political campaigning was more common. This took various forms. An important method was to support particular candidates in local or national elections. They did this because they felt their interests were totally ignored by governments. The NCT nationally, through the local chambers, issued a series of questions to local MPs and councillor candidates. Locally, the CoTs used these and other questions, which were often published in the local press so that the candidates had to respond publicly in the same way. At other times they arranged meetings or 'interviews' with the candidates. They then distributed the answers received to electors directly, or in the local press, with often quite explicit lobbying and advocacy for individual candidates. They also arranged for their own fellow traders to stand in council elections.

For example, in Bury (Lancs.) in a 1921 local election, a handbill was distributed to CoT members, stating,

> traders interests are the ratepayers interests. Heavy rates call for the utmost economy where possible, combined with efficiency, your chamber is not satisfied that we are getting efficiency and the best results from some of the corporation undertakings. If you will use your vote irrespective party politics and also influence your wives and friends to do the same you have the chance of returning three of your members on Tuesday next. . . . **Vote for Waterhouse (East Ward), Salter and Evans (Church Ward)**.[180]

Whilst the CoTs were not ratepayer associations (although two early NCT members were), they often worked closely with them. Similarly, the Reading chamber in 1921 organized a campaign in support of specific candidates in Poor Law Guardian and Municipal elections: 26,000 letters were sent to electors. Six out of eight Guardians, and eight out of nine municipal councillors that were supported were successful. The process was repeated in 1923 with 8000 letters for electors to the Board of Guardians (eight out of eight favoured candidates successful) and 20,000 letters for the municipal elections (five out of eight successful).[181] The effort to influence elections and get traders themselves to stand appears to have been coordinated by NCT from about 1905 until well after WW2.[182] The shop window offered the NCT a very visible and widespread presence across the country. Unlike the chambers of commerce voice, the NCT lobbying was 'on display'.

The trade protection societies, as far as can be determined, took a party political position only once: in the 1905 General Election. Then they issued a *Manifesto of the Association*, in which it is stated that 'we appeal to business men throughout the Kingdom to press upon candidates for parliamentary honours the necessity of supporting reforms advocated by this association'. Like the NCT there was a pamphlet with 21 questions for parliamentary candidates that all derive from

---

[180] Filed in Bury chamber minutes, 1921; bold text in original.
[181] Reading, *Annual Accounts* (1923); in chamber history, p. 36.
[182] Questions for parliamentary candidates, Seventh NCT National Conference (MS 29340/1, p. 27).

specific TPS campaigns.[183] After 1905 the NATPS seems to have left any party political activity to the NCT and chambers of trade.

3.9 SOCIETY AND DELIBERATION: NETWORKS, STATUS, AND 'BRAND CAPITAL'

Society itself, discourse, and meetings were also (and still are) major forces for joining and retaining membership drawing on the obsession of members with gaining commercial intelligence and market opportunities. There are both formal and informal aspects to this process: the meetings with formal resolutions and votes, and the scope for continuous informal exchanges. In later periods, discourse and deliberation largely fell to standing committees, subcommittees, and 'sections'. Modern equivalents operate through email and electronic meetings as well as face-to-face committees.

Society, acceptance, and 'politeness'

Socializing, discourse, and deliberation interact, to allow formulation of views. But the history of chambers was also bound up with an expression of status. From membership and networking came social acceptance and inclusion, as well as marketing opportunities, as in non-commercial societies with which chamber members heavily overlapped.[184]

'Politeness' was an 18th-century catchword for social acceptance.[185] This applied both to the person and to the place. Chambers were a significant element of this phenomenon, both contributing to local 'politeness' and drawing from the 'politeness' of the locality. This drew from 'the art of pleasing in company', as a part of harmonious communal and urban living, and as a developing concept of 'civilization' and good human behaviour.[186] This influenced the content of early reading rooms and book borrowing; e.g. Liverpool chamber member and Stamp Act protester Stephen Hayes was fined in 1775 for keeping overdue Lord Chesterfield's *Letters to his Son* and was not allowed further borrowing until it was returned. He was clearly an avid reader on how to behave![187]

The rhetoric of politeness strongly affected deliberation, so that conflicts were conceded or if possible reconciled.[188] This facilitated the development of unity, though it could encourage acquiescence and passiveness, or capture by elite interests.[189] Thus we find few examples in minutes or reports of chambers of

---

[183] NATPS minutes, *Manifesto* (1905); DE 3512/29.
[184] Clark (2000a), chapters 6 and 7.
[185] e.g. Chesterfield, *Letters to his Son*; Trusler, *Principles of Politeness*; quoted in Langford (1989).
[186] As associated respectively with the Earl of Shaftsbury, Addison, and Steele in the *Spectator*, overlapping with evangelical revivals; see e.g. Langford (1989, 2002); Borsay (1989); Sweet (2002, 2003).
[187] Liverpool Subscription Library minutes, 12 June 1775; Liverpool RO 027 LYC1/1/1.
[188] Langford (2002), p. 315.
[189] Nettl (1965); Castles (1969).

disputes or disagreements, and if recorded this is usually very discreet or opaque. Analysis of newspaper reports usually gives greater insights into significant disputes. The chambers generally appear remarkably unified externally. This, of course, is also the most effective lobbying strategy, but it undoubtedly owed much to a tradition that suppressed dissent as 'ungentlemanly'. Echoes of 'politeness' survived until very late: a correspondent to the Welwyn Garden City chamber lamented in 1949 that 'the age of even mild tolerance has gone' after 'slanders' by members of the chamber against the managers of local shops had been quoted in the *Welwyn Times*.[190]

'Polite' was not only a social label of a chamber member but also of a locality. Acquiring the trappings of genteel respectability, members would access a 'wider social universe'.[191] To be polite was to be acceptable among prominent local elites: originally the concern of the gentry, increasingly the upper middling sort also sought to be accepted. Analysis of travel guides and other topographical literature demonstrates the growth from the late 18th century through the 19th century of attributes that made a locality attractive for tourists offering status, interest, and activity.[192] This was also part of the movement for local improvement Acts and reform. The rapidly expanding provincial press were also significant in this 'place marketing'. To be a polite place meant acquiring accepted social standards among the local elite and having specific visible manifestations of politeness: parks, walks, museums, theatres, good schools, bookshops, libraries, exhibitions, urban squares, paved streets, bowling greens, and 'urban services', as well as the development of leading buildings and institutions, Assembly Rooms, Exchanges, coffee rooms, and respectable hotels.[193] These were social milieus, but also business milieus. The main users of the Newcastle Assembly Rooms were not the gentry (who may have thought it too narrow for politeness), but the merchants and traders who liked to jostle together.[194]

For chambers, stimulating the provision of such facilities became an important role, and the development of a suitable business society was itself a mark of an organized and engaged business elite. The chamber of commerce in the main commercial centres, and later the chamber of trade in smaller towns, also became an asset which a respectable city or town should have. The chambers themselves acquired a 'brand' value, and so did the towns that had them. They became part of the expected assemblage, listed in all guides usually with its council, often immediately after local government, portrayed as similar in status.

This in turn reinforced the desire for chambers to have as their president and vice-president those commanding instantly recognizable respect and status (usually those with titles, the local gentry, MPs, and members of the House of Lords), and having on their councils the local Mayor, burgesses, and JPs, who are usually

---

[190] John Eccles, director of the Howardsgate Trust, to F. J. Osborn, secretary of the chamber, 19 August 1949; Welwyn Library, FJO/K294.
[191] Clark (2000a), p. 230.
[192] Sweet (2002, 2003); see also Minchinton (1957); Borsay (1989); Thompson (1988).
[193] Sweet (2002), pp. 372–3; Ellis (2004); Minchinton (1957); and local sources in later chapters.
[194] Berry (2004), Table 8.1.

explicitly identified with these titles in local directory listings. The presence of the gentry confirmed status and betokened support from those with the divine 'right to govern'. Thus, in Cardiff, the chamber was very pleased to have the support of the Marquis of Bute, Cardiff's most eminent figure, to be president from 1888.[195] He also donated the largest subscription each year (10 guineas).[196] Newcastle in 1855 expressed satisfaction 'that the roll of the chamber now contains the names, not only of every parliamentary representative of the boroughs on the Tyne, . . . but those of the Lord Lieutenants of both Northumberland and Durham, the representatives of South Northumberland and North Durham, and several other persons of high rank in the state'.[197] This desire has continued up to the present; the Earls of Derby have been active presidents of the Liverpool chamber for the 100 years 1910–2010.

The chambers were thus active arenas for projecting status, with rules of polite conduct and criteria for membership. Although this is quite alien to the modern chamber, Langford notes for the early years 'deciding who to exclude . . . was as important as ensuring that it included the right people. Countless tiny elites throughout the land exercised this exclusive power, themselves arranged in hierarchies.'[198] For a chamber of commerce this meant having the prominent local dignitaries, but also focusing on the main employers and exercising effective control through a council that contained the pre-eminent elite of local business people.

Exclusiveness and elites

Early chambers certainly saw themselves as high-status organizations, which required a level of exclusiveness. Exclusiveness was primarily exercised by requiring application by letter or introduction by existing members, meeting the committee or president, and satisfying criteria for acceptance. A chamber could exclude through the chamber's committee or council, or by ballot. The formality of this process alone erected a barrier and sense of exclusiveness, whether or not it was ever used. However, it was also certainly employed into the 20th century by some chambers.

The most common expression of exclusiveness is contained in statements that the chamber was seeking members from the 'major' or 'leading' businesses. A few placed specific criteria on this; e.g. in Jersey in 1768 there was a restriction of membership to shippers who owned more than 20 tons of shipping, or the equivalent for other businesses, subsequently raised to 90 tons, though dropped in 1837.[199] In Limerick in 1807 membership of the committee was initially exclusive to those businesses with either export duties in excess of £1500, or import duties in excess of £3000. This was adjusted in 1811, chiefly to allow membership of the committee from corn dealers and brewers who had little export.[200]

[195] Cardiff history, p. 1.   [196] Cardiff chamber, *Annual Reports.*
[197] Newcastle-upon-Tyne, *Annual Report* (1855).
[198] Langford (2002), p. 314.
[199] Jersey chamber, founding *Deed*, Articles 13 and 21, February 1768; minutes 2 March 1837.
[200] Limerick Minutes, May 1807 and 19 April 1811.

More commonly applicants were 'discussed' by the committees/councils of chambers; in some cases this continued into the 1970s. Few were actually excluded, possibly because the process was self-selective in the first place. Typically various enquiries might be made to assess the worthiness of an individual. As Dublin observed, 'election is by ballot, and they were particular as to that. They would not admit anyone that was not of good standing and position, and that safeguard was exercised without giving personal offence.'[201] Only a few early chambers record active debates about particular applications to join, though the details of these, including the names of the potential members, are not always given. A few examples indicate the issues involved. The Salisbury chamber of trade refused membership in 1920 to 'Wiltshire's largest printing works', because union wages were not paid to workers. This has to be interpreted as a mixture of social leverage and restrictive practices as at least two of the Chamber's council at the time were also large local printers. In another case, in Kidderminster chamber of commerce in 1949, Robinson & Son of Fair St. 'applied for membership but failed to find a proposer'.[202] In Ipswich, the 1860 articles provided that any member prosecuted was suspended from the chamber.[203] If not explicit, this particular rule applied de facto to most other chambers.

Exclusiveness in some chambers was also fostered by restrictions on the number of members; this allowed a focus on the key firms in the business community. For example, Croydon's Rules and Regulations of 1891, only revised in 1929, stated that membership was 'not to exceed 500'. Coventry restricted its membership to 1000 in its 1918 Articles, which was increased in its 1949 by-laws to 2000, only removed in 1967.[204] The early New York chamber in 1768 geared the entrance fee so that it increased with membership size, which was a strong limitation on numbers to the most significant merchants.[205] These methods mirror evolution in non-commercial societies of the period. It was better for them to focus more on including the major interests than seeking to cater for all.[206]

Some early chambers also had explicit blackballing provisions. It is important not to overemphasize these, because their existence was probably more important as a symbol of exclusiveness than their use. However, on proposed election, many chambers allowed for a potential member to be excluded if a number of existing members voted against them. Jersey had extensive rules from its 1768 foundation for secret ballot to be held in a separate room where papers were put in two locked boxes (yes and no) and voters had 'to pledge his honour that he was not influenced by any [other] person'; i.e. campaigning was banned. This was used

---

[201] J. R. Wigham, Dublin chamber; quoted in London *CCJ*, 5 August (1886), p. 54.

[202] Salisbury chamber history, p. 7: Kidderminster chamber minutes, 1950.

[203] Ipswich chamber minutes, 1884.

[204] Coventry chamber; Memorandum and Articles of Association; *Bye-laws* (1919, 1949, 1967).

[205] Bishop (1918), pp. 6–7, 64–8, 230. Initially there was a flat rate entrance fee of $5 in 1768; but in 1770 it became $10 rising in $2.5 stages above 80, 100, and 120 members. In 1840–3 it was reduced to $1, but increased to $3 in 1856 and back to $10 in 1858, reflecting changing views about exclusiveness.

[206] Clark (2000a), chapters 6 and 7.

to vote on membership, resolutions, and election of committee and officers.[207] Manchester in 1794 had a 'black book' to identify 'swindlers, and exposing persons void of principle and honour'.[208] Although only one firm's name, a merchant in Naples, was entered, which was subsequently removed when that firm had paid the balance of their account, Helm, probably correctly, speculates that its importance was mainly to indicate exclusiveness.[209] In Dublin from 1783, the admission of new members was by ballot box into which were dropped black or white beans by each voting member; five negatives, or a majority of negatives, would reject the member.[210] The relaunched Dublin chamber of 1820 initially had no blackball procedure, but one year later amended its rules to introduce a ballot with 'one black bean in four to exclude'.[211] Waterford's 1805 rules specified one black bean in four to reject: two applications were rejected in 1806 (by 17 black to 13, and 23 black to 7), but there are few other rejections recorded.[212] Belfast also used beans until the 1830s; admission to membership of the chamber was 'by ballot of the council; the majority of black beans excluding'.[213]

An interesting variation, linked to chamber size, was in New York, which had a sliding scale of 'blackballs'. Three blackballs would disqualify a candidate when membership was 30 or less, with a rising number of blackballs needed as the membership increased (one blackball for every ten members). This survived until 1834, although it was not removed from the articles until much later.[214] Charleston required a vote of not less than two-thirds of the members present.[215] One of the latest references to this procedure is in Wolverhampton where a clause of 'three blackballs to exclude' was in their first by-laws (1856), though this was apparently never used.[216]

Checking between nominations and elections to membership is not usually possible in minutes, so that the extent of real exclusion is difficult to assess, but appears to have been infrequent. The exception is Dublin, where its amended rules of 1821 were used quite actively to exclude in the 1820s, and this seems to have reflected growing sectarian tensions. The first excluded applicants were Richard Dolland and John Hill in September 1823, then Thomas Kennan, John Tibthorp, and A. Nordblad in October, one more in December, six in March 1824, one or two in most meetings in the rest of 1824 and 1825, and three in March 1826.

[207] Jersey chamber, *Deed*, Articles 8–11, 24, 25; February 1768.
[208] Helm (1897), p. 2.
[209] Proceedings of the Manchester Commercial Society, 2 October 1794 ff., quoted in Helm (1897), p. 2; Redford (1934), pp. 22–3.
[210] Quoted in Prendeville (1930), p. 196.
[211] Dublin chamber, *Amended Rules*, General Meeting minutes, 4 December 1821.
[212] Waterford chamber minutes, *Rules*, 7 June 1805; 17 January 1806 (John Maher and Joseph Dwyer rejected).
[213] Belfast chamber, *Report to Council*, November 1832, p. 3; D1857/1/G/3.
[214] Sliding scale of blackballs replaced a decision to increase the number of blackballs from 3 to 6 one year after establishment; New York chamber minutes, 5 December 1769: Stevens (1867); Bishop (1918), pp. 7 and 59.
[215] Charleston chamber, *Rules*, Article 9, 1774; Library Company of Philadelphia 13194.
[216] Wolverhampton chamber history, p. 4.

Cullan interprets this period as one in which the membership was more conservative than the council, which contained Quakers and many with sympathy to Catholics, but Arthur Guinness and other unionists were keen to control the chamber resulting in many tensions, with elections of new members as one place to exert control.[217]

Exclusion also applied to visitors, who had to be introduced by a member. Jersey's articles allowed guests at their all-important dinners 'as a guest to those that bring them, but nobody else on any account whatsoever'.[218] For Dublin, a 'stranger' had to be from an address beyond the local area (beyond 14 miles), and their use of the chamber was restricted to no more than a week.[219] But external residents were usually permitted to become members of a chamber, often at reduced rates. Thus Dublin, Dundee, London, and other chambers had members at a reduced 'country rate'; in Cork and Waterford they were free after an introduction. But Jersey expected owners of ships from 'London, Southampton and other coasters' to pay the full subscription in 1768.

Exclusivity and fraternity was also encouraged in other ways. The portraits of presidents and secretaries would be commissioned and hung in chamber offices, just like societies,[220] and plate or other items were sometimes given or bequeathed in wills, or prizes for local schools administered by the chamber. Status was also enhanced by some use of regalia, such as chains, chairs, and badges of office. Death was often honoured by obituaries and mass attendance at funerals. These were well-established traditions carried forward from the guilds and non-commercial societies.[221]

In modern times chambers of trade and FSB use badges, letterheads, and window badges to allow members to advertise their membership. But the chambers of commerce have rarely allowed badging; e.g. in the 1913 Birmingham chamber, a proposal to have a certificate of membership for use abroad or to hang on a firm's wall was 'deferred sine die'.[222] It also rejected the use of 'member of Birmingham chamber of commerce' on member letterheads.[223] In 1923 an ABCC proposal to issue 'passports' to chamber members when they were travelling abroad to give access to foreign chambers was rejected.[224] Ipswich in 1931 sought to prevent use of the chamber name or title of office holders 'upon any printed or published document which does not deal with matters directly concerning the chamber'.[225] Where chambers have allowed use it has been exceptional; e.g. Westminster in 1949–50 issued window badges; but this chamber had a very high proportion of

---

[217] Cullen, Dublin chamber history, pp. 54–62.

[218] Jersey chamber minutes, *Deed*, Article 32; February 1768.

[219] Dublin chamber, general Meeting minutes, *Rules*, 7 November 1820.

[220] The New York chamber's first purpose-built offices had a portrait gallery as a central feature: Bishop (1918).

[221] Clark (2000a), p. 228.

[222] Birmingham chamber, GPC minutes, 5 May 1913.

[223] e.g. Birmingham chamber, GPC minutes, 26 October 1916; it acted to prevent unauthorized use of the chamber's name in 1924: GPC minutes, 20 October 1924.

[224] ABCC consultation on Improvement Committee recommendations, 1923; MS 14479.

[225] Ipswich chamber minutes, 29 September 1931.

retail members.[226] Wolverhampton in 1977 introduced a logo for use on letter-heads and members' publicity 'which it is hoped will be widely used by members'.[227] Generally chambers relied on the listing of membership in directories as the main signification of solidarity.

Exclusivity is not part of modern chambers. As a result most have a wide range of members, and many are not businesses; e.g. local government officers, college principals, school head teachers, and executives of public bodies. Of other modern associations, only the CBI and IoD maintain a level of exclusivity. The CBI requires members to be incorporated and trading in the UK; IoD 'full' membership is restricted to directors of companies that are solvent and of 'substance' (defined as a minimum turnover of £250,000).[228]

Social aspiration and economic change

Exclusiveness and 'politeness' were correlated with, if not in part caused by, the economic and commercial developments of the 18th and 19th centuries. The rising middle classes, and manufacturing and commercial elites, could acquire 'politeness' and thus rise to a position of status with the gentry, at least in their own eyes and those of peers.[229] Their numbers burgeoned with industrial and urban growth. This naturally resonated within chambers: as Meister argues, the greater the social changes occurring, the greater is the chance that associations will form, and the stronger will be their membership.[230]

'Politeness' was also interrelated with what we now would call 'customer care'. Quality of personal service became increasingly expected, with 'customers of rank' increasingly received as equals. The development of chambers coincides with the emergence of consumer society. Poor service and lack of politeness was associated with backwardness, 'politeness' with progressiveness.[231] It was natural for this to be linked in chambers with the emerging concept of free trade, openness, accessibility, and levelling of access.[232]

Hence, across the early concepts of 'gentlemanly' behaviour and the tradition of 'merchant trust', was a social process that linked the humble trader, the middling manufacturer, and the elite merchant into 'gentlemanly' cultural codes and appropriate business behaviour.[233] Membership of an appropriate body could increase personal status or indicate acceptance. Organizations like chambers acquired 'brand capital' by links to these concepts, and by having patrons from the elite that were the assured custodians of the standard. This was crucial to chambers as providers of

---

[226] Westminster chamber, *Annual Reports* (1949, 1950).
[227] Wolverhampton chamber, *Annual Report* (1977).
[228] Membership leaflets and websites (2010).
[229] Langford (2002), pp. 318–22; also Pocock (1985); Borsay (1989); Corfield (1995); Brewer (1997).
[230] Meister (1984).
[231] McKendrick, Brewer, and Plumb (1982); Weatherill (1996); Langford (2002), pp. 319–20.
[232] Rogers (1989); Cain and Hopkins (1980, 1986, 2002); Chapman (1992); Bowen (1996).
[233] Brewer (1997); Weatherill (1996).

'trust goods'. Chambers of commerce, more than any other business bodies, were interlinked with these codes, and remained regarded as 'respectable' bodies into modern times, with all the positives and negatives that now implies.

3.10 CONCLUSION

This chapter has outlined the varied forces that stimulate development of locally based general bodies such as chambers. This forms a framework for analysis of their evolution in the following chapters. For some parts of the discussion the 18th century is a key to understanding the present. This will surprise many current chamber of commerce managers, and their members, but the congruities are in many cases quite remarkable.

The discussion has emphasized that there are *multiple forces* acting on chambers. As a result, a wide range of different activities that offer individual, collective, and 'non-preferred' benefits have developed, which became complex '*bundles*' of roles offering to members and to association managers a mix of incentives and opportunities. The role of strategic resource support to individual businesses is often mixed with social opportunities, 'insurance', 'taster', and brand/reputation effects. Solidarity and support for a cause may offer further stimuli, as well as challenges, particularly during periods of 'great events' (transgressive contention), when there are opportunities for new frames and repertoires of discourse to be established—when rivals are most likely to form and chambers are most pressed to change. Running across each of these dimensions it is the localness of solidarity that underpins chambers.

In addition to their autonomous objectives, and the individual objectives of their members, leaders, or staff, is the external force of government and the state. The state is a passive and an active agent; it offers threats, and also opportunities for influence and benefit. The state is a resource that can be used by chambers, but it is also a source of distortion with dangers of co-option, recruitment, and 'capture'. The effect of party politics can also be a source of membership dissent, internal discord, and dissension, threatening existence. The tensions are usually overcome by the use of bundles at any one point of time, and flexibility of services development over time. The specific mix, or bundle, is not stable over time or place. This means that the tensions have to be renegotiated at each stage of development; contingency and local variety are likely to be the continuing orders of the day.

4

Concepts and Origins
Establishing the First Chambers

4.1 THE SEARCH FOR PROXIMATE CAUSE

The previous chapter has identified the multiple forces behind the foundation and growth of chambers. These tell us why chamber activity might be sought and sustained, but they do not explain *why it first arose where and when it did*. The search for proximate cause is the focus of this chapter. Such a search has not been systematically attempted before, and there have been some systematic misunderstandings; hence the extended discussion here. The chapter focuses on two interlocked aspects: the origins of *the concept* of a chamber that established the brand; and the forces of contention that were sufficient to get busy business leaders to act. The chapter breaks new ground in demonstrating the continuity of concepts and people from earlier protests (such over the 1765 Stamp Act) through to later chamber foundations, adapting 'protest' into organized and sustained voice.

The chambers were initially very limited in number. There were only four or five in the British Isles 1768–82. They then grew slowly to 11–18 by 1790 and about 23 by 1839.[1] In North America the earliest was New York in 1768, although there were earlier societies in Boston and Nova Scotia with similar characteristics; there were four or five chambers by 1795 and seven by 1806, a number that remained almost unchanged until the 1840s. There was a proposal and probable development in Quebec in 1776–89, and a Jamaica chamber over 1778–85. These phases of early development are shown in Figure 4.1.

It is clear that the new chamber phenomenon was initially very localized and, after its implant, early diffusion was relatively slow. But it was a phenomenon that traversed the Atlantic world. This was a key phase in the expansion of globalized trade and the establishment of the second British Empire.[2] This leads this chapter to investigate forces for local voice throughout this Atlantic world, and to explore concept and proximate cause within the threats from, and to, the imperial government deriving from the 'great events' of the period.

---

[1] All numbers approximate and refer to those actually operating at the time: see Table 2.1 and Appendix 1.

[2] e.g. Bargar (1956); Harlow (1952); Namier (1961); Minchinton (1971); Olson (1979); McCusker and Menard (1985); Morgan (1993, 2007); Bowen (1996, 2006).

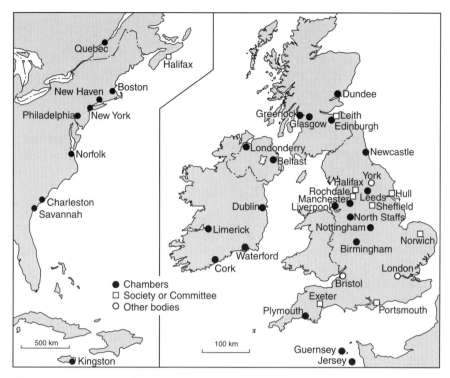

Fig. 4.1. The early chambers of commerce 1768–1819, and societies or committees that were local committees or delegates of 'national' chamber organizations.

4.2 ESTABLISHING THE CHAMBER CONCEPT OR 'BRAND'

The concept of a 'chamber', rather than starting as a single template, seems to have evolved from individual local initiatives as bottom-up or grass-roots organizations: collective organizational learning. Nevertheless, Whiston, Davenant, Postlethwayt, Mortimer, and other writers appear to have provided the conceptual skeleton that local leaders adapted to their own circumstances for organizations that could assert voices for colonial and provincial trade.

Whiston and Davenant's 1681–1696 proposal for a Council of Commerce

Probably the first concept of a *council of commerce* resembling a chamber of commerce, as a general, independent elected body, was a proposal promulgated by Charles Davenant at a time when it was feared that the king, William of

Orange, might undermine British trading interests for the benefit of the Dutch.[3] A Bill was presented to parliament to establish this council in 1695, supported by the Tories, and vigorous debate followed which was very nearly successful.[4] The proposal drew from an earlier Plan by James Whiston, who in writings in 1681, 1693, and 1695–6 conceived the concept of a 'commercial parliament' elected from leading merchants on the basis of field of foreign trade, region/county, and sector.

The parliamentary Bill was for a publicly backed, but independent body with seven key features outlined by Whiston,[5] most of which underpin the subsequent chamber concept. First, commercial advice to government should come from those involved in commerce: 'if sick we consult a physician: so when the trade of the nation is to be secured or advanced, the merchant's or tradesman's advice is questionless best able to accomplish the same'. Second, there were to be regular meetings with formal and public minutes. Third, there would be sector and regional representatives: in the first proposal this was 69 from named counties, sectors, or fields of foreign trade (chiefly two per field/region, but 12 places for shipmasters chosen by Trinity House), with others making a total of about 100, about 40 of whom were expected at any one meeting. Fourth, each member would be paid 10s. for attendance at meetings and there would be a salaried chief clerk and other officers, chosen by the members, providing a permanent professional secretariat. Fifth, decisions would be made by votes of members, with a register of votes kept, each proposal having to be read three times before rejection. Sixth, it was to receive all proposals regarding trade, to report on conditions of trade (to parliament and ministers), and suggest improvements in government policy or laws: to open 'a yet fairer light, and insight into trade . . . and thereby be better enabled to redress all those mal-administrations, and non-improvements of trade which . . . cannot so easily fall under sufficient parliamentary inquiry'.[6] Finally, it was proposed that part of the navy was set aside for commercial support and convoy duty, which should be subject to directions from the council of commerce, sent to the Board of Admiralty, subject to the king's control.

Within the Davenant–Whiston discourse is a deep concern to limit arbitrary rule, overcome ministerial and parliamentary incompetence, and improve

---

[3] Davenant, 1656–1714, MP 1685–8, 1698–1701, had strong political links, assisting Bills (through Robert Hanley 'the most important parliamentarian of his day'); an important pamphleteer and force behind the Council of Trade established in 1696: *History of Parliament*; *DNB*; *Biographical Dictionary of British Economists*.

[4] *A Memorial Concerning a Council of Trade*: BL Harleian papers MS 1223, vol. i, fos. 184–8. Lees (1939) gives a detailed account and sources for the parliamentary debate.

[5] Whiston *c.*1641–1706 was a broker to merchants at the Royal Exchange; he established *The Merchant's Weekly Remembrancer*, issued 1681–1707, an important four-page journal, which included price and trade information, short articles, and political commentary. In 1693 he published *A Discourse on the Decay of Trade*, which was rewritten as a lobby document for the Bill, published as *The Causes of our Present Calamities in Reference to the Trade of the Nation . . . with the most proper expedient to remedy the same . . .* (1695), BL 816.m.12(.5); repeated with modification in BL 816.m.12(.6); Lees (1939), pp. 44–7. See also *A Short Account of the Grievances of the Nation* and other pamphlets (e.g. BL 816. m.12(.7) and 816.m.12 (110–116)), which opposed taxation on commodities: a foretaste of later debates. *DNB*; *Biography of British Economists*.

[6] Whiston, *A Discourse on the Decay of Trade*; quoted in Lees (1939, p. 45).

negotiation of trade treaties and organization of the navy. Davenant gives a clear statement of the problems of information asymmetry: 'it is...impossible for noblemen and gentlemen [i.e. ministers and parliament] not educated in trade ever to arrive at a perfect knowledge of the matters in question; for want of which their judgements are abused by clamour, importunity, prejudice, partiality, or some other prevailing bias; and seldom...come to a right decision; to the manifest damage of the nation'.[7]

These proposals are important because they were prominent, raised expectations about reform, sought formal involvement of the major traders and the outports,[8] and placed into the public and commercial mind the concept of a new and independent mechanism for improving governmental decisions on trade. The actual result in 1696 was disappointing: the establishment of a Committee of Trade, which was a very different body appointed from the aristocracy. However, Davenant and Whiston's proposals continued to resonate in subsequent writing, but perhaps became most significant when Burke took them up in 1780.

Postlethwayt: the early recognition of competitive institutions

Possibly one of the most important early writers to provide widespread understanding of the chamber concept was Malachy Postlethwayt. He wrote extensively in the 1750s on trade and mercantile issues, raising the need for a new settlement for colonial trade.[9] He drew on Whiston and Davenant and made a key feature in most of his writings of the superior role of French institutions, which he argued had given competitive advantage: Britain needed to copy these changes 'to enable us the better to support such a rivalship against France'.[10] There were various aspects to this argument, including the role of bounties for exports, reduced import duties, and other regulatory advantages that France supposedly offered, as well as specific aids to manufacturing sectors,[11] control and effective use of public expenditure and taxation,[12] and restricting government intervention.[13] But a key element running throughout was the role of the French Council of Commerce, founded in 1664, and the local chambers of commerce, established in 1701.

[7] Davenant (*c*.1695), BL Harleian papers, MS 1223, vol. i.

[8] Bristol strongly supported the Bill through its leading merchants, and mayor: Lees (1939), pp. 57–60.

[9] Malachy Postlethwayt, 1707–67, was a prodigious author, who has been seen as a strong advocate of the slave trade and the African Company. But his intellectual influences were greatest through publications on trade and commercial rivalry with France. His *DNB* entries make no comment on his advocacy of French institutional models or representative routes such as chambers, yet these are key thrusts of his works. His brother, James Postlethwayt, 1711–61, was well connected to the secretary of the Royal Society, publishing significant books on *History of Public Revenue* (1753), and in 1759 on disease and mortality; credited as major sources for later writers Adam Smith and Jeremy Bentham, on public taxation and debt; see Bennett (2011a) for new genealogical coverage.

[10] As expressed in Postlethwayt, *Britain's Commercial Interest* (1757), p. 249.

[11] See especially Postlethwayt (1749, 1757).

[12] See Postlethwayt (1757), which has the subtitle 'that an increase of the public debts and taxes must...prove the ruin of the monied, the trading, and the landed interest'.

[13] Postlethwayt's wider influence on economic thought in *DNB*; Johnson (1937); Bennett (2011a).

A national council of commerce finds a key place in Postlethwayt's most widely circulated and reprinted book, his *Dictionary of Commerce*, first published in 1751–5 in instalments and then reissued in 1766 and 1774. This recalled Davenant, but also drew heavily on a French *Dictionaire universel de commerce* by Jacques Savary of 1720–30.[14] Information on the French Council is also a key part of the trailer and advertisement for Postlethwayt's *Dictionary* in 1749.[15] One of Postlethwayt's other heavily circulated books, *Great Britain's True System* (1757), describes and praises French chambers at greater length.[16] There, he states that 'the council of commerce was an admirable establishment for the benefit of trade, and has been productive of unspeakable advantages to France.... They are elected annually by the corporation and magistrates of the several towns, and every one of these towns has a distinct chamber of commerce.... Such like establishments, properly conducted, would certainly prove of inestimable advantage to the commerce of these kingdoms [Britain].'[17]

Postlethwayt was the Keynes of his day, the leading economist whose writings were universally known. He had been an adviser to Walpole during the Excise Tax crisis, also worked for several years for Henry Pelham, and was in contact with Pitt and Rockingham. Although his roles are shadowy, and his genealogy has been obscure, recent research has filled these gaps and highlighted his continuing intellectual influences behind the scenes: on the Africa Company 1744–6; probably helping Pelham with the 1749 Debt Act and 1751 Tobacco Act; as one of many economic advisers to Rockingham during the Stamp Act crisis in 1765–6; and possibly interlinked with leading members of the Liverpool Stamp Act committee.[18] Whilst chambers were only a small part of Postlethwayt's advocacy, his ideas found continued currency by being taken up politically and disseminated by others, especially Bolingbroke and Burgh, later by Wilkes and Burke, and by Brougham.

Postlethwayt stated the central *purpose* of chambers was to overcome information asymmetry: 'to confer together on the most proper measures requisite to be taken, to make not only the trade of their own town flourish, but to increase both the inland and foreign trade of the whole kingdom'; their *process of meeting*, 'twice a week'; their *method of operations* by receiving 'all informations and proposals to any branch of traffic whatsoever'; and *'managing disputes with the colonies* by hearing representations concerning abuses and difficulties in trade, and also complaints relating to impositions in trade, made by the governors,

---

[14] The *DNB* for Postlethwayt suggests that he was criticized for plagiarizing work in Richard Cantillon's *Essai sur la nature du commerce*, which was written in about 1734 but published in 1755; but there is little overlap with this; Savary's work, though, is heavily used, and is acknowledged in Postlethwayt's title: see Johnson (1937).

[15] Postlethwayt (1749).

[16] There is further enthusiastic praise for a national Council in Postlethwayt's *Short State of the Progress of the French Trade and Navigation* (1756), and *Britain's Commercial Interest* (1757), pp. 9–13, 34–45, 57–66, and 96.

[17] Postlethwayt (1757), pp. 247–9; emphases in original removed.

[18] Bennett (2011a); the Liverpool committee merchant partnership of Benson and Postlethwaite.

and other public officers . . . , which are represented by them to their respective deputies'.[19]

This model is very much a centralized structure, operating a two-way flow of information of resolutions and advice between the government, the main out-ports, and the colonies. It closely resembles aspects taken up later by the General Chamber of Manufacturers, and clearly lay behind some of the correspondence that exists in the 1760s between some early chamber figures, such as Garbett, Wedgwood, and Burke. Postlethwayt advocated using merchant deputies, 'well skilled and experienced in commerce' who could provide an input into legislation 'derived from a very exact and circumstantial state of commerce as carried out by the merchants and traders', which would allow legislators 'to adapt and conform their laws to the nature of peculiar branches [of different trades]'.[20] This argument was strengthened in a very angry piece in 1759, *The Merchants Advocate*, which argued that the Customs were preventing merchants claiming a 5% subsidy on exports 'without the consent of parliament'. He called for 'the united weight of the body of merchants [to] obtain such redress . . . as no private persons can do'.[21] In a period just preceding the Stamp Act, this reiterated a vision for a national collective voice that was to resonate through subsequent developments.

Postlethwayt also had a *Plan* for a merchant educational body, called a *Merchant's Public Counting House* (1750). This echoes the Whiston–Davenant concern with aristocratic ignorance. The *Plan* was to take in 'gentlemen' to teach them the skills of trade, including 'managing foreign currency transactions and exchange; understanding duties, subsidies, bounties, tariffs and drawbacks; double entry bookkeeping, accounts of sales'. A key aspect was experience of commercial discourse, 'pleasing conversable exercise, and argumentation', focused on 'remarkable cases, relating to the negotiation of bills of exchange; and curious points that regard insurances, . . . that arise in the course of practical business'.[22] The value of discourse, and the need for improved commercial training, is echoed in many later chamber developments. The *Plan* was implemented in 1751 as a mercantile academy in Hertfordshire.[23] Although it is unlikely that this survived for long, the ideas profoundly influenced two other authors: Thomas Mortimer and John Weskett.

---

[19] Postlethwayt (1757), pp. 248–9.

[20] Postlethwayt (1757), p. 259.

[21] Postlethwayt (1759), vol. ii, pp. 10, 13; see also pp. 19–20.

[22] Postlethwayt (1750), pp. 38 and 83–4. Charges were 100 guineas per year, to cover two years of training, minimum of one year, argued to be cheaper that assigning a trainee to a merchant house, which required a premium of 500–1000 guineas per year for five or six years.

[23] Based at Waterside, Hemel Hempstead (Postlethwayt (1751), second edition), showing a change in implementation: under pressure from London merchants 'practical merchandising be entirely laid aside'; instead 'little offices' simulated correspondence between the Custom House, insurers, banks, etc.

Thomas Mortimer's 'blueprint'

Like Postlethwayt, Mortimer gave considerable publicity to the European chambers, but he went further in offering a more developed proposal in his 1772 book, *The Elements of Commerce*.[24] This was widely disseminated, being reissued in 1780 and 1802 editions, translated into German in 1783, and enlarged as a *General Commercial Dictionary* in 1810, which went through three further editions by 1823.[25] Mortimer acknowledged earlier writers, and his use of Davenant and Postlethwayt was particularly close, thus providing a means for their ideas to continue to reverberate. It is likely that Mortimer's book was the source that stimulated Burke's revived interest in Whiston–Davenant in 1780.

Mortimer's proposal for chambers of commerce in 1772 was an intellectual case, but reflected continued political frustration with government. It also provides a vision for chambers across the Atlantic world. Mixing the two terms, 'council' and 'chamber' of commerce, he suggested that what was needed was an 'intelligent council of commerce in almost every county of England, and in every province of the American colonies'; i.e. across the empire of the time. 'It is true, we have a Board of Trade, but it takes no immediate cognisance of the commerce of the kingdom . . . almost merely . . . for political use. . . . We appear to be adrift in commercial matters, without pilot or compass, driving before the wind of accident . . . so that if we long escape shipwreck, we shall have wonderful good fortune.' Critically, he went on to assert that 'if only one council of commerce in this kingdom, and another in each of the American colonies, had subsisted on this plan, *we should never have heard of the Stamp Act*, nor some of the other Acts of parliament still unrepealed'.[26]

Mortimer drew on his experience as Vice-Consul to the Austrian Netherlands at Ostend 1763–8. In 1764 the Flemish government had suddenly laid a high duty on rock salt, which greatly affected the exports from Liverpool to Ostend. 'If a chamber of commerce had at this time subsisted in Liverpool, the memorial I sent home upon that subject should have been transmitted directly to such a chamber of commerce, instead of going to the Secretary of State's office where its fate was to be neglected . . . or to be sent to our present flimsy Board of Trade, to be laid on the shelf.'[27] Mortimer's period as Vice-Consul gave him direct experience of the local court powers of consuls, but when he failed to be reappointed to the post

---

[24] Thomas Mortimer, 1730–1810 was a well-placed son of the Master of the Rolls. He was an extensive author, and continued to advocate chambers into the 1800s, e.g. lecture 10 of *Lectures on the Elements of Commerce, Politics and Finance* (1801). His *Universal Director* (1763, p. 19) lists him as a compiler and author, private teacher of languages and 'the art of acquiring a correct style fit for the press'. He wrote *A Concise Account of the Rise . . . of the Society for the Encouragement of Arts* (1763), listed in its *Membership List* (1768) as a linen draper. He began as junior clerk to Court of Chancery, then merchant and consul, later clerk to the Chief Baron of Exchequer (1792) and to the Lord Chief Jurie of Common Pleas (1793–8). See also *DNB*, which ignores his chamber role.

[25] Thomas Mortimer (1772). He acknowledges that he drew on earlier sources (p. 196, note), such as Child, Cary, Man, Davenant, Postlethwayt, and others.

[26] Mortimer (1772), pp. 192–3 and note; emphasis added.

[27] Mortimer (1772), p. 200; his reference to Liverpool may also indicate that he was aware of early discussions there to found the chamber established in 1774.

in 1768, in what he claimed was a political move, he developed a deep feeling that the political system was corrupt and incompetent.[28] These convictions are evident in his 1772 book, where politicians are portrayed as ignorant (and corrupt) and needed better sources of information and advice. He felt they needed better education and he also set up an academy to teach young gentlemen and others about the world of commerce.[29]

In Mortimer's view the government was undermining the economy through incompetent and contentious legislation on trade, taxes, and the colonies:

> the errors of parliament may be rectified by amendments, or repeals of acts detrimental to commerce; but the effect of ignorance in commercial affairs becomes more fatal, when its gets in possession of the administration of government.... The history of England furnishes too many instances of the imbecility of entire administrations in this respect; the very department peculiarly charged with the inspection and care of commercial affairs [the Board of Trade], having often been filled with gentlemen, who could not claim to the least mercantile knowledge ... and (unhappily) the superior offices of state ... [are] likewise occupied by men equally deficient in this point.[30]

This view also finds resonance in Adam Smith, who in 1776 was writing about government bureaucrats being 'negligent, expensive, and oppressive ... idle and profligate', diverting funds from 'more necessary expenses'.[31]

Mortimer's concept of chambers was thus first and foremost a means to improve government. There were eight objectives:[32] (i) 'the chambers of commerce, in the counties of this kingdom, to make reports' at least quarterly on the state of the economy to 'the grand council of commerce in London' (i.e. the replacement of the Board of Trade); the members should be elected from the freemen of corporations by the principal traders; (ii) the chambers should act as commercial juries in seaports to report on, remonstrate, petition, or manage local grievances related to

[28] See: *Political Register* (1769); *The Remarkable Case of Thomas Mortimer* (1770); see also *Monthly Review*, 42 (1770), pp. 251–3; *Whisperer* No. 57, 16 March (1771). The *DNB* does not follow this up. He was appointed Vice-Consul in January 1764 by the incumbent (Mr Hatton), who had not visited the town in 15 years, and promised to transfer the post, which he did not do. Change of minister from Grenville, who Mortimer knew, to Grafton led to dismissal. He lobbied Jenkinson and many others in his cause: BL Add MS 34713, fos. 182, 206, 211–4, 221; 38211, fo. 84. His correspondence 1766–9 shows he was judged as inflaming a dispute between captains, using consular summary powers. Robert Wood, on behalf of Lord Weymouth stated that 'Mr. Mortimer has discovered a moment of temper and an impatience of contradiction in his manner of what he calls the rights of a British Consul, that is very alarming, and, if not soon moderated, may produce very unhappy consequences for himself and the King's service'; letter to William Gordon, consul at Brussels, 11 February 1768. Weymouth wrote that Mortimer acted with 'passion and petulance'; letter to Gordon, 12 February 1768. Weymouth later accepted Mortimer 'had been correct' in exercising his powers, as 'supported by the Admiralty solicitor', but he was caught up in political play: Weymouth letter to William Gordon, 1 March 1768. TNA: SP 77/104.
[29] End paper of Mortimer, *Elements* (1780 edition): he 'receives into his house up to ten young gentlemen', charging 100 guineas per year for each pupil—the same as Postlethwayt. Mortimer's academy appears to have been successful, as judged by continued advertisements.
[30] Mortimer (1772), Introduction, p. vi.
[31] Smith (1776), vol. ii, pp. 347, 357; vol. i, p. 468.
[32] Mortimer (1772), pp. 192–200.

Customs, trade flows, smuggling, etc.; (iii) they should frame a concise and complete mercantile code 'digested, approved by the majority of the chambers of commerce in the kingdom, ratified by the grand council at London, and legalised by Act of parliament, and to terminate mercantile disputes in a summary way'; (iv) they should devise a means for employing the poor in honest industry and support the police in preventing them becoming criminals; (v) they should find a means to settle outstanding debts with creditors, rather than use of prison; (vi) there was to be reform of the death penalty and transportation to put criminals to useful work; (vii) the chambers should establish marine societies for education of boys for sea service; and (viii) they should consider all commercial memorials to ministers and foreign-based consuls. This specification revived and developed earlier ideas, and acted as a medium for dissemination and popularization.

John Weskett's Plan and the first London chamber of commerce 1782–1800

John Weskett's *Plan of the Chamber of Commerce* in 1782 was established and actually ran over 1782–1800.[33] His *Plan* supplemented Mortimer's thinking and was in the form of 12 draft articles, many focusing on arbitrating and settling commercial disputes, discussed in Chapter 7. But its core was a 'council of *merchants* and *traders* of the first consideration, judgement, and experience, chosen annually; who meet weekly, or frequently, . . . to confer on, communicate to government the properest measures of promoting and regulating both foreign and inland trade of their own towns, and of the whole of the Kingdom; and to receive all information and proposals useful to every track of traffic'.[34]

Weskett also foresaw a role for chambers to offer advice: all business people 'may have a *constant*, or an *occasional* recourse to this office . . . in like manner as they might have to a confidential friend, agent or correspondent' (Article I); 'immediate, and confirmed appointments are given for *verbal* consultation and conference' (Article II); 'from consultation, opinion, advice and information naturally result' (Article III), which include representation to government and others. The chamber could also act as a legal representative or agent for 'attending or transacting with other people, bodies, courts, MPs, government', thus

---

[33] Little is known of John Weskett beyond his insurance and chamber publications. He must have lived approximately *c.*1730–1800, and his writings suggest that he was among other things an underwriter (Sutherland (1933), pp. 56–7). In 1783 he is listed in directories as a merchant. He was assistant secretary of the African Company in London from about 1751 until at least 1767, which suggests he was probably a participating African merchant; TNA: T 70/144–5; *The Court and City Kalender or Gentlemens Register*, London 1767, p. 239. He was legally trained, *Browne's General Law List*, 1787–1800. His *Plan* and *Treatise* are his major works, the latter is a very detailed and authoritative study offering an early codification of insurance law. Sutherland (1933), pp. 56–7, 264–5, 518–19, quotes various legal cases; some of these must have resulted from actions on behalf of others through the chamber.

[34] Weskett (1782), pp. 6–7, all emphases in original.

'forming and drawing of minutes, memorials, petitions, remonstrances, appeals, proposals, plans'.[35]

Weskett implemented the *Plan* establishing his chamber and becoming its director in 1782. Subscriptions were three guineas annual fee 'for constant resort for advice' (as described by Article II), or five guineas for a two-year service. Non-subscribers could receive the same service for a fee of not less than half a guinea for a first consultation, with a second consultation on the same matter free. The chamber was open all days 'Saturday afternoons and Sunday's excepted'.[36] Whatever its limitations, this was the first London chamber of commerce, and it appears to have lasted for 18 years.[37] His 1782 publication lists its address as 'near the Royal Exchange';[38] local directories place it at Cornhill (later the King's Arms Tavern) until 1800.[39] Weskett is also listed in the *Browne's General Law List* for all years 1787–1800 as having his address as director of the chamber of commerce, Cornhill.

It is difficult now to establish if Weskett's chamber was more than a one-man operation without wider impact. Despite its existence at the time, the only other chamber to refer to it is the Glasgow chamber where he sent a copy of his *Plan*, outlined his activities, and drew attention to his *Complete Digest on Insurance* (available at £2 5s.—'some captains of vessels, and other persons who sail from the Clyde, to the West Indies and North America, might be inclined to take a few copies with them for sale'). His letter suggests that his chamber was solely for dispute resolution: 'for enlarging the means of private utility (in default of all public commercial establishments, in this country for judicial purposes)'. But he offered to Glasgow 'to render you some acceptable and perhaps *material* services; of which you and your friends may freely and confidentially avail yourselves'.[40] Hence, it would appear that Weskett was not involved in the national lobby campaigns of the time. He was informed about provincial societies, corresponded with Glasgow chamber, and refers in his *Digest* to insurance bodies in Liverpool, Bristol, and Glasgow, offering bases for chambers based on local maritime courts.[41] He may thus have influenced the development of arbitration in Glasgow and other chambers.

Impact of the blueprint

Mortimer and Weskett provided an agenda that truly seems to have offered the blueprint for subsequent developments, although, like Whiston, Davenant, and Postlethwayt, their work is not cited in any of the chamber foundation statements or subsequent histories. Even Mortimer's concept of a marine society was taken up

[35] Weskett (1782), pp. 10, 13 and 15; emphases in original.
[36] Article XI, pp. 22–4; Article XII, p. 24.
[37] His proposals and activities are not covered in any of the London chamber's histories.
[38] Weskett (1782), p. 24.
[39] e.g. *The London Companion*; Wakefield, *General Directory*; Bowles, *New London Guide*.
[40] John Weskett to Gilbert Hamilton, secretary of the Glasgow chamber, 1 March 1783: Glasgow chamber papers TD 1670/4/15; emphasis in original.
[41] Weskett (1783), p. 83.

in many areas, with early chambers frequently in the vanguard, although all marine societies were founded as independent trust bodies. The impact of Mortimer and Weskett thus seems to have been through articulating what was already current. They may have been recorders of what was an emerging network of thought between national and local business leaders.

What we can be more certain of is that their writings were well known. They are listed in many libraries of the time.[42] Millar in 1787 states that of Mortimer's *Elements* 'it is unnecessary to give any account of a book so generally known'.[43] In Liverpool, Postlethwayt's and Mortimer's books were purchased for its subscription library[44] (to which most future chamber members belonged), and Postlethwayt had been given local resonance by being quoted in the campaign against the East India Company in 1768 for which two future chamber leaders (Heywood and Smythe) were the leading interlocutors.[45] We also know that Weskett was well connected and of status, being assistant secretary of the African Company 1750–67, which had local committees in London, Bristol, and Liverpool, giving him strong provincial networks.

Certainly Mortimer's ideas became recognized by the incumbent landed gentry as sufficient threat for his work later to be denigrated in the agricultural magazines of the day. For example, the comment on his *Lectures on the Elements of Commerce, Politics and Finance*, was that 'the establishment of a chamber of commerce . . . is spoilt by a recommendation of its interference with legislation. . . . Of course this is all visionary. Government is no longer real; the proposal of such a chamber of commerce is indeed to propose a revolution and government to be devolved, at Mr. Mortimer's request, into the hands of a select body of men after Mr. Mortimer's own heart.'[46] Attacks on chambers from the agricultural and landed interest were to continue into the 1840s.

The concept takes legs: Rockingham and Burke 1765–1783

Perhaps most significant of the impacts, however, was the network of thought that brought parliamentary leaders and early chamber writers together. Postlethwayt seems to have had a direct line to government through three prime ministers: Walpole, Pelham, and Rockingham. Rockingham remained a key focus of the opposition over the period when chambers were established and seems to have been at the centre of the knowledge networks for commercial reform at this time, together with Shelburne, Dartmouth, and others. Mortimer was writing in a period when the 'laws of trade' were being challenged, the government was becoming

---

[42] e.g. *Catalogue of the Manchester Circulatory Library* (1794) lists Weskett's *Digest* with only 25 other commercial titles, including Mortimer's *Elements* and De Foe's *Tracts*.

[43] Millar (1787), p. 17.

[44] Catalogue and purchases: Liverpool RO, 027 LYC 1/1/1, 1/1/2, and 3/1.

[45] Cross-membership of chamber and subscription library (Bennett (2010), tables A4 and A5); Postlethwayt quoted against East India by John Phillips, *Liverpool Gazette*, 23 and 30 June, 1 December 1768.

[46] Review of Mortimer's *Lectures*, in *The Council of Agriculture Magazine*, 6, July (1801), p. 46.

isolated, and the opposition offered a route for business influence. Rethinking trade and representing the merchant interests became important in the 1765–6 Stamp Act crisis; East India Company's crisis of 1767–8, in which Liverpool's subsequent chamber members, Rockingham (belatedly), and other opposition groups engaged; in the conflict over America; and in Burke's efforts for reform of parliamentary representation.

Burke's influential speech in February 1780 directed attention at the whole system of parliamentary representation, seeking suppression of offices. Its most substantial impact was to revive the discourse of Davenant, leading to abolition of the Board of Trade in 1782 in favour of direct representation by MPs and others, and starting a new attack on the charter companies like the African and East India. Burke noted that 'in 1695 . . . [parliament] attempted to form . . . a board for the protection of trade; which, as they planned it, was to draw to itself a great part, if not the whole, of the functions and powers, both of the admiralty, and of the treasury'.[47] What is significant here is that Burke renewed interest in Whiston and Davenant's idea of a national council of commerce as a preferable body to the then Board of Trade. This influenced, or was influenced by, Birmingham's Samuel Garbett, who had exchanged views with Burke on a national body in 1766. By 1780 the whole concept of a chamber of commerce system, with a national representative function, was very much in the front of attention. This was crucial for the General Chamber.

Other commentary and discourse: widening frames

There were also other intellectual currents. Voluntary organizations and societies were springing up on a large scale for social, charitable, and religious purposes; Langford and Clark refer to the period as an 'associational age'.[48] New societies for industry, invention, agriculture, and commerce were also very active. These societies were significant vehicles to bring together innovators across Britain and in the colonies, and included leading politicians. They also offered templates for formal governance, charters, and organization.

The Royal Society, founded in 1660, remained an important leader, and its history had been reprinted in the 1730s, as part of an active discussion of its influence on science and invention.[49] Malachy's brother James Postlethwayt was elected in 1754, and Thomas Butterworth Bayley (the first president of the Manchester chamber) was elected in 1773. There was also a wide network of other leading figures who had involvement with the Birmingham and North Staffordshire chambers: Joseph Priestley, Erasmus Darwin, and Benjamin Franklin were all elected members by 1766; Josiah Wedgwood, Matthew Boulton, and

---

[47] Edmund Burke, Speech on Economical Reform, 11 February 1780; reprinted in *The Writings of Edmund Burke*, vol. iii, pp. 481–551 (ed. P. Langford, Oxford: Clarendon Press, 1981); see also Klinge (1979).

[48] Langford (1989); Clark (2000a).

[49] T. Sprat's *History of the Royal Society*, of 1667, was reprinted in 1723 and 1734; quoted in Allan (1968), p. 12, n. 24.

James Watt were elected 1783–5; and there was another connection to Manchester through Thomas Percival, elected 1765, who led the Warrington Academy with Bayley, the Liverpool Heywoods, and others. The Royal Society played a key role linking individuals in the Midlands, through Wedgwood's Lunar Society friends and other circles (such as Samuel Garbett).[50] There were also the Royal Societies of Edinburgh and Dublin, both founded in 1731, Franklin's proposal for what became the American Philosophical Society in 1743, and the New York Society of Arts of 1765. These were all networking media for the early chamber members.

But probably most important for the chambers was the Society of Arts. Various schemes for a society had been proposed in 1722 and 1738; that in 1722 actually being called a Chamber of Arts.[51] These failed to take off, but in 1754 the Society for Encouragement of Arts and Manufactures and Commerce was established. This was a major vehicle to transfer information between localities, becoming prominent in the 1760s. All the conceptual leaders of chambers were members. Mortimer, as a member, published its first history in 1764. Postlethwayt became a member in 1758; John Weskett in 1762 (and a relative Robert Weskett was a member from 1769). Thomas Butterworth Bayley, and London-based Jersey merchant James Amicea Lemprière were members. Liverpool corporation was a significant supporter, granting the Society £100 in 1765.[52]

The Society of Arts was also used by Garbett and Wedgwood. Wedgwood's Liverpool agent Thomas Bentley stimulated discussion by the Society about inland navigation in support of the Trent–Mersey canal in 1765.[53] Importantly, its membership was wide, including the leading manufacturers, traders, bankers, and innovators, some leading political figures, some colonial figures and agronomists, as well as populists like John Wilkes.[54] It included most of Wedgwood's Lunar circle and many others, such as Jebediah Strutt in Derby. It was a rapidly developing networking medium, with 110 members in 1755, 708 in 1758, and nearly 2000 in 1760.[55]

The chamber concept thus had diffusion media into the world of practising merchants, which were in turn interlinked with politicians. From 1766 Garbett had made the idea of a national council or chamber more widely known,

[50] See Schofield (1963); Uglow (2002).
[51] Full text of the 1722 proposal for *Constitution and Regulations of the Proposed Chamber of Arts*, and 1738 proposal reproduced in Allan (1968), pp. 163–8: Royal Society Misc. MSS, vol. iv, No. 57.
[52] *The Annual Register* (1765), p. 111; Liverpool Town Books, 3 July 1765, Liverpool RO.
[53] Garbett letter to secretary of Society of Arts, October 1765, hoping that it would 'think the canal a proper subject for consideration and offer rewards' for choice of routes: Wedgwood correspondence: Farrer (1906).
[54] Among the politicians were Rockingham, Bedford, Portland, Grafton, Richmond, Bute, Dartmouth, Shelburne, Townshend, Pitt, Thomas Pownall, George Savile, and Edmund Burke; other members were Richard Arkwright, Joseph Banks, Jeremiah Bentham (father of Jeremy); bankers such as Francis Baring, and James, Thomas, and Patrick Coutts; leading colonials like Benjamin Franklin; and leading merchants and improvers like James Hanway, Arthur Young; John Wilkes was elected in 1758: see Wood (1913); Lists of members of 1758, 1762, 1769, and following.
[55] See Mortimer's own history of the society: *A Concise Account of the Rise, Progress and Present State of the Society...* (1763); see also Wood (1913); Allan (1968).

corresponding with Edmund Burke, whose support he had tried to enlist.[56] Garbett was well known to senior ministers through his expert commentary on the Birmingham metal industries, particularly issues related to metal coinage and military ordnance such as swords. He developed a particularly strong relationship with Shelburne, but also with Conway, Dartmouth, and Rockingham, whom he tried to imbue with a sense of obligation to the Birmingham manufacturers in general, and to Garbett himself in particular.[57] Rockingham proved most critical, as he used the provincial manufacturers and merchants, and American agents in London (which included Burke), in the 1765–6 Stamp Act crisis. There was thus a significant exchange of ideas about how to improve commercial advocacy, with the concept of local chambers beginning to emerge as a basis for voice and improving government information. Moreover this had made some limited headway by the time Mortimer was writing in 1772 (with the New York and Jersey chambers founded in 1768, Guernsey in 1769, and a North Staffordshire potters chamber by 1767).

The Society of Arts also encouraged many imitators, from local conversation and debating societies, to commercial and agricultural improvement bodies. Its *Transactions* became widely read and frequently reprinted, and the ideas widely diffused and copied.[58] There was local overlap of these societies with the early chambers. In Liverpool eight chamber committee members of the 1770s were also leading members of the Hundred of West Derby Agricultural (Improvement) Society, 13% of the known chamber committee.[59] In Manchester, 17 of the 29 chamber committee members (59%) were members of the Salford Hundred and Manchester Agricultural Societies, established in 1772 and 1774, respectively.[60] Thomas Butterworth Bayley FRS and FSA, president of the chamber, was vice-president of both Agricultural Societies. By 1781, when the Manchester chamber was re-established, there were still 33 Agricultural Society members among the chamber's 130 members (25%). This overlap between manufacturers and merchants with agriculture at first sight seems extraordinary, and is often explained as a common interest in reducing the costs of food to keep wages down. But inspection of the main activities of the Salford and Manchester Societies shows the initial aim was to feed horses (essential for transport) and to put straw on the streets to improve their cleanliness.[61]

There were also many other networks and societies between the leading businesses in the main localities at the time, which are discussed more fully in Chapter 14. These brought together Liverpool, Bristol, and the Midlands in particular, though

---

[56] Garbett letter to Edmund Burke, 29 October 1766; quoted in Norris (1957), p. 452.

[57] See Norris (1957), pp. 452–3; Langford (1973); Money (1977); Dietz (1991); fuller discussion in Chapter 9.

[58] See Bowden (1965), pp. 43–4 for a summary of these developments.

[59] See Bennett (2010), p. 106; source, LRO 630 WES.

[60] Derived from comparison of lists of both bodies: see *Manchester Mercury*, 21 June 1774, 28 November 1775 for members of the Salford and Manchester Agricultural Societies; 8 March 1774 for chamber members.

[61] *Manchester Mercury*, 4 January, 1 and 15 November (1774), and following issues.

these networks stretched to Yorkshire, Ireland, Scotland, and all major parts of the economy, including the colonies. This networking allowed transfer of ideas between the Rockingham party during the Stamp Act crisis, and local luminaries in the major centres across the Atlantic world. Wedgwood's extensive national political and personal networks were probably particularly significant. He had many business partners in Liverpool and the Midlands, among whom in the 1760s was the first chair of the Liverpool chamber in 1774, John Dobson. He also had associations with the first chair of the Manchester chamber, Butterworth Bayley, and the first chair of the Birmingham chamber in 1783, Samuel Garbett.[62] Wedgwood travelled the country frequently, using the Liverpool MP, William Meredith to promote his business in 1763, and to promote the Trent–Mersey Canal from 1765. Wedgwood, as a Unitarian, was involved with the Warrington Academy, which brought him into contact with Butterworth Bayley and the Liverpool Heywoods who were also Unitarians. Meredith was also a particularly important element of diffusion. Wedgwood and Richard Chaffers, another potter related to a leading Liverpool chamber member Edward Chaffers, had financially supported Meredith's highly contested election to become MP in 1761. A prominent Liverpool banker, William Ingram, father of chamber committee member Francis, was also a principal backer of Meredith, and used the strength of the potters to swing the election for Meredith.[63] Thomas Earle, brother of chamber member William Earle, was the main Liverpool member of the Society of Arts; whilst the Liverpool Rathbones, Darby's of Coalbrookdale, Reynolds of Bristol, Matthew Boulton in Birmingham were intermediaries and in wider intellectual and business exchanges with Wedgwood and Meredith's circle.

For the Merchant Venturers in Bristol, which sometimes acted like a chamber, Richard Champion and William Reeve were key members, with Champion a major merchant, banker, and potter in close contact with the Americans, lobbying hard in London in 1765–6 and 1774. He made celebratory porcelain likenesses of Franklin and Washington in 1776 and had unsuccessfully tried to rival Wedgwood's patronage by the queen and leading politicians. After a brief spell in politics as Burke's deputy as paymaster general in 1782 and 1783–4 (under Lord North, and then Fox–North), Champion emigrated to America in 1784.[64] Similarly the Bristol Venturer Henry Cruger, nephew of New York chamber president and Assembly leader John Cruger, was closely concerned with the London lobbies and a frequent correspondent of Rockingham.[65] There was thus a strong set of personal interconnections between politicians, the early thinkers and writers about chambers of commerce, and their early leaders.

---

[62] For further detail of Wedgwood's Liverpool links, see Bennett (2010), pp. 35 and 150; for Birmingham see Norris (1957), Bowden (1965), Money (1977); also Schofield (1963).

[63] This was a specific attack on the Tarleton family interests in the Corporation; see Hughes (1906), p. 132; Sanderson (1977); Boney (1957); Bennett (2010), pp. 98–9 and 118–19.

[64] Guttridge (1934), pp. 5–8.

[65] Langford (1973, 1986a, 1986b); see also Rockingham correspondence lists: Sheffield Archives, Wentworth Woodhouse Muniments.

A title for the concept

As well as the intellectual case, the title 'chamber' also offered other attractions: it had intertextual resonance as a brand name that conveyed status, formality, the impression of legal standing, and independence/judicial ability. A proximate series of events may have provided specific textual allusions: the re-establishment of the Paris chamber of assurance as the Royal Chamber of Assurance in 1750 (which Weskett wrote about, as well as related bodies in the other major ports); and the surviving Chamber of Assurance in London.[66] Similarly the chartered companies were sometimes referred to as chambers, especially that for the Herring fisheries, and this may account for a single stray reference to a fishing chamber of White-haven in *c*.1753.[67] These bodies may have made the title 'chamber' familiar in Britain.

However, the model of French chambers with business people servicing govern-ment-controlled and appointed committees, would have been repellent in Britain and America at the time, compared to a voluntary body.[68] But they offered an attractive comparative title, being standard features of many books from the 1750s.[69] They had become widely known beyond economic authors; favourably noted in various travel books of the period.[70] William Knox in 1789 referred to chambers as 'receptacle and deposit for commercial knowledge . . . the only means of collecting and bringing into use the information on which regulations ought to be founded'.[71] William Lord Newhaven in 1786 stated that 'the world is now one great chamber of commerce, of which each nation make a part, several striving by every possible means to supplant each other'.[72]

The title 'chamber of commerce' thus seems to have come to be preferred because it offered brand status that many of the founders were only groping towards. It was also very different from the other terms in use which reflected social and mass mobilization; e.g. 'assembly', 'gathering', 'movement', 'meeting',

---

[66] Weskett (1783), pp. 89 ff.; see also Magens (1755); Millar (1787), pp. 16–17; and Chapter 7.

[67] The *Encyclopaedia Britannica* edition of 1778–83 contained a brief definition of chambers, referring to France; for Britain it mentions only one chamber, the Company for herring-fishing. Whitehaven 'fishing chamber' petitioned over concerns with whaling, the French, salt, and bounties for Greenland; BL Add MS 38462 fo. 31.

[68] e.g. Braudel (1983), vol. ii, p. 81 quotes a 1710 comment from a merchant at Dunkerque: 'all the [French] chambers of commerce . . . are good for nothing but ruining general trade by making 5 or 6 individuals the absolute masters of shipping and commerce wherever they are established'. As a result some French chambers were shunned, and became inactive.

[69] For example, Country Gentleman (1753), *Reflections upon Nationalization, Corporations and Companies Supported by the Authorities of both Ancient and Modern Writers* (by William Pulteney, MP, William Johnstone); Goldsmiths-Kress papers. John Bennet, merchant (1736), *The National Merchant: A Discourse on Commerce and Colonies*, printed for the Royal Exchange, London, pp. 13–14, 24; John Ashley (probable author) (1745), *The Present State of the British and Foreign Trade to Africa and America Considered and Compared: With some Proposition in Favour of the Trade of Great Britain*, London, pp. 7–9.

[70] e.g. Lord Gordon Stone (1795), *Travelling Memorandums Made in a Tour upon the Continent of Europe in the Years 1786, 1787 and 1788*, vol. iii, pp. 68–9.

[71] William Knox (1789), *Extra Official State Papers, Addressed to Rt. Hon. Lord Rawdon etc.*, Debrett, London: Goldsmiths Kress.

[72] Newhaven, Baron William Mayne (1786), *A Short Address to the Public*, Debrett, London, p. 2.

'crowd',[73] or French 'councils' and 'syndicates'. Instead, 'chamber' reflected support for the existing formal and elite government, although challenging it, and for deliberated judgement, not spontaneity in response to a crowd, and not rebellion. In addition it suggested a permanent body, whilst social and political movements were almost definitionally short term.[74]

'Chamber' also recalled the meeting-chambers of the local corporations, which the commercial bodies sought to rival; and it also suggested an equivalence of the chambers of the Houses of Parliament. Hence, 'chamber' was part of an intertextual narrative that resonated with the idea that they were not only associations, but also formal meeting places, with weighty and elite membership, where expert deliberation took place, but with a status and permanence beyond a campaign or a coffee house. 'Chamber' also had legal resonance with the courts, and hence was aligned with the idea of a medium for commercial arbitration. However, the evolution of the chamber brand identity was predominantly empirical with the key attributes of differing personal visions, lack of template, organizational learning, and contingency, which indeed are general among voluntary associations.[75] Although all the first five chambers were called 'chamber' from their outset, as were most of the others established in the 1780s, the choice of title was not universally adopted until 1815; other names used were 'society', 'committee', and 'association'.[76]

4.3 THE FOUNDATIONS OF CONTENTION: TAXATION, 'PROTEST', AND THE AMERICAN COLONIES

An idea or concept was not enough to engage busy businessmen: they also required a proximate threat to spur action. The question assessed here is how a new 'discourse coalition' formed around the concept of chambers. Tilly and Tarrow, among others, have argued that the Stamp Act of 1765 and American War of 1775–81 were the two 'great events' that changed the frames of policy in late 18th century Britain and America, and introduced new repertoires of contention on a systemic scale, as *transgressive contention*: where incumbent and established agents, and the existing government machinery, were unable to resolve the issues of concern.[77] Historians since Sutherland have similarly argued that a change of repertoires and connectivity of government occurred in this period.[78] The chambers

---

[73] Tilly (1995, tables 4.4 and 4.5) lists these terms most frequently for political campaign bodies in 1758–81.

[74] Tilly (1978, 2004); Tarrow (1974).

[75] See Chapter 3; also Grant (1993, 2000); Langford (1989); Clark (2000a).

[76] As in Birmingham 1783–1813, and Manchester's second chamber 1781–1800.

[77] See Chapter 3; Tilly (1978, 1994, 2004); McAdam, Tarrow, and Tilly (2001); Tarrow (1994), pp. 45, 70–2.

[78] Sutherland (1933), p. 60; Morgan and Morgan (1962); Bradley (1986, 1990); Bargar (1956); Namier (1961); Countryman (1981); Jacobs (1992); Armitage (2003).

emerged as part of this political frame change.[79] This field has been written about by hundreds of authors; the purpose here is to relate this to the chambers and their leaders, for which some surprisingly neglected avenues can be opened.

The critical ingredients for chamber formation

Three crucial elements were needed to connect the chamber concept to the mainstream of political debate to ensure something happened: first, there had to be a medium through which to operate as an organized lobby and political opposition (both in parliament and in the larger Atlantic world); second, other routes had to be closed or made difficult to access, to require new modes of organization for those with grievances; and third, there had to be events that led to sufficient anger with the governing elite that the opposition was fuelled and local action sparked.

The relevance of the opposition was that it raised the mere circulation of the chamber idea to the political level. This was a period when political parties were only beginning to emerge, but an organized opposition was becoming significant in framing a diverse agenda of 'reform'. Of relevance here, the primary early organizer of the opposing parliamentary interests, Bolingbroke (in the 1732–3 Excise tax crisis, and the peddlers' agitation of 1730), had taken Davenant as a source of economic guidance on British *national economic interests*, and resistance to arbitrary extension of the state and its tax burdens. Over 60 ports and major centres had acted in concert by sending petitions giving fixed instructions to their MPs to vote against the Excise legislation.[80] Postlethwayt's first engagement with government was during this crisis as a covert adviser/pamphleteer for Walpole. The opposition similarly grasped Davenant and Postlethwayt under Rockingham's lead in the 1760s (especially during his period as prime minister, when the 'opposition' was in government 1765–66), and through Wilkes in his populist campaigns of 1769–76.[81] The ideas were also given great currency in publications by James Burgh over 1754–74, who argued that extra-parliamentary associations were a means to marshal collective opinion to counteract the power of government (particularly its patronage). Burgh's concept of a Grand National Association of representative interests was to have great currency in the subsequent political efforts for electoral reform by Wilkes, Wyvell's Counties Association, the slave trade abolition movement, and even the Gordon riots.[82] It was also a natural stimulus

---

[79] As political, not social movements; though recently Young (1995) and Smith (1995) have revived aspects of Jameson's (1926) interpretation of American developments as a form of social movement.

[80] Langford (1975); Price (1980, 1983); Pocock (1986) pp. 273–81.

[81] Wilkes quoted Postlethwayt's *Universal Dictionary* on taxes in particular: see e.g. Butterfield (1949), pp. 279–80.

[82] Burgh, J. (1754), *The Dignity of Human Nature*; pamphleteer in *Crito* (1764); and *Political Disquisitions* (1774–5). See Butterfield (1949), pp. 259–68; Langford (1975, 1991); Brewer (1976), pp. 342–4.

to the chambers. The concept of a national representative body with delegates had become mainstream opposition politics.

Associations and collective petitions of the aggrieved were the natural avenues to challenge the structure of the contemporary state through 'respectable' opposition. The politically excluded were obsessed about the institutionalized structure of power that entrenched aristocratic interests and prevented reform through control of places and patronage. The excluded contained many of the new merchant and manufacturing classes. At local level exclusion extended to the key local institutions: the common councils that controlled local government in the large cities. These exclusions were reflected in support for the Wilkes and later Counties Association, but also found reign in the contemporaneous so-called 'subscription movement' of 1772–9 that sought repeal of the religious exclusions of the Test Act and Corporation Act. Petitioning, the crowd, populism, and 'association' were now new orders of the day on a mass scale, with petition signatories on the major questions equalling or exceeding the voters at general elections.

Anger with the governing elite was brought to a new peak by a series of 'great events'. The underlying theme of the period is a crisis building up between the authority exercised by the aristocratic state, and local economic interests that wanted to ensure unimpeded freedom to trade and make entirely reasonable decisions in their own interests. The first great event to exhibit these tensions was Wilkes '45' in 1763, leading to Wilkes Middlesex election affair of 1768–9, itself part of the response to, and cause of, such events. A second critical event was the *organized collective* of businesses that in 1766 achieved repeal of the Stamp Act and legislation on Free Ports. This was followed by a series of further local economic associations seeking to enforce trade embargoes in Britain and America to prevent extensions of taxation and control. These bodies and their campaigns were all largely successful,[83] which of course encouraged more of the same. The first eight chambers were set up in the period 1767–74, and at least five were linked to committees for these legislative reforms.[84]

These lobbies were based on an Atlantic structure: nationally organized through local committees and delegates spanning the main provincial cities of Britain and the American colonies. It was from these essentially ad hoc beginnings that, among other things, more stable chamber structures emerged. But all this failed with the most significant of the 'great events', the American rebellion, and war of 1775–83. This shattered the economic as well as the political foundations of the Atlantic economy and Empire. It also split the business community; much initiative for new economic associations went into abeyance; and the early chamber members found themselves having to choose between being 'loyalists', 'revolutionaries', or trying to stay neutral. But cessation of hostilities in 1781 opened the way for a second phase of chamber foundations.

[83] Langford (1973, 1975, 1980); Olson (1973, 1979); Kammen (1968, 1970); Minchinton (1971); Doerflinger (1986).
[84] Boston, New York, Charleston, Liverpool, and Manchester. Kingston (Jamaica), Jersey, and Guernsey sought specific local reforms.

Access in the pre-Reform state

The whole thrust of the establishment of chambers assumes that they felt they were 'outsiders'. In the period up to the Reform Acts of 1832 for national elections, 1835 for local municipalities in England, Wales, and Ireland, and 1846 in Scotland,[85] most leading businesses were excluded from politics, and had weak influence on local municipal decisions. There were increasingly two nations, one aristocratic, static and shrinking, but in political control, the other rapidly growing. This other interest was itself in two parts, both of which were largely unenfranchised: first, the world of business was increasingly powerful in its own arena but had limited influence on national government, and patchy influence on local government; second, the broader population was usually powerless in all arenas.[86] The excluded saw government as corrupt and unreliable, and its intervention was increasingly to be resisted since it would lead to even more corruption through patronage. This view united both of the excluded categories, but inevitably there were tensions between the business leaders and the wider population. A related dimension of exclusion arose from religious dissent,[87] which was of some consequence for early chambers, particularly in Ireland.

In parliament in 1761 there were only about 15 businessmen within the 560 MPs; in 1780 there were about 18.[88] There were about 78 MPs with mercantile interests, but most were not independent, their influence diminished because any political advancement depended on the aristocratic establishment; 'their fortunes, their status, and their livelihood depended on coexistence with traditional groups . . . rather than hostility towards them'.[89] Intermarriage, close relations with the landed interests, and receipt of patronage were critical social objectives, and the only way to develop a political career and influence.

A key problem was how government manipulated local electoral franchises, which had come almost entirely under control of patrons and government. Various reforms narrowed the number of electors, making them easier to control, increased the security of a seat, and narrowed the candidates who could afford election expenses. The problem became steadily greater. In 1700 about 20% of MP seats were influenced by patronage; by 1741 it was 45%; 60% by 1780; and 82% in 1816.[90] In Ireland almost all were patronage seats.[91] Patronage assured an enduring control by the landed elite. It led to the common sobriquet, that parliament was

---

[85] Although the Scottish 1846 Reform had little effect in the larger towns and it was not until 1888 that the guildery and other aspects of corrupt Scottish Burghs were abolished.

[86] Langford (1973, 1991); Brewer (1976, 1989).

[87] See e.g. Checkland (1952, 1958); Bridenbaugh (1955, 1962); Hilton (1977); Hilton (1988, 2006); Bradley (1990); also Chapter 14.

[88] Namier and Booke (1964).

[89] O'Gorman (1989), p. 210; see also Innis and Rogers (2000).

[90] All figures quoted from O'Gorman (1982), pp. 18–21 who summarizes the sources of alternative estimates; see also Porritt and Porritt (1903), vol. ii, pp. 8–63.

[91] Only 11 out of 117 open; Porritt and Porritt (1903), vol. ii, pp. 339–41; James (1973). The chief open boroughs were Carrickfergus, Cork, Drogheda, Dublin, Londonderry, and Waterford (though there is doubt about Waterford).

filled by 'the indolent and ignorant Great', of the aristocracy and landed classes.[92] These concerns became increasingly important as parliament sat for much longer as the century progressed, became more intrusive into commerce, and information about its actions became more extensively covered in the press.

Barriers to local access

The systems of election for parliament and municipalities overlapped. The landed interests expected to be the leaders of municipal politics, and sought control via elections of freemen or held influence over them because freemen were the electors of MPs. As a result, 'the two systems, the parliamentary elections system and the system of corporation misrule, were so interwoven, so interdependent'.[93] This was particularly serious for larger city municipal government since the landed interests were usually not very interested in it; and hence led to the great neglect that chambers were to focus on, especially in Ireland.[94]

The more 'open' larger towns relevant to most chambers included leading businessmen among the freemen, but they rarely made it into the ruling bodies of the common councils.[95] The election of freemen, if not controlled by aristocratic patrons, was generally controlled by the smaller traders and artisans (the 'mechanics') under the patronage of government interests, or placemen appointed through patronage: Customs officers, Excise officers, surveyors, landwaiters, tidewaiters, etc., as well as military officers, who were usually all pro-government. In the major ports these placemen were numerous, and often odious, inefficient, and corrupt. They were a proximate cause of anger in almost all the early Irish chambers, as well as in Liverpool, Bristol, and the American ports.[96] The result was that the larger business interests could rarely prevail locally. Also in many important areas there was no municipal government, and businesses had to rely on county MPs to represent their voice; e.g. in Birmingham, Halifax, Manchester, and North Staffordshire.

Additionally, dissenters were formally debarred from local and national office. Although some participated if they kept their religion low key, this was nevertheless a significant barrier, and one with great symbolism. It was also a proximate issue. In 1767 scope for greater dissenter participation seemed to have been opened up by a legal judgement in The City, and in 1772 a Dissenter's Relief Bill had been initiated. But this, and a prominent Feathers Tavern petition in 1773, were all rejected. This encouraged many dissenters to engage in radical movements; for

---

[92] Kendrick, *Address c.*1780, quoted in Bowden (1965), p. 159.

[93] Porritt and Porritt (1903), vol. i, p. 55; also Municipal Corporation Commission, *Reports* (1835–9); Colley (1982); Brewer (1989).

[94] see e.g. Brewer (1976); O'Gorman (1982); Phillips (1992).

[95] O'Gorman (1989), pp. 55–62; Ireland from Porritt and Porritt (1903), vol. ii, pp. 339–41; James (1973). The degree of openness is disputed by Rogers (1989).

[96] There had been efforts to remove Customs officers from election rolls in 1770, 1780, and 1781. A parliamentary Act finally succeeded in 1782, 13 days after Rockingham had become prime minister; having effect for the 1784 election: Kemp (1953); Langford (1973, 1989, 1991); Bradley (1990).

many others it was a signal to develop quieter methods of reform. For both it encouraged a high dissenter involvement in petitioning campaigns.[97] For chambers, the dissenting supporters were mainly of the latter, 'reform', group but tensions with radicals were to become a significant aspect in America and Britain.

These patterns are vividly illustrated by one of Liverpool's chamber leaders, Benjamin Heywood, a dissenter but prominent banker and public figure, who analysed the 1775 petition for coercion against the Americans, noting those who were Council members or Customs officers. Indeed, Liverpool provides one of the best examples of the effect of pre-Reform oligarchic corruption. There were strong divisions between the 'ins' on the franchise and the 'outs', with strong control by an oligarchy of local 'families' linked to government.[98] The chamber was born from objections to the corporation's dock fees, and the mayor's 'public *breach of faith*', provocation of party feelings, and 'spreading abuse' against chamber leaders.[99] The corporation opposed the chamber, and after its foundation established its own committee of trade to compete with it.

Other locations where the local corporation actively tried to suppress chambers include Dublin in the 1780s, Cork in 1814, Bristol in the 1820–30s, London over 1780–1850,[100] and may have included Manchester in 1801, when a group of the members voted to suspend the chamber.[101] The chambers were a means to circumvent and rival the corporations' voice through an alternative status and weight of elite business membership. It is not surprising that some corporations resisted them.

Mechanisms for access through American and colonial agents

One way for the colonies to try to gain access was a network of agents in London. The American and West Indies merchants had organized societies or committees since the 1730s. These became very active in the 1760s, as well as the traders to Turkey, Spain, Ireland, Germany, and Muscovy. There was also the African Company, where Postlethwayt had been a key lobbyist over 1743–6, and Weskett assistant secretary *c*.1750–67.[102] Once the East India Company was under attack after 1767, this also had to lobby. Generally government ministers tried to find compromises through these agents. Olson describes the pattern as one where 'ministers continued to keep parliament from passing legislation unpalatable to the colonists, and to bypass the Board of Trade when important decisions were to be made. . . . Ministers worked out day-to-day compromises acceptable to political leaders on both sides of the Atlantic.'[103]

---

[97] Money (1977); Bradley (1986, 1990); see also Chapter 14.
[98] For detail on Liverpool, see Bennett (2010), pp. 67–90; see also Sanderson (1977).
[99] *Williamsons Advertiser*, 11 and 18 March 1774, emphases original; Bennett (2010), p. 74.
[100] See Chapter 5.
[101] The minutes, and discussion of Helm (1897) and Redford (1934), note the attempt to close the chamber.
[102] Penson (1924); Olson (1973, 1979); Dietz (1991); Bennett (2011a).
[103] Olson (1973), pp. 159–60.

The colonial agents and committees were extremely significant for chamber development because they offered a 'professionalized' model for managing deliberation and marshalling an effective voice in London. Their approach represented a step change from the ad hoc petitions and delegations used by British localities; the agents were a permanent presence, in continuous contact with senior members of the administration, and got wind of legislation before it was formalized, frequently being able to divert it or influence its modification to prevent extremes. This is very much akin to how modern lobbies work.

In addition, the American interests and their agents increasingly met in subscription coffee houses. The evolving model combined a London professional agent with a fixed meeting place, or *milieu for discourse*, which was copied as a core feature of many early chambers, as discussed in Chapter 11. The coffee clubs discussed colonial legislation between the American agents and local merchants, 'reworked' responses from the colonies into a form potentially more influential on the government, and drafted petitions that could then be posted up for other coffee club patrons to sign, thus gathering large-scale support and a level of unity of voice.[104] A specific club developed for each colony. Once a stable 'membership' and subscription base was established a chamber was only a step away. Although experiencing periods of threat and instability, this pattern of voice generally worked effectively to limit government excesses. The relation of the home metropolitan state and its right to rule was not seriously discussed.[105]

4.4 'GREAT EVENTS' 1: WILKES, THE STAMP ACT, AND RELATED ACTIVITY

It is from the accession of George III in 1760 that the subsequent great events are usually dated. The 'language of the court' changed, the young king and his followers more actively sought strong influence in parliament, and shook up previous cosy alliances within the aristocratic networks of the 'old Whigs'. However, the rights of local Assemblies in the colonies were initially reaffirmed, provided they worked within English laws.[106] Inadvertently this offered new opportunities for influence by the opposition and hence by the colonies. It also tended to strengthen the traditional forces in many of the crucial boroughs and counties (the landed aristocracy, and the borough common councillors), which the government relied on for electoral control of parliament. This intensified tensions at the local level.

There was also a revived drive to replace the Customs with Excise taxes as a source of revenues. The Customs had long been recognized as heavily evaded through smuggling. Excise taxes offered less scope for evasion on commodities

---

[104] Olson (1973), pp. 125–8; (1979, 1980).
[105] Christie and Labaree (1976), pp. 25 ff.
[106] Butterfield (1949, 1957), Brewer (1976); also Langford (1973, 1980, 1986a); Thomas (1975, 1991).

such as tobacco, wine, and spirits that were most prone to smuggling, but also suggested scope to increase revenue by extending taxation to an entirely new range of products. This may have been a rational modernization of taxation, but it was unlikely to be popular with merchants, nor with manufacturers, or their consumers. Most critically, it widened the potential for contention to the manufacturers, small artisans, retailers, and wider population. Excise administration was also intrusive, requiring local inspections; something the major merchants were used to, but which was newer to the manufacturer and small trader, and which the colonies were bound to resent. Customs modernization may have seemed politically innocent, but it contained seeds for enraging the whole community down to the humblest shopkeeper, and demonstrated to all the effect of tax expansion. It has been argued that Excise taxes led to a qualitative leap in political debates and change in frames, which linked taxation to representation and stimulated challenges to an electoral system that offered no representation to the bulk of those who paid; this meant that American claims had resonance beyond the elite merchants and manufacturers, to the whole population.[107]

The frame of discourse also began to change in other respects: the new ministry now saw the colonies increasingly not just as sources of supply (and hence self-sufficiency for Britain as generally perceived under the old 'laws of trade'), but (following Postlethwayt) as sources of demand for British products. This stimulated efforts to limit American manufactures and to tax the colonies, particularly to pay for colonial defence, a need demonstrated by the recent war.[108] For most British politicians the 'colonies had no raison d'être if they did not contribute to the economic well-being and so to the power of the metropolitan state'.[109] The language of government embraced a new mercantilist concern, to enhance the market for British manufactures and revenues, suppress smuggling, and prevent entry to the Empire's markets from other European states. The balance of trade became hotly debated; tonnages of shipping and cargoes inward and outward were more assiduously compared.[110] A new debate emerged about reinterpreting the 'laws of trade' as means to value the colonies. There were many reissues of major 17th-century commercial texts, including Davenant. Postlethwayt, Mortimer, and other authors fed this hungry demand for a new commercial view of the colonies.

Emergence of the new 'frame' of contention

In October 1760 the King replaced the 'old Whig' dynasty and the elder Pitt was replaced by Bute, who sought to stamp a new authority on the Commons. The war with France was brought to an end in 1763, but many saw the Treaty of Paris as a dishonourable settlement, giving back many conquests from France and

[107] Langford (1973, 1975, 1991); Brewer (1976).

[108] The Stamp Tax in particular was seen essentially as a means to raise revenue for the garrisoning of the American colonies: BL Add MS 33030, fo. 334–5. Summarized in Sosin (1965); Thomas (1975).

[109] Christie and Labaree (1976), p. 21.

[110] See Harlow (1952); Langford (1973); Christie and Labaree (1976); Bowen (1996, 2006).

Spain, only agreed to satisfy the king's foreign friends. Pitt saw it as an act of renunciation. The Liverpool merchants 'sent so many memorials against the peace, they found it very difficult to say anything respectful' when it was signed.[111] The exchange of Martinique and Guadeloupe for Canada was seen as a loss of prime sugar islands for the sake of a worthless territory with a large and troublesome French and Catholic population.[112] Contemporaneously religious worries were raised by attempts to establish bishops and extend Anglicanism through missionary work in America: religious liberty and civil liberty became synonymous for many Americans.[113]

The king's speech at the opening of parliament in 1763 praised the Treaty, but was immediately denounced by John Wilkes in edition 45 of his journal the *North Briton*.[114] In Liverpool feelings ran high and 'scraps of the *North Briton* are scattered all over the town.'[115] A continuing clash with the government ran through various elections in Middlesex 1768–9, where John Wilkes was repeatedly elected as MP, but the government found ways to declare his election void. This brought the corrupt control of the franchise to a new prominence of public attention.[116] Wilkes, heavily supported by both spontaneous and sponsored mobs (called the 'sons of liberty'), became identified as the leader of 'reform', his slogan 'Wilkes and Liberty' and his '45' celebrated in numerous publications and celebratory ceramic mugs, made in Staffordshire, Liverpool, and Bristol; the potters were closely aligned with Wilkes.[117]

Many subsequent 'reformers' in Britain and America first cut their teeth in the Wilkes campaigns, and became involved in his Society of the Supporters of the Bill of Rights. After the 1732–3 excise tax campaigns this was the next major extra-parliamentary political frenzy. Wilkes's campaign had thousands of activists, with many local 'committees of correspondence' and populist 'sons of liberty', a phrase copied in America, harnessing grass-roots local action. More significantly for business lobbies, it was also a campaign from which emerged some prominent intermediaries; these notably included later dramatis personae: William Meredith and Richard Pennant (later called Lord Penryn) the MPs for Liverpool; Edmund Burke, MP for Bristol who was also an American agent; Henry Cruger 'a hot Wilkite' Bristol merchant later also a Bristol MP and related to the New York Crugers; George Savile MP for Yorkshire; and Rockingham and his party.[118]

---

[111] William Meredith MP, letter to Lord Newcastle 27 May 1763; BL Add MS 38320 fo. 350.

[112] See Pitman (1917); Penson (1924); Price (1986, 1991).

[113] By the Episcopal Society for Propagation of the Gospel: Bridenbaugh (1962), chapters 8 and 9; also Bradley (1990).

[114] Rudé (1962), pp. 20–1.

[115] Bamber Gascoyne letter to Lord Newcastle 21 April 1763; BL Add MS 38320 fo. 312.

[116] Butterfield (1949); Rudé (1962); Brewer (1982); Colley (1982); Rogers (1989); Randall (2006).

[117] Butterfield (1949); Sutherland (1952); Brewer (1982); McKendrick (1982).

[118] Meredith is one of the most crucial of the group for chambers: he proposed the motion against the government on general warrants in 1764: Thomas (1975, p. 19); he also played a significant dramatic role in March 1771, when as a Wilkes supporter he helped mediate with 'a crowd of 50,000 in Palace Yard' to rescue Lord North whose carriage's glass, and then the whole carriage, was destroyed;

William Beckford, City mayor and MP, Barlow Trecothick a City alderman who became an MP in 1770, and many other prominent City merchants also played prominent roles in Wilkes's campaigns. The City was already tuned to extra-parliamentary activity: under Beckford over 1754–63 it had developed a vigorous petitioning campaign on reform of parliament and elections before Wilkes came on the scene.[119]

Wilkes stimulated involvement in politics, but business engagement was mixed. Many leading merchants supported Wilkes but also tried to work more moderately from the inside, chiefly through Rockingham who became the main opposition leader. Also support for Wilkes was dangerous, inevitably seen as opposition to the government. As claimed by Thomas Mortimer, the 'transient civilities I showed Mr. Wilkes in December 1767, while he was wind-bound at Ostend' lost him his consular post in 1768.[120]

In 1763 George Grenville became prime minister and took Bute's reforms forward, challenging the previous tenuous balance with the colonies; he ended earlier 'salutary neglect'.[121] Grenville shook up the Customs service, and ordered the navy to more closely control the American coast to prevent smuggling. There was also a series of Acts that sought to raise revenue from the American colonies and reassert the control of trade through the Navigation Acts. The Molasses Act of 1763 and Sugar Act of 1764 were a strong stimulus to action that led to committees of resistance in Boston, Philadelphia, New York, and other American ports. The Currency Act of 1764 and bullion discussion of 1765 sparked further resistance in America and lobbying in Britain, and had to be ignored in the face of the economic reality of a shortage of specie. Petitions from London, Glasgow, and Liverpool in 1762–3 on the Currency Act, and from Liverpool, Lancaster, Manchester, Halifax, Leicester, and Derby on bullion engaged local business leaders in organized campaigning.

The catalyst of the Stamp Act

The Stamp Act of 1765, which required the distribution of stamped documents and papers, and collection of stamp taxes, proved the strongest catalyst to action. On receiving the news of the Act almost all the American colonial Assemblies rejected it, and the first Congress was called in New York. The traditional rivalry between the colonies had been overcome by common external threat, and a process of coordination and resistance to imperial power was initiated

---

the crowd also took off North's hat and cut it into pieces; *Brickdale Diary*, vol. xlv, p. 52; quoted in Rudé (1962), p. 162 and n. 2.

[119] Sutherland (1933, 1956); Goodwin (1979).

[120] *The Remarkable Case of Thomas Mortimer* (1770), pp. 6 ff; also see above.

[121] Or, more properly, First Lord of the Treasury. The summary which follows is based on Laprade (1930); Butterfield (1949, 1957); Bargar (1956); Smith (1956); Watson (1957, 1968); Walsh (1959); Namier (1961); Morgan and Morgan (1962); Sosin (1965); Kammen (1968, 1970); Langford (1973, 1975, 1986a, 1986b); Maier (1973); Olson (1973); Steffan (1984); Dietz (1991); Thomas (1975, 1987, 1991).

which was set to run. Stamps were seen as an entirely new form of internal taxation, enforced by summary courts, viewed as asserting intrusive direct control over the colonies. Numerous American petitions against the Act were sent, and presented by the American agents in London. They were initially rejected by parliament. This itself was seen as a major affront. In the views of some contemporaries, it was this summary rejection that 'lost Britain the affection of all her colonies'.[122]

Mobs formed to intimidate the governors, judges, and distributors of the stamped papers, starting in Massachusetts and spreading rapidly to all the American colonies. This intimidation effectively prevented enforcement. The mobs were not so much popular mass uprisings, but at this stage often organized and orchestrated by the merchant elite, through intermediaries. However, they also had strong populist and radical support, and most merchants were very resistant to assemblies and riots, which were seen as a 'very injudicious method'[123] because they threatened the safety of the merchants and their property: most major American merchants remained resistant to revolution and rebellion up to the very end. Subsequently carrying the title 'sons of liberty', they chiefly drew from 'mechanics' bodies, which were associations of artisans. Nevertheless, it is important to recognize that at this stage mobs were seen as a traditional and legitimate means to influence an inattentive government, and were not confrontational if they were controlled and disciplined.[124] They provided reinforcement to the major merchants who sought to negotiate with the government.

The legacy of 1766: new local organization and repertoires following the Stamp Act

The Stamp Act crisis and associated legislation were critical to the emergence of chambers as they stimulated the emergence of new local leaders and organizations in both Britain and the colonies. In America these were the committees that represented each colony at the Congress, and local committees that sought to enforce American resistance through a non-importation embargo. In Britain there were local committees or leaders that lobbied for their areas directly to parliament.

After initiating the Stamp Act, Grenville was replaced as PM in July 1765, by Rockingham. He was a reluctant choice by the king because he was a leading 'opposition' figure. For commerce he was an important ally; he had major trading interests (through his estates, particularly in mining and pottery—Rockingham Ware), which gave him wide contact networks with other leading potters including Wedgwood and Bentley, export merchants, canal builders, improvers of the River

---

[122] William Smith, New York jurist, later a loyalist, letter 30 May 1765; in Christie and Labaree (1976), p. 53.

[123] Letterbook of Philadelphia merchants, James and Drinker, to David Barclay & Sons of London, 14 October 1765; quoted in Jensen (1963), p. 159, n. 17.

[124] Morgan and Morgan (1962); see also Walsh (1959); Langford (1973); Maier (1973); Christie and Labaree (1976); Olson (1973); Langford (1973); Randall (2006), p. 194.

Don, and manufacturing interests in Leeds and elsewhere. He also developed strong support from the dissenters.[125]

Rockingham was appointed just as news of the resistance and riots in America reached England. When he heard the news he realized that enforcement was impossible without military coercion, which in any case was not possible at the time, and he moved towards seeking modification, and then repeal of the Stamp Act: back to the traditional government response of concessions. But both the king and parliament were opposed. As a result, Rockingham sought to use external interests to bring pressures to bear on parliament.

The London merchants trading in America were to be particularly influential. Directly encouraged by Rockingham, following dinners with Barlow Trecothick in November,[126] a large-scale meeting of London merchants was held on 4 December 1765. The meeting elected a committee of 28, with Trecothick as chair; other key committee figures were George Aufrere MP, David Barclay, Capel and Osgood Hanbury, and Nicholas Ray, as well as some American agents, especially Benjamin Franklin and Edmund Burke. The London committee circulated a letter to 30 towns encouraging them to petition parliament, with 23 doing so,[127] and others sending petitions more spontaneously.[128] There were also petitions from the American agents in London. Although the petitions mostly called for amendment, the merchant stance rapidly shifted to immediate repeal because modification of the Act would be 'ineffective'; but they avoided any comment on constitutional issues, a position advised by Rockingham, and probably drafted by him into the London letter.[129] The leaders were able to engage directly with Rockingham through frequent dinner meetings with the senior members of his cabinet over November 1765–February 1766.[130] It is one of the most extraordinary episodes of direct exchange between a government and business interests, each gaining from the other.

Most of the local leaders to emerge played a crucial role in subsequent chamber development (or in the case of Bristol it sharpened the Merchant Venturers to act like a chamber). In Birmingham it marked the emergence of Samuel Garbett to prominence, as well as enhancing the positions of Matthew Boulton and, in the closely related potteries, Josiah Wedgwood. In Liverpool most of the local Stamp Act leaders subsequently became involved with the chamber's committee (especially important being the Heywood brothers, and Thomas Dunbar), with William Halliday acting as Liverpool's representative in London, and William Meredith, the local MP, a key intermediary. As a resident in Macclesfield, Meredith also sought to

---

[125] Cox and Cox (1983), Langford (1973), p. 117, Ditchfield (1988), pp. 56–7, Smith (1956), and Watson (1957, 1968) detail the links of Rockingham and the business people involved.

[126] Watson (1957), pp. 29–39; Trecothick knew Rockingham from earlier lobbying against the Mutiny Act.

[127] *Parliamentary History* (1766), vol. xvi, pp. 133–6; there were 24 petitions, two from Bristol (the merchants, tradesmen, and manufacturers; and the Merchant Venturers).

[128] Thomas (1975), pp. 187–8.

[129] Langford (1973, 1986a); Smith (1956).

[130] Smith (1956); Watson (1957).

engage Manchester, using fustian manufacturer Robert Hamilton, Lancaster West Indies merchant Abraham Rawlinson, and one of the Liverpool Heywood bankers, who subsequently sent their thanks to Rockingham.[131] In Bristol it was William Reeve the largest merchant and master of the Venturers, other Venturers (Henry Cruger and Richard Champion), with the support of Edmund Burke (who was a local MP, Rockingham's personal secretary, and also an American agent). In Yorkshire George Savile MP acted with Meredith as intermediary with Leeds, where textile manufacturers Emanuel Elam and Obadiah Dawson acted as representatives; in Wakefield they linked with woollen merchant and manufacturer John Milnes, and several of Milnes's family; and in Halifax with Benjamin Farrar, a textile manufacturer. In Leicester there was hosiery manufacturer Joseph Bunney, and in Nottingham hosier Thomas Morris. In Glasgow John Glassford, a leading tobacco merchant and banker, was the representative with support from Archibald Henderson and James McCall.

Some of these leaders were specifically contacted by Rockingham directly, or through Burke (who was responsible for Lancaster, Glasgow, and Birmingham), Meredith (for Liverpool, Manchester, and Dublin), and George Savile in Yorkshire.[132] Rockingham was also very fully informed about the issues involved through Burke as his personal secretary, and Burke's assistant (Joseph Harrison). Harrison appears to have been a critical source stimulating written materials to Rockingham, and preparing and synthesizing them for use. One aspect of this work was handling a series of 'dissertations' written by expert informants (and others). Among these dissertations probably most influential were those by Henry McCulloh, John Fothergill, Thomas Crowley, Nicholas Ray, and Malachy Postlethwayt. Although the effect is unknown, this was certainly another occasion when Postlethwayt's ideas came to the attention of a prime minister.[133]

The Committee of the Whole House

In January and February 1766 a Committee of the Whole House (of Commons) was appointed to resolve the impasse. This Committee was a major exercise, hearing about 23 hours of evidence over 13 days. Forty merchants, colonial agents, and American visitors presented arguments at the bar of the House.[134] Savile, Burke, and Meredith rehearsed and briefed many of them.[135] Most important were

---

[131] Sheffield Archives WWM R 58; quoted in Smith (1956), p. 248; it is unclear which Heywood.

[132] See Langford (1973, 1986b); additional material from Smith (1956); Watson (1957); and BL Add MS 33030.

[133] Watson (1957, 1968) details the role of each of these 'dissertationers'. Postlethwayt's argument to Rockingham (Sheffield Archives WWM/R/6/ fo. 55; miscellaneous writings: 'Mr Posslethwayt's schemes') chiefly concerned discouraging American manufactures as a quid pro quo for repealing the Stamp Act; this mirrors the approach he appears to have used with Walpole in the Excise tax affair of 1732.

[134] The recording of evidence from 25 representatives in given in BL Add MS 33030, fos. 78–204; see also Smith (1956) and Watson (1968); some appeared but were not called and did not speak.

[135] See Smith (1956), pp. 25–33; Watson (1957), pp. 47–9; Langford (1973), pp. 101–4; Thomas (1975).

Trecothick, as chair of the American merchants in London, and Benjamin Franklin, agent for Pennsylvania at that time, who both appeared for four hours. Franklin was also influential in reinforcing the view (quite misleadingly) that the Americans were only concerned about internal taxation, not external taxation or the right of Britain to tax and govern at all. The pressure of the petitions, together with other forces, particularly a resounding speech of support from the elder Pitt who was probably hoping to return to office,[136] was significant in leading to the repeal of the Stamp Act on 21 February 1766, with the political compromise of a Declaratory Act reasserting the right of parliament to tax the colonies following a few days later. The immediate celebrations of the merchants and colonies were considerable, and many of the petitioning cities in Britain sent memorials of thanks to Rockingham, their MPs, or other supporting representatives in London. Two American cities erected statues to Pitt: New York and Charleston.

The Stamp Act as a critical event

The Stamp Act crisis and concurrent Wilkesite activity was the first organized national lobby on such a scale. It extended connections and methods used in the Currency Act and bullion discussion of 1765, and gave many local individuals direct experience of national lobbying. It demonstrated to them at first hand the inadequacies of many political leaders and the Committee of Trade; and it exhibited to business leaders in the significant trading localities in Britain the scope for local collectively organized and moderated voices, working as a unity of interests, to circumvent the patronage of the landed interests in parliament and the local corporations. The well-rehearsed cases presented at the Commons gave experience of the language and processes of government and founded a method of approach that was previously mostly the preserve of the American agents and a few specialist parliamentary agents. This founded not just a new frame but a new method of professionalized campaigning. It also joined a group of business people who had strong connections to national politics with a new generation of emerging leaders aged 30–45 who were to maintain the momentum for the next 20 years.[137]

The strong links of many of the known leaders and signatories of the 1765–6 petitions in Britain to subsequent local chambers and/or the General Chamber and other major agitations are shown in Table 4.1. This traces the political activities of the provincial British Stamp Act leaders in subsequent chamber developments, and the involvement of later chamber leaders in the Stamp Act petition, including known 'delegates' of the General Chamber. It demonstrates a strong continuity from 1765 into the 1770s and 1780s. Reading the table left to right, almost all the Stamp Act leaders were subsequently involved in their local chambers and in the General Chamber (78%). Conversely, reading the table right to left, the known

---

[136] Langford (1973); Christie and Labaree (1976), pp. 74–6.

[137] Watson (1968), p. 386 argues that Rawlinson, Hamilton, Reeve, Glassford, and the London merchants like Trecothick and Beckford were most politically connected; these were also older; see Chapter 14.

Table 4.1. The known Stamp Act provincial campaign leaders, their relation to chambers founded 1774–85, Wilkes and peace petitions, General Chamber, and religion

Area	1766 Stamp Act leaders	Birth/death	1765–6 Stamp Act petition	1768–9 Wilkes petition	1775 peace petition	1774–83 Local chamber member	1785–7 General chamber delegate	Relig.
Birmingham	Samuel Garbett	1717–1803	√	–	–	√	√	A
	Matthew Boulton	1728–1809	√	–	–	√	√	A
Bristol	Richard Champion	1743–91	√	√leader	√presenter	SMV	emigrated	Q
	Henry Cruger (MP 1774–80, 1784–90)	1739–1827	√			SMV	n/a	A
Glasgow	William Reeve	c.1715–78	√	√	–	SMV	dead	Q
	John Glassford	c.1737	√	n/a	n/a but supporter	chair	n/a	A
	Archibald Henderson	c.1735–	√	n/a	n/a	chair	n/a	A
	James McCall	c.1725–	√	n/a	n/a	√	n/a	A
Between Halifax and Bradford	Benjamin Farrar	?1736–	√	n/a	√James	n/a	n/a	D?
Halifax			√	n/a	√	Samuel Waterhouse	√	A
			√	n/a	√	John Waterhouse	√	A
Lancaster	Abraham Rawlinson	1709–80	at Manchester	n/a	√jun. & senior	at Manchester	dead	Q
			at Manchester	n/a	√	–	Henry Tindall	A
Leeds	Obadiah Dawson	–1794	√	n/a			√	D
	Emmanuel Elam & bros.	1732–96	√	n/a	√Samuel & John Elam	√John Elam	√	Q
Leicester	Joseph Bunney	1715–82	√	n/a		dead	dead	Q
Liverpool	Thomas Dunbar	–1776	√	√	–	√George Dunbar	dead	A
	William Halliday	c.1725–1800	√	√	√	√Samuel Halliday	–	A

Location	Name	Dates						Religion
Manchester	Benjamin Heywood	1722–95	√	√	√		–	D
	Robert Hamilton	c.1725–81	√ at Lancaster	√ at Liverpool	√	√	dead	A
			–	n/a	√ at Lancaster	√	Thomas Richardson	A
		1749–1817	√ at Lancaster	n/a	–	√	Thomas Walker	D
			–	n/a		√	John Phillips	A
			√ at Lancaster	n/a	√ at Lancaster	√	William Barrow	D
Nottingham	Thomas Morris	c.1734–87	√	n/a	–	n/a	–	A
	George Robertson	c.1720–	√	n/a	–	n/a	–	A
		c.1730–	–	n/a	–	√	W. Northage	D?
		c.1739–	–	n/a	–	√	W. Hayne	A
		c.1729/34–	–	n/a	–	√	Sam Turner (sec)	A
Staffordshire/ potteries	Josiah Wedgwood	1730–95	√	–	√ potters petition	√		D
Wakefield	John Milnes	1709–71	√	dead	dead	dead	dead	D
	James Milnes	1721–92	√	n/a	n/a	√	Messrs Milnes rep. by Mr. Burrel	D
	Pemberton Milnes	1729–94	√	n/a	n/a	√	Messrs Milnes	D
				n/a	n/a	√	Messrs Milnes	D
				n/a	n/a	√	Holdsworth	D
				n/a	n/a	–	–	D

Notes: A, Anglican; D, dissenter; Q, Quaker. Names of business partners included where they sign petitions. Wakefield and Halifax chamber members were delegates to Leeds chamber. Other areas with later chambers either did not have petitions or were signed by one name for the whole city (as in Glasgow), marked n/a as not applicable;—did not sign or not a member.

Sources: Stamp Act leaders from Smith (1956) and Watson (1956, 1968); Wilkes and peace petitions, TNA HO 55 series: 6/8; 9/3; 4/3; 10/18; 11/9; 11/60; 11/64; 12/3; 21/39–40 and 43; chamber membership from Appendix 1; General Chamber from Chapter 9; religion from Chapter 9; religion from IGI and TNA RG 4 and 6.

leaders of delegate committees and the General Chamber had mostly been Stamp Act petitioners (71%). The Stamp Act leaders, where documented, were also active in the intervening Wilkes and peace petitions, respectively in 1768–9 and 1775. Hence they continued as political activists. An interesting element is the high proportion of dissenters: these were 52% of the Stamp Act leaders, of which 42% were Quakers. This is much higher than in the general population and shows Rockingham's choice of networks to engage, and the growing pressures from dissenters for reform. But the involvement also of many Anglicans demonstrates the generality of the campaigns. Thus, as discussed in Chapter 14, dissenter networks were important, but were one of many networks providing potential alliances.

Stamp Act–chamber continuities in Liverpool and Manchester

For the first two mainland chambers in Britain the analysis of continuous engagement can be demonstrated even more strongly. Liverpool has the only record of a substantial Stamp Act committee outside London. As shown in Table 4.2, of its 17 Stamp Act committee members, eight are known members of the subsequent chamber (or their surviving partner, who was a brother in each case): at least 50% of the surviving members by 1774. But excluding the aldermen in the corporation, 80% of the surviving Stamp Act committee were chamber members. The dissenters were again disproportionate (35%), or 50% excluding the aldermen, greatly exceeding the local dissenting population (of less than 10% in Liverpool at this time). This reflects the leadership of the Heywood brothers and the more general pressures for reforms. These committee members were almost all involved in the petition to improve the docks in 1766.[138]

However, whatever common ground with the corporation existed in 1765–6 started to break down with the Wilkes petition in 1769, since this challenged the constitution. Only two of the six aldermen on the Stamp Act committee signed the Wilkes petition, and the corporation sent a loyal address against Wilkes in March. The freemen and merchants sent a counter-petition favouring Wilkes with 1100 signatures through Meredith and fellow MP Richard Pennant, and the corporation sent a further loyal petition in January 1770 calling the counter-petition 'small, partial and inconsiderable'.[139] This revived earlier friction.

The Liverpool Stamp Act committee had been formed in December 1765, but when Trecothick's letter arrived in January 1766, Meredith MP noted that it 'was concealed from the merchants of Liverpool [by the corporation] until produced, on my informing them of it, and their *demand* to see it'.[140] In Leicester there were similar tensions between the Tory corporation and Whig hosiers, led by Joseph

---

[138] More explanation of these Liverpool petitions in Bennett (2010), pp. 120–8.
[139] Sources quoted in Rudé (1962), pp. 128, nn. 1–3.
[140] Meredith letter to Burke, 1 January 1766, emphasis in original: Sheffield Archives WWM 1/Bk P/1/76.

Table 4.2. Liverpool Stamp Act committee 1765–6 in order of signing: chamber membership, and petitioning activity 1765–1775

Stamp Act Committee	Birth/death	Religion	Chamber member 1774	1765 Stamp Act petition	1766 Docks	1768–9 Wilkes	1773 Free ports	1775 peace
John Crosbie (president)	1716–91	A	a	√	√			
Charles Goore (vice pres.)	1701–83	A	a	√	√	√		
George Campbell	c.1700–69	A	a, d	√	√	√	d	d
William Halliday	1725–96	D	√ Samuel	√	√	√ Samuel		√
Thomas Dunbar	–1776	A	√ George	√	√	√		
Arthur Heywood	1717–95	D	√	√	√	√	√	√
Benjamin Heywood	1722–95	D	√	√	√	√	√	√
John Sparling	1731–1800	A	a	√	√			
Thomas Falkner	1719–85	A	√	√	√	√	√	
John Brown	c.1740–	A	a	√	√			√
John Benson	c.1730–c.1793	A		√	√			√
John Postlethwaite	1725–1779	A		√	√			
Samuel Kilner (of Lancaster)	–1776	D	d	√				
John Crosbie jun.	1716–91	A	(a)	√				
John Walker	c.1733–	D?	√	√	√	√		√
Thomas Smythe	1737–1824	A	√	√	√	√	√	
Stephen Hayes	c.1747–	D	√	√	√		√	√
Total signers	17	17	8	16	15	9	5	7
Total as % (of those alive)		D=35.3	50.0	94.1	88.2	52.9	31.3	43.8

Notes: Religion: D—Dissenter; A—Anglican; 'd' indicates dead by that date, where known; 'a' indicates alderman.
Sources: Liverpool 'American [Stamp Act] committee', from letter to the Bristol Merchant Venturers, 31 December 1765, SMV/2/4/2/10 7(a), which contains 14 entries in which three are partnerships for which all partners are included here; other sources and other petitions in Bennett (2010).

Bunney.[141] In Liverpool, Meredith's action forced the corporation to open a wider response. As the resistance was pro-government stimulated by Rockingham, the corporation could be strong supporters: but they retained control—the current mayor of 1765–6 (Crosbie) was president of the committee, an upcoming mayor for 1768 was vice-president (Goore), and past mayor of 1763–4 (Campbell, the 'friend' of Meredith and Rockingham) asserted precedence by being the first to sign. The other committee members were not excluded from politics, since *all* were freemen and thus could vote (Kilner was a freeman at Lancaster), but they did not hold the real power as aldermen and common councillors.

The Wilkes petition and other disagreement between the chamber members and the corporation deepened; none of the aldermen supported the Free Ports petition in 1773, and there were further divisions over the American war; Sparling and several other aldermen became detested. With continuing friction the chamber was founded to circumvent the corporation in 1774.[142] By this time all the surviving aldermen on the Stamp Act Committee had moved to the other side of the fence to support the government.

The other early mainland chamber area, Manchester, did not have a known Stamp Act committee, but had many petitioners against the Act. Comparison of these with the members of the 1774 chamber shows that 59% of chamber members were petitioners. Even after many deaths, at least 22% of the 1781 chamber had petitioned against the Stamp Act in 1765.[143] The other early UK chamber locations, Jersey and Guernsey, did not petition.

Stamp Act–chamber continuities in America

In America, similar continuities developed. The local committees for non-importation were direct precursors of stronger bodies in the later revolution,[144] and of chambers in Boston, New York, and Charleston. In Boston the non-importation committee was based on an earlier society formed in 1733 to resist the Molasses Act. This was reconstituted in about 1760 to resist renewal of the Act and to be a general Boston Society for Encouraging Trade and Commerce within the preserve of Massachusetts Bay (BSETC). It had formal governance procedures and broad lobby objectives, in almost every respect acting as a *de facto chamber*, and was a direct forerunner of the first Boston chamber of 1785.[145] Similarly in New York, the local non-importation committee of 1765 evolved into the first formal chamber in 1768.[146] In Charleston the chamber was more hastily constituted in

---

[141] Smith (1956), pp. 203–3.

[142] See Bennett (2010), pp. 71–3, 77–80.

[143] Comparison of the membership lists in *Manchester Mercury*, 18 January and 18 March 1774, and 24 July 1781, with the Manchester Stamp Act petitioners, TNA T1/443/50.

[144] Jensen (1963); Oaks (1977); Tyler (1986); Langford (1986b).

[145] Andrews (1916), pp. 161–5; Tyler (1986).

[146] Stevens (1867); Bishop (1918). The relation to the non-importation committees was not direct elsewhere; in Charleston the chamber was founded in opposition to the committee of 1773; in other areas the committees did not evolve into chambers.

1773, but contained the same leading merchants as the non-importation committee.[147] A Philadelphia chamber was not attempted until 1784, but the same moderating forces operated over how the non-importation ban was implemented, and attempts at control by the major merchants,[148] with a strong overlap of the same names in the 1784 proposal and earlier Stamp Act and non-importation committees.[149]

The continuities have been most extensively analysed for the case of Boston. Tyler has demonstrated the continuing attempts of the merchant leaders in BSETC to moderate, even though the leadership of the resistance was increasingly taken over by radicals within town meetings, and by smaller and younger traders within BSETC. Table 4.3 shows the involvement of the members of the 1763 BSETC members in subsequent major activities. The developments over 1766–8 show interests aligned in non-importation, later petitions, and even with the 1769 formation of the 'sons of liberty' (which 36% of BSETC supported). But after 1774 this accommodation broke down, with the early members of BSETC reducing support. A 'Solemn League and Covenant' in 1774, which a 'radical' town meeting promulgated, forced taking sides. Most BSETC members found it unpalatable; only 15% were willing to sign. Overall, where known, 22% of BSETC members became 'loyalist', of which 16% supported British occupation under General Gage, 13% were declared to have been loyalists after British withdrawal, and 14% were banished by the State of Massachusetts.

Table 4.3. Members of the Boston 'chamber' (BSTEC) in 1763 and their subsequent involvement in other activities

	BSETC members signing	Total signers	BSETC % of total signing	% of BSETC signing
1767 BSETC petition to Commons	54	71	76.1	55.1
1768 non-importation subscribers	53	198	26.8	54.1
1769 Sons of Liberty	35	138	25.4	35.7
1774 members of Continental Association	10	33	30.3	11.5
1774 protestors against Solemn League and Covenant	16	86	18.6	15.1
1774 Welcome address to General Gage	14	88	15.9	16.1
1777–8 declared 'loyalist'	11	85	12.9	12.6
1778 banished by Massachusetts Act	12	81	14.8	13.8

Notes: Tyler traced 106 of the 146 BSETC members from 1763, which was reduced by deaths to about 98 by 1768, and 87 by 1775.
Source: Calculated from Tyler (1986), Appendix.

[147] Sellers (1934); Walsh (1959); Rogers (1974).
[148] Oaks (1977).
[149] Tench Coxe papers, 21 October 1784, Reel 46: Historical Society of Philadelphia.

Early tensions and regional differentiation

Despite the success of the Stamp Act protests, even in 1765 there were fundamental warnings of fracture. In the American cities this mainly focused on the divisions between the mechanics and the merchants; with the mechanics seeing the merchants as a force they would have to circumvent if they were to achieve their desire for independence,[150] as is clear for Boston in Table 4.3.

In Britain the Atlantic ports and centres of 'new' industries petitioned in favour of repeal, but many inland boroughs were passive.[151] Norwich specifically declined to act on Stamp Act repeal. Six other receivers of Trecothick's letter did not respond. Birmingham was a particularly complex case, where Garbett, who was an important lobbyist in private, withheld himself from appearing at the Commons committee; Boulton was careful to be unavailable, and Trecothick spoke for Birmingham noting that it 'was particularly affected'.[152]

The Stamp Act crisis thus demonstrated the places that were the leading players in the new economy: Rockingham's choice of locations to engage, and the self-declared group of those concerned to offer voice. It is notable that for Britain and Ireland, the only places with chambers (or delegates) established up to 1807 that had no major Stamp Act activity were Jersey, Guernsey, Londonderry, and Edinburgh. Thus the 1766 crisis was critical for planting seeds of a 'chamber movement' in the susceptible places.[153]

Reinforcement of the 'reform' agenda

Success in Stamp Act repeal opened the next phase of contention. The merchants and agents immediately began to plan 'a complete revision of the commercial laws' with the colonies, with further meetings taking place in March 1766 to develop a 'regular and digested scheme'. This was to lay down a blueprint[154] for the changes that, whilst primarily developed in London under Trecothick, Barclay, and others, increasingly interleaved with the provinces, and seemed to be building on Postlethwayt. The Free Port scheme of April 1766, again led by Rockingham and Meredith, brought together Bristol (SMV), Lancaster, Liverpool, and Manchester interests with the London American and West Indies merchants, with Beckford (London mayor and MP) and Rawlinson (Lancaster) as prime movers.[155] Although there was much division between these interests, success was achieved with the Free Ports Act in May 1766, covering Dominica and Jamaica, which may have encouraged the chamber there.

[150] Andrews (1916); Stevens (1867); Jensen (1963); Oaks (1977).
[151] See Bargar (1956); Langford (1973); Bradley (1986, 1990).
[152] Bargar (1956); Norris (1957); Money (1977); for Trecothick's comments, BL Add MS 33030, fo. 105.
[153] Price (1991, table 1) confirms the same listing of the most active centres of trade and political activism.
[154] Agreed 10 March at the Kings Arms Tavern; quoted in Sosin (1965), pp. 81–2.
[155] Watson (1968), pp. 416–42; Armytage (1953); Langford (1973); Thomas (1987), pp. 259–63; Hamilton (2005).

These business initiatives were part of a more general 'reform' agenda. 'Reform' might have meant different things to different people but, as noted by Innes, its strength was to provide scope for a general unity of interest for change.[156] For business interests, much of this turned into resistance to further extension of state activity, as chiefly signified by taxation and 'arbitrary' legislation. This was a popular cause, because the extension of the state meant expansion of government patronage and corruption in politics.[157] But there was also ideological resentment by merchants of intrusion by the state into commercial affairs that they saw as their province; and the two strands of reform of government and commercial autonomy were intricately mixed up in Postlethwayt's texts, as promulgated by Bolingbroke and Burgh, as noted above.

However, while the business lobbies continued to be influential, their position was to be progressively eroded by the demands and intransigence of the colonies.[158] 'Reform' began increasingly to collide with demands for more radical change and revolutionary movements. Rockingham, perceived as weak by the king, was almost immediately replaced and remained in opposition until after the colonies were lost. The merchants were marginalized and became divided between which political factions to support. For example, when the East India Company became a focus for government attention in 1767–8, Liverpool, Bristol, and other areas again pressed for reforms, but were unable to find a winning political alliance between the elder Pitt, Rockingham, and others, who were divided about how to proceed.[159]

4.5 'GREAT EVENTS' 2: THE AMERICAN REVOLUTION

The calm from Stamp Act repeal was soon disrupted by Townshend's extension of Excise duties over tea and other commodities in 1768 and the colonial response (calling these 'intolerable Acts').[160] Although there were again efforts to appease the Americans, with repeal of all the Townshend duties except tea in 1770, further efforts to assert parliamentary authority, and inflammatory actions by Hillsborough (American Secretary 1768–72) over Massachusetts continued to provoke the colonies.[161] Preoccupation of the government with the continuing Wilkes affair over 1767–71 and the East Indian Company also pushed America to the sidelines, which meant that mistakes were probably made. There was also the 1774 Quebec Act and appointment of a Catholic bishop in Canada in 1766, which appeared to threaten religious as well as civil liberty.[162]

---

[156] Innes (2003); Innes and Burns (2003).
[157] See e.g. Brewer (1976); Langford (1991).
[158] Sosin (1965); Kammen (1968); Olson (1973, 1979).
[159] Sutherland (1933); Black (1963); Watson (1968), pp. 46 ff.
[160] Although the Townshend duties were withdrawn after three years; Sosin (1965) and Langford (1991), pp. 43–5 argue that taxation was not itself significant, but seen as a political imposition.
[161] Thomas (1987), pp. 14, 206–10, for Hillsborough's obstruction of American agents by insisting on appointment letters from the colonies in 1768, toughening of instructions to Governors 1768–70, and redrafting of cabinet positions in 1770.
[162] Bridenbaugh (1962), chapter 11.

Most critically in the colonies, the Townshend duties led to a repeat of American mob intimidation through the 'sons of liberty', a new non-importation embargo in 1768–9, and merchant attempts at temperate petitioning in Britain. Under the provocation particularly of Boston, with the tea party of 1773 the last straw, a policy of military coercion on the American colonies was embarked on over 1774–5 leading to war with America 1775–1781. This period stimulated lobbies, but these were often marginal, with the merchants in London and the provinces frequently cautioned not to send petitions because this would only inflame or fix government views in the wrong direction.[163] But the king and parliament were not to be moved: indeed, Lord North's government felt militarily capable and held strong support in parliament and the country up to the time of emerging British military defeats.[164]

Divisions of opinion; forced to take sides

The period of 1767–75 was divisive, with many British and American merchants becoming unsympathetic to colonial rebellion.[165] The Boston tea party of 1773 (which directly challenged authority and destroyed property) hardened British opinion. But the first major bloodshed, at Lexington in April 1775, and then the Declaration of Independence in 1776, with powers of summary arrest of loyalists and confiscation of their property, were turning points that forced everyone to take sides. In America resistance to Britain now became compulsory; and in Britain support for the Americans could be interpreted as treason. This split the merchant communities, and many families, between loyalists and rebels. In America, by 1776 the committees of correspondence and inspection were in the hands of the radicals and forced the merchants to rebel or confiscated their property.

In Britain, a statement by William Meredith in 1778 summed up the position of many of the leaders forced to take sides. Referring back to Walpole's Excise scheme of the 1730s, he noted that although such a scheme of taxation might be right, it was so inflammatory he would advise the king to withdraw it; with the Townshend taxes, 'he would not be a minister to enforce taxes at the probable expense of blood'.[166] The colonial situation should not have come to this, and he was therefore keen, like others, to encourage conciliation to provide a peaceful solution.

Despite the divisions, the main British localities involved in the Atlantic trade copied the earlier models developed for the Stamp Act crisis: new committees and the existing chambers sent memorials on disrupted trade and debt with America. At least 75% of the known members of the Liverpool chamber in 1774–80 were traders in America, and the leaders of the Liverpool and Manchester chambers were also the leaders of local opposition to government through initiating the petition for

---

[163] Watson (1957); Langford (1973); Thomas (1987).
[164] Valentine (1967); Thomas (1975, 1991); Whitley (1996).
[165] Flick (1901) gives a detailed account of the complex situation in New York; also Stevens (1867).
[166] William Meredith, *Historical Reflections on the Taxation of Free Trade in a Series of Letters to a Friend*, London (1778), p. 81 (BL: 7660.c.3915).

concessions to the Americans in 1775.[167] Similar proportions of members in the Glasgow, Belfast, and Dublin chambers of 1783 were interlocked with the broader Atlantic economy.[168] Thus the run-up to the American rebellion, and coercive response was a further wake-up call activating early chamber leadership.

Economic as well as political stress

The 1774–5 crisis was not just political; it was also economic. The trade in America involved very extensive advances of credit, estimated as an export trade worth £3 million in 1766, with credit of up to £4.5 million.[169] There had been a rapid growth of Anglo-American trade after 1763, increasingly based on bills of exchange and credit for American cargoes, as well as a growing use of colonial paper money. The credits were transferable 'currencies' primarily held in London, but also by banks and the major merchants in Glasgow, Bristol, Dublin, Liverpool, as well as in America.[170] Even in Ireland, although much of the Irish trade was conducted through London factors, Irish merchants were heavily involved from Dublin, Limerick, Waterford, Cork, and Galway.[171] Dublin remained the second largest city in the British Isles throughout the 18th century, considerably greater in size than Bristol, Glasgow, Liverpool, and Edinburgh, while Cork ranked about sixth in the 1760s.

Like any credit surge, it is arguable how long this growth of debt could have been sustained, but the collapse of tobacco prices and a shortage of specie in America and to a lesser extent in Britain, leading to a reliance on devalued paper money, brought a crisis of liquidity. This was exacerbated by the ill-judged legislation against American paper in the Currency Act of 1764, which was a topic of petitioning in Liverpool. It also influenced credit between Glasgow and London, and between the American colonies themselves.[172] A new Currency Act in 1773 helped to ease pressure, and marked one of the last successes of the American agents. But this Act was inflammatory since it involved the colonial assemblies explicitly acknowledging the authority of parliament,[173] and the tea duties symbolically remained.

With the first shots of war in 1775, most credit was cut off, resulting in a debt crisis on both sides of the Atlantic. There is much argument about the extent of

---

[167] John Dobson in Liverpool, and Thomas Butterworth Bayley in Manchester; Bennett (2010), p. 125.

[168] In Jersey it was over 60%; see Chapter 14.

[169] House of Commons Committee of 1766: BL Add MS 33030, fos. 88 ff and fo. 204; these cannot be accepted fully at face value, but give reasonable estimates; see Price (1980), and Langford (1986b).

[170] Many politicians were heavily involved in business: Rockingham in W. Riding pottery and woollens; the Earl of Dartmouth (President of the Board of Trade) in Midlands metal trades; Lord Newcastle with the London merchants; see e.g. Christie and Labaree (1976), p. 63.

[171] Laprade (1930); Davis (1962); Papenfuse (1975); Price (1980); Morgan (1997). For Scotland see McCusker (1997); Devine (1971, 1975, 1978, 2003, 2004); Dickson (1980). For Ireland see Cullen (1968, 1977); James (1973); Truxes (1988); see also Wakeford (1812); Marmion (1855); McDowell (1944).

[172] Price (1980, 1992).

[173] Sosin (1965), pp. 138–40.

this;[174] but there is no doubt that transatlantic debt was a major cause of tensions between business and the government. Credits were central to the subsequent treaties between Britain and America in 1783, 1794, and 1802, establishing a means to resolve outstanding debts on both sides. They were the subject of strong lobbying, with unresolved claims pursued by the New York, Glasgow, and Liverpool chambers and London merchants until the 1790s.[175]

The political and economic challenges were not confined to the American Colonies and Britain, but also affected Canada (through the interrelated 1774 Quebec Act), Ireland, and the Channel Islands, as well as the interconnected West Indies and African trades. The Stamp Act crisis and the subsequent coercion of the colonies shook an interconnected world. As stated by Berg,[176] there was 'an intricate, objective and subtle structure... [within which] merchants in various parts of the empire spoke a business language mutually understood... [that] constituted a sort of community having its own regularised practices supported by its own code of ethics'; this was all thrown awry in 1774–5.

4.6 EARLY CHAMBERS IN AMERICA

In America, local commercial committees formed during the Stamp Act crisis and the non-importation embargo against British goods. There were also broader commercial societies in Boston in 1760, and in New York in 1765.[177] The Townshend Acts of 1768 stimulated a new non-importation movement, which revived merchant committees in Boston, Philadelphia, Baltimore, Charleston, Savannah, and New York, with some smaller places also having some sort of committee as well.[178] The two earliest chambers, in New York in 1768 and Charleston in 1773, were in the two places that erected a statue to Pitt in thanks for his role in repeal of the Stamp Act. They were also the two leading locations in support of Wilkes, with Charleston voting a grant of £1500 to his campaign, which led to British suspension of the Carolina Assembly.[179]

The New York chamber of commerce

In New York, a committee of about 20 leading merchants was formed in 1765 to take control of the Stamp Act non-importation embargo, rather than allow it to fall under the sons of liberty. This merchant committee was a critical precursor of the foundation of the chamber in 1768, although for a time the two maintained

---

[174] Jensen (1963), chapter 2; Langford (1973, 1986b); Price (1980).
[175] See Chapter 9.
[176] Berg (1943), p. 177; see also Haggerty (2006).
[177] BSETC and the New York Society for Promotion of the Arts: see Andrews (1916); Harrington (1935); Bridenbaugh (1955), p. 287; Tyler (1986).
[178] Schlesinger (1917), pp. 127–9; Andrews (1916); Harrington (1935); Walsh (1959); Steffan (1984).
[179] Weir (1983), pp. 306–312; Rogers (1974).

separate existence.[180] The Stamp Act organizers invited other members, and a chamber was formed with an initial 45 members. The chamber members wanted a more permanent presence, with a strong emphasis on providing physical premises that encouraged a milieu for discourse as well as a basis for lobbying.[181] The leading members, John Cruger, William Walton, Theophylacte Bache, Henry and Philip Cuyler, and William and Nicholas Bayard, were major merchants and manufacturers, and among the largest landholders of New York city.[182] This was an economic elite, closely linked with the pre-independence political elite. The first chamber president, John Cruger, had been city mayor and was speaker of the New York Assembly. In that role he attained prominence as a moderating voice during the 1765 Stamp Act protests: possessing a skill 'to moderate the passions of his fellow-men and to harmonize the widely differing opinions of the opposing parties'.[183] In the coercion protest, again he led the chamber to act as a moderating force, although by then the chamber presidency was filled by Theo Bache (1773–4), William Walton (1774–5), and Isaac Low (1775–6). The chamber leaders were largely Anglicans (some Episcopalian), many closely associated with the 'De Lancey' party, which supported loyalist reform of the relationship with Britain, but wished to maintain the colonial relationship. Leading chamber members such as the Waltons, Crugers, and De Puysters were intermarried with each other and the De Lanceys.[184] All the New York chamber leaders had strong trade connections with Britain, and Sir William Baker (the prominent London MP opponent of the Stamp Act, Quebec Act, and other coercive measures), the senior partner of Baker, Kilby and Baker, was the main trading partner of De Lancey and Watts in New York.[185]

Isaac Low, chamber president in 1775–6, became chair of the committee of inspection during the 1768–70 non-importation embargo, in which the chamber participated, and, with John Jay, he was the key figure representing New York at the Philadelphia Continental Congress in 1774. Low and Jay were important forces in the 'Olive Branch petition' from Congress on 5 July 1775, which was the last American effort for concessions; and Jay argued for defusing tensions by Congress paying for the lost tea (not acceptable to Congress or parliament). Low tried to achieve moderation, and managed to get three merchants (all members of the chamber)[186] elected among the five delegates to the New York provincial Congress in 1775. The result was that by April 1775 it was in New York alone that 'the shadow of royal government remained', with the chamber as a supporter.[187] At the

---

[180] Stevens (1867); Bishop (1918).

[181] Their first action was providing a supply of tobacco, with a fire and porter to tend it; see Chapter 11.

[182] See Stevens (1867), pp. 12–95; Harrington (1935), pp. 12–15; 349–351; Friedman (1947).

[183] Uncle to Henry Cruger, in Bristol, q.v. below.

[184] Flick (1901), pp. 18–22; Stevens (1867) pp. 14–16; Truxes (2001).

[185] Sosin (1965), p. 4; for other trading connections of American colonies and Stamp Act and later developments see Bargar (1956); Smith (1956); Watson (1957); Olson (1973); Thomas (1985, 1991).

[186] Isaac Low, John Alsop, and Philip Livingston; only Livingston subsequently supported independence; Stevens (1867); Harrington (1935), p. 349.

[187] Comment by Governor Josiah Martin of North Carolina, 7 April 1775; quoted in Thomas (1991), p. 222, n. 12; see also pp. 174–220.

same time the first chamber president John Cruger, as chair of the New York committee of correspondence, was communicating continuously with Burke in Britain to try to encourage concessions. He wrote as late as May 1774 on behalf of the New York committee that 'a desire of dissolving our connection with the parent country is an idea to which every good American is a stranger'. He encouraged using his nephew Henry Cruger jun. in Bristol, as a direct source of more detailed American information for Lord Dartmouth, who could give 'a full, precise and faithful communication of the general sentiments and wishes of the people of this colony'.[188]

Low represented the favoured position of the chamber, to negotiate a settlement. Analysis of the subsequent allegiances of the 104 chamber members living in 1775 shows that 57 were loyalists, 21 were neutral, and only 26 were sufficiently radical to fight Britain;[189] i.e. it was predominantly loyalist, but also reflected the divisions of the city more generally.[190] But as the crisis developed the chamber became more isolated, and the continual manoeuvres by the radicals progressively undermined the merchants and moderates. Thus, after the refusal of the New York Assembly (by 17 to 9) to appoint delegates to the Congress that met in mid-1775, the radicals polled the city directly to establish a provincial Convention (favoured by 825 to 163), which then nominated the 12 Congress representatives. From this point the Convention took effective local control from the Assembly, and the chamber was marginalized. However, it is notable that New York remained the colony least committed to independence up to the end: Low and Cruger were probably influential in the Congress on 17 May 1776 agreeing not to oppose British occupation of New York. The tensions continued when the New York delegates on 4 July were forbidden to assent to the Declaration of Independence: New York had to convene a special Convention, which ratified it on 9 July.[191]

The Boston Society and chamber

The Boston Society for Encouraging Trade and Commerce (BSETC) was reconstituted in about 1760 expressly to resist renewal of the Molasses Act. In 1763 it sent a statement of the 'State of Trade', written by Thomas Gray and Edward Payne, to all the other Northern colonies to engage them in lobbying their Assemblies:[192] a prelude to the Stamp Act resistance. Most BSETC members had strong trade connections with Britain, with John Hancock (perhaps the largest of

---

[188] Letter from New York committee of correspondence, 31 May 1774, signed John Cruger, jointly with James Jauncey, Jacob Walton, and J. Bocrum, who were all connected with the chamber; Sheffield Archives: WWM 1/Bk P/ 1/513, fos. 1 and 2–3.
[189] Harrington (1935), p. 349; using the records by Stevens (1867).
[190] e.g. as in the committee of inspection, and committee of fifty-one; Harrington (1935), p. 349; Stevens (1867).
[191] See e.g. Thomas (1991), p. 328.
[192] Sosin (1965), pp. 42–3; Tyler (1986).

the Boston merchants) using Henry Cruger in Bristol as his main agent, thus forming the strongest link of Boston with the networks of Stamp Act resisters in Britain and John Cruger in New York.

BSETC was a chamber-like body, with a 1763 formal 'charter'. Its format may have been suggestive for the New York chamber. It continued to act like a chamber, with many of its members seeking conciliation. But the control of the society became a battleground resulting in the society shifting from chamber to revolutionary body. Divisions initially emerged as a result of the perception of how far each centre adhered to the embargo on British imports and exports in 1768–70. The embargo itself collapsed. Boston considered itself to have held firm, with at least 109 of the 143 firms that imported English goods subscribing to the ban (76%), and most others resigned to supporting it.[193] But New York and Philadelphia merchants circumvented the embargo, 'enriching themselves at the expense of Massachusetts'.[194] In Carolina, the New York and Philadelphia merchants flaunting the ban were seen as 'traitors to their country, themselves, and ages yet unbound'. Philadelphia had the same mistrust of the others.[195]

BSETC became increasingly dominated by patriots. Of the main committee, patriots outnumbered loyalists four to one, although the membership and main attendees at meetings were roughly equal. Nevertheless the leading Boston merchants were suspected of colluding to limit the 1768–70 embargo, and there was a prominent campaign against the embargo run by merchant interests in the *Boston Gazette*. Thus, when the new importation ban emerged in 1773, Boston's radicals, anticipating the merchants' reluctance to uphold another embargo, staged a takeover of the committee of correspondence in 1772, with one of America's leading radicals, Samuel Adams, as leader. Even the strong patriot major merchants on BSETC, such as Thomas Cushing and John Hancock, refused to serve. On 1 June 1774 the Boston committee promulgated a Solemn League and Covenant for an immediate embargo. The leaders of BSETC, among 129 leading citizens, circulated a condemnation of the Covenant on 3 June, but found themselves ostracized and their businesses boycotted.[196] As shown in Table 4.3, only 15% of BSETC members were prepared to sign, and the leadership was under extreme pressure. BSETC was then taken over by the radicals, about 50% being subsequently identifiable as patriots, and only 13–16% loyalists, most of whom lost their property and were banished. It subsequently kept up a close exchange with New York interests to monitor and gather information, viewing Isaac Low's moderating activities as prevarication and betrayal.

[193] Langford (1986a, 1986b); Thomas (1987), pp. 122–7; Tyler (1986), pp. 112–13.
[194] Andrews (1916), pp. 247–59; Thomas (1987), pp. 204–6.
[195] Stevens (1867); Andrews (1916), pp. 251–2; Jensen (1963); Oaks (1973, 1977).
[196] From the names listed by Andrews (1916), p. 164, compared to the lists in Tyler (1986); Thomas (1991).

The tensions of rebellion

In each major centre, in addition to any 'chamber' or committee of the merchant elite, were the radicals and 'mechanics' (small traders and artisans). Although the merchants attempted, and generally succeeded, in maintaining control of the committees of inspection following the Townshend and Coercive Acts, as they had during the Stamp Act crisis, the mechanics steadily gained ground. The mechanics were able to move attention to the local Assemblies and then to the first Continental Congress, where they forced a progressively more radical agenda for complete independence from Britain. This forced the merchants to strengthen non-importation in 1774, and to supplement it by a non-export embargo.

For the radicals, non-payment of the duties and adherence to the embargos became part of general resistance to arbitrary rule and 'taxation without representation', which made protest and extra-legal activities by the 'sons of liberty' into a 'legitimate' rebellion justified by demands for fundamental rights. The new frame of contention had now been crystallized into commitment to rebellion. But most major merchants saw things differently, resisting until the end. Increasingly British merchants were in favour of repression of the colonial rebels, and this included (though more reluctantly) many American merchants. But they were not in favour of repression if it involved significant bloodshed; a rather contradictory position that proved untenable.[197] Charles Goore, a Liverpool Stamp Act committee member, by January 1775 had turned to the 'hope that the British Government will not submit to their arbitrary demands, . . . for it's evident they are resolved to be independent'; by June he felt 'God grant such measures may be taken that his Majesty may bring the Americans to be dutiful subjects'; 'the colonies assume an authority in several of their demands they have no right to'.[198]

The chamber in New York and BSETC in Boston in the early part of the 1770s were thus not themselves protest bodies, included both loyalists and patriots, and tried to dampen the radicals.[199] Their preoccupation was to articulate a general, moderate, and deliberated view, to follow traditional routes of influence, and to persuade government, not to overthrow it. The chamber concept was even seen in 1769–70 as sufficiently expedient, as a counterweight to protest, that the Lieutenant-Governor recommended the award of a charter to the New York chamber, to reward loyalty. This was, somewhat surprisingly, granted by George III in March 1770, making it the first incorporated chamber in the world.[200] The petition to the Lieutenant-Governor, and his reply, are couched in identical phrases of loyalty: 'so considerable a body of merchants of this City, united in principles of loyalty, afford the strongest assurance of zeal in support of the government and our happy

[197] Stevens (1867), pp. 78–90; Morgan and Morgan (1962); Christie and Labaree (1976); Langford (1986b); McCarthy (1986).
[198] Goore letters to William Meredith, 25 January 1775 and 13 June 1775; to J. McWhirter 3 July 1775; Goore letter book, W. L. Clements Library, University of Michigan; quoted in Langford (1986b), pp. 317–18.
[199] Countryman (1981); Harrington (1935), pp. 72 ff., p. 95, pp. 25–8.
[200] Bishop (1918); Schlesinger (1917).

constitution ... having the most favourable influence by promoting due obedience to the laws'.[201] This exchange demonstrates the desire by both sides to use the chamber as a moderating intermediary against the pressure of the radicals.

After the British occupied New York in 1777, offering certain trade privileges in return for loyalism, the chamber's leadership was exposed to challenge. Some chamber members had left to fight the British in 1775, and the chamber went into abeyance from May 1775, 'in the light of the present unnatural rebellion', until mid-1779. But some leaders returned in 1777 with the British only to flee in the face of Washington's advancing assault in 1778, and their properties were confiscated. The two British Peace Commissioners (Lord Howe and William Eden) were also forced to evacuate New York in 1778. The chamber was re-established in 1783 with patriot or neutral members. Isaac Low's experience demonstrates the dilemmas; his efforts to prevent separation in 1775–6 dubbed him a loyalist, but his brother was a leading rebel; he returned to New York with British occupation in 1777 but had his property confiscated in 1779 and went to the UK. Other leading members of the chamber, such as Hugh Wallace and Henry White, were also forced to leave and lost their properties, though White returned in 1776 with the English, tried to mediate, but was evacuated back to England in 1783. Others, such as Theo Bache and William Walton tried to stay neutral, with varying degrees of success, and were allowed to stay in New York after 1783. John Cruger withdrew from public life and stayed after 1783. The secretary of the chamber, Anthony van Dam, managed to remain neutral over the entire period, remaining as secretary 1768–83.[202]

The Charleston chamber of commerce

Charleston chamber in Carolina presents a complementary picture, formed after a general meeting on 8 December 1773, with rules similar to the New York chamber with a committee of 21.[203] It was formed by the 'larger merchants and gentlemen' not just as a specific response to the emerging crisis, but also as a more general body.[204] It sought a moderating role. This is not surprising as the Charleston trade (chiefly in indigo and rice) depended to the largest extent on British direction, capital, and markets; it was one of the most strongly interlinked with Britain.[205] The president, John Savage, was one of the most prosperous merchants in Carolina. The vice-president was Miles Brewton, a banker and very rich slave trader, who owned the best mansion in Charleston. The treasurer was David Deas, a Scottish merchant. Brewton and Deas had been elected members of the South Carolina

---

[201] Full text of address and reply of 24 March 1770; quoted in chamber minutes; Stevens (1867).
[202] Stevens (1867), pp. 78–95, 105; also *DAB*; though Friedman (1947) states van Dam was forced to emigrate.
[203] *Rules* of the Charleston chamber of commerce (1773): Library Company of Philadelphia, 13194.
[204] South Carolina, *General Gazette*, 13 and 24 December 1773; in Rogers (1974), pp. 161–2.
[205] Price (1974, 1978).

Assembly in February 1773.[206] John Hopton was secretary, who was a clerk to
Henry Laurens, one of the leading merchants of the South and an important
moderating voice in the Provincial Congress.[207] Laurens was a key figure behind
the precursors of the chamber, having been a strong supporter of the Stamp Tax
lobby, and was chair of the committee for non-importation in 1769–70, but he was
away in England in 1771–4;[208] a relative, James Laurens, was a chamber committee
member. Henry Laurens and Brewton had been key figures in the State Commons
(with Charles Pinckney and others), major supporters of the donation to Wilkes
and the statue for Pitt, and in the dispute with the Governor and Crown over the
power of the State Assembly over 1767–72, leading to its suspension in 1772. The
chamber was thus again a body of protesters and reformers, but from the economic
and political elite.

One of the chamber's first actions in December 1773 seems to have been an
attempt to moderate the measures to prevent the landing of tea, to overcome the
actions of the mechanics to prevent unloading of the recently arrived East India
ship, the *London*. Negotiations between all the parties led to the local council and
chamber offering protection to the collector of Customs, who seized and landed the
tea, storing it in the Exchange. Whilst seen as less criminal than in Boston, where
the tea was dumped overboard, or in New York and Philadelphia where the ships
were turned away, it was still judged as insulting by the British.

Nevertheless, the Charleston radicals were chagrined that theirs was the only
place where tea was actually landed, and the chamber was blamed. A meeting of
mechanics, called for 16 March 1774, established a standing committee to act in a
future crisis, and even discussed calling it a 'chamber of counterpoise'.[209] David
Deas, the chamber's treasurer, won a contested election for the Assembly in June,
which temporarily halted the mechanics. But the mechanics then called a more
general meeting on 6–8 July 1774, involving massed back-countrymen, at which
the delegates to the first Continental Congress were elected. The chamber's three
nominees were defeated (including Brewton); although to appease the merchants
there was a compromise on the delegates' instructions.

By now the chamber was in eclipse, although its presence helped to gain
representation among the 15 merchants on the committee of 99, which was to
handle future local meetings and ensure revolutionary commitment, but they were
outnumbered by 15 mechanics and 69 planters. Like New York, there were patriots
and loyalists within the same family, with the moderate Brewtons and radical
Pinckneys and Izards notably intermarried. Subsequently many of the chamber
leaders were branded as loyalists, expelled, and their property confiscated. John

---

[206] *Gaine's Universal Register of American and British Kalendar* (1775), Gaine New York.

[207] Laurens, a very wealthy merchant, became a leading member of the Assembly and Continental
Congress, with strong patriotic credentials after a notorious dispute in 1767 with British Customs
officers (pulling one's nose) and the Admiralty Court; he tried to moderate in the 1760s, and
again in 1775 until the Declaration of Independence, when forced to take sides: see Weir (1983),
pp. 299–302; *DNB*; *DAB*.

[208] McCrady (1899); Rogers (1974); Andrews (1916), p. 256; *DNB*; *DAB*.

[209] Bridenbaugh (1955), p. 288; Rogers (1974), pp. 162–6.

Savage and John Hopton fought for the British and were forced to flee to England. Miles Brewton was in a difficult position. He had been an early local leader, but was forced out of moderating roles. His wife was a cousin of the wife of the new Governor, Lord William Campbell, whom he accommodated in his house when he arrived in June 1775. Brewton is credited with influencing Campbell to take a moderate approach, and tried to mediate between him and the Assembly's leaders, entertaining them both in his mansion, but in 1776 he packed up his possessions and sailed for England with his family; his ship was lost and he was presumed drowned.[210] The Deas family suffered confiscations but were allowed to stay in the State and maintained links with the expelled. Laurens, who was a 'moderate' supporting opposition but not violence, felt the Declaration of Independence was an 'awful renunciation of what he strove to support', and that Congress was too hasty in shutting the door on reconciliation. But he fought for the Americans, was captured by the British and imprisoned in the Tower, and subsequently acted as a moderating influence on 'amercement'.[211]

   The chamber continued to act in local commercial matters up to 1780, with reluctant rebel Laurens a major force in the chamber, a member of the Carolina Congress in 1774 (and its president in 1775). The chamber chiefly tried to ameliorate the disruptions to credit and trade. In 1774 it gave support to the Carolina Assembly urging acceptance of local certificates of indebtedness issued by the Assembly against public credit, secured by the first tax bills that were to be passed by any newly independent State government; this provided for local liquidity, without the consent of the Crown. In 1775 it published a list of acceptable charges on protested bills of exchange.[212] In both cases it was the underwriting by the merchants through the chamber that made the credit instruments acceptable. The chamber went into abeyance with the occupation of Charleston by the British in 1780, but was revived in February 1784 with 70 initial subscribers, overwhelmingly patriot. One of its first actions was to try to open trade with France and Holland, though this was not very successful, and to promote trade in rice and cotton, the development of the port and local canals, and it helped defend the city against the French in the 1790s.

Subsequent developments

After 1781 both the New York and Charleston chambers were revived. Boston was re-established briefly in 1785–90, re-established again in 1794, and finally became a continuing body in 1815. A chamber in Philadelphia was attempted in 1784 by Tench Coxe, Anglican and low-profile loyalist. It seems to have failed, despite obtaining support from over 300 business people. It sought to promote

---

[210] McCrady (1899), p. 406; (1901), pp. 30–1, 183–4; Rogers (1974); Weir (1984).
[211] McCrady (1899), pp. 403–10; (1901), p. 179; Lambert (1988), pp. 291–5; *DAB*.
[212] Sellers (1934), pp. 72–3; McCrady (1899), pp. 408, 731; *Wells Almanac and Register*, from Bridenbaugh (1955), pp. 287–8; see also modern chamber: <www.charlestonchamber.net/about/history>.

manufactures and stimulate trade. It was an explicit attempt by the merchants to counterbalance the 'country' interests to influence Congress, support federalist Republicans, and counteract the Confederation.[213]

A spirit of cooperation or imitation had some influence on the foundation of subsequent chambers in most of the other major cities and trading centres: New Haven (1794), Philadelphia (1801), Norfolk (1803), and Savannah (1806). The agenda in this later period changed to attempts by the leading port cities to rebuild their economies after the war, respond to war with France after 1793, and renewed war with Britain in 1812, to recover British debts, and to develop local regulatory controls over navigation and trade (chiefly acting as State-wide bodies).[214] Chambers thus became part of the structures of economic promotion and policy development to emerge from independence.

4.7 EARLY CHAMBERS IN CANADA: HALIFAX AND QUEBEC

In Canada the local English population was predominantly loyalist, even though many had come from New England. The Stamp Act papers had been accepted in the two leading colonies of Quebec and Nova Scotia, with virtually no resistance. There was pride in this demonstration of loyalty, and there was widespread support from the farming and artisan classes as well as the merchants. Similarly there had been no support for the embargos of trade in 1768–9; and Nova Scotia had even accepted tea shipments in 1774, some of it rerouted from Portsmouth (New Hampshire). Indeed the Canadian colonies had been included in the exportation ban by the Continental Congress in May 1775. Halifax was a strong base for British military operations during the American rebellion, receiving cannons captured from Charleston and evacuees from Massachusetts, whilst invading American rebels attacked loyalist Canadians in Montreal and Quebec in 1775.[215]

Merchant committees and the first Halifax chamber initiative

The English merchants in Canada had their own discontents, however, which focused on the governors and other elements of the aristocratic state, and included anger with any appeasement of the majority French population. There was less concern about constitutions than practical governance. Both Quebec and Nova Scotia had seen active campaigns against governors and corrupt local officials. These had achieved recall of the governor in Nova Scotia in 1763, a purge on

---

[213] *Plan for a Chamber of Commerce*, Philadelphia, 21 October 1784: Tench Coxe Papers, reel 46, Historical Society of Pennsylvania; see also Doerflinger (1986), p. 275; Haggerty (2006), pp. 130–1.

[214] The two other leading cities of 18th-century America did not form chambers until much later. In Baltimore a board of trade was formed in 1821, and a Corn and Grain Exchange was the prime chamber-like body during the 19th century, which evolved to become the chamber in the 1890s; Walsh and Fox (1974), p. 698. In Wilmington the chamber was not formed until 1853.

[215] Kerr (1932); Thomas (1991); Reid (2004).

corrupt public accounts in Nova Scotia in 1774–6, and appeasements of local concerns elsewhere.

To press their concerns and to promote trade, the English merchants formed local committees in a number of centres during the 1750s, including Montreal, Quebec, and Halifax (Nova Scotia).[216] The Halifax committee formed in 1748–50 seems to have had the strongest early presence, and has been claimed as the first business group in North America, 'where the merchants of the town . . . formed themselves into an association to benefit trade'.[217] These committees continued in halting form for many years, largely in response to need. For example, it is claimed that the Halifax committee was active in securing a local Assembly in 1758, and was a major force behind the loyal petition of the Nova Scotia Assembly in 1775. It continued petitioning in the 1780s and 1790s, helping to form a Marine Insurance Association in 1794, and made attempts to initiate the Shubenacadie canal in 1798, and a bank in 1801. These initiatives have been seen as precursors of the Halifax Committee of Trade first formally established in 1803, which was a broad based and formal body, covering trade, agriculture, and fisheries. It went through various re-establishments before an explicit chamber of commerce was founded in 1822.[218]

The status of the early associations over 1750–90 is difficult to discover from surviving records. Most appear to have been primarily ad hoc, with little formal status or rules. Thus until the 1790s, and perhaps not until 1803, the Halifax initiative appears to have been essentially a small committee or group of leading merchants prepared to press the Governor or to petition London, rather than a general and broadly based chamber as defined in this book. If there was a more formal body, it worked very closely with the Assembly, since it was the Assembly that took the initiative in appointing the first Nova Scotia agent in London in 1762 and his successors. The first formal chamber at Halifax (of 1803) helped to stimulate the foundation of a Quebec chamber in 1808. However, well before this there was a significant initiative to develop a Quebec chamber.

The first Quebec chamber of commerce

Quebec City was Canada's only large urban centre at this time, and the main port of entry to the entire northern interior. The proposal for a Quebec chamber of commerce in 1776–7 was the direct outcome of the 1774 Quebec Act. This followed the success of the Seven Years War, which ceded Canada to Britain by the Treaty of Paris in 1763.

Soon after the Treaty, the King had made a *Proclamation* that in Quebec an assembly could make its own laws, provided they were 'as near as agreeable to the laws of England'. But an assembly was never granted, and instead legislation was placed under the Governor, James Murray, and council. Despite initially assuming

---

[216] Creighton (1937), pp. 32–55; Butler (1942), p. 1.
[217] Akins (1895), p. 27; 'The Halifax Board of Trade: An historical sketch 1748–1908', *49th Report of Halifax Board of Trade* (1908); Cuthbertson (2000), p. 3 n. 1.
[218] Butler (1942), pp. 1–4; Cuthbertson (2000), pp. 6–16.

that English law and institutions were to apply, there were many practical problems and a concern to placate and pacify the former French citizens, recognizing that they formed the overwhelming majority of the population, and the need for the 'conqueror to proceed gently'.[219] As a result, concessions were made in Murray's 1764–5 ordinances and subsequent evolution that allowed the use of the laws of *either* Britain or France, admitted Canadian jurors and advocates, and allowed either language to be used. Local usage and custom was to apply, formally agreed by the British Committee of Trade in 1766.[220] This was received sceptically by the British merchants in Canada and in England. But when built into the Quebec Act in 1774, Jefferson and others portrayed them as allowing absolute rule and the development of Papacy, by permitting free worship.[221] The evolution of discussions leading up to the Act stimulated a petitioning campaign by Protestant subjects and London Quebec merchants in 1768, revived in 1773–7, and continuing at least until 1789.[222]

The immediate stimulus to the Quebec chamber in 1776 was the imposition of French law under the Quebec Act by the Lieutenant-Governor (Louis/Lewis Cramahé). After 1775 Cramahé became a de facto parallel French governor,[223] with equal status under the provisions of Murray's ordinances. It was claimed that Cramahé was pushing to make French laws dominant. Particularly resented by the British merchants was the abolition of trial by jury except in criminal cases; i.e. covering all civil and commercial disputes (the same concerns as in America).

Sensing the impending constitutional settlement, both British and French communities in Canada began stirring in late 1773. British Protestant community meetings in October and November sought their own Assembly through two petitions: from Quebec (signed by 61) and Montreal (signed by 87). These reached the American Secretary (Dartmouth) on 6 April 1774. A French petition of December arrived in February 1774, from 65 *seigneurs* of Quebec who sought French criminal and civil laws, a share of government employment, restoration of former boundaries, and a Legislative Council, not an Assembly.[224] Given the developments in America, a Council was also favoured by ministers who did not

---

[219] Instructions to Murray from George III: BL Add MS 33030, fo. 240; see also Marshall (1971).
[220] BL Add MS 33030, fo. 17–49, 235–42; Add MS 32982, fo. 21, 79, 225.
[221] See e.g. Sosin (1965), pp. 183–4; Thomas (1991), pp. 97–117, 148–9, 232–3.
[222] Summarized in *Answer to an Introduction to the Observations Made by the Judges of the Court of Common Pleas for the District of Quebec...with Remarks on the Laws and Government of Quebec*, London 1790; hereafter referred to as *Answer* (18th Century online).
[223] Cramahé, born *c*.1720, was in fact a loyal British supporter who entered military service in 1740, fought under Lord Cathcart in the West Indies in 1740 and Flanders in 1745. He went to Quebec in 1759 under the military, but left to act as secretary to the Governor 1761–4. He went to England, but returned to Quebec in 1764 as secretary to General Guy Carleton who commanded the province. When Carleton left for England in August 1770, where he became one of the primary forces behind the Quebec Act, Cramahé who was then the senior member of the Council took over, and was made Lieutenant-Governor in 1771, becoming president of the Council until Carleton returned in 1775. He then reverted to secretary, but was elevated as the representative of the French. He petitioned Pitt for employment or a pension in April 1786, then aged 66: TNA PRO 30/8/220, fo. 76.
[224] Shortt and Doughty (1914), vol. i, pp. 486–98 and 504–11; Creighton (1937), pp. 75–8; Marshall (1971).

want a repeat of the American Assemblies.[225] The dual legal system might also discourage any American attempts to spread west or north.[226] The Quebec Act passed in June 1774 with a large majority. Like the contemporaneous American coercion Acts it was passed despite the efforts of opposition MPs, including Herbert Mackworth MP who in May presented a petition from the Quebec merchants in London. The Act was seen as a betrayal of the Whig settlement, and both Chatham and Walpole railed against it in the Lords.

Whatever its objectives, and Thomas claims it was an enlightened and conciliatory settlement,[227] the Protestants in Quebec (and the Americans) saw it very differently. Indeed they lost the right to an assembly offered in 1763, as well as the British protections of habeas corpus and trial by jury.[228] It was another example of high-handed aristocratic deals. For the French population it was appeasement of the *seigneurs*; the landless French gained nothing and their duty to pay tithes was reaffirmed. When the Americans invaded Canada in 1775, many Catholics and some protestants assisted the rebels, whilst the *seigneurs* defended Quebec until the arrival of the British troops.[229]

The Quebec merchants petitioned the king directly in November 1774, objecting to French law being imposed, and portraying this as having Papist intent.[230] The petition came from Quebec and Montreal committees, signed by 184 people. This was dismissed in London as a discontented minority encouraged by the American rebels. Wilkes took up the cause, calling for the repeal of the Quebec Act, which was said to be 'establishing Popery and French laws' in Canada.[231] It aroused parliamentary debate, with Savile a major supporter of repeal, but it was easily defeated. In 1776 the Quebec merchants petitioned again, with a related petition following in 1777 from the Quebec merchants in London, objecting to law reform that gave 'indefinite powers . . . to the Judges, and of the prejudice which prevails in them without exception'.[232] This was ignored.

The Quebec chamber was born out of these tensions. The merchants Charles Grant, James Johnston, and Robert Lester were deputed in 1776 to approach the governor to argue the case for juries to be used in civil commercial disputes. This was refused, but the three delegates then moved instead to propose 'a chamber of commerce in Quebec, which, they thought would, in some measure, compensate for the want of juries'. Clearly they had already conceived this proposal, and had in mind a chamber with arbitration powers, as already established in New York and Jersey, which would circumvent the French laws. With the governor's support a plan for a charter for a chamber was prepared. This was sent to England, discussed

---

[225] e.g. Edmund Burke speech on Quebec Bill, 10 June 1774; reprinted in *The Writings of Edmund Burke*, vol. ii, pp. 471–3 (ed. P. Langford, Oxford: Clarendon Press).

[226] Burke letter to New York; quoted in Thomas (1991), pp. 100–1 and ff.

[227] Thomas (1991), p. 113.

[228] Civil and criminal law of Quebec: Sheffield Archives; WMM 1/Bk P/1/517, fos. 8 and 522.

[229] Thomas (1991), pp. 115–16.

[230] *Parliamentary Register*, J. Almon, pp. 479–83, 18 May (1775) (petition of 12 November 1774).

[231] *Gentleman's Magazine* (1774), p. 444; quoted in Rudé (1962), p. 195; Thomas (1991), pp. 231–3.

[232] *The Remembrancer* (1775–84), 2 April 1778, pp. 186–8.

by the Committee of Trade in March–July 1777, which asked for a report, and then approved the proposal for a chamber as 'appearing to be a regulation both proper and advantageous, it was recommended to the care and consideration of the governor'.[233]

However, the governor left the chamber's charter in abeyance because of opposition expected from the parallel French Lieutenant-Governor (Cramahé) and the Council; i.e. again there was appeasement of the French *seigneurs*. The English merchants viewed them as 'all placemen or pensioners': their strategy has been '*always to keep the old and new subjects of the Crown, that is, the English and Canadians as disunited as possible*'. But even more inflammatory was a militia ordinance, which 'has given the finishing stroke to this discontentment. I really believe there is not a man of them now but would rebel ... except for a few of the gentry in places of profit, and such as have pensions, or hope to have them'.[234]

The chamber proposal was thus deeply interlinked with protest and search for independent English voice in Quebec, but with a specific twist towards arbitration to overcome the tensions between the two legal systems. The protests continued, with the merchants petitioning repeatedly into the 1780s through their London agent Adam Lymburner. The protests were probably from either a formal chamber for which no records survive, or a less formal committee acting like a chamber, as had operated behind the 1773, 1774, and 1775 petitions. There was probably a body called a chamber in 1787 and 1789, of which James Johnston and Robert Lester were leading members. This seems to have been behind the extensive listing and critique of 'incompetent' commercial judgements by the Court of Common Pleas over 1786–89,[235] with continuous lobbying to restructure the laws until 1790, and a vigorous effort to remove the judges and Canadian Attorney General in 1789.[236] It is probable therefore that a de facto chamber existed 1776–89, although it may never have established formal articles of association.

4.8 THE CARIBBEAN: THE FIRST KINGSTON CHAMBER OF COMMERCE

Great events affected the Caribbean in a different way. These colonies were strongly loyalist during the American rebellion, and viewed the Americans as disrupting the tranquillity of 'the nation'. Although the Stamp Act led to riots in St Kitts, and the

---

[233] *Journal of the Commissioners for Trade and Plantations*, 21 March and 24 July 1777; 13 April 1778.

[234] This account is based on a letter of 14 June 1777 from a Quebec merchant reported in *The Remembrancer* (1775–84), 2 April 1778, pp. 181–3; emphasis in original; see also Maier (1973).

[235] Along with G. Allsop, W. Goodall, John Young, L. Duniere, J. Blackwood, Matthew Lymburner, and John Painter: letter to James Monk, 9 November 1789, *Answer*, Appendix VII, pp. 71–2; see also *Charges brought by the* [missing words] *Commerce before the Legislative Council*, 14 April 1787, in *Answer*, Appendix XI, p. 77 and Appendix XIX, pp. 101–5, which implies a committee or chamber.

[236] *Answer*, Appendices V–XIX, pp. 64–105.

other Leeward Islands withheld payment, in Dominica, Jamaica, and the Windward Islands there was no resistance.[237] There was no local white equivalent of the 'mechanics' class of artisans that had interest in rebellion, and unlike America the population was strongly committed to Britain, many staying in the Caribbean for only a few years. The West Indies could also be dominated by the navy, needed defence from foreign invasion, and support from the British garrison against slave insurrections (which occurred in Jamaica in 1760, 1765, and 1776).

Local grievances

However, the scene was locally complex. There had been flurries of activity asserting the rights of local Assemblies, with 'riots' in the 1750s and 1760s in the Assembly rooms in Barbados, Dominica, and Jamaica. These arose from opposition to arbitrary or inflammatory actions by particular Governors. In Jamaica, the only Caribbean colony that seems to have developed a chamber, there were extended conflicts between the Governor and Assembly in 1751–6 and 1764–6, which both succeeded in having the Governor recalled.[238] These successes were somewhat resented by Kingston (which was the main commercial centre and port), whose merchants saw them as the outcome of corrupt interests of Spanish Town (the capital) and the planters. The Free Ports Act of May 1766, covering Dominica and Jamaica, was also locally divisive. In Jamaica the renewal of the Act in 1773 was delayed by a year as a result of the resistance by the Assembly, Governor, and interests in England who believed the Act encouraged smuggling and did little for trade. Similarly the Assembly in 1774 passed a Jamaica slave tax. The Kingston merchants, Liverpool chamber, Bristol Venturers, and London West Indies Committee coordinated lobbies against the opposition to Free Ports, and against the slave tax.[239] On 24 December 1774 the Kingston 'party' in the Assembly succeeded in passing a petition supporting the Americans. This was similar to other petitions against coercion, but went much further: calling for resistance to parliament's 'plan for enslaving the colonies', and criticizing 'the papist religion established by law' (through the Quebec Act) and the Massachusetts Acts.[240] Thus a pattern had developed, as in some of the American colonies, of trying to find a more effective voice for the main commercial centre than their often-unsympathetic Governors, as well as staving off local opposition from a planter 'aristocracy' that often controlled the Assembly.

The foundation of the chamber in 1778 certainly demonstrated Kingston's concern to assert its specific needs. Frustration and alarm had grown as a result of the inadequacy of the naval protection. The French overran Dominica in September 1778, and there was fear of an imminent invasion of Jamaica. St Vincent and

---

[237] Metcalf (1965); Clayton (1986); O'Shaughnessy (1994, 2000); Hamilton (2005), pp. 159–64.

[238] Metcalf (1965), pp. 187–91.

[239] Armytage (1953), p. 46; Metcalf (1965), pp. 185–6, 196; Clayton (1986); Bennett (2010), pp. 12, 36–7, 121–4.

[240] TNA CO 137/70. This was probably an attempt to appease the Americans. Indeed they received the thanks of the US Congress: Metcalf (1965), pp. 187–90; Clayton (1986), pp. 328–30.

Grenada fell in early 1779. The Governor, John Dalling, initially responded by declaring martial law on 4 September 1778, and laying an embargo on homebound ships. This was deemed unnecessary by the Assembly, who forced him to remove martial law and the embargo. James Pinnock's contemporary diary records that 'nobody knows any good reason for it [martial law]'; and when it was removed 'The governor was damnably disgruntled at its being taken off'.[241] Dalling was a military figure who wanted to 'command', whilst the Assembly judged him impulsive and sought to limit declarations of martial law to the Council of War (hence subject to the Assembly).

In response, the Kingston magistrates and merchants formed a 'committee of correspondence' in October, which may have been the proto-chamber. It initiated a system of convoying between the Island's ports and sent an address to the King through Lord Germain (American Secretary in London), via Stephen Fuller the Jamaica agent in London, stating that martial law was unnecessary and that the need for reinforcements 'may not be kept from the King's ear by the artifices of those who have already too long amused and deceived the good people of this Island'. This was a direct attack on Germain and Dalling. Fuller observed that 'want of protection will shake their loyalty to its roots'.[242] Dalling's response was to call for full military power and pay. Germain agreed to military rank, but without pay, and he supported martial law, which Dalling reimposed on 7 August 1779, with the Assembly now reluctantly acquiescing.[243] However, Dalling was to continue fruitless personal vendettas against Assembly members, the local naval commander, and the Attorney General, leading to paralysis of effective government. When local interests succeeded in having Dalling replaced in November 1781, invasion was imminent. The new Governor raced to prepare defensive redoubts and train the neglected militia. St Kitts fell to the French in February 1782, then Montserrat and Nevis. The threat was only removed at the battle of The Saintes in April 1782 with defeat of the French fleet, which was on its way to Jamaica.[244]

The Kingston chamber of commerce

Against this background the chamber was established in November 1778 with formal *Rules*, minutes for quarterly and annual meetings, and election of committee and officers.[245] The members of the chamber were mostly from Kingston, and it was referred to as the 'Kingston chamber of commerce', but it also had members

[241] *Assembly Journals*, CO 140/59; Pinnock, *Diary* BL Add MS 33316, 4 September and 1 November 1778.
[242] Fuller to Germain, 5 January 1779, enclosing Address of Committee of Correspondence of 22, 24, and 28 October, and Assembly meetings of 22 and 28 October; CO 137/74.
[243] Dalling to Germain 21 November and 12 December 1778, reply 6 March and 2 April 1779 CO 137/74; Pinnock, *Diary* 7 August 1779.
[244] Metcalf (1965), pp. 210–19.
[245] Referred to in reports in *Jamaica Mercury and Kingston Weekly Gazette*; general meetings held in November.

from Port Royal, St George, and probably other centres. It took over de facto arrangements for convoys, calling public meetings to fix the times for departure, and negotiating directly with naval commanders, profusely thanking them when successfully delivering shipping. The chamber also organized printing of blank books of bills of exchange in sets of 'four rather than the normal three' facilitating the circulation of paper,[246] and was probably behind a petition to London to allow printing of paper money (as undertaken by Charleston chamber). These were responses to the local specie crisis that became severe in 1778–9, exacerbated by the Governor, with Germain's resistance to paper money reinforcing the view that London was incompetent and out of touch.[247] The chamber did work with the Governor to send support to Westmorland parish after the disastrous hurricane in 1780,[248] and one chamber member, Richard Watt, was a Commissioner for distributing hurricane relief money.[249] The chamber survived until the end of the crisis, at least until 1785, and perhaps longer as a latent body.

Without further records it is difficult to be certain of the chamber's full role. However, listings of the committee for 1778–85 provide insights into its leadership.[250] Of 41 identifiable chamber members, at least nine became deeply involved in the island's government. Assembly members for Kingston were Paul Phipps senior 1778–87, Thomas Gray 1781 and 1796, Archibald Galbraith 1787–96, Robert Hibbert 1787–90, John McLean 1787–96, Eliphalet Fitch 1791–7, and John Jacques 1791. Thomas Hibbert jun., the first president, was Assembly member for St George 1770–80, and Archibald Thomson for Port Royal 1787–90, and Portland in 1790. Over 1776–91 ten members were judges of Chancery or other higher courts, 23 were JPs, five were members or wardens of the parish vestry (and John Hardware the chamber secretary 1778–82 was parish clerk); several were Commissioners of the local Board of Works and other committees (John Jacques was president of the Fire Wardens), and many were active members of the militia.[251] Only nine (22%) known members held no other public role. Six key figures (Alexander Allardyce, Moses Benson, Thomas Bond, Thomas Gray, Robert Hibbert, and Thomas Hibbert jun.) were president, vice-president, or treasurer for 90% of the possible opportunities over the chamber's known seven years of life. The chamber thus held considerable local power; it was not a body of 'outsiders'. The role of Archibald Galbraith as Commissary for Provisions may have helped the chamber become so closely involved in convoys.

---

[246] Quarterly meetings of 6, 20, and 27 November 1779, and *Jamaica Mercury* and *Royal Gazette*, 19 February, 20 May, 18 and 25 November 1780; *Jamaica Register and Almanac* (1783) states chamber founded in 1778.

[247] Germain's response 5 May 1779 (CO 137/74) was seen as totally inadequate, leading to a direct address to the King (Metcalf (1965), p. 209).

[248] Quoted in J. Fowler (1781), *A General Account of the Calamities Occasioned by the Late Tremendous Hurricanes and Earthquakes in the West Indies Islands* (London: J. Stockdale), p. 21.

[249] Commissioners listed in *Cornwall Gazette and Jamaica General Advertiser*, 1 September 1781.

[250] See e.g. *Jamaica Mercury and Kingston Weekly Advertiser*, and *Royal Gazette*; *Jamaica Register and Almanacs*; also see J. Morgan (1979) pp. 10–17 in Jamaica chamber of commerce, *The Bicentennial Handbook, 1779–1979*, <www.jamaicachamber.org.jm/history>.

[251] Attributions from *Jamaica Register and Almanac, 1776–91*.

There were also significant interlocks with Britain and America, which included connections with the early chambers. Of the most senior chamber figures, Robert Hibbert became largely an absentee in London, and he and Thomas Hibbert were connected to Hibbert family members of the first Manchester chamber. Moses Benson was related to Liverpool Stamp Act committee members Benson and Postlethwaite, Archibald Campbell was a partner of Liverpool Stamp Act committee member George Campbell (the 'friend' of Meredith and Rockingham), Richard Watt (hurricane Commissioner) was uncle of a member of Liverpool chamber, Richard Lake was related to two Liverpool chamber members, and there were many links of others with Barlow Trecothick and William Beckford who had led the London Stamp Act protests. There were also many links to the sugar merchants in the later Glasgow chamber, Greenock traders, Bristol Venturers, the prominent London traders, and with the New York and Charleston chambers.[252] Hence, there were many routes for transfer of the chamber concept, with local attitudes of the Kingston chamber leaders that can be discerned reflecting similar characteristics to the loyalist chamber members elsewhere. They wanted a counterweight to the disputes in the Assembly, were more concerned to get something done than argue about constitutional minutiae, and were aggrieved with Governor Dalling and inadequate attention from Germain. Its members were elite merchant activists, trying to ensure greater sensitivity to business needs by those in government, challenging the local 'aristocracy', precipitated by alarms (of invasion), but remaining loyal to the existing constitutional settlement.

4.9 CHAMBERS OF COMMERCE IN THE CHANNEL ISLANDS

Jersey and Guernsey were, and still are, governed by their own parliaments, the 'States', which are formally under the Crown, through William of Normandy's accession in 1066. Any relationships between them and the UK operated through the Privy Council (appointed by the Crown), which also appointed a non-resident Lieutenant-Governor, independently of parliament. The Jersey chamber, developed in May 1767, was founded in resistance to assertions by parliament over Customs and legal powers. This was a by-product of the Stamp Act debacle, which led the government increasingly to use parliament instead of Royal prerogative as a means of asserting its authority, in order to increase its legitimacy.[253] This was an affront to the American colonies and Quebec, who increasingly petitioned the king directly. In the Channel Isles it presented a new and 'unconstitutional' intrusion between them and the king. In 1762–3 Ordres Politiques issued by the Chefs Plaids d'Heritage changed the rules under which civil servants worked; in 1767 parliament sought to set up direct Customs inspection; and in 1771 an Order of King in Council asserted Crown control and required any States' laws in force for

[252] See Checkland (1958); Devine (1971, 1978); Hamilton (2005); Morgan (2007); Bennett (2010).
[253] See e.g. Thomas (1987), pp. 10–11.

more than three years to be sanctioned by the king in Council. In 1774 parliament sought to take control of duties on rum and spirits.[254] These actions were inflammatory and required the States to be active to defend local interests.

However, in Jersey the States was not active, being controlled by the resident deputy to the absentee Lieutenant-Governor, Charles Lemprière, who was Bailiff of Jersey from 1750 until 1781, and his family and supporters. Lemprière became very unpopular, exercising power arbitrarily, issuing 'ordinances through his Court and through the same Court punished all who protested'.[255] There was much discontent, and in 1769, there was rioting led by John Dumaresq against Lemprière, who as a corn trader was seen to be profiting from corn exports, which he was regulating when grain was short. Although the chamber was not openly involved in such protests, it later used John Dumaresq (or a presumed relative) as its London agent.[256] The pressure to reform the States, or even to get it to sit, continued, with Jersey chamber frequently petitioning the Governor for attention, or the King 'to request the president to summon the States at the earliest date'.[257]

As in the American colonies, the chamber's development was thus part of the intellectual and commercial ferment to find a more effective and legitimate voice for their concerns than their discredited unelected local representatives acting under aristocratic control. Lemprière was judged to have 'possessed no more idea than an oyster, and like that inert animal he seldom opened his mouth but to take in fluids'.[258] Nevertheless, the chamber sought the patronage of the Lieutenant-Governor, and relatives of Lemprière's became chamber members. This again shows the extraordinary ambiguity of the early chambers: they were vehicles for protest, but largely in an ordered and gentlemanly fashion recognizing established hierarchy, not through revolution.

The Jersey chamber began meeting in 1767, and has continuous minutes from 1768, but the first Guernsey chamber's establishment is only indicated by a badge of office dated 1769,[259] one reference in the Jersey minutes, and a record of its existence by Arthur Young in 1786, stating that 'a chamber of commerce has been lately established in Guernsey'.[260] From what we can now ascertain it worked closely with Jersey, taking joint action by having its own 'deputy' Havilland Le Meseurier in London, jointly with Jersey's agent Dumaresq, in July 1785.[261] However, the Jersey chamber minutes give little indication of other Guernsey chamber activities. The continuous records of the modern chamber begin in 1808.

Whilst it is tempting to believe that Jersey and Guernsey chambers may have been influenced to adopt a French model of chambers because of proximity to

---

[254] Bois (1970), Privileges documents 11/45–11/52, pp. 191–4.
[255] Syvret and Stevens (1998), p. 192; Jamieson (1986); and Jersey chamber histories.
[256] Syvret and Stevens (1998); not clear if the same man; Dumaresq acted as agent 1785–1790s, see Chapter 8.
[257] e.g. Jersey chamber minutes, letter 14 March 1768 to Governor praying for 'countenance and protection'; and petition to the king, 17 November 1786.
[258] Quoted in Syvret and Stevens (1998), p. 195.
[259] Gregory Cox (1983), Guernsey chamber history.
[260] Arthur Young, *Annals of Agriculture* (1786), p. 370.
[261] Jersey chamber minutes, 4 July 1785.

France, there is no evidence for this; and, as in Britain, the use of government-appointed business people to run French-style chamber committees would have been deeply resented. Moreover, French, the 'official' language of many transactions in the Islands, was not used in any of the chamber papers (except in some official letters). Indeed the chambers were not developed along French lines, and foreign influence was confined to the Dutch or Danish, with which both Islands had closer trading links, and who supported the chamber.

Proximate cause

The proximate stimulus to the Channel Island chambers was thus objective grievances similar to those in the colonies. First, there was deep resentment with the local administrator, so that appeal was sought to a voice that could provide a more effective lobby than that of corrupt local people and bodies. This motivation continued well into the 19th century with frequent dissenting voices between the Jersey States and chamber;[262] though the Guernsey States and chamber were more aligned. It appears to have been firmly believed in Jersey in 1767 that appeal directly to the Crown, around the locally inert, would provide redress. This has echoes from the Americans' approach over 1767–74. Second, there were major concerns about local political commitment to trade, particularly over harbours. Both the early Jersey and Guernsey chambers made harbour improvements their main immediate and sustained campaigns. This achieved faster success in Guernsey because of the support of their States, but continued in Jersey into the 1850s because of the dilatory attention by their States.[263] Third, there was dislike of the Navigation Acts, which required cumbersome clearance in England of Channel Islands ships proceeding to America and Newfoundland. Fourth, there was hindrance to the main trade, of Newfoundland and Greenland fishing, as a result of government interference. Jersey had, like the Liverpool fisheries, a triangular trade from Newfoundland with Europe for salt fish exports and wine imports. There was also a substantial ex-Jersey community, mainly in the Gaspée that, like the American colonies, had a spirit of independent self-reliance that resented intrusions by Westminster.[264] There was also a Jersey community in Carolina closely involved in its embargoes and resistance to Westminster.[265] Fifth, Jersey shipping businesses

---

[262] One of the more celebrated open disputes was in 1786, when the States was abruptly adjourned by the president leaving his seat and thus ignoring a petition from the chamber. This became a celebrated legal wrangle with further petitions and counter-petitions: see Jersey chamber minutes, e.g. 17 November 1786 ff; also *A Collection of the Several Petitions, Representations and Answers of the States and of the Royal Court of Jersey, Relative to Political Differences, Comprehending Transactions from the Year 1779 to 1788*, Jersey, 1788, e.g. pp. 210–12 (18th Century online).

[263] Jersey chamber minutes from 14 March 1767; Guernsey chamber minutes from 9 November 1838.

[264] e.g. remonstrance by fishermen in the Newfoundland trade, 3 December 1768, presented by Attorney General of the States, through a delegation sent to London objecting: Bois (1970), Privileges document 8/63, p. 132.

[265] e.g. another branch of the Lemprières, Clement Lemprière was subsequently one of the captains who captured British ships to obtain gunpowder and military supplies for the rebels in 1775: McCrady (1901), pp. 21–2.

resented paying 'sailors sixpences' to support Greenwich hospital. The first recorded action of the chamber was to take 'immediate steps for relieving the trade of the Island from the persecutions carried out by Thos. Jas. Gruchy, receiver of sixpences'; these were seen as a form of taxation without representation, which offered no local benefit.[266] Jersey subsequently initiated its own Marine Society as an alternative.

The precise timing of foundation of the Jersey chamber in 1767 appears to have been due to specific moves by the British government to exert more control over Channel Islands Customs duties. In January 1765 it was proposed that the Commissioners of Customs would establish their own Customs officers on the Islands. It was also proposed to levy a new duty on coal exported to them. Two petitions, from Jersey merchants and the Guernsey States Deputies, were sent to the Privy Council. Both petitions, though heard at the Council, were dismissed, and an Order in Council of February 1765 approved the establishment of Customs officers from 4 April 1767.[267] This is a precise analogue of the treatment of American petitions at the same time, with London asserting a control that the Islanders deemed unconstitutional.

It is clear from these activities that whilst the Guernsey States had resisted and lobbied on behalf of their merchants, the Jersey States had not. This inaction in Jersey was almost as inflammatory as the Orders themselves, and was seen as Bailiff Lemprière's indolence or subservience as placeman. That the Jersey chamber was founded a few days after this Order (in May 1767) is indicative of the concerns, which continued after the 1760s as the Jersey and Guernsey chambers tried to limit the power of the Customs officers. In 1785 one of the few records of the early Guernsey chamber shows that 'the chambers of commerce of both Islands sent two deputies with a memorial to the Lords of the Treasury' covering a wide range of grievances about restrictions on trade, Newfoundland fisheries, West Indies and American trade, privateering, smuggling, and the Irish Propositions. This continued into 1787.[268] Even by 1809 the Guernsey chamber was arguing that the government of the Island was being transferred to the Commission of Customs and their officers, 'and no mother and family returning home from market will be able to take their tea, salt, wine etc. without being exposed to the rude search of the Customs House officers; ... Revenue is the object, and the prevention of smuggling the pretext.'[269]

Seen from Britain, the Channel Islands were infested by smuggling. Seen from the Islands, it was convenient and part of their fundamental rights to import and re-

---

[266] Jersey chamber minutes, 8 March 1768. Guernsey was still objecting to sailors sixpences in 1835: minutes, 3 November 1835; it helped set up a Society for Merchant Seamen instead.
[267] Bois (1970), Privileges documents 8/60, 8/62, pp. 131–2.
[268] Arthur Young, *Annals of Agriculture* (1786), pp. 370–81; see also Jersey chamber minutes 4 July 1785 ff., joint action through their 'deputies' in London; also reported in 1787 Jersey petitions against the States in *A Collection of the Several Petitions...*, 1788, op. cit.
[269] Guernsey chamber minutes, 21 April 1809. A joint petition of the chamber and the States against the extension of Customs powers was mounted on 2 May 1809; lobbying continuing over the following years.

export independently of parliamentary control and duties. The concerns over the Customs, closely resembling the feelings in Boston, were probably also exacerbated by the establishment of the British government's American Department under Hillsborough. As part of the response to the growing Massachusetts rebellion, Hillsborough in 1768 developed strategies to take the fisheries under direct British control. A Royal charter company to exploit the Newfoundland and Gaspée fisheries was proposed to control exclusive fishing rights. This was perceived as the efforts of 'base, ungenerous, selfish . . . Great People pocketing these benefits'.[270] It directly challenged the Islands' shipping interests that depended heavily on free access to these fisheries. A vigorous chamber lobby followed.[271] In 1775 the Islands may have influenced the town of Poole to argue that it could take over the New England fisheries.[272] By 1786 parliament obliged the 'bankers' on the Grand Banks to operate under certificates, but the chamber won the right to be the issuer of these through its secretary,[273] in effect operating under delegated power from the jurats.[274]

Despite the Jersey chamber being the oldest in the British Isles, it had few links with other early chamber formations. There were probable links with Liverpool, which replicated its unusual subscription structure (and perhaps Manchester).[275] This could have been through merchant verbal exchanges, through a member of the Society of Arts (James Amicea Lemprière, who was one the London-based Jersey merchants appointed as a London political agent of the chamber in 1768),[276] or through Thomas Butterworth Bayley the president of the first Manchester chamber in 1774 who was FRS and FSA. However, there are almost no other traceable links with other British bodies: Jersey and Guernsey were not involved in the collaboration to lobby over American duties in 1768, or later agitations. The only early joint action with mainland chambers was a brief response to the General Chamber objecting to the French Treaty proposals of 1786.[277] There is also no reference to Jersey by the Bristol Venturers, or the Glasgow, Dublin, and Belfast chambers after 1783, which record many interactions with other early chambers. Thus Jersey's early development appears to have been an outcome of local grievances with its States government and Governor, but which drew on common origins and desire for 'reform'.

---

[270] Anonymous pamphlet: *The First Measures Necessary to be Taken in the American Department*, addressed to Earl of Hillsborough, London, 1768; p. 19.

[271] Jersey chamber minutes, Newfoundland fisheries, 14 March 1768, 8 February and 13 March 1769.

[272] Poole, quoted in Thomas (1991), pp. 206–7; see also oblique references in Jersey chamber minutes 1774–5.

[273] 'By Act of Parliament relative to the bounties passed 21 January 1786': Jersey chamber minutes, 19 March 1787.

[274] Bois (1970), Privileges documents 8/66, provided this power in 1771 in response to a protest from the States against the Registrar of Certificates.

[275] See Bennett (2010), pp. 17–18, 76, 135; and Chapter 6. The same structures may also have been copied by the Manchester 1774 foundation but there are no documents to prove this.

[276] Jersey minutes, 14 March 1768 'agents appointed to manage the affairs of the chamber in England'; see also Chapter 8. He was a member of the Society of Arts from the 1760s.

[277] Jersey chamber minutes, 9 November 1786; see Chapter 9.

4.10 THE EARLY CHAMBERS OF COMMERCE IN IRELAND

Ireland was also a 'colony', governed by an English Lord Lieutenant (or Viceroy from 1767). The constitution, like America, was ambiguous. Although the main legal source used in the 1770s (Molyneux) argued that Ireland and England were joined in a voluntary compact, and that only the Irish parliament could legislate locally,[278] London normally legislated for Ireland. As a result the Irish had to lobby London, with the London secretary of the Lord Lieutenant often acting as a counterpart of the American agents.[279] When Eden was Secretary in 1782 he was sometimes 'spending 13 hours a day' listening to Irish lobbyists and their concerns.[280] Ireland also had the added disadvantage that its main aristocracy was English, and it was exploited ruthlessly to place loyal supporters of the government; the boroughs were almost all 'venal'[281] and 'a large share of its profits, places, pensions and sinecures' were given to the English.[282] There had been no elections in Ireland between 1727 and 1760.

The Stamp Act and Townshend Acts had more effect in Ireland than anywhere except America in stimulating local committees of leading businesses to form: in Dublin in 1761, in Cork in 1769, and in Limerick and Waterford at about the same time.[283] Even more than the Stamp Act committees in England, these were chambers in all but name, having formal constitutions, a broad membership, election processes and subscriptions, and consequently greater breadth and stability. Meredith acted as an intermediary for the Dublin committee during the Stamp Act crisis, and in 1765 was lobbying for Irish appointments in the Lord Lieutenant's gift to support trading interests.[284] These became a natural foundation for Ireland's own non-importation movement in 1779. The Stamp Act and emerging American crisis led to a general thrust to settle colonial affairs in a way that would also advance Irish causes.

But the control of Irish politics by the English prevented immediate changes. The appointment of George Townshend as Lord Lieutenant in 1767 was specifically aimed at raising more revenue (including stamp duties), and was founded on developing a 'Castle' party that would wave the legislation through the Irish House of Commons. This stimulated a more organized 'patriot' opposition in the Irish parliament, but with little effect.[285] The American move to rebellion widened the groundswell of both popular and elite support for the opposition; the *Freeman's Journal*, a Dublin liberal paper, viewed the rebellion as inevitable (given the unjust

[278] William Molyneux (1698), *The Case of Ireland's being Bounded by Acts of Parliament in England Stated*, Dublin; see York (1998), pp. 207–8.
[279] James (1973); Cullen (1983).
[280] Auckland correspondence; BL Add MS 34418, fos. 144–5, 333–4; see also Lammey (1988).
[281] Porritt and Porritt (1903); Namier and Brooke (1964).
[282] McDowell (1944), p. 16; Powell (2003), p. 141.
[283] See Cullen (1983), pp. 34, 58; also see Chapter 5.
[284] See Powell (2003), p. 85; quoting letter from Meredith to Pery, 5 October 1765.
[285] O'Connell (1965); James (1973); Lammey (1988).

position of the colonies, and Ireland). The First Philadelphia Congress had sent messages to Ireland as well as other colonies seeking support,[286] which found strong sympathy in the Irish Commons, especially for resistance to trade restrictions and expansion of taxes, from all except those 'attached securely to the Castle or papists'.[287] However, the control of the Lieutenant (now Earl Harcourt) over the Irish Commons and Lords was never in doubt, ensuring strong defeat of patriot opposition to his October 1775 speech, and success for plans to send Irish troops to America.

However, as with Wilkes, there were movements to influence elections, notably an initiative by the Freeholders Society in favour of independents against placemen. Further political societies grew up to promote electoral reform, with the influential Society of Free Citizens of Dublin having strong patriot members but also strong cross-membership with the merchant committees of the city, who hoped to use the pressure for commercial benefit, as well as to moderate the activity (as in America).[288]

The British success in the Seven Years War removed immediate fears of a Catholic uprising in Ireland, and this gave scope for the loyal Irish to lobby for improved trading and political conditions. There was long-standing resentment by the loyalist Anglo-Irish merchants of restrictions on Irish trade as a result of the Navigation Acts, by which shipped goods had to pass through England to be exported elsewhere. The merchants also experienced many adverse tariffs and were ineligible for bounties. It was natural that there should emerge an economic, as well as a political alignment of many Irish with the Americans. It was strongest among the Protestants.[289] Shelburne observed in 1779: 'In every protestant or dissenter's house the established toast is success to the Americans.'[290] The Catholics opposed the American constitution, which excluded them, but the rebellion resonated with patriot causes and was widely reported in the Irish press, especially in the *Freeman's Journal.* There was also wide reprinting of pamphlets from both America and Britain, with a letter from Franklin of 4 November 1778 in the *Hibernian Journal,* 'the cause of America is that of Ireland', particularly influential.[291]

Merchant opinion

In October 1775 the Dublin merchants had organized a petition for concessions to promote peace, like those in Britain, and similar petitions were sent from Belfast and Cork.[292] The electors in Dublin, Cork, and Belfast instructed their MPs to

[286] York (1998), pp. 211–15; Townshend was the first *resident* Lieutenant for some decades.
[287] Contemporary comment, in McDowell (1944), p. 41; also James (1973); Lammey (1988); Powell (2003).
[288] McDowell (1944); Lammey (1988); Powell (2003), p. 143.
[289] Cullen (1968); James (1973); Truxes (1988).
[290] Letter from Shelburne to Price, 5 September 1779; quoted in Harlow (1952), vol. i, p. 522.
[291] McDowell (1944), pp. 41–3.
[292] *Parliamentary History* (1775).

promote peace and vote against any grant to fund war effort.[293] These petitions were forthright in stating that the American War was based on arbitrary claims by Britain and was ruining trade. The Irish were also worried that a British victory in America would lead to extension of similar taxes to Ireland. A last straw was the American embargo on imports and exports, which included Ireland, and the British embargo on Irish exports in 1776 in retaliation.

Resistance began to develop which led to threats from the Irish volunteer army. This had developed spontaneously in 1778 to resist the French threat during the American War when most of the normal garrison was in America, and to control internal unrest. By April 1779 the volunteers had reached 15,000 recruits, 40,000 by December, over 50,000 by 1780; far exceeding the English garrison of 8,000 at the time.[294] The Lieutenant had to allow them access to armouries, but when the French invasion fear faded, the arms were not returned. No one believed the rush to enlist reflected a desire to defend English supremacy.[295] Primarily composed of Protestant property holders, loyal, armed, and ready to redress grievances of the 'rule of one country by another', this was a major force in frightening the British government to make concessions.[296] As commented by John Scott, the Irish Attorney General in December 1779, 'we have government without strength, administration without numbers, and an armed populace without control'.[297] The volunteers carried repeated motions for an independent parliament, free trade with Britain, and repeal of the Irish Declaratory Act. They also imposed a 'buy Ireland' policy, which from April 1779 developed an Irish non-importation movement based mainly on the local merchant committees. These proved surprisingly effective.[298]

In 1778 Lord North had sought several reforms for more open trade, but was only able to achieve a limited Irish Trade Act by 1780 (although this had the significant effect of removing the Test Act for dissenting Protestants). According to some commentators, lobbying from British merchant interests was important in restricting concessions.[299] Certainly there was strong resistance from the City of London in 1778–9, and from manufacturers and corporations in Glasgow, Liverpool, and Manchester especially the sugar refiners in 1780. But this was led by the corporations rather than the wider business community; the Liverpool corporation's committee of trade circulated the other towns in Britain and seems to have acted as organizer of resistance to Lord North's proposals for Irish trade. The Liverpool chamber supported equalization of trade but opposed North's 1778 Act.[300] Resistance was also strong from senior government members and landed MPs.

---

[293] Powell (2003), p. 142.
[294] Quoted in Harlow (1952); Powell (2003); Whiteley (1996); York (1998).
[295] Valentine (1967), vol. ii, p. 113; Whiteley (1996), p. 177.
[296] McDowell (1944).
[297] Letter of Scott to Townshend, 3 December 1779; quoted in Powell (2003), p. 182.
[298] Harlow (1952), vol. i; Whiteley (1996); Powell (2003).
[299] This interpretation derives from Lecky (1903), *A History of Ireland in the Eighteenth Century*, vol. ii, pp. 178–9; see also Harlow (1952), vol. i, pp. 518–20; Powell (2003), p. 164.
[300] Bennett (2010), pp. 40–1, 57, 85–7; *Manchester Journal*, 11 July 1778.

To increase pressure on the government, there had been significant Dublin riots in 1779; an effigy of Lord Townshend was burnt, and John Scott (the Attorney General) was lucky to escape from an attack.[301] Like the riots in Boston and American cities during the Stamp Act crisis in 1765–6, there was suspicion of involvement from some of the larger business leaders.[302] But the concessions North's government was able to make, through an Act of 1780, were limited. When judged against the independence achieved by the Americans, Ireland had been severely short-changed.

After the British defeat at Yorktown in 1781 the volunteers held a Convention in February 1782 in Dungannon church, to force stronger reforms on England. This was a turning point for the merchants and propertied interests. For the patriots a speech in the Irish Commons by Henry Grattan on 16 April 1782 marked their new unity and ascendancy. Grattan argued that Yorktown meant that Ireland should also be given greater autonomy and 'redemption' as a 'nation', though continue to recognize one king for the two countries. Grattan's motion for an independent parliament was carried nem. con., engaging support well beyond the patriots.[303] The volunteer army and Convention forced the new and weak Rockingham government of 1782 to grant an independent Irish parliament and repeal the Irish Declaratory Act of 1720. This marked the transition from informal to formal empire as far as Britain and Ireland were concerned, 'an autonomous state inside an Empire'; it was one of the first key actions to safeguard the 'colonies' after the American war.[304]

The stimulus of an independent Irish parliament

The new independent parliament in Ireland was promising, and the appointment of Carlisle as Lord Lieutenant, and particularly his chief secretary William Eden, led it to be more open. However, these changes still left important areas of Irish trade unreformed, and there was the critical question of how the financial relationships between the two countries would be settled; these issues provided the background for the establishment of the Dublin and Belfast chambers of commerce in 1783.

These chambers were formed specifically in response to the development of the new Irish parliament, and were complemented by strengthened activities from the pre-existing merchant committees in Cork, Waterford, and Limerick. Subsequently, independent chambers were formed in Waterford (1787), Londonderry (1790), Limerick (1807), and Cork (1814–9). Their focus was strongly towards international trade interests and taxation, but also on improving local navigation, lighthouses, and overcoming local abuses in their corporations; the Londonderry and Cork chambers were formed specifically to resist their corporations. Indeed municipal activity was a major source of grievance in all the Irish chambers, as in England;

---

[301] See e.g. James (1973); O'Connell (1965).
[302] Powell (2003), p. 181.
[303] Summarized in York (1998), pp. 225–8.
[304] Harlow (1952); Whiteley (1996); Ridden (2003).

with continuous protests about harbour fees, wharfs, roads, bridges, markets, and the electoral franchise.

The effect of the 1780 repeal of the Test Act and the growth of the volunteers opened the way for the upper-middling traders and dissenters to play a fuller role in political and business life, and the chambers provided one route for them. In all areas the chambers or merchant committees contained a wide range of Catholics, Quakers, and other dissenters, as well as a dominance from the established Church because they were the most numerous of the major traders.[305] The chambers offered a new mechanism for voice to lobby the new Irish parliament, as well as interests in England.[306] The Dublin chamber was a vigorous opponent of Pitt's Irish propositions in 1785, which were seen as not going far enough towards full integration of trade, and it was a strong lobbyist for greater freedoms for merchants more generally. The Protestant freeholders also remained a powerful force. Their pressure led to transferring some of the rights over local markets and harbours from the local corporations to the chambers in Dublin, Limerick, and Waterford. Freeholder pressure also lay behind attacks in the 1790s by the Londonderry chamber on the legitimacy of its local freemen.[307]

The chambers were generally a moderating influence on the volunteer movement, from which the radicals split to form the Dublin Independent Volunteers in 1780; whilst in Belfast the merchants and manufacturers effectively sidelined the volunteer radicals who were dominated by Presbyterians. The Irish chambers were a spin-off from the radical effort to confront aristocratic electoral control and corrupt corporations, but as elsewhere they were generally reformist not revolutionary, and were multi-denominational. Even in the Irish rebellion of 1798, there was a mix of religious support and leadership in both North and South; it was not initially sectarian, though it later became so.[308] Hence, whilst not representing the full breadth of the community, the chambers were certainly aimed at counteracting the landed aristocracy, and seen as a challenge by them.[309]

4.11 THE EARLY CHAMBERS IN BRITAIN

In Britain prior to the establishment of chambers there was a range of precursors that undertook lobbying roles, like the Bristol Merchant Venturers, which played a major role on the Stamp Act and throughout the period.[310] The effect of these bodies, as support or resistance to chambers, is assessed in Chapter 5. In addition, the Excise tax crisis of 1732 had stimulated activities from London, Bristol,

---

[305] Cullen (1983); see also Ridden (2003), and Chapter 15.
[306] See Cullen (1968, 1983); Oakley (1983), Glasgow chamber history.
[307] See Chapters 5 and 9.
[308] McDowell (1944); Cullen (1983); Whiteley (1996); Powell (2003), pp. 191–3.
[309] Cullen (1983); see also Chapter 5.
[310] Minchinton (1965, 1971); Langford (1973); Morgan and Morgan (1962); Morgan (1993, 1997, 2007).

Liverpool, and Whitehaven, which drew on local committees.[311] The first Bute Acts of 1762 stimulated London, Glasgow, and Liverpool committee responses, and the Stamp Act crisis stimulated a wider round of committee formations, with at least 23 active local groups or delegates, as noted earlier. The African Company now had Bristol and Liverpool 'branches', and the West Indies Committee had Bristol, Dublin, Glasgow, and Liverpool branches. There were Glasgow and Edinburgh Merchants Houses, and merchant committees active in Greenock, Exeter, Great Yarmouth, Chester, Haverfordwest, Whitehaven, and Leicester.[312] More ambiguously there were also the Wilkes and Counties Association movements. There was thus widespread experience of voice in the 1760s and 1770s. Behind these lobbies was the growing demand for equality of trading opportunity for the outports; later to be framed as reciprocity of trade. The colonial system and its aristocratic control were being increasingly challenged.

The first phase of British chambers 1767–1780

The first mainland chambers were Liverpool, Manchester, and North Staffordshire. In Liverpool and Manchester the Stamp Act crisis and related developments stimulated new organizations that could be used when new needs or crises emerged. Both these chambers were interlinked with American concerns and objections to local municipal actions; in Liverpool this focused on disputes with the corporation over town dues on docks and shipping;[313] in Manchester it was linked to the need for municipal action on roads, lack of direct borough electoral status, concern with foreign spies stealing secrets, and patent protection. Critical to both were the Stamp Act and Wilkes leaders, which led to a coalition of reformers who were subsequently the leaders of the first chambers, as shown in Tables 4.1 and 4.2. Immediately after the Liverpool and Manchester chambers were founded in 1774 their respective chairs, John Dobson and Thomas Butterworth Bayley, were the joint organizers of the Lancashire petition for concessions with America, and the chambers sent concession petitions of their own.[314] For both cities this was against their corporation's petition for coercion; in Liverpool this must have seemed like a repeat of the 1766 Stamp Act frictions (when the corporation suppressed Trecothick's letter), and the divisions over Wilkes in 1769.

   The interlock of the local leadership with the opposition political response is most clearly evident for the case of Liverpool. Here the MP William Meredith, who had been elected in 1761 against strong opposition from the Corporation and government, was acting as close intermediary with Rockingham. Meredith's letters of 1763 show how he was formulating memorials, as well as receiving them. On the 1763 Irish proposals, he wrote that he would 'send the memorial about the Irish

---

[311] Langford (1975); Price (1980, 1983).

[312] i.e. before the General Chamber; see Chapter 5. Sources: chamber records give cross-references, particularly Glasgow, Manchester, Birmingham, Dublin, Waterford, and the Bristol Venturers; also Gross (1890); Helm (1897); Redford (1934); Wright (1913).

[313] Full account of Liverpool chamber's formation in Bennett (2010).

[314] Bennett (2010), p. 125; see also Bradley (1990), p. 343.

provisions after knowing the sense of the merchants [in Liverpool] more fully upon it'. He became deeply involved in shaping opinion and facilitating voice; for example in 1763 he wrote that 'I hear that [Bamber] Gascoyne is making interest in Liverpool, who is sure to be joined by a great part of the corporation, a majority of which consists of one family (the Gildarts) their relatives and friends. . . . But without a mayor the rest of the corporation is insignificant; and a Mr. Campbell, a friend of ours, is in nomination.' But the 'idea to adopt Gascoyne has put two or three of the corporation into our party'. When he arrived in Liverpool Meredith found that 'everything turned out . . . beyond our hopes. . . . My friend [Campbell] was elected mayor, and the division among the gentlemen who oppose me [was] so much greater than I expected, especially in the corporation, that no acts of power can be effected now, and the interest of my friends has now some reality.'[315] Later Gascoyne was to note Meredith's support for Wilkes and opposition to the Grenville taxes: 'ribbons with Liberty, property and no Excise are the ornament of my opponent's houses and carriages'.[316] Pennant's election in Liverpool in 1767 required similar support from Rockingham interests.[317]

Meredith went on to be an intermediary for Rockingham and Newcastle on the Stamp Act, as noted above; but already by 1763 the efforts of the Rockinghamites to create support in Liverpool is clear. Meredith wrote to Lord Newcastle in 1768 after being with Rockingham and his friends, noting their 'principle friends to be depended upon'.[318] From this grouping flowed the Liverpool Stamp Act Committee, and as Table 4.2 shows, the leaders who developed the chamber.

Similarly Meredith promoted the merchants' interests to seek reforms of the African Company and East India Company, against Gascoyne's opposition.[319] In 1767–8 these efforts were rebuffed. The East India Company had become a focus for political intervention for the first time. This stimulated pressure for reform from the outports, with a committee of merchants in Liverpool elected that proposed expanding the Company to have branches in the major outports. In some discussions these were even referred to as local 'chambers'.[320] The outports would raise new capital of £8 million, and lend this to the government at 2% in exchange for the exclusive privileges of trading with India and China (raising from London £3.2 million; Bristol and Liverpool £1.6 million each; Glasgow and Hull £0.8 million each). A Liverpool meeting of 28 January 1768 elected one of the Heywoods (probably Benjamin) and Thomas Smythe (both later leading chamber members) as their delegates, who were sent to negotiate in London.[321] There was early optimism when a letter was received from Heywood and Smythe 'expressive of

[315] Meredith to Charles Jenkinson, 14 September, 12 and 25 October 1763; BL Add MS 38201, fos. 110, 186–7, 205.
[316] Bamber Gascoyne to Lord Newcastle, 21 April 1763; BL Add MS 38320, fo. 312.
[317] Watson (1968), p. 540.
[318] Meredith to Lord Newcastle, 15 October 1768; BL Add MS 32911, fo. 252.
[319] See Klinge (1979); it is claimed Gascoyne and several of the Board of Trade members benefited personally from the Africa and East India Companies contracts.
[320] *Williamsons Advertiser*, 5 February 1768; Baines (1852), p. 441; a reflection of the Dutch EIC.
[321] *Liverpool Chronicle*, 4 February 1768.

great confidence in the utility of that design, and enlarging on the cordial and genteel reception they meet with from all they have occasion to treat with'. However, when they returned to Liverpool in late March they did 'not report so favourably on the matter as the town generally expected'.[322] They had not been able to overcome the intense national political machinations and resistance by Gascoyne and ministers. Reform was only modest, with Rockingham slow to give support and the provinces finding it difficult to find allies.[323]

North Staffordshire was the only other mainland chamber in the first phase of foundations. It is first noted in 1767 as a committee seeking higher duty on china imports, when Meredith was approached for help. This may have been a one-off action, since its next known activity was a general assembly in April 1773 to manage prices.[324] These specific actions would not be noteworthy, but it evolved to become a more general 'potters chamber' by 1774, and was also a major element of the General Chamber in the 1780s. The potters thus provided another learning milieu for chamber lobby activity. In 1775 the chamber was involved in its own petition for concessions in America. Wedgwood confirmed that because of this he did not sign a more general petition 'handed about here for several reasons. The chief was that we had very lately petitioned as a body of Staffordshire potters and I think we have in that and other respects distinguished ourselves as a particular body of men (though not corporate).'[325] This confirms the distinction of a temperate and measured petition by respectable business leaders through a formal body, from that of the masses. It also shows the preference for low-key actions, avoiding public attention and 'noise'. Over 1774–6 the chamber made a series of other lobbies on canals, access to foreign markets, protection from East India imports, china clay, and opposition to Richard Champion's porcelain patent;[326] it appointed a clerk in 1776.[327] These campaigns were led by Wedgwood, supported by John Turner in the potteries, drawing on Thomas Bentley's expertise. In 1784 it became a more formal chamber with minute book and constitution; Wedgwood became formally the chair, and it had significant inputs into the General Chamber.[328]

Divisions over America

The American rebellion led to two phases of petitioning in Britain. Both are distinguished from the Stamp Act period since now the opposition lobbyists were 'outsiders' with few direct friends in government. Though Meredith had joined

---

[322] *Liverpool Chronicle*, 3 and 17 March 1768.
[323] Sutherland (1952); Philips (1961); Watson (1968), pp. 466–80.
[324] Josiah Wedgwood to Thomas Bentley 14 February 1767; 14 April 1773: Wedgwood MS No. E. 18135-25; 18451-125; quoted in Thomas (1934), pp. 392–3.
[325] Wedgwood to Bentley, 14 November 1775; Wedgwood MS No. E. 18624-25; quoted in Thomas (1934), p. 393.
[326] All these lobbies were similar to Liverpool at the same time, indicating some collaboration; see Chapter 9.
[327] Wedgwood letters to Bentley, 5 March 1774, 23 June 1775, 7 February 1776; other issues quoted in Thomas, (1934), pp. 393–5, 163–70.
[328] Thomas (1934, 1935); see also Chapter 9.

Lord North in 1774–7, he and others were unable to shift a resolute government with little room for manoeuvre and continuing strong support in parliament; Rockingham was frozen out. The first phase of petitions in January–March 1775 sought concessions from parliament. This was initiated by London merchants, chaired by David Barclay (with William Baker another leading figure), who held a large meeting on 4 January at which Liverpool, Manchester, and Leeds (Samuel Elam) interests were involved, at least through correspondence. On 23 January the London petition was submitted to parliament at the same time as two from Bristol (from the Venturers and from other merchants and manufacturers). By the end of January there were petitions from Birmingham, Dudley, Glasgow, Liverpool, Manchester, Newcastle, Norwich, Wolverhampton, and the seven pottery towns. In February there were petitions from Leeds, Nottingham, Whitehaven, Bridport, four Yorkshire woollen towns (through Huddersfield), and the West Indies merchants; by March these were joined by Belfast and Waterford.[329] This is comparable to the 26 during the Stamp Act, and from many of the same places with most of the same leaders involved, as shown in Table 4.1.[330] The American agents were also again involved, but in a more low-key way. In London and Newcastle there was very explicit reference back to the Stamp Act, Townshend duties, and links to the Quebec Act (with Wilkesites strongly involved in both; Wilkes was mayor of London, October 1774–5). The London petition was passed by parliament to a Commons committee, a tactic proposed by Meredith; this may have sought to build support (as with the Committee of the Whole House in 1766), but Burke immediately denounced it as 'a committee of oblivion'. Indeed the committee sat for only a day and the government ignored it.[331]

The government this time organized counter-petitions for coercion in America, although some were also spontaneous. These came from local corporations (in Leeds, Liverpool, Nottingham, and other towns), the Church, Trinity House, and various interests that were mainly linked to government patronage.[332] On 7 February parliament declared the colonists in rebellion, chiefly as a response to the Massachusetts unrest and the tea party.

This raised the stakes, as any resistance to the government was now potentially treasonable. It was very divisive between the local interests, with most major merchants now being very cautious (for example Barclay and Baker, and the West Indies merchants in London now became reluctant leaders), though petitioning continued: for concessions, for repeal of the Quebec Act (led by Savile and Burke), and against the New England Fisheries Bill.[333] Initially charges of treason could be circumvented by petitioning the king rather than parliament. But after news of Lexington reached England on 28 May, a royal proclamation of rebellion was made on 23 August 1775.

---

[329] Thomas (1991), pp. 182–4; also Bradley (1986); Bargar (1956); Olson (1973, 1979).
[330] As well as Jamaica, Quebec, and the Quakers; *Parliamentary Register* (1775–80); Bargar (1986).
[331] Thomas (1991), pp. 188–90.
[332] Bradley (1986, 1990); Thomas (1991), pp. 185–7.
[333] Thomas (1991), pp. 191–235.

The declaration and proclamation made petitioning even more difficult, but a second wave of petitions seeking peace followed from September 1775 into early 1776. The 'Olive Branch petition' from Congress in July 1775 was debated in parliament in November, but rejected. The deadline for American compliance with their non-importation embargos expired on 10 September. News of its effects, the evacuation of loyalists, and the rebel invasion of Canada, reached England in November. The government had to raise money for war through a parliamentary vote and this offered an opportunity for more petitions. There were about 26 petitions for peace, with the county petitions often representing more towns; e.g. in Lancashire 29 towns contributed 4000 petitioners.[334] Rockingham and Richmond were again involved, leading a Lords' protest in November 1775. Again the government stimulated loyal addresses, though many were also spontaneous. More loyal addresses than petitions were sent (about 126), though many were from corporate bodies and hence unsigned and perhaps represented little; the peace petitions had many more signatures.[335] The loyal addresses were all printed in the official *London Gazette*, whilst none of the petitions for concessions was officially noted.

The peace petitions were often more radical than the earlier actions, with radicals and the Wilkesite Bill of Rights Society and London Association heavily involved in several. For the moderates the petitions now had to be couched in much more careful terms. Nevertheless the resistance was very large and on the same scale as the Wilkes Middlesex election campaign.[336] But this made the leading traders even more cautious: they were caught in the middle between radicals seeking revolution (or at least major changes to the constitutional structure of Britain and the colonies), and the aristocratic interest that actually ruled the country and would only be influenced by moderate and respectable opinion.

The chambers sought to be a moderating force. Liverpool *chamber's* resolution in late 1775 urged the government to improve trade with America.[337] In the wider Liverpool petitions the individual chamber *members* were divided almost equally between coercion (30%) and concessions (34%), with 26% neutral,[338] although the original Stamp Act committee members were heavily pro-concessions, as shown in Table 4.2 (and this was true of Stamp Act activists more generally, as shown in Table 4.1). Similarly in the Manchester chamber there were 25% for coercion and 24% for peace, with 51% neutral.[339] But the chamber *leaders* in Liverpool and Manchester were involved in the more aggressive Lancashire peace petition. Thomas Butterworth Bayley, the Manchester chamber's president, and his supporters John Dobson (Liverpool's president) and Col. Richard Townley

---

[334] *Humble Address and Petition . . . of the County Palatine of Lancaster, of 18 December 1775 . . . for Reestablishment of Peace and Harmony betwixt Great Britain and the Colonies in America* (Manchester: Wheeler).

[335] Bradley (1990), pp. 319–23; Thomas (1991).

[336] Bradley (1986, 1990).

[337] Liverpool chamber *Abstract*; Bennett (2010), pp. 30, 125.

[338] Bennett (2010), appendix tables A6 and A7.

[339] Comparison of chamber members of 1774 and 1781 signing concessions and loyal petitions.

(not a known chamber member), were denounced in the local press: Bayley was 'one of the declared champions of the opposition...[with] opinions totally inadmissible in an argument of this nature', and when he withdrew with 'other patriots' there were hisses and groans; theirs was 'the most insolent and impudent usurpation'.[340]

In Bristol the peace petition was drafted by Burke as part of his conciliatory plan; it sought to disassociate its signatories from coercion and was moderating. Those seeking a stronger drafting, such as Richard Champion, formed a 'secret committee', whilst Burke and the other MP Henry Cruger, continued to offer help to mediate. Burke also sought to use Bristol as a conduit to other towns, as he had done with Rockingham in 1766.[341] Cruger said he would 'not defend the violence of the colonists in word or deed'.[342] Others were more radical claiming fundamental rights (for example in Staffordshire, Leeds, Coventry, Worcester, Middlesex, and Southwark).[343] It was from this that Wedgwood sought to distance himself and the chamber in Staffordshire, as noted above.

The government held firm throughout this frenzy. There were several reasons why it could do so.[344] First the opposition was weaker and more disorganized: Trecothick was ill, Meredith and Pownall had changed sides (if only temporarily), Rockingham's MPs had been reduced from 55 to 43 in the 1774 election, his main Commons spokesman (Dowdeswell) was ill, and most of the American agents were in disarray. Second, there was resentment of a perceived lack of gratitude from the Americans for the effort and cost expended by the British lobbyists during the 1766 crisis or during the 1768–70 embargo.

Third, the increasing effectiveness of the radicals in both America and Britain was deeply worrying to the elite merchants. Boston seemed to be asking for complete freedom to trade, whilst American manufactures were clearly rapidly increasing and threatened the demand for home goods. A complete realignment of British trading conditions was unlikely to find favour with those whose wealth depended on it. The King and Lord North recognized this, handling 'the petitions astutely;...the government displayed a public face of tolerance, it appeared very menacing to radical leaders'.[345] The use of proclamations mirrored the use by American radicals of 'covenants', forcing opponents to support extra-legal positions.

Fourth, the stakes were raised by the increasing American violence. There were similarities to the Boston riots in Liverpool when mobs from a seamen's strike caused by reduced wages rioted over several days in August 1775, damaging ships and wrecking leading merchants' houses (including at least one chamber member William James); ships' cannons were drawn up and discharged in front of the Exchange, several people were killed. The disorder only subsided after the army

---

[340] *Manchester Mercury*, 7 July 1775, letter from 'a gentleman'.
[341] Quoted in Thomas (1991), p. 173.
[342] Stevens (1867); Harrington (1935).
[343] Bradley (1990), p. 322.
[344] The following summary follows Langford (1986b), pp. 310–18; Price (1986); Thomas (1991).
[345] Bradley (1990), p. 426.

arrived from Manchester. This suggested internal radical dangers similar to those in Massachusetts.[346] Indeed Liverpool had to be supported by the army and militia again in 1777, when a curfew was called; it had a permanent garrison of Yorkshire militia after 1779 chiefly to ward off American threats but also to exert local control.[347] Even Meredith's support was turned towards coercion by the tea party's destruction of property: 'now that the Americans had not only resisted the act of parliament but laid violent hands on the merchants' property, it was high time to regulate the course of justice, so that our merchants might trade hither with security', though it is also argued that he was influenced by pressure when he joined Lord North's government over 1774–7. Langford interprets this as the Liverpool merchants turning 'savagely anti-American', but this is an overstatement.[348] Meredith and many in Liverpool and Manchester, through their chambers and petitioning, were still seeking conciliation.

The final phase of events leading up to Lexington and open war with America was thus seen as a threat to a system of government that the merchants might have fervently wished to reform, but which they were forced to defend in order to protect their own economic interests. Up to the end they hoped to avoid actual conflict. But, with war, 'reform' went off the agenda, and no new chambers were founded between 1774 and 1783.

The second phase of British chambers 1783–1800

With humiliating defeats in America, cessation of hostilities in 1781, and the peace treaty of 1783, the same questions re-emerged for chambers and businesses as in 1775. The government was in a much weaker position to resist in 1781 and 1783, as in the Irish developments, noted above. In these circumstances, Postlethwayt's and Mortimer's vision for a chamber system must have seemed even more resonant and feasible. The reissued 1780 edition of Mortimer's 1772 book demonstrates renewed interest, and Burke's speech of 1780 revived Davenant's ideas. In 1779–86 there was a further set of so-called 'bill of rights' petitions to reform the electoral franchise of the counties, led by Wyvell, the City of London, and a Counties Association movement.[349] The 'crippling' taxes necessary to finance the debts following the American War, and the restrictions on trade resulting from the East India Company monopoly continued as sources of grievance. The Board of Trade was abolished in 1782 following Burke's intervention, widening the distance between the government and the merchant community. There was vigorous voicing of concern to resolve credit and debt issues between the two countries dating from 1776, for which London merchants, and the Glasgow and Liverpool chambers lobbied vigorously.[350]

---

[346] Brooke (1853), pp. 326–47; Rose (1958); Lemisch (1968).
[347] Brooke (1853); see also Bradley (1990), p. 281; Thomas (1991).
[348] Meredith speech in Parliament 1773; quoted in Langford (1986b), p. 316; see R. G. Thorne, *History of Parliament* (1986).
[349] Rudé (1962); Sutherland (1933); Black (1963).
[350] Sheridan (1960); Price (1991); see Chapter 9 for full discussion.

These pressures led to the revival of Garbett's ideas in Birmingham in 1782–3, with the establishment of a Birmingham chamber (Committee) in 1783. This immediately formed alliances with individuals and 'chamber' committees or 'societies' in Glasgow, Sheffield, Manchester, Norwich, Liverpool, and other areas, and with the North Staffordshire potters. Garbett's correspondence with other localities is voluminous in the period 1782–4. He was a de facto clearinghouse for information from all the main manufacturing areas, passing it on with commentary to Lord Shelburne (then briefly in government, and to whom Garbett was a financial adviser) and later Lord Lansdowne, with his activities certainly stimulating local groupings to form in some places.[351] This directly facilitated the establishment of the General Chamber of Manufacturers in 1785, and led to Wedgwood and Boulton becoming engaged. The General Chamber's discussions had indirect effects on Leeds and Nottingham. The necessity for a forum for deliberation under more ready management than open meetings was a force stimulating the establishment of Leeds chamber on 22 March 1785, although its first debates and lobbies were on the postal service, before turning to the Irish and later the French Treaty.[352] The precise date of establishing the 'Nottingham chamber of manufacturers' is not known, but by September 1785 it gave 'an elegant dinner to Daniel Parker Coke MP for his patriotic and manly exertions against the Irish propositions'.[353] Hence, its activities were closely interlocked with the General Chamber and its title suggests that it was more of a town committee using the new brand 'chamber'. Its only other known activity was 'as guardians and protectors of the interest, welfare, and prosperity of the trade and manufactures of this town' to offer a reward of 20 guineas for arrest of the rioting framework knitters who broke up hosiery frames in October 1787.[354]

Independently of Garbett, but stimulated by similar concerns, was the establishment of the chambers at Glasgow, Dublin, and Belfast, in 1783, and Edinburgh in 1785. Together with Birmingham, Leeds, Jersey, Guernsey, Manchester, Liverpool, and the North Staffordshire potters, there were now 11 chambers in Britain and Ireland; Waterford was founded in 1787, and Londonderry in 1790. They were complemented by strengthened activities from some pre-existing commercial committees and societies of merchants acting like chambers, in Leith, Dundee, Greenock (as well as those in Ireland at Cork and Limerick), and the Venturers in Bristol. There were important connections between the leaders in these centres, especially between Birmingham, Staffordshire, and Scotland. One link was the Carron Company based in Scotland. This had Sheffield's Roebuck and Birmingham's Samuel Garbett as initial partners (with William Cadell) in 1759. By the early 1780s Gilbert Hamilton (long-term secretary of the Glasgow chamber) was a major agent for the company (and also brother-in-law to James Watt, Boulton's

---

[351] Garbett-Lansdowne correspondence (Birmingham Archives, ZZ61B; and Clements Library, Michigan); see also material used in Wright (1913); Money (1977); Bowden (1965); Dietz (1991).

[352] Reported in *Leeds Mercury*, 22 and 29 March 1785; Leeds chamber minutes from 27April 1785.

[353] *Nottingham Journal*, 17 September 1785; *The Datebook of Remarkable and Memorable Events Connected with Nottingham*, 13 September 1785.

[354] *Nottingham Journal*, 3 November 1787; *The Datebook . . . Nottingham*, 26 October 1787.

partner);[355] Patrick Colquhoun (Glasgow chamber's first president) was another agent. Banking was a major part of the networks: John Glassford and James Dunlop were the Carron's bankers (Thistle and Greenock banks); other bankers were Edinburgh's Patrick Miller (deputy Governor, Bank of Scotland) and Walter Hog (British Linen Bank). Recapitalization of the Carron in 1769 brought in further links with the banks: Mansfield Hunter, Thistle, British Linen, and Ayr Bank.[356] All these named individuals and bankers were members of Glasgow or Edinburgh chambers when established in 1783 and 1785, respectively. Glassford was a Stamp Act leader, and Hamilton had become an active lobbyist on American concessions by at least April 1774, organizing a letter from 75 Glasgow merchants and merchants in Liverpool. There was thus intensive exchange about chamber concepts and lobby objectives between the first phase and second phase of chamber founders.

It is also important to note that in this phase several chambers used a 'correspondence committee', a strong echo of America. For example, such subcommittees were set up by Birmingham in 1784, which was in correspondence with similar committees in Manchester, Sheffield, Norwich, and Manchester, and through Gilbert Hamilton (secretary of the Glasgow chamber).[357] The North Staffordshire chamber used a correspondence committee of 21 people in 1785 to take actions with the General Chamber over Pitt's Irish proposals.[358] Birmingham was in contact with Samuel Green and the Liverpool chamber, which also formed a correspondence committee in 1786.[359] These committees were a small subgroup of the chamber, empowered to negotiate on behalf of their locality. This allowed individuals to meet at a national level and align their efforts with others, again an echo of the American continental Congresses and the Stamp Act actions. The General Chamber of 1785 was one immediate outcome of this, where 'delegates' from each area met to form a 'national' opinion, discussed in Chapter 9. This was short-lived, but was succeeded by a 'Union' of chambers in 1793.

The British chambers, like those in America, were bodies of the major businesses, 'reform' bodies, not populist or radical movements. They were certainly stimulated by the 'great events', but in a reverse of Tarrow's observation, noted in Chapter 3, that elites are challenged by new political movements, the chambers seem to have adapted the spirit of protests into an elite body with a more general and enduring structure than protest alone. Chamber members were strongly

---

[355] Gilbert Hamilton was the first secretary of the chamber (part time) over 1783–1808; he was also an agent for the Carron Iron Company (the Coalbrookdale concern of Darby), a merchant in liquor and vitriol, and a bill-collecting agent for the Bank of Scotland: *Glasgow Chamber of Commerce Journal*, May 1970, pp. 246–8.

[356] Campbell (1961), pp. 7–21; Bennett (2011b).

[357] Garbett letter to Lansdowne, 14 October 1784, enclosing letters from each of these places re Austrian trade restrictions; see also *Account of the Manner in which a Standing General Committee was Established*, 8 October 1784 (Birmingham Archives ZZ61B and C/19/27082).

[358] 14 February 1785; see Thomas (1934; 1935), pp. 20–1.

[359] Formed of George Case, John Gregson, Joseph Brooks jun., Thomas Earle, John Tarleton, and Thomas Staniforth, with Green as secretary: Garbett letter to Lansdowne, 31 August 1786; Garbett-Lansdowne letters, ZZ 618, Birmingham Archives.

interconnected with Wilkes attacks on parliamentary representation in 1768–71, and the Association movement of 1779–86. But the chambers were not founded with Wilkes's ideas in mind. The General Chamber and local chambers also ignored Wyvell's Association because they were more concerned with broader commercial questions than electoral reform.[360] Wilkes and Wyvell led popular mass campaigns. The terms of chamber actions, in Colquhoun's words, were 'temperate' or 'fair opposition', as discussed in Chapter 9. As today, chambers focused on approaches couched in terms that could persuade government to change policy. In the case of resolving outstanding debts with America, they *had* to work through government, achieving success in 1794–5 through the Jay Treaty, with which Glasgow chamber was particularly actively engaged. The chambers can thus be seen as one part of a 'reform' agenda. Not a revolutionary movement, but a movement that could support elite business interests when challenged by proximate threat. However, this period came to an end, like that in 1775, with war in 1793 against France, and even more stringent anti-sedition laws imposed by Pitt. This put further chamber development off the agenda in most areas until after the next cessation of hostilities in 1815.

The new chamber concept: Glasgow 1782–1784

The foundation of the chamber in Glasgow gives important insights into how the chamber concept had been *localized*, transformed from the earlier ideas of Post-lethwayt and Mortimer of a national chamber. The correspondence of its first president, Patrick Colquhoun, provides valuable insights into the new concepts, which must have echoed the early experiences of other areas where records have not survived. Colquhoun already had a substantial reputation as a lawyer and was Lord Provost of Glasgow in 1782. He had been a representative from Glasgow to Lord North in 1779.[361] He was not going to embark on establishing a chamber without substantial political support. He approached Henry Dundas, the weightiest Scottish politician of the time. Dundas initially assured Colquhoun only briefly of his support.[362] But in a later letter he notes: 'from the persons concerned I make no doubt of its [the chamber] being concluded upon the most beneficial principles. . . . It sometimes happens that in heats and jealousies get into institutions . . . ; these I hope will be your forceful case to prevent and if you do I flatter myself you will have much credit by the institution.'[363]

Colquhoun also prepared the ground well by obtaining support from the leading businesses of Glasgow at the time, and covering all the other areas of potential local objection, the chief justice in Edinburgh praising his attention to this detail.

---

[360] Black (1963), p. 118.
[361] Autobiographical note, *c*.1802; LMA AC 1230/7.
[362] Henry Dundas to Colquhoun, 11 November 1782; Colquhoun Glasgow chamber papers, TD 1670/4/12.
[363] Henry Dundas to Colquhoun, 8 January 1783; TD 1670/4/14.

At present, when the general system of commerce has undergone such a revolution, and our trade often suffering so much by the restraints of a complicated war, must now break out into new channels, under regulations, foreign and domestic, formerly unknown, . . . it must be of great importance, to have . . . the ablest advice: and the many respectable names which I read in the list of members and directors of the chamber of commerce offered me, from the personal knowledge I have of them, the most flattering hopes.[364]

In this and his use of Dundas, Colquhoun was drawing on his legal networks; and James Dennistoun, the leading member of the Merchants' House, became a strong supporter, although noting the troublesome practical difficulties of balancing interests: 'It will require some address to convince the small towns that the weight of Glasgow, where the meetings are to be held, does not too preponderate.'[365]

Again Colquhoun's legal background helped found the chamber with a role in commercial arbitration from the outset. A leading Glasgow merchant, William Wilson, took pleasure in the chamber proposals 'with a view to stop, or at least lessen that confusion, uncertainty and expenditure which has hitherto attended the discussion of mercantile questions before the courts of law. . . . [It] would save the community many thousands [of pounds] yearly in expenses, waste of labour and time . . . and anxiety.'[366] Another leading merchant, William Cunningham, recommended the formality of regular public reports and accounts, something that municipal corporations were notorious for either not maintaining or making public: 'accounts hastily read over and audited in this public manner are very liable to be objected to, and justly'. Accounts 'should be printed . . . and sent to each member. . . . This method will prevent any misapplication of money and give satisfaction.'[367]

Some of the most critical advice came from John Keppen, a leading merchant firm in Greenock, who praised Colquhoun's abilities to hold the new body together, a 'task undertaken by a chief magistrate of Glasgow whose abilities are equal to it; and whose zeal and exertions for the public welfare, do him such honour'. But he warned about the need for a broad governance structure beyond a few leaders. 'It has been observed that though such institutions are active and useful at their commencement, they usually degenerate either into faction, or listless indolence in the end—there can be no danger of the latter while you continue in the direction.' Keppen went on to propose a self-denying ordinance for members, to act in the common interest. Given the emergence of the General Chamber a couple of years later, this was very prophetic. He wrote:

differences of opinion will naturally arise even among those who have the same ends in view, and partial and selfish motives will sometimes influence the members; as a palliative it might perhaps be not improper to communicate an oath to every director on his appointment 'that he should to the best of his judgment act for no other motives

---

[364] Thomas Miller to Colquhoun, 11 February 1783; TD 1670/4/14.
[365] James Dennistoun to Colquhoun, November 1782; TD 1670/4/12.
[366] William Wilson to Colquhoun, 28 October 1782; TD 1670/4/11.
[367] William Cunningham to Colquhoun, 2 November, 1782; TD 1670/4/12.

but such as tended to promote in the most effective manner, the general interest of commerce and manufactures, . . . without prejudice to the general interest' . . . it may have the effect at least that it would keep the gentlemen awfully in mind of the original intent of the institution.[368]

Furthermore there was strong support for deliberated and reasoned voice, based on unity. John Dalrymple, a major Edinburgh merchant, noted that 'advantage will be to give *weight of truth* in applications to ministers. There are few mercantile favours that will be refused to the united voice of such a body of men. The Scotch members [MPs] are the worst channel in the world to get favours of trade, almost none of them are merchants. If they be men of straw they concentrate on getting places for themselves.'[369]

This correspondence to Colquhoun is significant in allowing us to see how the chamber concept had moved on from Mortimer, towards the definitions used in this book: it recognized the structure of transparent governance and discourse required, the practical means to achieve unity, and the need for respectful alliance with the key established political forces. By 1782–3 in Glasgow there was a deep understanding of what a *local chamber* could achieve, and how it should set about doing it. This was mirrored in the earlier Birmingham and Staffordshire correspondence of Garbett and Wedgwood,[370] and in the way in which chambers like Liverpool and Jersey operated. Garbett was a key networker, and Liverpool's activities appear to have had a lot of impact, but Glasgow has a special significance because it was a more durable body than Birmingham or Liverpool's. Its foundation deed was explicitly copied by Belfast, Dublin, Edinburgh, and other chambers, which also sought advice from Glasgow. Hence for the second phase of chamber establishment, Glasgow proved to be the leading example of best practice adopted by most others, extending previous experiences, and it offered a counterweight to the conceptual base of Postlethwayt, Mortimer, and Burgh, based on national centralization. Glasgow chamber's immediate link with a coffee house in 1783 was also copied by most other early chambers (see Chapter 11).

Glasgow was also the first chamber in Britain or Ireland to receive a charter. New York gained the first chamber charter in 1770, but Glasgow was the source for copying by Edinburgh in 1785, and attempted by Jersey in 1787; although charters were not achieved by other chambers for a long time, as discussed in Chapter 7. However, perhaps most extraordinary of Glasgow's contributions was that it seems to have been the force that introduced into chambers a deep commitment to abolish the Corn Laws. As well as its formal constitution covering governance, aims, and objectives, its sixth article commits the chamber explicitly 'to consider all matters affecting the Corn Laws'.[371] Liverpool chamber had lobbied in 1775 against Corn Law proposals. But commitment as a founding article is unique to Glasgow. The chambers as a whole came to be strong campaigners for Corn Law

---

[368] John Keppen to Colquhoun, 7 November 1782; TD 1670/4/12.
[369] Sir John Dalrymple to Colquhoun, 18 November 1782; TD 1670/4/12, emphasis in original.
[370] As reviewed by Norris (1957); Money (1977); Dietz (1991).
[371] Glasgow chamber, *Articles* (1783); also Glasgow chamber history.

abolition, as examined in Chapter 10. What is astonishing is that, although couched very carefully, this conflicts with all the other aspects of 'respectability' in Colquhoun's founding efforts; and it appears to have been accepted by Dundas. That this was possible seems to be derived from seeing the Corn Laws as inimical to Scotland; Dundas could accept this commitment to reform as a means to assert Scottish views, but it is nonetheless surprising.

4.12 CONCLUSION

This chapter has sought to understand how the chamber of commerce concept emerged as a 'brand' that offered attractions to a wide range of the major trading centres in Britain, Ireland, America, and the Caribbean from the 1760s. It seems to have evolved from grass-roots initiatives, but had significant intellectual fillip from Postlethwayt and Mortimer, who revived the Davenant/Whiston ideas. The concept circulated widely among the business leaders, and was popularized as a *national* initiative by Bolingbroke, Burgh, and Wilkes, and taken up by Rockingham and Burke, intermeshed with concerns about the Board of Trade: it became an element of the political opposition's 'discourse coalition'.

There were two waves of establishment: the first in 1767–75 was a response to immediate threats and opportunities for influence occasioned by the aftermath of the Stamp Act, and the challenges of managing opinion within and about America by local merchant elites. The second wave was a response to the end of the American war in 1783, and the related political settlement in Ireland with a more independent parliament. There were also renewed concerns in Britain with taxation, the need to reduce government spending, and to resolve outstanding debts across the Atlantic. Glasgow, led by Patrick Colquhoun, provided a new conceptual and practical guide for *local chambers*, transferred to most of the second phase of chambers, which endured and supplanted the ideas for centralized bodies at national level. As a result of these foundations, by the late 1780s both the concept and key practical characteristics of local chambers that were to run for the next 200 years were essentially defined.

Critical factors in establishment seem to have been the overwhelming sense of threat in the leading trading centres: threat to trade and threat to political stability. This was a period of 'transgressive contention' where old routes of influence were less open, but new opportunities arose and new coalitions of interests around new discourses had leverage. The chambers appear to have been one outcome of this transgressive period. In Britain the 'dog didn't bark': there was no revolution. Instead the aristocratic vested interests diverted opposition in the 1770s and 1780s, and used suppression in the 1790s, with the result that significant reform to political structures did not occur until the 1830s. However, the American debacle changed the mechanisms and repertoires for discourse within the Imperial policy community, in Ireland, and with the colonies: new frames were established. The chambers were a significant part of this evolution, reflecting a more general pattern that, in a period of significant change, economic campaigns are most intensely developed by those with greatest exposure to loss/risk, with highest aspiration, in milieus where there is greatest heterogeneity, and where there is a need for separate elite voice above the clamour.

The character of the chamber voice was thus simultaneously radical and traditional. The leadership and most of the members of chambers had a predominant concern to influence the government of the here and now. This did not mean that chamber leaders were happy with the status quo. The municipal corporations, burghs, and counties, and elsewhere the colonial governors, and States parliaments of Jersey and Guernsey, were sources for anger. However, the leading businesses and chambers generally sought government improvement and 'reform', within the realm of the achievable. This meant trying to adapt the existing frames and repertoires, even though these were clearly under challenge. In America the chambers generally had a strong presence of 'loyalists' and sought compromises not confrontation, trying to counterweight and limit the radicals.

The second wave of foundations after 1783 spread the chamber concept and stimulated new national coalitions. The greater number and regional differentiation of the chambers, and the disappearance of the American agents after the Declaration of Independence in 1776, required new models. Several experiments emerged: the General Chamber of 1785–7, the Union of chambers 1793–1805, and local bilateral coordination. A rather special hybrid body of an American chamber of commerce in Liverpool was established in 1802, stimulated by the American consul based there, James Maury. With London-based American traders, this kept alive the American focus in Britain for the next 100 years, acting as a national body and opening an important office in London from 1815; its secretary was to become the first secretary of the Association of Chambers in Britain in 1860, turning the wheel full circle, as discussed in Chapter 8.

5

Diffusion

5.1 THE DIFFUSION PROCESS

The emergence of protest, frustration with government, and the influence of the new models for voice, accounts for why chambers emerged in the form they did, when they did. It is also suggestive of why they emerged specifically *where* they did: in many of the leading centres of the Atlantic economy. However, whilst protest might be sufficient to get dedicated campaigners motivated, as discussed in Chapter 3, it is not usually enough to keep a more general body of interests engaged. To survive, chambers had to develop a continued mission and spread to all relevant locations so that their voice had national weight and credibility. This chapter examines that diffusion process.

Diffusion requires an idea, a range of susceptibles, and overcoming of barriers that prevent development occurring, as well as ability to adapt to different circumstances. The analysis that follows demonstrates the significance of population size as a key feature of chamber diffusion. The susceptibles were the largest cities, only later diffusing to smaller places. Particularly susceptible were the ports; hence a large city that was also a port was almost bound to have an early chamber. However, as in all diffusion processes, there were places that were late developers, where barriers to diffusion existed. Most notable of these locations were London and Bristol.

The first phase of chamber development implanted the concept, established the brand, and provided practical experience. The early brand was ambivalent: certainly locally well established and entrenched in some places, it also had some strong political negatives as a result of the General Chamber's campaigns. The French wars of 1796–1815 and anti-sedition laws after 1795–6 also put many commercial activities and lobbying on hold. Nevertheless, by 1839 about 23 were operating. This included the special case of the Liverpool American chamber (1802).

A more rapid development of chambers of commerce occurred from the 1840s, and by 1890 the structure was very similar to the 20th-century pattern, spreading more widely relatively slowly, reaching a steady number of 90–105 over 1900–90.[1] After 1990 in the UK there was a period of consolidation of smaller chambers and multiple chambers in close proximity, so that conceptually the chambers moved from representing the main cities, to covering larger geographical areas, for a whole conurbation, sub-region, or county. Mergers between

---

[1] See Appendix A.

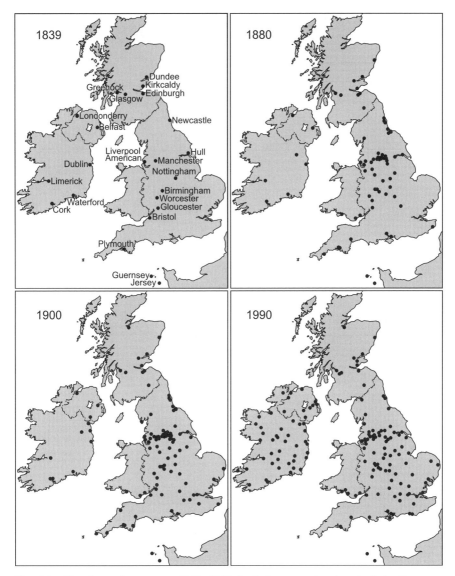

Fig. 5.1. Chambers of commerce 1839–1990 (includes town chambers in Ireland).

chambers of commerce, and merger of the BCC and NCT reduced the numbers after 1990 to reach 54 major accredited chambers of commerce in 2010, within which there were approximately 168 smaller 'affiliated' or 'associated' chambers of commerce.

The evolution, shown in Figure 5.1, highlights the spread of chambers to all the main manufacturing and port centres by 1880, with the chambers in Yorkshire and

Lancashire being particularly numerous, reflecting the large number of significant independent centres in these areas. London remained a notable gap until 1882, but by 1900 the diffusion was wide, with London and the South-East now having chambers, as well as further developments in the North and Midlands. Through the 20th century the spread became even wider, with many smaller places developing chambers, many of which were de facto chambers of trade.

In Ireland after 1922 the Irish chambers seceded along with the Irish state. Ireland was an early leader in chamber development, with chambers developing fairly rapidly to cover all the main ports. But development more widely was very limited up to 1900.[2] There were still only the original chambers in the Republic by 1890 (except for the second one in Cork which split in 1882), five in all. This number increased to seven when Dundalk was founded in 1892 and Drogheda in 1894. But there was no further increase in numbers until the 1920s. New Ross (1922), Galway and Sligo (both in 1923), Tralee (1929), and Wexford increased the number to 12 by 1930. Progress was then steady with 19 by 1952, 27 by 1960, 41 by 1970, with a similar number in the 1980s, but then expanded rapidly in the 1990s, to reach over 120 in 2010. This diffusion, shown in Figure 5.1, results from the spread of development from the major ports to many small towns after the 1970s, with even more rapid expansion from the mid-1980s, with multiple bodies called 'chambers' developed in the larger cities such as Dublin and Cork. Much of the recent expansion appears to have been stimulated by the need for local economic development partnerships, especially the need for business bodies to be associated with various local government and EU funding initiatives. The chambers are essentially based on the 123 urban districts and town councils, with the four counties in Dublin, each having a separate chamber.

Northern Ireland, where the chambers remained affiliated with ABCC and the British system after 1922, also showed considerable later expansion. From only three chambers in 1900 (Belfast, Londonderry, and Newry), this expanded to eight by 1950, but did not significantly increase again until the 1980s and 1990s, to reach about 25 in 2007. No distinction between chambers of commerce and chambers of trade ever took strong hold in Ireland, so that Figure 5.1 shows the total pattern of all 'chambers' over time.

The earlier discussion has included the first chambers in America because of their interrelations with those in the British Isles. After 1806 the American chambers were slow to develop and there were few additions to the map shown in Figure 4.1 until the 1840s. At this point the chambers diffused away from the Atlantic seaboard, with St Louis founded in 1842, New Orleans in 1845, Cleveland 1848, Cincinnati 1853, Milwaukee 1856, and St Paul in 1867. The American chambers then developed in a different way; State Boards of Trade become more

---

[2] There may have been other short-lived early chambers. Belfast chamber minutes refer to Sligo chamber in 1822 (minutes 13 February 1822) and talk of establishing a branch at Enniskillen (minutes 4 February 1822). An early Youghal body is mentioned in Limerick chamber minutes (letters 3, 6, and 15 February 1823). Galway chamber was based on merger with bodies that went back to 1791; see Chapter 11.

important. In 1858 there were ten American chambers in existence and 20 Boards of Trade.[3] These followed the war of 1812–15, with more rapid expansion occurring thereafter.[4] In Canada, Halifax was re-established in 1803, Quebec in 1809, and the Jamaica chamber in 1839.

5.2 DIFFUSION: 'EVERY TOWN SHOULD HAVE ONE'

The diffusion of the chamber concept also became conceptual: that a chamber was needed in any town that wanted to be taken seriously and make its voice heard by government. It was an entry in the travelling directories of the railway age; usually shown immediately after local government councillors: almost an acceptance of a complementary democratic base.[5] This had resonance for the landed gentry and elite, with whom the local business people sought alliance and support: chambers offered respectability and 'politeness', and a place could profit from 'politeness'.[6] At the end of the 19th century objectives were enlarged; place promotion by the smaller trade chambers became particularly important for mass tourism. Beyond the age of politeness in the late 19th and early 20th centuries, 'fashionable and cheap' became the common form of newspaper advertisements for resorts,[7] as the railway network took off and workers' holidays increased. As a result, the production of tourist guides, provision of accommodation bureaux, and the creation of tourist events and attractions such as dances and band concerts became important aspects of chamber activities: to support 'place competition' and 'place marketing'.

It also became the policy of the national chamber association to encourage development of chambers in all major towns. From 1883 the chambers began to see 50,000 or more as the population size of a place that would be expected to have a chamber, and 25,000 was also suggested as a threshold.[8] The modern target 'market' for a chamber is much larger, suggested at a minimum of about 10,000 businesses of one employee or greater,[9] which equates to a population of approximately 250,000 local residents.

An early local sense of the need to have a chamber is evidenced in Worcester in 1839 in the process of setting up its chamber:[10] 'There is now scarcely a *seaport* or *manufacturing* town in the kingdom of any importance that has not seen the advantage of forming a society from among its inhabitants for the protection of

---

[3] Sturges (1915); Lurie (1972).

[4] It has been argued by Rose (2000, see especially pp. 134–8) that American lobbying and business–government relations depended more on personal contacts until the late 1850s. Her case study of the cotton industry evidences this, but it is more likely that the small number of chambers and boards of trade up to the 1860s in the main cities adequately covered the needs.

[5] See Sweet (2002, 2003); also Chapter 3.

[6] Borsay (1989); Langford (1991), pp. 378–80.

[7] Barker (2004), pp. 182–3.

[8] London *CCJ*, 2 (12) December (1883); see Chapter 8.

[9] Bennett (1990); BCC (1990); see also Chapter 8.

[10] Worcester chamber minutes; *Report of a Provisional Committee*, appointed to promote the formation of the chamber, 7 May 1839; emphases added.

local interests, and the redress of its local grievances in trade, whether they arise from public or private causes.' Or as noted in attempts to set up a London chamber in 1867, 'every third-rate town in the kingdom has its chamber of commerce or some kindred institution'.[11] Similarly the NCT in the 1920s stated 'the imperative need for effective local trade organisations. . . . In every town and district we find organisations, religions, philanthropic, social, literary, athletic and scientific. . . . Thus do ideas grow and purposes become fulfilled by unity and collective action. . . . A competent, well-equipped and progressive chamber of trade should be a permanent feature in every town and district.'[12] Local government changes also encouraged competition: e.g. in 1960 in Hampshire the New Milton, Milford, and district chamber of trade competed with the Lymington chamber for the siting of the new local town hall.[13]

Of course there was no inevitability about these developments: a local leadership and membership had to be developed. This was not always possible; as in all chamber developments, local contingency came into play. Thus in Birstal (Yorkshire; 1881 population 6766) 'everybody believed it would be a good idea to establish a chamber, but nobody seemed to put the idea into shape'.[14] Nevertheless most places down to the size of Birstal did establish chambers of trade or commerce by the 1950s.

Competition for space and voice

As a result of these pressures the concept of 'chamber of commerce' was increasingly stretched. As noted in 1917 'there were more organisations . . . using the name "chambers of commerce" that were not in fact chambers of commerce than those affiliated with the [ACC]'.[15] This expansion of bodies became rapid in the later 19th century and early 20th centuries and, as shown in Figure 2.1, the chambers of trade, trade protection societies, and chambers of agriculture, as well as sector-based bodies, all grew rapidly in number. The geographical diffusion of the alternative systems was wide. Figure 5.2 shows the development of the chambers of trade in Britain from their formal inception in 1897 up to the 1950s. Their counterparts in Ireland and most of Scotland were the smaller chambers of commerce, but across England and Wales chambers of trade covered most of the small towns and included many of the large cities, particularly, like the chambers of commerce, in Lancashire, Yorkshire, and South-East England. Perhaps most notable is the very dense development of chambers of trade in two types of location. First, in South Wales, they clearly offered to the small but distinctive communities of the mining valleys a particular attraction. Second, in the coastal resort towns, they offered benefits of allying traders around tourist promotion: the main resort areas of the

---

[11] Scott (1867b), p. 10.
[12] NCT (1921), *Local Trade Organisation*, leaflet, p. 1. MS 29343/1.
[13] 'Fifty years ago': report in *Lymington Times*, 20 November 2010.
[14] E. W. Wainwright, Birstal chamber, in London *CCJ*, 5 August (1886), p. 54.
[15] Thomas Keens, Luton chamber secretary, in ACC *Monthly Proceedings*, 4 October (1917), p. 47; also London comment by Musgrave (1914), p. 43.

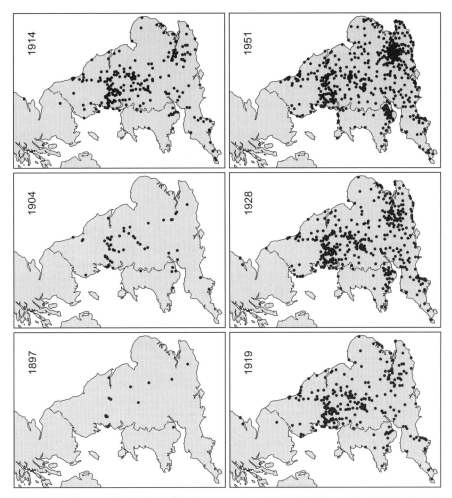

Fig. 5.2. Diffusion of chambers of trade 1897–1951. (*Source*: NCT membership books and directories.)

South, North Wales, and Lancashire coasts had almost continuous strings of chambers of trade.

Over the same period trade protection societies diffused to the larger centres. They had an early concentration in Lancashire, the Midlands, and South-East, but came to cover most of the main centres in England, Scotland, and Ireland, though never with much presence in Wales. In addition there were the chambers of agriculture that existed up to 1959, and a wide range of mainly national sector trade and professional bodies, numbering over 3000 since the 1950s. As indicated in Figure 2.1, the British Isles was covered by a wide diversity of competing brands and bodies, which reached a peak in the period 1930 to 1960.

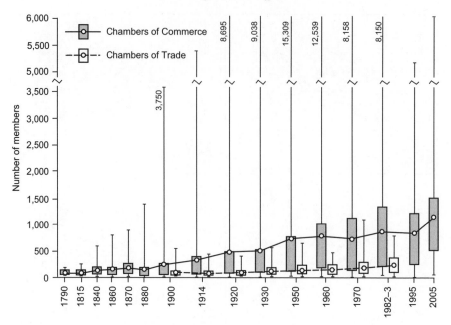

Fig. 5.3. Number of members in chambers of commerce and chambers of trade 1790–2005: mean, range (maximum to minimum), and 20%/80% box plots.

The effect of this growing spread and stretch of the chamber concept is clear from the increasing range of their size. All the early chambers were of moderate size, about 100–200 members, with only a small range between the largest and smallest. This is clear from Figure 5.3. The spread of chambers of commerce to the smaller towns kept the mean size small, even declining slightly in the 1880s, but the *range* of sizes greatly increased from 1900 as a result of a few chambers becoming very large. The mid-and late 19th century was a period when the chamber concept took hold in the large centres such as Manchester, Birmingham, and Glasgow, and from 1882 in London, so that by the 1870s the largest chambers were approaching 1000 members. By 1900 several had well over 1000 members; from 1960 over 20% of the system had more than 1000 members. But the invasion of the system by the smaller towns kept the majority of chambers of commerce small until 1990. The chambers of trade also expanded, but more slowly.

This is similar to the pattern of American chambers, which confirms that high variability is endemic in voluntary systems in which there is no public law to regulate market entry and use of title. As in Britain and Ireland, early chambers of commerce in the USA were concentrated, with only seven by 1807, and ten by 1858, plus 20 boards of trade.[16] By 1898 chamber numbers reached about 414,

[16] US boards of trade brought together the various sector interests into a single local body. They were mostly similar to chambers of commerce in the early years of development, but later included spin-offs of State or municipal regulatory activity; see Sabine (1859); Lurie (1972); and Chapter 4.

but there were also about 490 local boards of trade, and 868 other local bodies called variously 'communal club', 'commerce club', 'commerce league', or 'commercial association'. By 1920 there were about 950 local chambers of commerce and nine state-level chambers, but 'chambers' in the wide sense numbered about 8000, a figure that has been maintained up to the present.[17] There are some regional differences in this pattern, with most bodies called chambers of commerce or boards of trade in the East, commercial clubs in the Mid-West, and a more equal representation of both in the West. There was also a continuing association with the ports: the 68 leading US ports in 1913 all had a local chamber.[18]

5.3 EXPLAINING TAKE-OFF: SCALE AND WEIGHT

The start of the chamber diffusion process in Britain and Ireland was strongly focused on the large commercial centres that were regional agglomerations with extensive hinterlands, and almost all were ports or well connected to them by improved river navigations or canals. The chambers were *not* based on the traditional county towns that had become some sort of focus of markets or administration in the established central place system.[19] The large regional centres offered a critical mass sufficient to recognize a need, and to develop a resource of leadership and membership that could found and sustain chambers.

Following their origin in the largest centres, the diffusion of chambers across the rest of the urban system seems to have been essentially down the city-size hierarchy. This hierarchical diffusion process is illustrated very clearly by the rank-size distribution graphs shown in Figures 5.4 and 5.5.[20] These are plots of the population size of each place against its rank at each time period, both using logarithmic scales. The rank-size plots are statistical patterns that can be used to compare the evolution of cities in a single country over time, and to compare one country with another.[21] They allow the shape of the population distribution to be seen at a glance, with any pattern of primacy of the largest city, or development of distinct tiers and hierarchies of centres (several centres with similar populations), clearly evident. The rank distribution captures in a simple way the more complex interrelations between the cities and towns as a 'system of cities', since the rank of any centre can only increase at the expense of others. Superimposing on the rank-size plot the development of chambers demonstrates how their diffusion strongly interrelated with city size as the city system itself evolved.

[17] The American chambers in 1920 had a mean membership of 647 with a range from 10 to 17,500 (the largest in New York). This is only slightly higher than the UK mean at the same date (476), but the range of 1 : 1750 is wider than the UK 1 : 435. (Source: calculated from the listings in US Department of Commerce, 1923.)

[18] Jones (1916); for ports over 1m tons or $30m in volume in 1913; a few of the chambers were referred to as boards of trade or commercial associations.

[19] Langton (1984, pp. 147–9), (2000); see also Law (1967); Pred (1973, 1977); Robson (1973); Corfield (1982); Daunton (1995).

[20] These Figures, and subsequent analyses, use standardized population measures: see Appendix 3.

[21] Weber (1899); Berry (1967); Pred (1973, 1977).

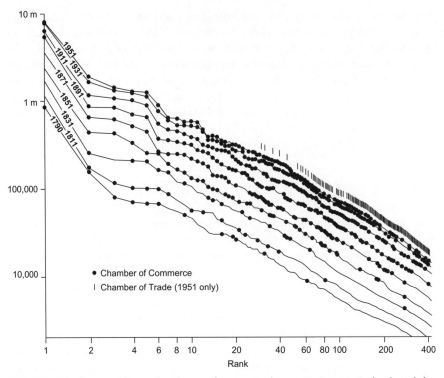

Fig. 5.4. Population rank-size distribution for cities and towns in Britain, Ireland, and the Channel Islands, 1790–1951, with chambers of commerce in any centre shown at each time period. Chambers of trade, which began to be established as identifiable organizations from 1897, are shown for 1951.

For the early period, shown in Figure 5.4, the number of chambers is small, and their development limited to the largest places, except for the special cases of Jersey and Guernsey. In 1790 the only large centre with no chamber is Bristol, the third largest city. After 1800 (when Weskett's chamber in London closed), both London and Bristol are the exceptions among the largest cities in having no chamber, until Bristol chamber was founded in 1823, and London in 1882. But apart from these two exceptions the relation of chamber development to city size and rank is remarkably close. From the 1860s there was a strengthening trend for some of the smaller places to also develop chambers, with chambers of trade after 1897 diffusing chambers to medium-sized towns of 25,000 population and smaller.[22] The result was two diffusion processes across the chamber system, with the two systems overlapping.

For the later period, shown in Figure 5.5, the underlying population information is re-based to reflect growing urbanization that merged many smaller places into

---

[22] Note that there are further chambers of trade in very small places (less than 2500 population) that are too small to be shown in Figure 5.4: there were 14 of these in 1911, 36 in 1931, and 113 in 1951.

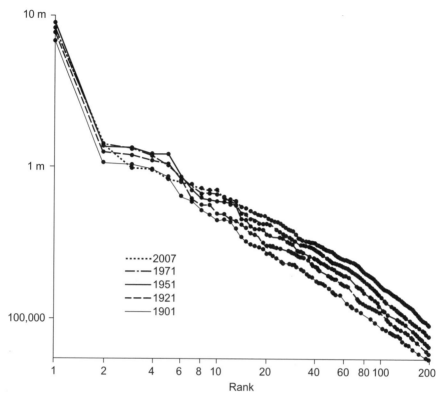

Fig. 5.5. Population rank-size distribution for cities and towns in Britain, Northern Ireland, and the Channel Islands, 1901–2001, with chambers of commerce and chambers of trade in any area shown at each time period.

large cities and conurbations that reduced the number of areas. The rapid expansion of the chamber of trade system in the 1950s brought in many expanding towns that were previously very small, as well as many small rural locations. Some counties such as Kent became almost entirely covered with small chambers from an early date. After 1960 a new phase of development occurred as some of the chambers of trade tried to become chambers of commerce.[23] For 1990 there is the maximum modern numerical extent of the chambers of commerce, where many still covered small and large towns, as well as many that covered wider areas such as Hertfordshire, North-East England, or the Three Counties of Gloucester, Hereford, and Worcester.

At first sight it is surprising that large size was so dominant in chamber of commerce development. It would be expected from most literature on collective

[23] For example, in the 1970s, chambers of commerce in Ayr, Dunfermline, and many Scottish centres developed as well as in Grantham, High Wycombe, Maidstone, Medway, Penzance, and St Austell.

action that the larger the group the more difficult it would be to come to a common view and to align interests.[24] But this demonstrates some of the misunderstandings. The process sought by chambers and most other local business bodies was not alignment of interests as in a political movement among people, but cohesion of major business interests around general needs, a 'unity' of interest among leading businesses (or those that chose to participate): unity meant agreement, not necessarily alignment, since most businesses remained competitive with each other and had varying reasons to support unity at different times. Hence, large size was not an impediment to chamber formation, though it provided challenges to unity. Rather size seems to have offered a large enough population of businesses of the right type for which a chamber had relevance. Once established, size also offered incumbent advantages.[25] In modern terms, size also offered what evolutionary economists call the advantage of 'contextual variety'.[26]

Indeed, it was becoming a commonplace among contemporary economists, such as Cantillon or Adam Smith, that city size was a critical determinant of weight and scope for other institutional developments; and that size in turn depended upon resources, cultural features, and technological innovativeness, which was increased further by foreign trade.[27] This has also underpinned modern interpretations of the geography of economic development and the role of institutions.[28] Large cities are the focus of agglomeration economies as well as diversity, as Marshall first noted.[29] Great cities are also linked to the benefits of patronage of the arts and openness to ideas and innovation.[30] Hall sees cities at the time of early chambers as the centres of creativity, art, and expression, as interlinked with business innovation; allowing 'a kind of cultural reproduction over generations', as social meeting points, 'fulcrums of ideas that were magnets for innovations in commerce, arts and sciences'.[31] City size and city growth were strong correlates of growth in international trade throughout the 18th and 19th centuries in the British Isles.[32]

In pre-Reform Britain, the cities had large electorates that tended to have the more open electoral contests, as they were more difficult for the government to control. It was thus more possible for them to influence their MP. This and their greater diversity made them more fertile ground for political dissent and development of political movements. This interlinked with the major ports; as Jackson notes, 'harbour works required Acts of parliament to authorise capital formation, compulsory purchase and dues. . . . Understandably, ports took their parliamentary representatives seriously and "organised" elections to satisfy their perceived economic needs.'[33] This meant the corporation, mayor, and MPs were under greater

---

[24] See Chapter 3 and e.g. Olson (1971); Chamberlain (1974); Tarrow (1994).
[25] Hansen (1985).
[26] Boschma (2009); see also Jacobs (1969); Pred (1977).
[27] On Cantillon, Malthus, Adam Smith, and Quesnay; see Taraschio (1981).
[28] See e.g. North (1990); Acemoglu, Johnson, and Robinson (2001); Boschma (2009).
[29] Marshall (1919); Jacobs (1969, 1984).
[30] Hall (1998), pp. 282–8; Pred (1973, 1977).
[31] Hall (1998), p. 20, quoting Taine (1865) recognizing the creative magnetism of the city.
[32] Jackson (2000); Langton (2000); O'Brien and Engerman (1991); Hall (1998).
[33] Jackson (2000), p. 723.

pressure from business interests in the major cities, and especially the ports. They also had more experience of seeking parliamentary influence in order to get improvements. The cases of Liverpool, Manchester, and Birmingham, so important in early chambers, and the Bristol Venturers, illustrate profoundly contentious elections.

5.4 HINTERLANDS

Interrelated with city size was evolution of hinterlands. In Europe from 1750, and Britain from earlier, city trade with hinterlands of medium-sized, smaller towns and rural areas grew rapidly.[34] The British economy was shifting to regional city dominance, where the large centres provided the economic stimulus for manufacturing and trade in smaller centres, whilst simultaneously their hinterlands offered an increasing market for the cities' products through production, warehousing, logistics, distribution, and commercial organization, particularly banking and market networks.

Something of the real economic spirit is captured in the contemporary comment about Manchester in 1815, by Archibald Prentice, a muslin distribution agent from Glasgow and subsequently a leader of the Manchester chamber: 'I found that I met in the street in one day, more country drapers than I could . . . meet in their own shops in two: if we kept our manufactured stock in Manchester, we could considerably increase our business, and at a great saving in travelling expenses'. Manchester also had 'centrality—[easily accessible to] Wigan, Preston, Blackburn, Bolton, Bury, Rochdale, Ashton, Stockport, and numerous fast-growing villages, all increasing in importance'.[35]

The dominance of the regional cities in early chamber formation also interlocked with international exporting and importing. This was why their role as ports, or as places with ready access to ports, was critical. As observed from an American perspective in the 1770s, London, Liverpool, and Glasgow merchants were dominant, buying up all the best goods for export, inhibiting the scope for smaller places to develop direct trade with the colonies.[36] This is not to underemphasize the increasing number of direct links of small centres in international trade, but the whole system depended on an increasing regional city concentration of commercial activity. As Berg observes for Europe more widely:[37] 'two urban systems coexisted and interpenetrated. One system was a hierarchy of central places, culminating in a regional capital and ultimately in the capital of a multi-region state. The other system related those cities involved in long-distance trading networks together with their secondary outposts or satellites.' This is reminiscent of Berry's observation on city growth as interrelations up,

[34] De Vries (1984); Wrigley (1987); Crafts (1984, 1985, 1997); Berg (1991); Langton (2000).
[35] Prentice (1851), pp. 66–7; further comment on Prentice in Chapter 10.
[36] See e.g. Papenfuse (1975), p. 60.
[37] Berg (1991), p. 179; in turn quoting Hohenberg and Lees (1985), p. 457.

down, and across the urban hierarchy, as a 'city system of systems of cities'; or as Jacobs has described it, the emergence of cities as the nexus of the national economy as a whole, combining export multipliers of local and regional connected places, with import substitution and reprocessing multipliers to further expand regional markets.[38]

For chambers the benefits were the same as for the cities: agglomeration economies of scale for membership (size, critical mass), as well as economies of scope to develop a general view (across diverse sectors, labour markets, skills, finance, and sources of innovation). They were also the focus of networks. Every area had its networks—what was distinctive about the large cities was that their networks were very powerful, and were nationally and internationally linked. Hence, city size was also a surrogate for network and chamber capacity.[39] Indeed, differences in size of hinterlands is used by Morgan to explain the rapid rise of Liverpool to eclipse Bristol in the 1770s,[40] and explains why Exeter, York, and Whitehaven (which had been prominent in earlier periods) had limited potential in the new conditions of the 19th century: they lacked sufficient hinterland. By 1801 many of these centres no longer had significance. Some remained relatively static; Norwich declined absolutely.

The regional centres were the emerging centres of the new global order, critical to the main focus of chamber concerns: international trade and national regulations. They were the focal points of what we would now call 'clusters'. The dominance of the regional centres is an enduring characteristic of the British economy up to the late 20th century, with market potential *within* the different regions of Britain being critical factors in explaining economic growth and competitiveness up to WW2,[41] through internal agglomeration economies and externalities to local businesses. But *between* regions, agglomeration had little benefit until nationally linked transport was widely available.[42] Thus the national and European-wide benefits of agglomeration in major centres, as emphasized by the 'new economic geography' literature,[43] were not significant until after a more radical decline in transport costs, particularly from the 1980s. Between-region differentiation, 'industrial districts', and diversity were the key characteristics of the British economy up to the 1970s,[44] and remain critical aspects of Ireland. The operative geographical market was thus the region, and its communications with oceanic trade, rather than the nation. Global influences now challenge the status and value of bodies rooted in localities and regions such as chambers, but this was not significant until the 1980s.

[38] Berry (1967); Jacobs (1969, 1984).
[39] See Chapter 14.
[40] Morgan (1993, 2007).
[41] Crafts (2005); Crafts and Mulatu (2005); in contrast to Lee (1971, 1981).
[42] Hudson (1989).
[43] e.g. Crafts (1985, 1997); Acemoglu, Johnson, and Robinson (2001); Boschma (2009).
[44] See also Langton (1984); Hudson (1989).

5.5 OVERSEAS TRADE AND THE FOCUS ON PORTS

From the 18th century a rapid change in the value, volume, and significance of foreign trade occurred in Britain. This had begun in the 17th century, but the changes became major and more rapid from the 1760s and through the 19th century. Overseas trade became an increasing driver of the whole national economy. The ratio of exports to GNP was 6% in 1660, 8% after 1688, and reached 12% by 1800. It is estimated that at least one-half of the increment in UK national industrial production from 1688 to 1815 was sold overseas, and about one-half of the non-agricultural and agricultural processing labour force depended directly or indirectly on exports. On the import side over 1790–1820, net imports of farm produce rose from about 20% to 40% of domestic farm output.[45]

The growth of chambers of commerce after 1767, therefore, coincided with a massive shift in the British economy towards overseas export, import, and entrepôt trade. This gives particular point to the comment by Clark, almost as an aside in an otherwise detailed study of non-commercial societies, that 'chambers of commerce... developed in various *port towns* under George III [i.e. 1760–1820], to represent and reconcile local business interests'.[46] Similarly in Ireland it was observed by contemporaries that 'at all the principal seaports of Ireland there is a "chamber of commerce"... consisting of... merchants who have formed themselves into an associated body for the protection and regulation of trade'.[47] As noted by O'Brien, government and commerce were strongly interlocked through joint concern with the ports.[48] Naval supremacy was a political objective, but also gave a unique commercial advantage of state-backed support for investment in international trade.[49] This further reinforced the ports as the main focus of chambers, not only in Britain and Ireland, but other parts of the Atlantic world.

Growing volumes of trade required port development. The 'ports were not at the end of the line but in the middle of a network... [serving] foreign economies as well as their own'; which included overseas credit.[50] Traditionally British foreign trade was dominated by London, and was controlled by the chartered companies based there, in later years particularly the East India and Levant Companies. Until the early 18th century, London controlled about 70% of all foreign trade. The next largest port was Bristol with about 5% of trade, then Dublin and Glasgow/Clyde, and then a wide dispersion of other ports, with Liverpool becoming significant by mid-century. This historic structure was the outcome of a dispersal of production across the country, difficulties of land transport that encouraged using the closest small port, the focus on woollens and the European market, and control by chartered companies based in London. A decisive shift had occurred by the

[45] Statistics quoted from O'Brien and Engerman (1991); Chapman (1992).
[46] Clark (2000a), p. 152, emphasis added.
[47] E. Wakefield (1812), *An Account of Ireland, Statistical and Political*, vol. ii, p. 30.
[48] O'Brian (1988); see also Rodger (2004); Morris (2004).
[49] O'Brien (2000), pp. 28–31.
[50] Jackson (2000), p. 24; Price (1974, 1978, 1980, 1992).

1750s. London, of course, also grew, and it remained dominant, but its relative dominance began to be eroded.[51]

A first critical shift was the relative freeing of trade from the chartered companies so that interlopers could participate directly, particularly in the African and West Indian trades. From 1750 the African Company was reconstituted into three 'branches' with freemen in the outports (Bristol and Liverpool) as well as London, paying a nominal membership fee of two guineas. Increasingly the government was forced to recognize that trade could not be regulated through chartered companies alone, and parliamentary challenges to the East India Company became frequent after 1767. By the 1780s and 1790s the old 'laws of trade',[52] based on the concept of a chartered company and the Navigation Acts, were being challenged or flouted, except in the more distant Far East (although even here 'interloper' challenges were emerging).

A second shift was the development of the Atlantic trade with America and the Caribbean, which favoured western ports over London, particularly Liverpool, Glasgow, Dublin, and Bristol. In this trade even East Coast ports in Scotland (such as Dundee and Leith) had an advantage over London in terms of speed in an era based on wind technology. Third, was the extension of the main ports through rapid growth of coast-wise trade to serve their regions, in Bristol, Glasgow, Dublin, Liverpool, Newcastle, and London. Fourth was transport improvements, which increasingly connected the major ports with the inland centres (such as Birmingham, Manchester, the West Riding, or Staffordshire). This allowed their participation in international exporting and thus they also became locations for early chamber development. They benefited first from improved river navigations (such as those on the Trent, Severn, Don, and Weaver in the early 1700s) and later the development of canals. Critical were the St Helens and Trent–Mersey canals for Liverpool and the Potteries from the 1760s; the Forth–Clyde canal for Glasgow in the 1770s; and the network of Yorkshire, Nottingham, and Staffordshire canals for Hull from the 1770s.[53] The East India Company was also restructured in this period. Whilst the primacy of London remained for East Indian operations, the company established an increasing number of agents in the outports (usually local merchants, attorneys, and town clerks). This influenced Portsmouth and Plymouth to diversify and become more general entrepôts, whilst Plymouth and Falmouth became increasingly important as first/last landfalls for mail, bullion transfer, and passengers.[54]

In addition, the greater needs for capital investment favoured those port locations that could support it, and this underpinned many early chamber preoccupations. Expanded piers necessary for unloading; the increasing demand for wet docks that allowed loading/unloading at all states of the tide; and dry docks permitting

---

[51] Davis (1962); French (1992).
[52] Child (1698); see Black (1985), pp. 94–113; Palmer (1990).
[53] Davis (1962); Jackson (2000).
[54] Sutherland (1952); Philips (1961); Thomas (2002).

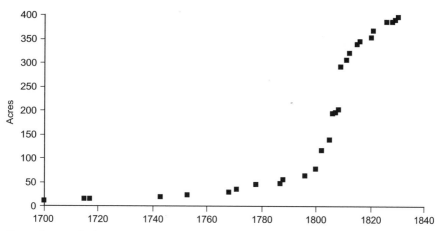

Fig. 5.6. Wet dock investment 1700–1839, cumulative total. (*Source*: Swann 1960, table 2 and text.)

maintenance, were accompanied by steam cranes and hydraulic equipment, and from the 1820s steam tugs and then coastal steam transport. With the volume of trade increasing, warehousing became more important for both outward and especially inward cargoes, which shifted ports from being rather casual facilities for beaching with small piers and harbours, to becoming large fixed infrastructures requiring massive investment and political campaigning for parliamentary improvement Bills.

The rapid take-off of major port investment in the early 1800s is indicated by the expansion of wet docks, shown in Figure 5.6. Wet docks are critical in the British Isles, which has high tidal ranges: at Liverpool, Bristol, most of Devon and Cornwall, and the Channel Isles the range is over 20 feet; and at Belfast, Dublin, and Cork 8–10 feet.[55] In many areas harbours and docks were major concerns of chambers at their foundation, and a frequent focus of their lobbies, locally and nationally. For example, in Bristol the need for wet dock development of the 'floating harbour' was a critical factor in the foundation of its chamber in 1823. In Jersey and Guernsey the need for harbour development was also a prime motive for establishment of their chambers and a perennial focus of their lobbying. For Liverpool, the administration of the docks and dock fees was the main catalyst for chamber establishment in 1774. For smaller places a recurrent focus of their chambers became their port status as 'head ports', 'member ports', or 'creeks/havens'; e.g. Falmouth. The Customs, Trinity House, and related administrative bodies all became focuses for chamber lobbies.

[55] Swann (1960), table 2, pp. 38–9; Bird (1963); Jackson (2000).

Testing the port and rank-size relationship

The population rank-size distribution for 1790 is shown in Figure 5.7 for the British Isles and the former American colonies. The figure also shows the ports and the cities that had chambers of commerce over the 1768–1819 period. Two features stand out. First is the dominance of the ports in the size distribution, and second, the concentration of the chambers in the port towns and the larger places. In America at this time, all significant population centres were on the coast because of their former colonial interdependence with Britain. This was also true of Ireland. Almost all of the largest of these centres established early chambers.

The order of chamber foundation dates also approximately followed the population rank-size distribution; and the relationship is statistically significant, for each of the cases of America, Britain, and Ireland, although in each case there are 'anomalies'.[56] The late development of a chamber in London and Bristol is extremely anomalous, discussed later below. In America, Philadelphia was dominant in population size well ahead of the next largest cities of New York, Boston,

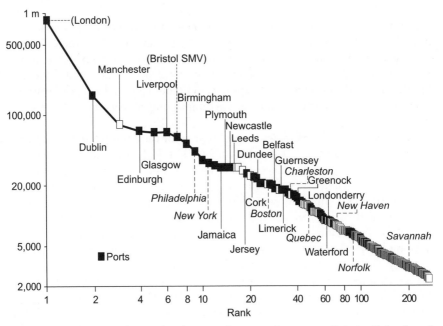

Fig. 5.7. Population rank-size distribution of cities and towns in Britain, Ireland, and America in 1790, showing the ports; chambers of commerce founded 1768–1819 shown by names.

---

[56] The association between population rank-size and chamber ranked foundation date gives a Mann–Whitney U test of statistical association of 8 for America; H1 accepted at $p = 0.01$. If ranked trade volumes are used, U is 12; H1 accepted at $p = 0.1$. For Ireland U is 34; H1 accepted at $p = 0.05$. For Britain U is 7 for N = 15; H1 accepted at $p = 0.01$, with Weskett's London chamber included.

and Charleston, which all had chambers by 1773. Although there was a proposal for a Philadelphia chamber in 1784 with 312 members,[57] establishment was delayed until 1801. Baltimore was even more anomalous; becoming the second largest port by trade volume and fifth in population in 1790, its late chamber foundation (1890) may be explained by its trade position: the depth of water in Chesapeake Bay allowed large ships to bypass Baltimore as an entrepôt, but it had a committee of manufacturers by 1805.[58]

Within America and Ireland all the major cities were also ports; so that city size, port status, and the presence of an early chamber of commerce all interrelate.[59] In Britain by 1839, 13 of the 15 largest places had chambers. There is a statistically significant relationship of rank-size and chamber foundation date for both the first seven and the first 13 chambers. Despite this, the pattern is more complex than America or Ireland, with many inland centres important: 11 of the earliest 25 British chambers were inland. Also the chambers had begun to be established in smaller places: the early special cases of Jersey and Guernsey, and Greenock (although this is explained by its role as outport of Glasgow). However, despite the complexity of Britain, it also has a significant match between the port size, population rank, commercial weight, and the ranked date of chamber foundation.

5.6 REGIONAL AND SECTOR DIFFERENTIATION

Within the general process of chamber diffusion down the city-size hierarchy and to the ports, there was also an important regional differentiation between the great commercial centres and the newly emerging manufacturing centres. As listed in Table 2.1, only three of the first 19 chambers founded up to 1819 were in inland manufacturing centres (Manchester, Birmingham, and Leeds), and none of these was stable, whilst most of the port chambers had continuous or near continuous existence. However, there were a further 12 areas where there was 'chamber' activity, but chiefly in the form of ad hoc committees and 'delegates' to national meetings, for which the General Chamber was a key stimulus to development. Of these, one-half were in inland manufacturing centres.

Regional differences

Recognizing the differentiation of these early chambers is critical. Most early chambers were in the ports, but the previous scholarly literature has focused almost exclusively on inland chambers in Manchester and Birmingham, and to a lesser

---

[57] Tench Coxe papers, 21 October 1784, Reel 46: Historical Society of Philadelphia.

[58] Price (1974), pp. 163–73; Price (1980); Oaks (1973); Haggerty (2006). Baltimore is complex; the 1890 chamber was created from the Grain and Flour Exchange. It had a correspondence committee in 1775, and by 1805 had a committee of manufacturers; it founded a Board of Trade in 1821, which lapsed in 1830, was re-established 1836–43, and continuous from 1869 (Sabine 1859; US Department of Commerce 1923).

[59] Marmion (1855), pp. 631–2; Truxes (1988); de Courcey Ireland (1986).

extent Leeds.[60] These three early chambers were essentially the 18th-century exceptions: they were inland (although increasingly connected to the ports by canals), and almost exclusively formed of manufacturers. This has distorted most scholarly accounts.[61] It is arguable whether the early chambers in Manchester and Birmingham fully satisfied the definitions of chamber adopted in this book: they were not strictly a general interest (being almost exclusively manufacturers), were often focused on protection and control, and may not have always been fully transparent and deliberated. For the early areas with delegates and committees rather than full chambers, there are similar issues about their generality, and they were certainly not open, transparent, and deliberated by a broad membership.

This distinction influenced the development of the General Chamber of *Manufacturers*, where the port-based chambers were less involved, and in the case of chambers like Glasgow, Liverpool, and Jersey, chose to maintain liaison with the General Chamber at arms' length. Similarly, when a Union of chambers operated over 1795–1805, the members were largely those concerned with manufacturing interests (Exeter, Birmingham, Halifax, Leeds, Rochdale, Nottingham, and Manchester; although London merchants and Greenock was also involved).[62]

The tensions between the manufacturing and the commercial interest were thus both sectoral and regional. A further tension was with the retailers, which were not a direct target for most chambers of commerce, and many early chambers despised or tried to exclude them. This left the way open for the diffusion of the 'chamber' concept to be taken over by alternative bodies for retailers and smaller traders within the chambers of trade. The chambers of agriculture also evidence the unwillingness of the chambers of commerce to embrace this sector, though in most cases this was born of a visceral distrust between them.

Regional identity

It is important to understand these tensions not just as differences in sector interests, although this was clearly important, but also the result of an increasingly important and growing self-consciousness of regional and local identity from the 1760s. This encouraged a demand for voice to articulate what were felt to be specific needs of each area. It was part of their 'place status'. For social movements, Langton argues that local identity made it more difficult for national organizations to operate effectively, and caused disunity in social protests; e.g. undermining the chartists and early general trade unions.[63] This also applied to business organizations. Advertisements developed for cities, smaller towns, and resorts that promoted their special features, distinctiveness, and quality.[64] Hence, whilst there was coalescence around the major regional agglomerations as the main centres of

[60] Helm (1897); Redford (1934); Bowden (1919–20, 1965); Norris (1957); Read (1964); Money (1977).
[61] e.g. Rose (2000) and Daunton (1995) rely heavily on the earlier studies listed above.
[62] See Chapter 9.
[63] Langton (1984); see also Black (1963); Innis and Rogers (2000).
[64] Barker (2004).

chamber voice, there was also the demand for smaller places and more rural areas also to have their own voices. These different voices became increasingly accepted as regional and local identities both inside and outside the regions themselves, and were even taken into regional novels.[65] As Clark sees it, the regional centres were the forces for both integration and diversification of the urban system in this period.[66]

This was reinforced by the special opportunities that chambers had to lobby, since they had local and county MPs as obvious targets for persuasion, and could also draw on other local officials and dignitaries to demonstrate a wider support of 'respectable' opinion. Politicians as well as chambers became concerned to promote their areas so that a natural alliance developed with them. In early, as well as modern lobbies, success is more likely through coalitions of sympathetic interests, demonstrating a greater 'public' interest.[67] This also helps lobbies to be focused on the achievable, and the political opportunities of the moment. As noted by the NCT acting for the chambers of trade in 1921: 'Those who sit in high authority have no ear for fugitive or unorganised opinion.'[68] The case or 'memorial' prepared by the chambers presented pre-digested arguments and evidenced them, and was a natural objective for MPs to seek to influence, as well as being influenced by them. Success of a chamber lobby 'depended on the clout and connections enjoyed by the lobby, . . . friends in high places . . . especially in high office was of incalculable benefit.'[69] 'Gentlemanly process' was important: the chambers delivered memorials in person, by senior members meeting their MPs.[70] Finer refers to the whole lobby process up to the early 20th century as one based on organization, riches, access, patronage, and surrogateship (business offering to act as a de facto agent for government).[71] The processes worked both ways, MPs and the government had to cultivate compliance and political acquiescence, as much as individual business and chambers wished to cultivate government willingness to modify burdensome regulations.[72]

This was further reinforced by the increasing importance of the regional and local newspapers. One of the most important challenges for giving voice is finding effective mechanisms for articulating it. The development of chambers coincides with the emergence of a vigorous local and national press: circulation increased in the late 18th century: from only a few million in 1700 to an estimated 7 million copies in 1750, 10.7 million in 1757, and 12–13 million after the 1770s.[73] The press offered a new avenue for influence, that of public opinion. It provided a

[65] Bowden (1919–20, 1965); Read (1964); Money (1971, 1977); Norris (1957); Langton (1984), p. 156.
[66] Clark (2000b), p. 15.
[67] Brewer (1989), pp. 243–9; also Mackenzie (1955); Greenwood (1997); Grant (2000).
[68] NCT, *Local Trade Organisation* (1921), publicity leaflet, MS 29343/1.
[69] Brewer (1989), p. 240.
[70] e.g. in Manchester in 1795; quoted in Helm (1897), pp. 23–5.
[71] Finer (1955), pp. 280–5.
[72] Brewer (1989), especially chapter 8; see also Mackenzie (1955); Stewart (1958); Eckstein (1960); Beer (1965); Finer (1955, 1966); Jordan and Richardson (1987); Greenwood (1997).
[73] Cranfield (1962), pp. 175–8; Aspinall (1973), p. 6; Harris and Lee (1986).

vehicle for chambers to publicize 'cases' and inform members of progress of a
campaign, helping to maintain commitment and solidarity of members, and
allowing claims of broader public support.[74] The press thus provided a campaign
mechanism to confront change in political frames and repertoires.

The press also underpinned the articulation of local and regional identity,
perhaps even helped it to emerge, adapt, and become defined,[75] by providing a
new and critical source of political and commercial information. Press reporting
became a major force stimulating greater local sensitivity by MPs: 'From the later
eighteenth century, MPs were only too aware that their speeches were public
statements . . . MPs found themselves forced to declare their principles in a very
public manner.'[76] This promulgated broader 'public debate' and provided opportunities for chambers to lobby.[77] Thus a new medium and the new chamber
movement developed in tandem, each supporting the other.

By 1780 all the main cities had a local newspaper or journal, and by the 1840s
this included all the medium-sized towns. The major provincial newspapers were
taken widely within their regions, and the papers from the major cities were taken
nationally; the chamber of commerce libraries and reading rooms, for example,
usually took the papers from all the main cities, normally London, Liverpool,
Manchester, Hull, Glasgow, and other centres.[78] The synergies were often even
more direct: the main owners and sometimes the editors of local newspapers were
leading chamber members. The chambers of all sizes used the press as a key
medium for dissemination of their views and activities locally; the press came to
be a critical element in their development of general and deliberated policy, with
reporters frequently invited to be present at meetings. Often the smaller chambers
were as strongly or more strongly interlinked with their local newspapers as the
large cities. The press in turn relied on local organizations, including the chambers,
to provide material that demonstrated that they were closely identified with local
concerns. Chamber debates and policy positions, dominated by international trade
and national politics, added lustre to the regional media by confirming their status
as international centres. Since the newspapers from the main centres were sent
around the British Isles and shipped abroad, this may have also been an important
force behind the chamber diffusion process.

5.7 BARRIERS TO DIFFUSION: 'NOT IN MY BACKYARD'

Whilst the early development of chambers of commerce was very closely related to
the hierarchy of major population centres and ports, there were some notable gaps:

[74] Aspinall (1973); Harris (1987).
[75] Jackson (1971); Aspinall (1973); Harris (1998).
[76] Harris (1998), p. 51.
[77] Brewer (1989); Harris (1998).
[78] See library holdings quoted in Chapter 11.

particularly London and Bristol. It is important to assess the counterfactual of why these did not develop early chambers.

The chambers were not launched into empty territory. Already business voice and lobbying were well developed. This could take place as ad hoc petitions from individuals or groups of merchants or manufacturers; and ad hoc committees were often formed to represent a more general interest. There were also important earlier local bodies that acted, or claimed to act, as a *general* interest representing the locality until the electoral Reform Acts, and in some cases until much later. Indeed the abolition of most of these bodies by the Reform Acts may have been a direct stimulus to forming some chambers, e.g. as in Leith. Some of these earlier bodies were municipal (corporations, guilds merchant, and the guilds), some the residual of old statute companies (the staplers and merchant adventurers), and some were alternative voluntary bodies established before chambers (merchant companies and committees). Each might or might not be sympathetic to the concept of developing the new 'brand' of a chamber with which they could work as a partner, merge into, or to which they could adapt themselves to become.

Thanks to the work of the Municipal Commission 1835–9 we have a reasonably systematic survey of the state of these earlier bodies in the 1830s, and this can be supplemented with other sources; although we must be careful about inferring their level of activity, since the Commission records are inconsistent and imperfect,[79] and many records of these bodies do not survive. However, an overall picture can be developed for the period 1790s–1830s, as shown in Figure 5.8. This shows the situation in England and Wales for all former bodies that can be identified as significant, and in Scotland and Ireland presents the position in the major cities and towns.

The figure shows the wide dispersion of bodies of different types. Although by the 1830s many were in disuse or not significant, they remained as a presence in several important locations, particularly major ports. For those believed to be still active over the period 1790–1835, Table 5.1 summarizes the position. The effect of each body on chambers is briefly reviewed below, beginning with the most significant, London.

London

The late development of a chamber of commerce in the City of London is at first sight quite extraordinary. Finally established in 1882, it was then approximately the 70th chamber in the country to be founded.[80] Yet London had always been by far the largest port and trade centre; its trade in the 1850s contributed one-half of all customs duties and had one-fifth of all the tonnage of shipping in England and

---

[79] The quality varies and several Commissioners had strong prejudices to record or not particular features, varying by region; see Finlayson (1963).

[80] This discussion refers to a London chamber with significant lobbying and voice. There was Weskett's London chamber 1782–1800, which was significant, but was not a voice body; see Chapters 4 and 7.

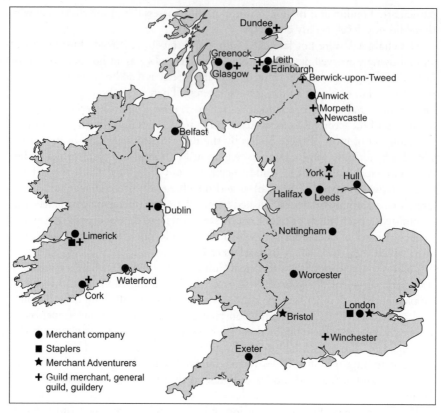

Fig. 5.8. Older merchant bodies active in 1790–1830.

Wales. 'The disadvantageous situation in which the commercial community of the metropolis were placed, from not having a representative body of their own' was noted in 1823.[81] As Scott, the Lord Chamberlain of the City, commented in 1867: 'to no community is legislative protection of its vast and legitimate interests more essential, . . . yet there is no city in the empire so entirely devoid of combined and organised commercial action'. Yet it 'is a matter of notoriety that every third-rate town in the kingdom has its chamber of commerce or some kindred institution'.[82]

There were attempts at establishing a London chamber before 1882. There were two serious and large-scale attempts: first in 1817–18, repeated in 1823–4; and second in 1867–72. There was also some effort to establish a chamber linked to the tribunal of commerce concept in the 1850s. Lord Brougham's Association for Promotion of the Social Sciences even considered in 1856 that it was increasingly acting 'in some degree as a chamber of commerce for the metropolis' as it had 'so

---

[81] R. Shaw, merchant, on establishment of a London chamber, *Morning Chronicle*, 29 August 1823.
[82] Scott (1867b), pp. 4–5 and 10; also Scott (1867a).

Table 5.1. Older merchant and business bodies exercising some form of *general* interest that were still active 1790–1830,[a] with their status

	Merchant Adventurers (MV)	Staplers	Guild Merchant, General Guild, Guildery	Merchant Company
Alnwick			Disused	✓ sections of Corporation
Berwick-upon-Tweed			✓	
Boston	Disused			
Bristol	✓		Transferred to Venturers	
Exeter	Disused	Disused	Disused	✓ probably only informal
Halifax				
Hull	Disused	Disused	Trinity House	✓ probably informal
Leeds				
London	✓	✓	Court of Common Council; also Livery companies	✓ several associations
Morpeth	✓		✓	
Newcastle-upon-Tyne	✓	Disused	Trinity House; general guild disused	
Nottingham				✓
Winchester			✓	
York	✓	Disused	✓	
Edinburgh			✓	✓
Dundee			✓	✓
Glasgow				✓
Greenock				✓
Leith			✓ Dissolved 1832; also Trinity House	
Belfast		Disused	Disused	✓
Cork		Disused	✓	✓
Dublin		Interrelated with guilds	✓	✓
Limerick		✓		✓
Londonderry			'Irish Society' of London	
Waterford				✓

[a] shown by ✓

Note: The Preston Guild is omitted as it was purely ceremonial.

Source: Municipal Commission (1835–39); Gross (1890); supplemented with local records.

many mercantile members'; it also had 14 provincial chamber members at the time. The Association's secretary thought of asking the Lord Mayor to establish a 'London Commercial Committee', 'to call a meeting to start it—I apprehend that we could get some hundred members in the City if the thing really took— there is no doubt that the want of something of the sort is much felt in London.'[83] This was never realistic but demonstrates the yawning gap that London was perceived to be in the chamber system. The late development in London arose from four challenges.

Meshing with other City interests

First, was the existing presence in London of many of the major national and international trading lobbies. As a result of their presence, most London chamber proposals suggested a chamber should have representatives from these bodies, as in 1823: 'to secure the permanent connexion of the chamber with the great commercial interests of the metropolis'.[84] The 1823–4 proposed chamber Board was to be made up of local MPs, and the serving chairs or governors of all the main London-based lobbies: the nine chartered companies (Bank of England, East India, London Assurance, etc.), as well as Trinity House, the six London dock companies, Lloyds, and the merchant societies for East India, West Indies, the Continent, North America, wine and spirits, and Ship Owners' Society. Although this proposal had significant support from the major merchants,[85] others opposed it. George Hibbert and Thomas Tooke felt that the chamber would be hostage to the protective 'exclusive interests' of the corporation, livery companies, and chartered companies.[86] They put a motion against the 1823–4 proposal, that it would 'be inexpedient to proceed further under any circumstances . . . which could not be useful or convenient, and might be mischievous'.[87] This tension and the lack of direct independent election from the membership remained critical flaws. Other chambers at the time would have struggled to see this structure as a valid partner (especially as most were campaigning vigorously against the monopolies of the chartered companies). The format of the 1823–4 proposals demonstrates both the special challenges of London and the blinkered view of many proponents. It was an attempt to link modern needs with past structures that contained so many contradictions it was doomed to fail.

A second challenge was the attitude of the City Corporation, which had often played a role as a direct voice and representational body, and had been

---

[83] George Woodyatt Hastings to Lord Brougham, 24 June 1856; HB/13051; UCL Special Collections. Further discussion of Brougham in Chapters 7 and 8.

[84] Report of committee on formation of a chamber of commerce, *Morning Chronicle*, 19 March 1823.

[85] 280 signed an 1823 petition that led to the chamber proposal: *Morning Chronicle,* 29 August 1823.

[86] Tooke was a major economic thinker of the 1820s, influential on Bank of England reform and reforming the Corn Laws. He correctly identified the deficiencies of the 1823–4 proposals.

[87] *Morning Chronicle*, 5 April 1824; also quoted in Musgrave (1913), appendix B; see also Hibbert in *Morning Chronicle*, 19 March 1824.

very independent and active, at times even a campaign body. During the 1770s and 1780s it was a leader in the Counties Association campaign for electoral reform.[88] It continued to be active, for example lobbying on the abolition of slavery, the freedom to import grain, and the Corn Laws in the 1820s. It was in many ways quite understandable, therefore, that many local business people felt that an additional local body was not needed. To try to solve this challenge the format of the 1867 proposal sought to bind in the City interests.

The 1867 proposal was made by Benjamin Scott, Lord Chamberlain of the City, and hence was one of the most serious efforts. It specifically sought to achieve a 'quasi amalgamation' of the City Corporation with the chamber concept by a membership structure with the mayor as president, five delegates from the Court of Aldermen, five delegates from the Court of Common Council (representing the City Corporation interests); ten merchants, ten brokers of shares and produce, ten warehousemen and wholesale dealers, five ship-owners and underwriters, five other insurance interests (fire, life, and guardian societies) (representing the business community); four representatives of the City in Parliament (ex officio); and other MPs trading in or commercially connected with mercantile, banking, or professional firms in the City (ex officio) which were estimated at 40. This gave a chamber council membership of 110 in all. To these could be added representatives of the 12 leading livery companies.[89] Scott went on to propose that the City Corporation made available space (at Gresham College) and provide for a small staff of a secretary and clerk.

Scott was particularly energized, as City Lord Chamberlain, by the need to revive City government, as well as offering a chamber voice. He saw the commitment to the City being eroded as a result of suburbanization: the leading merchants, brokers, and manufacturers now lived outside the City and were not, therefore, part of the City electorate: 'thus it happens that the conjoint action of merchant and municipal feelings and influences has, to a great extent, though not entirely ceased'. He also stated that earlier actions by the City to enforce membership of the livery at £40 (i.e. to become freemen) resulted 'not merely in estrangement, but even in antagonism'.[90] Many of these difficulties had been removed by the reforms of franchise in the City in 1835 and the reduction of registration fee for the livery to five shillings, but Scott argued it would still be difficult to attract active business people to act *both* for businesses' interests and for the municipal needs of the City Corporation. His proposed chamber attempted to provide a wider set of motives for commitment.

If achieved, Scott's proposal might have indeed been a powerful force in national politics. However, like the 1823–4 proposals, it was not a voluntary independently elected chamber, would have had difficulties working with the other chambers, and would have been unlikely to attract a wide membership, since they had no place in its governance. It was a different echo from the past, also doomed to failure.

---

[88] See e.g. Sutherland (1933, 1956); and earlier discussion in Chapter 4.
[89] Scott (1867b), p. 13.
[90] Scott (1867b), pp. 6–7.

Meshing with the other chambers

A third challenge for London's was how its chamber interrelated with the rest of the chambers. The City Corporation and the London interests that made the early attempts to found a chamber all seem to have had ambitions beyond establishing just a local chamber for London. They wanted it to embed the national trading organizations based in the capital, and to bolster a voluntary chamber by using the legal powers of the City. This became a particular focus of the 1870 and 1880 proposals that attempted to establish not just a chamber, but also a Court of Arbitration using the Corporation's powers. This introduced severe tensions: it suggested that London was trying to take over the whole chamber system, to found a national chamber somewhat on the lines of the former General Chamber. This would have been unacceptable to the other local chambers. This tension was to arise again in the 1890s and 1960s when London seemed to be attempting a takeover of the association. But most problematic, the London proposals collided with the government.

Meshing with government

The fourth challenge for London, which affected all the proposals of 1817, 1823–4, and 1867–72, was resistance from the national governments of the day. In each case it was this definitive critical resistance that killed the proposals, not local City interests. The 1817 proposal emanated from H. S. H. Woollaston, who had been in close contact with Frederick Robinson, who was vice-president, then president of the Board of Trade in 1812–23. Woollaston claimed that this proposal 'nearly succeeded', that the 'government was amicable to such an institution'. It had received support from Robinson, but the government was not going to initiate a chamber, or 'pledge itself on the subject; . . . it should stand or fall by its own respectability'.[91] Thomas Wilson MP believed that the proposal foundered 'principally for want of a sufficient number of respectable names to carry it on'.[92] However, as far as can be determined, the government was actually very resistant to this proposal. Commenting in 1819, it was stated that this was the *tenth* attempt to establish a chamber in London and that it had 'proceeded so far as to enter the names of members under the title of "The Equitable Trust Society" . . . [but] that it is not the kind of institution that is adapted to the temper and disposition of Englishmen—at least not in the metropolis'.[93] Further research is merited, but it appears that it was Henry Brougham that pressed for a London chamber in 1817; Robinson supported it, but then reneged.[94]

---

[91] H. S. H. Woollaston, referring to his earlier efforts, quoted in report on a 'metropolitan chamber of commerce', *Morning Chronicle*, 29 August 1823. It has not been possible to trace the early attempts.
[92] Quoted in *Morning Chronicle*, 19 March 1824.
[93] *The London Tradesman: A Familiar Treatise on the Rationale of Trade and Commerce* (1819) (London: Simpkin and Marshall), p. 322: Goldsmiths-Kress.
[94] Brougham's activities are covered in detail in Chapters 7 and 8.

The 1820s proposal was in many ways a follow-up to the 1817 effort, with Woollaston and John Smith still prime movers. It developed from a 'meeting of merchants, bankers, traders and others' on 1 May 1823, which had appointed a committee 'to consider the expediency of forming a chamber of commerce in the City of London'. This committee had emanated from an earlier meeting of 18 March 1823, which had been consulting with chambers in Glasgow, Dublin, Liverpool, Bristol, and Manchester over a successful lobby that had resulted in the Act on Merchant and Factors (1823).[95] Clearly the London merchants had seen the benefits of chambers elsewhere and were impressed. Brougham was probably again involved. The committee reported in August 1823, but unlike almost all other chambers it sought to found the chamber not just with local support, but also with government backing. It was argued 'the advantages to be derived from a chamber of commerce in the City of London, must greatly depend upon an unrestrained and cordial communication with the several branches of His Majesty's Government'.[96] Government support was also necessary because the chamber wanted a Royal Charter under which to operate 'so that your committee confidently hope that the same high and distinguished patronage will not be withheld'.[97]

But government support was not forthcoming. When the committee reported back in early April 1824 a letter was summarized by the chair of the committee (John Smith, MP) from the PM, the Earl of Liverpool, which terminated developments.[98] This letter informed them 'that strong objections are entertained by His Majesty's ministers to such an association being formed within the City'. As a result Smith seems to have lost interest and passed the chamber proposal to William Manning, MP. However, it was agreed 'to defer the consideration of the said report until it shall have been ascertained whether any . . . modifications of the project will obviate the inconvenience which it is apprehended might arise from such an institution in the metropolis distinguished from similar existing associations in several of the ports of the United Kingdom, some of which have received this special sanction of the Crown, and all of them enjoying the countenance of His Majesty's Government'.[99] The imperfections of local support, combined with the power of the government, and lack of powerful alternative support in parliament derailed any further development.

[95] Reported in *Morning Chronicle*, 19 March and 29 August 1823; for discussion of the lobby see Chapter 9.

[96] Motion passed by proposers of the 1823–4 chamber, *Morning Chronicle*, 5 April 1824.

[97] Report of the committee to develop a chamber, *Morning Chronicle*, 19 March 1824.

[98] This was a difficult period for Liverpool's government, with his cabinet fragile from 1822; support for chambers would have been contentious and peripheral to his main political objectives.

[99] *Morning Chronicle*, 5 April 1824. No trace of Lord Liverpool's letter has been found (e.g. in his outletters in the BL Add MS); Smith may have invented it but knew the government's opposition. He had been leading protagonist for the chamber. He was from a Nottingham banking family and reform minded. Manning was a West Indies merchant, who resisted downstream expansion of London Docks, and led resistance to Bank of England reforms. He was not a reformer likely to pressure the government; *DNB*; Thorne (1986), *History of Parliament*.

The government also succeeded in killing off the attempt of 1871–2. This followed Scott's 1867 efforts, but instead of his proposed structure, the City Corporation sought a tribunal of commerce to act as a chamber to resolve commercial disputes, discussed more fully in Chapter 7. Here, the critical aspect to note is that government managed to delay consideration by setting up a Queen's 'Indicative Commission' to consider the whole question of tribunals of commerce. This effectively sidetracked and stalled the national campaign for another 20 years. In the City, the Lord Mayor agreed to be appointed to the Commission and the Corporation took the advice of the government (via the Lord Chancellor) that 'it was not advisable to pass any measure' themselves until the Commission had reported. The Lord Mayor was leant on by government, and the plan for a London chamber collapsed as well as any support for tribunals.

The incorporation of a TPS in 1876, as the London and Provincial Chamber of Commerce, was one outcome of this debacle. There was no incumbent in London to defend the use of the chamber title, and the BoT agreed to grant it registration.[100] This chequered history of the London chamber is a tribute to the fear of the chamber's voice by successive governments that sought to suppress early chamber proposals. As long as London remained without a chamber the whole movement lacked important credibility, which offered advantage to government.

Bristol, Newcastle, and York: The Merchant Adventurers

Slow chamber development occurred in some other places because of the continuing role of the Merchant Adventurers. The Adventurers were a private company, not a state body, granted a Crown monopoly, originally covering specified finished goods, particularly cloth, generally for trade between England and the Low Counties. The company was based in London, and with three or four thousand members in total.[101] But other places became increasingly significant (as Marte Towns). The Adventurers were incorporated as separate societies in Bristol, Hull, Exeter, Norwich, Newcastle-upon-Tyne, York, Limerick, Belfast, and possibly in Kendal and Chester.[102] But by the time chambers were developed they were independently active in only four areas: Bristol, London, Newcastle-upon-Tyne, and York.[103]

---

[100] *Memorandum and Articles of London and Provincial Chamber of Commerce*, 11 February 1876. The Articles make no pretence to be a general chamber, covering only fraudulent dealings, debt collection, and lobbying for changes in commercial law: TNA BT 22/14/3.

[101] Gross (1890), p. 151.

[102] Gross (1890), pp. 151–2; Municipal Commission (1836) xxvii, pp. 348–9; xxviii, p. 698. Gross incorrectly states that the local companies were part of the London company. They were independent bodies and generally resisted London and the chartered companies (McGrath 1975).

[103] Municipal Commission (1835–9) xxiv, pp. 1761–2; iii, p. 1639; ii, pp. 1202–5; Surtees Society (1895, 1899).

Bristol

Bristol was the most significant. For a critical period the Bristol Society of Merchant Venturers acted like a chamber, lobbying nationally as it had done before the chamber concept came on the scene.[104] This activity continued in cooperation with other chambers from the 1770s, mainly with Liverpool over 1774–94,[105] but also Manchester and Glasgow.[106] It had 100–20 members over 1750–1830, and took an active political lead in electing many prominent or sympathetic politicians as honorary members; e.g. William Meredith, George Saville, Earl of Sandwich, Lord Sheffield.[107] The Venturers were also quite deeply embedded in local municipal government, including the local dock company, which they had helped to promote. Since the Venturers already comprised most of the major merchant interests of the day it is not surprising that Bristol is anomalous in having a relatively late chamber foundation in 1823, despite its population size and major role as a port.

However, once the Venturers became involved in the harbour scheme, chiefly after the 1780s, this dominated their minutes, with much less lobby activity and an unpredictability of views. As a result it was quite common to find petitions from Bristol coming from the 'merchants, principal traders and inhabitants', or from the mayor, rather than the Venturers. During the 1785 Irish Proposals lobby, Bristol sent three petitions: from the 'merchants, traders and inhabitants,' the Venturers, and from the sugar bakers. When the sugar bakers' petition was presented at parliament by Henry Cruger MP, he presented it as the position of 'the chamber of commerce at Bristol (and from the sugar bakers)'.[108] This record in one sense is typical of this period, in which many local commercial committees termed themselves 'chambers' or became delegates to the General Chamber.[109] But it is also indicative of the tensions that were emerging in Bristol, where the Venturers were no longer locally perceived as acting with a broad enough voice.

The tensions in Bristol were to surface much more vehemently in the 1820s. The chamber was founded initially as a campaigning body protesting against the dock company, particularly its high rate of harbour dues and inefficiencies. Whilst the unreformed corporation was the main target for this, the Venturers were also implicated, as it was claimed that the Venturers were granting relief from dues, which should have only applied to their members.[110] The early Bristol 'floating

---

[104] See Chapter 9, and Latimer (1903); McGrath (1975); Minchinton (1971); Morgan (1993).
[105] Bennett (2010) gives the full correspondence between the two bodies.
[106] Bristol RO: outletters to Glasgow: to Patrick Colquhoun, 31 May 1780 (SMV/2/1/2/3); Gilbert Hamilton, 12 April 1783 (SMV/2/4/1/2); reply to Gilbert Slater, Liverpool chamber, in response to his request from Manchester chamber, 7 December 1779 (SMV/2/4/1/1); Bristol RO.
[107] Elected, respectively in 1766, 1766, 1777, and 1790: Bristol RO: SMV/10/1/2/1.
[108] Briefing to Pitt, *The Opposition to the Irish Arrangements Traced*: PRO 30/8/321, fo. 196A; parentheses in original; nothing further seems to have developed from this 'chamber'.
[109] See Chapter 9.
[110] Letter from Robert Brush, master of Venturers: Bristol RO: Red Lodge papers 13748/5 (Bundle 4: fo. 7).

harbour', promoted by the Venturers from the 1770s, was completed in 1809. It closed the river to create a wet dock at low tide. This had been a source of strong local divisions of business opinion from the outset: the existing shippers on the river now had to pay dues for river frontage they had previously enjoyed free. The dues had to be set at a high level to recover the considerable costs. No dividend was paid to investors until 1823, but from that date the pressure built up to reduce the dues. The Venturers held eight of the 27 places as directors in the dock company, but the dues were mainly paid to the corporation. The dock company had been slow to respond to the increasing uproar, and the chamber, eventually with support from the Venturers, was founded mainly to take up this cause. The pressure began with petitions in 1822 to return revenues from the corporation to the freemen (which included most chamber members): 'that the property and the benefit of all the revenues of the corporation belong to your petitioners and their fellow burgesses for whom the common council are trustees call for investigation'.[111] A flurry of letters between the early chamber, the Venturers, mayor, and common council in 1822–4 led to no concessions: 'this corporation will not yield'.[112] Bills were presented to parliament; pamphlets by 'a disciple of Adam Smith' listed principles for setting dock fees, and some reduction was achieved in 1825. At this time it was claimed that the dues were at least 50% above those of London, Hull, and Liverpool.[113]

The battle between the corporation and the chamber was extended over many years, was typical of other port cities seeking improvements in the face of corporation opposition,[114] and was vitriolic. The Municipal Commission in 1835 recognized 'the chamber in collision with the corporate bodies of the city'.[115] A poem of *c.*1822 summarizes the council's position:[116]

A CHAMBER? Yes, A CHAMBER!

A Chamber of Commerce, presided by S—k,
To control the Comptroller, and open the Dock:
The fees of the Corporate Body to stint,
Whose gripe is as close as the closest to flint:
To silence all brawlers, who brawl for their dues,
Quay-wardens and Bailiffs—all water rat crews:
This Chamber has met its Directors to name,
When all are desirous that honour to claim. . . .
Forty Directors! By twenty too much . . .

---

[111] Petitions of burghers and resident merchants and traders of Bristol to House of Commons: Bristol RO: Red Lodge papers 13748/5 (Bundle 4: fos. 1 and 2).

[112] Common council memorial, 1 November 1823; full correspondence with the chamber chair, Thomas Stock, is preserved in Bristol RO: Red Lodge papers 13748/5 (Bundle 4: fos. 1–17).

[113] As claimed by 'A Burgess' (1833–6); see Bristol chamber history.

[114] See e.g. Innes (1998, 2003); Innes and Rogers (2000); Sweet (2002, 2003).

[115] Municipal Commission (1835), xxiv, p. 1208; it shied away from the detail and sought to extract what it needed from reports using sworn statements 'to gather . . . a collected narrative'.

[116] Printed paper, 'Miller Lines', signed 'For Tumblewayte and Co.—J. T.'; Bristol RO: Red Lodge papers 13748/5 (Bundle 8); it refers to Thomas Stock, president of the chamber. It is interesting also for its recognition of Glasgow as the other leading chamber at the time, with Liverpool in abeyance.

These jumbled together would make a hotch-potch,
Equal to any, so fam'd with the Scotch,
And Bristol may possibly rival Glasgow,
Tho' Liverpool long since has given it—the go.
Such a chamber as this will all Chambers surpass,
If its roof be of iron—its supporters are BRASS.

It appears that the corporation went on to try to subvert the chamber. The minutes for 1828–33 do not survive or never existed, although a combined annual report for 1833–4 claims the lobby against port dues was pursued.[117] However, reports by 'A. Burgess', which were reprinted from the *Bristol Mercury* of 1836, claimed that a group of leading members of the chamber had become suspect: the 'complainants have now become directors of the chamber' and had failed to press their views.[118] In the view of 'A Burgess', the chamber had been subverted to support the Port and corporation by various personal inducements. The chamber's position was split between the 'liberal' campaigners, those who supported the closed corporation, and those who were 'timid with dislike' of 'the nature of the mouvement' against the corporation and Venturers.[119]

Some reductions in dues were achieved in 1836,[120] but the final success of the chamber's campaign was not achieved until an 1848 Act. This passed responsibility for the docks to the reformed city corporation, removed the Venturers, and led to a steep reduction in dues. The chamber's campaign was in some ways an extension of the Free Trade Movement, and followed tactics similar to the Anti-Corn Law League. A primary force in the later reforms was the Free Port Association, formed in September 1846. The chamber effectively merged into this association for the next two years, with Leonard Bruton, the reputed author of the 'A. Burgess' letters of 1833–6, becoming the association's secretary. The chamber fell into difficulties once the 1848 Act was achieved, and was only revived when Bruton became chamber secretary in 1853.[121] The tension over dues continued, however, with reversion to heavy dues in 1856, only modified in 1863.[122]

The Bristol case is, therefore, complex. The Venturers were acting as a major lobby before chambers began, and cooperated with them in the 1770s and 1780s. The Venturers then became preoccupied with the local docks and their need to support benevolent expenditures. Some alternative activity to establish a chamber in 1785 was short-lived. When a chamber was founded in 1822–3, after early resistance, the Venturers became strongly involved in the chamber campaign over

---

[117] Bristol chamber, *Annual Reports* (1833, 1834).

[118] *Strictures on the Later Reports and Proceedings of the Bristol Chamber of Commerce*, A. Burgess (BL 8247.a.38); reputedly authored by Leonard Bruton; see also J. M. Gutch (1823), *Letters on the Impediments which Obstruct the Trade and Commerce of the City and Port of Bristol: from Felix Farley's Bristol Journal*, 'Cosmo': Goldsmiths-Kress.

[119] John Barnett Kington (1834), *Thirty Letters on the Trade of Bristol* (Bristol: John Wright), p. 17: Goldsmiths-Kress; spelling as original.

[120] Bristol chamber, *Annual Report* (1836), pp. 3–5.

[121] Little (1954); Wells (1909), pp. 79–101.

[122] See Latimer (1903), pp. 239–42; Wells (1909), pp. 58–66; Little (1954), p. 257.

the docks, against the corporation. Once the chamber was on a firm footing in the 1850s, the Venturers became chiefly a benevolent body. The Venturers master and wardens became ex-officio honorary members of the chamber, together with the mayor, MPs, and chair of the Bristol Docks Company. The financial relationship from at least 1859 was mainly in the form of a donation by the chamber to the Venturers, which seems to be recognition of their charitable role: £100 per year in most years, £50 in 1900–14, but back to £100 in 1920. The payments ceased by 1930.

Newcastle

In Newcastle there is evidence of a succession from the Society of Merchant Adventurers to the chamber in terms of voice role, although this is not commented on in the official history of the chamber. The Adventurers were active and still recruiting members up to at least 1875, and committees were active until at least 1834, but they made no lobbies after the chamber was founded in 1815. Their main meeting room and court was held in the Exchange, which also housed the Town Clerk's office, and was used by the chamber. Initially there were overlapping subscriptions between the chamber and the Adventurers, and some overlap of key individuals.[123] As the chamber developed the Adventurers shifted to become solely a benevolent body, and occasional references in chamber minutes to the Court Room suggest the chamber also sought to take over the residual regulatory role of the Adventurers until this was removed by the reforms of 1835.

York

In York the evidence suggests the Adventurers were resistant to a chamber. The city was late to develop a chamber (1896), and this was probably due to the semi-active role that the Adventurers played in some lobbying.[124] However, York was a town in economic eclipse from the 18th century, seen as backward in innovation where the West Riding was forward.[125] Hence, it was not a prime target for chamber development, about 43rd in population rank-size in 1890. However, a committee of the Adventurers was formed in 1895 to consider the formation of a chamber. They solicited a compendium of other chamber statements of objectives to see if they could develop the model. Whilst there was concern that 'the corporate integrity of the ancient Company of Merchant Adventurers must be strictly guarded and preserved', it was clear that a chamber might be useful for lobbying: 'there is evidently a strong feeling among the existing chambers in favour of strengthening by the further increase of such institutions the influence of the manufacturing, commercial and trading classes on legislation affecting their own

[123] See Chapter 11.
[124] Surtees Society (1918).
[125] See e.g. Sigsworth (1958).

interests'.[126] Nevertheless the chamber 'was originally composed of, and founded by, the members of the Company of Merchant Adventurers' and was opened to all only one year later, on 1 January 1896.[127]

In fact the role of the Merchant Adventurers continued unchanged in York. The rules of the chamber stated that the Adventurers 'are affiliated with the Associated Chambers of Commerce, being the chamber of commerce for the said city'. So that it was members of the Company who were the chamber of commerce members, with 'persons other than members of the Company' allowed to participate, as 'associates'. In 1899 it was reported that the Adventurers had 116 members and the associates had increased to 82, from 62 in 1896. In 1900, the earliest year separately to list associate and Adventurer members, there were 71 associates and 36 Adventurers. Initially only associates paid a subscription. However, between 1901 and 1909 a half-guinea subscription was introduced for members of the Adventurers as well. By 1910 the accounts show payments for only 61 members at 10s. 6d. and four associates at a guinea. By 1912 there were only three associates paying the full subscription.[128]

Clearly there were tensions in the relationship leading to a shift in support. In the early days the associates grew in size but began to leave as a result of their secondary status at double the cost. The annual income fell from £78 to £27 between 1900 and 1912 (excluding balances). This situation was unsustainable against annual expenditure of £37. It is at this point that the records of the chamber at the Adventurers cease and the chamber was established independently. There was also tension with the ACC, which was unhappy with the closed membership.[129] It appears that the Adventurers thought they could run a chamber as a sort of subsidiary operation, but their continued role limited the chamber's independence of action, undermined support from ACC, and the commitment of both groups of members was undermined by jealousy of each other.

The Merchant Staplers

These derived from the granting by the Crown of a monopoly to export the 'staple' wares of the realm: principally wool, but also leather, tin, and lead. The staple towns were those where the wares were sold or from which they were exported. Some staple towns were abroad (e.g. Bruges, Calais, Antwerp, Saint-Omer, and Middleburgh). The main home staple towns in later years were Newcastle, York, Hull, Norwich, Great Yarmouth, London, Southampton, Exeter, Dublin, Limerick, and Cork.[130]

---

[126] Letter from Joseph Wilkinson, secretary of Merchant Adventurers, 25 March 1895, in Minute book (York, Merchant Adventurers Company Archives).

[127] York Chamber, *Annual Report* (1896).

[128] York Chamber, *Annual Reports* (1897), p. 13; (1913), pp. 5–6; (1899), p. 10; (1901), p. 7; (1910), pp. 5–6.

[129] Merchant Adventurers, letters to ACC, 9 and 24 April 1895; reply from ACC 10 April 1895 (York, Merchant Adventurers Company Archives); no entry in ACC minutes.

[130] Gross (1890), pp. 140–3.

The staple towns developed a tradition of commercial leadership and self-regulation which may have stimulated early chambers. They were places of warehousing, where wares were weighed and sealed by the mayor of the staple, and regulated by the law of the staple, or law-merchant. The mayor and officers of the staple were elected by the body of merchants and were distinct from the mayor and officers of the town, and often undertook some functions that were normally the preserve of the town, e.g. keeping the peace, and the power of arrest for trespass, debt, or breach of contract. They were functionaries of the Crown, though as time progressed mayors of the town tended to act ex officio as mayor of the staple. In Ireland, the retiring mayors and bailiffs of the town were frequently appointed as the mayor and constables of the staple. In Britain the staplers were mainly a national body, but in Ireland each staple town was separately incorporated.[131]

Grants of charter in the Stuart era made many of these bodies primarily part of the control of the electoral franchise and any economic function disappeared; e.g. in Belfast[132] and to a lesser extent Limerick. As a result the staplers remained of significance in only three places by the 1780s, in each of which they resisted chambers; elsewhere they had fallen into disuse. The most important case is that of London, discussed separately above, where they seemed to have urged the corporation and government to resist a local chamber. In Dublin the staplers had become part of the guilds, and were also resistant to establishing a chamber, as discussed later below.

In the third case, Limerick, the staplers show an interesting dynamic. The chamber founded in 1807 was very active and took over many of the functions of the staplers and guilds, as well as some corporation functions such as organizing markets, quality inspection, and harbour management. In effect it took over the staplers' role who theoretically had a monopoly of exporting local goods under their 1609 charter. The staplers now never met, but in 1824, when forced by the Lord Lieutenant of Ireland to name their members (who numbered 32), it became clear that their sole purpose was electoral control, to send delegates to the common council of the city.[133] However, the publicity in 1824 led to some discussion as to whether they should seek to take back the rights to hold the butter and linen market, and other trading activities that had been developed by the chamber. The chamber minutes record some attempt to revive the staplers and exercise their charter, thus taking back functions from the chamber.[134] No effort was made, however, but an echo of this clash of formal expectations is given in the Municipal Commission Report of 1835. The commission recognized that the chamber was managing markets, but felt that 'the purposes of practical utility to which such a body [the staplers] might, from its title, be supposed properly to

[131] Gross (1890), pp. 143–6.
[132] Municipal Commission (1835), xxviii, p. 698.
[133] Municipal Commission, Ireland (1835), xxvi, p. 348.
[134] O'Connor (1938), p. 21; Lenihan (1866), *Limerick its History and Antiquities* (Dublin), p. 462.

be directed' should have been doing this.[135] As elsewhere, where the Commission found chambers active, it felt some 'formal' body would have been preferable.

The guilds merchant

The guild merchant was still active in several locations when chambers came on the scene. It was historically distinct from the borough corporation, but in many cases the two had amalgamated. Indeed, in many major towns the loss of the guild merchant can be seen as either an act of negligence by the corporation or may well have been a deliberate suppression of a rival body which was independent of the landed interest and was more concerned with 'vulgar' commerce and manufacture than the beauty of the environment and its 'politeness', as evident in Dublin.[136]

In the 1830s there were about 27 guilds merchant, hanse, or common guild assemblies in England, about 30 in Ireland, and over 60 in Scotland, that were in varying degrees active. Those that are chiefly relevant in the larger and medium-sized towns and ports, shown in Table 5.1, numbered about 18. After the Municipal Reform Act 1835 in England and Ireland they ceased to be relevant, but the Scottish 1846 Reform Act had little effect in the larger towns and it was not until 1888 that the guildery was abolished. In the discussion here it is important to be clear that we are dealing with the general guild assemblies, not individual craft guilds. Though Langford states that the guilds were in serious decline,[137] they had influence in a few places.

Dublin

The Dublin position is perhaps the most illuminative of the tensions. Here the guild merchant performed an important role to support trade, in opposition to the corporation. The merchants of Dublin, writing in 1768, had 'long experience of the utter inattention of corporate bodies to the interests of trade . . . and the generality of them [are] entirely taken up in contests for little distinctions or pre-eminence among themselves'.[138] A committee of merchants was formed for the purpose of erecting an Exchange building in 1761.[139] It overcame corporation resistance by gaining its own Irish parliamentary Act for the Exchange in 1765. However, the corporation tried to reassert its position by challenging the legal status of the committee; in 1786 it petitioned the Irish House of Commons to vest the Exchange in a body composed of the Wide Street Commission,[140] Aldermen, and

---

[135] Municipal Commission, Ireland (1835), xxv, p. 349.

[136] See e.g. Cullen (1983), pp. 42–4.

[137] Langford (1989).

[138] *The Case of the Merchants of Dublin*, 1768; quoted in Cullen (1983), p. 35; the statement was apparently written by Travers Hartley, q.v. later below.

[139] See later in this chapter.

[140] The Wide Street Commission, established by the Irish Parliament, had the aim of improving the environment of the city—its 'politeness'. It had no concern with commerce and consisted of the mayor and 20 landed gentry, none resident in Dublin, and mostly not in Ireland.

only one-third from the committee of merchants. The merchants' view of this was that the corporation 'wanted... the fruits of the merchants own labours'. The merchants counter-petitioned, promoting a Bill at the bar of the Westminster House of Commons using a London agent,[141] noting that 'the merchants never received the least assistance from the corporation... nor propose to lay out and expend money for carrying out and completing the work'. A parliamentary committee eventually upheld the merchants' view, but concluded 'that the ground should be vested in a body corporate, that the said body should not be the municipal corporation, but the guild of merchants', recommending a committee of 16 merchants, plus the mayor, city sheriffs, the two MPs, and the master of the guild of merchants.[142] Since the merchants' committee was not itself a chartered body in which land or property could vest, the use of the guild merchant was a device to circumvent the corporation.[143]

Wider Irish experiences

Probably the most significant contribution of the Irish guilds merchant to the chambers was supporting local trading activity. Most of the trades had come under local corporations despite their historic position under the guilds. The trades were often neglected by the corporations, or their administration corrupt. In Dublin the butter-tasters and weigh-masters traded also on their own account with resulting major conflicts of interest. Even by 1820, the main stimulus to re-establishing the Dublin chamber was the 'various abuses which had become rooted, the absence of regulations and responsibility, the inefficient performance of work and the range and arbitrary charges' of the personnel managing the porters, butter crane, coal meters, Customs House store, etc.[144] In 1823 a chamber member, Mr Brophy, took independent legal action against the Guilds and won; the chamber voted him £1000 towards his expenses.[145] In Waterford and Limerick the Guilds Merchant managed to persuade or force the corporation to pass responsibility for the butter market to the chamber. In Limerick this was achieved a year after the chamber's foundation of 1805, when there was effectively a takeover of the old guild merchant by the chamber in 1806.[146] Support from Belfast and Waterford chambers was also sought for protecting home butter from imports, and in 1820 Limerick instituted five levels of quality for butter, with a chamber quality mark for each level. Trade

[141] This was paid for by a very active financial campaign through 14 lotteries 1766–79, raising a profit of £49,441: Cullen (1983), pp. 35–40.
[142] This account is drawn from Prendeville (1930), pp. 50–9; Cullen (1983), pp. 38–41; see *Irish House of Commons Journal*, vi, p. 68; viii, p. 221 and appendix C.1; ix, p. 114 (1796 edition).
[143] The significance and status of bodies corporate is discussed further in Chapter 7. The Dublin guild was not an active body, except during elections; Municipal Commission, Ireland (1836), xxiv, pp. 269–72.
[144] Dublin chamber, *Report of Council* (1821), p. 7.
[145] Dublin chamber, *Report of Council* (1823), *Annual Report* and accounts, pp. 3–4.
[146] Municipal Commission, Ireland (1835), vol. iii, p. 349; this notes that the chamber was to a great degree composed of the same members as the guild of merchants.

greatly increased and the chamber had a major impact on agricultural development of the area, which was even conceded by the Municipal Commission.[147]

The Dublin, Waterford, and Limerick chambers also gained control of port management at various times during the 1780s and early 1800s. The Belfast chamber was not so fortunate; on several occasions in the 1790s they tried to gain some control of Custom House fees, and withheld quayage fees until harbour works were undertaken, but this was slow. They had more impact on the access canals and lighterage.[148]

Londonderry

In Londonderry there was a special case, with the local corporation being appointed by the City Corporation of London: the so-called 'Irish Society' of London, which derived from a charter of 1662 that constituted 26 citizens of London into a 'plantation society'. Most were absentee and never visited. The foundation of the chamber in 1790 may have reflected efforts by the Irish Society to exert stronger control, particularly with improved administration of rents and other privileges under its new secretary Robert Slade.[149] But this was also a time of great ferment in Ireland, with attacks by cottagers on their landlords in Donegal, and continuing rural unrest into the 1830s. In Londonderry there were concerns about the proposed construction of a new bridge over the River Loughfoyle, which was resisted by some key landed interests in the Irish parliament.[150] It also required a lease for tolls with consequent effects on ferries. This was essential for economic development but was a key aspect of contested elections for the parliament. There was also a continuing controversy over Lady Hamilton's unpaid dues for her fishing rights that dated back to 1788, which were being infringed.[151] But the chief concern of the chamber appears to have been over the way rights were deployed and the electoral franchise exercised, which was high-handed and ignored local business views, leaving control in the hands of two main families, the Hills and Alexanders.[152] The Municipal Commission in 1837 dubbed the Society anomalous and inordinately expensive, granting leases through patronage that were far too long, with too many absentee landlords who neglected their properties.[153]

The history of the early chamber in Londonderry is obscure, with only three records surviving before the foundation of the modern chamber in 1885.[154] The

---

[147] Municipal Commission, Ireland (1935), vol. iii; see also O'Connor (1938), pp. 27–33.

[148] Quayage: Belfast minutes 20 February and 3 March 1792; Custom House fees; inquiry set up 1791–4, revived 1802.

[149] See Curl (2000). For example, the warrants and receipts of the Society were missing 1787–90: Irish Society rough minutes, 10 August 1790; LMA: CLA/049/AD/03/01/008.

[150] e.g. Lord Abercorn and his followers: Murphy (1981), p. 3.

[151] Irish Society rough minutes 16 and 24 April 1790; 26 May 1790; 7 December 1790; LMA: CLA/049/AD/03/01/008. Lady Hamilton remained a concern until she agreed to assign her fishery rights in 1797, but legal actions continued into the 1820s: Irish Society (1842).

[152] Murphy (1981), chapter 1.

[153] Municipal Commission, Ireland (1837), xxvi, pp. 16 and 191–3; see also Murphy (1981).

[154] Unfortunately no record of the chamber occurs in the Irish Society; a letter from Londonderry to Dublin chamber, Council minutes, 1826, on duty of goods from England, may be from the chamber but is not explicit (LMA Archives 1064/3/1).

first chamber was founded in July 1790 'to promote the interests of trade . . . by the union of commercial knowledge',[155] with early actions calling for the simplification of Customs duties.[156] However, two of the three surviving records relate to concerns of the chamber with the local charter, which suggests that the Irish Society structure was a major cause of difficulty. In 1793 the chamber asserted 'the right of the citizens of Derry to enquire into their privileges' which resulted in the chamber deeming 'it their duty to provide an authentic copy of the charter . . . [to] strengthen that harmony, which so long prevailed in this city . . . [acting from] purity of motives and rectitude of their conduct'.[157] Again in July 1830 the chamber obtained a legal opinion on the charter, mainly because of disputes over a mayoral election.[158]

These records of the chamber's concerns reflect particular periods of higher tension, but there were also major tensions in 1815 with the high costs of rebuilding of the bridge which led to a reprinting and analysis of the charter, and in 1819 there was a citizens' address which involved at least one known chamber member.[159] After 1816 the City of London waged a campaign to take greater managerial control. This began with a motion to require the Irish Society to submit annual accounts to the City. The City prevailed, but only in 1825.[160] It is important to note that the Londonderry chamber did not reflect leading radical or Catholic sympathies, although there were some members of the more extreme Presbyterians.[161] Their principal concern seems to have been to reform the franchise; it was thus a predominantly loyalist body, as far as can be determined.

England and Scotland

In England, the Guilds Merchant were generally less relevant, as they had ceased to exist in the main centres. But in Scotland, the general guilds, or guildery, remained significant in Dundee. The guildery championed harbour improvements in 1814–15 forcing the town council to promote a private harbour Bill after years of criticism of its inactivity. This was initially opposed by the main business merchants, manufacturers, and ship-owners because the revenue would be applied to municipal as well as harbour purposes. A group within the guildery pressed for compromise, and the Act of 1815 placed the harbour under independent commissioners for 21 years. The commission had one-quarter of its members from the

---

[155] Londonderry chamber (1793), *Translation of the Charter Granted by King Charles II to the Mayor and Citizens of London-Derry*, published by the London-Derry chamber of commerce (ESTC T193966; reel 13715, fo. 23), p. 10.

[156] Printed resolution by Londonderry chamber in favour of the simplification of Customs duties, 6 November 1790, p. 10; PRONI D562/15425.

[157] Londonderry chamber (1793), *Translation of the Charter . . .* , p. 10.

[158] Londonderry chamber (1830), *Case Relative to the Elective Franchise in Londonderry, with the Opinion of Mr. Harrison, Taken on Behalf of the Chamber of Commerce*, BL: 8139.df.35/1(1.).

[159] William McClintock; listed among eight citizens in address of 7 September 1819; Irish Society (1842).

[160] Irish Society (1842), p, 143.

[161] Members are listed in the 1790 and 1793 documents.

guildery. This stimulated a case against the corporation to recover previously lost guildery rights that led to it having to frame a new corporation constitution in 1817. The existing provost, Alexander Riddoch, was ousted and replaced by Patrick Anderson, the dean of the guild. Riddoch was a phenomenon of the placement and control of Scottish burghs, holding or managing the post of provost since 1788, and was seen as the prime cause of lethargy and inefficiency. Anderson encouraged a chamber foundation, though the leadership came from an independent flax merchant and manufacturer Edward Baxter. Several of the leading chamber members were individuals who had served on the corporation but had not been favoured by Riddoch (e.g. Alexander Balfour and Thomas Bell).[162] The Forfarshire chamber founded in 1819 thus received support for the guildery against the corporation, as in Dublin, but a new model was favoured as a general voice. As Gross noted, 'the guilds [merchant] were being superseded by the stimulating measures of chambers of commerce'.[163]

Companies of Merchants

These were also fairly widespread when chambers emerged in Scotland and Ireland (Table 5.1), where they played significant roles. They were a successor body to the guild merchant in some places, although Gross argues that 'there seems to be no genetic between the two'.[164] They had similar powers: regulating trade (particularly watching over encroachment by retailing), checking weights and measures, prosecuting cases concerning trade infringement, and might engage in 'common town bargains' as in Dublin where officials purchased and distributed cargoes landed at the port.[165]

Chamber records show active merchant companies (often termed 'committees') in the 1780s in Edinburgh, Glasgow, Greenock, Leith, Exeter, and in Ireland, at Dublin, Cork, Waterford, Limerick and Belfast, with some overlap with the guilds merchant (see Table 5.1).[166] In Dublin, the staplers were related to the company of merchants, since a stapler had to have been for two years a merchant, but these were probably mainly or exclusively the wealthier merchants.

Scotland

The Edinburgh merchant company is probably fairly typical of the more major of the merchant companies. Its charter stated its aims as 'promotion of foreign trade and reducing abuses of trade for merchants, importers, or sellers'.[167] Merchant

---

[162] This account is derived from Terrell (2006), Dundee chamber history.
[163] Gross (1890), p. 164.
[164] Gross (1890), p. 129.
[165] Gross (1890), pp. 134–7. Town bargains not involving a merchants' company also occurred in Liverpool, Plymouth, Waterford, Kilkenny, Neath, Kenfig, and Thurso.
[166] Chamber records for each of these cities and cross-references; see also Manchester and Birmingham cross-references; Redford (1934); Wright (1913); Cullen (1983), p. 5.
[167] Edinburgh charter, 19 October 1681; quoted in Heron (1903), pp. 383–51.

companies were also benefit societies for members and their widows and orphans, and hospitals and schools.[168] A few of the Companies were also active lobbyists. The Edinburgh Merchants Company lobbied for promotion of bridges, development of hospitals, and later on railways and docks, establishment of schools; it lobbied against the Corn Law, income tax, banking law, and malt tax.[169] It was a major force for the repeal of the Corn Laws in 1846, and lobbied against agriculturists on many occasion. It was generally more active than the Edinburgh chamber at the time, which was reprimanded by the Glasgow chamber.[170] Similarly in Glasgow, the merchant company was an active lobbyist (for example resisting the extension of the Corn Laws in 1777).[171]

Elsewhere in Scotland, the merchant company at Leith, founded in 1593, held power under authority of the Edinburgh corporation. It was essentially a benevolent body for seamen with an income of £707 in 1833.[172] It had little if any involvement in voice. In Dundee the main concern of the merchants committee was with the Exchange, and no lobby seems to have taken place. The merchants house at Greenock, however, was clearly acting like a chamber of commerce in respect of representation and memorials in the 1790s, consulting with the Glasgow chamber on actions of the Commissioners of the Customs with respect to the loading of certain goods, and the two organizations cooperated to prepare memorials. There was further cooperation on Corn Law Reform.[173] The Greenock chamber formally succeeded the merchant committee in 1813.

Ireland

The Dublin committee of merchants established in 1761 was a significant force. It had its origin in grievances about the corporation's costs, aversion to taking account of trading interest, and interference in trade. As noted above, the committee was vigorous in organizing opposition to the corporation using the guild merchant via sympathetic members and supporters. The committee was also the leader in a further conflict with the Irish landed interest in 1774. The Revenue Commissioners, under the influence of the Lord Lieutenant of Ireland and the landed MPs, proposed the re-siting of the Custom House further down the River Liffey. This was seen as an attack on the merchants, undermining the close link of central Dublin and its businessmen. It was particularly inflammatory because the removal of the current Custom House was seen as a pretext so that a new bridge could be built across the river primarily for the convenience of the gentry to get to their properties. Indeed, the inadequate size and run-down nature of the Custom House was viewed as indolent neglect and a conspiracy by the landed interest to force the

[168] Municipal Commission (1836), xxix, pp. 320–1.
[169] Heron (1903), chapter 11.
[170] See Chapter 10.
[171] W. H. Hill (1866), *A View of the Merchant House of Glasgow* (Glasgow: Bell and Bain).
[172] Municipal Commission, (1836), xxiii, pp. 217–18.
[173] See e.g. Glasgow chamber minutes, 10 September 1790, p. 75; 31 December 1790, p. 85.

move. The Dublin committee favoured rebuilding on an adjacent site. It lobbied the Irish parliament vigorously and assembled a petition from other merchant committees in London, Bristol, Liverpool, Great Yarmouth, Chester, Haverford-west, Glasgow, Whitehaven, and Leicester (which incidentally gives the only evidence of the existence of some of these committees). They also contacted committees in Cork and Belfast.[174] However, the parliament, having set up a committee, finally agreed the Revenue Commissioners' proposal and a new bridge was built lower down the river (now O'Connell Bridge).[175] The merchants had to accept this conclusion, but had succeeded in holding back development for ten years.

These events, combined with the establishment of the new Irish Parliament in 1782, led the committee to consider establishing a more formal chamber: 'every consideration appearing to demand a general union among traders and a constant unwearied attention to their common interest'.[176] The first chamber chairman, Travers Hartley was the key committee member in the campaigns over 1768–90. He was MP in the first Irish parliament 1783–90, a radical who became very significant in the campaign against Pitt's Irish proposals in 1785–6.[177] The Dublin chamber from 1783 had some differences from the committee of merchants; most critically it had open membership, whereas the committee was a purely self-appointing group. There was thus a search for a broader legitimacy. Once the Dublin chamber was formed the committee merged into it.

Dublin also had the Ouzel Galley Society established in 1705 as a form of tribunal of commerce, to arbitrate disputes between merchants. This was unusual in being established as a permanent private tribunal, with a membership restricted to 40. It was also a dining club at least in the 1760–99 period and passed resolutions on free trade, and on a free parliament in 1782. After the chamber became established it tended to lose its significance, arbitration hearings tailed off after 1824, and meetings became infrequent; the society was wound up in 1888.[178] However, during some years, when the Dublin chamber was either dormant or divided, the Ouzel Galley acted as a general voice and was liaising with other chambers on an equal footing in the 1790s and 1812–20.[179] Hence, like the Edinburgh merchant company, it provided a fallback when the early chamber experienced difficulties.

Elsewhere in Ireland, there was also an active merchant committee in Waterford in the 1780s which lobbied on the salt tax, postal service, Corn Laws, and the

---

[174] Dublin merchants committee minutes; quoted in Prendeville (1930), pp. 61–7; Cullen (1983), pp. 41–4.

[175] Prendeville (1930); Cullen (1983); see *Irish House of Commons Journal*, vi, p. 86; ix, pp. 102–3; appendix CCCIII.

[176] Proposal to develop the Dublin Chamber 1783; see Cullen (1983), p. 43.

[177] See Chapter 9; brief political biographical details in Cullen (1983), pp. 35–57; Prendeville (1930).

[178] G. A. Little (1953), *The Ouzel Galley* (Dublin: Cahill); Cullen (1983), pp. 25–30; Prendeville (1930).

[179] See Belfast and Glasgow chamber minutes, which demonstrate frequent liaison with the Ouzel Society.

electoral franchise. It had particularly strong support from its chair (John Newport), who was also Chancellor of the Exchequer.[180] Waterford chamber seems to have evolved directly from this committee of merchants. The chamber president was authorized to write as the 'committee of merchants' in April 1787 only three weeks after the chamber's foundation.[181] There is no further record of the committee after that date. In Limerick the merchant company erected the 'Commercial Rooms' in 1805 by subscription of 100 shares at £65 per share (£6500), and occupied part of the building until 1833 when it became the Town Hall.

Cork

However, in Cork, defects in the committee of merchants formed in 1769 were a source of anger stimulating chamber development, although this has not been previously noted. The committee had become controlled by a small group who overlapped with the city aldermen and other officials, and was predominantly Protestant. The Cork merchants may have initially been alerted by correspondence received from the Waterford chamber for support for various lobbies, which appear to have been largely unanswered by the Cork committee. Indeed the committee refused to collaborate with the Waterford chamber on a lobby for a tax on foreign butter and cattle imports as the 'subject is more a political than a commercial one'. The committee also appeared inactive over convoying.[182] But the immediate cause of anger in Cork was excessive expenditure and inefficiency in the weighhouse.

The Cork weighhouse was managed by the committee, but was in disrepair in 1813. A fund was established for rebuilding it, calling for contributions from the corn and butter merchants and the committee. Work had begun in March 1814 but became a protracted business involving relocation of the weighhouse during rebuilding, and was delayed by the death of the committee's treasurer. Bills had to be drawn on the committee's members whilst funds from the former treasurer (which he clearly held personally, possibly an abuse of his office) were released.[183] Over the same period there were problems with the Customs House, which traditionally the committee would have resolved.

Perhaps most critical, however, the committee moved its meetings in 1813 from the Liverpool Arms Hotel, which involved minimal cost, to a committee room at the Commercial Buildings rented at £409 per year.[184] These buildings themselves were a major source of anger. On 19 July 1814 a local newspaper had reported that the Commercial Buildings Company was seeking an Act to allow it to tax local

[180] Prendeville (1930), pp. 26–30.
[181] Waterford chamber minutes, 20 April 1787.
[182] Waterford chamber letters, in Cork committee of merchants, minutes, 28 March 1814 over mail coaches; 14 September 1814 over taxation; committee in-letters 5 March 1814 (U401/258), 3 August 1814 (U401/ 1330), 28 October 1815 (U401/149), 10 April 1816 (U401/267); convoys in committee minutes, 23 July 1814 ff.: Cork Archives.
[183] Cork committee of merchants, minutes, 29 July and 11 August 1813; 5 March 1814.
[184] Cork committee of merchants, minutes, 31 August 1813.

citizens for every entry in the Customs House; this was to be 2s. per entry, 'one half for the private emolument of the company, the other half . . . for the improvement of the river and port of Cork'. The newspaper called for petitions against this impost by a 'junta' to be directed to a 'patriotic member' of parliament.[185]

A day later a meeting of merchants called for the establishment of a chamber of commerce as an alternative to the committee, 'to protect our rights, and to further the general trade of Cork, . . . [formed] from the merchants and traders at large, which will possess the public confidence'. The meeting also objected that the president of the committee of merchants (Gerard Callaghan) had agreed with the Customs House that it could work only one day per week at sampling and inspecting warehoused goods, that the committee was 'self-created', and no longer held authority to represent, not least over any obligation to pay increased fees for butter weighing.[186] The embryo chamber elected a chair, Sir Anthony Perrier, and secretary, Samuel Lane.

The committee was slow to respond to the threat, taking four months to note the chamber's initiation. It then set up a subcommittee, and on 26 November 1814 it produced its own resolution, which it sent to the newspapers. This defended its president, and its status as a 'self elected body . . . originally founded by the merchants and traders at large . . . and is since continued by an annual election'. But it was forced to admit that it drew its authority from the merchants and traders who could change its regulations as they saw fit. It stated that having two bodies was 'inconsistent and may prove injurious' and that the public authorities, admirals of the port, etc. should for the present send all communications to the mayor,[187] thus reasserting the traditional system and keeping control since the committee and city corporation overlapped.

It is unclear what happened to this early Cork chamber; five years later, in November 1819, the minutes of the modern chamber show it became formerly established. Only one of the chamber's founding committee (Francis J. Maloney) overlapped with members of the 1814 meeting; but the chamber immediately resumed its attack on the committee of merchants. Its main activities of the next five years were preoccupied with reforms to the committee. The committee retaliated. The chamber reported that 'those who were interested in the perpetuation of the old system, affected to despise our prospects'. The chamber then began a long exchange in January 1820 with the secretary of the committee, John Cotter.[188] This was aimed at obtaining an account of income of the butter weighhouse, hide and cask cranes, and expenditure. Though Cotter 'could not in any way recognise the committee of the chamber . . . [he] was ready to grant us individually, as respectable merchants, an inspection'. It was found that 'there is much room for alteration' and amendment in the accounts, there was no break down of income

---

[185] *The Freeholder*, 19 July 1814.
[186] Report of meeting held at the Commercial Buildings; *Cork Mercantile Chronicle*, 20 July 1814.
[187] Cork committee of merchants, minutes, 17, 21, and 16 November 1814; reported in *Cork Mercantile Chronicle*, 29 November 1814.
[188] Cork chamber minutes, 31 December 1819.

sources, and large expenditures were incurred 'for entertainments . . . and for documents made available to subscribers to the Commercial Buildings coffee room, both purposes wholly unconnected with butter and hide skins which should only be taxed to defray charges . . . incident thereto'. Cotter denied the charges, a meeting of the committee defended its activities, and it refused to reduce fees. It was at this point that harangues broke out in the chamber's reading room over two evenings, resulting in a Mr Hutchinson being expelled from the membership.[189]

From this point the chamber sought to remove the committee. In April 1820 it set up its own committee of 25 members to manage the butter, hide and skin cranes 'composed of 11 exporters of butter, 7 butter buyers, three dealers in hide and skin, and four country gentlemen being owners and occupiers of land'. It appears to have taken over the management, though the committee still managed the accounts. By June 1821 it sought that the committee provide weekly account of exports and imports, with which the committee complied.[190] The chamber continued as de facto manager until the municipal reforms of 1835.

5.8 CONCLUSION

This chapter has examined the diffusion process by which the 'chamber' concept came to spread across Britain and Ireland, so that by the mid-20th century virtually all small towns as well as large cities had a chamber. The leading early locations were almost all large commercial centres, most were regional agglomerations with extensive hinterlands, with heavy economic and political weight, and extensive involvement in international trade, and almost all were ports or connected to them by improved river navigations or canals. The diffusion from the major centres until the 1860s largely continued down the rank-size distribution of cities, with the ports remaining as major foci. But from the mid-19th century other bodies also calling themselves chambers, or related to them, emerged which spread the concept far more widely and competitively: the chambers of agriculture took the concept to the rural areas; the retail and local traders associations developed the concept in the small towns taking on the generic title of chambers of trade; the trade protection societies developed a related model. Brief comparison with the later evolution in the USA shows similar developments, with chambers, local boards of trade, and local 'communal clubs', 'commerce clubs', and 'commerce leagues'. The parallels with Britain and Ireland seem to suggest that competition and fragmentation are endemic in voluntary systems.

There was also an important regional differentiation reflecting local geographies: first, predominantly commercial and trade-based chambers of commerce in the major ports; second, manufacturing-based chambers of commerce, initially with a very narrow remit, in the new industrial areas; third, retail-based chambers of trade

---

[189] Cork chamber minutes, 3, 9, 16, and 17 February; 1, 8, and 13 March 1820; see Chapter 11.
[190] Cork chamber minutes, 5 April and 8 November 1820, 17 January, 22 June 1821; also Prendeville (1930), pp. 25–30.

in the smaller towns and resorts; and fourth, chambers of agriculture in the rural areas. As time went on virtually the whole space of Britain and Ireland was filled with these bodies, reaching a peak in the 1970s and 1980s.

The fragmentation of the diffusion process reflected a search for a new means to articulate voice to government and the wider public, and as a marketing tool for place status and place promotion. This in turn was an outcome of an increasing integration within regions focusing on ports that provided the key links with the global economy, search for regional and local identity, and promotion of the 'unique' characteristics of each place. Until the 1970s, integration of the economy was essentially limited to the regional level. National integration covered only a few industries; local industrial districts held the order of the day; and each area sought a chamber to express its own local distinctiveness within the national and international arena. Much of this desire still exists today, but since the 1980s national and global integration and shifts of major industries offshore has raised major challenges for locally based chambers just as it has done for firms.

The chapter has also examined the counterfactual: of why some key locations did not develop early chambers. In Bristol and York the local Merchant Adventurers seem to have held back developments by initially offering a reasonably effective alternative that was a hangover from the past. In some other areas merchant companies and merchant committees evolved into chambers, or worked with them. But in other areas resistance from older bodies made development of chambers difficult. Frustration with these bodies stimulated chambers. The very late development of a London chamber, however, whilst showing many influences resulting from the availability of alternatives in the City, seems to exhibit chiefly a visceral resistance by national government to a chamber on its doorstep. Efforts to establish a London chamber in 1817, 1823–4, and 1868–72 all demonstrate government interference to prevent chamber development.

PART 3
STRUCTURAL TENSIONS

6

Governance, Management, and Resources

6.1 INTRODUCTION

The governance of modern chambers is through elected councils and committees of unpaid volunteers, with detailed financial management, monitoring of membership, and other customer demands handled by professional staff. This is very different from the early chambers where the link to their members was direct: all discussions were in meetings, and these could be very frequent. The members managed the bodies directly, by collective deliberation. As time progressed the president, other officers, and the 'council' or executive committee became more critical to management. The links became more complex when staff were appointed, particularly as the number of staff grew. In turn, the staff became responsible for managing the routine processes of giving voice, recruiting members, and providing services. Voice became more marshalled, organized, and based on consultation rather than deliberated. A complex nexus, therefore, evolved in which information asymmetries could arise with inevitable tensions that had to be managed: tensions between the voluntary elected officers and the staff; and between the member activism of the few and the lethargy or apathy of the many. This chapter examines the developments and challenges offered by resourcing and governance issues surrounding the management of 'interests' in chambers, legitimizing them, and supporting them with professional management and services.

6.2 GOVERNANCE AND SOLIDARITY

The formal management of chambers falls on an elected council who, in modern terminology, are the trustees and directors of the incorporated body. The leading members, council, and president were, and are, the chief resources for lobbying. Most of the earliest chambers had both councils and elected officers. Jersey in 1768, and Liverpool and Manchester in 1774, had councils (or committees) of 21 including the chair/president, and additionally had a secretary.[1] This was a common committee size during the 19th century, though many were larger. For a sample of 55 chambers in 1892, the range of council size was from 8 (Dundee) to

---

[1] Jamieson (1986); Syvret and Stevens (1998); Helm (1897); Bennett (2010). Only 7 in New York in 1768–80: Stevens (1867).

48 (North Staffordshire).[2] There was some tendency for an increase in size; e.g. Belfast grew from 15 in the 1780s to 21 in the 1850s. By 1892 the average of 55 chambers was about 24.[3] By 1914 the average size of ACC chamber councils was 29.1, with a range from 4 (Aldershot), 5 (Letchworth), and 7 (Salt), to 53 (Bradford), 56 (Burnley), 112 (Liverpool) and 137 (London).[4] The size of councils was first monitored by ABCC in surveys in 1989 showing sizes to have increased further by the late 20th century. There were about 3105 members of chamber councils/boards in 1989, a mean of 30.1 per chamber. However, from about 1990 the mean began to fall: to 26.2 in 1992. Subsequently board size more significantly reduced as chambers have sought to focus on strategic leadership, have responded to the 'new age leadership model'; and other forces. Mean board size was 16.4 in 2005, and 12.7 by 2010.[5] The range in board size in 2010 was from 5 (Hereford and Worcester) to 31 (Glasgow, which was the only chamber over 24).

The emphasis on large sizes offered more opportunity to include a wider range of opinion, and also reflected attempts to include committee chairs and leading members in the deliberations of the main council; so some increase in council sizes resulted from the growth in committees. As in most organizations, boards are now normally supplemented by executive committees or senior management staff teams that make the main decisions. Executive Committees of chamber councils emerged in the late 19th century and grew in frequency among chambers as their membership became larger, their committees more complex, and as the time required for management grew. They usually consisted of no more than the senior officers and perhaps a few other committee chairs, normally 3–6 in size.

Some councils contained external advisers who were non-members. For example, in early years, often the MPs, mayor, town clerk, harbour master, local Customs officer, or similar local officials were honorary members (and many were very active attendees). In 1892, of 55 chambers, 26 had mayors as ex-officio members of their councils, 20 had local MPs, two had High Sheriffs (Dublin and Exeter); the Dock or Harbour Trust was represented on councils in four chambers as well as the Merchant Venturers in Bristol; and in London the council had the Chairs of the Stock Exchange, Lloyds, and the Bank of England.[6] This is less true of modern chambers, where external advisers are usually restricted to committee memberships.

Stability and turnover of committee members

The constitutions of modern chambers have rules limiting the period of office, usually requiring resignation for a period before re-election is possible. This was also used as a standard model in most of the earliest chambers. For example, in Jersey and Liverpool one third of the 'committee' of 21 were to resign each year. However,

---

[2] Royal Commission on Labour; *House of Commons Papers* (1892) xxxvi, part V, pp. xxxii–xxxiv.
[3] This evolution mirrors that in non-commercial societies; Clark (2000a).
[4] ACC list of members 1914; MS 14477/5.
[5] BCC *Census* and *Benchmarking* statistics; see Appendix 2.
[6] Analysis of Royal Commission on Labour, *House of Commons Papers* (1892) xxxvi, part V, pp. xxxiii ff.

there is, and was, always a tension between appropriate governance structures that required turnover, and maintaining sufficient voluntary commitment to get people to stand for election and do the necessary work once elected. For this reason, many early chamber councils had a remarkably permanent appearance to their committees, despite their constitution requiring turnover. Thus, in Liverpool, 16 members of the chamber's 21-strong council served for five of the first six years, and for the 12 years 1774–82 with records there were only 61 committee members (whereas there could have been 245); the Dublin chamber had essentially the same council from 1784 until 1794.[7] Limerick, which had a process of annual election from 1807, introduced a rule in 1810 that at least one-third of its committee must retire each year, but many of the same names re-emerged.[8] In Belfast the council had to stand for election annually from the outset in 1783, but most of the same names continued year after year in the 1780s and 1790s. However, when the chamber was re-established in 1802, its elections were more hotly contested, and in 1820, 35 candidates stood for 15 council places.[9]

Nevertheless, in the great majority of chambers, for most years, council members remained remarkably durable during the 19th century, and in some cases up to modern times. This was a major force for continuity, but also for inertia. It was a major influence on the 'politics of the bureau', by which decisions tend to follow a similar pattern year on year. This, combined with the low turnover of membership joining and lapsing in the early years (see Chapter 15), was a major force for stability, but could make the chambers slow to respond to new needs.[10] A rump committee could also be wayward. Jersey chamber had a constitution requiring reconstitution every three years. In the run-up to its third reconstitution there was a proposal to gamble the whole remaining assets on a lottery in 1773.[11] In Guernsey in February 1849 an attempt was made by a rump council to dissolve the chamber, with the assets passed to 'Collings Benevolent Fund' for the relief of destitute tradesmen, artisans, and sailors. At face value the minutes record this as due to a lack of active membership. However, a new minute book begun by a new committee shows that the dispute was over a policy stance taken by the president and the rump committee: 'the president and a majority of the [old] committee considered' that a petition should be sent to the Home Secretary to remove the power of local authorities to levy la petite coutume and other discriminatory duties. A general meeting rejected this, 'but the president and his friends . . . instead of retiring . . . resolved to break up the chamber and alienate its funds'. The remaining members called their own meeting and re-established the chamber, declaring the previous minutes and decisions invalid and its votes 'null and void'. New meetings of members were called, a new committee elected, new members sought, and a new

---

[7] Liverpool: Bennett (2010), table 1; Dublin, listed in local directories.
[8] Limerick chamber minutes, 1 May 1810, and comparison with earlier and later years.
[9] Belfast chamber, minutes; contest of 3 August 1820.
[10] See further discussion of membership trends and the 'bureau' in Chapter 16.
[11] Jersey chamber minutes, 12 May 1773.

statement of intent was published 29 March 1849. The old president John Valrent was replaced by Abraham Bishop.[12]

For the elected chairman[13] long-term continuity was also frequent in the early years. Some of these were clearly weighty and dominant figures that offered unique leadership skills, such as Patrick Colquhoun in Glasgow (president 1783–9), or Samuel Garbett in Birmingham (president 1783–95). They might also be difficult to overthrow. But Garbett probably sums up the more general problem: if he did not do it, no one else would! In 1785 he wrote:

> They would sign a petition, but they will neither give money or go from home on the occasion, nor voluntarily meet two or three times in a morning, and if I was to leave Town, I don't believe a tolerable meeting would be procured . . . for I don't see a man that would give himself the trouble to ask gentlemen to come, nor do I see one that would conduct what is absolutely necessary at public meetings.[14]

These challenges continue. As a result, Stewart concluded in 1984 that the chambers

> do not conform to an ideal model of representation and accountability. In broad terms a relatively small proportion of members are actively participant in chamber affairs (as opposed to making use of chamber services); the 'representatives' of individual firms are generally self-selected; elections for council or committees are rare. In short chambers are very similar to many organisations reliant on the active involvement of a few interested . . . members.[15]

This is of course no different from most voluntary bodies, as well as organizations such as local government committees, and public participation in local and general elections. Democracy in all forms has many challenges for engagement. For the chambers, this underlay the call for public law status in the 1970s and 1980s, so that chambers could be more broadly representative, as discussed in Chapter 7. Improved means of gaining active member involvement in decision taking have also underpinned the concern of modern chambers to become more inclusive and consultative. This has been greatly facilitated by the use of electronic communications since the 1990s.

6.3 COMMITTEE STRUCTURES

Effective governance requires a means to link the members, councils, committees, and staff. A chamber is not just a lobby organization or service provider; any consultancy or other business can offer this. Managing commitment, or 'interest', also requires supporting the officers and councils with sections, committees,

---

[12] Guernsey chamber minutes, 2 February 1849; new minute book, 6, 18, 26 February; 1, 25, 29 March 1849.
[13] As distinct from presidents, which were often honorary posts, which had even longer continuity.
[14] Garbett letter to Matthew Boulton, 12 March 1785; quoted in Money (1977), p. 36.
[15] Stewart (1984), p. 43.

subcommittees, and other groups that focus on specific specialized tasks. Many of these concern specific representational fields, such as taxation, international trade, and in earlier times, postal services, railways, and freight rates. In addition, there are frequently social committees, membership committees, and other specialized groups focusing on internal needs. The committees usually overlap with the councils in membership, in many cases with the committee chairs being ex-officio members of the council.

The committees draw in a wider range of the membership. As noted above, some committees may also contain external advisers who are non-members (and this has increased in recent years). Estimates by ABCC in 1989 suggest that there were 5570 committee members additional to those on councils, a mean of 54 per chamber. Although there may have been some double counting, this still indicates a formidable volunteer input; a total of about 8000 people involved in the voluntary governance of British chambers in 1989. It reflected major efforts to involve members, and create an 'active' cadre that could respond to the needs of policy deliberation and decision making. Indeed, ABCC refer to them as those concerned with 'policy' as a means to demonstrate the strength and breadth of knowledge in the chamber system.[16]

The committees and elected officers are the key conduit of deliberation, and of relationships with members, and often also are links to specialist external interests, including local government, and local economic development initiatives. Hence, an analysis of committees provides important insights into the structure and issues that activated chambers and influenced their governance. Setting up a committee was a reaction to the need for a specific mode of governance to negotiate with members in order to develop and/or legitimize representational strategies, or to manage the chamber itself and its membership.

Figure 6.1 shows the changes in number of committees over time; this excludes internal management committees, such as finance or the council. The earliest chambers had no committees; all policy questions were discussed and decided by the full council. Indeed in many deliberations the discussion was of the full membership.[17] For chambers with small membership, or with narrow interests such as chambers of trade or agriculture, this remained true into the 20th century. For example, in Barnsley even in 1914 the management committee was 'all the members', although by 1920 a formal council was established.[18] However, as time progressed, the number of committees has proliferated, with little indication that it is reducing in modern times. Committees are generally the stuff of associations.[19]

Before 1815 many specialist committees had a short life, and no chambers had long-lived standing committees. Thus Glasgow in 1784–5 had over 20 committees for particular policy discussions, but all were disbanded once they had reported,

[16] ABCC *Census*, 1989; see Appendix 2.
[17] Even where arbitration was offered there was not always a standing committee in early chambers.
[18] Barnsley chamber, *Annual Reports* (1914; 1920).
[19] For most non-commercial societies the number of committees grew, increasing to at least 20 by 1800. Clark (2000a), p. 255 interprets this as for publicity and as a way to engage members.

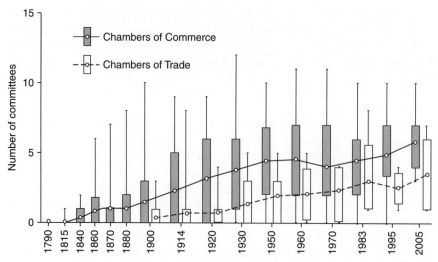

Fig. 6.1. Number of committees, mean, range, and 20/80% box plots, in chambers of commerce and chambers of trade 1790–2005 (excludes executive and management committees).

usually after only a few weeks. Similarly Birmingham in 1840–80 had many committees on specific lobbies which lasted no more than a year or two. Standing committees were not widely developed until the middle of the 19th century. As a result, as shown in Table 6.1, not until the 1860s did half the chambers have at least one committee. A major change occurred over WW1: whilst over 40% of chambers still had no standing committee structure in 1900 (other than for internal management), this was under 20% by 1920, and this proportion continued to decline. This reflects the growing influence of the corporatist state needing ever greater policy apparatus from the business community. By the 1960s almost all chambers of commerce had committees, but for chambers of trade Figure 6.1 shows this came a little later, and their total number of committees was always smaller.

Table 6.1 shows the character of the committees, for chambers of commerce only. Within the broad pattern of change, there is considerable diversity. Many of the older chambers evolved towards greater and greater complexity of committees, but others remained with none at all up to recent decades; yet others had many committees, and then abolished them, perhaps re-establishing a different structure at a later date. Some later chambers started out with numerous and complex committees, then simplified them. The overall pattern of evolution, therefore, hides much of the local dynamics.

Table 6.1 illustrates four key features. First, there was an increase in committee numbers in order to gain expertise for fields of lobbying and representation activities. Second, there was evolution to take account of differences between the members, chiefly by industrial sector. Moreover, these two elements developed at

Table 6.1. Number of standing committees of each title; chambers of commerce only

Committee Title	1840	1860	1870	1882	1900	1920	1930	1950	1960	1970	1982	1996
Arbitration	3	4	6	8	11	15	15	12	10	4	4	–
International trade/exports[a]		1	6	8	14	20	18	20	24	15	15	41
Postal/telecommunications[b]		1	6	6	9	20	28	24	22	14	9	–
Transport[c]	3	2	3	7	10	31	39	36	41	31	25	47
Parliament/law		1	3	5	13	20	25	25	17	11	9	17
Education (and training)		1		2	3	20	21	23	22	17	16	42
Taxation (central)			1	1	2	2	4	13	16	16	14	42
Local rates and valuation						1	1	3	5	3	4	–
Municipalism/town planning[d]		1			2	3	13	12	16	19	18	33
Local trade promotion/advertising[e]		1				4	13	9	12	5	4	23
Town development/infrastructure			2	1	1	2	1	2	–	1	1	8
Standards/designs[f]				3	3	3	4	5	1	1	–	–
Social/entertainments					1	5	10	13	13	9	9	n/a
Industry sections[g]	2	2	6	15	14	29	31	35	32	18	16	33
Retail		1			1	11	13	19	19	19	22	36
Wholesale		1			1	1	1	1	2	1	1	–
Agriculture						1	2	1	1	1	–	–
Sub-area geography					1	2	2	4	5	7	4	29
Small firms							–	–	–	–	2	28
Other	1	2	2	1	2	1	1	1	1	3	2	n/a
None	4	9	18	21	18	19	15	7	7	5	5	–
No. of chambers in sample	9	18	32	49	37	70	74	69	69	51	44	61

a. Often termed 'exports' from the 1950s.

b. As distinct from postal advisory committees (not shown), which were joint with other bodies after 1912.

c. Includes railways, canals, ports, roads, bridges, etc.

d. Includes parking from 1982.

e. Where separate from the specific sectors.

f. Includes patents and trademarks.

g. Includes tourism from 1982.

Note: excludes short-term committees of less than one year, and councils and internal management committees such as finance, GPC, and membership development. All information, except 1996, is derived from local chamber minutes and reports; 1996 is from BCC *Census* that is not strictly comparable, and probably contains some double counting between categories.

about the same rate, achieving a wide spread over the system from the 1920s. A third element, social and entertainment committees were slower to evolve, chiefly from the 1930s. Though dinners, banquets, and other meetings were frequent from the outset, they usually did not have standing committees to organize them. A fourth area, arbitration, reflects support for one of the chambers' early services, which grew to a peak of committee involvement over 1920–50.

An interesting feature of Table 6.1 is the key areas of representation where standing committees emerged. In early years these were primarily on international trade and transport issues, but rapidly postal and communications issues were also involved. Committees to scrutinize parliamentary and legal developments joined these from the 1860s. Postal and communication committees were given a boost by the government's 1912 establishment of Postal Advisory Committees, of which chambers were key members.[20] By 1914, education also became a major concern, as a result of the commercial education scheme developed by the London chamber, promoted by chambers through local scholarships and prizes. In recent years more specialist forums have usually replaced 'parliamentary' committees.

The ABCC in the 1920s, through its secretary Dunwoody, was calling for all chambers to have at least three committees dealing with: national and local taxation; home affairs, regulation and transport; and foreign and colonial.[21] In Table 6.1, there is not much evidence of this template. Rather the chambers were evolving a variety of structures in very varied directions, with WW1 proving an important period of change in which industry sections were developed and the number of chambers with no committees significantly reduced.

A surprising feature is that committees with a specific local concern developed rather late, particularly those scrutinizing local government activity; mainly after 1900, and particularly from the 1920s and 1930s. The developments appear to represent the response of chambers to growing municipal service development and intervention during the slump, and the establishment of the modern town planning system in 1947. Local rating and valuation issues also increased after WW1. Tourism committees became more frequent from the 1990s.

The development of section and sector committees was central to many 19th-century chambers, e.g. in Hull, Liverpool, Manchester, Belfast, and London the industry sections might perform as sector trade associations, and in some cases attempted to act as wage/price bodies. These industry sections were well developed by 1870, and were an effective means to manage tensions between competing interests. Sometimes there was only one, as with the straw-hat sector at Luton, or leather at Northamptonshire. In other cases there were many sections, as at Liverpool (23), Leicester (21), and London (29).[22] Manchester had seven sections

---

[20] Ilersic and Liddle (1960); see Chapter 10.
[21] R. B. Dunwoody, article in many chamber journals, e.g. Belfast chamber *Journal*, July (1924), pp. 51–2.
[22] Figures for 1890s; for example, Liverpool in the 1920s and 1930s had sections for Africa; West Africa; America South and Central; East India and China; Greece and Levant; Italy; Portugal; Russia; Spain; animals and meat; canned goods; bird food; coal; edible nuts and dried fruit; hide and leather; iron and metal trades; iron, steel, tinplate and metal merchants; motor trade; tea; timber; tobacco;

for different trading regions and eight industrial sector sections. Belfast had three by 1889: grain and flour milling; wholesale grocers, druggists, and tea merchants; and shipping.[23] This was increased to four in 1914 with an aerated water section. Glasgow started a paint and oil section in 1917, which was its longest lived; its merchants and provisions section began in 1918, textiles in 1938, engineering in 1940, shipping and forwarding in 1941, and yarn in 1948. Edinburgh had two sections by 1920: printing, and drapery and retail. Some chambers established sections very late; e.g. Guernsey had its first sections in 1991. Sections continue to be important structures for chambers.

Many sections were linked to national trade associations, sometimes as formal branches, more often through association membership of the chamber that then found a place in the relevant section. In Coventry membership by associations grew from 12 in the 1920s, to 17 in 1939.[24] By 1952 there were over 700 trade associations as members of local chambers,[25] and 719 in 1970, representing many thousands of individual businesses.[26] London quoted that 35 associations with 30,000 members had joined the chamber through associations in 1911, which had risen to 50,000 in the 1950s; it repeated this number into the 1980s.[27] Sector membership of chambers declined from the 1960s and especially in the 1970s, with growth of CBI and the shift of government consultation to a predominantly sector structure under NEDC and ITBs. Table 6.1 shows that this process of shift from local to national sector bodies was, however, surprisingly slow and late.

The development of stronger sections was one outcome of attempts to improve governance. Thus in Liverpool in 1878 sections were seen as a way of overcoming a debacle over political involvements.[28] London advocated sections as a more general governance mechanism in 1884, suggesting that 'wherever a certain trade is important enough to supply 15 or 20 members, a special section might be formed, with independent officers having a seat on the central board'. This would strengthen governance: 'the consideration of questions should be referred for study, analysis, and report, to specialist committees, but action should only be taken after discussion by the central board'.[29] By 1904–6 ACC was also strongly advocating sections. Bristol responded to this specific call by introducing sections in 1906, and other chambers also began to follow the ACC lead.[30] After 1920 the section became part of the improved efficiency drive within chambers. This had two facets: first to recruit new members across a wider spectrum of local businesses; and second, to improve governance by allowing a 'mixed model' of chamber

---

forage trade. There were also four trade associations as members. A summary of London sections is given in Chapter 11.

[23] Belfast chamber minutes; and subcommittee minute book.
[24] Coventry chamber, *Annual Reports* and minutes.
[25] Knowles (1952), p. 5.
[26] ABCC MS 17367/3, 1970; this was 1.6% of total ABCC membership.
[27] London chamber, *CCJ* (1911); *Annual Reports* (1956, 1957), and following.
[28] See Chapter 3.
[29] London *CCJ*, 5 February (1884), p. 27.
[30] Bristol chamber, *Annual Report* (1906), pp. 6–10.

responses. As stated in a 1954 ABCC publication, 'The interests of various trades and businesses represented in a chamber are not always identical.... Sections can act either separately, in their own interests, or seek the full weight and influence of the chamber. The chamber is looked upon as neutral ground on which all trades can meet when there are matters of common interest.'[31]

Committees or sections for the retail sector became significant in the run-up to WW1, and especially after WW2. It became ABCC policy to encourage these after 1928, although some pressure to include retailers began after 1917.[32] This evolution in part reflects the development of the NCT and local chambers of trade. Many of the larger chambers of commerce developed retail sections in an attempt to stymie the development of a local chamber of trade; in other cases they developed a section as a medium to cooperate with a local chamber of trade. ABCC itself began a retail committee in 1941, though it was still divided on the issue (of 31 replies, 6 were in favour of a retail committee, 18 against, and 7 neutral).[33] There is little evidence of any change after the merger of the NCT and ABCC in 1992. The two chambers with agricultural sections seem to reflect a local relationship with a chamber of agriculture (Aberdeen in 1920, and Leicester by 1914).

Conversely, some chambers of trade developed manufacturing sections, which served the membership that was linked to ABCC rather than NCT. Thus Barnstaple chamber of trade established a committee of manufacturers in 1941, which quickly became a separate section with an additional subscription. In 1949 the section was disbanded to become a formal subcommittee of the chamber, with its funds transferred;[34] and the chamber responded by joining ABCC in 1947 as well as NCT, though this was thrown awry when ABCC increased its subscriptions in the 1960s. When the chamber left ABCC in 1969 a North Devon Manufacturers Association then became more important.[35] Chambers of trade also sometimes had to develop sections for different parts of the distributive trades. Thus Hereford, after amalgamation with its local drapers association in 1932–3, went through significant upheavals that were only resolved by developing separate trades and commercial sections in 1936 with different subscriptions.[36]

Sections of chambers to cater for different geographical sub-areas began to develop from 1900. One of the first was Walsall's sections for Wednesbury, and Darlaston, allowing it to span a larger district than Walsall alone. Northamptonshire had sections for Kettering, Wellingborough, and Rushden. However, area sections remained few until the 1990s, with many chambers using a differentiation of 'city' and 'country' subscriptions to help bind different groups together. Sub-area sections expanded rapidly as an outcome of the ABCC accreditation strategy of the 1990s,

---

[31] ABCC, *Chambers of Commerce Manual* (1954–5), p. 3.
[32] See e.g. ACC *Monthly Proceedings*, 4 October, 1917, pp. 8–48; ABCC Executive committee 7 March 1928, which declared that 'where conditions are favourable a distributive section should be formed . . . as full members of the chamber'.
[33] ABCC, Council minutes, 1 October 1941.
[34] Barnstaple chamber, minutes, 8 January 1941, 11 February 1949.
[35] Barnstaple chamber, minutes, 9 February 1970.
[36] Hereford chamber minutes, 1 February 1932, 19 October 1936, 4 January 1937.

which encouraged chambers to merge and reach out over larger areas. Also, as a result of the merger of the ABCC with NCT in 1992, smaller affiliated mainly retail chambers were brought into the system. At the same time 'satellites' within Business Link often affiliated with larger chamber 'hubs'.

Small firm sections, mainly in response to discussions sparked by the Bolton Report in 1971, began first in Bristol and Croydon in the late 1970s, and then in Plymouth and Westminster, but were surprisingly little developed by 1992; however, there was a rapid growth by 1996 to cover nearly one-half of chambers, reflecting chamber involvement in Business Link.[37] In Ireland they became common after involvement with EU SME programmes since the 1990s.

6.4 PERSONNEL

Many early chambers were entirely voluntary bodies with no staff; the elected 'officers' of the chamber acted on all matters, sometimes recognized by an honorarium. However, as time progressed the roles became progressively more professionalized, and staff were employed to fill them. In a modern chamber of commerce, the elected officers of the council, including the president and vice-president(s), are still voluntary, but the chief executive (formerly the secretary), finance officer (formerly the treasurer), and other staff are all employees of the chamber. In the chambers of trade, voluntary executives remain the norm.

The evolution of the current position was quite slow and varied considerably between areas and types of chamber. As Finer observed, the evolution of this 'new and growing profession [of association staff] has been largely unnoticed and its history entirely unwritten'. Or as put by Dupree, such secretaries were neither businessmen nor civil servants, but 'professional secretaries'.[38] As early as 1788 the challenge of appropriate staff skills was recognized by Patrick Colquhoun as requiring 'a combination of information and experience';[39] i.e. not just administrative efficiency was required, but also a sensitivity to, and knowledge of, the world of business. This has proved a continuing challenge up to the present.

The general evolution of staff, shown in Figure 6.2, exhibits slow development until 1900. Early staff numbers were small, and often part timers, but there were exceptions such as Limerick, which was managing local markets and the harbour. By 1818 it had a secretary, assistant secretary, butter crane minder, fisheries warden, and various inspectors, some of whom were part time. The early Dublin chamber had a Mr Hughes as superintendent of porters at £2 per week, Mr Jones as receiver of harbour porterage charges at £70 per year, as well as a secretary at £60 (termed registrar until the 1860s), and later introduced staff to supervise fees for

---

[37] See Chapters 13 and 16.
[38] Finer (1966), p. 29; quoted in Dupree (1987), p. 29.
[39] *Plan of a Public Agency in London for Commercial Affairs*: Glasgow chamber papers, TD 1670/4/52, October 1788, p. 6.

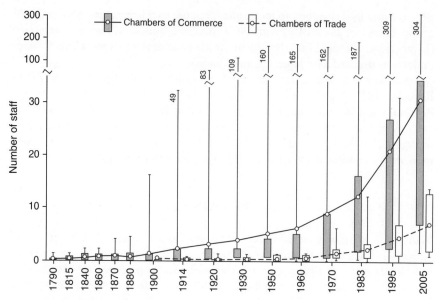

Fig. 6.2. Mean staff size, range, and 20%/80% box plots, in chambers of commerce and chambers of trade 1790–2005.

harbour cranes and wharfs, pier fees, and coal metering.[40] By 1840, nearly one-half of chambers had some staff: a mean of 0.45 full-time equivalent. Limerick had four (having lost its market functions it had a secretary, librarian, porter, and house-keeper). Bristol, Manchester, Leeds, and Glasgow all had equivalent to one full-time staff by the 1840s. Glasgow had a full-time librarian, part-time secretary, an 'officer [clerk] and part time porter to make up the fire' in the 1830s. The General Chamber had a full-time secretary in 1786. By 1850 about five chambers had full-time, or near full-time staff, by 1860 it was ten, with Salt (Northwich) having two full-time staff (one local secretary and an agent in London, who was the former secretary), Dublin two, and Limerick four. In the trade protection societies, the London TPS had two staff (a secretary and assistant) in 1850 and nine staff in 1861, and Leicester TPS had three staff in the 1860s, rising to 11 by 1900. Smaller TPSs, such as Beverley in 1834, used 'a solicitor employed as secretary of the society . . . to attend all committees and other meetings, record proceedings and give such advice and assistance as required'.[41]

By 1870, over 70% of chambers of commerce had some staff, with a mean of 0.7. The year 1900 is the point at which the chambers of commerce exceed a mean staff of one, but in the chambers of trade that were then emerging there were barely any staff. By 1920 the chambers of commerce had a mean of nearly 3, with a maximum of 83 (London), but the chambers of trade had a mean of only 0.14, over

[40] Dublin chamber, *Annual Reports* and minutes (1821, 1823).
[41] Beverley Guardian Society for protection of trade, *Rules* (1834); BL 1568/5809.

80% having no staff. When Knowles assessed the chambers of commerce in 1949, noting that 80% had only part-time staff, he was recognizing the gap between the small and the large chambers.[42]

Taylor describes the mid-to-late 19th century as a turning point where the modern chamber of commerce was rooted, arguing that the appointment of full-time staff made a critical difference: '1870–1900 became a watershed . . . marking the change from the powerful volunteer to the dedicated professional'.[43] There is no doubt that Taylor's observation carries weight, but he places this change at the wrong point. As shown in Figure 6.2, professionalization was not new in 1870. Several early chambers had full-time staff. In 1840, of 13 chambers with records available, only six were entirely voluntary; in 1860 it was about five out of 25. So professionalization was earlier and more widespread than Taylor attributes. It is also important not to write off volunteers, who remained critical to the lobbying activity well into the 20th century, and are still significant today. Professionalization has its limits: contacts and personal weight of leading members often counted (and still count) for as much as professionals.

But in the sense Taylor intended, professionalization was much later as a system-wide development. Professionalization, as might be understood today, with a chief executive leading and managing a professional service organization is really a phenomenon that developed more widely in the chamber of commerce system from the 1970s. Mean staff size reached ten in chambers of commerce only by the 1980s, but then rapidly increased to 27 in 1995, 43 in 2005, and 42 in 2010.

The secretary

The secretary became the critical individual as the chambers professionalized. The tasks of minute taking and managing the accounts was passed to the secretary, although overseen by the president and treasurer who would retain nominal and indeed legal responsibility as directors. As time progressed, it was natural for the burden of writing of reports, researching statistics, consulting with members, and day-to-day representational activities to gravitate towards an employee who had the time and skills to devote to the task.

The role of the early secretaries was normally chiefly clerical and administrative, though requiring care and attention to detail, and where they also managed the financial accounts, a level of financial experience and probity. Two early solutions to emerge to fill this role were either to provide an honorarium to a council member who might delegate the clerical and bookkeeping work to one of their staff, or to recruit a suitable person. Usually these early recruits were paid only part time, and their status varied a great deal. In many cases they were senior partners of their business, but in other cases they were junior clerks, either recruited by advertisement, or nominated from a member's solicitor or accounting practice. The first two secretaries of the Glasgow chamber were major public figures: Gilbert Hamilton

[42] Knowles (1949).   [43] Taylor (2007), pp. 30 and 42.

(secretary 1783–1808) was also Lord Provost of Glasgow 1792–3, agent of the Carron Iron Company, banker, and had many other significant trading interests; Dugald Bannatyne (secretary 1808–35) was postmaster in 1806.[44] Several others were significant merchants, as with Liverpool's Samuel Green 1774–92; or Jersey's Phillip Hamon 1773–c.1800. New York's Anthony van Dam in 1768–83 was a prominent insurance agent.[45] But others were more basic clerks.

It is important not to underestimate the role of these first staff appointments. Many volunteers and part-time secretaries were critical to professionalization. Green and van Dam were the linchpins that held their organizations together over periods of tumultuous and divisive change: such as the slave trade abolition movement in Liverpool, and the fracture between loyalists and rebels in New York. The appointment of Samuel Bruce as the secretary at Belfast in 1822, remaining up to 1833, wrought a remarkable change on the chamber. It had previously had periods of halting existence. Bruce regularized the membership lists, increased recruitment, reorganized the minutes and reporting, published reports for the first time, and increased exchanges with other chambers in Ireland and Britain. His example is followed in other chambers as professional administrators became engaged. Bruce and most of these early appointments were part time on small honoraria; for Bruce it was only £20 per year. But this did not mean they were lowly or ineffective. Indeed they generally came from relevant businesses. But voluntary and part-time secretaries also had profound limitations. As stated by the ACC president in 1917, 'will anyone admit that a body supposed to be representative . . . can be adequately served by a chief executive officer with a salary of £20 a year? It is impossible.'[46]

The secretary as focus

By the middle to late 19th century the role of secretary was recognized as crucial and had secured high status, though not always a high salary. With this came a new crop of recruits from business and the professions, with progressive moves towards full-time posts, and with support from assistants and clerks becoming essential in the larger chambers. A critical role of the secretary was as an interface between the elected council and the members, and between the members/council and the outside world, particularly government: termed 'the spinal column of the organisation and nerve centre' by Knowles.[47] Or, as recognized by ABCC in 1958, assessing why some chambers had apathy and small memberships: 'the prime cause is a bad secretary. Most things stem from that. The next worst cause is a bad president. He only comes second because he is transient.'[48]

---

[44] The first two secretaries, Glasgow chamber, *Journal*, May (1970), pp. 246–9.
[45] Liverpool from Bennett (2010); New York from Stevens (1867), p. 105.
[46] Algernon Firth, ACC president, quoted in ACC *Monthly Proceedings*, 4 October, 1917, p. 10.
[47] Knowles (1949), p. 8.
[48] Development Advisory Committee, minutes of first meeting, 3 September 1958; ABCC, GPC, minutes.

The role of the secretary in levering and organizing chamber councils is captured in the extensive diary of Raymond Streat, secretary of one of the largest chambers in the 1930s, Manchester.[49] First was the need to understand and manage disparate views and articulate them to the members: 'April 9th 1931: The level of debate was not really very good. I doubt if many present fully grasped the proposal . . . Barlow [the president] himself has not worked out in his own mind how the plan will operate in detail. Nor has Grey. Hughes has more concrete notions, but when I hear what he has in mind I feel sure the rank and file will never agree.' Second, it shows the need to anticipate and find means to develop a collective view: 'I recommended the Executive to set up a committee . . . as a means of securing for the chamber a little corps of well-informed men against the time . . . when some vital question . . . would present itself.'[50] Third, there was the need to marshal, facilitate, and support the president and leading members who usually made the main lobby presentations to government, though Streat increasingly himself became a leading figure in negotiations with government departments. Fourth, for Streat, more unusually, was the role of leadership and initiative. This is vividly summarized for the 'unqualified declaration in favour of tariffs' which the Manchester chamber published in 1931.[51] This was a clever capture of the reform moment, an act of opportunism and subtle leadership, which put Manchester chamber, and Streat, in the forefront of the national debate.

Streat also saw the secretary as the main lead on marketing and income raising as well as management: 'Are you a salesman? Can you work with a few girls and office boys, . . . where your bright ideas can be turned into cash by salesmen like brother Jones?' These were the skills he saw from his role in advising a young colleague whether to take the secretaryship at Leeds.[52]

For most of the new professionals, the chamber secretaryship became their career; many stayed in post for the rest of their working lives. Raymond Streat felt it was difficult to move between chambers: 'I feel convinced that there would always be a hidden but effective prejudice against taking a secretary to fill a secretaryship'. He quotes how 'Purt of Leicester has tried to move up and has failed'. Hence, advising one of his assistant secretaries whether to move to Leeds he noted 'Leeds will in all probability be your life'.[53] However, by the 1920s there was encouragement for chambers to look between each other for career development of their staff, and to notify other chambers where 'they had good assistants on their staff for whom there was no avenue for promotion'.[54] The ABCC secretary, Knowles, took this up again in 1949, noting that in his knowledge only five people had moved from one chamber to another in the previous 22 years. He argued that a special qualification should be required, with a summer school each year, and

---

[49] *Diary of Raymond Streat*, 2 vols., Dupree (1987).

[50] Streat *Diary*, Dupree (1987), vol. i, pp. 55 and 74, referring to Russian trade protection.

[51] Ibid., pp. 89–91 f.; also see Chapter 10.

[52] Ibid., p. 491; referring to S. J. Batchelder, see below.

[53] S. J. Batchelder was a section secretary in Manchester, promoted to assistant secretary in 1936, and moved as secretary to Leeds in 1937–70s: Dupree (1987), vol. i, p. 378 n. and p. 490.

[54] ABCC, Association of Chamber Secretaries, 3 October 1929.

periods of placement in several chambers.[55] In more recent years this has developed further, with more external appointments brought in at senior level, encouragement for chief executives to move up the chamber hierarchy, and for assistant secretaries to take posts as secretary elsewhere; e.g. W. J. Luxton moved from secretary of Birmingham to London, in the 1960s; Simon Sperryn, in the 1980s and 1990s, moved from Birmingham to Manchester and then to London; Bryan Carnes spent ten years at Birmingham before moving to North Staffordshire in 1994, continuing until 2011; David Frost in the 1990s moved from Walsall to Coventry and Warwickshire CCTE, and then to BCC in 2002. In Ireland J. R. Clark moved as secretary of the Irish chamber association to the Dublin chamber in 1928.

The challenge for small chambers was a 'chicken and egg' problem: without good secretaries, the chamber could not develop, but a small and weak chamber was not attractive as a career. The problem is well summed up by S. J. Batchelder, who moved from Manchester as Streat's assistant to become Leeds chamber secretary in 1937. Leeds then had three staff compared to Manchester's 20. Streat had warned him 'what Leeds chamber's funds may be capable of in the way of expansion I don't know ... it will be a grim business ... you will have to force yourself to be small minded'. A few months into the job Streat was replying to a 'melancholy letter' from Batchelder, and warned him: 'don't expect to rebuild Leeds in less that ten years .... Time is on your side so long as you are neither disheartened, disillusioned nor soured. Laugh and be patiently crafty.' Batchelder was encouraged by this: 'I knew I should have a sticky time here and in the first few weeks I found it worse than I ever suspected anything could be. Now after a couple of months I find the state of things is worse than I conceived when I came, but today the sun is shining and the world might be worse'. Batchelder found particular encouragement from 'successful ad hoc meetings' with members; he was unable to 'get my council to do anything'.[56] He went on to encourage grass-roots pressures for 'a bit of galvanising', and indeed successfully stayed as the Leeds secretary until the 1970s, becoming one of the key members of the ABCC, a member of the first attempt to reorganize ABCC under Knowles in 1947, and a member of the Dixon (1967) and Millichap (1976) Committees.[57]

From secretary to chief executive and contract manager

As chambers evolved, the secretary's role was recognized as more and more important, and the individuals sought were of higher experience, qualifications, seniority, and indeed salaries. The early secretarial job descriptions are often unspecified. Even in the 1930s the only *prescribed* duty of Streat in Manchester

[55] Knowles (1949), pp. 6–7.
[56] All quotations from Streat's *Diary*, Dupree (1987), vol. i, pp. 490–1, 521–2; letters from Streat to Batchelder, 2 May and 12 September 1937; Batchelder to Streat 15 September 1937.
[57] See Chapter 8.

was to record the proceedings of meetings of the chamber.[58] But as time progressed, fuller and more formal job specifications became more common, the expectations higher.

Southampton's well-cast but traditional job description of the 1870s stated: 'The secretary shall conduct the correspondence of the chamber, arrange the business of all its meetings, keep minutes of the proceedings of all of its committees, draw up reports, petitions, and memorials, and collect the subscriptions. He is also required to keep his attention constantly directed to all Bills before parliament affecting the intentions of trade and commerce.'[59] A later view is well summed up in 1956 in the forward to Wolverhampton's chamber history by their President:

> the general membership does not meet at frequent intervals and must largely rely on the council, honorary offices and the secretary to put forward their views and watch their interests. The honorary officers necessarily change at comparatively short intervals and so the reputation of the chamber and its mode of approach to problems must necessarily reflect in no small measure the personality of the secretary.[60]

Even in small chambers such as Jersey and Guernsey, the job description in 1984 included not only managing the staff, but monitoring the government, giving advice to members, and projecting the chamber.[61]

Thus, much of the activity of the chamber had moved from the voluntary model to a professional one relying on the secretary. The demands shifted from their clerical and minute-taking skills to their impact, business presence, personality, their networking capacity, and financial, marketing, and business development skills. In the modern chamber, communication skills and ability to develop services for members have strongly focused the individual sought. The terminology and title changed: from secretary to executive director, or chief executive. By 1998, 59% of chamber directors in line management fields had university or equivalent professional qualifications, with 67% coming from the private sector and 33% from the public sector.[62]

The shift of role in modern times is evident in the advertisement for a new London chamber chief executive in 2002, which called for 'senior leadership experience with successful private sector business . . . personal stature to command respect . . . and outstanding communication, managerial and personal skills, energy and commitment', with an advertised pay level of £120,000. The Derbyshire chamber in 2003 specified its need for a new chief executive as requiring 'energetic and visionary leadership . . . an ambassador for the business community'. A West London chamber set up in 2000 described the role as combining 'company direction, business development and strategic account management . . . building

---

[58] Streat, *Diary,* Dupree (1987), vol. i, p. xxvi.
[59] Southampton chamber, *Articles of Association* (1875), p. 15.
[60] In V. B. Beaumont, Wolverhampton chamber history, p. 2.
[61] Draft job specification for Jersey chamber secretary: letter from T. W. Gollop (Jersey director) to Guernsey chamber, in Guernsey minutes, 30 August 1984.
[62] *Survey of Local Economic Development in Chambers* (Bennett and BCC, 1998).

and developing close relationships with major businesses and key economic stake-holders to grow a 21st century organisation'.[63]

The transition to a modern form, in which service development has become a primary goal, was not always easy. In 1986 Swindon chamber went significantly into deficit, having appointed a much higher paid chief executive in place of their former secretary specifically to develop member services, but activity 'did not become as beneficial as soon as anticipated',[64] with resulting cost overruns. Cardiff's 2008 collapse, and crises in Mid Yorkshire, Sheffield, and Birmingham in 2009–10 were caused by similar difficulties.

In the 1980s and 1990s a further skill requirement was added to the secretary's job description: to manage contracts with government. An early demand for this had emerged from the first apprenticeship schemes developed in the early 1960s. But these were small and easily added to the secretary's portfolio. With the government New Training Initiative of 1981, especially the Youth Training Scheme, very large budgets suddenly became available to those chambers willing to act as managing agents, and which were located in areas of high youth unemployment—at which the scheme was directed. This expanded further with the launch of Training and Enterprise Councils in 1990 and Business Link in 1993.

The sort of chief executive now sought had to have the ability to run a medium-sized business, to be able to manage a significant staff, and to perform to externally set performance targets of both customer satisfaction and delivery of government demands; and all this had to be balanced with their role in managing the chamber's traditional business and membership. This brought in a different range of personnel, what some older chamber chief executives called 'quango types': attracted by high salaries, but expecting to move on in the medium term, and hence not deeply committed to the organization. This is a form of managerial 'staff sorting' that had some adverse consequences for other staff morale and membership retention, with traditional chamber staff often being treated as only fitting into second tier roles.

The abolition of TECs in 2001 and erosion of Business Link after 2006 brought this particular party to an end. Many of the expensive chief executives appointed in the 1990s chose to move on, were made redundant, or had to make a transition from growth to downsizing. Government as a major 'customer' had to be replaced by rethinking the needs of the core chamber business: the chamber member. New chief executives were needed, often on a lower salary package, with stronger local commitment, and more in the mould of the more modest ambitions of the early 1980s. A primary focus on serving chamber members, and developing direct services for them, have become again the principles needed.

Secretarial services

A common supportive role was for the chamber secretary to provide secretarial services to other local business associations. This helped the chamber financially

---

[63] Advertisements in *The Times*, 7 September 2000, 2 May 2002, and 11 September 2003.
[64] Swindon chamber, *Annual Accounts* (1987), p. 1.

since a fee could be charged for 'secretarial services', and it also helped build connections with other local bodies. This covered both area-wide bodies such as chambers of trade, and also sector bodies such as local trade associations. Thus, J. Jones was secretary of three of the local business associations when the chamber was founded at Middlesbrough in 1863: the chamber, the North of England Iron Masters Association, and the Royal Exchange.[65] In Birmingham the secretary had received £65 per year for acting as the secretary to the Builders Association, of which £40 was paid to the chamber; this was increased to £84 in 1912 with £50 paid to the chamber.[66] In Leicester the chamber's secretary in the 1930s, according to his own rather self-congratulatory account, founded many trade associations and other societies, and became engaged in other secretaryships.[67] This was also important in Liverpool, following restructuring in the 1870s, and Cardiff from 1943. In London and many of the other major chambers, secretarial services to sector associations became a major activity. In 1900 secretarial fees were £136 to the London chamber, rising to £27,527 in 1950 and were still £25,094 in 1960.

In principle, there was nothing wrong with the secretary or the chamber taking on other roles, which were often not only compatible with, but supportive of the chamber. Thus in Leeds in 1851 a part-time secretary at £100 was appointed, but they found they needed a full-time secretary. When he was appointed in 1856 at £150 per year, he was also allowed to maintain his agency for the Phoenix Fire and Pelican Life Assurance companies, and to act as secretary of the Woollen Association, charging £10 secretarial fee and £10 rent per year 'provided that the agency does not interfere with the discharge of duties of the chamber'.[68]

The advantage to chambers was that this brought obligational and solidarity benefits from a wider business community. It also allowed them to claim vastly larger memberships. However, these roles could compete for time and undermine chamber effectiveness. The first secretary of the Macclesfield chamber in 1867, George Clarke, certainly found it difficult to meet his personal financial demands through his salary as chamber secretary alone. He was continuously in arrears with payment of personal bills, his draper (Hucksell and Pattinson of Macclesfield), for example, writing numerous letters requesting outstanding payments.[69] Clarke had tried to combine his role as chamber secretary with his income as an insurance agent. But the Liverpool and London Globe Insurance Co. took a dim view of his involvement asking him 'how long you have been connected with the chamber of commerce and what grounds you have for supposing that you may be able to influence businesses [for the insurance company] of an acceptable character and the

---

[65] Middlesbrough *Business Directory* (1871).
[66] Birmingham chamber, GPC minutes, 12 February 1912.
[67] Purt (1961), p. 12, Leicester chamber history.
[68] Leeds chamber minutes, 27 August and 3 September 1856; Beresford (1951), Leeds chamber history, p. 33.
[69] Personal correspondence files 1867–8, Cheshire RO: D2950/30–2.

probable amount'.[70] Whatever the reason, Clarke quickly moved to become secretary of the North Cheshire chamber of agriculture in July 1868.[71]

Staff and salaries

As time progressed, further staff were needed additional to the secretary. Sometimes, indeed, other specialist or menial staff were employed before a secretary emerged. This was particularly true where early chambers managed reading rooms, libraries, or coffee rooms. Junior clerks, librarians, messengers, attendants, porters, housekeepers, waiters, cleaners, caretakers, 'boys', and similar staff emerge as early employees.[72] The Irish chambers with specific roles in local harbours and markets had crane minders, harbour wardens, fisheries wardens; roles usually undertaken by a member (or their staff) or a nominated individual paid an honorarium, with a bonus gratuity if the service was satisfactory. One of the most important early appointments was an agent in London. Such a lobbyist commonly cost £100 in the 18th century.[73]

Assistant secretaries emerged to support the efforts of increasingly overburdened secretaries. These were initially seen as fairly low-level posts in terms of skills. One of the first assistant secretaries, in Limerick, was appointed solely to collect the members' fees; the early subscriptions of the chamber from 1807 were based on a fee for imports and exports, using a Customs officer to collect the levy at a 5% fee; but he was found inefficient so that the secretary took this over in 1809 with the aid of an assistant.[74] When the Newcastle chamber moved to appoint its first assistant secretary as its second member of staff in 1932, it sought that an 'unemployed quaysider should be given preference'.[75] However, Glasgow paid its first librarian £75 in 1840 compared to the secretary's £52 10s. from 1852–3, before the secretary's salary was increased to £100 from 1854.[76]

Early secretaries were often part time, with salaries more akin to honoraria. In Dublin, the first secretary in 1783, William Shannon, a local notary, received £30. Belfast first started to pay its secretary £20 in 1822, increased to £50 in the 1850s, and £60 in 1857. Limerick paid its full-time secretary £140 from 1809.[77] The Birmingham secretary was supposedly full time over the 1850s–1880 and received £100. These were comparable, but probably better than in non-commercial societies, where £60 a year was paid for a senior secretary, with 20 guineas being common.[78] But basic clerks in the early 1800s at the Treasury were paid £90–500,

[70] Letter to Clarke of 17 April 1867: D2950/30.
[71] Letter to Clarke at the North Cheshire chamber of agriculture, 17 July 1868: D2950/31.
[72] New York's first member of staff was a doorman and messenger: minutes, June 1768: Stevens (1867).
[73] All salaries quoted as per annum below, unless otherwise stated; see Chapter 8 on agents.
[74] Limerick chamber minutes, 24 March 1809.
[75] Newcastle chamber minutes, 7 December 1932.
[76] Glasgow chamber accounts, *Annual Reports*.
[77] Limerick chamber minutes, 24 March 1809.
[78] Clark (2000a).

at London banks £100–280, and at the East India Company £70–300.[79] Hence, early chamber salaries were low, especially for experienced and responsible people.

Salaries remained low. Belfast paid its first full-time secretary £100–120 in 1898–9.[80] Oldham paid £100 in 1888, a similar level to that of many other chambers at this time. When Wolverhampton sought to appoint a full-time secretary in 1902 it expected it 'would cost at least £100'. The larger chambers were more generous, Manchester in 1870 paid its secretary £262 10s. plus £82 10s. honorarium. Liverpool paid its secretary £350 in the 1870s, £450 in the 1890s, raised to £500 in 1898, and its assistant secretary £150 in 1894.[81] Cardiff in 1900 was paying £250 for its secretary and £20 for a boy. When Birmingham reorganized its staff in 1917 it increased the secretary salary to £800, increased by £50 for four years, thereafter increased in relation to the chamber's income. But it paid its assistant secretary only £25 until 1917, when a minute clerk was employed at £130, and a 'Form K' clerk at £100. A buildings manager was appointed in 1919 at £300.[82] By 1908 London was paying its secretary £1000, and its assistant secretary £500. Of its 28 staff, nine received over £200 per year, and salaries ranged down to £20. By the 1930s Manchester had one of the highest salary rates. Despite the secretary (Raymond Streat) believing they could not afford his salary in 1932, his salary was raised from £2000 to £2250 in 1934. This was exceptional, as a permanent secretary's salary in the civil service was only £2000 at this time. Streat was anxious to raise and improve salaries and staff quality and skills, for example resisting attempts by the council to reduce staff salaries by 10% in the slump year of 1932. The deputy secretary at Manchester was paid £1450 in 1938.[83] But in 1930 Southampton was still only paying its secretary £425 plus bonus.[84] The other bodies also paid poorly. The central chamber of agriculture paid its full-time secretary £375 in 1912, rising to £450 in 1920.[85]

For comparison, the salary of a civil service intermediate division clerk in 1911 was £100, rising by £10 per year to £200, and then by £15 per year to £350 (minimum starting age 18).[86] Hence, chambers were commonly paying salaries at the lower-middle range of the clerical grade for a role that needed significantly more independence of action and leadership.

Other staff were paid even more poorly, though these were often part-time jobs, or were occupied by 'boys' or elderly retainers. Cork's two waiters were paid 9s. per week in 1819. Southampton in 1851 had a messenger at £3 per year and an attendant at 7d. per week (£1 10s. 4d. p.a.); in 1930 it was paying its clerks £2 per week; in 1960 clerks received £5 per week and the assistant secretary £13 10s. 10d.

---

[79] Booth (1886; Moses (1914)); range depending chiefly on years of service.

[80] Belfast chamber minutes.

[81] Liverpool chamber, Committee on Finance, Library and Members; 380 COM 2/7.

[82] Birmingham chamber Council minutes, 25 June 1917; GPC minutes, 26 October 1916, 8 March 1917, 26 May 1919.

[83] Streat *Diary*, Dupree (1987), vol. i, pp. 10–11, 142–3, 173, 351; vol. ii, pp. 10–11.

[84] Southampton chamber, *Annual Report*.

[85] *Annual Reports*, central chamber of agriculture; BL Ac. 3486.

[86] Moses (1914), pp. 306–7.

per month (£162 p.a.). Belfast had a porter at £13 in 1860, and a charlady and messenger both at £5 4s. in the 1870s and 1880s. Edinburgh's Assistant Secretary received only £50 per year in 1920.[87] Birmingham's 'lady clerk' was paid 3s. per week in 1913 (£7 16 s. p.a.).[88]

Staff and salaries since the 1970s

The very low salaries and traditional structures of chambers were challenged by the need to manage training contracts in the 1970s and 1980s in the larger chambers. This was followed by EU and other contracts from the 1980s. Much wider management skills were now required and much higher salaries were possible. For example Coventry went from a traditional well-established chamber of 19 staff in the 1980s into a large organization of 82 staff in 1993, and 200 in 1999 after it became a CCTE. For smaller chambers the changes were even greater. Shropshire went from 1.5 in 1980, to 14 in 1995, and to 103 in 2005; Wigan from 0.5 to 25 to 139; Derby from 5 to 6 to 178; Rotherham from 1.5 to 10 to 146. In Ireland over the same period staff changes were slower; Dublin grew from 7 to 15 to 18; Cork from 4 to 2 to 8; and Waterford from 1.5 to 3 to 10.

The larger staff, wider range of tasks, and higher salaries were mostly paid by government contracts. This became a major part of the incentives for the senior management to seek changes in chamber status in the UK: CCTEs and merged chambers and Business Links would never have attracted the support of chamber managers if they were paying salaries similar to chambers. In the mid-1990s a mean TEC chief executive salary was £100,000, and a Business Link chief executive £80,000. Operations directors of TECs and Business Links were receiving £35,000–50,000; personal business advisers were receiving £25,000–35,000, and were considered 'lowly paid'. Yet at this time the chamber chief executives were generally receiving less than £60,000, and operations directors were often paid no more than £30,000; e.g. in 2002 Birmingham partnership managers and project managers were paid £28,000–35,000. Average staff salaries (below chief executive level) in a representative group of the medium-sized chambers in 1992 were only £15,500.[89]

This radical change in remuneration was matched by radical change in role, to become large-scale service providers and partnership leaders with government. With the demise of CCTEs and downsizing of Business Link funds, there has been a major change. Whereas Finer and Dupree identified the need for new 'professionals', as noted above, the secretary of chambers until the 1980s retained a strong loyalty to the organization; non-profit bodies attract managers whose goals are different from those of the typical private company.[90] The CCTE and Business Link period reversed this 'managerial sorting' so that the chambers had managers

---

[87] Minutes and *Annual Reports* of each chamber.
[88] Birmingham chamber GPC minutes, 9 September 1913.
[89] Wage data derived from newspaper advertisements; see also Bennett and Krebs (1993a).
[90] Weisbrod (1988), pp. 31–3.

more like any other company with no specific interest, or commitment. This undermined bodies where the members had obligational links and solidarity, and were not just customers. In a world without CCTEs some of the older style chamber managers' characteristics may now be more appropriate.

Chamber 'departments', staff functions, and organization

The earliest chambers were unified bodies with the secretary and/or president as the focus. The concept of 'departments' within chambers was very slow to develop, and was usually associated with the growth in volume of activities and staff. London was probably the first to create administrative departments, establishing a separate membership department in 1896, and then other departments associated with its main service fields: employment agency, examinations, arbitration, export documents, enquiries, etc. The large TPS bodies were also early developers of departments, for enquiries and status reports, bankruptcy, and debt collection from the 1870s. Few chambers of trade were ever large enough to have departments.

London's departmentalization can be described as functional: by field of activity. This became the general model, but it was slow to develop more widely. Birmingham, when it considered internal staff reorganization in 1917, initially considered two divisions: 'secretarial' (minutes and reports, as well as advice to members, certificates, and trade association links; plus new functions of *Journal*, information, translation, and library), and 'commercial or business' (accounts, purchases, membership, social club, room hire and catering, advertising). However, this rather confusing structure proposed by the president (H. W. Sambidge) was not taken up, and instead a three-way division each with its own assistant secretary, suggested by the secretary, was developed. This separated (i) secretarial functions (for minutes and reports), (ii) bookkeeping, which shared a general pool of six clerks and an office boy, and (iii) a buildings manager who oversaw a clerk, caretaker, commissionaire, lift attendant, boy, and cleaners.[91] Thus of over 17 staff, only four (about 20%) were senior executive professionals, whilst the rest were clerks or functionaries. This was a slender resource for professional support for business advice and lobbying for a membership of nearly 3000 at the time; it demonstrates the dominance in even the larger chambers of the tasks of supporting committees, facilitating meetings, and managing rooms and facilities.

This pattern did not change significantly for most chambers until the 1970s, when inspection regimes for certificate issuing, and significant training departments for executive and youth training became the norm, often as specific cost centres or divisions. Business advice and support functions that began to grow in the late 1970s as a result of the Bolton Report, and after 1993 with Business Link were normally grafted on as a further functional division. The typical modern structure of staff is reflected in a 1998 survey. This showed that of an average 22 staff in BCC chambers: management, membership, and lobbying occupied 8.5, training staff or

---

[91] Birmingham chamber, GPC minutes, 26 January and 8 February 1917.

managers were 6.9, information advisers and certificates were 4.9, and liaison with partners in economic development and education were 1.1.[92]

A functional structure of chamber staff was the norm. But when chambers began to work with TECs, and especially when 16 of them merged with TECs after 1995, much more complex structures developed. The chambers, or the merged TEC-chambers and Business Link-chambers, had to manage a complex interplay of membership services, government contracts, and demands to act as business leadership bodies. Some did this through expanded departments. Others tried more integrated approaches.

The 'New Age' leadership model developed in the 1990s was the most ambitious attempt to integrate functions. It sought to use business bodies such as chambers as key inputs to more general restructuring of public services, especially through local partnerships and capacity building. This was often attempted by moving internal organization towards a more integrated structure, or 'matrix management', which sought to draw common approaches and methods across chamber departments, TECs, and Business Links. The aim was to join up initiatives, drawing in partners to work in a more integrated way, with different cross-department structures for different local initiatives. The staff size of TECs had a mode of 50 in 1992–4, rising to 100 by 2001. Chambers similarly became large organizations, with a mean staff of 50, ranging up to 200 by 2000, generally largest in the merged TEC-chambers. In effect, matrix management attempted to achieve for large organizations what the secretary did for the chambers when they were small bodies: to act as a unified entity. With the demise of TECs and Business Links many chambers had to downsize and restructure significantly, but the experience of matrix and other forms of integrated management have been important lessons to providing a more customer-focused modern chamber.

Managing the membership

An effective membership administration is one of the most critical elements of chamber management, since this maintains the link with members and their commitment through paying a subscription. This was the job of the secretary in early chambers; but as chambers grew they appointed specific staff to do this, developed membership departments, and employed specialist canvassers to recruit members. London chamber was the first to establish a 'membership department' in 1896, reorganized in 1910. This was copied by other major chambers, but in smaller chambers recruitment has relied on the secretary or a single member of staff up to the present.

The efficient management of the membership was a challenge to early chambers, and indeed remains so. To get members to renew requires their current addresses to be known, a letter and invoice to be sent out, and a payment received in reply. When the payment is received it is then necessary to record this in a database and

---

[92] *Survey of Local Economic Development* (Bennett and BCC, 1998).

remove those that do not pay. Birmingham and Manchester used a card index system for this in the 1910–20s period, making it easier to keep a running tally, which was cross-indexed as a source of sector and other information.[93] However, the monitoring and management of the membership of many chambers was often extremely casual. Many *Annual Reports* do not routinely quote membership numbers, and even fewer quote new joiners and resignations. It was fairly general to overstate membership and, until modern times, chambers were also reluctant to accept resignations, often allowing lapsing members to accumulate long periods of arrears in the hope that they would resume payment. This led to significant difficulties of chamber governance, and also contributed to a false sense of stability. The effect of membership administration on member joining and lapsing is fully explored in Chapter 16.

Many chambers also exaggerated their membership either for local boosterism, to influence the national association, or to gain more votes in ABCC proceedings. Birmingham noted in 1924 that Manchester used an inaccurate method to calculate its total membership: 'it was unsatisfactory that a chamber with a smaller membership than Birmingham should appear in publications of ABCC with a larger number'.[94] After the 1991 ABCC *Development Strategy* defined 1000 as a minimum membership requirement for accreditation, a remarkable number of chambers moved up to just meet that threshold! This problem was removed by BCC moving to accreditation of services rather than using size criteria after 1998.

6.5 FINANCIAL RESOURCES

The governance of chambers also depends on their financial wherewithal. Historically the link between governance and finance was direct, through paying a subscription. Subscription was the price of joining, and provided a further price comparison when decisions were made to remain a member when the next subscription fell due. For the chamber managers (paid or voluntary) the subscription was the key link to the membership: as stated by the ABCC secretary in 1949, 'finance is the controlling factor'.[95] The link was direct when subscriptions were the sole or main resource, as was the case in many early chambers. As stated by Liverpool in 1918: 'the truest test of a voluntary association . . . is the measure of financial support it receives'.[96] For most chambers this position did not change until the 1970s. Thus for the first 200 years, the subscription defined a key mechanism by which chambers were judged, by both members and managers. This is shown very clearly in Figure 6.3. The mean proportion of subscriptions within total chamber income never fell below 80% until the 1950s, only began to decline steeply after 1960 (reaching 44% in 1982), and was down to 24% by

[93] Birmingham chamber GPC minutes, exchange with Manchester, 7 January 1924.
[94] Birmingham chamber GPC minutes, 4 February 1924.
[95] Knowles (1949), p. 11.
[96] Liverpool chamber, *Handbook* (1918), p. 50.

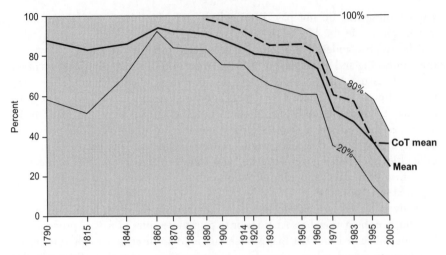

Fig. 6.3. Proportion of income derived from subscriptions in chambers of commerce 1790–2010. Mean, range, and 20%/80% box of subscriptions as a percentage of total income; only the mean shown for chambers of trade (CoT).

2005. Figure 6.3 also demonstrates that the range was generally narrow. A few chambers (such as Jersey and Limerick) had other significant income sources over 1790–1840, but the range remained narrow until the 1970s.[97] In chambers of trade the pattern was similar, although the shift from subscriptions has been slightly later and smaller in extent.

The period after the 1970s thus represents a fundamental shift of the chamber system. As the income from other sources steadily increased it became possible for the governance link between members and management through their subscriptions to be steadily diminished. The new sources of income were initially fees for services, a significant proportion of which came from members: fees for certificates were the main source of other income over 1920–60. However, from the 1970s other income was coming in large amounts not from fees, but from government contracts for services. It is this period that has most severely challenged the governance of chambers by introducing dangers of core chamber activities becoming by-products. It was also this period that saw greater diversity enter the system, between those chambers with large fee and government income and those without.

The evolution of chamber incomes is shown in Figure 6.4. It should be noted that in this figure the scale is logarithmic; this allows the actual contemporary values to be read off, but it compresses the upper range. Total chamber income ranges steadily widened over the period from the 1860s, but especially after the 1970s, where the high income of a few large chambers pulls the mean of the whole system

---

[97] Figure 6.3 is influenced by the small number of early chambers. The chambers with significant other incomes were Jersey, Limerick, Cork; to a lesser extent Edinburgh and Glasgow which had substantial interest income.

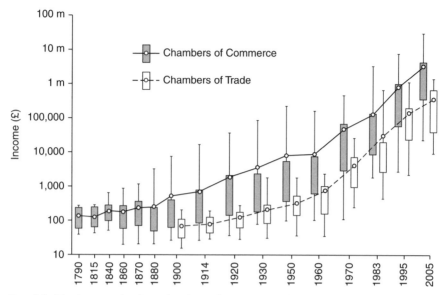

Fig. 6.4. Total income levels in chambers of commerce and chambers of trade 1790–2009 (log scale). Mean, range, and 20%/80% box plots at current prices.

heavily upwards, to the edge of the 80% box plot. The minimum income levels stayed remarkably constant over a long period, showing how some of the chambers remained very static.

The same was true in Ireland; in 1996 only five chambers had income over £400,000, whilst 65% had less than £100,000 and 40% less than £40,000.[98] The variability which is endemic to a voluntary system with no controls on market entry has thus tended to greatly increase; a pattern which is common with the USA where the range is even wider.[99] In the UK the chambers of trade, although evolving with a much lower level of total resources, also experienced a very rapid increase in range of resources between the poorest and richest, chiefly from the 1980s. This arose because, despite their small size, some also became important contractors for government services, chiefly under Business Link after 1993, whilst in Ireland EU funding was significant from the 1990s.

The dominant role of other (non-subscription) income in the total income pattern is clear from Figure 6.5. For most of the early system the range was small: 80% had £100 or less other income until 1840 (although some large chambers had acquired incomes from interest earned on assets, renting rooms, secretarial services to other associations, and in Ireland from markets). But up to

---

[98] Goodbody Associates (1996), Table 2.13.
[99] USA chambers in 1920 had mean income of about $10,600, and range from $85 to $130,000 (largest was New York); broadly comparable to the UK mean (of £1947) at the same date, but the range 1:1500 is higher than the UK 1:940, reflecting large State level chambers: calculated from the lists in US Department of Commerce (1923).

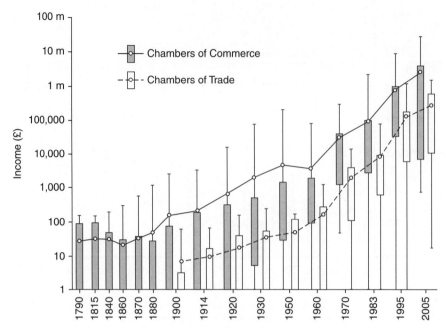

Fig. 6.5. Levels of other income in chambers of commerce and chambers of trade 1790–2009 (log scale). Mean, range, and 20%/80% box plots at current prices.

1920, over 20% of chambers had no income except subscriptions. WW1 saw some important changes as many chambers participated in the government's 'form K'. From the 1920s the fees from document certificates also became significant, and were responsible for most of the differentiation of income up to 1960. The lower maxima in 1960 and 1970 reflects drops in London's certificate income in this period. The system as a whole took off in the 1980s with increasing maxima being achieved each year and the range steadily increasing. But the minimum other income of the smallest chambers stayed very low until they merged into the larger chambers of commerce after 1995, or left the system to become chambers of trade. The budgets of the BCC chambers rose to an average of £2.9 million by 1998; for the larger chambers budgets had reached over £10 million by 2000,[100] with the largest at £33 million, at the peak of these developments.[101] In Ireland average non-subscription income exceeded 50% by the 1990s mainly through service fees, but after 1996 EU programmes also became significant. The chambers of trade showed some similar patterns, though as noted, the figures here reflect an upward bias towards the largest of these chambers. The vast majority had virtually no non-subscription income until the 1960s, after which the largest mirror the chambers of commerce.

---

[100] All of which were CCTEs.
[101] All statistics quoted in this paragraph from BCC *Benchmarking* data.

6.6 CONCLUSION

One of the greatest challenges for associations is to manage the process of cohesion and loyalty of their membership. This requires a subtle mix of leadership and grass-roots democracy. The governance regimes to achieve this were established from the earliest days of chambers, and essentially similar structures are used to this day. From the 1840s this increasingly involved the support of professional staff as a central resource for chamber development, but only from the 1950s was staff resource large enough, on a widespread scale, that staff rather than councils became the main input to the activities of chambers. Large-scale professional organizations, however, were the product of the 1970s and especially the 1980s. In contrast, most chambers of trade remained dependent mainly on voluntary input into the 1970s, and most are still entirely voluntary.

One of the greatest challenges has been, and remains, the activism of the few and the lethargy/apathy of the many. The limited number of volunteers coming forward, and the sometimes-restricted range of experience available among them, has often meant that leadership has fallen on a few shoulders within a locality. This means that chambers have been strongly subject to the 'politics of the bureau': the same people have remained involved, and their decisions have often been strongly influenced by what has gone before. This has strong implications for how chambers have been viewed by members, their commitment, potential detachment, and thus on joining and lapsing patterns, 'exit, voice, and loyalty', which is examined in detail in Chapter 16.

Over time, the committee structures became more numerous and complex, though tending to become simplified and streamlined since 1990. The structure of committees/sections also grew to reflect a varying range of policy agendas. All this sought to involve different groups of members in more effective ways. Committees and sections reflect the need for *deliberation*: for members, or representative groups of members, to be able to analyse and debate issues and then to develop policies, lobbies, and also to provide inputs to management. This is an essential part of how an association can relate to, and service the needs or wants of, its members. It is also an essential part of the way in which sound and well-evidenced policy documents can be developed, and lobbies mounted. Committee complexity is thus a natural outcome of the need for larger-scale efforts to deliberate, to lobby, and to involve members.

More generally, from the 1970s, and especially from the 1980s, the resources of chambers have shifted fundamentally: external income from fees and government contracts has become increasingly important to the major chambers. This has increased the differentiation of the large chambers from the rest, and has increasingly challenged the financial link between members and managers that had been more assured when subscriptions were the sole or main source of income. Even some of the chambers of trade became involved in this bonanza. As a result, after 1990, many of the chamber staff became increasingly dominated by the needs of government contract management. From the 1980s, therefore, the chambers became deeply implicated in by-product issues, with their USP challenged by the breadth of services they were providing, and in the 1990s their mission confused by providing 'non-preferred' services for government, with dangers of 'managerial sorting' that preferred government over member demands. This remains a major challenge for future development, as discussed in Chapter 17.

7

Recognition and Public Status

7.1 IS ANYONE LISTENING?

Chambers of commerce in Britain, Ireland, and America are governed under a common law system. They have had no specific public law or government status, such as those in countries like France or Germany. This chapter investigates the consequences of this institutional structure: how does a common law system present opportunities and threats to business voice, and how have chambers responded to this.

The core *raison d'être* and USP of voluntary chambers is independence of voice. But the challenge is to ensure that someone is listening. Rather than being a privileged interest, chambers have frequently felt ignored by government or excluded by the administrative departments of state. Initially aristocratic mores, then populism, and the clamour of special interest groups, have been countervailing powers that have squeezed out economic and business needs, particularly those of localities. It is natural, therefore, that chambers have sought to gain a specific status to be consulted and make their voice heard. Hubert Llewellyn Smith, permanent secretary to the BoT in 1914,[1] recognized chambers needed 'to discharge effectively that double function of keeping government departments in touch with trade, and of keeping traders in touch with government departments'. But this did not tackle the question of how this was to be achieved.

There have been various stages to the efforts by chambers to gain status from the state, detailed in this chapter. In pre-Reform Britain up to the 1830s, those entities that were not formal chartered or incorporated bodies had no *guaranteed* right to be listened to by parliament. This impediment led to efforts to gain charters and to incorporate, followed by efforts to gain a 'locus standi'. A separate line of argument called for 'tribunals of commerce' as alternatives, or supplements, to the law courts. The search for government backing for tribunals is one of the most significant, but previously almost entirely neglected, themes of chamber discourse. Some success was achieved in the 1880s and 1890s, but left chambers frustrated. As a result, a further wave of initiatives emerged, presaged in the 1850s, but primarily after 1900, towards a 'public law status': to gain the perceived advantages of European chamber systems. This objective recurred, always vigorously sought by some chambers, but equally vigorously

---

[1] ACC, *Proceedings* (1914), speeches at Annual Dinner; reprinted *The Value and Importance of the Work of Chambers of Commerce*, p. 3.

resisted by others. In the 1960s, public law status became the official objective of the national association, only to be abandoned in 1996. However, a significant advance was made in 1999 with a formal Act to protect the title of chambers and to define for the first time in British law their core form and functions. Similar protection has been afforded in Ireland.

7.2 THE 'RIGHT' TO BE HEARD: CHARTERS AND INCORPORATION

A frequent challenge to early chambers was that they were 'self-elected'; i.e. they had no formal status and their core values of voluntarism and independence were used as a source of weakness. Thus, in criticizing the General Chamber in 1787, *The Times* dismissed 'all stir of a *self-created* chamber of commerce, and disappointed patriots'.[2] There was thus a real challenge to demonstrate that a chamber had a standing beyond a few self-appointed people assembled to sign a petition. Most of all, it had to be demonstrated that the opinion was based on a legitimized process of general support from a defined community.

The government and critical press were familiar with models of businesses formally constituted by statute. Before the days of limited liability companies, the statute or chartered companies (East India, Levant, Royal Africa, etc.), and bodies like the Merchant Adventurers were the only formal legally defined business bodies other than the corporations of local government. They had an automatic *right* to be heard by government. That right extended to requiring a formal response from the BoT or others in government, to which they addressed correspondence and memorials. Most importantly there was a right to be heard by parliament; a chartered company could request to appear at the Bar of the Commons and be heard by the whole of parliament. This also applied to the municipal corporations, burghs, and counties. Moreover, a petition or correspondence from a formal body could, without raising objections, be addressed to parliament through one of its MPs; petitions from informal bodies could be refused.

The use of charters

This difference in status was recognized immediately as a key impediment to be overcome. The New York chamber managed to acquire approval for a charter from George III in 1770, two years after its foundation, which was granted in order to bolster loyalist support in the city. This was subsequently renewed by the governor of New York in 1784.[3] The Glasgow chamber was founded in 1783 under a Royal charter, largely due to the foresight of its first president, Patrick Colquhoun, his willingness and ability to finance the considerable cost, as well as

---

[2] *The Times*, 17 March 1787; emphasis added.
[3] Stevens (1867); Bishop (1918); see Chapter 4.

deploying his personal position in 1782–3 as the Provost of Glasgow as a route of access. Colquhoun was advised by London agent John Seton that 'a Royal charter will add permanency and weight to the establishment of your chamber of commerce and there can be no objection to your obtaining it as I presume you will neither ask for powers to purchase lands nor to borrow money in your corporate capacity which are the great objections to His Majesty granting powers of incorporation'. Seton advised that the only materials needed were a petition, which would be referred to the Attorney General and Lord Advocate, followed by a meeting: 'I should conceive a conversation with yourself explaining the plain meaning of the institution'.[4]

Edinburgh was able to follow a similar route in 1785–6, where the costs were £166.[5] But the request for a Royal charter from the Jersey chamber was refused in 1787, and repeatedly thereafter.[6] Dublin considered seeking a charter in 1823, but abandoned it.[7] The only other chambers able to obtain charters after 1785 all reflected the different circumstances of Scotland and Ireland: Greenock received a charter in 1813; Leith in 1852; Limerick, founded in 1807, gained a charter in 1815 largely as a result of its de facto licence as an arm of the local corporation;[8] and Waterford, founded in 1787, sought a charter in 1807, eventually granted in 1815 largely on the basis of the debenture structure of shareholders that it had developed for purchase of its building.[9]

Government resistance to charters

Jersey's efforts to obtain a charter in 1787 illustrate the barriers. To prevent early opposition from the local States and the British government 'it was unanimously agreed and resolved to keep secret among the members of the committee' the charter proposal until the final papers were ready to be laid before the whole membership of the chamber. This was 'particularly recommended' by John Dumaresq, their local member acting as London agent. The papers were agreed at a chamber meeting in August 1787, and a petition and letters then sent soliciting support from the Governor, Bailiff, and jurats.[10] However, by January 1788 a caveat had been lodged 'with the Attorney General by William Heythuyson one of 60 clerks in chancery against the petition'. The chamber resolved to fight this, raising new funds if necessary. Papers were prepared by the secretary evidencing the contribution of the chamber to the 'commercial advantage to this

---

[4] John Seton, letter to Colquhoun, 11 February 1783; TD 1670/4/14; also see Chapter 4.
[5] £101 for London solicitor William Suttie; £50 12s. 6d. Chancery Office, and £15 Great Seal Office: Edinburgh minutes and accounts, 1786.
[6] It was finally incorporated as a limited company in 1900.
[7] Dublin chamber, *Report of Council* (1823), p. 5.
[8] Quoted in Limerick entry in Bristol chamber, *Yearbook* (1908–9): Bristol RO 38605/Pu/35; for Ireland see O'Connor (1938).
[9] Waterford chamber minutes, 17 July 1807; *Charter text* (1815); discussion of debenture in Chapter 11.
[10] Jersey chamber minutes, 23 April and 18 August 1787.

country', and John Dumaresq was sent to England to assist the lobby.[11] Dumaresq pressed matters, and a hearing before the Attorney General was held at which the caveat lodged by various 'gentlemen of this Island' was supported by legal 'counsel for these gentlemen [who] was instructed to deny various facts and services alleged to have been done by the chamber for the good of trade and of the public in general ... [and] delivered in writing ... sundry objections and pretensions advanced against the chamber'. As a result the Attorney General suspended his report on the charter until he was further informed.[12] Dumaresq briefed the chamber on the objections, prepared a reply, which the chamber approved. He was then instructed to pursue the matter,[13] but no further developments are recorded. The Jersey experience shows how critical it was to obtain local support, or at least ensure that there were no local objections, and to have strong support from government, something that Colquhoun in Glasgow had painstakingly undertaken.

The lack of success of efforts to obtain charters in England and the Channel Islands was also probably the result of political resistance to the chamber concept by the younger Pitt and successive governments after the aggressive lobbying by the General Chamber in 1785–7. The unsuccessful efforts of the London chamber to gain a charter, or any other form of formal status, through the City Corporation in 1817, 1823, and 1850–70, discussed in Chapter 5, demonstrate a powerful resistance of successive governments to grant support for a chartered London chamber; and as discussed later below, related efforts to formally constitute chambers as local 'tribunals' also failed. This begs the question of whether developments might have been different if the General Chamber had never been established.

Josiah Wedgwood, the General Chamber's co-chair, certainly recognized that chartered status would make an important difference. By 1786 he was advocating that a charter or Act of parliament would confer 'an existence beside what we are often twitted with, a *self-delegated one*. We could answer the question—what is a chamber? which stood so much in our way last year.' It would most of all allow direct use of 'petition or remonstrance as a real and substantial body'.[14] At the end of 1786 he was optimistic that ministers would support chartered status, and Garbett sent him a copy of Glasgow chamber's charter of 1783, though Garbett was worried by the difficulties of getting agreement from the 'great variety' of the General Chamber's members.[15] Indeed the plan was killed by the eruption of discord within the Chamber over the 1787 French Treaty.

The difficulties experienced by lack of chartered status are well illustrated in the lobbies of the 1780s. When Thomas Stanley, MP for Lancashire, presented to

---

[11] Reported by Paul Le Mesurier; Jersey chamber minutes, 3, 9, and 24 January, 5 February 1788.
[12] Jersey chamber minutes, 3 December 1788; the names of the objectors are not recorded.
[13] Jersey chamber minutes, 12 January 1789; Dumaresq's summary and his response are not preserved.
[14] Wedgwood to Thomas Walker, 8 March 1786, emphasis added; Farrer (1906), p. 39; also Dietz (1991), p. 195.
[15] Garbett to Shelburne, 14 October 1786; quoted in Dietz (1991), pp. 195–6.

parliament the petition of manufacturers of Manchester concerning the fustian tax in 1785, the president of the BoT, Charles Jenkinson, was quick to note that 'undoubtedly the House could not recognise any meeting or aggregate body of men, who assembled without either the authority of the Crown or parliament'; i.e. they lacked a formal charter. This was all part of the political play, the 'twitting' as Wedgwood called it. However, after making the point, Jenkinson was nevertheless prepared to accept the petition in the name of one signatory, Thomas Walker, not the Manchester chamber, other associated bodies, or the claimed 50,000 signatories that had been involved.[16]

In the Irish parliament, similar issues raged. When Travers Hartley, president of the Dublin chamber, but also an MP, presented the petition of the chamber on the navigation laws in 1785, Mr Fitzgibbon, the Attorney General, could not 'consent to receive a petition from a body of men styling themselves—a council of a chamber of commerce—a title utterly unknown to this House, either as a chartered or a corporate body, and therefore however respectable the petitioners, this House can take no cognisance'. He went on: 'what is a chamber of commerce. Merely a self-elected body, and the name a title usurped.' This theme was continued by Mr Beresford MP, who said the 'House cannot recognise a body unknown to law . . . [but] they may come as a guild or merchants of the City of Dublin, or as individual merchants'; and John Scott MP argued: 'usurped titles of president and vice president of the chamber of commerce—titles that we in vain look for in the Statute Book . . . or in the charters of corporations',[17] should mean that their views could be set aside. There was no refusal to receive petitions from individuals, since everyone had the right to petition parliament and the Crown. But for bodies, the right to be heard rested on their formal status. Thus the Dublin case was resolved by accepting the petition from Hartley as MP and his cosignatories as individuals, not from the chamber.[18]

A similar problem arose when it was sought to ensure that chambers were informed about new legislation or parliamentary debates. Formal corporations such as the municipalities and East India Company received copies of Bills and Acts automatically; chambers and others could not immediately acquire them and had to use an agent or other intermediary. Thus in the 1790s, Glasgow chamber, with its charter, was routinely receiving Bills and Acts along with the Lord Provost of the city, as were the mayors and clerks of the other major cities. Edinburgh, the only other chartered chamber in Britain, was rarely as thrusting and seems to have never sought this right, so that material was sent to the Dean of the Edinburgh Guildery; in Bristol it was sent to the clerk of the Merchant Venturers.[19] It then relied on their attitude to chambers whether it was sent on locally.

---

[16] Thorne (1986), *History of Parliament*, 11 March 1785, p. 350.

[17] *Parliamentary Register or History of the House of Commons of Ireland*, October 1783–May 1784, pp. 205–7.

[18] Strangely, despite this the Dublin chamber decided not to attempt to acquire a charter in the early 1800s, as it was not going to have property, stock, or capital: Prendeville (1930), p. 101.

[19] e.g. House of Commons, Resolutions of a Committee of the Whole House, to whom the *Report from the Committee on the Promulgation of Statutes* was referred, 20 March 1797, p. 6.

These difficulties continued until the Reform Acts removed most of the special rights of guilds and restructured the corporations. But even with their reforming zeal, the Municipal Commissioners of 1835–9 were unhappy with the idea of chambers. They only deigned to notice chambers in two areas (Bristol and Limerick), whilst there were about 20 actually operating at the time, and in both areas they were critical of their role. In Bristol, they observed that the chamber founded in 1823, 'cannot be passed over in silence, in consequence of the important part it has taken in some affairs of the city. We think there is no doubt that the formation of such a society *ought to have been unnecessary*. . . . the functions which the chamber proposed to take on itself, making allowance for the alteration in modern habits and principles of trade, were precisely those for which the . . . Adventurers was originally incorporated'. Similarly in Limerick, the Commission noted with warmth that the Company of Merchants of the Staple had been replaced by a chartered chamber of commerce, which was 'very effectively and zealously' attending to its business, but it nevertheless stated that 'from its title, [it might] be supposed properly to be directed' by the Staplers.[20]

As a result of these perceived difficulties, many chambers sought to work jointly with their local corporations, even in Glasgow where they did not formally need to do so. And when Glasgow's chamber president proposed in 1788 that a London commercial office should be established for lobbying, he suggested status could only be achieved if a joint 'Commission' from the Royal Burghs, chamber, and commercial population could be produced.[21] However, working with local corporations was not a very powerful or reliable ambition, and was vulnerable to swings of the local political pendulum.

Incorporation

A different strand of approach followed recognition of the benefits of incorporation as limited companies. This was not possible until the Company Acts of 1844 and 1856. But, once these existed, a new route to formal legal status existed, and the chambers were among the earliest organizations to use it: 16 of the first 1000 companies in England and Wales.[22] There was also one early incorporated TPS (Notts. and Derby Traders Association).

Leone Levi, who is discussed more fully below, was one of the first to advocate incorporation as an option to provide chamber status. He drafted a Bill in 1857 for incorporating chambers of commerce as a special form of company registration. The objective was to gain status with government, but also to put chambers on a more secure footing. This did not initially receive overwhelming support. Worces-

---

[20] Municipal Commission (1835), vol. xxiv, p. 1208; vol. xxvii, p. 349.
[21] See Chapter 8; Patrick Colquhoun, *Plan*, pp. 7–11.
[22] See Richmond and Stockford (1986): the chambers were Oldham, Swansea, Newport, Ipswich, Bolton, Manchester, Lincoln, London, Leeds, Cardiff, Hull, Kendal, Spen Valley, Batley and Birstal, Liverpool, and Middlesbrough.

ter for example 'respectfully declined cooperating . . . believing they are more likely to effect their objects and retain their vitality by continuing as unprivileged voluntary associations'.[23] Once the ACC was established in 1860 it also considered chamber incorporation. Jacob Behrens (Bradford chamber) continued with Levi's proposal for a special Act of incorporation, and the ACC began to explore it with BoT. A move for a private Bill to have a separate incorporated status for chambers was begun in 1866, with support from Edward Baines and Edward Crossland MPs. Nothing came of this, but with limited support from BoT, the ACC began to press chambers to incorporate in 1866, reiterated in 1869.[24] The pressure from ACC led to a wave of chamber incorporations under the standard Company Acts in the 1874–84 period, with those in 1882–4 in part also stimulated by the pressures from the Royal Commission on Labour.[25] However, many chambers still resisted incorporation: Leeds considered it in 1862–8, rejected it, and left it as an open question, though it supported tribunals.[26] Worcester in 1874 was put off by the directors having unlimited liability.[27] From 1900 incorporation became more attractive, resulting in a second wave. Chambers were particularly attracted by *licensing* as result of company law reform; this allowed registration with limited liability but without the word 'Limited'. There were at least 14 incorporations under these terms 1900–19.[28]

Incorporation assured a fixed legal structure, and a form of governance through the company's memorandum and articles of association. In 1936 the stated benefits for chamber incorporation were claimed to be: a gain in stability; greater status (otherwise they had 'no more status than a sports club'); becoming a body corporate with perpetual succession; the ability to contract and take legal proceedings in its own right; its officers and members were freed of unlimited personal liability; and it offered the opportunity to prevent others from assuming the title.[29] Stockport in 1962 argued that incorporation was a means 'of converting a hitherto ad hoc group of industrialists into a properly constituted company'.[30] Incorporation obliged individual chambers to regularize accounting; no longer could they run for years in deficit supported by friendly bank overdrafts (which gave banks too much control), or topped up by donations (which could be distortionary and undermine incentives to cater for the majority of members).[31] From such discipline came the pressure to remain solvent and regularly inspect 'the business'. This opened the way to begin to impose standards related to revenues and services offered. Incorporation also facilitated some technical improvements: it was easier to receive bequests and donations, and deal with taxation (especially when VAT was introduced); and it

---

[23] Worcester chamber minutes, 7 July 1857.
[24] ACC, Standing Committee minutes, 24 February 1862, 20–2 February 1866, and following.
[25] See e.g. TNA BT 58/10/COS 1174A and 1211A following.
[26] Leeds chamber minutes, 29 January 1862, 4 February 1863, 5 February 1868, 7 January 1869.
[27] Worcester chamber minutes, 6 October, 3 November, 1 December 1874.
[28] See chamber Articles of Association, in TNA BT 22/11/10, BT 22/12/1–3, etc.
[29] ABCC, Home Affairs Committee, 1 July 1936.
[30] Stockport chamber, *Annual Report*, 4 June 1962, p. 14.
[31] See e.g. Taylor (1985), p. 97.

offered more ready redress in the courts against officers.[32] In the 20th century incorporation also became a key way of trying to differentiate the chambers of commerce from the chambers of trade.

Despite the benefits and pressures, by 1920, 21 (33%) of the smaller ABCC members were still unincorporated. Although it was possible for ABCC to refuse any application to affiliate from a chamber that was not incorporated,[33] by 1950 29% of ABCC chambers were still not incorporated.[34] The government, through the Board of Trade, had taken the view from 1917 that incorporation should be mandatory for chambers to receive any government support. Similar pressures were exerted on other business associations. A period of association reconstruction ensued, as discussed in Chapters 2 and 8, with varying degrees of success. But for the ABCC chambers in Britain, incorporation became universal only in the 1980s. However, incorporation was never sufficient for chambers to receive the special status they sought. As a result, the debate within chambers moved to formal 'locus standi'.

Chambers in Ireland began to be concerned about control of title in the late 1960s, and from 1969 urged all chambers to become incorporated. All the major chambers were incorporated by the late 1980s. But, as in the UK, small bodies that were not seeking incorporation continued to call themselves chambers, and in the 2000s a series of 'country chambers' emerged, some of which sought incorporation, with the Companies Registrar unsure how to deal with them.

7.3 FORMAL STATUS: 'LOCUS STANDI'

The concept of 'locus standi' emerged as a terminology in chamber debates in 1882, but had origins in the earlier tensions over charters, and also resonated with the efforts to establish tribunals of commerce. 'Locus standi' appears to have been first taken up by the London chamber in 1882, in an editorial in its *Chamber of Commerce Journal*, which had been launched that year. The argument presented was that British chambers were principally limited by their small size of membership, resources, and gaps on the geographical map. If they were not a national system in all prominent places, government would not take them seriously. Thus locus standi was bound up with the 'quality', size, resources, and geographical coverage of chambers. This underpinned the call for 'recognition' of chambers to overcome their limitations as purely voluntary bodies.[35]

The enthusiasm for this seems to have derived from Kenric Murray, the first secretary of the London chamber, who is the presumed author of the *CCJ* editorial articles. He put a resolution to the ACC later in 1882 calling for it to prepare a Bill that would 'confer locus standi upon chambers ... before Parliamentary

---

[32] Without incorporation, the courts often failed to protect societies from mismanagement and fraudulent conduct by their officers: Clark (2000a), p. 180.

[33] ABCC Home Affairs Committee, 3 June 1934.

[34] ABCC, GPC, 5 December 1956.

[35] The issue of resources and standards is discussed in Chapter 8; here the focus is on 'status'.

Committees, before the Railway Commission, and before all official or private or scientific committees or enquiries'. Murray also noted that it had been recorded on page 16 of the Railway Rates and Fares Committee that chambers of commerce and agriculture should have this right, and this should be pressed for careful consideration by the BoT.[36] Under pressure, the BoT did introduce a Bill in 1884 to make Incorporated Chambers of Commerce recognized complainants (with others) aggrieved by contravention of the Railway and Canal Traffic Act. A further degree of success was achieved in 1885 when a Standing Order of both Houses obliged any Railway Bill to receive petitions and objections on rates and fares from 'chambers of commerce or agriculture, or other similar body, representing a particular trade of business in a district'.[37]

These developments gave formal recognition to the representative function of chambers, and it was reaffirmed by House of Lords recognition in 1896.[38] But the dilemmas are made clear in the quotes above. It was difficult for government to grant chambers special recognition without including other similar bodies. The common law system and the political pressures of a pluralist system of governance made this an unlikely option for government to accede to. As a result, the recognition offered was deficient in various respects: first, it did not preclude individual business people petitioning directly, thus limiting the exclusiveness or 'privileged' access of chamber membership; second, it did not really enlarge on the recognition the chambers were already receiving, where they had received effective responses on the railway issue in particular;[39] third, it gave equal status to their rather detested and disparaged rivals, the chambers of agriculture. But limited recognition did open the door to government a little wider so that chambers were normally called on by parliamentary and other bodies in preference to individual traders, and it reinforced their position to be seen as the main representatives of broad local business interests. It also helped reinforce the avenues to the BoT where chambers became the main members of an Advisory Committee on commercial intelligence in 1898, as discussed in Chapter 10.

7.4 PUBLIC LAW STATUS

Government legislative support for chambers was an important issue within 18th-century commercial debates. As discussed in Chapter 4, a proposal by Whiston and Davenant in 1695 had suggested that a council of commerce be established by parliamentary Act: a formal public law national chamber. Postlethwayt and Mortimer also advocated a national association of local chambers that would undertake routine commercial surveillance *for government*, as a national adjunct to the BoT, to scrutinize legislation affecting business and suggesting improvements.

[36] London *CCJ*, 10 October (1882), p. 215.
[37] London *CCJ*, 5 June, and 5 August (1884), p. 219.
[38] ACC, *Proceedings*, 15–16 September (1896), p. 10.
[39] See Alderman (1973); Ilersic and Liddle (1960), pp. 107–16.

Chambers of commerce in France and Germany

Postlethwayt and Mortimer drew on foreign examples: chambers of assurance such as those existing around most of Europe at the time, and the French chambers derived from a national Superior Council of Commerce set up in 1601 to inquire into problems of commerce and advise the government. Although the French Council had a short life, it was revived in a General Council of Commerce in 1616 after petitions from merchants. This acted as an advisory committee with minister Richelieu as president. In 1664 a strengthened Council was set up by Colbert with much more power for economic promotion, and this was further developed in 1700 by establishing state-sponsored *local* councils/chambers of commerce, paid for by local municipalities, to give advice to the national council. These were the first 'public law' local chambers. Dunkerque was established in 1700, and Bayonne, Bordeaux, Lyons, Lille, Montpellier, Nantes, Rouen, Saint-Malo, and Toulouse in the years up to 1726. Municipal powers to regulate trade were passed to these chambers.

After the French Revolution the system was reconstructed by Napoleon, with 22 local chambers; to which were soon added nine others. Napoleon's reforms were also built into the German administrative structure for chambers, refined later by von Stein. By 1860 there were about 48 local chambers in mainland France; 143 by 1908; and 155 in 1913. The Marseilles chamber has a different history, being first established by voluntary municipal action in 1599, becoming independent of the municipality in 1650, and only brought into the public law structure in 1779, though it remained independently recognized and sanctioned by the King. Acts of 1803 and 1820 provided chambers with power to levy local business taxes (such as port dues) and to undertake various trading activities. In Germany this was a levy on the local government business tax (*Gewerbesteuer*). Structures for elections were defined by statute, with the business tax register providing the electorate and *compulsory* 'members'. Formal 'members', however, are only those elected, about 12–30 in number.[40]

French and German chambers are thus close to a 'corporatist' model with interests and resources defined by the state, which guarantees access, revenue, and a level of attention, but limits their capacity to act autonomously from the state's demands. As Herring concludes, 'their intimate relationship with the government is taken as a matter of course ... providing a recognised means [for] discussion', which aids 'in building up systematically a volume of opinion behind a measure'.[41] Public law is claimed to give French chambers some formidable benefits as local development agents.[42]

A comparison of the modern British and Irish chambers with public law systems, shown in Table 7.1 exposes the contrasts. The British and Irish chambers are often

---

[40] Herring (1928); Lefevre (1977); Magliulo (1980); ACFCI (1987, 1990); Wolfe (1915b); Waters (1995).

[41] Herring (1928), pp. 689–97.

[42] Waters (1995).

Table 7.1. Contrasts of public law with British and Irish chambers of commerce

Public law system	British and Irish private law system
• Compulsory membership	• Voluntary membership
• Membership fees seen as 'tax'	• Membership based on commitment
• Complete coverage of business	• Self-selective coverage of business
• National network in all areas	• Difficulty in spreading networks to low-density rural areas and small communities
• Assured size and critical mass	• Critical mass achieved only with fees and contracts tied to specific purposes
• Large organization	• Variable size with many small organizations
• Services with major staff resources underwritten by public finance to meet public needs	• Services and income based on sales and contracts to meet business demands
• Public control of status and internal management	• Freedom of action, but sometimes uneven quality
• Assured status and stability	• No special status and some instability
• Recognition of formal voice and representational role	• No formal representational role and recognition for voice
• Single organization in a given area (or one of a very few organizations)	• One of many organizations in an area with competition and overlap in a crowded domain
• Little internal policy conflict within a local area	• Potential for uncertainty about policy due to variable membership and lack of access routes to government

Source: Adapted from Bennett, Krebs, and Zimmermann (1993, table 1.1).

small, uneven in coverage, have to compete with other organizations, and have instability and uncertain resources. On the other hand they are closer to the market needs of their members, and they have a level of commitment from true members, not ones compelled to pay. The public law counterparts have size, permanence, complete coverage, and assured points of entry with government. As stated by German commentators: 'informing the state about the problems and interests of the business community is a function that both state and firms require from the chambers. By giving chambers a public law status, the state has forced itself to participate with business in the law-making process. This is an expression of the democratic right of the business community to be included in the political and legislative process.'[43] Hence, 'the chamber is . . . a platform for the exchange of know-how and experience to prevent the permanent reinvention of the wheel. But chambers are also quasi-political institutions that carry out economic politics in the interests of firms, e.g. by preventing laws being drawn up by bureaucrats which cannot be applied in reality, or by preventing high taxes or fees. The state has to inform business about its intentions and has to accept the chambers as competent partners.'[44]

[43] Hans-Georg Crone-Erdmann, director of Nordrhein-Westfalen chambers of commerce association; in Bennett, Krebs, and Zimmermann (1993), p. 176.
[44] Dieter Münker, chief executive of Augsburg chamber; in Bennett, Krebs, and Zimmermann (1993), p. 178.

Enter Mr Leone Levi

Comparisons with the public law alternatives in Europe hung over the voluntary chamber system evolving in Britain and Ireland, with revivals of the debate about the benefits of greater public support resurfacing every few decades. But nothing happened until the 1840s and 1850s, when the debate became strongly over-lapping with that about giving chambers authority as 'tribunals of commerce', discussed later. A clear early statement is that by Leone Levi in 1848. Chiefly associated with 'tribunals', he also argued that 'whilst party principles and feelings are allowed to interfere with general interests, and a total want of means is experienced to ascertain the requirements of commerce at large, there cannot exist a true and faithful representation of its power or a proper channel of representation with the legislature'. This could be overcome only if 'chambers of commerce, composed of commercial men, should be formed in every commercial town, which should send *representatives to form a standing committee attached to the Board of Trade*'. Thus the chamber's expertise would provide direct inputs to government, overcoming 'an evident deficiency of knowledge as to commercial requirements'.[45]

Levi's significance in the public law debate was that, as the successful proponent of the second Liverpool chamber in 1849–50, he managed to gain considerable support for his views.[46] Through his related activities arguing for alignment of commercial law, and his advocacy of 'tribunals of commerce', he was invited to lecture to chambers around the country in 1851–2,[47] and Leeds chamber pub-lished his lecture there. He was certainly perceived as having significant impact; his obituary at the Royal Statistical Society referred to him as the 'father' of chambers of commerce.[48] Indeed, Levi claimed that many of the chambers estab-lished by the 1880s were based on his Liverpool model. Whatever the truth of these statements, which is doubtful, his energy and activity at that time was certainly a major influence on the reception of the chamber concept at a high level. His work on commercial law found support and patronage from the Earl of Harrowby (then Lord Privy Seal), Lord Brougham, Henry Labouchere (President of BoT), and C. R. Porter (Secretary of BoT), and some support from Prince Albert.[49]

Harrowby's quoted response to Levi's proposals for incorporated chambers presages all future debates, as well as echoing all previous difficulties. Whilst

---

[45] *Liverpool Mercury*, 25 September 1849, emphasis added.
[46] Leone Levi, 1821–88, became a major influence on chambers. His 1849 proposal to Liverpool chamber appears to be his first published work, followed by his 1850 *Commercial Law*, later reissued as *International Commercial Law* (1863). He published a large scale *History of British Commerce* (1872) and many other works. He lectured widely to the local chambers and was appointed a lecturer at Kings College London in 1853, which published two of his lectures: *Shipping Law and Insurance* (1853), and *Richard Cobden* (1865). His early autobiography, published posthumously, covers some early chamber activities: Levi (1888). See also *DNB* (2004).
[47] He certainly addressed chambers in Liverpool, Edinburgh, Glasgow, Aberdeen, Manchester, London, Dublin, Leeds, Bradford, Hull, and Belfast: Levi (1888), pp. 46–71.
[48] *Journal of the Royal Statistical Society*, 51(2) (1888), pp. 340–2.
[49] Levi (1888), pp. 32 and 38.

generally supporting Levi's ideas, including that commercial questions should, before legislation, 'be submitted for the opinion of chambers of commerce. . . . The expediency of having a representation of traders at the Board of Trade he doubted.' Thus government should consult more widely, but Harrowby saw no privileged position for chambers over other bodies. Government was for politicians. Moreover, Levi found Manchester's John Hume and Thomas Bayley (president of the Manchester chamber[50]) even more hostile. Hume claimed, with some justification, that commercial people when in parliament or administration went native, and 'their votes more hostile to the true commercial interests of the county than any other portion of the House of Commons: commercial men have been the stoutest opposers to all improvement towards free trade as well as parliamentary reform . . . fully as selfish as the landed interests'.[51]

Nevertheless, Levi's lectures and activities influenced several chambers in the 1850s to favour formal recognition. When Levi became the 'metropolitan agent' for some of the chambers over 1856–9, he advocated incorporated status for chambers, and John Darlington, secretary of Bradford chamber, suggested in 1856 that a company charter be granted to all chambers in towns of over 100,000 population. The debate continued to run. In 1863 a memorial was presented by the Leeds chamber to the BoT asking for legislation to define chamber status.[52]

The Danson Report and Minister of Commerce proposals

The establishment of the national association (ACC) in 1860 gave a further fillip to thinking. The fact that one of its first actions was to appoint a Standing Committee to consider public law status, at its February meeting of 1860, demonstrates the prominence of the issue. One of the ACC representatives, John Danson, vice-president of the Liverpool chamber, prepared a booklet *Chambers of Commerce and the Government* in the same year, as 'pages addressed by a member of the Committee to his colleagues for circulation among the chambers of commerce of the UK'. It became viewed as an ACC paper, and it derived from earlier thinking of Danson and Sampson Lloyd as members of the Social Science Association, discussed later. The booklet drew directly on the French model and advocated that the ACC should be recognized by government as a formal body not only 'addressing its own proposals to government, but also the responsibility of examining in detail, and reporting upon, whatever measures affecting commerce the government may desire to bring before parliament'. The president of the ACC would then be one member of a reconstructed BoT, the other members of which would be business people nominated by government to represent the interests of agriculture, manufacturers,

---

[50] Not to be confused with the first Manchester president, Thomas Butterworth Bayley, 1744–1802.
[51] Quoted in Levi (1888), pp. 30–1.
[52] Quoted in Taylor (2007), p. 90; see Beresford (1951), Leeds chamber history.

and other sectors 'with the duty of assisting with their advice the President of the Board (or Minister of Commerce)'.[53]

Danson's proposal focused on what we would now call *information asymmetry:* government should have input from business at an early stage, before the legislation was finally digested and became generally public; government should 'be better informed . . . and sooner informed'. Danson's comments of 1860 could be equally well applied to the present: 'we now seldom learn what the government intends until the thing intended has been determined upon, . . . or is on the eve of accomplishment'. This could be improved by 'the chambers and the government . . . brought to act together . . . under the direct sanction of the government'. This was the only way of 'conveying information to government *prior* to the framing of particular law, or of communicating facts proper to guide, beforehand, the policy of the executive government'. Thus, from its earliest stage, some members of the ACC were considering it having a public law role 'as some arrangement for mutual action, and therefore for mutual recognition . . . a connection with the government'.[54]

Danson's proposal echoed Levi, perhaps not surprising as Levi knew Danson at Liverpool and found his way into the ACC Executive as the agent of the Staffordshire chamber in 1860. Danson's report is quite breathtaking for its time, since the ACC had just formed, had a membership at that time of less than half of the local chambers, and excluded two of the largest and most significant members, Manchester and Glasgow. It gave no explanation of how the local chambers would be affected by this proposal, except that each area would be represented in the Association. This problem of how the ACC and local chambers would interrelate was one of the strong issues for the ACC over the following years, and continues to be sensitive to this day. Interestingly, Harrowby's comment to Levi on this matter in 1851 proved correct: 'the establishment of a general chamber of commerce [the ACC], though useful, would not supersede the necessity of separate [local] associations'.[55]

Over the years similar ideas were revived in various forms. The call for a Minister of Commerce became almost an annual resolution at ACC conferences in the 1870s. In 1878 Sampson Lloyd, ACC president and MP, raised the matter in the Commons, and in 1879 managed to obtain a small majority to establish a Ministry of Commerce and Agriculture against government opposition. But nothing was done. Further action resulted in a memorandum and a successful further vote, followed by some agreement from Gladstone as prime minister to go ahead in 1882. The chambers of agriculture agreed with the establishment of such a ministry covering commerce and agriculture.[56] However, at the Annual Meeting of the chambers in 1883 there was considerable dissension, led by Nottingham chamber, and little support from other chambers, with the result that the initiative was lost. It

---

[53] Danson (1860), pp. 1 and 20; this does not survive in the ACC archive, but is at the Bodleian Library.
[54] Danson (1860), pp. 10, 13, and 16.
[55] Quoted in Levi (1888), p. 30.
[56] Major Craigie, secretary of Central Chamber of Agriculture; in London *CCJ,* 10 October (1882).

appears that ACC policy was ahead of its members, as indeed Danson's paper certainly was. In any case the proposal won no government support. The prime minister continued to assert that this was an 'inopportune time',[57] and Hicks-Beech, then president of BoT, stated that he was 'unable to concur' with the need for a minister within the Board of Trade: 'I do not think it would be for the advantage either of commerce or of agriculture that the care of these great interests should be entrusted to a single minister.'[58] However, in 1888 a Ministry of Agriculture was established, greeted with applause and self-congratulation by the chambers of agriculture. The chambers of commerce were now dismayed, saw Hicks-Beech as duplicitous, and renewed their efforts for a Minister of Commerce. Jacob Behrens from Bradford chamber led a new set of pressures, but again with no success.

With this lack of movement, attention switched to pressing for reorganization of the BoT and trying to ensure that its president was effective. It was suggested in 1904 that the president of the BoT should be better paid and given the title and status of minister.[59] However, the pressures for a Minister of Commerce were revived again in 1905, when Louis Sinclair and six other MPs unsuccessfully promoted a private member's Bill for a Minister, fixing the salary at £5000. This was revived again in 1914. Ilersic and Liddle interpret the efforts as an attempt to obtain protection and tariffs. The 'marked correlation between the state of trade and the pressure for a minister of commerce...was based not so much on the desire for a recognition within government, as for someone who might listen to commercial and manufacturing interests and persuade the government to assist them in their difficulties'.[60] This seems overstated, and ignores the persistence of the search for recognition.

Renewed pressure for public law status

Independently of the Minister of Commerce campaign, several chambers still pursued public law support in a wider form. The association, however, was strongly opposed up to the 1960s. London chamber in 1883 recorded that 'we do not envy the official status of Continental associations. Whatever compensations...these may enjoy, are amply compensated for by the limitation of their prerogative.... Chambers must remain free and voluntary institutions.'[61] An ACC Executive Committee report of 1905 took forward internal reorganization to improve status, but pointedly ignored recognition.[62] When asked to respond to three main areas of criticism of public recognition at the autumn meeting in 1905, the Executive Council response on each was completely opposed. First, on the issue that chambers should have *official* status, the meeting agreed on the value of incorporation

---

[57] ACC, Executive minutes, 10 April 1885; MS 14476/4.
[58] Letter from Hicks-Beech, 7 November 1888; reported in ACC, Executive minutes, 16 November 1888.
[59] ACC, Executive minutes, 14 June 1904; MS 14476/5.
[60] Ilersic and Liddle (1960), p. 37; see also pp. 33–6.
[61] London *CCJ*, 5 February (1883), p. 32.
[62] ACC, Executive Council report *Status of Chambers*, 6 June 1905: MS14476/5; q.v. below.

and Royal charters, but concluded that 'no artificial status would have any practical effect, . . . the influence and weight of a chamber depend largely upon the activity of its members, and the thoroughness and efficiency with which it carries out its operations'. On the second issue, that chambers ought to be maintained by national funds, as in France and Germany, the council calculated that the constitution of these European chambers was frequently misunderstood; that these chambers were de facto small committees appointed from a small electorate by government and could be disbanded by ministers. This could not be construed as an improvement on the British system and 'there is no likelihood of a system of taxation being imposed to provide for the maintenance of chambers, . . . and if it were, it would necessarily entail the loss of the voluntary principle'. On the third issue, that policy questions of commercial importance should be submitted to them for advice, the council noted this already happened extensively and quoted many recent examples.[63]

This debate in 1905 essentially laid the quest for public law status to rest. Some voices in individual chambers continued to raise the issue periodically; for example Bristol in 1908 noted that 'in the case of not a few towns, the annual reports [suggest] . . . hesitation is shown by some in joining . . . because no official status has been yet accorded. . . . We marvel much that chambers have not some kind of official status, equal to city councils, to which they might be usefully allied in Town Halls'.[64] Similarly, Liverpool in 1918 recognized that 'the weak spot in a chamber of commerce is its voluntary constitution. It has no powers to enforce its rulings. . . . Being voluntary associations they will always be handicapped.'[65] Birmingham's secretary, George Henry Wright, stated his preference in 1905: 'it was said that under an official status chambers would lose their independence. He ventured to assert they would gain their independence . . . [Now] they were dependent on an uncertain constituency . . . [resigning] if any section of members became dissatisfied with any opinion expressed by the council.'[66]

But these views never found widespread support and remained off the association's agenda. The Autumn meeting in 1906 summed up the ACC council position: they were 'concerned that their power and influence depended entirely upon the voluntary principle upon which they existed . . . They had nothing to gain by officialising chambers of commerce, and they had nothing to lose by going on as they had been doing in the past.'[67] Later, B. F. Stiebel (Nottingham chamber) commented that he had been in favour of official government status 'but having now given more study to the question, he concluded that our independence and freedom were worth more even than the Continental palaces with their government control'.[68] A call from North Staffordshire in 1957 asked for the continental system

---

[63] ACC, Executive Council minutes, 9 January 1906: MS14476/5.
[64] Quoted in Bristol chamber *Yearbook* (1908–9), pp. 5 and 20: Bristol RO 38605/Pu/35.
[65] Liverpool chamber, *Handbook* (1918), p. 34.
[66] Birmingham chamber, *Journal*, 30 September 1905, pp. 134–5; quoted in Marrison (1996), p. 106.
[67] Speech by Lord Amptill, reported in London *CCJ*, 25 (1906).
[68] Speech at Autumn Meeting of ACC, reported in *CCJ*, 26 (1907), p. 19.

to be investigated,[69] and visits between ABCC and the German chambers association did occur at this time, but with little tangible outcome.

The stimulus of state corporatism: public law status re-emerges

The public law issue came alive again in the late 1960s in the UK, but in Ireland there has never been a strong effort in this direction, perhaps because they were often more closely built into the corporate state. However, as discussed in Chapters 2 and 10, the UK sector trade associations, the FBI, and other manufacturing interests, were playing an increasingly direct role as agents supporting government policies after WW1; but the chambers, although becoming closely involved with government, were excluded from the national consultative machinery when NEDC was established in the 1960s, and were reduced to representation through the FBI.

Public law status re-emerged as a way to enter what was perceived to be this hallowed 'insider' status. The new stimulus came from the conclusion of the ABCC's Urwick Orr Report of 1968. This suggested that a regional 'focal' organization for chambers could form the basis of European-style public law chambers, essentially modelled on Germany. This would complement the government Regional Planning Boards and Councils. The achievement of public law status became accepted ABCC policy in 1971, which was very actively pursued by a working party charged with drafting legislation.[70] It was a major undercurrent within the Devlin Report of 1972 and continued in the Millichap Report of 1976. However, the responses at the outset from government were so discouraging that it is unclear why members of ABCC felt they could ever win the argument. *The Times* concluded that 'there will be hostility in industry towards any government that seeks to compel businessmen to subscribe'.[71] The civil service view was that the government would welcome developments to organize more and/or better export services, but questioned how far this needed public law status. The advice of the Solicitors Department was that public law status needed definition of functions, and that public law per se was irrelevant to status without knowing the 'specific powers' conferred.[72] These views were available informally to ABCC. A more confidential civil service note from a Deputy Secretary at BoT reported an informal exchange at a CBI meeting where the 'CBI had formed no view' on the ABCC proposals, but their immediate reaction is that 'this is a lot of impractical nonsense ... it is inconceivable that industry would accept such a statutory requirement or the government would be willing to enforce it'.[73]

[69] E. James Johnson, secretary of North Staffordshire chamber: quoted in ABCC, GPC, 6 November 1957.

[70] ABCC National Council, minutes 2 June–6 October 1971, reports the working group; also see Chapter 8.

[71] *The Times*, leader 'A voice for business', 3 January 1973.

[72] Memo from Peck, 22 September 1971; J. B. Evan, Solicitors Department, 13 March 1972: TNA BT 103/619.

[73] J. L. Rampton memo to Sir Max Brown, Secretary for Trade, 21 September 1971: TNA BT 103/619.

The Devlin report in 1972 was perhaps the best opportunity for change, since it looked at the whole issue of representation of business with government.[74] However, this large agenda also confused the possible outcomes. The ABCC view presented to Devlin was that qualifying chambers should have a public law status that would 'impose a basic measure of rationalisation of the total chamber of commerce and trade association structure. The effect would be to establish a completely representative network across Britain.'[75] The Devlin Report did not recommend public law status. It was encouraging about some its benefits, but emphasized the lack of any test by chambers of rank and file members' views; or as Taylor put it 'the absence of any ABCC evidence that compulsory contributions were acceptable to business and their established organisations'.[76] Instead, Devlin proposed merger of ABCC and CBI, as a Confederation of British Business. This was seen as 'somewhat tantalising' by the civil servants in BoT, but others were opposed, and it was only judged feasible if both organizations were reorganized.[77] In any case it was rejected by both.[78] For ABCC this seemed to further strengthen the arguments for public recognition as another route forward for chambers, to counteract the CBI. But the London chamber's position was that public law was a red herring diverting attention from the real issue of internal self-improvement.[79]

Probing scope for support in the early Thatcher years

A new opportunity seemed to open up with the Conservative government in 1979. As Taylor puts it, the ABCC took speeches by Michael Heseltine in 1980 and 1981, then Secretary of State for Environment, as encouragement that the government might support public law status. However, an approach to the prime minister (Thatcher) and Secretary of State for Industry (Tebbit) was rebuffed,[80] although important roles for chambers emerged under the Thatcher government in local regeneration and other initiatives.

A further opportunity emerged from a group of Conservative MEPs with links to ABCC who published a report in 1983 by Norvela Forster (a consultant and also an MEP). This argued that there was a 'case for giving chambers some form of enhanced status . . . The multiplier effect of giving chambers a minimum form of public law status and at the same time some increased powers by delegation from government or local authorities would make the case even stronger'.[81] The report

[74] Devlin Report (1972); Taylor (2007), pp. 90–3, describes the impact on subsequent developments.
[75] ABCC Discussion Paper, 1972; quoted in Taylor (2007), p. 91.
[76] Devlin (1972), p. 62; Taylor (2007), p. 91.
[77] Briefing letter from L. R. Hanson regarding Devlin Commission, March 1972: TNA BT 103/619.
[78] CBI response in ABCC National Council papers, 4 April 1973; see also 7 February and 5 March 1973.
[79] Comments by Sir Patrick Reilly, London chamber president, *Commerce International*, July 1973, p. 66; however, London advocated public law status to link it with ABCC in March 1973: see Chapter 8.
[80] Taylor (2007), p. 91.
[81] Forster (1983); quoted in Taylor (2007), p. 92.

proposed that chamber income could be supported by a levy collected via VAT or local business rates. An income of £30 million per year was sought, with the chambers taking over public roles for local authority trading standards, monitoring of toxic wastes, tourist promotion, and administration of airports.

The Forster Report's recommendation for public law status fell on deaf ears in 1983, although the role in local rates was taken up in part in the consultation mechanism of the 1984 Local Government Act. But ABCC began to develop other arguments for achieving similar benefits. One primary strategy, suggested in the Forster Report, was to seek delegation of government services into chambers. Forster had suggested that chambers could take on delivery of the Small Firms Service, the Industry-Education Unit, export promotion, and some role in vocational training. The ABCC developed these ideas further through exchanges with Norman Tebbit in 1984; some contracting did occur, as discussed in Chapter 13.

A second ABCC strategy was a proposal for a business registration scheme through chambers. Chambers had been early supporters of the Company Acts and developments in partnership law in the 19th century, as had TPS and chambers of trade. Similarly there had been strong support for the Business Names Act in 1916. The value of incorporation and registration of business names was a mechanism to limit fraud and misrepresentation. If chambers took over the registration scheme this would provide a way to a formal status; and echoed some European jurisdictions where chambers managed the business registration process. This agenda was initiated by a group of chambers, led by London, which sought to develop a voluntary system of business registration.[82] This followed the abolition of the statutory Business Names Register in 1979. The statutory register had never been complete, and had various defects, but was recognized to provide some limit on fraud. The chambers viewed a register as offering advantages to small businesses through recognition for bona fide traders, similar to the benefits of the Companies House register for incorporated businesses. However, its replacement by a voluntary register run by chambers collapsed; firms were unwilling to use it.

As a result the ABCC decided to evaluate the scope to strengthen two aspects: making the register compulsory for all businesses employing over five workers; and providing an office where businesses could register for all statutory purposes.[83] A survey of business attitudes to these proposals showed only a small majority of support for the first, but strong support for the second. ABCC produced a report in 1992 that was then discussed with Heseltine (president of the BoT), and the DTI.[84] Taylor's assessment of Heseltine's advice 'was that business registration would be perceived as adding to the bureaucratic burden on business at a time when the government was seeking to reduce that burden, that it would be opposed by other business groups, and would not be acceptable to government backbenchers . . . perceived as special pleading by chambers—an attempt to secure public law status by the back door': which indeed it was. However, civil service

[82] The others were Birmingham, Cardiff, and Liverpool; see Taylor (2007), p. 93.
[83] ABCC Council minutes, May 1992; quoted in Taylor (2007), p. 93.
[84] ABCC, *Business Registration Scheme* (1992); BCC, National Council minutes, 9 July 1992.

advice was that the 'single point of registration might be worth exploring'.[85]
The ABCC continued to work on the concept of centres, setting up a working
group in 1991, which reported in 1992 in favour of establishing Commercial
Formalities Centres.[86] This received some support from the NCT, and in 1993
BCC produced a lobby document advocating Business Registration Centres, with
compulsion for all economic entities to register, including the smallest firms.[87] But
Heseltine and government priorities moved to the development of Business Link,
which became, in effect, government's own attempt to provide single centres for
business contact with government; as discussed in Chapter 13.

Significant government funding and recognition under Thatcher

The strategy of using the rapidly developing role in contracting as the basis for a
form of recognition was initially more fruitful. As discussed in Chapter 13, various
roles were devolved onto chambers, and a major boost in 1990 was the establishment of Training and Enterprise Councils (TECs). A policy position emerged for
ABCC to support the idea of TECs as a step on a road to a form of public law
status. A group of eight chamber chief executives in 1992 issued an internal
consultation paper that advocated a range of options for public law and pressed
ABCC to pursue them. Taylor, as director general of ABCC 'urged that, whatever
the choice, it had to be properly researched and a professional campaign mounted'.
A detailed evaluation of the German public law system and a conference at
Sunningdale in 1992 also had some influence on the chamber debates: an opportunity seemed to open from the public support of the TECs which, when combined with chambers, could be equivalent to the German chamber structure.[88]

   This was encouraged by Michael Heseltine who, after 1992, appeared to support
the idea that TECs could evolve to become de facto public law chambers. One of
his books supported European style chambers in Britain.[89] Indeed, other commentators, including this author, supported this direction.[90] Heseltine facilitated an
evolution that saw merger of 16 TECs with chambers over 1994–7. He also
thought that chamber operations when combined with Business Link could offer
a route to equal the capacity of the European chambers.[91] However, whilst many
saw these developments as stepping-stones to more formal public recognition, this
was never achieved. Chambers remained, formally, just another contractor. Moreover, whilst encouragement from government, particularly through Heseltine, may
have led to expectations of an eventual public law position, this commitment was

---

[85] Quoted in Taylor (2007), p. 93.
[86] ABCC Working Group on Statutory Business Registration, 1992: *A Gateway to European
Competitiveness*; National Council Paper CL 5/92.
[87] BCC, *Business Registration Centres: The First Stop to Easing the Compliance Burden and Improving
Competitiveness* (1993).
[88] Bennett, Krebs, and Zimmermann (1993); Taylor (2007), pp. 138–40.
[89] Heseltine (1989); see Heseltine (2000); and interview with Heseltine, in Greaves (2008);
also Chapter 13.
[90] See Bennett, Krebs, and Zimmermann (1993); Bennett (1995); Fallon and Brown (2000).
[91] Heseltine (1992a, 1992b, 2000).

not shared or sustained by other senior members of the Conservative government, and disappeared after the election of Labour in 1997. Arguably, Heseltine's initiatives did more harm than good in raising expectations among the chambers, and making them very vulnerable to the political pendulum. Even Heseltine did nothing about public law status when in office. Indeed his retrospective comment was that 'a Tory government would never introduce public law status' and that 'there is no prospect of it coming about; culturally it would be seen as interference'.[92] Taylor argues: 'public law status remained a Holy Grail, an objective to be yearned for but with little prospect of attainment'.[93]

7.5 PROTECTION OF TITLE

Another way for chambers to gain advantages of public recognition, but without becoming 'public law' bodies, is for them to be embraced with a statutory framework of recognition. This could extend, as it does in Finland and Sweden, to recognition of defined local territories, with rules of governance and representation, and protection of title. This approach also echoes the modern Canadian chambers, and some aspects of early US Boards of Trade. The Finnish and Swedish models were among the options advocated by ABCC in 1992. One major outcome of the campaign was success in protection of the 'chamber' title in 1999.

Early concerns with chambers of trade

The earliest detailed discussion of restricting the use title appears to be in the 1920s when there was increasing concern about chambers of trade, and also that a 'Universal Chamber of Commerce' was being used as a subtitle by the TPS.[94] In 1920 Exeter proposed restricting the title 'chamber of commerce' to members of ABCC; Luton gave support. London commented that they had investigated this some years earlier but gave it up as any legal steps were 'hopeless'.[95] But London came round to the idea, and in 1922 the ABCC Executive Council agreed 'a Bill should be promoted . . . to link the use of title . . . on the lines of the Bill drafted by the London chamber'. The proposed title was 'British Empire Chambers of Commerce'. But this approach was quickly dropped in favour of an endeavour 'to argue with NCT so that their affiliated bodies call themselves chambers of trade',[96] with which NCT agreed in 1922. However, this resolved nothing and in 1924 there was another initiative to amend the Companies Act to protect the use of title, and a conference was arranged with NCT to seek their enforcement of the

---

[92] Heseltine comments (2005); in Greaves (2008), p. 1008. See also Heseltine (1987), p. 428; (1989), pp. 106–8.
[93] Taylor (2007), p. 93.
[94] ABCC Home Affairs Committee, 2 December 1925.
[95] ABCC, *Proceedings*, 10 November 1920, pp. 56–7.
[96] ABCC, Executive Council minutes, 2 August 1922 and 4 October 1922.

1922 agreement.[97] But by 1926 the unsurprising conclusion had been reached that this would only protect the title when applications were made for incorporation, which most NCT chambers were never likely to do. It also had no effect on controlling title of existing bodies.[98] Instead an Act of Parliament was necessary.[99]

Dunwoody, the ABCC secretary, drafted a possible framework for a Chamber of Commerce Act that he presented informally to civil servants in 1924. This proposed restriction of title through the BoT maintaining a register of those bodies that were permitted to be called chambers of commerce. Registration was to be renewed annually, for a nominal fee of no more than one guinea per year, subject to the BoT being satisfied that the chamber still existed.[100] Civil servants immediately poured cold water on the idea, which they thought 'loosely drafted'. They were concerned that the chief power was refusal of registration, which would 'rely largely on the ABCC, who will thus obtain a real control'. They were concerned about how this would interface with incorporation: how could the BoT remove an incorporated body? But they were also concerned with any inspection costs, particularly as Dunwoody wanted to include British chambers abroad.[101] But the fatal issue seems to have been that the BoT was not convinced that there was a significant problem from unregistered tradesmen's associations. They therefore suggested that Dunwoody made a stronger case, which 'does not appear to have been made out yet'. Dunwoody was reported to be consulting the ABCC members.[102]

The ABCC did indeed consult its members, and a committee was set up to consider the matter, with a deputation sent to the BoT in 1926. However, the concerns of the BoT appear to have remained the same, and nothing was achieved. The issue of how to handle NCT chambers rumbled on. The title issue re-emerged in 1933 when a letter on title to be sent to BoT was proposed, after further consultation with NCT;[103] but again nothing came of it.

Use of the Companies Register

Some means of control was eventually achieved under Section 17 of the 1948 Companies Act. This gave the Board of Trade power to prevent registration of any company with a name it thought undesirable.[104] Any application to register a company with the title of 'chamber of commerce', 'chamber of trade', 'chamber of industry', or variations of them, was referred by Companies House to the ABCC and NCT. The ABCC applied the rule that only a chamber satisfying ABCC criteria could be called a 'chamber of commerce and industry', others were called

[97] ABCC Home Affairs Committee, 7 May 1924.
[98] This was confirmed by the BoT: reported in ABCC Executive minutes, 6 January 1926.
[99] ABCC Home Affairs Committee, 8 January 1926.
[100] *Chambers of Commerce: An Act to Provide for the Registration of Chambers of Commerce*; a draft by R. B. Dunwoody 1924; TNA BT 60/7/1.
[101] Opening memo, 4 April 1924: TNA BT 60/7/1.
[102] BoT officers H. Winearls and R. Matthew memos, 12 and 14 April 1924: TNA BT 60/7/1.
[103] ABCC Home Affairs Committee, 5 May and 7 July 1926; 4 October 1933.
[104] Subsequently included in the Companies Act 1985 and Business Names Act 1985; see Taylor (2007), pp. 128–9 and n. 9.

either 'chambers of commerce' or 'chambers of trade'. But this did not control unincorporated bodies or existing bodies. Companies House was also unwilling to control title for a geographical territory; they argued that they could only judge whether an applicant was a bona fide chamber, not what area it covered. The control was therefore very limited.[105]

Significant problems also emerged from how Companies House operated. First, it acted on behalf of the government, which ultimately depended on the view of the Secretary of State, which could vary. Second, there was no guarantee that Companies House would consult ABCC; again this depended on government commitment. Third, Companies House continued to refuse to restrict geographical names. In 1994 they permitted incorporation of an East London chamber of commerce, even though an East London chamber was already registered; and ministers refused to intervene. The problem increased in the mid-1990s when many TECs and Business Links developed dubious marketing brands that competed with chambers. Disputes were also difficult to resolve if they were between ABCC member and non-member chambers. Thus, the large mid-Yorkshire chamber (usually not an ABCC member) wanted to use the title West Yorkshire, which was unacceptable to Leeds and Bradford (both ABCC members). The Walsall chamber (an ABCC member, subsequently called East Mercia) wanted to use the title Black Country without the approval of the other areas covered by this geographical name (which was resisted by the similar sized Wolverhampton ABCC chamber). A small Wessex chamber was approved by Companies House, even though it covered only a small part of Wiltshire and was falsely portraying itself as a much larger entity covering the territory of several large ABCC chambers.[106]

Similarly in Ireland, consultation by the Irish chambers association with the Companies Registry Office concluded that the title chamber of commerce could not be protected by patent.[107] But later the government supported the use of Companies Registry to protect the title of 'chamber of commerce'. A 2004 restatement of the principles was that the 'Registrar was not obliged to take advice, but must consider this advice in the context of government direction that it is important to have a coherent and effective chamber network throughout the country'.[108] But, as in the UK, this has not prevented a proliferation of small high street 'chambers' and other bodies, perhaps 200 in number in 2009.

New initiatives and success

Because of these difficulties, protection of title continued to re-emerge as an issue and, after the Novella Forster Report in 1983, one aspect of ABCC policy was directed at a further effort to get legislation; this effort was strengthened after the

---

[105] *Protection of Title*: ABCC Briefing note to chamber chief executives, 25 August 1995.

[106] ABCC (1993), *Code of Practice: Chamber Boundaries, Relationships and Titles*; see also Taylor (2007).

[107] Irish Chambers Association, *Report*; quoted in Cork chamber council minutes, 4 December 1969.

[108] Chambers Ireland, *Annual Report* (2004), p. 15.

failure of efforts for public law status. More research was undertaken. Initially a wider model was presented to government, similar to that in Finland and Sweden: government could officially recognize chambers as representatives in agreed territories, provide the right for them to be consulted on business issues, protect their title, and lay down their rules of governance.[109]

Despite the obvious problems of confused title, government remained unsupportive. However, a new opportunity to make progress arose when Andrew Lansley, Conservative MP for South Cambridgeshire and a former deputy director of ABCC in the mid-1980s, put a Bill into the Private Members Bill ballot. It was drawn 13th in 1997. Michael Trend, Conservative MP for Windsor, put it in again in 1998, again unsuccessfully. But in 1999 a further attempt by Lansley was drawn second, and succeeded in being enacted.

In arguing the case, BCC papers focused on confusion of brand name, complications of geographical coverage, and potential for fraud.[110] Lansley's arguments in parliament focused on the scope for abuse, particularly by individuals in the former Soviet states fraudulently establishing 'bilateral chambers' in the UK, by individuals claiming to be a chamber organization, the scope for geographical conflicts, and the need to improve mechanisms for formal consultations with the TECs and thus facilitate government objectives.[111] He was an effective advocate showing that chambers could do something for government, as well as being helped to strengthen themselves. The preparations for the Bill received government advice and support from the Labour Secretary of State (Stephen Byers) as well as Conservative party backing. Its main opponent was Eric Forth, Conservative MP for Bromley and Chislehurst. He was unhappy that a body seeking support for self-regulation relied on the role of the Secretary of State to control title. He also felt that government support let the chambers remain a 'cosy cartel' . . . 'to ensure that those whom the existing cosy collective disapprove of are not allowed in', and 'to avoid any thrusting, new, exciting, dynamic bodies being allowed in'. He also criticized the fact that the actual definition of what constituted an approved chamber, and its territory, was omitted from the Act, and left to DTI and ABCC to decide.[112] Forth's criticisms demonstrate the impediments to chamber development in the Thatcher years. Forth was still voicing the mantras of that time. The Labour government, through Byers, strongly supported the Bill at the third reading; Lansley patiently explained the issues involved, Forth's criticisms were withdrawn, and the Bill was passed without amendment.[113]

The Act gave the Secretary of State the power, through consulting with the BCC: to approve only those organizations that were 'genuinely representative of the business or other interests in that place or area'; that were independent and 'not under the direct control of government or a local authority'; that were

---

[109] Forster (1983); quoted in Taylor (2007), p. 92.
[110] BCC (1999), briefing note to chambers.
[111] *Hansard*, 26 February 1999, cols. 703–6.
[112] *Hansard*, 7 May 1999, cols. 1195–6.
[113] Company and Business Names (Chamber of Commerce etc.) Act, 1999.

'controlled only [by] its members... [with] not less than 75%... engaged in manufacturing, commerce, services, trade, shipping, distribution, agriculture, fishing or professional practice'; and promoted 'the interest of the whole business community of its area'. There is also the first statutory definition of chamber services in Britain:[114]

- To 'provide the local business community with information, advice and assistance'.

- To 'undertake, or encourage its members to undertake, joint promotional activities and to develop arrangements for mutual support'.

The significance of the Act can be overstated. It dealt only with controlling new interests, not the existing system, and it did nothing to ensure government listened any more closely to the chambers' voice. However, it is an important Act since, for the first time, it provided a statutory mechanism to control the brand, limit competition and fraud, and define a range of chamber characteristics and services. Crucially, it asserted the key definitions used in this book of a general, deliberated local voice, voluntary, independent, and covering a defined geographical area.

The implementation of the Act relies on guidance as to what constitutes a chamber, and this fell to BCC in consultation with DTI (and also the Department of Employment when TECs existed). This proved critical in giving a form of statutory backing to BCC accreditation standards, and reinforced the BCC's *Development Strategy*, as discussed in Chapter 8. The critical feature is that voluntary chambers are accorded the unique right to use the chamber title, and are consulted routinely on legislation and public policy. In Ireland, the Companies Registrar is used as the main protection. But watching UK developments,[115] a restructuring of the Canadian chamber association occurred in 1997, which followed a similar pattern. Canadian local chambers and boards of trade must seek incorporation under a Board of Trade Act. This provides similar advantages of protection of title for a given defined territory, and individual members are absolved of liabilities for the chamber (like a limited company), provided that it makes proper annual returns and follows an accreditation process similar to that in Britain. The Canadian chambers are very explicitly non-profits.[116]

7.6 TRIBUNALS OF COMMERCE

An overlapping, but separate approach to public recognition developed around tribunals of commerce, to facilitate and arbitrate in resolving commercial disputes. This theme is critical to chamber development, and continued to echo through

---

[114] Act and Schedules; Schedule 1, Purposes (b) and (c).
[115] This followed exchanges of BCC with consultants advising the government in Canada, and with the current author, in 1995–6.
[116] Canadian Chamber of Commerce, *Corporate Governance Manual* (2007); <www.chamber.ca>.

many of the subsequent debates on 'status of chambers' discussed above. Yet the history of this debate has been hardly recognized.[117]

In the 18th century there was general frustration with the quality of dispute resolution through the law, as expensive and costly, with the juries often dominated by smaller traders who were 'unreliable' or uninformed, and in front of whom the major merchants resented appearing. The old law merchant still existed, but was under pressure, not least from international wars and conflicts. There was also increasing dislike of the Admiralty Courts. These were concerned with adjudicating on salvage from wrecks, prizes, seizures from privateers, sale of flotsam, local fines and fees, and could also hear private suits.[118] They met in a wide range of ports, and, importantly, in the colonies. Many merchants had favoured these courts as they offered quick and cheap summary justice under the Admiral, with no jury. However, they were resented in the colonies, where they were used to collect and administer new taxes under the Stamp Act and Townshend duties, were seen as arbitrary intrusions by the Crown into local government and American legal structures, and were a major factor behind rebellion.[119] The Admiralty Courts were also increasingly disliked in Britain, as arbitrary and unpredictable. As a result many of the early chambers introduced their own arbitration services for commercial disputes. This was a chamber activity in Jersey from the outset in 1768 and New York from 1769. It steadily became embedded in the chamber system as a service.[120]

The call for a formal legal basis for chamber arbitration

Despite developing their own commercial arbitration service, chambers sought a more formal legal basis, as tribunals, from the outset. Probably the first significant general reference to commercial arbitration tribunals is that in Nicholas Magens's *Essay on Insurances* (1755), which was a widely known source. Chambers of assurance, acting under delegated government powers, were used in Europe for dispute resolution, and there were also at least 30 in America by 1795. There was also a London Chamber of Assurance that acted as a register of insurance, broker, and arbitrator; as well as Royal Exchange Insurance and London Assurance.[121] These activities did not absorb the whole market and may have offered a precedent for the idea of chamber of commerce arbitration.

---

[117] Ilersic and Liddle (1960), pp. 83–92, give brief cover from 1858; Taylor (2007) gives none.
[118] Cunningham (1919); Crump (1931). The Admiralty Court still exists, in England issuing over 1000 claim forms per year, hearing 70–90 cases, meeting in London and seven other centres (Birmingham, Bristol, Cardiff, Chester, Leeds, Liverpool, and Manchester); Commercial Court and Admiralty Court, *Annual Report* (2005–6).
[119] Cunningham (1919); Andrews (1929); Crump (1931).
[120] See Chapter 12 for a full discussion of the evolution of the service.
[121] Raynes (1964), pp. 42–59, 157–9, and 171–8; and evidence to Select Committee of the House of Commons on Marine Insurance (1810). The London Chamber of Assurance survived at the Royal Exchange at least until 1762, when it had three governors and 47 directors: *Almanach des Négocians* (Bruxelles: J. Jorrez, 1762), pp. 96–104; Goldsmiths-Kress.

At this time in Britain the main marine insurance body, Lloyds, was wrestling with internal conflicts in moving from being purely a coffee house to becoming an industry self-regulator of marine insurance trading and indemnity to reduce frauds. Marine insurances were also increasingly being undertaken in the outports, especially Bristol, Liverpool, and Glasgow, but all linked with London. The benefit of a system of merchant self-control was a crucial underpinning. There was extensive circulation of discussion about legal cases, widespread use of books for merchant instruction, and the emergence of a consolidated legal code that Weskett was influential in drawing together.[122] Thus, the concept of a court or tribunal run by merchants for merchants, was already well understood in the outports, and widely across Europe.

For chambers the key conceptual thrusts by Postlethwayt and Mortimer both suggested that broad-based chambers of commerce could act as tribunals. They drew on the law merchant, the councils of commerce in France (and elsewhere), and the insurance courts;[123] Postlethwayt himself had acted as an umpire in disputes. Mortimer's second objective for chambers referred to them as 'commercial juries'. His third objective was that 'they would frame a concise, complete mercantile code, or book of commercial laws'. His fifth objective was that 'they would alter the mode of satisfaction to be given by insolvent debtors to their creditors'.[124] John Weskett's influential *Complete Digest of the Theory, Law and Practice* of insurance (1781) proposed a 'chamber of assurance' based on the model of the Paris chamber, with fortnightly meetings for settling insurance disputes by use of arbitrators. England needed something similar: 'a court of select merchants (established by authority)'.[125] Weskett developed this further, as discussed in Chapter 4, forming the first London chamber 'to take *speedy* cognizance of, to *hear, compose, determine,* and register *all causes* and *controversies,* arising in *matters of trade, commerce, navigation, and insurance,* in the most *easy, summary,* and *inexpensive* manner:—and being always on the spot, and daily conversant with the *practice* of trade'.[126]

Diffusion of the tribunal concept

Magens, Postlethwayt, Mortimer, and Weskett thus provided early conceptual stimulus for chambers to act as tribunals. These influences were reinforced by a major work by Park on *Marine Insurances* in 1789 that used Magens heavily and went through multiple editions well into the 1800s,[127] and Mortimer's 1772 book was reprinted until 1815.

There was also some further development of the tribunal concept in the early part of the 19th century in the case of local marine insurance associations. For

---

[122] Martin (1876); Weskett (1783), p. 383; Sutherland (1933), pp. 46–65.
[123] See Gerard Malynes, *Lex Mercatoria* (1688); Charles Molloy, *De Jure Maritimo et Navali* (first edition 1670s repeatedly reprinted; tenth edition 1778), and the frequently reprinted *Discourse* of Josiah Child (1698).
[124] Mortimer (1772), pp. 195–200.
[125] Weskett (1783), pp. 149 and 321.
[126] Weskett (1782), pp. 6–7, all emphases and punctuation in original.
[127] J. A. Park (1789), A *System of the Law of Marine Insurances* (London: J. Cruickshank).

example, the Norwich chamber, founded in 1847, originated from a marine association 'which ought to serve [insure] trades from loss at sea' and which was formed in about 1840.[128] There was also 'Tom's Coffee House Arbitration Room' in London, which was frequently used in the early 1800s.[129] Some resonance of the tribunal concept also occurs in parliamentary reports of the 1810s and 1820s regarding securing payment of debt, reducing fraud, and establishing more uniform treatment across different jurisdictions;[130] a lobby by the chambers and local committees for changes in the laws of agents and factors was influential on early London chamber proposals.[131]

Lobbying for change: Lyne vs. Levi

However, the tribunal debate took on a new life in the late 1840s. The immediate cause was the effects of the 1847 Act reforming County Courts. These courts became rapidly established, but by 1848–9 were crowded, slow, and expensive; with lawyers who were ill-fitted to commercial matters. Independently of the chambers, the TPS took off in this period as a means to avoid the courts altogether, reducing costs to plaintiffs by 20–30%, and reducing the time taken to a few days.[132]

Recognizing these problems, the tribunal concept was raised to the political level as a result of independent initiatives of two different individuals. One was Francis Lyne,[133] who attempted to marshall support through meetings in London, Bristol, Dublin, and elsewhere, to form an Association for Promotion of Tribunals of Commerce, from about May 1851.[134] The second individual was Leone Levi. In 1849 he published a report calling for a 'local tribunal of commerce' in Liverpool, and also for tribunals to be established in all the principle towns for the settlement of commercial disputes like those in France.[135] Like Mortimer, Levi saw a wider role than just judicial (for example through informing and lobbying government);

---

[128] Unattributed newspaper cutting, 26 January 1848, in J. J. Coleman Collection 'Scrapbook'; Norfolk Local Studies Library: NFK/QC N 942.615.

[129] Quoted from Lord Chancellor, letter from Francis Lyne to Lord Brougham, 14 April 1851; HB/4171; UCL Special Collections.

[130] See Cannan (1919); Sutherland (1933); Select Committee on High Price of Bullion, *House of Commons Papers* (1810), vol. iii.

[131] Select Committee on the Law relating to Merchants, Agents and Factors (1823), pp. 265 ff, especially pp 281–3; p. 217 quotes petition from Dublin chamber in favour of reform; see Chapter 5.

[132] Calculated by Wood (1999), comparing the Leicester TPS records and county courts; see Chapter 2.

[133] Francis Lyne, *c*.1800–*c*.1887 was a prolific essayist, sometimes advocating chambers of commerce. He was a partner in Lyne, Dorie and Co., founded in 1826, wine and general merchants at 12 Mark Lane and then 6 Hunter Street, Brunswick Square, London. His father Joseph was a partner with Lewis Stephens and uncle Charles Lyne in the 1780s in Lisbon. His own partnership was put into bankruptcy in the late 1840s, which Lyne contested, still taking legal action in the 1850s and 60s. This coloured his view that lawyers padded time to raise costs. In *The Attorney's Own Book: or The Emancipation of Truth* (1850) he rails against lawyers. His work is often muddled and he could not have been easy to work with. He sought to ingratiate himself with Lord Brougham; in one letter he reviews his possible inheritance of £3m from a relative then living next door to Brougham (Brougham papers, especially HB/5971 memo, 9 October 1852; UCL Special Collections).

[134] Lyne to Brougham, 4 June 1853, HB/5975.

[135] Levi (1849), p. 5; from *Liverpool Albion*, 1849.

but he saw the judicial role as key to obtaining recognition. Given that Levi was working extensively on his major book at the time (*Commercial Law*, 1850), there seems little doubt that he had read Postlethwayt and Mortimer, but there is no acknowledgement of their thinking.

In 1849–50, Levi was engaged by Liverpool business people to help them establish their chamber, for which his 1849 report was commissioned. The chamber did not, however, appoint him as their secretary, which he was clearly seeking, but made him an honorary member.[136] However, it did establish a chamber arbitration committee, and adopted and published Levi's further report on tribunals in September 1852. In this report, Levi called for codification of the laws of trade and commerce. He stated that seven commissions had sat in the last 200 years but little progress towards codification had been made. The rapid expansion of trade and commerce had meant that the current laws were inadequate, 'existing in dispersed fragments', and this 'judge-made-law' was 'often not satisfactory'. Levi proposed that chambers of commerce and mercantile associations 'take the work into their own hands' to codify, and establish a tribunal body to operate, with compulsory powers to ensure permanent local bodies, with summary process, but informed and binding in law. At a meeting in September 1852, with Dublin and other chamber delegates in attendance, Levi's report was received, and the Liverpool chamber commended Levi to take the lead on this.[137]

Liverpool chamber wanted parliament to set up a 'small well-selected commission' to work on codification, including Levi. This should undertake the codification process. It would overcome the 'difficulties of obtaining the continuous support of changing bodies voluntarily associated, and the co-operation of the best qualified men in the seats of commercial activity for the lengthened period over which the work of codification must extend'.[138] However, at this point the initiatives of the two individuals, Lyne and Levi, began to collide. We only have Lyne's account of events, as Levi's autobiography and correspondence covering this period, surprisingly, make no mention of their exchanges.

The Association for Promotion of Tribunals of Commerce

Lyne launched his Association in 1851.[139] It published several reports and developed the role of 'agitating . . . to familiarise the subject of Commercial Law Reforms to the public mind'.[140] A considerable campaign of reports and exchange of letters occurred through the press, but *The Times* newspaper refused to report. This caused

---

[136] Liverpool chamber, second *Annual Report* (1851), p. 16 (BL 8247.bb.36): 'Your directors . . . would call to remembrance the services of Mr. Leone Levi, by whose exertions and appeals to the public, the general desire for the establishment of a chamber of commerce was successfully accomplished'. The *DNB* copies the *Journal of the Royal Statistical Society*, 51(2) (1888), pp. 340–2, which incorrectly states he was secretary of the chamber; he was actually secretary of the group that set up the chamber.

[137] Liverpool chamber (1852), pp. 5–7, 11, and 22.

[138] Ibid., p. 11.

[139] *Prospectus for Tribunals of Commerce Association*, 17 April 1851; Brougham papers BH/4170.

[140] Liverpool chamber (1852), pp. 5–7.

'hard words' to be used by Lyne to the *Times*, which Lord Beaumont and Mr Montague Gore lamented.[141] However, the Earl of Harrowby presented petitions for a Tribunals Bill from Liverpool and Bristol chambers to the House of Lords in June and July 1853. Interestingly, in support of this petition Lord Wharncliffe distinguished between tribunals and chambers of commerce: 'chambers of commerce were for the protection of the public interests in trade. Tribunals of commerce were for adjudicating upon matters of dispute'.[142] Hence, it was possible to support tribunals without supporting chambers, which was the conclusion that each of the subsequent legal reforms actually delivered. The Association marshalled further petitions: from the Lord Mayor of the City of London, senior aldermen, peers, the high bailiff of Southwark, and the mayors and senior magistrates of many towns, as well as the chambers of commerce in Liverpool, Bristol, Worcester, Plymouth, bankers in 12 of the largest towns, and many brokers and London traders.[143] The petitions were considered by parliament, the BoT prepared a memorandum to the Secretary of State for the Home Department on the Conseils in France and Belgium, and there is evidence of discreet lobbying, but the 1854–5 Bill was not proceeded with.[144]

Lyne claimed to have invited Levi to assist the Association, and indeed Levi joined its committee, which paid Levi's expenses from Edinburgh to meet Lyne in London. But when Levi arrived he withdrew his name. Levi is reported to have said that he had been with the Earl of Harrowby (MP for Liverpool), and Messrs Baring Bros.,[145] and that the leading houses would devise an appropriate plan for tribunals and take it out of Lyne's hands. Levi is then reported to have approached the rest of the members of the Association's committee to remove Lyne. Lyne claims that on 26 April 1853 Levi read a paper to the Law Amendment Society seeking them to condemn the establishment of tribunals. Two days later (28 and 29 of April) Levi made a further report at Liverpool, where Lyne told Levi 'that his conduct . . . was not such as commercial morality could or would approve'.[146] In fact, Levi's first appearance at the Law Amendment Society had been during the Great Exhibition, to give a lecture on 18 June 1851, chaired by Brougham. After Levi's lecture on the complexity of international commercial laws, there was a proposal put by Harrowby, seconded by William Ewart MP, that an international code should be established, with a committee to take it forward. Little happened immediately, but Levi's lectures to chambers and other bodies around the country (including local branches of the Law Amendment Society) in late 1851 and early 1852 led to motions from the chambers supporting commercial law reform. In 1852, on the

[141] Ibid., p. 7. Letters of Lyne to Brougham, 27 and 28 February 1852, 2 May 1853; HB/5968–9, 5973. There is also an extensive printed set of arguments, correspondence, and rebuttals; HB/5970.
[142] Quoted in Tribunals of Commerce Association (1856), p. 7 also (1854a).
[143] Liverpool chamber (1852), pp. 8–9.
[144] See *House of Commons Papers, Memorandum* (1854–5), L, p. 371.
[145] Thomas Baring, the leading City figure of the 1840s and 1850s, had been a major opponent of the Anti-Corn Law campaign; Howe (1997), p. 14. He had large landed interests and was deeply protectionist; an unlikely ally for Levi's cause, but a key member of the Law Amendment Society, and one of the committee who took forward proposals on arbitration.
[146] Tribunals of Commerce Association (1854b), pp. 2–3 and p. 22.

basis of his lectures and book, Levi was invited to present his arguments to Prince Albert.[147]

Law Amendment Society and the Common Law Procedure Act (1854)

Much in the Lyne-Levi conflict appears to hinge on the patronage of key figures, especially at the London Law Amendment Society. This was a prestigious body, formed in 1843, mainly of leading lawyers, but with other prominent members like Thomas Baring.[148] Levi, Lyne, and others appeared before it at a second meeting on codification of the law, and to seek support for Lyne's Association on 16 and 17 November 1852, arranged through Lord Harrowby and Henry Brougham.[149] Lyne felt that their response was discouraging and 'we all felt as we returned from the meeting that *effectual* law reform must come from commercial associations, and not from the Law Amendment Society'. Lyne goes on to comment that 'the idea of lawyers calling public meetings to promote law reform is a high joke ... there is a wolf in sheep's clothing'. However, in 1854, Lyne quotes support from the Society, particularly its president Lord Brougham, and vice-presidents Lords Warncliffe and Harrowby. Lyne claims 'that if I had not battled hard against my treacherous foes in the City of London, who had been listening to Mr Leone Levi, the tribunal of commerce movement would have been prematurely destroyed'.[150]

However, it is Levi, not Lyne who is credited with the legal reforms then achieved. According to the *DNB*, it was he who made the critical contribution to the law of arbitration in the Common Law Procedure Act (1854), which established improvements in legal decisions on commerce. Levi was also a major contributor to codification in the Mercantile Law Amendment Act (1856):[151] 'these remained lasting memorials to Levi's influence and industry'. Certainly any success in raising and having the tribunals issue more widely discussed, and amendments taken to parliament, at this point relied chiefly on the Law Amendment Society in collaboration with Levi.[152]

In these developments Brougham was a key figure of influence. He had begun his political career as an agent for Liverpool and Manchester chambers in 1808, as discussed in Chapter 4. He was a heavyweight political figure, but outsider to the aristocracy, a leading supporter of slave trade abolition and the Reform Act, a

---

[147] See *DNB*; Obituary, *Journal of the Royal Statistical Society*, 51(2) (1888), pp. 340–2; Levi (1888), pp. 45–56.

[148] Its president in this period was Brougham, with 19 vice-presidents including the Attorney General, Solicitor General, Lord Privy seal, ministers, and various foreign honorary members who were lawyers. It had about 230 individual members, which included three chambers in 1856 (Belfast, Plymouth, and Worcester); *13th Annual Report, Rules and List of Members*; Know. Pamph. 622 (11), Liverpool University Library.

[149] See *DNB* entry for Levi, p. 541.

[150] Tribunals of Commerce Association (1854b), pp. 12 and 20–7.

[151] *DNB*, pp. 541–2, by academic lawyer G. R. Rubin, interprets Levi as mainly a contributor to legal reform.

[152] Liverpool chamber (1852), pp. 24–6 and title-page commentary.

practising lawyer and judge, and leader of wider law reform (his law reform speech of 1828 still regarded as critical to modern debates), former Attorney General and Lord Chancellor, with good economic knowledge and a 'classical' free market view.[153] He was the founder of the Society for the Diffusion of Useful Knowledge in 1826 (closely associated with the economist Thomas Tooke, another chamber supporter), and in 1857 was the founder of the National Association for the Promotion of Social Science and its president 1857–65. He was a key figure in the Law Amendment Society and thus offered a prime target for the chambers.

Local chambers began to lobby the Law Amendment Society; for example, Leeds wrote to seven other chambers in July 1852 to urge support; Belfast established a tribunal of commerce committee in early 1852, responding to Levi's visit to the chamber, and had exchanges with the Society, joining in November 1852, the Society having agreed 'to admit various chambers of commerce to a voice in their proceedings'.[154] Most major chambers, including Dublin, Manchester, Liverpool, Newcastle, Birmingham, Belfast, and Worcester subscribed.[155] The National Association of Trade Protection Societies also met the Law Amendment Society in 1853; it raised its central concerns about improving the law of debtor and creditor. The NATPS recommended that local TPS became members of the Society,[156] and a few did. The Law Amendment Society had the benefit of substantial involvement from the lawyers in the House of Lords; as Darnton Lupton of the Leeds chamber stated, 'the more the aristocracy mixed with the thinking part of the people the more would they be held in the love and respect of the nation'.[157] The Society pressed for the Mercantile Law Amendment Act (1856), largely as a result of Levi's efforts, as well as the Joint Stock Companies Bill (1856), reform of statute law, and improvement to the property rights of married women. The Mercantile Law Amendment Act sought to align the commercial laws of the three kingdoms of England, Scotland, and Ireland through a Royal Commission established in 1853.

National Association for Promotion of Social Science

Brougham's initiative for a Social Science Association was another way to support law reform and had a wider remit: to discuss social and economic factors influencing behaviour that might then guide legal reform. Many chambers became involved in this from the outset; 14 attended its first national conference in October 1857. One of its earliest major reports was on the *Promotion of the Amendment of*

---

[153] A leading liberal within the Whigs, he had been in the government ousted at the 1837 election; he remained sympathetic to Manchester and the chamber concept: McCord (1958), p. 39. See also Stewart (1985), and *The Biographical Dictionary of British Economists*.

[154] Leeds chamber, minutes 7 July 1852; Belfast chamber, *Annual Report*, July–December (1852), pp. 5–6.

[155] The Jersey chamber lobbied the States to establish tribunals in 1850; chamber minutes, 24 December 1850.

[156] NATPS, minutes, 17 May 1853.

[157] Leeds chamber minutes, 7 July 1852.

Law in 1857. This mainly focused on bankruptcy and insolvency and had a committee of 31, drawn from 12 major chambers and seven TPS.[158] Neither Lyne nor Levi were members, and both fell out with Brougham over it[159] (although Levi appears to have been revived in Brougham's esteem by 1859).[160] Judging from the reports of the Social Science Association's debates, John Danson (Liverpool chamber) and Sampson Lloyd (Birmingham chamber) were the key chamber participants, and this initiated an agenda that led to the early adoption by ACC of tribunals and public law concepts for chambers, as discussed above. Danson and Lloyd's agenda split the ACC in 1861, as discussed in Chapter 8.

The evolution of the efforts to achieve reforms, including that for tribunals, shows that resistance from the lawyers, numerous in both Houses, had to be overcome. Levi's Common Law Procedure Act (1854) answered most of the lawyers' concerns, so that chambers acting as tribunals were not seen as needed. The development of chambers as elected legal adjudicatory bodies was also perceived as radical. It was unlikely to succeed as it sparked general alarms related to the Reform Bill of the time. In the Palmerston papers of 1851 a letter from James Wilson MP refers to a 'conversation on chambers of commerce or tribunals of commerce as they would more probably be', where 'the views of the larger commercial men . . . [who] speak chiefly of India, trade and navigation', raised concerns; he felt it was not easy to call 'for the election of members [of tribunals] without exciting the suspicion that it had anything to do with the Reform Bill'. Wilson was planning a visit to 'Liverpool, Manchester and some other chambers of commerce to investigate further'.[161]

The continuing campaign

Wherever the credit should lie for the Common Law Procedure Act (1854), the legal reforms were seen as inadequate by Lyne, and most of the chambers. The attempt to achieve more general tribunals carried on, and Lyne continued to chair the Tribunals Association. Continuing efforts can be traced through Worcester and Manchester's minutes. Both chambers sent delegations to the 7 October 1852 meeting of the Law Amendment Society, and the meeting at Liverpool in 1853. In

---

[158] National Association for the Promotion of Social Science (1857), *Promotion of the Amendment of Law;* Know. Pamph. 623 (12), Liverpool University Library.

[159] Levi resisted Brougham's Social Science Association in 1856–7; see Chapter 8; also letters of George Woodyatt Hastings (Secretary of the Association) to Lord Brougham, 6 February 1857 (HB/ 6078), and 2 April 1857 (HB/13086); Lyne made himself unacceptable by begging for money: 'Lyne is behaving in such a way that we have been obliged to write and tell him we cannot have him at the conference' of the Social Science in 1857; later, 'I have had another letter from that troublesome man, Lyne—three pages long—and containing with a good deal of nonsense, more than one absolute untruth', to which no reply was sent: Hastings to Brougham, 6 February 1857 HB/6078, and 2 April 1857, HB/13086.

[160] e.g. collaborating on codification of law and the metric system; Brougham papers: HB/4049, 12383, 12384, 12390 ff., 43581.

[161] Letter to Palmerston from James Wilson MP, Wiltshire, 16 November 1851; TNA PRO 30/ 22/94, fos. 127–8.

1853 Lyne widened the objectives of tribunals to 'arbitration ... of the numerous strikes of workmen'. In 1854 a new resolution on tribunals was sent from Lyne to Worcester chamber, which called for a Committee of Inquiry into Tribunals of Commerce. Worcester agreed to sign this.[162] Lyne's Tribunals Association continued to be financed by subscriptions from chambers and other bodies; e.g. Bristol chamber agreeing to raise a subscription for the petition by approaching the 100 largest firms in the city after Lyne's son had visited and spoken at the chamber.[163] The new petition to parliament was agreed in early 1856, with amended resolutions which 'appeared more practical and practicable' in mid-1856.[164] By May 1857 Lyne was asking all chambers to write to their MPs to press for a Committee of Inquiry.

After all these pressures a Commons Select Committee[165] was established in 1858, and Lyne asked chambers for evidence or examples where tribunals could act; but Worcester did not respond—'inasmuch as the Directors present do not concur in all the propositions advanced by Mr Lyne they do not think it will further Mr. Lyne's view to supply the marginal information he requires to be attended to the questions proposed to be asked by him to the Parliamentary Committee'. Again in May 1858, Lyne asked Worcester to take part in the Committee. Worcester agreed to support, but in June took no action as 'no agreement arrived at'. By 1859 Worcester's interest in Lyne was dead: 'an application from Mr Lyne for a contribution of five guineas to the Association was not complied with'.[166] Other chambers also seemed to have switched attention; for example Leeds took no action after 'some members of the committee entertained considerable doubts as to whether a regularly organised association really exists of which Mr. Lyne purports to be chairman'.[167] By 1861 Liverpool, on receiving a letter from Lyne seeking support for a London tribunal, declined to act.[168]

Worcester's experiences indicate Lyne's energy, but also demonstrate internal divisions in support. The lack of action via the 1858 Select Committee appears to have been the last straw for Worcester. The emergence of Levi as an agent for some of the chambers (including Worcester), and the foundation of the ACC in 1860 also provided a new leadership, though Worcester did not join until 1874. Worcester's minutes also indicate a very active involvement in other means to develop action. It was a member of the Society of Arts, and the Law Amendment Society, though it did not send delegates to meetings after 1853. But it became much more heavily involved in The Law Amendment Society's Mercantile Law

[162] Worcester chamber minutes, 1 November 1853; 3 March 1854; 2 and 9 January 1855.
[163] Bristol chamber, *Annual Report,* July (1854), p. 10 (visit of Francis Palmer Lyne); January 1855, p. 8.
[164] Worcester chamber minutes, 1 January 1856, 7 May 1856.
[165] Select Committee on Tribunals of Commerce, 1858. This met six times and gathered valuable evidence, which was published as parliament was dissolved.
[166] Worcester chamber minutes, 4 May and 1 June 1858; 3 May 1859.
[167] Leeds chamber minutes, 29 April 1857.
[168] Liverpool chamber received a paper from Lyne in 1861 to support a London tribunal of commerce; the chamber declined to sign the paper, but expressed gratification in hearing the proposal to establish a London chamber; Liverpool chamber, Council minutes, 28 January, 1861.

Conference of 3 February 1857, as well as Brougham's Social Science Association Conferences of 1857–66, which were pressing for law reform in a different way.

Tensions between the chambers

Some of the difficulties for the tribunal concept become clear in the Manchester minutes. In reply to a letter from Jos. Hall, of the Newcastle chamber on 3 February 1864, Manchester chamber records that 'on more than one occasion [it had] expressed an opinion adverse to such institutions [tribunals] and did not see any reason to change'.[169] Worcester also agreed to take 'no action' on a Newcastle proposal for courts for settlement of commercial disputes.[170] Observing the actions of the ACC, Manchester published a report in late 1865 by one of its members, H. J. Leppoc, who had been a Manchester delegate at various national meetings including the Social Science Conferences. After extensive discussion of tribunals in 1866 (with a press report filling five columns on 12 December 1866), an agreement was reached in Manchester to set up a *voluntary* tribunal, but it did not support compulsory tribunals. A list of 24 people from the chamber acted as arbiters to initiate the body.[171]

Similar tensions were evident in Dublin. It did not re-establish its arbitration service until the 1890s. Dublin received a proposal for William Richardson in 1858, a law agent of coastal vessels, probably influenced by Lyne, arguing for the chamber to establish an arbitration court, but the council concluded that there was nothing to recommend it.[172] This was all the more surprising as the chamber was then de facto merged with the Ouzel Galley society, which had been an arbitration court, though by then inactive. Dublin similarly left a letter from Levi in 1856 unanswered. But the chamber bought £10 worth of the stock of pamphlets on tribunals of commerce by Henry Dix Hutton of Dublin (approximately 300). This seems to have been stimulated by a statement by the Brussels Free Trade Congress.[173] Later the chamber supported the extension of the 1889 Arbitration Act to Ireland.[174]

The efforts of the Association of Chambers of Commerce

The ACC, founded in 1860, immediately took up the cause of the tribunals of commerce, probably as a result of John Danson and Sampson Lloyd's involvement in the earlier Social Science Association debates. In 1865 ACC helped sponsor a Bill

---

[169] Manchester chamber minutes, 8 February 1864.
[170] Worcester chamber minutes, 4 September 1866.
[171] Manchester chamber minutes, containing press report, 12 December 1866.
[172] Dublin chamber, Council minutes, 17 November 1858.
[173] Dublin chamber, Council minutes, 20 November 1856; 15 and 22 December 1856; the Ouzel Galley Society was wound up in 1888. Dix Hutton had addressed the London Tavern on 4 October 1856, and had received much press and other support.
[174] Dublin chamber, General Meeting minutes, 8 March 1909.

by Newcastle chamber for mercantile courts. This was sponsored again in 1866, but both failed. Hull chamber felt this was due to too many lawyers in parliament whose profits would suffer; they should be 'declared interested parties, and neither allowed to speak nor vote'.[175] The opposition from Manchester and other chambers was not helpful. Although Manchester was not a member of ACC until 1898, divisions between the main chambers, especially with one so prominent as Manchester, undermined the political case. The ACC marshalled its next campaign in 1867 around a paper by Jacob Behrens (vice-president of the Bradford chamber).[176] He echoed earlier themes about the cost, slowness, and competence of the courts, the need for a commercial code, and the effectiveness of continental models of tribunals such as those in France and Germany. The key feature of Behrens's new scheme was a proposal to establish tribunals in every town or borough of 15,000 inhabitants, through an 'application from an incorporated chamber of commerce . . . co-extensive with the district of the County Court. The jurisdiction must be compulsory . . . [in] trade transactions; . . . but not disputes between masters and workmen.' This was clearly more acceptable to the dissenting views in Manchester, Worcester, and other areas.

A key step was a Tribunals of Commerce Bill proposed in 1871 by ACC, with Behrens still a key influence. This was 'introduced into the Commons by four of the Association's MPs'.[177] This Bill reiterated the principle that tribunals were to be established by petition of incorporated chambers of commerce or from any city or borough council, with districts assigned by the Lord Chancellor (essentially, therefore, County Courts), with merchant judges and the County Courts acting as registrars.[178] This was referred by the Lord Chancellor to the Judicature Committee, which was then considering reform of the High Court; this was enlarged to become a Queen's 'Indicative Commission'. A Commons Select Committee was also established. However, no action was taken despite many deputations and lobbying efforts by ACC, although the Select Committee did recommend in its 1872 Report that in the centres of industry 'a permanent court of unlimited jurisdiction' should be established.[179] ACC reintroduced the Bill, as amended and another Select Committee took evidence in 1873.[180] The Bill was again reintroduced in 1874;[181] however, this again failed to progress. Lyne re-emerged to rail at 'the self-interested lawyers in this committee who prevent progress'.[182] In 1878 four further Bills were presented by ACC; in 1880 there was a memorial to the Lord Chancellor; and in 1884 a memorial to the Prime Minister

---

[175] Hull chamber, *Annual Report* (1867), p. 16.
[176] *Tribunals of Commerce*: paper read at Council of Bradford chamber, 29 October 1867; ABCC Executive paper; MS 14477/1.
[177] Ilersic and Liddle (1960), p. 85.
[178] Bills, VI, 477 (1871), p. 42; text of Bill as amended, ACC Executive Council minutes; MS 14776/2.
[179] Ilersic and Liddle (1960), p. 85; *House of Commons Papers* (1871–2), xii, p. 523.
[180] Bills VI, 199 (1873) p. 57; *House of Commons Papers* (1873), ix, p. 513.
[181] Bills, V, 425 (1874) p. 2.
[182] Lyne (1876), especially p. 50, where he castigates them as operating under an 'old Popish system'.

and Lord Chancellor. These unsuccessful efforts were mirrored by the failure of a second strategy in the 1890s: to campaign for wider jurisdiction of the County Courts to enable traders to recover small debts cheaply.[183] Typical of the efforts, as reported in the ACC minutes, is the comment after an ACC deputation met the Lord Chancellor in 1887: he recognized 'the very great importance' of the chambers' case, but provided nothing and referred them to the actions of Westminster Hall and City of London.[184] This is a further important acknowledgement of the government's strategy to focus attention on corporations and formal court processes, and to sideline the independent chambers.

Efforts in London 1871–1872

A serious attempt to establish a chamber in London had developed when the City Corporation adopted a proposal for a tribunal of commerce during the 1871–2 efforts by ACC.[185] This followed the Report of the Commons Select Committee on Tribunals of 1872. This Report was considered by the Court of Common Council, and subsequently sent to all its members. The City's Local Government and Taxation Committee was tasked with considering the Report and preparing a response. This committee came out strongly in favour of the concept of tribunals and produced a report listing 17 principles which parliamentary legislation should follow. It believed that only a parliamentary Act would achieve the necessary status for tribunals. The Common Council agreed to these recommendations, in effect, also agreeing to support a London chamber.[186]

At this point, however, the City was persuaded to step back, when the Lord Mayor was appointed a commissioner of the Queen's 'Indicative Commission' considering 'tribunals of commerce'. This proved fatal to the legislation and to the City's support for it. The Corporation took the line of appeasement: 'the Lord Chancellor advised . . . that it is not advisable to pass any measure establishing tribunals of commerce until the subject has undergone consideration . . . from the Indicative Commission'. The Corporation was therefore 'of the opinion that the steps taken . . . have resulted in obtaining an extension of the powers of the Indicative Commission and report to the Crown the desirability of establishing tribunals of commerce but we cannot hope that any legislation on the subject will take place this session'.[187] The ACC had reintroduced the Bill, as amended, through MPs in 1873, but the City's role in the Indicative Committee meant that it acquiesced when the Bill was withdrawn. The government had managed to delay and sidetrack both tribunals and the foundation of a London chamber, as discussed in Chapter 5.

[183] Ilersic and Liddle (1960), pp. 85–92.
[184] ACC minutes, 27 July 1887; MS 14477/2.
[185] See also Chapter 5; there is no coverage of the London materials in Ilersic and Liddle (1960).
[186] City Corporation, Court of Common Council, minutes, 14 November and 5 December 1872.
[187] Ibid., 1 May 1873.

The Arbitration Act 1889

As shown in Chapter 12, chambers had in fact developed arbitration as one of their services from an early date; they did not wait for formal legal tribunal powers. These local arbitration activities were given further encouragement by the establishment of the London chamber in 1882, and support from the City Corporation to establish a local arbitration court.[188] Lyne re-emerged to argue that the London chamber should become a national tribunal 'subjugating all the other chambers of commerce ... [so that] it could carry a mighty influence with the Board of Trade'.[189] Once London chamber had an arbitration court, working jointly with the powers of the City Corporation, it was then more straightforward to lobby for a more general Act. It introduced a Bill into the Lords in 1886, sponsored by Lord Bramwell, focused on consolidating arbitration law. This failed several times before the Arbitration Act 1889 was finally achieved.[190] This development largely laid to rest the debate on 'tribunals of commerce'. Although London initially referred to its Court of Arbitration as a tribunal of commerce, the term was never used again after 1891.[191]

Under this Act, a submission for adjudication was irrevocable, and the umpire had court powers, acting in effect under delegated powers from the High Court, to whom appeal could be made at various points in the process. The process of appointing umpires and the mode of procedure drew heavily on the processes established by London and Manchester chambers.[192] The Act gave chambers a significant victory in one sense. It established their position to operate local hearings within, but separate from, court processes. It thus gave them the tribunals of commerce that had been sought for over 100 years. But it did not transfer powers from the County or other courts. It was more akin to formal recognition by the courts, which had been used unsuccessfully in New York in the 1870s. The Arbitration Act thus led to a role that was an alternative to, not a replacement of, court processes; and the lawyers continued to resist its use. As a result, there was a relatively low take-up of chamber arbitration. Hence, the victory for the chambers was somewhat hollow, and it notably did not provide the general recognition that many chambers desperately sought. However, the existence of the Act had the effect of turning the debate away from tribunals to the issue of status and recognition. Hence, when 'costs of litigation' and similar problems in the courts later recurrently re-emerged, the chambers no longer voiced the need for tribunals, but argued for improvements in court processes.[193]

[188] London chamber, *Annual Report* (1883), pp. 73–81; City Corporation, Report of Coal, Corn and Finance Committee, 1888; LMA: COL/CC/04/04.
[189] Lyne (1882), p. 21.
[190] An Act for Amending and Consolidating the Enactments relating to Arbitration; 52 and 53 Vict. C. 49, 22 August 1889. It remained substantially unchanged in the subsequent Act of 17 May 1934; 24 and 25 Geo. 5 . 14. Elements continue today. These Acts are ignored by Ilersic and Liddle (1960). The Act did not apply to Ireland, which maintained voluntary schemes throughout.
[191] London chamber, *Annual Report* (1891), p. 4.
[192] As claimed by the London *CCJ*, 10 September (1892), pp. 211–12.
[193] e.g. in response to the 1935 Royal Commission on the King's Bench Division, although Newcastle and a few chambers pressed for a lobby, London chamber and the ACC took a low-key approach: ABCC Finance and Taxation Committee, 6 March 1935 and Executive Committee, 7

The tribunal debate is important since it shows how the independent and voluntary bodies in Britain and Ireland wrestled within a common law system to be accorded a stronger position with judicial powers. That they were ultimately successful, but in a rather limited way, is probably inevitable given the tensions inherent in the British and Irish legal and institutional structures. As a result, the contemporary assessment in Levi's obituary of 1888, is broadly correct: whilst 'chambers of commerce are thoroughly useful and practical institutions. Tribunals of commerce have, generally speaking, failed.'[194]

The tribunal debate is also important in demonstrating the deep resistance in parliament to recognizing external and independent business roles sanctioned by the state. Lyne was right to castigate the influence of the lawyers in both Houses as defending the vested interests of their own pockets. It is a different version of the experiences of the chambers against the landed gentry during the Anti-Corn Law campaign. The *DNB* comment on Levi, by a legal historian, makes the point well. It recognizes that Levi (and hence Mortimer and Weskett before him) was 'challenging whether law was the best framework regulating business and commercial affairs'. In commercial markets, contract provisions, as conceived in law, are often less important than experiences of promises made and honoured. Deals are honoured 'not because the law will impose sanctions for breach but because traders prefer to adhere to the values of the commercial community...promises were honoured in spite of the law... What was being promoted was the creation of the "local state", in this case a local commercial state... It was favoured by many commercial traders but crucially (and decisively) rejected by the lawyers on the Judicature Commission in 1874.'[195]

The tensions in the British debate, which led many chambers to prefer voluntary over government-backed schemes, are reflected in the American system. In New York chamber a voluntary arbitration system existed from the outset, but a dispute developed between those who wanted compulsory arbitration and those who did not.[196] Attempts to achieve government support for compulsory arbitration in 1770 and 1787 failed, and there was a prominent refusal to abide by an arbitration decision in 1844. However, in 1864 New York State acted to make decisions of the chamber committee the basis of court judgements, and in 1874 an Act created a Court of Arbitration. However, this compulsory approach was ineffective and a voluntary committee was re-established in 1911. Bishop, writing in 1918, observed that voluntary discussions were in practice binding, despite being only supported by 'a gentlemen's word of honour'. As a result he claimed, 'our chamber acts as an almost irresistible moral force'.[197]

August 1935. This resulted in a very generalized resolution at the 1936 ABCC Annual Meeting (MS 14476/13, Resolutions, p. 5).

[194] *Journal of the Royal Statistical Society*, 51(2) (1888), p. 341.

[195] *DNB* (2004), p. 542; author G. R. Rubin; see also Rubin and Sugarman (1984), especially pp. 102–3.

[196] Stevens (1867); Bishop (1918).

[197] Disputes were made the basis of court action: *Powers of the Arbitration Court of the Chambers of Commerce of the State of New York, 1864* (BL8247.cc.42(10)); Bishop (1918), pp. 121–4.

7.7 CONCLUSION

The quest for government recognition and status by the chambers has been a recurrent theme from their earliest days to the present. It will continue to recur and be re-examined as each change in government or economic activity throws up new demands. This chapter has shown the impact of this debate, which has given chambers many fillips to development. The early concepts of formal status led to initiatives by New York, Glasgow, Edinburgh, Waterford, and Limerick to gain Royal charters. For most of the rest of the system, however, formal status awaited company incorporation as a standard governance structure for chambers of commerce in both Britain and Ireland developed over 1850–1900. This was well ahead of other business associations, which did not begin to incorporate until WW1. A few chambers of trade followed suit in the 1920s, but TPS and most chambers of agriculture never incorporated.

However, this did not provide the recognition chambers sought, so that a quest for 'public law status' became an alternative route. In one manifestation this was outstandingly successful. The pressure to establish chambers as 'tribunals of commerce' achieved notable success in initiatives by early chambers on a voluntary local basis. Arbitration bodies grew into important activities in most major chambers over 1768–1914. Success was also achieved as a result of the initiatives of the 1850s for legal reform, led by Leone Levi and supported by Brougham, which opened the door for a level of chamber arbitration through the Common Law Procedure Act of 1854. Pressures for more general tribunals of commerce failed, but the 1889 Arbitration Act gave chambers a formal recognition for a more limited service.

This element of progress, however, did not assure chambers the guaranteed access to government that they desired. A more general public law status became the main target, pressed from the 1960s until the 1990s. This proved to be a major distraction, although some benefits were achieved through protection of title, which is now the basis for the legal position of chambers in both Britain and Ireland, with similar structures in Canada and elsewhere. For the first time in Britain, this laid down a statutory control of brand and a defined range of chamber characteristics and services, as a general, deliberated, and independently governed local voice. In one sense this marked the conclusion of 240 years of debate, and now underpins the BCC as a strengthened body empowered to develop accreditation and other controls. But in another sense it has opened a new chapter in which 'recognition' still has to be striven for. A local voice is now more assured, but the challenge remains to make sure that it is listened to.

8

National Voice and Local Voice

8.1 INTRODUCTION

Any organization seeking to influence government has to find a means to make its voice heard. Being local as their prime USP, the chambers faced major challenges from the outset: was their voice to be delivered by each chamber acting separately, or should they join together to unite their activity; but if they united, how could they manage the inevitable differences in emphasis and interests between different places; how much resource placed behind voice was to be based locally, and how much centrally; and how were expectations and pressure from government to be dealt with? When services also came into play, a further set of questions arose over how these were organized and marketed and any quality control undertaken between the national and local levels to ensure brand protection and enhancement.

This chapter focuses on the balance between the national and local chamber organizations. It first outlines the development of agents in London. It then assesses the evolution of models of organization, through various offices, unions, federations, and confederations, leading up to the associations of chambers founded in 1860 in Britain and 1923 in Ireland. The chapter gives particular attention to how the tensions between local and central organizations evolved, and between voluntary development and professionalization of staff. The emphasis on services to members led to new forms of influence over the local chambers by the professionals and the national association, based on benchmarking, accreditation, and control of 'status'. Government and EU funding also played a major role in association development. This has influenced mission and staff focus, just as it has in the local chambers.

8.2 EARLY USE OF EXTERNAL AGENTS

The most critical mechanism required for effective voice is a means to deliver and maintain influence. In modern times this has become a highly professionalized field, but its basis was not fundamentally different in the past: it has always needed a 'case' to be framed, a means found to present it, and maintenance of pressure. The mechanisms have remained essentially the same:[1] first, to develop a presence at the

---

[1] Useem (1984); Brewer (1989); Greenwood (1997); Grant (1993, 2000).

centre of power in London (or for Irish chambers in Dublin); second, to develop and use strong links to intermediaries, such as sympathetic MPs, who could present or draw attention to the case being lobbied; third, to seek direct routes to the decision makers—ministers and key officials; fourth, to use 'delegates' composed of the most influential and best-connected members to interact and draw attention at the highest levels possible; fifth, if possible to establish coalitions with other local interests and national organizations to reinforce the case. This could all be done from the local level; but increasingly a dedicated London presence was helpful. This was usually most cheaply achieved through appointing an agent.

Agents in London

One of the most important transitions from ad hoc to routine policy exchange was use of a London agent. This might be a specialist parliamentary agent, who could be their appointee or a solicitor-agent. An agent offered three possible services: providing information on upcoming legislation and administrative changes; drafting favoured changes, including drafting Bills; and supporting the orchestration of any campaign.[2] In the earliest lobby campaigns, the president or secretary of the chamber drafted the 'case' and then travelled to London to present it. They drew on trading connections to provide contacts, among which local MPs and dignitaries, banking partners, colonial agents, sector, or other groups were natural starting points. But this was haphazard and unreliable. From an early date, therefore, established professional agents were also used. For example, before the chambers, merchants in London, Glasgow, Whitehaven, and Liverpool had used solicitor-agents to present their case in the 1732–3 Excise crisis; again in the 1765–6 Stamp Act repeal campaign; and there was the model of the American and colonial agents.[3]

Jersey was the first chamber to develop its own agent. Initially in 1768, this was through Jersey merchants located in London (and interrelated with trusted Jersey families): Messrs James Amicea Lemprière,[4] Gruchy and Le Breton, and Le Gros and Le Gros (who were also asked to become members). These merchants were 'to fix among themselves one of them who may particularly receive instructions and remittances', and to hold a copy of the chamber's rules and list of subscribers 'for them to produce upon any occasion, to show the solidity of the chamber'. They were also to hold a list of the tonnage of the subscribers to the chamber 'which being produced to their Lordships will not a little strengthen our applications'.[5] This initiative shows how the chambers sought to use trusted intermediaries, and provided them with sufficient bona fide to underpin the status of the chamber; the

---

[2] See e.g. Rydz (1979); Brewer (1989).
[3] See Chapter 4; Sosin (1965); Kammen (1970), p. 105; Langford (1975); Olson (1979, 1980).
[4] Lemprière, a member of the Society of Arts, was a possible transmitter of Jersey papers: see Chapter 4.
[5] Jersey minutes, 14 March 1768 'agents appointed to manage the affairs of the chamber in England'; the 'Lordships' refers to the members of the Board of Trade and Privy Council.

reference to tonnage confirms how shipping and trade volume carried political weight, as argued in Chapter 5.

Jersey moved to appointing its own direct agent, termed their 'deputy in London', probably in the 1770s, but the first specific record is of John Dumaresq acting in this way from 1785. At the same time Guernsey chamber appointed Havilland le Meseurier as its deputy, and the two chambers acted jointly on issues such as Customs and harbours. Dumaresq spent most of his time after 1785 in London, making trips back to Jersey to be briefed, purchasing the Statutes of England, books and maps, and having meetings to negotiate over petitions.[6] He also appears to have been one of the main agents operating transfers of money between Jersey and the mainland, particularly when the chamber became immersed in the large-scale recovery of prize money from privateering from the 1790s. Dumaresq was receiving about £60 per year for his efforts in the 1780s and 1790s, but also handling an annual account of about £240 for lobbying expenses from 1786.[7] He appears to have primarily used Lord Beauchamp as a political intermediary.[8] Although he acted as the main lobbyist, a London solicitor was also used, and money to support activity was held in London by Francis Janvrin and John Triott, merchants who were also chamber members.[9] Other Jersey merchants in London were also used as supports and informants, particularly Paul Le Mesurier during the chamber's charter lobby.[10] Hence, the London agent was part of a complex network of activity to ensure the chamber's voice was heard in the capital. Guernsey tended to rely more on formal links in the States, but also used Thomas Le Breton, the King's Procureur of Jersey, in 1836.[11]

Other early chambers tended to rely on a London solicitor-agent. Over 1783–95, Glasgow used John Seton, who cost an average of £50–70 per year in agent's fees and expenses.[12] Dublin similarly used a London solicitor-agent, Charles Treadgold, costing them £10–15 per year in agent fees in the 1780s:[13] 'for English votes last session' as well as 'Irish votes'.[14] In both cases, the main roles were to keep an eye on potential legislation, send parliamentary papers to the chamber, record and send the votes in parliament, and present the chamber's memorials. In 1808, London, Liverpool, and Manchester merchants used Henry Brougham as their parliamentary agent to lobby against the government's Orders for embargo of trade to Europe in other than British or neutral ships. It was this activity, his strong writing in the reformist *Edinburgh Review*, and his 1828 law reform speech at the Bar of the House, that brought Brougham to the

---

[6] Jersey chamber minutes, e.g. 4 July 1785, 30 June 1786, 2 March 1787, etc.; see also his negotiations with Pitt in 1790; TNA PRO 30/8/131 fos. 29–32, 35.

[7] Jersey chamber, account books; the sums ran to £000s when prize money was received.

[8] Jersey chamber minutes, 23 May 1786; which records thanks and a gift to Beauchamp.

[9] Jersey chamber minutes, 30 June 1786; Jersey chamber account books.

[10] Jersey chamber minutes, 24 January 1788; also see Chapter 7.

[11] Guernsey chamber minutes, 22 March 1836.

[12] Glasgow chamber minute books; Seton, Gray's Inn solicitor, acted for many others; connected to the Touch, Forbes, and Coutts banking families, and related to Edinburgh merchants.

[13] Dublin minutes; see also Prendeville (1930).

[14] Prendeville (1930), p. 98; quoting Dublin chamber minutes.

attention of the leading Whigs and initiated his political career. It is from this period that Brougham's association with chambers seems to have become established.[15]

The detailed activity of these agents on behalf of the chambers can be seen in John Seton's work for Glasgow in 1787–8, for which a detailed financial account survives. Seton's general costs amounted to £21 for 'a year's salary as agent at London ... for correspondence', plus expenses of £3 11s. 2d. These general expenses covered the costs of procuring copies of printed Acts, making copies of one of Glasgow's memorials, plus postage, porters, and coach hire. It also involved an attendance fee to meet with the chamber's president (Patrick Colquhoun) 'to select the different glaring abuses' relating to their memorial on Customhouse fees 'previous to his going to the minister [Pitt]'.[16] The agent's general role was thus to provide a continuous information flow and more specialized support for any specific memorials from the chamber. Colquhoun accepted that it was very difficult for individual delegates visiting London to do this task, which was 'a business always very tedious and often ... irksome', for which they lacked experience.[17]

Glasgow's successful lobbies over 1787–8, for the White Ashes Act and the Thread Act, show Seton attending parliament and committees, assisting the parliamentary clerks' office, meeting ministers, 'writing and delivering cards to members' of parliamentary committees (numbering 50 members), and scrutinizing papers. Seton charged 13s. 4d. for each attendance, involving 17 itemized plus other attendances on the White Ashes Bill, and 15 attendances on the Thread Bill. This was an expert input, with Seton drawing draft Bills, 'drawing reasons in support thereof, ... perusing the Bill ... and making sundry alterations thereof'. As time progressed the role of agents like Seton became more formal after parliament imposed 'standing orders' with which agents had to comply. In 1827 there were about 10 external agents increasing to 47 by 1865.[18]

Most of the leading chambers maintained their own agents well into the 20th century, especially those that were not members of ACC. They clearly viewed this as more effective than the early years of the ACC, and their local voice carried more weight than being buried in a larger collective. Even the tiny Falmouth chamber employed its own parliamentary agent, rather than using the ACC in the 1860s, to lobby on its lifeboat and harbour Bills. Falmouth also, independently of ACC, joined in a lobby with the Salt chamber, sending a delegation to the Secretary of State for India to reduce Indian salt duties in 1877.[19]

[15] *DNB* entry; see Chapter 7 for further aspects of Brougham's activities.
[16] Account from John Seton dated 4 November 1788, Glasgow chamber letters, TD 1670/4/52.
[17] Glasgow chamber, *Plan of a Public Agency in London for Commercial Affairs*: October 1788, p. 2.
[18] Seton's account, op. cit.; see also Rydz (1979), pp. 50–8, 81, 208–11.
[19] Falmouth chamber minutes: see Falmouth chamber history, p. 20.

An office in London

A stage beyond contracting an agent was to establish an agency or office in London. Jersey's agent effectively evolved in this direction; but the most significant early example is Glasgow, which moved away from Seton and established its own agent in 1789–90. The Glasgow agency followed a *Plan* proposed by its chair, Patrick Colquhoun, in 1788. 'Almost every month, nay every week, something is occurring at the seat of government interesting to one or other of the numerous bodies of traders and manufacturers, who from their remote distance and from their inability often to act singly, may suffer extreme injury . . . from hasty regulations or laws not calculated for the general good.' The agency would allow 'all precedents with regard to commercial transactions with the state . . . [to] be accessible to mercantile and manufacturing bodies—where a collection of all public state papers relative to commercial affairs are to be found—where proper cases may be drawn, and [proposals] . . . may be watched and corrected . . . under the management of persons who will turn their whole attention to such subjects'.[20]

Colquhoun was clearly not fully satisfied with John Seton: 'a law solicitor who can have no accurate ideas on such subjects' results in 'enormous fees charged, it is the blind leading the blind' with the result that lobbies 'often fail'.[21] Colquhoun annotated Seton's bill for 1787–8, and there is a vigorous exchange of letters on costs.[22] Colquhoun concluded: 'When it is considered what an immense sum of money is expended yearly by the commercial and manufacturing bodies in transactions with government in state negotiations . . . it is easy to discern the utility and advantage as well as the great economy of the proposed institution . . . the same aggregate business might be done well and effectually at one third, perhaps one fourth of the present annual expense.'[23]

Colquhoun's London *Plan* covered nine objectives: collection of papers and documents; attendance at parliament; investigations at the Board of Trade; constant correspondence and transfer of information to all constituent member bodies; drafting Bills and cases; meeting the relevant ministers and public bodies; assisting all claims against public officers and for public money due (acting by 'power of attorney when necessary'); providing information of the state of manufactures and trade in foreign parts; and helping with advice and assistance to manufacturers when in London. It would also be a *Scottish National Office*, not just for Glasgow (although Edinburgh declined to join, stating they would continue their solicitor-agent). He also outlined the need to find a sub-agent to attend the progress of Bills through parliament; thus some use of existing solicitor-agents was still considered necessary.

Colquhoun recognized that an agent had to carry weight and status to be able to approach ministers, acknowledging the issue of locus standi that bedevilled

[20] *Plan of a Public Agency in London for Commercial Affairs*: Glasgow chamber papers, TD 1670/4/52, October 1788, 11 pp.
[21] *Plan*, pp. 1–3.
[22] Seton's account for 1787–8 and related letters; Glasgow chamber papers TD 1670/4/52.
[23] *Plan*, p. 4.

chambers. He suggested that this could be achieved by being appointed by a document declaring the support of the Scottish Royal Burghs, the Scottish chambers and committees of trade, and by a 'General Commission' signed by 'a combination of respectable individuals engaged in commerce and manufacturers'. This 'would at once stamp weight and dignity on the office'. In typical style he then circulated drafts of the declaration for each of these bodies to use.[24] With the *Plan* is inter-bound a letter of support from the local MP, Islay Campbell, who had 'long been of the opinion that such an institution properly conducted would be extremely useful'. Campbell argued that the agent needed

> good access ... and constant vigilance and attention ... to correspond with societies and individuals here, to convey information ... and in short to act as a solicitor in all commercial matters where the interest of Scotland ... is concerned. When great commercial points are agitated the traders of Scotland have not the advantage of being at hand, and they may not always have exactly the same interest or the same objects, with those of the same classes elsewhere.[25]

Campbell was a well-connected heavyweight politician with whom the chamber had worked closely in 1784–6 over several Bills.[26] Colquhoun was again using astute cultivation of national and local political figures.

Colquhoun was clearly designing the post of agent for himself, and could count on the support of the three constituencies he named, as he had been convenor of the Royal Burghs, was currently president of the Glasgow chamber, and commanded a wide following in commercial circles across Scotland. He must have been delighted with the closing sentence of Campbell's letter, that 'I know no person more fit than yourself to give it a beginning'. Colquhoun duly became the first incumbent. It lasted only two years, in part because of the cost to the chamber, but also because Colquhoun had other preoccupations.[27] Glasgow reverted to using the normal parliamentary agents.

The Liverpool office in London

The next ambitious early operation was the office in London of the Liverpool American chamber of commerce, jointly financed with other trade bodies in the town, and latterly with the corporation. This chamber had only been established in 1802, but on the instigation of the two Liverpool MPs, a London office was

---

[24] *Plan*, pp. 6–11.

[25] Letter from Islay Campbell to Colquhoun, 11 October 1788, bound into *Plan*, between pp. 10–11; Glasgow chamber papers, TD 1670/4/52. Campbell was Solicitor General in 1783; Lord Advocate in 1783–9 appointed by Pitt to succeed Dundas; then Lord President of the Court of Session 1789–1808; each on Dundas's recommendation. Although a dry speaker as MP and supporter of Pitt's government, he was an effective advocate for Glasgow interests: Thorne (1986), *History of Parliament*; *DNB*.

[26] e.g. printed linen duties, 1784; Irish propositions, 1785; Greenland fishery bounties, 1786; see Chapter 10.

[27] He became stipendiary magistrate in Shoreditch in 1792, an appointment influenced by Dundas: *DNB*.

established in 1814 with John Backhouse, a prominent merchant, as the first secretary.[28] The salary was £100, raised to £125 in 1828. The office continued until the 1930s, coming entirely under the city corporation's control in 1880. Henderson quotes it as the only municipal office of its kind.[29] The American chamber covered its main costs by paying £50–150 per year over 1815–27 (about half of its own total annual expenditure). The corporation, which had declined to support the office initially, gave £50 a year 1824–6, £100 a year 1827–42, and then £200 a year 1843–57.[30] The Dock Board, and associations of saltshippers, East India, West Indies, Portugal, Brazil, South America, and Mexican traders also contributed after 1823. The roles of the office were specified in an 1858 document which followed the appointment of Thomas Baines as the third secretary in 1857: first, to collect information (parliamentary Bills, votes, etc.); second, 'imparting information . . . to render to the chamber for general reference and to any other association specifically requiring them on paying their cost, copies of any Bills and Parliamentary papers'; third, assistance to Liverpool MPs; fourth, advice to Liverpool men who visit London to present memorials, arrange interviews and furtherance of their parliamentary business; and fifth, to visit Liverpool when required. The office could conduct 'no public business . . . but such as relates to the borough and port of Liverpool'.[31] Its main role became predominantly support to the Liverpool MPs, pressing for reforms of dock administration to remove the stranglehold of the corporation, engaging in correspondence and meetings at the highest levels.[32] Baines went on to be the first London 'secretary' of the ACC in 1860 (see below).

The other major early example of a London office was the Salt chamber, whose secretary became its London agent over 1853–73. This acted as a direct voice in addition to the ACC, of which it was a member. Salt also opened an office in Liverpool, in addition to its Northwich office, to ensure that it had an agent in the port to look after its interests with the merchants.[33]

Irish agents in London

The early Irish chambers had an additional challenge. They had to lobby Westminster, even when they had their own parliament up to 1800, but they had additionally to lobby the Dublin parliament and other interests. For the Irish chambers the lobby on Westminster had all the challenges of those on the

[28] Backhouse was secretary until 1823, when he was appointed to a government post; he had been private secretary to George Canning (MP for Liverpool) after 1816. He was succeeded by William Wainewright, who continued until 1857: Henderson (1933b), p. 474.
[29] Henderson (1933b), p. 479; the Liverpool American chamber merged into the Liverpool chamber in 1908.
[30] Henderson (1933b), pp. 473–5.
[31] Statement of *Duties to be Performed by the Secretary of 'The Liverpool Office in London'*, 15 January 1858; quoted in Henderson (1933a), pp. 21–2.
[32] Henderson (1933a, 1933b); Bennett (2010), pp. 135–6.
[33] See Chapter 14.

mainland, but like Jersey had an additional sea crossing. It was not surprising therefore that at an early stage they developed their own office in London to deal with 'remote legislation'.[34]

The proposal for this office came initially from Limerick, which circulated a plan to the other chambers on 27 December 1821. Subsequent discussions drew in Cork, Waterford, and Sligo, with Dublin and Belfast.[35] Dublin proposed electing a secretary for one year in the first instance, with an association of chambers of Ireland formed to manage the office, each chamber having one vote for every £25 of subscription contributed to the costs.[36] Belfast voted £80 and nominated William McQuoid to hold the post. A meeting of all the chambers in Dublin in May 1822 appointed McQuoid,[37] who in the meantime had written to William Tennant (a leading Belfast member) to use his influence with the members of the Dublin chamber on his behalf![38] By 1 June McQuoid was writing to the chambers suggesting that a 'greater collection might be made' for the costs involved, and he began the office soon afterwards. By April 1823 Belfast was taking the lead in negotiating with him, setting his salary at £100 for the first year 'provided such sum was collected from the contributing chambers', and was discussing the 'regulations of the office'. He was now referred to as the chambers' 'parliamentary agent'. Three leading Belfast members were deputed to communicate directly with McQuoid: Thomas Vance, John McCracken, and William Boyd.[39] In their report to the council at the end of 1823, the Belfast chamber was assured that 'by joining together with every other merchant association in Ireland, by their united influence, important objects have been obtained, which singly, were sought in vain'.[40] However, the initiative seems to have died after another year.

Limerick and Cork had dissented from McQuoid's appointment, and preferred James Roche instead. Roche was a Cork banker whose bank had failed in 1820 and was already based in London. Limerick described the role as 'facilitating transmission of applications for the chamber to the authorities in London and obtaining prompt answers thereto and generally in procuring information'. It also stated that an agent would be 'exempt from the inconveniences and possible abuses to which an establishment assuming a national character might . . . be liable'; i.e. Limerick was unhappy with Dublin's more collective approach of a general levy.[41] Roche was approached by Limerick and Cork, and agreed to serve for one year from February 1823; to hold 'the position of secretary for the proposed *Irish public officer in London of Irish affairs*'. By early 1823 his correspondence was from the 'Irish

[34] Prendeville (1930), p. 98.
[35] Limerick chamber minutes, 27 December 1981; 12 January, 29 May 1822; 7 April 1823. Belfast minutes, 12 January 1822; 29 May 1822; this is the first mention of a Sligo body, no further reference has been found.
[36] Belfast minutes, 10 April 1822.
[37] Belfast minutes, 29 May 1822; Dublin from Prendeville (1930), pp. 191–2.
[38] Letter from William McQuoid to William Tennant, PRONI D 1748/B/1/21.
[39] Belfast minutes, 7 April 1823.
[40] Report to Belfast chamber Council, 19 November 1823; PRONI D1857/1/G/3.
[41] Limerick minutes, letter to Joseph Harvey, 13 December 1822.

Commercial Office'.[42] The title used shows the ambition to extend beyond that of the chambers alone, and shows that the Irish chambers now had two London agents, each claiming to be the Irish representative; one for Dublin and Belfast (and perhaps some other chambers), and one for Limerick, Cork, and Youghal (which had agreed to co-finance Roche with Limerick in 1823). Roche opened his office at 20 Parliament Street and began approaching peers. Subsequent correspondence shows that Roche continued for the year but was not reappointed, despite his willingness. He received £100 per year, the same as McQuoid.[43]

Both Irish association offices in London seem to have disappeared after their first year, with chambers reverting to ad hoc London agents; Cork paid a London law agent £18 for services in 1858.[44] Once the ACC was established, Dublin and Belfast used it and were particularly active members; all the other major Irish chambers also belonged to ACC during most years. It provided a much less expensive and potentially more effective route for influence than their own office. This changed in 1923, when the Irish chambers seceded from ABCC with the foundation of the Irish Republic. Two separate associations were formed, of chambers in the Republic and Northern Ireland, with Dublin leading the initiative in the South, as discussed later. Subsequently the Republic's chambers focused exclusively on the Dublin government until accession to the EU in 1973 raised the need also for Brussels representation.

8.3 TOWARDS A NATIONAL-LOCAL ORGANIZATION

Gradually other models were explored that created a collective resource at the centre. With a central resource much of the effort could be concentrated on specialists, and there was the promise of increased effectiveness. Wootton identifies lobbying as significantly shifting after the 1760s, which saw the beginnings of specialist organizations where forms of 'political modernisation peep tentatively out', to the 1860s where grass-roots organizations became nationally integrated voices.[45] The chambers were in the vanguard of this transition.

There were various ways of achieving this, ranging from a loose collective vehicle or 'union', to an association of local bodies levying its own subscriptions with its own governance structure, council, formal delegates, and so on. A national association can also take on many forms: from a strong centre which has power to exercise executive authority and control over its local members, as the NCT and central chamber of agriculture were, and the General Chamber attempted to be, to a weak

[42] Limerick minutes, 12 March and 13 December 1822; letter from Cork chamber, 16 December 1822; letter from James Roche, 26 December 1822; Cork chamber council minutes, 9 February 1822; emphasis added.

[43] Limerick chamber minutes, letters from Roche, 3, 6, and 15 February, 22 September 1823. This is the only mention of an early Youghal body; referred to as the committee of merchants with James Ellis Keen as president.

[44] Cork chamber minutes, 28 May 1858.

[45] Wootton (1975), p. 11; pp. 35–54.

body where all decisions are made collectively in large meetings as with the NATPS. The chambers of commerce have tended to be positioned between these two extremes, with a moderately strong centre, but also strong local control.

From the General Chamber to a national 'Union' of chambers 1793–1803

The early chambers had liaised with each other from their outset. By 1783 this cooperation was widespread and included all the new chambers, many other local committees and 'delegates', and active individuals. These exchanges took on a particular focus after the formation of the General Chamber in early 1785. This was the first national chamber body, with delegates appointed by provincial committees (or by chambers where they existed), who paid one guinea per year. However, as noted in Chapter 9, this structure was doubly unstable: the individual members could outvote the chamber delegates, and the rotating chair introduced inconsistency and conflict. It survived only two years.

Notwithstanding the existence of the General Chamber the pattern of independent exchange and liaison had continued between the chambers over 1785–7.[46] This period is critical in showing continued attempts to align 'provincial' interests and develop 'national' representation that led to a 'Union' of chambers from 1793 until at least 1805. This was a loose agreement to meet, collaborate, and exchange, with an elected chair, but no formal constitution or subscription. As shown in Chapter 9, it mainly had members from the manufacturing towns and those engaged in European trades affected by the French wars. The nine or ten other chambers lobbied independently. This type of coordination continued, depending on the issues, well into the 1850s, as shown in Chapter 9. However, from 1855 more collective models began to be explored.

A metropolitan agent

The earliest collective model was a 'metropolitan' or 'town agent', which emerged in 1855. This was the result of a proposal put to two meetings convened at Birmingham chamber, chaired by Bristol, to which all other chambers were invited. The role of the agent agreed was:

1. To transmit to each of the 'united chambers' a weekly analysis in a circular letter of all Papers, Returns, Bills or Reports issued by the two Houses of parliament having a direct or indirect bearing on trade, commerce and navigation.
2. To despatch such Papers etc. as the chambers may order.
3. To inform of any movement in London of any commercial reform supported by the mercantile or trading classes or by law associations of mercantile societies.

---

[46] Local liaison did not collapse, as stated by Bowden (1919–20, 1965); Redford (1934); and followed by others.

4. To make arrangements for deputations sent to London by the chambers for holding of interviews with any Member [MP] or Department of government etc.[47]

This development reflects a step forward from both the earlier Union and independent use of agents. A single agent was now to act for a group of chambers, as attempted in Ireland in the 1820s. Bristol had circulated 23 chambers on 18 April and 6 June 1855 with this proposal. Nine were opposed 'on the grounds of them having already a town agent' (Liverpool, Manchester, Glasgow, Edinburgh, Newcastle, Southampton, Plymouth, Dublin, and Leeds); seven agreed to go ahead (Belfast, Birmingham, Bradford, Bristol, Hull, Stoke-on-Trent, and Worcester); and four were still considering and had not replied (Dundee, Leith, Waterford, and Cork). Those going ahead took on the title of 'united chambers', though Worcester referred to them as the 'associated chambers', and the agent himself referred to the 'metropolitan agency' and also the 'association of provincial chambers'. They clearly saw themselves as forming an embryonic national association to which the other chambers would eventually wish to belong. Indeed, six of the initial seven chambers were among the ten first subscribers to the ACC five years later; only Worcester was then absent. They agreed a simple constitution; to subscribe £10 per year from each chamber; to advertise the post in *The Times* and *The Economist*, with Bristol handling the applications; and to report proceedings to each chamber.[48]

Most of the chambers record only the formal decisions,[49] but Worcester highlights some of the tensions. The agent proposal seems to have emanated originally from Leone Levi, who was already well known to the chambers as a result of lectures and legal reform proposals, including tribunals of commerce, as discussed in Chapter 7; he had also helped to establish the second Liverpool chamber in 1849–50. The proposal was championed by Bristol, which described the agency as 'a medium of communication with parliament and the government offices'.[50] However, Worcester had suspicion that this was being set up for Levi; they recorded that 'two gentlemen Mr. Leone Levi and Mr. Henry Ayres had offered themselves as candidates for appointment'.[51] Bristol had been very impressed by a series of six highly successful lectures by Levi held 10–25 May 1855.[52] Perhaps for this reason, Worcester was divided about the concept: 'Mr. Aldrich thought that such an agent was not under the control of, or responsible to the united chambers and advocated the format of a Central Chamber of Commerce to which body [the agent] . . . should be more immediately responsible'. He was recognizing the difficulties of managing an agent representing many bodies by only a loose collective

---

[47] Minutes of Birmingham 'meeting of united chambers', 2 August 1855: in Worcester chamber minutes, slightly abbreviated; Birmingham chamber minutes do not survive for 1832–60.

[48] Worcester chamber minutes, 20 June 1855. This development is not included in Ilersic and Liddle (1960).

[49] e.g. for Birmingham there are only brief formal comments; see also Wright (1913), p. 134.

[50] Bristol chamber, *Annual Report*, 30 July 1855, p. 8.

[51] Worcester chamber minutes, 20 June 1855.

[52] Bristol chamber, *Annual Report*, 30 July 1855, p. 8.

agreement. 'Mr. J. W. Lea differed...and thought we should not aim at a dictatorial association...he feared we should lose our independence'. In any case, personalities intervened: 'Mr. Lea as well as Mr. Aldrich opposed the appointment of Mr. Levi', although they approved an agent 'in principle'.[53] This was one of the factors behind the call for a national advertisement for the post. A loose coordination risked loss of local control to the centre, especially if a strong personality like Levi was the agent in charge. It also appeared costly to a small chamber like Worcester; £10 per year was about one-third of their income. These themes of control, local individualism, and costs, continue throughout subsequent chamber association history.

The agent was appointed in late 1855. Twenty-two candidates applied, five were short-listed and, having seen their papers, Worcester delegated their president to vote for either Mr William Cote or Mr John Cannon at the appointing meeting in Birmingham on 12 November 1855. However, the president had to report 'the election of Mr Leone Levi by the majority of the associated chambers'. Cooperation in a national body led to the rule of the majority. After his appointment Levi soon approached the chambers for more support, first to subscribe to his new book *Annals of Legislation* and later to pay various of his expenses, including fees and travel costs to give his lectures.[54] He also continued to approach the non-subscribing chambers offering his services. The agent was already taking on a life of his own. Levi was an enthusiast and initially Worcester accommodated. The president had a 'conversation with Mr. Levi at the Mansion House which had removed the unfavourable impression that had existed with regard to the gentleman',[55] and the chamber generally welcomed his frequent missives and information. However, in 1856 Worcester opposed Levi's proposal that chambers should incorporate, and also opposed Levi's concept of tribunals of commerce. Worcester's disquiet with Levi grew, and on 1 January 1860 a resolution that the subscription should be terminated was proposed by Messrs Tymlis and Evans. This was opposed by Messrs Aldrich and Kerr, but after an equal vote the president cast his vote in favour of termination.[56] Similarly when the ACC was established in 1860, Worcester did not join. It became a member only in 1874 after its subscription was reduced to five guineas.

Leeds is one of the non-subscribing chambers that records its views. It attended the Birmingham meetings in 1855, but decided that it was 'undesirable for the present to take part'. When Levi approached Leeds for support for his application for the post of agent to the 'association of provincial chambers', the chamber replied that it was 'not united in that association'.[57] Personality again seems to have intruded. Leeds had hosted a very successful lecture by Levi on 'codification of

[53] Worcester chamber minutes, 6 & 16 November 1855; Bristol chamber, *Annual Report*, 30 January 1856, p. 3.
[54] Worcester chamber minutes, 20 June 1855; 4 December 1855; 4 November 1856; 3 January 1860.
[55] Worcester chamber minutes, 6 May 1856.
[56] Worcester chamber minutes, 1 January 1860; after earlier discussions in late 1859.
[57] Leeds chamber minutes, 30 July and 5 September 1855.

commercial law' in January 1852, of which it had printed 7000 copies at considerable cost jointly with Bradford and Hull, enthusiastically supporting Levi's argument that 'different chambers of commerce throughout the Empire should unitedly attempt the accomplishment of this object'. The printed lecture was sent to all MPs, Lords, and chambers of commerce in the Empire, with a record that 'the various chambers of commerce have cordially agreed to assist in this great national movement'. Leeds had also gone on to 'highly approve of suggestions for holding an annual meeting of deputation of chambers of commerce and other societies to consider amendment and consolidation of commercial law'.[58] But relations with Levi seem to have cooled: when he approached Leeds again in March 1853 offering a course of lectures, this was declined. Similarly he wrote on several occasions from 1855 'begging' their support for the metropolitan agency and the £10 fee, including 'several private letters' to the vice-president.[59] The substantive debate in Leeds on Levi took place in June 1855, when the chamber felt it could not afford the £10, and its secretary was doing the work already (as stated by Mr Banfield). The council reviewed an early example of Levi's periodic reports, and was not impressed: Mr Wilson stated that Levi had missed the most important Bill of the period, the Speciality and Simple Contract Debts Bill. Leeds decided to reply that the council could 'not see any immediate necessity of availing themselves of the service', and repeated this in ensuing correspondence.[60]

The 'metropolitan agent' was a significant development of cooperation. It showed the potential of the role, and it can probably be claimed that Levi's vision was a major stimulus for its development. The structural components of his vision, an association with a national agent, supported by subscriptions from incorporated member chambers, were principles taken up subsequently. But his vision for tribunals and a formal legal role was very divisive. At that time incorporation was also divisive, with many chamber leaders inexperienced and opposed to this new legal form. Levi's vision struck at the heart of the voluntary principles and local autonomy, jealously guarded by many in the system. The time was not right, but his personality also seems to have suggested to many that he could not be trusted to act as advocate of a collective view and was too keen to promote his own ideas.

8.4 THE EMERGENCE OF A NATIONAL ASSOCIATION

The experience of cooperation in the metropolitan agency undoubtedly paved the way for six of the seven chambers that collaborated to move ahead to found a stronger model in 1860, a national formalized association: the Association of Chambers of Commerce (ACC). Only Worcester dropped out of the initial

---

[58] Leeds chamber minutes, 2 February, 7 June, and 4 August 1852; minutes of 1 March record that it 'would be most effective without the prospectus of his works'.
[59] Leeds chamber minutes, 9 March 1853, 5 June 1855, 31 December 1856.
[60] Leeds chamber minutes, 5 June 1855; see also Beresford (1951), Leeds chamber history, pp. 39, 63.

seven chambers supporting the agent, and four other chambers joined: Coventry, Gloucester, Leeds, and Sheffield.[61] Although the initial minutes of the ACC show others attending, there were only ten paying members in 1860–1. It is suggested in several previous accounts that there were 16 founding members,[62] but the others did not pay initially. Since Manchester, Glasgow, and Edinburgh declined to join, and Liverpool withdrew in 1861, a pattern was established from the outset of patchy support for the association. Many chambers also continued to employ their own parliamentary agents, including most of the large chambers. Ireland was included from the outset through Belfast, but later all the major Irish chambers joined until 1923, in the case of Cork mainly through its second chamber (the Incorporated chamber), although both Cork chambers were members in the early 1900s.[63]

Establishment of the ACC

A history of the ACC has been written by Ilersic and Liddle covering the period 1860–1960. This is a useful base, to which the reader should refer, but it largely ignores the organizational aspects and the relationships with the local chambers highlighted here. The traditional account of the formation of the ACC draws on a speech by Charles Norwood during his second presidency of the association in 1885.[64] Norwood (from Hull) had also been the founding ACC president and claimed that it was a motion put to the 1859 meeting of the third Social Science Association Congress in Bradford that had kick-started the ACC. Frustrated by a very uninteresting Congress, several chamber leaders who were attending felt they should not depend on an external organization 'like the Social Sciences. Were they not important and powerful enough to have an association of their own?' They made a resolution to form an association, circulated it to other chambers, and a first meeting was held in February 1860.

This account captures Norwood's view, and it is also true that the Social Science Association, and Law Amendment Society, had stimulated chamber leaders to come together regularly, as discussed in Chapter 7.[65] The Association opened a special avenue to meet over legal reforms, with Lord Brougham (its president), and Lords Wharncliffe and Harrowby (its vice-presidents) as magnets. Brougham was a particular attraction as a heavyweight political animal, and the former agent for Liverpool and Manchester in 1808. There was even a point in 1856 when the Association considered it could become 'a chamber of commerce for the

---

[61] ACC; MS 14476/1, p. 62.

[62] Dunwoody (1935); *Chambers of Commerce Manual* (1954–5), p. 4; compared to ACC minutes 1860–2.

[63] The Cork Incorporated chamber was 'loyalist', pro-Union, whilst the Cork chamber became pro-independence; see Chapter 2. The Irish chambers in ABCC in 1912, with their votes were: Dublin (3), Cork (1), Cork Incorporated (2), Limerick (1). Waterford resigned in about 1890.

[64] Ilersic and Liddle (1960), pp. 1–2, 7–8; who were unaware of earlier chamber cooperations.

[65] Ilersic and Liddle (1960), pp. 7–8; about 14 chambers attended the Social Science Conference in 1857–9.

metropolis', echoing Brougham's ideas of 1817–23, although this was never likely.[66] However, the Social Science Association was always a rather broad body, including sector trade associations, colleges, labour unions, town councils, a church society, and links with the Reformatory Union.[67] It was unlikely to provide the sharpness of economic focus chambers wanted.

Hence, by 1860, something more was required. Levi's agency had provided some important experiences, and it was from this that ACC developed. But the link to Levi was abandoned, as he had become obstructive. The Brougham correspondence, setting up the first Social Science Association Congress in 1857, records that 'we are most displeased with Levi. He has written to more than one chamber of commerce, advising them *not* to attend the conference—He may keep away some by this, but he cannot prevent the conference—for we have enough to go on with.' Later it is recorded that 'we have the best of the chambers in England [attending, but] . . . I am sorry for the course Levi has adopted, because we should have been glad of his help.'[68] It would appear that Levi's need to develop his own agency prevented him supporting the potential for other collective models; he was removed from the council of the Social Science Association in 1857 and played no part in the establishment of the ACC. These fractures stimulated the chambers to start from a different position with a new structure and a new agent.

Early stages of ACC development

In many ways the ACC initially resembled a collective agency for assembling papers, and a talking shop; not a collective. It took ten years (1870) before it was raising subscriptions from the majority of chambers. When major delegations or campaigns were mounted it had to raise a special subscription from the members. Many of the largest chambers ignored it. For government ministers and the press, the credible expertise and comment was still at the local level, from the large provincial chambers. Norwood's view was that for the first 25 years the ACC had been 'snubbed by ministers and slightingly treated by the press, . . . that some of the subjects which occupied its members' attention were small'.[69]

Most of the limitations resulted from the ACC being a very lean organization. It appointed as its first part-time secretary Thomas Baines, already prominent as the agent for the Liverpool American chamber, and shared their office in 30 Parliament Street. The overlap with the Liverpool American chamber has not been previously noted. This offered economies, immediate expertise, and synergies, but had in-built limitations for a new collective vision. Baines was an experienced advocate, strongly

---

[66] Hastings letter to Brougham, 24 June 1856; HB/13051; UCL Special Collections; also see Chapter 5.

[67] See Brougham papers, especially correspondence of Hastings with Brougham and Frederic Hill: HB/13086–92, 13119; 8780–4; UCL Special Collections.

[68] Letters of George Woodyatt Hastings (Secretary of the Association for Promotion of Social Science) to Lord Brougham 8 December 1856, HB/13070; 11 December 1856, HB/13071; UCL Special Collections.

[69] Ilersic and Liddle (1960), p. 2.

supported the first Social Science Association Congress, and saw the need for a coalition of the provinces: 'the absurd bigotry of the City people ... [and the] great good by showing that the provincials' supported reforms'.[70] Baines served for three years, was succeeded by T. B. Simson for a further three years, and then by James Hole, who served 1867–94 and must be credited with the real establishment of the association. The salary was part time and only £100 per year in 1860, raised for Hole to £120 in 1873, and then £170 in 1877. These first three secretaries were called the 'agent in London', which signifies status as servants of the local chambers: this was a confederal structure with a weak centre. The role was to collect information, transmit it to chambers at cost price, and to assist local chambers in gaining interviews with MPs, officials etc.[71] As a result the ACC also continued to use specialist parliamentary agents (of whom Edward Fithian, who later became the first full-time secretary, was one). But the real power lay with the delegates from the local chambers, who were diverse, which meant that the president was crucial. Initially Levi was among the delegates, attending initial ACC meetings as 'agent' of the North Staffordshire chamber in 1860, but he was replaced by Godfrey Wedgwood and M. D. Hollins in 1861.

Despite its limitations, the ACC was of considerable benefit to the smaller chambers. As noted by Swansea in 1876, 'though by themselves they could not do much, the chamber was a unit of a very powerful federation ... which exercised considerable influence'.[72] The ACC also stimulated greater exchange of information between chambers. The publication of its *Report of Proceedings and Resolutions Adopted at the Annual Meeting*, begun in 1862, was an important early source for members, which continued into the 1930s.

But some in ACC quickly tried to assert a strong central leadership. The ACC established a central journal in 1868, the *Chambers of Commerce Journal*. This proclaimed that 'whilst the more active members of the chambers are fully conscious of the influence they exercise ... they are nevertheless conscious of a deficiency. There is a vigorous action at the heart, but in some cases the pulsations are less vigorous at the extremities. ... This weakness ... is *the localisation of the influence* of individual chambers.'[73] In the ensuing discussion the ACC view of the tensions to be overcome is made clear: 'the really important questions which chiefly engage the attention of chambers are national and local. It is necessary to discuss their local bearings, but their ultimate solution must be based upon a general consensus of opinion involving compromise between the conflicting trades and districts'. In other words, the ACC general view should override local dissenters. This was not the way to make friends among the local chambers, nor did it recognize the power differences between them, nor the reality of local contingency.

---

[70] Comment from Baines contained in letter Hastings to Brougham, 31 December 1856, HD/13076.

[71] ACC minutes 1860–1; see also Ilersic and Liddle (1960), p. 11.

[72] Charles Booth, president of Swansea chamber, at AGM, quoted in *The Cambrian*, 28 January 1876.

[73] London *CCJ*, 1(1), 29 February (1868) (emphasis added); 400 copies of this were printed at a cost of £45 (ACC Accounts, 1869).

The *Journal* collapsed after one issue. A later effort in 1876, the *Chambers of Commerce Chronicle*, voiced similar centralized control ambitions. It failed after one year (12 issues), and a combination with another journal, the *British Mail and Journal of the Chambers of Commerce of the UK*, ran for only six years 1880–6.[74] These ambitious statements must have derived either from Sampson Lloyd as president, or James Hole as agent. Although they were unrealistic self-propaganda with no chance of implementation, they confirmed the fears of Worcester and other chambers about central control.

Liverpool and the ACC Memorandum of 1861

The tensions are illustrated very clearly by Liverpool's early experiences, leading it to withdraw from the ACC in 1861. Liverpool had joined in 1860 and had been involved in efforts by the ACC to lobby over the Bankruptcy Act of 1861. In the legislation, the ACC's voice was completely ignored by government. Liverpool's delegate to the ACC, John Danson, then continued to support the association's efforts to reform the Act.[75] But the chamber clearly felt Danson was exceeding his mandate; and that the ACC approach to bankruptcy led by Sampson Lloyd, a Conservative MP, and a banker who held different positions on bankruptcy than many members, had led to the government rejection. The chamber also disliked an ACC report by Danson, which called for French-style public law chambers.[76] This echoed Levi's ideas, and Levi had been pointedly excluded from being appointed secretary of the Liverpool chamber despite his efforts to help the chamber become established. The ACC agent, Baines, may also have been significant; as the agent also for the Liverpool American chamber he would have been a source of information on Lloyd's performance. It was at this point also that Lloyd was moving to become the next president of ACC, replacing the more innocuous Norwood. For these varied reasons some leading Liverpool members were not happy to have their voice submerged into the ACC. The minutes of the chamber for 1860–1 are not full, but by 4 November 1861 the appointment of the delegate to represent the chamber at ACC was a heated topic, with 'the appointment deferred until . . . [the vice-president] will move that this chamber either withdraw from that association or take steps to *have its views more efficiently represented* at its meetings'.[77] At the next meeting on 22 November the council voted to withdraw from ACC. The ACC tried to temporize but clearly did not appreciate how far Danson had gone beyond his local support.

Of course personality was probably also involved,[78] but the incident echoed the concerns of other chambers such as Worcester, and struck at the heart of the ACC

---

[74] Information on journal survival derived from BL Newspaper catalogues and staff, Colindale.

[75] Ilersic and Liddle (1960), pp. 67–70 summarize the ACC actions on bankruptcy in the 1860s.

[76] See Chapter 7.

[77] Liverpool chamber, Council minutes, 4 November 1861; emphasis added.

[78] The relation of Danson with Liverpool in 1860–1 is unknown, but another dispute over 'commercial blockade and belligerent rights' proved very divisive, with resolutions and counter-resolutions put to the membership (Liverpool chamber, Council minutes, December 1862), and a

relations with the member chambers: could the delegates act independently of the local bodies that nominated them and develop 'an ACC view and voice', or was everything that ACC said subject to approval by its members. The ACC called a special general meeting to consider the matter, with the new vice-president from Liverpool (John Campbell) attending. It had referred to the ACC Standing Committee a reconsideration of the constitution. This resulted in a new preamble, or Memorandum, to the ACC rules. Campbell's view was that the new proposals 'would not meet the views of the chamber'; later he attended the 1863 annual meeting of the ACC ('as an individual and not in an official capacity') and confirmed the Liverpool view of the danger the association posed to the chamber: 'the association represents only 17 chambers of all those bodies in the Kingdom; . . . and that therefore the influence of the association was calculated to carry the weight of all of the chambers of commerce to the prejudice of the large chambers that had not joined it'.[79] Indeed the role of the Standing Committee was itself one of the bones of contention on how policies were determined.

The Standing Committee had overseen Sampson Lloyd's efforts to lead on the bankruptcy Bill. The Liverpool chamber stated that 'by the constitution of the ACC, no power is given to that [Standing] Committee thus to compromise the chambers comprising that Association'. When interrogated further by ACC, now with Lloyd as president, Liverpool stated that the committee 'do not seem to have any power to pass such a resolution as that inserted in the *Times* in June last [1861] on the Bankruptcy Bill'.[80] Liverpool had withdrawn because

> they had come to the conclusion that it was a mistake to ascertain and represent the opinions of the commercial classes of the country by a vote of delegates from different chambers. It seems hardly possible by any distribution of votes to give each chamber the power, on each question debated, to which its population, the extent and nature of its trade and manufactures, or its special knowledge of the particular subject entitled it . . . . and any chamber which might dissent from a resolution come to by a majority . . . would be held forth to the government . . . [which] it was actively protesting against.

The Standing Committee fell back on noting how it had followed agreed procedures and that John Danson and another Liverpool delegate (Mr Thrickman Finlay) had been in attendance when the Bankruptcy Bill was discussed. 'They attached almost equal importance to combined action where that is practical not as superseding but as very materially augmenting the force of separate action on the part of individual chambers.'[81]

The new ACC Memorandum had three clauses: (i) to focus ACC joint action where 'each chamber would separately have more difficulty in accomplishing'; (ii) to 'discuss and consider commercial questions . . . and to disseminate information';

'protest' entered in the minutes (8 January 1863). There were clearly different factions with Danson losing support.

[79] Liverpool chamber, Council minutes, 13 October 1862; 5 March 1863.
[80] Reported in ACC Standing Committee minutes, 13 February 1862; 10 April letter from Liverpool, quoted in the Committee minutes 8 May 1862.
[81] ACC Standing Committee minutes, letter to Liverpool chamber, 8 May 1862.

and (iii) 'to establish a London agency'.[82] It was also agreed that no resolutions could be voted on unless they had been previously circulated. But a blocking amendment by George Dixon and Arthur Ryland (Birmingham chamber) was *not* carried by 5 to 1 (6 abstentions): that the objects of the association should be to promote discussion and dissemination, but that 'no application be made to the government or parliament in the name of the association if any of the constituent chambers shall express disapproval'. However, in Campbell's opinion, neither the Memorandum nor even the blocking amendment satisfied Liverpool.[83]

Ilersic and Liddle's briefer interpretation of this episode was that there was a misunderstanding and the ACC 'not only saved itself from becoming a mere debating society without power of effective action but probably from an untimely end'.[84] But a more correct view is that it failed to address how the interests of the large and most significant chambers were to be safeguarded within an organization that was already becoming dominated by smaller chambers in small places. The regional differentiation of the system that had been present from the outset was essentially ignored. Liverpool and the three other major chambers remained out of the ACC for forty years, and the ACC moved on to include more and more of the smallest chambers. Indeed a further change to the rules in 1863 replaced 'one vote to chambers of 30–100 members' with a new definition giving 'one vote to chambers not exceeding 100 members'. This allowed chambers with less than 30 members to join the ACC, which was stimulated by Kendal's desire to join.[85]

Developments 1861–1880

As a result of these tensions, the early ACC might be seen most accurately as an additional conduit for local views, rather than establishing a central resource that was leading or independently promoting an agenda. The lack of some major provincial chambers as members, and the absence of any London chamber, undoubtedly contributed to a governmental view that the strength lay in the provinces. For this the role of MPs remained strong. The association took great care to develop strong links with sympathetic MPs to supplement those of the local chambers. All the eight early ACC presidents 1860–96 were MPs, the next presidents 1896–1912 were members of the Lords. Algernon Firth in 1912 was the first president who was not in Westminster.[86] In addition a number of the local chamber representatives at the ACC meetings were actually their local MPs; e.g. W. Forster (Bradford). In all, the ACC could usually count on at least eight MPs to

---

[82] Proposal drafted by Ripley (Bradford chamber) and Norwood (Hull chamber): Liverpool chamber, Council minutes, 13 October 1862.

[83] ACC Standing Committee minutes, 30 September 1862; Liverpool chamber, Council minutes, 13 October 1862.

[84] Ilersic and Liddle (1960), pp. 16–20.

[85] Subject to a resolution of a general meeting, or by unanimous resolution of the Standing Committee. New rule 2; ACC Standing Committee minutes, 30 September 1862; Ilersic and Liddle (1960), pp. 18–19.

[86] Listed in Ilersic and Liddle (1960), pp. 243–4.

exert parliamentary pressure, and they were able to garner other support. In many ways, then, the early ACC can be seen chiefly as a means to brief these MPs, and attempt to link their local views into a coherent agenda that could be pushed into government or parliamentary priorities. It was this that provided the influence, and it also defined the character of the early ACC, and demarked its limitations.

To expand these links the ACC chose in 1865 to set up a formal subcommittee of MPs to advise and participate in the association. This was constituted in 1866 as a 'sub-committee of MPs representing boroughs and counties whose chambers are branches of the association . . . [in order to help] bring forward legislation on commercial questions'.[87] To clarify their status a special subcommittee meeting stated they were honorary members of the ACC, which could 'express their opinions freely but not vote'.[88]

This initiative resulted in about 46 MPs becoming honorary members over 1866–9. Whilst the ACC executive suggested most of the initial names, the chambers were also asked to nominate. Of the ACC Executive's nominations 15 out of 17 were Liberals (88%), the other two being a Liberal Conservative and a Reformer. For the chambers the nominations were more diverse, but still 15 out of 29 were Liberals (54%), two were Liberal Conservatives, and three Liberal Unionists. But the local chambers also put up five Conservatives, three Radicals, and one Reformer. Given the instability and evolving form of many party loyalties at this time not too much should be read into this. Nevertheless it is clear that the main supporters of the chambers were Liberals in various forms (78%). Of these MPs, three represented Irish constituencies (all Liberals), one Conservative was a prominent protectionist; and one Liberal, one Liberal Unionist, and one Conservative had prominently campaigned against the Corn Law repeal. So there was also marked diversity. Of 28 with active and identifiable business interests, most were merchants (54%) or manufacturers (29%), but there were also a few lawyers, farmers, and a building contractor.

The early presidents were all Liberals, except Sampson Lloyd, the prominent MP and banker from Birmingham, who was a typical mid-century frugal Conservative. Since he served for 18 years from 1862 until 1880, this must have created tensions, although these are not revealed explicitly in the minutes. But it probably serves to account for some lack of focus over this period. All commentators have acknowledged that the ACC was trying to cover too many issues with too little resource.[89] This also resulted from the diversity of local views, but reading the minutes of the early ACC one is struck by the overwhelmingly random way in which many issues arise: from an MP, from other council members, from government agendas and activities of the time. The swings of government focus are particularly noticeable (as evident in Tables 10.1–10.4). Comparison of the independent chamber activities and how ACC responded is also suggestive of their differing capacities. Many of the chambers were pursuing very focused strategies for the development of their

---

[87] ACC Annual Meetings 1865, 1866; reported in Standing Committee minutes.
[88] Special subcommittee meeting 10 May 1866; reported in ACC Standing Committee minutes.
[89] See summaries in Ilersic and Liddle (1960); Taylor (2007).

localities. But for the ACC, London chamber's criticism in 1884 seems correct:[90] 'when we examine the programme of questions which our chambers meet annually to discuss, . . . we find . . . several resolutions which have appeared there bi-annually for the last eleven or twelve years, without a solution seeming any nearer.' Very little was being achieved, and Lloyd's frugal approach to Birmingham corporation seems to have been applied to ACC, resulting in a very meagre organization.

Establishing a stronger centre after 1880

Important changes in ACC occurred in the 1880s as a result of pressures from the London chamber after its establishment in 1882: particularly the more regular election of presidents that held office for only 2–4 years (reduced to annually after 1956), and the appointment of the first full-time 'secretary', Edward Fithian, in 1888 at a salary of £340, increased to £390 in 1890.[91]

The lack of development at ACC in the early period is evidenced by how London behaved when it joined in 1882. It was immediately critical and started to call for reforms. It noted that chambers 'have of late years developed a tendency to deal exclusively with the predominating local trade'. London chamber went on to propose that individual chambers should diversify their membership to smaller traders and professions, should establish specialized sections, increase their subscriptions and memberships, and called for official status for chambers and a minister of commerce. 'Had our requirements been properly centralised in responsible hands, would England in 1880 have been almost alone amongst nations without a Minister of Commerce?' In other words, the ACC and its members had not been effective. 'We are being left behind in chamber of commerce work, not only by the Continent, but by our own colonies.'[92] London also went on to report a survey that it had conducted of chamber incomes that it suggested demonstrated that 'their resources were insufficient to permit them to organise their work, their staff, their libraries, or offices on a fitting scale. . . . The united expenditure of the largest towns . . . hardly reaches £5000 per annum, less than was paid the other day for Marie Antoinette's writing-table.' Hence, for London the lack of leadership was a major problem: systematic change was needed across the system. By 1883 London was noting that 'the Association, we are glad to note, appears to be entering upon a period of self improvement'.[93] By 1884 it was welcoming 'as a good omen, the breeze of reform which appears to be passing over our chambers of commerce. . . . This movement was necessary and has come none too soon'.[94] These were all very negative comments on the leadership offered by Sampson Lloyd over 1862–80, who as a frugal Conservative was out of touch with the rise of the Liberals nationally, and their influence in the ACC.

---

[90] London *CCJ*, 5 February (1884), p. 27.
[91] ACC secretary, 1888–1912.
[92] London *CCJ*, 1(5), 1 July (1882), pp. 91–2.
[93] London *CCJ*, 5 February (1883), p. 32.
[94] London *CCJ*, February (1884), p. 27.

The 1880s also saw the Board of Trade (BoT) become more engaged with chambers. It had been instructed to call on chambers and other business associations for consultation on policy administration when the Liberal Joseph Chamberlain was president of BoT in 1880–5. It became well aware that the chambers 'differed in importance and efficiency'.[95] A stronger structural capacity was needed. Under the pressure from London and the BoT the 1880s mark the beginning of attempts to develop towards a national chamber system meeting particular standards. A special conference was called in 1883 as a result of London's efforts 'to discuss all the items of interior working reform. . . . Nothing will so much conduce to its stability, and to the increase of its influence as the reform of its component parts.'[96]

The first targets for 'filling the map'

Key outcomes from the 1883 conference were the first map of the chambers in Britain, with targets to 'fill the map' in untouched areas; and recognition that there was a need to attain a 'sufficient income'. London had stated this strategic weakness in 1882, and its *Chamber of Commerce Journal* (CCJ) began a campaign to change perceptions. The argument presented was that British chambers were principally limited by 'the smallness of their revenue', which in turn was a result of their small number of subscribers and the low subscriptions they paid. It compared this adversely with Europe and the rest of the world, quoting New York in particular as having a strong 'social and industrial status . . . [so] that it found possible to charge entrance of \$25 and an annual fee of \$20'.[97] New York had an income of about \$20,000 at the time and nearly 1000 members.[98]

As targets for filling the map London proposed that all towns over 50,000 population should have chambers. It identified 18 areas where this should be readily possible 'with no chamber but in which one should be organised'. It printed and distributed the first known map of chambers of commerce (enclosed with its first annual report in 1882), showing ACC members and where a chamber should be established. The map was issued 'with the special object of facilitating discussion upon the resolution which the London chamber placed on the programme' at the 1883 conference, 'with a view to bringing about the organisation of new chambers of commerce in the places indicated'. This is the first direct recognition of the problem of 'gaps on the map' that undermined the influence and authority of the ACC, and hence of the chambers as a whole. Chambers were found 'thickly sprinkled in Lancashire and Yorkshire—in the iron districts in particular—but wanting in other parts of the country'.[99]

---

[95] A. E. Bateman, standing in for BoT president at Manchester chamber meeting in 1897; in Helm (1897), p. 110.
[96] London *CCJ*, February (1883), p. 32.
[97] London *CCJ*, May (1882), pp. 1–2.
[98] Bishop (1918).
[99] London *CCJ*, December (1883); the map is archived in ABCC Executive papers, MS 14477/1.

These proposals were not followed up by ACC, which felt it did not have the resources or power to undertake development work in individual locations, but ACC strongly approved the principle (although the vote was nem. con. suggesting doubts remained) and handed over to local chambers the facilitation of development in other areas.[100] This had some influence on the next phase of chamber foundations: of the 18 towns identified on London's map, most had formed one by 1900. But there was a considerable problem of 'chicken and egg': how to get things started in centres that did not have a chamber. As Birstal (Yorks.) chamber observed, 'chambers of commerce was a business which belonged to anybody, and therefore, to nobody. Everybody believed it would be a good idea to establish a chamber at Birstal, but nobody seemed to put the idea into shape.' Similarly Bristol 'had attempted for some time to bring into its area some of the smaller surrounding towns; but the difficulty was knowing who to approach in a motion of this kind. . . . [and] none of them sent satisfactory replies.' However, as Worcester correctly and defensively observed, this proposal was 'not to create new chambers, . . . but to annex those towns. . . . [It was not likely] they would get any large number of towns, with a considerable population, to allow themselves to be annexed to local centres.'[101]

The views on 'sufficient income' were never unanimously shared. In 1886, when the London chamber pressed for all chambers to increase their resources, many smaller chambers argued for the importance of the voluntary input that many chambers received as being as important as money resources. This was of course correct. Voluntary inputs were critical, and bound in the council and members; volunteers also reduced the chamber's expenses by paying their own costs rather than charging the chamber for their travel, etc.; 'even canvassing for subscriptions was done for the love of the work'.[102] But lack of money was nevertheless a severe impediment to effectiveness. London made the first attempt to gather the information on local chamber resources, completing a table of all chamber information in 1884, which listed 71 chambers, not all of which were members of ACC. This was the first attempt to measure total chamber resources, and also market penetration, which began to be seen as linked to resources.[103]

Getting everyone on board

Drawing in the remaining major chambers that were outside the ACC became a major priority: 'the four large chambers . . . which have so far held aloof' were targeted. 'We trust that the example which the London chamber has given, in joining its authority to that of the Association, may not be without influence upon its sister organisations . . . [which are standing] aloof from the national trade

---

[100] London *CCJ*, August (1886), pp. 53–5.
[101] E. W. Wainwright, Birstal chamber; J. C. Godwin, Bristol chamber; F. Corbett, Worcester chamber: London *CCJ*, August (1886), p. 54.
[102] J. F. Oates, Heckmondwike chamber, London *CCJ*, 5 August (1886), p. 54.
[103] London *CCJ*, July (1882), p. 91; March (1886), p. 65; February (1884), p. 27.

conclave'.[104] London even proposed setting up chambers in the main towns near to Manchester, which 'might lead it to reconsider its decision as to joining the Association'.[105] The joining by the major chambers was a critical step, achieved with Edinburgh joining in 1893, Manchester in 1898, Liverpool rejoining in 1899, and Glasgow joining in 1910. Only then could the ACC really claim to be an organization representing the major cities in the country.

Interestingly, these chambers record virtually no comment or discussion on why they were persuaded to join; just a formal minute to do so. The only indicative comment is in Manchester, where Gustav Behrens (one of the council) pressed the case in 1898, arguing that the other various major textile centres were represented, and that there was 'substantial advantage which had attended the participation' of the chamber in the ACC congress held in 1896, which it had never previously attended. Behrens claimed that 'the influence of the chamber in the counsels of the association would be powerful and beneficial', also noting that he expected Liverpool and Glasgow to join. He also believed that 'certain matters which had arisen lately [in] the Manchester chamber would have secured a much-needed access of influences with the government if they had been united with the other chambers'.[106]

By the late 1890s, perhaps as a result of London's influence, the ACC was now regarded as more effective and provided a significant benefit through its congress. It is from 1898 that we can date the emergence of the ACC as a significant and accepted national voice for the chamber movement. However, behind this was also the change in attitude of government. In 1897 Salisbury's Unionist government had begun reform of the BoT by establishing a Committee on Commercial Intelligence to replace its Trade and Treaties Committee. Behind the scenes discussions were taking place between BoT and ACC that led to the important development of a government Advisory Committee (ACCI), to which chamber members were to be nominated through ACC. ACC was for the first time holding power as a recognized 'insider' to the policy process, as discussed in Chapter 10.[107] It was becoming difficult for the major chambers to stand outside ACC any longer.

For the ACC itself a major result was to become more ambitious, develop greater internal leadership, though its actual lobbying activities remained relatively similar, a 'continuation of the old'.[108] The internal changes were, however, considerable. After 1900, the ACC presidency was held by a series of high-profile and aggressive individuals, of which Lord Avebury and W. H. Holland (later Lord Rotherham) over 1900–7 were notably influential in parliament. A role as 'insiders' began to raise expectations, and from 1905 the issue of the 'status' of chambers and their 'standards' emerged. Negotiations began with government to have a subgroup of

---

[104] London *CCJ*, February (1883), p. 32.

[105] K. B. Murray, London secretary, London *CCJ*, August (1886), p. 54.

[106] Gustav Behrens, Manchester chamber, *Monthly Record*, October (1898), p. 250; December (1898), p. 301.

[107] Though Manchester had a place in ACCI only in 1906; and Glasgow not until 1910: see Table 10.5.

[108] Ilersic and Liddle (1960), p. 149.

chambers 'recognized' or 'accredited'. These critical developments, which are largely ignored by Ilersic and Liddle,[109] began the long process of detailed partnership with government that marks the rest of the chamber history, and profoundly changed the role of the national association, as discussed further below and in Chapter 13. Indeed, a significant change is recognized in the rhetoric by which ACC presented itself, with the Bristol chamber handbook of 1909 calling for the national association to be recognized, like the US 'House of Representatives' as a 'Parliament of Commerce', 'that might not unreasonably be established in some nobler building nearer to Whitehall, as a free tenant of the crown'.[110] The concept of parliament of commerce had first been coined in 1881, when it was suggested that 'commercial parliament . . . is a convenient and appropriate title by which the ACC is coming to be known'.[111] This was exaggerated, but it showed the new self-confidence of the ACC.

Tensions in the early subscriptions to the association

The early ACC relied on a model of member subscriptions related to the size of chamber, which then provided different numbers of votes. The first subscription schedule gave: one vote to chambers of 30–100 members (which became all chambers with less than 100 members in 1863), at five guineas; two votes to chambers of 100–250 members, at ten guineas; and three votes to chambers over 250 members, at 15 guineas.[112] This survived until 1881, when a new structure was adopted after controversies that began in 1878. The new structure still charged chambers of under 100 members five guineas for one vote; and ten guineas for those of 100–250 members for two votes; but a new range was adopted for chambers of 240–600 members at 15 guineas for three votes; and chambers of 600–1000 members at £21 for four votes; with every additional 500 members costing a further five guineas giving one further vote to a maximum of six votes. This structure sought to match resources and power in the ACC. But consultation on it in 1878 revealed the wide spread of opinions, as many new and small chambers sought to become members. Of 50 chambers consulted: nine could not afford to alter their subscription; two would pay five guineas only if they had two votes not one (Bradford and Hull); three rejected the principle of extra votes for additional subscriptions (Dundee, Falmouth, and Wolverhampton); 24 agreed to pay; and 16 did not reply.[113] The scale was increased in 1889, respectively to £8, £16, £24, and £32, with £8 per 500 additional members.[114]

[109] Except for brief comment on 'Form K': Ilersic and Liddle (1960), pp. 170–2.
[110] *Chamber of Commerce Yearbook*, Bristol chamber, 1908–9, p. 19 (Bristol RO: 38605/Pu/35).
[111] *Capital and Labour*, no. 364, vol. viii, 7 February 1881, p. 78 (copy at ABCC archive; MS 14477/1). The concept of commercial parliament bounced around for years, linked to the call for official status discussed in Chapter 7, and taken as the title of the Ilersic and Liddle official history. It found some support from Richard Haldane when minister in WW1 and in the 1920s: Johnson (1968); see also Chapter 10.
[112] These were the figures in 1861; in 1860 they paid at half these rates for the part year.
[113] ACC Executive minutes, 10 May and 14 June 1878; 9 December 1881.
[114] ACC Executive minutes, 12 April 1889.

The intricate balances within this structure show that although the major chambers held significant control, and paid most of the costs, they could not outvote the smaller chambers. Indeed, as the smaller chambers grew in number, and with a change that allowed the very small to have a special reduced subscription, the larger chambers were in an ever-smaller minority, even with their additional votes. Thus by 1912 London and Manchester were the only members with five votes (Manchester only increased its payment in 1912 to get five votes); eight had three votes;[115] 17 had two votes; and 93 had one vote. Hence, the chambers with less than 100 members could outvote everyone else. Even including the chambers with over 250 members the large chambers had only 33 votes. This had profound consequences for how the association developed.

First, the association found it very difficult to move towards imposing any standards on its members that the smallest chambers were unable to meet. This meant that there were effectively no minimum standards. Second, the brand was confused and eroded. Third, although the ACC was in a position to compete with the small chambers of trade as they emerged at this time, if it was to succeed in managing this competition it had to be ready to take in all small chambers, with the consequential erosion of the large chamber vision and reduction in capacity to be credible with government. Fourth, even with this structure, the ACC had perennial problems of actually getting member chambers to pay. Fifth, the structure was very unequal and did not match payment to inputs and weight; by 1949 Knowles could still quote that 64% of ABCC income was paid by only 10% (12) chambers, 'a most unhealthy position'.[116]

Thus when ACC raised its subscriptions in 1912 to £8 for the smallest chambers, and then £10 10s., £21, £31 10s., £42, and £52 10s. on the same basis as previously, this was agreed by the majority of ACC members, but anarchy broke out over payment. The demand from ACC was sent out, but 'many chambers, though they had expressed assent to increase, remitted their subscriptions on the old scale'.[117] When requested again, some then paid the increase, but others did not; about 65 (only 54%) had paid after nine months. Many chambers struggled or were unwilling to pay; others like Kidderminster paid but protested.[118] A committee was appointed to review the situation, to find a means that 'while increasing total income, would be equitable to large and small chambers alike'.[119]

This resulted in new rates emerging following a Leeds proposal;[120] but Birmingham chamber was very resistant, expressing 'its surprise and regret that so important

[115] Bradford, Cardiff, Dublin, Glasgow, Hull, Leeds, Liverpool, and Sheffield: Leeds gained 3 votes in 1911.
[116] Knowles (1949), p. 10.
[117] ACC Executive minutes, 14 May 1912.
[118] Kidderminster chamber minutes, 29 January 1912.
[119] ACC Executive minutes, 18 October 1912.
[120] ACC Executive minutes, 18 October, 12 November, and 10 December 1912; 11 February 1913.

a matter...should have been adopted simply by a show of hands and no numbers declared...the new scheme...reduces the subscriptions to be paid by as many as 45 of the present subscribing chambers'. Birmingham's council 'declines to be bound by a resolution so passed'.[121] A committee was formed to meet Birmingham, who were eventually mollified and acquiesced in the new rates, but there was a deeply divisive discussion within Birmingham. One of Birmingham's delegates on the ACC (J. S. Taylor) was so frustrated that he urged the chamber to resign. The chamber's GPC agreed a resolution that 'the Articles of the ACC are inimical to the true interests of the Association and of this chamber'. This resolution was withdrawn from the chamber's council, but an alternative was carried: 'that this chamber feels that the Executive Council of the ACC does not carry out with sufficient force the resolutions of the meetings of ACC, but with the hope of a change they desire to continue for their membership for one year'. With this decision, and acceptance of the new subscription levels, Taylor resigned as Birmingham's ACC delegate and was replaced by the president (H. W. Sambidge), though Taylor was requested to continue on the ACC Railways Committee.[122] This episode shows the defeat of the large chamber voice on ACC in favour of retaining the smallest chambers.[123]

When a further rise occurred in 1919, doubling the subscriptions across the board, with a new minimum of 20 guineas (£21), this was agreed by 230 votes to 57, but led to a vigorous debate and more squabbling. Dublin argued that its 801 members were paying proportionately more than London's 8371 members because the largest chamber fees were limited to a maximum.[124] Grimsby argued for a 'tax according to ability to pay scaled by membership size'. But 'a delegate' noted that Grimsby was 'a place that was simply rolling in wealth' and its amendment was defeated 235 to 32. Indeed some small chambers such as Wolverhampton and South of Scotland argued that the proposed increase was too small. Warrington was responsible for the first acknowledgement of the early influence of the FBI, which it stated 'was already doing more on foreign trade, so that the chambers should increase their efforts'.[125] These issues remained endemic tensions within the system.

---

[121] Letter from Birmingham chamber, 20 March 1913, in ACC Executive minutes, 8 April 1913.

[122] Birmingham chamber GPC minutes, 8 and 10 December 1913, 14 January 1914.

[123] Subscription change passed at a special meeting of chambers, 10 June 1913; ACC Executive minutes.

[124] The ABCC tried to persuade London to pay more, but only managed to get an extra £250 for a brief period 'as a war bonus' during WW2: London chamber, Council minutes, 9 May 1944; MS 16459/23.

[125] Warrington then had 75 members, but 8 members also joined FBI at £100 per year; other comments from ABCC Annual Meeting Report, 15–16 April 1919. Grimsby was supported by Kidderminster because of the 'unfairness as applying to small chambers'; Kidderminster minutes, 1 April 1919.

8.5 THE PERIOD OF 'RECONSTRUCTION' AND
DEVELOPMENT OF 'STANDARDS' 1904–36

New structural issues began to emerge from involvement with government: if the chambers were to become valued partners, then they had to have a national coverage and quality to respond in every area. The ACC began to respond through a series of debates in 1904. These were initially a spin-off from the government's ACCI and a search for government 'status' by chambers, as discussed in Chapters 7 and 10. One of the key ripostes from government was that if status was to be granted, the chamber system had to offer some assurances of its standards.

The debate about 'status' at the 1904 chamber meetings led to a committee, which reported in 1905. It suggested radical steps: first, it specified the *functions* 'they should as far as possible comprise'; second, it recognized *inadequate resources* as 'the great want of many of the chambers' that limited their ability to engage with officials to deal with growing demands; third, that chambers in a given area should *collaborate* more and 'act together'; fourth, that small chambers should *group together* 'in order to extend the representative character . . . and obtain greater influence and financial support'; and fifth, that proper *governance* required them to meet at least once per month, and all should establish trade sections.[126]

The specified functions envisaged that chambers would: provide information to the BoT; respond to requests for their views on 'means of increasing the prosperity of commerce and industry'; found and support technical schools, exchanges, testing houses; publish their proceedings and a survey of the local economy at least annually; collect and disseminate local commercial information; distribute information from consuls and the BoT, and respond to enquirers; establish arbitration and conciliation committees; and organize a commercial reference library. These recommendations provided the first definition of chamber services, and underpinned the debate on chamber structures for the next 100 years.

The report was generally accepted, leading to moves to establish sections, improved reporting and governance, development of libraries, information provision, technical education, and the spread of arbitration services.[127] But increased resources and collaboration between small chambers remained distant goals. Perhaps most important for immediate developments, however, was the emphasis on providing for a two-way flow of information with the BoT. This was a response to the role of ACC within the BoT's ACCI after 1898, which was given added shape by the pressures of WW1. Thus internal chamber standards and external government demands became intertwined.

The main outcome of the ACC's 1905 report was to enhance its status with BoT. From 1906 all external members of the BoT's ACCI members were chamber nominees. The ACC had moved to the 'preferred' insider and 'natural' partner of government on foreign trade. This position was maintained until 1918 when a

---

[126] ACC Executive minutes, 6 June 1905: report of committee on *Status of Chambers of Commerce*.
[127] See Chapters 6, 11, and 12.

successor committee to ACCI was formed: an Advisory Council to BoT that survived until 1938, as discussed in Chapters 10 and 13. Its significance here is the influence it had on the association's attitude to the member chambers.

Working with the BoT as an 'insider' put pressure on the chamber movement to address the question of which chambers were capable of acting as partners of government and which were not. It led to a new concept of 'approved chambers' that were to be used as conduits for BoT exchanges. This responded to recognition by the BoT permanent secretary, Hubert Llewellyn Smith that 'every step must be taken ... to improve the weaker chambers. ... He could not shut his eyes to the fact that ... there were still a few chambers ... whose organisation did not go beyond a brass plate and an annual banquet. He did not undervalue a brass plate, and he certainly did not undervalue an annual banquet. They were symbols of organisation ... [but] the legitimate influence exercised by the Association in the councils of the nation,' meant bringing up standards of the weakest.[128] The BoT was for the first time expressing a desire for those chambers to be 'reconstructed'. Becoming an 'insider' brought obligations and external pressures.

This pattern was repeated in the USA, with similar pressures from government. The US Department of Commerce undertook analyses of foreign chamber systems in 1913–15 through the work of Archibald Wolfe.[129] Similar responses to the British BoT were offered, demonstrating related responses of encouraging voluntary systems to improve their efforts in the face of changing patterns of international trade and tariffs. In 1912 a federation was formed, termed the Chamber of Commerce of the USA, 'for the purposes of encouraging trade and international discourse ... and of promoting cooperation between chambers of commerce, Department of Trade and other ... organisations of the United States, *increasing their efficiency* and extending their usefulness'.[130] This set about defining standards for chambers in 1914: proposing standardized by-laws; moving all chambers to annual subscriptions with expulsion from membership if unpaid after three months; publicly advertised office addresses; audited accounts; regular meetings (with a limit on speeches, allowing broader participation), and incorporation.[131]

The first 'approved chambers' 1917–1936

Under this stimulus, a major ACC report on 'status of chambers' in 1917 was circulated and debated very fully by 130 chamber representatives.[132] This can be

---

[128] Speech at Annual Dinner, ACC *Proceedings* (1914). See also ACC leaflet: *The Value and Importance of the Work of Chambers of Commerce*, p. 4.

[129] Wolfe (1915a, 1915b).

[130] *Articles of Chamber of Commerce of the USA*: Wolfe (1919), pp. 508–9, emphasis added. Previous initiatives to establish a National Council of Commerce in 1878 and 1907 lacked credibility and support from businesses and the local chambers: Sturges (1915), p. 55; Werking (1978).

[131] Sturges (1915), p. 85.

[132] 'The status of chambers of commerce': ACC *Monthly Proceedings*, 4 October (1917), pp. 7–48.

seen as a turning point in collective awareness of internal structural tensions between association members, and the launch of a new relationship with the BoT. The objective of the report was to identify those chambers that could meet the standards and be used as the key BoT contact points. These chambers would be *incorporated* by the BoT. Chambers 'unable to reach such a standard shall remain members of the association . . . [but with the] earnest hope that such chambers, by amalgamation or by increased local support, will be able to come into line at an early date'.[133] This approach foreshadows almost all subsequent efforts at obtaining government support up to the present.

The original proposal for BoT approval was prepared by a special committee of ACC, which suggested that four conditions should be met. A chamber must (i) be incorporated; (ii) have its own separate office (this was to remove the phenomenon of chambers being managed as part of another business, such as a solicitor or accountant); (iii) have 'a whole-time secretary, or an efficient second man'; and (iv) have sufficient income. Only chambers meeting these conditions could be affiliated to the ACC. British foreign chambers or British chambers abroad were to be excluded and dealt with by a different process, in order to preserve the confidentiality of papers from the eyes of members of the foreign chambers in Britain, and the British chambers abroad.[134] This was implemented in 1919 (hence the name change to ABCC). The debate on these conditions was vigorous, and from the first displayed very explicitly the wide gulf between the large and small chambers. As commented by Algernon Firth, ACC president at the time, 'there was a striking lack of unanimity among the chambers', with greatest objection to the fourth condition, of sufficient income.[135]

Firth went on to ask: 'do chambers do their work efficiently; are they representative of the interests of their districts; have they sufficient accommodation and staff; does their constitution assure proper representation; can they answer queries and disseminate information when government seeks this?' Whilst the performance of local chambers with part-time staff might be acceptable to their members, they often failed to provide proper support to the ACC: in some small chambers 'questions on which the Association has sought the views of chambers are never brought before the members of the chamber at all. They are decided by the part-time secretary. . . . How can this Association represent to the government that that chamber desires a certain course of action when . . . it has never considered the question at all?' Firth also observed that only 60 chambers had responded positively to the ACC request to participate in disseminating the government 'Form K' information; 40 had refused to do so or were lukewarm. 'Someone must pay for the cost of distribution, and, as the government have collected it free for us, it is our *duty* to distribute it. . . . Is it any wonder that the government asks that all chambers

---

[133] ACC Executive minutes, 3 October 1917.
[134] This was formerly voted as a change in articles of association at the Annual Meeting; see comments by Manville, president; ABCC April (1919), *Monthly Proceedings*, pp. 23, and 97.
[135] ACC *Monthly Proceedings*, 4 October (1917), pp. 8 and 16.

shall be made efficient bodies? . . . Rest assured that the government will force us to. Or establish some other body to do so.'[136]

The intrusion of government was also seen as an influencing voice within the association. Firth stated it unequivocally:

> It may be true, so far as local affairs are concerned, that the way in which a particular chamber is run is entirely a matter for itself, but when that chamber asks for a voice in directing legislation for the country as a whole . . . It has no right to have a voice . . . unless it conforms to the conditions which meet the approval of government. Consequently, those chambers which did not meet the new standards being not fitted to do the work of chambers of commerce should be prevented from calling themselves chambers of commerce (hear, hear), and so discrediting the rest . . . . We are . . . called upon to put our house in order . . . to raise the standard of all the chambers to the standard of the few good ones.[137]

Thus for the first time, using government BoT backing, the ACC was trying to remove small chambers from its membership and focus on those meeting a minimum level. Meeting the BoT standards was seen as preparing the way for the chambers to become 'the official representatives of the government',[138] thus providing a new route to the status so long sought. The standards suggested were fairly unchallenging, but the reaction was very divisive.

The debate mainly focused on how the very small chambers could raise sufficient income. It was noted that only mergers and expansions of territory could overcome small subscriber bases, but the ACC stood back from recommending specific proposals, noting 'it was not for the ACC council to make any suggestion, because it would mean virtually saying that certain chambers should close themselves out. . . . That was a matter for the chambers themselves.' Heckmondwike, Ossett, Cleckheaton, Hartlepool, Barrow-in-Furness, Plymouth, Preston, Warrington, and Luton defended their position as small chambers, with Preston taking the most reasonable line that 'the scheme put forward was quite sufficiently elastic for everyone to come in'. Warrington noted that federations of small chambers were possible. Plymouth and Cleckheaton called for flexibility over hours of attendance by staff, and this was supported by some of the larger chambers such as Leeds and Sheffield, but was resisted by Manchester, which said there must be a full time secretary. Ossett (Yorks.) simply stated it could not raise the money from its small membership in a small place. It was told 'Ossett ought to get itself in line' and charge two guineas. Luton's secretary, Thomas Keens, argued that small chambers like his own achieved high market penetration (he claimed 97% of the *major* traders), and that having a broader membership would only dilute the chamber. Traders' associations could be used as complementary bodies (a point supported by London chamber). Moreover, raising subscriptions would only deter members; it was better to raise charges for special services. Keens also argued strongly for the value of voluntary inputs: a full-time secretary was not needed where

[136] Firth, ACC president, in ACC *Monthly Proceedings*, 4 October (1917), pp. 10–12, emphasis added; 'Form K' is discussed in detail in Chapter 13.
[137] Firth, ACC president, in ACC *Monthly Proceedings*, 4 October 1917, pp. 15–17.
[138] H. W. Sambidge, Birmingham chamber, in ACC *Monthly Proceedings*, 4 October (1917), p. 19.

'secretaries looked upon their services to the town the same way as members of county councils, local boards etc. and were prepared to work to the last ounce in serving the town independent of the salary they received'.[139] After the meeting the manoeuvring continued, with Birmingham receiving requests from Batley and Luton to support their objections to specifying a minimum income of £500.[140] The strength of local feeling about the ACC proposal is captured by the unanimous resolution of the Worcester chamber sent to ACC in 1918: the 'chamber protests against the action of the executive council ... to differentiate between various chambers affiliated to the association on the ground of the amount of their annual income and approved fully of the steps taken by Luton chamber for a reconsideration'.[141]

As became normal in the ACC debates, a compromise was struck and an amended proposal was sent to the BoT for approval in early 1918, in which the income requirement was dropped. The final BoT conditions for an approved chamber became: (i) their own office; (ii) a 'permanent secretary' with adequate clerical assistance; (iii) a council holding regular meetings; and (iv) the 'requisite machinery for dissemination of information'.[142] The condition that only chambers meeting the BoT conditions could be affiliated to the ACC was withdrawn by Firth.[143] This was a significant watering down of the original conditions on the level of secretarial support, with the 'requisite machinery' condition the strongest assurance that could be agreed. As a result, few chambers that were active enough to put together an application were likely to be excluded, and the ACC continued to wrestle with the tensions between the very small and large chambers; as stated by Firth there should be nothing 'thought or said ... derogatory to the position of the smaller chambers'. Greenock in 1923, for example, asserted that 'they do not at present see their way to go for a reconstructed chamber and would rather bear the ills they have than lose their antiquity'.[144] In effect the ACC followed the advice offered by Musgrave from the London chamber, that the ACC council be given authority to recognize a chamber of commerce when it saw it, large or small, to protect the 'real' chambers of commerce from the chambers of trade.[145]

The first tranche of chamber applications for approval in 1918 numbered 70.[146] By April 1919 this had grown to 84, which were being 'carefully considered'. The ACC council began moving towards submitting a list to the BoT of 'only a few of the chief chambers in this country';[147] though in fact almost all were accepted. But the threat proved an important catalyst to some; e.g. for Preston the

---

[139] Firth, ACC president, in ACC *Monthly Proceedings*, 4 October (1917), p. 18; Sir George Toulmin, Preston chamber, p. 21; G. H. Wilson, Ossett chamber, and Firth's response, p. 30; Thomas Keens, Luton chamber secretary, p. 24; London comment by C. E. Musgrave, p. 43.
[140] Birmingham chamber, Council minutes, 21 December 1917; left to 'lie on the table'.
[141] Worcester chamber minutes, 11 January 1918.
[142] Letter from BoT; in ACC Executive minutes, 1 May 1918.
[143] Firth, in ACC *Monthly Proceedings*, 4 October (1917), pp. 38–9.
[144] Correspondence from Greenock, in ABCC Home Affairs Committee, 12 December 1923.
[145] C. E. Musgrave, in ACC *Monthly Proceedings*, 4 October (1917), p. 43.
[146] Listed in ACC Executive minutes, 2 October 1918.
[147] Report of Executive Council, April 1919, pp. 12–13.

approval exercise was the motive behind the appointment of its first full-time official in 1917, and the acquisition of its own accommodation, after moving out of an office donated by the Preston Gas Company in 1919.[148] Moreover, after the Customs Convention of 1923, government regulation of certificates of origin passed to the BoT, which used its power to support ABCC policy: only approved chambers could issue certificates.[149] This became an increasingly important lever as the certificates became numerous up to WW2, and then increased again after the war.

Controlling standards

In the UK over the period 1922–36 ABCC approval was policed by its Home Affairs Committee and moved off the council's agenda. After 1923 the chambers in the Irish Republic formed their own association, which eventually introduced its own standards, discussed later below. In the UK, the ABCC Committee quickly set about trying to impose standard reporting requirements, including accounting standards, governance requirements, and standard articles of association for chambers, for which the pressure from Dunwoody as ABCC secretary was critical.[150] Not all of this was followed through at local level, but the leverage of approval moved most of the 'real' chambers towards more common approaches. It is from this time that the ABCC moved to a position where it was able to put some pressure on the local level. This was only possible because it now controlled access to an increasingly important service backed by BoT: document certification.

It was at this point therefore that the partnership with the state began in earnest. It was catalysed by state-led initiatives of WW1, but was largely an outcome of the ABCC itself seeking state backing for its certificates and standards activities. The state did not lead, the voluntary bodies sought state support. Indeed, Dunwoody claims that it was pressure from the ACC during WW1 that led to the reorganization of the BoT and the development of a separate Department of Overseas Trade;[151] and it was this department that became a major link for chamber members through the 'Form K' service contracted by government from 1917. The role of ABCC, therefore, came to rest more strongly on its backing by the state, but the state was drawing on inputs that it required from the chambers. This was also the time that the ABCC moved into its first own major office complex, at 14 Queen Anne's Gate (in August 1920), where the British National Committee of the International Chamber of Commerce (established in 1919) was also located. The new offices were seen as significant in being closer to government, with the co-location increasing the ABCC weight.

---

[148] Preston chamber history, Heywood (1966), p. 13.
[149] The FBI (later CBI) regional offices could also issue certificates but were never large players; see Chapter 12; and Taylor (2007), chapter 5.
[150] R. B. Dunwoody was the second 'secretary' of ABCC, covering 1912–46.
[151] Dunwoody (1935), p. 17.

The first ABCC targets for filling the map

A separate strand of development came from an Improvements Committee of ABCC established in 1923, which developed an objective of 'filling the map', taking up London's mapping exercise of 1882. There had been other suggestions for the target market. For example, in 1856 John Darlington, secretary of Bradford chamber, suggested that a company charter be granted to all chambers in towns of over 100,000 population.[152] An 1867 ACC paper concerning public law status by Jacob Behrens, vice-president of the Bradford chamber, argued that tribunals should be established 'in every town or borough of 15,000 inhabitants, ... co-extensive with the district of the county court'.[153] London had suggested 50,000 in 1882.

The Improvements Committee aimed the first national target at towns of 25,000 population and over in 1923. The Committee made the most systematic survey of the map of market potential to be undertaken until the 1990s. It showed that there were 256 towns of over 25,000 population in England and Wales, plus 17 in Scotland. In these there were 80 chambers of commerce, 139 chambers of trade, 91 drapers chambers of trade, 44 TPS, 14 branches of the FBI, and 12 chambers of shipping. The findings are summarized in Figure 8.1. This shows significant competition in the main industrial areas and London, as well as gaps.

The Committee identified 108 target towns with over 25,000 population which had no chamber in England and Wales. In Scotland there were eight, plus three unaffiliated chambers; Ireland was not analysed. Of the 116 target locations, 45 in England and Wales had either a chamber of trade, drapers chamber of trade, or TPS; in Scotland there were no other major organizations in the target towns. This left 71 'towns with over 25,000 population in which it may be assumed that no responsible trade organisation exists', as well as 45 towns where a question arose of whether a chamber of commerce should be organized.[154] As shown in Figure 8.1, about two-thirds were within conurbations where in some cases a large local chamber might provide coverage, especially around London, Manchester, and Merseyside. But many were scattered across the country. Of these scattered locations, perhaps one-half were within the potential orbit of an established chamber that could have extended its coverage from a major town to cover the county area. But in some cases there were widely dispersed centres, such as those in Northumberland, Durham, the outer South-East, and Wales. It is notable that these proposals saw the target market in terms of towns and not areas: there was no recognition of the potential of 'county' chambers formed by expanding from the main centres, although by this time they had begun to exist (e.g. in Derbyshire and Leicestershire).

---

[152] Quoted in Taylor (2007), p. 90; also Beresford (1951), Leeds chamber history.
[153] *Tribunals of Commerce*: a paper to Council of Bradford chamber, 29 October 1867; MS 14477/1.
[154] ABCC, Improvement Committee, *Memorandum on Extension of Chambers of Commerce and Membership*, 6 June 1923, p. 1; report from Glasgow chamber on towns in Scotland; MS 14479.

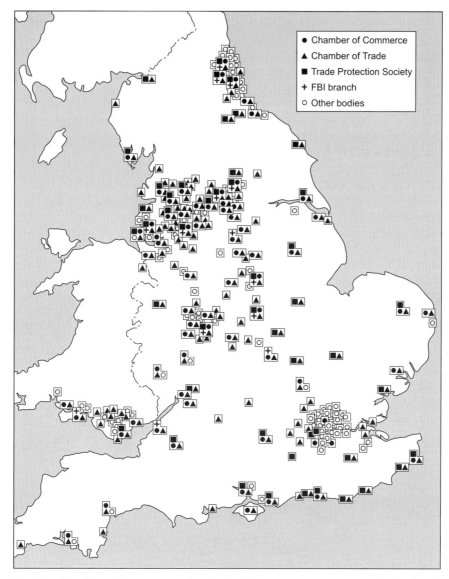

Fig. 8.1 Chambers of commerce and other local business organizations in England and Wales 1922, in towns of 25,000 population and over. (*Source*: ABCC, Improvement Committee: MS 14479.)

The Committee also proposed other means to extend the chambers by alteration of the articles of the association to allow organizations that were not called chambers of commerce to join ABCC. This was interlinked with a proposal that the minimum subscription to the association be abolished and replaced by a levy of 5s. per member. This would have been a great encouragement to small chambers:

for a chamber of 30 members this meant a reduction from £21 to £7 10s.; but was much greater than costs of affiliation to NCT (which moved from a charge of one guinea per association to 6d. per member in 1919, with a minimum of 1 guinea).[155] It might have encouraged integration with the regions of FBI, and thus attempted to control its potentially most dangerous competitor. If the committee's recommendations had been followed the ABCC would probably have swallowed many of the chambers of trade and the NCT would have merged with it. But they met considerable resistance, particularly from the larger chambers. London argued that the chamber brand would 'lose considerable prestige'; Luton wanted 'only genuine chambers'; and Northamptonshire forecast that a problem of supporting 'opposition bodies' would result; it suggested that the minimum population size should be 50,000.[156]

These developments mark a significant change to the internal debate. Although not all of its recommendations were followed, encouragement of chambers in smaller places resulted in expansion of the ABCC system in the 1920s and 1930s to its maximum extent down the town-size hierarchy (see also Figures 5.4, 5.5, and Table 14.5). But there remained a central ambiguity. On the one hand, the Home Affairs Committee often referred small chambers applying for membership to nearby existing members in order that they work together as joint members, or as a federation covering the larger area. Thus in 1924 an application from Fleet and Church Crookham (Hants.) was referred to Aldershot; and in 1932 it was agreed that 'where small chambers may be formed in the metropolitan area, the right plan would be for such chambers to seek affiliation with the London chamber'.[157] It also encouraged cooperation between chambers, and from this time some important developments occurred. Manchester established a 'regional chamber' in 1934, although Liverpool, Wigan, and Warrington were excluded because they did not have a major interest in cotton.[158] Chesterfield was reconstructed in 1924, and linked with Sheffield. In 1929 Sheffield also explored cooperation with Barnsley and Rotherham. Sheffield offered access to its services from these chambers, and collected subscriptions for Chesterfield until 1961.[159] Similarly, from 1935, Sheffield supplied copies of its journal to Barnsley members at 12s., and circulars at 10s. per year.[160] But these were difficult matters and often foundered on how income or subscriptions would be transferred between chambers. Kidderminster refused to amalgamate with Stratford-upon-Avon 'as the distance was too great and the means of communication difficult'.[161]

---

[155] NCT Executive minutes, 3 May 1919; MS 29340/2.

[156] Response to ABCC consultation on Improvement Committee recommendations, MS 14479.

[157] ABCC Home Affairs Committee, 6 April 1932.

[158] The regional chamber included Blackburn, Bolton, Burnley, Bury, Manchester, Oldham, Preston, and Stockport: Manchester chamber, *Monthly Record*, 27 (1934), pp. 156–9.

[159] Sheffield chamber, Council minutes and membership committee, 28 January 1929; which contain Chesterfield's subscription information 1924–61; Chesterfield chamber minutes, 28 November 1930.

[160] Sheffield chamber, Council minutes, 13 May 1935; memorandum by W. P. Pickering, 11 April 1935 (paper C.9–C.11).

[161] Kidderminster chamber minutes, 16 September 1919.

But on the other hand, the Home Affairs Committee was unwilling to encourage new chamber formation. Birmingham suggested in 1931 that 'investigations should be made with a view to widening of the area of existing chambers of commerce to take in districts not at present covered',[162] that all existing chambers be affiliated, and 'where practicable' a chamber should be 'set up in towns with a population exceeding 40,000'. But the Home Affairs Committee held that 'the organisation of new chambers must be left in the hands of local interests', and chambers of trade 'are not in a position to pay the requisite subscriptions to the association'.[163]

Much of the encouragement for chambers to work together was also unrealistic. It was particularly difficult for the more widely dispersed locations. Thus Barrow-in-Furness, Kendal, Carlisle, and Lancaster explored cooperation in 1917 in order to employ a joint secretariat, but abandoned it as 'absolutely impractical'.[164] The South of Scotland chamber was frequently quoted as a case overcoming these barriers,[165] but it was a special case of a very focused chamber (chiefly hosiery manufacture) with cooperation of several small towns that were relatively accessible to each other but cut off from everywhere else. There were perhaps better cases that were ignored: Walsall operated over a district that included Wednesbury and Darlaston; Southampton, Portsmouth, and Winchester had cooperated in the 1920s with a joint journal; and Bemrose publishers had developed joint journals for chambers in the 1920s; e.g. for Blackburn and Burnley, and Wolverhampton and Dudley.

Another strategy was to expand *individual* direct members of ABCC. This began in 1914, and expanded after 1925 as a result of a recommendation from the Home Affairs Committee, chiefly to increase ABCC income.[166] This offered some new blood and involvement, but was generally on a small scale (maximum 272 in 1930) with little chance to participate in ABCC decisions. Moreover between one-third and one-half came from one place, Glasgow.[167] There was nothing to approach the NCT's involvement of its individual members, and it was abolished in 1958.

8.6 THE BATTLE TO IMPOSE STANDARDS: 1947–1989

Despite the progress made, a report by the new secretary of the ABCC in 1949, Arthur Knowles, was scathing.[168] Labelled 'highly confidential and urgent', it

---

[162] ABCC Executive Council minutes, 7 January 1931.
[163] ABCC Home Affairs Committee, 3 December 1930.
[164] Mr Major, Barrow-in-Furness chamber, in ACC *Monthly Proceedings*, October (1917), pp. 30–1; in fact this coordination was implemented only after 2001.
[165] e.g. Algernon Firth, ACC president, and A. J. Hobson, Sheffield chamber, in ACC *Monthly Proceedings*, October (1917), pp. 18 and 33.
[166] Individuals received ABCC publications as their main benefit; but they had to remain a member of their local chamber: ABCC subscriptions document in MS 14478, 24 September 1925.
[167] In 1928 Glasgow accounted for 66 of 133 individual ABCC members; by 1929 it was 86 out of 200; ABCC Executive minutes, 7 November 1928; 6 November 1929.
[168] Knowles (1949); he was the third 'secretary' of ABCC, covering 1946–59.

recapped Algernon Firth's speech of 1917 and asked what had changed. Knowles stated that protection of title had improved but was inadequate; all chambers having separate offices 'is probably as far away from being implemented as it was three decades ago'; the aspiration for a full-time secretary 'has never been satisfied. At least 80% have a part-time secretary; in many cases . . . a spare-time secretary'; and the proposal for chambers to have sufficient income 'might as well never have been voiced. . . . Little progress has been made.'[169] An independent assessment of this period suggested that 'many constituent chambers were small, weak and incessantly suspicious of each other'.[170]

Assertion by the Association of Chamber Secretaries

Meetings of chamber secretaries had intensified over WW1, and in its aftermath they continued, sometimes developing views independently or ahead of the ABCC council. There had been an Association of Chamber Secretaries since 1922.[171] Its records were often kept deliberately confidential from the ABCC council. As a result its papers, other than minutes, are incomplete in the ABCC archive and have to be supplemented from local chambers that retained copies. In the 1950s the Association of Chamber Secretaries became the main force for reforms. This marks the point where the professionals began taking over from elected voluntary officers in steering ABCC, and where the ABCC secretary began to be a significant force for change. Knowles's paper in part reflects this shift of emphasis; and it also indicates a growing view that it was the elected chairs and councils of the (mainly smaller) chambers who were often holding back developments.

Knowles's 1949 paper seems to have been stimulated by a conference of the chamber secretaries in July 1947. This conference set about defining the role of the ABCC, seeking greater publicity, calling for improvements in the ABCC *Monthly Proceedings* (which they stated 'did less than justice to its deliberations' and could be rendered 'more enlightening'), reforming the ABCC subscription structure, and reviving the calls for improved chamber 'efficiency', chiefly through increased membership and increased subscriptions.[172] The proposed subscription structure should move from the flat rate of 5s. to 6s. 8d. per member, with a minimum payment of £21 (as then current) and a maximum of £2000. This rise was agreed in 1950. Three other critical decisions were that the ABCC should not receive a levy from the local fees for certificates of origin; that local canvassers for membership should be employed (though a proposal for the ABCC to do this and lend

---

[169] Knowles (1949), pp. 4–5.

[170] Alderman (1973), p. 100.

[171] A 'secretaries club' was established 1897: ABCC, *Chamber of Commerce Manual* (1954–5), p. 13.

[172] Report from the elected secretaries of affiliated chambers to ABCC Executive Council: *Organisation of the ABCC*; 16 September 1947; the elected secretaries from the 42 secretaries attending the July 1947 conference were H. Eyles (Birmingham), James Ainsley (Manchester), S. J. Batchelder (Leeds), R. P. Braund (Norwich), E.G. Harris (Portsmouth), and A. de. V. Leigh (London); copy at Croydon chamber.

canvassers to chambers was not followed); and that the ABCC executive should retain flexibility in making decisions on affiliation (i.e. chambers that did not meet the minimum subscriptions levels could still remain members after ABCC scrutiny of their case).

Knowles's paper can be seen as reflecting new grass-roots activism from the secretaries, which he had probably been instrumental in stimulating. Indeed, the 1949–50 ABCC *Annual Report*, presumably written by Knowles, noted how 'impressed' he was with the stronger support the secretaries were giving to the executive council.[173] His paper represents an attempt to bring the secretaries' discussions to the ABCC council table. Knowles suggested abandoning the requirements for separate offices and full-time secretaries, arguing that these deficiencies would be resolved by other development. He also argued that affiliation to ABCC could be made probationary for the first two years in order to encourage non-incorporated chambers to join and then bring themselves up to standard. This was accepted by ABCC, which allowed Ayr to join in 1949.[174] But Knowles argued that the chief focus should be changing the role of secretaries in small chambers through shared and collaborative structures, so that all chambers had the use of a full-time secretary, or service agreements with the large chambers.[175] This was particularly possible for small chambers located close to each other, or where small chambers were close to large ones. Without this improvement 'many chambers [will remain] centres for discussion but not hubs of service. Until membership is anchored in service in the smaller as well as in the larger chambers, there can be no marked increase in the total chamber of commerce membership; in too many places, membership will continue not to have the meaning it should have.'[176] Many chambers supported this; Coventry proposed that 'an attempt should be made to link small chambers with the larger ones, for the purpose of increased service to members of the small bodies'.[177]

It is from this date therefore that services became indelibly linked to wider chamber activities and aspirations for development. The national association was now not just about voice, but also about service standards; and it is from Knowles's report that the sponsored article in the *Financial Times* derives, summarized in Chapter 3, which states the *dual role* of chambers:[178] the USP of chambers became local voice, and *also* business services. As stated by Knowles, 'The big majority of chamber members are not really inspired by a sense of public duty towards their chamber as an instrument for the general good; they regard it as a servant, helping them in *their* business. The price of their favour will increasingly prove to be the *service* they are given. The alternatives before chambers are, therefore, *serve* or

---

[173] ABCC, *Annual Report* (1949–50), pp. 28–9.

[174] ABCC, Executive minutes, 7 December 1949.

[175] Knowles (1949), pp. 7–10.

[176] Knowles (1949), pp. 7, 11–13.

[177] ABCC Executive papers, 2 February 1949; MS 14477/7.

[178] This must have been crafted by Knowles, though signed off by the Council: 'British chambers of commerce: how they serve their members', *Financial Times*, 9 March 1949.

stagnate.'[179] Indeed in a subsequent memorandum Knowles comes close to ignoring the local voice function altogether, reserving this largely to the ABCC.[180]

Cautious steps forward

Knowles's vision began as an internal debate about the future of the ABCC. Leeds records its view that the ABCC council 'often seems to be overweighed with detail' and it supported more matters being delegated to a panel of secretaries whilst the council dealt with 'major points of principle or wide interest'. It proposed that a committee of chamber presidents should develop a future strategy for ABCC.[181] Other chambers also began to discuss a new relationship with the centre. A discussion began, which continues to this day, 'that if no ABCC was in being, it would be essential to form one',[182] although its role had to be reassessed.

But the follow-up was slow. Apart from the subscription increase from 5s. to 6s. 8d. per member, the main immediate outcomes were increases in central staff[183] and an appeal for a special fund for ABCC to improve its premises and reduce its deficit.[184] This raised £23,149 over 1951–6 from individual donors and chambers.[185] An effort was made to offer a template to local chambers and members of what a chamber stood for, with a *Chambers of Commerce Manual* published in 1954–5. This provided a useful summary, and is derived directly from parts of Knowles's paper, repeating some of the historical commentary (and inaccuracies). It lists local chamber services under three headings: (i) individual services (numbering 41 headings) of information and representational benefits; (ii) community services, to 'promote good conditions locally' in planning, education, transport, postal, telephone, civil defence, etc.; and (iii) national affairs 'in support of local interests', but 'most subjects of national character are dealt with through the ABCC'.[186] But it did not provide the kind of hands-on specific guidance on 'how to run a chamber' that the NCT offered in its *Handbook* of 1960.[187] And in terms of organizational change, progress was initially minimal. A survey of the small chambers in 1953 asked them to report 'how chambers with part time secretaries and small financial

---

[179] Knowles (1949), p. 20.

[180] Knowles (1952).

[181] Leeds chamber minutes, 6 September 1950: *Finance and Work of the ABCC.*

[182] e.g. Eric Carpenter, president of ABCC, confidential remarks at annual address; ABCC Executive minutes, 5 July 1955, p. 1.

[183] The most important appointments were two new deputies to Knowles: W. J. Luxton as legal and parliamentary secretary, and P. J. A. Bathurst as secretary of the overseas division.

[184] ABCC was still at the grand but old-fashioned building of 14 Queen Anne's Gate. It is described as built initially as a residence about 1760 with attractive ground and first floor rooms but much wasted space; and second and third floors with too little space. A move would need 4000 sq. ft., half for offices and 600 sq. ft. each for a council room and storage: *Report on ABCC* to conference of ABCC presidents and secretaries, 21 January 1959.

[185] Listed in ABCC annual accounts.

[186] *Chambers of Commerce Manual* (1954–5), pp. 2–3; this went through three editions in 1955, 1956, and 1957; the first two sold 7600 copies to chambers: ABCC GPC, 1 August 1956. By 1959 it is described as 'stone dead'; *Report on ABCC* to conference of ABCC presidents and secretaries, 21 January 1959.

[187] NCT, *Handbook* (1960); MS 29346; see Chapter 2.

resources could make the best of themselves within their inescapable limitations' (a classic case of a leading question!). The responses to this survey were to remain confidential solely to the ABCC secretary, and the Association of Secretaries of the chambers; they found that 'with regard to the consolidation of the chambers . . . the meeting expressed concern lest this might lead to the submerging of individual chamber identity and autonomy. . . . The development of coordinated activities in areas should be allowed to evolve out of demand and necessity rather than it should be forced.' The secretaries were also 'opposed to any idea of regionalisation'.[188]

The organizational issues crystallized only after the chamber secretaries prepared a report in 1954, sent to the then president, Sir Eric Carpenter, and presented to the ABCC executive by Ronald Walker, chamber secretary at Bolton.[189] This stated that 58 (53%) of the ABCC chambers provided only 14% of the membership, and they 'were the weak links in the chain'. Their main problems were: low subscriptions, which resulted in inadequate finance; insufficient drive to increase membership, which needed more canvassing; and there were inadequate links between ABCC and the small chambers. The key conclusion was that local chambers needed 'a full and constant review under ABCC auspices'. The ABCC agreed to set up a President's Advisory Committee to prepare a report on future organization, with W. V. Stevens, Edinburgh chamber secretary, as chair. A visit by the German chambers' national organization, DIHT, took place in March 1955, which fed into the thinking, particularly the need for increased income.[190]

The chief outcome of the President's Advisory Committee was a proposed revision of the articles of ABCC to levy a new subscription for each chamber at 10s. for each of its members, with a minimum of £21, maximum of £3000, and a general agreement to move forward. Carpenter, the ABCC President, added a confidential preface to the July 1955 ABCC Annual Report calling for various reforms which focused on making the ABCC more strategic; dividing volunteer from professional inputs ('members and staffs each have their contribution to make and the combination of the two provides the requisite service'); improving the flow of 'executives'; increasing staff and equipment of chambers; and 'pooling of resources . . . in geographical areas, [so that] chambers individually and as a whole could attain greater vitality and prosperity and thereby give better service', particularly libraries.[191] The latter remarks presaged the beginning of a debate on regionalization that was to run up to the present. The most tangible change was the establishment of an ABCC General Purpose Committee (GPC) from 1956, and a Development Committee from 1958, to which organizational issues were assigned. It is from this point that a new drive to tackle the tensions in the system began.

---

[188] ABCC, Association of Chamber Secretaries, minutes, 17 July 1953.
[189] ABCC, Council, minutes, 6 October 1954; Walker is a surprising advocate as Bolton had then only 200 members and £1000 in total income; it was one of the smaller chambers.
[190] ABCC, Council, minutes, 23 March 1955.
[191] Eric Carpenter, president of ABCC, confidential remarks at annual address; ABCC Executive minutes, 5 July 1955, pp. 2–4.

'Constant review' by the GPC[192]

The most crucial change of the period was the idea that ABCC had authority to keep local chambers under constant review. This was a considerable development from the ABCC approach to the first 'approved' chambers that began in 1918. Now chambers that did not conform were not merely to be left to their own initiatives, but were to be pressed to change. However, as always, progress was slow and halting. The new ABCC president, Frank Bower, 'personally felt that the council should not attempt to impose any specific plan of action for chambers to follow', and any plan for an 'agreed system of regionalisation should not be imposed'.[193] Moreover, when ABCC did try to move forward it was met with some trenchant criticism.

The main initial effect of the GPC was to be tougher on new applications from chambers for affiliation. Applicants had to quote their composition of membership from different sectors (usually broken down as manufacturing, merchant, retail, and professional). Newhaven (40% retail), Isle of Wight (20% retail), Reading (49% retail) were accepted, but Westbury (66% retail) and Rugely (85% retail) were rejected or asked to reapply after widening their membership, 'because a relatively high proportion of members were retailers'. It appears that a 50% maximum for retail membership was being used as a cut-off, though this is not explicit. Despite this, retail membership was increasingly accepted as necessary, but the line of competition with NCT was drawn by stating that 'chambers of commerce should be encouraged to take into membership the non-retail sections of chambers of trade in their area';[194] as in Birmingham which had a link with the industrial section of the Tamworth chamber of trade.

But the biggest early issue for the GPC over 1956–9 was how subscriptions should be levied between retailers and other members as far as the ABCC fees were concerned. With the new schedule of ABCC subscriptions many chambers faced what they deemed were large rises. In 1956, the GPC received 13 applications for reduced subscriptions, and agreed 12 of these for that year on the basis of their large retail presence.[195] More chambers asked for reductions in 1957 and 1958. But for subsequent years the GPC took the view that chambers with large retail membership should pay the same subscription as others.[196] The GPC became increasingly tough: when Forth Valley and Birkenhead asked for lower subscriptions in 1958, their accounts were scrutinized and they were told to raise their member

---

[192] The ABCC, GPC records deposited for 1956–64 are limited chiefly to formal minutes. Gaps have been filled as far as possible from local chamber holdings, as cited.

[193] ABCC, GPC, respectively, 2 July and 8 January 1958.

[194] ABCC, GPC, quote regarding Westbury; other applications cover 1958–63. Westbury was allowed to join in 1961 having increased its industrial membership to 31, which were claimed to be over 90% of the industrialists in the area; retailers still constituted 60% of the chamber: ABCC GPC, 1 March 1961.

[195] For Bath, Barnstaple, Croydon, Isle of Wight, Jersey, Poole, Rugby, Southampton, Trowbridge, Widnes, Worcester, and Coventry; ABCC GPC, 7 November 1956.

[196] ABCC, GPC, 5 November 1958.

subscriptions.[197] The scrutiny of the ABCC into the local was now at a level not previously seen. In response to this growing pressure, Barnstaple, Winchester, and Worcester said they would not ask members for the subscription needed and resigned, whilst Dudley said it would pay at two rates, and Southampton and Croydon campaigned for a two-rate model more generally. Brighton said it would pay no more than £50 (a fraction of what was due).[198] The GPC initially allowed Dudley and Croydon a reduced subscription for 1958, but its efforts were derailed by a more general resolution passed at the 1958 Annual meeting: that chambers paying a subscription to the NCT could reduce their capitation fee to the ABCC from 10s. to 5s. in respect of retail members.[199] A campaign led by Southampton and Croydon had won the day.

The Southampton and Croydon campaign

The GPC pressures resulted in a campaign of resistance led by Southampton and Croydon, supported by other chambers that had large retail membership.[200] Both chambers had large membership of about 1000, of which 35–40% were retailers. Croydon had left ABCC in 1926 to join NCT, only rejoining in 1934. Southampton was a member of both, and so were other chambers. These chambers took the view in 1957 that the ABCC was serving the retail sector poorly, the subscription was too high, and that unless a compromise was struck they would resign. For Croydon the subscription had risen from £44 in 1950, to £561 in 1958. They also argued that the new stance of ABCC to scrutinize individual chambers was unconstitutional. In its early history 'the relations between the association and the constituent chambers were … harmonious … without imposing an undue strain upon the financial resources of the constituent chambers…. Because the method was association, the parties within it had rights and duties to each other, and … nothing was done that might injure the financial tap-roots of the movement.' But now chambers that subscribed to the NCT were to be compelled to pay on their total membership 'on what grounds it is difficult to conceive'.[201]

Southampton and Croydon went on to blame the changes fully on Arthur Knowles. After his arrival at ABCC in 1947,

> the old under-manned secretariat began to branch like a living tree. Department after department came into being, … each in charge of a competent secretary, expenditure began to increase at such a rate as to evoke an uneasy feeling that the old constitutional

[197] ABCC, GPC, 5 February 1958; Birkenhead increased its subscriptions from £1 11s. 6d. and three guineas, to two guineas and four guineas in 1959; Forth Valley did not respond.
[198] Brighton and Hove chamber letter to Croydon; in Croydon Executive Council minute, 29 June 1956.
[199] ABCC, GPC, 2 October 1957; for implementation on 1 January 1959.
[200] Similar, though less vitriolic, minutes cover local views in Worcester and Luton.
[201] *Memorandum on the ABCC* by Bernard D. Knowles, secretary Southampton chamber, 1957, p. 4. This was the background document used at Croydon chamber annual meeting of the finance and GPC, April 1957. The paper does not survive in Southampton chamber archives; held at Croydon chamber.

principle that the association must cut its coat according to its cloth . . . had somehow gone by the board . . . and control had begun to pass from chambers to the association . . . . Far too little care has been exercised in determining the type of activities which are calculated to serve the best interests of chambers as a whole, and schemes . . . have been embarked upon . . . that have entailed much work, and consequently expenses which might have been avoided.

Donations to support the refurbishment of the ABCC offices were also resented.[202]

The issue had been rumbling for some time, since an attempt by Preston in 1953 to have *any* memorandum from ABCC agreed by all chambers was dismissed as impractical.[203] But 'the storm broke out at the 1956 Annual meeting' of ABCC, which Southampton claimed resulted from London's impatience at continuing to have to bear high costs for the ABCC.[204] London certainly threatened to withhold increases in subscriptions in 1956 if a GPC was not established with strong powers to 'control finance and administration'.[205] It was also at this point that London seems to have conceived a quasi-takeover; for the ABCC to move into London's offices. Indeed ABCC did move in with the chamber in February 1960 (in Queen St., and moved with it to Cannon St. in 1973). Although this was sensible in order to reduce costs, share bookkeeping, and postal support; and although ABCC had a separate entrance and its own room for up to eight staff, it led to jealousy from other chambers. It was a strategic mistake that gave away the authority and status of the association. In February 1976 ABCC moved out of the London chamber to sublet from CBI (in 6–14 Dean Farrer St.); which was also unwise in the aftermath of the failure of the Devlin Report.[206]

But the key conflict in 1956–7 was over the new subscriptions: these still allowed the large chambers to limit their total contributions at the expense of the rest, whilst the chambers with large retail memberships felt particularly penalized. For London, the maximum reduced payments from £6500 to £3000. Southampton argued that London had seen the ABCC as 'the "riderless horse" [that] must be brought under control' and had misused its position on the GPC to limit its own payments and increase those of other chambers. London was also blamed for introducing the power for GPC to scrutinize individual chamber accounts in order to 'impose' subscription levels: 'the London chamber succeeded in getting through their proposal that a GPC should be set up with power to control finance'.[207]

Southampton argued that it was not the purpose of ABCC to 'become a kind of supra-national authority . . . [rather than] an auxiliary institution whose function it was—to quote the Memorandum of the Association—"to attain by united action what each chamber would have difficulty in accomplishing in its separate capacity".' This was the very statement introduced in 1862 as a result of the concerns of Liverpool

[202] *Memorandum on the ABCC* by Bernard D. Knowles, Southampton, 1957, pp. 5–6; p. 12.
[203] ABCC, Council minutes, 15 May 1953.
[204] *Memorandum on the ABCC* by Bernard D. Knowles, Southampton, 1957, p. 6.
[205] ABCC, Council minutes, 11 April 1956.
[206] See below, and Chapters 2 and 10.
[207] *Memorandum on the ABCC* by Bernard D. Knowles, Southampton, 1957, p. 6.

that had led it to resign. The old tensions remained! Southampton made five proposals to ABCC: (i) ABCC expenditure should be reduced to a level that would not impair the activities of the local chambers; (ii) ABCC subscriptions should be revised immediately to a more equitable level of burden; (iii) subscriptions should be based on a scale of subscription incomes, not number of members; (iv) chambers of commerce also operating as CoTs should not pay on their CoT membership 'unless appropriate service was given in return'; and (v) ABCC should help and promote individual chambers e.g. through a 'national publicity week'. In conclusion, Southampton argued that ABCC should not regard local chambers as 'pigeons waiting to be plucked...', but as geese that lay the golden eggs and require tending and nurturing'.[208]

Croydon took up Southampton's campaign. It maintained membership of ABCC until 1959, being given a special rate of £300,[209] but since it was not allowed to continue the reduced rate it resigned, although it was still permitted to issue certificates.[210] It was reluctant to leave because it was worried about losing its certificate issuing powers; and also because 'any possible application in the future to re-affiliate to the Association would be harmed by the London chamber's claim to be the only chamber in affiliation within a radius of 20 miles of its address'.[211] By resigning 'at least we shall remain a functioning organisation. Accepting crippling commitments to the ABCC can only mean that this chamber will cease in a short time to exist at all.'[212] It did not rejoin until 1974. At about the same time a number of other chambers also left ABCC and joined NCT, including Aylesbury, Barrow-in-Furness, Dover, Ipswich, Port Talbot, and Winchester. Southampton claimed 'the movement [is] showing signs of disintegration'. It certainly marked the start of a cycle when Southampton was as frequently a non-member as a member of ABCC, which continued up to the present. At the same time other chambers joined FBI; e.g. Cambridge joined FBI in 1956 for its 16 manufacturing members.[213] Croydon joined the FBI on behalf of its manufacturing section of 260 members in 1958.[214] The ABCC responded by getting the FBI not to accept sections of chambers as members, which led to Croydon resigning from FBI in 1959.[215] However, Sussex, which joined ABCC soon after this period, found a loophole in 1974 when subscriptions were raised again; this allowed it to pay a reduced ABCC rate purely for issuing certificates, and it joined CBI instead.[216]

---

[208] Ibid., pp. 12–13.

[209] Bath, Birkenhead, Poole, and Forth Valley chambers also sought reduced rates, but were given reductions only for the current year; ABCC GPC, 5 November 1958.

[210] ABCC, GPC, 2 November 1960.

[211] Letter from Croydon secretary to ABCC, 3 February 1959; copy at Croydon chamber. In 1944 London claimed an area of 20 miles from the chamber, 'for over 30 years': London chamber, Council minutes, 9 May 1944: MS 16459/23.

[212] Letter from H. T. Halpern, 19 January 1959 (FB. HTH/WMW); at Croydon chamber.

[213] Letter from Cambridge chamber secretary to Croydon chamber, May 1956; at Croydon chamber.

[214] Although it was unhappy about the influence it could wield within FBI: Croydon Executive Council minutes, 29 June 1956; annual accounts 1958; 'Notes on affiliations' 1958.

[215] ABCC, GPC, 2 January 1959.

[216] Federation of Sussex Industries; Sussex chamber history, p. 9.

This was part of a trend of chambers coming and going from ABCC when they disagreed with it. For the small chambers each financial or other change at ABCC produced major questions. Taking Barnstaple as an example, it joined ABCC from its foundation in 1911, but lapsed over the 1920 changes, rejoined in 1930, but also joined NCT. It continued through WW2 mainly because of wartime manufacturers' needs, and founded a committee of manufacturers in 1941 (which had its own subscription and a membership of 33 in a chamber of only 100). It maintained ABCC membership when Croydon resigned in 1959, successfully raising its subscriptions to do so. But when the ABCC apprenticeship scheme provided little scope, it lapsed in 1969.[217] In Worcester the directors proposed resigning in 1957 'because of the further raising of affiliation fees . . . and the failure of our negotiations . . . to produce an equitable settlement'. This was defeated by one vote at a general meeting, with the *News and Times* reporter present agreeing not to publicize it.[218]

In this factious debate London was challenged to raise its subscriptions; as noted by Southampton, it was the only chamber for which the maximum of £3000 had any effect. But it steadfastly refused, noting that its maximum limit had been accepted since the 1920s, and it had agreed to pay more in 1944 only 'as a war bonus'. It also reasserted the agreement it had with ABCC, the 'London rule' of 1944, that no other chamber should be affiliated within 20 miles of the City, as a means to restrict Croydon and Westminster issuing certificates of origin.[219] ABCC reluctantly continued to support this, but only under pressure. As noted in a confidential letter from Slough chamber in 1957, 'who would propose making up the £3000 deficit to the ABCC if London resigned, which it had threatened to do?'[220] None of this was helpful to resolving the disputes.

A clash of models, resolved by compromise

The episode demonstrates the clash of chamber models: between, first, an all-embracing chamber of all sectors, with retail proportionately large (about 40% in chambers like Croydon, Southampton, Portsmouth, and even larger in smaller places); or second, a chamber that was still predominantly only the major commercial and manufacturing businesses. The first model had been advocated by ABCC as a means to increase membership, but the implications had not been thought through. The period also brought to light the stranglehold of London, and the deficiencies of BoT support. Whilst the chambers thought they could rely on BoT to prevent non-affiliated chambers issuing certificates of origin, the BoT would issue warnings but take no action. Thus Croydon was able to continue to issue certificates, Westminster became an important issuer, and Hammersmith also

---

[217] Barnstaple chamber, income and expenditure 8 January 1943; Council minutes, 11 February 1949; 20 April 1950; 4 September 1959; AGM minutes, 20 February 1969.
[218] Worcester chamber, minutes of General Meeting, 26 February 1957.
[219] London chamber, Council minutes, 9 May 1944.
[220] John Peck (Slough chamber secretary) letter to F. A. Moxley (Croydon secretary) April 1957; at Croydon chamber.

began in the 1960s. Barnstaple repeatedly considered issuing certificates and was only put off by the cost of the staff required, estimated at £150 per year in 1969, but not by BoT or ABCC restrictions.[221] This all undermined the authority of ABCC, and was a major worry in the case of Hammersmith which was believed to be 'in the pocket' of a few large companies.[222]

The ABCC had to reconsider its subscriptions, finally leading to a vote in favour of increases in 1959, as proposed by the president's advisory committee in 1955, but Croydon's resolution to reduce subscriptions where chambers also paid NCT subscriptions was also carried. The voting on the resolutions was analysed in detail by the GPC: 210 voted in favour, 179 against, and 39 abstained; it was carried by the medium-sized and smaller chambers. The six largest chamber votes were cast 121 against (by Liverpool, London, and Manchester), 49 in favour (Glasgow and Leeds) with 38 abstentions (by Birmingham's votes).[223] This is a vivid expression of the tension between the large and small chambers at the time. But even this decision was challenged. On the one hand, the ABCC sought a further increase in capitation fee to 12s. 6d. Various scenarios for the retail fee if capitation was increased were analysed, with losses from the Croydon resolution estimated at £777 from 3109 retailers in 28 chambers (28% of their membership; undoubtedly exaggerated in some cases).[224] These proposals were all voted down in the GPC; most members recognized that some stability was needed after a wounding period. On the other hand, several chambers lobbied for a delay in implementation of the 10s. subscription until economies were found in the costs of ABCC.[225] These were mainly sought by relocation of the association to the offices of the London chamber. A proposed development secretary was deferred. But there were also calls for further cuts in ABCC office staff by Liverpool and Manchester, questioning of the costs of overseas delegations, and reducing subscriptions by ABCC to outside bodies.[226] Further claims continued to be made for reduced subscriptions; e.g. by Brighton and Hove in 1961, Reading in 1962, which were both refused; although when Forth Valley was in financial difficulties in 1963 a reduced subscription was allowed for three years. This unhappy period made all the chambers uneasy, both large and small; London, Liverpool, and Manchester were increasingly feeling that they could do more on their own; others resigned.

The 'ideal chamber' of 1959

The GPC initially moved more cautiously after this. A Development Committee was established in 1958, which tried to re-establish what was the USP of chambers ('what . . . can or should they do which no other body can do so

---

[221] Barnstaple chamber, minutes, 20 February 1969, 3 December 1973.
[222] Interview comment to author from Ron Taylor, 21 November 2006.
[223] Votes were weighted by membership; ABCC GPC, 1 July 1959.
[224] ABCC, GPC, 2 December 1959.
[225] This was pressed by Manchester, Bristol, Southampton, Cardiff, Newport, and Preston; i.e. apart from Newport, larger-medium sized chambers: ABCC, GPC, 4 November 1959.
[226] ABCC, GPC, 4 November 1959.

effectively') and what was the 'root cause of apathy where it exists'.[227] Some effort went into improving public relations and publicity, particularly to overcome confusion with the NCT and its chambers;[228] consideration was given to improving the ABCC council, which was considered too large and might benefit from regional representation and postal voting;[229] but the main emphasis remained on trying to improve smaller chambers. The continuing opinion was that 'the small chamber is too small to be a viable unit'.[230] By 1959 developments were being discussed around four main themes: 'ideal chamber', communications, regional groupings, and role of ABCC.[231] These developments were increasingly made in conferences between presidents and secretaries, where a consensus was sought. The conference in 1959 succeeded in defining what it thought were the potential activities of large, medium, and small chambers. These are summarized in Table 8.1.

The concept of 'ideal chamber' now fell into three types, with the largest, and as far as possible the medium-sized, chambers offering coverage of most functions. The service specification is given by a leaflet, *Your Chamber of Commerce*, a copy of which does not seem to survive, but is summarized in the medium chambers draft. This lists certificates, translations, temporary assistance, and a wide range of information as 'direct services'; supplemented by 'first aid advice' on issues such as arbitration, law, taxation, non-domestic rates, town planning, patents, and copyright.[232] The main distinctions are for the concept of the small chamber, which had few services and a simplified management and committee structure. The surprising thing is the lack of emphasis on social functions in the small chamber ideal. 'The value of social occasions as an aid to membership and holding members' interest' was mentioned in some of the discussions in the January conference, but was not strongly followed up; a point that is analysed further in Chapter 11.

In addition, an effort was made to respond to governance issues, by having 12 ABCC Council places available for small chambers having fewer than 300 members to elect within 'parish' groups. By 1958, 31 chambers had formed into 11 'parishes' on a voluntary basis based on: Kidderminster, Grimsby, Burnley, Bolton, Warrington, Wakefield, Bury, Gloucester, Exeter, Newport, and Barnsley. The 12th parish became a disparate group covering the Channel Islands, Isle of Man, and various scattered chambers.[233] This helped the issue of regional cooperation to be more actively investigated. London, for example, explored with 'chambers in East Anglia and the Home Counties whether some arrangement could be reached under

---

[227] ABCC, Development Advisory Committee, minutes, 3 September 1958; in ABCC GPC minutes.

[228] Ibid.

[229] *Report on the ABCC*; Conference of ABCC presidents and secretaries, 21 January 1959.

[230] ABCC Development Advisory Committee, 3 September 1958.

[231] *Chambers of commerce today and tomorrow*: Conference of ABCC presidents and secretaries, 21 January 1959; copy at Croydon chamber.

[232] Papers for Conference of ABCC presidents and secretaries, 21 January 1959; copies at Croydon chamber.

[233] ABCC GPC, 2 July 1958.

Table 8.1. The functions of large, medium, and small chambers as conceived by the conference of ABCC presidents and secretaries, 21 January 1959

Large chambers (over 1000 members)	Medium chambers (generally 300–1000 members)	Small chambers (100–300 members)
Standing committees for internal management	Standing executive committee for internal management	Standing executive officers for internal management
Standing committees for	Standing committees for	
Education	Education	
Overseas trade	Overseas trade	
Transport	Transport	
Finance and taxation	Finance and taxation	
Other local needs	Other local needs	
Sections for trading regions of the world		
Sections for major local industries	Other local needs	
Services:	Services:	Services mainly by referral and cooperation with other chambers
Overseas trade	Certificates	
Home trade	Information	
Library	Library (in cooperation with municipal library)	
Translation bureau	Translation service	
Arbitration	Arbitration	
Junior chamber	Junior chamber	
Annual report	Annual report	Annual report
Journal and circulars to members	Journal and circulars to members	Newsletter to members using ABCC materials—monthly Council meeting reports
Publicity at 'every opportunity'	Publicity at 'every opportunity'	
Liaison with other organizations	Liaison with other organizations	'Link' with other organizations Liaison with chambers of trade
Social: Annual dinner, lunch meetings	Social: Annual dinner, lunch meetings	Forum for discussion
Entertainment of foreign missions and visitors	Entertainment of foreign missions and visitors	
Other activities	Other activities	Other activities
Temporary assistance	Temporary assistance	

Note: Drafted by William Luxton (London) for large chambers; V. N. Brailsford for medium chambers; and Duncan Mutch (Barnsley) for small chambers): copies at Croydon chamber. The original three drafts were independent of each other and an attempt has been made here to align language and structure to facilitate comparison.

which the services of the chamber can be made available to their members'.[234] The first mention of regionalization occurs in the papers of the ABCC GPC after 1956. It was generally ruled out as a means of trying to bring small chambers up to a common standard, but it was increasingly recognized that regional cooperation was beneficial to chambers either to share resources or personnel.

[234] Report of Annual Meeting held 5 May; London *CCJ*, June (1959), p. 8.

From 'movement' to 'network', and the dominance
of the professionals

Although the ABCC was moving more cautiously in the early 1960s, the underlying issues as perceived by the professional secretaries, and hence by the larger
chambers who mainly employed them, had not been resolved: weak total resources,
variable service cover, confusion of brand, and competition from other bodies. The
'ideal chamber' was no solution; it merely tried to better present the status quo. The
next phase saw the secretaries again taking the lead, after a vigorous exchange of
views at their June 1965 annual conference. They produced a report in September
1965, again drawing attention to the lack of a full-time secretary in 69 of 100
affiliated chambers, many of which 'do not have sufficient resources to compile and
maintain detailed records of their members' products, the markets with which they
deal, and the services they offer'. The 31 largest chambers now accounted for 80%
of the membership, 85% of total income, and 90% of staff resources.[235]

It is from this period that the terminology of chambers as a 'movement' seems to
disappear, replaced by 'network', sometimes by 'system' or 'structure'. The modern
use continues as 'the chamber network' of accredited chambers.[236] This terminological change is not trivial: it reflected a change in fundamental concept, from
chiefly personal commitments and solidarity to material benefits in the form of
services. This was associated with the contemporaneous shift in the nature of the
membership, from mainly individuals to primarily limited companies and partnerships. As outlined in Chapters 14 and 15, the nature of the underlying structure of
business and the economy had changed, and so had the 'interest' that chambers
were being called on to represent. The main problem, as perceived by the chamber
secretaries, was unequal service cover, which was a code for little or no services in
most small chambers. The solution suggested was 'that all or some of the chambers
with full-time secretaries and staff should be responsible for providing individual
services to all chamber of commerce members', based on 'regional organisations'
acting as 'foster chambers'. This would 'not impinge in any way on the activities of
chambers in local affairs', and would allow all chambers to offer a high level of
services, but subscriptions would have to rise across all chambers to pay for it. To
prevent free riding between chambers, a basic minimum 'capitation fee' of £10 per
member was recommended, part of which should be paid to 'foster chambers'. 'An
agreed minimum subscription regionally and ultimately nationally would ensure
that there was no danger of the facilities of the "foster chambers" being used by
members of the smaller chambers at a lower subscription, and it would also give the
"foster chambers" some assurances of continuity of income.'[237]

This was a very challenging agenda. First, for the service dimension, services
provided from 'selected centres' did not exist in several of the largest chambers at

---

[235] Association of Chamber Secretaries: *Report on the Role of Chambers of Commerce in the Changing
Economy,* September 1965; MS 17593.
[236] e.g. BCC website accessed over the period 2005–11.
[237] Association of Chamber Secretaries: *Report on the Role of Chambers,* September 1965.

the time; this was thus mainly a London vision. Second, regional cooperation recognized the threat from FBI regional branches, but ABCC made the unrealistic statement that local 'parochialism must not only be killed, it must be buried once and for all'. Consultations from government were to be sent only to the regional centres, with local chambers only involved directly where they had specific expertise. This might have recognized the reality that the small chambers rarely contributed; it was claimed that 'during the last five years . . . the average response [from local chambers] has been 27%, and many of those replies have not helped the association to advance a view'. But to tell the small chambers that their voice was to be ignored was unlikely to be popular. Third, the consultees that were sought were not so much the chambers, but the members: 'the names of individuals within a company who can be relied upon to provide an informed view on matters on which they are particularly knowledgeable'. The 1965 report thus not only challenged the capacity of small chamber leaders, but sought to bypass them. It was perceived as a step on the way to removing the small chambers altogether.

Fourth, for voice, 'chambers must accept the situation that the association acts for the whole movement in submitting views to government departments. . . . Chambers should not attempt to alter decisions which have had to be made.' Where there is disagreement, 'they should accept the situation of having their views incorporated in the representation as a minority opinion'. This was a complete reversal of the earlier situation. Although a more aggressive leadership position for a 'director general' of ABCC was rejected, it was clear that it was the major regional chambers that would rule the roost. Again, as in 1947, it is surprising that some of the smaller chambers agreed to this paper.[238]

The Dixon, Luxton, and Urwick Orr Reports

Momentum was maintained through a series of reports. The first of these, and perhaps most fundamental, was the 'Dixon Report' in 1967. Prepared by the treasurer of ABCC, Philip Dixon, and a group of chamber secretaries, this was the first joint report of the GPC and the chamber secretaries, and thus represents a stronger attempt to bind in the elected membership.[239] It considered three issues: (i) the treatment of disaffiliated chambers, where there was ready agreement to remove these from any ABCC representation, though regional groups might maintain liaison; (ii) the functions and structure of chambers, where for the first time the concept of a *minimum size* and *critical mass* for chambers covering larger territories was voiced; and (iii) that the ABCC should be reformed to become a national chamber, or British Chamber of Commerce (BCC) with a membership of ten regional groups, formed of the 26 'principal chambers', with the object of

---

[238] The 1965 paper was drafted by J. Peck (Slough) as chair, with S. J. Batchelder (Leeds), R. C. Booth (Birmingham), J. A. Lackey (Manchester), W. J. Luxton (London), H. L. Milliard (Leicester), D. Mutch (Barnsley), M. Neil (Glasgow), R. Walker (Bolton), and T. A. Wyatt (Bath).

[239] *The Functions and Structure of Chambers of Commerce*; Dixon Report; Association of Chamber Secretaries, paper G.155–67; copy at Ipswich/Suffolk chamber. Dixon was a Yorkshire accountant.

'advancement of private enterprise, . . . promotion and protection of trade, commerce and industry, and provision of help to all firms, particularly the medium and small', with the BCC National Council elected on a regionally weighted basis. Other chambers beyond the 26 'may become affiliated to the BCC providing that they agree to servicing and other arrangements with the principal chambers'. The list was 'drawn up after a study of the industrial conurbations in the country and indicates where the principal chambers ought to be'. It was envisaged that 'the gradual raising of standards . . . will result in time in more chambers coming up to the standard of the principal chambers', probably about 40 were possible.

Dixon also readdressed the target of filling the map in a more systematic way. Whilst the ABCC secretary, Knowles, in 1949 had a map on his wall 'bearing a peg where each chamber is located',[240] in 1967 Dixon suggested that 'to a very great extent a chamber by custom has been restricted in its area of recruitment and local activity by local authority boundaries which are becoming less and less relevant to the modern pattern of industrial and commercial activity'. Dixon proposed that a chamber needed to reach out to cover larger areas 'recognisable . . . either in terms of geography or economic/industrial structure or both'. Moreover, marking the first emergence of the *concept of critical mass*, it was recognized that without increased territory 'in many cases a chamber has been unable to draw for membership upon a sufficiently large area to derive the sort of income which is necessary to support' it. [241]

All these proposals worked their way forward over the years and provided the basis for the modern approach still in use. But their progress was, as always, slow. It was also suggested that the title 'chamber of commerce and industry' (or CCI) should be introduced as a means to distinguish them from other bodies.[242] This did tend to occur, and continued into discussions of the 1990s, but its effect was to introduce further terminological and brand confusion.

The regional chambers with their constituent principal chambers, membership, and representation on the National Council were specified as in Table 8.2. This was a radical change not just in organization of services, but also in representation according to membership and chamber size; it cut off the small chambers completely from formal membership and voice in the association. With the Dixon Report, a London chamber statement (the Luxton Report) was also circulated to chambers.[243] This supported the Dixon recommendations but dissented in urging a stronger central control by the ABCC (with external prominent business members); that principal and other chambers should not be distinguished (thus allowing smaller chambers to continue to play a role); that independent consultants should review the structure; and that the membership should be differentiated into production, commerce, and distribution (with a stronger emphasis on commerce). In addition there was a report from the board of the council of ICC (the

---

[240] Knowles (1949), p. 6.
[241] Dixon Report; paper G.155–67.
[242] The suggested title seems to have been drawn from the visit of the DIHT German chambers.
[243] W. J. Luxton was one of the deputies to Knowles in 1949, subsequently moving to Birmingham and then to London chamber.

Table 8.2. Dixon Report 1967: proposed structure of regional and principal chambers

Regional chambers	Other principal member chambers	Membership	National Council representation
Belfast	—	870	1
Birmingham	Coventry, North Staffs.	7781	1+2
Bristol	—	2314	1
Cardiff	—	986	1
Glasgow	Aberdeen, Dundee, Edinburgh	7915	1+2
Leeds	Bradford, Hull, Sheffield	6266	1+2
Leicester	Derby, Nottingham	4034	1+1
London	Luton, Norwich, Portsmouth with Southampton, Westminster	18714	1+6
Manchester	Liverpool, Preston	7078	1+2
Tyneside	—	1028	1
Total (10)	16	57986	10+15

International Chamber of Commerce). This placed strong emphasis on the need for each service area having separate income and expenditure budgets, particularly where there were commercial services and management of real estate; in a comment prescient of many future tensions, it also suggested as desirable that a reserve fund should be established against future exceptional expenses.[244]

Luxton's London proposal stimulated the ABCC to commission consultants Urwick Orr to look at how a final scheme should be designed; their terms of reference were to determine 'how best to create a strong, properly financed and competently staffed central organisation'. The Urwick Orr Report of 1968 was uncompromising:

> The movement is that of a large assembly of local organisations—some large, many small—each a separate, self-governing body and accountable only to itself. There are, in some quarters, attitudes of parochialism and unwillingness to co-operate . . . . If the movement is thought to be losing its influence in the higher counsels of this country it is not entirely because the association is weak but rather because the whole movement is itself weakly organised and inadequately financed.[245]

The consultants built on the Dixon Report. The regional chambers now became titled 'focal chambers', which should be the service delivery bodies, meeting *an agreed minimum range of services*, whilst the ABCC should shed all service activities and focus on voice.[246] The regional chambers should be financed by a levy per

---

[244] Model plan for the organization of the general secretariat of a chamber of commerce and industry: *Report from Council of the International Chamber of Commerce*: copy at Ipswich chamber.
[245] Urwick Orr (1968); quoted in Taylor (2007), p. 86.
[246] ABCC, GPC, paper G.126–68: copy at Ipswich chamber.

non-retail member on the other chambers. It also suggested that ABCC should
have additional sources of income beyond chamber subscriptions, and recommended that chambers seek European-style public law status.

These proposals were largely adopted, but were slow to diffuse across the whole
system. The six main enduring reforms were: (i) the regional restructuring of the
ABCC representation, which was now managed under a National Council from
1969 (with the regions brought in line with the number of government economic
planning regions: 12);[247] (ii) the secretary of ABCC was now to be called director
general; (iii) there was to be a structure of separate chairs and presidents of ABCC;
(iv) direct receipt by ABCC of a share of certificate-related income from 1968,
derived from providing training and administration. These direct receipts rose from
£525 in 1968 to reach £8,000–10,000 over 1981–95, increasing to over £25,000
per year after reforms in 1995.[248] (v) The large chambers had to pay much more;
London had to pay half the increase in ABCC income.[249] An increase of other
subscriptions to ABCC was also agreed, by 354 votes to 69, but Bath, Bootle,
Bristol, Gloucester, Liverpool, and Nottingham resigned (although for the last two
this was a protest and they quickly returned),[250] and a more intensive investigation
of European chambers began.[251] (vi) Service standards were now to be systematically assessed: ABCC was to organize inspections of chambers focusing on the staff
and procedures for certificate issuing. It was also proposed that small chambers be
no longer 'eligible for membership unless affiliated to a focal chamber and had paid
the relative affiliation fee'.[252] But this was not implemented: most small chambers
remained within the ABCC, provided they were willing to continue to pay.

Although the attitudes to these reforms varied between chambers, there was now
an acceptance for the first time among the medium-sized chambers of the need to
change, whilst more of the smaller chambers now disaffiliated, chiefly under the
financial pressures of continuing in ABCC and inspections. This was the point at
which Barnstaple left ABCC in 1969 and focused on NCT. Many other small
chambers did the same. Barnstaple had already been concerned about the costs of
affiliation when the subscription increased from 5s. per member to 6s. 8d. in 1950.
It had then raised its subscription from a flat rate one guinea, to a scale from one to
four guineas for 1951. It was also being pressed by the NCT in its appeal for
£50,000 for its new building, donating £25 in 1952.[253] It complied with further
ABCC increases in 1962 by raising its subscriptions almost exactly by the required
ABCC increase, with a new scale from £1 5s. to £4 14s. 6d.[254] It rejoined ABCC a

[247] ABCC, National Council minutes, 3 December 1969.
[248] By 1997 there were three schemes being run by BCC: Export Marketing Research Scheme; Language for Export Advisory Scheme; and Certificates of Experience; see Chapter 12.
[249] London *CCJ*, July (1973), p. 55.
[250] ABCC, *Annual Report* (1966–7), p. 1.
[251] Two conferences were held with European chambers, in 1963 and 1965.
[252] ABCC, National Council, minutes 29 May 1969.
[253] Barnstaple chamber minutes, 20 April 1950; 14 January 1952.
[254] Barnstaple chamber minutes, 1 January 1962, 4 September 1959; AGM minutes, 20 February 1969.

few years later, but then lapsed in 1980 joining the Confederation of Business Organizations instead, though retaining its NCT membership.

In Ipswich the chamber was providing most services called for by Dixon, but was concerned about 'special services' such as missions and apprenticeships, which were already supplied by others or 'were not demanded by members'. It drew attention instead to its active chamber luncheon meetings, nine per year, reasserting the need for informal opportunities to exchange views. It also dissented from the large weight of representation given to London.[255] The London chamber reiterated its concerns in the Luxton report to strengthen the centre by having independent external members of the ABCC council.[256] Westminster chamber noted that nothing in any of these reports really tackled the problems of the smaller chambers and how to bring them up to standard. Indeed the proposals would undermine the small chambers, reducing their membership and revenues, and thus undermine the whole system, including the principal chambers.[257] Coventry chamber felt that the regionalization was a good proposal, provided that it was used to help individual chambers improve their services, but any measure to weaken their autonomy must be resisted and there should be no promotion of focal chambers as superior; encroachment by larger chambers should be resisted; a Midlands focal chamber was not needed; and there should be no compulsion (otherwise Coventry would disaffiliate from ABCC).[258] Conversely a Council of Northern chambers was formed which was enthusiastic about regionalization, 'which has brought the four North Eastern chambers together and has assisted in the formation of a common opinion on many matters'.[259]

As a result, 'focal chambers' began to be established but were often fairly nominal entities. The practicalities also proved contentious, chiefly because of the charges made by the focal chambers on the other chambers. For example Ipswich strongly objected to the levy proposed by the Norwich chamber, which had become the focal chamber for East Anglia.[260] Similarly, Coventry objected to the Midlands structure, did not accept Birmingham as the focal chamber, and applied itself to become a focal chamber.[261] Teesside did not accept Tyneside. Few chambers would accept links to London, which they regarded as attempted takeovers. Similar disputes raged around the country with the outcome settling down in most cases to a loose liaison structure within the region, with most financial levies collapsing after the first year. This barely extended from the informal regional conferences established between many chambers much earlier.[262]

---

[255] Letter from Ipswich chamber to A. C. F. Hey, ABCC secretary, November 1967.
[256] Letter from Robin Booth, chair of London chamber, 14 November 1967; copy at Ipswich chamber.
[257] Letter from Westminster chamber president, November 1967; copy at Ipswich chamber.
[258] Memorandum on *Structure and Functions of UK Chambers of Commerce*; Coventry chamber council minutes, 29 July 1968.
[259] Teesside and SW Durham chamber, *Annual Report*, 31 December 1960, p. 13.
[260] Ipswich chamber, Executive Committee minutes, 13 January 1969.
[261] Coventry chamber, Council minutes, 20 October 1969.
[262] e.g. Birmingham helped establish a quarterly Midlands chambers' conference in 1917, which ran for many years: Birmingham chamber, Council minutes, 31 December 1917.

Inspection and standards

Dixon had begun to define service standards. This evolved largely into a tick list of offers that was easy for most medium-sized chambers to satisfy, or at least claim to satisfy. But for issuing of certificates a more rigorous regime of inspection was begun. This was undertaken by senior staff from member chambers, thus binding in and using the resources of the network. Assessment was against a common set of criteria: of staff size (at least one full time), staff training in certificate issuing, and an audit of issuing procedures. Whether or not the aim was to purge the small chambers from membership, it had this effect. For the first time the small chambers, particularly those relying on local solicitors and accountants as their 'staff', were called to account and the membership of ABCC began to narrow.

The inspection process took place over 1969–71, and many of the inspection reports survive. They offer considerable insights into how many chambers were operating, also providing statistical material on membership coverage and representativeness.[263] By September 1970 the inspectors had identified four weak chambers (Carlisle, Chester and North Wales, Oldham, and Ossett), plus two others (Halifax and Rugby) that were causing concern. Many of the smallest chambers had by this time withdrawn from inspections. These six chambers had each had two visits, and a third visit took place to satisfy inspectors. The type of problems that were uncovered were mainly of staff capacity. Carlisle was not observing Arab boycotts, and had gaps in procedure for verifying the origin of manufactures, last producer's declaration, and bought in goods. In Chester and North Wales the secretary Mr. G. B. Elphick had 'imperfect knowledge of procedures', and by the second visit had passed the work to his son (J. B.); a third visit found the procedures much improved. Halifax had quickly made the improvements required after advice from Bradford. Oldham was run by local accountants, and Ossett by solicitors. Reluctantly the inspectors accepted this, but ensured procedures were improved. Rugby was run from the premises of a member, C. H. Iven & Co. Again this was accepted after procedures were improved.

A further consequence of Dixon was collection of the first systematic data on chambers. The inspection reports were followed by collection of the first comparative financial data for each ABCC member chamber, organized through the Association of Secretaries in 1973.[264] This was to lead to a regular *Census* from 1988, and formal *Benchmarking* and accreditation from 1997. Similarly the chamber secretaries set up a working party to improve the training of chamber staff. This targeted training in focal chambers, with five-day courses based at Birmingham begun in June 1972.[265] Also an attempt was made to improve standards after 1973

---

[263] ABCC, Inspection Reports, MS 17556–7.

[264] Called *Some Basic Statistics*; see Appendix 2. John Batchelder was clearly the initiator with ABCC staff in 1973, but on his own in 1976 (ABCC, *Annual Report* (1976), p. 6); he was Raymond Streat's protégé at Manchester before moving to Leeds: see Chapter 6.

[265] Association of Chamber Secretaries, *Working Party Proposals on Training Chamber Staffs*, 18 January 1972; copy at Ipswich chamber.

through a Development Fund, which helped the improvement of facilities, committees, etc.

Challenges to the ABCC and the role of London

It became common whenever chambers were called on to change that the association was also reviewed. This was natural, since the changing structure of the membership potentially affected the organization, finance, and voting of the ABCC; but it was also tactical, with some chambers using this strategy to delay development, and others needing to be bound in by seeing the centre accepting some pain. Indeed, the Dixon, Luxton, and Urwick Orr Reports had resulted in several significant changes to ABCC, as noted above.

However, in 1972–3 a much more fundamental debate about the future of ABCC developed. This was sparked by its deteriorating financial position, its incapacity to increase its income in line with the ambitions that were being placed on it, the changes perceived to be needed as a result of UK entry into the EU (on 1 January 1973), and frustrations with the overall impact of the chambers compared with CBI. The Devlin Report of 1972, which had recommended merger of ABCC and CBI, was an attempt to address the latter. This was, however, an abject failure with no changes effected, as discussed in Chapters 2 and 10; and ABCC still remained outside the NEDC. Almost all the senior staff at ABCC left or retired after the Devlin debacle,[266] and this left it vulnerable.

The London chamber appears to have begun a debate at the National Council meeting on the ABCC budget in late 1972. After Devlin and the ABCC staff resignations a specification for the new director and staff was required. London suggested that the director had to be a more prominent leader and 'outstanding man'; he 'should be the "Alf Ramsey" of the movement [a legendary England football team manager]. He should know the capabilities of the key staff in the chambers and should be able to enlist their help when necessary'; routine matters could be handled by the London chamber on behalf of ABCC, offering cost savings.[267] The ABCC had been renting premises from the London chamber since 1960, but had remained independent; the new proposal was for integration. The outcome of the debate was to set up a working group.

The working group had a difficult task, with matters coming to a head in April 1973. London had prepared a paper on the *UK Chambers of Commerce in the Context of the Devlin Commission*; Birmingham produced a *Counter-proposal to London's Paper*; there was a *Rejoinder by the London Chamber on the Birmingham Chamber's Counter Proposals*; and various correspondence, of which perhaps the most significant was Bristol chamber's promise to rejoin the ABCC if significant reforms were made. The London paper suggested four alternatives: (i) formation of a British Chamber of Commerce and Industry through merger of ABCC, London,

---

[266] ABCC, *Annual Report* (1972–3), p. 1.
[267] ABCC, National Council minutes, 8 November 1972; Westminster was not consulted on these plans.

and Westminster chambers, with other chambers and their members becoming either direct or 'derivative members'; (ii) merger of London and Westminster, but continuing to host ABCC; (iii) ABCC abolished, and other chambers affiliated to a merged London and Westminster; and (iv) do nothing. The initial debate focused on option (i). In its paper and the discussion Birmingham questioned the need for a *new* body, and noted that the proposals did nothing to address finance. The president also noted that the estimated savings of £10,000, or 10%, coming from sharing staff did nothing to meet the needs for an expanded organization. There was also much debate about the confused position of the membership of the provincial chambers within the new body.[268] In effect, although some of the National Council members were prepared to move in the direction of the first option, most opinion saw this as an attempted takeover by London, which would not solve the fundamental problems and would create many new tensions. Indeed the complex structure and lead role of London and Westminster in the new body never offered a realistic option for a voluntary system of independent local chambers.

The final outcome in June 1973 was the inevitable fudge. It was agreed that the capitation fee to ABCC would remain unchanged at £1.20; the London chamber would continue to waive rent and other costs for the ABCC offices, and not pay a capitation; the Development Fund would continue; and a plan would be developed to improve ABCC activities in Europe.[269] This is sometimes confusingly referred to as the Booth–Luxton report, but there was no such report: the conclusion was the National Council's based on the inputs from Booth (Birmingham) and Luxton (London). It was effectively no change, left ABCC with its financial tensions, but raised the alarm of provincial chambers as to London's long-term objectives. After some further tensions, ABCC moved out of the London chamber in 1976.

Public law status: the Millichap and Norvela Forster Reports

Running alongside the discussion of Urwick Orr and Devlin had been the re-emergence of the idea that chambers should seek public law status. This had received a particularly large commentary in Devlin and was emerging as the chosen option by many chambers. It was embedded in the London proposals for a new national body, though it argued that this body could be developed anyway as a preparatory stage before public law status was achieved. It became the formal policy of ABCC in 1971. The development of the debates about public law has been discussed fully in Chapter 7. Here the concern is how the debate affected ABCC.

The Millichap Report of 1976 provided the next impetus.[270] This was the outcome of a working party that adopted the position that to prepare their bid to government for public law status, the chamber system had first to reform itself. This

---

[268] ABCC, National Council minutes, 1 May 1973.
[269] ABCC, National Council minutes, 6 June 1973.
[270] *Report of the ABCC Working Party on Chamber Development*: chair K. A. Millichap, 1976, NAT. CL (76) 19; copy at Worcester chamber.

required there to be rationalization so that all recognized chambers achieved minimum standards; other chambers could join ABCC only as affiliates through the larger chambers. Millichap largely followed Dixon. Within focal chambers, all associated chambers should harmonize subscription rates. Regrouping and amalgamation was required into 30–40 chambers. Millichap identified 29 current chambers as meeting the standards and 11 more that might. It recommended an expanded inspection procedure that focused less on facilities than 'functional performance', such as response rates to consultations, number of policy initiatives, quality of contacts, effectiveness of getting member problems resolved, level of press coverage, etc. Millichap asserted that the variability of the system did not match 'the needs of business [which] did not vary in this way'. The attitude of government was anticipated to be that it 'could be persuaded in respect of the validity [of views] of the major chamber operation [but] is by no means prepared to extend such thinking to the smaller chambers which it tends to regard as a markedly inferior operation'. Hence Millichap used the supposed demands of public law status to put uncompromising pressure on the member chambers: 'any chamber which continues to fail in its duty by perpetuating low subscriptions and low standards will, one would hope, not remain in being much longer to debase the name, chamber of commerce'.[271]

The effect of Millichap was to increase the internal pressures for reform, and it certainly levered many chambers to increase their income and service offers; e.g. in Worcester it was the final pressure that led to a full-time member of staff and move of premises.[272] But the effort to strengthen the power of ABCC and intrusion of inspections raised resistance. The lack of support from government for public law also undermined the capacity of ABCC to achieve other reforms. This was not recognized sufficiently quickly, and public law continued as the main ABCC objective long after it was transparent it had no hope of success. A further report, by Norvela Forster in 1983, also advocated public law status. Taylor argues that the emphasis on standards, inspection, and affiliation for small chambers was correct. But the linking to public law status introduced a blind alley, a search for a 'holy grail' to solve the basic financial and structural problems.[273] As discussed in Chapter 7, the search for status has to be seen within the dominant paradigm of the corporatist state to gain a place on the NEDC, which all proved fruitless. This paradigm was collapsing and not until the ABCC re-initiated its *Development Strategy* in 1989–91 was the tension over public law resolved: by focusing on internal development using the chambers' own resources.

Structures in Northern Ireland and Scotland

The regional structure may have been patchy across England and Wales up to the 1990s, but in Northern Ireland and Scotland a more committed structure

---

[271] ABCC, *Annual Report* (1977), p. 3.
[272] Worcester chamber minutes, 31 October 1978.
[273] Taylor (2007), p. 91.

developed. A Northern Ireland Association of chambers was established in 1923 as a result of the creation of the Irish Republic in the South (which also developed its own association in 1923, as discussed below). This included Belfast, Londonderry, Newry, Coleraine, Ballymena, Ballymoney, Portadown, 'and others'. The ambition was to cover the eight counties by a chamber in each. In the initial structure, any votes and decisions were based on each chamber having a minimum of two representatives, with one additional representative for every 50 members in excess of 50. A majority of three-quarters of those voting was needed. This gave Belfast a dominant voice over the whole. The association was keen to retain cooperation with Dublin and chambers in the South. However, Dublin initially proposed an all-Ireland association, which Belfast felt it could not support given the differences in legislation and distinct 'community of interest, fiscal and otherwise'.[274]

The main chambers in more recent years have been Belfast and Londonderry, and these were normally the only ABCC members. In 2001, the structure was reformed so that Belfast called itself the Northern Ireland chamber, and it now claims the whole territory of the province as its catchment. But there remain about 20 other small chambers that have a variety of relations with it, ranging from formal affiliation to occasional contact.

The Scottish chambers have had an association since 1942.[275] Formed originally as a central committee, it became more formally established as an association in 1970. Prior to this Glasgow or Edinburgh usually provided a Scotland-wide view, if it was needed. Its chief initial role was liaison within Scotland, and to present a more unified and organized presence on ABCC. However, it 'did not work to the entire satisfaction of all chambers and its operational cost did not appear to chambers to be justified by the results achieved'. As a result it was replaced in 1973 by a consulting body, serviced by the Glasgow chamber; an application for Edinburgh to be the regional body for Scotland to which the other chambers would affiliate was not accepted by ABCC, nor by many of the chambers.[276] At this stage therefore Scotland had some of the halting development and fluctuating commitment of the English regions. A broad Scottish Association has, however, re-emerged since the 1980s, which does provide a level of collective marketing to members and to Scottish institutions, which became more significant after re-establishment of the Scottish parliament in 2001.

8.7 FROM THE 1991 DEVELOPMENT STRATEGY TO THE 21ST CENTURY

There is an argument that the search for public law status represents the pinnacle of the influence of the professional staff of chambers. They sought to increase membership by compulsion that they were unable to achieve by voluntary efforts,

---

[274] Belfast, *Chamber of Commerce Journal*, April (1923), p. 13.
[275] ABCC, Council minutes, 7 October 1942.
[276] Comment in South of Scotland chamber, *Annual Report* (1974), p. 7.

perhaps not understanding the 'natural' limits that seem to apply to membership market penetration (examined in Chapter 14). However, with no support from government for public law, the UK chambers have had to fall back on voluntarism: that they could convince members that they wanted to pay to join. It was the major challenge for Ron Taylor, who became the ABCC director general in July 1984, to resolve this tension. Taylor has written on his response in his 2007 book; the discussion here focuses on the overarching themes.

One critical change by the time of Taylor's appointment was that another route to chamber riches was beginning to develop. The New Training Initiative, launched by the government in 1981, had introduced schemes for which many chambers were acting as managing agents. As discussed in Chapter 13, this set on course a pattern of rapid growth of external income to many chambers that at last began to deliver the resources sought without any public law legislation. ABCC began to see this as the obviously preferred route. A second critical change achieved in the late 1980s was the reform of the articles of the ABCC to become a smaller Board rather than a very large National Council. This offered a tighter regime able to make decisions more quickly. Third, Taylor significantly expanded central ABCC staff, backed by the local chambers that were experiencing major expansions of their income. This produced the first major 'surge' in staff (from 13 to 23 over 1985–9) since that under Knowles over 1947–60. Fourth, there was the development of a separate ABCC office in Coventry, from 1989, specifically tasked with 'delivering income earning services to government, businesses and individuals', with a staff that had reached 15 by 1996.[277] This remains a key element of the BCC service and income structure. Fifth, there was the initiation of the BCC *Quarterly Economic Survey* (QES), largely the brainchild of ABCC assistant director Andrew Lansley.[278] This remains one of the key economic surveys, and was the only survey correctly to call the recessions in 1992 and 2007. Sixth, there was significant enhancement of data collection, starting with the *Census* in 1989, becoming the modern system of *Benchmarking* in 1998. But the most critical initiative was the *Development Strategy* of 1991 with a related accreditation process, which fundamentally changed the relations between the centre and localities.

The 1991 *Development Strategy*

Taylor's account of the emergence of the *Development Strategy* credits a report written in 1989 by Tony Platt, the recently appointed chief executive of the London chamber, as stimulating the then DTI Secretary of State, Nicholas Ridley, to consider the future of government support to business. Ridley called a meeting of Taylor, Roger Burman the ABCC president, and John Banham the director general of the CBI. Platt's report had argued that European businesses were advantaged by a chamber system that provided a universal and professional business information

---

[277] BCC National Council, September 1996: *Business Plan 1997*, pp. 22–6.
[278] The only previous effort was a 1960s *Commercial or Merchanting Trends Survey,* which ran for 4 years, using a sample of 500 members; ABCC, GPC minutes, 26 March 1962, 14 August 1963.

service wherever they were located which improved their competitiveness compared to the UK. Ridley asked what the ABCC and CBI were doing about this. The ABCC saw this as an opportunity, and set up a task force composed of a 'Group of Eight', which included Taylor and his deputy, Andrew Lansley, and six chief executives of the major chambers.[279] For a while this group toyed with arguments to lobby for hypothecated revenue from the non-domestic rates or other taxes, but was persuaded instead to look for transition support from DTI to encourage chamber development.[280] This period of 1989–90 was a critical one in the Thatcher government, and Lansley argues that a much more ambitious opportunity for chambers had been opening, but was closed when Nicholas Ridley was forced to resign over unrelated matters.[281]

Instead of major government support, the chambers had to establish their own *Development Strategy*. The Group of Eight, chiefly drawing on Taylor's vision, focused on: defining standards, accrediting chambers that met the standards, bringing all major chambers back into membership (ten important chambers were unaffiliated in 1989–90),[282] encouraging merger or collaboration between large and small chambers, and drawing up a map of the geographical shape of the network. The first phase of developments was based on concepts of 'critical mass' and filling the map, which were provided by a consultancy report commissioned from the current author: the so-called 'Bennett Report' of 1991.[283] Subsequently, critical mass was moderated to emphasize service effectiveness and delivery. Another part of the vision was improving inter-chamber electronic cooperation through a 'Chambernet', which was extremely innovative for the period before the universal internet. The DTI was persuaded to put £2.3 million into helping this development, about half of which went into Chambernet, with the rest going into a 'certification training fund', which amounted to about £200,000 per year over 1991–6.[284] As noted by Taylor, this was 'miserly' compared to the £1.3 billion then being put into TECs, or the £117 million initially invested in Business Link in 1993. But for a poorly resourced system like chambers it was critical.

The strategy was implemented from 1991, and was built into the ABCC constitution through amendment to its articles. The most critical change was to replace earlier rather bland statements of the service cover necessary for a chamber

---

[279] Lansley subsequently became an MP in 1986, and Secretary of State for Health in 2010; he was promoter of the Chamber Title Bill in 1999 (see Chapter 7); the others were Geoffrey Hulse (Nottingham), Ewan Marwick (Glasgow), Tony Platt (London), Leslie Robinson (Thames-Chiltern), Simon Sperryn (Manchester), and John Warburton (Birmingham): see Taylor (2007), p. 116; Ridley makes no mention of this in his autobiography.

[280] See Taylor (2007), pp. 116–18; advice from Edmund Dell, MP and former Treasury Minister, president of London chamber, persuaded the group that the Treasury would never agree hypothecation.

[281] Comment to author, June 2009; see Chapter 13.

[282] Bristol, Dorset, Dundee, Gloucester, Kirklees, Leicester, Milton Keynes, Southampton, Sussex (FSI), and Swindon.

[283] Bennett (1991); ABCC (1991) *Effective Business Support: A UK Strategy*; and ABCC (1992) *Effective Business Support: A UK Strategy: Phase 2. Financial Times*, 26 February 1991; also Grant (1993), pp. 119–21.

[284] Taylor (2007), p. 119; and ABCC/BCC Company Accounts.

to be affiliated with a more precise definition set by the council, with failure to meet standards met by a review by a senior member of staff at the ABCC, with recommended steps for improvement.[285] An important further support was a manual for *Managing the Accredited Chamber*, disseminated in October 1992, and a draft *Memorandum and Articles for a Core Chamber*.[286] The new articles of association from 1994, when the title was also changed from ABCC to BCC, set standards covering five points: a chamber must demonstrate its ability to: (i) represent the views of its business community; (ii) supply information, advice, and assistance; (iii) encourage member companies to join together in promotional activity and systems for mutual support; (iv) aid the development of international trade; and (v) participate in activities to develop and improve the general prosperity of its area, e.g. cooperation with local authorities, education, training, and urban regeneration.[287] This was significantly further strengthened in 1996 when revision of the articles introduced an approval and accreditation process, and restricted members of the association to only those chambers that were accredited from 1997.[288]

The *Development Strategy*'s successes and failures

There were many successes from this strategy. First, most of the major non-affiliated chambers joined the ABCC. Second, and most important, the development of standards and accreditation took shape, beginning in 1992–4 with the new standards statement, and has become embedded in the system since 1998, once the initial accreditation process had been completed. The initial accreditation standards were based on size criteria, with a capacity to grow, and minimum services of: information, representation, international trade, training, membership services, business development, marketing, and staff development.[289] The process was based on a mixture of documentary materials and inspection (covering 1–3 days involving scrutiny of paper records, interviews with staff, written agreements with adjacent chambers on agreed boundaries, and evidence of customer satisfaction surveys).[290] These reflected the Bennett Report, with the addition of important pressures to sort out boundary overlaps and focus on members' satisfaction.

Third, there were many mergers and new collaborations between chambers that, for the first time, systematically changed the national map and provided more uniform services over larger areas, covering the whole country (see Figure 14.3). Some of the mergers occurred soon after 1990 (of which the most significant were

---

[285] *Memorandum and Articles of Association of ABCC*, 5 December 1993; earlier service standards in ABCC: *Minimum Requirements for Chamber of Commerce Services*, 14 December 1992.

[286] Manual prepared by David Senior (formerly deputy director London chamber), and Brian Armatys (hon. legal adviser Sheffield chamber); Armatys also prepared the *Memorandum* earlier in 1992.

[287] Slightly abbreviated from revised BCC *Byelaws of National Council, Explanatory Memorandum*, 8 September 1994; these were essentially the same as used in the 1999 Title Act, see Chapter 7.

[288] *Memorandum and Articles of Association of BCC*, as adopted 23 January 1997.

[289] BCC, *Accreditation and Approval Guidance to Chambers*, 17 February 1994.

[290] BCC, *Accreditation and Approval Guidance to Chambers*, approved 5 December 1996.

the North East chamber formed by merger of Tyneside and Teesside; London and Westminster; Thames-Chiltern, Guildford, Reading, Oxford, and Surrey).[291] Some occurred later, such as Greater Manchester chamber embracing most of the metropolitan area, the North-East Lancashire chamber (Blackburn and Burnley), West Lancashire (Lancaster and Preston), Black Country (Wolverhampton, Walsall, Dudley, and Sandwell); and some were stimulated by TEC/Business Link boundaries (such as Hereford and Worcester, or Coventry and Warwickshire), or the abolition of TECs and Business Link (as for many of the Manchester mergers, and London with Croydon). Despite some de-mergers after the abolition of TECs, there had been a reduction of chamber numbers from about 90–100 in 1990, to about 65 by 2000, and 54 in 2010.

Fourth, there was the first real effort by BCC to fill some 'gaps on the map': a problem first identified in 1882. The most significant of these were initiatives in Kent and London. In Kent, with DTI and Kent County Council support, and involving the current author, a new Kent-wide chamber was established in 1995. Although this was disbanded in 1998, three groupings of sub-regional Kent chambers have emerged as a stronger network. In London, the Westminster and London chambers merged in 1994, and a structure of small local chambers linked to London was established, again adapting consultancy inputs from the current author.[292] For the first time this gave a structure that tried to cover the whole metropolis. In other areas the main efforts were to use existing larger chambers to reach out. Thus after the failure of the Cardiff chamber in 2006, and difficulties of the North Hampshire chamber in 2009, bids were invited from other chambers to run the chambers there.

Fifth, the accreditation process showed adaptability to cover the increasing number of arrangements that were being negotiated between chambers, TECs, and Business Links. The shape of the system itself, under plans to merge these organizations together, led to a new *'Future Chamber'* strategy over 1995–7. The *Future Chamber* was essentially a means to encourage mergers of TECs and chambers (to form CCTEs). This was succeeded by the *'21ˢᵗ Century Chamber'*, over 1997–2001, which developed the strong vision of a chamber-plus-TEC-plus-Business Link as the desired model. These visions, which are discussed at length in Chapter 13, collapsed in 2001 with the abolition of TECs, and in retrospect the most lasting contribution of this period was to find a way to help embed the accreditation processes in all affiliated chambers. But as Taylor notes, the debate was very divisive, over the role of TECs and other matters, and 'deeply held differences had to be reconciled'.[293] These differences saw some chambers leaving BCC after 2000, some of which had only recently joined. The critical debates were over: how chamber standards were defined; should government schemes be

---

[291] See Appendix 1; Taylor (2007), p. 125 covers mergers and changes 1989–99.
[292] *Kent Chamber of Commerce Development Study* (DTI, Kent TEC, Kent County Council, and Kent Federation of Chambers of Commerce, 1992); *London Chambers of Commerce Development Study* (LSE for Chambers of London, Westminster, and Croydon).
[293] Taylor (2007), p. 150.

included and become mandatory; and should measurement be based on abstract criteria of size and activities, or through assessment of service performance? The abolition of TECs closed the former debate; for BCC accreditation the emphasis moved towards greater emphasis on performance, which was a repeat of the evolution after the Dixon Report of 1967.

But Chambernet UK Ltd was a failure. It was set up as a separate company, with shares held by chambers and the BCC, but went into liquidation in September 1995. It proved incapable of building the IT network between members originally envisaged and was delivered too late and over cost. The project foundered on inadequate local chamber databases that were incompatible, and over-optimistic timetables and mis-design of bespoke software (familiar in IT procurement projects). Taylor argues that it was critical mistake because the chambers 'lost not only money; they lost credibility with government ministers at a time when ministers were promoting Business Links'.[294] Given the disparity of resources involved, and the limited achievements of Business Link databases, this was not a fair comparison, but it left BCC and chambers in a weakened position, absorbing £500,000 of losses.[295] But most critically it removed a database initiative at a time when chambers had been trying to build their capacity against challenges from Business Link. BCC and chambers were then forced to rely on whatever Business Link began to provide, which was often not fit for purpose, and was in any case lost when Business Link was absorbed into regional structures after 2005.

The concept of 'critical mass'

The first phase of chamber development after 1991 drew on a concept of 'critical mass'. This had been in Taylor's mind, and perhaps drew from his earlier experience of the Dixon and subsequent reports. The 'Bennett Report' was commissioned to define what it meant. As noted earlier, the concept of a 'sufficient income' to assure 'effectiveness' had been first stated by London chamber in 1882. But the issue of sufficiency of resource was ducked in 1917; dropped from the conditions for chamber approval over 1918–36; and did not re-emerge until Knowles raised it in 1949. The first explicit ABCC statement of a critical mass target is in the 1967 Dixon Report: 'We are convinced that there is a minimum size below which a chamber cannot command the resources to provide adequate facilities and staff to function properly. For this reason we believe that mergers must be brought about or that small chambers must be required to make properly financed serving arrangements with larger chambers in the area.'[296]

This history was not known to the author at the time he undertook the study for ABCC.[297] Hence, starting from scratch, an attempt was first made to identify from

---

[294] Taylor (2007), p. 129.
[295] See e.g. *The Times*, 7 February 1995: 'Chambernet of horrors'.
[296] *The Functions and Structure of Chambers of Commerce*; Dixon Report.
[297] When the author's research on chamber history began in 2005 the earliest data available was from the chamber secretary surveys of 1976 and 1982: see Appendix 2.

the 1989–90 ABCC *Census* data, and new surveys, whether there was any pattern in the provision of services, income or chamber staff that suggested there was a threshold which defined a minimum critical mass to operate an effective chamber. Using the data from the 94 affiliated and ten major non-affiliated chambers, various frequency distributions and statistical analyses were undertaken. The conclusion was remarkably similar to that deriving from the numerous previous commentaries reviewed above: that chambers were highly varied, there was a distinction between small and large, but many chambers defied classification! To make progress the Bennett Report used multiple criteria, finding that, although the thresholds were fuzzy, it was possible to define an approximate minimum critical mass based on a combination of staff numbers, income, office accommodation, and membership size.

A further significant step was, however, required. A clear part of the ABCC objective was to define a proposed new map for the chamber network, meeting the need for chambers to cooperate, merge, or expand their territorial coverage to the whole UK land mass. This brought to light a new set of issues that had been largely neglected in earlier chamber discussions: market penetration, scope for market development, and how territories should be fitted together; and whether local authority boundaries should be used, or some other basis. A survey of the chambers produced what became the first map of the chambers to display catchment areas; shown in Figure 14.2. It demonstrated that chambers focused on the individual towns and cities in which they had existed from their outset. This was their 'core' territory. Many chambers claimed much wider areas, sometimes entirely unrealistically, which in many cases related to local government at the upper tier of counties. But there was overlapping and competition between chambers in some areas, notably the conurbations; some chambers were entirely surrounded by others; and there were blank areas, chiefly in parts of Wales, Scotland, South-West England, and rural areas. This pattern was a deficiency, but it also provided an opportunity, since there were many potential businesses that were currently largely untapped as members. The territorial cover is discussed in detail in Chapter 14. In 1990 the outcome was a proposed chamber map for the whole country, with a detailed transition strategy for each area, recognizing that detailed negotiations would have to take place between chambers in each area over potential collaboration or merger, and how marketing could be expanded effectively into the 'empty spaces'.[298]

As a result of this analysis, multiple criteria for 'critical mass' were defined, including the extent of market penetration. This was coupled with a new call to raise subscriptions to more realistic levels. The final set of minimum criteria were:

(i) Staff of 30–4 full time equivalent (excluding government funded posts)
(ii) Gross income of £1 million (excluding government support)
(iii) Accommodation of 8000 sq. ft.

[298] Given in full in appendix to Bennett (1991).

(iv) Membership of 1000, with scope to reach at least 2000–3000
(v) Catchment area of 10,000–50,000 businesses.

Given the total size of the British business population, the last two criteria would provide scope for a chamber system of about 50–5, with 30 of the current chambers coming close to meeting the full set of criteria, plus two of special status for the Channel Islands and Isle of Man. The remaining 60 needed significant developments, especially in areas with no current chamber strong enough to build on: notably Kent, Devon, and Cornwall. The criteria were based on a 'self-sustaining' system, without government support. If government support was available, then it might be possible for smaller chambers in some areas to reach the standard in a non-self-sustaining way. This proved to be the case, as TECs and Business Links developed, but proved to be a short-term pot of gold.

As noted above, the concept of a critical mass experienced valid criticism that it was crude and measured inputs not performance; but at the time it was the most ready way forward. The first four criteria were used initially in the accreditation standards, but the accommodation test was soon dropped, and after 1995 the other criteria were replaced by detailed inspection of service performance.[299] The proposed map also suffered trenchant criticism. Although in many presentations around the country in individual chambers, the author found little objection to the need to extend markets, chambers found collaboration, and especially merger, very difficult to accept. It was nevertheless pressed hard by BCC, with continuous assessments made of local developments, and continued pressures from central staff. The formation of the North-East chamber in 1995 was a prominent step forward, providing experience to the whole system. However, many boundary issues became convolved with TEC and Business Link developments. This gave some small chambers a lifeline. It also muddied the waters of a 'self-sustaining' system, and only after the collapse of Business Link contracts after 2005 was a start made on re-confronting a self-sustaining map. Subsequent analysis by the author developed some of the critical mass concepts further, whilst a PhD thesis by Will Bratton in 2000, in collaboration with BCC, provided a number of scenarios for improving the definition of critical mass and defining a chamber map based on optimal market area algorithms.[300] The negotiations on the ground over local structures continue up to present and, as is characteristic of a voluntary system, will doubtless be subject to redefinition into the future.

Mission tensions 1997–2001

After Labour was elected in 1997 initial commitment to TECs soon evaporated, resulting in their abolition in 2001. Business Link was merged into Regional Development Agencies (RDAs) in phases after 2005. The budgets for contracts

---

[299] BCC, *Revised Accreditation Criteria*, 5 September 1995; BCC, *Report of Accreditation Standards Working Party*, November 1999.
[300] Bratton (2000); also see Bratton, Bennett, and Robson (2003); and Chapters 14 and 15.

to chambers increased rapidly until 2001, and then diminished radically. After 2010, the RDAs were abolished and replaced by LEPs. These were crisis points for many individual chambers, as outlined in Chapter 13, but the BCC also found itself in a difficult position. Its new director general, following Ron Taylor's retirement in July 1998, had been Chris Humphries, a former Hertfordshire TEC chief executive, and former chair of the TEC National Council since it was formed in 1993. He was attuned to the *21st Century Chamber* strategy, which was itself tuned to TECs. He embedded BCC in many TEC and related projects, and was seen as particularly supportive of CCTEs—perhaps to the disadvantage of independent chambers.

Humphries was very much an appointment to satisfy the new chief executives of the CCTEs. Indeed Taylor's retirement was a few years early in order to satisfy CCTE demands for higher profile and someone who was 'one of them'. The CCTE executives were largely new to chambers; less concerned with 'membership' and more attuned to services, especially government contracted services, and with large public-sector backed salaries.[301] When Humphries left, David Lennan was recruited as the new director general in June 2001, specifically tasked to get the *21st Century Chamber* underway, raise the chambers' profile, and manage the change process.[302] From a background in large bank and local authority organizations, he recruited two project managers to assist, replacing previous posts in London and Coventry. He also tried to act in a directive way, 'commanding' chambers to respond. This was bound to raise antagonisms. It led to an eruption from the grass roots, where even the mildest local chamber personalities called for Lennan's resignation. Bill Midgeley and Isabella Moore (respective presidents in the North-East and Coventry and Warwickshire) forced the issue.

In any case the whole previous strategy was blown awry by the abolition of TECs, and hence CCTEs, at this time. No longer was there a platform of major government support available, much of the *21st Century Chamber* became obsolete overnight, and many new chamber staff were ill-suited to the more traditional role of managing a slim-line organization where voluntarism and a much lower level of government income were to become the order of the day; a good example of managerial 'sorting' as discussed in Chapter 3. Some chambers resigned from BCC, or threatened to do so. Lennan and BCC agreed a severance package in April 2002, four days before the BCC annual conference, over 'disagreements about the speed and direction of change'.[303] The press cover at the time stated that 'his downfall was due to his inability to raise the chambers profile as effectively' as the CBI's Digby Jones, and his slow progress with modernizing BCC.[304] Lennan blamed lack of support from the Board and president, Anthony Goldstone. He acknowledged that he had devoted too little time to the BCC board, perhaps only 5%, whilst he

---

[301] Comments to author by David Frost, 19 January 2010; also see Chapter 6.
[302] BCC job specification, 2001; also *Financial Times*, 'Champion of joined-up thinking', 28 June 2001.
[303] Quoted from John Lockett, BCC president; in Taylor (2007), p. 156.
[304] *Financial Times*, 'Sacked chambers chief "eclipsed" by media-savvy rival', 20 April 2002; also *Financial Times*, 22 August 2002, 'Business chief sacked for not moving quickly to cut costs'.

estimated that Humphries had given about 10–25%, and Taylor about 30–40%. This was in line with his understanding that he was in a command position, and had to develop more income for BCC independently of subscriptions and accreditation fees.[305]

Looking back at this unhappy episode, two forces were at work: first, a victory of those local chambers who viewed reliance on government as dangerous; second, some reversal of the pattern of developments since Arthur Knowles took charge in 1947, which had seen the professionals at the centre progressively take over from the elected board representatives: a great deal of the revolt from the grass-roots local level was led by chamber presidents as much as local chief executives who wanted more value for money from the centre, to cut its budget, and resented government involvement. Press comment focused on the reforms of the chambers being 'perceived as too radical by the "bunch of old fogeys" on the board'.[306]

Reconstruction after 2002

The new director general of BCC from May 2002 was David Frost.[307] As a former chief executive of the chamber at Walsall, he was used to managing on a shoestring, but he had then become chief executive at Coventry and Warwickshire CCTE, a very large organization. He represented both camps, and was a reliable pair of hands when the BCC could no longer take risks. Frost rapidly responded to the concerns of chambers, immediately consulting them on what was wanted. They jointly identified: the need for a much higher profile for BCC and its policy work; a small but effective range of commercial services; and an end to the 'us and them' which had been felt to enter the network. The first female president of BCC, from September 2003, Isabella Moore and former Coventry and Warwickshire chamber president, also breathed fresh air into the organization, de facto taking over from Goldstone a year early in August 2002.[308] All but one of the BCC board members left at the same time. Frost was confronted with a financial crisis.[309] He immediately cut costs at the centre of BCC, the staff was slimmed from 42 to 32, cheaper offices were found, and the Coventry office was reconstituted to generate more income for the network.

Frost and Moore can be credited with rescuing BCC from collapse. In 2002 and 2003, 18 of the local chambers had been withholding subscriptions or had been granted discounts. Some had been openly threatening to affiliate with CBI.[310] By 2004 most were back in membership, and by the end of 2009 all major chambers had rejoined, including Plymouth and Exeter through a Bristol-led South West Group, Southampton, Mid Yorkshire, and Northern Ireland. In 2005 a

[305] Comments to author by David Lennan, 20 August 2002.
[306] *Financial Times*, 20 April 2002.
[307] Initially Frost's was as a short-term part-time appointment to rescue BCC; but he subsequently applied for the full-time post when it was advertised, and was appointed in January 2003.
[308] *Financial Times*, 23 August 2002, 'Sent from Coventry'.
[309] *Financial Times*, 23 May 2002, 'Fresh blow hits chamber lobby as commercial partner fails'.
[310] *Financial Times*, 30 August 2002, 'BCC faces wave of defections'.

development fund of £70,000 for local initiatives was being offered by BCC. Although not unprecedented as claimed, it was much more significant than an earlier initiative offered over 1973–6.[311] The central staff could again be increased, to 37 by 2008. Frost initiated a highly successful national competition and awards ceremony in 2004 to stimulate both chamber development and local businesses, with categories for best membership services, best campaign, best international trade services, etc., and overall best chamber. This performed critical roles in strengthening bonds across the network, raising the profile of chambers, and encouraging the standards and accreditation process. The overall best chambers in 2004–10 were, respectively, North East, Rotherham, Thames Valley, St Helens, Sheffield, Edinburgh, and St Helens again in 2010—demonstrating the diverse range of chamber quality. A 'Young Chamber' organization was established in 2008 to encourage school-aged interest in representation. Further mergers and developments along the lines of the 1991 *Development Strategy* have occurred.

The tensions of national and local continue, as they have since the foundation of the Association in 1860. One of the key challenges has been to manage an increasingly independent group of chambers that represented the 'core cities' chosen by government as the key locations for a range of promotional activities. The core city programme, discussed in Chapter 13, led a new group of chambers to ask 'why do we need BCC'. With the reduced number of member chambers (as a result of accreditation and merger processes), each member chamber has had to pay more. Even if they have a larger membership combining several previous chambers, core city and large chambers still looked at the absolute sum and began baulking at having to pay individual subscriptions of £60,000–75,000 to BCC.

Partly responding to these pressures, in 2009 a new corporate governance structure for BCC was implemented,[312] which has the main features of: (i) a reduced board size (down to 9, from 24), made up of six business members (mainly from chamber membership; nominated by a nominations committee) capable of taking on the role of vice-presidency, plus the president and two executive directors from the BCC staff (the director general and director of finance); and (ii) an advisory council, made up of local business members (one elected from each region, and excluding chamber staff and executives), plus three elected chief executives, and the president and vice-president. These changes partly responded to the 2006 Companies Act over the role of non-executive directors and conflicts of interests. However, the aim was to radically refocus BCC activities: the board is chiefly tasked with legal director responsibilities, planning, and overseeing management of BCC; whilst the advisory council is the connection with the network. The staff was also restructured in 2010, with new directors of operations, international trade, and policy. Five main roles, or 'pillars', for BCC have been specified: international trade, accreditation, policy, governance, and commercial services.

It remains to be seen how far these changes will satisfy the local chambers and their members. The restructuring has delivered what many chambers wanted, with

---

[311] For a summary of the period 2001–7, see John Lockett, in Taylor (2007), pp. 156–8.
[312] *Articles of Association of BCC* (2009).

all disaffiliated chambers rejoining by 2010. But the structure contains dangers of disconnecting the BCC from the underlying chamber structure. It is potentially more highly centralized than at any time in the past. Also, as recognized at the 2009 AGM, the nominations committee process for 'parachuting' new blood experienced early difficulties. The commitment of the new BCC board will be tested against future challenges.

With the demise of TECs and major Business Link funding, the chambers and BCC have been re-confronted with the challenges they faced in 1990–3: to find resources from their own self-sustainable efforts, under greater pressure from reduced government support. In studies of management strategy, enterprises in difficulties frequently take wrong routes. Collins argues that often decline is self-inflicted. Enterprises seek salvation in merger or acquisition, trying to transform the business at a stroke; embark on a radical restructuring that ignores the underlying strengths and weaknesses; undermine momentum by constant change; try to make dramatic leaps in strategy or technology; or recruit new visionary leaders who have no understanding of the business. All these strategies usually fail, compared with determination and discipline to focus on the core business using the innovative components of insider knowledge. The best leaders able to halt a downward spiral are usually insiders who know the strengths of the business and rebuild it by eradicating the weaknesses and innovate within the existing framework.[313]

In developments of BCC after 1992, the strategies of radical change, acquisition of NCT (see below), and 'visionary' leaders have all failed to deliver. In retrospect the evolution chimes with Collins's stages of decline: stages 1 and 2 the 'hubris born of success' and 'undisciplined pursuit of more' quite nicely fit the period of CCTEs driven by government largesse. The period 1998–2002 under Humphries and Lennan fits the 'denial of risk and peril'. In effect, the period under Frost and Moore after 2002 offered 'insider' reconstruction; and it was successful, as suggested by Collins's model. But the new BCC structure since 2009 appears to have some dangers of turning the clock back, into Collins's stage 4: 'grasping for salvation', with radical change and new visionary leaders who fail to work from the membership and network using the strengths of the local level. With the appointment of a new president, and a new director general, in mid-2011, a challenging period looms. Despite these difficulties, the lasting contribution of 1990–2011 has been that accreditation of service performance has become well established, the map is covered, and the chambers have gained a higher profile in lobbying and influence.

8.8 MERGER OF ABCC AND NCT

Separately from the changes within ABCC itself was another debate about how it might work more closely with NCT and the chambers of trade. Talks about closer

[313] See Collins (2009); and more detailed examples in Baden-Fuller and Stopford (1994).

cooperation had been ongoing since the 1950s, and more actively in the 1970s around the Devlin and Bolton reports. The ABCC and NCT had generally maintained a working relationship often with mutual support to each other's campaigns. The 1920s ABCC Improvement Committee defined the relationships at the local level, reiterated by Urwick Orr, that 'where no chamber of trade existed the chamber of commence should recruit, elsewhere they should meet and work together where necessary but not compete'.[314] Merger was considered on several occasions, probably most strongly in 1969, but always rejected.

The first serious proposals for merger developed in 1983–4.[315] However, information about discussions leaked out in 1985, which sparked internal resistance, and both organizations were forced to put discussions on hold.[316] However, the worsening financial situation of NCT, perhaps exacerbated by the leaked press reports that encouraged some CoTs to lapse from NCT, and the growing financial strength and restructuring of ABCC, made further explorations attractive. Moreover, Ron Taylor, the director general of ABCC, who had been involved in the 1984 talks, was a plausible and inviting magnet, and the ABCC *Development Strategy* foresaw smaller chambers affiliating to BCC chambers. It seemed as if all the advantages of a national organization could be gained at little cost to CoTs, and the local bodies could carry on more or less as before. At one level this was an unchallenging offer. Merger of ABCC and NCT was agreed in 1992 and redrafted Articles of the BCC permitted any NCT chamber to join. But at another level, the new ABCC Articles required that by 1994 CoTs had to be incorporated, had to pay the ABCC affiliation fee, have salaried staff, and had to satisfy minimum service standards for information provision, export assistance, business advice, and contacts with government departments and other bodies; demands which most CoTs could never meet.[317]

Taylor's retrospective comments on these developments emphasize the rationality of the process. 'With the benefit of hindsight the development of the two streams is a matter of regret. The NCT Chambers were undoubtedly serving the needs of local small businesses but in the long term the proliferation of small underresourced chambers of commerce/trade damaged the standing of the entire chamber of commerce movement. The similarities in title . . . served to confuse not only potential member businesses, but also the politicians and the journalists'.[318] His subsequent private view was that 'the NCT was a dying organisation in the 1980s. Its decision to sell its offices in Henley and buy another in Reading wrapped up needed assets in buildings; it was losing members, and was losing its clout politically after a very good period; it had high staff and pension costs from the past; and the ABCC appealed to the ambitious executives of the NCT chambers, of which there were a growing number, e.g. in Colchester.' Taylor also had no doubt about the

[314] ABCC National Council, minutes, 28 July and 6 August 1969.
[315] *Possible Merger of ABCC and NCT*: NCT Minutes, 20 November 1984; MS 29343/15.
[316] 'Business Chambers may unite', *Times*, 9 January 1985; 'Small business groups may merge', *Financial Times*, 10 January 1985 (with NCT Minutes; MS 29343/15).
[317] *Memorandum and Articles of Association of ABCC*, with amendments, 5 December 1993.
[318] Taylor (2007), pp. 65–7.

character of the merger as a 'takeover', as seen by ABCC. It had the desired effect of 'taking out a competitor', which would lead to a strengthened position for ABCC. 'The plan was that over 4–5 years the NCT would fold into ABCC and local CoTs would join local groups of chambers of commerce, thus strengthening the whole chamber system. The NCT was an asset; which without the merger would have wasted.'[319] It did indeed fold into the ABCC and transferred assets of £116,457 in investments and £220,000 in property.[320] This was a critical resource to overcome subsequent financial crises at ABCC/BCC.

How far was Taylor's analysis correct? Have the small chambers strengthened the BCC, did they fold successfully into a single national body, and have the small chambers been strengthened or weakened as a result? Two outcomes are clear. First, whilst the merger took the entirety of the NCT into the BCC, at a local level CoT affiliation has been patchy. By 2010 BCC had 168 affiliates through its local chambers. This is an important resource, delivering 23,600 members in contact (or over 20% additional to the membership of BCC's own chambers).[321] For the affiliates, membership of BCC offers a link with an organization of national status, and a wider network of services; it also fosters local cooperation with the larger BCC chambers.[322]

However, many small local chambers remain outside formal contact with BCC. No BCC data exist on other non-affiliated chambers, nor is it possible to be sure how many of these are former NCT chambers. They probably numbered about 400–500 in 2010. Hence a level of local competition and confusion has continued. Moreover, the distinctions between accredited, affiliated, and other chambers remain unclear to the outsider: most MPs and local councillors cannot distinguish between accredited and non-accredited chambers.[323] Thus whilst the merger with NCT certainly strengthened BCC as a single national chamber voice, at local level the two systems of chambers often still remain, as before. Even smaller BCC chambers, such as the historic Jersey and Guernsey chambers, 'could exist without the BCC but, as the issues are similar, BCC provides a good sounding board, and is also important for certification services'.[324] Hence for the future there is still much to be played for at the local level.

8.9 THE IRISH CHAMBERS ASSOCIATION

The development of the Irish chambers association after 1923 also demonstrates the dynamics of voluntary chamber systems, the tensions between the centre and local, and between the larger and smaller chambers. Before 1923, development of

---

[319] Ron Taylor comments to author, November 2006.
[320] But with about £60,000 in legal and other costs; ABCC, *Accounts* (1992, 1993); Companies House.
[321] BCC, *Benchmarking* statistics.
[322] e.g. comments to author from Simon Judd, chair of Lymington town chamber, June 2005.
[323] Mekic (2007), chapter 7; also see Chapter 17 below.
[324] Comments to author by Clive Spears, president of the Jersey chamber, April 2009.

Irish chambers was aligned with the UK, with most of the historic and major chambers becoming active members of the ACC. The Irish chambers participated in the UK government's 'Form K' scheme until 1921. Even after Irish independence there were frequent exchanges and consultations with the UK chambers, which have continued up to the present. Particularly prominent was coordination in the late 1960s and early 1970s over entry to the European Community, and threats by the UK government subsequently to withdraw.[325] Bilateral relations between individual chambers also continued; for example, Cork benchmarked itself against both Dublin and Bristol in the 1960s in terms of its expenditure and income;[326] Dublin established a connection with Glasgow, Manchester, Birmingham, and Liverpool in 1998, so that members could use services on a reciprocal basis (information, events, room hire, courses, libraries, databases, and credit checks).[327] Also there have been a growing number of all-Ireland initiatives. Although most have been mainly symbolic developments from the peace process, the border-region chambers have engaged in significant collaboration, and the two chamber systems have jointly pressed for improvements of trunk roads and rail links.

Early Irish development

With the establishment of the Irish Republic, the Dublin chamber set about stimulating an Irish association, which was founded in 1923 as the Association of Chambers of Commerce of the Irish Free State, referred to as Chambers of Commerce of Ireland (CCI), and after 2005 as Chambers Ireland (CI). There had been attempts at Irish cooperation before: their London agent in 1822–3; and in 1907 there was a proposed Association of Irish Chambers, but this collapsed— the Waterford chamber for one 'disagreed with the lines proposed'.[328] The initial Association proposals made by Dublin in 1923 were also not acceptable to the other Irish chambers; seen as too ambitious and centred on Dublin. The amended format focused on providing voice for the chambers as a whole 'separately or unitedly', to prepare Bills for parliament, establish a Dublin Office with secretary, 'to attain those advantages by united action which each chamber would have difficulty in accomplishing in its separate capacity'.[329] Both Cork chambers and most other major chambers joined. The first secretary J. R. Clark, stayed until 1928, when he moved to become secretary of the Dublin chamber.[330] The subscriptions for chambers were tiered, and derived from the ABCC history. There was a minimum of IR£21 for chambers with a membership of up to 50

---

[325] Minutes of Dublin and Cork chambers; e.g. in 1974 the Dublin, Cork, and London chambers liaised closely over harmonization of EEC law and other issues.
[326] Cork chamber, financial accounts and treasurer's minute book, 1960–8.
[327] Dublin chamber, *Annual Report* (1998).
[328] Waterford chamber minutes, 14 January and 16 December 1907.
[329] *Memorandum and Articles of the Association of Chambers of Commerce of the Irish Free State*, 12 July 1923: Articles 3(c)–(g).
[330] Dublin chamber, *Report of Council* (1929).

(though this could be varied by the Council to a final minimum of 10 guineas for very small chambers). The general scale was based on a capitation fee of 5s. for the first 200 chamber members, 2s. 6d. for the next 200–500 members, and 1s. 3d. for members over 500, with an adjustment for life members, with numbers based on audited accounts submitted to the CCI. The different fee levels and chamber sizes provided a scaled representation of up to 25 members (one vote), 25–50 (two votes), 50–200 (three votes), 200–500 (four votes), every additional 100 members (one vote), with the same scale for number of representatives on the CCI council. Individual firms and business members could join as associate members at a fee of one guinea per year if they were members of local chambers, or in locations where no chamber existed, with the intent that this might stimulate chamber formation.[331]

Tensions over costs emerged quickly, and continue to the present: an endemic pattern in any voluntary system. Local chambers might want the Association to do things, but they were frequently unwilling to pay for it. The new association was criticized by Cork[332] as requiring 'subscriptions in excess of the absolute necessities of the moment'. Cork proposed a reduced schedule of subscriptions: of 2s. 6d. for the first 100 members, 1s. 3d. for 100–200 members, and 1s. for over 200 members, and that 'the expenditure of the association be regulated'. However no change was made and the Cork chamber had to double its subscriptions to two guineas in 1926.[333] Limerick thought its £21 subscription 'rather large' in 1933, but reluctantly agreed to pay.[334] The first revision of the formal structure was new articles of association in 1953. The same minimum IR£21 was used, but the capitation scale was increased to 5s. for membership up to 200, 2s. 6d. for 200–500 members, and 1s. 3d. for membership over 500. The voting and representatives remained unchanged for the smallest chambers, but three votes and three representatives now covered memberships of 50–100, with four votes and representatives for 100–200, and then one vote and representative for each additional 100 members.[335] The scales of 1923 and 1953 favoured the smaller chambers.

The association was initially chiefly a means to organise meetings and exchange views. But in 1952 it launched a *Chamber of Commerce Journal* as an organ of the association, as a 'regular means of keeping in touch with all chamber activities in Ireland . . . and for the expression of the opinions of the association and of individual chambers'.[336] However, this stated that it was 'issued by the Dublin chamber of commerce' on its title-page, and it rapidly evolved to become the chamber's journal, since it was the host and main financier of the project. The association's

---

[331] *Memorandum and Articles*, Articles 10 (a)–(h).

[332] Cork chamber, Council minutes, 3 May 1928; the chamber had an overdraft of IR£490 at the time, with income from assets withheld by its trustees; see Chapter 11.

[333] Cork chamber, Council minutes, 24 February 1926; by 1930 the subscription was reduced back to one guinea when the Cork trustees released more of the asset income.

[334] Limerick chamber minutes, 30 October 1933.

[335] *Articles of Association of Chambers of Commerce of the Irish Free State*, 1953.

[336] President of the association, J. O'Keefe, Dublin *Chamber of Commerce Journal*, 1(1) January (1952), p. 3.

own journal was relaunched in the 1990s to differentiate it from the Dublin *Journal*, most recently titled *In Business* (a quarterly). A *Yearbook* has been produced since 1993, which is a publicity document and synopsis of activity and awards.

The association was not a strong lobby in its early years. Even in 1969 Cork chamber felt that its only major submission on national policy was on the government's annual budget, and 'the collection and preparation of this submission appears to be carried out in the most perfunctory way' with little or no involvement from member chambers.[337] The tensions in the Irish association were/are similar to those in the UK: to maintain coherence when there is such a range of size and capacity between the chambers, and to avoid disaffiliation of the main local chambers. Like London's dominance in the UK, Dublin dominates in the Irish Republic, and there were (and still are) only five or six other chambers of major substance: Cork, Limerick, Waterford, Galway, Drogheda, and Dundalk. But there are about 25 other significant chambers, and 60–70 other chambers, mostly very small, as well as many town traders' chambers. The structure of Irish politics means that all 164 MPs tend to want a chamber in their area and, as in the UK, usually cannot distinguish between accredited and other chambers. Also, with a proportional system of electoral representation, the last candidate elected often depends on as little as 100 votes. Business organizations, such as chambers, are viewed as very important influences on marginal voters. This has kept a spirit of smallness strongly alive within the Irish chamber system.

The first serious attempt to assert greater quality control on the system was initiated in 1970–1. This again proved controversial, with the initial plans criticized by Cork, which noted that 'the chief impression ... so far has been one of vagueness' with the new request for IR£5000 income not explained. Cork suggested that IR£1800 was sufficient for the association,[338] and also criticized the lack of support they had received for their local concerns, which at that time focused on restructuring of the Aer Lingus airline and AnCo (a state training body that still exists as FÁS). Moreover, Cork objected to the IR£500 that was to be paid to the Dublin chamber for secretarial services; they thought only IR£200 was justified.[339]

The most significant change in 1970 was the introduction of a chamber recognition process, to distinguish 'accredited members' of the association from other chambers.[340] It was at this time also that the Irish chambers began seriously to develop concerns about control of chamber title, and to urge incorporation as the normal model for accredited chambers, as discussed in Chapter 7. The aim of accreditation had been to reduce the number of chambers from 41 to about 32 county/city chambers and eight regional chambers, with smaller chambers affiliated via the larger ones. However, the effectiveness of the accreditation was not onerous

---

[337] Cork chamber, Council minutes, 4 December 1969.
[338] The CCI subscription income in 1969 was IR£639 from member chambers, with an additional grant from the Irish government for membership of the International Chamber of Commerce; expenditure was IR£946: Cork chamber minutes.
[339] Cork chamber, Council minutes, 4 December 1969.
[340] Dublin chamber of commerce *Journal*, September 1970, p. 11; Dublin's secretarial fee rose to IR£1550 by 1974–5.

since the number of chambers remained at 40 in 1980, with Cork (maintaining its doubts) deciding 'to go slow on' any regional structure.[341] By 1986 the number of association members had reached 50 and 'a source of great joy to the association is the fact that the number of member chambers continues to rise. . . . New chambers are being formed and thus more local communities are benefiting from inputs from local business.'[342] Indeed up to the 1990s, the primary object of the association remained increasing chambers in membership and not quality controls.

A strengthened Irish association after 1989

The first full-time member of staff at the association was appointed only in 1987, when it moved out of the Dublin chamber.[343] With its own 'professional secretariat', the 1990s saw a strengthened focus on accreditation, standards, and a search for critical mass. This adapted many of the ideas from the 1991 ABCC *Development Strategy*, with a *Best Practice Manual* for chambers launched at its annual conference in May 1993.[344] Subscriptions based on a single per capita levy for each chamber member were instituted in the 1980s, together with individual corporate subscriptions introduced in 1990. The Association's subscription income from the chambers based on the former tiered system was IR£3081 in 1975. This increased to IR £90,860 in 1992 from a mix of chamber subscriptions (56%) and individual corporate subscriptions at IR£1000 per firm (44%). In 2003 the subscription was 310,000 Euros, 79% from chambers and 21% from corporates. Corporate subscriptions were adjusted to €1500 in 2000, and raised to €2000 in 2003. A steady rise of the chamber subscriptions occurred in the 1990s as the association made efforts to improve its network support, from IR£6 per capita in 1991, to IR £10 in 1999 (subject to a minimum for the smallest chambers). It stood at about €30 per member in 2010, constituting about 15% of association income. As in the UK, there were cycles of chambers in arrears and threatening to disaffiliate, which increased when finances were tight, or when there were tensions with the association.

A rebranding exercise in 2005 reorganized the association as Chambers Ireland (CI). This was a crucial relaunch that sought to abandon its 'fuddy duddy' image, provided a uniform logo (adopted by all accredited chambers except Dublin by 2010), and also embedded a firmer set of accreditation criteria.[345] The 2005 relaunch introduced four levels, with standards that had to be met by each:[346] (i) *City chambers*; which must have active lobbying (at least five campaigns a year), represent their whole area, run at least three network events a year outside their city location (and at least ten in total), minimum membership of 300, at least two full-time staff, office open five days per week, updated website, full participation in CI

---

[341] Cork chamber, Council minutes, 4 December 1969.
[342] *Ireland Today, Bulletin of the Department of Foreign Affairs*, No. 1027 (April 1986).
[343] Reported in Chambers of Commerce Ireland, *Annual Report* (2004), p. 10.
[344] Chambers of Commerce Ireland, *Annual Report* (1992).
[345] Chambers of Commerce Ireland, *Annual Report* (2004), p. 17.
[346] Summarized from Chambers Ireland: *Best Practice Manual* (2009 edition).

activities; (ii) *County chambers*, with the same requirements as cities, but must have at least five campaigns, have 400 members, and three full-time staff; (iii) *Local or District chambers*—at least 100 members, one part-time member of staff, a chamber office, website, and at least five events per year; (iv) *Associate chambers*—minimum 50 members, run at least two network events a year, and participate in local chamber relationships. All types of chamber also must have a membership charter, and cover a defined geographical area agreed with CI (and hence with other chambers). Service specification beyond this is limited, with the smallest chambers only having to offer the services that CI provides, with local 'custom and practice' limiting full buy-in to the CI design. Irish accreditation thus resembles the BCC *Development Strategy* model of 1991–5, based on abstract criteria, rather than the later emphasis on chamber capacity and service outcomes, with the smallest chambers remaining non-affiliated and operating in their own way.

There have been 59 full members of CI over 2006–10, within which 42 are accredited to issue certificates of origin.[347] As in the UK, government (through the Department of Enterprise, Trade and Employment) license CI to maintain the certificate system (18,900 issued nationally in 1992). The strongest 30 county/city chambers offer the main base of the system. Some of the larger chambers cover wider territories; for example the South-East chamber has eight or nine participants from four counties, based on Cork; and the Galway chamber maintains a contact with many small chambers in its area. This allows for affiliated as well as non-affiliated chambers to have some involvement in the chamber system as a whole; but it does not cover all 'chambers' even in these areas, and in other areas connections with the smaller chambers vary. The government's spatial strategy has encouraged sub-regions and regions based on groups of counties to develop, in part derived from EU level II and III regionalization, with the chamber groupings able to act as participants in local strategic partnerships, as in the UK.

The CI office is based in Dublin, but efforts are made to arrange events in all areas. All the Irish chambers are incorporated, with Limerick the sole remaining chartered chamber.[348] The total system is claimed to have 13,000 members and 200 full-time staff. The association in 2010 had a chief executive, 12 staff, a *Journal*, *Yearbook*, and *Weekly Digest*. Its main activities are national lobbying, network and brand management, trade training and development, acting as the Irish committee of the International Chamber of Commerce (most significant on arbitration and banking activities), corporate responsibility schemes and awards, and local government awards.

Each of the full members has theoretically equal voice through a consultative committee, but since the 1970s CI has been governed by a Board of 11, only three of whom are chamber executives, plus the chief executive of CI itself. Thus the majority are business people, nominated by the chambers, although there is no

---

[347] Chambers Ireland, *Yearbook* (2009); and *Exporting Internationally: A Smarter Business Guide to Certificates of Origin* (2010).
[348] There are perhaps another 100 chambers that are informal and ephemeral local traders associations.

nominations committee. This narrow board seems to have served CI well until the 2000s, when the finances got out of control. CI had a rapid growth from 11 staff in 2003 with income of €900,000, to a peak of 28 staff and €5.1m income in 2007.

The pressures on the system were extreme through the 2007–10 global financial crisis, but the main challenge came internally. CI sought to capture a large value and volume of government and EU-funded activity, with the DAWN[349] project over 2001–5 significantly increasing the scale of activity and risks. This was run in conjunction with the local chambers who rolled it out to SMEs, but was managed centrally by CI staff. This was succeeded by even larger programmes. As discussed in Chapter 13, a major deficit accumulated which had to be tackled in 2007. The CI chief executive resigned in 2008, across the board cuts in expenses were made, and staff reduced from 28 to 12. The shift in staff numbers has been accompanied by a shift in activity. Indeed since 2008 CI has had to redefine its mission, focus more strongly on the network, and rebuild trust with the member chambers, which have generally proved more robust. There is a strong parallel to the experience of the UK system with the CCTEs, but with mission distortion in Ireland from government/EU schemes focused in the central association more than the local chambers. The refocusing of CI since 2008 offers some valuable lessons that are assessed further in Chapter 17.

8.10 CONCLUSION

A national organization for chambers started through bilateral exchanges and cooperation, but first took a meaningful form through the General Chamber, the early 'Union' of chambers, and various specialist agency appointments. A London agent or office was initiated from an early date by several chambers using their own resources, notably Jersey, Glasgow, Liverpool, and the Irish chambers. The first effort to develop a national collective was the Irish agent over 1822–3, followed by the English metropolitan agent of 1855–60 supported by seven chambers. Conferences and exchanges in the 1850s, such as the Social Sciences Association, the Law Amendment Society, and the Tribunals of Commerce Association facilitated developments. But the critical step of founding a national association was taken only in 1860, followed by the Irish association in 1923, which have continued up to the present.

Within a formal association there are many tensions of balancing different interests, resolving the relative central and local roles, raising the resources required, and making the national body effective. As the discussion has shown these tensions were resolved by progressive strengthening of the central level and the development of standards that eventually excluded some chambers from direct membership. Critical points occurred in 1917–19 when the first process for approving chambers was established. A second stage was achieved in the UK when Arthur Knowles and

---

[349] DAWN: EU Diversity At Work Network, which was part of the wider EQUAL initiative.

the chamber secretaries developed a structure for central–local relationships that provided a much stronger central capacity and personnel over 1947—60. This overlapped with the emergence of services as a key complement to voice. Many further reports were prepared, and pressures exerted for improving member chambers and resourcing which culminated in the first inspections under the Dixon Report requirements in 1969–71. But in the UK it was only with the expansion of government contracts and then the 'Ron Taylor surge' in central personnel in 1985–90 that the next critical change occurred, culminating in the 1991 *Development Strategy* in the UK, and the 1993 *Best Practice Manual* in Ireland. A formal accreditation process began in 1995 in both Britain and Ireland.

Since the late 1990s there have been many developments in detail, notably around the fluctuating targets and levels of government and EU contract funds available locally and nationally, but from about 2001 major changes have occurred that have challenged the continued development of centralization. In England this chiefly resulted from reduced government support and finance following the abolition of TECs and changes in Business Link financing, resulting in the 2001–2 crisis when the director general of the BCC was replaced. In Scotland, Wales, and Northern Ireland associations between the chambers have been considerably strengthened by the impact of devolution of government. In the Irish Republic the attractions of government and EU funding programmes were more focused in the national association, resulting in mission distortion over 2004–7, followed by a retrenchment. In both the UK and Ireland the financial crisis of 2007–10 has accelerated the pressures to rebalance the centre and localities, and to readdress the model of a self-sustaining chamber system where the level of government support has to be treated as shrinking, and unreliable. The influence of government is the subject of Chapter 13, whilst Chapter 17 takes the discussion forward to address the future of chambers.

PART 4

ACTIVITIES

9

Early Chamber Voice

9.1 SEARCHING FOR VOICE AND IMPACT

Part 4 of this book covers the activities of chambers, of which lobbying, to present voice, was and still remains the USP and core function. Early chamber lobbying reflected a significant change in how voice was organized after the 1760s: shifting from independent, ad hoc, and local, to coordinated bodies, acting nationally, making greater use of professional parliamentary agents, and increasingly using the much expanded role of the newspapers.[1] This resulted in a shift from relatively rare campaigns, protests, or petitions, to more common and routine exchanges between government and business, which is essentially how the modern chambers operate.

In this chapter the focus is on the lobbies voiced up to the early 1800s. As seen in earlier chapters, this period covers a landscape of local and national government that was dominated by patronage and corruption by the governing interests at Westminster, and some local organizations preserved from the past. It was essential for many chamber lobbies to work with others, or limit their damage. Lobbies had to develop coalitions, particularly with MPs and sympathetic peers or local corporations and counties.[2] Part of these coalitions was often international: colonial interests and local ones could ally with, and use, each other: 'English and American politics . . . [were] a vast system of pressures and counter pressures'.[3] If chambers achieved success it was often a result of alignment with other pressures that won policy changes.

This chapter outlines the earliest examples of local independent chamber voice, but also the experiments with building national chamber consensus, leading up to the national 'Union' of chambers after 1793. The early focus of the chapter on the individual chambers is an important antidote to earlier literature, since it demonstrates the evolution of an enduring structure based on locally distributed independent chamber organizations. However, the period is also critical in seeing the development of a short-lived national body, the General Chamber, which offered a different model and a challenge to the local chamber system. The chapter devotes

---

[1] See Chapter 8, and Kammen (1970); Wootton (1975), pp. 11 and 35–54; Olson (1979), pp. 371–2.
[2] Innes and Rogers (2000); Innes (2003); Hoppit (2003); Innes and Burns (2003).
[3] Olson (1979), pp. 385–6.

considerable attention to the activities of the General Chamber over 1784–7, since this became one of the most significant forces in shaping the minds of local organizers and national government of the time, and has distorted much academic comment. It offered critical lessons in how to voice, and what to avoid, and arguably constrained the chamber movement for the next generation.

9.2 AN OVERVIEW OF VOICE 1767–1819

The different chambers of the early period did not behave as a uniform set of entities, even when they collaborated together. Rather, their lobbies reflected local interest and contingency, and the degree of local interconnection with national and international political and trading conditions. The contrasts can be seen in Table 9.1, which depicts the main categories of lobby activity for 14 of the early chambers plus the special case of the Bristol Venturers (and for Manchester shows two contrasted periods of development). For all these chambers there is a major focus of concern with international trade, national government taxes and regulations, and navigation and communications (chiefly harbours, lighthouses, and postal service). These three categories account for 75% of all chamber lobbies.

Behind these international concerns was the growing demand for equality of trading opportunity. The colonial system was removed for the Americans and restructured for Ireland and elsewhere. The major chamber interest was moving towards a frame of *reciprocity*, or a *level playing field*, in trade. This was given stimulus by Postlethwayt and other economic writers, but was significantly strengthened by Burke's various confused salvos, and especially by Adam Smith's 1776 *Wealth of Nations*. It found continuing life through Henry Brougham, and was later transformed as 'free trade'. The concept of reciprocity underpinned most of the chamber approaches to international trade and treaty negotiations. But this new frame was not uniformly shared: it was concentrated in the ports, and this put them on something of a collision course with the traditional manufacturers and those benefiting from the old laws of trade, especially those in London and the chartered companies. For chambers like Manchester, Birmingham, and Leeds, it was divisive within the membership between the 'old' and the 'new'.

A leading example was attacks on the protected interests of the chartered companies. In Liverpool concerns with the Africa Company in London led to coordination with Bristol in April 1779 to jointly resist the London interest. Liverpool chamber was 'much alarmed at the advantages the advocates for monopoly were likely to receive from the abuse of the present establishment' and were 'working with the different members [MPs] in this and the neighbouring counties'.[4] But the main target was the East India Company where abuses were

---

[4] Gill Slater to SMV, 12 April 1779; SMV/2/4/2/22 (18); SMV out-letters, SMV/2/4/1/1, 8 April 1779; Slater re. Africa Company; SMV proceedings, 8 April 1779, SMV/2/1/10: Bristol RO.

notorious, and provincial interests were excluded.[5] Two leading chamber members in Liverpool led the city's campaign against the East India Company in 1768 (Heywood and Smythe).[6] These lobbies were revived with each opportunity of renewal of the Company's charter: in 1792 by Glasgow and Liverpool chambers and Bristol SMV,[7] and in 1812 by Birmingham and Glasgow.[8]

Beyond the concern with international trade, Table 9.1 shows three broad groups of chambers. First, a group of six chambers (including Bristol SMV) heavily dominated by international trade, treaties, and problems with naval convoys or naval commanders, together with national taxation or regulations (especially Customs and the Post Office); their only other major concerns were issues of navigation such as lighthouses, harbours, roads, and canals. In many ways these were the most 'typical' chambers, reflecting the emerging frame of reciprocal trade and reforming old structures; these were the underpinnings of later chamber movement as a whole.

Table 9.1 Classification of the lobby activities in a sample of the earliest chambers, by group and date: proportion of each chamber's lobbies engaging with each type of issue

Chamber (and period covered)	International Trade	Tariffs/ bounties	Tax, Customs, regulations	Local navigation and postal service	Protection/ patents	Local
Bristol SMV 1780–90	40	—	30	25	—	5
Liverpool 1774–96	50	12	24	9	2	3
Jersey 1768–95	36	20	24	16	—	4
Greenock 1815–19	33	—	45	22	—	—
Guernsey 1808–19	24	—	38	38	—	—
Waterford 1787–1819	20	—	37	40	—	3
Manchester (2) 1792–9	72	—	11	—	—	17
Glasgow 1783–1819	42	8	19	12	—	19
Edinburgh 1785–1819	23	8	23	23	—	23
Cork 1819–30	13	—	7	20	—	60
Limerick 1807–19	16	10	16	10	—	48
Belfast 1783–1819	13	9	17	44	—	17
Dundee 1819–25	15	20	20	20	5	20
Birmingham 1783–1812	30	15	10	5	30	10
Manchester (1) 1774–86	40	—	10	—	40	10
Leeds 1785–92	46	—	15	8	31	—
Total	34	5	23	18	6	14

Notes: Total is average weighted by membership. SMV: Bristol Society of Merchant Venturers.

[5] See Philips (1961) and Sutherland (1952) for discussion of the various campaigns against the company.
[6] *Liverpool Gazette*, 4 February 1768; see also Chapter 4.
[7] Glasgow minutes and chamber papers TD 1670/4/74; Report of Committee on the East India Trade, 25 December 1792; Liverpool in Bennett (2010), pp. 63–4.
[8] Speech of Thomas Attwood, High Bailiff of Birmingham, 4 March 1812; Bruce (1811) *Report of the Negotiation between the Hon. East India Company and the Public*...; Goldsmiths-Kress.

A second group of seven chambers was again focused on international trade and national taxation/regulation, but also had an important concern with local markets. The local market focus spanned two subgroups: for the Irish chambers it reflected their concerns to develop a trade that had previously been controlled by England. Provision trades (chiefly butter, hides, flax) were sectors where Irish chambers developed new forms of marketing, product promotion, and quality regulation. For other chambers the concern was with promoting the industries and interests of local sectors; the new 'industrial districts'.

The third group of chambers shared the common ground of international trade, navigation, and national taxation as a major focus, but also gave significant attention to protection of their industries by limiting foreign espionage, 'seduction' of workers to move abroad, limiting exports of new tools and machinery, and patent rights. The three chambers in this group (Manchester, Birmingham, and Leeds) all tried to achieve government backing for a level of control over local markets through various lobbies in the 1780s: e.g. width of cloth (Manchester); quality of swords (Birmingham); control of quality stamping of cloth, moisture content of wool, and methods of dyeing (Leeds); or by trying to stimulate cooperation between the industries in their areas (as in Manchester's efforts to enforce controls through patents on velveteen); and Birmingham's attempts to overcome high prices and shortages on brass and copper. These were attempts less at combinations than forms of market protection. Although the information is scantier, the North Staffordshire potters chamber also fell into this group, mainly seeking trade protection.[9]

The distinctiveness of this group explains how the early Manchester and Birmingham chambers became so involved in the General Chamber: the preoccupation was very much for manufacturing and protection of markets. Leeds is similar, but with more characteristics that resemble the broader-based chambers focused on international trade and national taxations/regulation. Of the chambers involved in the General Chamber, it was one of the first to disengage. Two other chambers lobbied briefly on protection issues: Liverpool attacked Richard Champion's patents for porcelain; and Dundee sought help for the jute industry.

The third group was not seeking to preserve the old laws of trade, but it was not unequivocally committed to more open trade. It was also ahead of a fourth group that did not have chambers at all: the older industrial areas that resisted the new policy frames—small manufacturers in London, and places like Norwich, and Exeter.

The concept of three broad groupings is overgeneralized; local contingency and priorities are also evident in Table 9.1. Liverpool's very high concern with international matters related to its burgeoning trade in Africa, the West Indies, and America. Greenock, Guernsey, Jersey, Edinburgh, Dundee, and especially Bristol and Belfast, reflect major concerns with the deficiency of local harbours,

[9] Thomas (1934, 1935).

dock dues, and navigation lights, and Belfast developed several vigorous campaigns to improve inland canal connections to feed the port. Perhaps most surprising is the low degree of focus of all the chambers, except Cork, on specifically local issues other than navigation. The only early examples were: improvement of gaols (Liverpool), local state appointments and patronage (Jersey and Liverpool), construction of the Linen Exchange and local banking (Belfast), and street paving (Waterford). For Cork the heavy early emphasis on local issues relates primarily to intense efforts to reform and challenge the local Committee of Merchants (discussed in Chapter 5). The small focus on local issues in most chambers is all the more surprising given the origin of many in anger with their local corporations. This evidences the origin of the chambers not as mere protest bodies, although that was what activated members, but a broader-based reform movement from the 'provinces' and outports.

9.3 EVOLUTION OF EARLY VOICE

The early lobbies of 18th-century chambers have not been previously properly documented. They covered a wide range of fields, and developed over an increasing range of provincial centres. Dominant themes were treaties and trade, but an increasing issue was also public expenditure and taxation. From 1685 to 1819 the national debt grew from £2 million to £854 million, reaching 2.7 times national income, largely as a result of wars. The share of national taxation required to service this debt increased from 2–3% in 1685 to 60% after 1815.[10] This understandably created concerns by business about tax burden, particularly in 1783–1815.

The period 1767–1782

This period covers the frame change of the early years of George III and the war with America, in which the first five chambers of commerce emerged in the British Isles, in 1768 in Jersey, about 1769 in Guernsey, in 1774 in Manchester and Liverpool, and the North Staffordshire potters. These coexisted with the other mercantile societies, earlier bodies, and ad hoc lobbies, of which the Bristol Venturers were most important.

International and national focus

For the Liverpool chamber, the full record of its activities 1774–7 contained in its *Abstract*, and the more fragmentary evidence for later periods, gives a good overview of the main concerns of the other early chambers. Over 1774–7 there were 34 lobby, petition, or representational activities recorded. This is a high level of activity

[10] O'Brian (1988); see also Rodger (2004); Morris (2004).

by contemporary or even modern standards: its early leaders John Dobson, Gill Slater, Benjamin Heywood, and Thomas Staniforth were clearly critical forces locally and in raising concerns nationally, primarily through a very supportive MP, William Meredith. After 1774 Meredith seems to have been as critical a link for the chamber as he was for the Stamp Act lobby; and indeed the strong overlap of the chamber leaders and Liverpool's Stamp Act committee has already been shown in Chapter 4; after about 1780 other MPs such as Richard Pennant and Banastre Tarleton were also used.

As shown in Table 9.1, the Liverpool lobbies primarily concerned international trade, and related to the American war: ten involved convoys, privateering, and protection of shipping; four involved embargoes on arms, provisions, or other trading; three concerned the slave tax imposed by Jamaica in 1774–5; two related to trade and debt in America; and one each related to the Greenland fishing bounty, unfair trading, and forts in the Gold Coast. National issues were also important for the early Liverpool chamber. However, most of these also concerned trade, one-half with the costs of lighthouses; other national issues concerned the Corn Laws, and Champion's patent on porcelain. The local issues also mainly concerned trade and communications: the postal service, port facilities, national regulations on vulnerability to the pressgangs for the navy, and rum bond rules. These remained major running concerns of Liverpool into the 1780s and 1790s,[11] with efforts to gain compensation from privateering by the French and Americans, how captured prizes were dealt with, and convoying.

One of the most important trade issues was over proposals for open trade with Ireland and the West Indies. This had begun under Lord North's government in 1778, when Liverpool corporation opposed developments and marshalled other towns to follow suit.[12] The chamber also opposed Lord North but later favoured open trade on a reciprocal basis. The Customs service also became an important issue, where Liverpool and Bristol cooperated after 1782 to oppose new fees, further expansion of personnel, and unauthorized perks.[13] The Customs service was the subject of 11 joint meetings of the chamber with Liverpool corporation's committee of trade between December 1781 and March 1782, with William Gregson (for the corporation) and Gill Slater (for the chamber) as joint chairs. New sets of rules were produced which specified the hours when Customs officers should be in attendance, allowed the consolidation of goods from one business transaction into a single Customs entry (overcoming the abuse that officers were levying on individual items to benefit their pockets), and set fees for every transaction in 43 categories. As always, success was slow and it was not until 1785, when a new local Controller of Customs was appointed, that reforms got

[11] See Liverpool chamber *Abstract*; and full discussion in Bennett (2010), pp. 26–66.
[12] Corporation minutes; Committee of Trade minutes, 28 March, 6, 15, and 18 April, 2 November, 24 December 1778; 22 February and 15 March 1779.
[13] Bennett (2010), pp. 41–2; also letter from Gilbert Slater, Liverpool chamber chair, 4 January 1782; Bristol RO, SMV/2/4/2/24 (1); out-letter, 21 January 1782 to Henry Cruger MP supporting Liverpool request, SMV/2/4/1/1.

fully under way.[14] There are many resemblances of the topics of these campaigns with those of the North Staffordshire potters,[15] indicating a level of liaison.

In Manchester, the chief concerns were removal of restrictions on use of cotton goods, import duties on cotton, the Navigation Laws (especially the use of neutral ships during the American War), and naval convoys.[16] It would appear that both Liverpool and Manchester had to work hard to improve inconvenient convoy arrangements that mainly assembled in London or Portsmouth. The chambers' efforts were one of many of the period that evidence the growing importance of the outports against a dominance of traditional London and East India trading interests. Manchester also promoted a wide range of protective measures: to prevent foreign spies gaining manufacturing secrets (with which Robert Peel, father of the later prime minister, was notably involved during 1781), to facilitate the punishment of receivers of stolen goods, improve the supply of cotton including reducing restrictions on imports, remove restrictions on the use of cotton goods, aid employers fighting worker combinations, and limit emigration by foreign workers.[17] There was a major campaign against extending the patent rights on spinning machinery (particularly Arkwright's jenny). When Arkwright defended his patents by serving writs on the spinners, a special chamber subscription was invited to resist his actions, with 22 firms contributing at a rate of one shilling per spindle.[18] This agenda mixed the concerns of the large merchants with those of the smaller manufacturers, became convolved with manoeuvring for positions in the corporation (especially the key position of borough Reeve), which led to a far more populist approach in Manchester than in the other early chambers.

Liverpool and Manchester also campaigned in a coordinated way in 1775 to improve trading conditions with America, developed in coordination with the national assembly in London of 300–400 merchants trading in America as well as over 200 West Indies merchants, who met in London as a 'resistance . . . couched in decent and manly terms' against the government's action against the American colonies.[19] The chambers worked with these interests, though they also acted independently, sending their own delegations and working through their local MPs. This was in addition to chamber involvement with the 1775 conciliatory petitions from Liverpool and Manchester noted in Chapter 4.

If we judge the seriousness of the concerns by the efforts made, and likely costs expended, three issues stand out in Liverpool: the condition of American trade and debt, where William Meredith MP was used and three delegates from the chamber 'attended several weeks in London'; the Jamaican slave duty, when, 'a numerous deputation from hence attended the Board of Trade'; a petition against the

---

[14] Corporation Committee of Trade, minutes 25 March 1782 and 27 July 1787; Liverpool RO 352 MIN/COM I 2/1.
[15] See Thomas (1934, 1935).
[16] Redford (1934), pp. 2 ff.
[17] See e.g. Bowden (1919–20, 1965); Redford (1934); Norris (1957).
[18] See summary in Redford (1934), pp. 3–6.
[19] *Williamsons Liverpool Advertiser*, 20 and 27 January 1775; Baines (1852), pp. 449–50; Bradley (1986), p. 22.

lighthouse general tax, where two delegates 'attended and gave evidence in the House of Commons' in coordination with the Bristol Venturers. Liverpool's *Abstract* for 1774–7 provides an unusual self-assessment of its effectiveness on the issues lobbied, judging 66% to have some positive outcome.[20] This is probably as good as, or better than, any modern lobby organization.

The Jersey chamber was pre-eminently concerned with harbour improvements in this early period. Concerns that echoed the other chambers related to Customs, smuggling, convoys, embargoes, and trade. As far as is known, these were also the issues concerning the Guernsey chamber. As noted in Chapter 4, events in America were particularly inflammatory to Jersey, as they affected trade, fisheries, and settlements in Newfoundland and the Gaspée.

First attacks on the Corn Laws

This period is also notable for the beginnings of attacks on the Corn Laws, which continued into subsequent periods. Reform was a founding article of the Glasgow chamber in 1783, and it became a leading organizer. Jersey's chamber members had been inflamed by the Island's Bailiff paying himself corn bounties in the 1760s, as discussed in Chapter 4; and Liverpool had been the first chamber to lobby against the Corn Laws, opposing Pownall's proposals in 1775.[21]

Glasgow had been alert to an attempt by the landed interest to extend the Corn Laws in 1777, before the chamber was established. There was a joint lobby of the merchants, the Lord Provosts of Glasgow and Edinburgh,[22] and the Burghs Convention; an agent was employed at six guineas. This is significant for its scale, methods, coordination with local government, and alignment of merchants with manufacturers and small traders. Glasgow also attempted to engage with the landed interests: a formal meeting was held with the Scottish gentry to explain the economic and political problems of the 1777 Bill which would 'render the import of oatmeal as difficult as possible', a critical issue for Scotland.[23] The chamber took up these concerns with a Corn Law committee 1786–91, seeing new Corn Law proposals coming 'from the same quarter [as 1777] . . . the landed proprietors'.[24] Its main campaigns were in 1786–7 and 1789, with memorials and publicity mounted in 1790 when its first president (Colquhoun) presented the chamber's petition at the Commons.[25] The 1787 lobby drew directly on the 1777 activities, and followed a meeting that included the landed proprietors, and sought an improved

---

[20] Liverpool chamber, *Abstract*, p. 5, January 1775; p. 6, February 1775; p. 7, March 1775; Bennett (2010).

[21] Liverpool chamber, *Abstract*, 7 December 1775; Bennett (2010), p. 34.

[22] Memorial of merchants, traders and manufacturers of Glasgow, 2 May 1777; *Thoughts Representing the New Corn Bills*, Edinburgh 1777; Resolution of the Convention at Edinburgh, 10 July 1777; Act of Glasgow corporation, 19 November 1777 (Glasgow Archives, TD 1670/4/2).

[23] Minutes of the Committee appointed by a meeting of landed Gentlemen, 17 November 1777, Edinburgh (Glasgow Archives, TD 1670/4/2).

[24] Glasgow chamber minutes, 2 January 1787.

[25] e.g. Glasgow chamber minutes, 10 October 1786 and 2 January 1787; minutes and accounts 1790, especially 4 May 1790.

means to regulate import and export in ten districts to provide a rational basis for regulations.[26] In Liverpool, a large correspondence over 1790–2 from Edgar Corrie, probable chamber president, attacked Lord Sheffield, and the role of local JPs in Corn Law administration.[27] The Union of chambers in 1795 also lobbied on the low taxation of the landed interest; 'there is a large description of men who escape from all contributions for the protection of the immense wealth which they possess'.[28]

The Edinburgh chamber, founded in 1785 and based in a city with a strong government and aristocratic concentration, was initially supportive of the Corn Laws. The landowners had proposed that the 'prices of grain at Mid Lothian should hereafter be the rule for opening and shutting the ports of Scotland' for imports. Glasgow's campaign received support from commercial committees or magistrates and councils of 'Paisley, Greenock, Port Glasgow, Saltcoats, Hamilton, Kilmarnock, Anderston and others'. But Edinburgh chamber had developed a plan with the landed proprietors for a single Scottish schedule 'such as we [Glasgow] cannot but disapprove . . . we are persuaded, that, on reconsideration they will see sense to abandon it'.[29] Edinburgh subsequently joined Glasgow's lobby. This campaign was judged sufficiently dangerous for the agricultural interest to take on a running criticism of the Glasgow chamber.[30]

The period 1783–1793

This period covers the cessation of hostilities with America and France, the Treaty of Versailles in 1785, up to the renewed war with France in 1793. With Pitt's government of 1784, which was to survive until 1801, a period of more stable trading conditions appeared to be promised, although his government was initially extremely vulnerable. The re-establishment of the Board of Trade by Pitt in 1786, with higher status and permanent secretariat who became a long-serving and expert staff, opened the way for an engagement of business interests with government in a more effective way. The period saw the establishment of a rash of local chambers: Glasgow, Dublin, Belfast, and Birmingham in 1783; North Staffordshire more formally in 1784; Edinburgh, Leeds, and Nottingham in 1785; Waterford 1787; and Londonderry in 1790. There were also bodies that were primarily delegates in Exeter, Halifax, Huddersfield, Hull, Sheffield, and Norwich founded in the mid-1780s.[31] Putting to one side the issues that absorbed the General Chamber of

---

[26] See Glasgow chamber minutes, *Report of Committee Discussion Relating to Corn Laws, for Consideration of General Meeting of the Chamber of Commerce and Manufacturers of Glasgow* (1787).

[27] Letter from Edgar Corrie 1 March 1791; BL Add MS 38226, fo. 73. Letters and pamphlet from Edgar Corrie: BL Add MS 38226, fos. 290–338, 25 September 1791; letters: BL Add MS 38227 fos. 14, 21–6, 98; 15 and 25 August 1791, 18 October 1791. See also Liverpool Athenaeum, Misc. Papers 38, pp. 5 ff.

[28] John Turnbull to Pitt on behalf of the Union of chambers, 11 May 1798: TNA PRO 30/8/184, fos. 183–4.

[29] Glasgow Chamber (1787), *Report of Committee of Directors Relating to Corn Laws*.

[30] e.g. *Farmers Magazine* (1804), p. 370; (1814), pp. 206, 254; (1823), p. 200.

[31] See Table 2.1. John Weskett's chamber of 1782–1800 undertook no lobbying.

1784–7, this period saw considerable other activity. To put the General Chamber's concerns with Pitt's Irish proposals in perspective, after these had been briefly (and vigorously) discussed in the Belfast chamber in June 1985, the next major issues were the 'shameful deficiency in the size of British bricks', the Customs, salt trade, sugar permits, and postal mails.[32]

Renegotiating the 'laws of trade'

A significant continuing concern of this period was foreign export duties and access to markets. After the Eden Treaty with France in 1786, the immediate concern was Spain. Eden was again involved, negotiating directly in Spain from late 1787 soon after he concluded the French Treaty. Among local delegate bodies there were lobbies from 1788 by Exeter merchants and MPs,[33] as well as MPs and representatives of other committees in Leeds, Norwich, and Manchester,[34] which continued under the Union of chambers after 1793. The concerns were similar to the French Treaty: to reduce inward duties and retain outward bounties where possible. Pitt saw rationalization in the same terms as the French agreement, but the trade with Spain was more significant at the time and had been less disrupted by the war with France. However, the negotiations were protracted, and by December 1794 the Manchester chamber debated whether to lobby Pitt for increased effort, deciding to defer consideration. Indeed the terms of the Treaty became overrun by the worsening situation of the war with France, leading to Spain declaring war on Britain in 1796.

For the Irish chambers, key concerns were to achieve an 'unequivocal reciprocity of trade' between Britain and Ireland, with the woollen and textile manufacturers in Ireland particularly aggrieved by British duties and restrictions. Also of concern was quickly reopening markets after the American war, especially in the provision trades (beef, butter, bacon, and fishing); applying the same Navigation laws to both countries to facilitate the tobacco and wine trades; opening direct trade with Portugal and Spain for both wine and manufactures (particularly woollens); reforming Irish laws on credits, bankruptcy, and the post office; and reducing or removing Corn Law restrictions which required licences for movement between Irish ports to be obtained in Dublin. The Corn Law Act of 1784 was a key focus of chamber lobbies against local aristocratic interests. It resulted in a scarcity of corn in Ireland, especially Dublin, and was eventually repealed in 1797, allowing equalization of bounties between all Irish ports.[35] However, trade equality remained a key issue in Ireland, even after Union in 1800.

---

[32] Belfast chamber minutes, 15 June 1785 and 2 January 1786.

[33] See Samuel Tremlett, Exeter merchant, letter to Pitt, 13 May 1789: TNA PRO 30/8/184, fo. 107; John Rolle MP letter to Pitt, 11 November 1788: PRO 30/8/173, fos. 20–3.

[34] Adams (1904); *Newcastle Courant*, 15 January 1791, reprinting an item in the *Norfolk Chronicle*, no. 111; quoted in Black (1994), p. 496.

[35] See Dublin and Belfast chamber minutes; also Prendeville (1930), pp. 80–95; Cullen (1983).

As well as trade, more detailed manufacturing concerns also became prominent as a result of the new mix of chamber bodies. Birmingham came to immediate prominence, where there was a concern similar to that in Manchester, with spies stealing manufacturing secrets in 1785. In 1786 the chamber appealed against legislation that allowed the export of manufacturing tools, specifying those tools which it thought prudent to prohibit from export; it made efforts to circumvent combinations of copper and brass producers that were pushing up prices; to remove the export duty on silver wares; and for an export bounty on ironware to combat growing European competition. In 1790 it lobbied to prevent the export of brass.[36] These all related to the leading members of the Birmingham chamber, especially Samuel Garbett and Mathew Boulton, who were major producers and users of metal goods.[37] Birmingham chamber was also immersed deeply in the concerns of Garbett (its president), with BoT tests of the quality of swords as a result of a dispute with the East India Company over quality and cost. This dispute was divisive between Garbett and some of the other Birmingham sword manufacturers, notably James Woolley, which was probably a major factor in a decline in visibility of the chamber at this time.[38] Other correspondence from Garbett also shows concerns with counterfeiting of foreign coins, arguing against the introduction of copper coins, and in favour of a plan to sell Birmingham manufactures free of monopoly beyond the Cape of Good Hope; i.e. competing with the East India Company.[39] In North Staffordshire the chief concerns were protection and promotion of pottery exports.[40]

In Liverpool there were lobbies against a Bill to encourage whale fishing in the Southern hemisphere; continuing concerns with American trade and debt; export quotas on grain to the West Indies; whether barley and beans could be exported to Gibraltar;[41] issues of navigation at North Shields; the need for better records of ships, tonnage, and duties at Liverpool; and a major effort to get improvements in the postal service, led by Gill Slater the chair. The chamber was involved in extensive correspondence in 1786–7 with the president of the Board of Trade on the need to rectify Irish 'trifling duties' on imported fish, as unfair in comparison to Greenland fishery imports into Britain; the exports of salt and its smuggling from Ireland to Wales and South-West England; the proposed duty on fir balk staves; the Treaty with France and the Ordinances of the port of Dunkirk that prevented the export of corn in other than French vessels; the need to codify insurance laws, where Britain is 'most behind other countries: and suffers from 'fickle,

[36] Wright (1913), pp. 11–23.
[37] See Chapter 4; Bowden (1965); Olson (1979); Norris (1957); Money (1977).
[38] Wright (1913), pp. 26–37; Money (1977).
[39] Letters from Garbett to Pitt, 17 December 1786; 29 November 1788; 8 March 1789; 31 October 1791; TNA: PRO 30/8/138, fos. 39 ff.
[40] Thomas (1934, 1935).
[41] See Bennett (2010), pp. 42, 55–7; also minutes of the Committee on Trade in response to Samuel Green secretary of the Liverpool chamber of commerce; 19 October 1790, fo. 179; 22 November 1790, fo. 185 (BL Add MS 38392); 23 March 1791, fos. 49–50; 28 March 1791, fo. 56 (BL Add MS 38393).

indeterminate and even frequently quite opposite law decisions, ... which has given a plentiful harvest to pettifoggers'.[42]

In Jersey, there were continuing concerns with restrictions on navigation by the French at the Normandy port of Granville, the president William Patriarche writing to Pitt in 1787 for support; and in 1790 lobbying over the appointment of a chief magistrate.[43] In Dublin, Belfast, and Edinburgh there were concerns with reconstructing Atlantic trade after the war, and with lobbies on American debts.[44] Edinburgh approached Pitt directly over alignment of the wheat import regulations between England and Scotland. In Glasgow, one of the most active chambers of the period, there were numerous lobbies and memorials. Examples over 1783–90 were: on bankruptcy law, the sugar and tobacco trades, tax on banknotes, iron manufacture, importation of liquor casks, customs regulations to have goods proved at Glasgow (rather than having to do so at Port Glasgow or Greenock), regulations for appointment of offices (Customs), the Corn Laws of 1787, the Thread Bill, fisheries, handkerchiefs, salt laws, Shetland wool, tobacco tax, American debt, and against East India Company imports. Even when participating in the national lobby on the Irish proposals in 1785, Glasgow was also pressing for reform of the tobacco law, the regulations on thread manufacture, duties on warehousing of sugar, and American debts.[45] In Manchester, apart from continuing concerns with convoys, there were some general lobbies developed, but most activity focused on the fustian tax and General Chamber activities, with which the chamber became intimately linked through its leading members.

The Post Office

The quality of the postal service was a major concern to most chambers. Almost all the early chambers raised voice for local improvements; it was the *first* lobby mounted by Liverpool in 1774, and Leeds in 1784.[46] In the 1780s the chambers supported a plan to introduce mail coaches, proposed by John Palmer. Liverpool stated that 'complaints against the mode of management ... had long been great and frequent'; the chamber 'supported the methods ... instituted by John Palmer at Bath'.[47] Palmer proposed the first national mail coach service (replacing post boys on horseback). Pitt allowed this to begin on 2 August 1784 as an experiment from Bath and Bristol to London. The Post Office had opposed Palmer, raising 'three volumes of objections' in July 1783 declaring it 'absolutely impractical'. With a change in government to Fox and North the plan was postponed, but was taken up again in December 1783 when Pitt became prime minister; the Post

---

[42] See Bennett (2010), p. 48; Henry Wilckens letters to Lord Hawkesbury: 8 December 1786, 7 January 1787, 19 March 1787: BL Add MS 38221, fos. 11, 98–9, 292–3.

[43] Jersey chamber minutes; also TNA PRO 30/80/134, fos. 22–7, 5 September 1787; PRO 30/80/131, fos. 29–32; PRO 30/80/148, fos. 150–1, 6 August 1790.

[44] See chamber histories and minutes.

[45] Glasgow chamber minutes, 1783–90.

[46] Leeds chamber minutes, 27 April 1784.

[47] Memorandum, 17 August 1784; Liverpool RO MD/2.

Office lodged another volume of objections, but Pitt overrode them to allow the trial.[48] It was very successful; by mid-1785 Palmer's mail coaches covered all the main centres in England, and later Scotland. Liverpool's began on 5 July 1785;[49] but Leeds was still lobbying to improve the service into 1788.[50]

Coordination of local campaigns 1783–1793

This period also saw a widespread development of grass-roots coordination between the independent local chambers. Although these actions were necessarily dispersed, the well-maintained minute books at Glasgow evidence many examples:[51]

- 1783, 18 February: coordination with merchants in London and 'chambers' of commerce in Bristol and Liverpool on the sugar and tobacco trades.
- 1783, 3 March:
  - Coordination with iron manufacturers in Scotland
  - Correspondence with chambers of commerce in Bristol, Liverpool, and manufacturing towns in England
  - Support for a chamber of commerce in Dublin.
- 1786, 7 June: qualified support for foundation of a chamber of commerce in Edinburgh.
- 1786, 1 September: receiving exchanges with manufacturers of Paisley.
- 1785–8: continual lobbying for Act exempting British manufactures from auction duty; followed by plan for a Cotton Hall in London free of duty.
- 1789: urged renewal of 1783 Act on bleaching.
- 1790, 9 April: coordinating with Edinburgh chamber and Merchant Society on Corn Laws.
- 1790, 10 September: coordinating grievances with Merchants House at Greenock on memorial on Customs on landing goods.
- 1790, 21 December: coordinating with Greenock merchants committee on Corn Laws.
- 1790, 21 December: coordinating with Highland Society to start an association for improvement of British wool, donating 50 guineas.

---

[48] John Palmer (1782), *Plan for the Reform and Improvement of the General Post Office*; see also (1792), *Papers Relative to the Agreement Made by the Government with Mr. Palmer for the Reform and Improvement of the Posts*, London; also Vale (1967), pp. 10–38.
[49] Letter from Samuel Green, secretary of the Liverpool chamber of commerce thanking Bamber Gascoyne MP and John Palmer Esq., 31 December 1786; Liverpool RO MD/3; see also Bennett (2010), pp. 43–4.
[50] Leeds chamber minutes, 24 November and 20 December 1788.
[51] Glasgow chamber minutes; see also personal accounts by Yeats (1818), and Colquhoun (1802).

- 1790–1: maintaining a coordinating committee between Glasgow and Edinburgh chambers.[52]
- 1791–2: extensive lobbying campaign with other chambers for reform of the Corn Laws; correspondence with Liverpool, Manchester, and Irish chambers.

These exchanges evidence a strong and diversified lobby structure developing between the chambers that extended earlier efforts. Pitt's re-established Board of Trade offered improved liaison after the defeat of his Irish proposals. There was also an emerging mechanism of general meetings of local chambers, other delegates, and merchants in London, who were in contact with the Treasury recurrently over at least 1786–90 independently of the General Chamber; Ehrman refers to this as a semi-permanent association.[53] Leeds chamber, together with Exeter's chamber committee and Mr Baring in London, activated its MPs Wilberforce and Duncombe in 1788 over Spanish prohibitions of exports. In 1789 they were in contact with Wedgwood, and activated their two MPs again, together with Garbett in Birmingham and the Manchester chamber over problems in Leghorn.[54] This was a predecessor of the 'Union' operating after 1793, discussed further below.

The period 1793–1835

The early part of this period has long been seen as one where commercial reforms were to some extent put on hold.[55] The Revolutionary and Napoleonic Wars with France put great pressures on trade, and after the renewal of war with France 1793, the first 'Great War', there was deepening disruption as Britain was progressively shut out of European markets by French military occupation. Although there was a lull in 1802–3, following the Peace of Amiens, hostilities were renewed and Britain became ever more isolated. There was some relief to maritime trade after the Battle of Trafalgar in October 1805, which reduced the capacity of the French navy. But after 1807 Napoleon controlled the whole European coastline and was able to close it to British imports. In retaliation, in 1807 the British government introduced an embargo on trade to Europe in other than British or neutral ships. This was a significant international challenge, met by an American embargo on shipping to Britain and prohibition of many goods entering the United States, which led to renewed war with America 1812–15. French privateering continued, and the war economy dominated Britain, leading to enlistment by many chamber members to create a large European land army, and trade disruptions, with no relief until the Battle of Waterloo followed by Napoleon's surrender in July 1815. Fear of

---

[52] See e.g. Glasgow chamber minutes, 21 December 1790.
[53] Ehrman (1969), p. 289.
[54] Leeds chamber minutes, 27 and 29 October 1788; 11 September, 2 November, and 21 December 1789.
[55] See e.g. Ehrman (1962, 1969); Black (1994); Rodger (2004).

revolution led to Pitt's anti-sedition laws of 1796, which made it more difficult to hold meetings, which constrained chamber organization.

Convoys, trade, and taxes

Despite the constraints, there were many important developments for the chambers over this period, although there was less attempt by the government to use business organizations to facilitate the planning and delivery of the government's war effort, in strong contrast to WW1 and WW2. Convoys were a major issue from 1793, then the embargo on coastal trade introduced in 1795, and a tax levied on merchants to pay for the convoys introduced in 1798. The Admiralty issued various instructions calling for cooperation from 'the merchants of London and other principle towns', which included involvement by those chambers in existence.[56] Conferences were called on particular trade routes, with Lloyds emerging as crucial to inducing cooperation by insisting on convoying in order to provide insurance cover. The bottlenecks caused by convoys increased the pressure for a stronger voice from the outports and for larger-scale port facilities.[57]

In this period, the Manchester chamber, which fell into disuse in 1787–8, appears to have been reactivated in part to handle convoy negotiations. Its minutes after 1793 provide an important record of the continuous exchanges on convoy problems, and evidence of coordination with Exeter, Hull, Halifax, Wakefield, Norwich, Birmingham, Liverpool, and London.[58] Problems of coordinating with the Mediterranean and East India convoys, which generally came from London but also from Portsmouth and Exeter, were particularly resented, as shipping from Lancashire, the Midlands, and Bristol generally had to wait at Falmouth. London and East India interests were viewed as riding roughshod over the western outports. The Manchester chamber minutes also record similar concerns from Hull, where convoys to Hamburg and Russia began in 1795.[59]

Customs services remained major irritants. Waterford began a long campaign for improvement in fee schedules in 1796, coordinating with Dublin, Cork, Limerick, and Belfast.[60] But in August 1796 it took the extraordinary action of threatening extra-legal activity: withholding payment of Customs fees. The minute is unusual for having a list of specific signatories below, but they have been cut from the book. Clearly there were second thoughts and concerns that they could be treated as seditious. Instead the chamber resumed its war of attrition, sending a deputation to negotiate with the Customs Controller in September 1796, reaching a further impasse with no agreement in December.[61] The chamber then proposed a new fee

---

[56] For example, letter from Lords of the Admiralty, received by Manchester chamber, minutes, 9 June 1796.
[57] Davis (1962); Crowhurst (1977); Ville (1987), pp. 10–13; Rodger (2004), pp. 559–60.
[58] Reviewed in Helm (1897) and Redford (1934).
[59] e.g. Manchester chamber minutes 15 March 1794; see also Redford (1934), pp. 27, 29–32.
[60] Waterford chamber minutes, 29 April, 13 and 14 July 1796.
[61] Waterford chamber minutes, 10 August, 15 September, 6, 23, 24, 28, and 31 December 1796.

schedule, with members 'not to pay any other' in January 1797.[62] There is then a break in the chamber's minutes until 1804, though meetings clearly continued. It would appear that the formalities of the chamber were abandoned because agreement could not be recorded. In December 1796 committee members had been directed to have 'no conversation . . . with Custom House officers out of this room', so that separate factions were clearly present.[63] It is an interesting case where those favouring extra-legal activity clashed with those trying to negotiate reforms; echoing the American chamber experiences in 1773–5.

Another major concern of this period was with credit and bills of exchange. The financial crisis of 1792–3 led to a number of local actions, particularly in London, Bristol, and Liverpool. In Liverpool, following the failure of Caldwell's bank in 1793 (a chamber member), the chamber members were deeply involved in a rescue, forming a committee with the corporation to seek a Parliamentary Act to issue local corporation loan notes.[64] Elsewhere debt problems led a London Committee of Merchants in 1797 to urge the Bank of England and government to extend the period for discount from 18 to 24 or 30 months.[65] Liverpool chamber had similar concerns,[66] and this was a key part of regulation of foreign debts proposed by the Union of chambers in 1797, involving committees in Birmingham, Exeter, Halifax, Huddersfield, Leeds, and Manchester. The problems arose from war interference with trading in Spain and Italy, and the needs in America to purchase warehouses for the next crop of imports, with the Bank refusing to provide additional credits. The issue moved on to cover the general difficulties of bills drawn on foreign locations, such as Grenada and the West Indies,[67] and later, in 1810–20, was rolled up in a range of pressures from London and other locations during debates on the bullion crisis, to which a few chambers contributed (notably Dublin).[68]

Other issues of trade of continual concern for the Irish chambers were arguments about reciprocity and a level playing field of trade. The chambers at Dublin and Limerick in the early 1800s, and the committee of merchants at Cork in 1803, were concerned that the projected Treaty with the USA excluded American ships from convoy duty, whilst cheap land there reduced their production costs. They called for equal treatment for the Irish provision trade.[69] The Jersey chamber was concerned about the renewal of the Russian trade Treaty in 1815–16.[70]

[62] Waterford chamber minutes, 4 and 11 January 1797.
[63] Waterford chamber minutes, 17 December 1796.
[64] The rescue committee was formed entirely of chamber members: see Bennett (2010), pp. 61–2.
[65] Letter to Pitt from Stephen Lushington MP, 1 April 1797, enclosing resolutions of Committee of London Merchants; TNA PRO 30/8/153, fos. 216–19.
[66] Letter from John Tarleton to Pitt, 5 June 1795; TNA PRO 30/8/182, fos. 34–8.
[67] Letters to Pitt; TNA PRO 30/8/153, fos. 212–13; PRO 30/8/182, fo. 38; Lushington letter to Pitt 1797; TNA PRO 30/8/153, fo. 229.
[68] See Cannan (1919); Sutherland (1933); Select Committee on High Price of Bullion, *House of Commons Papers* (1810), vol. iii. Some local committees quoted in the Committee may or may not have been chambers.
[69] See Prendeville (1930); O'Connor (1938); letter to Pitt, 15 February 1805; TNA PRO 30/8/173, fos. 297 ff.
[70] Letters from Dr J. Dumaresq (Jersey chamber agent) to Pitt, c.1816; TNA PRO 30/8/131, fo. 35.

A further area of concern was the increasing number of Pitt's new taxes on different products. The new tax on glazed paper in 1794, which was used heavily by woollen manufacturers, fell particularly on a few counties. Exeter delegates estimated that costs on glazed paper increased from £206 to £311.[71] The Liverpool, Manchester, and Glasgow chambers were similarly exercised about the impact of the Salt Tax in 1795. The English chambers sought an equal playing field with tax in Scotland. Glasgow sought abolition. Liverpool was exercised about the arbitrary distinction between white salt and rock salt, and unequal treatment by Scottish distillery laws.[72] Resistance to the extension of the Stamp Tax raised further concerns in 1804, when Halifax merchants and manufacturers objected to the extension of payments below £30, 'which will fall hard on small clothiers and Cloth Halls'. The tax required stamps on bills of exchange and promissory notes, which Halifax called 'unjust'. Petitions were initiated in a meeting at the Talbot Inn on 14 July 1804, and at Huddersfield at the George Inn on the same day.[73] Pitt's Land Tax, introduced in early 1798, and income tax proposal of 1799, stimulated large-scale protests. The involvement of chambers in these is unclear, and may merit further research, but these taxes certainly kept alive large-scale lobbying from numerous localities. However, chambers were certainly involved in other representations to parliamentary committees; e.g. the Committee on Use of Rock Salt in Fisheries 1817, and the Committee on the Law Relating to Merchants, Agents and Factors 1823, and related developments.[74]

Despite all these efforts, with such a huge collective commitment to war, commercial negotiation of contracts with government Victualling and Ordnance Boards replaced lobbying for many leading merchants and manufacturers. The BoT became preoccupied with the issuing of licences during the war. These preoccupations increased significantly with a change of government in 1807–8, and were not to be overcome until the restoration of peace in 1815. Thus, for example, the major campaign by Liverpool and Manchester merchants in 1808 (and the American chamber in Liverpool), against the government's orders for embargo on trade to Europe in other than British or neutral ships, which was led by Henry Brougham as their parliamentary agent, but was ignored despite its recognized weight. With the government preoccupied and impervious, it is not surprising that some chambers became relatively dormant or disappeared in the early 1800s. Re-establishment, and new bodies, then became of significance from about 1813 onwards.

[71] Letter from John Cole and J. N. Kennaway, the merchants and manufacturers of Exeter to Pitt, 1 March 1794; TNA PRO 30/8/133, fos. 322–4.

[72] Letter from John Tarleton to Pitt, 17 December 1795, TNA PRO 30/8/182, fos. 42–44; Manchester chamber minutes, 9 and 22 November 1796; Oakley, Glasgow chamber history (1983), p. 26.

[73] Letter from Henry Lascalles MP to Pitt, 19 July 1804, enclosing petitions; on request of Edward Swaine, John Edwards (chair at Halifax), Thomas Atkinson (chair at Huddersfield); TNA PRO 30/8/150, fos. 116–21.

[74] See also Clapham (1926), p. 200.

Activities

Managing divisions: response to slave trade abolition 1787–1788

A critical period for the chambers was the emergence of the slave trade abolition movement in 1787. Given that many of the early chamber members were involved, abolition was a major challenge. The chambers in Liverpool and Glasgow had a large membership of slave traders; the same was true of the Bristol Venturers, the London, American, African, and West Indies merchants; and to lesser centres such as Lancaster and Whitehaven.

Handling the emergence of the slave trade abolition campaign was thus potentially an explosive and deeply divisive issue for the chambers. It is also one where the explicit records become unreliable, as many of those opposed to abolition in the major trading ports were reluctant to give public voice.[75] For example, Liverpool's chamber member Edgar Corrie wrote secretly to the president of the BoT in February 1788 supporting abolition:[76] 'I am a merchant of Liverpool, and it might be attended with irreparable prejudice to some branches of the business in which I am engaged, that I stood forth with any opinion that could favour the abolition of the slave trade.' Therefore he 'begs that this private letter may not be communicated to any person unless to Mr. Pitt' and that 'my name must remain an invisible secret'. As Corrie was writing, many other chamber members were joining with the corporation in vigorously opposing abolition, led by member John Tarleton.[77] The Liverpool chamber's secretary also played an active role in opposing abolition, but he did this from the Liverpool Africa Committee Room with his salary paid by the corporation.[78] As a result the Liverpool chamber itself appears to have made no statement on the slave trade either way.

In Glasgow, with similar divisions, the abolition debates were simply avoided. A committee was set up in 1788 that reported

> having attentively considered the papers communicated from London, and individually formed opinions on the subject; but finding that there are different opinions, not only in the committee but among the directors and in the corporation [chamber] at large, they do not think it expedient that the directors as a chamber should take any decisive resolution on this occasion; leaving it to every member to take such part in the question as to each for himself shall deem proper.[79]

The formal minute records agreement with this recommendation, leaving developments to the 'wisdom of parliament'.[80] Hence Glasgow and Liverpool simply avoided inevitable division on abolition. For chambers in areas with less at stake it

---

[75] Sanderson (1977); (1989), p. 197.

[76] Edgar Corrie to Hawkesbury 24 February 1788; and 'memorandum by M.J.'; BL Add MS 38416, fos. 35–6, 37–44.

[77] R. G. Thorne (1986), *History of Parliament*; the other members of the delegation were Robert Norris, James Parry, John Matthews, and Archibald Dalzell, none of whom was a known chamber member; Bennett (2010).

[78] Samuel Green to Hawkesbury 21 and 30 May 1788; BL Add MS 38416, fos. 93, 96; Bennett (2010), pp. 49–53.

[79] Report of the Committee on the Slave Trade, convener Archibald Grahame, members John Gordon and James Gordon; Glasgow chamber papers, 14 October 1788; TD 1670/4/52.

[80] Glasgow chamber minutes, 14 October 1788; TD 76/1.

was possible to strongly support abolition, as in the case of Dublin, where Travers Hartley and Alexander Jaffray led the chamber to press for repeal measures in the Irish parliament,[81] and Edinburgh where the chamber petitioned for abolition.

This episode is important in showing how unity was maintained and managed in these early chamber bodies. Similar concerns arose again when abolition became a major issue in the 1830s; Dundee chamber passed a resolution supporting abolition, 'but as this chamber is properly intended for the protection of commercial interests . . . the meeting do not think it expedient to petition parliament on the subject of slavery'.[82] It took no formal position as a result.

Campaigns on American debts and the Jay Treaty

Debts held between Britain and America, but unpaid since the American rebellion, had been a running sore since 1774–5. It was claimed that the pre-1776 debts were ruining some of the merchants and were estimated in 1791 at £3 million.[83] By 1804, post-1776 debts were estimated at £5.36 million, with another £5.21 million to be discussed.[84] The governments would have liked to forget about the issue, but chambers and merchants in both countries maintained pressures. When the possibility of resolving the issue with the Americans began to emerge in the 1790s, a new campaign was mounted, particularly by the London merchants, and the traders in Glasgow, Bristol, and Liverpool, in which the representations by Glasgow chamber and the Union of chambers were significant.

The Jay Treaty, signed in Britain on 19 November 1794 and named after its negotiator John Jay for the Americans, mainly concerned debts and commercial settlement, and also settled the border with Canada.[85] Jay was highly regarded in America, then the elected governor of New York, but was also well regarded in Britain, having been one of the New York delegates to the Continental Congress who had argued for conciliation.[86] He also proved to be an accomplished and pragmatic negotiator, after his arrival in Britain proposing to Grenville that they initially find a framework for settlement by negotiating directly without secretaries and formalities.[87] It was in this context that Grenville and Jay drew on advisers from the merchant communities, including the chambers. The key commercial clauses of the Treaty were Articles VI and VII: to adjudicate claims for compensation through commissions. Although the commissions when established had a

---

[81] Resolution of the Dublin chamber for abolishing the slave trade, 29 March 1788; see also T. Clarkson, (1808) *The History of the Rise, Progress and Accomplishments of the Abolition of the African Slave Trade*, vol. i, pp. 496–7.

[82] Dundee chamber minutes, directors meeting, December 1830.

[83] Some debts were dealt with by loyalist compensation law in 1789, e.g. some by William Bolden and others in Liverpool: Schofield (1964), pp. 126–7; PRO AO 12/54, pp. 353–70. There was no chamber involvement in this.

[84] Bemis (1924), p. 315; Kellock (1974); full details in BL Add MS 38358.

[85] Treaty of Amity, Commerce and Navigation (Jay Treaty) 1794; see Bemis (1924); Morris (1967); Ehrman (1969); Schofield (1964).

[86] See Stevens (1867), pp. 78–90; Morgan and Morgan (1962); Morris (1967); also see Chapter 4.

[87] See Trumbull (1841), p. 181, who was Jay's secretary.

variety of tensions, and discussions were interrupted, with commercial settlements not finally resolved until 1804, and distribution of compensation continuing until 1811, they were eventually judged a success by both sides.[88]

In Liverpool the chamber had lobbied the government about American debts in 1777, and this was revived in a series of approaches directly to Pitt beginning in March 1795.[89] In Glasgow American debts had been one of the earliest concerns of the chamber. The chamber's continuing campaign used the provost and MPs. Colquhoun wrote as provost in 1782 urging that the peace Treaty should include commercial settlement.[90] Islay Campbell MP (who had been a key supporter of Glasgow chamber's foundation) renewed the campaign in 1789, writing to Pitt calling for action.[91] The impeding Treaty negotiations between the two countries stimulated more exchanges in 1794.

Grenville (president of the BoT), on Jay's arrival in June 1794, established two committees of merchants to advise him on whether the settling of claims should be through the courts, or by other means, and how evidence of claims should be dealt with.[92] These pre-dated the formal commissions under the Treaty, and were used to design the technical procedures to be followed. One was formed largely of London merchants trading in America, chaired by Duncan Campbell, with William Molleson and John Nutt; this focused on debts after 1776. The second was a separate body to focus on American debts before 1776. The second committee had two Glasgow chamber activists as the main members: Gilbert Hamilton and Robert Findlay. The other members were James Ritchie and Alexander Oswald. The working between the two committees was not always easy, with the second repeatedly trying to contact Duncan Campbell 'to know the London gentlemen's opinion'.[93]

The role of Glasgow chamber in the Treaty negotiations has been neglected. According to Patrick Colquhoun, first president of the chamber, now in London, he was 'instrumental, after great exertions at a very critical moment, in procuring the insertion of the names of merchants in Glasgow, who had property confiscated in America' in the early draft of the Jay Treaty.[94] Robert Findlay (current chamber president) and Gilbert Hamilton (chamber secretary) were used as key informants by Grenville, met directly with Jay and his secretary John Trumbull from July 1794, and were instrumental in arguing for the use of factors' and other traders' accounts, which would not normally be admissible in English courts. John Glassford (another leading Glasgow chamber member, banker, and Stamp Act protester), marshalled the evidence in Glasgow whilst Hamilton and Findlay negotiated in

[88] Bemis (1924); Moore (1931).
[89] Liverpool chamber *Abstract* 1774–7; letters from Clayton and John Tarleton to Pitt, 23 and 26 June 1794; 24 March 1795; 18 May 1795; 5 June 1795; 21 July 1795, TNA PRO 30/8/182, fos. 19, 26–7, 34–8; Bennett (2010), pp. 59–66.
[90] See Devine (1975), p. 153.
[91] Islay Campbell letters to Pitt, 22 April 1789: TNA PRO 30/8/120, fos. 90–1.
[92] 23 July 1794, TNA FO 95/512.
[93] Letters of Gilbert Hamilton and Robert Findlay to Pitt and Grenville, 2 July 1794; 8 August 1794; TNA PRO 30/8/141, fos. 145, 167–71.
[94] Quoted in Yeats (1818), p. 15.

London.[95] Subsequent negotiations led to an agreed framework for assessing deductions, depreciation, interest rates, and commission fees on the debts. These meetings made new estimates of the pre-1776 debts, of about £2.78 million. Dundas and the Duke of Hamilton were part of the flow of negotiations, with correspondence continuing until December 1794, when Pitt assured Findlay (for Glasgow) and William Molleson (for the London merchants) that 'HM ministers have thought under all circumstances of the case, [now] fit to be agreed to on the part of this country'.[96]

The chambers and local delegates played a further role through John Turnbull representing the Union of chambers (discussed further below), jointly with US representative Samuel Bayard, to resolve claims in the courts over ships captured by each side during the war. This helped to simplify other elements in the Jay Treaty. Similarly to Glasgow's efforts on debt, this laid the framework for how claims were settled, but actually adjudicated most of the outstanding cases, making decisions over about 286 vessels.[97]

Despite the pragmatism, many Americans regarded the treaty as too favourable to the British, chiefly on the Canadian border issue and Article XII on the West Indies trade; there was also criticism that it rewarded those who had speculated by buying up old debts at steep discounts.[98] It met considerable resistance from Republican (pro-French) interests; and the Assemblies in New York, Philadelphia, Portsmouth, Baltimore, and Charleston all protested against Article XII. It was not finally ratified in the Senate until 8 June 1795, with the New York chamber playing a significant role in support.[99] George Washington sent a letter of thanks to the chamber, regretting 'the diversity of opinion which has been manifested on this subject', but noting that 'it is a satisfaction to learn, that the commercial part of my fellow citizens . . . so generally consider the Treaty as calculated, on the whole, to promote important advantages to our country'.[100] In fact the chamber resolved in favour by 70 to 10 of those attending.[101] Thomas Paine referred to New York chamber's support as a 'snivelling address', with similar comments on the merchants of Philadelphia.[102] Boston chamber's efforts to support the Jay Treaty led to significant internal divisions, with dissent from 182 of its members who were

[95] TNA FO 915/512, fo. 35 appointing Findlay and Hamilton; fos. 45–75 negotiations; fo. 106 Glassford letter of 29 July 1794. Gilbert Hamilton and Robert Findlay, 25 June 1794, through the Duke of Hamilton, 8 August 1794; TNA PRO 30/8/141, fos. 143–8, 169–74; 26 June 1794; PRO 30/8/154, fos. 158–9.
[96] TNA FO 915/512, fos. 181–302 covers the correspondence of Findlay, Hamilton, and London negotiators; Pitt to Molleson and Findlay 3 December 1794, fo. 304.
[97] Cases adjudicated 18 September 1794 to 25 February 1795; BL Add MS 79526, fos. 1–22.
[98] Bowden (1930), pp. 122–4.
[99] Labaree (1963), p. 111; Stevens (1867); Bishop (1918).
[100] Washington to Comfort Sands, President of the New York chamber, 20 August 1795; in Annex to *Treaty of Amity . . . etc.* (Philadelphia: Lang and Ustick), second edition, pp. 178–9.
[101] Minutes of the New York chamber, 21 July 1795; Stevens (1867); Bishop (1918), pp. 37 and 45–8.
[102] *Letters from Thomas Paine to George Washington*, second edition, 1795.

'unwilling to be implicated' in the 'ignominious' vote to accept the Treaty. Thomas Russell, the president, voted both for the Treaty and the vote of dissent.[103]

Jay had anticipated problems in 1794: 'the steam I hope will soon ease, but the agitation of the waters will naturally take some time to subside'. This required continuous exchanges between Jay and Grenville up to 1801, including agreeing the names of Commissioners. Jay noted in 1795 that 'where so much heat has prevailed irritation will remain amongst individuals, and will occasionally produce inconvenience and embarrassment to both governments'; but they must maintain 'uniform and steady conduct on great points':[104] the two governments were not again going to allow the radicals to intervene.

Analysis of the claimants to the two commissions shows most British claims to be from London, with Bristol, and Glasgow the next major centres. There were many claims linking the early chamber members in America to British creditors. In Britain, prominent chamber claimants were: in Glasgow Colquhoun himself, his family firm, John Glassford, Alexander McCall, Duncan and Dugald Campbell, and Todd and Menzies (for which Gilbert Hamilton was an assignee); Liverpool had only about six of the British claims, all associated with chamber members, of which the major firms were Backhouse, William Bolden, Sparling and Bolden, and Joseph Dalterra (of Dobson, Dalterra and Walker; where Matthew Dobson was administrator for John Dobson, who had been the first chair of the chamber).[105]

9.4 THE NATIONAL 'UNION' OF CHAMBERS 1793–C.1805

Previous collaborations, and then the need to organize collective action between areas over convoying and American debt, seem to have stimulated a wider concern to coordinate activity through the establishment of a 'Union' of chambers from 1793. This probably followed the semi-permanent association developed in 1783–90, and represents the first 'association' of independent chambers. The important points to note here are: first, it shows many subtleties of activity to negotiate alignments of interests between the different areas: if the government, particularly Pitt himself, could find its way to modify policy, the Union (through its chair John Turnbull) hoped to deliver agreement; second, most actions were being done very quietly behind the scenes with an attempt to reach a negotiated agreement outside the public eye; and third, this led to an abhorrence of publicity, with fewer records made, which makes it more difficult to trace and be confident of levels of activity. The particular interest of this period is the subtlety it shows and assiduous efforts to

---

[103] Boston chamber, 11 August 1795: *The [Jay] Treaty, its Merits and Demerits Discussed*, Goldsmiths-Kress.
[104] Jay to Grenville, 22 November 1794, 9 July 1795; BL Add Ms 59049, fos. 78 and 90; fos. 1–107 cover other correspondence over 1794–1801; see also correspondence with US commissioners, especially John Anstey: TNA FO 915/514; and FO 304/31.
[105] See claimant listings for USA (Moore, 1931); for UK (Kellock, 1974); for Glasgow (Devine 1975, pp. 153–60); and web-based *Cozens/Byrnes Merchants Networks Project*, accessed February 2007.

keep campaigns out of the press, recognizing Finer's point, 'that fuss, noise, mass lobbying' may be counter-productive.

The activities of the Union of Chambers

The Union was stimulated initially by negotiations over the Spanish Treaty of 1793, and problems of naval convoying. A first chamber conference was held in London in 1793 over the convoy question; and then in 1796–7, stimulated by the effects of the French occupation of Leghorn and the expanding effects of the war, another conference focused on Spanish and Italian trade; at this point the meeting became a more formal 'Union of Chambers', though this was never more than an agreement to meet, collaborate, and exchange. John Turnbull was chair of the first conference, became the facilitator of intervening exchanges, and became formally the chair of the Union from 1796.[106]

His coordinating role projected Turnbull into the position of joint adjudicator with Samuel Bayard, representing the United States, over 1794–5 certifying claims in the Admiralty Court from agents regarding vessels captured or condemned as part of the efforts to resolve disputes leading up to the Jay Treaty; discussed above. The sequestration of British property in Spain in 1796 led to a vigorous campaign by the Union, which continued at least until 1805, when delegates or chambers in Birmingham, Bristol, Exeter, Halifax, Leeds, London, Manchester, Norwich, Rochdale, and Sheffield lobbied to receive the proceeds of sale of a Spanish frigate and other captured prizes.[107] Outside the Union, Liverpool was now liaising through individuals, as its chamber appears to have lapsed.[108] Other communications with Pitt led in 1801 to a national meeting called to allow the Union to contribute to the peace negotiations of the Treaty of Amiens. Turnbull was able to write to Lord Spencer as 'chairman of the respective bodies of the merchants and manufacturers of England trading with southern ports of Europe and with South America'. Hence, as well as trying to emulate aspects of the General Chamber, but without its noise, the Union was emerging as a body for particular southern trading markets.[109]

John Turnbull's involvement as a major figure is intriguing, since his links with Quebec through Alexander Davison (a leading agent in Quebec, then in

---

[106] John Turnbull was a merchant partner in Turnbull and Macaulay in 1793, trading in Quebec; a successor firm to Macaulay, Gregory and Turnbull which had at least 1500 tons of shipping in 1786 when tendering for Australian convict transportation. Later he was a partner in Turnbull and Forbes, with trade in Leghorn in 1797–8; most of his partnerships had links to naval victualling. Turnbull had debts of about £10,000 in Italy in 1793 for which he sought Pitt's help in recovery; Pitt passed the request to the Treasury for action, releasing £4800 two days later; Turnbull to Pitt, 8 and 10 April 1793: TNA PRO 30/8/184, fos. 174–5. He also sought Pitt's help over advances of £9256 to estate proprietors in St Domingo on 6 July 1798; PRO 30/8/222, fos. 55–6.

[107] Henry Lascalles MP, letter to Pitt, 20 February 1805, enclosing petitions of deputies of various towns; also November 1804 and 18 February 1805; TNA PRO 30/8/150, fos. 122–5.

[108] e.g. Thomas and William Earle of Liverpool approach to Duke of Portland over the problems in Corsica and Leghorn; letters 2 September and 1 October 1796; William was a major chamber member.

[109] Redford (1934), pp. 56–62.

London),[110] and liaison with Boulton and Wedgwood, suggest continuity with key General Chamber members. But he chose to act very differently, as a coordinator and facilitator, not a prominent public figure, and operating quietly without attention, drawing on some of the chambers and local committees involved with the General Chamber. He also drew together 'selected' London merchants.[111] Turnbull proved to be energetic with considerable political subtlety. As a merchant he dealt with the local representatives on equal terms, was adroit at managing the tension between areas, and had sufficient political connections to allow him ready access, providing Pitt with an important sounding board for his policies.

Reciprocal trade

Turnbull chose to emphasize the need for 'reciprocity' or level playing field of trading duties in order to persuade Pitt and his government. He managed to manipulate the disparate views of the local areas very cleverly. The tensions are evident in the Manchester chamber minutes.[112] The Manchester responses were often critical of Turnbull, or when they had less direct interest (as in many of the Mediterranean issues) they were laggard. But Turnbull was generally able to overcome these tensions. A good example is provided by his approach to Pitt in March 1798, which related to new taxes laid on convoys. He states that he could not 'presume to anticipate the result of the general sentiments of the different bodies of merchants in London . . . and the request of the great manufacturing towns, in submitting to you, the resolutions of their different general meetings';[113] here is unity in diversity, not unlike many modern BCC submissions. Turnbull goes on: if it is

> expedient even incumbent on the government to prevent any British vessel sailing from a British port with convoy, more frequent convoys will necessarily be required; but from Manchester, Leeds and Exeter, they are decidedly of the opinion that the manufacturers' interest in this country . . . would be greatly injured . . . by the new duty which is proposed to be laid on exports and imports. From Birmingham, they also disapprove of it, but appear to be moderate, and that they would be satisfied with certain modifications. At Halifax they greatly approve of the plan, but with the duty on exports to Hamburg should not exceed 1 percent. These I believe, are generally the sentiments of the manufacturing towns.

Turnbull transmitted to Pitt the original letters from each town, in order to secure his own position, but goes on:

> although four of these towns seem to be adverse to the measure, . . . I am inclined to hope that I may be able, on representing the matter in a favourable, and just point of

---

[110] Turnbull and Macaulay used Davison as agent in Quebec. Davison was closely connected with Nelson and the Treasury, back in London in the 1790s he was closely involved with Huskisson and Dundas in the government, and arranged Matthew Boulton to strike Nelson's Nile victory medal in 1798; he also knew Wedgwood and had trading interests in Italy: Downer (2004).

[111] e.g. Manchester chamber minutes, 14 April 1794; see also Redford (1934), pp. 27–38.

[112] Redford (1934), pp. 25–62.

[113] Turnbull to Pitt, 2 March 1798; TNA PRO 30/8/184, fos. 180–1.

view, to reconcile them to it, provided that you are pleased to authorise me to say, that
it is your intention, as I have always understood it to be, that the duties in question are
only to continue during the continuance of the war.

Turnbull's negotiations were not easy. He reported to Pitt two weeks later that the
government's proposal 'will meet with very decided opposition from all the
manufacturing towns, which I am extremely sorry for, since I sincerely think,
that its principle is just, and with proper modifications it might have been
serviceable', though at Norwich 'their chairman has been with me, and I have
endeavoured to reconcile him to the duties in question, when properly modified'.[114] But by May he was optimistic that 'Mr. Pitt appeared to have led with
attention and maturely considered the letters and resolutions' which Turnbull had
presented.[115] By June, Turnbull was able to present 'resolutions which have been
today unanimously agreed to by a general meeting of the merchants of London and
delegates of the principal manufacturing towns of England'. The paper of resolutions can be paraphrased:[116] (i) much merchandise could be had only from Spain;
(ii) the Order of 27 April 1798 had granted licences to neutral ships, but no neutral
vessels would risk the French; (iii) a new model was needed, where licences were
granted to those who swore before the Privy Council that goods travelling to a
neutral port from Spain (actually from England, Ireland, or the colonies) should
not be detained by the navy; and (iv) there was also concern with the Act
prohibiting British subjects residing in the enemy's country or any correspondence
being held with them except by licence, when most such subjects were ignorant of
the need for a licence. These resolutions indicate the intricacy of the two-way
information exchange, and were sent not only to Pitt, but also to the Duke of
Portland, Earl Spencer, and Lord Liverpool. Turnbull sought Pitt's advice on how
to bring this wider group of ministers into agreement, through the BoT.

The Union pursued a range of policies, including means to resolve outstanding
credits with Spain in 1796–7, and in January 1797 issued a *Notice of the Commercial Societies of Manchester, Leeds, Halifax, Birmingham and Exeter*, proposing a set
of 'fundamental principles of trade': (i) once goods were shipped, an English House
was not responsible for delays; (ii) unless otherwise specified, contracts were to be
understood to be in English money and weights and measures; (iii) no abatement
could be admitted as a result of variations in exchange rates or detention of vessels;
(iv) no forced debts to hostile armies or governments would be accepted as acquittal
of debts; and (v) the commercial societies were to communicate with each other the
names of any houses abroad acting 'contrary to the honour expected among
merchants'. This proposal had come from Exeter, and this chamber (perhaps to
make recompense for its earlier misdemeanours—see below) undertook to arrange
the translation of the regulations as a 'circular letter of the Union of Commercial
Societies into French, Spanish and Italian'. Several thousand copies of the *Notice*

---

[114] Turnbull to Pitt, 15 March 1798. TNA PRO 30/8/184, fo. 182.
[115] Turnbull, probably to Pitt's secretary, 11 May 1798; TNA PRO 30/8/184, fos. 183–4.
[116] Turnbull to Pitt, 6 June 1798, with resolutions; TNA PRO 30/8/184, fos. 185–6; see also BL
Add MS 38231–2, 38235.

were printed and distributed.[117] These regulations reflect a much more ambitious agenda than earlier joint chamber efforts, not only to lobby, but also to establish rules for international trade, debt recovery, and communication of information on unreliable foreign traders. The initiative was probably influenced by the contemporaneous Jay Treaty commissions, and made an attempt to avoid some of the credit problems of the American war during the current one.

The Union did not collapse in 1802, and nor did Turnbull give up, as suggested by Redford.[118] There was a particularly vigorous lobby in 1805 over the sequestration of British property in Spain, which had occurred in 1796. This lobby sought to acquire the proceeds of sale of a Spanish frigate and other vessels detained at the time as prizes. The lobby was unsuccessful, but provides important evidence of continued meetings of the provincial chambers and committees; in this case in November 1804 and February 1805, with Turnbull 'waiting in London for Mr. Pitt',[119] with the following deputies:

John Milford (London)	Samuel Oates (Leeds)
John Startin (Birmingham)	John Rapp (Manchester)
John Ebsworth (Bristol)	James Hamer (Rochdale)
James Banfill (Exeter)	William Brittain (Sheffield)
John Bramley (Halifax)	J. G. Bazeley (Norwich)

These names differ completely from the representatives of 1795–6,[120] although they are all in the same line of business as merchants, or combined manufacturers and merchants, and the locations are the same. There was also activity by Colquhoun in 1800 (the founding president of the Glasgow chamber, and then stipendiary magistrate in London's Shoreditch), who used a London committee to support extension of police powers to set up the first marine police force on the Thames. His committee appears to have been part of the London committee of merchants and Union of chambers. The redoubtable John Turnbull was chair, and its other members were the leading London merchants, most of whom were linked to the main merchant committees: Thomas Bonar, John Brickwood, John Dumage, Edward Foster, Beeston Long, Albert Roberts, and Robert Thornton.[121]

Marshalling opinion, avoiding 'noise'

Turnbull's activities and the Union of chambers evidence several important developments. First, his letters show him to be claiming no more unity than it was

---

[117] Manchester chamber minutes, 5 and 10 January 1797; Helm (1897), pp. 42–4; Redford (1934), pp. 58–9.

[118] Redford (1934), pp. 61–2.

[119] Henry Lascalles MP, letter to Pitt, 20 February 1805, enclosing petitions of deputies of various towns of 18 February 1805 and November 1804; TNA PRO 30/8/150, fos. 122–5.

[120] Except Startin, who was involved in the early Birmingham chambers, in both 1783 and 1790.

[121] Quoted in Yeats (1818), p. 29.

possible to achieve, but also appearing to have the ability to negotiate alignments of interests between the different areas: if Pitt could see his way to modifying policy, Turnbull hoped to deliver agreement. This was a reversal of Rockingham's style, but with similar formats of exchange. Second, all these actions were being done very quietly behind the scenes. They had the flavour of modern policy exchanges outside the public eye, where neither lobbying body nor politicians want to be seen to make concessions. The chambers were not becoming an insider interest, but they had a direct line of access. As Ehrman noted, Pitt was becoming very personally involved and directive in trade negotiations,[122] and this was being done very discreetly; the Union made little attempt to use MPs or petition parliament.

Further evidence of the importance accorded to discreteness is provided by an incident in November 1796, when some information leaked into the press about a proposed memorial from the chambers regarding compensation for lost property in Italy and Spain. The leak appeared in a major opposition paper, the *Courier*, and was blamed on the Exeter chamber. The Manchester minutes record that 'they are acting on different grounds to other manufacturing towns and are more politicians than merchants'. They were directly warned that any publication 'may influence our application' to the government for attention. This occasioned an exchange with the Exeter president (probably Mr Cole), who replied to James Edge and Thomas Richardson (the past and current presidents of the Manchester chamber) that 'Exeter disavows any publication which occurred without their knowledge and has asked the editor to say who inserted the entry'. The significance of this exchange is that it demonstrates the strong desire to avoid the noisy campaigns of the General Chamber, all the more so as Thomas Richardson was the man who stood with Thomas Walker when the Manchester crowd was raised against the fustian tax in 1784–5.[123] Walker's activities had convinced the Manchester men to eschew party politics and public attention. This concern may also explain why it has been impossible to find a copy of this issue of the *Courier*; it is missing from otherwise continuous runs from all newspaper collections in Britain and America. It is tempting to believe that the chambers organized its removal. But in any case it demonstrates the impact of the popular press and the sensitivities of the new chamber leadership to any possible association with the former General Chamber, and exposing their campaign, and Pitt, to the opposition. Subsequently, Exeter was invited back into Union, but their delegates were forced to eat humble pie: the Manchester minutes report that the Exeter delegates (Mr Cole, Mr Kennaway, and Mr Tremlett) affirmed that 'they have no intention of interfering or appearing in a political light, but merely as commercial men'.[124] Subsequently Kennaway was one of those negotiating with Grenville and 'delegates of the various manufacturing towns' regarding Exeter ships held up at Gibraltar awaiting convoys.[125]

---

[122] Ehrman (1962, 1969).
[123] Manchester chamber minutes, 22 and 23 November 1796; noted by Redford (1934), pp. 18, 57–8; but its significance is not drawn out.
[124] Manchester chamber minutes, 29 November 1796.
[125] William Kennaway to Grenville, 10 December 1796; TNA FO 95/5/8, fo. 623.

It is also important to note that the Glasgow, Edinburgh, Dublin, Waterford, the Liverpool American chamber, and other local chambers were not involved in the national Union, nor were the Bristol Venturers. Thus one group of chambers was seeking organized joint working, whilst another group acted separately, though sometimes in cooperation with each other. The main focus of the Union was on manufacturing and the European trades, whilst the chambers outside the Union were chiefly concerned with America, Africa, and the West Indies.[126] Strong regional differences between chambers derived from different roles in international trade led to different commitments to working with a 'national' lobby based in London.

9.5 NATIONAL ORGANIZATION, 'NOISE', AND THE GENERAL CHAMBER 1784–7

The key argument of this chapter is that a routine and well-developed and continuing structure of lobbying government and exchanging information to provide voice developed in *local* chambers from 1768. This model of independent *local* bodies provided the enduring organizations of the next 200 years, even though some fell by the wayside. But from late 1784 until mid-1787 an additional phenomenon developed: the General Chamber of Manufacturers. It has received much more academic attention than the local chambers, but it is the exception and has thus distorted understanding. By 1784 there were seven active chambers in existence, plus Guernsey in some form and Weskett's London chamber; and in 1785 Edinburgh and Leeds chambers were founded for reasons linked, but unrelated, to the General Chamber. Hence the General Chamber entered an existing market.

The General Chamber was a different model from the local chambers: it was a national body from the outset, based in London, drawing support from local 'delegates', but also individuals who only in some cases represented local chambers. It also made protest a key objective, becoming as much a political movement as a lobby organization. The discussion here is divided into three sections for the three main lobby campaigns with which it is associated: the fustian tax, the Irish proposals, and the French Treaty.

The fustian tax, 1784–1785

The new government of Pitt in 1783, beset by urgent financial difficulties, introduced many new taxes. All were likely to raise objections. A tax on dyed stuffs, cotton and linen mixed with cotton, which became known as the 'fustian tax', was not in a different league, but was one of the first to affect the burgeoning

---

[126] Devine (1975); Olson (1973, 1979); also see McCusker and Menard (1985); Morgan (1993, 2007) on the emergence of the British-American merchant interest; also Checkland (1952, 1958).

cotton industry. Like many other Excise taxes, it was to be collected by special commissioners, which incensed the manufacturers as much as the tax itself.[127]

When announced in 1784, the tax immediately caused alarm in Manchester and Glasgow, as well as other areas. In Glasgow the chamber of commerce set up a committee, and offered support to Lancashire, issuing a memorial on the inefficiency of the 'tax on fustians'. In both centres additional subscriptions were raised; in Manchester there were 350 subscribers by August 1784, and a protest petition purportedly gathered 50,000 signatures. Manchester immediately began to coordinate with Birmingham.[128] A strong link between Manchester, Birmingham, and the Staffordshire potteries had been developing over the previous 15 years, as evidenced in Samuel Garbett's exchanges noted in the Stamp Act period (Chapter 4), and in several campaigns by potters.[129] The fustian campaign had the support of other manufacturers, unaffected by the fustian tax, but fearing new taxes on all raw materials and manufactures: e.g. the iron founders in Shropshire, Worcester, Stafford, and Warwick; and the Birmingham commercial committee (the chamber). Garbett's view, communicated to his friend Lord Shelburne, stated that 'none but enemies of our country could *rationally* devise taxes upon exportable manufacturers' when what was needed was a more equal sharing of tax burden by the non-industrial population.[130]

The campaign started in a similar way to others, and Manchester's view echoed earlier approaches of respectable opposition:[131] 'however disagreeable, and ever burdensome and oppressive that law may be, it is the duty of good and loyal subjects not obstinately to resist it . . . [but to] write with manly business, decency and decorum in petitioning for repeal, and setting forth in a proper manner, the inconvenience, disadvantages and mischief that arise from it'; i.e. an appeal to reason. But the scale of the petition in Manchester is also indicative that this had some different undercurrents, with numerous small artisans being engaged. Subsequently it is evident that this was a key part of the Manchester leader's approach, Thomas Walker: to seek 'noise' and use populism. Manchester's fustian protest was more of a Wilkesite constitutional challenge, and had only superficial resemblance to the lobby mechanisms used by the established chambers.

The voluble Manchester lobby sent a delegation to London, led by Thomas Walker and Thomas Richardson. They were asked to testify before the BoT on 31 January 1785. Throughout their first day of testimony they did not realize that the Board was actually consulting on the contemporaneous Irish proposals (q.v. below); they felt manipulated and angered.[132] The fustian concerns were not considered until they appeared on 21 March, when Walker's efforts appear as confused as the

---

[127] Bowden (1965), p. 170.
[128] Garbett letter to Shelburne, 14 October 1784; quoted in Norris (1957), pp. 454 f.
[129] Thomas (1934, 1935); Norris (1957); Money (1977).
[130] Quoted in Norris (1957).
[131] From the *Manchester Mercury* and *Harrops General Advertiser*, 28 September 1784, but probably a direct quote from Thomas Walker; quoted in Martin (2002), p. 8.
[132] Harlow (1952); Dietz (1991), p. 115; Read (1964), pp. 30–6.

committee's.[133] But again Walker felt treated with condescension. Opinion in Manchester was incensed at the reported treatment, and on 12 April 1785 many thousands of weavers from Oldham and other surrounding towns marched on Manchester. News of the unrest was sent to London. On 20 April the Commons voted for repeal, and on 21 April Walker and Richardson returned to Manchester believing themselves victors:

> the repeal of the fustian tax had been moved by the Prime Minister, seconded by Mr. Fox, the leader of the Opposition, and carried without a division. The delegates . . . alighted at the Bull's Head in the Market Place, which was filled with people. After a short speech from Mr. Walker, the two deputies were placed upon chairs and carried through the streets. . . . and on 17 May, after the Repeal Bill has received the Royal Assent, there was a great procession of fustian cutters, after which a silver cup was presented to each delegate in recognition of his services.[134]

The Manchester delegates were heroes; Walker was launched as a major force in the region and was led to believe he had a role as a national leader; a new Wilkes.

The view from the established chambers was rather different. Glasgow was chiefly concerned about other proposals, but had been also pressing Pitt about burdens on fustian manufacturers.[135] Their agent in London (John Seton) had advised no progress was being made, despite the hearings in January 1785.[136] The Glasgow delegates went to London and then got swept into the fustian tax frenzy. The Glasgow delegates began by preparing a 'system of temperate opposition' to the fustian tax on 26 March, but finding no hopes from the minister, joined with the Lancashire delegates who had already appeared at the Bar of the Commons.[137] Glasgow's petition was brought to the Bar on 13 April. A further case was prepared which was put into the hands of almost every member of the House, impressing on them the necessity of repeal. The vote on 20 April indeed repealed the fustian tax, but this only tackled a small part of the manufacturers' concerns, and only a fraction of the cotton interests. Walker left before the success of the main tax campaigns and mistook what had been achieved; final success relied more on Glasgow and other Lancashire delegates (notably Robert Peel and Thomas Smith).[138] This makes clear the rather different role and effectiveness of Walker and Richardson, compared with the more persevering approach needed.

---

[133] *Merchants and Manufacturers Magazine of Trade and Commerce* (London: J. Almon, 1785), pp. 113–33, 221–95.

[134] Helm (1897), p. 14; Knight (1957): the silver cups were from the corporation of Bolton (inscribed as 'the original seat of the fustian industry').

[135] Glasgow minutes, *Report of Committee on Burdens of Manufacturers*, 28 December 1784.

[136] Letter from John Seton to Patrick Colquhoun, 2 March 1785, TD/1670/4/26.

[137] The rest of this account quotes from the *Report of the Delegates of the City of Glasgow, Commissioners of the Chamber of Commerce and Manufacturers to Proceed to London in the Month of March 1785*, Glasgow chamber minutes, June 1785, TD 76/1, pp. 136–45.

[138] Joseph Smith in some papers; Peel was the father of the future PM. The fustian tax repeal still needed pressure in the Lords when Walker left: Bowden (1965), pp. 170–2; Helm (1897), p. 14.

Continued efforts on other taxes

After Walker left, Glasgow delegates continued to press for the repeal of a tax on printed goods and proposals to reform Irish trade. The Printed Goods Tax was not discussed in the Commons, but the Earl of Surrey raised it in the Lords on behalf of Glasgow. It was initially lost, 'but by a great and steady exertion in bringing forward and in uniting the English printers—not a moment was therefore lost—a new case . . . was drawn and submitted, agreed with Lancashire members . . . [and] a most perfect union of interests and executions established between the English and Scotch printers and manufacturers'. On 25 April an interview was held with Pitt, and senior ministers: Houghton, Pultney, Stanley, Blackburn, and the Lord Advocate (Eden). Patrick Colquhoun, the Glasgow president, explained the case and left samples of various low-priced substitute printed goods. Two days later Colquhoun, with Alexander Brown (the other Glasgow delegate and Lord Provost), again met Pitt in the company of six MPs and 18 Lancashire and Cheshire printers and manufacturers of whom Robert Peel and Thomas Smith were the persistent leaders. Pitt agreed to exempt low-priced goods and the committee immediately met with the Board of Excise to settle the details. By 2 May a compromise set of resolutions was agreed, but immediately 'the London wholesale drapers and printers . . . brought forward a most powerful opposition—delayed the progress in the interim and created infinite trouble'. The Glasgow delegates 'holding the minister [Pitt] as pledged' continued to negotiate and eventually a further compromise was agreed. Colquhoun's report makes it clear the huge 'labour and cost in conciliating . . . and removing these differences, and bringing the London and Lancashire gentlemen to hold one opinion and to act in concert'.

Lessons from the fustian tax lobby

There are four aspects from the fustian tax lobby that are significant. First, it demonstrates the emergence and importance of a growing manufacturing lobby that had already been evident in the Stamp Act repeal of 1765–6. Bowden interprets this lobby as based in 'new' industrial areas; though it is important to recognize that many of the weavers and fustian manufacturers were not actually using 'new' forms of manufacture. Second, it reinforced views of the arrogance of the aristocracy and corruption of electoral representation. As seen by James Watt and others in the Midlands, the landed gentlemen see us as 'poor mechanics and slaves to be looked down on with contempt'.[139] Third, it demonstrates differentiation between areas and interests, and with this the need for lengthy negotiation and deliberation to attain a 'unity of interests'. In this Colquhoun and Brown from Glasgow, and Peel and Smith from Lancashire, were clearly critical. Alignment of interests took time and required leadership, dedication, and commitment, and 'painful' negotiations with 'the solicitor to the Board of Excise—the solicitor to the

---

[139] Quoted in Bowden (1965), pp. 155–6 ff.

Customs—then to the Treasury'.[140] Walker didn't bother with this, but went back to Manchester to gain immediate publicity with the crowd.

Fourth, the campaign showed the vulnerability of Pitt's government and how the opposition and independents in the Commons could be used to gain concessions. After the American debacle, it suggested 'business as usual', back to the 1766 Stamp Act cave in. Indeed Pitt certainly recognized the problems. But the message of Pitt's climb-down was confused. It certainly showed the value of lobbying; but did it confirm, as Walker believed, that success was best achieved by noise and populism, using the opposition, and becoming 'party political'? The tensions became clear in the next phases of development.

The Irish proposals 1784–5: The General Chamber triumphant

Ireland had been granted a more independent parliament in 1782, partly as a response to the American debacle.[141] This settlement had left open whether the same commercial laws, duties, and bounties applied (and which government was responsible). Pitt took this up in 1784, and had similar objectives to Lord North: that the Irish parliament should be independent over internal affairs but must work within a common understanding with the rest of Britain on trade and external affairs; 'we must, in order to make a permanent and tranquil system, find some line according to which the Parliaments of the two countries may exercise their right of legislation, without clashing with each other'. Pitt's aim was to introduce as strong a unity of trade as possible, in return for which growth in the size of the Irish economy would allow it to pay increasing contributions towards 'the common exigencies of the empire' (chiefly the costs of the navy).[142]

Over the turn of 1784/5 Pitt formulated the specific plan of taking any future surplus of the Irish hereditary revenues (chiefly Customs and Excise) to pay towards the costs of naval defence, with any deficit reducing the contribution required. However, when this proposal was introduced into the Irish parliament on 7 February 1785 the clamour against it forced modifications by reducing the revenues taken, except in wartime. Pitt was forced to introduce the proposal at Westminster on 22 February, when a compromise was still being worked on.

Pitt had sought to consult business interests in Britain involved in the Irish trade. He followed the established procedure: at the end of January 1785 ordering the BoT to report on the settling of reciprocal duties with Ireland, and continuing Irish import preferences from abroad. The committee's consultation brought a large number of merchants and manufacturers together in London. The evidence of Josiah Wedgwood from the potteries was probably typical of the other industries:[143] the proposals were acceptable 'if earthenware was allowed to be imported free of all duties into both countries'; i.e. he wanted a level playing field, or

[140] *Report*, op. cit., Glasgow chamber minutes, June 1785.
[141] Ehrman (1969), pp. 50 and 196; see Chapter 4.
[142] Pitt letter to Duke of Rutland, 1784; quoted in Ehrman (1969), p. 200.
[143] Meteyard (1866), ii, p. 538.

reciprocity, between the two countries. Indeed the BoT believed that there was general support for genuinely equal trade.

Pitt interpreted the consultation in late February to be that 'the manufacturers had not been alarmed' by the proposals, and by 3 March he still believed that 'there seems no reason to expect delay from addresses sent from commercial towns'.[144] Pitt had an advanced and shortened version of the BoT's report published on 1 March, although this was largely ignored. At this point, possibly through the encouragement of William Eden and Lord Sheffield, key opposition leaders, the business deputations began to be alarmed. The BoT had been demoted to being a part of the Privy Council after 1780, and the business leaders were reportedly treated with condescension by its aristocratic members.[145] The unwillingness of the government to negotiate on the fustian tax and Irish proposals also echoed obduracy during the American War.

Formation of the General Chamber

On 7 March a meeting of manufacturers was called in the London Tavern. There were delegates from over 20 areas, who agreed various critical resolutions against the Irish proposals, and at a meeting on 10 March with Sir Herbert Mackworth MP in the chair Wedgwood proposed the formation of a chamber of manufacturers; this was seconded by Matthew Boulton and, after 'considerable debate', resulted in agreement to establish the General Chamber of Manufacturers of Great Britain 'to act as a permanent representative industrial association, to watch over their interests as one aggregate'. A special committee met on 12 March chaired by Wedgwood, and a further general meeting on 14 March formally adopted its constitution and elected its officers. Ironically it was the consultations by the BoT in January–March that brought all these interests together that led to the formulation of the General Chamber. Pitt's consultation had set up an explosive combination. In addition a number of prominent business leaders were also in London in March and April for the politicking around another vexed election of directors to the East India Company.

Ehrman's account implies that Pitt had developed his Irish proposals largely out of public view and the BoT was an inefficient sounding board. But business interests certainly got wind of it early. Glasgow chamber established a committee on the Irish proposals on 28 December 1784. Patrick Colquhoun, its president, originally made arrangements to go privately to London in January–February. But after the proposals were presented in the Irish parliament on 7 February, the Glasgow chamber agreed on 22 February that Colquhoun should go together with the Glasgow provost Alexander Brown, to 'attend the sundry interests of the

---

[144] Committee on Trade, and Pitt correspondence, quoted in Ehrman (1969), pp. 205–6.

[145] Harlow (1952), p. 604, Ehrman (1969), pp. 207–8, and Dietz (1991), pp. 112–34 rightly question how far opposition orchestration was necessary. The account of how the BoT operated confirms that the business people who appeared were alienated and did not need encouragement. Indeed, detailed exchanges between Wedgwood and the opposition only began after the proposals were presented in February: see Meteyard (1866), ii, p. 542 ff.

trades and manufacturers of this country' (Scotland). Their agent in London, John Seton, informed them on 2 March that Mr Pitt 'was not wanting to make rapid progress on the Irish business' but wanted to meet the Glasgow delegates.[146] Similarly Wedgwood in January 1785 had been so concerned about the Irish proposals that he rented 'spacious and handsome rooms at 10 George St., Westminster' specifically to be on hand to lobby.[147]

Whatever the interpretation of events and the degree of Pitt's freedom of manoeuvre, as Ehrman concludes, the establishment of the General Chamber was 'the turning point'. It met Pitt on 10 March asking him to delay the Irish proposals, but received no concessions. The Chamber's meeting on 12 March agreed to a petitioning campaign to demonstrate wider support and sought wide publicity to undermine the government's position. The press gave extensive coverage on a daily basis, and gave the impression that the Chamber was working with the opposition and that the government was threatened. This was divisive,[148] but petitions, reports, and further lobbies poured in: 31 petitions were presented to the Commons by April 1785, and 85 by the end of the Committee hearings on 12 May.[149] Pitt was forced quickly to make concessions to agree the continuation of the Navigation Acts, to restrict carriage of French and Spanish imports on Irish ships, and a range of other details that moved away from the general principles of a unity of trade that he had originally sought. The new Bill introduced in May now had 16 propositions, and was an object lesson in the impossibility of regulating trade item by item. It was made more difficult because the joint British-Irish issues were to be considered at one level as a 'unity' but at another level were regulated by two parliaments.

Pitt was forced to concede that a Committee of the Whole House of Commons would be handed the job of enquiring afresh. This gave both the opposition and the Chamber new opportunities for influence, though they saw the dangers of this dividing and bypassing them; Colquhoun suggested that 'a number of questions would be artfully put, to draw answers contradictory to each other, and those answers would be used against them'.[150] The ensuing hearings increased the propositions to 20, then to 31, as various special interests were taken into account. By 25 July they had been agreed by both Houses at Westminster, and then proceeded to the Irish parliament. Pitt hoped that a conciliatory address reaffirming Irish independence, and a great deal of lobbying by Irish landed interests, would assure passage. But in Ireland both patriots and business interests were unconvinced; and the sharing of costs was seen as a 'tax at the discretion of a foreign

---

[146] Glasgow chamber minutes, 28 December 1784; 20 February 1785; letter from John Seton to Colquhoun, 2 March 1785.
[147] Meteyard (1866) ii, p. 538.
[148] See acrimonious debate recorded in *Merchants and Manufacturers Magazine of Trade and Commerce* (London: J. Almon, 1785), pp. 31–41.
[149] Listed in TNA PRO 30/8/321.
[150] *Merchants and Manufacturers Magazine of Trade and Commerce* (op. cit.), pp. 59–60.

parliament'.[151] The General Chamber correctly judged that the concessions forced on Pitt would be unacceptable in Ireland and commenced their celebrations on 25 July. When it became clear that it would be defeated the Bill was withdrawn from the Irish parliament, and in effect then died. 'Dublin was illuminated that night, and the crowds thronged the streets'. It was Pitt's most 'serious failure in his first two years of office' and his vision of a unity of Britain and Ireland in external affairs was destroyed in 'quibblings and mistrust'.[152]

The role of existing local chambers

The role of the existing chambers in this resistance has previously been largely overlooked. In Ireland the two chambers, established in 1783 in Belfast and Dublin, circulated the reports of the General Chamber and were active opponents of the proposals in the Irish parliament.[153] The Belfast chamber organized a large-scale town meeting, for which reports and other materials were prepared and published in the press; resistance to the Irish proposals was agreed to a tumultuous crowd.[154] In Dublin, several of the leading MPs were chamber members, including its president, Travers Hartley. With Hartley's pressure, a chamber petition was forced into the parliament critical of the proposals, despite challenges to the chamber's status to make such a petition.[155] The chamber's attitude was that the proposals were inadequate, with Irish woollens, worsted, silk, and mixed good manufacturers receiving no benefit to end the previous period where they had been suppressed. British goods were still to enter Ireland free or at low duty, whilst most goods traded to Britain attracted high duties. Indeed this reiterated the chamber's concern in 1783, when it proposed operating controls on imports on similar lines to the non-importation agreement during the American war.[156]

The Dublin chamber took the view that the proposals offered 'very unequal and unjust terms' and instead called for a Treaty based on 'permanent and equitable principles . . . and unequivocal reciprocity': the terms, indeed, which Pitt claimed to be seeking. Moreover, the chamber claimed that the propositions 'subverted the independence of the Irish parliament'.[157] The chamber's approach followed an address it had organized to be sent from all 'the trading towns of Ireland', which urged them to oppose Pitt's proposals.[158] Dublin chamber was acting as a voice for

[151] Thomas Lewis O'Beirne (1785), *A Letter from an Irish Gentleman in London to his Friend in Dublin on the Proposed System of Commerce* (London: J. Debrett); Dublin City Library.
[152] Ehrman (1969), pp. 209–16.
[153] See e.g. *The Report of the Resolutions of the Committee on the Affairs of Ireland with Remarks on the General Chamber . . . together with an Authentic and Copious Sketch of the Elegant Speech of the Rt. Hon Charles James Fox, on Monday 30th May 1784* (Dublin: P. Cooney): London Senate House Library.
[154] Belfast chamber minutes, 25 May and 15 June 1785.
[155] See Chapter 7.
[156] Reported in *Parliamentary Register of the Irish House of Commons*, col. 3 (1783), p. 138.
[157] Dublin chamber minutes; *Votes of the Irish Commons* (1785), pp. 120–1 refers to the chamber's opposition; also see Prendeville (1930), pp. 80–3; Cullen (1983); *Parliamentary Register of the House of Commons of Ireland*, vol. iii.
[158] *Address to the Trading Towns of Ireland*, from Council of Dublin chamber, 9 June 1785: *Annual Register* (1784 and 1785), London, p. 337.

the whole Irish national position, in the same way the General Chamber was acting for England. The chamber also seems to have engineered letters to the English press, arguing that 'no commercial or other regulations can be beneficial to any nation that invade its constitution, [or] restrict its trade'.[159] This was a clear follow-on from the Anglo-Irish freeholder movement; but also has resonance with the way the Edinburgh chamber initially sought to call itself the General Chamber of Manufacturers for Scotland in 1784—which was successfully resisted by Glasgow.[160] Pitt's proposals thus not only stimulated activities in Britain but also in Ireland; and the Dublin chamber's members were leading participants in the celebrations in the city when the Bill was withdrawn. Travers Hartley, together with the chamber as a whole, took the credit for the withdrawal: the chamber congratulated itself, its brand had been launched only two years after its foundation, and the chamber voted its thanks to the Irish parliament.[161]

As noted above, Glasgow was perhaps the most active of the other chambers, and its two delegates, Colquhoun and Brown, made a personal record of their experiences.[162] They reported arriving in London on 17 March and, after many discussions with MPs and advisers, on 26 March 1785 they had an hour with Mr Pitt, 'who after a full hearing, candidly declined giving the least hopes' of revision of the propositions or relief of 'duty on handkerchiefs and other Scottish manufactures sent to Ireland'. It this situation they had 'no alternative but to establish a regular and fair system of opposition'. They 'strengthened their interest' by participating in the Report of the General Chamber, presented the Glasgow chamber's petition, and prepared and published queries in answer to various comments by Scottish MPs. When the propositions were delayed until May there was continued negotiation with Pitt over the details, with a further meeting secured on 26 May in association with London and Lancashire drapers and printers. On 25 June Henry Dundas provided a promise to Colquhoun that 'every assistance would be given and every exertion made to remove all future cause of complaint'.

The labours of the Glasgow delegates absorbed 15 weeks. They had a profound effect on Pitt, and occupy a major part of his personal folio of briefings.[163] As well as the specific revisions of the Irish propositions, Glasgow also secured the other concessions noted above (on printed goods, etc.), and strengthened their links with Dundas. But the cooperation with the General Chamber was on limited terms: the 'Glasgow chamber, being a body corporate of merchants as well as manufacturers, cannot as a society form any regular junction with the General Chamber in London'; it would maintain links and exchange of information but at arms'

---

[159] e.g. Letter from 'A constant reader in Dublin', reporting the Dublin chamber petition against the Irish proposals: *Nottingham Journal*, 27 August 1785.

[160] Glasgow chamber minutes, 1784.

[161] Cullen (1983), p. 51.

[162] This seems to have been neglected in previous analyses. The following summary follows their *Report of the Delegates for the City of Glasgow, Commissioners of the Chamber of Commerce and Manufacturers to Proceed to London in the Month of March 1785*; Glasgow chamber minutes, June 1785; TD 76/1, pp. 136–45.

[163] TNA PRO 30/8/321, fos. 197–201, 211–14, 217–18, 231–44.

length.[164] Colquhoun had already been made very aware of the politicization of the General Chamber, when on 25 March he 'pointed out the necessity . . . for the Chamber to steer clear of party; . . . he particularly advised no resolutions to be hastily drawn up or agreed until they had been maturely considered'.[165]

In Liverpool, as far as can be ascertained, its chamber was not a member of the General Chamber and worked through its MPs. The chamber appears to be included in the 'gentlemen, merchants, traders and other inhabitants' of Liverpool, which was the *first* petition presented to parliament on the Irish proposals, presented by Bamber Gascoyne sen. MP on 3 March 1785. It was phrased in temperate terms, supporting Pitt's own concept of more open trade, but drew attention to the large and open coast of Ireland which facilitated smuggling, and legal importation from the plantations which could then be clandestinely introduced to England. It concluded by 'praying that the privilege of supplying her own markets with the produce of her own colonies may be preserved inviolate to this kingdom, and that every farther extension of trade between Great Britain and Ireland may be established upon such equitable principles, as will redound equally to the mutual benefit of both countries'.[166] This was much more temperate than the corporation's opposition to open trade with Ireland and the West Indies in 1778–9; the chamber had begun to shift the local terms of debate in Liverpool.[167] Pitt marked the phrase 'mutual obligations', and underlined 'due proportions' in his copy of the full text.[168] These are the only marks on Pitt's copy of the petitions except for 'costs of labour' underlined in the Wigan petition, and various notes on the Bristol merchants' petition similar to Liverpool's.[169]

The text of Liverpool's 'conciliatory' petition was seized on by Pitt as support for his proposals; he 'congratulated the House on a Petition presented from an enlightened body of men, the merchants of one of the first trading towns of the kingdom'. But the Liverpool text was also seized on and used by opposition leader Fox, who accused Pitt of taking the 'opportunity to abuse the petitioners in so gross a style. Every word he had uttered was a direct attack upon their understandings'. Liverpool's petition was not 'conciliatory . . . [and] he certainly was not prepared to treat the merchants of Liverpool with so much disrespect'.[170] Liverpool was thus in the centre of the fray, and misused by both sides! As Pitt or his secretary noted: 'the manufacturers are assembled from every town in London and such a force is

---

[164] Glasgow chamber minutes, 14 February 1786. Colquhoun formed a negative impression of the capacity of the General Chamber, despite its success in the Irish Proposals, q.v. above.

[165] *Merchants and Manufacturers Magazine of Trade and Commerce* (op. cit.), pp. 59–60.

[166] *House of Commons Journal*, xxv, col. 348.

[167] Bennett (2010).

[168] Liverpool text in TNA PRO 30/8/321, fo. 125; prepared by Pitt's secretary but with Pitt's annotations.

[169] Wigan petition, fos. 141–3; Bristol merchants, manufacturers, and traders, fos. 170–1; TNA PRO 30/8/321.

[170] *House of Commons Journal*, xxv, cols. 348–9.

preparing a means to crush it [the propositions].—What dreadful consequences arising from the rough politics of the day!!'[171]

In Bristol one of the petitions was presented by Henry Cruger from 'the chamber of commerce at Bristol (and sugar bakers)' indicating how the brand was diffusing.[172] The Venturers also petitioned separately, choosing to maintain an arms' length relation with the General Chamber, like Glasgow. Their delegates attended the early meeting of the Chamber in March 1785, and responded separately to the French Treaty (in liaison with Liverpool 'deputies'), but reported no other coordination.[173] In Birmingham, although Garbett was involved indirectly in the General Chamber (mainly through Wedgwood), he had separate correspondence with Lansdowne and Eden, maintaining the key role as a clearing house for other areas that he filled in earlier years. He forwarded letters to Lansdowne from Glasgow coming from Islay Campbell and Dundas regarding Customs on boring machines; the definition of hardware and inclusion of buttons in the French Treaty; on port dues in Liverpool and Hull; the Poor Law; the mint; corn shortages, etc.[174] In Leeds the chamber was stimulated to form on 22 March 1785, in part by the need to manage the deliberation on the fustian and the Irish proposals following a series of open meetings held in the city.[175]

These neglected episodes demonstrate that existing chambers, and Colquhoun, as well as the more widely referenced Wedgwood, Garbett, and Boulton, were critical in influencing the new government's policies. It also shows how Glasgow, Bristol, Dublin, and Belfast chambers formed a working relationship with the General Chamber, but also acted independently to keep it at arms' length. Thus the General Chamber did not absorb all the independent chambers around the country as implied in some earlier accounts. The significance of the developments also shows that the Atlantic trading interests were developing a different approach to chamber representations from the 'new manufacturers'. North Staffordshire, Birmingham, and Manchester were the leaders in the General Chamber, and their local chamber leaders (respectively, Josiah Wedgwood; Samuel Garbett and Matthew Boulton; and Thomas Walker) were among its joint vice-presidents. For these chambers the close association created problems of separating local and national interest that became critical in the next years

The General Chamber develops

The General Chamber as a concept seems to have been in the minds of several Birmingham industrialists in the 1760s when Samuel Garbett canvassed the concept of a national body, sanctioned with the authority of both Houses of

[171] TNA PRO 30/8/321, fo. 194A.
[172] Ibid., fo. 196A; other roles of Cruger discussed in Chapter 4.
[173] Proceedings and Index of Bristol Venturers; SMV 2/1/2/3 etc. 12, 19, and 26 March 1785; letter from Liverpool, 24 July 1788.
[174] Garbett-Landsdowne letters; Birmingham Archives, ZZ 618; also Norris (1957); Money (1977), pp. 35–47.
[175] Reported in *Leeds Mercury*, 8, 22, and 29 March, 12, 24 May, 5 July 1785.

Parliament, to combine the functions of being a committee of experts and a parliamentary pressure group for manufacturers.[176] This proposal had not progressed, but in 1783 Garbett became the first chair of the Birmingham commercial committee (or chamber). In Staffordshire, Wedgwood had become the leader of the potters chamber and appears to have been influenced by Garbett's ideas. But it was Garbett who stimulated committees to form in other areas who provided delegates: he and the Birmingham chamber were in contact with Sheffield, Nottingham, Leeds, Norwich, Wolverhampton, Walsall, Dudley, and Stourbridge.[177]

For Thomas Walker in Manchester, the General Chamber seems to have offered a chance to put into practice some of the ideas he had been formulating. He was a leading dissenter and was strongly influenced by James Burgh's *Political Disquisitions*, which as noted in Chapter 4 served to revive interest in Davenant and Postlethwayt, and had been recently used by Burke in 1780. Burgh suggested extra-parliamentary associations as a means to counteract government, under a Grand National Association. Walker had been deeply involved with Wyvell's contemporaneous Counties Association since 1779 and was linked with Fox in the opposition. He was a radical close to Wilkes in spirit, and had ability to raise the crowd, later being elected as Borough Reeve in 1790, and was a great publicist (later editing the *Manchester Herald*).[178]

At its first formal meeting on 14 March 1785, the Chamber elected Josiah Wedgwood as chair. Wedgwood, though known as sympathetic to radical views and friendly with opposition leaders, was also an independent and important member of the establishment. With a commission to make Queen Charlotte's tea service in 1765, and the subsequent launch of Queen's Ware, Wedgwood had very effectively cultivated the patronage of the Royal family, the aristocracy, and the crowned heads of Europe.[179] He was also considered as a hugely successful businessman, with known market connections in all the significant locations of the world, listened to with seriousness and expectation.[180] His Etruria factory and involvement with the Trent–Mersey canal made him the model of the 'new' industries and an experienced lobbyist, with extensive connections with the key ministers and opposition leaders.[181] Aged 55 in 1785 he was at the height of his powers and a heavyweight that could not be ignored. As recently as April 1783 he

[176] Following Postlethwayt and Burgh; Garbett to Burke, 29 October 1766; quoted in Norris (1957), p. 452.

[177] In October 1784; *Account of Birmingham Commercial Committee 1784*; Birmingham Archives C/19/27082.

[178] See *DNB*, which wrongly credits him with 'founding' the General Chamber; he was one of several vice-presidents. Walker was a small cotton weaver who became a prosperous merchant, and had close links with Matthew Boulton, and offered an apprenticeship to James Watt's son, who became Walker's agent for Europe. He later rejoiced in the revolution in France, and was tried unsuccessfully for sedition in 1793–4; see Knight (1957); Walker (1794). He had high spirits, becoming involved in a very public row with local barrister William Roberts at a Revolution Society dinner in 1788; Roberts published a pamphlet calling Walker a bully, fool, scoundrel, and blackguard 'unworthy of association with, or notice of gentlemen'; Walker successfully sued for libel; Gurney (1791).

[179] Reilly (1992), pp. 275–6; Meteyard (1866); also *DNB*.

[180] McKendrick (1982); Brewer (1982).

[181] Meteyard (1866); Ehrman (1962, 1969); Reilly (1992).

had been in close contact with Fox to seek reductions in import duties for pottery in Europe whilst Fox's brief government was negotiating the Treaty of Utrecht with France and Spain. He, with the similarly well-connected Boulton, was the major asset of the Chamber, dwarfing other members, and a formidable opponent for Pitt.

The Chamber initially developed strongly. Pitt was lucky to survive the challenge, acted quickly to reduce other areas of possible defeat, and quickly reconstituted the BoT with new members. As Arthur Young observed:[182] 'when the manufacturers of the Kingdom, with the Chamber for a centre of union, raised so violent an out-cry; when parliament was filled in consequence by opposition to them; and when the minister was burnt in effigy . . . can any man imagine he would be free with making experiments'. The Irish proposals had been a humbling experience that Pitt was not going to forget quickly.

The Chamber had an executive of 21 manufacturers resident in London or willing to travel there, meeting once per month. It appointed a president, Sir Herbert Mackworth, a leading independent MP, a large landowner, banker, and coal and copper mine proprietor in Neath and Glamorgan.[183] There were rotating vice-presidents (mainly Wedgwood, Boulton, Walker; also John Wilkinson) and a full-time employed secretary who collected the subscriptions of one guinea (William Nicholson, once an agent for Wedgwood in Amsterdam). The funds were pump-primed by early personal subscriptions; e.g. Matthew Boulton's was one of the largest (£100); Jebediah Strutt gave £30. It began a monthly journal at 1s. per copy in April–May 1784: the *Merchants and Manufacturers Magazine of Trade and Commerce*.[184] A major aim of the Chamber was to stimulate other bodies: it 'got the raw materials, a lawyer and a skin of parchment ready' for any area to set up a committee and join; it developed a motto, 'every petition has its weight'.[185] The issue of weight had a particular resonance, since among the most controversial of the petitions used in the Irish campaign was one which claimed 80,000 signatures from Lancashire, presented on 14 March by the county MP Thomas Stanley. This was a petition against the fustian tax (about 50,000 names) supplemented by those objecting to the Irish proposals. Pitt acknowledged 'the sentiments of so very serious a body of men, called for the most serious attention of the House'.[186]

However, many individuals were concerned about the use of mass petitions and disapproved of the Chamber's noisy approach, notably Garbett, who felt that it would be more effective to influence 'eminent men', by 'acting a more manly and friendly part towards the Administration' and keep above politics.[187] By sounding a 'dawn bell we should not only have raised thousands to sign petitions but have

---

[182] Young, *Annals of Agriculture*, 4 (1785), p. 118; Dietz (1991), pp. 157–8.
[183] *DNB* (2004).
[184] This became a review of the meetings of the chamber, cited above; copies at Goldsmiths-Kress. First advertised, e.g. in the *Leeds Intelligencer*, 19 April 1785.
[185] Wedgwood letters to Boulton 29 April and 27 May 1785; quoted in Dietz (1991).
[186] Pitt, *Parliamentary Register*, xvii, pp. 425–6; quoted in Dietz (1991), p. 144.
[187] Garbett letters to Boulton, 1785, quoted in Money (1977), pp. 41–3; instructions to Warwickshire members, quoted in Dietz (1991), pp. 146–7.

found difficulty to allay the frenzy that would have been the consequence'.[188] Garbett also played a critical role in maintaining cohesion in Birmingham, Sheffield, and Staffordshire.[189] But he was reluctant to testify at the Bar of the House 'and throwing themselves into the arms of Mr. Fox, Mr Eden etc.'[190] The Irish parliament's decision removed the dilemma and Garbett, who had been thinking of resigning from the Chamber, conceded, 'it is wonderful they [the Chamber] have not done more wrong'.[191] The use of petitions, the press, and the opposition was a direct challenge to authority; it was difficult to ignore, but also difficult to agree to.

The structure of the Chamber as a loose federation of provincial delegates from local committees and existing chambers, as well as individual members was unstable. The individuals were supposed to be from districts that did not have provincial chambers or committees; but of 300 members by August 1785, 93 of those paying came from Manchester (i.e. about one-third), most of the rest were from London, whilst other areas only 'promised' large memberships.[192] This gave dominance to Manchester and London, and no new provincial chambers or committees that had not already been in contact with Garbett in 1783 were established as a result of the Chamber's activities. The tensions inherent in the structure and regional divisions of approach were fatal in the next stage of development.

Internal tensions and the Eden Treaty 1785–1787: the General Chamber collapses

With success over the Irish proposals the General Chamber began to engage in other fields of lobbying and activity. In late 1785 it began a campaign against foreign spies attempting to steal manufacturing secrets (a particular concern of Manchester, and Garbett, Boulton, and Wedgwood in Birmingham); it also publicized changes in foreign trade conditions, such as those in the Netherlands restricting British imports; initiated an investigation to help prevent smuggling; and began an investigation of the Excise laws to improve their administration.[193] They were also aware that the Irish question would not go away: James Watt wrote to Boulton expecting the Irish proposals to be revived 'as soon as parliament meets, as the Minister has by no means dropped the idea'.[194] Wedgwood was also coming to share Garbett's views about the dangers of becoming too close to the opposition and thus being seen 'as sons of faction and our Chamber as a party meeting'.[195]

---

[188] Garbett, quoted in Dietz (1991), p. 146.
[189] Without his effort the Chamber might have had no support from the West Midlands; Money (1977), p. 35.
[190] Garbett letter to Lansdowne, 20 May 1785; quoted in Dietz (1991), p. 149.
[191] Garbett; quoted in Dietz (1991), pp. 158–9.
[192] *Plan of the General Chamber of Manufacturers of Great Britain.*
[193] Dietz (1991), pp. 160–3.
[194] Watt letter to Boulton, 20 September 1785; quoted in Dietz (1991), p. 163.
[195] Wedgwood letter to Boulton, 21 May 1785; quoted in Money (1977), p. 43.

The critical issue to emerge, however, was a new Treaty with France. At the cessation of hostilities between the two countries in 1783, the Treaty of Utrecht had *temporarily* renewed commercial provisions for bilateral trade, with one Article that called for a commercial Treaty to be concluded by 1 January 1786. This was an issue of consequence, since duties during the wars had been estimated by Adam Smith to be at 75%, and trade between the two countries had virtually ceased, except in smuggling. The diplomatic negotiations were protracted but led to a Treaty being signed by 26 September 1786, with a supplementary convention to the Treaty signed 15 January 1787, and transmitted to the House of Commons on 26 January 1787, with further conventions negotiated in April, coming into effect on 10 May 1787 when British ports were opened to French trade.

Pitt had attempted various consultations with business interests as the negotiations progressed, and he believed the Treaty represented a reciprocal liberalization of navigation and commerce, with also freedom to travel, reside, purchase, and use goods between the two. The French gained concessions that wine, vinegar, brandy, and olive oil could be imported to England on favourable terms (equivalent to that enjoyed by Britain's long-term ally Portugal); also included were French cambrics, linens, millinery, and other finely wrought goods. Britain gained access for export to France of cabinet ware and articles of iron, copper, and brass (at a duty of no more than 10% of value) and of cotton and certain woollens, porcelain, earthenware, and pottery (at no more than 12% of value). There were also limitations on other duties and bounties on exports, and the extension of 'most favoured European nation status' to the ships of each country.[196]

The General Chamber sidelined?

Pitt had appointed a new minister specifically to lead the negotiations on this Treaty, on 9 December 1785. This was none other than one of his chief opposition opponents to the Irish proposals, William Eden: hence the term the 'Eden Treaty'. As Ehrman notes, there was nothing unusual in individuals changing sides in a period where political parties were still emerging. But Eden was so identified with the opposition and the events leading to Pitt's humiliation on the Irish proposals, that it was a remarkable choice; and Eden was seen as careerist, condemned or shunned by his former opposition colleagues.[197] However, Pitt judged that he would be able to draw back into his support the business interests that had been alienated during the Irish problems, 'it would disarm the opposition at least as much as it exasperated them'.[198] Pitt's choice of Eden also sought to circumvent the General Chamber by using Eden's networks to deal directly with business leaders, and Pitt instructed Eden[199] 'that our sole object is to collect, from all parts of the Kingdom, a just representation of the interests of the various branches of trade and

[196] See Bowden (1919–20); Ehrman (1969).
[197] Meteyard (1866), ii, pp. 554–6; Ehrman (1969), pp. 484–5.
[198] Pitt letter to Rutland, 14 January 1786; quoted in Dietz (1991), p. 166.
[199] Pitt letter to Eden, 16 December 1785, quoted in Bowden (1919–20), p. 28, emphasis added.

manufacture which can be affected by the French arrangement . . . I probably need hardly add, however, that there are many reasons which make it *desirable to give as little employment or encouragement as possible to the Chamber of Commerce* taken collectively.' This quotation, frequently used, is often misinterpreted: it was a warning to Eden as a former opponent as much as it was an indication of Pitt's dislike of the General Chamber.[200]

The manufacturers were indeed delighted by Eden's appointment. Wedgwood wrote to Eden, whom he knew personally, that 'the manufacturers in general rejoice with me on your appointment',[201] and Boulton stated that he would himself have appointed Eden. Eden was known for his constant attention to the views of the manufacturers, and 'cordiality' with them.[202] Eden indeed did consult widely with individual leaders of business across the country: 'passing *every* morning and all morning in examination of merchants and manufacturers'.[203] This was a wide consultation, though it excluded, probably deliberately, some interests expected to be hostile (e.g. agriculture, and the Spitalfields weavers).[204] It also seems that Thomas Walker was not invited or refused to attend Eden's consultations, since other Manchester delegates appeared (again Robert Peel and Thomas Smith).[205]

Ehrman summarizes the interests on the Treaty as those in favour, divided, and doubtful.[206] Eden and Pitt clearly favoured the 'new' manufacturers as contributing most to future national wealth. The exchanges included many leading members of the General Chamber. Indeed it is clear Eden maintained an exchange with Wedgwood, for whom both he and Pitt had enormous respect, independently of his role in the Chamber.[207] This is also evidenced in Pitt's reply to Eden when seeing Wedgwood's congratulatory letter, where he noted,[208] 'I am very glad that you will have the opportunity of following his [Wedgwood's] suggestions'. Wedgwood also espoused Pitt and Eden's principle of reciprocity:[209] 'we only wish for a fair and simple reciprocity, and I suppose (but I speak without any authority), that our Manchester and Birmingham friends would be willing to give and take in the same way'. Other chambers were also consulted; e.g. Leeds discussed the matter vigorously, sent delegate Alexander Turner in January 1786, liaised with Wakefield

---

[200] See e.g. Ehrman (1962), p. 45.

[201] Wedgwood letter to Eden, 5 January 1786, quoted in Dietz (1991), p. 166. Eden was already highly regarded by business people after his role in Ireland and efforts at conciliation in America (see Chapter 4).

[202] Bowden (1919–20), p. 29.

[203] Eden letter January 1786, emphases in original; evidence in TNA BT 6/111–14: in Ehrman (1962), p. 45.

[204] The full list of attendees and summary minutes are at BL Add MS 34462.

[205] Meteyard (1866), ii, p. 554; BL Add MS 34462, fo. 69.

[206] Ehrman (1962), pp. 46–8.

[207] Indeed Pitt's father, Lord Chatham, and Wedgwood had a close association: Meteyard (1866), ii, pp. 542–3.

[208] Pitt letter to Eden with Wedgwood's congratulatory letter, 16 December 1785; in Wedgwood (1915), p. 240.

[209] Wedgwood letter to Eden, 5 January 1786; quoted in Wedgwood (1915), p. 240.

(Messrs Milnes) and Halifax (Messrs Samuel and John Waterhouse), and strongly supported the Treaty as a basis for 'reciprocal trade'.[210]

Eden continued to consult with business leaders after he left for France in March 1786, with Wedgwood and Eden maintaining correspondence, and many manufacturers meeting Eden in Paris in June and July.[211] Indeed, Eden wrote to Pitt, headed 'private and secret', 'that the delay which has unavoidably taken place subjects me to numerous applications from various people here [in Paris], several of whom come from Sheffield, Birmingham etc., on the speculation of being near at hand to take any advantage in the opening of trade'.[212] Contemporaries recognized that the Treaty was 'framed in concert with the manufacturers themselves', with the manufacturers of cotton, hardware, and pottery industries benefiting most. Edmund Burke, for example, warned that 'the opinion of two counties [Lancashire and Staffordshire], however extensive and commercial, should not be taken for the sense of the people of England'. Lord Landsdowne, who had condemned the manufacturers over the Irish proposals, stated on the French Treaty that he 'was proud of the conduct of the manufacturers'.[213] The French view also suggested that the British had done well: 'the Treaty secured incontestable advantage for our agriculture . . . [but] crisis in our industries'.[214] Some observers even viewed the following French industrial crisis as due to the Treaty and a contributor to the French Revolution three years later.[215] The most affected areas of cloth manufacture, Normandy, Picardy, and Champagne felt 'the Treaty is preponderantly favourable to the English', and they complained that they had not been informed and consulted until the Treaty was signed.[216]

Both Jersey and Guernsey chambers lobbied for modifications of the Treaty, where Arthur Young noted that whilst 'party and prejudice may have misrepresented the motives of a similar institution' (the General Chamber), 'the chambers of commerce of both Islands sent two deputies with a memorial to the hands of the Treasury', with the aim of restructuring trade also for the Channel Islands.[217] However, for the Jersey chamber there were echoes of older animosities with the States, which broke up prematurely before considering the chamber's memorial. The chamber found nothing in the Treaty 'prejudicial to this Island except that we

---

[210] Leeds chamber minutes, 5, 13, and 28 December 1785; 3, 4, 21 January; 9, 17, and 26 October 1786. See Table 4.1.

[211] Ehrman (1962, pp. 183–4; 1969, pp. 491–2) claims there was only slight contact; but letters to Pitt from Eden meeting the Birmingham merchants in Paris suggest otherwise, 1 July 1786; TNA PRO 30/80/110, fos. 88–92.

[212] Eden to Pitt, 6 June 1786, PRO 30/8/110, fos. 127–30; that Eden was believed by Pitt to be in contact with these interests also follows Grenville's role overseeing the negotiations on behalf of Pitt: see Adams (1904), pp. 6–7.

[213] Views summarized and quoted in Bowden (1919–20), pp. 30–1; and Ehrman (1969), pp. 486–90.

[214] Dumas, *Etude sur la Traité*, p. 191; quoted in Bowden (1919–20), p. 32.

[215] Schmidt (1908), 'Le Traité de 1786 et la crise au rière en France', *Revue historique*, xcvii, pp. 78–94.

[216] *Observations préliminaires de la Chambre de Commerce de Normandie sur le Traité de Commerce qve l'Angleterre*, quoted in Sée (1930).

[217] A. Young, *Annals of Agriculture* (1786), p. 370; refers to 1785; one of the few records of Guernsey chamber.

are not allowed the same leave of importing all French manufactures in England as we hitherto have enjoyed with respect to articles of wines etc.' The chamber approached the Lieutenant-Governor to approach Lord Beauchamp to raise this in the Lords, and also instructed its London agents John Dumaresq, and Mesurier and Trott, 'to obtain the privileges of importing French goods from this Island as of directly from France'.[218] A later memorial raised further concerns over olive oil and manufactures.[219] There is some evidence here that the States was responding to Pitt's desire to sideline chambers, but this was also part of the chamber's continuing dispute with the States over harbours.

Divisions within the General Chamber

Pitt and Eden appear to have sought an acceptable commercial compromise, with Pitt achieving his objective of *formally* sidelining the General Chamber, and Eden consulting directly with Wedgwood. But the Chamber was not content to rely on Wedgwood or be left out. In late 1786, after the Treaty was signed on 26 September, the Chamber held a number of meetings of its executive committee to consider the Treaty, and exchanged letters and enquiries with Eden who was wise enough to respond politely. The Chamber's committee received general reassurance both from Eden and from its own members/delegates that it had provided 'the best information it can collect from the chambers of commerce and manufacturers' (its member bodies).[220] As a result, on 7 December 1786 the Chamber's committee, under the chairmanship of Wedgwood, adopted resolutions supporting the Treaty.

However, when published, the Chamber's resolutions aroused strong press condemnation and attacks by an alternative faction, led by Manchester's Thomas Walker. The press accused those who were favourable to the Treaty of gaining control of the Chamber and misrepresenting the views of other manufacturers.[221] Various new meetings were called in February and March 1787, but the disagreement could not be resolved. The discussion was to prove fatal and the Chamber was disbanded in acrimony by mid-1787.

Historians have tended to interpret the break-up of the General Chamber as an inevitable consequence of divisions between different business interests. Redford concluded that subsequent chamber inactivity was the result of these discords.[222] Bowden concluded that the division of the Chamber reflected a deep disagreement between the old 'craft'-based manufacturers (who needed monopoly) and the new factory-based producers (who were more supportive of open trade)', an interpretation also followed by Ehrman.[223] These interpretations seem to miss the main

[218] Jersey chamber minutes, 9 November 1786; Beauchamp (William Lygon) was a supporter of Pitt: *DNB*.

[219] Jersey chamber minutes, 17 November 1786 and 30 January 1787.

[220] Wedgwood letter to Eden, 5 January 1786, quoted in Wedgwood (1915), p. 240.

[221] *Gazetteer at New Daily Advertiser*, 12 January 1787; quoted in Bowden (1919–20), p. 22.

[222] Redford (1934), pp. 11–13.

[223] Bowden (1919–20); Ehrman (1969), pp. 491–2.

point of personality, tactics, and the uniqueness of the national Chamber compared to other interests, particularly the provincial chambers.

Wedgwood had been strongly involved in the original discussions leading up to the 9 December 1786 meeting resolutions.[224] Walker had refused to be involved early in 1786, or had been ignored, but he called and chaired the general meeting of 6 February 1787 to reconsider the Treaty. This appointed a new committee and on 10 February another general meeting strongly criticized the original committee, and in effect Wedgwood. It stated that the December resolutions had been made without all relevant parties being notified (two committee members and one chair were not summoned) and the resolution was phrased too decisively, 'failing to acknowledge the great diversity of opinion expressed at the committee meetings'.[225] There was deep dispute over the earlier resolutions, with a majority vote to change them, resisted by Wedgwood's supporters.

Walker led this revolt, and in so doing broke ranks with Manchester chamber. He appears to have packed the General Chamber meetings with London artisans and to have been motivated primarily by links with the opposition to cause Pitt as many problems as possible. It is also possible he was positioning himself to take over as Borough Reeve for which an election campaign was developing, and to prevent Wedgwood becoming the leader of the northern section of the Slavery Abolition Society in 1787.[226] Meteyard interprets Walker's behaviour on this 'point to have cleaved to party, rather than distinguished principles;... to have been as prejudiced and hasty as Wedgwood, on the other hand, was petulant and complaining'.[227] Read interprets him as 'probably... motivated by mere political partisanship'.[228] Wedgwood himself felt that 'great pains have been taken by little-minded men, to clothe the manufacturers with party coloured robes'.[229] After the dust settled, Wedgwood wrote to Eden: 'my late antagonist, Mr Walker, has quite lost himself in Manchester, and I may add through the whole island'. He was pleased with Eden's approval for snubbing Walker in June 1787: 'my last answer to him, which in my opinion was the wisest and the best because it was the shortest I had made. I am told my conduct has been approved at Manchester in particular. I rejoice to find that all croaking against the Treaty is at an end.'[230]

Walker was a relative outsider, except in Manchester, and linked with the opposition. He 'felt it was only through political action that anything of social importance or for the public good could be achieved, and so he... continued to "act upon hazard"'.[231] He was thus happier fighting government than working with it, the converse of Wedgwood. Press cover and the new petition of the

[224] Meteyard (1866), ii, pp. 553–6; Ehrman (1969).
[225] *Public Proceedings of the General Chamber . . . on the French Treaty* (1787), p. 6.
[226] Martin (2002), Chapters 4 and 5.
[227] Meteyard (1866), ii, p. 561.
[228] Read (1964), p. 32.
[229] Auckland (1861), *Correspondence*: Wedgwood letter to Eden, 5 January 1786; Meteyard (1866), ii, p. 556.
[230] Ibid.: Wedgwood letter to Eden, 16 June 1787.
[231] Knight (1957), p. 174

Chamber presented to the Commons on 12 February 1787 by opposition MP Nathaniel Newnham publicized the discord in the Chamber.[232] Many leading members resigned from the Chamber, including Manchester. Pitt's view was that the views of the manufacturers 'merited every respectful attention' but not when it came from 'a few manufacturers collected in a certain chamber of commerce', which had not procured 'all the lights they might require'; i.e. it did not have the support of the leading industrialists. Walker's leadership was defended by the opposition leader Fox: 'a more respectable name than that of Thomas Walker did not exist', who also invoked support from Messrs Milnes of Wakefield.[233] But these parliamentary conflicts only served to sour others in the Chamber further.[234]

On 17 February, with Wedgwood now back in the chair of the Chamber, but not in control, a new set of resolutions was passed. These recollected the original principles of the Chamber 'to watch over their interests at large as one AGGRE-GATE tend to be prepared to furnish government, if required, with such IMPAR-TIAL and *true information*... for want of which, or by relying upon the *information given by interested individuals,* the true interest... has been often unavoidably mistaken'.[235] The emphases in this resolution all pointed to Wedgwood, who was portrayed as tainted. The resolutions went on to call for 'all reasonable delay' in order to allow 'deep consideration' of the Treaty.[236] For Wedgwood this was a humiliation. It had been achieved because Walker had again managed to pack the meeting with large numbers of individual members who far outnumbered the delegates of the provincial chambers. Wedgwood sought to regain control and in March 1787 tried to pass a rule based on proportional representation to prevent future defeats by 'the tooth brush manufacturers of London'.[237] A group of his 'friends' drew up reforms to restrict the number of delegates from any chamber, ensure they had support of a fixed number of existing members, and only those could speak who held voting rights.

Disintegration and recrimination

None of Wedgwood's reforms or the petitions of the provincial chambers progressed. When the Chamber next met on 27 March, with Walker in the chair, Wedgwood avoided going.[238] The meeting considered a report of its new committee on the Treaty. The report went into great detail on the rate of duty on each

---

[232] Newnham was a banker, merchant, and independent member of the Commons, generally opposed to Pitt.
[233] *Parliamentary Register XXI*, pp. 163–4; Dietz (1991), p. 191; *Annual Register* (1878), pp. 65–90; see also Bowden (1965), pp. 187–8.
[234] Wedgwood himself felt that the chamber had come to be seen as 'a mere party affair... of Mr Fox and his party.... I have great aversion to putting my name to such things... and have never waited on Mr. Fox, nor even exchanged a single word with him on the subject'; Wedgwood to Walker 15 January 1786, quoted by Walker (1794), pp. 96–7.
[235] General Chamber, Resolution I, 17 February 1787, all emphases and capitals in original.
[236] Resolution IV, op. cit.
[237] Wedgwood letter to James Watt, 20 March 1787, quoted in Dietz (1991), p. 191.
[238] Wedgwood letter to Watt 20 March 1787, quoted in Dietz (1991), p. 193.

main trade (cotton, beer, silk, etc.) and concluded that it was an unequal Treaty. The report and *Proceedings* were published and widely distributed, with an inflammatory introduction by Walker.[239] The provincial chambers were furious. The Birmingham committee, under the chairmanship of Matthew Boulton, resolved that the parliamentary petition and publication of sundry resolutions disapproving of the Treaty were 'exceeding impolitic', not authorized by the Birmingham committee or delegates, and that a new constitution for the General Chamber should be drawn up with 'regulations made as may tend to prevent such conduct in the future, and also prevent improper persons from being admitted members of that Chamber'. It would no longer send delegates or consider itself regulated by the Chamber.[240] Wakefield (through Milnes) came behind Walker, but Leeds reaffirmed its support for the Treaty (only Stamp Act protester Obadiah Dawson dissenting).[241] Even the Manchester fustian manufacturers declared that 'no person has been appointed by us as a delegate to the General Chamber' and they supported the Treaty; voting 441 to 78 to reject Walker. Sheffield and Staffordshire also withdrew.[242] Glasgow, Dublin, Edinburgh, and Liverpool chambers had in any case acted independently and supported the Treaty. The General Chamber fell into abeyance in mid-1787 after passage of the Treaty.

Walker was isolated, but Wedgwood suffered numerous personal attacks. One, which bears all the hallmarks of Walker, on 28 March 1787 in the *Morning Chronicle*, the day after the Chamber's general meeting, was a piece from the 'ghost of Friar Bacon of Brazen Nose College':[243]

> Mr Wedgwood *was* united with men of principle and honour—He *was* a principal informing the Chamber of Commerce.—He *was* the promoter of harmony and union among them . . . Mr Wedgwood *is* connected with, and became the tool of Administration.—He *is* their instrument in attempting to dissolve the Chamber of Commerce, so much dreaded by them.—He *is* artfully attempting to sow dissensions . . . .—He is the faithless and artful underminer of the *general*, and advowed advocate of partial interests. . . . Mr Wedgwood *will be* detested and despised by the manufacturers of the Kingdom.

A lampoon must have been equally distasteful.[244]

> Last year little Josi, and Dobson & Co.
> Erected a Chamber of Commerce we know,
> The reason they gave, I had almost forgot,
> But I think that it was about a *basin or pot*

---

[239] *Public Proceedings of the General Meeting*, 27 March 1787; see also Dietz (1991), pp. 188-9.
[240] Wright (1913), pp. 25–6.
[241] Leeds chamber minutes, 16 and 19 February, 15 June 1787.
[242] Redford (1934), pp. 12–14; Norris (1957); Money (1977).
[243] Quoted in Wedgwood (1915), pp. 243–4, all punctuation and emphases in original.
[244] *The Chamber of Commerce* (*c.*1787), attributed to George Villiers (Bodleian, 13 Theta 6(22)), some verses omitted, emphases in original. This is also significant as it perhaps indicates John Dobson, president of Liverpool chamber, and business partner of Wedgwood in the 1760s, was involved in the General Chamber.

They made such a talking as carry'd an alarm
And kept Mr. P. [Pitt] and his friends very warm!
So London at length was fix'd on for the spot,
Where they met ev'ry ev'ning to talk *o'er a pot*

They thought it was proper to meet and debate
On what they should come to as well as to state,
So jointly as soon as a Chamber they'd got
They wanted to furnish a real *chamber pot*

... The Treaty for Commerce he likes very well,
If from his own party he'd clear'd to rebel ...

Hawkesbury and Sydney ...
Ordered a service of pots.

All this meant to show that a free Navigation,
Exists in the narrowest part of the Nation!
And since a new Treaty of Commerce we've got,
We wish all the Frenchmen were drowned *in the Pot*

The personal animosity to Walker continued and was deeply party-linked. In 1788 when Walker was at a meeting in Manchester about how to unite opposition to the East India Company 'Mr Thomas Walker (fond of popularity) took the lead and speeched away for the fustian makers; Mr Robert Peel and others for the printers; at last they were so warm that Mr Lawrence Peel and Mr Walker collared each other, and all was violence.'[245]

Contemporary lessons drawn from the General Chamber

The General Chamber died in recriminations. But the provincial chambers continued and others developed. The 1784–7 period must be seen, therefore, as the unfolding of an experiment of a national business association that failed. The lessons for the provincial chambers were complex. First, the Chamber had reaffirmed the power of lobbying under a general national umbrella of broad interests,[246] but forcefully exhibited the limitations of a national body with loosely federated societies and floating individual members. As Gilbert Hamilton, the Glasgow chamber's secretary, noted: 'one extensive plan ... to comprehend the whole commercial and manufacturing interest ... is of great difficulty and must be well digested'.[247] The original plan was a national body with provincial chambers as its members; the model advocated by Davenant, Postlethwayt, and Burgh. Instead it became a national body trying to facilitate and organize a very varied range of different individuals, local

---

[245] TNA BT 6/140/45 'Letter from Manchester about calico and muslin business'; also quoted in Bowden (1965), p. 168; parentheses in original.
[246] Norris (1957), p. 460; Money (1977), p. 45.
[247] Gilbert Hamilton letter to James Watt, *c.*28 January 1784; quoted in Schofield (1964), p. 102, n. 74.

committees, societies, and genuine chambers. National bodies henceforth were built from the bottom up; ambitions to build from the centre, and affiliate local bodies to a cause, would never be resurrected except for specific campaigns.

Second, it certainly sullied the brand of 'chamber' and confused local bodies with the General Chamber, which Pitt himself, as we have seen, took to calling 'that chamber of commerce'. This was a setback to the established bodies that retained that brand. Third, the developments re-emphasized the need for formality and constitutions that would ensure a formal and transparent process for making decisions representing the generality of members. This in turn, fourth, suggested the need to formalize the membership and those that could vote. Fifth, Glasgow expressed the wider view that merchants and manufacturers were equally to be included; i.e. chambers should be *general* bodies. The General Chamber's view was exclusively of the manufacturers. But sixth, a clear lesson was that the small trader and craftsman was an unreliable member. Opening membership to smaller businesses exposed chambers to mass public involvement and populism. As in America, local chambers when confronted with a choice, opted for elitism over the masses, and reform over radicalism.

Seventh, the experiences confirmed Garbett's views, that the preferable way to influence government was discreetly. A lot of 'noise' made it more difficult to gain concessions from politicians: quiet influence was likely to be more successful, provided the avenues for consultation in government were open. After the failure of Pitt's Irish proposals, reassurance seems to have been given that this was now possible, as evident in the exchanges of Pitt with Turnbull and the Union of chambers. Eighth, Walker's capture of the Chamber and work with the opposition exhibited the dangers of becoming politically aligned. It was divisive between members, and it risked manipulation and abuse that left businesses exposed. The way in which Wedgwood suffered vilification and abuse in the opposition popular press was salutary: it was off-putting to others to come forward, and it reinforced the need to be exclusive and operate through quiet lobbying, and avoidance of political partisanship.

Finally, the Chamber evidences the conservatism, resistance, and power of London guilds and livery companies, and the difficult ground for liaison with organized groups in the capital. They had little involvement with the Irish lobby, none with the fustian tax, and equivocal positions on the French Treaty. Wedgwood stated the problem: 'The principal glover has a contract under government and does not appear [at meetings]. The button-maker makes buttons for his majesty and therefore he is tied fast to his Majesty's minister's button-hole. . . . few of the principal manufacturers are left at liberty to serve their country.'[248] A new union of local bodies planned after the break-up of the General Chamber specifically excluded London, except for the major trading interests (such as West Indies, etc.). The Birmingham leaders were planning a union to include Manchester, the iron makers and cutlers of Sheffield, the potters of Staffordshire, the association of hosiery makers in Nottingham and other commercial combinations in the Midlands. It would meet at Manchester, Birmingham, and Stoke-on-Trent in

---

[248] Wedgwood to Boulton on the Irish proposals, 1 May 1785; quoted in Meteyard (1866), ii, p. 547.

rotation. It was 'to have nothing to do with Londoners except on particular occasions'.[249] This did not come about, but Wedgwood continued to maintain the possibility of revival if needed: 'the Chamber sleepeth for the present, but may be awakened at any time';[250] it became explicitly a latent chamber.

The lesson for government was the danger of not consulting important provincial business interests: the General Chamber demonstrated the power of organized business to embarrass government, particularly if allied with the opposition. Hence the critical development achieved was that routine consultation with business and exchange of information was re-established, primarily through the Board of Trade. The government recognized that it was dependent on listening and welcomed using deliberated information gathered by semi-permanent bodies such as chambers.[251] The modern form of business lobby had been created. The changes wrought by the Stamp Act protests had become embedded and diffused to a wider canvas. Everyone was aware, including Pitt, that this was a change in national representational processes, and that London and the chartered companies were no longer the only voices that should be heard. The General Chamber thus simultaneously sullied but reinforced the chamber brand.

9.6 CONCLUSION

This chapter has reviewed the early development of the voice of chambers of commerce over a period in which they became a leading business lobby. They remained one of many voices, but became an organized force of the main 'provincial' centres and ports, often working with London, sometimes against it. The breadth of chamber lobbies was wide, as it is today, but was already focused on international trade, and national taxation and regulation, as well as a range of issues specific to each area. However, in 1786–7 there was a crisis of brand. On the one hand, Pitt's re-establishment of the BoT, with a stronger status and permanent secretariat than its predecessor abolished in 1782, opened the way for more effective routine communications with chambers and other business voices. On the other hand, the break-up and dissension within the General Chamber sullied the 'chamber' brand. Other commentators have observed this crisis, but twin-tracking of chamber activity beyond the General Chamber has not been previously recognized. The result is a very different interpretation of the chambers over this period.

The chapter has sought to show that, whilst the 1787 General Chamber failed, the concept of local chambers did not die. Helm, Bowden, Redford, and Beresford have all argued that there was a split between protectionists and free traders in this period.[252] This is a misinterpretation, which is why the term 'reciprocity' and level

---

[249] James Watt letter to Wedgwood, 25 July 1787; quoted in Ashton (1963), p. 173; Norris (1957), p. 460.

[250] Wedgwood letter to Eden, 16 June 1787; Auckland (1861), *Correspondence*; also Wedgwood (1915), p. 244.

[251] See Ehrman (1962), pp. 81–2.

[252] Bowden (1919–20, 1965); Clapham (1926); Ashton (1963).

playing field (the contemporary terms used) have been employed here. There was no concept of free trade at this time in the meaning to be developed later. Thus the conclusion by Helm, that the Manchester merchants were 'not yet emancipated from the thraldom of protection'[253] is misleading. Similarly, Redford's conclusion that there was growing 'apathy', so that 'the commercial societies of the 1790s met with little success, and there can be no doubt that their failure to secure substantial and tangible benefits for their members contributed largely to the general decline of the movement after 1798' is incorrect. Beresford and others have misleadingly restated Redford's assertions.[254]

In contrast, it has been demonstrated here that many chambers remained very active, had significant impact in many fields (often in coalition with others), but from the 1790s often took a deliberately low profile and kept out of the press. The anti-sedition laws may have further encouraged this after 1796. Notable successes of this period were lobbies on American debt, the Spanish Treaty, attempts to maintain trade during French expansion in Leghorn and elsewhere, various taxation, banking, and other matters. The chambers (mainly through Glasgow) played a leading role in the legal process leading up to adjudication of claims on American debt. If, as Clapham states, this was a 'subordinate part',[255] it was collectively greater than any other provincial business lobbies at the time, and the participants appear to have, in general, been pleased with the outcomes they achieved.

The period is important not only for the birth of a sustained chambers' voice, but also for the evidence it gives of lessons learnt about the lobbying process: the balance to be stuck between 'noise' and subtle activity is the most obvious. It also reaffirmed, as in America, that local chambers when confronted with a choice, should opt for elitism over populism, and reform over radicalism. But also critical was the experience of attempts at national organizations that went beyond using London agents. National bodies were valuable, but in future would only be built from the bottom up based on federations of local bodies, like the first 'Union'. The concept of a national chamber as derived from Davenant, Postlethwayt, and Mortimer, and pressed as a political engine by Burgh and Burke, would only be resurrected for campaign organizations. The importance of maintaining 'unity' of interests for successful lobbying was now fully recognized. The value of *deliberation* to achieve unity, with transparent governance, and well-argued briefing papers, is perhaps most evident of all in the profuse paperwork of the Glasgow chamber, and the role of effective leaders like Patrick Colquhoun. The re-establishment of the Board of Trade also encouraged some chambers to enhance routine representational activity, seeking exchange and involvement with departments and ministers when opinions were being formed. This formed the main working method when the Board was under Robinson and Huskisson 1815–27.

[253] Helm (1897), p. 60.
[254] Redford (1934), p. 51; Beresford (1951), pp. 13, 62, Leeds chamber history; Rose (2000), p. 135.
[255] Clapham (1926), pp. 309–10 states that chambers 'played only a subordinate part in the life of the country'.

10

Chamber Voice from the Corn Laws to the Twenty-First Century

10.1 INTRODUCTION

The previous chapter has shown how early chamber voice emerged. This chapter brings the analysis up to the present. The early part of this period was one in which 'reform' became a mainstream political cause,[1] within which chambers were often leaders; notably in continued anti-Corn Law campaigns and the lobby against the East India Company monopoly. However, chambers were less directly involved in the most fundamental reform: the parliamentary Reform Acts of 1832 in Britain and Ireland, and the Municipal Corporation Act of 1835 (1846 in Scotland). These reforms had fundamental effects on how chambers lobbied, since they brought new interests and new membership. For example, campaigns for municipal incorporation and electoral reform in Birmingham and Manchester were critical underpinnings of the Anti-Corn Law League in 1838, and leading reform members on town councils were often also members of the chambers.[2]

Once municipal reform had been achieved, albeit imperfectly, there were new avenues for local interests to take voice to Westminster. In some ways this opened a heyday of local business leadership through opportunities to take on civic roles and improvements. 'Reform' helped chambers by providing a more extensive system of 'open boroughs', and there was a less corrupt, more efficient, and receptive state structure with reduced scope for patronage. Nevertheless, patronage remained important,[3] until further reforms to the electoral franchise at the end of the 19th century, and in the early 20th century, which widened the countervailing interests and introduced a much more active state, so that chambers had to contend with a much wider and more complex structure.

This chapter begins with an overview of chamber voice activities as received in parliament. This broad overview is complemented by detailed assessment of the major issues and lobbies that had most significance for the chambers themselves. Many of these over 1860–1960 have been covered in some detail by Ilersic and Liddle, which remains an important complementary source. Here the aim is to assess the most critical campaigns. The best publicized and most important was the

---

[1] Innes (2003); Innes and Burns (2003).
[2] e.g. Sturge in Birmingham, and Cobden in Manchester in 1838; Read (1964), p. 131.
[3] See e.g. Gash (1977).

anti-Corn Law agitation, which shifted the political economic debate towards a 'paradigm' of free trade. The Corn Laws, free trade, and tariffs thus naturally form major focuses of the chapter. The rest of the chapter then deals with the overarching themes of 20th-century chambers: foreign trade and consular support; the local state and rate campaigns; and efforts to link voice between the chambers and CBI.

10.2 OVERVIEW OF LOBBIES 1800–1913

The period after 1800 saw two critical trends for chambers: first, an expanding voice through the increase in number of chambers, particularly after 1850; second the emergence of a national structure in the 1850s through a national agent, and after 1860 through a national association (the ACC/ABCC). From 1897 for chambers of trade there was also the NCT; and after 1923 a national chamber association for Ireland. Ilersic and Liddle identify the chief targets for ACC lobbying up to WW1 as reforms of the Foreign Office, international trade and treaties, legal reforms, patent law and trade marks, railways and canals, shipping, the post office and telegraph, and education (particularly technical education). Their assessment is broadly correct, but can be put in wider context.

Fields of lobby activity

The recently assembled online parliamentary papers allow a systematic search and classification of the totality of chamber voice directed at parliament. Although there are deficiencies, this offers a systematic way of grasping the evolving pattern.[4] For the period up to the 1880s private Bills and parliament itself remained the chief target of lobbyists; after this government departments became much more significant, but parliament remained important through its committees, commissions, reports, and inquiries. Chambers became less able to initiate legislation themselves, but they were always active when parliament was considering or consulting on changes.

The overall pattern of lobbies, shown in Table 10.1, demonstrates this shift. Although the number of chambers became much larger in the 1880s, and government more significant, the totality of chamber voice to parliament tended to stabilize 1870–1900, before increasing in the run-up to WW1, where tariffs and favoured nation status increased the lobbies relating to geographical markets. Table 10.1 classifies chamber voice into four groups: directed at (i) general trade issues, regulations, and laws; (ii) tariffs; (iii) trade in specific international geographical markets; and (iv) specific business sectors. The efforts around the Corn Laws in 1830–48 are excluded as this would swamp the rest. The analysis splits around the

[4] It provides a reasonably consistent index from the point of view of the recipient. It excludes Jersey, Guernsey, and the Isle of Man (which directly lobby the States, Crown, and Privy Council). Dates are referred to end years where parliamentary sessions are split. All the figures in the following tables are approximate as lobbies sometimes overlap, classification is difficult and tends to reflect government terminology; unfortunately other databases on parliamentary papers do not have codes for lobbyists; e.g. Hoppit (2003).

Table 10.1. The focus of parliamentary lobbies by chambers of commerce 1801–1913 (percentage for each period)

Focus	1801–15	1816–35	1836–48	1849–60	1861–70	1871–80	1881–90	1891–1900	1900–1913
International trade and government regulations	53.4	65.3	63.9	52.0	59.1	59.6	54.1	52.3	36.1
Tariffs and duties	—	0.8	1.7	2.8	1.2	0.6	2.1	3.8	5.8
Geographical markets	37.0	21.0	28.7	36.9	37.4	31.9	38.8	38.6	51.7
Business sectors	9.6	12.9	5.7	8.3	2.3	7.9	5.0	5.3	6.4
Number	73	248	296	230	262	354	441	330	720
No. per year	12.0	12.4	24.7	20.9	26.2	35.4	44.1	33.0	55.3

Note. Excludes Corn Law campaign 1836–48.

Reform Acts of 1835, and the immediate aftermath of abolition of the Corn Laws in 1848.

The overall trend shows particularly active lobbying in the 1836–48 period, especially given the small number of chambers in existence (and on top of the Corn Law campaign), and after 1871. Throughout the period there was a dominance of concern with trade and government regulation, accounting for over one-half of all voice activities up to 1900. This was, and is, the core concern of chambers. Within this there was an increasing focus on tariffs, leading up to the Cobden–Chevalier French Treaty in 1860, and from the 1870s. This became a major focus for chambers, but Table 10.1 puts this in perspective: tariffs were one significant concern among many. The chambers never had a mission to develop sector objectives so that it is not surprising that lobbies about individual industries were only a minor part of chamber voice. Generally chambers voiced against specific sector support; combinations such as the sugar and shipping conferences were particularly resisted.

The trends in chamber voice activity can be compared with more general analyses of parliamentary pressure. Innes and Hoppit show how, after earlier surges of parliamentary Acts and lobbies, the 1820s marked an important take-off of the volume of legislation through the 19th century, with the 1870s marking another period of rapid increase that initiated a wide range of government initiatives in taxation, local government, and public services, and a stronger role of Party government.[5] The chambers demonstrate this trend, from being primarily independently proactive to having to develop a major capacity to respond to government. This shift also affected how lobbying took place: a speech by Charles Monk, Liberal Unionist MP, ACC president in 1883, noted that 15 years ago a private member's bill could carry through parliament against the united opposition of the government, but that was now impossible.[6]

This period also saw the chamber's association (ACC) widen activity, a response that became criticized for pursuing too many goals and diluting the chamber message.[7] Indeed, Michael Hicks-Beach, president of the Board of Trade in 1904, commented on the ACC's 'great many resolutions on a great many subjects . . . sometimes with quite inadequate discussion'. They should 'confine themselves to a few subjects, rather than . . . frittering away the influence they might possess'.[8] With the agenda now increasingly set elsewhere, the chambers found it more difficult to focus, a challenge that remains up to the present.

More detail on each of these lobby fields is given in the following Tables. It is clear that the agenda of voice changed as the external need or threat changed. In Table 10.2 the range of voice on trade and regulation shows the ebbing of some early concerns, such as the slave trade, transport, Customs, bankruptcy/debtors, and the East India Company (after it was forced to open trade to China in 1833 and

[5] Hoppit (2003); Innes (2003); Innes and Burns (2003); see also Cain and Hopkins (2002).
[6] ACC Autumn Meeting, London *CCJ*, 10 October (1883), pp. 1–2.
[7] See Ilersic and Liddle (1960); Taylor (2007).
[8] Speech at Bristol chamber Annual Meeting, 1904; quoted in London *CCJ*, May (1904).

lost control of government in India in 1857). In the early years the Board of Trade was a major force under Lord Liverpool's government, with Frederick Robinson and William Huskisson as respective presidents in 1817–23, and 1823–27, and Brougham as Attorney General. This period saw the chambers supporting revision of the Navigation Acts and, through the Reciprocity Duties Act 1823, winning the critical battle that Britain should move to low duties and protection, as long as other countries could be persuaded to reciprocate.[9] This led to chamber actions on bilateral trade treaties, equalization of British and Irish duties in 1823, demands for budget surpluses to lower tariffs in 1824 and 1825, and revival of further trade lobbies in the 1840s.

Towards the end of the period the main concerns were trade unions and labour issues, education, taxation and public expenditure, local government, and local rates taxation. Some issues remained significant throughout: ports and shipping, patents, standards, combinations, the post office. Others had points of attention when significant government or international action was occurring, such as exhibitions, the navy, law courts, company and partnership law. Trade and tariffs were major features of the period after 1880 as tariff reform gained traction. Also notable was the very prominent attention given to consuls and embassies in the 1860–1900 period. The tariff reform and consular campaigns are discussed further below.

The international geographical markets on which government was lobbied all related to specific trade objectives or disruptions. It is remarkable that after the dominance of American issues in the 18th century, the USA hardly figures: the key regions were Ireland, Europe, Africa, India, and the West Indies; with India becoming the most significant single region for chamber attention over most of the period.[10] As noted by many commentators, India (accounting for 17–36% of geographically focused lobbies 1849–1913) replaced America as the focus of empire. Africa became more important after the activities of Livingstone and Stanley in the 1870s[11] (accounting for 10–17% of chamber geographical lobbies 1871–1913). Wider ranging legislation and voice embracing concepts of 'the colonies' or 'the empire' fluctuated in importance, with most lobbies focused on specific countries or regions.

Local chamber roles

The early period is instructive of how the chambers operated before they developed a national agent or association. There were five key features. First, Irish chambers were very active, accounting for 40% of all lobbies over 1830–50, with Dublin the single largest source of activity for the whole UK, and Limerick and Belfast also prominent voices. Second, among the non-Irish chambers, the effort was led by five chambers (Edinburgh, Glasgow, Manchester, Greenock, and Hull), which

[9] See e.g. Llewellyn-Smith (1928); Lingelbach (1938); Brown (1958); Palmer (1990); the role of the chambers in these debates deserves more attention than has been possible here.
[10] As also noted for chambers by Davis and Huttenback (1984), pp. 256–60.
[11] Good overview, but with little comment on the role of chambers, in Cain and Hopkins (2002).

Table 10.2. The trade and regulatory focus of parliamentary lobbies by chambers of commerce 1801–1913 (percentage for each period)

Focus	1801–15	1816–35	1836–48	1849–60	1861–70	1871–80	1881–90	1891–1900	1900–1913
Public expenditure and taxes	2.2	3.7	0.5	1.6	1.3	0.9	0.9	1.2	4.8
Customs/duties	17.6	3.6	1.0	7.1	0.6	0.5	—	—	—
Navigation laws/trade treaties/tariffs	4.4	3.7	22.5	8.7	2.5	4.2	8.5	10.8	11.3
Consuls/embassies/FO	—	—	0.5	0.8	24.0	40.0	41.1	18.9	1.6
Ports/coasts/pilots/lights/shipping	13.7	11.7	9.0	28.5	22.7	13.6	9.8	2.7	11.3
Roads/bridges/canals/rivers/railways	11.1	13.4	12.0	7.9	4.4	8.9	6.3	1.4	11.3
E. India Co.	24.4	1.8	3.5	2.5	—	—	—	—	—
Slave trade	6.7	23.8	16.5	2.4	—	0.5	—	—	—
Navy/prizes	11.1	1.2	0.5	—	—	—	0.4	—	1.1
Exhibitions/museums	—	—	—	4.8	1.3	0.5	0.4	1.4	1.6
Trade unions/employment law	—	—	4.0	1.6	10.8	3.3	1.3	25.7	16.1
Education/universities/apprenticeship	—	0.6	2.5	—	7.6	0.9	11.2	24.5	19.8
Weights and measures/standards	2.2	0.6	—	—	1.3	0.5	0.9	—	0.5
Patents/trade marks	—	0.6	—	—	1.3	4.7	2.2	1.4	4.4
Post office/telephone/telegraph	4.4	1.8	4.0	8.7	5.1	0.9	1.8	2.7	1.1
Bankruptcy/debtors	—	19.5	8.0	2.4	1.9	2.3	0.9	1.4	0.5
Company & partnership law	—	—	2.0	16.7	1.9	4.2	3.6	1.4	1.1
Combinations	2.2	1.2	—	—	0.6	—	0.9	—	1.1
Law courts	—	5.5	4.5	—	5.1	5.6	0.4	1.4	1.6
Local government/poor law	—	7.3	9.0	6.3	5.1	3.3	8.5	5.0	9.6
Local government rates	—	—	—	—	—	—	—	0.4	1.2
Tribunals of commerce	—	—	—	—	2.5	5.2	0.9	—	—

accounted for 42% of all lobbies, and 70% of those in Britain. Third, among these, Scotland was very prominent, with its four chambers accounting for 30% of all lobbies. Fourth, foundation date was significant to the level of activity; the newest chambers had the least voice activities, with Bristol, Plymouth, Dundee, and Cork relatively inactive. Fifth, already over this period there were many rival voices: the parliamentary papers shows that none of the lobbies had less than ten other interest groups involved, some from the same city, and some legislation had very large numbers of lobbyists. So at this stage the chambers were in no sense the only local voice even in the localities in which they existed.

Hence, before the advent of a national agent or association there was a significant level of individual chamber voice activity, but it was unequally shared. Moreover, the issues lobbied were highly varied; none involved more than three chambers. Up to 1855 the widest were the Mercantile Marine Bill (1850), by Belfast, Hull, and Plymouth; for an inquiry into East India Cotton (1850), by Glasgow and Manchester; Arrest of Absconding Debtors Bill (1851), by Liverpool and Manchester; Patent Law Amendment (1851), by Belfast and Greenock; for placing home-made spirits in bond (1851), by Edinburgh and Leith; and for an Ocean Penny Post (1851–2), by Bradford and Manchester. Also, the coalitions between chambers did not have a stable pattern of cooperation. Local need reflected the lobbies mounted. A clear example is Worcester in 1862 when it sought to acquire the status of a bonded port; it went straight to the Chancellor of the Exchequer to press for a parliamentary Bill independently of other chambers.[12] The same occurred with all local improvement Bills. Local priority and contingency were the order of the day.

10.3 OVERVIEW OF LOBBIES 1914–2010

For the later period Ilersic and Liddle's analysis up to 1960 identifies the key themes of chamber voice as: public finance and government services, economic slump and recovery, WW1 and WW2, and politics of industrial intervention. The more systematic analysis of chamber activity in parliament (which excludes Ireland after 1923) demonstrates that these themes were significant, but there were many others.

This was the period in which government became a dominant element in the economy. Public expenditure as a proportion of GNP had run at 9–15% of GNP over the period from the 1830s up to WW1, but expanded beyond 20% from the 1920s, reaching 30% in 1960, 41% in 2006, and 48% in 2010 (after the financial crisis).[13] Government agendas now dominated: scope for private Bills all but disappeared by WW2, and working through the machinery of government departments became the main avenue for influence. Commenting on the latter part of this period, David Frost, director general of BCC 2001–11, noted that direct lobbies on parliament were few, but chambers would always seek to be influential contributors

---

[12] Worcester chamber minutes, report of meeting with Chancellor, 28 May 1862.
[13] ONS statistics; and sources in Daunton (2001), p. 23.

to select committees, inquiries, respond to significant parliamentary consultation exercises, or be quoted in debates.

Fields of lobby activity

Table 10.3 carries forward the general classification of chamber voice by main field up to 2009. In this and the following tables there are the same caveats about difficulties of classification; and the two world wars are excluded, since Ilersic and Liddle give good coverage, and they are atypical periods of voice. The Tables are split into the main spans of each Party regime, though some regimes are aggregated to reduce space.[14]

One of the most notable aspects is the recent massive increase in parliamentary lobby activity undertaken: whilst the 1870s represented a shift to an 'active' state regime, this declined in the 1920s (and chambers also perhaps were less active), but from the 1950s the lobbies per year steadily increased, surpassing any previous levels of activity from the 1980s. This was a period of chamber revival, and under Labour 1997–2010 business faced a massive and technically meddlesome legislative agenda (the Finance Acts and tax codes over this period, for example, increased in size by a factor of ten).

Up to WW2 the chamber lobbies show a continuation of earlier trends, with specific geographical markets remaining prominent, and trade and tariffs becoming increasingly important as government policy evolved. However, WW2 marks a clear watershed, after which the decline of empire and independence of the colonies reduced the focus of parliamentary exchanges related to specific markets. National regulations and trade policy became dominant, with business sectors emerging as significant policy foci during post-WW1 reconstruction, and the Labour regimes of 1945–51 and 1997–2010.

The shifting priorities of chambers within trade, tariffs, and regulatory lobbies, shown in Table 10.4, demonstrate a range of effects. First, a dominant theme was resistance to increasing government taxation, expenditure, and regulatory intrusion, with interlinked campaigns over local rates. An ABCC report in 1925 on *The Industrial Situation* came to 11 recommendations, the most important of which were: cutting national and local government expenditure; reducing local authority wages to those in line with the private sector; steps to reduce industrial unrest; and a hold on state legislation affecting working conditions (chiefly working hours).[15] By the 1930s business was on the defensive; nationalization was resisted in all forms. Whilst there was support for 'safeguarding', this was in a limited form that supported, not replaced, business management and profit motives. The ABCC wrote to the PM Atlee, stating that 'nationalisation in itself will achieve nothing', but its continued objections were ignored.[16] The ABCC view was that 'the

---

[14] Notably the Wilson, Heath, and Wilson–Callaghan governments of 1965–79; in line with recent assessment that suggest Heath (Conservative) made little change from Labour agendas: Sandbrook (2010).

[15] ABCC, letter to BoT, reported in *Proceedings*, August 1925.

[16] ABCC, Executive Committee minutes, letter to Atlee, 5 December 1945.

Table 10.3. The focus of parliamentary lobbies by chambers of commerce 1917–2009 (percentage for each period)

Focus	1917–22	1923–9	1930–9	1945–51	1952–64	1965–79	1980–97	1998–2009
International trade and government regulations (incl. energy)	50.5	50.0	40.8	63.7	70.6	82.6	72.4	75.5
Tariffs and treaties (excl. EU)	2.9	11.1	14.5	3.8	4.2	1.3	1.1	3.6
Geographical markets (incl. EU)	31.4	33.3	39.4	24.8	18.7	12.1	21.0	8.9
Business sectors (excl. energy)	15.2	5.6	5.3	7.6	6.5	4.0	5.6	12.0
Number over period	288	183	302	178	443	733	486	1036
No. per year	48.0	26.1	30.2	25.4	34.1	52.4	65.9	86.3

Table 10.4. The trade and regulatory focus of parliamentary lobbies by chambers of commerce 1917–2009 (percentage for each period)

Focus	1917–22	1923–9	1930–9	1945–51	1952–64	1965–79	1980–97	1998–2009
Public expenditure and taxes	12.6	15.9	16.5	17.0	10.0	14.4	6.4	14.5
Customs/tariffs/treaties (excl. EU) and FDI	5.4	18.3	26.1	5.7	5.7	1.6	1.5	4.6
Consuls/embassies/FCO	2.7	—	—	0.9	0.7	0.6	5.8	0.5
Ports/coasts/pilots/lights/shipping	3.6	11.5	15.5	20.0	1.3	4.8	0.8	0.5
Transport	16.2	6.8	6.0	6.6	9.3	9.3	11.7	6.0
Energy and fuel	0.8	—	1.1	10.5	47.9	14.7	7.0	2.6
Environment	1.8	—	—	—	0.7	0.9	5.0	4.3
Public admin., civil service, red tape	0.8	—	—	1.9	0.7	0.6	1.4	10.3
Welfare/health/housing/police, etc.	2.7	4.5	2.3	4.8	0.7	8.0	5.7	9.1
Defence and security	—	—	4.8	1.9	1.3	1.0	1.5	2.9
Exhibitions/museums/heritage/sports	1.8	4.5	1.1	0.9	—	0.6	1.2	2.2
Trade unions/employment law/wages/prices	21.4	4.5	3.5	6.6	1.3	5.1	8.7	2.6
Education and apprenticeships	8.9	4.5	1.1	2.8	0.7	3.5	3.5	14.2
Universities	3.6	—	—	0.9	2.1	0.6	0.6	0.8
Weights and measures/time/decimalization	2.7	—	—	0.9	0.7	0.3	0.3	—
Patents/trade marks	0.8	6.8	9.5	—	2.1	1.6	0.8	0.2
Post office/telephone/radio/media	2.7	4.5	2.3	6.6	2.1	8.3	3.2	1.2
Bankruptcy/debtors	—	—	—	—	—	—	—	0.5
Company & partnership law	—	6.8	1.1	0.9	0.7	1.0	0.3	1.2
Competition and monopolies	—	—	—	0.9	5.9	4.2	9.0	1.4
Law courts	5.4	2.3	3.5	3.8	3.6	4.8	5.2	3.6
Local government	2.7	2.3	1.1	0.9	0.7	1.0	1.7	1.4
Local government rates	0.8	4.5	2.3	0.9	0.7	0.3	1.5	0.5
Business associations	0.8	—	—	0.9	—	0.6	1.2	0.5
Science and research	1.8	2.3	1.1	0.9	0.7	4.5	0.8	1.2
Planning, urban and regional development (incl. local business support)	—	—	1.1	2.8	0.7	7.7	15.2	13.2

government devoted too much time ... to translating its political theories and too little time to attacking national economic problems'.[17] A focal point was the ACC annual meeting in 1958, where a campaign fund against further nationalization was developed in liaison with the IoD, resulting in a leaflet, *Free Enterprise or Nationalisation*, with 20,000 copies distributed.[18] The taboo on discussions of nationalization as 'too political' was abandoned.[19]

The chambers were not opposed to welfare and other reforms per se; indeed business leaders were supportive, and often stimulators of legislation. For example, Sheffield chamber and ACC initiatives for technical education, Hull chamber's call for complete revision of the Poor Law and old age support, and Birmingham's continued initiatives for sickness insurance, labour exchanges, and other unemployment support had strong influence on Churchill and Beveridge and the legislation of 1908. The ACC proceedings show widespread support for other social initiatives of this period. The chambers could not be termed 'illiberal',[20] but were concerned with practicalities and costs. Indeed Tables 10.2 and 10.4 show that chambers were increasingly engaged in voice about social programmes, bureaucratic burden, and economic impact.

Tariffs and treaties, whilst an increasingly major focus up to WW2, ebbed in the face of growing European concerns, 'overseas development', and emphasis on GATT. The early emphasis of chambers on navigation, ports, and transport continued, but expanded to a much wider engagement in 'transport policy' across an increasing spectrum of government actions. Energy (particularly gas and electricity for most of the period) became a major concern as these sectors shifted from private to public; then from municipal to nationalized industries, with much chamber lobbying involving responding to local or regional consultative committees; and then to privatization. Interrelated with energy was the emergence of the environment, initially mainly through pollution control legislation, and then more specific modern concerns with wider controls and carbon regulation. Traditional specialized lobbies in fields such as patents, trademarks, and coinage also continued; as did lobbies related to the post office, communications, and the modern media.

Education lobbies by chambers, always an important theme, show a marked upturn after 1997 mainly because each of Labour's local Education Action Zones required separate legislation, which produced a lot of involvement over 2000–2. The concern of chambers with trade unions and employment law, whilst undiminished among members, shifted to other organizations after WW1, so that the chamber lobbies mainly focused on local elements: the consequences for wages and prices (particularly in the 1950s and 60s), aggregate reform in the Thatcher period, and regulatory burdens on employers. Other more recent focuses have been lobbies on the heavy burdens of regulation and red tape during the Labour government of 1997–2010, and the emergence of monopolies and competition

---

[17] ABCC, Executive Committee report (1947), p. 4.
[18] ABCC, GPC, 1 October 1958.
[19] See e.g. ABCC, GPC minutes, 2 July 1958; London *CCJ*, 89, July (1958), pp. 7–13.
[20] Ilersic and Liddle (1960); Hay (1977).

regulation since the 1950s. Perhaps surprisingly, compared with their earlier history, the chambers have exhibited little concern with universities and research. The main exception was over 1965–79, reflecting the appointment of the first science minister in 1960, and the efforts of the Wilson government to link with industrial development. Interestingly, there is no evidence that the growth of chamber voice was primarily a response to the growth of organized labour, as sometimes claimed.[21] The main effects of unions were more indirect, through the rise of the Labour Party in the House of Commons, which was to be a much greater long-term threat than militancy.[22]

Perhaps the most notable shift of the later period, however, was the emergence of local, urban, and regional development. Until the 1960s, this was wrapped up in sector legislation for industries (cotton, shipbuilding, coal, etc.) and then nationalization. The Town and Country Planning Act of 1947 led to engagement of chambers in this new regulatory field. This expanded under the Wilson Labour regime of 1964–70 with the development of regional policy and planning, then urban regeneration initiatives of the 1970s and 1980s, followed by local training boards and councils, local business support, and other initiatives. Chambers were strongly influenced by these developments, and naturally engaged in related lobby efforts. Infrastructure also became a steadily more significant part of these regional and local concerns, reiterated in recent reports.[23] After 2001 devolution of government to Scotland, Wales, and Northern Ireland, and development of the English RDAs, also engaged chamber lobbies.

The counterpart to the strengthening focus of chambers on UK internal development was some reduction of concern with legislation on specific overseas markets. There was a marked shift in parliamentary attention, and chamber concern, away from India, Africa, and the West Indies after the 1950s. From being the single largest overseas focus of attention, India moved to a minor concern after independence in 1948. More general colonial independence widened government concerns to other countries in the world; international aid and overseas development policies replaced the empire after 1965 (except in the Thatcher period, when government activity in this area, and hence chamber attention, was very meagre). The League of Nations, established in 1919, was an important focus for chambers in its early years, and this continued for the early evolution of the UN, and now for overseas aid.

Recently, the most marked shift of chambers' geographical focus has been the emergence of the EU. This began in the 1960s, and increased markedly after the UK joined the EU on 1 January 1973. The EU accounted for over 60% of all geographically focused lobbies by chambers in the Thatcher period 1979–97, and remains the single largest geographical focus. In addition, and excluded from this analysis, has been direct European lobbying by chambers to Brussels and other EU institutions, activity through Eurochambres (the European Association of

[21] e.g. Yarmie (1980); Clapham (1932), pp. 145, 153.
[22] Ilersic and Liddle (1960); Jennings (1962).
[23] e.g. BCC (2010), *Reconnecting Britain: A Business Infrastructure Survey*.

Chambers of Commerce), and other pan-European institutions.[24] Much of this has been focused through ABCC/BCC. Ireland was no longer a focus for specific legislative concern after independence in 1923.

Ireland

It is possible in the space here only to summarize briefly the lobbying efforts by the Irish chambers and national association after independence in 1923; clearly further research is merited. The major individual Irish chambers, perhaps more than in the UK, have remained as key chamber voices. This is the result both of the smallness of the Irish state that gives more access to local interests, but is also an outcome of the attitude of the chambers to their association, which restricted it to a few voice activities. Indeed, the criticism by Cork chamber in 1969, that the national association did nothing more than mount a 'perfunctory' lobby on the government's annual budget settlement,[25] was largely accurate, but was mostly a result of the limits placed on it by the chambers.

Thus the major chambers in Dublin, Cork, Limerick, Waterford, Galway, Drogheda, and Dundalk could usually gain direct access for their views. Their main attention focused on local needs, especially infrastructure (ports, airports, roads) and development needs, including schools, colleges, universities, and inward investment initiatives. This remains the pattern, but after the chamber association moved out of the Dublin chamber and employed its own staff in 1987, the association developed greater ambition. This mainly bore fruit after about 1991–2 when government funding (backed by EU initiatives) engaged the chambers in regional economic development, and related lobbying activity. In 2006 there was great interest in plans to give local government powers over Business Improvement Districts, similar to those in the USA and planned in the UK. With growing partnership with government came avenues for direct lobbying so that, from about 2000, the Irish chambers association has become a major lobby body alongside the major individual chambers. Text searches of Irish parliamentary papers and general media for 1990–2010 years suggest that the most frequent lobbies are similar to the UK, in rank order: taxation, expenditure, and the national budget; local rates; education, training and manpower; inward investment, trade and exports; infrastructure, transport, and regional development needs.

Assessment

The analysis here has provided an overview of the wide range and shifting priorities of chamber voice. From a position of having small government and a modest state,

---

[24] Significant involvement with Europe and other international partners began through the International Chamber of Commerce when this was founded in 1919, and this was strengthened in 1962 through ABCC membership of the Conference Permanente of the Common Market, which became the Europartneriat in 1973. Eurochambres was founded in 1958 on a wider basis, having 45 member countries in 2010.

[25] See Chapter 8.

the UK and Ireland moved to a proactive state influencing all areas of business activity, as a consequence of which the chambers had to mount an increasing range of lobby activity. The focus developed and changed chiefly through shifts in government activity and evolution of international relations with the rest of the world. By the 1990s Taylor had no doubt that 'the ABCC tended to react to government action rather than influence the trend in government thinking',[26] but this had probably been true since WW1. As time developed the role of *local* chamber lobbies significantly diminished: with few lobbies on parliament directly by local chambers after 1945. The chambers' national association became the main national voice to government. Local voice activity diminished throughout the 20th century, though the devolution of powers to Scotland, Wales, and Northern Ireland after 2001, the Core Cities approach since 1995, and increased localism since 2010 have begun modest reversals of this trend. In the Irish Republic a similar range of lobby priorities has emerged, but a stronger local voice has remained in addition to the national association.

This overview, of course, only captures the broad emphasis, it does not attempt to analyse mechanisms, motivations, or the degree of influence exerted and its effects. In order to delve more deeply the rest of the chapter focuses on a range of the key lobby fields, which have significance for the evolution of the chambers as a whole, individually, and as a network of voices.

10.4 THE ANTI-CORN LAW CAMPAIGN

The most important chamber campaign of the 1800s was the abolition of the Corn Laws. This was frame changing for the chambers, and for politics as a whole. It also laid the foundation for much subsequent development. As noted in Chapter 9, although associated chiefly with the 1830s and 1840s, the Corn Laws were a focus for chamber lobbying from their outset in the 1770s and 1780s. But severe collapses of corn supply in the period immediately following the French war in 1813 led to the hated legislation of 1815.

The 1815 Corn Laws were seen by both contemporaries, and in most modern interpretation, as a flagrant Act by the landed interest to raise prices and hence rents. The Laws initially imposed an outright ban on corn imports at prices below a certain level, later revised to a scale of duty. The aim was to stimulate price stability and self-sufficiency (an autarky policy stimulated by the previous war). However, it ensured prices remained high and supplies sometimes short, which became acute during the Irish famine; for ever associated with the 'hungry forties'. Repeal attracted support from those opposed to 'aristocratic misrule', dissenters, and the working classes, as well as business interests. Repeal was also associated with internationalism, reduced taxation, peace as opposed to wars between rival aristocracies, and opening of trade.[27] The Customs officers levying the duty, or turning

---

[26] Taylor (2007), p. 133.
[27] e.g. Hilton (1977); Spall (1988); Howe (1997).

away laden ships from the ports, were also seen as odious. As stated by the Dublin chamber in 1824: there were 'defective regulations, illegal fees at the Customs House and patronage in regulatory offices. . . . all legislative interference to regulate the prices of commodities of general consumption not only fail but act contrary to their purposes.'[28] However, the forces of resistance to repeal were formidable: the landed classes held substantial majorities in both the Commons and Lords.[29]

It can be claimed that reforms to remove restrictions on trade such as the Corn Laws began in 1786, when both the Treaty with France was agreed that had caused such divisions in the General Chamber, and the Board of Trade was re-established. This Treaty provided the diplomatic model for trade expansion and cemented diplomacy as an adjunct to commercial policy; whilst the BoT became the primary mechanism for consulting business interests. Wars against France over 1793–1815 postponed development, but Liberal Tory governments of the 1820s under Lord Liverpool and George Canning, and with Frederick Robinson and William Huskisson as Presidents of the BoT, revised the Navigation Acts to introduce a principle of *reciprocal trade*. They also introduced new administrators to the BoT, most of the leading members of which wanted further reform,[30] who began to open links with the provinces, the chambers, and other interests, and developed close relations with Cobden.[31] Among the most prominent of BoT reformers was George Richardson Porter, who became a significant pamphleteer advocating wider reforms. Over 1826–34 these policies had been in retreat under protectionist pressures, and it was Richard Cobden's inspiration to see that BoT and other pro-reform ideas focused solely on the Corn Laws provided a better chance of success than a more general campaign against protection that would have alarmed more opponents.

The significance of the Corn Laws to chambers

The significance of the Corn Law campaigns has attracted many hundreds of academic papers and books, particularly on the politics of opinion formation and who deserves credit for repeal. However, what is important here is: how the business interest was framed; what institutions and methods were important in the campaign; how relatively important were chambers; and what were the consequences for the chambers?

First, although the concern of chambers with the Corn Law was of long standing, the priorities were not uniform, with chambers having a diversity of view on import/export duties and tariffs, which was not surprising since different industries benefited from different tariffs. The Corn Law campaign transformed that diversity into a broad view for repeal and for free trade. Though this was never shared by all

---

[28] Dublin chamber minutes, March 1824; quoted in Cullen (1983), p. 60.

[29] See McKeown (1989). Much academic debate focuses on whether it was government leaders, particular Peel, who were resistant to reform, or MPs. The view followed here interprets resistance to be chiefly from MPs and Lords. This is the view of Hilton (1977); Searle (1993); Daunton (1995); Howe (1997); Marrison (1998).

[30] See Chapter 9, and Llewellyn-Smith (1928); Lingelbach (1938); Brown (1958).

[31] Brown (1958), pp. 34–64, 158–86; Platt (1968), pp. xxxvii–xxxix.; Howe (1997).

chamber members, even in Manchester,[32] it was to dominate subsequent chamber voice activities.

In retrospect it is easy to see the Corn Laws as a simple target: few agriculturists were chamber members, though a few prominent aristocrats were honorary presidents. In addition, those businesses that were members, predominantly merchants, manufacturers, and local traders, had experienced some reductions of tariffs in the 1820s, Peel's Liberal Tories promised more reforms (indeed reducing 750 duties and abolishing 450 others in 1842), and international traders found a total ban on grain imports incomprehensible when the prices would support importation. The 1815 Law was also seen as a continuation of wartime restrictions on trade in conditions that no longer applied, part of government wartime expenditure ratchets that could be removed by a more commercial approach.[33]

There was nevertheless great initial diversity. Thus when Glasgow took an early lead on the 1815 Act, seeking to draw Birmingham chamber into its campaign to resist the legislation, and then to seek to repeal, it received only lukewarm support:[34] Birmingham and Manchester both initially favoured reform of the tariff scales rather than repeal.[35] Chamber pressure was episodic, there were many other issues in this post-war period, and the Corn Laws were only one of several. However, in Manchester, abolition was pressed continuously by a minority of leading members. They were unable to gain a chamber majority in votes in 1820, and proponent John Benjamin Smith lost motions in favour of repeal at every annual meeting over 1828–35, with Archibald Prentice (as editor of the *Gazette*, and later the *Manchester Times*) publicizing the chamber's equivocal position.[36]

In Ireland, however, Westminster parliamentary interests had imposed a very restrictive set of controls on all agricultural products. Hence, it is not surprising that all the early Irish chambers opposed aspects of the Corn Laws, particularly the differential bounties between ports (The Irish Foster Act), and inequalities in treatment with England. Petitions were sent in the 1790s by Dublin and Belfast chambers; and by these chambers again, as well as Limerick and Waterford in the 1820s. After union with Britain in 1800, there was a major concern that free trade between the two countries would destroy Irish agricultural and manufacturing industries. A 20-year period was allowed for full implementation of free trade, and when this ended in 1825 major concerns were again raised.[37]

---

[32] Redford (1934); Lloyd-Jones and Lewis (1988).

[33] This was one of Cobden's central arguments: that armaments raised the costs of business, required high taxation, and distorted decision making: see summary in Spall (1988), pp. 426–9.

[34] Glasgow chamber minutes 1812–15; major expenditure on memorials and anti-Corn Law leaflets covered this four-year period; for Birmingham see Wright (1913), pp. 62–4.

[35] For Manchester, see Redford (1934), pp. 134–5; and Lloyd-Jones and Lewis (1988); for Birmingham, Wright (1913).

[36] Turner (1994), pp. 239–40; Pickering and Tyrell (2000).

[37] But when the 1838 campaign got under way in England the Irish chambers lobbied hard to ask for protection if the Corn Law was repealed. In this they were unsuccessful.

Manchester takes the lead

Despite the efforts by other chambers, and its earlier equivocation, the Anti-Corn Law campaign will forever be associated with Manchester after 1837–8. A contemporary account by Henry Ashworth is borne out by the other records and the Manchester chamber's minutes.[38] Ashworth and Richard Cobden, two members of the chamber's Board, went together to the Liverpool meeting of the British Association in late 1837, where they spent much time together in conversation, but also heard and discussed a presentation by George Richardson Porter, then head of the statistical department at the BoT. Porter represented continuity from the 1820s reforms of Robinson and Huskisson. He was well known for his authorship of *Progress of the Nation*, released in sections from 1836,[39] arguing to remove the whole system of protection and tariffs that had grown up during the wars, reducing the size of the state and developing a properly balanced budget.

Ashworth recounts how Cobden, who had begun to write pamphlets on free trade in 1835, was excited by the exchanges and vowed: 'we'll use the Manchester Chamber of Commerce for an agitation to repeal the Corn Law'. Ashworth, who was well aware of the chamber's earlier equivocation, replied that the chamber would not take this up and, if there were to be an agitation, it would need major new funds and have to develop independently.[40] Cobden then began to meet with others to develop the concept of a national organization, which became the Anti-Corn League (founded in October 1838).

However, neither Cobden nor the proponents of repeal in the chamber gave up hope of bringing it into the campaign. With other members, Ashworth and Cobden pressed the chamber in a meeting on 13 December 1838 to draft a strong memorial for repeal. A draft under discussion was detailed in its critique, but fell short of calling for repeal. The attendees of what was the chamber's largest ever meeting were as deeply divided over calling for modification or repeal as they had been for the previous 20 years. The meeting was adjourned after five hours of discussion, until 20 December. In the meantime municipal elections took place that saw Cobden elected Alderman. When the chamber reassembled, a further five-hour discussion led to a vote six to one in favour of an amended motion and memorial for repeal, drafted by Cobden, Ashworth, and J. B. Smith.[41]

The president during these discussions was George William Wood, MP for Kendal, and a Manchester cotton dealer and manufacturer. He was a leading light in the chamber's refoundation in 1820, but after becoming MP progressively saw his public career more in terms of government than the chamber. He had sought to moderate the Corn Law motions, but was now asked to present the chamber's repeal motion to parliament. Wood largely evaded the issue in the Commons

---

[38] Ashworth (1876); Prentice (1853); McCord (1958); Turner (1994). Ashworth and Prentice were leading members of the League so not entirely unbiased. Prentice was also editor of the *Manchester Times*.

[39] Porter (1851) is a consolidated edition.

[40] Ashworth (1876), pp. 14–15; Helm (1897), pp. 74–5.

[41] Ashworth (1876), pp. 20–2; Redford (1934), pp. 154–7; Helm (1897), pp. 75–7.

debate on 5 February 1839. In Prentice's account, 'Wood had been flattered and softened up by Peel's government by being asked to second the debate on the Queen's speech. Wood noted the effects of distress, but sought to belittle them and even attribute some of the distress to attempts of manufacturers to reduce wages.'[42] Peel thanked him for the account he had given from the chamber of 'the stable and secure position of the commerce and manufactures of this country'.[43]

Cobden and his Leaguers were furious, both for the misrepresentation of the memorial and for the misattribution of motives to what they saw as a moral cause. The contemporary comment in the *London Examiner* called Wood's speech 'painful and ludicrous'.[44] Comments in a letter to Cobden sum up the tension:[45]

> Well, your President of the Manchester chamber of commerce is a darling! He can't defend the Straits of Thermopylae but opens his flanks to the enemy. 'Dilly, Dilly, come and be killed', was almost Peel's dealing with him. . . . He looked 'very foolish'. It was as if he designed to break the Corn Question . . . If you can you must depose him. . . . He has made himself not only mischievous but ridiculous.[46]

Wood was deemed to have gone 'native' with the government. He and his supporters on the chamber Board were thoroughly discredited for compromising Manchester's voice. In the week following the Commons debate, a public meeting in his Kendal constituency strongly condemned his conduct. At the general meeting of the chamber in the following week 15 of the chamber's board were replaced by members more favourable to repeal, and Wood was replaced as president by J. B. Smith.[47]

These incidents demonstrate the seriousness of the chamber deliberations, which were treated with 'deep and concentrated interest, amounting even to a feeling of solemnity' in the words of one of the successor chamber presidents, Henry Ashworth;[48] how divisive the issues were; and how the chamber was 'captured' by new progressive members, the free traders. The removal of the old guard was most of all a power shift with great symbolism.[49] Whatever the role of Cobden's League, Manchester chamber was also now thoroughly associated with Corn Law repeal.

The Anti-Corn Law League

The subsequent campaign did not achieve repeal until 1846 and over the intervening period the dominant activities were through a special-purpose lobby body established for the purpose: the Anti-Corn Law League. The League is an

---

[42] Prentice (1853), p. 108.
[43] *Hansard*, 5 February 1839, p. 106; Wood's comments p. 59.
[44] Prentice (1853), p. 108.
[45] Letter from Joseph Parkes, London legal agent for the League, to Cobden 8 February 1839, quoted in McCord (1958), pp. 46–7.
[46] Quoted in Prentice (1853), p. 109.
[47] Manchester chamber minutes; Prentice (1853), pp. 110–12.
[48] Ashworth (1876), pp. 20–1.
[49] It had previously been chiefly concerned with cotton and import tariffs, with a wide range of campaigns 1820–50.

important historical phenomenon. It made a lot of noise. It raised over £200,000 of support from various rounds of subscriptions, produced over 20 million pamphlets, a range of newsletters and journals with circulation in the hundreds of thousands (the weekly paper of the League circulated 200,000 copies in 1845), it established *The Economist* at arm's length, held thousands of meetings, and arranged many lectures (650 lectures in 1843 alone) as well as other presentations all over the country through networks of affiliated local associations.[50] It engaged the working classes, women, and many previously uncommitted business people, and even some rural areas and gentry. It sought to contest parliamentary elections, to swing electoral opinion by various registration exercises of voters, and won several by-elections and general election seats. It was acknowledged as 'The Great Fact' of electoral politics after winning a City by-election of 1843.[51] Its support and funds were used to help build the Manchester Free Trade Hall. This was all new territory in lobbying and politics. However much debate there may be between historians about why it was so outstandingly successful, its key lessons were clear: whilst gathering support from wide interests, working classes, evangelicals, tradesmen, and others, it was pre-eminently an economic campaign to further business interests as a foundation for national prosperity and thus was seen as critical in order to support wages and social reform.

The strongest link with previous experience was probably the anti-slavery campaign. This also had had a strong Manchester presence and many of its methods were similar. Critical also was the absolutism and evangelical aspect of both campaigns.[52] For the Corn Law campaign, repeal was the only acceptable strategy, otherwise it could be distracted into negotiations and complexity. But most of all, the lesson of anti-slavery, as relayed to Cobden, was the 'necessity of taking a stand on the rock of abstract truth and justice'.[53] This also echoed the strategy of the 1766 Stamp Act abolition campaign and the American rebellion. A moral high ground was sought that had intellectual foundations.

The Manchester chamber remained important in developments and was radically affected by the campaign. Redford's comment is misleading that 'after adoption of this petition [in December 1838] the Manchester chamber of commerce ceased to take any prominent part'.[54] As Redford's own account, and that of Helm and Ashworth demonstrate, the chamber was transformed. The old guard were removed: the president was replaced and Cobden's supporters were elected to the Board in place of the official list of nominations.[55] The chamber helped organize many meetings with the League in Manchester, published many pamphlets on the

---

[50] See Prentice (1853); McCord (1958); Pickering and Tyrell (2000).

[51] *The Times*, 18 November 1843, quoted in Redford (1934), p. 153; McCord (1958), etc.

[52] See e.g. Hilton (1988); Martin (2002).

[53] A contemporary comment by Joseph Sturge who had been active in both campaigns: H. Richard (1864), *Memoirs of Joseph Sturge* (London: S. W. Partridge).

[54] Redford (1934), p. 155.

[55] A Board subsequently viewed by the chamber as 'not so enlightened': Lord Rosebery; in Helm (1897), p. 91.

Corn Laws,[56] it supplied the first League president (again J. B. Smith), the first committee of the League included about forty prominent chamber members,[57] the chamber subscribed substantial money and facilitated access to solicit subscriptions from its members, it was formally part of meetings with Peel the prime minister where it provided a force of 'respectable opinion' in 1840–1 to complement the League's more ambiguous position,[58] and it continued to pass memorials critical of the government's lack of action or inadequate efforts to repeal.

But the key impact on the chamber was on brand: the chamber would forever be associated with the Corn -Law repeal and free trade: the foundation of the so-called 'Manchester School'. Although this was never a uniform body, the League was viewed nationally as an 'offshoot' of the chamber. Partly as a result, 'Manchester became something fine among business centres of the world, permeated by a cosmopolitanism'.[59] The League claimed there were now two parliaments 'one in London and one in Manchester'.[60] As Cobden stated:[61] 'just as Jerusalem was with the origin of our faith, ... so would Manchester be identified in the eyes of historians as the birthplace and the centre of the greatest moral movement since the introduction of printing. ... It saved you not merely from starvation, but it saved you from revolution.' Indeed it was Disraeli who is credited with inventing the title 'Manchester School' to describe the ascendant new doctrine,[62] and this was a statement about the chamber as much as the League.

Impact on chambers

The impact on the chamber movement as a whole was also profound. The broadest commentaries on why the campaign succeeded suggest that the post-Reform structure of parliament had shifted interests towards factors favourable to repeal.[63] But these influences only made repeal feasible; Peel was an important agent, and the

[56] The 1837–8 debate at the chamber was part of the popular reading of the period, and published in various forms for wider dissemination; e.g. *The Corn Laws: An Authentic Report of the late Important Discussions in the Manchester Chamber of Commerce ...* (1839); T. Perronet Thompson, *Catechism on the Corn Laws* (1838); and *Corn-Law Fallacies, with Answers: With a Dedication to the Manchester Chamber of Commerce* (1839).

[57] Redford (1934), p. 154.

[58] e.g. Ashworth presented himself to Peel as from the Manchester chamber in the meeting in which he participated in 1840: Ashworth (1876), pp. 27–8. Other delegates from the chamber met Peel in 1841, and in the following years. Ashworth's account suggests the chamber was particularly important in demonstrating to Peel the daily miseries of the people and business as a result of the workings of the Corn Laws. Peel, from nearby Bury, was addressed by Mr Edmund Grundy of Bury 'plainly and powerfully' about the distress of Peel's own lessees in the area during the 1841 delegation: Ashworth (1876), pp. 29–30.

[59] Marrison (1998), p. 3.

[60] *Norfolk News*, 10 February 1849; quoted in Searle (1993), p. 1.

[61] Quoted by Lord Rosebery; in Helm (1897), pp. 94 and 97.

[62] See Howe (1997), p. 5.

[63] McKeown (1989), pp. 378–9, who summarizes the other parliamentary analyses; see also Jennings (1962), pp. 352–67; Howe (1997), pp. 23–8; Pickering and Tyrell (2000); Trentmann (2008).

lobby campaign was critical to actually achieving change, with Manchester and the chambers indelibly associated with it.

As a result, the whole country, parliament, government, and the civil service became aware of the *Chamber* concept, especially that in Manchester. The League's immense publicity campaign launched not just themselves and free trade, but the chamber brand. It also associated chambers indelibly with free trade (whatever their diversity of opinion on the issue). This acted as a new take-off for the chamber movement. The Corn Law campaign crystallized the chamber as the 'modern' means for cities to marshal business opinion and to successfully lobby. It was a body that no significant place could do without if it meant to be counted as a major business centre; it represented the coming of age of the outports and provincial manufacturing centres against London and aristocratic interests. It also bound them together in a common agenda. Indirectly this also stimulated their national organization in 1855–60.

The deposing of the 'old guard' in Manchester also carried a significant national message. Here was a signal to other long-established chambers of the need to be progressive and to reform themselves—it was an invitation to new members to become active as campaigners. According to one of the campaign leaders, Prentice, the debate in the Manchester chamber in December 1838 was followed by the whole nation, through the local and London papers. It demonstrated how the chamber 'had been overtaken by the vice of old corporation inaptitude to move'; and the president Wood was seen as representing 'standstill'.[64] 'Gentlemanliness' and 'politeness' might still be the order of the day in Victorian relations, but this need not stand in the way of reforming, professionalizing, and, if necessary, through proper debate, removing those preventing change. There was also the danger that, if resistance to change from 'protectionists' was not dealt with, it would divide the chambers. An Anti-League had sought to do this and, in Preston for example, had publicized divisions between the manufacturers claiming that the major firms supported the Anti-League.[65]

The other chamber that experienced most hiatus was Newcastle. This had sent a petition in 1838 calling for modest modifications of the Corn Laws: to use bonded warehouses for flour that would allow British shipping to enter the trade between Europe and other parts of the world, and allowing foreign wheat to be ground in bond at Newcastle and re-exported.[66] The then president, Sir Matthew White Ridley, Bart., had accommodated to this petition. But a special meeting in February 1839, a few days after Wood was removed in Manchester, unanimously adopted a petition to *repeal* the Corn Laws, referring to the landed property class as 'favoured' and 'free of burdens', calling the Laws a 'matter of notoriety'. The president absented himself from this meeting, and the vice-president Joseph Lamb chaired.

---

[64] Prentice (1853), p. 84; see also Checkland (1983).

[65] Including the largest firm, Horrocks Miller & Co.: Anti-League: *A Short Letter to Richard Cookson on ... the North Lancashire Agricultural Protection Society*, quoting the *London Standard*, 20 March 1844 (BL RB.23.a.12747(1)).

[66] Newcastle chamber, minutes: Petition, 3 March 1838.

Subsequently Ridley declared himself unaware of the resolutions,[67] even though they were published in the local newspapers,[68] and distributed throughout Northern England and to Parliament.

The view of the iniquity of the Corn Laws as class-based is clear from the third motion of Newcastle's 1839 petition: 'that the landed property of this country, being free from any particular burdens for the exclusive benefit of the land-owners, at the expense of every other class of the community, must be manifestly unjust'.[69] The general tenor was tough. This was a considerable advance from Newcastle's resolution a year earlier for bonded warehouses for flour.

As developments became more serious nationally, and the chamber adopted a new petition for repeal in March 1841, the Newcastle president was 'the only dissentient' and he felt obliged to resign. He was even more isolated than the Manchester president Wood in 1839 who had managed to raise the support of 16% of his meeting. Ridley could not 'tacitly consent to compromise my own [views], or by lending a silent sanction to resolutions or petitions for that body embracing the repeal of the present Corn Law, to promote indirectly the advancement of any such system, as would in my opinion be fatal to the best interests of this country'.[70] The chamber respectfully accepted the resignation, publicized Ridley's letter in the press, and elected Lamb president in his place;[71] the membership of the chamber increased. Interestingly, by the mid-1850s all the local Lords, MPs, and gentry were back in membership; the chamber had become accepted as a legitimate progressive element of society.[72]

Whilst progressive reform occurred in Manchester and Newcastle, in several other chambers the impact of the Anti-Corn Law campaign may have precipitated demise. Of 13 chambers in some form of existence in the period 1813–35,[73] three went into abeyance after 1835 (North Staffordshire, Wolverhampton, and Birmingham), and in London a proposal for a chamber collapsed. In Birmingham and North Staffordshire there are no records that give unequivocal evidence for why demise occurred. But in Birmingham the chamber became dormant between 1832 and 1841. The precursors of this period saw an 1814 petition in favour of modification of the Corn Laws delivered to both Houses. However, the directors of the chamber were thinly supported in public meetings, and by the end of 1816 there was already a debate about the continuance of the chamber. In 1817 Birmingham chamber moved more radically to call for abolition of the corn duty. But in 1819–24 few meetings were held. Resolutions in 1824 and 1825 again supported repeal, and in 1826 a special meeting agreed a new petition in favour of repeal, but by 1827 the membership of the chamber was dropping.[74] The

---

[67] Letter of Resignation from M.W. Ridley, 29 March 1841; Newcastle chamber minutes.
[68] e.g. *Newcastle Courant*, 15 February 1839.
[69] Minutes of Special Meeting of 14 February 1839, Newcastle minutes.
[70] Resignation letter, Newcastle chamber minutes.
[71] Newcastle chamber minutes, 29 March 1841.
[72] Newcastle chamber minutes, *Annual Report* (1855).
[73] Excluding chambers in Ireland.
[74] Wright (1913), pp. 62, 72–3, 90, 97–8, 105.

evidence suggests a peripheralization of the chamber during a period where debate on reform focused on the corporations (the Reform Acts of 1832 and 1835). Wright infers that this period was associated with 'serious internal trouble' in the chamber, and it would appear that the Corn Laws and the 1832 Reform Act were factors reducing the scope for the chamber to develop. It was not re-established until 1841 and played little role on the Corn Laws.

In other chambers, the Corn Law issue was too divisive to be taken on to the table and campaigning was left to the League. Thus, in Worcester, Mr Hardy attempted to put a motion for Corn Law repeal.[75] But the chamber directors would not accept the motion, as it was 'not within their province'. Even in Glasgow, conservative directors held sway. Whilst previously in the vanguard on reform, there was a protest in 1839 against the directors of the chamber for 'not supporting the Manchester petition against the Corn Laws'.[76] In this, and a similar issue on sugar refining, it was resolved that members would protest and petition in their own names but the chamber would hold back, and it seems to have played no significant part in the Corn Law campaign of the 1840s. Indeed, in 1842 the chamber sent a fulsome petition to Peel approving his actions (of delay). Peel equally fulsomely replied, calling the chamber the 'chosen guardian and organ of such conservative interests'. This nevertheless led to strong dissension, with Walter Buchanan challenging the directors of the chamber in 1840, and moving a change in constitution in 1841 to allow general meetings to determine policy, not the directors.[77] But none of this was successful.

We thus have three varied chamber responses to the Corn Law campaign, removal of the old guard (at least two of the chambers); dissension and resistance encouraging dormancy (probably three of the chambers); and putting the issue off the agenda (probably about six of the chambers). The sidelining of the issue by about half of the chambers at the time suggests that Prentice's comment on Manchester noted earlier, that the 'vice of old corporations—inaptitude to move' was telling. The chambers were caught between respectable gentlemanly behaviour and the landed interests on the one hand, and progressive economic opinion on the other.

Other implications

Corn Law abolition had implications far beyond local chambers. The League stimulated all sorts of local interests to develop, ranging across the labouring classes to the leading manufacturers and merchants. Thus as well as strengthening chambers, it also led to competition. In Scotland the traditional bodies of the Glasgow and Edinburgh Companies of Merchants in Edinburgh were as significant in the Corn Law agitation as the chambers.[78] Similarly in Bristol and York the Merchant

[75] Worcester chamber Report 1840; quoted in Clarke (1989), Worcester chamber history, p. 12.
[76] Glasgow chamber minutes, 2 January 1839.
[77] Oakley (1983), Glasgow chamber history, pp. 98–9.
[78] Heron (1903), chapter XI.

Adventurers were of some significance.[79] In Manchester chamber dissidents formed a Commercial Association.[80] Some municipal Corporations also provided important support.

Some competition was more systematic. Anti-League campaigns were initially established in 1843 under the title of Agricultural Protection Society. As discussed in Chapter 2, these adopted the title 'chambers of agriculture' from 1865. These became a competitor to the chambers of commerce, as well as occasionally working with them. Hence, the Anti-Corn Law campaign stimulated the creation of rival rural organizations.

Related spin-offs for chambers, and indeed other interest groups, was recognition of the new potential to organize and influence government policy, and mechanisms to achieve this. The League 'removed the assumption that government was some arcane mystery best left to a hereditary caste of landowners'.[81] Large-scale electoral registration by traders capable of buying small freeholds was stimulated. Lobbying was not just the preserve of the rich merchants in chambers or the landed gentry in Parliament. The League showed how to become an 'all-powerful interest group able to exert irresistible pressure within Parliament'. It showed how 'mass fervency could be stimulated; it turned free trade into a popular moral crusade . . . [with the result that] the cult [and] myth of Cobden . . . cast a far longer shadow over the terrain of Victorian and Edwardian politics'.[82]

The chambers of commerce rarely sought to operate through loud and noisy campaigns again, generally returning to the low-key and insider routes favoured after the 1780s debacle of the General Chamber. But they learnt the lesson of the need to apply continual pressure, the need for greater resources to achieve their goals (including more professional staff),[83] the benefits of working with insiders in parliament (such as Cobden and Bright as MPs), and the advantage of alliances with other interests in the workplace, church, and wider society. However, they were never fully aligned with Cobden, Bright, and other politicians, with whom there were disagreements on many technical issues.[84] They emerged as modern lobbyists trying to disseminate, influence, and win opinion.

10.5 FREE TRADE AND TARIFFS

The success of the Anti-Corn Law campaign marked the point of frame change where free trade became 'the single most distinctive characteristic of the British state';[85] and

[79] Wells (1909); Little (1954); Surtees Society (1918); York Merchants Adventurers, minute book.
[80] Turner (1994), pp. 239–40; Pickering and Tyrell (2000).
[81] Searle (1993), p. 2; Clark (2000a), pp. 467–8.
[82] Howe (1997), p. 30: see also Chapter 3, and Hajer and Wagenaar (2003), on discourse coalitions.
[83] The League's budget of £200,000 dwarfed the chambers. The 1786–90 and 1814–15 Corn Law campaigns saw only a few hundred pounds spent by all the chambers involved.
[84] See Searle (1993), e.g. pp. 195–8.
[85] Saul (1960); Howe (1997), p. 1; see also Trentmann (2008).

where Manchester's local 'epistemic community' developed global reach.[86] As a result, after 1846 the next phase of reforms passed parliament without major controversy, including abolition of the 'sacred' Navigation Acts in 1849. The Liberals became staunch free traders, and hence natural allies for chambers, with one of Gladstone's prominent speeches in support of free trade delivered at the Leeds chamber in 1881.[87] The rapid growth of trade after 1850 seemed to vindicate all the reforms.[88] Because of its significance, as with the Corn Laws, free trade has seen hundreds of previous studies. The purpose here is to trace how chambers influenced debates, and the effect on the chambers themselves.

Defence and the early challenges from fair trade

One follow-on from the ascent of free trade was the establishment of a number of organizations that sought to keep Cobden's flame alight (he died in 1865) and to head off any emerging threat. Most important was the Cobden Club, established in 1866, and modelled on Brougham's Association for Social Science, as a public arena for discussion and promotion of ideas.[89] It was Cobden's belief from the outset that pressures for protection would always be strong in a state with large expenditure that stimulated special pleading, and patchy business representation in parliament.

For the chambers, free trade was critical in reinforcing the 'general' interests of their localities and resisting special pleading or legislation for particular industries, underpinning the patterns shown in Tables 10.1–10.4. But from the 1870s various challenges to free trade began to emerge, with a number of organizations beginning to probe the strength of free trade commitments: the Association of 'Revivers' of British Industry (1869), Fiscal Reform League (1870), and Reciprocity Free Trade Association (1871). Generically these began to coalesce around *fair trade* as a political leitmotif, with a National Fair Trade League founded in 1881 (surviving until 1891, and succeeded by the United Empire Trade League, 1891–1901). This had Sampson Lloyd as its first president, a leading member of the Birmingham chamber and ACC president. It became an influential body against which the Cobden Club mounted major electoral campaigns in 1880–1 and for the 1885 general election.

The fair traders gave voice to increasing concerns about unfair foreign competition. These had been growing as a result of colonial barriers (particularly those in Canada after 1859, later developed further in the 1870s; and Australia after 1866). Other important challenges were the US McKinley tariff of 1890; German tariff increases in 1902; and German pressures on central Europe. The Royal Commission on the Depression of Trade and Industry in 1886 was an initial turning point

---

[86] Sheppard (2005); Trentmann (2008).

[87] Leeds chamber, pamphlet: *Free trade*, speech by Rt. Hon W. E. Gladstone, 8 October 1881.

[88] There has been much argument about economic impact; this is a brief summary: see Matthias (1983); Trentmann (2008) for further discussion.

[89] Howe (1997), pp. 116–52.

in establishing a strong alternative position to that of Cobden, responding to the depression of the 1880s. It favoured government support for home industries in distress through tariffs, a duty on sugar, a retaliatory 10–15% ad varolem tariff on manufactures from protectionist countries, and 10% duties of foreign foodstuffs (but with imperial preference).[90] Similarly, the emergence of Irish Home Rule, particularly Parnell's rhetoric, claimed protection for Irish industries and compensation for past disadvantages, which all undermined free trade notions.

Some chambers and their members began to be influenced by these arguments, and there began to be calls at ACC conferences in the 1880s for more attention to problems arising from action by foreign governments. However, the 'Eastern vision' of Palmerston, focusing on developing trade with India, China, and Japan, provided alternative opportunities which some chambers supported, although in the case of India it introduced further worries for home industries (that engaged Manchester in focused lobbies).

An imperial vision of the empire as a commercial union became a key demand of the Fair Trade League, receiving support from Disraeli's Conservatives (1874–80). These campaigns found some support from chambers; for example, Macclesfield chamber was one of the earliest to debate the issue, in 1872 stating that whilst free trade was correct as a general principle, 'it should not be applied to the particular industry with which Macclesfield was concerned [silk]'; however, a conference in May 1879 called by the chamber had only nine people attending, who held divergent views.[91]

The chambers generally continued to support free trade, but not on abstract Cobdenite grounds. They were pragmatic, and in Europe focused on treaty negotiations as the best option if other countries failed to open trade unilaterally. Thus most chamber foreign policy lobbies focused on specific treaties, foreign commercial negotiations, including limited support for proposals for a 'European common market' under Disraeli's government in the mid-1870s.[92] Indeed, *Realpolitik* saw expansion of treaties with Europe that gave Britain MFN status in almost all countries over the period up to WW1, despite the strengthening of foreign tariffs. But MFN began to be a weak strategy as bilateral treaties grew, since with few import tariffs Britain had little bargaining power. As a result chamber members began to test fair trade in motions at chamber meetings, with Birmingham being one of the first and most prominent to air and vote on a motion proposed by Sampson Lloyd in 1881 (which was defeated). Bradford also reviewed its policy several times after 1875.[93] Fair trade motions also became increasingly important in Conferences of the Chambers of Commerce of the Empire, which began in the 1890s. However, only the South of Scotland chamber had developed a strong pro-tariff policy before the 1890s. Its president, Craig Brown, a prominent fair trader, called for reciprocity or retaliation as early as 1886. He attacked the

[90] Brown (1943); Howe (1997), pp. 108–52.
[91] Macclesfield chamber, in *Macclesfield Courier*, 1872 and 1879; in chamber history: Davies (1976, p. 201).
[92] ACC, *Proceedings*; Ilersic and Liddle (1960), pp. 38–65; Howe (1997), p. 163–70; see Table 10.2.
[93] Sigsworth (1958), pp. 105–7.

ACC, asking how it was possible for 40 out of 48 member chambers to 'cry against unfair and ruinous exclusions of British goods' and the association 'do nothing'.[94]

Chamberlain's attacks on free trade 1895–1910

Despite growing attacks, free trade was not seriously challenged until Chamberlain's period in office as Secretary of State for the Colonies in 1895–1902 under Salisbury as prime minister.[95] Chamberlain, a Liberal Radical, had split from the party (with others) over Gladstone's support for Irish Home Rule. He joined the Unionist government in 1895, as the leading Liberal Unionist. He was already a well-established charismatic figure that had transformed Birmingham's local politics and served as president of the BoT; in Churchill's words he was 'the most live, sparkling, insurgent, compulsive figure in British affairs'. However, as observed by others 'all our British affairs today are tangled, biased, or inspired by his actions'.[96] Daunton concludes that Chamberlain's campaign removed 'the possibility of pragmatic, technical revisions . . . Instead the debate was dominated by a much more divisive and controversial ideology of tariff reform . . . [that] was to constrain both the Liberals and Conservatives'.[97] For chambers he was a mixed blessing: Chamberlain understood chambers better than many, having been a member of Birmingham chamber's council as a young man, but as a politician saw them as 'erratic in their actions', was sometimes critical of the value of their opinion,[98] and his use of chambers was chiefly for political ends.

Chamberlain began advocating an imperial free trade zone with external tariffs in 1896, culminating in a speech at Birmingham chamber in November 1896.[99] His pressures had strong influence on the third Congress of Chambers of Commerce of the Empire earlier in 1896, which called for an imperial union. However, at ACC the resolution of support for a union (from South of Scotland chamber) received little support and was withdrawn to await the outcome of an inquiry.[100] Similarly the ACC annual meeting of 1901 called on the government to appoint a Royal Commission, though it supported MFN within the empire; a debate at a 1901 special meeting to back 'fiscal policy based on expediency', was opposed by London and withdrawn.[101]

[94] T. Craig-Brown (1886), *Foreign Trade and Tariffs: Their Effect on British Commerce* (Edinburgh: William Blackwood), pp. 4–11; he was later a member of ACCI, q.v. below.
[95] For a detailed discussion of Chamberlain's thinking and its interface with other political developments see Gollin (1965); Amery (1969); Searle (1971, 2001); Rempel (1972); Matthew (1973).
[96] Churchill's *Great Contemporaries*; and Garvin's *Life of Joseph Chamberlain*; quoted in Dahrendorf (1995), p. 44.
[97] Daunton (2001), p. 318; see also Trentmann (1996), pp. 1016–19.
[98] Quoted in Chamberlain letters to Charles Monk, 29 December 1881; 10 May 1883: Cambridge University Library, Monk and Sanford papers, C6/69; C6/73.
[99] Reported in London *CCJ*, November (1896), pp. 291–2.
[100] ACC, *Proceedings*, September (1896), pp. 17–22; moved by T. Craig Brown, a prominent fair trader.
[101] ACC, *Proceedings*, special meeting report (1901), p. 25; proposed by Stiebel (Nottingham) ACC Executive member.

The Boer War (dubbed 'Joe's war' by contemporaries) gave Chamberlain his first chance to encourage substantive government policy change. A corn duty was introduced in 1901 to help satisfy wartime revenue needs, as well as duties on sugar and coal exports. The corn duty raised hopes at the Colonial Conference in 1902 that it might be used as the basis for concessions to the colonies and colonial reductions of tariffs to Britain as a step to establishing 'free trade within the empire'. But Britain's need for revenue and colonial commitment to tariffs made this impossible.

Chastened by the intransigence of the colonies and others, Chamberlain moved towards the option of imperial preference combined with tariff protection.[102] He opened a campaign in a prominent Birmingham Town Hall speech of 15 May 1903. This was the first time when an explicit and outright attack on free trade was made by a government minister, with the sacred cow of Cobden denounced for restricting British power and influence and impairing economic development. Chamberlain advocated tariffs imposed on selected imports to raise revenue for needed welfare reforms, such as pensions, and encourage home industries by limiting imports and enhancing the empire through imperial preference. He set up a Tariff Reform League to popularize and act as a lobby for reform, with Arthur Pearson as chair. This was very destabilizing for the government of which he was still a member, and he was forced to resign in September 1903, in order to devote himself to the campaign. He retained strong support from Arthur Balfour, Conservative PM of the Unionist government of 1902–5, both because of Balfour's sympathies on pragmatic grounds with at least the need for tariff retaliation, and also because Chamberlain commanded a significant degree of party support. Balfour also supported the establishment of a Tariff Commission, as an advisory body of experts to design a 'scientific tariff'.

These developments were an attack on the policy frame of the previous 60 years, and a revolutionary challenge for both Conservatives and Liberals in the Unionist government. Chamberlain's policy had the aim of linking the Conservatives to the aspirations of the working classes by arguing, simplistically put, that tariffs would allow increases in welfare services by 'taxing the foreigner' without increasing domestic prices. Chamberlain's speeches culminated in the general election of 1905, when the choice between free trade and tariff reform was focal. The election was fought out through one of the largest effusions of pamphlets, speeches, meetings, posters, and some of the earliest political films. It culminated in the defeat of the Conservative Unionists by an overwhelming Liberal majority, which put tariff reform off the agenda.

The growing shift of opinion had profound implications for how chambers were to represent a 'unity' of interests, but on the ground they were faced with the reality of a Liberal government from 1906 until 1915. The Liberals retained free trade as a central policy plank to court the working classes and hold prices down, but sought

[102] There had been modest developments of imperial preference since the second Colonial Conference in 1894, but they were slow and limited; see summary in Belfast chamber, *Journal*, October (1923), p. 104.

increased taxation by other means. They set up the Free Trade Union as a supposedly non-partisan body to counterweight Chamberlain's Tariff Reform League. The support for free trade by the Liberals also allowed them to ally with the growing strength of the Labour Party: including offering expansion of welfare benefits, maintaining cheap food (with the motto that free trade prevented a return to the 'hungry forties'), redistributive taxation of land, and nationalization of canals and other undertakings.[103] It also offered scope to win over Irish free traders. This challenged business interests, many of whom turned against the Liberals after 1908 because of dislike of increasing links with socialism and support for high taxation to support rapid welfare expansion (pensions 1908, health and unemployment insurance 1911), culminating in Lloyd George's 1909 budget which introduced a graduated income tax, supertax, and land tax.[104] But the consequence of these developments was that, from 1903, free trade vs. tariffs became an issue that strongly divided the political parties, and for many chambers became 'too political'.

The chamber response 1900–1914

Chamberlain's speech had a major impact on chambers. Indeed Birmingham was chosen as the location for the launch as his constituency, and because of his links with the chamber and city corporation. He also had strong links with the ACC following his period as president of the BoT 1880–5.

However, before Chamberlain's public launch, there had already been other major developments. Salisbury's government had established a Committee on Commercial Intelligence in the BoT in 1897, and from 1898 an Advisory Committee on Commercial Intelligence (ACCI) had included chamber nominees and other business people, to improve government's working with industry. This was a development of enormous significance for chambers, as discussed later below under trade promotion lobbies. With respect to free trade, it meant that chambers had become favoured 'insiders' to some of the important debates about possible tariff protection. The chamber position by 1901 was to ask government to press foreign governments to reduce tariffs, whilst some chambers (notably Huddersfield and South of Scotland) supported retaliation if necessary.[105] Leeds had rejected retaliation, but in 1902 its president Jonathan Peate took the position that 'I am not so wedded to free trade... that I would not adopt any measure if it was calculated to forward the commercial interests of the country'.[106] Leeds also hosted

---

[103] e.g. Gollin (1965); Rempel (1972); Matthew (1973); Howe (1997), pp. 230–73; Trentmann (2008).

[104] Searle (1971), pp. 142–70; Rempel (1972); Marrison (1996); Trentmann (1996, 2008); Cain and Hopkins (2002).

[105] ACC, *Proceedings* (1901), and memorial to BoT; also TNA CO 323/475 and FO 881/7937, quoted in Trentmann (1996), pp. 1011–12, nn. 15 and 20. South of Scotland had undertaken an extensive survey of European and US tariffs, noting that it was leading to 'ruinous competition', and trade was being 'cut to pieces'; Gulvin (1973), pp. 141–4. In very limited cases ACC had since the 1870s supported restricting imports of bountied goods such as sugar, and was urging less reliance on MFN clauses.

[106] Leeds chamber, report of Peate's speech at 29 January 1902 AGM.

G. W. Balfour at its 1903 AGM, where it received a speech in cautious support of Chamberlain.[107] Similarly, in April 1903 the London chamber had hosted a national meeting that had aired opinion on the new German tariff. The chair had concluded by advocating the need for special tariff conventions with protectionist countries; MFN clauses were no longer adequate.[108] By 1904 this also became the early position of the ACCI, favouring retaliation if bilateral treaties could not be negotiated.[109] But these were internal debates conducted cautiously and pragmatically, influencing government approaches to treaty negotiations, with no need for the chambers to adopt a public stance.

Hence, when Chamberlain made his speech he would already have believed he had some support from chambers and other business leaders; 'businessmen had already come to question fiscal orthodoxy before Chamberlain's tariff reform crusade'.[110] But Chamberlain's explicit advocacy of a vague *general* tariff structure coupled with direct party trappings for state pensions and other expenditure went far beyond any chamber position; it sought to force and politicize change.

Several previous assessments of the subsequent developments within the chambers have been made,[111] so that it is necessary here only to summarize and supplement. The Birmingham chamber's council passed a motion supporting Chamberlain's policy only 12 days after its launch, on 27 May, reiterated on 22 July, and reinforced by a vote based on a survey of members on 23 September with virtually no dissent. It established a Tariff Committee in 1903. Birmingham had already been in the vanguard of embracing aspects of fair trade. A motion supporting selective protective duties had been narrowly defeated in October 1885 in response to the discussions of the Royal Commission on the Depression of Trade and Industry. But in 1887 a large majority supported a Fair Trade League motion, and in 1889 the chamber supported the Empire Customs Union proposals. A few other chambers also quickly passed motions in support of Chamberlain, including Kidderminster and Macclesfield.

However, most chambers responded with calls for an inquiry or Royal Commission to consider the matter; whilst Leeds, Burnley, Manchester, and Newcastle passed opposing motions, in favour of free trade. Chamberlain's policy thus immediately revealed the differences of opinion between chambers, and between their members. The considerable majority of chambers advocating an inquiry reflected in many cases strong divisions between members; and in the case of Dublin, Limerick, and others was a healing strategy of compromise resulting from defeat of motions supporting Chamberlain.

Chamberlain's policy was also divisive outside chambers, resisted by the Treasury, failed to convince many in the City (particularly finance and bankers), and was criticized by many leading economists including Alfred Marshall (who objected

---

[107] Leeds chamber, report of AGM 23 January 1903; *Leeds Mercury*, 24 January 1903.
[108] London *CCJ*, 108, April (1903), p. 86.
[109] See analysis of early ACCI proceedings by Trentmann (1996), pp. 1013–14.
[110] Trentmann (1996), p. 1016.
[111] Marrison (1996), pp. 79–116; Trentmann (1996); also Ilersic and Liddle (1960), pp. 154–6.

to his concept of economies of scale being used by tariff reformers to argue for aid to industries). A group of 14 economists wrote a letter to *The Times* in August 1903 refuting the claim that tariffs were a free tax on foreigners, stating that they would be fully shifted into higher prices. Pigou, one of the experts on such topics, criticized this estimate, but nevertheless suggested that 80% would shift to prices. Expert opinion thus pitted tariffs against cheap food and other goods.[112] Chamberlain was also strongly criticized and lampooned in a partisan press for the lack of any detail. There was no initial reason for chambers to jump onto a very divisive bandwagon.

However, the moves to develop the Tariff Commission, Balfour's commitment at least to retaliation, and further speeches by Chamberlain seemed to indicate a growing momentum. The appointment of the head of the Tariff Commission, announced in December 1903 also provided a fillip: Professor William Hewins, the founding director of the LSE since 1895.[113] Hewins provided important intellectual championing of tariffs as a modernization and departure from 'Little Englandism'. Similarly the credibility and connections of many of the members of the Commission, although attacked by the press, provided a counterweight to resistance to the 'scientific tariff'.[114] Chamber members began to see that a new political settlement might be emerging and were under pressure by some of their leading members. Ivan Levinstein (a major dyestuff manufacturer) conspicuously resigned as president of Manchester chamber to become a Commissioner. The Commission began to sit in 1904 and set up a lengthy process that provided a momentum behind tariffs, as Chamberlain had intended.[115]

Between the end of 1903 and early 1904 many chambers reconsidered their position, with motions passed supporting a tariff, at least as a retaliation, in Bristol, Leeds, London, North Staffordshire, Wolverhampton, Edinburgh, Belfast, Nottingham, Walsall, Dundee, Grimsby, Leith, Dover, Southampton, Barrow, Sheffield, Bradford, Greenock, South of Scotland, Swansea, Morley, and Halifax.[116] The Leeds discussion was typical. At a large meeting in November 1903 a free trade motion was proposed by Nottingham Conservative MP and chamber member Ernest W. Beckett, who spoke at length to head off Chamberlain's campaign; but an amendment to modify fiscal policy by Col. Tennant Walker was carried by 76 to 65 with about 100 remaining neutral.[117] This was support for reform, but hardly

---

[112] *The Times*, letters 15 and 18 August 1903; see also Marrison (1996), pp. 26–9.

[113] He was a supporter of imperial preference with some links to the London chamber, and author of a series of 'an economist' letters to *The Times* in 1903 that responded to criticisms of the tariff proposal.

[114] Important members were Vincent Caillard (Vickers Sons and Maxim), Alexander Henderson (stockbroker), William Lewis (coal), Andrew Noble (Armstrong Whitworth), Charles Tennant (St Rollux and United Alkali), Alfred Jones (Elder Dempster), Joseph Rank (milling), and Charles Parsons (marine engineering); see Marrison (1996); on Hewins, see Dahrendorf (1995).

[115] The Tariff Commission continued until 1921; but it could not agree on banking and finance, produced useful single-industry studies, but failed to agree a single scientific tariff or produce an integrated final report: Marrison (1996), chapter 7.

[116] Marrison (1996), pp. 80–2, based on reports in London *CCJ*; with additions.

[117] Leeds chamber, Special Meeting; minutes, 3 November 1903.

unequivocal and overwhelming. Similarly in Dublin in 1910 a long debate over two days resulted in a tariff reform amendment being lost by 67 to 17, and a free trade proposal being won by 23 to 17, but there were at least 80 who expressed no opinion either way.[118]

The London chamber was forced into debating the issue after prominent speeches at the Guildhall by Chamberlain in early 1904. Its council had proposed a policy of 'conditional retaliation' on tariffs in 1903, which had been put to ACC; however, internal dissent forced it to test the views of the membership. The poll in early 1904 was on a proposal for retaliatory tariffs only if other courses had been tried, if they had a reasonable chance of success, and if other branches of British industry were not harmed: 207 votes supported the council's policy, 33 supported it with removal of the provisos; 5 were in favour of Chamberlain's more ambitious policy, and 126 disapproved of the chamber's policy, although non-respondents outweighed all defined views. This was strong enough support for the chamber to put the 'conditional retaliation' policy to ACC again (where it was again lost).[119] With continued internal rumblings, London took matters further in 1907 when it put a motion to members 'that the present fiscal system is no longer suited to the needs of the country, and that it should be altered . . . first to promote the commercial union of the empire on a preferential basis, and second, to raise a proportion of our revenue from the imports of foreign manufactures'. This was carried by 1077 to 472 (69.5%), a slightly larger majority than in 1904, but with a much larger vote of 48% response from the membership.[120] From this point London began cautious pressure towards tariffs. Other chambers became more strident in ACC meetings. Derby in 1909 resolved by 46 to 9 that 'this country should release itself from the rigid system of so-called free trade . . . and that by broadening the basis of taxation and reforming the fiscal system, should place itself in a position to meet foreign competition on equal terms'.[121]

'Active neutrality'

The level of support for reform as an *explicit* policy that should be publicly voiced and advocated by ACC thus grew, but many chambers preferred that ACC lobby discreetly as 'insiders' and avoid taking an open stand; advocated particularly by Leeds, Birmingham, Manchester, and London. This favoured a public stance of 'neutrality'. The reasons behind this seem to be sevenfold.

First, there were still many chambers that were formally opposed to tariffs, especially the powerful Manchester, Liverpool, Dublin, and Newcastle chambers. Manchester had only joined the association in 1898 and Liverpool in 1899; this had required significant effort, discussed in Chapter 8, so that there were strong

[118] Dublin chamber, General Meeting minutes, 7 March and 11 April 1910.
[119] London chamber, *Annual Report* (1903), pp. 15–16; 1904, p. 17; see also discussion of ACC below.
[120] London chamber, meeting 21 March 1907; London *CCJ*, May (1907), p. 130.
[121] Quoted in Derby chamber history (1916), p. 39.

incentives to maintain a unity across the ACC. Second, even where motions supporting tariffs were won, this was often by small majorities, with many members abstaining, neutral, or not replying, and very prominent business leaders pitted against equally prominent leaders with contrary opinions. Chamberlain's approach was divisive and offered a sterile debate. The historical culture of chambers had been 'unity' of voice, and if strong divisions occurred they held back from direct involvement (they were 'neutral'). This was the effective position of Leeds, Manchester, Sheffield, and several other chambers. Chambers such as Wakefield, York, and Londonderry, which had only advocated an inquiry as the preferred policy, and the many chambers that had passed motions supporting tariffs but sought an inquiry as the best way forward, were also de facto 'neutral'.

Third, Marrison has argued that many chamber councils were dominated by free traders who were reluctant to acknowledge the votes against. He suggests a control by a minority of residual free trade liberals. The detailed examination of Manchester below both confirms this but also demonstrates more subtlety. Fourth, for many businesses and their chamber areas, imperial preference had too little value, either because the colonial market was too small, or compared to the increasing costs of duties and restrictions imposed by the colonies (e.g. for Aberdeen, Newcastle, and Plymouth). Hence, Chamberlain's imperial preference had little appeal. Moreover, fifth, the linkage between tariff reform and the expansion of government welfare spending jarred with the chambers' historic commitment to low taxation and a limited state. Sixth, there was also concern that countries like India could use preferential tariffs as a benefit behind which to build up their home industries (especially textiles) to the detriment of Britain.[122]

But the seventh, and perhaps primary, reason was that the issue was strongly party political. Chamberlain's campaign had put the Liberal Unionist position unashamedly. Birmingham noted that the fact that fiscal policy had been 'drawn into the whirlpool of party politics' made it 'practically impossible' for the ACC to discuss it.[123] Hull's position was typical of many chambers. In 1903 its council 'exercised a wise reticence' in not polling its members since 'the question is a national one and ought not to be made one of party politics'. Despite the dominance of free traders in the chamber, it did not want its divisions publicized: 'to maintain its legitimate influence ... [it was] wise to avoid questions on which they differed'.[124] Politics in turn raised the threat of member resignations; this was a further constraint encouraging 'neutrality' where 'unity' could not be achieved. Several chambers noted that their voluntary structure inhibited them taking a position where party politics were concerned. Birmingham's secretary, George Henry Wright, felt 'resignations would be bound to follow ... if any section of members became dissatisfied with any opinion expressed by the council'.[125]

---

[122] ACC Annual Meeting, 1905; London *CCJ*, August and October (1905).

[123] Birmingham chamber *Journal*, 31 January (1905), pp. 13–14; quoted in Marrison (1996), p. 105.

[124] Hull chamber, *Annual Report* (November 1903), p. 13; *Annual Report* (November 1908), p. 85; quoted in Marrison (1996), pp. 92–3.

[125] Birmingham chamber *Journal*, 30 September (1905), pp. 134–5; quoted in Marrison (1996), p. 106.

Indeed Lloyd George on 16 October 1907, as president of the BoT, told the Manchester chamber 'that chambers of commerce ought to keep politics outside (hear, hear). They will cease to have the slightest influence with government if they do not (hear, hear).'[126] Moreover, Chamberlain himself noted in a 1896 Birmingham speech to the chamber that it was 'by disseminating information, and by giving expert advice' that chambers best served their interests; and 'not by academic discussion upon highly controversial points of legislation and policy'.[127] So he must never have expected chambers to do more than test business opinion.

The role of the Association (ACC) 1903–1914

Another important dimension of the chambers' response was the behaviour of the association, particularly its presidents over 1903–10. When Chamberlain gave his 1903 speeches, the ACC president (1900–4) was Lord Avebury, a prominent free trader as MP 1870–1900, and then Liberal peer. He had been associated with the Liberty and Property Defence League in 1890–1900, and was founder of the Industrial Freedom League (1902) that campaigned against socialism and the expansion of the state. He presciently observed that no other issue would 'engender so much heat because views were so strongly held on each side'.[128] It should also be noted that the ACC since 1867, although non-aligned, had developed its strongest links with the Liberal Party.

In the ACC annual meeting of March 1904 Avebury attempted to shape the ACC view into one of 'conditional retaliation', following London chamber's resolution. As a former London chamber president (1888–93), Avebury was a strong influence on the drafting of the chamber's motion. Marrison has argued that Avebury's strategy was to contain and divert the challenge from Chamberlain,[129] but he also voiced the preference that was then emerging from ACCI. Avebury was one of the first members of the ACCI and well acquainted with how government and business interests were evolving towards limited modifications of free trade policy. However, at the 1904 ACC meeting Avebury's motion and a stronger retaliatory demand were both defeated, and Dublin's motion for a Royal Commission became the agreed ACC policy (voted 58 to 45).[130] In 1904–7 William Holland became ACC president (Liberal MP for Rotherham; later Lord Rotherham), and then in 1907–12 Earl Brassey; both Liberal free traders.

Holland had to oversee the 1905 ACC annual conference where tariffs and fiscal policy became the major debating item. The debate produced some of the deepest divisions between chambers in the ACC history. It was followed by similar debates up to 1910 in which tariff reform motions were put by the most forthright chambers, to be opposed by others, with a large number of chambers abstaining

---

[126] Quoted in Trentmann (1996), p. 1031, n. 91; from House of Lords RO, B/5/1/25.
[127] Speech at Birmingham chamber; London *CCJ*, November (1896), pp. 291–2.
[128] Quoted in Ilersic and Liddle (1960), p. 154; Marrison (1996), p. 82; see *DNB* for John Lubbock; he was a member of the Royal Commission on Depression of Trade and Industry (1886).
[129] Marrison (1996), pp. 82–5.
[130] ACC, *Proceedings* (1904); Marrison (1996), pp. 82–3.

or remaining 'neutral'. Marrison[131] has analysed the annual votes in ACC over 1904–10, showing that whilst the support for tariff reform grew (40–5 chambers in favour 1904–8; increasing to 46 in 1909, and 51 in 1910), and votes against reform very significantly reduced (from 58 to 12 over 1904–10), there was also a major increase in those seeking to remain 'neutral' (from 20 in 1905 to 41 by 1910). From 1911 to 1914 the tariff reform motions took the form of resolutions in favour of a Royal Commission. Thus, the ACC settled for the position of unity around a compromise that would allow them to speak with varied voices. However, this was in effect a policy of inaction, and dismissed by PM Herbert Asquith: 'no advantage would be served by a Commission'.[132]

Except for the first vote in 1904, which gave a majority against tariff reform, all the other ACC votes saw reform gain the greatest number of votes, but there was never an overall majority over those that abstained or remained neutral. Despite this, the presidency and ACC council interpreted them as continued support for free trade. In 1904 the initial vote was 41 to 40 against reform, with 20 chambers neutral. This was challenged by Samuel Boulton, one of London's delegates and now a Trade Commissioner. However, Holland took the neutral votes to count against the motion, with the result that it was deemed that the chambers continued to support free trade.[133] The same approach was followed in all the subsequent votes up to 1910, with the result that tariff reform never became ACC policy.

In 1904 there was much discussion about 'neutral' votes; continued in the 1905 meeting. In 1909 the president (Brassey) stated that it needed 'a two-thirds majority to justify the council going with the resolution', which required neutral votes to be included.[134] In 1910 a subcommittee of ACC examined the question of 'neutral' votes and concluded that they were not abstentions but 'a desire on the part of the chamber not to commit itself or the association for or against the resolution'. Although this was rejected by the ACC council,[135] it represented the reality of the desires by many chambers and their members to stand back from divisive issues. Brassey noted that chamber members had other campaign organizations 'through which those who had strong views could more properly gain the ear of the public and win the contest at the election'.[136]

In retrospect, whilst Avebury, Holland, and Brassey may have seemed high-handed, they managed to keep the chamber system together when it would otherwise have been hopelessly divided—the association would probably have split in two. In any case its voice would not have influenced the political outcome. Brassey's presidential address at the 1908 ACC meeting stated this clearly: 'Speaking as a free trader... the association should continue to speak with one voice at the BoT... if we go to a vote... there may be secessions and they will be

---

[131] Marrison (1996), pp. 83–5.

[132] Letter to ACC from Herbert Asquith, 1911; quoted in Ilersic and Liddle (1960), p. 156.

[133] ACC, *Annual Meeting Report* (1904), pp. 78–87, 92–105.

[134] ACC, *Annual Meeting Report* (1909), p. 66.

[135] ACC, Council minutes, 8 November 1910; London Council minutes, 1903–5; Marrison (1996), pp. 83–8, 93–7.

[136] Brassey, in ACC, *Annual Meeting Report* (1909), pp. 54–5.

regretted.'[137] The economist Alfred Marshall's comment in the light of the 1910 election provides crucial insight into the chambers' dilemma: 'the division between the districts … does not run with the interests of the population in T. R. or F. T. [Tariff Reform or Free Trade]'. It was far more confused. Marshall ascribed this to the outlook of the local press,[138] but it would be fairer to put this down to the effects of local contingency, and differentiation between businesses: a phenomenon familiar to chambers from their outset. For government to expect a simpler message was naive: 'as ever, business waited on politics.'[139] Moreover there were other things for chambers to act on; as Brassey stated, tariff reform 'took them away from matters which came more properly within their control and where their labours were more usefully applied'.[140]

But a significant consequence of this period is that it convinced many leading industrialists that the chambers were inadequate to provide the protectionist policies they wanted for their industries. The Tariff Commission was providing an alternative, testing a (weak) coalescence of opinion between many industrialists within and across sectors. It is from this period, therefore, that an alternative national voice for leading industrial businesses began to crystallize, which was to become the FBI.[141] The events of this period therefore mark a major watershed for chambers between the small state and active state, and the sector and local.

The Tariff Commission and Wartime Reconstruction Committees

The Tariff Commission was designed to build a consensus around a scientific tariff. It consulted hundreds of witnesses, undertook detailed inquiries and investigations, and received survey responses from over 15,000 firms. As an exercise in testing business opinion it was therefore unequalled up to that time. However, it failed to reach an integrated conclusion and some sectors (notably finance and cotton) largely withheld collaboration. Detailed assessments of its work are critical,[142] but the assessment of Trentmann seems to best capture the position of the chambers: 'the failure of tariff reform can be related to the open political system and the fragmented nature of the business community'.[143]

This pattern changed radically over WW1. A focus of forward thinking occurred through a Reconstruction Committee established in March 1916, which developed detailed industry reports. Analysis of these and of the wartime inquires into

[137] ACC, *Annual Meeting Report* (1908); quoted in Ilersic and Liddle (1960), p. 155.
[138] Marshall papers, 14 April 1911; Cambridge Marshall Library: quoted in Trentmann (1996) p. 1008.
[139] See e.g. Beer (1965); Marrison (1996).
[140] ACC, *Annual Meeting Report* (1909), p. 55; see also Table 10.4.
[141] Dudley Docker formed a Business League in 1911, supported by many of the Tariff Commission's members. Charles Macara launched the Employers' Parliamentary Association in 1912; he was president of the Federation of Cotton Spinners, associated with Employers' Parliamentary Council founded in 1890, and organized the free trade resistance to Chamberlain at the Manchester chamber.
[142] Saul (1960); Amery (1969); Marrison (1996); Trentmann (1996, 2008).
[143] Trentmann (1996), p. 1030.

economic conditions in 1916–17 show that all industrial sectors (even cotton) now wanted some form of protection after the war, with little support (14%) for a return to free trade.[144] Trentmann concludes that this was due, first, to a shift from an 'exogenous logic' (to respond to foreign tariffs) to an endogenous logic (that successful exports needed large and stable home markets). Second, it resulted from a rapid increase in the interdependence and integration between firms and sectors as a result of wartime needs, and accelerating industrial concentration through amalgamation and acceptance of cartels and cooperation that 'controlled' competition. Tariff reform thus had evolved from a defensive strategy 'to beat the foreigner' to supporting home industries and encouraging needed adaptation of the economy. The discussions leading up to the 1918 Balfour Committee's *Report on Commercial and Industrial Policy after the War* were a turning point for many leading industrialists; e.g. for Alfred Mond, this marked conversion from free trader.[145]

In this period the chambers moved very largely to a position of accepting change towards protection, with the ACC offering several motions in favour of a new approach to the empire; in 1915 ACC supported the McKenna tariffs,[146] and was hoping that chamber certificates of origin would allow 'preferential treatment under tariffs of the Dominions'.[147] By 1916 ACC was directly involved in the government's wartime reconstruction committees, particularly with relation to consular support, as discussed below. The 1916 annual meeting of ACC passed two crucial resolutions: (i) that the 'government be urged to enquire into the desirability of subsidising, or otherwise protecting, those industries' affected by the war or that had 'suffered seriously from German and Austrian competition'; and (ii) a resolution in support of some form of limited tariffs, noting 'that the cleavage of opinion ... was not so wide as marked such discussions prior to the war'.[148] The London chamber supported a 'tentative ad valorem tariff' with preference for the empire and allies as a temporary policy pending a more elaborate scientific tariff.[149] Symbolically, Manchester also appeared to abandon laissez-faire in 1916.

Reassessing Manchester chamber's 1916 'policy reversal'

Manchester's position in these debates deserves particular attention, both because after Corn Law abolition it was a conspicuous *national* political bell-wether for business as a whole, and because a vote in 1916 in favour of tariffs has been hailed as an apparent historical reversal for free trade. Manchester had resisted votes from the Fair Trade League in 1886, and in an 1888 postal vote, members supported free trade by 397 members (with 556 votes) to 187 (with 221 votes), 37 neutral, with

[144] Trentmann (1996), pp. 1045–7; using TNA BT 55/20–4; 38–41; 112–21.
[145] Marrison (1996); Trentmann (1996, 2008).
[146] Ilersic and Liddle (1960), pp. 168–9; 180–3.
[147] ACC, *Monthly Proceedings*; *Annual Meeting Report* (1915), p. 41.
[148] ACC, *Annual Meeting Report* (1916).
[149] Memorandum from London chamber, sent to BoT Committee on Commercial and Industrial Policy, 22 August 1916, reporting London's special committee on trade duty after the war: TNA BT 55/9 (CIP 5).

the high response rate of 62% of the membership.[150] Another test of opinion produced defeat for protectionism in 1892.

Chamberlain's 1903 Birmingham speech forced the next Manchester poll, which reaffirmed free trade by 300 to 120. Similar majorities of about 65% were achieved in votes in 1904, 1909, and 1910. However, the minority of about one-third of the chamber opposed to free trade was becoming more vociferous: the 1909 vote occurred at a 'tumultuous meeting' where the chamber's directors were attacked by the tariff reformers who claimed the result unrepresentative and the vote unconstitutional, resulting in challenges at further meetings in 1909 and 1910, which included a confidence vote on the president, Francis Ashworth.[151] The general elections of 1905 and 1910, and a by-election in 1908 also saw national attention directed at Manchester politics, especially in the seat of Manchester North-West, though the results, like that in the chamber, were complex.[152]

The extent of division put further chamber votes off the agenda until an annual meeting on 14 February 1916 where Manchester's unqualified free trade stance was indeed reversed. This vote was initially held on a resolution the council was hoping to present at the ACC; it was a restatement on free trade adapted to the needs of the post-war era. However, the resolution was attacked by fair traders, referred back to the council, and a postal poll had to be taken. The poll was 988 to 527 for reference back, with 975 not replying. This was taken as a vote of no confidence in the council, 30 of the 33 of whom resigned, and the resolution to the ACC was withdrawn with the chamber unrepresented.[153]

Clarke has made much of this as the reversal of free trade thought in Manchester.[154] His claims may have been true for the major cotton interests led by Charles Macara (now a leading FBI voice), but for the chamber (representing a more general interest) the change was subtler. The chamber's secretary indeed states that '*the first unqualified declaration in favour of tariffs*' was not until 1931.[155] Goodwin has interpreted the 1916 vote as opposition to a ruling clique by the independent-minded members, and reluctance to follow a resolution that was seen as anti-German and vindictive.[156] As stated by H. Derwent Simpson, who proposed the amendment for referral in 1916, 'every matter of importance upon which their opinion was required should be laid before the members and not kept back as the directors had done in the past'.[157] The pressure came from protectionists, but

[150] *Manchester Guardian*, 20 December 1888; see also Brown (1943), p. 132; Redford and Clapp (1956), pp. 106–7; Smith (1955); Clarke (1972); Marrison (1996), p. 89; note members had votes according to company size.
[151] Clarke (1972); Marrison (1996). Francis was a descendant of Henry Ashworth, who played a role in Cobden's campaign, as noted earlier.
[152] Clarke (1971, 1972).
[153] Manchester chamber, *Monthly Record*, 17 (1916), pp. 3, 15–17, 50–2, 66; Redford and Clapp (1956), pp. 203–5.
[154] Clarke (1972), pp. 501–2; Searle (2001).
[155] Raymond Streat, *Diary*; Dupree (1987), p. 90, emphasis in original.
[156] 'venting our spleen on ... Germany to cut off our nose to spite our face', in the president's words, *Monthly Record*, 17 (1916), p. 49; see Goodwin (1982), pp. 257–8.
[157] Manchester chamber, *Monthly Record*, 17 (1916), p. 51.

they achieved leverage only because the board was high handed. Moreover the change in the council can be exaggerated: the new council (of 38) had 14 from the previous 33.

Goodwin goes on to argue that the internal collective memory was of the council losing touch with the members, and this influenced subsequent behaviour by making the chamber avoid any resolution that was divisive. Its response to the 1916 vote was to reorganize the council and its committees, aiming to 'democratize' the chamber. It replaced the previous subcommittees (which were all appointed by and answerable to the council), and allowed the establishment of stronger sections (whose resolutions were adopted by the chamber in the name of the section), which allowed the involvement of several hundred people in chamber decision making. Any 25 members could now form a section, with its chair representing it on the council. By July 1916, 15 section chairs elected by the sections were members of the council, which the new president argued answered the challenge of the 1916 vote.[158]

Transition and confusion, 1918–1929

After WW1 many controls were quickly removed, but continued political fracture characterized more general tariff discussions. In September 1918 the Balfour Committee *Report on Commercial and Industrial Policy after the War* forced chambers to confront the issue again. The Report called for sustained government support to industry through loans, subsidies, and tariffs (with some form of imperial preference), and protection against dumping. A minority report called for a general ad valorem duty of 10% on all manufactured and semi-manufactured goods. The ABCC favoured sustained support, and came behind the concept and vocabulary of 'safeguarding' (which focused on key industries) rather than general protection.[159] Manchester chamber took a poll, which had a low response rate of only 22%; of these 193 opposed both reports, 303 favoured the main report, 165 the minority report, and 26 both reports. Whilst free traders were clearly defeated (by 72% to 28%), the chamber agreed to take no action given the low response and divisions shown.[160] The next big tariff debate occurred over the 1919 Exports and Imports Bill, which was designed to introduce anti-dumping duties. After referral to sections, Manchester's opinion was sufficiently uniform in criticism that the chamber was able to call for the government to open consultations to revise it. The Birmingham chamber rejected the Bill as 'an objectionable system of bureaucratic control and interference'. But the London chamber and ABCC firmly supported it by a large majority.[161]

The Safeguarding of Industries Act (1921) marked a new turning point. Whilst this obtained general support from the ABCC, many chambers were opposed, and

[158] Goodwin (1982), pp. 52–5; *Monthly Record*, 17 (1916), pp. 167, 217; 18 (1917), p. 34.
[159] Ilersic and Liddle (1960), pp. 181–3.
[160] Redford and Clapp (1956), p. 200; Goodwin (1982), pp. 267–8.
[161] Marrison (1996).

London set up 'Vigilance Committees' in a range of sectors, the purpose of which was to review each sector proposal and object to its operations if needed, as allowed under the Act. The Dyestuffs Act (1920) led to similar actions. The result was support for safeguarding where a case was strong and where other industries did not suffer. Similarly, ABCC supported maintaining the McKenna duties in 1924 on grounds of protecting industries and reducing unemployment.[162]

Thus opinion among chambers remained strongly divided on protection measures. The West Riding chamber, giving evidence in 1925 to the Balfour Committee on Industry and Trade (of 1927), was instructed to give no opinion on tariffs.[163] Manchester undertook major polls in 1923 and 1930 to sound member opinion, in both cases reporting the results to government and publicizing them in the press, but remaining neutral as a chamber: this was Manchester maintaining its role as national bell-wether, but not getting involved in 'politics'. The June 1930 poll was complex, showing 26% in favour of free trade, 42% in favour of safeguarding, 10% for general protection, 8% for protection except for some raw materials, 1% for protection except foodstuffs, and 13% for protection except raw materials and foodstuffs.[164] This showed the strength of opinion in different directions, but as the president argued it 'can do no more because decisions on fiscal matters can only be taken by governments, instructed by the electorate of the country'. With a substantial body of members, even if a minority, opposed to a given policy, 'who deserve equally well of the chamber', the chamber stood back.[165] As Goodwin observed, the membership generally supported the council's approach to handling divisive maters and leaving decisions to government. In this they took a line in common with most other chambers in the 1920s. Birmingham also initially imposed restrictions on its discussions of the 'political' issue of safeguarding, but reviewed this in 1924.[166] Cardiff still judged the issue too political in 1931.[167] However, Manchester had shifted its position by October 1930 to cautious support for fiscal reforms within a policy of encouragement for inter-empire trade; and in September 1931 the council voted 17 to 5 in favour of an immediate system of tariffs.[168]

The confused position of the chambers continued until 1930–1. The ABCC, under pressure from many chambers and its large industrial members generally acquiesced in or supported government intervention, once the politics were clear. With the Conservatives in office under Baldwin (1924–9), chamber opinion was too evenly divided, resulting in a quasi-embargo on discussion of tariffs over 1926–8. Marrison compares the Birmingham and Sheffield chambers in this period; the former became a strong advocate of well-designed safeguarding measures; whilst the latter was reluctant to express an opinion. Like Manchester, Sheffield was awaiting

[162] ABCC, *Annual Report* (1924), p. 18.
[163] Quoted in Rooth (1992), pp. 39–40.
[164] Manchester, *Monthly Record* (1923), p. 5; (1930); quoted in Goodwin (1982), pp. 271–90.
[165] Manchester, *Monthly Record* (1930), p. 212; Goodwin (1982), p. 290.
[166] Marrison (1996), p. 285.
[167] Cardiff chamber, Council minutes, 9 November 1931; see also discussion on politics in Chapter 3.
[168] Manchester chamber, proceedings, 13 October 1930; *Monthly Record,* September (1931); Redford and Clapp (1954), pp. 240–3; Dupree (1987), pp. 88–91.

clearer signals from politicians. However, it became concerned about 'falling off of membership' after it failed to press for import restrictions on iron and steel in 1927, and was forced to reverse its position by a poll in 1929 showing 515 to 46 in favour of safeguarding.[169]

Politically the period produced confused positions. Safeguarding and consular reforms had been the Coalition government's policies under Lloyd George (1916–22). The Liberals and Labour, however, remained committed to free trade. The Conservatives were reluctant to revive their explicit support for tariffs; the shadow of the 1905 election defeat remained strong. The Empire Industries Association (1924–32), which superseded the Tariff Reform League, was a means to maintain pressures on the Conservatives and try to convert others. It was formed by Leopold Amery and Neville Chamberlain after Baldwin's electoral defeat to Labour in 1924, but ran independently.

Rival business organizations

Other business initiatives produced pressures on ABCC from rivals. A Business League was developed to install more businesspeople in parliament to break the political limbo. It fought an abortive election campaign in December 1909, promoting extensive protectionism for industry. Dudley Docker took this up in February 1910 to launch the Business League of Wednesbury, with the aim of putting businessmen in the Exchequer and Board of Trade, with a Minister of Commerce who would hold office independent of government party. Other branches of the Business League were launched in the Midlands from 1911. The chambers saw the moves as significant enough to invite Docker to participate in their discussions with Asquith's government in 1911–12 on labour unrest. ABCC's recognized MPs also exerted pressure for change: e.g. Hallewell Rogers (Unionist in Birmingham) and Edward Manville (Conservative in Coventry) were aligned with the League's interests.[170] Manville went on to become ABCC President 1918–20.

Birmingham chamber also made overtures to Docker. As a major local industrialist Docker and the Business League were invited to the chamber in September 1911, but it 'could not fall in with the proposals', though it was sympathetic. Docker particularly wanted the chamber to elicit from election candidates their views on business matters, and 'let the League put certain matters through for the chamber to assist them'.[171] In 1916 the chamber made a request to Docker to chair its import and export committee, but received no reply; in 1917 he was invited by the chamber to the British Industries Federation in Birmingham, but did not reply.[172]

---

[169] Sheffield chamber, Membership Committee minutes, 21 May 1928; see also Marrison (1996), pp. 288–9.

[170] Davenport-Hines (1984), pp. 67–9.

[171] Birmingham chamber, GPC, 25 September and 17 October 1911. The other League delegates were Lincoln Chandler, A. Warne-Browne, W. Till (a workman), W. Roberts, S. Taylor, J. P. Achurch.

[172] Birmingham chamber, GPC, 18 September 1916, 24 April 1917.

Docker was an individualist and had other plans as founding president of FBI in 1917. But the FBI was also divided over tariffs. As a result a British Commonwealth Union (BCU) was formed in December 1916 as a break-away from the FBI, originally called a 'British Imperialists' party. The BCU had some powerful backers and was a vehement critic of free trade. Vincent Caillard at its foundation argued that it would 'discredit for ever the comfortable doctrine of laissez faire' and install a force in parliament with better knowledge of trade and industry.[173] It received sympathetic support from the Australian and New Zealand prime ministers, who favoured imperial preference and argued that laissez-faire had opened the door to Germany.[174]

In the 1918 election 18 of 24 BCU candidates were elected. Although many were not dedicated supporters, it introduced some new and vociferous advocates to parliament, most of whom were ABCC MPs, such as Manville. As a result the ABCC was supportive of BCU, though not directly. However, the BCU was not able to make much impact on the Lloyd George Coalition government over 1922–3.[175] It contested the 1923 election with less success and its activities then transferred to the Empire Industries Association, which was important in the tariff election of 1931. The ABCC was thus able to contain and assimilate the rivalry of the BCU, and its relation to an external League shows similarities to the Corn Law period.

The end of free trade 1929–32

The uncertainties changed after 1929. A Labour government had taken power in 1929 as a minority, determined to demonstrate Labour's ability to govern. After initial successes it was soon beset by difficulties of economic slump and budget limitations. The pillars of Victorian and Edwardian politics were under severe stress: the gold standard, pressures to balance the budget, and most of all the commitment to free trade. Labour had been committed to free trade from its 19th-century radical origins: as a support for cheap food, improved wages, international peace, and after 1918 as a means to expand exports. As a government its first approach over 1929–30 was to negotiate a tariff truce through the League of Nations, and in mid-1930 to seek import limitations through an Imperial Conference. But these were only holding policies, and they were generally thought inadequate by the chambers. As the slump deepened it became clear to many Labour leaders (particularly the PM Ramsay MacDonald, Dominions Secretary J. H. Thomas, and Employment Minister Vernon Hartshorn) that protection for home industries was the only way out of the impasse. But this was vetoed by the Treasury, led by Chancellor Philip Snowden, although supported by many other cabinet members.

Because of its significance, the subsequent unfolding of events has been subject to enormous literature and debate.[176] Labour survived until 1931, and was able to

---

[173] V. Caillard, 'A new force in industrial legislation', *Empire Review* (1918), 32, 383–8.
[174] W. M. Hughes, 'The organisation of industry' and W. F. Massey, 'The war and after', *Empire Review*, 32 (1918), 253–61, 262–7.
[175] Turner (1978), pp. 541–6; Davenport-Hines (1984).
[176] For fuller discussion, see e.g. Ball (1988); Williamson (1992); Searle (2001).

pass the Coal Act to nationalize the industry, as well as encouraging reorganization of cotton and some other industries, and developing a first limited Keynesian stimulus package. The chambers provided support for some of these developments. Involvement in the Cotton Board and other industrial reorganization played fairly naturally to their strong presence in the traditional industrial districts in which many of the depressed industries were concentrated; but the chambers were uniformly opposed to any form of nationalization. Labour's other policies, particularly its Unemployment Fund (which was being increasingly used to finance general government debt) and Education Bill, were opposed by most chambers because they were regarded as financially unsustainable.

On free trade the Conservatives had been riven and wary since the earlier debates. But a rapid shift back to support for imperial preference and tariffs was achieved in October 1930, chiefly as a result of the opportunity offered by a statement from the Canadian PM, that he would be willing to operate with imperial tariffs if the UK would meet his concerns halfway. Neville Chamberlain responded immediately, and was able to carry the leader Baldwin, shadow cabinet colleagues, and a largely willing grass roots, converting the Conservatives to protection. This became a dividing issue with the Labour and Liberal parties. However, with deepening financial pressures on the pound King George V forced the formation of an emergency national government in August 1931, with MacDonald remaining as PM, supported by Baldwin, Neville, and Austen Chamberlain and other selected Conservatives, and the Liberals. This was a temporary expedient and unstable. Labour ministers who were unwilling to support tariffs and other policies resigned in August, and MacDonald was expelled from the Labour Party in September, though remaining as PM. The national government's main achievement was to pass an emergency Economies Bill and renegotiate UK overseas loans. This provided only temporary relief, and the gold standard had to be abandoned in September.

Divisions on policy within the government forced a general election, held on 27 October 1931, fought on a National Coalition platform of 'considering all proposals likely to help', including tariffs, commercial treaties, and imperial structures. This is often called 'the tariff election': the Empire Industries Association held over 2,600 meetings in 1930–1; the FBI and League of Industry distributed over 1 million leaflets and 30,000 posters outside factory gates.[177] The result left the Conservatives as the majority party (473 seats) and main element of a new National Coalition government (of 554), with MacDonald still as PM, with a mandate for tariffs. However, they had to negotiate with a group of Liberals who were still reluctant to abandon free trade; although opposition from Labour was minor as they had only 52 seats. Nevertheless, the government was able to impose new Customs duties in November 1931, and introduce a revenue tariff in January 1932 through an Import Duties Bill (which led to the resignation of the Liberals in September). Further moves to 'fair trade' followed through a series of bilateral trade

---

[177] Marrison (1996), pp. 418–19; Trentmann (2008), p. 346.

treaties over 1932–3, with MFN clauses progressively abandoned during these negotiations, although full imperial preference was slow to take hold.

This was very much in accord with ABCC policy, reinforced by many local votes in the preceding period to extend safeguarding; e.g. by Leeds in 1928, Bradford and Kidderminster in 1930, and Manchester's 1930 poll (and Manchester gave full support to immediate tariffs in September 1931).[178] The ABCC was able publicly to call free trade a 'fetish' in 1928.[179] In their summer meeting in 1930 the ABCC strongly adopted 'safeguarding', and at their 25 September 1931 general meeting there was a critical vote with a 'practically solid vote for tariffs. London and Manchester, the pillars of free trade in years gone by . . . came round. Clare Lees gave a brilliant presidential address'.[180] The politics were now clear; business had 'waited on politics', and now rallied to what was felt to be unavoidable legislation.

Tariff machinery and the eclipse of chambers

Ironically, whilst the ACC implicitly accepted protection from about 1916, its influence on government policy was steadily diminished, as sectors became the basis for action rather than geographical areas. This began with WW1 output and price controls, where government tried to encourage sector bodies to develop or reconstruct themselves. This had some spin-offs for chambers like Manchester that had a strong sector presence (e.g. in the Cotton Board, and in negotiations with India).[181] But generally the BoT sought to stimulate national sector organizations. The Conservative president of the Board of Trade, Philip Cunliffe-Lister, stated in 1929: 'we must have rationalisation. It is necessary for economic efficiency and it inevitably involves the creation of larger units and making agreements . . . to combine . . . in the most efficient units.'[182] In the 1930s an all-party Industrial Reconstruction League, and the Next Five Years Group, recommended an enabling Act to give associations the powers to develop combines. Harold Macmillan was deeply involved in these discussions, and in related banking reform debates, and this experience led to later Conservative support for industrial organization in the 1950s when Macmillan became prime minister.[183]

Once the national government embraced protection, associations were used as key sources of information on the levels of tariffs and restrictions to impose; sectors were 'brought in line' by the BoT. The Import Duties Advisory Committee (IDAC) of BoT became the chief mechanism for this, requiring associations to speak for whole industries[184] and it 'acquired a dignity and sense of responsibility . . . for

---

[178] Quoted in Rooth (1992), pp. 45–6.

[179] Sir Walter Raine, as deputy president ABCC, letter to *The Times*, 6 October 1928; quoted in Trentmann (2008), p. 334.

[180] ABCC, *Annual Meeting Reports* (1930, 1931); Beer (1965); Raymond Streat, secretary of Manchester chamber, *Diary*: Dupree (1987), p. 95.

[181] Goodwin (1982); Rooth (1992), pp. 183–7; see also Raymond Streat, in Dupree (1987), pp. 87–114.

[182] Speech in House of Commons, 6 May 1929; quoted in PEP (1957), p. 21.

[183] Turner (1988), pp. 189 f.; Middlemas (1979).

[184] IDAC, quoted in PEP (1957), pp. 22–3; Marrison (1996), p. 323.

industrial self-discipline and self-government'. Turner sees this period of high ambitions for trade associations as 'hopes unfulfilled' since, with notable exceptions, often associations could not exert the pressures needed to restructure their sectors. Indeed, where association action did not work, the government was prepared to legislate; as in the 1930 Coal Mines Act, several Agricultural Marketing Acts in the 1930s, and the Cotton Reorganization Act.

Within a free trade structure the views of the localities were valuable inputs to governments. Some of that value continued under protection; for example the ABCC appointed an industrial adviser to the Ottawa Imperial Conference in 1932, appointed a member of the panel of advisers to the UK delegation at the World Monetary and Economic Conference in 1933, strongly influenced the establishment of Committees on the Restriction of Exchange in Europe and South America in 1933, and in 1934 was a strong influence on MFN clauses in commercial treaties.[185] However, the chambers were placed increasingly at the margins by the focused needs for government to look at whole industries and develop national policies for sector tariffs. This in turn underpinned subsequent government attachment to sector planning as part of national planning, which was eventually directed through NEDC and left chambers as second level advisers to CBI. The 'discourse coalition' had shifted over 1918–32, and became entrenched after WW2, leaving the chambers more peripheral to government's policy concerns.

10.6. TRADE SUPPORT AND CONSULAR SERVICES

Consular services provided a different influence on chamber development. As shown in Tables 10.2 and 10.4, they were among the largest recurrent concerns of the chambers from the 1830s. A remarkable degree of success for chamber lobbies was achieved after 1897 on improved trade support, and on consular services in 1916–17. But this success took years to achieve.

Until the 1820s the civil service and diplomats and consuls were largely appointed by patronage and were not well regarded. Moreover, in the East, the administration of foreign policy was de facto delegated to the East India and Levant Companies, which had the added odium of monopoly as well as inefficiency.[186] It was natural therefore that the Foreign Office (FO, which was created as a separate department in 1782), the consuls, and the BoT all became targets for chambers seeking reform. Some reform had occurred in the 1820s under Canning to improve civil service recruitment and qualifications, and again in the 1860s. But the diplomatic and consular services remained largely untouched, having a high patronage content until WW1. As recognized by Platt,[187] it was a reminder 'that reform seldom follows from the spontaneous recognition of injustice by those in authority'. Chamber lobbying indeed had to be persistent.

---

[185] Dunwoody (1935), ABCC secretary.
[186] Horn (1961); Platt (1963, 1971); Homer (1971); Middleton (1977).
[187] Platt (1971), p. 1.

The chamber criticisms were that the FO did not consult the BoT, and vice versa; the FO, India Office, and Colonial Office did not consult each other; and none adequately consulted with businesses before making diplomatic decisions. The Colonial Office concluded treaties between the colonies and other countries without including British goods; the India Office was notorious for ignoring the concerns of British manufacturers; and the Foreign Office was perceived as marked with ignorant and arrogant staff who neglected overseas consular functions.

The specific criticisms of the consular service focused on three main areas.[188] First, there was a lack of resources; the whole service was 'utterly inadequately staffed and paid and overwhelmed by its duties', with the consular positions often considered as 'a refuge for the destitute' (in Gladstone's words) rather than based on expertise,[189] of low status in an FO where social status was very important.[190] Second there was concern over conflict of interests. Because their pay was so low, consuls frequently traded on their own account and thus might not be objective in dealing with other businesses, and their fees were seen as arbitrary and excessive. Third, for some chamber members, there was inadequate 'pushing' by FO staff and consuls of British export opportunities. This was partly the result of laissez-faire policy, but also of consular staff ignorance of British manufactures, or diplomatic staff having gone native (more concerned with the sensitivities of the foreign country than with British business).

Early chamber lobbies on foreign trade support

Chamber concerns with foreign policy and the Foreign Office became more severe as the 19th century progressed, largely in direct proportion to the growing importance of foreign competition as the scope of 'free trade' was redefined. A Select Committee in 1864[191] highlighted concerns with treaties, consuls, and duties. Despite resistance from the FO, this resulted in the establishment of a separate commercial department within the FO in 1864 to administer the consular service. The former commercial department within the BoT was transferred to the FO over 1872–83. The new head of the FO department (Charles M. Kennedy) was initially well regarded by the chambers,[192] but this view soon changed. Kennedy resisted reforms, the FO commercial department acted as no more than a post box to the BoT, and concern with FO staff at home and consuls abroad continued.[193]

Rivalry between the Departments also continued. When Joseph Chamberlain became president of the BoT over 1880–5, he brought back the commercial

---

[188] See excellent summary by Platt (1963); also Middleton (1977).

[189] Platt (1963), pp. 496–7; quoting Gladstone speech 8 March 1842, and *Report of the Committee on Commercial Intelligence in Foreign Countries*, 1917–18, *House of Commons Papers*, XXIX, p. 711.

[190] Platt (1971), p. 1.

[191] W. E. Foster chair, Cobden a member; House of Commons Select Committee on Trade with Foreign Nations, *Parliamentary Papers* (1864), vii.

[192] Evidence to 1864 Select Committee on Relations of the Board of Trade and the Foreign Office, 1864; see also Ilersic and Liddle (1960), pp. 23–4.

[193] Discussed at length by Homer (1971), pp. 27–34.

department to the BoT, and the chambers mounted a very vigorous lobby for change in 1886, with numerous letters from the chambers and ACC to improve consular support.[194] The FO still saw no need to change, adhering to a doctrine of laissez-faire, but most of all was unwilling to modify its cherished political/diplomatic functions: James Bryce (parliamentary under-secretary) writing for Rosebery stated that foreign business efforts 'must be left to, and can be better discharged by private enterprise'.[195] Indeed, at this point the chambers themselves were divided about how far government should go. All supported improvement in consular services, but in 1886 Southampton and others were opposed to government 'pushing' for trade; and in 1897 Blackburn, Glasgow, and Manchester were opposed.[196] This reflected the emerging divisions over 'free trade' and tariffs. In any case the Gladstone and Rosebery Liberal governments opposed any 'pushing' activity and no reform of trade support occurred.

However, a significant change occurred under Salisbury's Unionist government 1895–1902. This significantly reformed the BoT and established it as a stronger force for trade support. The former BoT Committee on Trade and Treaties was replaced by a Committee on Commercial Intelligence in 1897, with chair Lord Inchcape (Courtney Boyle), permanent secretary of the BoT. This immediately began to consult with business interests on improving trade support. It proposed a new BoT Commercial Intelligence Department, the development of foreign missions, commercial museums, and improved dissemination of foreign trade information. The committee took the opinion of leading chambers, 39 giving strong support for its proposals.[197] The result was the establishment of the Commercial Intelligence Branch (CIB) of the BoT in 1899, and an Advisory Committee on Commercial Intelligence (ACCI) in 1898 to bring in external business expertise. The CIB was to focus the government's trade promotion efforts, and the ACCI was to advise the government on overall trade support policy. This was a radical step away from free trade, but within a very constrained remit. These reforms had two profound implications for chambers: first, as members of the ACCI, chambers had their first opportunity to become 'insiders' to policy; second, it provided the route by which reform of the consular service was finally achieved, with chambers gaining a role as partners of government in disseminating commercial intelligence.

Chambers as 'chosen' policy advisers on ACCI

The ACCI was an important innovation and represents one of the first occasions where government sought to work with business interests in a *formally constituted*

---

[194] e.g. Kenric Murray (London chamber secretary) to Lord Rosebery, 10 June 1886, and other letters: *Parliamentary Papers* (1886), (C. 4779) lx, pp. 14 ff.; quoted in Homer (1971) pp. 27 ff.

[195] Rosebery to ACC, 31 July 1886; *Parliamentary Papers* (1886), (C. 4779) lx, pp. 14 ff; quoted in Homer (1971) pp. 27 ff.

[196] Platt (1968), pp.113–14, pp. xxxv–xxxvi, quoting evidence by chambers to various committees.

[197] Though as usual some chambers offered dissenting views (including Huddersfield and Worcester which were opposed; Manchester, Glasgow, Bradford, and Liverpool opposed some elements, related to museums).

and continuous relationship. It was a forerunner of later corporatism. But in contrast to later developments chambers became the lead source of advice. The BoT asked chambers to nominate 'persons actively associated with the principal industries and trades—more particularly the export trades—of the country, and that they should also be conversant with general conditions affecting business in the principal industrial localities'.[198] At this point local contingency was recognized as important to the policy process. It was a major coup for chambers' lobbying pressure. Over the life of ACCI from 1898 to 1917 the chambers were the sole or primary external members. Their significance as the first formal conduit of government corporatism has been previously little recognized.

Initially the ACCI was constituted of 11 members: most chosen from government departments, but four chosen from nominations requested by BoT from the ACC; the chair was Lord Inchcape (secretary of the BoT), deputy chair Alfred Bateman (BoT Statistics branch, but also seen as a business representative), and the only non-chamber external member was the director of the Imperial Institute. Hence, from the outset chambers were the largest group of business members. However, the chamber role increased in 1900 to seven of nine business members, and after 1906 it supplied all external members chosen from ACC nominations. The ACC president became a member ex officio from 1912.[199]

Not all the names nominated by ACC are recorded. However, in 1910 there is a full list of nominations sent by ACC. These included three names from London; two each from Glasgow, Manchester, and Birmingham; and one each from Liverpool, Sheffield, Belfast, Bristol, Bradford, Hull, Newcastle, Nottingham, North Staffordshire, Leicester, and Cardiff. This more or less assured the four large chambers of a place. The BoT accepted two each from London, Manchester, and Birmingham, and one each from Liverpool, Glasgow, Sheffield, Belfast, Newcastle, and Cardiff. It is clear therefore that both ACC and the BoT were seeking to ensure a strong coverage from the large cities. Many ACC nominees were MPs, Lords, or Knights, all of whom were included except W. E. P. Priestley, MP for Bradford.[200] Thus those nominated were almost all already significantly recognized for their public service, and many were highly politically active. ACC chose to use as 'insiders' those who it deemed had most influence as already established 'insiders'.

Table 10.5 lists the full business-nominated membership of the ACCI, together with their known positions as MP, Lords, and chamber membership. Of the 30 names, the table shows that the membership had a high presence of politicians (40%), most of whom were Liberal Unionists. Of those with known political views, most were free traders. But the choices ranged beyond mainstream opinion at the time; most of this group moved to a conditional policy, similar to fair trade, which became the ACCI stance. Concerning geographical presence, it is clear that the BoT and ACC were seeking to represent the main manufacturing areas of England,

---

[198] BoT letter to ACC; ACC, Executive minutes, 10 June 1913.

[199] Algernon Firth joined the ACCI in 1912, filling a vacancy, then becoming ex-officio member as ACC president: ACCI minutes, 24 October 1912; TNA BT 55/1/1.

[200] ACC, Executive Committee minutes 1910; compared with appointees TNA BT 55/1/1.

Table 10.5. Business representatives on ACCI 1898–1917 (excluding civil service members)

Name	Chamber	1898–9	1900–5	1906–9	1910–13	1914–17	Politics
Abel Sir Fred	Dir. Imperial Institute	X d. 1904					
Adam Forbes F.	Manchester			X	X	X	
Bateman Alfred	BOT, bus rep	X	X	X	X	X	
Bell Hugh	London			X	X	X	
Birchenough Henry	Macclesfield and S. Africa			X	X	X	
Blackwell Thos. F.	London			X	d. c. 1906	Replaced by Spicer	
Brittain Frederick	Sheffield		X	X	X	X	
Brock Henry	Glasgow			X	X	X d. 1915	
Cox George H.	Liverpool		X	X	X	X	
Craig-Brown T	S. of Scotland		X	X	X	X	
Dunstan Wyndham R. Prof	Dir. Imperial Institute		X replaced Abel				
Firth Algernon	Halifax, pres ACC				X 1912–	X	
Hallewell Rogers	Birmingham						MP Coalition Unionist
Hickman Alfred	Staffs and Wolverhampton		X	d. 1910		X	MP Cons
Hobson Albert J.	Sheffield					X	
Holland W. H.	Rotherham, pres ACC	X	X	X	X	X	MP, Lord Rotherham, Lib
Joicey Lord	Newcastle					X res 1916	MP, Lord, Lib
Langdon Edward H.	Manchester					X	
Lubbock John	London, pres ACC		X	X	X		MP, Lord Avebury, Lib Unionist
Machin Stanley	Ex-BOT London rep				X	X	
Mitchell William H.	Bradford, ex VP ACC			X	X	X	
Murray James	Glasgow					X 1915 replaced Brock	
Northcote Stafford	Newcastle, pres ACC	X					MP Cons
Parkes E.	Birmingham and hon. sec. ACC			X	X	X	MP Lib Unionist
Patterson Lloyd R.	Belfast			X	d. c.1906	Replaced by Thompson	
Rollit Albert	Hull and London	X	X	X	X–1912		MP, Progressive Ind Cons/Lib
Spicer Albert	London				X	X	MP, Lib
Thomas David Alfred	Cardiff			X	X	X	MP, Lord Rhondda, Lib
Thompson Robert	Belfast				X	X res 1916	MP, Unionist
Wolff Gustav Wm.	Belfast		X	d. 1913		X	MP, Cons

Source: ACC, *Proceedings*; ACCI, *Reports* (Cd. 8962, 1898; Cd. 2044, 1904; Cd. 4917, 1909; Cd. 6779, 1913); and TNA BT 55/1/1.

London, Scotland, and Northern Ireland; Dublin never figured, and Wales appeared only briefly. When a member died or resigned they were replaced by another member from the same chamber; thus, de facto, ACC was controlling the committee's membership and geographical representation.

The work of ACCI

The ACCI received routine trade reports, discussed tariffs, and conducted inquiries into trade opportunities.[201] It is difficult to be sure of the effect of the ACCI, but it was clearly significant in the period before WW1; after 1914 it became part of the general planning of industry. The analysis by Marrison and Trentmann focuses on its role in the free trade debate, discussed above.[202] For this the ACCI was a significant forum for the government to manage a process of policy change in close consultation with business representatives in the critical period after 1900. For the interests involved it was critical in helping found, in effect, a 'conditional trade policy', as partly debated by the London chamber and advocated by Avebury (an ACCI member) to the ACC in 1904. This demonstrates one of the dilemmas of lobby organizations: whilst they may have significant influence on policy, the final outcome may differ from the 'preferred' option and this may cause tensions with the members. For many chamber leaders, 'conditional trade policy' had become the de facto preferred option, but this could not be explicit because of the divisions within their membership.

Beyond this role, the ACCI was also of significance in opening government ears to the continued problems of foreign trade, which offered an opportunity for chambers to become involved in the first foreign missions, dissemination of foreign commercial intelligence, and a range of other openings. Some role was played by the experiences of the committee in feeding the thinking behind the government's Reconstruction Committee set up in March 1916 by Asquith. Although Asquith resigned in December 1916, Lloyd George continued to use external advisers and was willing to support the establishment of the Advisory Council that succeeded ACCI in 1918. This was a period of great debate on the role of business in government, with Docker, Cailliard, and others moving for business MPs and ministers. Another line of thought from Richard Haldane was for a 'general staff' on economic affairs, which directly fed ideas about a 'parliament of industry'.[203] This held deep resonance with chamber assertions to be a 'parliament of commerce'. The ideas shaped later thoughts by Harold Macmillan and Philip Kerr, and emerged in a different form in the NEDC.[204]

The ACCI provided chambers with a uniquely powerful position as the 'chosen' insiders to the BoT, but it did not satisfy the broader aims they sought. In 1913 the

[201] The ACC was asked to nominate 10 names from which BoT chose 6; ACC, *Annual Meeting Report* (1901), pp. 21–3; Llewellyn Smith (1928), pp. 73–80; see e.g. *Report of the Committee on Commercial Intelligence* (1901).
[202] Marrison (1996); Trentmann (1996, 2008).
[203] Haldane was Secretary of State for War 1905–12, then Lord Chancellor 1912–15 and 1924.
[204] Johnson (1968), pp. 302 and 500; Beer (1965); Middlemas (1979, 1983); Dahrendorf (1995).

ACC tried to expand the committee to become a much more general body, asking for an extension to the terms of reference. This was linked to its campaign for a Minister of Commerce and a stronger business voice with government. However, the BoT stuck to its own terms, but did allow 'general commercial matters to be raised under AOB' at meetings.[205] As a result the revised terms of reference from 1914 were: to advise BoT on the work of its Commercial Intelligence Branch with respect to commercial missions and information; advise on matters relating to tariffs and commercial questions; or *any commercial question*.[206] This partially satisfied chambers, but was of little practical value. As stated by Edward Manville MP, when president of ABCC in 1919, the BoT itself was limited because it had too many other responsibilities to be effective, though it had been improved by the restructuring between departments after WW1 shifting some responsibilities away from the BoT.[207]

After 1918 the ACCI was replaced by an Advisory Council (initially called Committee) to the BoT, which survived until 1938. Initially it was proposed that this would have 14 members, composed of 3 merchants (including one ABCC representative), three manufacturers, three bankers/financiers/accountants, a shipowner, plus an economist, member of the press, and representatives of labour and the BTC. Steel-Maitland at BoT argued that this would not seek to represent all trades, but would be able to 'give an opinion that is really valuable as regards the different aspects of foreign trade'. The press was to be a member to aid 'commercial propaganda' and to advise on the BoT *Journal* to avoid 'mistakes' in the future, to help diffuse public understanding to help 'support measures which may be clearly necessary'; i.e. an effort at shifting frames. Only the ABCC, TUC, and 'possibly the FBI' were to act as nominating bodies, all the other members were invited by the BoT. The ABCC deserved this exceptional treatment because they were 'not a sectional but a comprehensive organisation'.[208]

However, the actual membership was drawn from a wide range of business interests, with the ABCC nominating only one, its president (Algernon Firth) although Faringdon was also a member. For the chambers the new Council, though welcome, was a significant erosion of their former privileged position as the sole/ primary adviser in the ACCI. The change marked a shift to a national policy structure where local interests were to become ever more eclipsed. However, even more concerning was the effectiveness of the Council. The minister's annotation of Steel-Maitland's proposals was prescient of the future of this committee: Lord Robert Cecil thought the committee was 'so large that I foresee it is not intended to consult them except on "broad questions of policy" . . . too numerous to be of use for executive purposes'.[209] Clearly many of the prominent names felt the same,

---

[205] ACC, Executive minutes, 8 July 1913; see also discussion in Chapters 8 and 10.
[206] ACC, *Annual Meeting Report* (1910), pp. 8–10; *Annual Meeting Report* (1914), pp. 8–1, emphasis addcd.
[207] Speech, ABCC, *Annual Meeting Report*, 15–16 April (1919), p. 22.
[208] Memoranda by Sir Arthur Steel-Maitland, 5 and 12 November 1917: TNA BT 60/1/1.
[209] Lord Robert Cecil annotation to memorandum by Steel-Maitland, 12 November 1917: TNA BT 60/1/1.

since several declined to join the committee (including Lord Inchcape, former chair of ACCI, W. G. Goeschen, and Frank Wedgwood).[210]

A regular feature of the committee became the 'commercial and economic outlook', which gave the ABCC an opportunity to input local views from across the country that clearly influenced government,[211] and which in turn underpinned a growing chamber commitment to economic surveys which has continued up to the present. It also allowed the ABCC to head off dangers. For example, in 1922 there were 'rumours of curtailing' the Department of Overseas Trade. Algernon Firth stated that 'there would be great opposition from the chambers, . . . it represented a development which the chambers had urged for years past when advocating a Minister of Commerce which could do initiative work for British trade'. Firth's role as an 'insider', and support from the committee, saw off this early threat from Treasury which was repeated in 1927.[212] Membership of the committee also provided opportunities. Thus, as a result of the 1923 International Customs Convention, government regulation of certificates of origin was introduced. This responsibility was passed to the BoT, which used its power to support ABCC policy: only approved chambers could issue certificates.[213]

However, Cecil's comments were correct, the Advisory Committee was chiefly receiving policy material from government and making observations and comments (much of which appears very brief, constrained, and formulaic in the minutes), there was limited scope to influence. It was not the main conduit through which government was now operating. WW1 had changed everything. Now there were a plethora of other avenues by which different interests influenced government trade and industry policy.

Commercial intelligence and reform of the Consular Service

The second major reform of the period following 1900 was the Consular Service. This had remained a chamber concern, but despite some improvements, by the start of WW1 no systematic reforms had occurred.[214] Helm, secretary of the Manchester chamber, received widespread support in 1903 when he stated that with few exceptions consular reports were 'useless'.[215]

The persistent concern of the chambers with consuls was commercial intelligence. The FO and government view was that consuls should be centres of commercial information abroad, which was then transmitted to British businesses. The ACC lobby for improvements met with some support from Joseph Chamberlain as president of the BoT over 1880–5. The most positive reform was the launch of the *Board of Trade Journal* in 1886. Consular reports had been essentially

[210] See correspondence and papers in TNA BT 60/1/1.
[211] BoT Advisory Council minutes, 1918–38: TNA BT 197/1.
[212] Algernon Firth comments: BoT Advisory Council minutes, 18 January 1922: TNA BT 197/1.
[213] The FBI (later CBI) London and regional offices could also issue certificates; see Chapter 12.
[214] Platt (1963, 1971); Homer (1971).
[215] Elijah Helm (1903), *Report of the Fifth Congress of Chambers of Commerce of the Empire* (Montreal), p. 38; quoted in Platt (1968), p. 113.

internal documents to the FO or published through various parliamentary routes (Blue Books and statistical abstracts), which were not even indexed until the 1880s, and were of little use to businesses. If any useful information was actually provided, it was not effectively disseminated, could not be readily found, was usually backward looking, and transparent to foreign competitors. Moreover, the reports were usually sent late, were too lengthy, and had insufficient interpretation: in 1904 only 9% of the Consular Annual Trade Reports were received on time.[216] Indeed, the chambers often used British-based foreign sources and travellers, particularly the Germans, Austrians, and Belgians, as they were better informed, and most critically, they were allowed to give confidential credit information.[217] The consuls were not permitted officially to give this by the FO, as they must 'not risk making enemies in a place where it is an important duty to cultivate good relations with his foreign neighbours'.[218]

The BoT *Journal* was launched to overcome these defects. It followed an internal memorandum of 1886. Commercial intelligence became the favoured policy by which consuls could help British business through the *Journal*, rather than 'pushing' for trade. However the Journal was a limited medium, and only as good as the consular reports it used. The first real change followed the Commercial Intelligence Committee's recommendation of 1897, when the BoT established its own Commercial Intelligence Branch (CIB) in 1899. This led to the creation of a register of British businesses in contact with BoT, and the gathering of specific intelligence which was distributed to businesses through the chambers. This was an early coup for the chambers, although by 1907 tensions led to BoT also consulting other leading businesses (that were not chamber members). The new approach was effective: the volume of enquiries to the CIB increased dramatically from 1244 in 1900, to 16,000 by 1914, and 40,000 by 1916.[219] The CIB also won a modest budget of £1000 to send foreign trade missions; the first went to South America in 1897. Chamber pressure through the ACCI also led to setting up a Special Register by CIB in May–June 1910, 'of firms desiring to receive confidential consular intelligence', with 1189 members. Also critical, the BoT began appointing its own trade commissioners in the colonies from 1908, introducing a parallel to the FO consuls, but aiming at a more useful system for businesses.

However, the main process of appointing consuls was still unreformed. The ACC made what turned out to be an important step in 1912 under its new secretary (Dunwoody) for sight of internal BoT proposals for reorganizing the Consular Service, which resulted in receiving a list of functions, with the request referred to Lord Jersey's committee on consuls, which was then sitting.[220] The

---

[216] Platt (1963), p. 500.

[217] Mr Brittain, past president of Sheffield chamber of commerce; letter of 16 March 1886 to FO/83/932; quoted in Platt (1963), p. 503.

[218] Foreign Office Report, February 1897, Appendix of Opinions etc., *House of Commons Papers* (1899), xcvi, p. 667; quoted in Platt (1963), p. 503.

[219] Report of the Advisory Committee on Commercial Intelligence, *Parliamentary Papers*, 1917–18 (Cd. 8815) xviii, p. 13; also Platt (1963), pp. 506–8.

[220] Response to request from A. R. Dunwoody, ACC 25 September 1912: TNA BT 13/51/5.

larger chambers increased the pressure: in 1912 Birmingham proposed to BoT that chambers should distribute more consular information, which they had already been doing in a limited way. The BoT replied that there was its 'Special Register at the Commercial Intelligence Branch of the BoT' and any business could subscribe to the BoT *Journal* to access this, which contained information from consuls and others. There was a charge of one guinea, but it was proposed that the Register could be accessed for 7s. 6d. for one year and 2s. 6d. per year thereafter.[221]

This was not very helpful, but continuing pressure from the ACCI membership was important during WW1 in helping engage the FO (now in the form of the Foreign Trade Department) to cooperate with the chambers. Of the ACCI members, Algernon Firth (ACC president), E. Parkes MP (hon. sec. of ACC), and ACC executive member Sir Hallewell Rogers MP seem to have been most critical in this period.[222] The cooperation between BoT and the FO led to a 'black list' of firms with whom trade should be suspended (because of German links), and a 'white list' of other firms. The chambers were relied on to check these lists. Subsequent close cooperation with the chambers through 'Form K' was a development from these 'white list' opportunities.[223]

A major fillip for reform came from the Royal Commission on Consular Services of 1915, set up following Lord Jersey's committee. The ACC prepared a large and detailed report, authored by Dunwoody and Stanley Machin (ex BoT, now London chamber president), calling for 18 specified improvements to the service, focusing especially on consuls as 'commercial intelligence officers' that should have a standard of qualifications and provide a flow of material covering a specified range of topics.[224]

Faringdon Committee 1917

The chambers maintained pressure for improvements. Following the 1915 Royal Commission and War Cabinet's Huth Jackson 'Reconstruction Committee' in 1916, a discussion between Runciman as head of BoT and Grey as head of FO had agreed a solution; but Wellesley the permanent secretary at the FO managed to manoeuvre for another committee to look at the details. This was the 'Future Organisation of Commercial Intelligence' (Faringdon Committee) of 1917. Its five members included Lord Faringdon (Tariff Commissioner and a protectionist, though a supporter of chambers),[225] Victor Wellesley (Secretary of the Foreign Office), Sir William Clark (Secretary of the Board of Trade), Dudley Docker (the

[221] Birmingham chamber GPC minutes, 4 November 1912, 9 September 1913.
[222] Advisory Committee on Commercial Intelligence, minutes, 14 April 1910 ff.: TNA BT 55/1/1. Hallewell Rogers was a Birmingham MP and member of the BSA board, a close associate of Docker.
[223] Foreign Trade Department, Circular, 20 January 1916 (TNA FO 833/16/52963, fo. 10618) and Memorandum, December 1916 (TNA FO 833/16/98245); quoted in Homer (1971), chapter 2.
[224] ACC, *Monthly Proceedings* (1916–17), pp. 318–27; Birmingham chamber, Council minutes, 29 January 1917.
[225] Sir Alexander Henderson, a strong Conservative, newspaper proprietor, stockbroker, and railway company chairman.

major Midlands manufacturer and president of the FBI), and Sir de F. Pennefather MP (a Liverpool chamber member and cotton merchant). A suggestion that Stanley Baldwin MP be a member was rejected by the FO, and Pennefather was a suggestion by the ABCC.

Faringdon reported in April 1917 after numerous exchanges between the FO and the BoT over which should head the reorganized structure. Faringdon and Clark submitted a minority report and wanted the BoT to lead; Wellesley and Pennefather, with Docker, submitted the majority report for the FO to lead. Faringdon complained that the committee was unfairly loaded with FBI sympathizers;[226] though Pennefather was a chamber nominee he did not behave like one. In any case Wellesley was dismissive of chambers ('got together for the glorification of one or two individuals') as well as commercial attachés.[227] The final compromise was that the FO should be the lead department, but that the two departments would operate together under one roof, with the FO the line of reporting for commercial counsellors/attachés abroad (who were to be given diplomatic status), and the BoT to be concerned with how intelligence was distributed and used in the UK.[228] This two-headed structure was attacked by Docker in a dissenting minute in yet another Report in 1919, and by William Clark at the time, who reserved the BoT's position, supporting the reforms only because he did not want to 'prejudice the claim of the BoT to have direct representation for trade purposes in foreign countries by officers of their own'.[229]

Despite the civil service resistance, the Faringdon Committee laid the basis for the following years, and had profound effects on the chambers and its rival the FBI.[230] For the chambers, there were two critical developments. One was to establish a new government Department of Commercial Intelligence, later named Department of Overseas Trade (DOT).[231] Its first head was Sir Arthur Steel-Maitland, a close associate of Docker and MP for Birmingham East. The Department was not very successful and Steel-Maitland resigned in June 1919 in frustration and disgust at the limitations put on him by the FO. *The Times* commented that 'the most important reconstructive work [was] brought to nought by the

[226] Faringdon letter to Balfour and Sir Albert Stanley, 18 April 1917; Wellesley minute 26 April 1917; FO 368/1855; see also Davenport-Hines (1984), pp. 134–5.

[227] Wellesley evidence to Huth Jackson committee 17 March 1916; BL Add MS 42245; quoted in Davenport-Hines (1984), p. 69.

[228] This was a typical ministerial compromise, negotiated between Lords Grey (FO) and Runciman (BoT): Committee on Commercial Intelligence in Foreign Countries, 1917: TNA BT 55/1/3–5 (ACCI 18); see also FO 881/10/29; FO 336/787; *Parliamentary Papers* (1917–18) (Cd. 8715) xxix. Runciman supported the chamber and BoT position, but his letter to Grey was refuted line by line by Wellesley, and the Cabinet stood back (TNA: FO 368/1672/195787); also Homer (1971), chapter 3.

[229] Dudley Docker, Faringdon Committee dissenting minute: letter of 10 July 1919 to Lord Curzon re Report on the Consular Service: BT 13/135; Memo by W. H. Cark, p. 13 of Committee report (1917): BT 55/1/3–5.

[230] For FBI see discussion in Davenport-Hines (1984), pp. 137–49.

[231] ACC, *Monthly Proceedings* (1917), pp. 96, 108. An Overseas Trade Board under BoT, that overlapped with the DOT, was created following a report from Sir Archibald Geddes in 1919: TNA BT 13/135 (G253); see also A. Steel-Maitland, 'The government and foreign trade', *The Nineteenth Century*, 85 (1919), pp. 409–20.

jealousies of state officials'; but a replacement was eventually appointed.[232] It was given poor accommodation, inadequate staff, and was resented by both BoT and FO. The FO sought to limit it; the successive presidents at the BoT (Sir Albert Stanley and Sir Auckland Geddes) were intent on absorbing it. The Treasury was intent on abolishing it, making strong efforts in 1922 and 1927.[233] The interdepartmental warfare continued until 1946 when it was absorbed back into BoT and FO. Whatever these defects, however, the DOT was a strong ally of the chambers.

The second development following Faringdon was reform of the consular service and to move it under DOT. This was again resisted and delayed by the FO; reform eventually taking place in 1919 following another survey, by Lord Curzon.[234] This finally shifted the goals of consuls towards trade promotion, and modified appointments, pay, and the geographical arrangement of the service. A key member of Curzon's committee, and FBI founder, Dudley Docker, again objected to the double-headed structure and supported the FO as a single lead. However, the crucial outcome for the chambers was that consuls now had to provide information that chambers distributed as 'Form K' across Britain. This opened the way for the first chamber contract arrangement with government which lasted until 1935, as discussed in Chapter 13. However, the issue of consular and diplomatic effectiveness has never gone away, the FO remaining stubbornly resistant (introducing its own economic relations section 1930–7),[235] and most recently the Coalition government since 2010 has tried to inject into the FO a new commercial focus to support exports. The old arguments against this, concerning conflicts of interest and 'pushing', were revived by diplomats![236]

10.7 THE LOCAL STATE: MUNICIPAL ENTERPRISE, AND THE RATES

Resistance by chambers to the advancement of the state and burden of public expenditure had been present from the outset and has continued up to the current day; e.g. Liverpool had started with concerns about corporation dock fees; and Bristol set up a local taxation committee in 1822 which campaigned against its corporation into the 1840s. However, local taxation became a leading issue for most chambers only after 1880, and primarily after WW1, as indicated in the overview Tables 10.1–10.4. The heightened concerns focused first on municipal enterprise and municipal trading; next, on the burden of the main local tax (the rates); and later, on town planning and other aspects of local government.

---

[232] *The Times*, 9 July 1919; quoted in Homer (1971).
[233] Davenport-Hines (1984), pp. 135–7.
[234] Report on the Consular Service, chair Lord Curzon; dissenting minute by Dudley Docker: TNA BT 13/135. Further support for chambers came from evidence to the BoT Commercial and Industrial Policy Committee of 1916–17: TNA BT 55/9–13.
[235] See Boadle (1977).
[236] *Financial Times*, 22 July and 5 August 2010; quoting resistance from ambassadors; but with high hopes from business that the new FO permanent secretary, Simon Fraser, would facilitate change.

Municipal enterprise

Chambers and other business groups had often been the main promoters of early municipal improvements, as discussed in Chapter 13. From the 1860s, and especially the 1870s, the scale of these developments took off, and a municipal vision developed not just to fill gaps or meet immediate social needs, but also to take over areas from successful businesses. These initiatives were led by radical reformers of local finance, and not initially by collectivist or socialist thought. The arguments were for the 'greater good', usually captured in language such as using profits or surpluses to 'reduce costs' of 'wasteful market competition', or 'provide benefits to the wider community'. Initially supported by most chambers, by the 1890s these became alarming, opening a major debate on 'creeping socialism'.

A survey in 1900 by Fowler grouped municipal services in three categories: (i) those where there was 'no option' but to use public action (such as roads, lighting, sewerage, hospitals, and support for the poor); (ii) categories that enhanced cultural facilities and civilization (such as education, libraries, museums and galleries, parks); and (iii) fields such as water, gas, markets, trams, electricity, piers, and harbours where there were high capital costs and/or monopolies that suggested public action, or leadership, franchising or support for private provision.[237] Generally municipal services in the first and second categories received support from local chambers, but it was expansion into the third category that led to growing controversy by the 1890s.

Chamberlain and 'gas and water socialism'

One of the most prominent expansions of municipal initiatives was under Joseph Chamberlain in Birmingham who, with a group of Liberal supporters, gained control of the council in 1873. Mayor in 1973–6, Chamberlain became an MP in 1876, and rapidly came to influence national debates on social reform, stimulating the 'Liberal Radicals' by the 1880s, tariff reform, and much else. In Birmingham many of his supporters were entrepreneurs and major businessmen. Chamberlain himself was a major screw manufacturer (Nettlefold and Chamberlain). These interests were aligned with, and chiefly members of, the local chamber; owners/managers of large enterprises, who had demonstrated integrity and financial probity, and 'better understood how to run a large organisation like the council than the shopkeepers'. They saw expansion of municipal services as an opportunity to bring efficiency and deliver better services. This approach marginalized opposition from the Conservatives (led by Sampson Lloyd, ACC president 1862–80) and other business groups that had been important since the 1850s (that had 'let the city founder' and sought to 'keep down the rates').[238] Indeed the election of Chamberlain to Birmingham's town council in 1868 and his re-election in 1872

---

[237] Fowler (1900), pp. 383–7; Ilersic and Liddle (1960) give no discussion of municipal issues until the 1920s.
[238] Dolman (1895); Hennock (1963, 1973); Jones (1983), pp. 242–4.

482   *Activities*

was seen as a local turning point as the first 'party political' election, and began the eclipse of Sampson Lloyd's national influence (and with it a difficult period for ACC): Chamberlain's slogan had been 'High Rates and a Healthy City'.[239]

Although dubbed 'gas and water socialism', Chamberlain's successful takeovers under the Birmingham Gas and Water Bills of 1873 and 1874, did not have socialist purpose. Chamberlain saw the objective as running municipalities like 'a joint stock company of co-operative enterprise in which the dividends are received in the improved health and . . . increased comfort and happiness of the community. The members of the council are the directors of this great business, and their fees consist in the confidence, the consideration, and the gratitude of those amongst whom they live'.[240] Public supply may have in any case been necessary to ensure access to all with rapidly expanding population and urban needs. More generally, shifts in technology towards large-scale production increased the pressure to do this, particularly for gas, water, tramways, and electricity. Less typically, Chamberlain managed to turn slum clearance and redevelopment into a profitable exercise by recouping speculative gains to the council, and taking a tough approach to compulsory purchase prices.

Birmingham had followed Glasgow, Manchester, and Bradford, but it became the touchstone for many other cities, including Bolton, Cardiff, Dudley, Leeds, Nottingham, Rochdale, and Salford.[241] In the Black Country, Walsall, Wolverhampton, and Dudley directly copied many of Birmingham's initiatives. In Liverpool, council leader Arthur Forwood controlled an even stronger caucus than Chamberlain, and took over water, trams, health, and other utilities. The local chambers and other business groups were heavily involved in supporting all these initiatives, and indeed it was synergetic with chamber efforts to promote localities.[242] By the 1860–80s about 170 of the major towns had engaged in developments. By 1906 water, harbours, highways, schools, sewerage, and gas were activities of most of the larger local councils, and accounted for 83% of all outstanding debt, with *private* water, gas, and electricity supply largely disappearing.[243]

Both Chamberlain and Forwood settled policy in personal caucuses, outside the respective Liverpool and Birmingham councils. Chamberlain used this model as the foundation for the National Liberal Foundation in 1877, which influenced the constitution of the Liberal Party for years to come. Initially this allowed close control by a business elite, and allowed chambers among many business interests to become heavily involved in municipal improvements, and inevitably closely aligned with the Liberals. But although essentially pragmatic, Chamberlain's policies opened any enterprise to takeover, which was the source of the conflagration with Forwood in the Liverpool chamber over 'politics' in 1878, discussed in Chapter 3. Chamberlain had used compulsory purchase powers not because

[239] Although Hennock shows that income from gas actually allowed rates to remain stable over the next ten years.
[240] Chamberlain, quoted in Kellett (1978), p. 42; see also Dolman (1895).
[241] Hennock (1963, 1973, 1982); Daunton (1977, 1995, 2008); Jones (1983).
[242] Jones (1983); Trainor (1993).
[243] Fowler (1900).

water and gas were inefficient, but because profits could be used in a wider way. His influence nationally, through his political campaigns in 1885 and period as president of the Board of Trade 1880–5, stimulated further expansion of municipal enterprise, especially to electricity supply. His approach may not have been socialist, but it opened the door to any ideology of collectivization. This became the battleground of the following years.

Municipal enterprise and 'municipal socialism'

Alarm at the expansion of municipal enterprise was present from the outset, but grew as local enthusiasts sought powers in new fields, extended in scope after the Local Government Acts of 1882, 1888, and 1894. The issue became a national political concern, mainly as a result of high-profile conflicts in the London County Council (LCC), and London School Board, both established in 1888. The LCC, controlled over 1888–91 by an alliance of radicals and socialists, became a battleground between the 'rads', 'cads', and 'fabs', involving conflicts between nationally prominent individuals such as the Liberals Lord Rosebery and John Lubbock (later Lord Avebury), Fabians such as Sidney and Beatrice Webb, and Bernard Shaw, and radicals like John Burns. Efforts to bring the 40 London MPs together into a radical parliamentary block vote particularly frightened the London chamber of commerce.[244]

Underlying these concerns was the emergence of growing socialist and collectivist influences, the trade unions, and the Labour Party (a parliamentary force from 1874 within the Liberals). The trade unions had a growing component dedicated to socialist ideas, and a small but vocal component dedicated to 'syndicalism' that was beginning to influence some local councils. This was copied from French concepts using the general strike as a weapon to undermine capitalism and transfer all industry to workers within cooperative production federations. The Fabian Society (founded in 1884) was another major platform, used by Sidney Webb, G. B. Shaw, and others to promulgate collectivist ideas; it published widely read pamphlets in two 'municipal series' in 1891 and 1897–1900. These explicitly advocated municipalities as avenues to gain state control in a wide range of areas of business; e.g. the drink trade, milk supply, slaughterhouses, bakeries, hospitals, insurance, Thames steamboats. In Manchester, Glasgow, and Bradford councils made efforts to extend trading to coal mining and distribution, and insurance; in Sheffield to establish pawnshops; and in Bradford sterilized milk supply.

John Burns MP, amongst the most radical on the LCC (member 1889–1907), portrayed municipal and trade union development as a class war, promoted by his leadership of the London dock strike of 1887–9 (which was a major stimulus to membership growth of the London chamber). By 1902 the agenda was widely referred to as 'municipal socialism'. Burns sought ownership of the docks, direct works departments, fair wage obligations, council housing, takeover of all voluntary

---

[244] Porter (1907); Grove (1962), pp. 24–7; Soldon (1974); Bristow (1975); Falkus (1977); Morris (1992).

charitable welfare bodies, syndicalist labour bureaux that managed communal workshops in each sector with representatives to the 'civic commune', and replacement of private shops in which 'men and women dawdled away useless hours' by more efficient municipal or cooperative shops. Lubbock (Lord Avebury), initially a supporter of limited municipal enterprise, broke with the 'rads' in the LCC after his experiences there.[245]

The chambers' concern with municipal enterprise

The chambers, along with other business organizations, responded to these perceived threats with varied concern. Rumbling discontent in the chambers in the 1880s had been voiced in several chamber meetings, but the chambers were divided with resolutions often quite muted. Many chambers continued to be strong supporters of municipal activity. But with the conflicts and dangers of collectivism now self-evident in the LCC, the London chamber became a leading voice of concern. The direct experience of its president Lord Avebury (LCC chair 1890–2, and chamber president 1888–93) was critical to this. London and a few other chambers also began to develop alliances with the more prominent campaigners against municipal enterprise. These were led by the Liberty and Property Defence League (LPDL) (president Earl Wemyss) founded in 1882, and a growing number of employer bodies concerned to combat the advance of trade unionism, of which the Employers Parliamentary Council (EPC; founded 1898) and Engineering Employers Federation (EEF; founded 1896) were the most significant. Wemyss and most of the leaders of these bodies saw municipal trading as only one element to be resisted as part of a more general war against socialism;[246] e.g. the London Municipal Society founded in 1894 published *The Case against Socialism* (1908) and supported a book by Towler (1909). All these bodies worked in a complex, and sometimes conflicting alliance, to combat and promote legislation, primarily in the Commons, with the LPDL also having a strong presence in the Lords. In most cases the chambers preferred to let these bodies exert the pressure, rather than antagonize their local authorities which they usually regarded as partners.

The London chamber, however, felt itself in the firing line of the LCC, and was under strong pressure from the electricity supply industry, especially the British Electrical Traction Company (BETC). Electrical suppliers were a target for takeover in the 1890s and 1900s. The LPDL was given prominent opportunities in chamber events, such as the London chamber's dinner in April 1900. Most of the leaders of BETC and the LPDL were members of the London chamber's Electrical Trades section, and its Municipal Trading committee formed in 1899, both chaired by Sidney Morse, within which a campaign had been hatched. The chamber's section passed a resolution in February 1899 'that the scope and scale

---

[245] Towler (1909); Bristow (1975); Roberts (1984); Kellett (1978), p. 44.
[246] e.g. Earl Wemyss (1899), *The Dangers of Municipal Trading* (London: Liberty and Property Defence League); D. H. Davies (1903), *The Costs of Municipal Trading* (London: Industrial Defence League); see Soldon (1974); Bristow (1975); Roberts (1984).

of municipal enterprise in opposition to and exclusion of private enterprise should be defined', with London's chamber council calling for a moratorium on any further parliamentary orders supporting local government powers.[247]

Through Morse, the London chamber became the leading pressure within ACC for resolutions. Within ACC there was resistance to a high-profile campaign; e.g. Lord Rosebery continued to argue the positive experiences of local municipal support. When Morse spoke to the London chamber resolution in 1900 calling on government 'to define the limits to municipal trading' and prevent any further extensions until this had happened, the ACC would support only a watered down version that was criticized by London as 'amounting to nothing'.[248] Hence, given the chambers' diversity of view, the main campaigning was left to other organizations. The London chamber, however, continued direct involvement with the LPDL: it organized 500 petitions (including many from chambers and local ratepayers' associations) to parliament between 21 February and 3 March 1899 calling for an inquiry into municipal trading. Arthur Balfour, leader of the House in Salisbury's Unionist government (subsequently PM 1902–5), was forced to promise a committee. However, meeting strong lobbying from the municipalities, Balfour prevaricated and the committee was not established until April 1900.

The committee reported quickly, and was critical, noting that anything seemed justified to municipalities, suggesting that 30 clauses per year could be struck from local Bills and Orders where they made attempts to provide services or manufactures that could or were being supplied by private enterprises. But the committee failed to do what London chamber and the Leaguers had sought: to define prescriptive limits. Instead it asked for more time and to be reappointed. This fell back on the Conservative/Unionist government that had prevaricated earlier, and was not enthusiastic. The committee was not re-established until 1903, when it again ducked the issue of defining limits on municipal enterprise, and focused instead on local authority accounting practices.[249]

The smaller local chambers and TPS were often the most vociferous and strongest supporters of the London chamber. Many were members of EPC that attacked conditions for contracts with local authorities. The TPS bodies were vigorous members, and disseminated EPC surveys in 1899 that showed that 163 local authorities in England and Wales and 17 in Scotland included conditions in contracts as to wages; 219 (24 in Scotland) had conditions on employment and wages. Due to their concentration in the large cities, these groups covered nearly 80% of the population, with West Ham (the first socialist borough) imposing these conditions 'to an unprecedented extent'. This was accompanied by a call to resist the contracts, otherwise 'the trade unions will become masters of the municipalities, and then it will be the employers' turn to be dominated by the trade unions. . . . It

---

[247] London *CCJ*, April (1899), p. 22; Roberts (1984), pp. 22–9.
[248] London *CCJ*, April (1900), supplement, p. 23.
[249] Joint Select Committee on Municipal Trading, 1900, Report and evidence, *House of Commons Papers*, vii; quoted in Kellett (1978), p. 44; Joint Select Committee on Municipal Trading (1903), vii.

begins in Tooley Street and ends in Tammany.'[250] The comments demonstrate the significance of the London boroughs, some of which became socialist, as were their MPs (e.g. West Ham, Poplar, Battersea), but elsewhere there were similar concerns where socialists held power (e.g. in Halifax and Glasgow).[251] It was from this period that many small London chambers outside the City were founded, some of which like West Ham and Woolwich briefly became members of ACC. The NATPS continued to lobby on this issue into the 1930s. The NCT was vigorously against municipal trading and, unlike ACC, was unabashed by referring to this as 'socialistic regimes' and 'socialism'.[252]

Although the ACC stayed neutral, many chambers apart from London (especially the smaller ones) were very active in the campaigning; and the ACC was strongly implicated through its president over 1900–4, Lord Avebury. He was one of the most conspicuous opposition leaders to municipal trading in the Commons, and after 1900 in the Lords. He published a major critique of state trading and its implications in 1906.[253] But his most important impact was in 1902 to found the Industrial Freedom League, of which he became president. This used a network of local groups and organized thousands of meetings and leaflets.

The LPDL, with London chamber, campaigned to increase the scope for private tramways, and in two Bills to limit municipal powers in 1904 and 1905; on each occasion there was some ACC support.[254] These efforts failed, but over 20 local (*private*) electricity supply Acts were achieved, mainly for smaller towns. There was no majority in parliament to limit municipal action, and wide support for reasonable initiative by local municipalities. Any effort to curb municipalities died with the election of the Liberal government in 1905, Prime Minister Campbell Bannerman stating that municipalities should 'not be hampered and hindered by obsolete, or unnecessary or galling restrictions'.[255] However, the BoT was stiffened in its resistance, and began refusing municipal requests to raise loans for electricity supply. The Local Government Board also began using its discretionary powers to reduce local authority loan repayment periods and disallow some undertakings.[256]

Although these campaigns failed to do more than slow the tide, they paved the way for subsequent efforts to limit local expenditures, stimulated greater central government and Treasury oversight of local government debt, and shifted the focus to rate levels and returning any surpluses from trading through reduced rates. This

[250] The Employers' Parliamentary Council, *Municipal Trading: Conditions for Contracts with Local Authorities*; contained in NATPS papers, DE 3512/28, May 1899. Other estimates are given in Gibbons (1901) and Towler (1909).
[251] Bristow (1975), p. 784.
[252] e.g. NCT (1921), *Local Trade Organisation*, leaflet (1921); MS 29343/1.
[253] Lord Avebury (1906), *On Municipal and National Trading* (London: Macmillan); London chamber had published one of his major speeches, *Municipal Trading*, in January 1903.
[254] e.g. the 1902 effort to renew Light Railways Act, 1896; Electricity Supply Bill, 1904; Municipal Borrowing Bill, 1905: quoted in Roberts (1984), p. 30; see also Soldon (1974); Bristow (1975); Falkus (1977).
[255] Sir Henry Campbell Bannerman, quoted in *The Economist*, 19 May 1906; Roberts (1984), pp. 30–2.
[256] Bristow (1975), pp. 785–6.

gave significant stimulus to local ratepayers' associations. These had begun in the 1850s, but expanded rapidly in the 1890s and 1900s. They indirectly stimulated the establishment of local chambers of trade and TPS, and developed concepts that fed into subsequent debates about the role of the central state as well as the municipalities.

National campaigns against local government enterprises were revived at various points, especially by the chambers of trade and NCT.[257] But for chambers of commerce the issue became less a national than a local concern, contingent on local council activities. For example, Wolverhampton chamber opposed the issue of Housing Bonds in 1919, believing this was no business of government.[258] In Birmingham in 1920 a resolution was passed stating 'that government and/or municipal trading, except public utility services, is wrong in principle, and in operation is destructive of initiative, paralysing in effect on trade of the empire, and inimical to the well-being of the community'.[259] In Croydon in 1927 the chamber petitioned against municipal trading, noting that a chimney sweep was the only private firm to secure a contract from the council. Again in 1931 it complained about schools selling clothing, and 1933 and 1935 protested against the council's electricity department which was exclusively using direct labour and also selling domestic appliances. Birkenhead and Portsmouth opposed the selling of coal by local councils in 1930.[260]

Municipal campaigns 1918–1970: the burden of the rates

After WW1 whilst municipal trading remained a concern, this was surpassed by concern with local expenditure and hence level of local rates. The chambers had supported 'limited government' from their outset, and Sampson Lloyd's long presidency had ensured that the ACC had tended towards policies to 'keep down the rates' as their central plank in the 1860s.

With the expansion of social policy after 1906 the chambers, together with most business interests, moved to policies to oppose increases in government expenditure.[261] These concerns reached levels of alarm after WW1, with continuous calls by ABCC, NCT, FBI, and other bodies to reduce national expenditure, and with it taxation. By the 1920s the rates became a central target, and one where the chambers had a distinctive voice since the burden was a local tax. Baldwin's Conservative government was the first to try to get a grip on this and set up a Committee on National Debt and Taxation, under Lord Colwyn in 1924. This stimulated thinking, but resulted in little action: a minor amendment on income surtax was achieved as a result of ACC and other pressure in 1928. However, the ACC was one of several important forces behind the Rating and Valuation Act

---

[257] NCT Council Minutes; e.g. 16 February 1927; NCT papers 1921–3.
[258] Beaumont, Wolverhampton chamber history, pp. 124–5.
[259] Birmingham chamber, *Journal*, 15 May 1920.
[260] Croydon chamber minutes, 22 March, 4 April 1927; 20 October 1931; 3 April 1933; 31 July 1935; Croydon history, p. 6; Portsmouth chamber, also quoting Birkenhead, *Annual Report* (1930).
[261] e.g. NCT Annual Conference, May 1911.

1925. This enforced a uniform structure of local rates, with revaluation every five years, and a reduction in the number of rating authorities from 15,546 to 1708 by removing direct parish and poor law levies. The Balfour Royal Commission on Local Taxation in 1896–1902 had provided an early focus for objections to valuation practices.[262] Hence, the legislation in 1925 was the culmination of a long period of pressure from London chamber, taken up by ABCC only at a late stage. The chambers were also influential in prescribing a standardized form of local government accounts, to aid assessment of burdens and whether rate levels were reasonable. This was influential on a parliamentary committee that recommended in favour of standardization in 1907.[263]

However, whilst standardization removed some local abuses and complexity,[264] it did not reduce burdens. Following the 1925 Act, the ABCC attempted to orchestrate a national campaign to achieve 'very large reductions in local expenditure of all local authorities'. Stanley Machin, president in July 1925, stated the national position that, 'in view of the importance of local rates in manufacturing costs, chambers of commerce should take the initiative in securing a larger representation on city and town councils and boards of guardians in order to check all extravagances and introduce necessary economies in administration'.[265] Belfast had already started action: on 27 February 1925, where the City Council was forced to see a delegation of 15 of the chamber of commerce's major employers, members of the chamber of trade, and five members of the Wholesale Merchants and Manufacturers Association. The Council was courteous but increased its rates just the same. The chamber set up a standing committee with the other two organizations, but continued to receive a series of excuses why expenditure increase could not be avoided.[266] This was typical of most local responses.

An important victory was achieved in the 1929 Local Government Act. For the chambers the main benefit was the introduction of de-rating for some manufactures in order to reduce the pressure on 'productive industry'. This opened a divide with the chambers of trade, who felt shops and non-manufacturing should not have to bear unequal burdens (agriculture was already de-rated). The NCT opened a vigorous campaign in 1928, sent a deputation to the minister, and continued to 'protest', but was isolated as the only business organization to oppose de-rating at a time of economic crisis.[267] The NCT continued to attack rating valuation principles, with a vigorous campaign in the 1950s credited with a large increase in its membership. Some success was achieved with partial de-rating for shops and offices in 1957.[268]

---

[262] London *CCJ*, 16, April (1897), p. 80.
[263] London *CCJ*, 25, April (1906), pp. 31–2; 26, September (1907); Committee report, Cd. 3614.
[264] In fact fully uniform valuation practice was not achieved until 1956; and in the 1980s in Scotland; Bennett (1982), p. 50.
[265] Letter from ABCC to presidents of local chambers, e.g. Belfast *Journal*, August (1925), p. 69.
[266] Belfast chamber, *Journal*, March (1925), p. 181; April (1925), p. 12.
[267] NCT circular No. 450, *The Government's Rate Relief Scheme*, 16 July 1928; *Rate Relief: Retailers' Protest*, NCT Annual Conference Proceedings, May 1929, p. 26.
[268] e.g. NCT, Annual Conference Report, March (1956); minutes 27 June 1956, 22 October 1957.

The 1925 Act also introduced the first *general* block grant for local government, which allocated support to each area based on a measure of local rate resources, and local needs (mainly based on total population, but with male unemployment, and (for Counties) miles of road as additional indicators). This grant had been preceded by previous efforts to allocate support to Education Boards since 1917, but the new block grant launched a new battleground to argue about the measures of resources and needs, and the total level of grant required.[269]

However, these changes did little to *reduce* local expenditure, and the savings from de-rating were considered small. The ACC continued to press for economies, in 1930 stating 'local expenditure is a burden and indefinitely increases costs of production... while the rate of wages paid and other expenditure in municipal trading departments affects prices'.[270] Again in 1933 the ABCC called for cuts in local expenditure, as 'local rates are a direct addition to manufacturing costs, while taxation is a charge on profits'. It sent a delegation to the chancellor and set up a committee to investigate local government expenditure, calling on chambers to provide information.[271] NCT also swung behind this approach from 1930.[272]

These developments, WW2, and subsequent developments of the welfare state at national and local level, never resulted in limiting local expenditure, since local government was essentially autonomous. In times of economic stress, the government put pressures on local government, which generally resulted in some adjustments, but in general the long-term trend was increased local expenditure, with the pressures on the rates absorbed by ever increasing levels of central government grants. This trend was arrested briefly by reduced grants during WW2, in the mid-1950s, and in 1970; but up to 1980 the fundamental compromise was to shift the burden of the local state on to central taxation. The result was that rates fell to only 22% of local income by 1978; it was even lower in most of the poorer cities; the rest was grants.[273] This created a dangerous pattern of fiscal illusion: that local expenditure came essentially free to local consumers and voters.

In Ireland after 1923 local government continued with a largely unreformed rating system. Lack of space prevents coverage of the details, but as central and local government expenditures grew this resulted in similar concerns to those in the UK, with local rates being the major perennial lobby issue of local chambers. Waterford tried to put forward its own councillors as early as 1919, though none came forward; but it did put forward councillors in the elections of 1925, 1931, and as late as 1979. Rates were a concern of campaigns in Waterford in 1927, 1937, and continue to this day. Limerick was legally represented at an inquiry into the local council's budget in 1932, together with the Ratepayers Society and Development Association.[274] In 1930 the Dublin chamber, with the Mercantile Association, decided not to put forward its own candidates, but supported

---

[269] See Bennett (1982). NCT had supported shifting the burden to central taxes from 1911.
[270] ABCC *Proceedings*, September (1930); also quoted in Ilersic and Liddle (1960), p. 187.
[271] ABCC *Proceedings* (1933); quoted in Ilersic and Liddle (1960), p. 202.
[272] NCT minutes, 4 October 1930, and following discussions; *NCT Journal* July (1936), p. 62.
[273] Summarized in Bennett (1982).
[274] Limerick chamber minutes, 19 September 1932.

named candidates, of whom three were elected: 'the first election at which the commercial community is given direct representation on the city council'.[275] Similarly Cork was supporting business candidates in the 1927 general election and 1930 local election. In 1955–6 it ran a vigorous campaign against the council on excessive rates and expenditure. It submitted a questionnaire to corporation candidates in the 1955 local election with limited success. In 1956 it sought to require the council to provide information on rates and expenditures (since financial reporting was not obliged), but was refused. It made a new request in 1957 as representing the principal ratepayers, but was again refused.[276] The concern of Irish chambers with the national budget and local rates and municipal expenditure has been prominent up to the present.

Rates campaigns and the 'new left' 1970–1987

Whilst ABCC and local ratepayers' associations had long campaigned against local government's perceived excesses, the issue reached its most prominent level after 1970. This arose from rapid inflation that forced continuous rises in nominal rate levels, and the development of greater central government concern to limit local expenditures, which reached a climax when the Labour government was forced to seek support from the International Monetary Fund in 1976. But also critical was development of an alternative political vision by a group of local authorities, generally termed 'new urban left' within the Labour Party. Both ABCC and NCT started continuous monitoring of local rate rises through surveys of their local members from about 1970. In 1975 NCT developed a prominent poster campaign for 'Rate Rebate Now' as a means to reduce burdens, which had the significant impact of getting the attention and support of Margaret Thatcher.[277]

The 'new urban left' became the most focused issue for many chambers. The left sought to exploit to the full the benefits of the fiscal illusion created by the grant system, keeping council rents very low in order to maximize government grants, maintaining high expenditures to offset constraints from central government, developing alternative local visions of 'caring' and economic intervention when central government sought cuts. When Labour was in opposition it supported a wide range of minority interests in order to create a potential 'rainbow coalition' of clientalist voters that could defeat the Conservatives. This movement began in 1970–4 when the Conservatives were in office, and continued under the Labour government of James Callaghan 1974–9 which was perceived as too centrist. But the greatest momentum was after the election of Margaret Thatcher in 1979.[278] 'New left' authorities developed the concept of a 'local state' as an autarchy from the policies of central

---

[275] Dublin chamber, Report of Council, 1930, pp. 23–4.
[276] Cork chamber, Committee book, 1 September 1927, 4 July 1930, 29 August 1955, 31 December 1956, 13 February 1957.
[277] NCT minutes, 1975; NCT Newsletter, *Intercom*, March (1975).
[278] Gyford (1985), p. 18.

government. The chambers were in the firing line as most such areas were in the major old industrial cities that formed the core of ABCC membership.

Most of these 'new left' councils were self-identifying, with a core group of about 24.[279] These councils steadily increased their rates from the 1970s, to an average of 30% above the overall government mean, with some reaching 50% above the mean in 1984–5.[280] Central government retaliated with powers to cap local rates, and compel consultation with local businesses in the Local Government Rates Act 1984; 18 councils were capped in 1985–6, almost all of the new left. The ABCC was one of the leading bodies to resist the development of 'extreme' rate rises, and lobbied hard through the 1970s and 1980s, supported by NCT, CBI, and others.[281]

At local level the example of Sheffield is typical, and one of the most significant because of its national impact, and the fact that its council leader over 1980–7, David Blunkett, became a local MP in 1987, Secretary of State for Education in the Labour government 1997–2001, and then Home secretary. The 'new left' became prominent in Sheffield over a council rent rebate scheme introduced in 1966. This split the Labour ruling group, caused immense popular dissent, and allowed the Conservatives to gain control in 1967. When Labour regained power in 1969, Blunkett became one of the leaders of a new group of activists. They reasserted 'socialist' values, tried to de-select their Labour MP, and became important within the national debate within the Labour Party. Blunkett with Geoffrey Green produced an important statement of the new left objectives in a 1983 Fabian Society booklet.[282] The traditional policy of keeping down rents was re-established, to which was added low bus fares, raising rates, and setting up an employment department: to prevent job losses, alleviate unemployment, stimulate investment, and develop industrial democracy and cooperative control of employment.[283] Decisions were increasingly taken out of the council into a party caucus supposedly involving a wider democracy. This was all rather reminiscent of the LCC after 1888. The city developed its own autarchy policy rather than applying for Enterprise Zone status in 1981; later it resisted the establishment of an Urban Development Corporation (both Thatcher government initiatives that brought resources). The city took on a national significance, self-publicizing itself as 'Red Sheffield'.[284]

Sheffield's chamber had long resisted municipal enterprise, but in the 1970s its concern was heightened by the council's new policies. Most of this opposition was low key, but in 1972 it publicly opposed a council private Bill to empower it to invest in industry and give grants in aid.[285] Rates began to emerge as the main issue

---

[279] Bennett and Krebs (1988), pp. 293–5; Gyford (1985). Nine in London, nine in metropolitan districts (including Birmingham, Leeds, Liverpool, Manchester, Sheffield, Walsall, and N. Tyneside), and six large non-metropolitan cities (Leicester, Nottingham, Harlow, Basildon, Scunthorpe, and Cleveland).

[280] Bennett and Krebs (1988), pp. 73–5, 87–8.

[281] e.g. NCT minutes, and newsletter, *NCT News*, September 1984.

[282] D. Blunkett and G. Green (1983), *Building from the Bottom: The Sheffield Experience* (London: Fabian Society).

[283] Sheffield City Council (1982), *Employment Department: An Initial Outline*; later called Employment and Economic Development Department (1985).

[284] Seyd (1993), p. 158.

[285] *Quality*, Sheffield chamber Journal, March–April (1972), p. 20; the Bill was unsuccessful.

when Blunkett became leader. In 1981 and in 1982 the chamber began to object openly to council spending: 'we fully support their endeavours to provide essential services at competitive prices, but we resist their use of the wealth we create to produce social and political change, and to this end will continue to press for rates reform'.[286] By 1983 it was 'concerned about the reputation Sheffield was earning by virtue of the policies pursued by the local authority, with the negative publicity that arose'.[287] The chamber was strongly supported, indeed pressed, by the business community; the 'new left' was a strong stimulus to membership.

Voluble criticism appeared in the press. In 1985 prominent national coverage in *The Observer* quoted the chamber chair, Peter Ford, that the Sheffield rates were 'crippling', and that Blunkett had 'a most unfavourable impact on the industrial and commercial life of the city' with policies that were 'unrealistic' and had 'done much to exacerbate a difficult economic situation'.[288] The previous chair asserted that 'money had to be earned before it could be spent; and attempting to create revenue by policies that drive businesses from the city... was sheer self-destruction.... The chamber wholeheartedly supported rate capping.' The chamber also criticized the council no-redundancy policy, lack of inward investment policy, and expenditure of around £3 million on its employment department.[289] The next chair of the chamber in 1986, Richard Field, described the situation as one in which businesses had to cut jobs to survive, whilst the city wanted to stimulate the economy and care for the unemployed. The inevitable result was that each 'shouted' and turned their backs on each other.[290]

Rapprochement and partnership since the late 1980s

The high-profile local conflicts between chambers and local government of the 1980s, and the continuing pressures by ABCC which helped to produce changes in national legislation, were in many ways an 'unnatural' period. The long-term history had been for strong local collaborations between municipalities and chambers jointly to promote their area. Even during this period, cordial joint meetings between the various local government associations and ABCC were maintained.

Indeed the evolution of Sheffield illustrates how chambers began to play an important role in assisting adjustment in 'new left' areas. Richard Field quotes the local legend that the director of the Sheffield chamber (John Hambidge) and leader of a council delegation (Clive Betts), whilst on a promotional visit to China in 1983, began to explore a new common way forward. A convention was agreed in 1986, under Field, that criticisms between the chamber and council would no longer be voiced in public, and a joint Sheffield Economic Regeneration

[286] John Harvey, president; *Quality*, May–June (1982), p. 26; see also May–June (1981), pp. 17–18.
[287] Allen Goodall, president; *Quality*, May–June (1983), p. 17.
[288] Peter Ford, *The Observer*, 27 October 1985; quoted in Seyd (1993), pp. 169–70.
[289] Hugh Neill, president; *Quality*, May–June (1985), pp. 11–12.
[290] Field (1991), pp. 50–2.

Committee, which included the city and chamber, was established as a 'kind of board of directors for the city'.[291] The red flag, annual Marx memorial lecture, city nuclear-free zone, etc. were removed, and a joint presentation in 1988 at the Mansion House sought to woo City and potential investors to Sheffield. The third successive general election defeat of Labour in 1987 also initiated a change in approach nationally towards a new realism leading, eventually, to 'new Labour' that embraced some of the changes of the Thatcher period. In Sheffield this led to a more positive approach to public–private collaboration, including support for its Urban Development Corporation in 1988 (very reluctantly), and the local TEC when this was launched in 1990 with Field, former chamber president, as chair.[292] This was largely down to Clive Betts's leadership in the council after 1987. Blunkett became MP in 1987 and embraced these changes openly, forming part of the national platform for 'new Labour'; however, it became clear that he remained viscerally opposed to TECs and some other forms of partnership (as discussed in Chapter 13).

With reforms of local government finance after 1987, particularly setting a uniform national level for business rates, the chamber positions were strengthened and they became more prominent partners for local government, as discussed in Chapter 13. Some of this collaboration was forced, but generally close collaboration between chambers and local authorities has continued. A more 'natural' set of relationships has been re-established. Whilst BCC was not able to support local government calls for re-empowering them to set local rates in 2006 or 2011, chambers strongly supported proposals then being mooted by government for Business Improvement Districts, and Local Government Business Growth Incentives which gave local authorities part of the rates proceeds of new economic developments in their areas.[293] These ideas were only modestly pursued by Labour, but have been reconsidered more positively under the Coalition government since 2010. However, resistance to the Coalition's cutbacks in public expenditure has revived local Labour party activism to confront central government; some repeat of the 1980s stand-offs is expected by chambers in Labour-controlled areas.

10.8 REGULATORY BURDEN

Earlier chamber lobbies tended to focus on public expenditure, taxation, and rates. Regulatory burden and the design of government programmes were always significant sources of tension as a response to pervasive information asymmetry and the lack of expertise in government, as discussed in Chapter 3. But regulation became a major element of chamber voice in the 21st century. As shown in Table 10.4, civil service efficiency and 'red tape' accounted for 10.3% of chamber voice concerns

---

[291] Ibid.

[292] Seyd (1993), pp. 167–83 gives a good review.

[293] BCC (July 2006), *Building Communities: Business Rates and Local Government*, report for BCC prepared by the Institute of Public Finance.

after 1997. The modern state, pressed by a wide range of countervailing interests beyond those of business, is frequently subject to demands to 'do something' about every market or social problem, even when there may be no state solution, there may be better non-state alternatives, or the costs of action far outweigh the benefits.

Regulatory burden first emerged as a major issue under the Conservative regime of 1979–97. That government responded with a Deregulation Task Force. This was superseded by a Better Regulation Executive (BRE) under Labour after 1997, which in turn led to introduction of regulatory impact assessments by Departments, audited by the NAO. However, the BRE became progressively dominated by consumer and trade union interests, with many of its later reports having no direct business input.

For the chambers, regulations became the most persistent campaign initiative of the 21st century. From the point at which the Labour government began to develop its high spending-large state approach in 2001, BCC recognized the dangers for business and began publishing a 'Burdens Barometer'. This charted the cumulative cost of new regulations and legislation introduced by government, using departmental impact assessments, as shown in Table 10.6. The campaign aimed 'to free business from the burdens of red tape and enable them to create new jobs and growth'. It also sought to ensure that future regulations 'did not stifle the business community's ability to drive economic recovery'.[294]

The barometer was backed up by a series of detailed reports commissioned from the London and Manchester Business Schools, which gave the campaign added credibility and took the economic analysis further. These have been hard-hitting for a chamber movement that is often perceived as staid. As concluded in 2010, 'much of the claimed overall benefit of regulation is no more than "bread and circuses"; giving attractive rewards to citizens and penalising productivity in the process. Transferring wealth from business to citizens, whatever the arithmetic, can be made to seem beneficial. In reality, however, it is a form of business taxation and damaging for competitiveness and the economy, and therefore UK citizens'. The reports have also directly engaged in a critique of government, for example attacking the BRE claim that regulatory benefits out-weighed costs as 'lacking credibility . . . [and] concealing the transfer of money from the wealth producing sector', and ignoring the impact on competitiveness and productivity.[295]

Some chambers saw the barometer as 'too political', but there is no doubt that it represented a major and sustained campaign success. It began to draw attention to the fundamental failing of Labour, as an intrusive, high-intervention, high-spend government, long before this met widespread criticism; and it gave chambers a strong platform from which to address specific legislation. It was mirrored in the Channel Islands where chambers had to respond to Labour's civil service reforms and rapid expansion of intrusive regulations.[296]

---

[294] Quoted from BCC Burdens Barometer (2009).
[295] e.g. Ambler, Chittenden, and Miccini (2010); quotes from pp. 2, 17–18.
[296] Comments to author by Clive Spears, Jersey chamber president, 30 April 2009.

Table 10.6. The BCC Business Barometer, measure of cumulative costs of new regulations 2001–2010

Year	Cumulative cost (£bn.)	Annual increase (£bn.)
2001	10.0	—
2002	15.0	5.0
2003	20.6	5.6
2004	30.0	9.4
2005	38.9	8.9
2006	50.3	11.4
2007	55.7	5.4
2008	66.0	10.3
2009	76.8	10.8
2010	88.3	11.5

Source: BCC Barometer, from BCC website.

The details of the barometer, naturally, have been controversial, despite being based on the government's own figures. It was deeply resented by Labour, and the BRE jumped to its own defence, in 2010 claiming that the benefits of regulation outweighed the costs by 2:1.[297] However, the Regulatory Policy Committee has backed up the general findings of the barometer. This was set up as an independent assessor of burdens by Labour in 2009 late in its term because of the continuing criticisms, but strengthened under the Coalition government in 2010. Its first report, covering the last six months of the Labour government, found that many departmental regulatory impact assessments 'lacked analytical rigour' and appeared 'to be produced as an afterthought . . . to obtain approval'. Too much weight was placed on preferred policy options, with insufficient assessment of the alternatives of 'doing nothing' or 'doing the minimum', with poor assessments of costs and benefits. From a first sample of 107 impact assessments, 21% had serious defects; of these 91% had defects on at least three of the six indicators assessed, and half had four or more defects.[298] The NAO has confirmed the same conclusions, reductions in regulatory burden has been slow, the majority of impact assessments have been perfunctory, and 'the majority of businesses think that government does not understand them well enough to regulate'.[299]

The BCC barometer continued under the Coalition government after 2010, but was re-based to reset the clock for assessment of the next period. The BCC has continued to argue for more attention to be paid by legislators to impact assessments, for improved impact measures, greater measurement at an earlier stage in the policy design process, greater care in implementing EU aspects to meet genuine UK

[297] <www.berr.gov.uk/what%20wedo/bre/benefits/page44019.html>; January 2010.
[298] Regulatory Policy Committee (August 2010), *Reviewing Regulation: An Independent Report on the Analysis Supporting Regulatory Proposals December 2009—May 2010*, pp. 16–17.
[299] National Audit Office (2011), *Delivering Regulatory Reform*.

needs, and greater post-implementation review.[300] The RPC's second report covering the first sixth months of the Coalition concluded that not much improvement
had been made; whilst Business Secretary Vince Cable was forced to launch a new
attack on red tape in March 2011, to which the BCC response was that 'real action'
was needed 'rather than words'.[301] The Barometer has been a powerful tool that has
kept chambers at the centre of the debate on 'red tape'. Indeed it has resonated with
the core concerns of chambers from their outset, noted in Chapter 4: poor legislation
and the 'ignorance' of legislators.

10.9 COMBINING VOICE? THE DEVLIN
REPORT AND AFTER

Following tariff reforms and WW2 the focus of government fell increasingly on
peak organizations to deliver sector partnerships with government to assist central
planning and 'Keynesian' demand management. Tripartism became the dominant
frame of the 'system of industrial relations'. In 1961–2 the Conservative government established a National Economic Development Council (NEDC) and sector
committees ('little Neddies'): 'to seek agreement on ways of improving economic
performance, competitive power and efficiency'.[302] By 1964 there were nine little
Neddies; by 1966 there were 21 covering 60% of manufacturing industry, each
with a tripartite structure, comprising the unions, business, and government.
Government departments, and divisions within them, were generally matched
with their relevant industrial sectors, as 'sponsors'.

The FBI became the main industry member of the NEDC, and had been
instrumental in several aspects of its formation following its conference in Brighton
in 1960.[303] The government accepted much of this, influenced by Conservative
corporatist thinking of the 1930s, with which the PM Harold Macmillan had been
involved.[304] With the return to power of Labour in the Wilson governments of
1964–70, tripartism was brought even closer to the centre of government's agenda.
The sector committees of NEDC were strengthened; further industries nationalized. A National Plan for the economy was developed, with regional economic
strategies drawn up by Regional Economic Planning Councils (tripartite), with
Planning Boards (of civil servants) responsible for implementation.

The establishment of NEDC alarmed the chambers. During its establishment
government used two commissioners to hold discussions with business bodies: Sir
Samuel Brown and Henry Benson. The chambers argued they had been important
parts of the former NPACI, which was subsumed into NEDC, and should

---

[300] Ambler, Chittenden, and Miccini (2010), pp. 19–20.
[301] Regulatory Policy Committee (February 2011), *Challenging Regulation*; Vince Cable statement,
18 March 2011, BIS; BCC press release, 17 March 2011.
[302] Selwyn Lloyd, Chancellor of the Exchequer, 1962; quoted in Middlemas (1983), p. ix.
[303] 'Next Five Years' or the 'Brighton Convention'; Blank (1973), pp. 85–90, 153 f.; Middlemas
(1983), pp. 8–19.
[304] Middlemas (1983), pp. 12–15.

maintain their role. Their case was ignored. Benson and Brown were commissioned again in 1963 by the presidents of FBI, BEC, and NUM to look at merger. This found strong support from the Labour Secretary of State, George Brown, who stated that he wanted to have one body to pursue the government's economic plan, particularly to bring together the wage (BEC) and non-wage issues (FBI/NUM). Following the Benson–Brown report of 1963, the three bodies merged in 1965 to form the Confederation of British Industry (CBI).[305] This provided a structure through which the Wilson government sought to control wages and prices. The first form of this policy was a tripartite structure involving a 'Statement of Intent' by industry, the unions, and government. But when this proved ineffective, the government imposed statutory prices and incomes policies in 1966 and 1968.[306]

The consolidated FBI/CBI position effectively froze out the ABCC. The independent members of the NEDC took no regard of views other than the CBI.[307] The ABCC continued pressure for a position on NEDC, but was always rebuffed. The CBI (with the TUC) had shifted to become an 'insider' body. When Blank wrote in 1973 that 'the powers of the state have expanded vastly (and that) ... the key factor in modern society (is) the obliteration of the border between public and private authority', he was referring to the CBI's new role.[308] It provided 'a new opportunity and a new challenge ... to provide continuous transfusion of a proper industrial awareness into the formative processes of government'.[309] Or as Nettl observed, industrial representation had largely become government sponsored: consensus was formed around the government's agenda.[310]

As Middlemas stated, 'what had been merely interest groups crossed the political threshold and became part of the extended state: ... dictated almost entirely by the needs of governments'. This inevitably led to 'a *corporate bias*' that restricted scope for other views, such as the chambers.[311] The exclusion of the chambers from corporate government led to the development of a continuing discussion about whether the CBI and ABCC should merge. To tackle this question, a report was commissioned by the CBI and ABCC in 1971 from Lord Devlin.

The Devlin Report

Devlin's Report in 1972 developed a vision of creating a Confederation of British Business (CBB) to represent 'industry and commerce in every form', including financial services, shipping, and the distributive and retail trades. The vision was very much of a combine, with vertical divisions aligned into one strategy at senior

---

[305] NPACI (National Productivity Advisory Council for Industry); Blank (1973), p. 198; Middlemas (1983).

[306] Fraser (1967); Blank (1973); Beer (1965); Wootton (1975); Devlin (1972); Grant and Marsh (1977).

[307] ABCC, GPC, 7 March, 7 November 1962; 3 July 1963.

[308] Blank (1973), p. 5.

[309] The comments of a major trade association director: Fraser (1967), pp. 166–7.

[310] Nettl (1965).

[311] Middlemas (1979), pp. 373–4; Grant and Marsh (1977).

board level, like a large company. It argued for the merger of ABCC and CBI, and preferably also the retailers (BRC). The CBB would become the general peak lead body, with members joining the general body and the relevant sector and/or local association. The chambers would take on the local and regional role of coordinating views leading up to a lobby, where Devlin viewed the CBI as weak, and also providing local services (where the CBI had few activities). Although taking a neutral position, Devlin in effect also gave impetus to the arguments for public law status for chambers, comparing the benefits of such status in Germany and recommended that 'every individual business should . . . belong to a chamber of commerce'.[312]

The vision was to overcome the fragmentation of business voices. As the secretary of the Devlin Commission, McDonald, wrote in 1973: 'if the Commission's recommendations are implemented . . . the relative order and simplicity of the pre-1914 era will have been restored'.[313] This proved wildly optimistic, and was unrealistic, given the forces of endemic business fragmentation. Moreover, it was echoing a centralized planning and coordination strategy between businesses and government, just when this approach was breaking down. More successfully Devlin also recommended setting up an Advice Centre to act as a 'clearing house' for information and support for the development of associations and representative bodies. Whilst having a rather halting history, this has found a continuing modern development in the Trade Association Forum, hosted by CBI, but independent of it. This acts as a guide on governance and management issues of associations, and helps to transfer best practice.[314]

The Devlin Report was seen as a major opportunity by the chambers, particularly the larger ones. It offered the chance at last to come in from the cold, and use the perceived weight and status of the CBI to enhance local chamber presence. The smaller chambers were, however, generally opposed, and even some of the large chambers were unenthusiastic. The NCT thought it irrelevant to distribution and trade services.[315] Like the CBI's Benson–Brown Report, the presidents of the organizations had commissioned Devlin, and there was little attempt to take along the grass-roots members until the report was published. The leading members of the CBI were fairly uniformly opposed; the chambers were now perceived as too peripheral to the mainstream of industrial relations, and their members generally too unimportant to be a concern to the 'captains of industry' at the centre of the CBI. The CBI rejected Devlin almost in its entirety. Comments received from CBI members by Grant and Marsh in 1976 sum up the problem: 'the Devlin Report was biased in the direction of the chambers of commerce'; 'I was a chairman of a chamber of commerce ten years ago. My successor was an ice cream merchant, followed by a furniture trader . . . I wouldn't be prepared to sit under that sort of

---

[312] Devlin Report (1972), pp. 15–16.
[313] McDonald (1973), p. 36.
[314] See e.g. Boleat (2000, 2003); Bennett (1997); Greaves (2008).
[315] NCT opposed CBB throughout the discussions: NCT minutes, 23 February 1971–22 April 1972.

chairmanship'; 'the chamber of commerce is the place for retailers, garage proprietors, service industry. They should do more about local things, like the adequacy of roads... The CBI [is] the place where manufacturers meet'.[316] Almost all the recommendations of Devlin died within a few months of publication, though increased alliance and working together was encouraged for some specific issues, which has continued up to the present.[317]

Merger returns to the table

The desire for merger of CBI and ABCC/BCC has been revived periodically, usually as a result of discussions between specific presidents or chief executives who have close personal relationships. Thus, in 1994–5, the BCC very actively pursued merger at a time when TECs, CCTEs, and other initiatives were drawing it closer to CBI. Again in 1999, under Chris Humphries as director general of BCC, merger was put to the membership, but as before was rejected in favour of continuing close cooperation.[318] After Humphries's departure merger was off the table, and looks unlikely to be a realistic option in future unless one or other body becomes too fragile to survive. However, the BCC did merge with the NCT in 1992, as outlined in Chapter 8.8. This had a profound impact on consolidating the national voice of the chamber movement. Generally the small chambers now address their national lobbies through BCC accredited chambers, which in turn operate through BCC.

10.10 CONCLUSION: MAKING AN IMPACT IN THE 21ST CENTURY?

This chapter has charted the course of the chambers' voice from 1800 up to the present. The influence of that voice grew rapidly from the 1840s as a result of the Anti-Corn Law campaign, which relaunched the chamber brand, crystallized the policy frames towards free trade, and stimulated many new chambers to form, which strengthened resources and breadth of representation. WW1 marked both a peak and a major shift in fortunes as other rival voices emerged and fitted better to the tune of emerging state control. Whilst Prime Minister Herbert Asquith had been able to say in 1914 that the chambers were 'the most authoritative and trustworthy exponent of the commercial interests of the United Kingdom',[319] by 1918 that had begun to change. Sector bodies and the FBI/CBI became progressively more favoured as government moved into sector planning, 'safeguarding' strategic and declining industries, nationalization, and then tripartite planning.

---

[316] Grant and Marsh (1977), pp. 72–7.
[317] Discussed further in Chapters 7 and 13.
[318] Taylor (2007), p. 107.
[319] Speech at Annual Dinner; ACC, *Monthly Proceedings* (1914).

The chambers had ridden high on the back of the free trade paradigm. But with concerns over retaliatory tariffs, national security, strategic industries, war effort, and planning systems, they were increasingly trapped in rearguard efforts to limit the advance of the statist paradigm, and to reassert the local when sector and national leadership was being sought. When systems of national economic planning became significant, during WW1, for the tariff negotiations in the 1930s, and in the NEDC in the 1960s and 1970s, the chambers were not only signally left out, but they also found it difficult to make headway at the local level as local government became increasingly dominated by central government dictats and finance.

A shift of fortunes emerged from the Thatcher period when state planning was in retreat, and local government emerged as an increasing national political concern. Ironically the main opposition to the Thatcher government, from the efforts of 'new left' local government in the 1980s through high local rates, acted as a clarion call for many business to join their chambers. Local voice was strengthened in the affected areas. Labour's Blair/Brown government of 1997–2010 tried to put the clock back, renewing national strategic planning and top-down targets, as well as shifting government programmes at local level away from private sector-led partnership towards state agencies funded by expanding state largesse. But the financial crash of 2007–9 and re-emergence of concerns over government indebtedness introduced an era of Coalition government from 2010 that has been more willing to seek partners that take on responsibilities formerly sought by government. Similarly in Ireland continuing financial crisis has cut the ambitions of government spending programmes. At the time of writing these influences are still unfolding. But it is clear that independent voices from outside the historic 'big government' apparatus are becoming increasingly important. This offers chambers new opportunities.

11

Milieus for Discourse and Deliberation

11.1 MILIEUS AS PART OF THE CHAMBER 'BUNDLE'

Whilst collective voice and lobbying was the core activity of chambers, these functioned largely as a result of exchanging information and views among members in order to develop a 'unity' of interests. Hence a milieu was required for discourse, discussions, and gathering news; what would now be called a means for 'interest mediation'. Musgrave in 1914, secretary of the London chamber, focused on the central role of discourse as 'deliberation': a means by which chambers could debate and apply the technical knowledge of their members to current policy issues. By this means chambers could become a local 'clearing house' of commercial intelligence and deploy their expertise in their lobby activity.[1] 'Deliberation' is contained in many of the founding objects of chambers, and is the frequent vocabulary used to describe their means of reaching decisions. The president of ACC in 1917 stated that 'we want places to which anybody can go and meet his friends and discuss any matter of interest that arises'.[2] This is also important in modern times, where milieus for meetings, and both social and market exchange, lie behind many member-joining and retention decisions.[3] Moreover, milieus are a key service of several other business organizations, particularly the IoD and private business clubs. In trade associations it is claimed that a major function is 'to provide a meeting place, a club function for those who want it, where they can talk to people with common interests'.[4]

Despite this, discourse and deliberation are not prominent in the formal policy statements by ABCC, BCC, or CI, and it has also been ignored in policy debates by government. There has always been resistance by chamber managers to being perceived as 'just a talking shop', and for the small chambers and chambers of trade there was definitely an image they sought to overcome of 'the tea-stained table cloth'.[5] This chapter, therefore, represents something of a challenge to earlier received wisdom.

Chamber milieus are themselves a 'bundled' offer filling several needs: a place to transact business; to deliberate and form views; to pick up gossip, news, and commercial intelligence; and to be able to consult major sources of printed or

---

[1] Musgrave (1914), p. 61.

[2] Algernon Firth, ACC president, quoted in ACC *Monthly Proceedings*, 4 October, 1917, p. 15.

[3] See Chapters 14–16, and Mekic (2007), chapter 6.

[4] Comment by Martin Hall, chief executive of Finance and Leasing Association; in Bennett, Krebs, and Zimmermann (1997), p. 109.

[5] Comment to author from the board of the very small Enfield (N. London) chamber of commerce, 1991.

distributed information such as newspapers, statistical information, listings, and pamphlets, and to talk about them. Also, as noted in Chapter 3, society and discourse in early chambers were seen as part of social positioning of the entrepreneur, 'meeting together ... they developed common social attitudes and forms of behaviour; by intermarriage they [members] became close-knit as a group'.[6]

Historically, milieus also became part of the projection of chamber values and status. When they acquired buildings these were in prominent sites, with generous proportions, often with formal architecture akin to town halls, with a grand entrance and often with a council room resembling a town council chamber. They sought to signify their presence as a voice of status with local government. It betokened solidity, with the objective of challenging government for the foreseeable future. It also provided some exclusivity to members as a 'home' or trusted environment for exchange and communication with like-minded other business people that were members. Buildings were and still are a means to project power and status into urban society.[7] However, this all changed after the 1970s; most modern chambers moved to business parks. Nevertheless a meeting place and supportive milieu continue to be important business needs. Although sources of information have changed, first with the introduction of cables and telegrams, then telephone and fax, and now emails, websites, and other electronic communications, the need for face-to-face meeting continues into the 21st century.

11.2 FORMAL MEETINGS

The most basic need for a milieu was a place to bring people together to be informed, discuss, and form the 'case' for a policy prior to lobbying and voice. Taverns, hotels, exchanges, and especially coffee houses were usually the venues where this occurred before chambers had their own buildings. These often had very large facilities. As seen in Chapters 4 and 9, the Kings Arms Tavern and London Tavern in the City were regular venues for meetings of 300 or 400 merchants in the 1770s to 1790s when they were discussing their responses and petitions to government. They were crammed 'tempestuous mass rallies'.[8] The atmosphere would have been electric. They were the milieu for the orator. It is easy to see how strong personalities such as Josiah Wedgwood, Thomas Walker, or Patrick Colquhoun could come to play such leading advocacy roles in this period. Those attending clearly came away enthused.[9] Later flavours of the discussions can be seen in the *Proceedings* of the ACC/ABCC, and some of the NCT congresses.

---

[6] See Fox Bourne (1886), pp. 396–7; also Minchinton (1957), p. 67; Olson (1971), p. 61; Clark (2000a).

[7] Morris (1986, 1990); Hall (1998).

[8] Olson (1991), p. 35.

[9] No good first-hand account survives, but the report of the London meetings of 1784–5 by Colquhoun to Glasgow chamber gives some flavour of the occasion: Glasgow chamber minutes, TD76/1, pp. 136 f.

Meetings in early chambers combined the functions of formal governance with providing reportage/information dissemination, and seeking inputs to lobbying positions. In many cases formal votes were taken on major policy stances, so that legitimation was a key role of meetings up to the 1920s, and indeed later. Through the 18th and 19th centuries, meetings were essentially the central means by which chambers operated, both as closed meetings of committees and the chamber's council or board, and as open meetings to which all members and perhaps the public and press were invited.

Most chamber records preserve papers of only the formal meetings for which minutes were taken. In some cases these might be as limited as the single annual meeting/AGM, and in the case of Salt chamber in the 1890s the general meeting to receive accounts became a three-yearly event for which three-yearly accounts and reports were prepared. For most chambers, however, there were quarterly, monthly, and weekly formal meetings of the council or its major committee,[10] punctuated by open meetings to garner wider views. In addition there were specialist meetings of committees or informal meetings of officers. Where necessary, meetings might become very frequent, even daily or twice daily, as occurred in parts of the 1780s and 1790s, when trade policy, treaties, and war effort were discussed; in the 1830s when the Corn Laws, and other local or national events demanded it; and again during the world wars. The chambers demonstrate some remarkable periods of commitment by their voluntary members.

As time progressed and the functions of meetings expanded, both formal governance and voting increasingly became more the preserve of annual meetings and the AGM, with other forms of member involvement mainly via committees and publications. These in turn became consolidated into annual reports by the 1850s and 1860s, or the national *Monthly Proceedings* of the ACC from the 1860s. Information collection and dissemination through meetings and publications became the major activity of most chambers by the time the chamber system was widespread across the UK.

The only chamber that appears to have kept a fairly complete record of its total number of formal meetings appears to be London. From the establishment of the modern chamber in 1882 meetings grew from 65 per year to 248 in 1890, to 872 in 1922, 1651 in 1932, 1190 in 1950, and 967 in 1960. The peaks appear to have been in 1946 and in 1964; since then there has been a steady decline. The general trend shown in Figure 11.1 demonstrates the effect of the 1930s growth of sector trade issues and the two world wars. Other exchanges of a more informal nature reflecting both member–chamber contacts, and chamber–government representation, is indicated by London's 'letters received' and 'circulars printed', which, as shown in Figure 11.1, follow similar trends, with a peak in the 1960s. As a comparator, Coventry chamber reports its circular letters in 1948 as 8000.[11]

---

[10] An 1892 sample of 55 chambers: 65% held formal meetings annually; 5% half-yearly; 22% quarterly; and 7% monthly: Royal Commission on Labour, *House of Commons Papers* (1892), xxxvi, part V, p. xxxiii.

[11] Coventry chamber, *Annual Report* (1948).

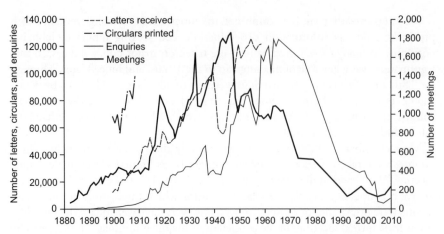

Fig. 11.1. An example of information exchange: number of meetings, circulars, letters, and enquiries for the London chamber of commerce 1882–2010. (*Source*: London chamber reports, and BCC *Benchmarking*.)

Economic cycles are evident in these data to some extent. The decline in London's inquiries after 1970 reflects declines in membership, and after 1999 the impact of government services developed through Business Link.

An analysis of the nature of the meetings held in London is given for early years in its annual reports and its *CCJ*. The most frequent were for governance (the executive, council, and general meetings), over 46% of all meetings in 1883, with four sections (textiles, chemicals, printing, and gold and silver) accounting for 29% of the rest. By 1884 governance meetings were down to 26%, and 13% in 1892. Table 11.1 for 1889 shows that most meetings concerned sector-specific sections and committees. This pattern was maintained into the current period and probably gives a good indication of the general pattern in most chambers. For example, Coventry in the 1940s and 1950s had about 49–58 sector meetings per year, plus another 12–15 per year of the council.[12]

Detailed modern statistics of the role of different meetings in chambers show that 30% of chamber's representation costs (essentially staff time) went to servicing member committees and working groups; other recurrent responses occupied 12%; meetings and contacts with local government 10%; ABCC and national surveys 10%; school, colleges, and education authority liaison 9%; liaison with training providers (including TECs) 8.5%; support to foreign visitors and missions 6%; and then 14.5% on a wide range of other interactions.[13] This suggests that the membership involves about one-third of the chambers' resources (not dissimilar to London in the 1880s), and liaison with other bodies about two-thirds. Chamber meetings are thus directed both internally and externally.

---

[12] Coventry chamber, *Annual Reports* (1948–58).
[13] Bennett and Krebs (1993a).

Table 11.1. Types of meetings held by London Chamber of Commerce 1889 (total 201)

Meetings	Number Held
AGM (1) and special general meetings (8)	9
Council meetings	15
Executive committee	20
Commercial Education committee	6
Labour Conciliation committee	9
Sector Associations (18),[a] of which	87
Chemical	(14)
Electrical	(11)
Other sector meetings (6),[b] of which	20
Grocery Trade	(9)
Area Sections (5),[c] of which	23
South Africa	(10)
East India and China	(6)
'Conferences'[d]	19
Other[e]	3

[a] Full list is cement, chemical, coffee and cocoa, diamond, electrical, engineering, furnishing, gold and silver, leather, metal, music, preserved food, printing, provisions, photographic, textile, tobacco, watchmakers.
[b] Candle trade, grocery trade, insurance trade, linoleum trade, timber trade, and wine and spirits trade.
[c] East India and China, South Africa, South America, West Africa, Australia.
[d] Dock strike (13), Railway rates (6).
[e] Dock Trust, Bill of Lading, Railway Rates and Fares Committee.
Source: London *CCJ*, March (1890).

Another measure of the scale of chamber meetings is available from the late 1980s, on events such as conferences and seminars.[14] They demonstrate expansion of a successful range of events, such as Glasgow's monthly current business affairs conferences started in 1966 (numbering about 10 per year), which continue in a modified form up to the present. As shown in Table 11.2, meetings increased to a peak in 1998, before rising to a new peak in 2010, with a narrowing of the range of variation between chambers. We cannot compare these figures for the whole system for the historical past, but it is probably the case that the level of meetings is now at a post-WW2 high. Despite the decline in London's meetings, shown in Figure 11.1, other chambers have expanded significantly.

The number of participants in these meetings, shown in Table 11.3, also demonstrates a rising trend. The mean of 3812 per chamber in 2010, or 3.01 per member, shows a very active modern role for meetings despite the expansion of e-commerce. These trends exhibit the influence of various factors: the role of the BCC *Development Strategy* to bring all chambers up to an accredited level of contact and activity with members, which had a major impact on the total activity, especially in the smallest chambers; the narrowing of the network by reduction of the number of chambers through mergers; and involvement with Business Link

---

[14] Excludes business training courses.

Table 11.2. Number of conference and seminar meetings per year held by chambers of commerce in BCC membership 1988–2010: mean, maximum, minimum, and 20%/80% percentiles

Year	Number	Mean	Max	Min	80%	20%
1988	2,729	26.5	292	0	36	2
1992	3,492	34.6	253	0	52	2
1994	3,810	42.3	479	0	33	3
1996	3,775	59.9	342	0	66	12
1998	4,024	54.4	300	8	90	15
2000	3,668	46.4	230	4	89	18
2002	3,434	50.2	170	10	74	24
2004	4,424	73.7	213	10	107	36
2006	4,729	84.4	240	17	93	43
2008	4,535	82.5	352	15	108	44
2010	5,068	93.8	269	17	153	39

Source: BCC, *Census* and *Benchmarking*.

over the 1990s. Whereas some of chambers held few or no events in the period up to 1990, now all BCC chambers are active in offering meetings and networking opportunities. Clearly meetings remain a significant part of the modern chamber service bundle.

11.3 ORIGINS OF MILIEUS: COMMERCIAL INFORMATION, OPPORTUNITY, AND STATUS

Chamber milieus originated to fulfil the most basic business needs. Early businesses often did not have offices and administrative personnel. The most significant members, the merchants, were normally not themselves producers requiring workshops or factories, whilst in any case manufacturing was often by 'putting out'. As a result, much business activity and many transactions were executed in meeting rooms, exchanges, assembly rooms, taverns, coffee houses, piazzas, or other locations that were not specific business addresses; indeed, many businesses had no address other than that of the residence of the owner, who might not wish to use it for business purposes. Many 18th- and 19th-century businesses were thus almost virtual, and in many respects resembled many modern small businesses. A typical merchant's day is summarized by the Dublin chamber in 1787: 'the merchant's entire morning must be devoted to the attendance on public markets in the sale or purchase of goods, executing the orders received by post of the day, effecting insurances and to other necessary avocations'.[15] As a result of this virtual trading environment, venues to meet that were respectable and convenient were sought

---

[15] Quoted in Cullen (1983), p. 24.

Table 11.3. Number of participants per year at conferences and seminars held by chambers of commerce in BCC membership 1988–2010: mean, maximum, minimum, and 20%/80% percentiles

Year	No.	Mean	Max	Min	80%	20%
1988	56,475	548	4,500	0	820	40
1992	50,306	498	5,660	0	790	30
1994	48,180	535	5,691	0	800	60
1996	81,800	1,298	10,000	0	2,200	198
1998	183,848	2,484	13,000	98	4,220	795
2000	175,977	2,444	9,513	0	3,665	900
2002	191,168	2,619	10,498	182	3,958	900
2004	202,783	3,379	13,795	500	5,025	2,325
2006	210,052	3,751	12,876	870	4,680	2,100
2008	188,228	3,422	10,228	781	4,539	1,818
2010	205,853	3,812	13,836	740	5,214	1,860

Source: BCC, *Census* and *Benchmarking*.

out, with a range of meeting places themselves developing as commercial businesses to meet the need.

This was a role chambers could fill, but the concept already had some important precedents on to which chambers could graft their additional objectives of voice, governance, and a membership for deliberating. During the 18th century many locally important institutions were established which were prominent in providing milieus for discourse among business people. An early and particularly prominent group were Commercial Exchanges. These usually involved the development of a physical building to act as an exchange and market, with piazzas and individual stalls. They were erected by subscribers who became the shareholders of the exchange or owned the freehold of the stalls, which could be sold on. Coffee houses became even more important milieus.

Commercial exchanges

Some of the most important exchanges were in London, where links with coffee houses were strong. Indeed Lloyds and many insurance companies originated in this way. A major early example was The Royal Exchange, which was one of the largest and longest lived, where 'traders from across Europe and round the globe met to set prices, arrange cargoes, settle bills and make deals'.[16] There were separate 'walks' for each national or major trading area, which helped to concentrate people together. The exchange had counterparts in other cities, 'where merchants and tradesmen . . . meet . . . to confer and treat together concerning merchandizing, shipping, buying,

---

[16] Ellis (2004), p. 166.

selling and the like'.[17] Business people might also use the area outside: 'Bristol merchants who had built themselves a fine Exchange Building . . . preferred to continue to conduct their business in the traditional manner, standing outside'.[18]

Outside London, commercial exchanges were developed in most major cities, at an early date in Liverpool and Manchester. In Limerick the Exchange was erected under the stimulus of the chamber members. In Yorkshire, 18th-century cloth halls played a similar role; e.g. in Leeds and Wakefield. The Exchange continued to develop as a model well into the 20th century, being established in Middlesbrough and Swansea in 1915, and Newcastle in 1920. Many of the later ones were developed by, or in conjunction with, chambers of commerce. They were all private initiatives of groups of merchants and traders, usually the most wealthy. They were run by committees of trustees, levied subscriptions, operated under formal rules, and depended for their launch on public meetings and calls for public subscription through local advertisement.

Coffee houses

By 1700 commercial taverns and coffee houses were numerous in London and had spread to every major town. The chambers used them extensively for advertising and holding their meetings, and distributing their petitions and memorials; thus Newcastle sent copies of its memorials over to Batrans coffee house to garner support and to disseminate information on its activities.[19] The commercial coffee houses and chambers of commerce subsequently developed overlapping memberships; some chambers developed their own coffee houses, and some became joint bodies. Indeed, some of the decline of coffee houses after 1850 was due to emergence of the chambers, as well as other more 'respectable' premises such as hotels.[20]

Taverns and coffee houses played a critical role as mediums for meetings and the circulation of business intelligence before and after the chambers were established. 'The coffee house became an extension of the trading floor . . . offering a warm and dry place where business could continue'.[21] It became the main source of intelligence, and the place to consult published newssheets and pamphlets. As commented by Fraser, 'the coffee-houses that sprung up in London and numerous other cities and towns marked the progress of a veritable plague of newsmongering'.[22] Some coffee houses, such as London's Baltic, developed wider services, such as interpreting a contract, confirming a debt, and facilitating arbitration. Many were the sites of auctions of bulk imported goods and cargoes, for promoting launches of

---

[17] Lewes Roberts (1671), *The Merchants Map of Commerce*, p. 12; quoted in Ellis (2004), p. 166.
[18] Quoted in Sweet (2002), p. 364; New York chamber used the Tontine Coffee House 1793–1827, and Merchants Exchange 1827–35 with open piazza space; Bishop (1918), pp. 151–4.
[19] Newcastle chamber, minute book listings, 1815–20.
[20] Lillywhite (1963), p. 27; see also Olson (1991), pp. 40–1.
[21] Ellis (2004), p. 169.
[22] Fraser (1956), p. 114.

joint stock companies, buying and selling insurance, receiving mail, and were often linked with the publishers of newssheets, listings, and newspapers.[23]

Coffee houses in the ports were also extensively used as post offices from the 1690s into the 1840s, with bags to receive overseas letters hung inside and then taken to outgoing ships; a service that was deemed more efficient than the 'state protected post office'.[24] This coffee house postal service was a cheap and self-maintained service by business, for business, which continued to resonate with chambers of commerce through the rest of the 19th century. There were continuous complaints, memorials, and lobbies about the cost and inefficiency of the state postal service, and criticism of the Post Office monopoly.[25] The criticisms have continued into the 21st century, and some chambers have provided an alternative service of mailboxes (such as Dundee and Waterford into the later 20th century), and also have substituted for the Post Office during strikes (e.g. in the 1970s).

Coffee houses were thus natural milieus for founding lobby campaigns and use by chambers. They also tended to be anti-aristocratic and anti-government, and hence offered a precedent for objectors to form views. They particularly suited the mechanism of lobbying founded on a large-scale meeting that reached agreement on general principles, that was then developed into a petition signed by those present or those who might visit and sign in the following days. 'At Alice's Coffee House, Hell Coffee House and at Waghornes's in New Palace Yard, the committees plotted and intrigued.' They 'coached witnesses before they appeared before the House or select committee, treated officials and MPs to food and drink, and met the most important figure of the eighteenth century lobby, the solicitor-agent'.[26] They were also used routinely by the BoT throughout the 18th century, to gather information and views on colonial laws and foreign developments.[27]

National and local newspapers, listings of prices at commodity auctions, prices of joint stock trades, rates of exchange, prices of government stocks and naval bills, listings of customs bills of entry (listing all goods imported), and marine lists of shipping arrivals and departures at English and foreign ports were all key publication innovations of the 18th century. The coffee house was the main milieu where they could be consulted. 'Coffee house owners vied with each other' to supply the latest news. The major ones had an open room able to seat up to 100–200 people, with a central counter and large 'communal tables and smaller ones where individual merchants worked or groups of four or five shared a newspaper'.[28]

Commercial coffee houses were not open to all. Increasingly they levied subscriptions and sought to become exclusive to specific business groups. The specialist American trade bodies in London changed from using open coffee houses to become subscription houses for Carolina, Virginia, Pennsylvania, New York, and New England, in the 1720s and 1730s. This allowed a focus by those attending,

---

[23] Barty-King (1977), p. 167; McCusker and Gravesteijn (1991).
[24] Lillywhite (1963), p. 20
[25] Ilersic and Liddle (1960).
[26] Lillywhite (1963); quoted in Brewer (1989), p. 239.
[27] Kammen (1970); Olson (1973, 1982, 1991).
[28] Lillywhite (1963), pp. 19–27; Ellis (2004); Olson (1991), p. 38.

but also imposed exclusiveness. It is clear from many local accounts that member-ship of the commercial coffee house was a sought-after and valued asset.

The coffee house was a critical commercial development of the period preceding, and overlapping with, the development of the chambers of commerce. It resonated with the 18th-century format of gentlemanly exchange—'a polite and commercial people' as Langford called it; as venues to demonstrate one's acceptance and to enlarge one's influence,[29] discussed in Chapter 3. It was an obvious model for chambers to utilize.

11.4 THE CHAMBER LINK TO COFFEE HOUSES AND HOTELS

The coffee houses were a major milieu that could be used by chambers in an ad hoc way, without allegiance to a particular one. For Jersey, dining as an activity was a key part of its founding articles and exclusiveness,[30] but this was not in a dedicated building until well after its early years. However, as the formality of chambers developed, a defined and relatively stable membership, formal governance, and the need to form a continuing platform for voice suggested a more permanent location for their meetings. Additionally the attraction of a drop-in facility to meet other members had all the advantages of a club, but with the added opportunity to help shape the latest deliberation and lobby. It was thus natural for chambers to look to developing their own dedicated milieu, and to look at the highly successful coffee houses and exchanges as models to adapt. Also, as Olson argues, coffee houses were less able to combine general with specific technical discussion, even if they were subscription bodies. Thus, when all the American colonies were affected, as with the legislation after 1760, separate coffee houses were less effective, and less relevant to government or the BoT as sources of advice.[31] Hence the search for a 'general' interest also stimulated chambers' search for a different model. Money and Wilson, respectively for Liverpool and Birmingham, argue that coffee houses and societies were major ways in which local identity was developed at this time.[32]

The Tontine and debenture models

The chambers set up coffee houses in a rather different way from most previous foundations. Many used a separate subscription to raise capital from individuals who then became the shareholders and trustees of the chamber's building. The subscribers may not have had a one-to-one overlap with the chamber's members since some members did not or could not find the shareholder contribution needed. Two models for this seem to have been used: a debenture structure, and Tontines. The debenture provided a continuing capital structure, but Tontines

---

[29] Langford (1989); see also Clark (2000a); Morris (1983), pp. 104–5.
[30] Jersey chamber minutes, founding articles, February 1768, article 32.
[31] Olson (1973, 1982, 1991).
[32] Wilson (1997); Money (1977).

strictly came to an end with the death of the last survivor.[33] Tontine coffee houses may have been adopted as a model because of their reputation for superior rooms, facilities, and status. They also had similarities to lotteries that were very popular at this time. The link of the chambers to these shareholder models has not been previously recognized; the structure is important for understanding the dynamics of several of the early chambers.

The use of Tontine and debenture structures, or linkage to a coffee house with similar structures, seems to have been close for most early chambers: in New York,[34] Boston,[35] Liverpool, Glasgow, Dublin, Waterford, Cork, Newcastle, and Dundee. The coffee house was also important in later foundations such as Lancaster (1897) and Galway (1923). In Limerick the Exchange provided parallel facilities. In Birmingham there are tantalizing indications that a coffee house may have been linked with the chamber.[36] Thus at least ten of the earliest 19 chambers had some relationship of this kind. For the earliest chambers perhaps New York's experience may have been copied. Its founding Articles of 1768 required a room for conversation with 'bread and cheese, beer, punch, pipes and tobacco, provided at the expense of the members present'.[37] Each chamber's approach was, however, slightly different and interacted with the dynamics of the rest of the chamber in different ways, as examined below in date order for the main British and Irish chambers linked to coffee houses.

Glasgow

The earliest UK chambers in Jersey, Guernsey, and Manchester do not appear to have had a specific link with coffee houses, and Liverpool did not develop this until 1783–4, so that Glasgow was the first UK chamber where a close interlock developed. Glasgow's chamber used the Tontine and Hotel from its outset in 1783, and this may have been important for getting the chamber under way. This coffee house/hotel was erected in 1781 following the initiative of Patrick Colquhoun, who became the chamber's first president, with other merchants. The coffee house was a true Tontine independent of the chamber, with rents distributed among the subscribers as long as they lived, the last survivor becoming the owner of the building. The Tontine was divided into 107 shares of £50 each, and the shares became traded entities having a value of about £100 by 1797. In addition annual subscribers at one guinea per year had use of the room, newspapers, and

---

[33] Tontines were developed by Laurentio Tonti, an Italian who founded the first in 1658 at Naples. His coffee house concept spread across Europe and parts of the New World. He became an adviser to Cardinal Mazarin, to whom he proposed an annuity scheme, rejected by the French parliament in 1653. It was later taken up by Louis XIV and others; see *The Lounger's Common Place Book,* vol. ii (1796), pp. 224–5; Dr Johnson's *Dictionary,* etc.

[34] New York used the Tontine Coffee House 1793–1827; Bishop (1918), pp. 151–3.

[35] David Greene, *Letterbook,* refers to the relationship (William Clements Library, University of Michigan).

[36] Styles Tontine Hotel, and Lloyds New Hotel in 1800 may have been linked to chamber members; further research required; they are not mentioned in Money (1977), pp. 98–120.

[37] Bishop (1918), p. 6.

magazines.[38] Its hotel apartments were critical to the overall popularity and finances.[39] The chamber used its main reading room and meeting rooms. The coffee room was 72 feet long, 'the largest and most elegant of the kind in Britain'.[40]

There are first-hand accounts of Glasgow chamber's rooms that demonstrate their value for information and discourse: 'here every man meets his friends, or his acquaintance; here he learns whatever is new or interesting at home or abroad, in politics, commerce; and often in literature. His mind recovers, or acquires here tone and elasticity; and each returns to his family or his business with new vigour'.[41] The Glasgow chamber was thus as much a club and source of commercial gossip as it was a pressure group. 'The manufacturers and merchants, . . . make a point . . . of appropriating the afternoon and evening to convivial enjoyment,—with the abstraction of a short interval, in which rising, in gay spirits, from the table, they rejoin to the tontine coffee house to talk over the news of the day, and the transactions of the week, and to make up parties for supper.'[42] Brown's 1787 account states that the coffee house was critical to the early life of the Glasgow chamber, 'and brought . . . a style superior to anything of the kind that we have seen in the three capitals of the Empire'.[43]

Liverpool

Liverpool's Exchange and two main commercial coffee houses (The Merchants and Pontacks) were the venues for merchants to meet in the 1770–1800 period, and both had large newsrooms.[44] Most chamber members (71%) were also members of the Subscription Library, established in 1758, and other societies, and thus clearly sought out venues to meet, network, and exchange views.[45] However, the chamber had an early desire to have a milieu of its own: 'a room . . . in the neighbourhood of the Exchange, where all the books, and letters of this Society [chamber] should be open to the inspection of the subscribers every day during 'Change hours; and a suitable allowance made to the secretary for the additional care and attendance';[46] i.e. to have a 'drop-in' meeting room.

This seems to have been provided ten years after the chamber's establishment in 1783–4, when a 'Tontine Coffee Room, Hotel and Tavern' was launched by four of the known or probable chamber members, with its accounts held by Arthur

---

[38] James Denholm (1797), *An Historical Account of the City of Glasgow* (Glasgow: R. Chapman), pp. 107–9.

[39] Oakley (1983), Glasgow chamber history.

[40] J. McNayr (1797), *A Guide to Glasgow* (Glasgow: Courier Office), p. 198.

[41] I. Lettice (1794), *Letters in a Tour through Various Parts of Scotland in the Year 1792* (London: T. Cadell), pp. 87–8.

[42] Robert Heron (1799), *Observations Made in a Journal through the Western Counties of Scotland in 1792* (Glasgow: Morrison, Perch), vol. i, p. 382.

[43] A. Brown (1787), *History of Glasgow* (Glasgow: William Paton), ii, p. 159; the others were London and Dublin.

[44] Brooke (1853), pp. 164, 269.

[45] Bennett (2010), appendix tables, shows the extensive cross-memberships.

[46] Liverpool chamber *Abstract*, pp. 15–16; Bennett (2010).

Heywood, another member.[47] They were to act as trustees, with rents and profits distributed annually to shareholders. Five thousand guineas was initially sought to finance this scheme. It may have been copied from Glasgow. It was very successful financially, occupying a prominent site on the north-east corner of Lord St. with Whitechapel, and opened by 1784 and called Bates Hotel.[48] It had a coffee room 80 by 28 feet, which became the main newspaper room of the city, three dining rooms, several smaller rooms and parlours, lodging rooms, kitchen, laundry, brew-house, rooms for servants, and good cellars. It became 'the first' of inns, with 'fifty or sixty bedrooms'.[49] Its reading room was the largest available for meetings until the Athenaeum was built in 1797.

Bates was not itself a chamber building, since a separate body of about 200 subscribers was sought, both women and men. But its link with the chamber's members was close, becoming in effect a partnership of the chamber through the initiative of four of its members. It seems unlikely that the chamber had a dedicated room in Bates; rather, as in Glasgow, the chamber rented the reading and meeting rooms.

Dublin

The earliest Dublin chamber had a close link to the Commercial Buildings in Dame St., which many members had helped establish, and where the coffee room was used to meet. When the chamber was re-established in 1820, one of its earliest objectives was 'to obtain the present coffee room (or part thereof)' in the Commercial Buildings and to hire its own attendant. The managers of the Commercial Buildings were initially reluctant to engage with the chamber, and it appears to have rented the adjacent building at £50 per year in 1821, which also allowed the establishment of a library. But by 1823 some compromise was reached with the chamber 'opening of a passage between the coffee room and the house they occupy'.[50] The chamber also had other staff, for porters superintending porterage charges, pier fees, and coal metering, which were based at the Customs House Long Room.[51] By 1846 the chamber was developing a 'merchants room', which was 'an office or waiting room... [used by those] requiring to write letters or transact private business arising out of visits to the reading room'. A counter and desks, with new gas lighting, were added to the reading room in 1846. The reading room and library was integrated as a coffee room and place of meeting and discourse, so that the merchants' room provided a quieter and more private area. Even in 1922

---

[47] Richard Heywood, Thomas Ryan, John Gregson, and Gill Slater (the second chamber president); advertisement in *Williamson's Advertiser*, 5 June 1783; sale of Tontine shares 4 February 1784 (Liverpool RO, Holt Gregson papers 942 HOL/8, p. 127).

[48] Accounts for the 'Hotel Coffee Room of Thomas Ryan': Heywood Bank ledger 1791–4, Barclays Bank Archives, pp. 97, 110; see also Brooke (1853), pp. 269, 37; Bennett (2010), pp. 10–12.

[49] From a visitor to Bates Hotel in 1798; p. 31 in N. Gay (1799), *Strictures on the Proposed Union between Great Britain and Ireland* (London), also *Williamson's Advertiser*, 5 June 1783.

[50] Dublin chamber, Council minutes, 21 June 1823.

[51] Dublin chamber, General Meeting minutes, 1821.

the main reading room was called a 'conversation room'.[52] The chamber made further improvements to the building, and later took over the Ouzel Galley room, which it rented out. The chamber saw the coffee room and other facilities, from the outset, as a source of revenue 'less burdensome than that of voluntary individual subscription'.[53]

The facilities at the chamber proved very popular, with various expansions of rooms and staff, open all days of the week (though Sunday opening was briefly curtailed in December 1846). The rooms included the staff offices of the registrar, and also after 1846 of the two assistant clerks (Mr Heron and Mr Russell). For Russell, at least, it became his family residence, and he acted as de facto caretaker. But he was asked to live elsewhere in 1858 when the staff was expanded to include a resident porter and caretaker.[54] From the outset the rooms contained a book for 'suggestions or hints or observations of subscribers for the interest of the association or benefit of trade and commerce' which were then laid before council.[55] This is the only record of such a book within a chamber, though others may have existed. For Dublin it proved an important source of information on lobby issues that were of concern, as well as comments on the rooms and services. But given the tensions within the chamber, it is also clear that it was sometimes used for political or abusive comment.

Dublin's rooms remained valuable assets: 'it has a well appointed reading room, considerable accommodation in the matter of free stationery, comfortable, if not luxurious seats and well-ventilated rooms. In Dublin they tried to do everything well.'[56] Dublin seems to be the only example in early chambers of dividing the rooms between a 'conversation-room' and a 'reading room'.[57]

Waterford

Waterford developed one of the most ambitious early plans for chamber buildings, like Glasgow and Liverpool, centred on a hotel. They had rented their own meeting room and coffee room from their outset in 1787. This was converted from the Old Assembly Room, and had a housekeeper (Mary Hartley) to provide refreshments, a clerk or member of the committee to transact bill business in attendance Tuesday to Friday 1.30–2.30, and arbitration committee meeting every Friday. Thus Waterford was one of first chambers to provide a composite range of services, as well as lobbying.[58] These rooms continued until 1797, and probably over the period until 1804, when the chamber considered a purchase. But it first rented a room in the Commercial Buildings 1805–7 for 50 guineas, and then two parlours in Ramsey's

[52] Dublin chamber, Report of Council, 1922.
[53] e.g. Dublin chamber, Council minutes, 28 July 1846; General Meeting minutes, 12 October 1820.
[54] Dublin chamber, Council minutes, 23 June 1846; 8 November 1858.
[55] Dublin chamber, General Meeting minutes, 12 October 1820.
[56] J. R. Wigham, president Dublin chamber, in London *CCJ*, 5 August 1886, p. 54.
[57] See Aspinall (1973), pp. 27–8.
[58] Waterford chamber minutes, 20 and 27 April, 26 October 1787; 11 December 1795.

House 1807–12 for 70 guineas. However, by 1812 it decided to raise £3000 to purchase its own building, initially on an eight-year lease with option to buy, which was exercised in August 1812. This was the house of George Morris (also referred to as the House of Concerns) in George Street.[59] It had four floors, basement, and loft and a prominent location opposite an important road junction leading directly from the quays; where the chamber was still located in 2011. It was of a size and on a site that offered immediate prominence and prestige.

The chamber made use of a debenture structure, offering shares of £50 for subscribers to become 'proprietors'. A deposit of £10 was requested with the final shareholding ranging from £25 to £100; 87 shareholders in all contributed £3525. This provided a return to shareholders, with the first interest paid in February 1815. The debenture was managed by three trustees, with a management committee of seven who would 'dispose of the rest of the house to best advantage but not for more than one year without a general meeting'. Unlike Liverpool and Glasgow, the trust was interlocked with the chamber by a clause stating that no proprietor could transfer shares except to a member of the chamber. This was maintained in the chamber's 1815 charter.[60] Its accounts were combined with the chamber, showing the sale and issue of debentures, and interest payments. However, chamber members subscribed annually and need not be debenture holders.

The size of the building purchased was designed to offer income to the chamber. The chamber occupied the premier first floor rooms, the upper two floors became a hotel, and the ground floor was used initially as a coffee shop and later let to the Harbour Board (with which the chamber had close relations, nominating 12 of its 24 members; it still occupied the ground floor in 2011). The chamber had maintained a reading room since 1804 with a wide range of newspapers, almanacs, and directories. This had a separate subscription of one guinea after the opening of the chamber's building. It became referred to as the newsroom, not open to the public, but non-residents could be admitted after introduction by a member.[61] It continued until 1958. In addition the Library Society (a lending library) moved into the chamber buildings in 1820, with a separate subscription open to all local residents and paying rent; it remained until 1926.[62]

The hotel had 11 bedrooms, two public rooms, kitchen, and cellar; seen as an addition rather than an essential part of the chamber's functions, unlike the newsroom. It was a useful source of income until taken over by Richard Free in 1823. He agreed to pay rent of £40 per year as well as providing porterage, making the fires, supplying candles, and maintaining the building. But in 1824 his rent was waived because of the losses he claimed he made. The chamber neglected to review

---

[59] Waterford chamber minutes, 2, 8, and 14 January, 6 May 1805; 5 October 1807; 2 February 1812; lease; list of debenture holders and interest payments, 2 May 1815; also Cowman (1988), Waterford chamber history, pp. 13, 16–17.

[60] Waterford chamber minutes, 10 and 21 February, and 12 April 1812.

[61] Waterford chamber minutes, 30 September 1808 (this continued the 20 April 1787 rules); contents of newsroom in *Annual Reports* in the 1900s.

[62] Waterford chamber minutes, 7 February 1820, annual accounts; also Cowman (1988), Waterford chamber history, p. 25.

this arrangement until 1841 when it set up an inquiry into Free's affairs. He had paid no rent since 1823 and was charging the chamber various fees, as well as subletting the hotel to another manager. As Cowman remarks, Richard Free was like a character from an Irish Victorian novel. But the final decision to evict only followed his action in letting the building for a political meeting in the 1841 general election, which he had been expressly forbidden to do.[63] The building never seems to have yielded rent as a hotel again. Its tenants over most of the 19th century were the Harbour Board (£80), Library (£31), a bank and another minor tenant (£43).[64] After the 1950s rents disappeared altogether and much of the building became difficult to maintain. After discovering dry rot in 1954, the chamber decided to hand the whole building to the Harbour Commissioners for a nominal IR£5, leasing its committee and reading rooms back at IR£1 per year.

Cork

Cork set itself up with exclusive use of a coffee room from its outset in 1819 (Shinkwin's), who also provided furniture, light, and candles for the year. It was open from 8.00 to 11.00 in winter and 7.00 to 10.00 in summer, providing a complete venue for conversation, reading, and meetings. There were two inkstands, pen and ink, a 'posting board' for messages, over 20 newspapers and almanacs, two waiters, and a porter. The room was 'useful to the merchant, instructive to the politician, and amazing to the stranger and light reader'.[65] It was clearly a very active discussion milieu: a restraining notice in 1820 had to be posted after 'occurrences' in the room on two preceding evenings, that whilst the committee 'do not attempt to restrain the free expression of sentiments and opinions, they are convinced that the subscribers will distinguish between such free communications and the public harangues of any individuals... [and] will promote order and propriety in the room'.[66] In what was a very factious environment, the chamber also had to compete with the older committee of merchants that had erected its own Commercial Buildings and coffee room. Conflicts with this committee since 1814 had lain behind the chamber's foundation, as discussed in Chapter 5. The chamber felt itself under pressure, so that when Shinkwin became insolvent they bought his furniture (£37 13s. 6d.) and moved to a larger venue in 1820 at Hobbs House in Patrick St., with two rooms and closet on the first floor, a small room on the second floor and kitchen, coal hole and WC, costing £6 per month.[67]

The need for a stronger statement of status led the chamber to want its own building; on foundation in 1819 it offered 100 shares in a debenture at £25, with the full subscription proceeds put on deposit after only 6 weeks. It appears that the target was a takeover of the committee of merchants and the Commercial

[63] Cowman (1988), Waterford chamber history, discusses this entertainingly, pp. 31–6.
[64] Yearly rents in 1900; Waterford chamber minutes, 2 November, 6 December 1954.
[65] Cork chamber minutes, 29 January, 8 November, and 31 December 1819.
[66] Cork chamber minutes, 8 March 1820. The problem was probably caused by Mr Hutchinson, who was expelled five days later and his subscription returned: minutes 13 March 1820.
[67] Cork chamber minutes, 18 and 19 August; 16 and 19 September 1820.

Buildings. This was unsuccessful, but by September 1822 it was able to issue its debenture, with later shares costing £30; unpaid shareholders were struck off and their shares bought by others. There appear to have been 120 shares, held by 98 shareholders, providing a total capital of £3410.[68] The precise timing is unclear, but work was begun to erect the building, later to become the Victoria Hotel in Patrick St., which was occupied by about 1824. In 1836 the hotel part of the enterprise was leased to Thomas McCormack for 21 years at £80 per year, who had a reduction in the first two years 'to put the premises in repair and paint the establishment'. His rent was increased to £200 per year in 1857, but later reduced to £170 when the shops in the hotel were let separately.[69]

Within the hotel the chamber maintained its offices and reading room, subletting a billiard room in 1836. This provided the chamber with a unique presence in the centre of the city, which became the premier venue for meetings. Its reading and meeting room was 'equal if not superior to any other of the kind'.[70] It held a wide range of newspapers and other reading matter, employed two waiters and a porter. Its value as a meeting room drew great interest for political meetings, and this was the source of tensions that led to the split of the chamber in 1882. Two separate chambers then continued in Cork until merged in December 1951.[71] The continuing chamber controlled the building and all-important reading room. It reasserted its freedom to use it as it wished, new rules stating that 'this room shall be the property of the subscribers, in virtue whereof the right is exclusively theirs of either refusing or consenting to grant the use of it on any public occasion';[72] i.e. the departing members lost their access and the continuing ones could continue to offer a political platform.

The possession of such valuable premises led to the chamber's structure being more complex than a normal subscriber membership. The building's debenture was managed by a separate trust, two or three holders of whom acted as trustees, paying some surpluses to the chamber, as in Waterford. But unlike Waterford there was a weaker link between the two, with the chamber managing its accounts separately with an annual subscription. In the early years the two groups were identical, but after 1823 it became possible for the trustee group and the chamber's committee to become disjointed. This possibility increased as shareholders died or wished to realize their capital and shares were sold on; indeed there was concern in 1860 that the hotel leaseholder Thomas McCormack was buying shares.[73] When the chamber split, some shareholders were members of the new Cork Incorporated chamber. This allowed tensions and conflicts to be maintained. The trust appears to have increasingly taken on a life of its own. When the chamber experienced financial difficulties in 1925, the trustees were unwilling to increase their support. The

---

[68] Cork chamber minutes, 31 December 1819, 25 September 1822; and list of shareholders 1836.
[69] Cork chamber minutes 10 May 1838; 2 May 1839; 23 and 28 January 1857.
[70] Cork chamber, General Meeting report, 2 January 1832.
[71] See Chapters 3 and 5.
[72] *New Rules of Chamber of Commerce Room*, Cork, 1881; poster in ABCC loose papers; MS 14477/1.
[73] Cork chamber shareholders book, transfers after 1836; chamber minutes, 1 January 1823, 9 March 1860.

chamber called on the trust to give more financial information, noting that there had never been any annual accounts submitted. The trustees sought legal advice on whether they had to comply and managed to resist the chamber for some time.[74] But the chamber found that it could assert some control over the trust by working with the more progressive trustees: in 1927 it was able to require accounts to be produced, and to force it to share its office and typist resulting in a saving of IR£52 per year on salaries.[75] After this date the financial support to the chamber became clearer, although the surpluses from the trust were small.

The tensions with the trustees in the 1920s echoed some of the earlier political clashes, and ran across the establishment of the Irish Republic in 1920–3. The two separate chambers had been discussing amalgamating since 1920, which was pressed by the new Irish Minister of Commerce and the mayor in 1923. A special meeting in December 1924 had agreed amalgamation. The Cork Incorporated chamber also agreed to wind itself up and form a new joint chamber.[76] But the trustees of the debenture noted that 'a substantial minority of the members opposed the proposed scheme of amalgamation. . . . The absence of a unanimous direction from the members and the legal expenses incident.' They refused to wind up the trust. There was both conservatism and political tension still at work, with one trustee able to hold back the developments. A further vote on amalgamation was rejected in 1930.[77] Moreover the chamber continued political activity. After amalgamation of the two chambers eventually was achieved in 1955, the hotel was sold and the chamber moved to new premises.

Newcastle

The coffee house was an important medium through which the chamber was created in Newcastle. A commercial coffee house had existed from at least 1801.[78] This seems to have folded into the chamber on its foundation in 1815, its formal minutes terminating when the chamber was established. The chamber minutes refer to it as one of their facilities after 1815. However, the coffee house continued somewhat independently until at least the 1820s, with its minute book containing copies of a few normal out-letters with complaints about the punctuality of delivery of newspapers until 1823.[79]

Analysis of the membership of the coffee house shows that at least 8 of the 14 members of the coffee house committee of 1810–15 were among the first 53 members of the chamber in 1815, and two were members of the chamber's

---

[74] Cork chamber, committee book, containing AGM press reports November 1925 and November 1926.

[75] Cork chamber, committee book, report of special council meeting 24 February 1927.

[76] Cork Incorporated chamber of commerce and shipping, minutes, 15 January 1925.

[77] Cork chamber, committee book, reports of AGM 21 November 1923, 5 December 1924, 1 November 1925; special meeting, 4 July 1930.

[78] See W. Whellan (1856), *Directory*, p. 956; full sources in Tyne and Wear Archives Catalogues.

[79] See e.g. out-letter 21 April 1823; the Secretary notes 'it is painful to me to complain again', minutes and accounts of the coffee house 1801–1823 (Tyne and Wear Archives SX/2/1).

Table 11.4. Membership of the Newcastle coffee house (1801–13) and the chamber of commerce, percentage of each type by sector and legal form (1816)

	Commercial Coffee House	Chamber of Commerce
Extraction and manufacturing	37	39
Services and commerce	42	53
Retail	11	4
Other	10	4
Individuals/Sole traders	79	34
Partnerships	21	66

Source: analysis of coffee house committee and chamber membership lists; Tyne and Wear Archives SX 12/1 and 2401/1/1.

12 strong committee.[80] The memberships also drew on similar cross-sections of leading local businessmen (see Table 11.4). However, the coffee house had an additional and wider membership than the chamber, with more members who were individual tradesmen rather than partners or company owners.

No trace of the coffee room exists after 1825, although there was discussion about opening an exchange and newsroom in the 1880s.[81] It would seem that after absorbing the coffee house, the chamber closed the function down by the late 1820s. Indeed, when a new Commercial Exchange was established in 1920, the chamber rented accommodation in it for a period, e.g. in 1950. The chamber probably missed an important opportunity to offer newspaper and coffee room facilities in the 1920–60 period. The Commercial Exchange grew rapidly into a large and successful organization having many hundreds of members. It was clearly a rival to the chamber as a meeting point and provider of journals and information, continuing into the 1960s.

Dundee

Dundee is another case where the chamber evolved from a coffee house. Although there was an early chamber of Forfarshire founded in 1819, this had fallen into a state of informal meetings, becoming a 'latent' chamber.[82] In March 1835 a Baltic Coffee House was set up with 48 subscribers who guaranteed the rent, with 28 more subscribers added later. This had a very chamber-like feel, its chief objectives being 'to facilitate the obtaining of correct commercial and shipping intelligence. . . . [and for subscribers to communicate] their latest advices regarding the state of the different markets.' A shipping book, monitored by a keeper, was to be kept. The coffee room was quickly successful. An earlier Exchange Coffee House in a Trades Hall of 1776 had raised a £3000 subscription for a new building which was opened in 1828, but this closed in 1845 as a result of competition from the Baltic.[83] The opening hours were 9.00–16.00.

[80] Analysis of minutes and accounts of the coffee house 1801–23 and Newcastle chamber minutes.
[81] Newcastle chamber minutes.
[82] See Forfarshire chamber minutes.
[83] Harry Terrell, retired chief executive of Dundee chamber, letter to the author, 3 March 2006.

Only one year later, by May 1836, the Baltic Coffee House 'subscribers agreed to resolve themselves into a chamber of commerce in addition to the present objects'.[84] A subscription of one and a half guineas (country members half price) for the coffee house was carried over to include the chamber and the 'Baltic' name was quickly dropped. This arrangement continued until the 1860s when the coffee house and the chamber moved to having separate subscription rates. The coffee house was now called a reading room, but the main staff of the chamber was still two waiters. By 1860 it was called the Merchants' Exchange and Reading Room. The reading room subscription became two guineas (one guinea country) when the chamber subscription was one guinea (10s. 6d. country) in 1900. The reading room had considerably more members (463) and raised a considerably larger income (£991) than the chamber (145 members and £149 subscription income) in 1870. This pattern continued into 1890s when the chamber subscription level surpassed that of the reading room for the first time (£2 12s. 6d. in 1900 for the chamber compared to £2 for the reading room; £1 6s. compared to £1 for country members).[85] This shift was achieved by offering to chamber members a combined package of reading room plus chamber at only a slightly higher price.

The Dundee minutes show continued financial friction between the two interests in the 19th and early 20th centuries. But in the end the higher and integrated subscription in the 1890s allowed the chamber interests to exert control: it became first a chamber, and second a reading room. Throughout, however, the chamber wisely recognized the importance not only of the income stream but the service that the reading room and coffee house provided. It was converted into a separate members social club paying rent to the chamber in the 1970s, although it had to be rescued financially by the chamber in the 1980s.[86] The coffee room gave the chamber a significant presence in the local community, which delivered a very substantial member base.

Lancaster

Another transition from a coffee house to a chamber was Lancaster at the end of the 19th century. A commercial coffee room had existed in Lancaster at the King's Arms from at least 1750 where merchants met and traded. The taverns were also used for sales from slave ships, other sales, and merchant meetings in the 1750s. During the 1780s a merchant's reading and coffee room was founded and this continued under the title Merchants Coffee Room until 1897, when it was handed over to the newly formed chamber of commerce.[87]

The Lancaster coffee room was very successful, and this may have held back development of a chamber in a city that should have had an early chamber given its size and trading history (cf. Chapter 5). Paull suggests the coffee room was 'the centre of a highly developed network which acquired and distributed information

---

[84] Dundee chamber, centenary history, p. 65, quoting the 25 May 1836 minutes.
[85] Dundee chamber, minute book and accounts.
[86] Harry Terrell, letter to the author, 3 March 2006.
[87] Jenny Paull's (1996) chamber history gives a detailed analysis which is extended here.

Table 11.5. Membership of the Lancaster Merchants Coffee Room and chamber of commerce 1808–1930, percentage of each business type by sector and legal form

	Merchants Coffee Room			Chamber of commerce			
	1808	1880	1893	1900	1914	1920	1930
Extraction and manufacturing	29	21	19	17	16	18	29
Services and commerce	38	37	19	25	38	18	23
Retail	8	15	44	32	27	35	31
Other	25	27	18	26	19	29	17
Individuals	58	52	74	60	62	65	49
Partnerships	38	42	23	31	22	29	20
Ltd. companies	4	6	3	9	16	6	31
Total no. of members	44	78	64	73	45	58	99

Sources: Analysis of Merchants Coffee Room subscriptions book and chamber membership lists (held at chamber).

on the whereabouts and condition of Lancaster shipping during the Napoleonic Wars . . . [with] merchandise being traded among the membership . . . such as coal, tobacco, timber, wines and spirits'.[88] From the early 1800s lawyers and professionals became more numerous as members, and the membership in general was wide, including tradesmen, clerics, and headmasters, as well as all the most notable merchants, landowners, the mayor, and MPs. Analysis of its subscribers shows that its membership was approximately 44 in 1808 rising to 63 in 1860, 76 in 1870, and 78 in 1880. It also had broad sector membership and included companies as well as individuals. Table 11.5 shows the evolution of its membership by business type and sector, and the transition to the chamber. The major trend is a shift towards a significant retail presence, a continuing dominance by individuals and sole traders, and a shift from partnerships to limited companies in the 20th century.

Paull suggests that there were two types of members in the coffee room's later days: the long-established that regarded the room as a gentlemen's club, and new professionals who sought change towards a broader business body with a stronger representative voice—a role they saw as only possible through the development of a chamber and its affiliations to the ACC. Paull describes a power struggle between these two groups of members in the 1880s. The newer members frequently resigned (though later rejoined), but by 1893 pressure from the new members, financial difficulty occasioned by lapsing and rising costs, and the establishment of the rival chamber gave little alternative to the coffee room committee, who handed the accounts and premises to the chamber in January 1897.[89] The coffee room continued as a chamber reading room and library into the 1930s. This constrained the chamber in the 1920s because it felt that raising the subscriptions required for ABCC membership would alienate coffee room members.[90]

---

[88] Ibid., p. 8.   [89] Ibid., pp. 16–19.
[90] ABCC, Home Affairs Committee, 7 January 1925.

The Lancaster evolution is important because it shows the tensions between the business people who wanted a mere meeting venue in the old style, and those who wanted a broader-based body able to voice a business view with wider authority and as part of a national organization of chambers. The fact that this transition occurred so late may be part of a generational shift that resisted the dissolution of their social chat; but it may also reflect typical grass-roots reluctance to abandon a favoured milieu in order to conform with ABCC objectives, a tension explored in Chapter 8.

Galway

In Galway the experience of other major Irish chambers suggested to the chamber founders in 1923 that they should also have a coffee room. The chamber developed out of the Royal Galway Institution which had operated from 1839–1923, and its predecessor (the Amicable Society) that had existed from 1791 to 1839. These bodies existed for the purpose of meetings, lectures, coffee, and bars. The chamber merged with the Royal Galway Institution in October 1923, only seven months after its own foundation, demonstrating the close association between the two from the outset. Moreover there was no desire to replace the former body's activities: whilst the chamber appointed a part-time secretary, it also appointed a full-time steward/caretaker from the outset, and a billiard room attendant. The Institution's rooms originally consisted of two ground floor reading rooms, one 36 ft. long and the other 18 ft., with a second floor library 36 ft. long, smoking room and caretaker's room, basement kitchen, cellars, servants quarters, and other rooms.[91]

The concept of a chamber in Galway was thus an amalgamation of deliberation, meetings, lectures, social functions, reading and newspaper room; the president in his 1932 address referred to the chamber explicitly as 'the club'. Early discussion at council meetings was often as much about billiard table repairs and bar accounts as commercial issues.[92] It is clear that for the business community the benefit of this was that the chamber became *the* focus of discussion and meetings in the city, so that it was natural for it later to take on many local economic development functions for the area. For most years the bar functions also provided the chamber with significant income; profits on whisky sales over 1924–32 never fell below £200 per year, with annual bar takings of £1400–2000 over the 1920s. The social facilities continued into the 1970s.

11.5. THE EVOLUTION OF PREMISES

The early chambers had few if any administrative personnel; this was mainly done by the voluntary elected officers. Thus the employees were often the waiters, porters, and librarians who maintained the coffee and reading rooms. Where chambers did not have their own coffee rooms, their facilities were generally a

[91] Galway chamber history, Woodman (2000), p. 117.
[92] See Galway chamber history, Woodman (2000), pp. 159, 178, 188.

rented meeting/reading room. Thus Jersey used a tavern from its outset, but in 1835, after an abortive discussion to erect its own building, it leased three rooms for £50.[93] Guernsey rented a room from its outset in 1809 'for meetings of the committee and general daily use of all the members ... where the books and papers ... may be referred to'.[94] Nottingham established a reading room from the 1860s, and had to look for a larger one in 1896.[95] The Sunderland chamber rented its own rooms from 1908, from the Fishery's Board.[96] Some chambers developed special areas: e.g. Leeds and Manchester had rooms with samples of local products; Walsall had a pattern room from 1907.

Other chambers had no dedicated rooms and continued holding meetings in hotels and taverns. Thus Belfast chamber used the Crown tavern in the 1780s, the Exchange Coffee Room in 1792, the Donegal Arms in 1793, and the Druids Tavern in 1794, but was back to the Donegal Arms from 1795. The Aberdeen chamber initially met at the Lemon Tree Tavern 1853–6, and then moved to the Royal Hotel.[97] In other cases, chambers met at the offices or rooms of related business organizations. Leeds chamber met at the Rotation Office and hotels in the 1780s.[98] Several chambers used Exchanges, e.g. Limerick 1805–33.

Local Town Halls were also used for meetings. For example, Wolverhampton met in the Town Hall 1856–61 before moving to rented premises.[99] Oldham used the Town Hall from its foundation in 1883 until 1989, moving with it when the Town Hall moved in the 1960s.[100] Barnstaple chamber had used the Guildhall for meetings until 1939; but when the meeting costs were raised to 10s. 6d. per meeting plus 2s. 6d. per hour for heating, and the chamber's offer of three guineas for its six meetings including heating was refused, it moved to the premises of one of its members (North Devon Bakeries) with the AGM held at Bromley's Café (owned by another member).[101] Hereford met in the YMCA, then the Town Hall, and then in hotels in the 1920s.

The chambers of trade, agriculture, and smaller trade protection societies most frequently used a local solicitor, accountant, or member business to host the organization. But the large trade protection societies were major bodies of 8–10 staff at an early date, and thus needed their own premises. Leicester TPS by 1874 had a general business office of 37 by 30 feet containing its staff, with 'two separate entrances, one for members and the other for general purposes'. In addition, there was 'an office, committee or board room' available, of 31 by 17 feet, which was used for meetings, particularly for creditors meetings.[102] A strong room was added to the general office in September 1886, 'built on space adjoining the office side wall' in

[93] Jersey chamber minutes, 10 August 1835; prior to this taverns were used.
[94] Guernsey chamber minutes, 21 January 1809.
[95] R. G. Walton, Nottingham chamber history, pp. 49–50.
[96] Sunderland chamber minutes.
[97] Aberdeen chamber, *Journal*, 1(1), October 1919, p. 1.
[98] Beresford (1951), Leeds chamber history, p. 8.
[99] V. B. Beaumont, Wolverhampton chamber history, p. 4.
[100] Oldham Archives, notes on *Accession of Oldham Chamber Archives*, D-ABJ, p. 5.
[101] Barnstaple chamber minutes, 18 April 1939; it rented its own offices only from the 1970s.
[102] Leicester TPS, *Annual Report* (1874), p. 2; in minutes, Leicester RO, DE3848/5.

an adjoining yard.[103] The board room, also referred to as a members room containing armchairs in which to relax, is listed as housing a library by 1880, mainly containing county court proceedings, circulars, lists of judgements in bankruptcy, deeds of assignment, etc.[104] The site, next to the county court, reinforced its quasi-legal status in debt recovery and regulation of creditworthiness.

Later initiatives for buildings

Later initiatives for their own buildings came in Birmingham in 1916, when £50,000 was raised from members. London moved several times before building on its current site, its aim in 1894 to ensure that its offices should be 'not inferior' to chambers in Glasgow, Dublin, Dundee, or New York and Chicago.[105] Other chambers developed buildings by linking with other organizations or services; e.g. Cardiff (from 1911) and Swansea (from 1915) launched an Exchange in which they occupied the prime space. Cardiff chamber rented offices in the Cardiff Exchange 1886–1994, which was the centre of the South Wales coal trade, where the chamber members used the Exchange itself and its newsroom (for an extra guinea per year in 1920). After many tensions, it assumed a senior role in the affairs of the Exchange after it was refurbished and extended in 1911.[106] The Swansea chamber developed the Exchange Buildings; it occupied the ground floor together with a docks post office, let the upper floors, and used the basement as an attractive restaurant.[107]

Smaller, and even some larger, chambers tended to move into the offices of one of their members (often an accountant or solicitor), of a related organization, or sometimes into a local council office or town hall. Only later did most lease or build their own accommodation. For example, Sheffield was located in different member's offices 1857–1903, before moving to the Cutlers Hall, 1903–57, and only in 1957 to its own offices.[108] At Middlesborough in the 1910–14 period, the Board Room of a local firm, Messrs. Bell Bros. Ltd., was donated for use of chamber meetings.[109] At Coventry, a local solicitors' office was used 1902–8, then a small office leased; in 1919, premises including a meeting room and two small offices were leased above a tobacconist and newspaper office; using similar premises until the 1970s, when a more prestigious location was found.[110] The Burnley chamber had been hosted by local accountancy firms from its inception in 1902, but in the late 1960s it rented its own offices when there was friction with the then host firm, as 'the chamber did not contribute to fees'.[111]

[103] Leicester TPS, minutes, DE3848/6.
[104] Leicester TPS, *Annual Report* (1890), minutes DE3848/6.
[105] London chamber, *Annual Report* (1894), p. 35.
[106] Cardiff chamber history, p. 3.
[107] Swansea chamber, *Yearbook* (1915), pp. 47–8.
[108] Sheffield chamber history.
[109] Middlesbrough chamber, *Annual Reports*.
[110] Andrew (1978), Coventry chamber history, pp. 4 and 6.
[111] Comments to author by Doreen Hitchcock, retired chamber chief executive, September 2005.

Those chambers that had no accommodation or limited premises considered themselves at a disadvantage. Barnsley in 1882 was 'considering forming a Coal and Iron Exchange in the Assembly Rooms of Barnsley Public Hall Buildings', but nothing seems to have come of this.[112] Before developing its own building Swansea felt that a major problem was 'the lack of the possession of a home of its own . . . which would be a visible existence of the chamber and a constant reminder of the objects it sought to attain'.[113] Much later, when Westminster chamber was established in 1949, it hoped to have 'its own clubroom and restaurant and a library, with sufficient staff to collect and issue the information required by members'.[114]

Kidderminster in 1902 felt that 'what was wanted at Kidderminster was an Exchange on a small scale . . . it would be an advantage to have a place where people could meet, not having to go to hotel rooms'.[115] In 1903 a discussion about establishing a reading room led to no effective action (the chamber never had its own premises). A room was considered to cost about £30 per year. 'The room was asked for by three or four members, and perhaps if they did not get a room they might lose one or two members. At the outside this would cost above £4 in (lost) subscriptions a year; they could not undertake to spend £30 to save £4. . . . While they would gladly spend £10 a year on papers, they could not undertake an expenditure of £30 or £35 a year.'[116]

For many of the small chambers the costs of a meeting room and/or library/ reading room was the major concern. North Staffordshire chamber was very worried about the costs in 1874 when it was paying £10 per year in fees for the library for its members and paid a further £5 per year for newspapers.[117] Worcester considered the possibility of establishing a new library and reading room in 1924 (it had had a library in the 1850s) and set up a committee 'to spend no more than £5 in establishing a commercial library at the chambers offices for use of members'.[118] However, it seems that this was not established because it was considered too expensive.

By 1917, the ACC was calling for all chambers to have their own offices 'where anybody can go . . . [and] to which members may resort for guidance and information, and from which the work of the chamber itself may be properly conducted'.[119] Pressures from ABCC continued for the chambers to have their own offices into the 1970s, as discussed in Chapter 8. Chambers gradually began to acquire these, even if the offices were often no more than a single room for the secretary. However, continued pressures from ABCC for dedicated offices, linked

[112] Barnsley chamber, *Annual Report* (1882).
[113] Swansea chamber, *Yearbook* (1915), p. 47.
[114] Westminster chamber chairman's statement, in *Annual Report* (1949), p. 28.
[115] Kidderminster, Annual Meeting, 1903.
[116] Kidderminster chamber minutes, containing newspaper report of meeting of 7 September 1903.
[117] North Staffordshire chamber minutes, 1874.
[118] Worcester chamber minutes, 10 December 1924.
[119] Algernon Firth, ACC president, quoted in ACC *Monthly Proceedings*, 4 October (1917), pp. 15–16.

526 Activities

to staff training and inspections, forced many small chambers to leave ABCC after 1976.

11.6. LIBRARIES

The coffee room and meeting room remained as a desired facility well into the 20th century, but most chambers moved to adopt libraries as the preferred concept for a meeting and reading place. The general evolution is shown in Figure 11.2. As with all the analysis, we must be careful about interpretation, as the survival of records, or the detail that they record, is often limited. But the pattern is clear; the facility was widespread by the 1870s, with over 50% of chambers having a facility, a figure that rose from 29% in 1840, and included almost all the large chambers. But the number then tended to decline slowly to about 30% over 1900–14 and 20% by 1950. Very few chambers of trade developed libraries. The financial difficulties of the 1930s, changes in the form of supply of information, and further economic pressures after WW2, seem to have steadily eroded their use in the 20th century.

Evolution of libraries

There is ambiguity in the form of early libraries; some were no more than collections for administrative purposes. Thus, when Limerick first built up a collection of materials, it was specialized and kept in the board room; by 1809, two years after its foundation, the contents were contained in one bookcase and consisted of Marshall on *Insurance*, Abbott on *Shipping*, Cooke's *Bankrupts Laws*, Watson on *Partnership*, Kyd on *Awards*, Baylee on *Bills*, Hautenville on *Duties, Lloyds List, Almanac and Register, Acts of Parliament* and *Votes* for current

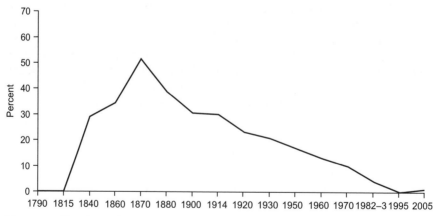

Fig. 11.2. Chambers of commerce with a library or reading room, 1790–2005 (percentage of chambers at each time period).

sessions.[120] It was only in 1830 that Limerick's Library was fully established and extended as a resource for members (see Table 11.6 below). In Belfast the first library in 1852 was an administrative reference collection, stocking Parliamentary papers and reports, reports of commissions, the *Journal of Trade*; its first two books ordered were Tooke's *History of Prices*, and Lindsay's *Navigation Laws*.[121] London's first 'library' in 1882 seems to have been only a few bookcases in the boardroom.[122]

However, whilst some libraries evolved from administrative collections, most emerged from reading/coffee rooms. Both demonstrate the shift towards more tailored services, offering a bundling of a facilitative environment for personal exchange of information with consultation of documents and more technical material, as well as the popular newspapers, with increasing scope to obtain help from specialist staff. 'Libraries' were never purely for information; they all seem to have been used also for networking and social functions. Thus in Norwich in 1847 it is explicit that personal meetings remained the key objective as well as access to library materials. Norwich chamber used the local Corn Exchange which was 'in all respects adapted to the purposes of the association, and whether, as a *rendezvous* for members, or as a newsroom, it combines most, if not all, the advantages which characterise the buildings in Newcastle and other towns, specially erected for the like object'.[123] Its critical importance was reiterated in the first annual dinner report of the chamber in 1848: 'Too many imagined it was merely a reading or a lounging room, that was not the case. The reading room was a secondary consideration' to that of meetings and deliberation.[124]

Despite the wider functions, the information value of libraries was their critical underpinning. Glasgow moved its member room into a new area in 1950 to offer 'a regular meeting place, [and] an *enquiry centre*'.[125] London linked its establishment of a reading room to the initiation of an information department in 1892, to which donations of books were encouraged.[126] A members' room was added in 1895.[127] There was some criticism of London's facilities as they were inconveniently spread across three rooms on three floors, and in 1897 it was noted that they were 'visited by a fair number of members, but not as many as hoped ... [and have] been encroached upon for storage'.[128] It moved to a ground floor room in 1903 as a 'members' room' for reading, writing, and personal interviews; the 'library' contained documents and a 'small room for personal discussion'.[129] Some members felt more was needed to attract new members, but others disagreed about the

[120] Limerick chamber minute book, accounts, 1807–8.
[121] Belfast chamber, subcommittee book, 10 April 1852.
[122] London chamber, *Annual Report* (1891), p. 37; reorganized in 1891 to make it 'accessible to members'.
[123] Letter from 'Norvicencis', April 1847; in J. J. Coleman collection, *Scrapbook of News Cuttings* NFK/QC, N942.615, Norfolk Local Studies Library.
[124] President's address at first annual dinner, 26 January 1848; NFK/QC, N942.615, op. cit.
[125] Glasgow chamber, *Journal*, February 1950, *Annual Report*; emphasis added.
[126] London chamber Executive minutes, 8 October 1891.
[127] London chamber, *Annual Report* (1895).
[128] London chamber, *Annual Report* (1897), p. 68.
[129] London chamber, *Annual Report* (1903), p. 20; Musgrave (1914), p. 70.

need for 'tea, coffee and smoking rooms, because we are all busy men'.[130] Coffee remained unavailable: it 'was for use for appointments, letter writing and reclining, and consulting books and papers'.[131]

The provision of libraries was significant enough for chambers to be wary of an initiative by an Association of Special Libraries and Information Bureaux in 1927, for public libraries 'to promote the use of sources in science, industry, commerce and public affairs and foster cooperation with translation and abstracting'. This was a direct competition from the public sector, and the ABCC declined to join.[132]

Resourcing libraries

Many chambers founded libraries through additional subscriptions; e.g. Limerick established its library in 1830 with a foundation subscription from 47 of its members, which rose to 51 by 1832, after which the costs were consolidated with the general accounts.[133] In Cardiff in the 1890s the Exchange offered a commercial library and reading room, and the service was subscribed to by a large percentage of the chamber members (98–9%). Since it yielded about £400 per year in subscriptions, the rent of about £28 and other costs allowed substantial surplus for the Exchange. This tension, and the frequently missing papers from the rooms,[134] led the chamber to set up its own and exclusive library in 1901 (perhaps overlapping with the Exchange, it is not entirely clear), and doubled its subscription to two guineas 'for which a comfortable, well furnished commercial library and reading room would be provided and files of the principal papers kept for the use of members. The secretary also to keep an index of all commercial cases likely to be of interest.'[135] The central problem was that the Exchange at one guinea undercut the chamber at two guineas, and exclusiveness of access could not be assured.[136] However, by 1903 'better control of it' was sought and proposals by the Exchange were thought 'most unsatisfactory' and were never resolved.[137] This continued until 1911, when 'a syndicate of commercial gentlemen was formed . . . leased . . . the whole of the offices on the second floor . . . including a separate corridor entrance. . . . [with] a spacious conference hall, with an attached council room and secretary's office'.[138]

---

[130] Exchange between Mr Urquahart Fisher and Mr Thomas Brooke-Hitching at London AGM; London, *CCJ*, May (1905), p. 110.

[131] *Annual Report* (1891), p. 37.

[132] ABCC, Home Affairs Committee, 5 January and 13 July 1927.

[133] Limerick chamber, Library Committee book, P1/56.

[134] Letter from Mr C. E. Evans, reported in Cardiff chamber Council minutes, 12 July 1899, complaining that 'newspapers . . . were often missing' from the reading room.

[135] Cardiff chamber, Council minutes, 7 December 1900.

[136] Cardiff chamber, Council minutes, 14 October 1903.

[137] Cardiff chamber, Council minutes, 29 October 1903; Report to council by subcommittee and deputation to the Exchange, 13 November 1903.

[138] Cardiff chamber, *Annual Report* (1911), p. 17.

This arrangement of joint membership, or reduced subscription relationships, with other bodies offering meeting room/reading room facilities, was used elsewhere, as for Cork, Waterford, Dundee, and Lancaster discussed above. The Manchester chamber of the 1820s used the local Exchange building, which since 1729 had been the main meeting place for manufacturers and merchants. The new building of 1808 initially had a bar with a barkeeper whose duties included 'supply and preserve files of newspapers, but also supply waiters', although the catering duties were abolished after one year. Its membership in 1809 numbered 1543, with most of the chamber also members of it.[139] Newport chamber (Mon.) had a system of additional subscriptions to the Daily Exchange Room. In 1884 there were 148 chamber subscribers to the Exchange Room at 10s. 6d. when the chamber subscription was one guinea, with a membership of 187 (79%). This arrangement operated from the early 1880s and closed before 1897.[140]

However, there were often tensions of joint memberships, particularly over different subscription levels and the level of benefits and use by chamber members. For example, the Derby chamber 'made an amalgamation with the Athenaeum News Room' in about 1864 shortly after the chamber was formed, and this suggests a close link between the two in the foundation process. But the two demerged in 1871 when it 'was found impossible satisfactorily to carry on the societies as amalgamated'. However, the News Room was taken over again in 1888, but after 1894 'was not sufficiently used to warrant its continuance' and was closed.[141]

The Belfast chamber used the Commercial Newsroom in the 1880s, available to members at an additional charge of two guineas (at a time when the chamber subscription was £1), although a proposal to merge the two organizations was voted down by the members, as 'not many of the chamber members were members of the newsroom and the costs were seen as too high'.[142] The office of the York chamber was first located with The Merchant Adventurers, which provided a reading room. In 1897 they found their own premises, but by 1900 gave it up, as 'so little use has been made of the reading room', and moved back to the Merchants Hall.[143] Guernsey had an active reading room from 1858, with some papers (such as the *Globe*) taken specifically to attract new members. The sale of papers was a useful income to the chamber.[144] But the opening by the States of the Guille-Allès library in 1894 caused a decline in use of the chamber's reading room, though it continued for a few more years.[145]

The ABCC also developed its own members' area after 1949 under the inspiration of its secretary Arthur Knowles. He proposed a lounge hall, the council room

---

[139] See Helm (1897), pp. 7–8.
[140] Newport chamber minutes.
[141] Quoted in Derby chamber minutes, 1916, p. 37.
[142] Belfast chambers history, pp. 216–17.
[143] York chamber, *Annual Report* (1897), p. 15 and (1901), p. 4.
[144] Guernsey chamber, minutes 15 and 28 December 1858; General Meeting, 27 January 1863.
[145] Guernsey chamber, General Meeting 28 August 1896, reports a long discussion on retaining the room.

used as a clubroom with writing facilities and 'something of a library', use of a telephone, and use of the postal address for overseas visitors.[146] It was directed towards individual subscribing members, but did not take off. The individual member scheme, revived under Knowles, increased the members to only 206 in 1949 from 137 in 1948, and then numbers steadily declined until the scheme was cancelled in 1958. It appears that only the executive committee members used the ABCC members' area. When the ABCC moved to the London chamber in 1960 the room disappeared.

Libraries as a chamber offer

The high price of publications, particularly newspapers and journals, and the bother of getting them delivered as speedily as possible offered an opportunity for a chamber to take on: there is a considerable volume of minutes in all cases of these reading rooms relating to trying to improve the performance of delivery agents; this was clearly a time-consuming hassle which was willingly passed to the chamber or other organizations.

The journals and even newspapers were expensive, particularly as a daily or weekly item of expenditure (newspapers cost 2½d. in the 1750s: equal to about £2 today), which included a hated ½d. Stamp Tax. This meant that a tradition developed of selling-on, handing-on, and holding them in communal premises (such as coffee houses). The chambers took on this market opportunity. The costs were indeed considerable; in 1850 Limerick chamber was paying £106 per year for library costs, of which £66 was for newspapers, £9 for magazines, 10 guineas for Lloyds List, and £20 for the Attorney List, plus books ordered. This rose to £133 in 1860 plus the costs of a librarian (about £30). For smaller traders a commercial library offered great advantages of costs and effort; and for both the large and small trader there was the convenience of an association getting this material, and combining the library with functions of society, discourse, and cohesion. Thus, for the rich merchant Falk family in Liverpool and Northwich in the 1860s–1920s period, the Salt chamber was less important for the cost savings on publications than for the cohesion and potential influence it offered over the other salt merchants.[147] The same is replicated among the Sheffield cutlers and steel makers, Bradford woollen merchants and manufacturers, Birmingham gun makers and metal industries, and so on in other areas.[148]

Costs also had an impact on how chambers had to manage their reading rooms, with chamber minutes recording continuous changes of rules over resale of papers and limiting theft. For example, Guernsey in 1809 instituted a fine of one guinea on a member removing any book or paper.[149] Cork's foundation rule in 1819 was

---

[146] Knowles (1949), pp. 11–12.
[147] See Chaloner (1961), Salt chamber history; Clapham (1926), p. 200; and analysis of the Salt chamber in Chapter 12.
[148] See e.g. Wright (1913); Money (1977); Hamilton (1967); Clapham (1926, 1932); Ashton (1963).
[149] Guernsey chamber minutes, 21 January 1809.

repeated as rule VIII in 1881: that 'any person taking away, tearing, or defacing any newspaper or paper belonging to the room shall be forthwith expelled'. In 1819 no newspaper was to be held by the reader for more than 15 minutes after being requested by another reader. Small locks were purchased for the lockers holding the newspapers and books, administered by the reading room waiters.[150] When *The Examiner* newspaper was missing from Cork's reading room in January 1820, a notice was put up asking for aid to 'the committee in the discovery of any person' and the waiters were fined 5s. When the paper was returned the waiters' fine was revoked.[151] Rules against lending newspapers continued to be enforced by the attending waiters.[152] The plethora of rules and minutes of discussions about library behaviour indicate that the papers were well read and heavily in demand. Libraries also combined readily into a service bundle with meetings and tailored support, with the positive by-product of involvement through very active bidding for selling on copies of newspapers.

Thus a library was a significant chamber opportunity, with the largest chambers having considerable collections. The 18th-century Glasgow Tontine Coffee House, linked with the chamber, took all the Scottish newspapers, 'but also the greatest part of those published in London, as well as some from Ireland, France, etc, beside reviews, magazines, and other periodical publications'.[153] The Glasgow chamber held 3,000 volumes by 1881.[154] By the end of the 19th century the London chamber had an extensive library, which was costing it £67 per year to maintain in 1899. Its full list of periodicals was first published in 1901.[155] It then contained 106 British newspapers and other periodicals, 87 foreign and colonial, 74 books of reference (mostly technical manuals and foreign information source books), 55 directories (mostly foreign), and 72 official trade returns and statistical volumes (almost all foreign except for six UK government annual reports). This was 394 items, far more than the smaller chambers listed in Table 11.6, though even then it is referred to as a 'selected list' in the case of books, directories, and statistical volumes. London had 7000 volumes in 1961.[156] By 1975 it was taking over 1500 trade journals and magazines.

In addition, many chambers also tried to gather information that was directly relevant to locally concentrated industries, e.g. Newcastle, Cardiff, Newport, and Swansea for the coal industry; Birmingham for metals; London, Liverpool, and Manchester for various foreign companies, banking, and financial concerns. A crucial activity of the Salt Chamber was the purchase of the Customs' returns for the major ports through which salt was shipped (e.g. in 1870 for the ports of

---

[150] Cork chamber minutes; committee meeting, 29 January 1819; rules 8 and 10, General Meeting 13 November 1819; *New Rules of Chamber of Commerce Room*, Cork, 1881 in ABCC loose papers MS 14477/1.
[151] Cork chamber minutes, 7 and 12 January 1820.
[152] Cork chamber minutes, 6 April 1852.
[153] James Denholm (1797), *An Historical Account of the City of Glasgow* (Glasgow: R. Chapman), p. 109.
[154] See Oakley (1983), Glasgow chamber history.
[155] Glasgow chamber, *Annual Report* (1901), pp. 128–33.
[156] London chamber, *Annual Report* (1961).

Liverpool, Runcorn, Weston, Middlesbrough, Stockton-on-Tees, West Hartle-pool, Gloucester, Bristol, Sharpness, Carrickfergus, London, and Fleetwood), costing £94 per year in 1929 and the main expenditure.

We should also remember that reading matter was not viewed in the 18th or 19th centuries as a purely individual or personal matter: 'For the majority of the literate, reading was ... often a communal activity.'[157] Thus the items in news-papers, latest goods inward, parliamentary, or other reports would frequently be read out loud and discussed in the library. In Glasgow, we have the comment that in the 1750s–1790s 'the principal merchants ... resorted to the coffee house or tavern to read the newspapers, which they generally did in companies of four or five in separate rooms'.[158] The Leeds subscription library society afforded 'materials for general conversation';[159] like Liverpool's this had substantial overlap with chamber members. A first-hand account of the Glasgow Tontine Coffee House in 1797, the chamber's home, gives a vivid view:

> At the daily arrival of the mail (bringing the newspapers and journals), a more stirring, lively and anxious scene can hardly be imagined. Indeed, no part of the day passes without some concourse of subscribers, or of strangers ... At those hours when the news of the morning may be said to have grown cold, the monthly publications claim attention in their turn, or people meet for the sake of looking out their acquaintance, or of engaging in casual parties of conversation.[160]

Similarly New York chamber had a meeting room from the outset and a library from 1840, where meetings were recognized as occasions when 'pleasure and business were joined together in the gatherings of the solid men'.[161]

As well as informal discourse, the formal meetings frequently involved reading out reports, letters received, and replies sent. The formal papers clearly derived in many cases from earlier casual discussions at the chamber. The published reports of local chambers sought to disseminate the discussion to the wider membership, and to other chambers and, after 1860, to ACC. Most were included in local news-papers (until the mid-20th century) becoming available to non-members as well. The ACC/ABCC *Monthly Proceedings* and *Annual Reports* have the same discursive format. They record meetings of papers read aloud, discussions of them, and reportage that is meant to convey the nature of the discourse to those who were not present.

Indeed, those chambers that provided merely a library without a social milieu, or offered merely a point of access in their offices where documents could be consulted, found them less used. To be effective, a library had to be combined

---

[157] Cambers and Wolfe (2004), p. 890.

[158] Carlyle (1805; 1910 edition), *The Autobiography of Dr. Alexander Carlyle of Inveresk, 1722–1805* (London: T. N. Foulis), p. 84.

[159] R. Thoresby (1816), *Ducartus Leodiensis*, p. 86 (ed. T. D. Whitaker); quoted in Morris (1990), p. 171.

[160] James Denholm (1797), *An Historical Account of the City of Glasgow* (Glasgow: R. Chapman), p. 109.

[161] John Austin Stevens jnr. (1867), looking back at early meetings; in Bishop (1918), p. 9.

with the scope for drop-in meetings and discussion opportunities. Thus, many chambers might state in annual reports and other papers that documents were available at the chamber; for example, Preston in 1921 noted 'a large amount of information is filed at the offices of the Chamber. Many trade and other journals, foreign and colonial trade catalogues . . . may be seen on application'.[162] The Worcester chamber library was theoretically available to the whole local business community in the 1850s, but in practice had a very cumbersome process of consultation: it was open to 'any respectable citizen . . . [with] a letter of introduction from one of the members or the secretary, and the member is accountable for the book [that was borrowed]'.[163] These were not convenient drop-in facilities; as stated by London, they had to be 'accessible to members'.[164]

In more modern times chambers have rediscovered some of the concepts lying behind meeting rooms and the library. The 'library' may no longer be the appropriate concept, but many chambers and most other business organizations have established networking opportunities, business breakfasts, and other social or marketing events to facilitate member-to-member exchanges. For the IoD drop-in meeting rooms are a core function. Birmingham had a social 'club' with catering and bar from c.1900 up to WW2. One of the more successful modern chamber examples was Croydon, which ran a licensed club/bar in the 1980s and 1990s,[165] which was a successor to its 1960s golfing society and car club, themselves following a bowls and sports club of the 1930s. Croydon appears to be the only modern chamber to have had a bar. Its financial success was mixed, but new staff and management controls turned losses of £16,000 per year on the bar and catering in 1982 to a surplus of £20,000 per year by 1985, and this was linked with a major period of increased membership after previous declines;[166] (membership grew in Croydon from a steady level of 965–85 in 1979–83, to 1227 in 1985).[167] In 2006, now merged as a section of the London chamber, Croydon re-established its golf club. Most other chambers have social sections, golf days, or other similar events.[168] In 2009 St Helens chamber established a drop-in café facility.

Content of libraries

The content of the reading rooms/libraries in the early period tells us something of the motivations, associations, and social categorization of the members.[169] Table 11.6 gives five examples from contrasted local situations, and ranging from small to

---

[162] Preston chamber, *Annual Report* (1921), p. 28.
[163] Worcester chamber, *Library Rules*, Minute Book, 4 October 1853.
[164] *Annual Report* (1891), p. 37.
[165] Croydon chamber, *Directories* and *Annual Reports* (1930–95).
[166] Croydon history, p. 13.
[167] Croydon, *Annual Reports and Accounts*.
[168] e.g. Barnstaple since the 1960s up to the present: Sheffield had a Golf Committee 1936–76 and a General Entertainments Committee 1947–62; it also had a canteen 1950–60.
[169] Langford (1989); Ellis (2004).

larger chambers across the 19th century. This demonstrates a strong emphasis on daily and weekly newspapers, which dominate the lists, and these newspapers come from a variety of the major commercial cities and ports, not just local or London papers. These examples appear typical, and are corroborated by the briefer information in other chambers.

The active chamber reading rooms clearly served a general purpose as well as a commercial library, with the daily newspapers being critical. The focus on foreign trade and parliamentary information is also clear. As stated in Falmouth, the chamber in 1866–22 'stocked all the papers on shipping and world news for the convenience of ships captains'.[170] This reflects the specific demand of early chamber members for up-to-date trade and overseas shipping and commercial intelligence. The primary motive for stocking reading material was topical information (primarily the newspapers), and other commercial sources. The Jersey chamber in the 1890s differentiated the eight main newspapers (including the French *Semaine financière*) that were filed in its reading room, from the other 25 papers and journals in the library.[171] This demonstrates the different styles of room, as well as the need to police to prevent theft.

In addition to the newspapers and journals listed in Table 11.6, the other main items were commercial listings (chiefly annual lists), commercial directories, railway timetables, and more popular weekly magazines, and books.[172] BoT papers, Blue Books, House of Commons *Journal*, *Labour Gazette*, monthly reports of consuls in foreign ports, reports of other government departments, annual reports of other chambers in the UK and overseas, various yearbooks and directories, and official lists of Bills in parliament were often obtained on exchange in many cases. Hence policy and statistical materials were also important. The York chamber argued when it set up a small library in 1899 that 'members (should) . . . gain considerable advantages from a personal provision of the various papers whereby they would ascertain the opinion of the commercial world at large on the important commercial questions of the day'.[173] Some chambers held a wide range of general books as well as purely commercial texts; e.g. in Limerick early book orders were *Wild Sports of the West*, *Adventures of a Younger Son*, *Traits of Irish Character*, *Humboldt's Travels*, *Southey's Lives of Uneducated Poets*, etc., as well as a number of accounts of voyages and reports on individual countries.[174] Hence, general information and broader education were parts of member demand, with many chamber minutes recording considerable debate over purchase of particular items.

---

[170] Falmouth chamber history, p. 30.
[171] e.g. listing in Jersey chamber *Annual Report*, 1891.
[172] See e.g. Plymouth chamber, *Annual Report* (1920, 1930); Kidderminster chamber, *Annual Report* (1923); Oldham chamber, *Annual Report* (1930); Dublin chamber, *Reference Library List*, 1925, 1950 (listed in *Annual Reports*); Cork and Waterford chamber minutes also record book and paper purchases.
[173] York chamber, *Annual Report* (1899), p. 9.
[174] Limerick chamber, Library Committee Book, P 1/56, 1831–2.

Table 11.6. Main items on regular subscriptions for the reading rooms of five chambers 1813–1898

Newcastle-upon-Tyne 1813[a]	Limerick 1837[b]	Dundee 1835–9[c]	Norwich 1847[d]	Lancaster 1898[e]
Courier (London Daily)	Times (London Daily)	The Globe (London Daily)	The Times	The Times (3 copies)
Star (London Daily)	Globe (London Daily)	The Sun & Public Ledger (London Daily)	Morning Herald	Standard
Globe (London Daily)	Sun (London Daily)	The Observer (London, Sunday)	Morning Chronicle	Daily News
Statesman (London Daily) Stopped 1814	Standard (London Daily)	Courant & Advertiser (Edinburgh)	Daily News	Daily Graphic
Pilot (London Daily) Stopped 1815	Shipping Gazette (London Daily)	Chronicle (Glasgow) 1836 replaced by Glasgow Courier	Standard	Daily Mail
Public Ledger (weekly; 3 times per week 1814)	Examiner (weekly)	Chronicle (Liverpool)	Gleaner	Manchester Guardian
Examiner (Sunday paper)	Bell's Messenger (weekly)	Advertiser (Liverpool)	Sun	Manchester Courier
Drakards (Sunday paper)	Naval and Military Gazette (weekly)	7 Dundee papers	London Stock Exchange List	York Post
Walkers (Newcastle paper)	Times (Liverpool weekly)	Daily shipping List (London)	Norfolk Chronicle	Leeds Mercury
Hodgsons (Newcastle paper)	Myres Advertiser (Liverpool weekly)	Price Current (London)	Norwich Mercury	Liverpool Post
Mitchells (Newcastle paper)	Chronicle (Glasgow 3 per week)	1836 Onwards Standard (London)	Norfolk News	Manchester Evening Mail
Humbles (Newcastle paper)	Clyde Commercial (Glasgow 3 per week)	Shipping Gazette (London Daily)	Mark Lane Express	Manchester Evening News
Liverpool (Daily)	Mercantile Register (Belfast weekly)	Fraser's Magazine (Monthly)	Railway Times	Lancaster Daily Post (4 copies)
Hull (Daily)	Constitution (Cork 3 per week)	Hull Advertiser	Law List	Lancaster Daily Spectator

(*continued*)

Table 11.6. Continued

Newcastle-upon-Tyne 1813[a]	Limerick 1837[b]	Dundee 1835–9[c]	Norwich 1847[d]	Lancaster 1898[e]
Leith (Daily)	South Reporter (Cork 3 per week)	Courier (London)	Economist	Western Gazette
New Price Current Stopped 1814	Chronicle (Waterford 3 per week)	The Spectator	Price Current (Tuesdays and Fridays)	Mid Herald
Lloyds List	Import and Export List (Waterford 3 per week)	Anti-Corn Law Circular		Illustrated London News
Shipping List	5 Dublin papers	Custom House List of Exports and Imports (London)		Graphic
Newcastle Gazette	5 Limerick papers	Various Dundee Newspapers		

Sources: [a] Newcastle, Commercial Coffee House/Reading Room (Tyne & Wear Archives);
[b] Limerick chamber, Library Committee book (Limerick Archives P1/55);
[c] Dundee Baltic Coffee House and chamber minutes (Dundee Archives);
[d] Norwich chamber *Annual Report* 1847 (J. J. Coleman Collection NFK/QC N942.615; Norwich Local Studies Library);
[e] Lancaster Merchants Reading Room (Account books, at Lancaster chamber).

11.7. CONCLUSION

The earliest chambers and other commercial societies had no doubts or inhibitions about their activities demanding a social as well as a formal dimension. Meetings, votes, arbitration, and other services all joined together to demand informal society as well as formal discourse and deliberation. Discourse in turn offered involvement, commitment, and loyalty; discourse was also the means by which the chamber's members deliberated, underpinned its key lobbying services, and made its decisions. Discourse was also the means for members to gain social involvement in the network of business relations in the local community as a whole, and develop links to raise capital, manage wealth and inheritance, and balance credit and debt, as noted in Chapter 14.

Discourse and deliberation remained an important part of the way chambers operated well into the 20th century. However, this was increasingly challenged by, first, the pressures to conform to the templates pressed by the ACC/ABCC for chambers to grow in size beyond the scale for intimate involvement—the national versus the local view; and second, to develop significant service activities that required the management to move towards professional staff. Thus, a report by the chamber secretaries in 1967 noted with criticism 'that a firm becomes a member of its local chamber not to obtain detailed services but simply out of a sense of loyalty to be a "member of a club", and to be able, in case of need, to cooperate with other like-minded businessmen in dealings with central and local government.... [This] is an outlook that has developed over the years because it has been found that the chambers concerned have been incapable of doing more.'[175] This became unacceptable to the national association and was squeezed from the template and inspection regime of chambers in the 1970s. This was a strong contrast to the small NCT chambers, which remained focused on social and networking functions throughout the 20th century, as they still are.

The traditional chambers might be dismissed as a 'talking shop' or 'club' by others, especially government. But this is to miss a key point—chambers were in existence to facilitate talk! Business operations required discourse with others. From this flowed marketing and business opportunities, but also mechanisms to form views and to lobby, through deliberation. Those chambers with coffee rooms could offer a major service that members wanted, with a library, newspapers, and conversation. It gave these chambers a comfortable resource base, allowed finance of a fine building, which became a central focus of local activity, and allowed them to do many other things for their members which other chambers were unable to do.

In modern times there have been many challenges to this nexus of discourse–involvement–deliberation–solidarity–society–milieu–organization. But the basic concept seemed to hold together until the 1980s, at which point the lapsing and turnover of membership has moved to a new level. Increasing numbers of lapsers

[175] *The Functions and Structure of Chambers of Commerce*, Dixon Report; Association of Chamber Secretaries, paper G.155–67; copy at Ipswich/Suffolk chamber; see Chapter 8.

have had to be matched by recruiting new joiners, who have to be assimilated.[176] Achieving involvement with such rapid turnover is challenging. But even in the 21st century, and with the dominance of the Internet, social exchange remains important. A large-scale survey of chambers in 2006 showed 58% of members valued social events as a major or minor motive for membership, and 93% valued chambers to keep them informed. Even among lapsers from chamber membership, social events accounted for 39%, and information/news for 66% of motives for joining. Events and access to information are among the most significant explanatory factors in statistical tests of member motivation.[177]

However, whilst all modern chambers have activities such as networking events, dinners, and business breakfasts, only one modern chamber runs a WIFI and café service, St Helens, which established this in 2009. Other chambers have conference suites, but St Helens is the only drop-in offer that mirrors earlier chamber facilities: it has been very successful, providing a hub for the whole chamber building and the membership: 'the fact that it is at the chamber itself, people know where it is—and they can park there—really makes it more attractive for businesses to come in'; networking and other events 'have never had so much take-up'.[178] The meeting rooms provided by IoD at its central and regional offices are a rival offer, and in the 21st century a key aspect of the services of business clubs has been provision of meeting rooms, offices, and desks where people can meet and work. Both IoD and clubs charge much higher subscriptions than chambers for individual members.[179] They, and St Helens, show the scope for this additional chamber service. The analysis of milieus for discourse provided in this chapter thus lays down challenges to those policies that see the future of business associations in narrower service terms. This is a challenge both to BCC and some of its accreditation standards, and to government policy in how it sees and values business bodies.

---

[176] See Chapter 16.

[177] Mekic (2007), tables 17-12, 17-17.

[178] Comments to author by Kath Boullen, St Helens chamber chief executive, 2 February 2010.

[179] Typically a top London suite costs £1500 p.a., whilst IoD membership was over £300 in 2010: see 'Private member clubs enjoy upside of downturn', *Financial Times*, 7 February 2009; compared to chamber membership for individuals in 2010 which ranged from £75 (Isle of Wight and St Helens) to £302 (Northants.), with most £120–220.

12

Services

12.1 INTRODUCTION

Modern chambers offer a wide range of services. Table 12.1 summarizes the position in 1996. It illustrates the service bundle in six broad groups: meetings, networking and information exchange; delivery of information and advice; support for international trade; managerial and workforce training; specific market services offered at a discount; and member communications. These services were variable across the chamber system, with not all chambers offering all elements. Since 1996 the system has become more uniform as a result of national accreditation and inspection, instituted fully from 1998 in the UK and 2005 in Ireland. Government-supported services draw on groups 2–4, but are excluded from the table.

The chamber services discussed in this chapter focus on the most important of those listed in the Table. They are delivered to individual businesses, directly contributing to strategy and resources. They are a mixture of excludable and non-excludable activities, some of which relate strongly from the collective aspect of chambers (their trust and 'mutuality'), and others that are largely free-standing 'entrepreneurial' activities. This offers scope for (i) reduced transaction costs deriving from improved tailoring and quality, or from the unique environments of trust enjoyed by chambers; (ii) links to local networks between members, experiential learning and search; and (iii) joint service bundles that mitigate free-rider problems and prevent collective action becoming a by-product. These services are part of the chambers 'bundled' offer (see Table 3.1), complementing lobbying and milieus (discussed in Chapter 9–11), and are the main fields used for contracting and service support to government (discussed in Chapter 13).

It is easy to see how the modern pattern of chamber services evolved. Interaction with members to respond to enquiries for specific information and help was a natural extension of using a chamber as a meeting room, becoming common chiefly from the 1920s coinciding with the period when export document certification became more widespread. Indeed the two aspects were interlinked in most cases. Subsequently, the latter half of the 20th century saw much more extensive service developments.

Table 12.1. The main services offered by chambers of commerce in 1996 and percentage of 62 BCC chambers offering each service

Service	%	Service	%
1. Meetings/groups		**4. Training**	
Networking events	98	Member company training	77
Conferences	69	Youth and adult training	56
Seminars	60	**5. Discounted Services**	
Room hire	53	Translation	34
Exhibitions	87	Fax bureau	23
Export club	68	British Standards sales	29
SME group	47	Health and safety schemes	53
Ethnic minority group	18	Fleet hire	50
Women in business	44	Book discounts	40
2. Advice		Health care	34
Information/enquiry service	90	Telecom discounts	56
International trade advice	95	Insurance schemes	24
Euro Info Centre	21	Direct mail	69
Consultancy on exports	55	Member-to-member discounts	71
Legal advice	53		
3. International trade support		**6. Communications**	
Missions outward	47	Electronic data interchange	37
Missions inward	53	Website	32
Trade fair visits outward	24	Internet	58
Certificates of origin	97	Newsletter	98
Arab certificates of origin	87	Members directory	98
ATA carnets	37		

Note: The table is specific to UK chambers but would be similar for Ireland.
Source: BCC *Directory* (1996).

12.2 EARLY SERVICES

The earliest chamber services beyond those of lobbying and deliberation were usually highly specialist. For example, New York chamber began from its outset in 1768 to operate as a standards body, to set a standard ton weight, standard rate for coins, and it intervened in the local flour and baking trade to ensure stable supply and quality.[1] The early Irish chambers all became involved in regulating butter, hide, flax, or provision markets to ensure weight and quality standards. Edinburgh employed a lighthouseman in 1786, and Glasgow an arbiter of thread in the 1790s. Manchester chamber was managing a testing house and laboratory for cotton goods in the early 1900s.[2] Leeds sought to regulate the moisture content of

---

[1] See Stevens (1867); Bishop (1918), pp. 17–22.
[2] *Manchester chamber, Handbook and Rules*, 1918; John Rylands Library.

wool in the 1880s.[3] In Luton a plait measurer regulated quality and size of the plaits used in the production of straw hats. These controls were at the most personal level, demonstrating efforts to maintain quality circles and networks; e.g. in 1881 in Luton the chamber's 'plait measurer...stated that he had seen certain plaits... which although it should be measured 20 yards to the score only measured 16 yards to the score—such plait had been made by Emma Ellis of Flitwick'.[4]

The Irish chambers became the most deeply involved in local market regulation. Limerick appears to have had the largest scale. This came from taking on regulatory and marketing functions that had been exercised by earlier guilds (especially the Staplers) and the local corporation, which had fallen into disuse. From its foundation in 1805, Limerick became involved in the potato and butter market (introducing five levels and quality marks on butter in 1820). It also regulated slaughterhouses and gave quality marks to hides and skins, for which it charged fees. These activities yielded considerable income, as well as requiring expenditure and administrative staff. By 1810 it was receiving £2823 income, with £377 from the import and export fund, £2302 from the toll and custom fund, £144 from the hide and skin fund, £472 from the butter fund, and a net loss on the seed fund. Expenditure was £2082, leaving a profit of over £700; by 1811 it had accumulated reserves of £2000, which had increased to £4000 by 1815. It spent £1000 of its reserves on constructing a Linen Hall within which it organized a weekly market, and established premiums for quality cloth, yarn, and flax, erected scutching mills, and imported flax seeds. This was taken over by the Limerick Agricultural Association in the 1820s. Limerick was a very entrepreneurial chamber. It also issued £500 in silver tokens in 1808 when there was a coin shortage.[5] In 1819 it tried to establish more scutching mills, and erected a flax mill.[6] By 1819–22 it was seeking stronger representation at the Irish Linen Board.[7]

Many chambers were also active in improvement of local harbour board administration, which was frequently corrupt and considered expensive. Dublin, Waterford, and Limerick at various times over 1807–1840s employed the harbour master. One of Belfast's earliest activities in 1783 sought a navigation light on the South Rock at the entrance to its harbour, and raised a fund of £2000 to commission a feasibility study to ascertain how best to straighten the River Lagan from the Quay to Garmoyle. It also raised a fund of £4000 in 1783 to build and fit new fishing vessels to improve local supplies, with shares offered first to the chamber members (up to a maximum of ten shares at £25, to limit dominance) then opened to the public. In 1784 it commissioned a survey of the harbour, and in

---

[3] Beresford (1951), Leeds chamber history.

[4] Luton chamber, Council minutes, 13 January 1881, p. 64.

[5] Limerick minutes and accounts; see Wakeford (1812); Lenihan (1866), *Limerick History and Antiquities* (Dublin); Prendeville (1930), p. 28; O'Connor (1938).

[6] Letter from Limerick chamber, 6 March 1819; PRONI D562/6947.

[7] Letters from Limerick chamber, 30 December 1819, 3 January 1820; memorial 27 February 1822: PRONI D562/7317, 7490, 7491.

1785 led cooperation to raise subscriptions to build the Linen Hall, setting up a lottery in 1787 to design and complete the construction. In 1792 it set up an inquiry into improving the quays and widening the Limekiln Dock; it also waged a campaign to clean up the quays from clutter, and threatened that its members would withhold their quayage dues from the freeholders, the Ballast Corporation, and Mr Grey (who were the offenders in cluttering the quays), if they did not comply.[8] In 1802 it was investigating improvements to the canal to Loch Neagh, and set up a subscription of £2000 in shares of £10 to buy 3–4 lighters to improve movement of cargoes.[9] Other activities to improve the docks and canals continued throughout the early 19th century; one of its most ambitious undertakings, in 1825, called a public meeting to lay a duty of either 1d. per ton on coal imports at Belfast, or 1s. per entry of inward and outward entries at the custom house, to pay £10,000 for the cost of a canal from Loch Erne to Loch Neagh.[10]

In Jersey, harbour improvements were a major source of friction with the States from 1768 until the 1900s! In Guernsey the States were more supportive, but it was again the chamber that created the pressure for change. Falmouth was continually pressing for harbour and navigation improvements. Londonderry was still receiving £22,000 per year from its involvement in improvements though the Harbour Trust in 1907.[11] Jersey, Belfast, and Liverpool chambers were all involved in taking the lead in developing marine societies to relieve the distress of seamen and their families, a role that Thomas Mortimer had advocated in 1772.[12] Falmouth chamber committed a considerable time and proportion of its income to procuring and installing a Time Ball in 1895, overhauling it in 1902. It was also a prime mover in installing a bell buoy on the Manacle Rocks, and promotion of pilotage, lifeboats, and lighthouses.[13] Limerick paid for clearing rocks from the harbour in 1808 and erecting a beacon on the Reeves Rock in 1815.[14] Waterford was pressing for improvements in the Hook Tower light from its foundation in 1787, with the harbour quays being continuing concerns into 1811 and 1816.[15] Similar harbour, lighthouse, and navigation services occupied other port-based chambers whether actually undertaking works, getting others to do so, or seeking effective management and economical costs. Trinity House was often criticized. Voluntary and possibly less serious services were those of the chaplain in the Edinburgh chamber in 1789–93, a consulting chemist in

[8] Belfast chamber minutes, 6 and 12 November 1783; 8 December 1784; 13 March 1785, 3 March 1787; 20 February–3 March 1792.
[9] Belfast chamber minutes, 20 April 1802.
[10] Belfast chamber minutes, 31 March 1825.
[11] Relevant chamber minutes; Londonderry entry in *Chamber of Commerce Handbook* (1908), Bristol chamber.
[12] Jersey: Syvret and Stevens (1998); Belfast chamber, minutes 10 November 1784; Liverpool: Bennett (2010).
[13] Falmouth chamber history, pp. 29–31, 36.
[14] O'Connor (1938).
[15] Waterford chamber minutes; Cowman (1988), Waterford chamber history.

Norwich, and meteorologist in Lancaster chamber in the 1930s,[16] each of which seem to have existed for only a few years. An offer for a volunteer honorary translator at Birmingham was declined in 1916.[17]

12.3 PUBLICATIONS AND COMMUNICATIONS

The earliest publications by chambers, apart from their 'memorials' and petitions, were usually various forms of annual reports. After this, journals, and then a wide range of handbooks and other publications were developed. The overall evolution is shown in Figure 12.1, demonstrating the shift from one-off pamphlets in the early period toward synoptic annual reports, then journals, in turn to be superseded by a barrage of specialist leaflets and reports from the 1980s. The chambers of trade show similar but later evolution.

Annual reports

By the 1880s most established chambers were publishing an annual report of at least 20 pages, but some were several hundred pages long. These usually consisted of a review of the year's activities, often including transcripts of the main letters sent, any memorials, and in some cases the replies received. The report could also contain a message or address by the president, a report by the secretary, or a report of the formal AGM. Most reports also contained financial accounts from the 1890s,

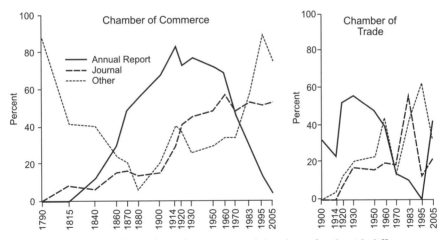

Fig. 12.1. Percentage of chambers of commerce and chambers of trade with different types of publications, 1790–2005.

---

[16] Edinburgh chamber history; Lancaster chamber, minutes 1930.
[17] Birmingham chamber GPC minutes, 26 October 1916.

though frustratingly many restrict this to a brief comment from the treasurer on the balances held.

Some annual reports also contain a list of members, at least for some years. Other reports contain significant amounts of statistical material, either national information (e.g. import and export volumes) or local information (such as their port statistics, or local freight volumes).[18] The Blackburn and Burnley chambers from the 1890s into the 1930s listed the number of spindles and looms for each firm in North-East Lancashire. In the 1820s Cork reported the statistics of all articles coming into or out of the port, with each committee member taking turns to make entries for one month.[19] Dundee published a shipping report from its earliest days, employing a keeper for this purpose at a salary of £8 in 1835. The service was only stopped in 1935 now that 'full shipping information is available in the morning and evening newspapers'.[20] Cardiff recorded coal export volumes. Local newspapers were also frequently used to publish memorials, annual reports, minutes of meetings, and other reports. Particularly in the smaller chambers, the cost of publishing their own reports was avoided, and the newspapers provided the main means of publicity; e.g. in Kidderminster and Goole into the early 1900s.

Once annual reports became established, for the period up to the 1950s and 1960s, many retained a similar and very formal format. This resulted from the efforts of the ACC after the 1880s to standardize and improve chamber presentation. Their format sought to give the clear stamp of representing authority and status. However, they increasingly became more stylish publicity documents and many became chiefly an advertisement and directory of members, or a listing of all local businesses, with members identified in some way (e.g. by bold type). Directories of members were a way of projecting status and encouraging other businesses to join. The shift from being purely brand or status documents towards local 'place marketing' and information sources widened their appeal. Advertisements by member firms became increasingly popular within these formats, in some cases turning the directories from a cost burden into providing a modest surplus. In many cases a printer or publisher took on the publications and shared any surplus. Bemrose, publishers of Derby, played a major early role in this over 1914–25, offering to produce and distribute yearbooks and journals for all chambers and being responsible for almost all chamber handbooks of this period.

Journals

From early years chambers also experimented with various formats of journal or newsletter on a more frequent basis. The earliest appear to be Glasgow in the 1790s, and Birmingham in the 1840s. Salt had a specialized journal containing price, customs landing statistics of salt, and shipping information on the salt

---

[18] New York published its first *Annual Report* in 1858 of 400 pages with national as well as local statistical coverage, filling a gap that no US government publications covered; Bishop (1918), p. 69.
[19] Cork chamber minutes, 7 January 1820. The practice does not seemed to have survived long.
[20] Dundee chamber history (2006), p. 64.

industry over the 1860–80 period. Worcester experimented with a journal to supplement its annual report in the 1860s–1870s. Aberdeen and Edinburgh began journals in the 1860s, which continue into modern times. Journals became popular in chambers from the 1920s up to the present, with Bemrose as an early stimulus. For example, in 1920 the Bradford chamber agreed with Bemrose the circulation of 2500 journals each month, with 2500 additional issues twice yearly, one in French and one in Spanish, for £3000 per year. The chamber was to receive 25% of the profit.[21] Bemrose was producing journals on similar arrangements for at least 20 chambers in the early 1920s.

In many cases journals replaced annual reports and directories, embodying in one issue each year a statement of the chamber's AGM, accounts, other formal information, and/or member lists. They also sometimes contained reports of major chamber meetings. Indeed the journals often began with the deliberations of the chamber's council and its lobbying activities; many also listed and welcomed new members. Later the content was supplemented by general economic commentary, specific local business discussions, features on individual firms, examples of good business practice, advertisements, the views of individual entrepreneurs or managers, and other content familiar in modern business magazines.

The view of the journal as a chief medium for communication with members is encapsulated in comments by Manchester when it began its journal (*Monthly Record*) in 1890: its purpose was to provide a medium 'through which the members of the chamber may express their views, . . . to note prominent changes taking place in the commercial world; to record important current events arising at home and in other lands, and their bearing on trade . . .'. It also sought to encourage member-to-member exchanges: 'to afford opportunity, within reasonable limits, for correspondence on . . . trade, and to publish such portions of communications between the chamber and the administrative departments as may be of service'.[22]

Journals began to become promotional documents. Thus Belfast saw its journal in 1934 as not only providing information to its members but also to help 'make Belfast and Northern Ireland and their commercial activities better known'.[23] The work of the Teesside and SW Durham chamber Publicity Committee, for example, was chiefly the supervision of the chamber's *Journal of Commerce*, whilst also monitoring all publications in the area, and initiating the first local classified trade directory.[24] Many chambers developed trade directories, and this was also a central activity of trade protection societies from the 1870s, which used directories as a means to give greater exposure to traders and hence more easily to identify those that were bona fide. The move for journals to become a medium for publicity gathered pace after WW2. In modern times many have been replaced by more frequent and briefer newsletters, which were almost universal within chambers of

[21] Bradford chamber, Journal Subcommittee minutes, 23 January 1920.
[22] Manchester chamber, *Monthly Record*, 20 January 1890, inaugural issue, p. 1.
[23] Belfast chamber, *Journal*, April (1934), p. 7.
[24] Teesside and SW Durham chamber, *Annual Report*, 31 December (1960), p. 27.

commerce by 1996, after which they increasingly became electronic (in 92% of BCC chambers by 2010).

In London, the chamber's journal took on a national as well as local significance. Launched in 1882 at the time the chamber itself was founded, it provided about £500 per year of income to the chamber from 1885. Its title, *Chamber of Commerce Journal* (*CCJ*), showed its ambition to be a national periodical, potentially used by all chambers and their members. It showed a very aggressive ambition in having a topical, catchy, and often 'political' editorial, a series of major articles on national policy issues or concerns of the business community, frequent reportage of statistical material, and a section on 'work of the chambers'. This last item could be used by each chamber to disseminate information to all other chambers, but most frequently it was a survey by the *CCJ* staff of other chamber reports they had received. The *CCJ* narrowed to a London and general business journal after 1900 with the reportage of other chambers becoming minimal. Attempts to broaden its appeal resulted in renaming it as *Commerce* in 1962 and *Commerce International* in 1970. The attempt by the London chamber to use *CCJ* over 1882–97 as an organ for all local chambers undoubtedly reflects an attempt to gain significant control over the national body (ACC), as well as a genuine attempt to contribute to chamber development nationwide. Its style and format was widely copied and certainly encouraged the launch of other chamber journals.

The publication of a national journal by the chambers association (ACC) was first tried in 1868 with *Chambers of Commerce*, a journal that appears to have had only one issue, although Macclesfield was still trying to use this for promotion in 1869: 'the Council particularly recommend that every member should be a subscriber to the Journal, which offered timely and accurate information of the several chambers of commerce of Great Britain and some foreign parts'.[25] There were two further short-lived attempts at a national journal in 1876 and 1886.[26] But the London *CCJ* tested the model most thoroughly and its experience appears to have confirmed that a national journal could not successfully cover local issues sufficiently for all members.

Other national publications by ACC/ABCC were more successful. The *Monthly Proceedings* was published from 1860 until 1958, and *Annual Report* from 1860 until 1978. Although criticized in later ABCC discussions, the *Proceedings* were a valuable publicity and information medium; Southampton chamber for example distributed 2000 copies to its members and others over 1915–20.[27] Supplements of national newspapers were also often used, such as *The Times Trade Supplement* of 1917, where 11,000 copies were distributed through the chambers.[28] But other efforts foundered under pressure from the larger local chambers that wanted to do their own thing. For example a *National Directory* of members proposed by ACC in

---

[25] Macclesfield chamber, *Half Yearly Report* (1869), p. 368 (Cheshire RO, D6615/3).
[26] See Chapter 8.
[27] See comments on the ABCC *Proceedings* after 1949 in Chapter 8; Southampton reported in *Monthly Proceedings* (1915).
[28] ABCC, *Monthly Proceedings* (1917), p. 361.

1915–16, which was aimed at 15,000 chamber members and 'buyers throughout the world', was cancelled because 'there is so much opposition to the project on the part of important centres', and London chamber was resistant throughout the discussions; it 'retained its entire liberty of action to stay out if they wished'.[29] The efforts by Bemrose of Derby tried to fill this gap. An *ABCC Newsletter* was tried 1958–63 in order to reach a wider membership, but with only limited success. The replacement for the *Proceedings* and *Report*, by *ABCC Newsline* attempted to reach a wide audience as well as chamber managers, but lasted only over 1979–80. There were also *Parliamentary Papers* over much of the 1950s and 1960s; these were increasingly important to chambers managers and their Councils, but were of little value to ordinary members. More recently *Business Briefing* was developed by ABCC over 1989–90, with initial issues underpinned by finance from DTI to replace a government statistical bulletin of business statistics; but when it had to be financed solely by subscriptions it quickly foundered. It was superseded by the *ABCC National Review* 1995–8. No regular major national publication has been attempted since then, and the web has become the core link of BCC with member chambers and member businesses. The difficult evolution of these national journals is in stark contrast to the success of the NCT's *National Chamber Journal*, and the NATPS *Circular*, though these also evolved to cover less local detail.

In Ireland, the launch of the *Dublin Chamber of Commerce Journal* in 1952 had some characteristics similar to London's *CCJ* of 1882. It aimed to

> represent not only the Dublin Chamber, but also, as its official organ, the Association of Chambers of Commerce of Ireland, and so every chamber affiliated to it [which numbered 19 at the time]. It will speak for them and it will strengthen the common bond between them, providing a useful means of communication . . . But there is a greater function . . . It will be sent to all chambers of commerce in Britain . . . and throughout the world . . . and lead to a better understanding at home and abroad both in human relations and trade.[30]

Its subsequent evolution mirrored that of *CCJ*: since the 1980s it covered little from other chambers, usually no more than one page, and became essentially a Dublin business magazine.

Other publications

As well as annual reports and journals, chambers have embarked on a wide range of other publications. The most common of these are 'yearbooks', 'directories', and 'handbooks', mainly after 1910, often published by Bemrose. These tended to have a common format of brief coverage of the local chamber's activities and history, a more extensive coverage of the local economy, a membership list, and many pages of advertisements that helped to underwrite the cost of production.

The distribution of these handbooks is recorded in the Bemrose editions; e.g. the Halifax Yearbook of 1917 was sent to members of that chamber, foreign chambers

[29] ABCC, *Monthly Proceedings* (1915–16), pp. 54 and 127.
[30] *Chamber of Commerce Journal (Dublin)* 3(1), January (1952), p. 4.

of commerce, Board of Trade Canada, British consuls and consular agents, British ambassadors, clubs (colonial and foreign), and merchants in the home, colonial, and foreign markets. The Yearbook states its aim as encouraging links by foreign traders to Halifax firms, but unfortunately, no records attempt to assess the success of these efforts. The *Chamber of Commerce Register* produced by Bemrose (1919–20) and edited by Thomas Keens[31] was an attempt to do the same thing in three volumes for groups of smaller chambers, with similar distribution. The lack of repeat or follow-up volumes in this format suggests that their success was limited. Similarly a *Yearbook of Commerce* experiment by London chamber in conjunction with ACC in 1892 was not repeated.

These handbooks overlap with the attempts by chambers to publish a wide range of other booklets that focused more on trade promotion for visitors and tourists. Usually labelled as 'guidebooks' in later years, these became a very frequent activity of all chambers, including the smallest ones, as shown in Figure 12.1. They were advocated by the NCT as one of the main outputs that CoT bodies should produce. Often chambers of commerce would work with chambers of trade to produce these guidebooks; for example, the Newport chamber (Wales) published a joint local business directory with its local chamber of trade from 1913 until the late 1920s. Guidebooks were also a source of frequent close collaboration with local government, and many guidebooks initiated by chambers were subsidized or taken over by local government in subsequent years, e.g. Dover in the 1920s. Jersey and Guernsey had a very active set of guides, posters, and leaflets to promote tourist visitors and the Islands' produce (tomatoes, flowers, etc.) from the 1880s; Guernsey supplemented this with a set of photographic slides in 1889 for use at talks.[32] More specialist guidebooks were also produced; for example Southampton in 1900 produced a handbook of local information similar to other guidebooks, but also containing a large range of shipping and local transport information 'to meet the requirements of the shipping companies [and] for distribution on board the vessels of the steamship companies using the port of Southampton'.[33] Over 10,000 copies were printed. By the 1990s paper handbooks had largely disappeared, to be replaced by web-based directories of members.

The electronic era

In modern times, paper communications with members and external publicity have been almost entirely replaced by electronic newsletters and member areas of websites. As shown in Table 12.1, by 1996 paper newsletters were almost universal across all chambers of commerce, but there was already substantial transfer to electronic formats. Chambers were early adopters of the web compared with most small businesses: by 1996, 32% had websites, 57% used email, and 37%

---

[31] Secretary of the Luton chamber; see Appendix 2.

[32] Guernsey chamber minutes, November 1899; a special subscription was raised to pay for the costs.

[33] Southampton chamber, Council minutes, 19 February 1900.

were involved in electronic data interchange with members. By 2000 these systems were universal; fax services continued in only 22%. The website and emails are now the main medium for news and communication with members, a means of gaining information on members' views on policy positions and their concerns, a mechanism for web-based surveys, marketing to non-members, and providing a 'directory' of members available to members and non-members with considerable marketing benefits.

By 2010, 92% of BCC chambers had moved to electronic newsletters. For 2008 there were 57 million hits on chamber websites, which included 45,000 transactions with a value of £1.8 million; which was more than double the 2006 figures. However, as the web has become more focused, website hits declined in 2010 to 41 million, but transactions increased to 59,500 with a value of £2.1 million. E-communication has also provided a new medium for 'deliberation', which has opened new potential for alignment of interests that has not yet been fully exploited. The BCC Quarterly Economic Survey has moved progressively to this medium, and had contact with 89,682 businesses in 2010. Social networking has also expanded via electronic methods as well as chamber events. In 2010 48% of chambers used Facebook, 67% Linkedin, and 29% Twitter. However chamber-based blogs were rarer (in only 4% of chambers), and YouTube was used in only one chamber. This is a rapidly evolving field likely to expand in the future.[34]

Websites have also provided an important medium for marketing groups of chambers, particularly cooperations between larger and smaller chambers; e.g. in South-West England; Scotland; counties such as Somerset and Sussex; and smaller areas such as North Norfolk, North Hampshire, South Hampshire, East Hampshire, and within London. In other cases BCC chambers have developed listings that cover larger areas at the county or sub-region level: notably Manchester. In yet other cases BCC chambers have sought to occupy the web-based search space for their areas by offering links to the smaller chambers (e.g. Black Country, Birmingham, Bristol, London, Nottingham, and Northern Ireland). This offers considerable scope for future development of services and member support.

12.4 COMMERCIAL ARBITRATION

The use of arbiters to resolve commercial disputes was a key feature of the 'law merchant' dating from centuries earlier. The involvement of chambers was a natural conceptual development.[35] Indeed, the development of arbitration through 'tribunals of commerce' became one of the key concepts behind early chamber initiatives in the 1780s, and was a major objective of chamber political lobbying from the 1850s until 1889 (see Chapter 7). As Taylor states, 'the great advantage

---

[34] All information from BCC, *Benchmarking* (1996) and following.

[35] A predecessor of the Dublin chamber instituted an arbitration body of merchants in 1705, the Ouzel Galley Society, which worked with the chamber from 1783 until it was wound up in 1888: see G. A. Little (1953), *The Ouzel Galley* (Dublin: Cahill); also Dublin chamber history.

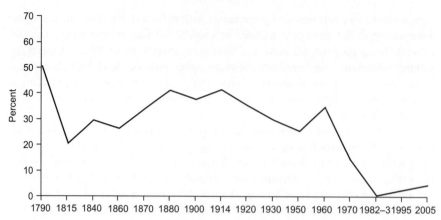

Fig. 12.2. Percentage of chambers of commerce offering commercial arbitration, 1790–2005.

possessed by chambers was their ability to appoint arbiters who knew "the custom of the trade".[36]

The first chamber arbitration services began soon after foundation in New York, in 1769; Dublin from the 1780s; Waterford in 1787; London (through John Weskett) in 1782;[37] Glasgow 1783–1820; Jersey from 1785; Edinburgh 1792–1820; Leeds acted ad hoc in one dispute in 1789; Dundee, Belfast, and Bristol began in the early 19th century; Limerick in 1840; Bradford in 1851; and Hull, Liverpool, and Leeds in 1852. Manchester became a model for other chambers after 1881.[38] London also had national significance as a model after it established its Arbitration Court in 1892;[39] e.g. Sunderland sought permission from the City Corporation to copy the London scheme, and the Sheffield Master Cutler made a similar request, both in 1893. Birmingham, which was surprisingly slow to develop arbitration, made a request in 1894.[40]

The spread of chamber commercial arbitration services is shown in Figure 12.2. From this figure it is clear that the service was quite widespread across the earliest chambers, but was not adopted by all later foundations; however, it increased again in the run-up to the 1889 Arbitration Act. In 1860 26% of chambers offered commercial arbitration, but this had grown to about 40% over 1880–1914,[41] a figure that slowly declined, relatively, with the increasing number of small chambers, enjoying a brief revival in the 1960s, after which it has almost disappeared as a service.

---

[36] Taylor (2007), p. 41.
[37] Weskett operated as an arbiter in his London chamber 1782–1800; see Chapter 7.
[38] Bradford chamber, *Annual Reports*; Manchester chamber, Tribunal of Arbitration, established 7 February 1881, Annual Meeting minutes.
[39] ACC, *Proceedings*, 21–3 March 1893, pp. 90–2.
[40] City Corporation, Court of Common Council, 1893, p. 43; 1894, p. 159; LMA: COL/CC/04/04.
[41] These estimates are based on those where there is local evidence of a service in existence. Royal Commission on Labour, *House of Commons Papers* (1892), xxxvi, gives 39 chambers providing arbitration.

The 1889 Arbitration Act, won after considerable lobby efforts discussed in Chapter 7, was important chiefly in providing a more readily recognised status; it did little to change processes. As noted in Liverpool's 1852 assessment, most of the major chambers then in existence offered arbitration services, but there was little take-up. The service was impeded by lack of recognition: 'experience shows that unauthoritative tribunals are rarely resorted to: the reports of the chambers of commerce of New York, Liverpool, Glasgow, Belfast, Hull and the Ouzel Galley Society at Dublin, are all uniform in their testimony of the rarity of the call for the exercise of this function . . . while County Courts are crowded.'[42] Even after 1889, as in other service developments, progress was slow and frustrating. The ACC commented in 1908 that 'chambers of commerce appeared to have shown a singular neglect in establishing the machinery to put the procedure of arbitration in place' following the 1889 Act.[43]

The arbitration service

The aim of the chamber arbitration service was speed and cheapness. A contemporary comment on London's was that it 'is to have all the virtues which the law lacks. It is to be expeditious where the law is slow, cheaper where the law is costly, simple where the law is technical, a peacemaker instead of a stirrer-up of strife.'[44] The exclusiveness of chambers was used in a few cases; in 1892 in five out of 39 chambers arbitration applications could be made only when one of the disputants was a member, but in the rest it was unrestricted.[45] Overall the service drew on the access the chambers had to people who knew the trade in which the disputes arose. The appointed arbiters drew either from a specific committee, or from the chamber's council as a whole. In 1892, of 39 chambers, 14 appointed an arbitration committee for each case when requested, which then laid its report before the secretary. London's first scheme in 1884 had 180–200 arbiters who were nominated chamber members in different specialist trades.[46] This was modified when the chamber established an Arbitration Court, which had a membership of only 24; 12 appointed by the chamber and 12 appointed by the City Corporation.

An individual reference to arbitration could arise because an arbitration clause had been inserted into a contract stipulating, 'the continuation, validity and performance of this contract . . . and all disputes which may arise . . . shall be submitted to the arbitration' of a particular chamber,[47] or could be referred from any other commercial contract dispute. Once initiated the process operated by appointing an arbitrator or 'umpire' (usually a single person, but could be a panel, if

[42] Liverpool chamber (1852). This is also clear from the Royal Commission on Labour, *House of Commons Papers* (1892), xxxvi.

[43] ACC Report, quoted in London *CCJ* (1908), pp. 25–6.

[44] *Law Quarterly Review*, 9 (1893), p. 86, quoted in <www.lcia.org/history>.

[45] Royal Commission on Labour (1892), part v, p. xxxiii.

[46] London chamber, *Annual Reports*, e.g. (1886), p. 26.

[47] Abbreviated from the recorded contractual clause used in the 1950s; quoted in London chamber *Annual Report* (1956), p. 38.

the parties were willing to bear the additional cost). The arbitrator would then request copies of statements and documents from each party, which were then exchanged between the parties. An oral hearing took place (though this could be waived, especially in international disputes), which might involve solicitors and counsel, and could include inspection of goods as to quality, etc.[48] The advantage was its speed of hearings and low costs. This led some chambers to specify rules for maximum periods for decisions of three to 21 days, the latter in Bradford.[49] However, there were clearly sometimes delays since provision is made in many sets of rules for new arbiters to be appointed if there were delays. The London arbitration book shows some complex cases taking over a year, but most took a few days.[50]

Initially the fees could be high; e.g. in Waterford in 1787–8 they ranged from £1 2s. 9d. to £6 17s. 4d.; after 1808 they were set at 1 guinea each to the chamber and the umpires for the first sitting, half a guinea each for each subsequent sitting to a maximum of 10 guineas, to be deposited at the chamber at the start of the session.[51] But generally fees were more modest: in Glasgow it was £2 from the 1780s until the 1920s. At the outset in London, Manchester, Belfast, and Leeds in the 1880s–90s the fee was one guinea per case. For non-members it was five guineas, with a fee for any appeal at 15 guineas (£21 for non-members), plus the costs of rooms, etc.[52] In 1892 the range of fees across the chamber system was from one to five guineas for members, and two to ten guineas for non-members.[53]

Subsequently fees were put on an hourly rate. In Liverpool over 1916–45 the fee was two guineas for the first hour of a hearing, one guinea for each subsequent hour, or four guineas in total for parties agreeing to handle a case entirely in writing.[54] London moved to this in 1920, where cases for disputes of less than £1000 were at a fee of three guineas for the first hour and two guineas for each subsequent hour; disputes of over £1000 were at a rate of six guineas and four guineas, respectively. This rate was held for 45 years. A proposal to raise the 'small dispute' rate to three guineas and four guineas in December 1953 was not agreed; an increase was not put in place until 1965.[55] It is clear from these fees that incentives were sought to limit the time (and hence cost) in order to preserve the desire for a forum for dispute resolution that was cheap, speedy, and simple.

The specifics of London offered it considerable advantages in establishing a more formal Arbitration Court in 1892. Not only was it a large business community and national centre, but also the City Corporation was (and is) an elected body principally comprising business and trades people. It, therefore, had a sympathetic local government environment, although even here there were tensions. The court

[48] e.g. London chamber, *Annual Reports*.
[49] Royal Commission on Labour, *House of Commons Papers* (1892), xxxvi, part v, p. xxxiii.
[50] London chamber; MS 16559.
[51] Waterford chamber, accounts for 1788 at rear of first minute book; arbitration rules, 30 September 1808.
[52] See e.g. Manchester chamber minutes; London Executive minutes, *Articles of Association* (1897).
[53] Royal Commission on Labour (1892), part v, p. xxxiii.
[54] Liverpool chamber, Arbitration Book, *Rules*; Liverpool RO 380 COM 2/1.
[55] London Court of Arbitration, minutes; MS 16559.

was under negotiation with the City's Local Government and Taxation Committee from 1887 until 1892.[56] The City's Common Council considered a report on the scheme in 1888, reconsidered it in 1891, and only in 1892 did the Coal, Corn and Finance Committee agree to vote funds of £300 per year for two years to initiate the scheme.[57] The City Solicitor was still slow in agreeing the final form of the joint court, expressing (perhaps validly, or perhaps obstructively) concern about how the arbiters were selected.[58] The court initially, in 1892, met at the Guildhall, but after 1909 met at the chamber. After 1981 it moved to independent premises. Up to 1921 the City Corporation had given £50 per year to help with its expenses, which rose to £100 in 1922 and £200 in 1938, but it discontinued all support in 1943;[59] the link with the Corporation became tenuous in the post-war period, and disappeared after 1981. Only one other chamber seems to have attempted to use local government to facilitate the foundation process—Nottingham. This involved several discussions with the local council, with the chamber's arbitration committee eventually agreed in 1893.[60]

Volumes of activity

Few chambers quote statistics for the number of hearings, and it appears that in most localities they were never large, and tended to diminish over time as other court processes became more favoured (despite costs and delays). In most chambers, annual reports record only one hearing a year, or one every three or four years. In the 1890s, many chambers claiming to offer arbitration may never have had a case to consider. The earliest chambers, Jersey and Waterford, had one or two cases per year in the 1780s and 1790s;[61] New York had 15 cases over 1769–71 (seven per year).[62] Belfast over 1850–80 had about 4–13 cases per year.[63] But the Limerick arbitration scheme introduced in 1840 appears to have never been invoked.[64] In some chambers the process was very ad hoc: in Birmingham the president acted as an arbitrator in a one-off case in 1868, but this seems to be the only example for many years; the next reported was in 1919.[65] In Cardiff, although arbitration is listed as a service from 1870, it was established on a more formal basis only in 1907,

---

[56] London chamber, *Annual Report* (1891), pp. 21–2.

[57] City Corporation, Court of Common Council minutes, 1888–91, 1892 p. 156; LMA: COL/CC/04/04.

[58] London chamber, Executive minutes, 1891.

[59] London Court of Arbitration, minutes (MS 16559); City Corporation, Court of Common Council minutes.

[60] See *Records of Borough of Nottingham*, Vol. IX, (Nottingham: Forman & Sons, 1956), pp. 362 and 365, which reports meetings from 2 January 1893 to 10 April 1893.

[61] Jersey chamber minutes, 23 and 29 April, and 8 and 21 May 1789; Waterford chamber minutes, 18 May and 20 September 1787, 4 April 1788.

[62] Bishop (1918).

[63] Inferred from arbitration income, with peaks in 1852–3, 1869, and 1875–9; Belfast chamber, *Annual Reports and Accounts*, 1851–1914.

[64] O'Connor (1938), pp. 95–6.

[65] Dispute between Worcester Supplies Co. and Green's Patent Tube Co.; Birmingham chamber, Council minutes, 30 December 1868; one arbitration reported 14 January 1919.

and heard its first two cases in 1908.[66] Bristol reported in 1902 that it was 'worthy of note that the first reference under the [arbitration] rules of the chamber since 1876 has been held'.[67] The Liverpool chamber arbitration book records only 13 cases over 1916–45: 3 in 1916; 3 in 1917; 2 in 1919; 2 in 1920; and one each in 1921, 1922, and 1945, with no cases in the other years.[68] Dublin established its court in 1927 (though it had the earlier Ouzel Galley scheme), but regretted it had no cases by 1929, which it adduced to 'conservative habits'.[69] Coventry received 'a few' cases in the 1950s.[70] Edinburgh acted to settle one dispute in 1959 'after a lengthy period of inactivity'.[71] Even in London there appear to have been only one or two cases per year 1883–1891.[72] Typical of many chambers is the example of a report in the Preston chamber of 1933, which refers to the details of one case that was clearly the first for a long time. It involved the interpretation of insurance policy conditions.[73]

However, a few chambers handled a significant number of cases. Statistics are not generally available, but it appears that Glasgow, Manchester, Belfast, Bradford, Leeds, and London became the main centres. The Manchester chamber was probably the largest provider; it had an average of 50–60 cases per year in the early 1900s, reaching a maximum of 103 in 1919, and gave 70–80 certified opinions in the late 1920s and many less formal ones each year.[74] Most cases concerned the quality of goods delivered under contracts, and alleged defects of printing and dyeing (of cotton goods), with many disputes being settled after the start of arbitration, resulting in a large number of cases not completed.[75] In Glasgow the records show an average of one case every two years up to 1918, after which numbers rose to four in 1919, and seven in 1921, with an average of about four per year thereafter.[76] In the case of Bradford, annual arbitration fee income, which was two guineas in 1870, had risen to £35 14s. in 1900, £101 19s. 6d. in 1923, £300 in 1950, and was £483 in 1960[77] (implying approximately 4–10 cases per year). In 1960, the ABCC formed an expert arbitration panel, stating that four chambers were involved in international arbitration.[78]

London has the best records, though volumes were about 50–70% of those in Manchester. The evolution of its work is shown in Figure 12.3. Cases ranged up to 63 per year at the highest in 1921, and after 2000. It was clearly most active in the

---

[66] Cardiff chamber, *Annual Report* (1908); the formal rules are in *Annual Report* (1912), pp. 25–7.
[67] Bristol chamber, *Annual Report* (1902), p. 35.
[68] Liverpool chamber, Arbitration Book; LRO 380 COM 2/1.
[69] Dublin chamber, Report of Council 1929.
[70] Coventry chamber, *Annual Reports* (1951, 1952).
[71] Edinburgh chamber, *Yearbook* (1960), p. 31.
[72] London chamber, *Annual Reports* note two enquiries and one case in 1883 for a fee of three guineas, and one case in 1890. The committee sat a maximum of five times in 1884 and 1885 indicating 3–5 cases.
[73] Preston chamber, *Annual Report* (1933), pp. 14–15.
[74] Manchester chamber, *Monthly Record*, February (1920), p. 56; Dupree (1987), p. 621.
[75] See report in Manchester chamber, *Monthly Record*, 31 January (1898), p. 6.
[76] Glasgow chamber, *Annual Reports and Accounts*.
[77] Bradford chamber, *Annual Reports*.
[78] ABCC, *Annual Report* (1959/60): London, Manchester, Glasgow, and probably Bradford.

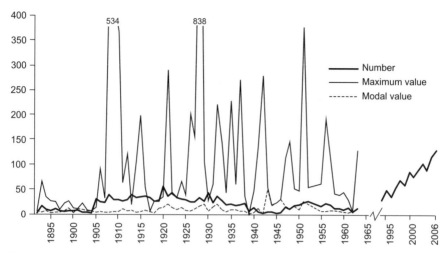

Fig. 12.3. London chamber Court of Arbitration, 1892–1968, and LCIA 1993–2006. Number of cases dealt with, maximum costs, and average (modal) costs charged. (*Sources*: London chamber, arbitration book MS/6559, with some information added from chamber minutes; after 1993 from LCIA *Annual Reports*.)

period 1905–38, in 1947–1950s, and in recent years. From the 1970s the service was used chiefly for international arbitration. The decline from the 1960s appears to be a result of the role of the International Chamber of Commerce, the reluctance of foreign companies or governments to use a London-based court, and the establishment of rival bodies.[79]

Figure 12.3 shows that the London court was indeed offering a cheap service, with many cases resolved for one or two guineas, even in the 1930s and 1940s.[80] Some cases involved much more substantial costs, though these seem to be concentrated chiefly in the 1908–10 period, in the late 1920s, and in other occasional years up to the 1950s. The modal cost of settlement stayed remarkably stable up to 1940 at £3–8, rising above this level in the 1920s, early 1930s, and after 1943. The impact of the economic slump and wartime trading difficulties seem to explain higher levels of use; but even then the modal costs show the court to be generally inexpensive. This remains true today where, although fee rates of £150–350 per hour and a registration fee of £1500 are charged, the total time involved is generally much less than court proceedings.[81] The arbiters involved are now generally lawyers, appointed from mainstream commercial firms. In Ireland, the Arbitration Act of 1954, and subsequent legislation, similarly turned arbitration into a more

[79] Comment in London chamber, *Annual Reports* (1964 and 1965).
[80] London quotes a time from lodging a case to a hearing as nine days, and 13 days for an award, with average fees of £5 12s. in 1893: PACC, 21–3 March (1893), pp. 90–2.
[81] <www.lcia.org/ARB-folder/arb-english-main.htm>, accessed 23 May 2007.

formal legal process based on professionals, with chambers withdrawing from any residual service by 1960.

After 1981 the London court was significantly altered; the name was changed to the London Court of International Arbitration (LCIA) to reflect the emphasis on international work; a new set of rules and procedures was adopted; and the court became a fully independent body from both the City and the chamber.[82] Initially, numbers of cases remained low, but by the 1990s steady growth was being experienced, and arbitration cases grew from 49 in 1995, to 75 in 2000, 130 in 2006, and 260 in 2009.[83] Interestingly, it is only with this modern development that the London court became a national (as well as an international) court, when all other UK chamber arbitration services effectively ceased. International arbitration had become established as a result of the activities of the International Chamber of Commerce in the 1920s, and an International Commercial Arbitration Code, Protocol, drawn up by the Economic Committee of the League of Nations in 1923.[84] A leading member of this committee for the UK was Raymond Streat, secretary of the Manchester chamber. He emphasized the importance of determination within the country of arbitration (not the countries of origin of the parties), and the resistance that had to be overcome from lawyers, especially in countries like France where local laws made the use of arbitration difficult.[85] The LCIA depends on a modern form of this Protocol.

12.5 DEBT COLLECTION

Debt collection, usually combined with a service to check the creditworthiness of potential business partners or creditors, became the core service of the trade protection societies (TPSs). But it was also linked with many chambers. It drew on the capacity of local agents to research and assess local risk. The TPSs began from about 1776 in London, but grew in numbers rapidly in the 1850s, probably as a result of the development of the County Courts after 1847. The local societies were the main bodies for the enquiries and debt collection, but the national association acted as coordinator, distributed a list of corresponding agents who could answer enquiries, and provided a circular of information about defaulters, bankrupts, and County Court cases across the British Isles (including Ireland and the Channel Isles). Even at its outset in 1776 the service was apparently very heavily used, with 'numerous cautions and notices issued'.[86] By the 1850s it had become

---

[82] City of London, Court of Common Council minutes, 26 February 1981, p. 55; <www.lcia.org/LCI_folder/lcia-history.htm>.
[83] <www.lcia.org/News_folder/news-main.htm>, accessed 23 May 2007; 1994–2000 provided to the author by LCIA.
[84] International arbitration by the International Chamber of Commerce was lauded in the 1920s and 1930s as 'business diplomacy', and a contribution to peace: Ridgeway (1938).
[85] Raymond Streat, 'Arbitration in international commerce', a commentary provided at the ABCC Association of Secretaries, reported in several chamber journals, e.g. Belfast *Journal*, July (1923), pp. 62–5; final text of the Protocol is in the Belfast *Journal*, October (1923), p. 108.
[86] London society for protection of trade against swindlers; BL 8246.a.15; p. 29.

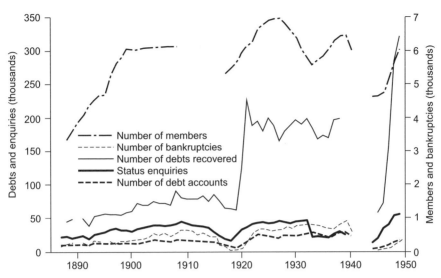

Fig. 12.4. Membership, debt collection, and status enquiries handled by Manchester trade protection society, 1887–1949.

an enormous service operation. As shown for Manchester TPS in Figure 12.4, many hundreds of thousands of status enquiries were made and debts collected with peaks of activity over 1920–40, a decline in WW1 and WW2, with a new peak in the 1950s.

Involvement by chambers

Several early chambers responded to the demand for a debt collection service. Later this became a key service undertaken by many chambers of trade. Weskett's first London chamber had offered the service over 1783–1800 in return for a three-guinea subscription, or a half-guinea for single matters.[87] One of the earliest references to a wider chamber service is by Aberdeen, which started a debt recovery service in 1851. In 1871 it recovered £19,445 from 9013 claims valued at £56,716, a recovery rate of 35% for 300–450 claims per year.[88] The recovery rate increased to around 50% in later years. The chamber's service was relabelled as a 'Trade Protection Department' in 1907. The Rochdale chamber of trade debt collecting service in 1871 dealt with 87,161 claims and recovered £286,036. As in Aberdeen, this was a major local service.[89] Leeds chamber considered a service in 1855, led by member Thomas Wilson who argued that the TPS only acted for retailers and that manufacturers and merchants needed a tailored service; however, after much discussion, with several dissenters, no action was taken.[90] But in 1879 Leeds and

---

[87] Weskett (1782), article XI, pp. 22–4.
[88] Aberdeen chamber, minutes and *Annual Accounts*.
[89] Rochdale Merchant and Tradesmen's Association, *Annual Report* (1871), p. 10.
[90] Leeds chamber minutes, 18 January and 1 February 1855.

four other chambers set up a creditors' association with offices in Leeds and Huddersfield to share the 'enormous cost of realising insolvent estates'.[91] Goole chamber acted as a TPS in the 1890s, had a differentiated subscription by number of status reports offered, and was publishing a weekly gazette with the 'latest information as to bankruptcies, bills of sale etc., together with lists of creditors in principal failures, supplied to subscribers, if required'. The chamber's enquiry department also offered a 'list of traders in good credit in any town or district'.[92]

Debt collection was (and is) by no means a simple undertaking. It required staff, and hence costs. St Helens chamber advertised in 1914 for a 'young accountant' to work on behalf of the chamber of trade to run the service.[93] As well as costs, there were tensions about how a service that pursued debtors was managed for a body that was seeking to support and represent all businesses in its area. St Helens shows some of these tensions. Its original title had been the 'St Helens chamber of commerce and guardian society', which reflected the priorities of some of the members. Mr A. Dodd, who became a key voice in the chamber, had been attempting to form a TPS, and would only combine his efforts with the new chamber provided that it 'included a blacklist [of debtors] for use of the members'. There were similar tensions in Leicester at its foundation in 1849. Subsequent discussions about the St Helens service showed the members to be split into two groups: Dodd and some who wanted a debt collection service; and others who felt the chamber should be established first, and then a service set up to 'work as an auxiliary in the prevention and collection of bad debts'.[94] The debate over the founding rules continued, and the eventual service was based on 'the duty of every member to furnish to the secretary all the information in his power that may conduce to the benefit and protection from fraud of the members; and especially to transmit . . . notice of all cases within their knowledge of attempts to obtain goods on fraudulent pretences'.[95] Within a few weeks this was being referred to as a 'cautionary list' of bad debts transacted, with an incentive provided to members that 'the secretary shall refuse information to any member, who in his opinion, or from information received, has not contributed such information as is within his knowledge'.[96] After six months the service was large enough to advertise for the young accountant.[97]

Colchester was another example, over 1923–49, indicating how the chambers linked with TPS bodies.[98] For the TPS, a link with a chamber provided a wider source of demand. As a result many TPS evolved to become small chambers, merged into them, or offered the service as a subcontract to a larger chamber. It

[91] Leeds chamber minutes, 5 May and 14 July 1879; the other chambers were Batley, Dewsbury, Heckmondwike, Huddersfield, and the Yorkshire Woollen Association.
[92] Subscription leaflet, Goole Library; YW/GOO/380; details of its subscriptions in Chapter 15.
[93] St Helens chamber minutes, 28 July 1914.
[94] St Helens chamber minutes, 10 December 1913, 30 December 1913.
[95] Rules agreed: proposed by Mr Dodd, seconded by Mr Pickavance, and supported by Mr Balshaw (who was now hon. secretary); St Helens chamber minutes, 6 January 1914.
[96] St Helens chamber minutes, 28 January 1914.
[97] The appointee was probably William E. Smith who is listed as a member of the chamber, and 'debt collector, Hardshaw St.'; St Helens chamber minutes, 1914.
[98] *East Anglia Daily Times,* April 1923; *Essex Telegraph,* 8 April 1949; and *Annual Accounts.*

remained a key service in some areas up to the 1990s. In general, the ACC/ABCC were not enthusiastic about debt collection services, because this was seen as a concern primarily of the small business and trade supplier, which were not historically viewed as the main membership targets. In 1925 there was a very sniffy ABCC minute: 'it was no business of chambers of commerce to answer enquiries as to financial status of firms'.[99] However, in the 1940s the London chamber initiated an overseas debt collection service following a proposal that had originated from the Association of Secretaries of Chambers.[100] The NCT attitude was different, and urged small chambers to establish debt collection.

12.6 INFORMATION AND ENQUIRIES

Answering of enquiries by chambers was an early adjunct of their establishment. When the staff was entirely voluntary, enquiries were handled directly by the president or other officers, who might refer to other chamber members. The volumes were clearly very low and occasional for this mode of working, though it had the benefit of direct member-to-member exchange that undoubtedly contributed to collective identification of interests as well as social exchanges, and might prove very effective.

Volume

Once chamber staff were appointed, they became the natural channel through which enquiries were answered, although referral to the council or to other members appears to have been frequent, and still occurs today. However, it is only in the late 19th century, and especially during and after WW1, that enquiries appear to have grown to an extent of consuming a large proportion of the secretary's and other staff time. As shown in Figure 12.5, development was slower and less widespread for chambers of trade.

Less than 20% of chambers offered an enquiry service until 1930, but it then increased rapidly. In Birmingham, enquiries increased to 10,800 over 1913–14, of which 3600 (33%) were estimated to be the result of the war.[101] After WW1 the growth seems to have come chiefly from two sources: first, the expansion of state regulation for which chambers' help in interpretation was requested; and second, from the development of document certification services (q.v.). The war years stimulated a major involvement of chambers in dealing with regulatory enquiries. Thus in 1940 Leicester quotes that 92% of its members were in contact during the year (13,000 enquiries).[102] Nottingham developed a Customs enquiries department immediately following the war.[103] Coventry wrote 3750 individual letters to

---

[99] ABCC Home Affairs Committee, 7 January 1925; MS 14482/1.
[100] London *CCJ*, July (1940), p. 360.
[101] Birmingham chamber, GPC minutes, 19 November 1914.
[102] Leicester chamber history.
[103] Walton, Nottingham chamber history.

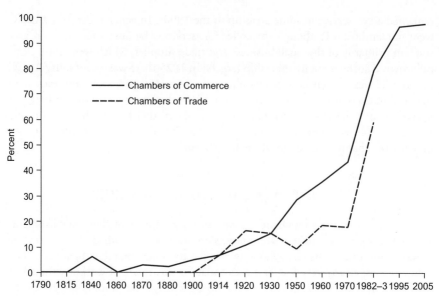

Fig. 12.5. Percentage of chambers of commerce and chambers of trade offering an enquiry service 1790–2005.

help members with specific problems in 1948; in addition to which it responded to 2000 other enquiries.[104] In general, chambers did not initially charge fees for handling enquiries, unless they involved extensive time and research. But they might charge non-members; e.g. Colchester charged enquiries at 1s. 6d. to non-members in the 1920–50 period.[105]

Analysis of the statistics for London (in Figure 11.1) may be indicative of the national trends until the 1970s: once recording began in 1891, numbers of enquiries grew rapidly up to the end of WW1, expanded more slowly in the 1920s and 1930s, declined significantly in the run up to and over WW2, but then expanded again to reach a peak in the early 1960s. Declines in the mid-1950s seem to reflect economic recession. The decline after the 1970s, however, appears to be structural and relates to the decline in London membership (which is not matched in other chambers). Declines from 2000 reflect competition from government Business Links.

From the 1970s statistics become available on the number of enquiries handled by the system as a whole, shown in Table 12.2 (which demonstrates London's aberrant statistics over 1970–90). An increase in enquiry activity in the late 1980s, rising to 802,783 in 1989, was offset by a steep reduction in the early 1990s, down to 260,371 by 1997. This is probably accounted for by two factors: first the severe recession of 1991–3 that removed many businesses; and second, the emergence of

---

[104] Coventry chamber, *Annual Report* (1948).
[105] Colchester chamber, *Annual Accounts*.

Table 12.2. Number of enquiries per year answered by chambers of commerce in BCC membership, 1972–2006: mean, maximum, minimum and 20/80% percentiles. Business Link (BL): number of additional enquiries handled within chambers for BL or third parties

Year	No.	Mean	Max.	Min.	80%	20%	Additional no. via BL
1971	38,019	418	115,000	0	7,480	100	—
1988	608,490	6,024	77,500	1	9,000	500	—
1992	578,891	5,732	70,000	6	8,250	600	—
1994	419,242	4,658	42,000	0	6,000	1,200	—
1996	306,047	4,138	27,743	39	7,772	940	—
1998	310,335	4,194	38,966	0	12,461	640	99,582
2000	307,230	4,177	31,090	0	11,148	1,117	102,448
2002	389,007	5,629	28,000	0	10,019	480	108,199
2004	398,981	7,764	50,599	150	13,650	2,156	66,885
2006	395,281	7,059	61,906	0	11,574	699	79,032
2008	393,522	5,957	41,385	0	6,396	0	51,088
2010	333,807	6,181	42,790	0	9,550	150	40,722

Source: BCC *Census* and *Benchmarking*; 1971 from ABCC MS 17548/3.

TECs in 1990 and then Business Link in 1993. From 1998, separate figures are given in Table 12.2 for chambers, and Business Link enquiries answered through chambers. In the Table the mean number of enquiries per chamber is affected by the amalgamation of chambers into larger bodies; down from 101 in 1992 to 90 in 1994, 74 in 1996, 61 in 2003, and 54–6 in 2004–10. The later enquiries are thus more concentrated than in earlier years. The range is also distorted by the emergence of Business Link and other third parties, as a result of which some chambers offered no enquiry service after 1994.

Character of enquiries

The nature of the enquiries being handled by chambers varies considerably in terms of the complexity (and cost) of dealing with them, and whether chamber staff can handle them in-house, or require referral outside. There are great differences in what constitutes an enquiry—a brief telephone call, letter, or email seeking a direction to other sources clearly differs significantly from an enquiry that takes time to consult sources or provide a level of specific assessment in-house. They 'vary from routine information which can be supplied over the telephone to highly complex questions on, for example, tariff classification, which requires considerable research, and really unusual queries such as the definition of a "day old" chick'.[106] This resulted in definitional problems. For example, in London, statistics on enquiries were amended in 1951 by the then secretary Max Leigh, who stated that 'he thought many of these [enquiries listed in the *Annual Report*] were

---

[106] London chamber, *Annual Report* (1962), typescript p. 11; MS/6459/32.

Table 12.3. Topics of enquiries as listed in London chamber *Annual Reports* (1956, 1957)

1	Parliamentary Acts & Statutory Instruments	10	Availability of government surplus stores
2	Agency agreements with overseas firms and individuals as selling agents	11	Letters of introduction
3	Enquiries for agents in the UK from overseas	12	Library and reference
4	Buying and Selling agents	13	Openings for trade
5	Complaints (mostly about payments of bills)	14	Overseas visits
6	Commercial representatives	15	Wording of contracts
7	Debts	16	Statistics
8	Examination of goods not up to standard	17	Subcontractors
9	Export agencies	18	Owners of trademarks and brands

undignified and had already given instructions for three-quarters of them to be deleted'.[107] It seems from this that they were more a record of any contact with members (and outsiders) rather than business enquiries in a strict sense. This problem of definition also beset government schemes such as Business Link.

In its *Annual Reports* of the 1950s, London lists the main topics covered by enquiries, which is instructive of the broad spread of demand, though no numbers are attached to each field so one cannot judge their relative importance. However, from the more anecdotal commentary in the London minutes and reports it is clear that the first five or six elements of Table 12.3 are among the most frequent fields covered. Overseas links became critical parts of enquiries by members from the 1950s, and government legislation became the other key area of concern. Some enquiries also specifically related to creditworthiness of individual businesses, or debt collection (as noted above).

In the smaller chambers enquiries related more to helping local visitors, commercial travellers, and those in transit. The early relationship of chambers with town guides and other publicity material has been noted above; but some of the chambers went much further by having local information bureaux, precursors of modern tourist offices. This was chiefly associated with the smaller chambers and was often undertaken in partnership with, and subsidized by, the local authority. For example, Cheltenham ran an information bureau in the 1930s and 1950s–1960s, mostly to facilitate hotel bookings. In 1938 it had an income of £631 and expenditure of £627; in 1950 income was £940 and expenditure £1358 with the deficit made up by donations.[108] It is clear, therefore, that they were not money-raising enterprises but chiefly a general support to the local economy (Cheltenham's membership of about 100 at this time had only five hoteliers).

The only assessment of chamber of commerce enquiries to analyse their transaction cost characteristics has been in 1992, using staff diaries. It showed that 54% of enquiries were on domestic and 46% on foreign matters, involving a similar division of staff time. The major topics of enquiries were specific clients, suppliers,

[107] London chamber, Council minutes, 13 February 1951; MS 16459/26.
[108] Colchester chamber, *Annual Accounts*.

and distributors (36% of all domestic enquiries, and 27% of foreign matters). Referral to other agents accounted for 13.5%. Other enquiries involved a very wide range, no category being more than 4% of the total. The general conclusion to be drawn is that chambers need to offer a broad range of expertise, but capable of being tailored to each business need, and drawing on the interconnectedness of the information expertise. Enquiries generally have relatively low transaction costs, and draw on the chamber's status as a trusted source for referral to other agents or as a local one-stop shop.[109]

12.7 CERTIFICATION OF COMMERCIAL DOCUMENTS

The certification of commercial documents was undertaken by a variety of individuals in the 18th and 19th centuries: by lawyers, town mayors, merchant organizations, and a variety of bodies. However, the chambers of commerce became a natural focus for certification once they were established. The volumes dealt with were initially probably very small, most trade relying primarily on the traditional methods of letters or contract notes exchanged directly between merchants, their agents or factors.

Origins

The significant development of certificates as a chamber-wide service originated in the late 1880s and followed the emergence of tariff wars. As noted by London chamber in 1890, certificates arose 'from the unfortunate prevalence of differential custom tariffs, and the necessity ... of checking ... that to which they are really entitled'.[110] London began issuing certificates on a very small scale for Serbia in about 1885–6;[111] the main service began in 1888. This grew rapidly. In that half-year alone it issued 1159 certificates. By 1893 the chamber was issuing over 10,000 per year. Numbers dropped back in the 1899–1911 period, before steadily growing, to over 300,000 per year from the 1960s. The world wars resulted in severe drops in certificate issuing, though from the middle of WW1 certification schemes to control trade with every nation resulted in a major increase in issuing.

The 1888 certificates resulted from action by the Italian government. London noted 'our staff was amongst the first to notice, and take advantage of, the permission given by the Italian government to chambers of commerce, to issue certificates of origin'. Spanish, French, Swiss, Austrian, and Bulgarian certificates were introduced in 1892, and in the same year Swiss commercial travellers' certificates as well as certificates for goods were required 'since the tariff war

---

[109] Bennett (1996b). See wider role of transaction costs in Chapter 3 (Table 3.2).
[110] London *CCJ*, 5 May (1890).
[111] Quoted in ACC, *Proceedings*, 13–15 March (1894), pp. 111–13.

between Switzerland and France'. In 1894, 5450 Swiss commercial travellers' certificates were issued by London, 41% of all certificates.[112]

The influence of foreign government tariff and other regulatory decisions dominates this early period. A large reduction in number of certificates issued in 1896 was the result of 'settlement of the tariff dispute between Switzerland and France'. The introduction of Canadian certificates in 1897 led to a large increase in that year, but reduction in numbers in 1898 was a result of changes in Canada and Spain. However, new tariffs imposed by Germany, Russia, Austria, Hungary, and Romania in the early 1900s led to increases. In 1912 the war between Turkey and Italy stimulated a further increase, whilst in 1915 the Russian government demanded certificates. After WW1 certificates were important in proving the nationality of firms, e.g. those of Belgium and Luxembourg introduced in 1922 were used to demonstrate 'non-German' origin.[113]

The initial system of authentication of certificates was cumbersome. Thus in 1888 London was issuing certificates to members only (soon dropped as a constraint). The business 'signed a stamped agreement, prepared by [the chamber's] solicitors, by which they undertake to indemnify the chamber for any mistake, omission, or false declaration'. These documents soon came under a British government regulatory regime, administered by the Inland Revenue. Then each chamber had to seek approval for its certificate issuing. This could be slow, and it is clear (though not explicit in ACC records) that at some times London was resistant to other chambers participating. For example, Leeds began stamping documents in 1891, but until formally recognized by the Commissioners of Inland Revenue in 1901, they had to be forwarded to London to be stamped.[114] At this time the Nottingham chamber had to have its certificates for Spain sworn before the Mayor or magistrate.[115]

The recognition of chamber certification by the government, through the Inland Revenue, was at first only an informal agreement, so that by 1893, London was calling for 'legislation to authorise the practice' more formally.[116] The first more formal regularization was by the Customs Convention of 1923, with administration by the BoT. This led to an agreement between BoT and ABCC that only designated chambers could issue certificates.[117] In 1937 the ABCC imposed rules for the issuing of certificates, which have continued through various revisions, subsequently overseen by the DTI. A further important development was the issuing of ATA Carnets (certificates to facilitate the transit of commercial

---

[112] London chamber, *Annual Report* (1888), p. 41; (1892), p. 7; (1894).
[113] London chamber *Annual Reports* for respective years.
[114] Noted in Leeds chamber *Yearbook* (1920), p. 44.
[115] Quoted in Taylor (2007), p. 54.
[116] ACC, *Proceedings*, 13–15 March (1893), pp. 111–13.
[117] In addition, the 1923 convention allowed the FBI (later CBI) London and regional offices to issue certificates. FBI was never a large player in issuing, but its role had some effect on ABCC negotiations with its members; see e.g. Chapter 8, and Taylor (2007), Chapter 5.

samples and exhibits to trade fairs), where London has acted as the national authority for the UK.[118]

Volumes and fees

Certificates were usually charged at a fee by chambers. London's initial rate was 2d., a significant saving on previous consular rates;[119] Russian consular fees were quoted as 3s. 3d. in 1892, rising to 9s. 9d. in 1893.[120] Certificates thus represent one of the earliest fee-based services for many chambers. Fees were, however, initially seen as fairly nominal, and Nottingham chamber kept the same fee for issuing of an export certificate from the 1890s until the 1960s.[121] In Ipswich, the first certificate of origin, issued to the major local company of Ransom, Sims and Jefferies Ltd, was issued 30 April 1901 for goods to Prussia. No charge was made for this, or subsequent certificates issued until 1918,[122] when a fee of 1s. was introduced, yielding an income of £1 18s. in 1920, rising to £3 18s. in 1930. London's fees, however, rose from 2d. in 1888 to average levels of 2s. over 1900–1940s.

The income stream became quite significant for those chambers that had a large number of exporting members, even from an early date. For example, certificates of origin gave Bradford chamber an income of £149 in 1900, rising to £1303 in 1923, £3247 in 1950, and £7207 in 1960.[123] This was, respectively, 21%, 20%, 27%, and 36% of total income in each year. In London, fee income levels were the largest of any chamber in most years, reaching £815 in 1893, but reducing to £84 in 1900. By 1950 they were £71,914, which was then 15% of total income. By 1960 the income was £48,368 (28% of all income); in 1970 £163,530 (41%); 1980 £1.2 million (43%); and 1998 £3.02 million (50%). In 1971 London was issuing 300,000 per year, claiming that this was 'over six times the next chamber of commerce in Great Britain and larger than any similar chamber in the world'.[124] For some small chambers with a large export sector, certificates became the major motive for membership and a dominant source of income. Thus in the South of Scotland chamber, with major local hosiery exporters from an early date, certificates had reached 38% of income in 1961, and 62% by 1977.[125] 'It was what kept us alive' in the view of the secretary of the chamber in the 1980s and 1990s.[126] For many chambers certificate income saved them from severe

[118] Taylor (2007), p. 54.
[119] Consular rates were confused, quoted as between 1s. 7d. and 2s. 1d.: London chamber *Annual Report* (1888), p. 41; and 7s. and 10s.: *Annual Report* (1892), p. 42.
[120] Quoted in ACC, *Proceedings*, 13–15 March (1893), pp. 111–13.
[121] Nottingham chamber history, p. 48.
[122] Ipswich chamber, minutes 30 April 1901, 26 February 1918.
[123] Bradford chamber, *Annual Reports and Accounts*.
[124] London chamber, *Annual Report* (1971).
[125] South of Scotland chamber, *Annual Reports*.
[126] Comment to author by Alan Rintoul, retired chamber secretary, April 2009; also see Chapter 16.

income shortages in the 1920s and 1930s,[127] and was their main service income until the early 1980s.

There was continued pressure in ACC/ABCC to standardize fee levels between chambers, or at least bring all up to an acceptable minimum level. In 1936 ABCC set up a 'special committee to act in cooperation with the Board of Trade', in cooperation with the FBI, to offer advice and guidance to the BoT and ensure that the chambers 'possess the means to organise united and uniform action'.[128] Extensive exchanges then followed in 1936–7 between the chambers, and between the chambers and ABCC, which sought to create a new regime of charges and a process to agree them. These exchanges proved largely fruitless.[129] The London chamber was reluctant to increase fees without a lower fee for small value consign-ments. The small traders were reported as critical of the high costs of certificates and the lack of justification for fees.[130] In 1939, Manchester chamber announced a new scale of fees without consultation with ABCC or other chambers. The FBI was unhappy that Manchester had moved without consulting the Certificates of Origin Advisory Committee of which they were members, and the FBI were critical of the 'low level of uniformity . . . in chamber of commerce procedures'.[131] Further align-ment was postponed during WW2. However, in 1956 a standard minimum national rate was generally in use of 1s. for members and 5s. for non-members; but in 1959 London again resisted a proposal from Manchester, supported by Glasgow and Belfast, to increase fees to 3s. 6d. and 7s. London was supported by Leeds and Bolton.[132] London's concern always carried great sway as the largest issuer of certificates, and was driven by the number of non-members using their services. The fees were eventually raised to 3s. 6d. and 6s. in 1963, to 5s. and 6s. in 1968, to 50p and £1 in 1970, and reached £2.40 and £3 in 1978. London's fees averaged 10s. in the 1950s and 1960s, rising to £5.60 in 1980, and ranged from £14.28 to £247.28 (incl. VAT) in 2007 depending on the type of certificate and country involved.

Variation between chambers

Comparative national statistics on the issuing of certificates do not exist for early years, and cannot be reliably constructed from local records. However, it is clear

[127] See e.g. Streat *Diary* for 1935 in Manchester, Dupree (1987), vol. i, p. 400: 'our income exceeded our present expenditure, largely because of the fees we are receiving for certificates of origin'.
[128] ABCC Executive Council, 4 March 1936; this consisted initially of the chair of the Overseas Trade Committee, the secretary of ABCC, the secretaries of the chambers at London, Manchester, Birmingham, Glasgow, Bradford, and Leicester, and two representatives of the FBI. In 1957 the structure was modified to have 5 chambers with over 2000 members, 3 chambers with 1000–2000 members, and 2 chambers with less than 1000 members: ABCC, GPC, 2 October 1957.
[129] London chamber, Certificates of Origin Committee; MS 16483/1.
[130] London chamber, Certificates of Origin Committee, quoting *Draper and Drapery Times*, 25 July 1936.
[131] London chamber, Certificates of Origin Committee, quoting FBI letter of 3 May, 1939; MS 16483/1.
[132] ABCC, GPC, 6 May 1959.

that although the major chambers dominated, many small chambers were also involved, albeit only issuing a handful of certificates. Figure 12.6 shows the range of certificate issuing of chambers around the country. Generally, this demonstrates the importance of ports of entry and export in 1972 (the earliest year with data), but with increasing concentration by 1991, and a stronger emphasis on airports in 2005. The pattern has become even more concentrated since 2005 as the number of chambers has consolidated further.

Developments after the 1970s make clear the shift from a very wide spread up to the 1990s, to a service concentrated within the main accredited chambers after 2000. The wide spread in the earlier period highlights the difficulties of maintaining a common standard and training staff to a minimum level. In many cases document issuing was only part of the local clerk or secretary's job. In earlier years these difficulties would have been even greater as the numbers of documents and fees charged were small. By the 2000s the highly concentrated system was able to develop and impose much stronger training and quality control standards. This is one of the most beneficial outcomes of an agreement of ABCC with the DTI in 1991, and the *Development Strategy* of the same period.

Government recognition

Document certification is an important case of autonomous chamber service development, but one that relies heavily on government support in both the UK and Ireland. It demonstrates how some of the weaknesses of a voluntary system can be overcome by a level of stable government support. This support has operated from the Customs Convention of 1923 up to the present. It is a good example of government working with commercial interests, backing procedures defined by business.

With government recognition, certificate issuing also became an important instrument of ABCC/BCC and CI policy. Recognition, controlled by ABCC and CI through a special committee composed of experts from leading chambers, was used as a means to encourage chambers to develop themselves, or to meet certain standards of size or quality. In the UK, efforts to raise the average quality of service resulted in a new staff training *Handbook* and national schedules of fees from 1963.[133] Inspection of chamber certificate-issuing staff and processes was inaugurated in 1967 following the Dixon Report, with 23 chambers inspected in 1967, 19 in 1968, and 42 in 1969.[134] However, the BoT allowed extension to new bodies, if conforming to ABCC inspection standards. This allowed Colchester, Tunbridge Wells, and Medway to issue certificates in 1967; and Paisley and North Lindsey in 1968. The inspection regime thus strengthened but also weakened ABCC controls, and it was forced to accept that Croydon and Westminster chambers would issue, even though they lapsed from ABCC in some years. From the 1990s recognition of

---

[133] Quoted in ABCC *Annual Report* (1963–4).
[134] ABCC *Annual Reports* (1967–8 to 1969–70); individual inspection reports 1969–70 in MS 17556.

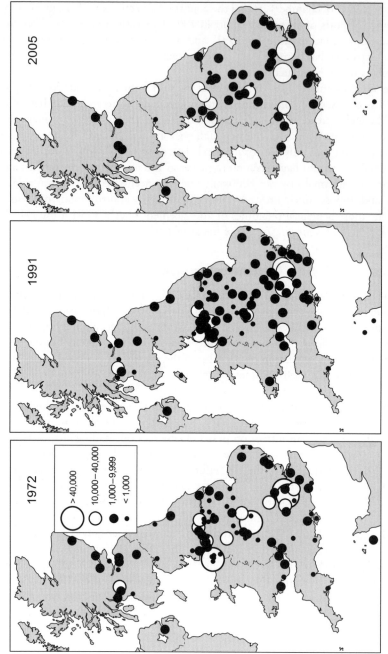

Fig. 12.6. Numbers of certificates issued by chambers of commerce in 1972, 1991, and 2005.

certificate-issuing powers was a means for BCC to lever chambers into mergers. Certificates are thus intimately bound up with the evolution of the national benchmarks and policy for the BCC chambers as a whole.

The modern development of the UK chamber export documentation and advice service dates from January 1991. This followed early joint working between the ABCC and DTI, in which the DTI had sponsored an Active Exporting Scheme. The 1991 scheme introduced a support system of research, market intelligence, export training, export clubs, and Single European Market information.[135] The initiative was linked to the European single market initiative introduced in 1992, which was intended to reduce internal tariff and trade barriers between the members of the European Community (now EU). The scheme operated under the Certification and International Trade Formalities Committee of the ABCC. This committee was a separate body from the ABCC as a whole, with 'Chinese walls' between it and the local chamber chief executives. It provided an important fillip to the chamber system and increased the role and central control by ABCC.[136] It also gave to ABCC significant new resources, about £200,000 per year in the early 1990s.[137]

12.8 CONCILIATION IN LABOUR DISPUTES

There are only isolated examples of chambers being involved in early attempts to mediate or conciliate in labour disputes. One example was in Belfast in 1802 where the chamber called on local JPs to 'suppress combination among the working tradespeople'; it organized a successful deputation to mediate between the muslin weavers, who agreed to improve the promptness of their delivery, and the employers, who agreed to pay cash instead of bank notes (which had been the main source of the grievance).[138] But there were few other cases. The increasing difficulties experienced by businesses deriving from the emergence of organized labour in trade unions and similar bodies were not, on the whole, something that chambers involved themselves in directly. Most employers instead used sector 'employer associations' whose specific purpose was to act as a negotiating and conciliation body.

Growth of Boards

However, in the late 19th century a move was made to try to engage chambers in labour dispute conciliation and some took an active role. The Trades Unions Commission of 1867–9 had recommended that local Boards of Conciliation should be developed; it was particularly impressed by one in Nottingham for the

---

[135] ABCC (1992), *British Chambers of Commerce Export Services 1992/3*.
[136] Taylor (2007), chapter 5.
[137] ABCC *Annual Accounts*.
[138] Belfast chamber minutes, 11 May and 12 May 1802.

lace and hosiery trades, which had a major effect on reducing strikes. 'The great point is to bring the masters and men face-to-face to discuss their differences before their feelings have become embittered . . . an expedient for bringing employers and members together to discuss in a friendly manner questions of wages, and other points of difference, . . . if possible, to come to an amicable understanding.' It was composed of seven employers and seven workmen, elected by each constituency, meeting quarterly or more frequently by demand.[139] The only other significant example the Commission found at this time was an arbitration board under a local judge at Worcester. As far as can be determined, neither of these conciliation bodies was linked directly to the local chamber.

According to the Webbs, employers were slow to see the advantages of these Boards, and the Commission was important in encouraging their more widespread development. In fact the evidence for their benefits is equivocal, and even the Webbs admit that many workers were reluctant to accept that wages were linked to prices and trade as, of course, the employers argued.[140] However, the 1867–9 Commission's recommendation for the development of Boards did have a major impact in supporting a purely voluntary system with no Act or legal powers; this was 'the essence of the system'. A legal approach was believed to lead to 'jealousy or distrust . . . of either party'. Although voluntary 'agreement is not legally binding, it is considered morally binding' and is the result of 'free discussion and, in most case, some degree of mutual concession, [which leads to] an understanding satisfactory to both parties'.[141]

By the time of the Royal Commission on Labour 1892, 32 chambers were listed as providing for dispute conciliation in their rules, and eight specifically listed as offering the service actively. The London chamber in its evidence stated that Conciliation Boards either existed or were being set up in 21 chambers.[142] The fullest list of chambers with some activity is:

Aberdeen	Dewsbury	Greenock	Morley
Barnsley	Dublin	Grimsby	Newport
Birmingham	Dudley	Halifax	Nottingham
Bradford	Dundee	Hull	Plymouth
Bristol	Edinburgh	Leeds	Rochdale
Cardiff	Exeter	Liverpool	Walsall
Cleckheaton	Glasgow	London	Wolverhampton
Derby	Gloucester	Manchester	Worcester
			Yeadon and Guisley

---

[139] Royal Commission on Trades Unions, *House of Commons Papers* (1867–9), xxxi, p. xxvii.
[140] Webb and Webb (1920), pp. 338–45; Phelps Brown (1959).
[141] Royal Commission on Trades Unions (1867–9), *House of Commons Papers*, xxxi, pp. xxvii–xxviii; Ilersic and Liddle (1960), pp. 156–7.
[142] Royal Commission on Labour, *House of Commons Papers* (1892), xxxvi, part V, pp. xxxii–xxxiv; (1892), xxxvi, part IV, p. 833.

This represents about 30–40% of the chambers in existence at that time. This is, however, an overestimate of activism. Some of these chambers never moved beyond considering setting up a Board. Only a few, particularly London, Leeds, Nottingham, Bristol, and Bradford seem to have definitely had active Boards, though two section committees named in Hull (for oil and for timber) acted as active Boards in setting wages.

The London chamber urged other chambers to follow the example of its Board of Conciliation over the 1890s.[143] The Belfast chamber, probably following this lead, set up its Conciliation Board, with rules governing 16 different trades in 1895, but there is no record of it having sat.[144] At that time there was disagreement between chambers on whether a voluntary or compulsory system of arbitration should be developed. In 1890 the ACC had held a vote on Aberdeen's motion in favour of voluntary Boards. But in 1893 Nottingham's motion in favour of compulsory arbitration was more favoured, with the final vote being in favour of the BoT being given legal powers 'to settle labour disputes by arbitration, conciliation and mediation'.[145]

Links to trades councils

Conciliation Boards were local and covered a range of trades rather than a single sector. This made chambers a natural base, but trade unions also required a means for coordination, which developed as trades councils. 'Boards have in almost every case formed under the auspices, and on the initiative, of the local chamber of commerce, and generally with the co-operation of the local trades council'.[146] It was stated that trades councils were formed to represent, 'advance and protect the rights of labour . . . by endeavouring to settle disputes . . . by petitioning parliament . . . by watching over the proceedings of local boards and law courts'.[147] By 1860 there were five established trades councils, in Glasgow, Liverpool, London, Sheffield, and Edinburgh, and about 24 by 1870–3. But like the chamber Boards, they did not really develop more widely until the late 1880s. There were over 60 by 1889–91, and by 1900 over 100.[148] The growth of chamber conciliation boards and trades councils was thus closely associated in time and in many areas they worked closely together, as in Birmingham, Dudley, South Staffordshire, and Walsall.[149] In Walsall the chamber acted in an ad hoc way to resolve a bit-makers' strike in 1888, but when it formed its formal Board in 1890, this was not accepted

---

[143] London *CCJ*, 5 July (1890), 10 February (1892), September (1894), March (1895).
[144] Belfast chamber minutes, 24 October 1895.
[145] Discussion in ACC, *Proceedings*, 26–7 September (1893), pp. 92–4; and 13–15 March (1894), p. 47.
[146] Royal Commission on Labour (1892), p. xxxviii.
[147] As stated in Aberdeen United Trades Council, *Rules*, 1889; in Royal Commission (1892), p. 325.
[148] Webb and Webb (1920), pp. 242–4 and p. 557 n.; Phelps Brown (1959).
[149] Trainor (1993), pp. 163–4.

by the unions. It was given a new constitution in 1900, after which it was used several times per year, working with the trades council.[150]

The trades councils could organize collective negotiations for a whole area, and provide shared support in times of crisis (e.g. strikes); but they increasingly took on roles and collective organization of a populist or political character (e.g. against slavery), arranged local demonstrations, began to lobby directly to ministers, and also lobbied within the trade union movement itself. For the Webbs 'the trades council represents the larger world of labour politics . . . working for the election of labour men in the local governing bodies . . . (of the) School Board, or the Town Council, or perhaps even as far as Parliament itself'. Their main role became a political organization, especially in the larger urban centres. From 1900 they played a formal role within Labour Party machinery. This party role steadily undermined their value as Conciliation Bodies.[151]

Later evolution

To overcome some of the deficiencies of Conciliation Boards, development was encouraged by the Conciliation Act (1896), which followed lobbying by the ACC and others. In 1907 the BoT was given power to set up a 'permanent Court of Arbitration for dealing with trade disputes . . . not in anyway departing from its voluntary character',[152] formed of three panels (of eminent people, employers, and employees). It urged the chambers of commerce to become strongly involved in this. This had some success in increasing the number of cases settled by Boards,[153] but trade depression in 1908–9 and the Trades Dispute Act of 1906, which considerably strengthened union powers, undermined it.

The ACC in 1912 still urged local chambers to assist in the formation of voluntary Boards.[154] But in 1914 a resolution from Dudley for chambers to establish Labour Tribunals in all areas was voted down, and ACC withheld from drawing up a template scheme, though it would supply chambers with copies of other chamber schemes.[155] Dublin declined ever to establish a scheme,[156] and many local Boards disappeared during WW1. The Aberdeen Conciliation Board, established in 1889, lapsed during WW1;[157] Leeds chamber's Board established in 1890, lasted until c.1910;[158] in Bradford only two disputes were settled, in 1891–2;[159]

[150] Walsall chamber, *Commercial Yearbook* (1916).
[151] Webb and Webb (1920), pp. 244–9, 454, and 557–561; Clinton (1977).
[152] See ACC, Proceedings (1907); also local chamber discussions; e.g. Barnsley chamber minutes, 1908, pp. 9–10.
[153] e.g. *Seventh Report of the BoT of Proceedings under the Conciliation (Trade Disputes) Act 1896* (1907–9).
[154] ACC, minutes, 1912.
[155] ACC, *Monthly Proceedings*, July (1914), p. 18.
[156] Dublin chamber, *Report of Council*, 1914.
[157] Aberdeen chamber, *Journal* (1) October (1919), p. 3.
[158] Leeds chamber history.
[159] Royal Commission (1892), p. xxxviii.

Warrington chamber's Board proposed in 1900[160] appears to have never operated; Birmingham considered re-establishing a Board in 1912 but decided not to go ahead;[161] Rotherham's Board existed up to 1919, but then lapsed.[162] The London chamber's Labour Conciliation and Arbitration Board operated from 1890 but closed in 1922[163] when it was costing £20–5 per year.[164] In 1907 the London Board considered 15 disputes, but this was down to nine in 1908 and 1909.[165] In 1916 it considered three disputes and acted in only one. The London Board, as well as providing 'amicable methods' for settling labour disputes, also promoted much wider activities such as voluntary agreements covering a whole workplace. In 1916 there were 18 of these under the Board, and 40 awards.[166]

Most chamber involvement faded with WW1 regulations. However, there were a few later examples, although their use was small. Winchester included such a Board in its Memorandum and Articles when it was established in 1918. Coventry's revised Articles in 1923 specifically allowed a conciliation Board to be set up, to negotiate on behalf of employers 'hours, wages or conditions of employment'.[167] In 1957 North Staffordshire chamber stated that it would have liked to be more active in dispute resolution, and suggested that ABCC should encourage this as a way of being more closely involved with government, like the FBI and NUM.[168] A different concept, of a Board of Conciliation between employers and the public was established in Croydon chamber in 1974, which continued until its merger with London chamber in 2007, though it was apparently used only very occasionally. Croydon drew this up in liaison with the Office of Fair Trading, with 'the basic intention to offer to conciliate between [chamber] members and the public wherever disagreements existed'. The scheme was launched at a lunch by John Methven, then director general of the OFT.[169]

12.9 LABOUR MARKET INFORMATION AND RECRUITMENT

Rather than attempting labour market regulation or conciliation, more chambers were involved in supplying labour market intelligence. The BoT relied on chambers

---

[160] Warrington chamber, *Annual Report* (1900), p. 11.

[161] Birmingham chamber, GPC minutes, 30 September 1912.

[162] Listed in *Industrial Sheffield and Rotherham Yearbook* (1919), but not mentioned thereafter.

[163] London chamber minutes, MS 16560; Labour Conciliation and Arbitration Board Report, 1916, MS 16459/7.

[164] London chamber, Finance Committee minutes, MS16465.

[165] London chamber, *Annual Report* in *CCJ*, 30 (1910), p. 130.

[166] London, Labour Conciliation and Arbitration Board, *26ᵗʰ Annual Report* (1916), p. 174; MS 16459/7.

[167] Coventry chamber, *Memorandum and Articles of Association* (1918), p. 4; pencil annotations by the chamber secretary preparatory to redraft of 1923 Memorandum. The first chamber opposed labour conciliation in 1856 (chamber history, Andrew, 1978, p. 2).

[168] E. James Johnson, secretary of North Staffordshire chamber: quoted in ABCC, GPC, 6 November 1957.

[169] Croydon chamber, *Journal* (1976), pp. 32–5, quoted in Croydon history, p. 12.

as a major source of information on wage rates in the 19th century, to monitor national trends, regional differences, and sector development. This was a key activity of Leicester chamber in the 1860s in the leather and hosiery industries. Macclesfield played a similar role in the silk industry, Nottingham in footwear, Manchester in cotton, Leeds in worsted, and so on in other industrial districts. This became a major input into Commercial Intelligence Committees of the BoT from the 1890s up to WW2.

Given their position in the local labour market, a few chambers also developed employment departments. One of the largest and most successful of these was in London, initiated in 1894. This sought to link employers needing recruits to employees who needed a job. Employers who were members received a discount on the recruitment fee (in the 1940s and 1950s this was £3 for members and £3 10s. for non-members for lower wage jobs of less than £5 per week; and £5 for members compared to £6 for non-members for the higher paid jobs with wages of £5 or more per week). The scheme also registered candidates who had passed commercial education examinations held by the chamber (there were 1672 of these in 1903)[170] and, since the list was published monthly in the CCJ (held by many libraries), allowed other employers to use the service.

It was a very successful activity, having over 5000 advertisements per year in the 1920s. In 1913 it had 4865 applicants and was involved with 4608 employers, rising to a peak of 13,347 applicants in 1932, and a peak of 5022 employers in 1915. The general evolution of the scheme is shown in Figure 12.7. The popularity clearly depended on the economic cycle, being higher for applicants when unemployment was high, and higher for employers when the economy was booming. It was severely reduced in both World Wars.[171] Although it delivered relatively small net revenue to the chamber (£165 in 1913, rising to £169 in 1920 and £735 in 1930), it was important in stimulating employer involvement, and hence membership, and reinforced the initiative by London for commercial education certificates (q.v. below). It also seems to have had a strong effect in encouraging membership retention (see Chapter 16). The London scheme was closed in 1953 due to reduced demand and competition from government Labour Exchanges.

Only three chambers developed large-scale and effective employment departments: when Derby chamber was considering developing its own employment department in 1933, it quoted that only three already existed: in London, Glasgow, and Manchester.[172] In other chambers some more informal activity may have existed, and a few chambers used it as a possible service to members which they advertised in their annual reports or publicity leaflets; e.g. Trowbridge chamber in 1910 claimed to use information from members requiring casual labour to find employment for the unemployed.[173] Also, as a response to calls from government, most chambers in 1918–20 actively circulated lists of unemployed ex-servicemen

[170] Musgrave (1914), pp. 69–70.
[171] London chamber, *Annual Reports*.
[172] Derby chamber minutes, October 1930.
[173] Trowbridge chamber, *Annual Report* (1910), p. 6.

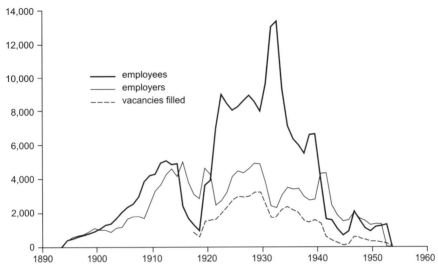

Fig. 12.7. London chamber of commerce employment agency: employees placed, employers involved, and vacancies filled, 1894–1953. (*Source*: London chamber *Annual Reports* and minutes.)

who were seeking vacancies. A special link between Welwyn Garden City chamber and Jarrow was established in 1933–4, after the Jarrow March, to transfer unemployed families in order to increase the availability of 'juvenile' labour.[174] But it is not clear, other than London, Glasgow, and Manchester, that any of these services offered substantial volumes. Large-scale involvement of most chambers to help the unemployed awaited the development of government training schemes in the 1960s. However, in modern times Mid Yorkshire chamber ran a significant local employment agency in the 1980s and 1990s.

12.10 COMMERCIAL EXAMINATIONS

From the 1850s there had been a widespread debate in Britain about the need for improved technical and commercial education. Much of this was focused on the need for clerks and administrators. Lyssons quotes the Census data of the period showing how the numbers of commercial clerks had increased from 43,741 in 1851 to 89,630 in 1871, further doubling to 175,468 in 1881, and rising to 307,889 in 1901 in England and Wales. Similar growth was also evident among commercial travellers, from 9,395 in 1851 to 63,940 in 1901, and also for accountants, banking, and insurance.[175] This spectacular rise, at a time of falling prices and

[174] Welwyn Garden City chamber, *Annual Reports* (1933 and 1934).
[175] Lyssons (1988), p. 4.

profits, but increasing output, emphasized the need for capability of office and business services support, particularly against foreign competition. As a result, improved technical education, and language training to deal with foreign markets, became widely recognized as urgent needs. The chambers had been strong advocates of the need for improvement from the 1860s. In 1867 the Vice-President of the Privy Council, as chair of a Council Committee on Education, received chambers' detailed summary of local deficiencies, which mainly focused on gaps in science skills.[176] Chambers contributed strongly to the Royal Commission on Technical Instruction (1881), and the Royal Commission on the Depression of Trade and Industry (1886), which provided further evidence of the need for improvements in technical education. In a survey in 1887, the London chamber found that up to 40% of staff in many city offices were foreign, chiefly German, and were mainly employed because of their superior training.[177]

Reform of the educational system began, through the Local Government Act 1888 and Technical Instruction Act 1889. But these were recognized as ineffective for technical education since they only enabled local Education Boards to act; few appeared interested in doing so, particularly for technical needs. Some developments occurred as a result of the activities of the Society of Arts in the 1850s; and the City and Guilds of London Institute was established in 1879. But there was still a gap that chambers felt they could fill. After considerable debate, which had begun in the ACC in the 1870s, the London chamber instituted commercial examination certificates in 1889, in conjunction with the Oxford and Cambridge School Examination Boards. The only other attempt to set up such a scheme was by Manchester chamber also in 1889, but this was discontinued in 1893 because of a lack of entries (only 110 in 1891 and 19 in 1892).[178]

The London chamber examination scheme

The London chamber scheme was very successful, with take-up deriving from pressure from local chambers and employers. Examination centres were provided at chambers or other local centres; and many chambers offered scholarships, prizes, and medals. By 1892 Ipswich, and by 1895 Portsmouth, joined London in providing local centres. These were followed by Aberdeen and Hull in 1897; and Southampton, Croydon, Cardiff, Luton, and Swansea in 1898. In these early days the start-up costs were heavy and off-putting. In Ipswich the implementation of the London chamber examinations cost £14 in 1893 with only £5 5s. recouped in fees from five candidates. In 1894 the cost was £13 12s. 4d. with fees of £8 15s. In the early days, therefore, the examinations were run at a loss for the early adopters.[179]

[176] Answers from chambers to queries from the Vice-President of the Privy Council; coordinated by ACC, *House of Commons Papers* (1867–8), liv, 23, pp. 1–24.
[177] Lyssons (1988), pp. 4–8; Ilersic and Liddle (1960), chapter 12; Musgrave (1914), p. 64.
[178] Ilersic and Liddle (1960), pp. 134–6; Lyssons (1988), p. 27.
[179] Ipswich chamber minutes, 1893 and 1894.

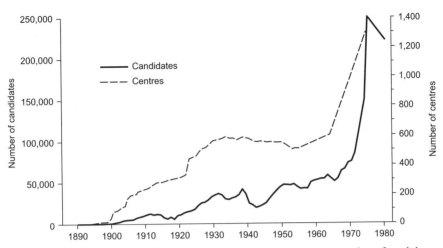

Fig. 12.8. London chamber of commerce commercial examinations: number of candidates and number of examination centres, 1890–1982. (*Source*: London chamber *Annual Reports* and minutes.)

As the numbers grew the unit costs reduced. By 1900 the number of centres had risen to 38; 233 in 1910; 315 in 1920; and 564 in 1930. The number jumped to over 1300 in the 1970s. These centres involved local colleges as well as chambers, and spread widely overseas.[180] With the development of local centres, so the number of candidates also grew, though examinees often travelled to London and other large centres to take examinations (e.g. in 1957, examinations were held in 11 centres). Total examination entries grew from 65 in 1890, to 922 in 1900, 11,605 in 1910, and 34,874 in 1930, with the numbers staying at between 20,000 and 46,000 up to the 1960s, after which it increased rapidly again. The evolution is shown in Figure 12.8. This reflects only the entries; the enquiries and stimulus of the scheme was much wider. For example, in 1896 in addition to 123 candidates, there were 1281 requests for papers; this rose to 3186 in 1897, and 7243 in 1898. The examination scheme became a registered charity in 1965; it was re-established as the Commercial Education Trust in 1989, as a company limited by guarantee. In 2002 the London chamber, as trustees, sold the trust to AIM Education and Development International plc, but retained 49% of the issued equity. In March 2006 the chamber's final holding was sold, though the chamber's name is still used for the scheme.

The entries were spread between elementary (about 30% in 1950), intermediate (about 50%), and higher stages (15%). Pass rates were, respectively, 62%, 59%, and 52% at each level in 1950. In addition, certificates for teachers were offered over 1905–25 (providing a total of 9400 entries and 4501 awards for these years), and secretarial diplomas were initiated in 1956.[181] Employers were strongly

---

[180] Bombay (Mumbai) was the first overseas centre, in 1900.
[181] All statistics from London chamber, *Annual Reports*.

involved in curriculum design from the outset, and were encouraged to develop adaptations and options designed for specific sectors (though by 1913 only one sector—textile trade—had done so). As an inducement to teachers and examiners, members of chambers, led by London, undertook that they would give preference to holders of certificates in filling vacancies, other things being equal among candidates. The register of the London chamber's employment department was a means to encourage this further[182] (q.v. above). By the 1920s and 1930s the established status of the examination (as well as comparable City and Guilds, Society of Arts, etc.) was widely used by employers as a guide to screen job applicants.

The certificates not only served, and continue to serve, an important commercial need, but also proved to be an extremely successful financial venture for the London chamber. Although it maintained separate accounts and sought to balance its income and expenditure, it gave the chamber immense national visibility, and in this field developed a very real sense in which the London chamber could act as a national lead in the collective interest. The involvement of most chambers as local centres, and the donation by many local chambers of prizes and scholarships, was a very tangible manifestation of a strengthening national chamber system across Britain. This success undoubtedly coloured London's approach to other chamber activities, in which its attempts to provide leadership were sometimes less successful. The service also supported a significant staff that had some limited spillover benefits to other service provision, contributing to London's early achievement of a critical mass of resources, staff, and services. From a comparatively late foundation in 1882, the London chamber staff had grown from 2 in 1883, to 16 in 1900, and 47 in 1914, overtaking all other chambers in staff and income by 1900. It appears that, with its employment agency service, to which there was a link, commercial examinations were a significant influence on membership retention in the London chamber (see Chapter 16). The modern involvement of chambers in 'commercial education', now largely through training programmes at chambers, colleges, and on employers' premises, continues up to the present.

12.11 OPPORTUNISTIC SERVICE DEVELOPMENTS

The spotting of specific market opportunities or pressure from particular members for a specific service led to several locally important services. Dundee innovated a post box service in the 1890s. These boxes were housed along one side of the reading room and yielded £59 per year in rent in 1900. This rose to £82 by the 1960s and was still £81 in 1970.[183] They were only disbanded in about 1995 when the last user withdrew. Their initial purpose was 'to provide a quick way for the manufacturers and merchants to receive and distribute price lists, which were deposited four times a day'. They became an important supplementary local mail

[182] Musgrave (1914), pp. 69–70.
[183] Dundee chamber, minutes and *Accounts*.

office up to the 1950s, with 'office boys having to call into collect mail on their way to work every day'.[184] Waterford had a similar post box service that continued until the 1950s (and they still survived in its entrance hall in 2011). Manchester had a testing house and laboratory that ran for many years and raised a considerable £1791 per year in 1914. Falmouth chamber had attempted, apparently unsuccessfully, to rent drawers in the desk in its reading room at 10s. 6d. per year in 1867.

Perhaps the most successful of these opportunistic developments were group telegraph, telex, and fax facilities. Dublin and Limerick were among the first to provide magnetic telegraph access in the 1840s, which they provided for many years. In the 1960s and 1970s group telex and then fax played a similar role. The income could be considerable. Dublin ran its telegraph service on a subscription basis, raising £175 in 1860. Telex income for Glasgow in 1970 was £877. Telegraph and telex machines were expensive, required skilled staff, and so were mainly confined to larger companies. This offered the chambers an opportunity to supply to small firms that were relatively small users and/or had only a few customers with machines. The group facility was a natural adjoint to chamber membership. A 'club' was usually formed for telex and telegrams, with an extra subscription; the telex messages received were phoned through to members. Whilst only a few early chambers had telegraph facilities, many developed telex, with membership of 'clubs' exceeding 100 in some cases; the chambers were important contributors to developing the telex network.[185]

The cost of telex machines fell and so many firms bought their own. But by the early 1970s, they were superseded by fax machines. These were given an enormous fillip by the postal strike of 1971, and for a time chambers offered group fax facilities, which were an important source of income. For example, income from telex and fax machines was yielding £32,836 for Ipswich chamber in 1986, but reduced to £9,498 in 1990.[186] In 1989, ABCC statistics show that the chambers handled 560,128 telexes and faxes on behalf of members, a mean of 5438 per chamber.[187] The costs of fax machines also fell quickly and chambers withdrew this service; only 22% retaining it by 1996. A similar rapid expansion of group email-internet access arrived in the mid-1990s, but was even more quickly superseded as the technology became cheaper and its use became universal.

Another opportunistic initiative was translation services, which filled an important gap. It remains a valuable, though minor service. The London chamber's translation bureau handled 1900 demands in 1926–7 (the first 16 months of operation), rising to 2200 in 1928, and 1386 in 1930.[188] Coventry undertook 300 translations in 1949, and 237 for 39 members in 1951.[189] By 1996, 57% of UK chambers offered translation services, but an effort by the Irish chambers

---

[184] Harry Terrell, retired Chief Executive, personal letter to author, 3 March 2006.
[185] Taylor (2007), p. 83.
[186] Ipswich chamber minutes.
[187] ABCC, *Census*; see Appendix 3.
[188] London chamber, *Annual Reports*.
[189] Coventry chamber, *Annual Reports* (1949 and 1951).

association, which sought to stimulate this service across Ireland following their 2005 relaunch, failed to take off because of a lack of demand.

London also initiated a very successful programme of foreign language courses in the 1960s and 1970s. Like commercial examinations this operated in many centres (mostly other chambers, but also colleges). In 1967 there were 2122 candidates in 45 centres, increased to 2212 candidates in 55 centres in 1969.[190] This was one of many schemes for courses, both for workforces and managers, which have continued in various forms to the present day.

12.12 FILLING GAPS IN A CRISIS

The chamber was a natural gathering point for intelligence about local problems, so that when major crises or disruptions occurred, the chamber often played a role in establishing some sort of stop-gap service. This was systemic during the two world wars, even in the occupied Channel Islands in 1940–5, when the chambers facilitated distribution and rationing systems.[191] There have also been many examples of localized actions at particular times of stress. For example, concerns about the local supply of glass bottles caused Portsmouth chamber to consider establishing a glass bottle manufacturer in the city in 1914, because of 'the costs and difficulties of getting supplies'.[192] During a severe drought in 1959 Leeds and Stockport chambers organized priority water supplies to particular firms, and the sharing of supplies from firms with their own boreholes.[193]

Strikes were a further example where chamber organization came into play. The London dock strike of 1887 is attributed as one stimulus to the growth of membership of the London chamber and the establishment of its labour Conciliation Board.[194] But it also provided a fillip to the chamber's organizational leadership. The chamber formed a conciliation committee to try to avoid future disputes reaching the stage of a strike. The coal strike and General Strike of the 1920s led many chambers to become the organizers of alternative sources of supply. For example, during the coal strike in 1920, Preston chamber organized fuel distribution from Preston Dock through a special subcommittee. This operated for two months.[195]

Whilst there are many early examples of chambers trying to conciliate in local disputes, the 1926 General Strike stimulated the most widespread chamber response. The London chamber and ABCC convened an emergency meeting the morning after the midnight deadline declared by the TUC for the strike. It was resolved to place the chamber network at the disposal of the government in order to maintain trade. They urged that the docks be kept open with government force.

---

[190] ABCC, *Annual Reports* (1967–8 and 1969–70).
[191] See Ilersic and Liddle (1960), chapters 15 and 18.
[192] Portsmouth chamber, *Annual Report* (1914).
[193] Taylor (2007), p. 98.
[194] See Smith (1982), London chamber history, p. 166.
[195] See Preston chamber history, 1966, p. 9.

The government used this (and other initiatives) by employers to keep some trade moving. The London chamber arranged a depot in London to which goods could be delivered and return loads accumulated from member companies and other chambers, with police protection. The ABCC maintained a telephone coordination for many chambers, and this also provided situation reports to the government. Preston organized local distribution, Liverpool housed an emergency Haulage Committee, Nottingham helped organize transport and the swearing-in of special constables and superintendents (the chamber president was a commander and the secretary a superintendent).[196] This may have endeared the chambers to government in the short term, but undoubtedly stimulated a visceral dislike from the trade unions.[197] Although all other employer bodies were also involved in a similar way, the chambers' role was critical locally and put them on the wrong side of the emerging radical leaders of the Labour Party.

Whatever the political impact, similar support to local business was an inevitable chamber activity in later strikes. For example, in the postal strike of 1971 many chambers organized alternative mail delivery systems, those in the North-West being particularly active using Manchester airport as a centre for foreign mail delivery.[198] On the initiative of Liverpool, London, and Birmingham, a network of collection and delivery points was established, linking the main chambers of the North, South, and Midlands, as collection and delivery points. Mail for Europe was ferried to Rotterdam and posted there; the Sussex chamber (FSI), though not an ABCC member, took 20,000 items of chamber members' mail to France over the period. This was also a time when many chambers used their telex, or installed fax machines, and offered group electronic transmission of messages chamber to chamber, with members calling in to send or receive. It was particularly heavily used by importers and exporters.[199]

The coal and train drivers' strikes of 1974 resulted in a government-enforced three-day working week. An interconnected telex system linking 70 of the chambers was established in order to circulate information about the resulting regulations. In January the government was issuing 5–6 Statutory Instruments a day that often changed industrial operations at a day's notice. By late January 1974 chambers were managing a daily information network capable of disseminating news of government orders and local conditions within 1–2 hours, using telex machinery through primary, secondary, and feeder relays based on linking London with hubs in Edinburgh, Manchester, Huddersfield, Birmingham, Norwich, and Southampton. As a result it was possible to give reports of the local coal strikes and problems faced by business, which were fed to government well ahead of any information they received from government regional offices. It was subsequently hoped to build this into a more permanent structure, but this never occurred, and became redundant with modern e-communications. However, in 1974 ABCC

---

[196] See Preston chamber history, 1966; Ilersic and Liddle (1960); Taylor (2007), p. 72.
[197] See especially Burns (1926); also Mowatt (1969); Clinton (1977).
[198] Comment to author by Doreen Hitchcock, retired chief executive of Burnley chamber, 2005.
[199] Taylor (2007), pp. 98–9.

was included in the frequent crisis management talks with CBI, TUC, and government, and it was pressure from the chambers that led to 'elimination of notorious Thursday–Saturday three-day ration of electricity' in favour of a more flexible approach.[200]

Similar responses were taken by the chambers in Ireland. For example, during the September 1922 postal strike the chambers set up a substitute postal service.[201] During the national strike in 1950, the chambers tried to mediate locally, but were unsuccessful, and tried to support local firms as much as possible. Similarly, in the 1979 postal strike, the chambers managed a courier service between the major cities and towns, increased their telex services, and were picketed in many cases because of their efforts.[202]

12.13 COMBINATIONS AND CARTELS

Combinations and cartels[203] are a specific form of activity to benefit members by trying to control markets by fixing prices, wages, output, quality, or other features of trade. They are one of the most rigorous collective services, needing all members to conform. Combinations and cartels were not explicitly illegal in Britain until the Restrictive Practices Act (1956).[204] Even then, it was not until the Enterprise Act (2003) and the establishment of more effective competition bodies in Britain and Europe that cartels became more fully policed. Before this combinations were accepted by government, and often explicitly encouraged, particularly during the world wars. The late 19th century and early 20th century is usually seen as their main period of economic significance, with evolution into large-scale corporations during the 20th century.[205] It is important to address the interconnection of chambers and combinations because the earlier literature has misinterpreted activity, which has continued to confuse modern accounts. The discussion here shows that the links of chambers to combinations was limited and exceptional.

Chambers of commerce

Apart from attempts to form Conciliation Boards to settle labour disputes, the involvement of chambers of commerce in market control was rare. Early examples to use the combined action of members were Jersey's efforts to control carpenters wages in 1787, and Belfast's efforts to regulate the pay of carters in the 1790s.[206]

---

[200] ABCC, *Annual Report* (1973), pp. 4–5; Taylor (2007), pp. 98–9.
[201] See e.g. Dublin chamber, *Report of Council* (1922).
[202] Galway chamber history, Woodman (2000), pp. 289–90.
[203] Also called price and product associations, rings, 'conferences', see e.g. Bowman (1989); Schneiberg and Hollingsworth (1991); Lindberg, Campbell, and Hollingsworth (1991).
[204] Macrosty (1907) suggests that there was, even before 1956, considerable case law that declared restraint on trade 'unlawful', quoting cases across the 19th century; see also Horn and Kocka (1979). However, significant combinations certainly did exist.
[205] Hannah (1983); see also Macgregor (1906, 1934); Rees (1922).
[206] Jersey chamber minutes, 2 and 6 March 1787; Belfast chamber history, p. 117.

The Staffordshire potters chamber in the 1760s was primarily focused on regulating trade.[207] Manchester chamber in the 1770s and 1780s tried to assert patent and other controls over velveteen and cotton manufacturers;[208] and in the 1790s the Glasgow chamber called together the dealers and manufacturers of thread to agree a common standard of length, count, and weight to prevent fraud. The problems of fraud, underweight, and inconsistency were becoming a problem for trade and the action of the chamber as a facilitator and arbiter appears to have been welcomed, and led to successful legislation.[209] In 1895 the Manchester testing house, and Leeds regulation of the moisture content of wool, were similar attempts at market control.

However, these were limited early cases. Membership bodies constituted for general purposes, such as chambers, are not well suited to be cartel bodies, failing because differences between individuals lead them to break ranks, thus undermining the control needed. Indeed, rather than organizing cartels most chambers have been concerned to break them; the early Birmingham chamber was involved in initiatives to break cartels in the copper smelting industry in 1790;[210] and Manchester was very energetic against shipping rings in the 1890s.[211] There were, however, two exceptional cases.

Macclesfield chamber

A collective silk body in Macclesfield had been mooted in 1827, and a Macclesfield Board of Trade was established over 1849–52.[212] The Board was a response to increased foreign competition, aiming to produce a list price for silk weaving, which was to be binding on each party (the employees and manufacturers). It was financed by levies on both employer and employee. The model appears to have directly copied the French example of the Conseil de Prud' Hommes at Lyons, with which Macclesfield was closely in touch as another major silk town. The Macclesfield Board broke down after only three years. In 1850 'Smith's weavers were willingly working under-price' and in 1851 'Brocklehurst's was forcing lower rates on their weavers'. The Macclesfield case illustrates many of the general problems of such collective regulatory action, John Brocklehurst being heavily criticized: 'he sits in the Board [of Trade of Macclesfield] and he, of all men, does the most to violate its regulations . . . How do you expect us to go along with the Board when Brocklehurst does not pay list prices?'[213] A similar effort for an Artisans Chamber of Commerce had been attempted by Gravener Henson in Nottingham in 1838, copying French Conseils, which was also short-lived.[214]

---

[207] Thomas (1934, 1935).
[208] Redford (1934).
[209] A. Brown, *History of Glasgow*, vol. iii, pp. 278–9.
[210] Hamilton (1967), p. 233; Money (1977).
[211] Manchester chamber, *Monthly Record*, 28 February (1898); Ilersic and Liddle (1960), pp. 117–23.
[212] See Austin (2000), Macclesfield chamber history, chapter 13, on which this account is based.
[213] Quoted in Austin (2000), p. 164.
[214] See Church and Chapman (1967), pp. 154–5.

Further development of free trade with France as a result of the Cobden Chevalier Treaty of 1860 allowed French woven silk duty free, but a 30% duty was paid on silk exports to France. This was a disaster for the industry, directly feeding into the foundation objectives of the Macclesfield chamber in 1867. The chamber immediately sought to become the negotiating body for the manufacturers to ensure a 'fair price' for labour. It successfully negotiated with the Handloom Weavers' Association from 1867 into the 20th century, and led to a 'sensible and friendly accommodation' in employment negotiations.[215]

The silk industry was a major victim of 'one-sided free trade' and was a strong influence on the overwhelming support for protection in the chamber after 1900. The chamber regularly held joint meetings with the Silk Trade Protection Association, and the president in 1903 saw tariff reform as the 'means we might hit our opponents . . . hardest'.[216] The chamber voted overwhelmingly in favour of tariff protection in 1903–4 with about 80–90% in favour, although the turnout for the meeting was only approximately 40% of the membership.[217] Marrison suggests its approach was characteristic of the smaller industrial districts and towns, but the evidence on other areas is equivocal, except for Salt chamber. Interestingly, the vice-presidents of the Salt chamber were the only attendees from other chambers at the Macclesfield chamber's inaugural dinner in 1867.[218] Given the local prominence of Manchester and Liverpool, two far older and more significant chambers than Salt, this attendance suggests a strong exchange of information on the issues of price, wage, and output regulation. Salt chamber had, with some effect, regulated the salt industry since the 1850s.

Salt (Northwich) chamber

The Salt chamber was focused on Northwich and the surrounding salt district, but also had membership of agents and shippers in Liverpool, the Midlands, Middlesbrough, London, and Ireland. It started as a locally based sector body, but joined the ACC, and became a chamber in a general sense, as well as a sector regulatory body. It followed a series of other salt associations: in 1815–25 'The Coalition',[219] and in 1841–83 the White Salt Trade Association.[220] The Salt chamber took on similar activities through its Salt Trade Committee formed in 1864, which was joint with the Association.[221] Thus in 1867 the chamber notes, 'the labours of the chamber, as usual, have been directed at the steady maintenance of prices'. A year earlier it notes that 'one of the most gratifying results . . . , consequent on the

---

[215] Davies (1976), Macclesfield chamber history, p. 195.
[216] *Macclesfield Courier*, 20 June 1903; this discussion follows Marrison (1996), pp. 110–12 who analysed the local newspapers for this period. No records of the chamber survive for this date.
[217] Marrison (1996), pp. 111–12; comparison with membership numbers from London *CCJ* reports.
[218] Quoted in Davies (1976), p. 198.
[219] See Chaloner (1961), Salt chamber history.
[220] The Falk family held the coalition of interests together: see Chaloner (1961).
[221] White Salt Trade Association, adjourned AGM, 4 April 1882; D6917/553, Cheshire RO.

labours of the chamber, has been the unanimity amongst the members of the salt trade, which has led to a steady maintenance of remunerative prices . . . unity is strength'.[222]

Salt chamber never had more than 50–60 members, making coordination easier. It opened a Liverpool office in the 1859–62, and had a London agent in the 1870s. This was the most successful period of price control and profitability for the industry, the chamber unashamedly advertising its efforts to control and open new markets, e.g. in 1870 in India, China, Japan, Belgium, France, and else-where.[223] In 1874 the president (H. E. Falk) visited India on behalf of the chamber. In 1886 he stated that 'this year has been signalised by the most unanimous association which the trade has ever yet achieved'.[224] This period also saw some diversification of membership to include traders in salt, and even two retailers.

The Salt chamber illustrates the problem of holding together a small organization with differing views and power among members. The energy and personal subsidy from H. E. Falk was clearly critical in the early years, but commercial fractures and differing interests continued. After 1888, with the formation of the Salt Union Ltd., the industry became more concentrated and controllable. The Salt Union was a combine formed by raising capital to buy out existing owners of salt works: £3.3 million of capital was raised and 67 owners were bought out.[225] The only other major surviving firms were Brunner Mond & Co., and the United Alkali Co.

The chamber's constitution was relaunched in 1889 after the formation of the Salt Union, with clause 1 stating that to qualify a member should have a 'holding of £1000 in the Salt Union or possessing a salt works existing or hereafter to be established'. Clause 4 stated that no servants of the Salt Union should serve on the chamber's council, 'making the Council a thoroughly impartial body', which implies that it was viewed as previously not impartial. The new constitution sought to ensure that 'the chamber hereforward be considered an efficient medium wherein members ventilate, debate, and by collective representation, correct any grievances or abuses which may locally or generally affect the interest of the district or the property of the members',[226] and all members paid the same subscription of one guinea.

However, by 1891, after only two years, this new constitution was significantly amended. Clause 1 was generalized so that 'all firms and individuals connected to salt trade and all shareholders in salt companies be eligible as members', and Clause 4 was 'expunged'. The Salt Union was asked to nominate three members to the council and the United Alkali Company one. As a result, the larger companies took a more dominant role, in return for which they had to pay more. Three subscribers now paid 5 guineas (the Weaver Navigation Trustees; the United Alkali Co., and Brunner Mond), the Salt Union paid 10 guineas, and all other members paid 1 guinea. The chamber became more reliant on the large companies; an attempt to

---

[222] Salt chamber, *Annual Reports* (1865–6), p. 5; (1866–7), p. 5.
[223] Salt chamber, *Annual Report* (1870).
[224] Salt chamber *Annual Report* (1885–6), p. 5 (but only 22 from 32 members actually paid their subscriptions).
[225] Calvert (1913), pp. 1–9.
[226] Salt chamber, *Constitution*, 15 August 1889; D6917/562, Cheshire RO.

raise subscriptions in 1891 failed, with medium-sized firms asked to pay more, the 'basis of subscriptions objected to by many members'.[227] Further discussions resulted in the Salt Union paying £50, the other three large companies paying £25 each, and the rest one guinea.

Despite these changes the finances of the chamber remained precarious. Whereas in 1859–62 the chamber had an annual income of £250–450, a well-paid secretary and two offices, by the 1890s the income was £45–95 per year. The secretary could not be paid over 1912–17, and arrears of subscriptions became a perennial problem, especially from the largest companies. In June 1907 there was £136 outstanding in unpaid subscriptions, and the bankers (Parr) were holding a debit balance of over £100. After WW1 there was a brief revival, which reduced the overdraft, but the following years showed an accumulating overdraft, which made the chamber's demise inevitable: £255 in 1927, £336 in 1928, and £409 in 1929.[228] A resolution in 1926 that members should 'double their subscriptions' to wipe out the deficit was unsuccessful, and in 1930 the chamber was wound up. The Salt Union continued to dominate the industry, and further consolidation left it as the only producer in the area, as it is in 2011.

Other chambers of commerce

There may have been de facto price rings and attempts to control prices and wages by other chambers. For example, in Newcastle, Cardiff, Swansea, and Newport the coal traders were very strong interests; in Dundee the jute industry was a major voice; in Glasgow the tobacco industry; in Kendal the cloth industry; in Luton the straw hat manufacturers; and so on. But if price rings and regulation existed, there is little or no evidence that the chamber as a body played a significant direct role in them. Indeed, in most cases, chambers sought to stay out of any role where they might be perceived as acting as employer associations, preferring to leave this to other bodies.

However, price and wage setting were certainly part of some of the London chamber's many sector sections in the 1880s and 1890s. Indeed this was acknowledged in their response to Royal Commission on Labour in 1892. Similarly, Hull chamber identified its oil and timber sections as involved in setting wage rates.[229] In Luton in 1914, meetings at the chamber of the Men's Straw Hat Manufacturers Trade Section resolved on a variety of wage issues; e.g. the minimum wage for sewing, stiffening, sweating, and panning; and the minimum prices for trimming. These issues had been part of an earlier meeting of the Luton chamber with the Felt Hat Association leading to resolutions on: the price of special stamping; how carriage should be charged; and the cost charged for boxes.[230] Further research

---

[227] Salt chamber, *Constitution*, amended 4 September 1891; Council draft minutes, 13 May 1907; D6917/562, Cheshire RO.

[228] All financial data from Salt chamber, *Annual Accounts*; D6917/565, Cheshire RO.

[229] *House of Commons Papers* (1812), xxxvi, part V, pp. xxxii–xxxiv.

[230] Luton chamber, Council minutes, 30 October 1914, pp. 174–7; reporting minutes of meeting of Committee appointed by Men's Straw Hat Manufacturers Trade Section, 8 October 1914, p. 160.

might reveal more section-based cartels linked to chambers. However, this could never have been a mainstream activity of the chambers as a whole. It conflicted with their more general mission, to act in a 'general' interest, through 'unity'.

Chambers of trade

The chambers of trade, with a membership mainly of retailers and distributors, and traders mainly (but not exclusively) selling directly to the public, had considerable interest in self-regulation of shop opening hours and holidays so that the general high street was enhanced for all. Since most shops were sole traders or small concerns, setting reasonable limits on hours was also important to both employers and employees. It was a classic collective action opportunity. Whilst any individual trader might gain some advantage by opening earlier or later than others, in general, all traders gained benefit from there being coordinated shopping hours when all the shops could be relied on to be open, and thus the shopper was more likely to visit. As a result, coordination arose fairly naturally in many towns and was vigorously led nationally by NCT.

The concern with shopping hours, early closing days, weekend, and holiday opening periods, also brought into play a need to work with local government. Indeed the traders' self-regulation generally had the support of local councils who used their powers to reinforce the traders' voluntary agreements. Some chambers of trade were also able to take on associated local functions; for example, Salisbury chamber of trade managed the allocation of market stalls on behalf of the council in the 1950s and 1960s.[231]

There were issues of overlap with the working hours in mills and factories, transport, and so on. Chambers of commerce were generally the milieus for any discussion in this area, but few became involved in regulation; and when they did they met with little success. This was the preserve of firms and involvement by external bodies was not generally welcome. However, there was limited coordination of holiday closure by chambers such as Sheffield, Southampton, and Portsmouth, which each had traditions of overlap of retail and manufacturing interests. Perhaps this is best summed up in discussion at Luton chamber in 1914, which was both a CoT and chamber of commerce: 'closing takes place at 5.30 on each day for selling departments only, subject to this being unanimous throughout the trade. It was further resolved that the closing of factories be a matter for individual discretion'.[232]

Readdressing the literature

Combinations were a very restricted aspect of a few chambers. Indeed, local chambers of commerce and trade were not well equipped to regulate their members, or restrict opting out. Despite this, a significant modern literature has implied that chambers were involved.[233] It is necessary here to remove this confusion.

---

[231] Salisbury chamber, *Annual Report* (1960), p. 6.
[232] Luton chamber, Council minutes, 14 September 1914, pp. 149 and 153.
[233] Yarmie (1980); Rose (2000), p. 135; Pearson (2004), p. 150.

The main source of misunderstanding derives from Clapham and Ashton.[234] Both quote Adam Smith, after all a perceptive contemporary observer, that 'masters are always and everywhere in a sort of tacit, but constant and uniform combination, not to raise the wages of labour above their actual rate'. Smith goes on to state that 'people of the same trade seldom meet together, even for merriment and diversion, but the conversation ends in a conspiracy against the public, or in some contrivance to raise prices'. However, Smith was referring specifically to corporations (including chartered companies), guilds, and wage fixing. Smith was very resistant to legal obligation to join anything, having membership lists (which facilitated coopera- tion), or majority votes that bound all to a single policy. Hence, he concluded that 'the pretence that corporations are necessary for the better government of trade, is without any foundation'.[235] Clapham and Ashton are important studies since they review a large body of evidence on combinations covering many industries. But they mis-apply Smith and, most confusingly, both quote as combinations the activity of the General Chamber 1785–6, the early chambers of commerce, and local commercial committees. This is inaccurate. Certainly these early chambers aimed 'to protect trade', but this meant lobbying government over Treaties. The debate was therefore about open and reciprocal trade versus protection, not about combination and coordination. This is a fundamental distinction. General interest local bodies such as chambers are quite different from employer associations and sector trade associations that seek to control markets.

12.14 CONCLUSION: BALANCING THE BUNDLE

This chapter has presented the evolution of chamber services. This service portfolio has to be seen against the other chapters of Part 3 covering other chamber activities. The services covered here represent some of the most important activities of the modern chamber, and are a key part of the offer that motivates membership.

Early services evolved chiefly from the interaction with members to answer enquiries. This led to a natural development of information and document certifi- cation services, which became the core offers of most chambers of commerce, large and small, by the 1920s. In a few of these chambers, chiefly London, Manchester, and Birmingham, there was also development of employment agencies, and com- mercial examinations. For the large and medium-sized chambers, arbitration be- came an important offer, probably a form of 'trust' or 'status good' for chambers demonstrating their stature, though the volume of take-up for all but the largest chambers was always small. The chambers of trade more strongly developed other offers, such as publicity and tourist promotion, debt collection, and credit enqui- ries, often in association with the trade protection societies. From the 1960s more extensive service development occurred, which marks the turning point of the

---

[234] Clapham (1926), pp. 200–5, 307–10; Ashton (1963), p. 185 and chapter 7; also Redford (1934); Bowden (1919–20).
[235] Smith (1776), vol. i, pp. 100 and 200–1.

chamber of commerce system into its modern form. Internal development focused on strengthened responses to enquiries, consultancy support, and involvement in work-based training and apprenticeships, often linked to government schemes, as discussed in Chapter 13.

As noted at the outset of this chapter, these developments have required careful management of the tensions that run across service bundles. This chapter has shown how the tensions have been managed within individual services. Service development has raised the need to keep an appropriate limit on services, first by not competing with the businesses of members, and second, by managing the by-product problem so that the core function of voice is maintained. This management of in-house service development was largely organic and the tensions accommodated. However, the greatest modern tension has come from the challenge of managing competition for resources from government-sponsored activities, which is the focus of the next chapter.

13

Partner and Contractor to Government

13.1 CHAMBERS: NATURAL PARTNERS

Activity with and for government has become a dominant aspect of the modern chambers, in both Britain and Ireland. Is this for members or for government purposes? The two may significantly overlap, but that mapping is often imperfect. Herein lies the modern dilemma for chamber management and members. Partnering government risks a special form of crowding out by 'non-preferred' services that undermine altruistic and donor behaviour. Also, as discussed in Chapter 3, there is a 'Samaritan's dilemma': if government is prepared to finance chambers, why should the members pay? As a result, reduced member involvement, loss of chamber independence, distorted mission focus, over-bureaucratization, and distortion of recruitment of personnel or behaviour through 'sorting' may all occur. The by-product problem may become extreme, so distortionary that the purpose of chambers as traditionally understood is entirely lost. The worst result is that the staff and leadership of the chamber are so distorted to meet government needs that they no longer fit the core mission. Finer refers to this as 'surrogateship'.[1] Despite the risks, chambers have readily embarked on working with government in increasingly large contractual relationships. In the 2010s the chambers sit at a cusp where they are wrestling with the resulting dilemmas. But within the span of their history, the issue is wholly recent, and primarily since the late 1980s.

It is easy to see why government has used chambers. As the voice of local businesses they offer a number of advantages that are unique and make them 'natural' partners for some purposes. First, most critically, chambers provide a network of connections to most of the businesses that are committed to the local economy: as shown in Chapter 15, most chamber members join for the joint bundle of individual services *and* to support the objectives of representing local interests and contributing to local initiatives. There is some obligation, and this extends to a network of localities across the country. This network offers to government a wide range of possibilities to co-opt local support for public programmes, or to recruit members, or the chamber organization, to operate government activities.

Second, chambers offer an organization that can be contracted to provide public services. This is not unique, since many other private and not-for-profits can offer

---

[1] Finer (1955), pp. 280–5.

similar capacity. But for chambers (and other independent associations) there is the scope for government to build its contracts on the back of an organization that has three distinctive advantages: (i) brand recognition and trust, which increases the potential legitimacy and repute of a government programme; (ii) scope to use the obligational support of chamber membership networks to encourage business involvement; and (iii) combining trust and obligation, it offers scope for the local business community to take ownership of a programme and improve its design and implementation so that it meets real economic needs rather than remaining a programme designed by civil servants.

Finally, chambers offer a specifically local expertise that is founded on drawing together local business views for a community. They have transparent governance and are democratically accountable to their members. This provides a locally legitimized partner that can help tailor government programmes and inform policy makers. Chambers can also input knowledge about local contingency. Too often ministers see an example of good practice and then say, 'let's have some of that everywhere', forgetting that local needs, structures, and capacities vary, requiring different solutions.

From 'outsider' to partial 'insider'

Historically the chambers mainly operated as 'outsiders' to the policy process—acting as lobbyists and advocates—although they were also important early initiators of local interventions through private Bills and other initiatives. Before 1917 they received no direct support or income from government (national or local), except for short-term individual local initiatives, and some ad hoc payments for occasional collaboration with exhibitions or missions.[2] From 1917, however, chambers began to become involved with operating some services directly for government, either through grants and subsidies, or later by contracts. Partnerships became most significant after 1967 when chambers began taking on government training contracts. This formed a base for rapid expansion from the 1980s until the 2000s, when government sought significant participation in local policy interventions, which chambers provided in many areas. This has continued since 2010, with chambers becoming leading agents in many Local Enterprise Partnerships (LEPs).

Whilst constitutional differences remain very important between Scotland, Wales, Northern Ireland, the Channel Isles, and England, and increased significantly in some directions after devolution in 2001, pressures from Westminster under the Blair/Brown government 1997–2010 tended to align each through a common civil service ethos; e.g. in Jersey civil servants tend to be recruited from Westminster or local government experiences 'who are used to a population of 60 million not 80,000, who tell us what we need, follow silo management, and introduce many ideas totally inappropriate to the Island'.[3] The devolved countries

---

[2] And the early role in local markets and harbours administered by chambers under corporation powers, chiefly in Ireland (which mostly disappeared after 1835).

[3] Comments to author by Clive Spears, president of the Jersey chamber, April 2009.

also became accustomed under Labour to high public spending solutions to problems, which have become unsustainable.

In Ireland, after significant early support to chambers to administer local markets and harbours, there was little government funding until the 1980s, after which chambers were increasingly used to assist national and local government economic development initiatives for their areas. European financial support was critical to many of these initiatives, with Ireland eligible for the maximum levels of support through EU Objective 1 status after accession to the European Community from 1 January 1973 (at the same time as the UK). But again after the financial crisis of 2007 severe downward pressures have made this unsustainable.

Shifting supports

An overview of UK developments in Table 13.1 shows the scale of government income to chambers over time. The table makes clear that the period from the 1980s was exceptional and frame changing for chambers. Involvement with government went from a small element added to the independent core chamber functions, to become the majority of funding. This began in the 1970s for chambers involved heavily in training, such as Birmingham, Chesterfield, Coventry, Glasgow, Hull, and Mid Yorkshire; but for the system as a whole the main impact followed the development of Business Link in 1993 and mergers to form CCTEs after 1995. Effected under a Conservative government that was intent on contracting out and privatizing services, this initially continued under the Labour government after 1997. At its height in 2001 government funding represented 76% of all chamber income, from which it shrank back to 52% in 2010.

These changes have had a profound effect on the chambers receiving the funds, and on the system as a whole. First, government funding has introduced significant financial uncertainty and instability. Rapid rises in the late 1990s and mid-2000s were matched by severe drops in 2002–3 and after 2008. Second, as Table 13.1 makes clear, those involved with the government funding were not the whole of the system; some chambers never participated (either through choice or inability to meet government criteria), and for others the amount of funding was relatively minor. The proportion of those receiving funds grew from 16% to a peak of 96% over 1970–2005, after which it has declined back to about 87%. This was chiefly the result of chamber mergers, in part to cope with the managerial needs and wider geographical coverage required by government programmes. In 2005 about 30% of the chambers received 87% of the government income, declining to 78% in 2010. The diverse agendas between chambers that have resulted have created tensions within the BCC.

In the Irish Republic, excluded from Table 13.1, a similar growth in partnership with government occurred after 1974, but with the main growth in the 1980s when EU programmes became very significant. This provided over 30% of income to the participating chambers by the mid-1980s, where it remained until *c*.2006–7. The Irish chambers association also became a lead partner with the EU and Irish government, receiving over 75% of funds from these sources by 2007. But after

Table 13.1. Government income to UK chambers of commerce 1920–2010 (£000s at current prices); mean, range, and 80/20% values for participating chambers

Date	Total	Mean	Max.	80%	20%	Govt. income % of total	ABCC/BCC chambers receiving govt. funds (number/ total)	ABCC/BCC chambers receiving govt. funds (%)
1920	7	0.7	—	—	0	5.4	49/103	47.6
1930	3	0.3	—	—	0	1.3	49/99	49.5
1950	0	0	—	—	0	0	0/98	0
1960	0	0	—	—	0	0	0/99	0
1970	900*	60*	—	—	0	25.8*	15/92	16.3
1982	2,426*	125*	—	—	0	26.5*	20*/82	24.4*
1991	27,000	450	4,049	—	0	28.3	60/99	60.6
1992	30,107	494	4,049	450	0	39.4	61/101	60.4
1994	31,667	422	12,510	71	0	37.0	75/90	83.3
1996	28,348	603	4,400	587	0	39.0	47/63	74.6
1999	160,852	2,822	24,874	2,063	0	64.2	57/74	77.0
2001	252,667	4,075	32,641	8,422	9	76.1	62/73	84.9
2003	93,453	1,416	15,928	2,315	24	52.4	66/74	89.2
2005	131,632	2,484	23,378	3,965	105	58.8	51/53	96.2
2007	122,081	2,654	23,380	2,988	44	63.7	46/49	93.9
2009	90,209	1,961	19,097	1,479	33	54.0	46/53	86.8
2010	89,087	1,895	18,028	1,702	78	51.8	47/54	87.0

* Estimate.

Notes: Minimum is always zero as some chambers never participated. Programmatic funding only, ad hoc payments and war periods omitted; year-on-year comparisons are not precise because membership of BCC changes and mergers occur; not all early data complete; CCTEs included only from 1999.
Sources: Estimated from local *Accounts* for 1920–82; 1991 from Bennett and Krebs (1993b); BCC *Census* and *Benchmarking* after 1992.

the widening of the EU to many new and poorer countries, Ireland lost its EU Objective 1 status. This, combined with the financial crisis of 2007–11, has seen heavy cutbacks of public support to Irish chambers, with the national association of Irish chambers suffering particularly severely.

This chapter provides an overview of the different approaches to government–chamber relations that have developed. The detailed involvement of chambers with each scheme is discussed in a broadly historical sequence. For each scheme a brief assessment is made in terms of the key criteria of: (i) value added (costs and benefits); (ii) additionality (added outcome effects, above what would have happened anyway, and therefore overcoming deadweight effects); and (iii) leverage (response of recipients to government support). The schemes are also assessed for: (i) strategic fit to chamber missions; and (ii) value to members, and where relevant to non-members, and thus support for chamber recruitment, commitment, and retention.

13.2 MODELS OF GOVERNMENT SUPPORT

There is a wide range of ways in which government can draw on chambers, and it is inevitable that over the long sweep of chamber history various different methods have been used. Chambers have also sought different means to co-opt government. Recognizing Liverpool's comment of 1918, that 'being voluntary associations, they will always be handicapped by lack of financial resources until the public properly appreciate their possibilities'[4], has led chambers actively to seek government support. Thus co-option has worked both ways.

The main contrasting models are depicted in Table 13.2. This classifies the types of cooperation on two dimensions: (i) the degree of relation between business interests themselves (whether drawing on individual businesses; groups and formally

Table 13.2. Categories of government involvement in terms of formality of inter-business relations and type of government commitment, with examples of the main chamber involvements discussed in this chapter

Relations between businesses	Co-option of/by government	Recruitment of/by government
Informal (individuals and members acting alone or as representatives)	• Advisers • Task forces • ACCI	• Executive agencies, development bodies outside chambers; e.g. UDCs, TECs/LECs, LSC, RDAs • Area Manpower Boards
Obligational (chambers and/or members as host, perhaps with others)	• Peer pressure; civic leadership, private Bills • Local strategic partnerships, Core Cities, LEPs • Interlocks/networks e.g. trade missions, exhibitions e.g. urban regeneration, local strategic partnerships e.g. ethnic minority, small firms, and other networks	• Leadership bodies, acting as 'hosts' e.g. LENs, BiTC • LEPs • In-house standards accredited by government ('approved chambers'—see Chapter 8) • Brokerage e.g. partnerships in college training schemes, crime prevention, etc.
Formal (contracts to chambers)	• Dissemination of information e.g. consular reports 'Form K' • Recognition of in-house schemes e.g. apprenticeships, certificates • Formal consultation e.g. on local Rates, manpower planning, advisory committees	• Contracts e.g. training schemes (YT, ET, etc.); Business Link • Grant schemes and other supports • EU Social Fund and ERDF • Wartime planning • CCTEs

[4] Liverpool chamber, *Handbook* (1918), p. 34.

organized structures that carry a level of commitment and obligation to the chamber/locality; or formal contracts); and (ii) the relation with government: co-option, or recruitment.

Co-option occurs when government delegates to others to deliver, usually within broad objectives: to act as an *executive* within an agreed framework, or to provide information or advice to government. Co-option allows development of new outlooks and approaches, and helps gain support for changing former policies. Government gains the advantage of using the existing practices, obligations, and leadership. Co-option is usually considerably cheaper, since it draws on goodwill and obligation, whilst recruitment and contracting rely on payments and compliance. It is generally the favoured model by chambers themselves, since it allows maximum freedom, provides status, and reinforces their relations with their members.

Recruitment involves using resources and control to *lever* change, usually through a specific contract, grant, or other support, for *a government purpose*, although a chamber can seek to be recruited. Sometimes the chamber can be used as a 'broker' to facilitate the links between the government objective and businesses; at other times a chamber can act as a 'host'. Support does not depend on voluntary action: the recruited management is levered to change through new resources and status, as with LENs and TECs. It can be used to develop new outlooks but is primarily a means to implement and legitimize pre-defined government programmes. The extent of any leverage depends on the efficiency of the design, the freedom of the business leadership to operate effectively, and the scale of resources. Recruitment suffers dangers from mis-specification of the rules and objectives, which alienate the individuals and bodies involved, and can undermine the networks that connect them with their members. There is a strong danger from the 'law of unintended consequences'—or 'perverse policy syndrome'—that government assistance undermines voluntarism. The level of commitment required is also usually greater than co-option, because of government bureaucratic processes and accountability. Since senior level inputs are required, it needs a high degree of altruism, political alignment, or more intangible personal benefits to the individuals involved. This can be very distortionary.

Contracting has similar tensions. Contracting allows government to outsource, offers to business little or no right to shape the agenda, but provides leverage through finance to deliver services. Self-enforcement is not involved so that the potential to diffuse practices is limited, although good practice can be copied. Moreover, the impact on business can be negative as well as positive: the highly specific nature of much government contracting, and the high level of bureaucracy involved, and hence overheads, mean that usually only very large or specialist concerns can afford to become involved. This may crowd out other activities and is distortionary between different businesses and chambers, as occurred with CCTEs. The difficulty of defining effective contracts makes them most appropriate when applied to narrow programmes with clearly definable objectives that can be measured and monitored. If the objectives are unclear or un-measurable (as with many TEC, Business Link, and RDA programmes) there are pervasive difficulties resulting in moral hazard, adverse selection, high cost, and perverse policy outcomes.

13.3 MUNICIPAL IMPROVEMENT AND LOCAL PARTNERSHIPS

As locally rooted bodies, it is not surprising that the earliest examples of chambers working with government arose at local level (national cooperation arose much later). The chief examples of these local partnerships have been municipal improvement, local advisory committees, and local strategic partnerships.

Municipal improvement

From their outset the chambers sought local improvements and economic development of their areas: civic leadership was a natural extension of their mission to promote the local economy. Some of their earliest activities involved taking on the management of local markets (especially in the Irish chambers); working with local harbour, lighthouse, and navigation interests (in almost all the port-based chambers); and promotion of improvements in transport, highways, policing, public health and hospitals, schools and colleges, housing and social support (chiefly in the larger cities).

Chambers were among the most frequent and prominent promoters or partners in Improvement Acts in 18th- and 19th-century urban areas, with the result that chamber leadership and civic leadership became strongly entwined. This was most prominent in Birmingham under the Chamberlains, and Liverpool under the Forwoods, leaders in both the chamber and local government, but was common in almost all major urban centres, as well as some smaller towns.[5] The 1875 Artisan and Labourers' Dwelling Act strengthened municipal powers, and had a significant effect on stimulating many chamber leaders to become involved in efforts to improve housing, for example in Wolverhampton. Almost uniformly the chambers also became involved in efforts at 'place promotion' and marketing for industrial development, commerce, and tourism. There was a collective interest for business and municipal leaders in the facilities, infrastructure, and reputation of their town or city, which made chambers key leaders and partners with local government;[6] a process that continues to the present day.

With reforms of local government in the UK, first through the Reform Acts of the 1830s, and especially with the Municipal Corporation Act 1882, and Local Government Acts of 1888 and 1894, more active urban government developed.

---

[5] See many of the chamber histories and discussion in Chapter 10; also Daunton (1995, 1996, 2008); Daunton (1977) for Cardiff; Trainor (1993) for Dudley, Walsall, Wolverhampton; Trainor (1996), Devine and Jackson (1995) for Glasgow; Lloyd-Jones and Lewis (1988) for Manchester; Hudson (1986, 1989), Smail (1994) for Halifax and W. Riding; more generally Garrard (1983); Morris (1986, 1990); Innes (1998, 2003); Innes and Rogers (2000); Sweet (2003).

[6] Morris (1986, 1990, 1992) reviews many earlier studies; see also Daunton (2008).

After the 1880s there was a two-tier structure of counties and districts, with 61 County Boroughs in the main cities (82 by 1922), and the Improvement Act districts all disappeared.[7] With these changes the chambers became less the initiators and promoters of improvements against laggard municipalities, and more the partners of stronger local authorities. They now had a smaller number of local bodies to lobby or work with, which facilitated closer partnerships, but also a more formidable local foe when conflicts arose. The main focus for the chambers was the county boroughs and those municipal boroughs that covered larger populations (generally over 20,000–25,000 population: see Chapter 5), though chambers of trade stretched much further down the size hierarchy. Generally the chambers were less concerned with the counties until the 1990s, which in any case were usually conservative and resisted city expansion and interests. This structure continued in Ireland from 1923 up to the present, where lack of local government reform has left chambers largely focused on cities and towns.

However, in the UK, the counties became considerably more powerful after reforms in 1964 in London, 1974 in England and Wales, and 1976 in Scotland, to create a uniform two-tier structure with no County Boroughs. The growing role of county spending and planning decisions influenced the chambers to spread their lobbying and representations to larger territories, although expanding local labour market areas also influenced this (see Chapters 5 and 14). The structure in the UK changed again after 1994, when single-tier counties were set up in Scotland, Wales, and Northern Ireland, and de facto County Boroughs were progressively re-established in England as unitary authorities.[8] This led to the emergence of the Core City concept after 1995, to the benefit of the chambers located there.

The consequences of these changes for UK chambers were profound. First, there was expansion of the geographical area of the major local authorities, with steady expansion of the boundaries of the major cities, and mergers between government units which encouraged the expansion of chamber territories, and hence their membership and breadth of interests. Second, there was a significant shift away from ad hoc and highly varied local responses, with a basic principle of 'local provision, for local wants, locally identified' over which chambers and other local leaders had exerted considerable leverage. This was replaced by a more uniform, formalized, and centralized structure where professional local government officers, national inspectors, and countless circulars and requirements for statistical returns increasingly sanctioned or disallowed local expenditures.[9] This tended to reduce the influence of independent 'outsider' lobbies such as chambers.

Third, with the shift towards a wider political franchise where party politics progressively held greater sway, local politics in the major cities often became

---

[7] Except for School Boards, which survived until compulsory education in 1909, and Poor Law boards, which were superseded in 1929: Lipman (1949); Keith-Lucas (1977); Hennock (1982).

[8] Begun under Michael Heseltine at Department of Environment 1990–2; notable for his later role; q.v. below.

[9] Hennock (1963); (1982), pp. 40–2.

more antagonistic to chamber and local business interests, which was particularly overt in the 1920–87 period. Fourth, local government finance was fundamentally changed. The main local tax (the rates), rose inexorably, and often rapidly, producing increasing tensions with the local business community. In addition the increase in central government grants to become over 70% of local revenue in metropolitan areas reduced the significance of local decision making, and hence connectivity with local businesses and the chambers.

These pressures transformed the relationship of local government with businesses and chambers to one where economic interests tended to become peripheralized; with chambers one of many 'partners' with, or contractors to, an ever-stronger local state. As noted even by Hereford chamber in 1936, in one of the least progressive and radical cities, 'the formation of the City Council Development Committee . . . is performing several of the functions that were formerly dealt with by this chamber'. As a consequence membership had fallen off and attendance at meetings was very low. This led to a vigorous debate about whether there was a need for a chamber at all. The chamber responded by developing a new structure of sections, which resulted in significant revival.[10] Daunton's description of the effects of state takeover of welfare services applies equally well to the economy: the erosion of voluntarism and weakening the local competitive environment of firms through a demand for uniformity of planning and state control.[11] This paradigm has been challenged by the Coalition government since 2010 with a reassertion of 'localism'.

Advisory committees

A counterweight to the ever-expanding role of the local and central state was advisory committees. The chambers argued vigorously for a place in local decisions, not just of local government, but also central government activities affecting the local level. These advisory committees did not put business interests in a lead position, but attempted to reassure that their views were heard. The chambers of commerce and chambers of trade became key representative groups on many of these advisory committees, often acting as the de facto committee, or nominating a substantial number of its members. These external committee roles were often listed in chamber annual reports and leaflets, to demonstrate the weight and status of the chamber. The chambers sought to become perceived as the privileged advisers to the state. The most prominent committees in the earlier period were:

Postal, Telephone and Telegram services. The chambers had been exercised about the postal service and its cost from the 18th century. From the 1860s there was continuous pressure for reform and cost reductions from the ACC. This was succeeded by concerns about the telegram and then the telephone system, over

---

[10] Hereford chamber, letter on members' referendum, August 1936; *Annual Report*, September 1936: *Hereford Times*, 14 and 19 September 1936; *Hereford Bulletin*, 19 September 1936; in chamber minutes, 14 September 1936–4 January 1937.
[11] Daunton (2008), pp. 33–8, 254–89.

which the Post Office acquired a monopoly by 1895.[12] Post Office Advisory Committees were established by the Post Office in the 1920s in some of the major cities (primarily London, Liverpool, Glasgow, and Manchester). Chambers set up their own committees on a wider scale following a call from the ABCC Executive in 1924 to set up a postal committee in every chamber. This influenced committee structures (see Table 6.1). When Sir Kingsley Wood became Postmaster General he encouraged the extension of the Post Office's Advisory Committees to all the major towns. By 1933 16 had been established, 'reconstituted or formed under the auspices of the chambers'; by 1938 there were about 42, and 53 by 1939.[13] They ceased to exist when the Post Office was turned into a public corporation in 1969.

Railway Rates. Local Traders' Coordinating Committees were established following the 1921 Railways Act and ran until rail nationalization in 1947. They provided for local consultation, and were given strong powers to comment to a national Railway Rates Advisory Committee (later titled Tribunal) that set tariffs and charges. Chambers were the major source of membership and expert comment in these committees, with almost all chambers involved. They sought reduced rates and limitations of railway monopolies (particularly resisting attempts by the railways to run ancillary road services). The committees were the culmination of efforts by chambers dating from the 1830s, and campaigns by ACC from its outset in 1861, often supported by local government.[14] Dunwoody, the ABCC Secretary viewed their establishment as a result of the united chamber effort: 'union is strength'.[15] The chambers' involvement gave critical expertise in local transport that was utilized by the government, in mitigating the 1926 General Strike, and at other times.[16] However by the 1930s Liverpool commented that 'in view of the very limited power . . . such meetings serve very little useful purpose', and Middlesbrough felt 'there has not been anything of interest'.[17] In Ireland there were similar Railway Wages Committees involving chambers.

National Certificates of Commerce. Certificates were initiated by chambers independently in 1935, but in 1939 ABCC became a joint awarding body with the Board of Education, and they took on the title 'National'. The ABCC secretary (Dunwoody) acted as secretary, and ABCC members formed a majority of the joint committee.[18] The initiative was only modestly successful, depending heavily on the involvement of two key chamber members acting as chairs (Lord Herbert Scott 1939–44, and Sir Geoffrey Clarke 1944–50s). Certificates struggled during the war, became re-established, and then merged into the Commercial Apprenticeship

[12] Ilersic and Liddle (1960), pp. 124–8.
[13] ABCC, Executive Committee report, 1933–4, pp. 40–1; and following years.
[14] See Ilersic and Liddle (1960), pp. 103–16, 151–3, 189–90; Beer (1965), pp. 65–8; Kellett (1968); Alderman (1973), pp. 99 ff.; ABCC, Executive Committee report, 1920–1, pp. 35–45.
[15] Article on 'Chambers of commerce' carried by most local journals; e.g. Belfast, July 1924, p. 52.
[16] See Chapter 12.
[17] ABCC, Transport Committee minutes, comments at railway rates conference, 11 February 1936.
[18] ABCC, Executive minutes, 11 January 1939; Executive report, 1946–7, p. 10.

Table 13.3. National Certificates of Commerce, 1939–1950

	1939	1940	1941	1942	1943	1949	1950
No. of schools	63	49	39	33	25	—	—
No. of candidates	310	184	138	110	66	49	150
No. of passes	172	141	102	88	49	43	92
Pass rate (%)	55	76	73	80	74	88	—

Sources: ABCC Executive minutes 6 November 1940, 3 January 1951; *Monthly Proceedings*, 1943–4; some data incomplete.

scheme after 1956 (see Table 13.3, and later discussion below). Efforts to establish similar certificates in Higher Education met resistance from universities.

Local Education Authorities (LEAs). Local chambers became members of LEAs when these were established in 1944. Initiative was left to local chambers to press for places on LEAs, and initially it was reported that many had become members. However, by 1949 resistance was already being met in some areas, and there was no support from the government for wider involvement of chambers and other 'outsiders' to the education interest.[19] Any involvement was token in what became essentially local government bodies. This resulted in a wide range of subsequent initiatives to build school–business partnerships, especially from the mid-1970s (see below).

National Insurance Local Committees. These were established in 1949 to advise on local administration of unemployment support. There were 186 in England, 26 in Scotland, and 18 in Wales, each with 20 members including 6 employers, 6 employees (usually unions), 2–3 local authorities, and 1–2 friendly societies. ABCC and NCT were invited to nominate members, and had members in most areas.[20] The Committees had a minimal role but laid foundations for later MSC District Committees and Area Manpower Boards.

Area Consultative Councils. The government established these in some of the nationalized industries, mainly after pressure from ABCC and FBI/CBI, one of the few concessions within the nationalization programme. They were probably most significant in electricity and gas, where they were set up in 1952, with 12 chambers involved on a regional basis. Similar councils, involving chambers, were established for the National Ports Authority in 1969, and for nationalized airports and road haulage.

Local Productivity Councils. These were set up following the establishment of the British Productivity Council (BPC) in 1953 (later called the National Productivity Advisory Council for Industry (NPACI)); the BPC established local councils, with 80 by 1953, 97 by 1954, 105 by 1957, and 130 by 1965.[21] Chambers became

---

[19] ABCC, Executive minutes, 9 January and 4 September 1946; 6 July 1949.
[20] ABCC, Home Affairs Committee, 2 November 1949.
[21] ABCC, Executive minutes, 15 May, 2 September 1953; and Executive reports for following years.

involved in most of these, which acted as advisory committees for improving manufacturing in Britain. This involvement diminished in the 1960s and was terminated with the abolition of NPACI in 1965, when NEDC and the Regional Economic Planning Councils were set up.

Regional Economic Planning Councils (REPCs). These were an outcome of Labour's 1964 National Plan, which established Economic Planning *Boards* (staffed by civil servants) and *Councils* in the English regions, Scotland, Wales, and Northern Ireland. The chambers had a member on all of the REPCs, together with many other interests. The chambers were generally positive about the enlarged scope REPCs offered for exchange between government and business at the regional level, although this challenged the regional structure of ABCC. The REPCs as a whole were criticized as relatively ineffective, never living up to expectations to strongly influence national policy, but they profoundly influenced strategic planning decisions on some issues (e.g. on airports and new towns). They were abolished in 1979.

Local Community Relations Councils. These were established as a means to engage local organizations in local improvement strategies, mainly with young people and ethnic minorities, as part of the national efforts of the Community Relations Council established in 1970. Chambers were involved in 26 areas by December 1970, but the initiative engaged only 11 major chambers; more numerous were chambers of trade, which were members in 18 areas, of which 11 were in individual London boroughs. Interestingly, it is one of the few government initiatives in which junior chambers became involved, in four areas (Bedford, Derby, Newcastle, and Nottingham).[22]

Rates consultation. From 1984 local government was obliged to consult with business in setting the local non-domestic rates. The chambers became the 'natural partner' to do this, although other bodies were also used. This became an important force that stimulated engagement, though resented by many in local government. After 1990 the power of local government to levy their own level of non-domestic rates was replaced by a centrally set uniform business rate. The consultation obligation was continued, focusing on expenditure levels, but it was inevitably weakened, with some claiming it to be meaningless; although ABCC and CBI felt it had some benefits by removing conflicts over rate levels.[23] It was often combined into local strategic partnerships after 2001, though consultation meetings were frequently poorly attended.

Business Improvement Districts. After 2005–6 a Business Growth Incentive scheme replaced rates consultation, with chambers as consultees. These could enact Business Improvement Districts (BIDs), provided they were supported by a majority vote from those affected; a proportion of business rates was assigned to the BID for five years. There was little take-up, but where implemented they have been

---

[22] List of areas contained in a letter from Community Relations Council: ABCC, Executive minutes, 19 December 1970.

[23] *A National or a Local Tax? A Study of Non-domestic Rates* (London: Chartered Institute for Public Finance and Accountancy, 1990); Bennett, Fuller, and Ramsden (2004), pp. 220–2.

successful: e.g. in Liverpool a 2009–14 BID has covered 250 retailers in Liverpool One; and a 2010 BID has been developed for the commercial district. Since 2010 the Coalition government has proposed extending BID powers, and tax increment financing, for which chambers are likely to be crucial partners. The 2011 Budget introduced 21 Enterprise Zones which retain the increment in business rates deriving from development to invest in further development, with chambers and local government deciding how this is used through the LEP (q.v. below).

Local Business Partnerships (LBPs). These were established from about 1990 between local authorities and chambers, mainly under pressure from chambers, as a means to develop a more 'business friendly' approach to regulation of environmental health, safety, and trading standards by local government inspectors. The aim was to encourage compliance and reduce enforcement and court action; about 24% expanded to cover economic development, and 9% finance (Rates). The initiative grew fastest up to 1996, when about 13 had been established. By 2001 there were about 27.[24] These were superseded by Local Better Regulation Offices (at county level), which are arms of the central government's Better Regulation Executive (BRE).

Chamber involvement with advisory committees continues to the present, mainly covering economic development promotion and/or regeneration; rates and local expenditure consultation, BIDs and Enterprise Zones; health, safety, trading standards (through BRE); schools, education, and learning; crime and disorder reduction; transport and parking; tourism; transport, airports, and other major infrastructure; hospital and health administration. There is great variety at local level with chambers involved in most local committees where there is a significant economic interest, usually along with sector associations and other local business groups. Over 2001–10, some of these structures became more formalized into local strategic partnerships, but since 2010 the Coalition government has tried to encourage more bottom-up efforts, centred on LEPs. Chambers offer considerable benefit to these as centres for local business networks.

Local Strategic Partnerships (LSPs)

Chambers and local government are usually the two key strategic bodies that are concerned about the local economy. Partnerships with local government existed for the earliest chambers in an ad hoc way, reflecting local contingency, need, and the extent of mutual cooperation. For example, Walsall developed a joint local promotion committee with the town council over 1907–16; Dover made a number of joint promotion efforts with its town council in the 1920s and 30s; Jersey and Guernsey were actively promoting tourism and local produce from about 1901, in conjunction with their States, and became especially active from the 1930s. Most chambers of trade were involved in similar schemes. There have been marked differences between three sources of these partnerships: local government led

---

[24] Statistics from survey in Bennett, Fuller, and Ramsden (2004), p. 245.

(where chamber and other business interests were recruited to give a view); genuine mutual partnerships; and central government initiatives. In the early period all were locally led; even in the 1970s and 1980s, surveys in the UK showed local government still as the major force in economic development partnerships;[25] but central government funding of initiatives became the critical stimulus in the 1990s.

In Ireland EU funding has been significant in expanding the role of local partnerships of chambers with government. EU Objective 1 status provided the whole of Ireland with a high level of support through EU Social Fund, ERDF, and Agricultural Funds. This underpinned County Enterprise Boards from 1992, which were under local government and drew on ERDF money. The chambers have been involved in many of the EU local initiatives, and have been recipients of substantial grants and supports for particular service delivery, especially as part of development projects, training schemes, and SME supports. In some cases these have been very substantial. For example, Galway chamber became the major development initiator of its airport, and its chief shareholder. This was based on the purchase of 29 acres of land in 1982, with a debenture offer to members and others, and large government grants.[26]

In the UK a modern assessment of chamber involvement in local partnerships is summarized in Table 13.4. This covers mid-1998, prior to significant change under the Labour government of 1997–2010. The main fields of chamber activities in these partnerships were in their core areas of exports, networking, and business support, but extended to key aspects of local infrastructure and environment. In almost all areas chambers were the main business members. Chambers were usually the leaders for individual projects, thus mainly furthering their own projects within a wider strategy with local government. However, central government and the EU

Table 13.4. Types of local strategic partnership in which chambers were involved in 1998

Field of activity	% of projects
Exports/international trade	27
Business networks	20
Business development/competitiveness	13
Lobby projects	13
Regeneration	7
Town centre schemes (including pedestrianization, security)	7
Infrastructure and environmental improvement	7

Note: 'Other' was 6%.
Source: Bennett and BCC (1998), *Survey of Local Economic Development*.

[25] Sellgren (1987, 1989); Bennett, Fuller, and Ramsden (2004), Table 2; the Local Government Act (1972) stimulated the appointment of economic development staff and established municipal enterprises.
[26] Corrib Airport Ltd.; see Galway chamber history, Woodman (2000), Chapter 8; the chamber rejected offers to buy its 90% share in 2004; Irish *Daily Mirror*, 11 May 2004.

were the stimulus to action in 73% of cases, indicating how both chambers and local government were being driven chiefly by external agendas.

In 2001, establishment of 'local strategic partnerships' became requirements in 88 areas receiving Neighbourhood Renewal Funds, with encouragement for them in other areas. This was pressed as part of local government's obligations under Labour's Local Government Act (2000), which sought 'to empower local government to lead their communities'.[27] There was a requirement for a Local Community Strategy, and within this an LSP was expected to lead to a more 'holistic' approach. Chambers were the major contributors and most frequent private sector interests for these strategies: in over 83% of areas in England and Scotland, and 67% in Wales.[28]

Many assessments of LSPs have been made. For chambers, the main outcome has been a widespread involvement: by 2002 chambers participated in 94% of LSP areas in the UK and Ireland, north and south. But, as in other partnerships, this is alongside other bodies, which in rank order of frequency in the UK have been local business clubs, FSB, regional CBI, IoD, and Business in the Community.[29] Quasi-business bodies receiving major government funding were also seen as partners by government, and they were frequently prominent (such as Business Link, enterprise agencies, and Universities; and County Enterprise Boards in Ireland). This undermined independent business interests. Analysis of LSPs demonstrates that most used relatively minor inputs from business, frequently relying on consultation through postal surveys, seminars, and newsletters. One-to-one meetings, or joint executives with chambers or any other private sector partners, were rare. Where intensive links occurred they were seen as disproportionately time consuming compared to the tiny sums expended or significance of activity by LSPs.

In the UK, formal LSPs under Labour healed some wounds among local government interests, but it is doubtful that they offered more than a means to help bring a business view to some government spending programmes. In many areas the avalanche of government money over 2001–9 squeezed out former joint actions and competed with chamber and private sector activity; e.g. in fields such as networks, business support, directories, and economic promotion.[30] Moreover, LSPs were not used as the main vehicle for many government schemes. An assessment of chamber involvement by BCC in 2006 concluded that 'engagement and consultation . . . is not always substantive or has any bearing on subsequent course of action', and that 'a more dynamic and accountable governance structure' was needed, with concerns 'about the effectiveness of these bodies and the limits of what they are able to achieve'.[31] LSPs also made excessive demands on private

---

[27] Department of Environment, Transport and the Regions (2001), *Power to Promote or Improve Economic, Social or Environmental Well-Being: Guidance*, p. 1.
[28] Bennett, Fuller, and Ramsden (2004), table 12.
[29] Bennett, Fuller, and Ramsden (2004), table 19.
[30] Chamber role is shown in Bennett, Fuller, and Ramsden (2004), tables 12–19; see also Office of Deputy Prime Minister (2003), *Evaluation of Local Strategic Partnerships*; Department of Environment, Transport and the Regions (2001), *Local Strategic Partnerships: Government Guidance*.
[31] BCC (January 2006), *Local Strategic Partnerships—Views of Chambers of Commerce*, p. 1.

sector time, and were frequently bogged down in settling 'turf wars' between public agents. Some improvement emerged from *Local Area Agreements*, initiated as another government requirement after 2006, which offered yet more government money; and this extended to include business support over 2008–10.[32] In 2009 a statutory duty for local 'Whole Place' strategies was introduced, but local initiatives continued to be swamped by central government agendas and targets, leaving the private sector as peripheral, and dependent on the high spending of the Labour years.

The BCC in 2007 and 2008 launched reports to establish a stronger engagement between chambers and local government.[33] These established best practice and effective models for facilitating engagement.[34] The theme was developed further in a BCC report jointly with the Local Government Association in 2009, which sought to develop a joint strategy for improved local collaboration.[35] These initiatives were stimulated by Labour's strategy to bind local authorities into stronger relationships with RDAs.[36] Since the 2010 general election the abolition of RDAs and the strengthening of local government as the only local strategy bodies (through Local Leaders' Boards) have encouraged stronger ties with chambers, which have been further reinforced by Local Enterprise Partnerships (LEPs), discussed later. Most LSPs have now folded into LEPs, or have disappeared. A period of tight public expenditure also began to encourage stronger collaboration by local government since chambers offer shared effort within tighter budgets.

Core cities

For some of the most important chambers, involvement in a Core Cities Group of local government cooperation, established in 1995, has been significant. This consists of London and the eight major regional centres: Birmingham, Bristol, Leeds, Liverpool, Manchester, Newcastle, Nottingham, and Sheffield. The aim of the group has been to develop a shared agenda and to stimulate greater government funding through locally chosen priorities. It is an interesting mix of bottom-up initiative and top-down opportunities, trying to bend government initiatives in more effective directions across eight main fields, of which transport, business support, skills, and sustainability were the major up to 2010.[37] Core cities developed close links with the Labour administration and received greater support based on an argument that they provide services and act as 'economic power houses' to their regions. They particularly sought to prevent RDA and government funds

[32] Department of Business, Enterprise and Regulatory Reform (May 2008), *Business Support Simplification Programme*.
[33] BCC (2007), *A Tale of the Cities: The Best of Times?*; BCC (2008), *Raising the Bar: Driving Local Authority and Private Sector Engagement*, joint report with Centre for Enterprise.
[34] See Chapter 13.
[35] BCC and Local Government Association (2009), *Back to Business: Local Solutions*.
[36] e.g. joint report by HM Treasury, DBERR, and Department of Communities and Local Government (2007), *Sub-national Economic Development and Regeneration Review*.
[37] <www.corecities.com>: provides a summary of priorities and activities (accessed June 2010).

being spread thinly across regions, targeted in penny parcels at micro-neighbour-hood levels. They focused on infrastructure and core city needs, which generally favoured Labour-controlled councils. The strong involvement of the chambers was an effective way of developing more meaningful partnerships than most other central government formal partner initiatives of the period. Core cities found a major role in the Coalition's LEPs, forming seven of the first 24 (only Newcastle was not initially successful), and in all core cities by March 2011; each bringing the city together with a larger sub-region.

For chambers the Core Cities also became a strong internal interest group within BCC. This had an important consequence on the governance of BCC, where the nine-chamber group, together with some of the other large chambers, have pushed for reforms, as discussed in Chapter 8. This created some tensions with the other chambers in the 2000s.

Assessment

Involvements with local committees and local government have potentially given chambers something of a privileged adviser or 'insider' role, co-opted to help government interests; but the perception was often very different from the reality. The minutes of the chambers show continued concern as to their ability to influence the agenda. The postal committees and REPCs were generally relatively successful, but the railway rates committees were a source of continuous friction. Involvement with LEAs, the NPACI, nationalized industries, and most LSPs was generally frustrating. Working with local government has often proved challenging, with different experiences in different locations at different times. With many committee involvements there was (and continues to be) a high level of tokenism, with chambers often expressing exasperation about the paucity of their influence on local or national government decisions and the time involved.

Because of dissatisfaction, chambers frequently consider the same matters within their own committees (which usually have similar titles and overlapping member-ship with any involvement with external committees), as shown in Table 6.1. The growth of internal postal and telecommunications committees after 1920, for example, reflects the growing importance of the issues discussed in postal advisory committees. Similar patterns are evident later, for transport, education, planning, town development, crime prevention, tourism, etc.

For government (local and national; UK and Ireland) the involvement of chambers in advisory committees represents potential for high value added (since almost all the costs are borne by chambers and their members); additionality should be high where the decisions improve economic competitiveness or public service efficiency. The purpose has not been leverage, but the effect for chambers has levered internal committee development, whilst providing direct mission fit with chamber lobby objectives and supporting member demands. The tensions in the advisory role derive from chambers being seen to be involved but unable actually to deliver change due to government intransigence. This has inevitably occurred, particularly with regard to nationalized industries, local authority planning and rates, some transport committees, and recent local strategic partnerships. Better results have been achieved from involvement in local economic development, regeneration, and tourism advisory committees where the mainstream services of local authorities have been less challenged, and from bottom-up initiatives such as the recent Core Cities Group.

13.4 WARS

Wars have been long recognized as producing a 'ratchet effect', whereby increasing government expenditure, and higher levels of state control during wartime, are not fully unwound afterwards.[38] This is partly a result of government momentum/ inertia in being slow to respond; but chiefly the result of political pressures for a 'peace dividend' of continued civil government expenditures. This occurred after each of the great wars of 1796–1815, 1914–18, and 1939–45, where government promised a 'land fit for heroes', 'new Jerusalem', 'we've planned the war, now we'll plan the peace', and so forth.

The ratchet can work for all interests. Many businesses gained directly from wars in terms of increased demand, and also greater certainty of orders from an economy that was subject to high levels of state planning and regulation. Chambers also gained from wars. They gained financial aid, benefits of contacts, and experience as a result of stronger direct involvement with the government machine. As observed by ABCC president, Algernon Firth in 1917, 'war has altered everything, and unless the chambers of commerce seize the opportunity which is now afforded them by government they cannot hope to keep their place as authoritative and trustworthy exponents of the commercial interests of the UK'.[39] Indeed the membership of ABCC chambers increased from 19,800 to 34,535 over 1914– 20, and from 34,950 to 48,868 over 1939–47, though the experiences differed considerably between chambers (see Figure 2.2). The increases in chamber membership during WW1 and WW2 resulted from businesses seeking greater help and advice, particularly over compliance with government regulations. For the Channel Islands, enemy occupied during 1940–5, German wartime directives prevented chamber meetings, but the chamber membership was drawn into helping islanders through the German Controlling Committee and Essential Commodities Committee; as in the UK these were concerned with rationing, trading conditions, and distribution.

The world wars were also a stimulus to the formation of several chambers of commerce and chambers of trade, although some also failed in this period so that overall numbers remained stable. For example, the Preston chamber was specifically initiated in 1916 to provide 'a powerful, representative organisation of industrialists and businessmen . . . to deal with the day-to-day complications and problems

---

[38] Pigou (1947); Peacock and Wiseman (1961); Johnson (1968).
[39] Algernon Firth, ACC president, quoted in ACC, *Monthly Proceedings*, 4 October (1917), pp. 16–17.

arising from increasing government direction of production and distribution in pursuit of victory'.[40]

Wars can also break deadlocks. For the chambers, WW1 deliberations of the Wartime Reconstruction Committee led to breaking the deadlock between the FO and BoT on consular support, discussed further below. Ilersic and Liddle review at length the effects of WW1 and WW2 on the chambers, and only a summary is needed here.[41] Chambers became involved in organizing production and distribution quotas; providing massively increased flows of information on business needs for supplies and contracts, licences, price controls; interpreting government regulations; advising members and non-members;[42] supporting insurance schemes and air raid precautions; promoting exports to friendly and neutral nations; replacing male by female workers; and helping find jobs for de-mobbed personnel after the armistice. As the ABCC put it in a *Financial Times* article: 'regulations drawn on general lines did not fit particular cases . . . and the spread of licenses to almost every business activity made it necessary for chambers to intervene with the government either on behalf of groups of members or of individuals so as to prevent the whole industrial machine coming to a stop'.[43] Planning for trade development after each war was also prominent, as was resistance to the continuing post-war burdens of state regulation and taxation, and after WW2, proposals for nationalization.

Despite the benefits of increased income and increased membership, the chambers vigorously sought a rolling back of the ratchet after each war. For example, after the American war in 1775–83 the chambers were leading advocates for the general business view of the need to reduce government expenditure and find acceptable taxes that would not inhibit economic growth. After the French wars of 1796–1815, there was the same concern to cut back government expenditures and controls. After WW1 concerns were just as strong, with the then ACC president, Firth, stating that 'during the war businessmen have to submit, but when peace comes it will need a strong action and cooperation amongst us all to limit the interference that now exists, and to reduce all these departments to their proper activities. . . . It will be far more difficult to abolish them than to create them'.[44] Or, as stated by the president of the Preston chamber in 1919: 'demobilise the officials . . . and give us the freedom we were used to. . . . The government can safely leave the conduct of the trade of this country in the hands of those who are most qualified by experience and training to continue running it.'[45] After WW2, the chambers focused on limiting government expenditure, and attacking nationalization as irrelevant. Westminster chamber stated the challenge of changing from 'no longer [going] to Whitehall, but we must go into the markets and get business'.[46]

[40] Preston chamber history: Heywood (1966), p. 7.
[41] Ilersic and Liddle (1960), chapters 15 and 18; see also Grant (1991).
[42] Purt, the Leicester chamber secretary, estimated that he had personally signed 'upwards of half a million certificates' over WW2: Leicester chamber history (1961), p. 22.
[43] *Financial Times*, 9 March 1949; reproduced in Westminster chamber, *Yearbook* (1949), p. 42.
[44] Algernon Firth, president's address, *Annual Conference Report* (1917).
[45] Quoted in Heywood (1966), Preston chamber history, p. 12.
[46] Westminster chamber *Journal*, October/November (1954), pp. 20–1.

13.5 EARLY NATIONAL PARTNERSHIP

The earliest example of chambers being co-opted to help central government occurred during WW1. After much pressure and many reviews, the Faringdon Committee on consular services of 1917, discussed in Chapter 10, marks a watershed. Faringdon's recommendations led to the first national partnership of government with chambers. A first effort was a proposal to set up government branches around the UK; this was superseded by a collaboration with chambers to distribute information through 'Form K'.

Government information branches

The BoT's first response to Faringdon was a proposal for commercial intelligence *branches* of its new Department of Overseas Trade (DOT) in eight major cities (Birmingham, Bradford, Leeds, Liverpool, Manchester, Sheffield, Dublin or Belfast, and Glasgow).[47] The purpose was to extract information from general government intelligence, particularly consular reports on foreign market opportunities, to draw to the attention of local businesses. This was the first serious threat by government to compete with chambers. The ACC responded vigorously that the branches should be staffed by chambers, since they were already doing this work; government branches 'would only create overlapping and confusion'. The president Firth argued that 'it would be better that they were located in a chamber of commerce than independently: it would militate against the position of chambers of commerce and would not be getting the most efficient work. . . . [since they] would not know the local conditions.' He also told the chambers that several options were being considered by officials and that 'if the Association did not give a lead, the lead would be forced upon it. Therefore it was up to the chambers to put things straight and reform themselves before they were reformed from outside'.[48] Thus Firth used the opportunity offered to try to stimulate change; in this he turned some pressures inward and initiated the first government approval process for chambers, as discussed in Chapter 8.

The BoT was forced to back down, accepting that 'the Department did not wish to force proposals on unwilling towns'; but it refused to delegate the work to the chambers.[49] It was then proposed that DOT staff should be based in chambers, working 'in close cooperation with chambers', though controlled by DOT.[50] This aspect of discussion closely mirrors some of the later discussion of Business Link (q.v. below). But, in the event, the BoT would not accept chamber staff as their

---

[47] ACC *Monthly Proceedings*; letter from DOT to ACC, 15 November (1917).

[48] Algernon Firth, ACC president, quoted in ACC, *Monthly Proceedings*, October (1917), p. 23.

[49] Report of delegation of ACC, meeting with BoT: Birmingham chamber Council minutes, 25 February 1918.

[50] See e.g. Birmingham chamber Council minutes, 31 December 1917; see also letter from BoT to Treasury, 3 December 1917: TNA BT 13/84.

local staff, only civil servant officials;[51] and the Treasury vetoed all local staffing proposals as too costly (the total cost was £12,000 p.a.). The Treasury also argued 'that the objects . . . are likely to be secured in a markedly more efficient manner . . . if a central organisation in London keeps in constant touch with chambers'. They also doubted that one officer located in each city could acquire enough local knowledge, such that 'the local office [would] merely perform the function of a clearing post office'; which was another observation prescient of subsequent TEC and Business Link discussions.[52] This would have been a great opportunity for chambers to have become 'offices for government'. But whilst the chambers were unsuccessful in this bid, a programme of visits to chambers by BoT personnel and consuls was begun, which continued until WW2, and was revived again after 1946.

Consular information and 'Form K'

With the demise of the proposal for DOT branches, the Faringdon Committee recommendations were instead implemented using the chambers to disseminate information from consular agents, distributed as Key Forms (later rather strangely abbreviated to 'Form K'). Form K had lasting impact on the chambers. They were the outcome of the influence of Dunwoody and Firth (president over 1912–18) through the ACCI and then the BoT Advisory Council. It is not correct to state that the proposal came from the BoT, which wanted recognized chambers to provide this scheme.[53] Rather it was influence from Dunwoody and Firth who managed to persuade the BoT they were the way for government to operate with businesses for the purposes of trade promotion, and that chambers were an ally against the Foreign Office. A process of chamber approval operated by ACC (but supported by BoT) could deliver a quality-controlled outcome. This in turn supported the ACC view that many chambers needed to be pressed to raise their game. This was identical to the way in which the BoT was used to support subsequent chamber development strategies, especially by Ron Taylor after 1990, as outlined in Chapter 8. To Dunwoody and Firth, therefore, falls the credit for the first vision of chambers as service delivery bodies to businesses in partnership with government; and Form K was the first such scheme.

Form K sought to lay before manufacturers and exporters information from 600 consular areas in the world (later expanded to over 800), on: (i) recommended foreign firms for the development of trading links, and (ii) competing firms that were not recommended. The forms contained a template of questions on each foreign firm, listing its commodity, track record of imports, whether recommended for direct trade or not, and the answers to 13 specific questions, a so-called K classification, devised by Admiral Henry Campbell.[54] Newcastle chamber found

[51] Quoted by Algernon Firth, ACC president; ACC, *Monthly Proceedings*, October (1917), pp. 31–2.
[52] Secretary of Treasury to BoT, 15 February 1918: TNA BT 13/84.
[53] As suggested by Ilersic and Liddle (1960), p. 171.
[54] Memorandum by R. B. Dunwoody, ACC Secretary, September 1917: *Distribution of Commercial Intelligence (Form K) Supplied by the Department of Commercial Intelligence*. Contained

'considerable difficulty in dealing with the sheets' of K information received, and that they were initially 'of little practical value to the members of the chambers'. After pressure from ACC they were revised to become a 'K code' in 1918.[55] This is an early example of the general incapacity of government to design activities in partnership with the users.

The forms were sent by the consuls to the Foreign Trade Department in London, who passed them to the ACC, who in turn sent them, either: (i) directly to individual businesses who were members of chambers (in five varied cases: Barrow-in-Furness, Greenock, Edinburgh, Halifax, and Hull); or (ii) to local chambers, who then identified suitable local businesses, copied the reports and sent them on (in 30 chambers, including Birmingham, Coventry, Liverpool, and Nottingham); or (iii) chambers received copies made by ACC and then distributed them (19 chambers, including Belfast, Manchester, Dublin, and London).[56] Businesses receiving the forms then decided on any actions. This process was labour intensive, with costs supported by the BoT, based on the number of forms processed. But these costs were very heavy in the initial design. For example, Birmingham employed a Form K clerk at £100 but found that over the first year the costs were £1600 in total for 1918, with the expectation that this would rise to £3000 in 1919. The chamber proposed reducing the very high costs of copying by having a cross-referenced index of opportunities available at the chamber that members could then access. The BoT would not accept this, as it wanted the forms to go direct to members. Birmingham requested other chambers to hold a conference on this, which took place in January 1919 after an ACC meeting with 20 secretaries present. The compromise offered to the BoT was that a subscription scheme would be offered to members so that they could receive the forms directly if they paid an extra 2d. per sheet.[57] Birmingham implemented this and was followed by many other chambers.

The scheme ran for 18 years, until 1935. As a result the association and some local chambers received substantial income flows. Though the costs remained high, the benefit was to significantly increase the visibility of chambers to their members, and to privilege businesses that received the forms over those that did not, thus offering a significant incentive for membership.

The result was a very extensive service. Up to June 1918, 536,858 sheets, 62,000 jackets, 7000 consular district lists, and 8000 memoranda had been processed by ACC.[58] By 1925 ABCC had processed 63,790 reports and made 4.4 million copies. London alone processed 388,000 reports in 1919, and 311,000 in 1920.

in various local chamber records, e.g. Westminster minutes, Newcastle and Cardiff *Annual Reports*; see also Ilersic and Liddle (1960), p. 183.

[55] Reported in Newcastle chamber, *Annual Report* (1918), p. 43; and other local chamber proceedings.
[56] ABCC, *Monthly Proceedings*, March (1918–19), pp. 49–50; January (1920–1), pp. 71–3; Dublin was excluded after 1921.
[57] Birmingham chamber, Council minutes 28 October and 30 December 1918, 27 January 1919.
[58] ABCC, *Monthly Proceedings*, June (1918), p. 33.

Table 13.5. 'Form K' 1917–1935; number of reports, copies made by ABCC, and income to ABCC from BoT Department of Overseas Trade

Year	'Form K' reports	Copies made	Income to ABCC (£)
1917–18	196	196,052	n/a
1918–19	4,556	1,695,328	5,109
1919–20	11,719	1,193,092	6,781
1920–1	17,349	1,034,511	5,090
1921–2	11,404	190,955	1,808
1922–3	6,802	64,745	475
1923–4	5,847	58,547	245
1924–5	2,492	23,157	99
1925–6	8,445	67,541	281
1926–7	8,881	51,425	197
1927–8	6,467	28,356	137
1928–9	6,659	24,792	114
1929–30	4,283	14,383	63
1930–1	2,887	9,228	43
1931–2	3,709	10,852	49
1932–3	2,247	5,747	31
1933–4	2,176	8,213	28
1934–5	518	1,710	5
Total	106,637	4,678,634	over 15,446

Source: reports and copies reported in ABCC *Monthly Proceedings*; income in ABCC Accounts and loose papers.

For medium-sized chambers the income was £30–90 per year in the early period, as in Leicester, Newcastle, and Edinburgh. As shown in Table 13.5, the scheme processed its largest volumes in 1919–22, after which volumes reduced, but revived again in the mid-1920s with the slump in trade. The income to ABCC was significant, representing 68% of total income 1919–20; but after 1922, the value became minor.

The Form K episode provided important experience to the chamber system: first it helped cement ABCC and its member chambers at an early stage just after the largest chambers had joined; second, it opened the eyes of the ABCC council to the potential for wider services to be provided from the centre, as well as from the local chambers; and this model provided an example of a successful cooperation between the association and the member chambers. But most important, it offered an example of how chambers could develop more strongly with a level of government support. It also introduced the first application and approval process for local chambers, under BoT agreed criteria. This paved the way for subsequent accreditation processes.

It has not been sufficiently recognized that one of the most significant of the WW1 effects on chambers was this Form K relationship: it provided chambers with a privileged 'insider' position working with government for the first time. As the *Times* commented: the chambers 'have now a great opportunity to identify themselves with the government work for the promotion of trade . . . They have in this instance received recognition up to the hilt'.[59] Similar use of chambers was not developed after WW2, when the government instead used its own regional offices in attempts to promote trade. The Form K experience provided additionality to chambers and to government; it was aligned with the chamber mission; it leveraged change in the chamber system by stimulating accreditation, and opened an important new dimension of chamber services based on enquiries and information provision. There was close strategic fit, giving direct support to members (and encouragement to non-members to join). It also offered potential to shift the frame of internal debate from the polar positions of either independence or public law status, towards a mixed model of partnering the state.

Industrial and commercial organization

As well as promoting foreign trade, the War Cabinet in 1916 had identified the 'organization of industry' in Britain as deficient, especially when compared to Germany and the USA. A committee was established to consider the question, taking evidence over 1916–17, reporting in 1917 (the Balfour Committee).[60] This defined much of the frame of policy development up to the 1970s, and was to marginalize the chambers. The focus was on trade conditions; tariffs; finance; and how to deal in future with allies, the enemy, neutrals, and the countries of the empire. The chambers' evidence to the committee, given by Firth and Dunwoody, concentrated on the metric system, which they advocated as a simplification of accounting and stimulus to trade, and pressure for a Minister of Commerce. The focus that chambers adopted looks ill-chosen in retrospect, since none of these concerns became focal for the committee, though the committee did support consular reform.

The Balfour committee is now most remembered for the avenue it opened for industrial amalgamation, government reorganization of industry, and 'reconstruction' of trade associations. These topics covered one-third of Firth's questioning, yet it is clear that he was ill-prepared for most of the questions, drawing on his personal experiences and having no chamber back-up paperwork; whereas his comments on metrication and Minister of Commerce in the other two-thirds of his evidence were all based on earlier chamber lobby papers. Firth used the example of the Bradford Dyers' Association, of which he was a member, and his own tapestry carpet and blanket businesses as the main experience he could draw on.[61]

Firth was only one of many individuals questioned, and it would be wrong to overemphasize his influence on the committee. But it was he who was the chamber's voice, even though he said he was not an official representative of the

[59] *Times* leader 1917; quoted in Ilersic and Liddle (1960), p. 171.
[60] *Commercial and Industrial Policy Committee*: evidence, TNA BT 55/9–13; final report, BT 55/13. Critical members were Lord Faringdon, Sir Alfred Mond, Sir Charles Parsons, and Arthur Balfour.
[61] Firth's evidence is pp. 443–91: TNA BT 55/10. His main business was T. F. Firth and Sons Ltd., Brighouse rug and blanket manufacturers, established 1867, incorporated 1889; subscriber capital paid in 1918 £652,000: TNA BT 60/1/1, notes on composition of BoT Advisory Committee.

ACC; Dunwoody made only one comment (on metrication). Firth could have articulated the importance of local supply chains and regional networks, the need for innovation and entrepreneurship, and the value of small firms. He was caught on the hop; the ACC had apparently never considered any of these issues; and Firth's comments reinforced all the other evidence gathered. The committee's conclusions were that (i) British industry needed to develop in future through amalgamations and combines so that it could compete more effectively with US corporations and German Kartells to gain economies of scale; and (ii) national trade associations were the best source of support for price, marketing and producer alliances, and rings. Or as Firth himself put it, the government 'should legalise combinations' in order to make inter-firm agreements enforceable.

It is not right to criticize Firth and the chambers, with the benefit of hindsight, that they did not see modern concepts of small firms and networks, and the re-emergence of the local within new global trading systems. But there were some profound gaps in Firth's understanding of sectors beyond traditional manufacturing, with some quotations that now read as excessively narrow. It is probably best to interpret these as generally held by the manufacturers of the time. But it did not help to move the chambers into a position where they were well equipped to deal with the emerging policy frame of the next 50 years. Firth's statement that 'the number of small firms is simply ridiculous' would have reinforced all the prejudices within the chambers that small traders could be marginalized or excluded. His experience of the Bradford Dyers' Association, that individuals would always opt out so that it was impossible to hold price and product associations together (the free-rider problem), reinforced the view that government leadership was required: 'Government investigation and if necessary government assistance should be given'. His concurrence with the committee's view, that *merchants* had de facto operated combinations which should be replaced by combines of producers, directly attacked the core chamber merchant members and the historic commitment to free trade. And he readily agreed that combination allowed 'the producer to get closer to the consumer and improve customer satisfaction', and 'for furthering our trade in foreign markets'.[62]

The new policy frame saw sector trade bodies and employers' associations as the favoured partners of government to deal with wage negotiations, plan large industries, and develop combines; with national peak bodies such as the FBI/CBI as a means to draw the sectors together. These bodies emerged to rule the roost. In answer to a direct question whether there 'should be associations of traders wherever they are in the country, rather than associations of commercial people confined to one location', Firth answered with the simple and unqualified 'Yes'. He made no attempt to defend the local chambers. As noted in Chapter 10, the free trade vision held by chambers since the 1850s had evaporated, and they had no policy frame to replace it. They were now hostage to other voices: the sector bodies,

[62] Algernon Firth, evidence to Commercial and Industrial Policy Committee, pp. 475–91: TNA BT 55/10.

FBI/CBI, combines, and employer associations dealing with labour. Indeed the FBI was often more open market in its views than the ABCC.

13.6 PARTNERSHIP IN TRADE PROMOTION

International trade and promotion were at the forefront of chamber concerns throughout the 19th and 20th centuries, as shown in Chapter 10. Historically chambers focused on treaty negotiations; but from the 1820s they increasingly also embraced overseas trade support. This evolved into efforts to 'push for trade' through foreign missions, exhibitions, and export research support and training. Each of these activities eventually became jointly financed with government, but their origins were in chamber initiatives.

Missions and exhibitions

Foreign missions by chambers, and involvement in exhibitions at home and abroad, had occurred from an early date, both as small-scale exploratory efforts, and at a larger scale. Early examples were the trips made by Macclesfield in the 1850s to the silk manufacturers of Lyons, and the visit by the president of the Salt chamber to India in 1874 to report on market opportunities. The 1851 Great Exhibition was a catalyst to more general chamber involvement with missions and exhibitions in the UK and abroad. These efforts became significant features for the BoT, which ran the first government supported mission in 1897. Its budget then was only £1000, but this increased to £12,000 by 1919 after formation of the Department of Overseas Trade. This allowed about four larger missions per year to be organized, chiefly for sector trade groups.[63] Chambers were involved in nominating some members, and this began an important process. They were terminated in the 1922 severe budget cuts, but revived again on an occasional basis.

Enthusiasm for missions took on a new form in 1964, when the Labour government gave greater support: government subsidies of 50% to identified costs were offered for missions organized by chambers and trade associations. By 1965 there were 48 outward, 32 inward, and 30 fact-finding missions. These continue to the present, through the DTI/BIS, and have found particular favour since 2010, with Prime Minister David Cameron as a frequent leader. They represent, in effect, a co-opting of government by chambers, although many other bodies also access the support (especially sector trade associations and large firms).[64] The first mission under this framework was organized by Birmingham, which claims that it was critical in developing relations with the Wilson government that led to support.[65] By 1967–8, 18 chambers had been involved, mainly the

---

[63] TNA BT/61/3/DOT/E735; see also Homer (1971).
[64] There were 220 bodies involved in 1975, including chambers: ABCC *Annual Report* (1976).
[65] Quoted in Taylor (2007), pp. 53–5.

Table 13.6. Outward missions organized by chambers 1965–2010

Date	No. of outward missions	No. of businesses involved	Value of business generated (£000s)	No. of inward missions	No. of businesses involved	No. of overseas trade fairs	No. of businesses involved
1965	48	—	—	32	—	—	—
1967	41	—	26,009	—	—	—	—
1970	49	—	—	—	—	—	—
1988	116	—	—	—	—	—	—
1992	149	—	199,808	—	—	—	—
1994	171	—	558,179	—	—	—	—
1996	149	—	264,627	249	—	46	—
1998	178	2135	373,651	261	2704	60	859
2000	191	2236	404,317	167	2566	68	496
2002	173	1889	151,179	167	1825	44	524
2004	158	1772	164,357	138	1877	60	667
2006	127	970	36,804	114	1129	47	454
2008	108	749	63,920	142	1591	77	417
2010	130	1038	39,832	134	1323	54	632

Note: Not all data available.
Source: ABCC annual reports and minutes before 1988, and MS 17559; BCC *Census* and *Benchmarking* from 1992.

larger ones.[66] The 1960s also saw the development of a more committed structure from government to exhibitions, through the British National Export Council, though support for actual events remained, and still remains, based on case-by-case bids.

The trade mission support from government still underpins an important service provided by chambers (and other business associations) to member *and* non-member businesses. It has encouraged membership, and has provided state subsidy to promote exports. The volume of missions organized by chambers is summarized in Table 13.6. The number grew steadily up to the 1990s, fluctuating around 150, with peaks in 1995 and in 1999–2000. Since 2004 there has been some decline, which reflects a reducing number of chambers in the system (so that one mission can cover the needs of a wider group of local businesses). To reverse this pattern, BCC has put international trade development and missions as one of its key priorities since 2009.

Export research support/training

Beyond missions and exhibitions, a broader platform developed when the DTI agreed to support an Export Marketing Research Scheme in 1989. This subsequently became part of UK Trade and Investment (UKTI), but run by chambers.

---

[66] Birmingham, Coventry, Dundee, Edinburgh, Glasgow, Leicester, Liverpool, London, Manchester, Northants., N. Staffordshire, Northern Ireland, Portsmouth, Sheffield, Slough, Walsall, Westminster, Wolverhampton: ABCC papers, MS 17559.

The scheme supports several hundred exporters per year, encouraging export projects and offering small grants to businesses to help with their first year of export development. Over 1989–2009, 6000 projects were supported through £11 million of grants, with £300 million of additional trade claimed to have been developed. This is a small but significant scheme. A related scheme, also initiated in 1989 through UKTI, is for Export Communications Reviews, which again offer support for exporters to review their activities. This supports about 100 reviews per year.[67] Both these schemes are managed by BCC centrally, and are among the most successful UKTI schemes judged by their satisfaction levels and assessment of business performance.

These schemes run from the BCC office in Coventry, established as one of Ron Taylor's earliest initiatives. As incoming director general in 1985 he sought to reposition the association as a partner of government. The schemes represent the first substantial service to the individual chambers since Form K. They thus presaged the more substantial developments that followed. The government expenditure on these schemes and missions is small, but the value for money, additionality, and leverage is high. For the chambers they provide close strategic fit, and direct support to members (and non-members) and are a stimulus to recruitment.

13.7 FROM APPRENTICESHIPS TO NATIONAL NETWORKS

The chambers had been concerned with technical education from an early date, reflecting concern about the commercial ignorance of the gentlemanly class. But the most urgent concerns emerged in the mid to late 19th century with the need for clerks and others technically able to fill the growing number of jobs in trading administration and more advanced production skills. This was a key part of lobbying from the 1870s, and chambers also began to establish their own scholarships and prizes for local technical schools.[68] The London chamber began its commercial examination scheme in 1894, as discussed in Chapter 12. But all of these were efforts to provide services or to influence from the outside. Working with government provided another opportunity.

Chamber commercial apprenticeships

The earliest efforts to work with government appear to have been in 1926, when the Wakefield chamber proposed a certificate of training for foremen. This was submitted to the Board of Education and was taken up in government initiatives to stimulate more training of craft teachers. The government was also supportive of commercial apprenticeships. These were first proposed by ABCC in 1938, delayed by the war, and finally established in 1957. They marked a major step for some chambers to develop experience that later allowed involvement with larger training

---

[67] BCC, *Annual Report* (2009).
[68] Summarized in Ilersic and Liddle (1960), chapters 12 and 14.

schemes. The scheme followed from earlier National Certificates of Commerce (see above), but offered a much more extensive three-year academic and practical training for employees aged 16–30. The ABCC launched the scheme with two area apprenticeship boards for England and Wales, and Scotland, and published a booklet, *A Better Career in Commerce*.[69] It was particularly designed to cope with the post-war baby boom school leavers of 1960–3. The schemes received recognition and support from the Ministries of Education and Labour, thus representing some co-option by chambers of government.

By 1960 the scheme was taking off. Whilst it did not prove to be as successful, or the money-spinner, as hoped, ABCC had received £500 in fees in 1958–9, and local chambers about £750. It was at its greatest extent over 1961–8 (see Table 13.7). It had greatest appeal to large manufacturers but some smaller businesses also became involved. The most successful chamber involvement was that of Glasgow; it accounted for almost all the Scottish enrolments, e.g. 41 of 48 in 1962–3, 59 of 61 in 1965–6. Glasgow also accounted for 45% of apprentices nationally (231 of 519 in 1965–6). This was the result of hiring a training consultant who acted as manager of the schemes and actively marketed them to employers. This was a model recommended by ABCC, but not copied by other

Table 13.7. ABCC Apprenticeship Scheme 1957–1969

Year	No. of new schemes approved per year	No. of new apprentices enrolled (England, Wales, NI)	No. of new apprentices enrolled (Scotland)	Total enrolled	No. of apprentices completed (total)	No. of companies registered	No. of chambers involved
1957–8	75	—	—	—	—	43	33
1958–9	34	120	90	210	—	115	37*
1960–1	73	118	80*	—	—	—	45
1961–2	24	182	103	—	31	500	45
1962–3	22	88	48	—	108	550	46
1963–4	18	119	46	515	84	—	46
1964–5	16	93	78	567	97	—	47
1965–6	17	114	61	528	86	—	49
1966–7	12	105	70	579	115	170	50
1967–8	13	134	82	576	66	83	50
1968–9	4	97	66*	470	240	—	50
1969–70	2*	75*	60*	—	200*	—	50*
Total	310*	1245*	784*	—	1027*	—	—

* Estimated.
Note: Not all data available for all years.
Source: ABCC *Annual Reports* and minutes; MS 17480/1–4; MS 17478/3.

[69] ABCC, Home Affairs Committee, 11 May 1938; MS 14482/3. ABCC, GPC minutes, 1 May 1957, 1 October 1958; ABCC, Education Committee, 2 June 1971.

Table 13.8 Variation between chambers in scale of ABCC
Apprenticeship Scheme in 1965–6

Total apprentices enrolled	Number of chambers	Completions
0	22	—
1–6	13	1
7–12	6	1
13–30	4	20
Over 30	4	27

Note: 1965–6 is the last year for which information is available.
Source: ABCC MS 17480/4.

chambers because of its costs. However, it was a major lesson for subsequent
thinking.

The scheme spread to the majority of larger chambers, offered in 50 chambers by
1966. But for most chambers the number of apprentices was very small, and in
many the scheme was only an offer. In 1965–6, for example, 45% of these
chambers had no apprentices on the scheme, and 71% had six or less. As shown
in Table 13.8, only 8–10 chambers were deeply involved, and of these it was only
Glasgow, London, Birmingham, Coventry, and Manchester that were significant
(each having 28 or more apprentices): these five accounted for 75% of all apprentices. The scheme tended to depend on a few committed firms; e.g. in Teesside the
first seven apprentices graduated in 1960, but all came from the same firm, with
only one other firm participating.[70]

ABCC apprenticeships were voluntary commitments from local employers
through their chambers. They were not always popular. For example, London
chamber did become heavily involved, but was very critical at the outset, 'even with
modifications and amendments, the council remained of the opinion that the
scheme was not a practical one'.[71] London wanted firms that were already running
schemes to be recognized, but the ABCC Education Committee had considered
applications under the scheme only where a firm's scheme had been in existence for
less than a year.[72] Indeed ABCC was forced to admit that many firms that were
training apprentices were not registering with ABCC.[73]

But the major tensions resulted from government setting up its own structures
and its unwillingness to include the chamber scheme. Whilst government had been
willing to be co-opted to support the start of the scheme, when it initiated its own
training structure in 1965 it invented its own scheme. This also demonstrated the
difficulties of overcoming the education lobby. The chamber scheme relied heavily
on working with local education providers, who were often reluctant to cooperate.

[70] Teesside and South West Durham chamber, *Annual Report*, 31 December (1960), p. 18.
[71] London chamber, *Annual Report* (1956), p. 10.
[72] London chamber, *Annual Report* (1957), p. 9.
[73] ABCC, GPC minutes, 7 February 1962.

For example, Barnstaple considered commercial apprenticeships in 1959, but did not proceed as there was 'little scope in Barnstaple', and the North Devon College was very resistant.[74] The lack of government backing encouraged some large employers to withdraw in favour of degree courses, but most smaller firms remained strongly committed.[75] The chambers' apprenticeships continued in a patchy fashion around the country, and became absorbed into the wider chamber training activities that developed after 1972.

Government training and apprenticeship schemes

The Labour government's Industrial Training Act 1964 essentially killed the ABCC apprentice initiative; it established a tripartite National Training Council and sector Industrial Training Boards (ITBs), with 13 ITBs established by 1966 covering 7.5m workers, and 27 by 1969 covering 15.5m employees (62% of the national workforce). These focused on sector planning and skills, not *local* employer involvement; and there was a level of compulsion as ITBs were able to exact a training levy from employers, unless they offered in-house training themselves. Voluntary schemes like the ABCC's could not easily compete, but they could assimilate within the new structure, and some chambers continued with a variety of cooperations between themselves and local employers through ITBs.

Nationally the ABCC received friendly words from the National Training Council after its establishment in 1965; and J. A. Hunt, who was a member of the ABCC Education Committee, became a member of the Training Council and chair of their Commercial and Clerical Training Committee. The Council produced a positive report in September 1966, which suggested that chambers organizing their training activity on a sector basis could work with ITBs, and organize training consultants that could be supported by ITBs (the Glasgow model).[76] To push matters, the Glasgow chamber formally requested five ITBs to recognize its scheme.[77] But rather than accept an existing scheme, the Training Council and ITBs wanted it to become part of a wider training arrangement, and developed their own rival Certificate in Office Studies to be provided in colleges, mostly at a lower level of junior clerk. By 1969 initial promises from the Council had turned into rebuffs. This period of limbo prevented the chambers publicizing their own scheme as fully as they wished, although they continued to receive many enquiries from employees and employers.[78]

---

[74] Barnstaple chamber minutes, 4 September 1959.

[75] ABCC, *Annual Report* (1969–70).

[76] National Training Council (1966), *Training for Commerce and the Office*; quoted in ABCC, *Annual Report* (1966–7), p. 11.

[77] The Engineering, Construction, Shipbuilding, Iron and Steel, and Carpet Industry ITBs; see ABCC, *Annual Report* (1967–8), p. 10; correspondence file MS 17488/1–2.

[78] In ABCC, *Annual Reports* (1966–7), p. 11; (1967–8), p. 10; (1968–9); Education Committee MS 17478/2–3.

Despite their drawbacks, the ITBs were an important opportunity for some chambers to participate, with about 15 becoming involved in a significant way.[79] For example, Walsall's president saw this as a major opportunity and fought hard with his council for the chamber to become involved. He was able to develop a strong relationship with the Leather Manufacturing ITB, indeed facilitating its development. This allowed the chamber to become a major training agent.[80] But the tensions of the ITBs with the chamber mission were always severe: a sector structure vs. a general chamber mission. Exploratory meetings showed that the Ministry of Labour wanted chambers to form sector links; e.g. Manchester with cotton, Leicester with knitting, lace, and net: the fossilized view of industrial districts that were disappearing at the time. Twelve ITBs were explored, but there was no adaptation to use chambers as the training body rather than business establishments.[81] Strong efforts to gain support for consultancy services and advisers were turned down.[82] There was some greater flexibility after the election of the Conservatives in 1970, who relabelled the Council as a Skills Training Agency in 1972 (relabelled again as the Manpower Services Commission (MSC) in 1973), and remodelled it as a contractor to a wider range of providers, which were developed as group training associations (GTAs—although still sector based).

The ITBs and GTAs represented the start of a wider training market in which government provided support for employer-based training, though continued pressure from the education lobby ensured that a preference existed for funding most training provision through local colleges. Many Northern and Midlands chambers were quick to become involved from 1966–7, but London chamber, having failed to gain support for a commercial ITB in 1969, established a group training association only in 1979. Although the direct income to the chambers was usually limited, with the training accounts managed through the ITBs or GTAs, involvement radically changed the participating chambers. It opened eyes to a new partnership potential with government.

A further change occurred in 1975 when the Labour government strengthened the MSC local level through 125 District Manpower Committees; later rationalized under the Conservatives and renamed as 58 Local Area Manpower Boards in 1983 (across Britain), and merged into TECs in 1990. These were initially tripartite structures (one-third each of employers, trade unions, and local government), with civil service administration through Area Offices. They were the first serious attempt to develop a *local delivery* structure for training. Chambers as well as many other providers became increasingly involved as board members, and as

---

[79] The main chambers involved in ITB schemes in 1967–8 were Aberdeen, Birmingham, Coventry, Dundee, Glasgow, Leeds, Leicester, London, Manchester, N. Ireland, Portsmouth, Slough, Southampton, Tyneside, and Walsall; MS 17488.

[80] Information from David Frost, former manager from 1979, and then chief executive of Walsall.

[81] Meeting report 21 February 1967; letter to ABCC, 25 August 1967; letter from W. R. Thompson, Department of Employment and Productivity to ABCC, 27 January 1969: correspondence file; ABCC MS 17488/1–2.

[82] ABCC, paper HA.13-67, January 1967: MS 17488/1.

local managing and/or delivery agents: collectively termed 'non-statutory training organizations' (NSTOs).

After the New Training Initiative of 1981

The NSTOs gathered stronger pace after the re-election of the Conservatives in 1979, and the launch of the New Training Initiative in 1981, which abolished the compulsory levy for ITBs, and launched the Youth Training Scheme (YTS).[83] For most chambers their main period of involvement in training started with YTS, launched in the face of a deep recession in 1981, and Adult Training for the long-term unemployed (initially called Employment Training) introduced in 1988. Both schemes have continued in different forms up to the present.[84] They required job placements with employers to encourage the unemployed to be better placed for subsequent long-term employment. This was a shift from the former approach of 'training for stock' that had favoured the colleges and education courses. It derived from the MSC's new chair, David Young, who was convinced that educational 'low achievers' needed alternative vocational routes.[85]

Many chambers were well placed to offer immediate support to these government schemes, since they had successful experience of workforce schemes. Many chambers developed training centres, training subsidiaries, and became involved in other government schemes such as Restart and Jobclub. By 1991 the largest 19 chambers had an average of 32 training staff (53% of total staff), whilst even the medium-sized chambers had an average of 9 training staff (62% of all staff).[86] Training schemes were becoming a dominant chamber function.

Table 13.8 shows the volume of places from government contracts that went to chambers from this period from the different training schemes. The earliest contracts were modest; for example Mid Yorkshire started with 120 places in 1982, and Glasgow with 200 in 1983. But the scheme grew rapidly. By 1985, 31 chambers were acting as managing agents and 17 were developing the related Adult Training scheme; over 2000 specialist staff were being employed by chambers and they were working more closely than ever directly with employers in order to provide placements and ensure effective training outcomes. By 1999 the chambers were the single largest independent training provider, delivering over 6500 courses per year for over 100,000 people (on government and private schemes).[87]

The most recent figures show fluctuations as a result of the needs of the unemployed (and hence are cyclical), as well as the restructuring to reduce the number of contract holders following the abolition of TECs and CCTEs in 2001.

---

[83] ITBs were not themselves abolished, but most collapsed without government funding; two continued to raise levies on their sectors voluntarily: the CITB and EITB.

[84] Called Train to Gain, Entry to Employment, apprenticeships, and other programmes in the period 2005–10; then Work Programme from 2011.

[85] Young (1990), pp. 73–102; Later Lord Young of Graffam (briefly brought back as adviser in 2010).

[86] Bennett and Krebs (1993b), table 14.

[87] Statistics from Taylor (2007), pp. 99, 101.

Table 13.8. Number of government training places contracted to chambers of commerce in Britain (combines youth and adult schemes), 1985–2010

Year	No. of places	Mean places	Max. places	Min. places	80% places	20% places	No. of chambers contracted	% of BCC chambers contracted
1985	14,500	468	1,000*	—	—	—	31	34.8
1991	23,169	482	7,000	12	350	12	49	47.5
1992	29,820	596	7,000	3	550	143	48	47.5
1994	36,589	851	6,542	6	992	258	43	47.8
1998	60,233	1,469	13,319	17	3,780	100	41	55.4
2000	62,137	2,071	12,500	3	3,600	168	42	56.8
2002	15,908	737	2,975	2	1,500	14	27	36.5
2004	18,252	760	12,674	27	2,228	50	24	39.3
2006	16,155	702	3,877	1	955	46	23	41.1
2008	12,024	668	2,235	98	1,267	127	18	32.7
2010	12,919	680	2,520	55	960	134	19	35.1

* Estimated.

Note: Non-participating chambers excluded from mean and range; year-on-year comparisons not precise because BCC membership changes.

Sources: 1985 from Taylor (2007), p. 99; 1991 from Bennett and Krebs (1993b); after 1992 from BCC, *Census* and *Benchmarking*.

With the passing of contractual management for some schemes to local authorities in the last months of Labour in April 2010, the market for external involvement was thrown into question. The local government 'Commissioning Framework' was fragmented, leading to massive complexity, variation in capability and approach between areas, with little capacity to manage cross-border and national demands and targets, and a bias against the use of outside providers.[88] Since 2010 the Coalition government has begun to restructure these schemes under a central funding council, with increased numbers of apprenticeships, but still with strong pressure from colleges.

The involvement of chambers in government training schemes showed a willingness to be recruited for government objectives. It also allowed some support for schemes the chambers had created. The objectives were synergetic with chamber missions, but the scale of the resources involved began to distort and challenge the independence of chambers. They also created a new internal tension, between the generally larger chambers involved in training, and the smaller ones that were not. This had begun under Labour, but it was the New Training Initiative, where the Conservatives tried to involve the private sector to a greater extent, that shifted the scale and tensions that had to be managed. The Conservatives created further challenges in the next period of development.

[88] Association of Learning Providers (January 2010), *National Commissioning Framework: Consultation Response*.

13.8 BUSINESS LEADERSHIP: LOCAL ECONOMIC
DEVELOPMENT, THE LENS, AND TECS

The Thatcher government, elected in 1979, experienced deep recession in the early
1980s with significant industrial collapse largely focused in the major urban areas.
This stimulated a series of initiatives which all focused on trying to give the private
sector a greater role in government programmes, within which chambers were seen
as a key partner. In addition to the New Training Initiative discussed above, there
were (i) urban regeneration and inner city programmes through the 1980s, including local government reforms; (ii) enterprise agencies; (iii) improvements in linkage
of education to the labour market and employers; and (iv) leadership structures to
empower businesses to take a major role in managing government programmes,
chiefly from 1989 (the LENs and TECs). Each of the initiatives led to new
government-funded bodies in the localities. From a position in which in 1979
there were only chambers and local authorities, there rapidly developed a multitude
of overlapping government-supported local agencies, which created competition for
chambers and confusion for businesses. The Audit Commission (1989, p. 1)
referred to it as a 'patchwork quilt of complexity and idiosyncrasy'.

The chambers had been involved in some of the thinking behind these initiatives
from 1976, when the Conservatives were in opposition, particularly with Michael
Heseltine, who became Secretary of State for the Environment 1979–86. This had
led to a statement by ABCC in 1976 that, whilst maintaining its traditional role of
working with all governments, 'nevertheless, especially when the government
majority is precarious, it is important that the ABCC should establish effective
links with the opposition shadow ministers as well as with ministers in office',
particularly to influence manifestos.[89] Heseltine proved to be one of the greatest
supporters of chambers, but also caused them great difficulties.

For understanding these developments, the chamber history written by Ron
Taylor, who was director general of ABCC/BCC over 1984–98, provides valuable
internal insight. In addition, the author has made several studies that show how the
major government initiatives of this period influenced external agents.[90] Here, the
focus is on the main tensions for the voluntary structure of chambers.

Inner city and regeneration initiatives

The new vision for the government's inner city programmes was Heseltine's first
foray into using chambers of commerce as a part of private sector-led approaches to
urban regeneration. In a Guildhall speech in 1980 he stated: 'representatives of the

[89] ABCC, *Annual Report* (1977), pp. 1–2; there was also experience of working with the
Conservatives in the Heath government of 1970–4, in which Heseltine and some other later
ministers were members.
[90] Taylor (2007); Bennett and McCoshan (1993); Bennett, Wicks, and McCoshan (1994);
Bennett and Payne (2000).

industrial and commercial world should devise ways in which they can have a proper dialogue and make an effective contribution to the decisions that local authorities and central government have to take. This organisation will *often be based on the chambers of commerce.*'[91] A similar statement was included in the July 1981 guidelines for local government in receipt of Inner City programme money. This was a central government scheme initiated by the Labour administration in 1977, but which was given a new priority: 'Ministers see a role for the private sector not only as a source of investment but also as influencing the scope and content of inner area programmes . . . [and] will expect, before giving approval . . . to be satisfied that the voice of the private sector has been heard and that detailed consultation has taken place. This will *normally be through members of the local chamber of commerce.*'[92] Never before had a government minister sought such a close cooperation with chambers: this was co-option or recruitment at its most extreme: but who was being co-opted—independent bodies helping government, or independent bodies bent to government targets?

Initially co-option of local businesses seemed to be the main approach. The government created an entirely new raft of its own agencies and programmes to tackle inner city and industrial decline. Most significant were Urban Development Corporations (UDCs), Task Forces, City Action Teams, and tax breaks via Enterprise Zones. These were central government initiatives taking direct action locally through new centrally appointed bodies, or in the case of Urban Programme Areas, setting down strong targets for local government priorities. Local government was seen as part of the cause of the problem of economic decline, and was to be circumvented, restricted, or forced to include in its decision making the views of local private sector partners, particularly the chambers. In the case of UDCs, even planning powers were wrested from local government, although by the 1990s local government was being strongly built into local regeneration initiatives.

These new bodies needed leadership, as well as involvement from investors and local businesses. In some areas this rested on central appointees alone; and UDCs in particular were often criticized for being 'parachuted' into localities with no local involvement. In other areas business leadership was stimulated through a new body supported by the Prince of Wales, and heavily influenced by Heseltine: Business in the Community (BiTC).[93] The CBI was also sucked into involvement.[94] The chambers became heavily involved, and with BiTC, and other business leaders, were given 'insider' routes as partners and advisers of government. There were uneasy relationships between chambers and BiTC when it tried to develop new business leadership teams in the larger cities (such as Sheffield and Teesside), which had strong chambers, but generally the two bodies operated in different areas and

---

[91] Text of Heseltine speech at London Guildhall (1980), *Cooperation between Business and Local Government*, Department of Environment, Press Notice 228; emphasis added.

[92] Department of Environment (1981), *Prospectus for Local Initiatives on Community Involvement*, emphasis added; see also Department of Environment (1982), *Bringing in Business*.

[93] See e.g. BiTC (1989), *Leadership in the Community* (London: Business in the Community).

[94] See e.g. CBI (1988), *Initiatives beyond Charity: Report of the CBI Task Force on Business and Urban Regeneration*.

acted as alternative means to develop action. Ironically, under a government that abolished corporatist machinery at national level, this brought chambers into an increasingly corporatist relationship with local government and central government through local funding initiatives. Though, as noted by Grant, the trade unions were no longer usually involved:[95] this was bipartite rather than tripartite corporatism.

A related aspect of these developments was a new requirement in the Local Government Act 1984: that local authorities had to consult businesses when setting their non-domestic rates. Chambers were again the natural body through which this could be achieved, although it put a considerable strain on their local resources.[96] A statement made by ABCC in 1989 encapsulates the new model: 'in order to pursue shared objectives in support of business, British chambers of commerce have established close links with government in relation to chamber activities and services ... to act as a delivery mechanism, at the local level, for government schemes. For schemes to work, the business participation has to be practical, local and genuine. The involvement of chambers at the outset, both in design of schemes and their delivery, helps to ensure the schemes' relevance and effectiveness.' The structure needed for effective cooperation, as seen by ABCC was

> firstly, a local presence, closely integrated with the business community. Second, the presence must have a staff infrastructure and support capability strong enough to organise, promote and maintain an initiative at the local level. Third, that presence must be permanent. That is to say, it must not melt away after the first enthusiasm of a new initiative has worn off. Chambers of commerce, uniquely, can offer that local presence and a very significant support capability, ... that is locally-owned—that has the authentic support of the local business community because it is *their* chamber.[97]

Participation by chambers provided something government desperately needed: legitimacy with the businesses located in local communities. For chambers there was natural willingness to be co-opted to a role to which they always aspired: civic leadership.

The interest in chambers as a 'natural' partner encouraged the DoE to commission a report in 1983 to investigate the role of chambers in local affairs. This report, undertaken by Murray Stewart,[98] provides a valuable insight since it included a survey of chamber views at the time these changes were beginning. This survey captures the chambers at the point of frame change: wrestling to determine how, and how far, they should become involved.

Stewart's report concluded that, indeed, chambers were a natural partner in the sense of being a locally based employers' movement. But it also concluded that many chambers were 'puzzled by the role thrust upon [them] over the last couple of years. ... [and were] going along with the Heseltine initiative because they have been asked rather than because they believe it to be necessarily the best course of

---

[95] Grant (1983).
[96] Stewart (1984).
[97] ABCC (1989), *We Mean Business*, emphasis added.
[98] Then professor of politics at Bristol University: Stewart (1984); see also Grant (1983). Both studies fail to distinguish chambers of commerce and chambers of trade.

action'. Many chambers wanted 'to be distinct from a system which in many respects they believe to be inefficient, bureaucratic and restrictive to local business'.[99] There was thus uncertainty about how the new relationship would operate, how it would influence chamber status and finance, and how it would influence their members who might feel they were paying for servicing government.

Most significantly, however, Stewart's 1984 report summed up the perception by government that was to bedevil development through the next period of initiatives: that chambers were best able to contribute detail and expertise to technical aspects of programme implementation, rather than the strategic vision needed to rebuild communities and regenerate whole economies. This was an understandable view, since central government had largely excluded chambers from the corporatist state, and chambers themselves generally saw involvement with specific projects or initiatives as more productive than debates about policy. There was also concern that effective chambers existed only in some areas. This was a major factor that caused government to look wider for partners.[100] As Heseltine himself noted, 'chambers are not all equally strong . . . too many have seen their role as representing the lowest common denominator . . . [and] failed to claim a clear and respected public posture'.[101] Stewart concluded, 'that any change would require action from central government to increase the formal position and/or resources' of chambers, through greater recognition, stronger access to policy debates, and formal incorporation of views into the relevant government decisions.[102]

These dilemmas were to remain, but it was already clear that the chambers were more comfortable with co-option (to work with government programmes), or contracts to deliver schemes, than recruitment (to undertake and legitimize government-designed programmes). In some chambers this rapidly changed, with an ABCC report in 1995 concluding that 'it is not appropriate for initiatives to be parachuted into individual cities from the outside . . . [it] requires long-term local leadership [from chambers]'.[103] However, Heseltine does not appear to have moved from a view he held in 1980, when he took over urban initiatives in Liverpool and wanted private sector involvement: 'I cannot pretend that I regarded chambers of commerce as the ideal vehicle, but they were the only vehicle available'.[104] This underpinned his support for BiTC, which should have been a warning to the chambers.

---

[99] Stewart (1984), p. 20.
[100] See Bennett and McCoshan (1993); Bennett, Wicks, and McCoshan (1994).
[101] Heseltine speech at London Guildhall (1980), *Cooperation between Business and Local Government*.
[102] Stewart (1984), pp. 44–51; see also Grant (1983).
[103] This echoed earlier reports: ABCC (1988) *A Tale of Four Cities*; BCC (1995) *Partnerships in Progress*; BCC (2007), *A Tale of the Cities: The Best of Times?*
[104] Heseltine (2000), p. 209.

Enterprise agencies and BiTC

Contemporaneous with the urban regeneration initiatives, Heseltine was also a strong advocate of enterprise agencies. These had begun independently of government from 1975, supported by leading local businesses (e.g. in St Helens by Pilkington Glass; Runcorn by ICI Mond; Bristol by Wills Tobacco; and Glasgow by British Steel), and by some local authorities (e.g. Hackney).[105] The London Enterprise Agency (LEntA) became the largest and was established in 1978 by a section of the London chamber under article 38 of its charter, with the purpose 'to promote growth of the small business sector and to contribute to inner city regeneration'. Its income grew to £295,000 by 1983, which was deployed to support small firms, but also to facilitate local education and regeneration schemes.[106] It was quickly copied by chambers in Birmingham and Leeds in 1979, by Norwich, Kirklees, Manchester, Bristol, and Leicester in 1980, and North Staffordshire and Luton in 1981. By 1982 there were 23 chamber-based enterprise agencies.[107]

Having made a visit to the London, Leeds, and Birmingham chamber-based agencies, Heseltine saw the scope to diffuse the idea more widely and provided a series of grant schemes from 1982, which were expanded to cover rural areas after 1987.[108] The grants required matching by private sector sponsors (although local government was included, in part, in later years). The schemes continued until 2007 through funding from unemployment training programmes. The effect of the grant schemes led to rapid diffusion across the country: from only 23 agencies in 1981 (all developed prior to Heseltine's initiatives) to 102 in 1983, 245 in 1985, and 421 by 1991. This included Scotland, where government support rather than private sponsorship was the key resource. They covered many small centres as well as urban regeneration areas, with the large cities often having several agencies. Private sponsorship chiefly consisted of seconded staff. Chamber sponsorship usually took the agency in-house under existing management, and used member companies and sponsorship to provide business counselling, finance, and other support.[109]

Many enterprise agencies were interrelated with chambers, chiefly in the major cities (in 1990 about 40 depended on chambers for management, finance, or leadership). But, as with the other government initiatives of this period, chambers were just one of many possible partners used. Indeed, Heseltine primarily worked with BiTC, which took over promotion and set up an association of agencies; this meant that many enterprise agencies tended to compete with chambers. The initiative increased confusion of actors on the ground and laid the foundation for subsequent need for rationalization.

---

[105] There were also foreign examples, particularly US Community Development Corporations.
[106] London chamber, *Annual Reports* (1979–83).
[107] Taylor (2007), p. 101.
[108] Local Enterprise Agency Grant Scheme (LEAGS) and Local Enterprise Agency Project Scheme (LEAPS), and Rural Project Grants (RPGs), each valued at about £5m per year: Bennett and McCoshan (1993), pp. 114–18.
[109] Bennett and McCoshan (1993), pp. 114–18.

Education initiatives and Local Employer Networks (LENs)

A further stream of initiatives developed after 1979 to better link education to the world of work. In many ways, conceptually these had modern origins in 1976, following a speech from the Labour Prime Minister, James Callaghan, at Ruskin College Oxford, which set off a 'Great Debate' on how education and business interests could be better integrated. However, vested education interests prevented any significant development under Labour, treating the curriculum and education process as a 'secret garden' impervious to the needs of the world of work. Callaghan framed the issue as the need to rebalance between equipping for 'a lively constructive place in society' and being fitted 'to do a job of work'.[110] The Labour policy on the ground relied on School-Industry Liaison Officers, the Careers Service, and, after 1978, a Schools Council Industry Project. This was all very localized and ad hoc; it developed useful experience, but had marginal impact.

The first significant initiatives to encourage system-wide change came from the Conservatives. First, there was the Technical and Vocational Education Initiative (TVEI), launched in 1983, which has been called arguably the most important curriculum initiative since the 1944 Education Act.[111] It was the brainchild of David Young, chair of the Manpower Services Commission (an arm of the Department of Employment). It was launched by MSC not the Department of Education, but it used LEAs, giving them considerable resources to develop new curricula and links with employers. The LEAs were generally enthusiastic, as were many teachers, but it was bitterly opposed by the education establishment, the committed far-left local authorities, and the Labour party, led by their education spokesman Neil Kinnock, who referred to vocational education as 'factory fodder'.[112] It was followed by a second, even larger initiative, school-business *Compacts,* begun in London in 1987 (and initially begun by the chamber via LEntA). Compacts covered 57 Urban Programme areas, but were subsequently subsumed within larger Education-Business Partnerships (EBPs), which covered all LEAs by 1989. A third initiative came from the DTI, after Young moved there. This scheme, of Enterprise and Education Advisers, was launched in 1988, seeking to improve student work experience, and teacher placements.

These three initiatives followed a recruitment model using chambers (and other bodies) as 'hosts' so that their membership, status, and networks could provide the critical ingredients needed for the programmes. Chambers were major partners for TVEI,[113] and played a dominant role in Compacts. Chambers were the sole

[110] James Callaghan, Ruskin College speech; in *Times Educational Supplement*, 22 October 1976, p. 72.
[111] See discussion in Bennett and McCoshan (1993), pp. 59–61, 138–46.
[112] See Young (1990), pp. 89–98; see Chapter 10 for far-left local government; Kinnock subsequently became Labour leader.
[113] David Young had originally sought to work with the CBI, but Terence Beckett (CBI director general) could give no assurances that CBI could deliver, so Young looked elsewhere: Young (1990), p. 92.

partner in 56% of the first Compacts, and the main partner in 11% more. With the wider coverage of EBPs, chambers remained in a lead position in those areas where they were strong (such as Birmingham, Manchester, and Sheffield).[114] Enterprise and Education Advisers were also disproportionately based in chambers: of 105 advisers established by 1989, one-third were hosted in chambers.[115] School-industry links have continued up to the present, with 76% of chambers involved in 2010, covering £13.6 million of funded activity.

In addition to attempts at reforming the schools, this period also saw a major onslaught on further education (FE) colleges to improve vocational skills for the 14–19 and older age groups, initially led by David Young when he became Secretary of State for Employment. The most critical change occurred when Young succeeded in transferring 16% of the LEA budget for work-related education from the Department of Education to the MSC. As a result of the *Training for Jobs* White Paper, 1984, LEAs now received this budget back only after completing a three-year rolling Non-Advanced Further Education (NAFE) Plan.[116] These plans required consultation with employers; 31% used solely chambers for this purpose, whilst many more used chambers together with others.[117] The plans also encouraged FE colleges to develop direct links with employers and employer bodies, independently of the LEAs.

A critical aspect of *NAFE Plans* was the development of a national network of employer liaison bodies for colleges and LEAs to work with: termed Local Employer Networks (LENs). These developed as an outcome of an ABCC/MSC Collaborative Project over 1985–6, set up as a further result of the 1984 *Training for Jobs* White Paper.[118] The project concluded that chambers should be the focal point, information centre, and major source of influence on employers to get them engaged with the needs of FE and schools. It also gained strong CBI support.

The LENs had ambitious objectives: to gather and interpret local labour market information; represent employers; and to consult and advise employers and Area Manpower Boards on employer needs through NAFE Plans.[119] This was a very ambitious agenda for an initiative that was only given £3.2 million to cover 132 LENs across Britain (about £20,000 per LEN, enough to do no more than employ one LEN manager; there was one LEN for each LEA). LENs were based on host organizations that were expected to provide additional resources; the chambers provided 60% of hosts.[120]

---

[114] Bennett and McCoshan (1993), pp. 152–67.
[115] Analysis of 1989 hosts from DTI database; Bennett and McCoshan (1993), pp. 146–8; DTI (1991), *The Enterprise and Education Adviser Service 1988–91: Achievements, Lessons and Good Practice.*
[116] This was later placed under TECs, q.v. below; Bennett, Wicks, and McCoshan (1994), pp. 193–5.
[117] Wicks (1990), p. 267; Bennett and McCoshan (1993), pp. 178– 9.
[118] MSC/ABCC (1986), *National Collaborative Project: Final Report*, Manpower Services Commission, Sheffield; the project was managed by Kirklees and Wakefield chamber, a leading training provider, and led at ABCC by Alan Bartlett, assistant director for education and training.
[119] *A Foundation for the Future* (1987), LEN UK Network Head Office, Sheffield.
[120] Bennett, McCoshan, and Sellgren (1990); Bennett and McCoshan (1993), pp. 180–5.

The education initiatives of the 1970s and 1980s sought chambers to act as training providers, and to become involved in planning and strategy for education and training. This produced a sea-change in chamber attitudes over the 1980s. Whilst chambers still differed in size and effectiveness, and there were divisions between them about the general policy to follow, most major chambers were now heavily involved with government. This led chambers deeper into being recruited for government purposes, with Young's use of chambers as 'hosts' being as important as Heseltine's vision for local consultations, and having a better strategic fit with chambers. The influence of the Department of Employment was to increase further in the next phase.

Training and Enterprise Councils (TECs)

The LENs and other initiatives by the MSC did not fully satisfy the government's desire to increase employer involvement in training and education. This was perceived to be a result of both the reluctance of education and training providers to adapt, and the reluctance of employers to get involved. Various influential reports called for a culture change on both sides.[121] A vigorous debate ensued on whether to continue to recruit 'hosts' for government schemes or launch government's own agencies.

Chambers offered an attractive, even a 'natural', partner to take on the role of host, and LENs and Compacts demonstrated their potential. But it was clear that chambers could offer sufficient support in only about 60% of areas. Other areas could have been developed, but the alternative chosen was close to the BiTC model of new leadership bodies: Training and Enterprise Councils (TECs) in England and Wales, and Local Enterprise Companies (LECs) in Scotland. David Young and others had pressed Mrs Thatcher hard for chambers to be the main hosts of TECs. She had been reluctant and was only won over by the support of major business figures, but her support was for a more limited scheme than originally envisaged. This was not a privatization, but delegation to an arm's length agency, with the civil service still in control. If she had wanted to go further, she was limited by her weakening leadership within the party after the Poll Tax debacle.[122] The outcome was a watered-down structure under the civil service that left the TECs struggling for independence and vulnerable to abolition, which a full privatization would have prevented.

TECs were announced in 1989[123] and established in phases over 1990–3, with a network of 104 replacing MSC Area offices covering Britain. They were generously financed with over £2.3 billion in 1993/4, an average of £18 million per TEC, and

[121] NEDO/MSC (1984), *Competence and Competition*; MSC (1985), *A Challenge to Complacency*; CBI (1989), *Towards a Skills Revolution*; NEDO (1991), *Training and Competitiveness*. See Bennett and McCoshan (1993), pp. 168–76.

[122] Young (1990); also comments to author from Sir Geoffrey Holland, 21 January 1998: formerly head of the MSC, permanent secretary at the Department of Employment at the time.

[123] Department of Employment (1989), *Training for Employment*. This was the last influence from David Young, though Fowler was minister; TECs also had support from Holland then permanent secretary at DE.

£32 million per Lowland LEC, initially staffed mainly by former civil servants from the former MSC Area Offices. Their boards had two-thirds of members drawn from chief executive or chair level of private companies, with chamber leaders not considered unless they met this criterion. They were to be 'the nation's top business leaders'; 'the cream of the local community'. But they were also to have a 'network of contacts' and 'act as ambassadors', recruiting 'people with the power to create change in their communities'.[124]

TECs presented a major challenge for chambers. They were set up explicitly to fill a gap that many chambers considered they already occupied: to offer business leadership and employer representation in the local community. They were recruited bodies, with a formal contract, and leadership picked by government with no specified local community links. This design prevented TECs from aligning too closely with chambers (or other bodies), and most new leaders of TECs acted very independently—they had been newly empowered to act as local leaders, although by government, not by the local business community. The CBI and BiTC were also heavily involved in TEC Board recruitment, and they sought a different type of leader from that of many chambers.

It was difficult for chambers to assimilate too closely with them: first, because board members were acting independently, not as delegates of organizations; and second, because TECs were set up explicitly to reduce local government involvement in economic development. This was an uncomfortable challenge for chambers since local government was a partner with whom they knew they had to maintain long-term working relationships. The TECs were in many ways 'too political', typical of the Thatcher period in which there was a determination to reset the government policy frames to move away from the education lobbies, LEAs, and local government. As a result chambers and TECs had mutually suspicious relationships in their early years.

The challenge for chambers became even greater when several TECs began to set up membership schemes. TECs had recognized from the outset that they had little legitimacy in their local communities, being appointed by a central government process. As a result, by 1993 the majority had either set up a membership scheme or were considering doing so, with only 32% joint with a chamber. The main objective was recruiting the major firms as members. Low subscription levels (average £32, maximum £200), and large membership targets added further concern that TECs were directly competing with chambers, using government largesse as a subsidy.[125] A BCC survey highlighted TECs undercutting the fees of chamber services,[126] and BCC pressed the DTI hard for TEC membership schemes to be suppressed.[127]

[124] Quotes from David Main, Cay Stratton, and Norman Fowler, Secretary of State for Employment, in BiTC (1989), *Leadership in the Community* (London: Business in the Community). See also Bennett, Wicks, and McCoshan (1994).
[125] Survey of TECs and LECs in 1993: multiple responses; Bennett, Wicks, and McCoshan (1994), pp. 67–73.
[126] BCC (April 1992), *Survey of TEC/Chamber Relationships*.
[127] Ron Taylor (BCC) letter to Jim Reid, Small Firms Division, DTI, 17 November 1992.

The TECs were also given responsibility for economic development and business support programmes, which also cut across the chamber's leadership. The TEC *Operating Manual* made business support the second main objective of TECs: to 'expand opportunities for local people to start their own business and to progress through training to new careers and greater prosperity'. For local economic development the TEC mandate was to serve as a 'forum for local leaders . . . to contribute to the regeneration of the communities they serve'.[128]

After a slow start, and despite the dangers, many chambers became heavily involved with TECs and LECs. With a few exceptions, local relations were eventually generally cordial. Chambers remained one of the larger providers for government training schemes, and offered benefits of access to important employer networks of members. Chambers were also important partners in many TEC/LEC projects, but the main TEC partners were local government, central government departments, and agencies. Hence, whilst TECs/LECs proved to be key partners for chambers, chambers were only part of a broad portfolio of partners for TECs, which increasingly became dominated by government funding streams.[129]

The CCTEs: TEC–chamber mergers

The TEC initiative resulted in two local business bodies, one publicly funded (TECs/LECs) and one privately funded (chambers); and there were also the enterprise agencies. It was difficult for a Conservative government to live with the criticism that it was setting up government rivals to the private sector. Yet it was reluctant to rein TECs in.[130] Strong lobbying from BCC eventually resulted in a compromise in 1995. This produced a protocol that sought to limit TEC membership schemes and other competition with existing business organizations. But most important, it also allowed mergers to develop between chambers and TECs to create Chambers of Commerce, Training and Enterprise (CCTEs).[131]

The chambers had initially developed a strategy that sought to take over the TECs, by converting them into chamber-like bodies, owned by members and independent.[132] However, takeover was impossible, and convergence leading to merger became the key objective of Ron Taylor at BCC, in which he worked very closely with Chris Humphries, who became head of the TEC National Council (an association to coordinate TECs). A process of convergence had been taking place in some places from the outset, and gathered pace after 1994. For example in 1990 Wigan began a process, completed in 1993, where the local authority, the TEC, chamber, education business partnership, and the main FE college had formed one of the most ambitious local partnerships for integrated local economic development.

---

[128] DE (1988), p. 1 and para 6.22; TEC, *Operating Manual* (1989), para. 1.2.

[129] Bennett, Wicks, and McCoshan (1994), pp. 249–56; 2001 situation in Ramsden and Bennett (2007), Bennett, Fuller, and Ramsden (2004).

[130] See the extended assessment of TECs and LECs in Bennett, Wicks, and McCoshan (1994).

[131] These were permitted by the government only in England, not Scotland or Wales.

[132] BCC review team, *National Strategy*, Annex 1, September 1993.

A similar model was developed in St Helens. These were *de facto* mergers. *De jure* merger of TECs and chambers was explored in five early cases in 1994: Milton Keynes, Northamptonshire, and Oldham, as well as Wigan and St Helens. A joint briefing on 'convergence' was provided in March 1994, with a checklist of aims, constitution, boundaries, functions, and transition.[133] This had the support of some key government ministers (notably Michael Heseltine after he returned to government in 1990).[134] It also had (qualified) support from senior civil servants (particularly Geoffrey Holland, permanent secretary at the DE, but was resisted by most others). The protocol in 1995 finally allowed mergers, to form CCTEs, if they satisfied criteria specified by the two government departments (DTI, and Department for Education and Employment), as well as BCC and the TEC National Council. Each merger required individual ministerial approval: CCTEs were definitely targeted contracting and compliance models. The BCC's criteria included an elected board, use of the chamber name, a membership operated on business disciplines, independence of member views, meeting BCC accreditation standards, and requiring a majority vote of members supporting merger.[135]

The aftermath of the 1995 protocol was 16 CCTEs created between 1995 and 1997, with others to follow. But after Labour's 1997 election there was an uncertain period. By May 1998 Ron Taylor was still optimistic, but control of TECs was passed to the Department of Education under David Blunkett, and in late 1998 he introduced a moratorium on further mergers until TECs were reconsidered. The final 16 CCTEs and expected mergers were:

1995	Northamptonshire		1997	Greater Peterborough
	Milton Keynes			Coventry and Warwickshire
	Oldham			
1996	Sussex		1998	Bedfordshire
	South Derbyshire			Bolton and Bury
	St Helens			Rochdale
	Shropshire			
	Wolverhampton			*Likely early mergers after 1998*:
	Wigan			Lincolnshire
	Hereford and Worcester			Norfolk and Waveney
	Rotherham			Isle of Wight
				Kent
				Gloucestershire

Seizing the initiative in 1995, the BCC had built CCTEs into a new vision, as its 1995 *Future Chamber* strategy. This sought explicitly to encourage mergers of chambers with TECs and so turn the TEC system into a chamber system. Even

---

[133] *Convergence of Chambers and TECs,* joint briefing from ABCC and TEC National Council (March 1994).

[134] BCC briefing notes for 'Meeting with Michael Heseltine, Deputy prime minister', 17 September 1996, a joint delegation of BCC and TEC National Council; this records that it was Heseltine who had pressed for mergers.

[135] BCC *Annual Report* (1997–8), pp. 6–7.

after Labour's 1997 election, early indications suggested some scope to expect that mergers might offer an attractive option, perhaps as part of an exit strategy of the government from TECs. This approach led to BCC's *21ˢᵗ Century Chamber* strategy, used over 1997–2001 to appeal to Labour. Despite the uncertainty, this facilitated mergers to include Business Link (q.v. below). A new local body of chamber-plus-TEC-plus-Business Link became the desired model for the future chamber. This brought the recruitment story to its ultimate climax: the chambers were trying to take over government bodies, but the extent of strings, targets, and controls attached dwarfed most chambers, and the wholesale recruitment of new chief executives to the new bodies rather than existing chamber staff, ensured that it was the chambers that were taken over by government objectives rather than vice versa. Whether CCTEs were 'chamber-like' bodies, or government agencies, swung like a pendulum (with each swing dependent on the latest ministerial change or new initiative).

The *Future Chamber* and *21ˢᵗ Century Chamber* strategies were very divisive. They were carried within BCC because they were supported by the largest and most powerful chambers, and the money on offer was an order of magnitude greater than independent chambers had ever been able to access. But CCTEs were correctly perceived as takeovers. Although two reviews of the structure by BCC in 1997 concluded in favour of CCTEs and assessed that voice had been strengthened, not weakened, by mergers,[136] the central BCC staff were instructed to 'adopt a stringently neutral position to new merger proposals'; Ron Taylor was reined in.[137] David Frost (Walsall), Peter Coles Johnston (Leeds), and others led a campaign against TEC–chamber mergers; Bristol was totally opposed. Meetings of chambers were held in Birmingham at the NEC, with Ron Taylor invited as a courtesy. Many chambers correctly assessed that CCTEs 'could be brought to an end by the click of the government's fingers', and also objected to government approval of board members.[138] This, and the continued uncertainty about Labour's support, ensured that no further mergers occurred. Labour's moratorium was imposed in 1998 just after Chris Humphries had been appointed to succeed Ron Taylor as director general of BCC; as discussed in Chapter 8, the moratorium immediately undermined the logic of that specific appointment.

CCTEs certainly offered some potential benefits: providing huge new resources; reducing confusion about who provided what business support services, with a single point of access; eliminating some wasteful competition; reducing excessive calls on the time of business people to lead and participate in similar yet separate local organizations; speaking with a single voice. Most CCTE chambers became stronger than when they went in: notably Hereford and Worcester, Northamptonshire, Lincolnshire, and Wigan, which had all been previously very small. Wolverhampton,

---

[136] Both conducted jointly with TEC National Council, the national body for TECs, and Department of Employment: Taylor (2007), pp. 145–7.

[137] Taylor (2007), p. 147.

[138] Comments to author, David Frost, June 2010; and Ian Kelly (Hull & Humberside chamber) September 2010.

which had worked from a converted (through grand) house now had a large office complex, with a high-profile chief executive and a president who was managing director of one of the largest local companies who developed an entirely new vision for the area.[139]

But there were also significant disadvantages: government contracts for TECs (and hence CCTEs) remained mis-designed and pervaded with principal-agent problems producing perverse outcomes; hence, merger had the danger of discrediting and perverting the chamber. Merger did expand membership, but there was doubt about its quality, depth, and commitment; membership in CCTEs increased greatly, but the lapse rate soon rocketed: see Chapter 16. There was also evidence that the scale of government involvement discouraged volunteers, as CCTEs became perceived to be an arm of government. Since they were dominated by government funding and guidance, CCTEs could not be fully independent, and indeed were compelled by their government contract to separate representation and lobbying from government contracted services, which undermined all synergies between the 'membership association' and programmes that the merger was supposed to offer. It was thus a very confused brand.

As an overall assessment, especially with the benefit of hindsight, CCTEs were a major distraction from the core challenge that chambers faced, and had always faced, of how to develop strengthened self-sustaining financial and obligational links with their members. CCTEs also split the chambers into two groups, of 'us and them'. The 'purist' group was as vocal as the CCTEs: 'we must not be sullied by government money'. The BCC had recognized the dangers of lack of cross-party support: a powerful group of Labour MPs and the TUC were viscerally opposed to CCTEs, and they lacked fit with Labour's regional and other ambitions.[140] But BCC nevertheless embarked on a very exposed strategy. It probably had no alternative; once TECs were invented chambers had to respond. But another potential avenue opened, which confused the issues still further: small firm support and Business Link.

13.9 LOCAL BUSINESS SUPPORT: BUREAUX AND BUSINESS LINK

Another stream of overlapping government policy sought to support businesses directly, to improve performance and hence the nation's competitiveness. Before the 1970s government had encouraged amalgamations to create large corporations, rescue packages, or direct nationalization (with the last major nationalization being the steel industry in 1967 under the Labour government of Harold Wilson). Relations between government and business were dominated by these massive industries, and on-off price/wage controls in other sectors. General government

---

[139] Views stated by David Frost to the author, 19 January 2010.
[140] Comment to author by Alan Bartlett, ABCC deputy director, 16 August 1994.

support to businesses, other than nationalized or aided industries, and through regional grants to 'depressed areas', was minimal.

Bolton Report, Bureaux, and the Small Firms Service

A major change occurred with the Bolton Report of 1971, which directed attention for the first time to the smaller firm: this was frame changing for policy at a time when the economy itself was also changing radically towards small firm growth. Keynes had succeeded in having small firms ignored, because of their 'animal behaviour' and the inability of government to control them (see Chapter 10).

Bolton put small firms in the context of the general need to improve economic growth and competitiveness, and argued that the economy as a whole suffered because small firms experienced barriers to market entry, finance, and acquisition of information that government could help to overcome. In general, Bolton followed a 'market failure' argument that justified government action in a limited way to fill gaps, but also emphasized the importance of recognizing that small firms must be given much greater policy attention. This was sympathetically received by the Conservative's DTI small firms minister of the time, Nicholas Ridley. The chief outcomes were: efforts to enhance competition to improve market entry by smaller firms; establishment of a Small Firms Division in DTI; pressure on banks to provide better support to small firms; and government initiatives in two areas: (i) a Small Firm Loan Guarantee Scheme (SFLGS) that sought to work with banks to reduce the risk levels of lending and hence improve financing,[141] and (ii) a Small Firms Service (SFS) that offered information to business enquirers.

The major impact on chambers was the SFS. Bolton initially suggested Small Firm Bureaux, established under the DTI Small Firms Division to 'provide information and assessment on technological, financial and management problems by providing introductions to the appropriate sources... of advice'. They were to be locally based and staffed by voluntary local personal advisers. The aim was a 'new localised information and signposting service'.[142] The chambers objected strongly that this was 'duplicating' their efforts and competing unfairly with them. They sent many protests, and a delegation went to the DTI to see ministers on 16 December 1971. There are some uncanny resemblances to early DOT branches proposed in 1917 (see above), and later Business Links, although the Bureaux were limited to first response, and the redirection of enquiries; i.e. chiefly a referral service. But here was the first sign that government under the Conservatives might set itself up in competition with chambers.

In trying to head off the Bureaux, the chambers claimed that their surveys showed they were already active suppliers of information and support to small firms, and that no government intervention was needed. The ABCC research produced some of the first useful information on chamber membership by firm size. This showed that small firms under 50 employees composed 76% of the

[141] Which still existed in 2011, and was strengthened during the 2007–9 financial crisis.
[142] Summary of specification in DTI note P73204, November 1971; in ABCC papers MS 17548/2.

chamber membership; 86.7% of members had used chambers to answer enquiries, 75.2% thought the service adequate; only 10.8% thought it lacked some adequacy, and 3.4% thought it inadequate. This was better than other organizations, where those lacking adequacy were 26.5% for trade associations; 24% for local productivity associations; 20% for CBI; and 26% for the British National Economic Committee. The most likely organization to which members would turn if they needed help was: accountants (75% of cases), solicitors (30%), banks (29%), and then chambers of commerce (27%) and trade associations (26%).[143] This was a self-selective sample of chamber members, but the *rank order* is little different from more modern surveys of uses of business support by the whole small firm population.[144] It certainly showed that chambers were already filling an important part of any gap in the market. On the question of whether a new organization could help with signposting, 80% said that it was not difficult to know where to turn to for advice; but 39.5% thought that a new specialist agency for small firms was necessary, and 70% desirable. However, asked whether government should create its own Bureaux, only 15% agreed.[145]

The surveys supported the chamber case that the government scheme would duplicate and compete with chambers and other existing providers; they confirmed that a gap existed which small firms wanted filled; but it did not give strong support for a government entity. To overcome this conundrum, the chambers argued that any scheme should be based in chambers. But the government was determined to do something itself, and the SFS was created as relabelled Bureaux. This was a cut-down format, based on a telephone help-line with referral and signposting staffed by civil servants, but no personal advisers. However, a separate scheme was developed for business advice through a Business Development Service. The SFS became a successful scheme, dealing with 250,000 enquiries per year, rising to 700,000 by 1990, and achieved 95% satisfaction levels. The Business Development Service was also more modestly successful, with 20,000 requests per year for its more intensive low-cost counselling service provided by secondees from larger businesses.[146]

This episode resolved the small firm issue for a while, but it was to return with the Conservatives in the 1980s. Despite their efforts in 1971, the chambers had remained relatively slow to respond to the new emphasis on small firms. The ABCC 1971 surveys showed that their explicit support for small firms was very patchy: only the large chambers had a significant enquiry answering service (44% of chambers; defined by answering 1000 or more enquiries per year), 30% had a small firms club, and none had a small firms committee or section. By 1982 there were still only two chambers with small firm sections/committees, increasing to

---

[143] Survey by Aston University, Small Business Centre, for ABCC (N=1842; quoted percentages exclude non-respondents): MS 17548/1.
[144] See summaries in Bennett (2006, 2008).
[145] Aston survey, op. cit.; separate questions, non-cumulative responses.
[146] See Bolton (1971); and overview in Bennett (2006, 2008).

four by 1992,[147] and most small chambers had not developed their enquiry services much further.

After the Conservatives returned in 1979 the SFS was continued, and additional schemes were added. A scheme to help the unemployed start businesses was launched by the MSC in 1981 (Enterprise Allowance Scheme), to allow the self-employed to receive welfare allowances.[148] The Enterprise Allowance Scheme used intermediaries as advisers or supporters, of which the chambers and enterprise agencies were most significant. Another was an EU-wide scheme of Euro Info Centres, which provided contracts to business enquiry centres. Some of these were based at major libraries, but chambers won contracts for most of these Centres, 65% of the British total of 20 (and almost all in Ireland). The chambers offered the widest of the services available in the Centres, because they could link with their other activities. In 1991, 64% of UK chambers used the contract to provide a library service; 34% a databank or online data access; 41% offered a call-back service on technical queries; 61% offered export counselling, 50% export consultancy; and 72% linked enquirers to further DTI support acting as a sort of clearing house.[149] It was an important initiative that stimulated chamber expertise, and many medium-sized chambers developed a European information centre even though they had not won a contract.

A critical change occurred in January 1988 when the Enterprise Initiative was launched, and the DTI itself was rebranded as *DTI: the Department of Enterprise.* This was the brainchild of David Young, who had moved as minister to DTI. It was the first attempt to combine DTI's disparate programmes. It added to the SFS helpline a subsidy scheme for small firms to use consultants to frame business plans, or improve design, financial, and information systems, manufacturing, marketing, and quality. This was the first large-scale national scheme of advice, at government expense. Support varied by region but was available everywhere. It remains one of the best-advertised and most successful business schemes that British governments have ever launched. It did not challenge chambers, but it raised the government's game. However, when TECs/LECs came on the scene, the SFS and Enterprise Initiative were rolled into them, and relabelled, with both schemes being moved from the DTI to the Department of Employment. This was a foolish error, destroying brand value at a stroke. Into this walked a new set of ministers at the DTI.

A government vision for chambers?

A significant opportunity opened for chambers under the Secretary of State at the DTI 1989–90, Nicholas Ridley, who had set up Bolton. As outlined in Chapter 8, the ABCC and a 'Group of Eight' were invited by Ridley to consider the future of

---

[147] ABCC papers on Bolton Report, MS 17548; also see Chapter 2, and Table 6.2 above.
[148] Young (1990), pp. 92–3.
[149] Bennett and Krebs (1993b), p. 10 and table 26.

government support to business.[150] This period was a critical one in the Thatcher government, following the debacle over the Poll Tax, and Ridley and Young appear to have looked on chambers as a new means of gaining local legitimacy through a chamber development strategy that would have provided significant support to all areas (i.e. establishing new chambers in areas where chambers were weak or absent, and strengthening others). This never had a chance to develop, as Ridley was forced to resign over unrelated matters in July 1990, David Young was moved, and Mrs Thatcher was forced out of office as Prime Minister in November 1990 in favour of John Major.

Instead of the Ridley/Young vision, the DTI came under Michael Heseltine when John Major moved him from the Department of Environment to DTI in 1992: this included responsibility for the unsteady relationship between chambers and TECs. As discussed above, chambers had already been used in Heseltine's initiatives for urban regeneration, and his support was re-expressed in a 1989 book written when he was 'in the wilderness' on the backbenches after he resigned from Mrs Thatcher's government in 1986. He argued that business representation in Britain was weak compared to the main competitors in Europe; it could be improved by merging CBI and ABCC (as suggested by Devlin), with a unified national voice and chambers providing local service delivery; this in turn would allow government 'to privatise or delegate training programmes completely'; with TECs 'built around the local chambers' and financial support through 'a hypothe-cated charge . . . collected by the local chamber of commerce'. 'Government, in its growing and necessary quest for support from the private sector in so many fields, would have an effective local body to back it and to help find and train the people whose help it needs . . . [to] back-up the essential part-time and voluntary contri-bution of public-spirited but increasingly hard-pressed managers.'[151]

This helped provide a vision for TEC–chamber mergers, and was the strongest support the chambers had ever received from a government minister. As with other forms of government support, however, it can be a poisoned chalice. As commen-ted by Mark Boleat with respect to Heseltine's related initiatives with trade associations in 1993–4, his 'analysis of what was wrong was absolutely right, but his prescription for putting it right was absolutely wrong'.[152]

The competitiveness agenda and Business Links

Heseltine set about implementing his vision, aiming to stay long enough at DTI to make the changes enduring. In the event he had three years in post, 1992–5, longer than any previous incumbent since 1979, then becoming deputy prime minister 1995–7 with influence over the structures he created. Arriving at the DTI he set

---

[150] Taylor (2007), p. 116.
[151] Heseltine (1989), pp. 106–9. The is reaffirmed in a 2005 interview with Heseltine: see Greaves (2008), pp. 1005–6; he believed 'officials had a better understanding of associations than the associations themselves'.
[152] Boleat comments 2004; quoted in Greaves (2008), p. 1010.

about building a strategy around what became a 'competitiveness agenda' along three dimensions: (i) reforming internal organization into sponsoring divisions for each major industrial sector; this led to structures of support to sector initiatives and the development of a 'model trade association' document that sought to lever change among associations;[153] (ii) improving export support, to separate officials involved in treaty negotiation from those promoting exports; and (iii) to improve support to SMEs. The chambers were affected indirectly by the first two of these elements, but the third brought them into a key role with DTI.

Heseltine's vision for SME support was a local delivery structure, purportedly with chambers at its centre. He acknowledged that 'once the TECs were in existence... we had two local organizations competing for the attention of local companies, as there was no coordination with chambers, [and] to make matters worse, some of the TECs were about to move into the business of recruiting individual members, thus intensifying the rivalry with the chambers'. There were also enterprise agencies, local authorities, and other bodies also involved in support to SMEs and local economies producing an 'overlapping and confusing pattern'.[154] Part of Heseltine's review of the DTI included setting up a Steering Group that included chambers, TECs, CBI, local authorities, and Business in the Community. The Group criticized confusion between providers, lack of strong involvement of the private sector, a lack of customer focus, and a low level of awareness of the services that were available.[155] This recognized the 'patchwork quilt' of local initiatives, already highlighted by the Audit Commission and others,[156] and paved the way for an integrating initiative.

The result was to set up 'One Stop Shops', almost immediately relabelled Business Link, launched in 1992.[157] They combined TEC business support with the consultancy support of the Enterprise Initiative, to 'glue' together local partners into a unified local organization.[158] A bidding process was opened in which chambers and other agents would put forward a plan for a partnership in each area. Originally the chambers believed that Heseltine wanted Business Link contracted solely to chambers, to offer a succession strategy that would allow TECs to be rolled into chambers based on 'co-location of premises': his 1989 book, and a 1992 speech to a TEC conference suggested this strongly.[159] This was critical in leading to the chamber's *Future Chamber* and *21ˢᵗ Century Chamber* strategies. But the chambers were wrong. As noted above, Heseltine never showed genuine willingness to provide them with preferred status, and had recognized in his

---

[153] See Bennett (1997); Boleat (2000, 2003); Greaves (2008).
[154] Heseltine (2000), p. 419; see also Audit Commission (1989, 1999).
[155] See Heseltine (2000), pp. 429–30; also senior DTI official Alan Titchener (1996), quoted in Priest (1999).
[156] Audit Commission (1989, 1999); also Bennett and McCoshan (1993); Bennett and Payne (2000).
[157] DTI (1992), *Business Link Prospectus, Department of Trade and Industry*, London; see also comments by Taylor (2007); Heseltine (2000), pp. 429–30; Bennett and Payne (2000).
[158] Heseltine (2000), p. 429.
[159] Heseltine, speech at TEC conference, 10 July 1992; circulated to chambers by BCC, 15 July 1992.

regeneration initiatives in the 1980s that they were only used because there was no other vehicle. He regarded chambers as patchy, with gaps in some areas where there was no local chamber, or only 'more backward chambers'.[160] He could have deployed funds for chamber development to fill local gaps, as Ridley and Young had been considering. From 1991, the chambers had a *Development Strategy* that offered this.

Heseltine's approach is all the more confusing since, contemporaneous with the launch of Business Link, he launched an initiative for trade association improvement in 1993–4, based on a 'model association', for which DTI gave development funds. For this there was no desire for competitive alternatives: the associations were encouraged to improve themselves with government support, which was subsequently managed through a Trade Association Forum, hosted within CBI.[161] This model could have been used for chambers under BCC, was indicated in Heseltine's 1989 book, but was not followed for reasons that remain opaque. Probably he was in too much rush; was devoted to smaller local initiatives that he also wanted to support (the enterprise agencies);[162] was influenced by the banks that saw detailed adviser advice as helpful to them;[163] and he certainly met resistance from civil servants and other ministers who would lose control.

Chamber involvement in Business Link: and the case of Leeds

The local Business Links were based on partnerships that varied greatly. By 1997, when the first phase of the system was fully established, there were 89, with over 260 satellites based on a 'hub and spoke' principle of cooperating local agencies. Chambers were involved in all of the hubs, but the lead partners in 42 cases were independent companies; 36 were subsidiaries or operating divisions of TECs; and only 11 were direct subsidiaries of chambers (all of which were CCTEs),[164] although some TEC links included chambers as managing partners. Hence, rather than supporting chambers, Business Link became another initiative that introduced new competition. As put by Robin Geldard, president of BCC in 1995: 'The road to heaven is paved with good intentions... If anything we have too many solutions... Chambers embarked on a *Development Strategy*... Government set up TECs... Now we have Business Links. And we have a major role for local authorities and enterprise agencies.... These responses are laudable but they are also expensive and confusing.... We all speak of networking, is it not in many cases duplication of effort'.[165]

[160] Heseltine (2000), pp. 430.
[161] Heseltine (1993), *Speech on Trade Associations*, CBI, 17 June, DTI text; DTI (1996), *A Best Practice Guide for the Model Trade Association*; see also Boleat (2000).
[162] Letter from David Grayson, BiTC, 'Heseltine proposals for first stop shops', *Financial Times*, 12 August 1992, makes clear his view that Heseltine was committed to continuing support for enterprise agencies as separate, though linked bodies. Grayson subsequently became Heseltine's trusted chair of the ISG.
[163] Banks quoted in Bennett and Payne (2000), p. 187.
[164] TEC National Council Survey (1997); ISG notes 272.
[165] Robin Geldard, text of speech at Milton Keynes, Annual KPMG Lecture, 19 September 1995.

Some chambers naturally saw it as essential to become the Business Link operator; but others saw it as a distortion to their mainstream activities. In the case of Stockport and some other areas the Business Link attempted to take over a small chamber, leaving the chamber as only a board and membership. This was rejected by BCC and the chamber was threatened with suspension, with its area offered to adjacent chambers.[166]

The most celebrated case was Leeds, which was the last Business Link to be established, where the chamber refused to become involved. Its president, David Richardson, wrote in 1993 that the chamber was concerned about the sustainability of Business Link finances and competition with chamber services confusing and eroding membership. He wrote again in 1994 objecting to the confusion of a city-based Business Link area when Leeds was then merging with Bradford, York, and North Yorkshire chambers, following the ABCC *Development Strategy*, which had been given DTI support. The DTI 'was talking with two voices'. Richardson reiterated doubts about 'unrealistic business plans, lack of market need and questionable financial viability'. He also noted the unhelpful 'bombastic' approach of the TEC, the 'overly prescriptive approach of the DTI,' and that 'Business Link will "crowd out" and undercut high quality commercially priced services that the private sector already provides'. The chamber specifically rejected co-location, presciently anticipating the brand confusion, and financial risk, this brought.[167] At Leeds' annual dinner in January 1994, with Prime Minister John Major as guest, Richardson raised the stakes higher, by stating that the chamber was 'in the middle of a confused struggle between government departments to provide an ill thought out scheme. . . . it illustrates the wider issue. Commerce and industry is being burdened with new schemes and initiatives which are dreamed up by civil servants and politicians when they take on a new post and which often get forgotten once they move on.'[168]

However, Heseltine was not to be so easily put down, and became personally involved, pulling all the levers he could. Ian Kelly captures the detail.[169] Heseltine's exasperation, after many personal efforts, is encapsulated in a November 1994 letter: that he wanted Leeds chamber, and other partners 'to demonstrate that you are willing to embrace changes in the way in which business support services are delivered in Leeds.' In a handwritten addition to this formal letter he noted that 'I attach particular importance to achieving a successful launch of a B.L. in Leeds. . . . It would look awfully silly to have a national chain of 250 B.L.s . . . with a hole in the middle called Leeds'.[170] Leeds finally assented, but at arms length from the

[166] BCC, National Council minutes, 10 December 1996.

[167] David Richardson to C. W. Leach (chair Leeds TEC), and Brian Walker (leader Leeds City Council), 13 January 1993; David Richardson to Sir Giles Shaw (Leeds MP) 12 July 1994.

[168] David Richardson, text of speech at Leeds chamber annual dinner.

[169] Kelly (1995); Ian Kelly, then Head of policy at Leeds chamber, became chief executive at Hull and Humberside chamber. Heseltine referred to chambers as 'vultures', *The Times* 4 June 1991.

[170] Heseltine to Edward Holroyd, president of Leeds chamber, 14 November 1994; the jibe 'a hole called Leeds' must have been intended in what became very personalized exchanges; it was certainly read that way by the chamber: see commentary by Kelly (1995).

chamber. Heseltine's letter demonstrates not only his inadaptability to the needs of the chambers, but also his rigid and contradictory vision of a large number of small centres, completely at odds with his mission of a single system of TECs and chambers.

The advantages and disadvantages for chambers

Business Links offered a range of services: those decentralized from DTI; the combined services of local partners; and the former SFS information and advice that TECs had offered. Heseltine also envisaged a new 'core service', acting rather like a local doctor. These were Personal Business Advisers, appointed as account managers, to which small firms were expected to turn for help at each stage of their development. This was an in-house extension of the Bolton scheme for advisers. The budget per Business Link was about £200,000, which was increased to about £600,000 if all TEC small firm resources were also used; it rose to over £1m on average in later years. But more important than the Business Link contract itself were other government schemes that were showered on them, from DTI, ERDF, and other schemes, with funding of up to £10 million in some local cases.

For those chambers that held Business Link contracts, like CCTEs, there were profound effects on local chamber management (which was very burdensome) and membership. Surveys by BCC showed that the management costs averaged £85,000. Savings from shared systems might be considerable, but no one identified net revenue increases. There was brand confusion and ambiguous effects on membership, with the most marked membership increases resulting from chamber campaigns.[171] Often the operation had to be 'dual-headed', to keep the two sets of interests balanced and to secure a possible exit. The initiative did bring the TECs and chambers closer together, because now TECs could not develop independent SME support and had to work through partners within Business Link. This was the key design feature sought by Heseltine.[172]

For the ABCC/BCC there were mixed outcomes. Many small chambers that ABCC had been trying to suppress were strengthened by Heseltine's vision. He wanted about 200 local 'shop fronts' as the access points,[173] 'as close a point of contact as possible—hence the largest possible number of outlets'.[174] Because of this, small chambers of trade could participate as one of the many satellites along with enterprise agencies and other bodies, and some now received significant sums of money. This continued the brand confusion in some areas. In other cases chambers were able to grow rapidly where they were previously weak (e.g. Hereford and Worcester, Luton and Bedfordshire, Northamptonshire, Sussex). This allowed them to attain critical mass and service performance standards of the accredited chamber network that they would otherwise have never achieved. 'Dual headed'

---

[171] *The Impact of Business Link on Chambers of Commerce* (1996), IFF Research for BCC; also Priest (1998, 1999).
[172] Heseltine, in *Hansard*, 3 December 1992, col. 414; see also Heseltine (1992a), p. 9; (1992b); (2000), p. 429.
[173] His vision was for offices in all the largest towns; Heseltine (2000), p. 429.
[174] Letter from Heseltine to author, 30 September 1999.

structures developed through de facto merger, as in Coventry and Warwickshire, or wider inter-linkages as in St Helens. This introduced some new chambers into the big league. Overall, Taylor felt that the public money 'had been beneficial in raising standards in chambers': even 'personal business advisors had been beneficial in bringing new people in, although they were not sustainable'.[175] Even after all the subsequent problems the view in many chambers was that this period gave the most fundamental leap forward for the chamber network.

Most symbolically important was that the BCC became a key national partner with DTI, closely involved in the launch of Business Link. BCC became a member of the Implementation Group to encourage local cooperation, the Assessment Panel that scrutinized bids, and the Implementation Strategy Group (ISG). This marked the formal entry of the BCC to a new 'insider' status. Through this involvement BCC contributed to drafting the *Operating Manual* and *Service Guide*, and through the ISG (which met with Heseltine) it had direct input to ongoing development of the initiative.[176] Taylor saw this as 'a critical step in drawing chambers and TECs together, with DTI as the common enemy, as the voice of the local partners/deliverers'.[177] The BCC was particularly crucial at an ISG meeting on 24 May 1995, persuading Heseltine to reshape the initiative to reduce government prescription on branding and self-financing targets.

However, there were many tensions. The ISG was never really influential: Heseltine remained intractable on the main issues, and the chair of the ISG (David Grayson) had been the national advocate of enterprise agencies and was not likely to overcome conflicting interests. There were insufficient resources (Heseltine envisaged that the DTI support would be only pump-priming, but Business Links were never self-supporting); considerable resources were needed in management, and the client's needs could be forgotten; there were concerns over 'branding' which could lose chamber identity within Business Link; and DTI requirements to raise fees for the service, and to offer it to all businesses, stimulated membership of chambers, but also undermined their USP.[178] The issue of fees remained the most confused throughout.[179] Business Link had the effect of substantially increasing chamber membership, particularly in CCTEs; but in many cases these were not committed members but customers that had merely been in contact; there was considerable optimistic use of statistics.[180] Heseltine's vision for over 200 local 'shops' was always questionable, based on favouring small entities and the enterprise agencies. The drive for small centres now looks even more short-sighted compared to electronic and other virtual interfaces with

---

[175] Comments of Ron Taylor to author, 17 December 1997.

[176] Together with the TECs, local authorities, and the DTI; see Bennett and Payne (2000).

[177] Comments of Ron Taylor to author, 17 December 1997.

[178] See e.g. BCC, *Annual Report* (1997–8), p. 7, which focused on brand damage and service competition; see also Bennett and Robson (1999b, 2004a, 2005); Bennett and Payne (2000); Bennett and Ramsden (2007); Taylor (2007), pp. 140–7.

[179] David Grayson as ISG chair always favoured fee emphasis, in line with Heseltine's desire and the enterprise agency model; it was retained under the next two directors of the Small Business Service, David Irwin and Martin Wyn Griffiths: see Bennett and Robson (2003).

[180] See Chapters 15 and 16.

business. The result was to spread the resource too thinly and undermine the aim of local coordination. David Grayson, as chair of the ISG, managed to convince Heseltine that Business Link (and hence chambers) was for SMEs, and enterprise agencies for start-ups. This division meant that any genuine aim for a single point of delivery was unachievable. Heseltine was either confused or willingly misled. The ISG minutes make clear that the chambers made little headway with their concerns, essentially being directed to do things to help Business Links whose chief executives increasingly acted as an effective lobby of their own.

Market penetration of SMEs by the highly complex architecture of Business Link reached only slightly higher levels than achieved, at one-tenth of the cost, by the centralized system of the SFS and Enterprise Initiative of the 1970s and 1980s. But satisfaction with intensive advice plummeted (60% in 1995), with high variability between areas and advisers (ranging from 20% to 90%). Overall satisfaction increased to about 85% after 2001, still lower than the services of the DTI in the 1980s. Moreover, the design concept of government providing large-scale intensive support to individual businesses, through PBA advisers and diagnostic assessments, was never justified by the costs and results achieved. It might have suited banks (by pre-screening business plans), and helped Business in the Community (by locating secondees and retirees), but it was never clear how a government-defined scheme could contribute more effectively than the abundant market suppliers (of lawyers, accountants, and consultants) or non-profits like chambers. The prescriptive design, targets, and quality measurement were all areas of continuing dispute, and caused all the classic outcomes of principal-agent problems: adverse selection, moral hazard, perverse policy outcomes, and high costs. Client satisfaction was initially far poorer than any of the contributing partners, although it climbed to comparable levels by 2000 when the system was reformed.[181]

Tensions between chambers

Business Links were also very divisive. This was already apparent from David Richardson's views at Leeds in 1994–5, noted above. He was at that time a vice-president of BCC, becoming president in 1996. When president he was forced to bow to pressure from the CCTEs and other interests, but this did not suppress the divisions within the system. As with CCTE mergers, there was resistance from many chambers.

BCC was forced to make a survey of 61 chambers in 1995 in order to find a common view on how to deal with DTI (and inform BCC discussions in the ISG). This showed that 51% of chambers were satisfied with the form of Business Link at that time (of which 12% were very satisfied), 49% dissatisfied (of which 7% very dissatisfied), and 60% felt there was too little influence over DTI decisions. Overall 35% felt that chamber involvement in Business Link was positive, 40% were

---

[181] Priest (1999); Bennett (2006, 2008).

negative, and 25% withheld judgement. Hardly a resounding endorsement; but the BCC was loath to openly criticize DTI.[182] Instead, a report by the author in 1995, commissioned by BCC, but independent of it, did criticize the whole structure in the terms summarized in the preceding paragraphs.[183] Some chambers were critical of Ron Taylor (then BCC director general) for deciding to publish it, as was Heseltine: government always finds it difficult to accept criticism; policy termination of failed programmes is difficult for ministers. However, it was in ISG meetings of 1995 following this report that the ruckus from chambers convinced Heseltine that prescription had to be reduced.

The chambers came out of the service evaluations relatively well. Business Links based on them systematically performed slightly better than those based on the only private provider (A4E), which were both far better than independent franchisees. But even the chamber performances were very variable (both within and between chambers), which was the dominant characteristic of the whole system (and has been attributed chiefly to variable adviser quality).[184] Business Link is one of the best examples of an area where government support may be positive, the leverage on external agents such as the chambers was very high (as Heseltine intended), but where the empirical experience suggests that additionality was low with many outcomes negative or having deadweight.[185] Much of the intensive help to start-ups and SMEs was zero-sum (policy winners created losers). Information delivery was much better, but at much greater cost than the SFS, with poor programme design and execution; and much of the initiative undermined private and non-profit sector provision, such as chambers.[186] It was never financially viable as intended, and the ISG, even after 1995, continued to resist programme improvements, or remove confusion over branding. BCC's desire that 'Business Link should never be the dominant brand' was never accepted.[187] Even the Treasury recognized in 2002 that 'A variant of Gresham's Law might operate, in that bad services drive out good'.[188] With such assessments the chambers inevitably suffered brand damage.

[182] *The Impact of Business Link on Chambers of Commerce* (1996) IFF Research for BCC; also see Taylor (2007), p. 142. As recognized by Rose (1989), becoming insiders makes a group a 'prisoner'; see Chapter 3.
[183] Bennett (1995); see also comments in Taylor (2007), p. 143: *Daily Telegraph* 17 July 1995.
[184] Comparison of different providers is given by Bennett and Robson (2003, 2004a); see also Mole et al. (2008).
[185] House of Commons Trade and Industry Committee (1996), *Business Links* Fifth Report, Session 1995–6, HC302; Bennett (2006, 2008); note that there are significant flaws in many evaluation studies of Business Link by the TECs as a result of not controlling for businesses that were not affected by their use.
[186] As also voiced by trade associations; British Printing Industries Federation the most voluble; the ISG was forced to issue a protocol in 1996 to prevent competition with business associations (ISG 33/96).
[187] Review of Business Link branding (ISG 32/93). The 'Response' by BCC (National Council papers, 12 January 1996), rehearsed again the problems of letterhead, business cards, advertisements, etc. with sole and dual branding. This met with only limited response from DTI.
[188] Treasury/SBS (2002), *Cross-Cutting Review* (London: HM Treasury), p. 153.

13.10 FROM CONTRACTS AND CENTRAL TARGETS
TO THE BIG SOCIETY: 1997–2011

The election of a Labour government in 1997 was bound to change the chamber role. Although vaunting a so-called 'third way' that attempted to link public and private objectives and processes, Labour was primarily concerned about reinserting the state into people's lives, so that the former concept of offering leadership to businesses or business organizations like chambers was bound to disappear. In addition, education interests became very powerful. Over half of the Labour MPs elected in 1997 came from education and local government backgrounds, many as trade union convenors in schools and FE colleges; of new Labour MPs, 56 were directly from FE and over 40 from local government with a strong FE commitment, and many carried deep resentment from the reforms of the Thatcher/Major years. This made the links with agents outside education's 'secret garden' very vulnerable. It inevitably put TECs/LECs, CCTEs, work-based training providers, FE college and school governors, and Business Links in the firing line.

But despite this fundamental shift, Labour still needed partners and agents to deliver. Thus chambers and other private sector structures offered the same attractions as they had for earlier governments. They were still able to offer themselves as contractors, but were unlikely to retain leadership positions. Any concept of the chambers as a 'natural partner' was unlikely to have traction against state-based interests, and at the local level, Labour was always going to favour local government over chambers for delivery. The result was to be a stream of challenges as each pre-1997 programme or agency came under scrutiny. This became most critical after 2001, when victory in a second election gave confidence to Labour to throw away its early public expenditure restraint and create a wave of spending, and it also increasingly looked inwards, particularly to reward its educationalist and union grass roots. A detailed 'barometer' of change over the 1997–2001 period shows Labour systematically moving away from using businesses as key decision takers in favour of public agents and centralized government controls.[189] This accelerated significantly after 2001.

Abolition of TECs and CCTEs

Labour was very sceptical about TECs from the outset, reflecting deep-seated opposition that had existed in local government. Some ministers immediately started looking for an exit route to abolish them, although PM Tony Blair had tended to be supportive, seeing their problems as ones of flexibility and funding.[190] The minister initially responsible for TECs, Kim Howells, was also guardedly supportive. But the oversight of TECs had passed to the Education Department

---

[189] Bennett and Payne (2000), pp. 234–6.
[190] Tony Blair (1992), *Training in Crisis: A Report on the Under-Funding of TECs* (London: Labour Party).

in 1998, under a Secretary of State, David Blunkett, who had undergone only a partial conversion to public–private collaboration in his days as leader at Sheffield Council, discussed in Chapter 10. He pressed very hard a Blair government that was reluctant to abolish TECs and did not want to lose the business community. But Blunkett's 1998 moratorium on chamber–TEC mergers demonstrated the emerging agenda. This was followed by warnings in March 1999 that an ongoing review of TECs was likely to be more radical than originally expected. Various scheduled changes to TECs, such as longer-term commitments through licences, were put on hold. The end was reached in the 1999 *Learning to Succeed* White Paper, in which Blunkett announced that TECs would be closed at the end of their contracts by 2001. Leadership of work-based training was passed to an Education Department agency (the Learning and Skills Council (LSC), which had two levels: central and local), with an increased role for local government and FE colleges. Blunkett ensured that the education interest won back control, with business roles reduced, and central targets increasingly limiting what flexibility had previously existed. The involvement of work-based training providers like chambers became increasingly uphill.

For the 16 merged CCTE chambers the world collapsed in 2001. Government decreed that de-merger should occur, and independent chambers had to be reconstituted from the ashes, often with new leadership of both staff and board. Many former chief executives just decamped, sometimes to local LSCs, whilst some board members were only interested in the TEC aspects, and in any case different skills were now required. Eleven CCTEs reconstituted as chambers. Of the remainder, Oldham, Rochdale, Wigan, Peterborough, and Bolton and Bury disappeared with their areas taken over by adjacent chambers.

For the non-CCTE chambers the pattern was complex, some retaining major contracts, others not, and all having to significantly retrench their training or other staff. Whilst the local LSCs had to retain close links to deliver training using chambers (and other private sector agents), the pressure from FE colleges steadily increased. Many strong links with chambers were extinguished when the local LSCs were absorbed into the RDAs in 2007, and some contracting roles passed to local government in April 2010. This shift had the political purpose of ending the structures established since the 1981 New Training Initiative. The old powers of local government were returned, and with it the concerns of the previous 100 years about involvement of training with the workplace re-emerged.

Loss of Business Link

Business Link initially survived the 1997 and 2001 changes. Labour was committed to it in opposition, and reaffirmed its commitment soon after the 1997 election with a new 'Vision'.[191] However, most managers of Business Links saw this Vision as essentially a quality control initiative, and indeed it became a means

---

[191] See e.g. Margaret Beckett, Secretary of State DTI, and Barbara Roche, Small Firms Minister (1997), *Enhanced Business Links: A Vision from the 21st Century* (London: DTI).

to impose stronger central targets. By 1999 a strongly centralized approach (specifically sought by then Chancellor, Gordon Brown) was imposed within a newly formed Small Business Service (SBS: an arm of the DTI). Business Link contracts had been managed through TECs so that when they were abolished in 2001 the structure had to be modified. This led to a 're-franchising' process in 2001, with a reduced number and new geography of 45 Business Link areas (mostly at county level that fitted with new government subregional goals within RDAs), plus many satellites.

These changes threw parts of the chamber system into further disarray, with some forced to terminate direct involvement. One of the most severely affected was Bedfordshire and Luton (which had been a CCTE and an integrated Business Link): it had to de-merge, and then lost the Business Link contract. The chamber budget dropped over 2000–9 from £15.4m to £1.3m, and the staff from 124 to 28. But other chambers remained more closely involved; the number controlling the franchises through director interlocks initially stayed about the same at 12 (formerly 11) in 2001, and their proportion within the smaller system increased to 26% (from 12%).[192] This proved only a brief respite, as Business Link contracts were thrown into fresh disarray when the budget and contractual oversight shifted to the RDAs over 2005–9. Although initially there was variety between regions, with strong support for chambers in some (such as the West Midlands where chambers operated all the six local Business Link outlets until 2009), in other regions the chambers were progressively squeezed out; Sussex (a former CCTE) and Birmingham lost their contracts in 2009. In effect, RDAs brought England in line with Scotland and Wales to have a single integrated state-led structure at regional level,[193] which offered little favour to chambers. They were no longer 'natural' partners.

The result of this period was a series of changes, to which chambers had to adapt to survive. Some chambers failed to adapt and collapsed; most of these were taken over by adjacent chambers (de facto mergers as with the five former CCTEs that disappeared). Others suffered funding crises (as in Cardiff, which was taken over by Newport to form a wider South Wales chamber); and some areas initially lost a strong chamber presence (notably Exeter and Swindon). In other places EU financial structures or lack of redundancy provisions provided challenges; e.g. as well as Cardiff, this affected Sheffield, and even Birmingham. Mid Yorkshire came under intense pressure and went into creditor voluntary administration in 2009 fighting to survive.[194]

In other areas new management and holding companies emerged which sometimes involved chambers. These companies introduced new competition, generally managed to achieve higher profit margins than chambers obtained, and were more

---

[192] Bennett and Robson (1999b, 2004a).
[193] In Wales, brought under the WDA in 1999 and then the Welsh Assembly. In Scotland, initially branded as 'Business Shop', rebranded in 1998 as Small Business Gateway, and brought under the Scottish Executive after 2001.
[194] Appendix 1 gives the full chronology in each area.

nimble in responding because they did not have to carry other chambers in their region with them. For example, after 1997 a not-for-profit company A4E successfully won two contracts for Business Link (in Durham and Humberside). Though it later failed to retain these, A4E continued as a well-supported training provider elsewhere. In Hertfordshire a non-profit company, Exemplas, took on the Business Link contract, former TEC/LSC training schemes, and other initiatives. Its shareholding includes the University, County Council, and chamber of commerce.[195] This provided a platform to take on Business Link contracts in several other areas: the rest of the Eastern region, Yorkshire and Humberside region, and London. Exemplas wisely put each contract into separate subsidiary companies in order to manage risk if contracts were not renewed. These companies have suffered considerable stress since the 2010 change of government and budget cuts, but have remained robust models competing with chambers on training contracts.

The local and regional state

Not all of Labour's developments were bad for chambers. Some of the objectives of the BCC chamber *Development Strategy* of the 1990s were achieved under the financial pressures. As Taylor observed, the abolition of TECs and the reduction of the Business Link system had the positive effect of removing complex external agents through which chambers had to negotiate; although this came at a price.[196] The regional structure of BCC was also strengthened. Over 1997–2011 an increasing number of programmes that were routed through local government and RDAs involved chambers, so that they remained an important partner of government, and government contracts remained important to the chamber system, and indirectly to members, although on a reducing scale.

The regional dimension presented challenges for a chamber system largely unused to effective regional coordination, although it had been continuously sought since the 1960s. However, the chambers adapted to RDAs, and the RDAs found chamber involvement not only necessary for delivery (initially especially for business support and training contracts), but also for legitimacy. As a result, chamber representatives became members of all boards and many subgroups in RDAs. But there were anomalies as to which chambers were involved. Generally the large city chambers had board membership (Birmingham, Manchester, London), but CCTEs were also frequently chosen, as with the Wigan chamber for the North-West RDA. Former CCTEs were also far more likely to be represented on the local LSCs; with chambers having 23 members in 2002 and 25 in 2003, after which statistics were not gathered. Large and small chambers were equally likely to be members of local strategic partnerships, 54 in 2002, and 56 in 2003.[197] These patterns demonstrate the chambers remaining in important positions under Labour

---

[195] See Companies House register: <www.exemplas.com>. One of its board members was Neville Rayner, chair of the Hertfordshire chamber, former TEC chair, and president of BCC over 2005–11.
[196] Taylor (2007), p. 147.
[197] From BCC, *Benchmarking*.

structures, but as one among many, with government-funded bodies often favoured as 'partners' within the RDA system.

Budget shift and budget decline

The receipts by the chambers from the main government schemes after 1997, shown in Table 13.9, demonstrate that total government income remained significant (it was still over 50% of chamber income in 2010).[198] Chambers remain important partners of government for delivery of local and regional programmes. But Table 13.9 also shows the stresses: income from government almost halved over 2005–10. As is clear from the table, the shift from TECs to LSC in 2001 was very significant overall (and catastrophic for the CCTEs), but the shift of Business Link funds after 2006 continued turning the screw. The means of payment also shifted, with many funds now directed through RDAs, with reduced value per contract received. Some of the changes arose from ERDF programmes, but most resulted from realignment of RDAs, like TECs before them, to become increasingly partners of other government funding rather than the private sector. It is important to note in this table, however, that some shifts are exaggerated since systematic data are only available on BCC chambers. Some major chambers remained outside the association over 2001–8, but were recipients of government funding.

The Coalition, LEPs, and chambers since 2010–11

When the tectonic plates shifted again after the June 2010 election, new and significant changes were required from chambers. Although it is early days for the

Table 13.9. Income from the main government contracts to chambers of commerce in England 1997–2010 (£000s at current prices)

Year	BL/SBS	TEC/LSC	Via SRB/RDA
1997		189,050[a]	
2000	33,484	20,308	36,867
2002	26,055	21,560	36,374
2004	36,407	34,867	34,851
2006	45,699	30,434	51,844
2008	13,450	30,756	24,512
2010	14,156	38,842	16,375

[a] 1997 disaggregated data not available.
Note: LSC includes New Deal, Job Centre Plus, schools funding including work experience, LEA schemes, and Young Chamber.
Source: BCC, *Benchmarking.*

[198] See Table 13.1; Table 13.8 shows the evolution of the training places funded by LSC and TECs.

Coalition government, the dominant initial themes have been retrenchment to reduce government funding; new localism to permit greater flexibility by local government and other agents; and stimulating the revival of voluntary inputs under the narrative of 'Big Society'. Key early changes were the abolition of RDAs (with transition, effective from 2012) and replacement by Local Enterprise Partnerships (LEPs); the reversal of the local commissioning framework for training, and development of an integrated Work Programme for the unemployed; and intensified pressure on local government to contract out and partner the private sector and encourage voluntarism. Old war horses were brought back, such as Lord Heseltine to chair the Regional Growth Fund that replaced RDA budgets, and Lord Young to advise the PM on SME policy (although he quickly resigned).

For chambers the most significant change has been the LEPs that replaced RDAs, phased in over 2010–12. These have required new partnerships with local government to be developed, formed across groups of local authorities in most cases, with no template from central government, so that structures vary. Whilst Eric Pickles, the Coalition local government minister, has suggested that they are a natural milieu for chambers to play a key role, they have produced another set of geographical tensions for the chamber movement. The chambers have been the natural partners in many areas, but were given no special status, mentioned in the White Paper announcing LEPs in only one context—to help maintain former RDA functions of business advice.[199]

The bidding process for LEPs was opened soon after the June 2010 election, with bids due in by September. The first 24 were announced in late October, with 35 by June 2011,[200] and a final tally of about 38 expected for England. Early indications are that local authorities are playing the lead role in most of LEPs, just as in LSPs, because they have the stronger core finance to support the management demands involved, often assigning one or two staff to support their development. Within the first 24 LEPs, in the early stages up to early 2011, chambers became the lead or senior co-partners in nine (37.5%), but were reduced to a 'tick box' or minor player behind local government in the remainder.[201] It is unclear whether, when LEPs develop further, they will involve businesses in a more meaningful way to give chambers more opportunity to shape local agendas, or whether they will be just another advisory committee, like LSPs, driven by external public funding streams. The BCC view is that if they do not have a meaningful role, then 'businesses will just walk away from LEPs'.[202]

In the 38 bids for LEPs that were not immediately approved there were major conflicts over the extent of business involvement, and between local authorities. The proposed geographical structure was inadequate in many of these areas, with local authorities each tending to want one for their district, instead of cooperating with others over larger and more meaningful economic areas: North and West

[199] *Local Growth: Realising Every Place's Potential*, Cm. 7961, October 2010, p. 17.
[200] Ibid., p. 39; BIS (2011) *LEPs: Coverage and Statistics*.
[201] BCC (November 2010), *Survey of LEPs*.
[202] David Frost, BCC director general, quoted in *Financial Times*, 14 February 2011.

Lancashire local authorities were a prime example of this, wanting three LEPs where business leaders felt one was appropriate; Humberside–North Yorkshire–North Lincolnshire another; North-East England except Teesside another; and most of South-West England. All these, except North-East England, remained without LEPs by March 2011. The process was criticized as a shambles by the CBI.[203] The BCC and chambers have been careful to engage in lobbying for positive change; most critically they persuaded ministers to put bids into three categories of green, amber, and red, so that defective bids could be improved. The first tranche of 24 LEPs were those judged green; but BCC remained worried that local government and other pressures would lead ministers to accept amber and red bids. BCC was made the network lead in April 2011 with Frost as chair.

The main fillip of LEPs to chambers has been to reinforce a core city region and subregional structure that is more in tune with how local economies really work than RDAs, and hence much better fitted to chamber geography. David Frost, director general at BCC, felt that LEPs needed to allow chambers and business interests to play a greater role in local planning decisions, help local transport strategy, as well as taking on the remaining support for business advice.[204] The abolition of RDAs also removed a competitor structure that had largely given up cooperating with chambers; hence their abolition left a clearer field. LEPs are potentially synergetic with the BCC *Development Strategy*: similar geographical areas; convergent mission emphasizing local voice and business leadership; support for economic growth, international trade and exports; and linking directly with local government rather than through ethereal and centrally driven local strategic partnerships or RDAs. The flexible geography of LEPs also offers some advantages, with 23 local authorities being covered by two LEPs within the first 31, some of which reflects chamber coverage; not all local authorities in an area need be included within a LEP area, only those that sign into the LEP agreement; and it is envisaged that not all areas may be eventually covered.

Most problematic for chambers is the lack of dedicated core funding for LEPs; hence involvement has to be financed from other income streams, which is challenging and potentially distortionary. Since March 2011 LEPs have been given a role in Enterprise Zones, which has potentially enhanced chamber voice and resources available, although initial resources have been judged inadequate.[205] There is also scope for LEPs to play a significant role in the strategy for how any increased flexibility of business rates revenue is used. Hence, LEPs may be positive in drawing on the core function and USP of chambers as voice, providing potential for high value added, additionality, and leverage; but they appear to leave a major gap in funding overheads that has tended to put local authorities in the lead. A small fund of £4 million (about £100,000 for each LEP) to help LEPs

---

[203] Richard Lambert, CBI director general; *Financial Times*, 22 October 2010; see also 31 August, 6 September, and 29 October 2010.

[204] David Frost, comments to author, June 2010; and BCC, press release, 28 October 2010.

[205] Gary Williamson, chief executive of Leeds, York, and N. Yorks. chamber: in *Financial Times*, 24 March 2011.

'understand the issues they face' was initiated in January 2011,[206] but only partly meets the need. It is also unclear whether the legal structure for LEPs will be supportive of chambers and other local partners, or compete with them (like TECs); how effective will be the eventual structure for amber and red areas; how LEPs will get beyond engaging with government on a contract-by-contract basis to offer scope for sustained local strategies; and how EU funding will be managed.[207] But the greatest challenge is whether government will heed business voice on local needs, or load LEPs with government objectives.

The Coalition government has also launched a Regional Growth Fund, as a part substitute for the RDAs, for which LEPs can bid. This was given a small budget of £1.4 billion for 2011–12. For chambers it has been somewhat suspect because the membership of the advisory panel allocating the Fund is mostly 'captains of industry' from large businesses (chiefly CBI members), including the CBI director general, chaired by Lord Heseltine, with little local economic experience. Membership proposals for chamber representatives were rejected. This has familiar tones from the NEDC and early stages of TECs.

The Coalition has also proposed power for local government to extend BIDs, vary local business rates, and raise tax increment financing from economic development.[208] Meeting resistance from BCC and other business bodies for a full return of business rates to local government, a compromise has been examined to allow local authorities to retain the increment in tax base from new business developments, after 'buying themselves out' of the central grant system for periods of five years.[209] If this is enacted it will inevitably involve chambers as lead business representatives (with others), as they are the only significant body now remaining that offers a system of locally based business representation. But there is a danger that government will again invent its own local bodies, with the excessive costs and inefficiencies that has always brought. There are also many dangers for businesses lurking in the details, with the experience of 1970–87 'new left' authorities providing a warning of the dangers of populist fiscal illusion when local government has control of business rates that allows costs to be passed from voters to businesses.

Since 2010 the chambers have entered a new phase of partnership with government. In many ways they are stronger than in the past, with a more consolidated structure of about 55 chambers, with 150–70 smaller affiliate chambers providing an adaptable network at different scales. They also have the experience of mission confusion of the previous 20 years to draw on, which should exert realism and

[206] BIS (2011), *Local Enterprise Partnerships Gather to Showcase Action Plans for Local Growth*.

[207] e.g. Mark Prisk, Minister for LEPs; answers to BIS *Parliamentary Inquiry into LEPs*, 12 October 2010.

[208] *Local Growth: Realising Every Place's Potential*, Cm. 7961, October 2010; *Localism Bill*, December 2010.

[209] Ernst & Young report on 'Business Rates' (2011) for Department of Communities and Local Government; and lobby efforts by Localis (a local government think tank); reported in *Financial Times*, 28 March 2011.

keep excessive optimism in check: it is unlikely that merger of chambers with government-financed bodies will ever again be on anyone's agenda. The greatest potential benefits, and challenges, will be to bring members into an understanding of the important new roles chambers will be playing as the business voice in LEPs: to engage the commitment of members to support the resources and networks needed for LEPs to be successful; and to keep chambers focused on their core mission, for which LEPs are only the latest in a history of potential government distractions.

13.11 GOVERNMENT SUPPORT TO CHAMBERS IN IRELAND

Apart from the active local activities of Irish chambers, which are included above, the first role of Irish chambers with the national government was the same as that in the UK, with participation in the 'Form K' consular reports over 1919–21. With Irish independence in 1922 'Form K' was terminated, and there does not seem to have been any effort by the Irish government to replace it or work with chambers as a whole until after accession to the EU on 1 January 1973. Ad hoc involvements locally, however, were very significant prior to this date, with government efforts to develop the regions of Ireland very active through industrial estates and subsidies, airports, infrastructure, and tourist promotion. In each case it was the local chambers that were active in this involvement, not the Association.

After joining the EU

This changed with accession to the EU. This provided access to very considerable money through ERDF, Social Fund, agricultural subsidies, and many other programmes. For many schemes, local partners were needed, and the government was forced to draw on chambers and other bodies. Generally, however, it sought to do this through state-led agencies, piggy-backing its own objectives on the EU schemes. The County Enterprise Boards were established in 1992. These were, and still are, funded under local government to support early stage companies. They resemble UK enterprise agencies and TECs, and have competed directly with chambers for attention. Local chambers have been involved, but have not generally received significant funds. The Industrial Development Association (now IDA Ireland), which is a national inward investment body, and Enterprise Ireland, which is an export promotion body, have also acted under government departments, and have had only limited chamber involvement. As in the UK there has been reluctance in government to use chambers as a major point of delivery, instead setting up competitor schemes of its own.

The most successful schemes (from a chamber point of view) have been those actually based on chambers, of which the five Irish Euro-Info Centres set up in 1989–90 were the first and most effective, becoming parts of the European

Enterprise Network, which continues to the present.[210] Later developments used chambers to deliver small business training, help to the unemployed, and local economic development programmes. But most of these have been short-term contracts with no agenda to build a specific chamber capacity, for which the County Enterprise Boards have been preferred. All the schemes have presented challenges of stable commitment, like those in the UK. Already by 1994 chambers like Galway were recognizing that they were becoming over-dependent on EU grants and contracts[211] (when it stood at 24% of income); by 2005 they were receiving 3.6% of income direct from EU grants and another 22% from functions and events part-related to EU support, some through CI.[212] In Limerick chamber project funding and management fees based on EU and government supports were 15% of income in 1999, but jumped to 25% in 2000, and reached 37% in 2006 where they remained.

The dependence on the EU shifted dramatically in 2007 after its expansion to include many new and much poorer nations. At a time when the Irish economy was being referred to as a 'Celtic Tiger', it became less able to access many EU programmes. This led to contraction of income for some individual chambers. But the main challenge came for the Association, which had also taken on a major role in EU programme delivery, a situation very different from the UK where the ABCC/BCC had never become involved in similar programmes.

Chambers Ireland (CI) became involved in EU programmes from the outset of Irish EU membership. By 1974 it was receiving grants to contribute to the Irish Business Bureau in Brussels (IR£4,000 in 1974). Even this small involvement made the character of EU involvement clear from the outset: that few margins were to be made, income was always balanced by costs, and the management overheads were not recoverable so that greater burden was placed on the small executive team (which was then serviced by the Dublin chamber in return for a secretarial fee). The EU programmes began to take off in the early 1990s, with CI 'regional development activities' growing from IR£8820 in 1991 to IR£18,107 in 1992, (chiefly through the EU programmes of LEADER, and also involvement with Northern Ireland through INTERREG). EU funding to CI reached IR£179,828 by 1999, when it was 38.5% of total income, and was covered by assets. But it rapidly increased after 2001 to reach a peak in 2007, when EU and government income reached about €3.9 million (76% of total income). CI staff dedicated to EU and related projects numbered only one in 2000, increased to 4 in 2001 and remained at 3–4 over 2002–4. But project staff then jumped to 9 in 2005, and reached about 19 in 2007, far outnumbering the core staff of CI (which remained at about 9 over 1999–2007). Turnover itself became what the 2005 accounts called a 'key performance indicator'.

---

[210] Regionally spread: in Dublin, Cork, Galway, Sligo, and Waterford.
[211] Woodman (2000), Galway chamber history, p. 323.
[212] Galway chamber, *Annual Accounts* (1995, 2005); Companies Registry Ireland.

The end of the party?

The risks took off between 2001 and 2005 with the Diversity At Work Network (DAWN) programme promoted through chambers, drawing on the obligational networks at the centre of chambers to engage with SMEs. From 2005 the scale of activity jumped again, mainly from the EU Human Resource Development (HRD) Programme, further DAWN/EQUAL activities, and other projects. These schemes were administered by the government's department (Enterprise Ireland), but contracted to CI. Already in 2001 the warning signs were clear: there was a major leap in turnover, but much of the money was passed through to providers, with high project management costs, and high risk deriving from inflation and any unexpected costs, with no cushion because surplus over costs was not permitted. This works for EU public law chambers, but is difficult to operate in a voluntary private law system. Despite CI having a strong record of programme delivery, deficits on most programmes built up. The association was on an escalator, similar to the Irish economy as a whole in these extraordinary boom years. The deficit jumped from €34,000 in 2005 to an accounting loss of €338,167 in 2008, and at the end of that year its 'current liabilities exceeded its total assets by €1.4 million'. The 2008 accounts state that losses had been reduced from €817,005 in 2007, but there was 'a material uncertainty which may cast significant doubt about the company's ability to continue as a going concern'. The 2007 accounts recorded 'significant uncertainty about the outcome of a grant of over €519,000 which [the government] . . . claims is repayable in full. . . . The directors are challenging this'.[213] Despite a subsequent agreement with Enterprise Ireland, significant losses had to be provided for, and this led to major retrenchment and restructuring in 2008.

The focus of CI on deliverables offered high value added and additionality to government, but stretched the strategic fit and mission for the chambers. Despite having completely valid project expenditures and a strong emphasis on outputs, this contrasted with EU auditors' concern with bureaucratic minutiae, and with civil servants focused on retrenchment and clawing back funds.[214] The board conducted a series of independent reviews and a major restructuring took place during 2008–9. A new chief executive joined in July 2008 and CI has since had to focus on services that meet core chamber objectives at low risk. The focus on EU and government projects created high activity, but with high management costs and mission distortion for the association, and no scope to cover risks from unexpected delivery costs or to make any surplus over cost recovery. It was also divisive between

[213] All financial data from Chambers of Commerce Ireland, *Annual Reports and Accounts*: Companies Registry Ireland. See also *Irish Times*, 21 February 2007, 'EU scheme contributes to chambers' loss'.

[214] The CI (2007) accounts state that the Department of Enterprise, Trade and Employment 'raised queries regarding the programme's audit trail and has sought reimbursement of all funds advanced. . . . [CI] have had an independent audit conducted on the claims, which confirms the existence of an audit trail in respect of the amount included in the accounts. The directors are challenging this . . . [and] continue to act proactively with DETE to reach a satisfactory conclusion'.

the chambers (the 'us and them' of those 20–30 working on EU project activities and those that were not), and between the chambers and CI. The EU programmes were run in conjunction with the local chambers, but managed centrally by the association staff. The local chambers benefited directly through activities run in partnership with them, and also received some financial transfers from CI, which for many was beginning to almost fully offset the subscription paid to the association by 2003. This was profoundly destabilizing since it suggested to participating chambers that CI activity could essentially be free to them, and also shifted the emphasis from network activity to project delivery for government/EU targets (which whilst valid, were not necessarily the main primary objectives of the chamber system).

The new CI chief executive has had to move away from involvements where risk cannot be priced into activity through appropriate margins, and to reinvigorate the relations of CI with the chambers.[215] There is a strong parallel to the problems of the UK system (as in Cardiff chamber and the CCTEs), but in this case with the distortion and risks chiefly affecting the central association rather than the chambers. Whilst CI has recovered, as in the UK, extreme financial pressure on central government in Ireland after 2007 has created problems for all government contracts based on the former largesse derived from the boom years. The future is thus even more challenging in Ireland than the UK.

13.12 CONCLUSION: HERE AND NOW

This chapter has demonstrated how chambers have come to play critical roles for government, in both Britain and Ireland: as obligational structures that can be recruited, individual members and structures that can be co-opted, and delivery bodies that can be contracted. In many cases co-option and recruitment has actually been sought by the chambers, in other cases forced on them, or was unavoidable in order to limit the damage that a government initiative might otherwise inflict. Up to the early 1980s the relative influence of government on chambers was minor, and generally fitted with core chamber missions. However, ironically, in the UK under a Conservative government during the Thatcher period that was committed to 'rolling back the state', chambers became progressively more involved in government interventions. These were first focused on urban and other economic regeneration initiatives, and then on training for the workforce and unemployed. In the 1990s this involvement expanded to business advice and support services.

The main periods of expansion in the UK, over 1980–5, and then 1989–97, derived from the influence of David Young, Nicholas Ridley, and the (often confused) vision of Michael Heseltine, who all felt that chambers had the potential to be significant partners of government. Never had chambers received such committed support from government. Taylor felt that 'the 1980s were in effect a

---

[215] Comments to author from Ian Talbot, chief executive of CI, 1 February 2010.

race to establish chambers as a national network fast enough for the government to want to invest in them'.[216] However, because chambers were felt to offer too 'patchy' a cover, all government initiatives were opened to many other partners as well as chambers. Ian Kelly, chief executive of Hull and Humberside, likens it to a three-card trick: 'we [government] need local support, chambers can do it, but are not available everywhere, so we will start something new'.[217]

The government could have used its initiatives to build chamber capacity in the areas where they were weak or non-existent, and then build on to these a 'privatized' system; but it didn't. As Taylor comments, a fraction of the money thrown at Business Link, TECs, and RDAs would have built a *durable* structure of chambers available for a full range of government purposes. Chamber involvement with government also proved very divisive. Even at the height of government support, the chambers never managed to summon more than a slim majority in favour of it: many chambers preferred to remain outside, or become involved in a limited and guarded way (as with the Leeds Business Link); they wisely had their eye on future swings of the pendulum and wisely secured exit routes for when the need arose.

The experience of recent history has demonstrated the dilemmas endemic in a voluntary chamber system: that the sustainable base of services from internal resources is limited, and that to over-expand or raise excessive expectations will lead to disappointment, retrenchment, and brand damage. Voluntary systems are vulnerable to mission confusion as a result of becoming 'prisoners' or 'surrogates' of government: and to instability when the party pendulum swings, when ministerial priorities change, or when the programmes designed by the civil service fail to meet the needs they are supposed to serve on the ground. The withdrawal of CI from Irish EU programmes, and in England the collapse of the CCTE brand, and memory of the questionable quality of Business Links, has left chambers with challenges of rebuilding brand, and adapting, frequently at short notice, to changing funding levels and priorities.

Much of the destiny of chambers has come to depend on the fluctuating support of others. As David Frost, the Director General of BCC, has observed reviewing the swings of the pendulum for the chambers since 1970:[218] 'ITBs *good*; TECs *bad*; CCTEs *good* though some very weak; de-merger of CCTEs and chambers *terrible*; LSC *bad*; Business Link *bad* then (eventually) *good*; RDAs *mixed*'. Although there is some systematic party political influence in this, both main parties have had equally varied results; with the period since the 1980s opening the chambers to extreme buffeting. It remains an open question at the time of writing whether the Coalition government will provide more stable and effective support, or will invent new initiatives and local bodies of its own. It is ironic that whilst some academics have called early chambers unstable and short-lived, even the most unstable chamber has had longer existence than most government initiatives.

---

[216] Taylor (2007), p. 122.
[217] Personal comments to author, April 2010.
[218] Personal comments to author, 22 June 2009.

For the membership, government involvement has confused the chamber brand and mission; it is often less the government that is blamed for short-termism, failures, and caprices, than the delivery body. This has in turn undermined some donor and obligational commitments to chamber membership: they can be seen as just another arm of government. *The Future Chamber* strategy of 1995 had even reached the conclusion that the brand 'Chamber of Commerce' should be retained 'if for only one reason. It is a trade name in international currency built up over 200 years'.[219] Perhaps the new concept of 'Big Society' offers more scope to participate in partnerships with government with less potential harm, but this remains to be seen.

[219] BCC (1995) *Future Chamber Strategy*, pp. 9–10.

PART 5

THE MEMBERS

14

Members and Interests

14.1 MEMBER TYPES AND INTERESTS

What type of businesses became members of chambers, why, and how stable was their commitment? The earlier discussion in this book has treated the chambers mainly from the supply side, as organizations making an offering. But their fundamental characteristic is that they are associations of members: there is thus a critical *demand side*, of what was (and is) sought from membership. The three chapters in Part 5 of this book examine demand: in this chapter the characteristics of the members and how far they covered localities; in Chapter 15 their motives; and in Chapter 16 their stability, of joining, remaining, or lapsing.

Business voice is necessarily based on an 'interest'. Identification with this interest is important to the organization (to know whom they are serving), to the members and potential members (who have to recognize that this is 'the body for them'), and to government (who want to know who is being represented). Clarity of the membership and their interests is thus critical to all. Interest can be defined exogenously or endogenously.[1] *Exogenous interests* lead members to share an 'identity set', based on objective characteristics, such as their location, business sector, firm size, trading markets, etc. *Endogenous interests* bring together 'like-minded people', who share a cause. These different types of interest lead to different ways of identifying members.

Exogenous interests, such as location and sector, bring together businesses with similarities that can be recognized by members, potential members, and government; and can be readily marketed and targeted. Success can also be readily assessed against those target groups: measured by market penetration or membership 'density'. Because these interests are objectively perceptible to all, membership choices are more likely to be based on economic rationality of costs and benefits, and are usually relevant to large and small businesses alike. This was and remains a key aspect of the chambers.

For endogenous interests aligned to a cause, targeting and marketing is more difficult since commitment is spread through the population of businesses. There may be underlying influences, such as social class, geographical affinities, and so on. But generally potential members have to be found by more general marketing, advertising, web, and email-based campaigns. Such groups are essentially self-

---

[1] e.g. Rothenberg (1988); Dunleavy (1991); Jordan and Maloney (1997).

defining. As a result, assessment of success in terms of market penetration is often impossible; instead total size and measures of retention/loyalty are often the only measures available. Since these groups reflect personal priorities, they are most relevant to individual entrepreneurs, owner-managed smaller firms, and to the management/board/personnel of larger firms. Decisions are more likely to be based on personal and psychological factors as well as any economic cost-benefit evaluation.

Chambers primarily have an exogenous definition of interest: to represent their locality. A substantial part of this chapter examines how far the chambers were and are based on local, general, or sector characteristics influenced by trends in corporate organization; how far different firm sizes have been involved; and what level of market penetration has been achieved. However, the chapter also attempts to assess the significance of endogenous forces of like-minded people, focusing on 'leadership' and networking among businesses within and between areas. This helps to better understand the modern context of 'clusters' that have become a key focus of policy debate.

The focus on locality is the chamber USP: this assumes that there is a 'certain type' of business person that becomes a chamber member who is committed to their locality. ACC/ABCC assumed that this was the case; in debates often referring to creating a 'chamber atmosphere' in an area, with members that have a wider 'local interest' than their business alone, and are energized by trying to change (or support others to change) some of the external influences on their business (such as local planning, national taxation etc.).[2] As Exeter stated in 1930, the chamber relies on 'a number of able, public spirited men willing to devote much time and energy to matters in which their own personal interest is slight, but which are of great public importance';[3] or as Worcester noted in 1839, its members recognized 'that a body of individuals, associated for one common object, is far more likely to succeed than one individual'.[4] How is this 'certain type' of business interest defined; and is it as influential now as in the past?

14.2 MEMBERSHIP 'INTERESTS' IN THE EARLY CHAMBERS

Assessing the characteristics of the members of the first chambers is crucial to understanding the 'interests' that underpinned the initial chamber brand, and how chamber members overlapped or were distinguished from other organizations and interests. The detailed annotation in 1775 by Benjamin Heywood, a key figure in

---

[2] e.g. statement by H. W. Sambidge, Birmingham chamber secretary, ACC, *Monthly Proceedings*, October (1917), pp. 18–19.
[3] e.g. Exeter chamber, *Annual Report* (1930), p. 20.
[4] Worcester chamber, *Report of a Provisional Committee Appointed to Promote the Formation of the Chamber*, 7 May 1939, p. 4.

the first Liverpool chamber, of the petition for coercion in America demonstrates how 'interest' was perceived: he noted the local councillors, those employed by government (such as Customs officials), and also began to annotate the business sectors of other signatories. We thus have critical early evidence of the identification by the chamber leaders of interests based on both business type (exogenous factors) and allegiances (due to patronage/employment, which constrained freedom of expression).

Analysing the members requires the painstaking construction of a database of both the membership and other involvements, at particular points of time. This has proved possible for 18 of the chambers established up to 1819 plus the special case of Bristol, where the Venturers (SMV) sometimes acted like a chamber: 19 locations in all.[5] These cover diverse environments in England (7), Scotland (4), Ireland (6), and the Channel Islands (2). The complex cases of Manchester and Birmingham are split into periods of development.

Geography

As we have seen in Chapter 5, the early chambers were located in the major cities, and especially the ports. But how focused was their membership on these centres, or were the centres surrogates for wider regional or national 'interests'? The location of members is shown in Figure 14.1. This exhibits the broad geographical extent of some of chamber memberships. Many were not based exclusively on historic core cities and narrow municipalities of pre-Reform Britain, but drew members from their region, and indeed in some cases from other parts of the country, and abroad. As noted in Chapter 5, two urban systems coexisted and interpenetrated: one system was a hierarchy of central places based on local and regional demands; the other underpinned the major regional hubs, based on long-distance trade.[6]

The chambers such as Manchester, Liverpool, Edinburgh, and Glasgow were notably regional hubs, with Manchester's membership widening geographically at its second foundation. Dundee was a 'regional' chamber for Forfarshire from its foundation in 1819, and even after 1836 when it became the Dundee chamber it still had members from further afield, with 'country' and 'town' subscriptions. The regional leadership of these chambers reflects the character of their industry; they were centres that acted as trading and commercial hubs for regional hinterlands and smaller towns. This was also true of Leeds, which had strong links through attendance at Leeds chamber meetings by 'representatives' from the nearby towns of Wakefield, Halifax, Huddersfield, and Rochdale. Many other chambers had membership more localized to their own cities, notably Birmingham, most Irish

---

[5] There are uncertainties with the information. Formal membership lists have been used where possible, but membership is not always recorded fully, the signatures or handwriting of names can introduce uncertainties, the transcription of names in print contains flaws, there is a variety of spellings of names (e.g. in the Channel Islands where French and Anglicized spellings can be inconsistent), and where partnerships sign it may be unclear who is the subscribing member; see Appendix 2.

[6] Berg (1991), p. 179; in turn quoting Hohenberg and Lees (1985), p. 457.

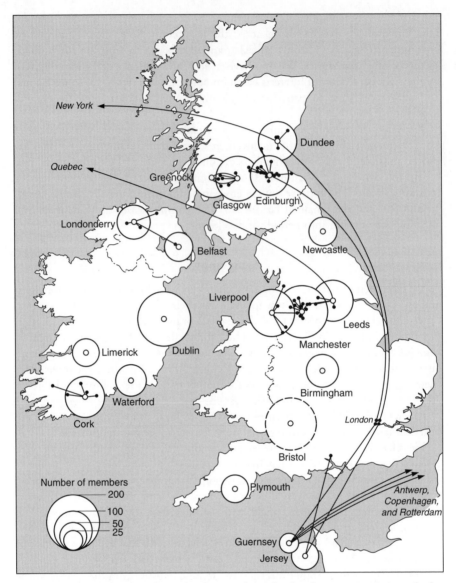

Fig. 14.1. The geography of membership in the early chambers 1770–1819; each dot represents one member from outside the core centre; from analysis of membership lists.

chambers, Plymouth, and Newcastle. In Bristol, the members were highly focused on the city as a result of the traditions and statute of the Venturers.

Five chambers drew membership from well beyond their regions. The expansive networks of Edinburgh (as a major banking centre interlinked with London) and the Channel Islands (linked to banking associates in London, and communication partners in Poole and Southampton) are particularly notable. By the 1830s

Guernsey was able to draw support even from foreign-based interests in Denmark and Holland, and almost all of the early chambers had a significant foreign involvement from merchants who also acted as local consuls or representatives of different countries. Leeds had a member from Quebec; Dundee had a member from New York. The broad geographical spreads of membership are an enduring characteristic of chambers of commerce, distinct from chambers of trade, and many other organizations.

Sectors

Sectors are often argued to be one of the most fundamental ways in which businesses align their interests. For chambers, as 'general' interest bodies, sector was clearly secondary to location. But chamber membership was strongly interdependent with sector, and in early periods sector carried with it levels of status and class differentiation, as well as political power. The sector composition of the early chambers is shown in Table 14.1, using a simplification of modern sector categories. Sectors are often difficult to identify because many business entities, as today, were diversified across several types of trade, and the entrepreneur (who was usually a personal member of the chamber) might have many businesses across several sectors (and locations). Hence the analysis can at best be only approximate, as noted in Appendix 2.

Merchants and shippers

The most notable feature of Table 14.1 is the preponderance, and increasing proportion, of merchants in all but three chambers. 'Merchants' were different from their modern usage. They were entrepreneurs and leaders in financing and trading the products of a wide range of businesses, and had the highest status among business people, major power brokers in the national and local economy.[7] Thus the chamber 'interest' was very much that of the business elite. The merchants became, by the mid to later 18th century, the central figures of what would now be called global trading companies. Their involvement in chambers was thus natural since their activities relied on, and radically influenced, the gross activity and development of the ports.[8] They were the leading independent capitalists and entrepreneurs of the day, many evolving into banking.

The merchants together with shippers were particularly numerous in chambers such as Jersey, Liverpool, Glasgow, Greenock, Leeds, Cork, Limerick, and Guernsey. But notable exceptions to the dominance by merchants are Manchester, the later Birmingham chamber, and Dundee, where the manufacturers make up the majority of the membership, 55–90%. Other chambers such as Belfast and Newcastle have a more equal mix of merchants and manufacturers, and it is notable that even those chambers that have a preponderance of merchants also have some

[7] Bowden (1965), pp. 136 and 140.   [8] See e.g. Jones (2000).

Table 14.1. Sector composition of members of chambers of commerce 1767–1825: percentage of members from each sector at each period

Chamber	Date	Agric. & primary	Construction & utilities	Manufacturing	Merchant/ wholesaler	Law, finance, bus. services	Transport, communications	Retail, hotels
Jersey	1767–78	—	—	4.3	34.8	13.1	47.9	—
Manchester	1774–80	3.6	—	89.2	3.6	3.6	—	—
	1781–89	—	—	91.9	2.7	0.9	0.9	—
Liverpool	1774–84	1.2	—	9.3	46.5	9.3	33.7	—
Bristol SMV	1774–84	2.5	—	25.0	47.5	17.5	—	7.5
Glasgow	1783–95	—	—	6.7	57.9	24.4	4.4	2.2
Birmingham	1783–89	—	—	42.5	55.0	2.5	—	—
	1790–99	—	—	70.0	20.0	5.0	—	5.0
	1813	—	—	76.6	12.2	8.2	—	—
Dublin	1783–99	—	—	20.0	48.9	24.4	—	6.7
Belfast	1783–90	—	3.6	32.7	38.3	10.9	—	14.5
Edinburgh	1785–95	0.9	8.0	20.5	48.2	13.4	3.6	5.4
Leeds	1785–92	—	—	23.0	68.9	3.3	—	4.8
Londonderry	1790–99	—	—	14.3	51.4	5.7	25.7	2.9
Guernsey	1808–26	—	4.8	16.7	59.5	4.8	4.8	9.4
Limerick	1807–15	—	—	6.7	60.0	20.0	6.7	6.7
Waterford	1804–10	4.2	—	12.5	37.5	16.7	12.5	16.7
Plymouth	1813–20	—	—	18.7	43.8	12.7	12.5	6.3
Greenock	1813–20	—	—	5.0	70.0	10.0	10.0	5.0
Newcastle	1815–25	—	11.9	21.4	42.8	14.3	4.8	4.8
Cork	1819	2.6	5.3	2.6	79.0	2.6	5.3	2.6
Dundee	1819–25	—	3.4	55.2	22.5	10.3	6.9	1.7
Total (%) 1768–89		0.4	1.9	22.1	47.6	14.9	8.8	4.3
Total (%) 1790–1825		0.5	2.9	18.8	50.7	14.2	8.1	4.8

Note: Total is for two time periods, weighted by numbers in each chamber, excluding Birmingham in 1813.

manufacturers. Thus the two main exceptions from chambers as 'general bodies' were Manchester and Birmingham.

An attempt to analyse more systematically the complexity of sector composition for Liverpool demonstrates that most chamber member businesses were sectorally diversified, particularly between simple merchanting and shipping, but also into manufacturing: pottery, salt, sugar baking, brewing, and trades associated with shipbuilding and maintenance such as rope manufacture. This diversification is also evident in Bristol, where again the sugar bakers were important members of the Venturers along with the merchants, and Glasgow for sugar, textiles, and tobacco manufacture.

The main trading markets of the chamber members also offers important indications of their 'interest' in government activities and the threats imposed. There was generally a strong inter-linkage with the Atlantic economy and the complex triangular trades between Africa, America, Greenland fisheries, the West Indies, Europe, and Britain. In Liverpool over 70% of the chamber members were primarily in Atlantic trades, and about 90% had some involvement; 21% were involved in Europe, and only 7% primarily focused on the UK or Ireland. The focus of the Liverpool chamber members on these long-range trades was also much greater than the port's shipping as a whole.[9] Since the long-range trades generally needed larger and longer-term credits, were more exposed to risk, and had greater exposure to losses from government 'bads', it is understandable that the chamber had more 'interest' in threats to the Atlantic trade in the 1770s than the city as a whole, as noted in Chapters 4 and 9. A similar pattern is found in Glasgow, Bristol, and Dublin.

What proportion of the merchants did the chambers encompass? Estimates by Massie in 1759 and Colquhoun in 1800s put total merchant numbers in Britain at between 3000 and 15,000, of the large traders.[10] The chamber merchant members numbered about 800, and hence represent 5–27% of the whole. But about two-thirds of the major merchants were in London, where there was no 'general' chamber. Excluding London, the merchant members of the chambers thus represented 16–80% of the major merchant population in the outports. For Liverpool, chamber members were about 85% of all shippers and merchants, whereas they were only 37% of the city's businesses.[11] Whilst the ranges are wide, they demonstrate that even at the minimum, the chambers had a very high market penetration of the total merchant population outside London.

'New' manufacturers

It has been argued that the 'new manufactures' emerging in 'new' locations were un-represented by an 18th-century political system dominated by the landed gentry, the large merchants, and the Church, and that this was a stimulus for the

---

[9] Which was about 14–18%: Bennett (2010), pp. 96–8.
[10] See estimates in Chapman (1992), pp. 22–4; Colquhoun was former Glasgow chamber chair.
[11] Bennett (2010), table 6, p. 95.

search for a new voice, particularly through the General Chamber.[12] Birmingham and Manchester have been the main examples for this argument. Indeed it is clear from Table 14.1 that these early chambers were different, with the strongest sector focus on manufactures, respectively, or cottons/fustians, and metal trades (especially buttons, guns, swords, and cutlery).[13] For the majority of chambers, manufacturers were an important sector, but were second or third after merchants and shippers.

The emphasis on 'new manufactures' has distorted understanding by focusing on the two exceptional chambers. More detailed analysis also reveals the diversity. Garbett's correspondence over 1760–90, and particularly over the 1780s, is voluminous and shows him acting as a 'clearing house' for lobbies of the manufacturers. But these are not just from 'new manufactures'; they cover all major industries, and in 'new' as well as 'old' locations such as Norwich and Exeter. As shown in Chapter 9, these were key members of the 'committees of correspondence' that developed in 1784 immediately prior to the General Chamber.[14] His most systematic effort in 1784 was a listing of the entire key manufacturing towns and ports, and their industries.[15] The locations fall both within and outside Trinder's listing of 'new' locations.[16]

It may be that it was the more innovative manufacturers in each location that were key parts of the chambers. In Liverpool it was the newly expanding coal, salt, and metal trades that provided members; even Londonderry, with a tiny manufacturing base, had one of its most innovative as a chamber member, James Atcheson's new brewery.[17] But the general pattern was chamber manufacturing involvement from the *export* industries where the merchant economy was interrelated with the manufacturer; or in Ireland it interrelated merchants with the provisions industry driven by exports. The manufacturers (and even some Irish farm producers) generally had common concerns with the merchants, rather than being opposed to them: to respond to threats to international trade, particularly in the Atlantic economy, and other government 'bads' such as extensions of Customs and taxation. They were jointly excluded: the merchants and manufacturers together made up only 5% of the electorate in the pre-Reform period, compared to 21% for retailers, 14% for the gentry, and 60% for skilled, unskilled, and agricultural occupations.[18] Hence, as in the earlier discussions, it is essential to

---

[12] Bowden (1919–20, 1965); Clapham (1926); see also Redford (1934); Norris (1957), Money (1977).

[13] The exceptionalism of Birmingham and Manchester is also evident in their lobbies (Chapter 9).

[14] e.g. Garbett letter to Shelburne 14 October 1784, enclosing copies of correspondence with Manchester, Sheffield, Glasgow, Norwich, Exeter, Leeds, Sheffield: Garbett–Lansdowne correspondence ZZ 61B; Birmingham Archives.

[15] Extensive listing enclosed in Garbett letter to Boulton and copy to Lord Rawdon, 21 May 1784: Garbett–Lansdowne correspondence ZZ 61B.

[16] Trinder (2000).

[17] G. V. Sampson (1802), *Statistical Survey of the County of Londonderry* (London: Graisberry & Campbell).

[18] Though the proportion of merchants was higher in the main ports it was never dominant; O'Gorman (1989), pp. 200–16; from a sample of poll books.

see chamber formation as embedded in the structure of British foreign trade and exports, particularly across the Atlantic economy.

Banking: a leading sector?

Before 1826, when joint stock banks were introduced, banks were predominantly local institutions ('country banks') strongly interlinked with major local businesses. Country banks grew rapidly in England, Wales, and Scotland at the same time as chambers, although this growth was punctuated by crises and closures. In Britain, there were about 12 in 1750, 300 in the early 1790s, reaching over 600 in 1803.[19] In Ireland the numbers grew from about 5 in 1780, to 10 in 1797, and over 70 by 1810.[20]

The banks were critical new economic institutions of this period, and also key investment and information sources.[21] Many country banks had origins among the larger merchants or manufacturers, and it was natural that they would already be, or seek to be, strongly networked to other local businesses and commercial bodies like chambers. The main business of the country banks was 'essentially note issue', to provide liquidity for local payments, turning the merchant bill of exchange into a 'currency'.[22] Hence, it should be expected that banks would become *a leading sector* within chamber membership.

Banking connections were also critical to how chambers linked to London (or the banking centres of Edinburgh and Dublin) and to each other. Country banking required clearance through the Bank of England and the London private banks, many of which were from prominent provincial banking families. This provided long-established and trusted informants in the metropolis, so that lobbying by chambers could draw on an initial platform of expertise. It was critical to the issue of loan notes in Liverpool through Heywoods bank (chamber members) in 1793.[23] It was also a source of advice on seeking charters for chambers by Glasgow, Edinburgh, Jersey, and Limerick. When Glasgow chamber used Gray's Inn solicitor John Seton as their agent in 1783–90, he seems to have been introduced through the banking connections of the Touch, Forbes, and Coutts banking families in Edinburgh.[24]

Similarly, country bankers needed to network with each other, which was also a strong symmetry with chambers. Thus the Heywoods bank in Liverpool and Manchester, run by Liverpool chamber members, cleared thousands of pounds over 1791–3 for the Thistle Bank in Glasgow (of which chamber members John Glassford, John McCall, and John Campbell were leading directors) and for the

---

[19] Clapham (1944); Powell (1966).

[20] Cullen (1968).

[21] Checkland (1975); Hudson (1986, 1989); see also Clapham (1926).

[22] Clapham (1926), pp. 265–6; Pressnell (1956); Devine (1975, 1977, 2003); Powell (1966), p. 118; Price (1991), pp. 283 and 288.

[23] Bennett (2010), pp. 61–2.

[24] See W. Forbes (1860), *Memoirs of a Banking House* (London: Chambers); and Colquhoun correspondence.

Merchant Bank (in which Glasgow chamber member Archibald Graham was cashier and the main counterparty).[25] Heywoods also cleared for the Manchester Bank before setting up their own branch.[26]

The local and national significance of country banking networks meant that, in most cases, *almost all* the major local banking interests of the time were among the leading members of early chambers. Analysis of all local banks and their partners and the members of the 18 earliest chambers and Bristol Venturers shows an overall average of over 70% of local banks having at least one chamber member. Of the banking partners, over 40% were founding or early chamber members. Excluding three exceptional cases that had no chamber–bank interlock, in the other 16 areas 77% of banks and 49% of individual bank partners were chamber members.[27] This is a remarkably high overlap, evidencing strong mutual interest. Since over 40% of country banks were located in chamber areas, chamber banking members accounted for nearly 30% of all country banks. Bankers were also crucial innovators; for example for the insurance industry, covering the main risks to business clients (particularly marine and fire).[28] Again many early chamber members were interlinked with insurance. This is most notable for the foundation of Liverpool Fire Insurance in February 1777, where all eight initial directors were chamber members.[29] Banks and chambers thus appear to be closely interlocked innovations of the late 18th century.

Moreover bank partners were much likely to be 'inner circle' senior figures in the chambers: 38.6% of bank partners that were chamber members held chamber offices, of which at least 14% were presidents or vice-presidents. This leading position was disproportionate to their numbers, of only 4–6% of the average membership and less than 0.5% of the business community. Also, in many chambers the treasurer was a bank partner; e.g. in Liverpool, Limerick, Jersey, Guernsey, and Plymouth. Glasgow's first secretary was a banker, Gilbert Hamilton. In Belfast the interlocks were exceptionally close. The chamber members took the initiative in 1784 to found the Discount Office (which was a quasi-bank, discounting bills), in direct response to the needs of the linen merchants and the establishment of the Bank of Ireland. Its 12 directors were entirely chamber members. Three of the partners from this Office then went on to establish the Belfast Bank in 1787, and a further three went on to establish Cunningham's Bank also in 1787; all continuing as chamber members.[30] In Liverpool, all the local banks were involved in membership of the chamber, making up 25% of the chamber's committee.[31] Dublin chamber members were dominant in the Bank of Ireland. In general, the

---

[25] Heywood Ledgers, Doc. C; Barclays Bank Archives.

[26] Quoted in Chandler (1964); Heywood ledger (now missing from Barclays Archives).

[27] Full details in Bennett (2011b), tables 1–3.

[28] Hudson (1986, 1989); Price (1991), pp. 288–94; Pearson (2004); Pearson and Richardson (2001).

[29] *Williamsons Advertiser*, 28 February 1777; Bennett (2010), p. 103.

[30] The Discount Office was a quasi-bank, and an agent for BoI; Millin (1927), pp. 11–12 and 184–6.

[31] Bennett (2010), pp. 94–5.

exceptions of bank partners who were not chamber members were the small and ephemeral banks; banks that served mainly the gentry and private needs rather than businesses; or where partners were not active in the business (providing only the capital).[32]

However, there were three chambers with no discernible interlock with banks: Manchester, Birmingham, and Newcastle. Although the lack of full membership lists means that further research is needed, this shows the clear exceptionalism of the manufacturing-based chambers. The Manchester chamber had no local bank partners, yet there were three to five established banks.[33] Birmingham also had well-developed banks, but over 1783–90 there was no active bank member of the chamber.[34] The chamber's position is in marked contrast to banking involvement in other Birmingham initiatives; for example, the Assay Office (established in 1773) and the Birmingham Improvement Acts.[35] In Newcastle, when the chamber was founded in 1815, there were several strong banks, and 29 potential partners and managers who might have become members of the chamber. None of them did so. Bank membership of the chamber only began to change in the late 1830s, and even then was slow to develop.

A further aspect of the contrasts between areas is the role of the chartered banks in Scotland and Ireland (in England there were no chartered banks other than the Bank of England). In Scotland, there were three chartered banks, the Bank of Scotland (BoS), Royal Bank (RBS), and British Linen Bank Co.; and in Ireland the Bank of Ireland (BoI). Because of their close interrelation with government grandees, their boards and appointments were normally dominated by political and other patronage. This made them unlikely organizations to link with chambers, yet in most cases they did.

In Edinburgh, there were two chamber members from RBS (a major shareholder William Ramsey, and the cashier William Simpson), and the Linen Bank had the general manager of 1785–1801, Walter Hog as a chamber member. In Glasgow, there was a strong link through the very prominent Gilbert Hamilton,[36] who became a BoS agent in 1802, and was the chamber secretary and established his own bank in 1795. In Dublin, although none of the formal governors were chamber members, 12 of the 15 directors of the BoI were; the only exceptions were Patrick Lawless and two members of the La Touche family (each of whom was strongly connected with landed interests).[37] This strong interlock arose from the complex politics of the time. The BoI was initially resisted by the merchants, with Travers Hartley organizing a petition of the Dublin merchants against the Bank on 4 March 1782, with a similar petition from the Belfast merchants, calling for its

[32] As was the case for the two major banks in Dublin that were not chamber members: La Touche, and Gleadows: see further below; Tenison (1894); Cullen (1968, 1983).

[33] Grindon (1877); Chandler (1964).

[34] The 1790 Birmingham chamber had Robert Coales as a member of the chamber's committee, but this was after his bank had closed.

[35] Tann (1993, appendix 1) lists Guardians; Dent (1973), pp. 158–61.

[36] See Chapters 6 and 9 for other roles of Hamilton; but he was the only BoS-chamber connection.

[37] Tenison (1894).

'postponement', for 'consideration'.[38] This was a ploy by Hartley and members of the Committee of Merchants, who were already planning a chamber for Dublin. Hartley was an experienced operator trying to circumvent the aristocratic interests in Dublin.[39] The dominance of BoI by chamber members was thus a coup that reduced the influence of the La Touche family and its aristocratic supporters. However, links with the La Touches had to be accepted for passage of the Bill and to provide sufficient security for the Bank. In this, William Eden (Lieutenant of Ireland 1780–2), was a critical intermediary between the warring interests, drafting and introducing the Bill in parliament. Banks were thus natural members and a leading sector within chambers, even for most charter banks, strongly linked to other businesses and hence critical parts of local networks.

Business organization and control

Business organization can be legally distinguished into three categories, which are one of the few examples of definitions that remain relatively unchanged from the 1700s until today: (i) sole traders and individual entrepreneurs; (ii) unincorporated business partnerships; and (iii) incorporated business, initially formed either by Royal charter or letters patent—chartered companies; or formed by Act of Parliament—statutory companies; but after Acts of 1844 and 1856 formed by incorporation of limited liability companies, as used today. These categories allow the main distinctions of management control underpinning the 'interest' of the chamber member to be assessed. They are also indicators of business size (in the absence of other information).

As shown in Table 14.2, many members of chambers were individuals trading alone, like most businesses in the country as a whole; they made up 48% overall, but were a much larger proportion in some chambers such as Glasgow, Edinburgh, Dundee, and Greenock. This indicates why the early chambers were so focused on activities that benefited individuals directly: such as discourse and service supports. It also confirms why there was so much focus on large-scale general meetings: all individuals wanted involvement. Businesses had much of the individual personality of their owners.

Partnerships were the slight majority of the membership, 52% overall, and much larger in Liverpool, Leeds, Newcastle, and Jersey. This is an extraordinarily high proportion for this early date, much higher than for the country as a whole, demonstrating that chambers were milieus for some of the largest, most advanced, and often most diversified businesses. The 89% of members from partnerships in Liverpool is particularly striking and reflects its very advanced trading structures interlocked with extensive Atlantic trade. The larger partnership businesses were

---

[38] Hall (1949), pp. 30–5; Millin (1927), p. 184.
[39] Cullen (1983), pp. 34–45 gives an account; see Chapters 4, 5, and 9 for other roles played by Hartley.

Table 14.2. Legal form of members of chambers of commerce 1767–1825: percentage of members of each type at each period

Chamber	Date of founding	Individuals	Companies/ partnerships	Limited/ chartered	Cos. as % of total businesses in area	Chamber Co. members as % of all Cos.
Jersey	1767	33	67	—	17.0	70.1
Manchester	1774	54	46	—	20.7	66.1
	1781	48	52	—	20.7	74.8
	1790	44	55	1	20.7	77.1
Liverpool	1774	17	89	—	21.0	62.0
Bristol MV	1774	54	46	—	21.7	16.6
Glasgow	1783	82	17	1	29.4	4.9
Birmingham	1783	42.5	57.5	—	19.5	13.7
	1790	55	45	—	19.5	22.7
	1813	61	39	—	19.5	19.6
Dublin	1783	59	37	4	14.0	8.5
Belfast	1783	55	45	—	21.3	42.1
Edinburgh	1785	78	21	1	10.4	27.3
Leeds	1785	16	84	—	24.7	34.5
Londonderry	1790	56	44	—	10.6	41.7
Guernsey	1808	41	59	—	10.0	68.4
Limerick	1807	62	38	—	7.7	43.6
Waterford	1804	74	26	—	7.6	42.3
Plymouth	1813	69	31	—	5.9	64.5
Greenock	1813	85	15	—	19.6	28.8
Newcastle	1815	33	67	—	27.5	63.4
Cork	1817	67	33	—	9.0	46.1
Dundee	1819	93	7	—	12.6	25.2
Total (%)		47.9	51.6	0.5	17.2	37.9

Note: Total is weighed by numbers in each chamber (for earliest date, where multiple dates).

generally the most identifiable to others, provided greater assurance of stability (particularly against death), and often indicated lower risk as there was a larger number of people to share burdens and against whom to make claims. However, even for partnerships the individual was the focus, and it is common to find all partners becoming chamber members. The chamber interest was thus predominantly from independent businesses, led by individual entrepreneurs and partnerships. But there were also a few incorporated concerns, 0.5% overall, in six chambers. These came from a canal company and the chartered banks in Scotland and Ireland.

Table 14.2 also compares chamber membership with the business structure of their areas. Whilst all these estimates can at best be treated only as indicative because of data constraints, the dominant pattern is for chambers to have over twice the proportion of partnerships as members than the locality as a whole. This is particularly true in the Channel Islands, Manchester, Liverpool, Plymouth, and Newcastle. A notable group of chambers had much lower partnership proportions, Glasgow and most of Scotland, Dublin and most of Ireland. Although further research is clearly needed, this appears to derive from the very large numbers, and higher proportions, of individual traders in these areas, and the search these chambers initially made to obtain large memberships.[40]

Firm size and status

The size of the businesses that were members of the early chambers, and their relationship to the rest of the local economy, is a crucial factor defining their interests. The statement by most chambers in their petitions and correspondence with government almost always stated that they were representing the 'principal' businesses. There is no reason to doubt this assertion, since if it were not true it would have been readily apparent to government and any local critics.

Unfortunately, there is no systematic information on firm size that allows comparisons for this early period, although the high proportion of partnership businesses is a key indicator of membership by many larger businesses, as noted above. However for Liverpool other information and contemporary sources confirms that the leading chamber members were also mostly the major businesses in their fields. At least 40% of the merchants were referred to as 'major' in contemporary records. Of the 330 local merchants 'men of substance with extensive overseas connection' in the 1790s, the chamber contained 19%. The merchants in the chamber were 51% of the major merchant flags shown on contemporary pottery mugs and jugs.[41] All the chambers with extant local chamber histories where more detailed analysis has been undertaken also confirm that many or most of the leading businesses of the time were involved in the chamber. Further confirmation is provided in studies of the broader elites, which show a significant later chamber presence, as discussed for civic improvement in Chapter 10. Moreover, in cases like Jersey, the chamber had a qualification for membership that sought to limit membership to the larger businesses.[42]

---

[40] The limited development of Irish partnerships arose from restrictions favouring the Irish aristocracy and limits on Irish trade. Both import and export was mostly held in English accounts, dominated by English factors in London, Bristol, Liverpool, and Whitehaven; Cullen (1968), pp. 92–9, 170–4; (1977); (1983). Even after the 1780s, many businesses and banks had to act mainly through their London correspondents, or the local houses of London banks, because drawings were chiefly on English banks or merchants with Irish business: Gilbart (1836); Hall (1949); Cullen (1968). French and other European businesses in Ireland also used London agents (Cullen (1968), pp. 159–65).
[41] See Baines (1852); Brooke (1853); Gatty (1882): Mugs 43, 44, etc.; also Bennett (2010), p. 95; these are underestimates since not all Liverpool chambers are known.
[42] Jersey chamber minutes, *Rules*, 1768; see Chapter 15.

Gender, age, and origins

In the 18 early chambers examined, there is only *one* instance of a female member, in the 1781 Manchester chamber (Mrs Norton, probably a fustian manufacturer). It is also probable that Sarah Clayton in Liverpool was a chamber member, since she was one of the most highly networked and interconnected business owners with chamber members; but without the full membership list we cannot be sure.[43] Thus, the female participation in early chambers is extraordinarily low, reflecting the wider social and economic constraints of the day.

There were few opportunities for women to enter into business on their own account until the 20th century. Women were therefore normally of employee status, mainly contracted for 'putting out' in manufacturing, or small traders in retailing. But there were some participants, particularly as a result of inheriting a business. Chamber membership lists do not necessarily reliably record these, since the business may still be referred to as 'Messrs', or as '& Co.' There is some evidence in later chambers that women were not welcomed,[44] but in early bodies, the objective of representing both the major businesses (principal traders), and having a preponderance of the major businesses, militated against women.[45] Hence, the early chambers were essentially a male preserve, and the language of their founding documents, minutes, and petitions is almost always couched in terms of 'gentlemen' of the city; as clear in the earlier chapters, which have not attempted to change the contemporary gendered language.

Age is an interesting further aspect, because it has been suggested that in periods of rapid social change and instability the intensity of activism is greatest in the age groups of 30–55, coinciding with the most intense period of professional activity.[46] Table 14.3 shows the age of the chamber leaders and members, and the earlier Stamp Act leaders, for a sample of the members for the first chambers in Britain and America. It clearly demonstrates that most were in the 30s and 40s age groups, with New York being slightly older. Surprisingly the delegates mainly involved in British Stamp Act lobbying, making demanding high-profile appearances at the House of Commons, had the youngest age profile. The age profiles in Liverpool and Manchester chambers were similar to the Stamp Act activists. But the moderate force exerted by Boston and New York during the rebellion was by people on average nearly ten years older than in the 1760s (mainly the same people). Thus these early chambers had not renewed (indeed New York limited its membership), and had become potentially more cautious bodies. Charleston, Manchester, and Liverpool, newly founded in 1773–4, attracted a younger range of ages.

---

[43] She was a proprietor of the Sankey canal, and ran a major coal and shipping business; the wife of chamber member David Tuoy, d. 1788, may also have been a member; see Bennett (2010), pp. 98–9.

[44] Although the only explicit statement found is that by Mr Hunter of Hartlepool in 1917, who claimed that a female clerk would not be able to answer commercial questions, and he was strongly disagreed with: quoted in ACC, *Monthly Proceedings*, 4 October (1917), p. 33.

[45] See e.g. Haggerty (2002, 2006).

[46] Meister (1984), p. 88.

Table 14.3. Approximate average age and 20/80% percentiles of a sample of Stamp Act groups and early chambers in Britain and America 1763–1775

	Mean age	20%	80%	N
British Stamp Act lobby 1765	35	31	40	23
Liverpool Stamp Act Committee 1765	41	28	49	17
Boston BSETC 1763	45	34	56	57
Liverpool chamber 1775	39	29	48	83
Manchester chamber 1777–81	38	32	44	25
Manchester chamber 1781–90	44	31	54	75
New York chamber 1770	50	30	60	13
Charleston chamber 1773	39	28	50	20
Boston BSETC 1775	55	44	66	57

Sources: Tables 4.1 and 4.2 Bennett (2010) for Liverpool; Tyler (1986) for Boston; Manchester, New York, and Charleston calculated from those traceable using IGI and other sources.

Origins of chamber members are also a valuable indicator, since it has been suggested that many of the leading entrepreneurs and political activists were foreign immigrants.[47] It is difficult to trace all the members (especially the most mobile), but it is notable that a high proportion were born locally or from nearby in all cases. Charleston had the highest recent immigrant membership, with about one-third from outside Carolina; but Manchester and Liverpool had less than 7% from outside Lancashire and Cheshire. It is also notable that although banking in general had a high dissenter and immigrant community component, the country bankers that were members of most chambers were not recent immigrants but locals (at least in their parents' generation), although the dissenter proportion was relatively high.

14.3 EARLY SOLIDARITY AND 'ENDOGENOUS' MEMBER CHARACTERISTICS

The early chambers were established not to serve just the specific demands of localities, but also to respond to threats and anger. Therefore personal, endogenous characteristics of the members were of great significance. This personal activism was part of an explosion of associations in the late 18th century that offered new opportunities to 'belong', based on self-selection, self-effort, and new leadership.[48]

The chambers offered particular attractions as one of the few organizations where business people were the leading figures; they were only minor participants in most

---

[47] Bowden (1919–20, 1965); Checkland (1952, 1958).
[48] See e.g. Langford (1989); Clark (2000a); Hall (1998), pp. 282–8.

other societies in the 18th century.[49] Chambers were also highly focused on economic concerns and, despite exclusiveness, had fewer barriers to access than most other politically powerful organizations (such as corporations).[50] The only rivals to the chambers as economic bodies were sector-based organizations, and societies for improvement, invention, or 'philosophical' discourse (scientific and technological discussions): as in the case of the Society of Arts, Royal Society, Agricultural Improvement Societies, some of the literary societies that had broader remits. The chambers were thus one outcome, but also contributors, to emerging associational action.

Meister has suggested that campaign bodies are most intensely developed by those most affected, those with greatest aspiration, and where there is greatest heterogeneity of the milieu so that voice has greater need for separate representation.[51] Chambers seem to reflect this more general pattern of membership by those with high exposure to loss/risk, aspiration, and need for separate voice above the clamour. Clearly it is not possible at this distance in time to know the allegiances and personal commitments of all the members of the early chambers. But it is possible to assess three critical dimensions using case studies: campaigners, religion, and wider networks.

Campaign activists

Campaigners can be identified in a number of ways, but one of the most clear-cut for chambers is to cross-relate political petitioning with chamber membership, since both petitioners and chambers were based in a locality. Petitions were very important in this period, and those on economic matters were almost always responses to potential economic harm, losses, and government 'bads'; hence, they are key reflections of anger and alarm, and a good indicator of endogenous political commitments.[52] As shown in Chapter 4, petitions were a major activity of early chamber leaders. Two case studies, of the first British mainland chambers, Liverpool and Manchester, are used to take understanding of chamber activism further.

For Liverpool we can cross-relate the chamber and petitioning movements at five critical junctures: the 1765 Stamp Act lobby; a 1766 petition thanking the Liverpool MP, William Meredith, for his 'endeavours in obtaining the repeal of the Stamp Act'; a petition for Free Ports in Jamaica and Dominica in 1773; the conciliatory petition in 1775 on America; and a 1780 attack on offices following Burke's attempt at electoral Reform.[53] The Stamp Act and Free Ports activity indicate the political activism of chamber members before they had the chamber as an outlet.

---

[49] Clark (2000a), p. 152.

[50] See Rogers (1989); O'Gorman (1989); Langford (1991).

[51] See Chapter 4; also Meister (1984), chapter 4.

[52] Of course economic alarms may be exaggerated; they are distinct from general petitions that sought desirable reforms, where losses and risks for the petitioner were usually minimal: see Hansen (1985); Kahnemann and Tversky (1979); Bargar (1956); Olson (1973, 1979); Bradley (1986, 1990).

[53] Fuller discussion, and listing of which members signed each petition, in Bennett (2010).

The totals of the Liverpool petitioners in 1765, 1766, 1773, 1775, and 1780 were, respectively, 115, 164, 55, 215, and 177. This gives some measure of the scale of campaign activism among the general Liverpool population at the time over major but specialized economic issues; it constituted only about 1–2% of the city's business population, and less than 10% of the freeman electors. But the chamber members were among the most active: they were 24%, 18%, 53%, 10%, and 18% of the signatures in each respective case. The chamber activists were also large proportions of the chamber membership: 45%, 47%, 45%, 34%, and 34% of the members signed each of these respective petitions. The campaign activism is also indicated by the chamber itself petitioning separately from the general city petition on peace in 1775, and later again on Free Ports. Hence the early Liverpool chamber was composed of some of the most politically active. Further analysis shows that the merchants and bankers were the most politically active in both the chamber and in the city, and were a much higher proportion of the partnership businesses petitioning (25–40%, depending on petition) compared to the petitioners as a whole (20% and in line with the city businesses as a whole: see Table 14.2). This confirms the expectation that the most active are likely to be those exposed to the largest risk of losses and with the most at stake.

For Manchester we can compare two campaigns: the Stamp Act petition in 1765, and 1775 petitioning for conciliation in America. Two comparisons are made: to the 1774 known membership, and to the full 1781 membership. The chamber petitioners as a proportion of the signatories in each case were: 38/21% in 1765 and 3/10% in 1775. The proportion of members signing was high: 59/25% in 1765 and 24/24% in 1775. The chamber members were thus highly politically active, with similar proportions as in Liverpool. The Manchester chamber petitioners were also more commonly from partnership businesses than the petitioners as a whole (59/32% in 1765, and 46/52% partnerships in 1775, compared to about 21% partnership petitioners from the city, the same as the city proportion of businesses).

The close similarity of these proportions in Manchester and Liverpool is suggestive that a more general pattern of chamber campaign activism may have been present. It has not been possible to trace petitioning in all the chambers, but a further indicator is for Belfast, where a petition of 1777 regarding flax seed was signed by 22 of the chamber members of 1783 (33%), which form 61% of the petitioners. Similarly in 1780, 35% of the chamber members signed a petition about export bounties on linen, forming 68% of the petitioners.[54] The proportions are even higher than Liverpool and Manchester. The strong relation of activists to the chambers, and the chambers' members being more active than the general population, especially for larger businesses, confirms the role of leadership from business elites. This phenomenon of a 'politically activist elite' is rather a different political movement from that investigated in most academic studies reviewed in

---

[54] Comparison of chamber subscribers list 1783, with 1777 petition reproduced in Belfast chamber *Journal*, March (1927), p. 184; 1780 petition in Chambers (1983), chamber history, p. 2.

Chapter 3, and reiterates the favour of chambers for 'reform activism' noted in Chapter 4.

Religion and dissenters

Religious dissenters have been claimed to be the critical leaders of many of the protests and reform initiatives of the 18th and 19th centuries. They were certainly leading figures in many more populist campaigns (such as Wilkes's activities 1769–76, Wyvell's County Association 1780, and the anti-slavery movement of 1787–1807). Dissenters were also very active in societies, which provided access and opportunities as 'a neutral arena: territory where political and social contact between landed and elite families could be maintained . . . without risk of political acrimony'.[55]

One set of explanations for the emergence of chambers and similar bodies is that they were part of a search for political expression by groups that felt unrepresented by the political system,[56] and that chambers offered opportunities for dissenters, and for Catholics in the Irish chambers.[57] The general pattern for the earliest chambers and Stamp Act movement is shown in Table 14.4. This demonstrates that dissenters were indeed disproportionately large in membership in all cases examined, and especially in the Stamp Act protests, as noted in Chapter 4.

This disproportionate representation needs careful interpretation. It is easy to be misled by the language of government supporters, which routinely claimed dangers from 'papists' or 'radicals' (often a synonym for dissenters) because this resonated with the fears at Westminster. The argument that dissenters and Catholics were excluded from other societies is also exaggerated; only the most voluble and fervent were excluded.[58] For the Stamp Act and other lobbies of 1765–75 Watson argues that dissenters were disintegrating as a unified group, and were used as a set of networks by Rockingham and others, rather than as a specific 'interest' that had to be mediated.[59] Moreover the evidence adduced of dissenters as key forces is patchy. Bradley's large-scale study, which shows strong dissenter support for petitioning in favour of concessions to America among shopkeepers and artisans, in only a few cases demonstrates this for merchants who were the main chamber members. Merchants generally formed similar proportions of dissenting (10.9%) and other denominations (11%) in favour of conciliation in America, and also for coercion (19.3% and 17.1% respectively).[60] This does not justify claims of striking contrasts as far as the significant business community was concerned.

Indeed the central criticism of the claim that dissenters were a dominant force in chambers is that they needed a *general unity* requiring a level of inclusiveness in

---

[55] Clark (2000a), p. 80; also Black (1963); Christie (1962, 1982); Bradley (1990); Langford (1989).
[56] Checkland (1952, 1958); Hilton (1977, 2006); Bradley (1986, 1990).
[57] See chamber histories for Birmingham; and Cork, Dublin, Belfast, Waterford.
[58] Butterfield (1957); Olson (1973); Langford (1991), pp. 76 and 82.
[59] Watson (1968), pp. 65 ff.
[60] Bradley (1990), table 10.5.

Table 14.4. Percentage of dissenters in a sample of Stamp Act groups and early chambers in Britain and America 1763–1775

	%	N
British Stamp Act delegates 1765	52.2	23
Liverpool Stamp Act Committee 1765	35.3	17
Boston BSETC 1763	56.9	42
Liverpool chamber 1774–84	31.4	88
Manchester chamber 1775–81	31.5	130
New York and Charleston chambers 1775	30.8	13

Note: These are approximate maxima in each case as all affiliations are not certain.
Sources: As in Table 14.3; and TNA RG 4-6.

their area for credible lobbying. Thus in Liverpool, where Checkland argued that the corporation and established Church were aligned, and dissenters worked from outside to challenge slavery, the corporation, and established mercantilist positions,[61] the chamber members were associated with both points of view: involving a high proportion of dissenters and a few Catholics but also working for reform of the Anglican vestry, and containing both pro and anti-slave trade abolitionists.[62] Similarly in Birmingham, much emphasis has been put on the role of the dissenters,[63] but detailed examination of the chamber shows it tempered dissenting views with the needs of businesses (especially through Matthew Boulton).[64] Whilst the closely linked Lunar Society had ambitious dissenter objectives, particularly through the uncompromising Joseph Priestley, Garbett (an Anglican) and other chamber leaders tried to establish 'unity' whatever their personal views. Of the identifiable members of the Birmingham chamber in 1783, and after 1790, only a minority can be identified as dissenters. In Manchester, the extreme and uncompromising views of the dissenter Thomas Walker led to his ostracism from the chamber.[65] In Belfast, Waddell Cunningham, chamber president in 1783–91, was a prominent radical, chair of the subscribers to celebrate the anniversary of the French Revolution in 1791, but was also leader of the Belfast volunteers to resist the French landing at Bantry Bay in 1796. He and the chamber were protesters, but loyalists.

More recent analysis of Liverpool shows where the role of dissenters chiefly lay. About 31% of the chamber's known and probable members were dissenters, much higher than the city's population of about 10%, and their networks were interwoven with other societies and trading structures. The first chair, John Dobson, and treasurer, Arthur Heywood, were dissenters. But the main effect seems to have been

---

[61] Checkland (1952), especially pp. 61–7.
[62] Bennett (2010), pp. 49–53, 113–16; 44% of chamber dissenter members were slave traders.
[63] Bowden (1919–20, 1965); Norris (1957), Money (1977).
[64] See discussion by Uglow (2002).
[65] See Chapter 9.

through their activism: dissenters were between one and a half and two times more likely to petition than Anglicans.[66] Within the chamber their role appears to have been primarily catalytic on the general body; they provided one of many important networks of trusted relationships, and were one of the main forces stimulating, but not controlling, the chamber's activism.

In the case of the American chambers, it was Anglicans who were primarily involved in leadership of early chambers and concerned with moderating the radicals to maintain links with England. There may even be a case that in New York the established Church interests to some extent put off the dissenters from the chamber. The chamber's leaders were closely associated with the 'De Lancey' party and Episcopalianism, which led to extreme local disputes.[67] But the chamber as a whole had a diverse make-up, including Anglican reformers and Huguenots.

Those cases where religion did play a significant role were almost entirely confined to Ireland, with its unique community tensions. In Dublin, there were many dissenters and radicals, including the president Travers Hartley, as well as a few Catholics. After the 1800 Act of Union tensions became progressively more acute. The attempt to revive the Dublin chamber in 1805, for example, was seen as sectarian by the ministers of the time: 'some advertisers [for the chamber] are Catholics and some of violent politics'.[68] Sectarian tensions, convolved with politics, contributed to Cork's foundation in 1819, but caused increasing tensions after 1852, leading to a split of the chamber in 1882. Although both Cork chambers were nominally non-sectarian, the old chamber was predominantly at least 'patriotic' (i.e. in favour of independence) and the new Incorporated chamber more loyalist. In Waterford and Limerick, although having large Catholic member-ships, the chambers also included protestants, dissenters, and Quakers. Hence, even in Ireland, the chambers generally attempted to stay above sectarian pressures, working for a general 'unity'.

Business networks

One aspect of solidarity needs further investigation: whether the networks of relationships between the businesses that were members of chambers existed in sufficient density to have facilitated chamber development. There has been exten-sive academic discussion of business networks, as both formal (i.e. contractual) and informal (resting on personal and untraded dependencies). As reviewed in Chapter 3, it has been claimed that such networks facilitate innovation, lend competitive advantage by reducing search and information costs, may facilitate knowledge transfer and financial intermediation, and may have provided chambers with 'trust goods'. A chamber may enhance all these possibilities. Chambers are concerned with not just individuals but also with the *system* of transactions: the horizontal and *collective relations* between firms, for close competitors and in

---

[66] A statistically significant difference: Bennett (2010), pp. 113–16 and 126–8.
[67] Flick (1901), pp. 18–22; also Stevens (1867).
[68] Letter from Rochfort to John Foster MP, 1 April 1805; PRONI D207/33/24.

The Members

unrelated industries. This offers advantages from the collectively reduced costs of the environment of decisions affecting local contracts and trading decisions, particularly information costs. This is a critical distinction between a general association that interlocks with many networks, such as a chamber, and a specific industry combination that seeks to control markets and prices.[69]

Historically, at the core of many chamber networks was the concept of the 'industrial district'. Originally recognized by Marshall in 1919, 'districts' were a commonplace of contemporary views. Sheffield cutlery, West Riding textiles, Manchester cotton, and so forth, were all well-known 'local district brands' that marketed the industrial character and products of their area.[70] Marshall argued that they were locations for rapid diffusion of innovations, and external agglomeration economies.[71] These were the locations where chambers could be readily grafted onto the 'district' brand; and the two should have been mutually self-reinforcing. This was very important in the manufacturing areas as the chambers developed.

Many chamber histories comment selectively on the networks that underpinned their districts, but the only systematic analysis of chamber interlocks is that for Liverpool. The first Liverpool chamber demonstrates that both formal and informal networks were important between the chamber members, and were particularly dense between the main committee members, having multiple links and chains of ties directly, and through other chamber members and their families.[72] This was through both open societies (such as the Subscription Library, Sefton Mock Corporation, Philharmonic Society) and the most exclusive societies in the city (such as the Ugly Face Society and Unanimous Society). There were also many links through families and intermarriages, through religious affiliations, and most frequent of all through formal economic ties of formal business partnerships and apprenticeships.

Indeed, analysis of other historical networks also suggests that economic ties and formal partnerships were as important as personal relationships.[73] In cases such as Yorkshire textiles or Lancashire cotton, for example, adaptive networking rather than sustained social structures was critical to stimulation of competition in order to obtain competitive advantage to link to market needs, and produce in the right quantities, to the specific technical specification required to meet time demands for shipment and delivery,[74] with these formal relationships also underpinning credit networks between producers, intermediaries, and consumers.[75]

This is a field where further research is required, but local chamber histories and the analysis presented here show that the early activists that established chambers

[69] See Chapter 3, and e.g. Williamson (1985, 1993); Langlois and Robertson (1995); Jones (1997).
[70] e.g. Norris (1957); Money (1977); Pearson and Richardson (2001); Sunley (1992); Mathias (2000); Morgan (2000); Popp (2003, 2005); Wilson and Popp (2003a, 2003b).
[71] Marshall (1919).
[72] Detailed interlocks for Liverpool chamber members are given in Bennett (2010), pp. 91–128; see also Haggerty (2002, 2006); Haggerty and Haggerty (2010).
[73] Popp and Wilson (2003, 2007, 2009); see also Daunton (1977, 1996); Haggerty (2006).
[74] Sigsworth (1958); Heaton (1965), pp. 293–393; Smail (1994, 1999), pp. 149–51; Hudson (1986).
[75] Price (1978, 1980); Langford (1991).

drew on a wide range of close economic and social networks which would have made it easier to form opinion, frame a 'unity' of views, and manage internal dissent. But these networks were not the sole preserve of the chambers. Many networks existed with no strong chamber interlock, and many leading members of the chambers were not interlocked through networks to other members. Hence, networks and interlocked allegiances were important in early chambers, but were not sufficient to explain the whole membership structure of interests. In Liverpool, the networks (both economic and social) probably linked about one-half of the chamber members, although were strongest among the most significant committee members.

14.4 MEMBER CHARACTERISTICS UP TO THE PRESENT 1: GEOGRAPHY

How did the membership of chambers develop to become the modern structure? The early chambers established a brand strongly identified with the locality, the *general* interests of the area, and a unity that sought to be above sectors and other distinctions. This evolved with the changing geography of local economies and other aspects of member interests.

Area and territory

The fundamental definition of membership of chambers has remained the locality or region: their geography. But as the *system* of chambers evolved critical questions emerged about the extent of local recruitment and involvement: for what territory was the interest defined? At the same time, the national system of chambers had to manage an increasingly diverse range of differently constituted bodies reflecting increasingly diverse local views. This inevitably raised the question of boundaries: where did one locality stop and another begin? As shown in Chapter 8, the national bodies were largely unable to control boundaries; the number of chambers and their size range continued to increase, and their purpose diversified. If there was a 'certain type' of interest that defined a chamber, it was becoming differentiated and competed for. In a voluntary system, until the more effective efforts following the ABCC *Development Strategy* from 1991, and control of title after 1999, a chamber was where a local group of leaders wanted it to be, doing what they wanted it to do.

The earliest enunciation of the principle by which a chamber defined its territory compared to other chambers was spelled out by London in 1886: 'if any area was to be fixed, in order that the chambers could cover a greater surface than at present, that was a matter to be settled by the delegates of the various districts. The principle town in which chambers existed might form the nucleus of the extensions.'[76] This

---

[76] K. B. Murray, quoted in London *CCJ*, August (1886), p. 54.

specified the definition as local, voluntary, and town or city based. This remained the dominant view until the 1990s.

The evolving 'geography of interest'

A simple way of grasping the evolving 'geography of interest' is shown in Table 14.5, which classifies geographical catchments claimed by chambers into cities and towns on the one hand, and counties or larger regions on the other. To this simple classification is added a split of the city/town chambers into three groups depending on the size of their local population at the specified date.[77] The 25,000 population criterion was suggested by the ABCC Improvements Committee in 1922; the 100,000 population criterion is approximately equal to the threshold of 10,000 businesses suggested in the 1991 ABCC *Development Strategy*.

Table 14.5 shows that for a long period the chambers were based largely on the cities and towns. Even though some had 'country' members from further afield, the 'interest' was places not areas; and chambers were open to those 'interested in the prosperity of that district'.[78] Few chambers claimed a territory that stretched as large as a county, and none covered an area larger than one county until the 1990s. A few titles used 'and district', and some brought together two small towns (Aldershot and Farnborough in the 1930s), but these all related to very small towns. Thus Swindon was defined as 'businesses in or near Swindon interested in the commercial prosperity of the borough' in 1920;[79] Burnley was defined as the Poor Law union district in 1902.[80] Indeed, some city chambers were under pressure not to move beyond their boundaries and embrace wider areas: when Coventry was considering new office accommodation in 1969, a possible move outside the city 'caused concern to our members and the local authority alike'.[81] Birmingham was the exception in the 1860s, sometimes claiming to be the 'chamber of commerce for Birmingham and the Midland District', especially when it was writing to ministers, but this was based on only limited regional cover.[82] Similarly London began to claim a much larger territory and to seek members from the whole country from *c.*1902, but its market penetration outside the capital was always thin.

This pattern was even truer in Ireland, where there has been no modern reform of local government. Chambers have remained largely city and town based, with county and regional chambers generally resisted. Efforts by the association to widen catchments to embrace smaller affiliate chambers have accelerated since the 1990s,

---

[77] All population data are standardized, as described in Appendix 3.

[78] As defined by Kendal chamber, minutes 9 February 1857.

[79] Swindon chamber, *Annual Report* (1920), inside front cover.

[80] Report of meeting, 22 March 1902; papers in Burnley history, at Burnley library.

[81] Coventry chamber, *Annual Report* (1969).

[82] Title used in inviting the Chancellor of Exchequer (Gladstone) to a banquet: letter reported in Birmingham chamber, Council minutes, 16 November 1862. Jackson (1950, figure 74) shows that the Birmingham membership in 1947 was essentially in Birmingham, plus West Bromwich, Stourbridge, and Redditich.

Table 14.5. Number of chambers of commerce (CC) and chambers of trade (CoT) with different geographical definitions at each time period, 1790–2010

	Counties or larger areas (CC only)	Channel Isles and IoM (CC only)	Towns/cities over 100,000 population		Towns of 25,000–100,000 population		Towns less than 25,000 population	
			CC	CoT	CC	CoT	CC	CoT
1790	—	2	— (1)	—	7 (1)	—	0	—
1815	—	2	4 (1)	—	5 (2)	—	2	—
1860	2	3	10 (1)	—	20 (3)	—	7 (1)	—
1900	2	3	27 (1)	4	30 (4)	23	18 (2)	41
1920	5	3	44 (1)	8	40 (4)	70	20 (4)	220
1930	7	3	53 (1)	10	39 (4)	80	15 (7)	266
1950	10	3	52 (2)	12	34 (5)	126	13 (20)	457
1983	13	3	56 (2)	n/a	28 (6)	n/a	3 (34)	n/a
1995	29	3	38 (2)	n/a	4 (7)	n/a	— (61)	n/a
2010	30	3	19 (2)	c.41	1 (8)	c.230	— (80)	c.320

Notes: Irish Republic chambers shown in brackets (not differentiated into CC or CoT). All numbers approximate. General Chamber, and Weskett's London chamber of 1782–1800, excluded.

and became more formalized since 2005 (see Chapter 8), but have met with little success. Dublin is covered by four county chambers (at least two of which are large bodies), and efforts to consolidate these have been resisted, though the chambers have strongly supported proposals for a mayor for the whole metropolitan area.[83] The 123 Irish Urban Districts and Town Councils continue to be the chief focus of the main chambers.

Before and after the 1991 Development Strategy

The only early UK cases of larger chamber territories were special cases: Staffordshire, which really only covered the pottery towns and was later called North Staffordshire up to the present; South of Scotland covered a network of small manufacturing towns in an otherwise rural area (Hawick, Galashiels, and Peebles) from the 1850s until the 1990s. After about 1910 some larger areas developed. The first two county chambers were the special case of Isle of Wight (1910), then Northamptonshire (1916), which had subsections for Kettering, Wellingborough, and Rushden, as a focused manufacturing association for boot and shoe manufacture (which constituted 60% of members, and 83% if related heel, polish, hide, and cardboard box manufacture are included).

[83] See e.g. *Irish Times*, 23 October 2007, 'Electing a mayor'; 24 February 2010, 'Will Dublin's new boss be a total mayor'.

By 1930 a few city chambers started to target their counties (Derby and Derby-shire, Leicester and County), a few larger places merged (Newcastle and Gateshead in about 1917), and Chester and North Wales (in 1921). Hereford proposed forming a Three-Counties chamber with Worcester and Gloucester in 1937.[84] But by 1960 only two county chambers had been added: Gloucester and County, Newport and Monmouth; though there were many of the smaller chambers that had added 'and district' to their titles. By 1970 the only further county-sized additions were Burton-on-Trent and South Derbyshire; Inverness and Highland; Luton, Dunstable, and District; Northern Ireland, covering the whole Province; and Perthshire.

The situation is shown clearly in the map used for the 1991 ABCC *Development Strategy*, shown in Figure 14.2. This can be compared with the early period in Figure 14.1. Based on a survey of statements by chief executives who drew their boundaries on maps, Figure 14.2 shows that even in 1990 chambers were chiefly focused on individual towns and cities as their 'core' territory, and for the largest cities little had changed from 1790. Many chambers claimed wider areas as their 'outer limits', mainly related to local government at the second tier level of counties.[85] But it was unclear that these were areas of marketing or 'interest' representation; they appeared to be chiefly more passive territories that were sometimes addressed when needed. Moreover, some of the map had no chamber coverage at all, whilst other areas had overlap and competition between chambers. In several places quite important and large chambers were encircled by others; Greenock, and Paisley, by Glasgow; Croydon, and Westminster, by London.

The anomalies between core and wider claimed catchments were greatest for London, which claimed a territory out to the M25, historically defined as 'a radius of 25 miles from its address', but was really only effectively covering the main business districts of central London, where it competed with chambers at West-minster and Croydon. Taking London's M25 claim, it only managed a 2.9% market penetration in 1990; restricting it to a more realistic core area of central London raised this to 27%. Moreover, the unrealistic claims of many chambers undermined the capacity to understand where the gaps in market lay. If London was really to cover the territory to the M25, to achieve a national target market penetration of 10% required it to increase membership by over 13,000: triple its membership at the time, and over half of the total new members needed from the whole of Britain to bring the chambers up to a target of 10% coverage. London's ambitious claims therefore held back understanding of the system's needs. As shown in Figure 14.2, the main gaps were for the more dispersed areas based on smaller towns, and the rural areas. This coverage remains challenging.

In contrast, the geography of the chambers of trade was unambiguous: all were based in towns and cities and none claimed county or large territories.[86] The

---

[84] Reported in Worcester chamber minutes, 28 September 1937, who supported the idea.

[85] This survey was constructed by sending to all chambers a large-scale map of Britain and asking them to mark on it their core areas for representation and service activities.

[86] There were some larger chamber of trade areas, but these were federations of smaller chambers; as in Yorkshire, and South Wales; these are excluded from Table 14.5; see Chapter 2.

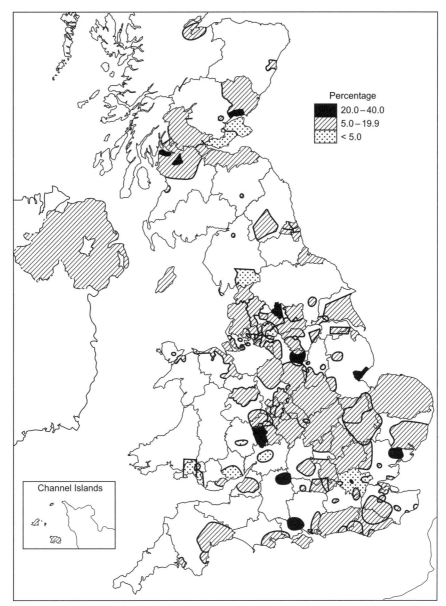

Fig. 14.2. Chamber 'core' territories in 1990, and density of market penetration as a percentage of local businesses of one employee or greater. (*Source*: survey of chamber chief executives, in ABCC *Development Strategy*: Bennett 1991).

resulting geography was a system of chambers that by the 1920s–1930s had a strongly developed presence in almost all settlements of 25,000 and upward (see Figure 5.5), but with overlaps and competition developing between the different chamber concepts. This is comparable to the pattern in the US, where again there was great variety, with complex names and territories, ranging from the very large to the very small, down to settlements of 300 in population (e.g. in several Nebraska 'villages').[87] These developments demonstrate the endemic fragmentation of a voluntary system with no controls on market entry.

A fundamental change towards a systematic structure based on larger areas began in the 1990s, chiefly as a result of the ABCC *Development Strategy* of 1991, and pressure from TECs and Business Links to merge boundaries using different territories after 1991–3.[88] The result has been that from 1998 the whole country has been covered mainly by chambers at the level of county, or groups of counties, as shown in Figure 14.3 for 2003. An analysis of 'optimal' chamber territories by Bratton confirms that counties or groups of counties generally provided the strongest basis for coverage at the levels of market penetration chambers achieve.[89]

The ABCC 1991 Development Strategy showed that with no systematic link of chambers to a single type of territory it was very difficult to assess chamber market penetration. Indeed when chambers wanted to quote high penetration rates they generally quoted their narrower 'core' areas. The market penetration shown in 1990 in Figure 14.2 demonstrates that often the densest development was in the smallest areas, with county and other larger areas generally achieving a more intermediate level close to the national average of 6–8%.

Figure 14.3 shows the later development of chamber areas and market penetration in 2003. The consolidation of the chambers into predominantly county areas is notable; the map is now mainly covered; and market penetration has become more uniform. Since 2003, further consolidation has occurred, chiefly in the metropolitan areas, with a single Manchester chamber formed for the whole conurbation, and smaller mergers elsewhere. Though in other places de-consolidation has also occurred, with Kent and Hampshire having more chambers operating than in 2003.[90]

Trading across boundaries

The convention between chambers was that they did not compete with each other: interest was defined by territory and a business from another area approaching a chamber would be cross-referred. The ABCC rule was that 'a member desiring information should go to the secretary of his own chamber, who if he had not the desired information would go to other chambers. . . . These sources of information failing, he should then address his enquiries to this Association. It was not considered

---

[87] See listings in US Department of Commerce (1923).
[88] See Chapters 8 and 13.
[89] Bratton (2000).
[90] The contemporary position can be viewed on the BCC website.

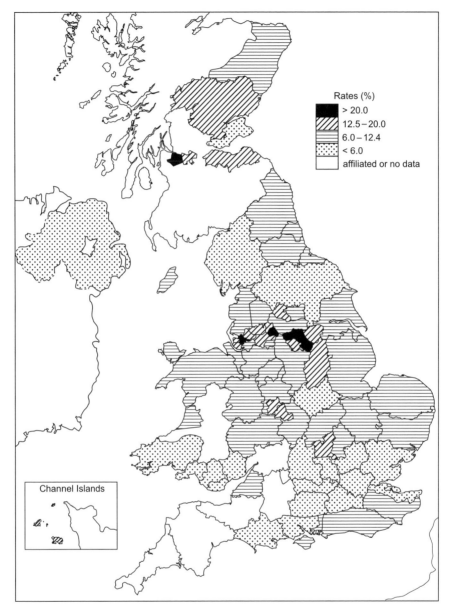

Fig. 14.3. Territories of accredited BCC chambers in 2003, and density of market penetration as a percentage of local businesses of one employee or greater.

desirable that a member of one chamber of commerce should apply direct to others
. . . of which he is not a member.'[91] The same rules were (and are) used in Ireland.

There was also a 'London rule' established in 1944, that the ABCC agreed not to
admit any chamber into membership within 20 miles radius of the City;[92] later
extended to 25 miles. This limited the efforts of Westminster to join ABCC in
1955, when the London chamber pushed the ABCC council to refuse.[93] But there
was much reluctance to support London's claims, and several ABCC council
members 'expressed doubts whether an area so large as London could efficiently
be served by [only] one chamber'.[94] Confidentially to the ABCC council, it was
agreed to allow Westminster to issue certificates of origin.[95]

If the space was uncontested (by an ABCC affiliate), then a chamber could
generally move into it. Although there were some conventions between the NCT
and ABCC, these were generally ineffective. As a result some chambers did set out
on more aggressive strategies. The Huddersfield chamber, under a very entrepreneurial chief executive in the 1980s–90s, Keith Welton, became the Kirklees and
Wakefield chamber, and then the Mid Yorkshire chamber, expanded its territory
wherever it could, steadily closed in on Barnsley, Leeds, and Bradford and took over
many small historic chambers. The Walsall chamber under another aggressive chief
executive, David Frost, later to become BCC director general, expanded into
Staffordshire and Shropshire in the 1980s and 1990s, and tried to move into
many other areas: other chambers in the region called Walsall the 'great white
whale' that could turn up anywhere.[96]

London was particularly aggressive in its early years, recruiting from all over the
country in 1911. Birmingham accused it of 'systematic canvassing' in its area as
well as in Newcastle, Manchester, and other places, and making 'derogatory
statements' about its *Journal* compared with London's. London agreed to withdraw
derogatory advertisements by its canvasser, and claimed it was not undertaking
systematic canvassing, though it did not apologize.[97] Other areas arranged boundary demarcation agreements: e.g. Coventry managed to achieve a 'gradual increase
[in membership] following the agreement on boundaries with the Birmingham
chamber' in 1969.[98]

Careful co-working also developed. Collaboration was advocated by ABCC from
the 1920s, but was difficult and often foundered on problems of sharing subscriptions and members. When pressure from Burton-on-Trent grew in 1936 for its
own chamber, Derby (which had covered the area) initially resisted but was not able

[91] ABCC, Home Affairs Committee, minutes, 3 October 1923.
[92] London chamber, Council minutes, 9 May 1944; this noted that for over 30 years the chamber had claimed this area regarding certificate issuing; MS 16459/23.
[93] ABCC, Executive minutes, 6 April and 4 May 1955; London chamber, Council minutes, 16 June 1955; MS 16459/28.
[94] ABCC, Executive minutes, 6 April 1955.
[95] ABCC, Executive minutes, 7 September 1955.
[96] Interview comments at Birmingham chamber 1989.
[97] Birmingham chamber, Council minutes, 7 and 11 November 1911.
[98] Coventry chamber, *Annual Report* (1929), p. 2.

to continue to make an effective offer and so had to permit a separate chamber to develop; it initially suffered only 9 resignations (3% of its membership), showing that a more local presence stimulated recruitment. It came to a management agreement with Burton to offer services.[99] Other successful management agreements were for Dudley, Kidderminster, and Worcester with Birmingham for subscription collection and some other services in the 1970s, 1980s, and 1990s; Sheffield administered Chesterfield in 1930s; Manchester ran a Salford chamber in the 1980s; and London ran an East London chamber in the 1990s. Some were very successful. Birmingham's agreement with Dudley began in 1974 when it had 200 members; this increased to 900 members in 1978 as a result of using a recruitment agent and offering Birmingham's services.[100] But there were tensions of identity. Some lasted but others were less successful. Thus Sheffield's exploration with Chesterfield, Rotherham, and Barnsley in 1929 offered Sheffield's services to firms that joined the chamber from the other areas; they remained members of their local chamber, with Sheffield paying back to the other chambers their local subscription. This only appealed to Chesterfield.[101]

The modern format was established in both Britain and Ireland in the 1993 *Codes of Practice*.[102] These accepted that a business could join any chamber, but chambers should not canvass outside their core areas. When approached by a business from another area, a chamber was to make the other chamber's presence known, and a check made with the other chamber to confirm that there were no outstanding subscriptions or misdemeanours. Boundaries were to be mutually agreed, with the association resolving disputes as part of the accreditation process, and would accept only one accredited chamber for any area, which ABCC/CI would then defend.

Chamber size and market penetration

Once chamber territories were defined it becomes possible to assess how successful they were in recruiting the businesses in their areas; in modern terminology what is their market penetration, the 'local interest' they encompass, and hence their credibility or legitimacy.[103] Market penetration became an explicit governmental concern following BoT involvement in 'approving' chambers after 1917, with each chamber asked to provide information on 'the extent to which they are representative of their district'.[104] As noted by Exeter in 1930, 'the failure of so many important firms to take an active part in local chambers . . . render these bodies

---

[99] Derby chamber minutes, 1936–7.

[100] Worcester chamber minutes, reporting on a visit to Dudley chamber, 3 August 1978.

[101] Sheffield chamber, Council minutes and Membership Committee, 28 January 1929.

[102] ABCC (1993), *Code of Practice: Chamber Boundaries, Relationships and Titles;* Chambers Ireland (1993), *Chamber Development Manual.*

[103] Cohen and Rogers (1992, pp. 433–6) argue that deep market penetration is essential to be called a *representative* body; also Bowman (1989); Coleman (1988); Sadowski and Jacobi (1991); Greenwood, Grote, and Ronit (1992); McLaughlin, Jordan, and Maloney (1993); Bennett (1996a, 1998a).

[104] Quoted in Birmingham chamber, Council minutes, 26 February 1917.

less effective'.[105] Bristol in 1903 sought increases in membership 'thereby enlarging the sphere of the chamber's usefulness'.[106] Galway in 1924 saw a ratio of one member for every 200 inhabitants as a target all chambers should reach, which it had already achieved.[107]

Figure 14.4 shows the evolution of market penetration by chambers of commerce, and the sample of major chambers of trade. In this comparison market penetration is not calculated against the total potential business population of an area, because no long-term data exist on business population. Instead a surrogate, the Census population, is used, since this is available over the whole period. Most remarkable about Figure 14.4 is the relatively constant proportions that cover a period of over 200 years. Chambers achieved 1.4–2.2 penetration on this index over 1790–1900; this changed only slightly to 1.6–2.4% for the re-based population index for 1914–2005. The only difference from this narrow pattern has been in 1995–2005. The dominant trend is therefore for the chamber membership to expand as the population has expanded, maintaining a relatively constant proportionality: 'organic growth'.

Across this trend there are four points to note. First, as populations expanded rapidly in the early 19th century, chamber memberships lagged up to 1840, but then expanded as many more chambers emerged in smaller locations where deeper

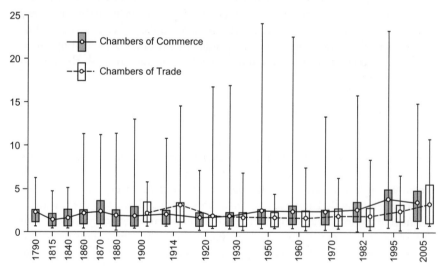

Fig. 14.4. Market penetration of chambers of commerce and chambers of trade 1790–2005. Chamber members per 1000 of the local Census population mean, range from minimum to maximum, and 20%/80% box plots. (Note re-basing of population in 1914; see Appendix 3.)

[105] Exeter chamber, *Annual Report* (1930), p. 20.
[106] Bristol chamber, *Annual Report* (1903), p. 44.
[107] Galway chamber history, Woodman (2000), p. 163.

penetration was possible in the 1860s and 1870s. There was, however, a small decline in the 1880–1900, with market penetration picking up again through the 20th century. Second, the larger chambers of trade had higher market penetration than other chambers in early years (1900–1920). Third, the range of market penetration widened until the 1950s, but has narrowed over 1914–20, and after 1960; with the chambers of trade generally having a much narrower range than the chambers of commerce reflecting the wider diversity of the latter. Fourth, the take-off in market penetration in 1995–2005 seems to have been short-lived; calculations on the BCC chambers for 2010 indicate a return to about 2.4%. As noted in later discussion, the period 1995–2005 was exceptional in many ways for chambers.

The index of market penetration used above, of chamber members per thousand local population, is somewhat unsatisfactory since it does not directly measure penetration of the business population. For the modern period it is possible to calculate direct market penetration of the business population, as shown in Table 14.6. This confirms the remarkable stability of market penetration, even over the shorter period available. There was a period of significant expansion in the 1990s as a result of two factors: the internal reorganization and development of the chambers; and chamber alignment with TECs and Business Links. But the benefits were short-lived, returning to 1970s levels after 2008, and suffering further during the 2007–9 recession. The recent trends are challenging, but taking a long view, it appears that chambers are in some sort of equilibrium of the market penetration they can achieve. Indeed, for Liverpool chamber it has been suggested that there is an apparent ceiling, whatever the chamber does (although achieving 15–16% of businesses employing one person over the 2000s is high compared to many other chambers). John Entwistle, chair in the 1990s, also believed that the chamber could not grow unless local businesses or population grew.[108]

The fact that the chambers have had similar market penetration rates over most of their existence is quite extraordinary. Over these years the chamber system has fundamentally changed, businesses have profoundly changed, and the nature of the demand for voice has been reordered numerous times with changing government agendas and repertoires of contention; yet the 'interest' in the chambers has remained at a remarkably similar level. If this is a meaningful comparison, it suggests that an equilibrium of the chamber 'interest' has been maintained: *either* by a stable and enduring commitment of businesses to local territory, *and/or* that there has been a dynamic feedback between demand and supply whereby the chambers have adapted to new member demands and 'interests' by a changed supply mix. Can this be tested?

Adaptive interests, adaptive services, adaptive territories?

For the modern period, analyses of cross-sections of chamber membership in 1994 and 2006 have shown that there is a close relationship between the market

---

[108] Cherpeau (2010); and Entwistle, quoted in Cherpeau (2010), p. 66.

Table 14.6. Market penetration of members of chambers of commerce: chamber members as a percentage of local businesses that employ one person or more

Year	Market penetration (%)
1976	5.3
1979	5.9
1982	6.5
1989	7.9
1994	7.5
1998	7.9
2001	6.8
2005	5.9
2007	6.1
2010	4.5

Sources: chamber members from ABCC/BCC; ONS business population, earlier years estimated, see *Employment Gazette*, May (1990); Bennett (1991).

penetration of chambers and their type of service offer. There is a close association of market penetration with membership size only up to a certain area, generally about 1000 sq. km.[109] This is the area of the city of Bristol or the Isle of Wight. Up to this area, market penetration generally increases, but after 1000 sq. km. there is a decline of market penetration with increasing size of territory. This distinction seems to underpin two types of chambers. First, for geographically large markets (i.e. generally over 1000 sq. km.), penetration is influenced chiefly by the scale and range of services offered, though settlement concentration and local market potential have important secondary explanatory effects. Second, for small chamber areas, service range has little influence, but the compactness of geographical area is very important to achieving high penetration. For large cities in compact areas there are advantages of compactness, scale, and ability to make wide service offers; hence the high penetration of a city like Liverpool. But for large places over more dispersed catchments, it is more difficult to achieve deep penetration, as for many County areas. Thus compact area and services can be substitutes for each other in achieving market penetration for small and large chambers, respectively.

This distinction influences service potential. For large chambers, market penetration increases chiefly in association with increasing service volume and quality. For small chambers, intensity appears to derive from effective voice. These area differences reflect both environmental influences of how businesses and settlements are spread around the country, and endogenous choices by chambers to develop particular service mixes. The tension is evident in the case of Falmouth. A historic

---

[109] Bennett (1996a; 1996b; 1998a); Mekic (2007).

chamber of commerce in a very compact area, it was criticized in 1905 for too much concern with distant places and 'subjects from across the seas . . . without the funds to promote the welfare of anything'. What was needed instead was a 'body of men interested in the welfare of the town, who will not only talk . . . but do something to make the town more attractive to visitors'.[110]

Modern analyses suggest that that there are two types of member interest in chambers, which differentiates them into two categories, by service range and geographical area,[111] as shown in Table 14.7. This distinction was partially recognized in 1959 when ABCC attempted to differentiate the functions of large, medium, and small chambers, as shown in Table 8.1. It also reflects other analyses where the level of demand has been found to be a determinant of the extent of division of labour within clusters of firms.[112]

Type 1 are generally the large chambers offering a wide bundle of service, achieving moderate market penetration unless in compact areas; they achieve high total membership as a result of their large market areas. Their member 'type' responds to a wide bundle of services as well as local voice activism. This is the high demand type of chamber. *Type 2* are generally the small chambers that mainly supply voice. Their member 'type' will not support significant services; the chamber achieves high market penetration over a compact geographic area.

The distinctions between these two types are not always clear-cut, and will be affected by greater chamber-to-chamber cooperation, and federal or affiliated structures. Also, in a voluntary system, it is likely that chamber managers will seek to maximize on both criteria, with the two strategies not mutually exclusive; e.g. large chambers can introduce sections, sub-area groups, and localized networking events to try and achieve the benefits of compactness. The result may be attempts to achieve a third type of chamber, shown in the middle of the table.

Table 14.7. Different possible chamber types in relation to territory, services, membership size, and market penetration

	Type 1	Type 3	Type 2
	Wide service bundle	Narrow service bundle	No service bundle (only voice and social/peer support)
Large territory	Membership high Penetration medium	Membership low Penetration low	Membership low Penetration low
Small territory	Membership medium Penetration medium	Membership low Penetration low	Membership medium Penetration high

[110] *Falmouth Packet*, April 1905; Falmouth chamber, *Annual Report* (1901); quoted in Falmouth chamber history, pp. 36 and 33.
[111] Bennett (1996a, 1998b); Mekic (2007), chapters 5 and 6.
[112] e.g. Scott (1998); Wolfe and Gertler (2004); De Propris and Lazzeretti (2009).

Type 3 has a narrow service range extending over either large or small areas. This is usually an unsuccessful strategy, but it may exist for some locations and time periods. It may reflect protected chamber markets due to isolation (as in Isle of Wight, Shetland, Inverness, or South of Scotland), or inertia. As noted by the ABCC president in 1955, chambers 'cannot even be classified into two groups, large chambers and small chambers'.[113]

These conclusions reflect strongly the more general discussion in the literature. Olson has observed that the extent to which businesses have common interests or want to access collective services governs the size of membership and territories over which collective action occurs.[114] He argues that the smaller an area the greater is the potential for agreement on what constitutes common local needs and hence the higher the potential market penetration among the local constituency. Conversely, the larger the area the greater will be the total number of businesses, the greater will be the potential diversity of interests, hence the greater will be the number of businesses that will not benefit from a particular service or lobby position; thus membership size will be lower as a proportion of total potential membership.[115] An expansion of Olson's argument is that there may evolve separate chamber areas for different service or voice mixes. This is indeed confirmed by the historical evolution, and is a version of Olson's principle of 'fiscal equivalence'; each area is defined so that services offered are broadly in line with demand and the costs that can be borne (of membership subscriptions). Hence, fragmentation into different local chambers, even rival local chambers, expresses different potentials to mix voice and service offers. The chambers of trade and the chambers of commerce thus represent the coalescence around two 'systems' meeting both aspects of Olson's thesis.

14.5 MEMBER CHARACTERISTICS UP TO THE PRESENT 2: SECTOR, ORGANIZATION, AND SIZE

The early chamber brand was common *general* interests but depended heavily on the largest firms, leadership from the leading entrepreneurs, and chiefly the major merchants, banks, and manufacturers. As time progressed chambers were challenged in a wide range of directions, and had to evolve new means to define their membership (their 'interest'), and hence who was their target for marketing.

Sector demands, sector trends

The sector has become a well-recognized and widely used categorization of how business 'interest' is defined. It was particularly favoured after WW1 in the subsequent organization of the corporatist state, and this led to favour for sector-

---

[113] Sir Eric Carpenter, president of ABCC, confidential remarks at Annual Address, ABCC *Proceedings*, 5 July (1955), pp. 2–4; ABCC Executive minutes.
[114] Olson (1971), p. 171.
[115] Bennett (1998b), p. 506.

based over geographically based organizations by NEDC in the 1960s–70s, and often continues up to the present. These developments presented many challenges to how the chambers identified interests.

However, the chambers have adhered throughout to representing the general interest. In the 1920s, in a statement repeated frequently by Dunwoody, secretary of ABCC, it was asserted that chambers supported 'every class in the community . . . open to all good citizens, firms and corporations'.[116] As a result chambers continued to try to rise above sectors. Thus in the 1824 attempt to establish a London chamber, it was recognized that the chamber should 'not be exposed to the suspicion of interested or partial motives; . . . and resisting importunities which have for their object undue protection in favour of particular classes', where the 'exclusive interests' from specific sectors and large corporations must be avoided.[117] The Newport chamber in 1876 recognized the danger that 'for many years past it had almost been limited to one class of person. In fact it had almost become a marine board . . . [but] it was a society that ought to be encouraged by all parties engaged in trade'.[118] The Belfast chamber repeatedly quoted in its journal in the 1920s a statement by one of the American chambers, that a chamber was 'made up of numerous special interests, and is rightly the advocate of those interests up to the point where they claim more than a community can give them. Then and always a great chamber of commerce will represent the interest of the people as a whole rather than the interest of the (particular) groups.'[119]

Major changes in sector composition thus presented challenges for chambers. Even in mercantile trades there were extensive shifts in the balance between merchants and shippers from the 1820s. Expensive port infrastructure and the growth of steam motive power expanded into the coastal and European trades, and then from the 1850s began to make progressive inroads into long distance trades, requiring larger investment in shipping and docks. This also encouraged development of an 'industrialized' workforce to service the ports, ships, and related industries, which in turn induced a different membership 'interest' and priorities for local chamber voices. There was a shift from local elites led by merchants, to one led by ship-owners, shipbrokers and agents, dock industries, and others down the supply chain (such as mining industries).[120]

Good examples of the transitions are Cardiff and Liverpool, where chamber membership and leadership moved to the shippers and producers from the earlier merchants over 1850–1900.[121] In Dublin the shift in dominance of the chamber's council from the merchant, banker, and trader also led to a shift to a broader

---

[116] An article on 'Chambers of Commerce', carried in many chamber journals, e.g. Belfast chamber *Journal*, July (1924), pp. 51–2.

[117] Report of committee to form a London chamber, *Morning Chronicle*, 19 March 1824; see also comment within this report by George Hibbert.

[118] Newport chamber, minute book press cutting, report of meeting, 12 April 1876.

[119] Randolph Coolidge, president to the Providence (Rhode Island) chamber, quoted e.g. in Belfast chamber *Journal*, September (1923) p. 96, and subsequently.

[120] Jackson (2000).

[121] Daunton (1977); Cherpeau (2010).

business base and away from the strong conservatism and loyalism of the 1820–70 chamber.[122] Similarly in Leeds there was a shift in control from merchant to manufacturer over the 1850s–70s,[123] and the chamber rejected opening to retail members in 1856.[124] A vivid expression of the new muscle presented by the manufacturers is provided by the refounding statement of the Birmingham chamber in 1813, which saw the merchant and landed interests as more or less equal enemies in terms of lobbying: 'the members of that class of society of which the legislature is composed have seldom a personal acquaintance with trade. . . . Hence it has frequently happened that the interests of the manufacturing districts have been unintentionally sacrificed to erroneous commercial and political regulations, whilst the landed, the shipping, the colonial, and other . . . interests have been protected by their advocates in parliament'.[125]

In many places the industrial district came to dominate. Thus Kidderminster in 1900 made its test of market penetration that it 'believed that all carpet manufacturers and spinners in Kidderminster, Stourport and Bridgnorth with two exceptions . . . subscribe to the chamber'.[126] Luton in 1917 quoted 97% market penetration, whilst Barrow-in-Furness stated that only four or five significant firms were not members, which again equates to about 95% penetration.[127] Northamptonshire in 1919 sought to represent the shoe, hide, and leather industries as its main target.[128] North Staffordshire in the 1920s had 77% of members from pottery and earthenware manufacture, and linked its activities to all the national pottery bodies, hosting the National Council for the Pottery Industry.[129] Walsall had 92% manufacturing members in 1916, chiefly from diverse harness makers and small metal industries.[130] The strong focus of the industrial district chambers led to increasing pressures from the manufacturers for chambers to do more for them, and in some places there was rivalry or affiliation with the CBI.

Evolution of sector membership

But most chambers had complex mixes of sectors they had to manage. Figure 14.5 shows the evolution of sector composition of the chambers. Because of the imperfect character of information only four aggregate categories are shown. The dominance of commerce evident in the early years continued through most of the 19th century, becoming less than 50% of the average membership only by 1860, and manufacturing became the largest sector only by 1914. Manufacturing then remained the largest sector (averaging 42–8%) until the 1980s, when

---

[122] Cullen (1983), pp. 73–9.
[123] Beresford (1951), Leeds chamber history.
[124] Leeds chamber minutes, 13 February 1856.
[125] *Prospectus for Birmingham Chamber of Commerce*, 19 July 1813 (reproduced in Wright, *Chronicles of Birmingham Chamber*, pp. 49–50).
[126] Kidderminster chamber minutes, 10 April 1900.
[127] ACC, *Monthly Proceedings*, 4 October (1917), pp. 23–4, 31.
[128] Northamptonshire chamber, *Yearbook* (1916, 1919) (LSE Library).
[129] North Staffordshire chamber, *Yearbook* (1920–8).
[130] Walsall chamber, *Annual Report* (1917).

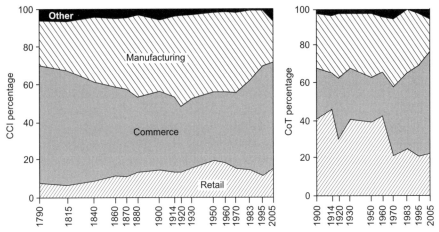

Fig. 14.5. Aggregate sector composition of members in chambers of commerce (CCI) and chambers of trade (CoT) 1790–2005.

commerce again became larger as a result of the decline of manufacturing, and expansion of professional and business services, which reached 56% in 2005. The sector composition within manufacturing in 1917 is reported in a rare survey for all chambers: the largest groups were textiles (55%), vehicles (30%), food provisions (18%), machinery (10%) and coal (10%), chemicals (9%), and building materials (8%), in which multiple classifications were allowed.[131] The 'other' category in Figure 14.5, which usually contained members from among local dignitaries up to the 1980s (such as the mayor, local MPs, the head of local Harbour Boards, Customs, or other major undertakings), never exceeded 5–6%. It has increased since the 1990s reaching 7.4% in 2005 as a result of including college principals, local government officials, and other public sector employees.

Retailers, although spurned in some chambers, nevertheless were always present in the system. The average proportion steadily increased from 7–8% in the early years to a maximum in 1950 of 20%, then declining; 16% in 2005. In some chambers it was considerable; for example, Southampton, Stockport, Croydon, and Portsmouth had 35–40% retail members in the 1950s and 1960s. Even a large industrial area like Coventry, which had only 44 retail members in 1920 (15% of the members), increased to 275 by 1956 (34%), and remained at over 20% into the 1970s after its total membership reached over 1000. Most of these chambers also supported local retail associations; for example, Coventry also had 20 small retail associations as members in 1945.[132] Some chambers of trade and commerce shared the same secretary, as in Stockport; they shared offices in Leeds; and over 20 chambers of commerce had a retail section by 1957.[133] Bernard Knowles, the

---

[131] ABCC, *Annual Report* (1917); covering 97 chambers and 24,000 members.
[132] Coventry chamber, *Annual Report* (1945), p. 4.
[133] ABCC, Home Affairs Committee, survey 4 June 1941; GPC minutes, 2 October 1957.

Southampton chamber secretary, in 1952 celebrated the chamber as combining the functions of a chamber of commerce and trade, with retailers as a distributive trades section. He noted that from its inception the chamber membership was always available to every section of the town's business community.[134]

The different balance of interests in the chambers of commerce that had large retail presence explains their different attitude to ABCC: it was Southampton (with Croydon) that led the revolt against the ABCC in 1957, discussed in Chapter 8. Ironically, retailers were most neglected in the smallest chambers of commerce, since these were usually the most dominated by manufacturing. Thus in the major debate in 1917–20 about the status of chambers and approval, it was the small manufacturing areas that were most indignant about including retailers: the tiny Barrow-in-Furness chamber asked if the proposals meant they 'should throw open their membership to shopkeepers'. The large chambers were relaxed, with Birmingham and London offering soothing comments about the need to broaden, and the increased strength of representation and resources this would offer.[135]

Figure 14.5 shows that in the chambers of trade, as expected, retailers were the largest proportion of members up to 1960; but subsequently this changed rapidly. Commerce was also always an important sector, averaging 20–30% over 1900–60, but reached 37% in 1970, and 55% in 2005. The focus of the chambers of trade was thus local traders in both retail and commercial services (among which estate agents, solicitors, consultants, and business service firms became increasingly prominent). The average combined commerce and retail proportions always exceeded that in chambers of commerce, with the difference steadily increasing over 1900–50, but narrowing from the 1980s as the chambers of commerce attracted many more commercial members. It is important to note that the large chambers of trade also had many manufacturers, averaging 27–32% over 1900–60, increasing to a peak in 1970 of 37%, before dropping back to reach 18% in 2005. The steep declines in manufacturing in both types of chambers since 1980 reflects the shift in the total economy.

The range of sector composition, as for most chamber characteristics, has always been very wide. Figure 14.6 shows the mean and range of manufacturing membership, which stretched from under 10% to over 80% between chambers over most of their history. This demonstrates the differences between the 'industrial district' chambers, and more diversified areas where manufacturing was one of several sectors. The range is narrowest in the most recent period, largely as a result of consolidation of the small chambers into larger bodies and the decline of manufacturing.

More detailed assessment of sector membership is possible using the few early studies made by ABCC, shown in Table 14.8. These data are not fully consistent, but they indicate the continuing dominance of the merchant, wholesaling, and trading sector in the chambers of commerce into modern times, with notable recent

---

[134] B. D. Knowles, *Southern Gateway*, Southampton chamber magazine, June (1952), pp. 19–20.
[135] Comments in ACC *Monthly Proceedings*, 4 October (1917); e.g. Barrow, p. 17; Birmingham pp. 18–21; London, pp. 42–3.

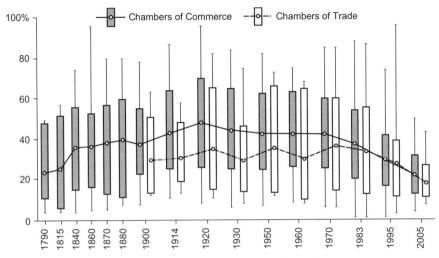

Fig. 14.6. Proportions of manufacturing members in chambers of commerce and chambers of trade 1790–2005: average proportions, range, and 20%/80% box plots.

Table 14.8. Detailed sector composition of members in chambers of commerce 1917–2009, aligned as far as data allow; percentage of membership at each date, recalculated excluding unclassified and 'other'

Sector	1917	1929	1970	1996	2010
Agric., mining				0.8	0.8
Manufacturers and producers[a]	48.1	46.1	47.4	27.8	16.7
Construction, utilities				6.9	6.8
Merchants	25.5	25.6			
Banks, financial	2.5	2.5	13.4	5.5	7.9
Insurance		1.8			1.0
Agents, brokers	5.0	4.5			
Other professional, business services	6.1	7.4		23.2	34.9
Transport, communications		1.9	18.6	7.7	6.1
Ship-owners	3.3	1.6			
Retail/distributors, hotels	7.2	8.6	10.3	12.7	16.6
Public admin., education, health			10.3	15.4	9.2

[a] Includes manufacturers who undertook their own merchanting in 1929.
Sources: ABCC, *Annual Report* (1917), *Monthly Proceedings*, 6 November (1929), p. 228; ABCC MS 14367/3, 17556, and 17478/3 for 1970; ABCC *Benchmarking* from 1996.

growth of business service professionals and retailers. From the 1960s banks, building societies, insurance companies, estate agents, auctioneers, solicitors, architects, and accountants become a very large group.

The agricultural, primary, and utility sectors remained small proportions throughout the history of chambers. In part this is due to small numbers of primary and utility firms in most areas; in many cases they are members, but there are not many of them to join. For agriculture, however, the number of firms is large, but their low membership of chambers is due to the fact that they were mostly small firms. Agriculture was also often seen as an enemy. Although Beresford argues that questions of agricultural policy were settled by repeal of the Corn Laws in 1846, there was continued friction between the chambers of commerce and the chambers of agriculture, which usually resulted in them opposing or ignoring each other.[136] Only Aberdeen and Leicester chambers had agricultural sections, both of which arose from taking over the local chamber of agriculture for a period.

Corporate organization, corporate trends

Changes in corporate organization also presented new challenges for chambers. With the availability of general incorporation from the Company Acts of 1844 and 1856, limited liability companies became an increasingly important model. They were slow to develop in many sectors, evolving initially for larger companies and riskier ventures by the end of the 19th century, and became a major vehicle for mergers and industrial consolidation.[137] However, they became numerically important after WW1. The chambers had grown up from the leadership of independent entrepreneurs and the major partners of family and other closely held concerns where the personality, networks, and priorities of the owner meant that there was no separation of the business and its management: an individual thus could speak for the firm in chamber deliberations. This changed when corporations became more important.

The changes in the character of firms belonging to the chambers is shown in Figure 14.7. This demonstrates the clear transition from individuals and partnerships in the first 100 years, to a dominance by limited companies by 1930, but after the 1980s this changes again. Recent evolution shows the emergence of the smaller and medium-sized firm based on partnerships. For the larger chambers of trade individuals and partnerships were larger proportions, but the evolution was similar.

These changes have had profound effects on chamber 'interests'. The growing role of incorporation led to a number of challenges to who represented a business in a chamber: the owner or senior managers; and membership of chambers became dictated by Head Office corporate policies for an increasing proportion of members that were branches or agencies for large national or international firms with no local HQ or senior managerial functions.[138] As a result, membership of chambers has been increasingly tested against shareholder value and 'ownership-disciplined alignment'.[139] Hence, although becoming an increasing proportion of chamber members, the contribution of larger limited companies to deliberation and framing

---

[136] One of the few references to agriculture is by Leeds chamber, which declined to support an approach from the Cheshire chamber of agriculture in 1868 in their campaign for public compensation to farmers for losses caused by cattle plague; Beresford (1951), Leeds chamber history, pp. 62–3.
[137] Hannah (1983); Jones (2000).
[138] Jones (2000), p. 42; see Chapter 16.
[139] Useem (1993).

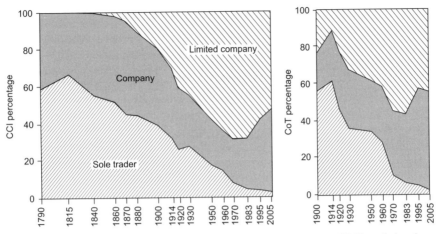

Fig. 14.7. Legal form of business members in chambers of commerce (CCI) and chambers of trade (CoT) 1790–2005.

policy is often circumscribed. And many did not see the point of joining a local body; as Liverpool chamber noted in 1953, there were in Liverpool 'about 450 firms with HQs in London which were not members . . . there was no real answer to what seemed to be a common problem'.[140]

Similarly, after joint stock banks were introduced in 1826, banks declined from being the 'leading sector' in chambers they once were. Banking became a highly consolidated sector, where local presence was based on a branch network. In 1851 there were about 961 branches (roughly equal to the number of locations exceeding 2500 population),[141] but this increased to 2008 by 1858, 6521 in 1900, and 9316 in 1914.[142] Banks thus moved from predominantly local institutions, with mutual benefits for the leadership of chambers, to businesses that were branches of national companies. Similarly the shift from local capital markets to a nationally integrated market undermined the relevance of chamber networks. Although the bank manager retained important social status, and usually joined the chamber of commerce or chamber of trade, they were of less relevance for forming a local voice.

These problems of identification of firms with chambers increased in three further phases. First, many merchant firms by 1914 had become multinational 'business groups' with large-scale trading, financial, resource extraction, and manufacturing undertakings in several continents. London became the favoured base for these, especially as a result of British investment abroad that made sterling the major international currency and London the focus for the finance of world

---

[140] Liverpool chamber secretary, comment to ABCC, Association of Chamber Secretaries minutes, 30 April 1953.
[141] Settlement sizes from Law (1967); Robson (1973); Clark (2000b); see Appendix 3.
[142] All banking figures from Powell (1966), pp. 310–11; quoting Easton (1836), *Banks and Banking*; and the *Bankers Magazine* at relevant dates.

trade.[143] The views of local chambers on their specific locality were increasingly irrelevant to developments.

Second, consolidation also occurred in manufacturing in waves immediately before, during, and after WW1 and WW2.[144] Industrial combines dominated the domestic economy, and were favoured by government. Although still relevant to industrial reconstruction in the main industrial areas up to WW2, the chambers became increasingly eclipsed. A final blow to manufacturing was dealt with the sharp contractions of the 1980s which severely curtailed membership of many chambers and was probably a critical initial force leading to the more unstable membership of chambers after this period. It also brought in many foreign owners of UK-based companies that, with notable exceptions, generally had less capacity to articulate local voice within chambers.

Third, after the 1980s, and particularly the 'big bang' reforms to the City in 1986, the financial and business service sectors went through a massive phase of consolidation and internationalization. This undermined the relevance and availability of local leadership. An equivalent and rather different form of big bang had similar effects in Ireland with its accession to the Euro. Again instability and ebbing commitment to chambers has resulted.

Whilst the data are not fully available, it is probably true that the members of chambers from their outset up to WW1 usually included most of the largest employers in their areas, and the ABCC as well as the local chambers could draw on key business figures of their day as presidents and council members. This became increasingly less true. Even in 1918 Liverpool chamber was commenting that a 'serious obstacle in the way of progress and strength . . . is the increasing difficulty of attracting suitable men of proven energy and ability, able to spare the time'.[145] There was a decline in ability 'to attract high profile . . . figures . . . [and those with] an ability to "open doors".'[146]

As a result, since the 1960s the chambers have not usually been able to attract leadership or involvement from the very largest companies because these are generally too widely spread to focus on single localities. Reliance therefore usually has to be placed on more localized companies which are smaller and have less national political clout. A survey of chamber members in 1991 showed that the seniority of chamber representatives within firms was high (as owners, directors, senior managers), they were closely involved in purchasing decisions, and were well informed (as judged by their readership of key media), but they were relatively more poorly paid and in smaller and more localized firms with single establishments.[147]

---

[143] Jones (2000).   [144] Hannah (1983).
[145] Liverpool chamber, *Handbook* (1918), p. 34.   [146] Taylor (2007), p. 83.
[147] Guy Consterdine Associates (1991), for ABCC: *Chambers of Commerce, Managing Directors of Member Businesses*; comparison with businessman readership survey, N = 416 telephone interviews in 19 representative chambers.

Firm size: the emergence of the SME

The small firm was generally ignored as an explicit interest by early chambers. However, many small firms were members. As shown in Figure 14.5, individual sole traders were the majority members of the chambers over their first 100 years, and only declined to a small minority of membership after WW2. But of course, many sole traders were large businesses in the early period, particularly before the advent of limited liability. Most merchanting was an entrepreneurial business that required only a small number of direct employees, and manufacturing was largely undertaken by 'putting out', which had few employees. The individual entrepreneur held his own easily up to the 1870s, in Clapham's view. The exceptions where large 'mills' developed were clothing, lace and textiles, metal and engine manufacture, tanning, building, brewing, earthenware, and rail and coal transport.[148] Hence the distinction between 'small' and 'large' firms was not so readily apparent as a phenomenon for the first hundred years or so of chamber development. Instead the distinction was of 'principal' traders and others, which wrapped up the quality and quantity of their trade or capital, rather than the size of the firm they directly controlled.

During the 20th century the small firm became a more prominent concern. Early indications of this within the chambers was the differentiation of subscription rates between the individual and larger partnership. This began from some of the earliest foundations, but became widespread from the 1920s; later subscription scales were differentiated to more complex measures of firm size or trading volumes. From the 1920s there was even thought about how size of member affected how they used the chamber, and how this influenced motives to join or remain as members; see Chapter 15. But in chambers, like national politics, the small firm was eclipsed. In the evidence given to the Committee on Commercial and Industrial Policy in 1917, Firth's statement that 'the number of small firms is simply ridiculous' demonstrated that the chambers did not really understand the sector at all. Firth went on to describe the dilemma for chambers: 'There are many difficulties . . . There are a number of small firms and a number of large firms; the small firm resents any suggestion which will hamper his efforts to capture the trade of his big competitor—he gets his trade by pricking the eyes out of his big competitors.'[149] This view was one from manufacturing, and from a large employer. How to balance this view with that of the smaller business remained a continuing challenge which was scarcely considered by ABCC; and the response in local chambers was piecemeal.

The Bolton report of 1971 changed this and stimulated a major readjustment of government thinking, launching a new policy 'frame', and with it the need for a new 'repertoire' of response by business lobbies. By the 1970s small firms were already a major national phenomenon. By the 1990s they were becoming dominant. In 2011, of the 4.8m businesses in Britain, only 10,000 or 0.2% were large

---

[148] Clapham (1932), p. 5.
[149] Algernon Firth, ABCC president, evidence, pp. 475–91: TNA BT 55/10; see also Chapter 13.

(employing more that 500 people) whilst small firms were 99.8% of all businesses, employed 50% of the workforce, and contributed 60% of total national output (turnover).[150]

The actual composition of chamber membership among firms of different sizes is difficult to establish for the early period since there are no national sources of firm-size information. However, for 1971 there is an ABCC estimate from the Bolton Report period. Subsequently there are ABCC *Census* and *Benchmarking*, as summarized in Table 14.9. This shows that a significant shift has occurred in recent years; firms of 1–9 employees have changed from being one of the main groups (with just over 40% of the membership in 1988), to become the *majority* of the membership.[151] Conversely, the larger and medium-sized firms have contracted in proportion of the membership, though their absolute number in membership has stayed approximately the same. A rapid growth in chamber membership in the 1990s and 2000s came mainly from the smallest firms, but this has introduced considerably more instability, as these members tend to be less stable as businesses, and less loyal and committed as members.

Chamber market penetration by firm size is shown in Table 14.10. This demonstrates that market penetration has declined for all firm size categories. Underlying these changes has been a major increase in the total number of businesses in the UK, from 2.4 million in 1980, to 3.8 million in 1990, and 4.8 million in 2010, within which almost all the growth has come in the smallest size groups. Hence, the chambers, like other business organizations, are chasing a fast-moving target when trying to recruit the smallest firms. But there has also been a

Table 14.9. The composition of chamber membership by employment size: percentage of total ABCC/BCC chamber membership by firm size 1971–2010

Firm Size	1–9	10–49	50–249	>250
1971[a]	(76.0)		[24.0]	
1988[a]	41.3	30.6	19.2	8.8
1993[a]	49.1	31.7	14.2	5.0
1996	50.3	32.4	12.8	4.5
2002	53.6	30.0	12.6	3.8
2005	56.8	28.2	11.4	3.5
2010	59.1	26.3	11.2	3.4

[a] Estimated because different size categories were used; data for 1971 too coarse to disaggregate.

Sources: 1971 from ABCC MS 17548/3, list of small firms in affiliated chambers (numbering 38,019); ABCC *Census* and BCC *Benchmarking*

[150] DTI and BIS, *Small Firm Statistics*.
[151] Note that the 1989 data have to be interpolated to be comparable to the size bands used by BCC at later dates, but any approximations do not affect the smallest size category.

steady erosion of their large and medium-sized firm members, at a faster rate than these size categories have been diminishing within the economy as a whole. Tables 14.8 and 14.9 show that the 'average' chamber member is now much more likely to be an SME owner-manager (of a business of less than 250 employees) than at any time in the previous 50 or more years. However, there is still a strong and continuing membership of the larger and medium-sized firms for which the chambers provide the strongest market penetration.

These changes have profound implications. For small firms there is typically much more diversity of policy view. For larger firms a unity of interests is usually easier to achieve, and government often uses their networks as sounding boards and sources of information and strategic guidance. For large firms the voice process may work both ways: 'key business associations serve as the stepping stones for inner-circle entry into the world of advisory boards and administrative appointments',[152] which act as incentives for both members and chambers. This is much less common for small firms. Hence, the attractions of the high-level information and contacts that large firms can offer is invaluable in forming and presenting 'interest', but, given the dominance of the membership by small firms, it is only one part of the influences that should form a chamber voice.

Nationalized industries and 'other' members

With the advance of the state into the realm of business from the late 19th century a debate emerged as to whether public sector industries and agencies should be allowed to become chamber members. This reached a climax in 1947 when the pros and cons were assessed. It was agreed that Coal Boards and other government

Table 14.10. The market penetration of chamber membership by firm employment size: chamber members as percentage of ONS business population of firms with one or more employee 1971–2010

Firm Size	1–9	10–49	50–249	>250
1971[a]	(35.0)		[65.0]	
1988[a]	5.0	20.5	38.2	58.6
1996	4.7	17.6	38.5	51.3
2000	4.8	17.6	37.8	48.4
2005	4.6	16.0	36.5	37.7
2010	2.9	10.2	24.9	28.1

[a] Estimated because different size categories were used; data for 1971 too coarse to disaggregate.
Sources: ABCC *Census* and BCC *Benchmarking*; Bennett (1991).

[152] Useem (1984), p. 101; Mizruchi (1982).

agencies could join at the normal subscription rates for each chamber, but that the 'position should be watched' and modified if problems arose.[153] The chief concerns were that having government-sponsored members would dilute independence, the ability to criticize government, and would undermine 'those who speak for free enterprise'. The ABCC accepted that some chambers already had local authority members, that the nationalized industries and agencies covered important sectors from which views were important, and that their other members were so numerous that state industries could always be outvoted. It was also felt that to exclude them might be judged politically partisan and might encourage government to set up its own committees and bodies to compete with chambers. Thus Barnstaple voted to include nationalized industries, even though its council recommended against.[154] Here was a vivid acceptance that to remain outside the corporate state risked being marginalized; chambers had to accept the government's agenda. A similar debate occurred over membership of chambers by TECs and Business Link.

Gender

Only a few women were members of early chambers, and numbers were never large until the modern period. It is impossible to construct historic trends, since the gender of the members is often not shown. With the increasing membership by companies and partnerships that had general not personal names, it is very difficult to identify gender after the 1930s. However, at least into the 1950s and 1960s, women members were rare, especially on chamber committees. Doreen Hitchcock, chief executive of the Burnley chamber, was usually the only woman attending most ABCC meetings in the 1960s, and felt as if she was being treated as 'an oddity'.[155]

Despite the male-dominated history, chambers are used more or less equally by both genders since the 1990s, although within Business Link partnerships there was some evidence of a decreased female participation in the early 2000s (another area of perverse government leverage).[156] Gender has become an explicit concern in membership recruitment. For Board membership, chambers had moved to 18% female by 2010, and were 48% of the senior management staff, after steadily increasing from the 1990s.[157]

Networking, and endogenous interests in the modern chamber

Across their history chambers have been strongly interlinked with local and regional networks of contracts, formal business alliances, and informal social relations. For the commercial centres these were trading networks; for the industrial centres they

---

[153] ABCC Executive minutes, confidential report by Arthur Knowles, 7 July 1947.
[154] Barnstaple chamber, AGM minutes, 30 March 1951.
[155] Comments to author, September 2005.
[156] Bennett (2008), table 9.
[157] BCC, *Benchmarking*.

were 'industrial districts'. In both types these were locations for rapid diffusion of innovations, and external agglomeration economies.[158] Chambers used and were grafted onto these networks, and the two were mutually self-reinforcing. But does the 'district' interlock survive for the modern chamber?

Reviews of historical networks demonstrates their significance in a range of varied industries and locations which were critical to the major historic chambers;[159] for example, in the Potteries; Sheffield cutlery and steel; Coventry bicycles; Manchester cottons; Darlington, Blackburn, and Derby engineering; Worcester gloves; Birmingham buttons, jewellery, and guns; Dudley, Wolverhampton, and Walsall metal industries; Nottingham and Leicester knitwear, lace, and hosiery; Kidderminster carpets; Northwich salt; Widnes salt and chemicals; Cardiff, Swansea, and Newcastle-upon-Tyne coal and shipping; Hawick–Galashiels–Peebles hosiery; Dundee jute and jam; or linen in Limerick, Belfast, and Dublin. District-based networks made a ready membership base for chambers; e.g. Dudley essentially 'consisted of meetings of friends' from its beginnings in 1881 until it developed services in 1974.[160]

Popp and Wilson provide some important overarching generalizations from historical case studies.[161] First, local social structures in districts were an addition to the market, not a necessary or sufficient condition, nor always or even often providing effective support, but were sometimes an important additional contribution to competitive advantage. Second, technological change and innovation was a key driver of the initial clusters and development of a critical mass, but then became less relevant. Third, development covered very long time periods, as did adaptation and any decline/regeneration. Fourth, the wide development of formal contracted partnerships was always the key organizational basis of economic relationships, between unrelated business people as well as kin, that drew on and reinforced other informal relationships.[162]

Additionally, business structure was critical: successful districts usually relied on a few leading firms; and key institutions (such as chambers) relied on the leadership of a small, committed, and effective group of individuals. This is perhaps the most critical of the Popp and Wilson findings:[163] 'networks were largely driven by small cohorts of leading actors . . . It is not network structure per se—or even network presence, . . . but instead the quality of entrepreneurship for which networks serve as a vehicle'.

These structures appear to have been critical to business environments in Britain and Ireland up to the 1970s, but a major change seems to have begun after WW2, which became increasingly important. Crafts dates the 1970s and 1980s as the period when communications in Britain became sufficiently integrated that

---

[158] Marshall (1919).
[159] Popp and Wilson (2003, 2007, 2009); Wilson and Popp (2003a, b); Becattini, Bellandi and de Propis (2009); see also Daunton (1977); Hudson (1986, 1989).
[160] Quoted in Worcester chamber minutes, report on visit to Dudley chamber, 3 August 1978.
[161] Popp and Wilson (2007); Popp (2003, 2005).
[162] Checkland (1952, 1958); Pearson (2004); Bennett (2010).
[163] Popp and Wilson (2007), p. 2986.

agglomeration economies and externalities to local businesses were significant *between* regions (as well as within them). This introduced global competition as a determinant of local economic growth potential, as emphasized by the 'new economic geography' literature.[164] Together with the contextual variety of a place, and the contingency of each local situation,[165] agglomeration economies and externalities are now judged to provide key elements of local competitiveness, providing strengths or deficiencies that influence wages and profits, innovation, and attractiveness for the highly mobile knowledge workers and knowledge creators that are likely to be key contributors to future local competitive success.[166] In addition, the emergence of supra-national regulation and multi-state jurisdictions for financial instruments has made bodies such as the EU, international standards bodies, and international dispute resolution increasingly relevant.

A major academic debate has raged over whether the connections that are important to locations depend on formal or informal alliances, or on the clustering of like industries that draw on common 'exogenous' factors. The cluster concept is complex and confused, but captures the joint location of businesses and factors of production in a location that collectively offers competitive benefits.[167] It has been argued that these interrelate with the city as context; however, many successful clusters are not in urban areas.[168] Governments since the 1990s have tried to encourage clusters.[169]

These developments have led to new challenges for chambers beyond their traditional roots in localities and regions. There may be advantages: if a chamber covers an area with strong cluster characteristics, it should be easier to develop membership and interest representation than in a more dispersed area, but this requires adaptation of chamber areas to new circumstances, generally over wider territories. Particularly challenging has been the emergence of global recruitment for company chief executives and directors, with local operations increasingly managed in a way that undermines their scope to provide useful inputs to a chamber's policies, or means that they are uninterested in contributing.[170] It also restricts the calibre and freedom of local managers due to the setting of policy at a corporate level elsewhere and the preference of the global elites within HQs to negotiate directly with governments and international institutions directly because this usually confers greater influence. Also challenging is that lobbies have to be targeted not just at local or even national government, but also at international

---

[164] Crafts (2005); Crafts and Mutatu (2005); see also Hudson (1986, 1989); Phelps and Ozawa (2003); Haggerty (2006); Popp and Wilson (2007, 2009); see Acemoglu, Johnson, and Robinson (2001), and Becattini, Bellandi, and de Propis (2009) for long-term historical trends.
[165] Jacobs (1969); Sunley (1992); Markussen (1996); Borschma (2009).
[166] Dixit and Stiglitz (1977); Fujita and Krugman (2004); Borschma (2009).
[167] Markussen (1996); Phelps (2004).
[168] Sunley (1992); Jacobs (1969); Glaeser, Scheinkman, and Schleifer (1995); Phelps and Ozawa (2003); Phelps (2004).
[169] DTI (2001), *Business Clusters in the UK: A First Assessment*; De Propris (2005).
[170] e.g. Useem (1984, 1993); Glaeser, Scheinkman, and Schleifer (1995); Storper (1997); Scott (1998); Stokman and Stokman (1995).

regulatory bodies, which requires working alliances beyond national associations; usually through Eurochambres and EU-wide industry associations.

14.6 INFLUENCES ON MARKET PENETRATION

The question of whether market penetration evolved in different ways over time cannot be fully assessed over the longer historical period, because not all data can be reliably reconstructed. But, a more limited analysis is possible for chambers of commerce only. Our prior expectations are that market penetration will increase as service benefits increase, but decline with increasing subscription costs. Other sources of chamber income may work either way: to reduce members as they feel their support is not needed; or increase membership because services are subsidized. A series of comparisons can be made, not all of which can be shown here, and on which further research is being developed. But a preliminary set of estimates is summarized in Table 14.11, for regression estimates of the four main features expected, with proportions of sector and business organization of members tested as additional features.

The main conclusion to be drawn from these results is that over time there is considerable stability, but the statistical relationships are often weak. This is to be expected given the small sample sizes in early years, considerable difficulties with some data, and the variety of local responses. Subscriptions rates have had a significant negative association with market penetration for almost all time periods, despite their relatively low cost; indicating a continued close scrutiny by members and potential members of costs. Other sources of income have not usually been significant, perhaps indicating that the two possible reactions cancel out between chambers, and members: they undermine commitment for some; whilst for others they indicate better value for money. Services are difficult to compare over time because of their variety and evolution. Tests of various services have been made, which are all consistent in direction, but with library/reading rooms being the most significantly associated with increased membership penetration in early periods (especially in the 1920s and 1930s), and the size of bundle (number of services) being most significant after 1960. Whilst the effect of CCTEs was positive in increasing market penetration, this was not statistically significantly greater than other chambers in the two cross-sections for 1995 and 2005 (whichever measure of penetration is used).

The main indications from these estimates (although preliminary pending further research) are clear: that there is some sort of equilibrium of supply and demand for chamber membership, with subscription rates carrying the main price message, and the most desired services offering the main stimulus for increased density of market penetration.[171] These are the main specific effects; otherwise the growth in membership of chambers has been essentially organic,

---

[171] Also see Chapter 16; and also indicated in other research, e.g. De Propris and Lazzeretti (2009).

Table 14.11. Statistical estimation of influences on market penetration 1790–2005

Year	R²	Mean subs. rate	Other chamber income per member	Services	Publications	Sector	Company or Ltd.
1790	0.18	−.100	−.276	.410	n/a	—	—
1815	0.10	−.198	*−.098*	*.014*	n/a	√	—
1840	0.21	−.509	.252	.524	*.017*	—	—
1860	0.15	*.344*	−.182	.393	−.278	√	—
1870	0.05	−.032	−.186	.107	−.156	—	—
1882	0.09	*−.617*	*.478*	.077	.103	—	—
1900	0.21	*−.418*	.289	−.141	−.058	—	—
1914	**0.20**	−.010	*.280*	.267	*−.214*	—	—
1920	**0.25**	*−.182*	.083	.453	−.062	—	√
1930	**0.24**	*−.232*	.029	*.421*	*−.223*	—	√
1950	0.05	−.183	.022	.066	−.106	—	—
1960	*0.13*	*−.380*	−.100	.073	.254	√	√
1970	*0.22*	*−.310*	.154	*.058*	−.078	—	—
1982	0.12	−.265	−.023	.273	−.058	—	—
1995	**0.18**	−.073	.013	*.223*	*−.459*	—	—
2005	0.07	.001	.099	−.079	n/a	—	—
1995	*0.15*	*−.347*	.062	.162	.129	—	—
2005	*0.15*	*−.303*	.050	.272	n/a	—	—

Notes: Independent results for cross-sections for each point in time (members per 1000 local population; members per business population, last two rows); (bold: significant at $p = 0.01$; bold italics: significant at $p = 0.1$; √ significant at least at $p = 0.1$). Services defined as library or not 1815–1950; number of services 1790, and 1960–2005. Publications defined as Annual Report 1815–1960; Journal 1970– (all chambers have journals for 2005, and none have publications in 1790). Sector measured by retail %; business organization by partnerships % 1790–1900; Ltd. Company % 1914–2005.

growing with the size of the business and general population: maintaining a relatively stable market penetration ratio with the possible customer base. This has also been indicated in Figure 14.4, and is confirmed by joining and lapsing behaviour assessed in Chapter 16.

14.7 CONCLUSION: EVOLVING 'INTEREST'

This chapter has assessed how the chamber 'interest' has depended on changing territories, sector composition, firm sizes, corporate organization, and other features. Whilst the contrasts over time are considerable, there is a common thread among the chambers of commerce of an adapting system with expanding territory, increasingly diversified across sectors, firm sizes, and corporate organizational structures. Of these trends, the modern chamber is most distinct in its very broad sector spread and in having a majority of small firms *as well as* a strong representation from medium-sized and larger firms. The earliest chambers, in contrast, were mostly dominated by international traders and exporting manufacturers, with membership heavily skewed towards the largest and 'elite' enterprises, within which banking seems to have acted as a crucial 'leading sector' both within and between areas. From being a relatively simple structure, for which 'unity' might have been easier to achieve, the modern chamber has a much more diverse range of interests.

Because of greater diversity, it is far more difficult for modern chambers to define a sector or firm-size 'interest'. Shifts in the nature of economies towards wider networks, globalization, and international regulatory structures have challenged local context even further. In response to these challenges, perhaps even more than in the past, it is critical to recognize that the key USP of the chambers is the 'certain type' of local interest they cover. Across the variety of their membership the critical feature remains the locality or region. This was interlocked historically with commercial trading foci and the ports, and with 'industrial districts', and may have modern interrelations with 'clusters'. Dunwoody in the 1920s defined chamber 'interest' as an 'obligation upon all qualified men as soon as their livelihood is assured, to devote some of their ability to the common welfare . . . take under their purview service to the entire community . . . devote themselves to making their towns attractive and satisfactory to live in'.[172] The modern challenge is to find whether this type of commitment and bond can be maintained.

A considerable emphasis of this chapter has been on how representative the chambers are/were of the interests of the members. This has focused on the market penetration of their 'geography of interest'. An extraordinary finding is that, as far as the data allow, the market penetration of chambers is almost the same now as it has been over the past 240 years, and that over the intervening years the fluctuations have been relatively small. Chambers have always had an average penetration about 1.4–2.4 per thousand of local population, or since the 1970s, 6–8% of established businesses. However, there are strong contrasts across the chamber system; as with all other chamber features, there is a dominance of local context and historical contingency. Despite recent efforts from the national association, territory remains largely self-defined and is still highly varied. Across the system run two types of chamber: the large, with voice and large-scale service delivery (the historic and modern BCC chambers of commerce); and the small, with voice and networks as their main activities (the CoTs and modern town chambers).

The differences in market penetration define two different types of chamber member 'interest' as well as two types of chamber. The large chambers have generally a moderate market penetration over a large area, whilst small chambers often have higher market penetration over a small area. The chapter shows that scale/area of coverage and service bundling are mutually interdependent features for members that influence the size of territory, activity offered, and the market penetration achieved. They also influence how the local 'geography of interest' is defined, the form of involvement with other local bodies (such as local government), the level of regional or national coordination possible with other chambers, the choice of geographical 'brand' name utilized (the town, city, county, or region),

---

[172] Dunwoody, 'Chambers of Commerce'; e.g. in Belfast chamber *Journal*, July (1924), pp. 51–2.

and the degree to which national bodies can adequately represent their varied voices to government. The concepts of these 'large' and 'small' chambers are essentially the same: deliberated, general voice; but they evolved into separate but overlapping systems as chambers of commerce and chambers of trade. A continuing challenge for the chamber voice remains bringing these different types of chamber into greater cooperation.

The stability of market penetration by chambers is in many ways surprising, compared with other business associations. The wider 'association market' has a high degree of fragmentation, a low degree of homogeneity within any business subgroup, a dominance by small bodies, with the emergence of large-scale all-encompassing business organizations with high market penetration relatively rare, and usually restricted to specialist sectors which have significant government subsidy, regulation, or leverage, or where there is a low degree of technical content (so that 'the lowest common denominator' is an economically optimal and useful outcome).[173] The chambers of commerce represent a contrast, of a successful national system based on larger entities and an enduring stability of market penetration. But chambers also mirror the tensions evident in sector bodies, where the smaller associations also tend to have highest market penetration.[174]

---

[173] Streeck and Schmitter (1985); McLaughlin, Jordan, and Maloney (1993); Grant (1987, 2000).
[174] Van Waarden (1991); Streeck and Schmitter (1985); Bennett (1996a, 1998a, 1998b).

15

Membership Motives: Benefits and Costs

15.1 INTRODUCTION

Motives for chamber membership interrelate with all aspects of chamber activity: how voice is formed and deployed; how services are bundled; how partnerships with government are developed and marketed; and how crucial management decisions are made about pricing through subscriptions and fees. Despite this critical importance, however, understanding of membership motives was little developed in early chambers. Membership was largely taken for granted as a self-evident 'status good' supporting chamber brand, or was a natural expectation because of allegiance to locality. Since lapse rates were historically low this was perhaps the result of a perception that there was no problem to monitor. However, in modern times lapse rates have become much higher and hence understanding of motives is now critically important. There is a vigorous contemporary debate about the character of the chamber member and 'interest', whether the commitment to locality still exists, and how to balance member services with government partnering, and the cost-benefit ratios this involves. In the discussion here the available evidence of membership motivation is interrogated: for joining, retention, and lapsing.

15.2 JOINING

The discussion in Chapter 3 of the forces underlying the foundation and growth of chambers suggests that there was a range of often multiple and overlapping motives for membership. Subsequent chapters have shown that 'protest', campaigns, and allegiance to a cause to lobby government were of critical importance. This developed into more routine policy monitoring and representation. It is clear, however, that in most cases the demand for collective political activity and lobbying preceded, or dominated, any attempt to develop individual services or other activities. It would appear that services developed more as a by-product of lobbying, not the other way round.[1]

Subsequently, support services to individual members began to become important, and from the 20th century chambers helped government in war efforts, and then a wide range of government services. Dunwoody, secretary of ABCC in the 1920s, stated that WW1 'gave great impetus to the formation and work of

---

[1] This is in line with the expectations argued more generally by Marsh (1978) and Hansen (1985).

chambers of commerce and many who had not hitherto supported them found it essential to do so in order to secure help and assistance in carrying out the regulations and orders which governments found necessary to impose'.[2] As multiple offers developed, multiple motives could come to govern the joining decision. These have the advantage to members and chamber managers of 'bundling'. They also help chamber managers to mitigate free-rider behaviour. Underlying much of this is also the 'brand capital' and status provided by membership, social obligation, 'taster' behaviour (experiential search), and 'insurance' principles. A range of partially collective, individual, and other benefits therefore developed.

The joining decision has, therefore, frequently been complex and involves both economic and social calculus. However, without the solidarity to the cause, social, brand, positional, or 'psychic' benefits of membership, the economic offer alone has probably never been sufficient historically, or in modern times, to explain why any individual business person joins. As Jordan and Maloney put it, a membership decision is a mix of inclination, plus opportunities, economic and non-economic calculation, and the persuasiveness of the membership offering.[3] Modern interpretations of why businesses join associations has generated an enormous literature, which can be grouped into four main categories:[4]

(i) *Purposive/expressive benefits:* the desire to give voice, 'protest', and the satisfaction from supporting a particular cause or ideology.[5] This in turn will be influenced by the level and form of government activity, and especially the perceived levels of threat:[6] threats of potential losses may be more significant than potential benefits (avoiding collective 'bads', rather than seeking goods).[7]

(ii) *Solidarity benefits:* status, socialization/social acceptance/involvement, social activity, and the 'brand capital' provided by membership;[8] sometimes termed normative conformity, which may be encouraged by personal and other ties (affective commitment).[9] This also covers the obligation to support local projects and the locality as a whole. This may vary for different groups, with elites encouraging other membership; e.g. through charismatic individuals, recognized leader personalities, large prestigious firms,[10] 'opinion-formers',[11] or 'movers and shakers'.[12] Elites can be a 'signalling' device. 'Patrons' have been used as a special subscription category in modern

---

[2] Dunwoody, 'Chambers of Commerce', e.g. in Belfast chamber *Journal*, July (1924), pp. 51–2.
[3] Jordan and Maloney (1997), pp. 169–71.
[4] Bennett (1996b, 2000) and Mekic (2007); see also Hansen (1985); Dunleavy (1991); Jordan and Maloney (1997).
[5] Moe (1980). These benefits may be strongest when interests are most threatened (King and Walker 1992), as in social movements—they are strongest when most under attack (Wootton 1975; Tarrow 1994).
[6] Blank (1973); Hansen (1985); Grant (2000).
[7] Hansen (1985); Opp (1986); Dunleavy (1991); Jordan and Maloney (1997).
[8] Marsh (1978); Berry (1977); Bennett (1996a); Grant (2000).
[9] Knoke (1983).
[10] Walker (1983); Useem (1993).
[11] SE Hertfordshire chamber, *Marketing Project* (1990), p. 14.
[12] e.g. Business in the Community (1989), *Leadership in the Community* (London).

chambers, both to reward those involved and also to clearly identify them so as to increase their impact on recruitment.[13]

(iii) *Material selective benefits:* the specific goods and services offered to individual member businesses that help reduce costs or improve business efficiency and ability to manage.[14] This is the rational choice basis for motivation: of costs and benefits. These contribute to the resource capacity of the firm by providing supports that may be unavailable internally;[15] which may be particularly relevant for smaller firms that are too resource limited to supply themselves.[16] 'Collective' and 'not-for-profit' services can also be important signals of low costs and high effectiveness, reducing search costs,[17] offer a range of lower transaction costs,[18] some based on 'trust goods', or other benefits that chambers enjoy relative to other suppliers.[19]

(iv) *Insurance benefits:* access to a range of services that may be needed, 'just in case';[20] or 'if you don't join, you will never know what you are missing'.[21] This may be encouraged by low subscriptions/service fee rates that make insurance a cheap good.

These benefits may be sought for the *individual* owner or manager, particularly in a small firm and/or they may be sought for the *firm as a whole*, to provide service support to managers and administrators of member firms. Membership may also be sought as potential *benefits for personnel* of a member's business: to express corporate social or political commitment to help motivate employees. This may also offer local status or legitimacy; e.g. many chain and branch businesses, such as banks, insurance offices, and major retailers join chambers to show local solidarity for what are otherwise perceived as 'outsider' interests. For *elites* or patrons, Useem has highlighted how 'those in the highest levels of corporate leadership' share common agendas and operate through interlocking directorates and networks that allow them to benefit from 'strategic locations' such as on the councils of bodies like chambers. This may lead to strong influence over government policy beyond their numbers, but may alienate the rank and file members, especially of smaller businesses.[22] Hence, different motivations may operate for different businesses, which may not be aligned at any one time, nor always consciously and explicitly evident; and there may be tensions between them.

---

[13] Mekic (2007).

[14] Olson (1971); see also Marsh (1978); Dunleavy (1991); Bennett (1996a, 1998b); Bennett and Ramsden (2007).

[15] From the resource theory of the firm: see e.g. Priem and Butler (2001); Edwards et al. (2002).

[16] Storey (1994); Bennett and Robson (1999a); Bennett and Ramsden (2007).

[17] Jones (2003, 2004); Bernhagen and Bräuninger (2005).

[18] Schneiberg and Hollingsworth (1991); Taylor and Singleton (1993); Jones (1997); Bennett (1996b).

[19] Lane (1997); Bennett and Robson (1999a, 2004b); see also Hansen (1985), p. 94.

[20] Bennett (1996a); Bennett and Ramsden (2007).

[21] Hansen (1985), p. 81.

[22] Useem (1984), pp. 6, 45, 70–5, and 101.

Contemporary statements

The motives for joining early chambers have to be inferred from statements by chamber managers and leaders; there were no early surveys of member views. Most early contemporary statements in chamber documents focus primarily on the lobbying function, especially when making membership drives. They emphasize the importance of achieving a large scale and representative coverage of membership from their locality, and the obligation on members to join and help. Business solidarity was seen, and is still seen, as a key aspect for underpinning legitimacy with national and local government interests, aligning local business interests, and encouraging other agents to work with the chamber.

Representativeness and legitimacy to outsiders, and stimulation to membership through encouraging local solidarity, were viewed as interlocked. One of the best statements is by Newcastle in 1855: 'The committee strongly urge upon every individual connected by membership with the chamber to exert himself, in order, by enlarging the list, not only to enable the institution to meet its expenses, but to claim to be the commercial representative, actually and fully, of the entire district whose name it bears.'[23] Similarly, in Greenock in 1901: 'all questions vitally affecting the commercial interests of the town and district... [are] the primary work of the chamber... Sympathy and support can be best manifested by businessmen joining the chamber... To maintain and promote the efficiency of the chamber, a much larger addition ought to be made to the membership.'[24] Also in Teesside in 1930: 'the council trusts that after the demonstration of virility [of lobbying] which has been given during the past year, more firms in the area will realise the advantages of a well-supported chamber of commerce'.[25] Similarly, the rather plaintive tone of North Staffordshire's 1883 report, recognizes the need to make impact to get members: the council 'while hoping that the claims of the chamber are gradually receiving more acknowledgement and support at the hands of the trading community, feel that much is still wanting to make it worthy of the district, and would very gratefully welcome suggestions'.[26]

The issue of political impact or legitimacy and size of membership were often conflated, and this continues to be the case in modern times. Thus, for Nottingham in the 1860s, it felt that its standing would be improved by increasing its membership and in 1868 asked its 'members to use their influence in increasing the number of subscribers, and consequently its standing and position compared with other chambers'.[27] This appeal had some success since membership did increase from 82 in 1868 to 130 in 1869. Blackburn saw as critical the interaction between chamber political influence and number of members: 'The council would like to see this number [of members] largely augmented, whereby the utility of the Chamber would be increased. The great increase in the influence of your chamber in

---

[23] Newcastle chamber, *Annual Report* (1855).
[24] Greenock chamber, *Annual Report* (1901), pp. 6–7.
[25] Teesside chamber, *Annual Report*, 31 December (1930), p. 6.
[26] North Staffordshire chamber, *Annual Report* (1883), p. 15.
[27] R. G. Walton, Nottingham chamber history, p. 39.

furthering the interests of the members should lead to an increased membership.'[28] Cardiff in 1951 hoped that

> members individually will use every endeavour to secure an increase in membership in the ensuing year. Today, governments tend more and more to organise the life of the businessman. No apology is needed for re-iterating that the voice of any individual is a cry in the wilderness; only by welding together the strength of the individual in its many forms and on the broadest possible plane can the requirements of free enterprise trade be protected adequately. The chamber of commence provides the means whereby this position can be achieved.[29]

A recent statement is that by Southampton in 2006: 'the larger and more diverse our membership the more influential we can be. Our main objective for this year, therefore, is to increase our membership'.[30]

Behind the lobbying function was also the concept of the chamber being a centre of excellence in credible technical expertise. This goes back to Postlethwayt and Mortimer's views, echoed in modern interpretations, of the information asymmetry that exists between business and government.[31] As expressed by Musgrave in London in 1914, the members provide technical expertise: 'trained business people who have to bear the financial consequences of their own decisions'. The chamber could be 'a clearing house for commercial ideas' where membership made available 'the views and opinions of experts who *use* the chamber as a centre for obtaining information on technical and trade matters or for determining important questions of business policy'. This expertise provided support to the chamber staff and council who sought to marshal the ideas, and to other members; so that solicitation, deliberation, and agreed opinion was the key function of the chamber as 'a practical deliberative body'.[32]

The historical mix of lobby and support for the business community as a 'solidarity good' gave their brand a position of trust in the community. As noted by North, historical status is itself a focus for present and future membership, as a path-dependent process.[33] Similarly, to the extent that associations offer a 'trust' relation between members, they provide a forum for implicit relationships that help overcome contractual problems and facilitate trade.

Among the other motives for chamber membership, the service benefits are largely a more recent marketing tool. North Staffordshire in 1957 noted that members were divided into three groups: those who consistently use services; those who pay subscriptions as a matter of course either because they might need assistance, or believe it is a 'public duty'; and those who do not know why. The services argument was estimated at about two-thirds of the membership.[34] Another

---

[28] Blackburn chamber, *Annual Report* (1914), p. 92.
[29] Cardiff, *Annual Report* (1951), p. 22.
[30] Southampton and Fareham chamber, *Directory* (2006), p. 7.
[31] See Chapters 3 and 4.
[32] Musgrave (1914), p. 61; emphasis in original.
[33] North (1990); see also Bennett (1996b), p. 659; (1998b).
[34] 'Notes on possible improvements of chamber services': E. James Johnson, secretary of North Staffordshire chambers: quoted in ABCC, GPC minutes, 6 November 1957.

example of quoted service benefits is that by Teesside in 1960: 'those members who have availed themselves of the *services* of the chamber and who have found them of value, could greatly assist in increasing membership, and thereby the influence of the chamber, by introducing to membership those of the associates who are not already members'.[35] A more recent statement is the chairman's message at Southampton in 2006: 'if you are already part of the Chamber of Commerce, you know that through your membership you gain access to a powerful range of exclusive services, information and opportunities'.[36]

Inter-firm marketing, information exchange, and networking are seldom commented on in historical records. A 1960 statement by Teesside is rare and reflects the rather special industrial structure of the area where two giant firms (ICI and British Steel) dominated the employment over most of the 20th century: 'stress should be laid upon the way in which the large industrial members so willingly co-operate in providing valuable information for the use of smaller manufacturing firms'.[37] Inter-firm marketing and networking became prominent with the emergence of Business Link in the 1990s, where chambers came to embrace not only their members, but any businesses in their areas as potential clients. The tensions in this are discussed in Chapters 13 and 16.

The chamber as an insurance against the need for services that might be used is chiefly seen as an insurance against adverse government policy (potential 'bads'). For example, Musgrave in London in 1914, viewed the subscription at least in part as 'an "insurance premium" [by which] thousands of firms still outside the chamber profit indirectly, and sometimes directly, from the work it performs for the benefit of the entire commercial world'.[38] More recently Southampton, in a 1972 marketing campaign, states that: 'Membership of the chamber is an insurance and the subscription is a very small premium for the assistance and protection it affords.'[39]

The problem of free riders, those businesses in an area that benefit from the chamber's activities without paying by becoming a member, is recognized in a plaintive statement by Southampton in 1961: 'it is disappointing to have to report that a number of firms take the chamber's existence for granted by trying to use our services and sources of information without first taking up membership'.[40] Similarly, Sheffield in 1929, assessing why it was so difficult to recruit, noted that there was a 'lack of appreciation of the importance of the chamber's work . . . many firms deliberately refuse to admit that they can receive any benefits from the chamber, nor do they believe that even if they are not members they are still benefiting'.[41] Liverpool's chair commented in 1989 that lapsing members needed 'to see what

---

[35] Teesside and South West Durham chamber, *Annual Report*, 31 December (1960), p. 9; emphasis added.
[36] Southampton and Fareham chamber, *Directory* (2006), p. 6.
[37] Teesside and South-West Durham chamber, *Annual Report*, 31 December (1960), p. 9.
[38] Musgrave (1914), p. 60.
[39] Southampton chamber, 1972 publicity leaflet (Southampton Local Studies Library, Misc. papers).
[40] Southampton chamber, *Annual Report* (1961/2), p. 7.
[41] Sheffield Chamber, Council and Membership Committee minutes, 28 January 1929, p. H12.

they could contribute to the chamber . . . rather than what they can take from it'.[42] This free riding overlaps with apathy or lack of awareness. The NCT in 1957 summed up the apathy of non-members as 'ignorance . . . of dangerous and adverse developments' [of government policy], and 'a lack of knowledge of the services [of the NCT]'.[43] Musgrave for London recognized free-rider issues in the comment: that given the low level of subscription, membership 'may be acquired on such nominal terms there is no excuse for accepting as a favour that which on election [to membership] may be had as a right by any reputable person or firm'.[44]

Where meetings were the main source of benefits, as in early chambers, exclusion from the meeting could be a way to deal with free riders, though this could lead to tensions and unpleasantness. There are few records of this, but that for Newport (Mon.) in 1876 is vivid: 'Mr. West said he felt some little interest in the chamber, but unfortunately he had been . . . kept outside the door of the chamber because he had not paid his annual subscription. He had purposely refrained from doing so until he saw some evidence that the chamber was going on actively. He had spoken to other members . . . and found they had abstained from paying [for the same reason]'.[45] The same minutes reveal that only 24 out of 100 members had actually paid in that year! In modern organizations, membership benefits are managed through swipe cards, use of membership registration numbers in booking events, and similar means to limit free riding and avoid lockouts!

Systematic surveys

Since the 1980s there have been surveys of the motives for joining which allow us to put these rather fugitive historical comments into an order of relative importance. Although it is unlikely that the same ranking will apply for all periods, modern surveys give important indicators to help interpret the past. Modern surveys of joining tend to show dominance by specific service benefits (about one-half of all motives in most surveys), and gaining marketing opportunities and contacts (about one-third of all motives).[46] Contributing to the local social good, solidarity, or the desire for lobbying and representation are very small joining motives (about 10% in total). However, in all surveys it is recognized that there are multiple reasons for joining, and that solidarity goods link with more individual service benefits. Indeed modern surveys find 77% of chamber members, and 25% of lapsers give representation at least as a minor motive.[47]

For example an Aberdeen survey for 1993 indicated that the five most important reasons for joining were, in rank order: opportunities to make business contacts, public relations activities, representation (locally and nationally), to support the

---

[42] George Alcock, in Liverpool chamber *Annual Report* (1989); quoted in Cherpeau (2010), p. 46.
[43] NCT, Report of Membership Subcommittee, 27 August 1957, p. 3 (BCC Store L55).
[44] Musgrave (1914), p. 60.
[45] Newport (Mon.) chamber, minutes, 22 April 1876.
[46] See summaries of other surveys and large-scale contemporary surveys in Bennett (1996a, 2000); Bennett and Robson (2001); Bennett and Ramsden (2007); Mekic (2007).
[47] Mekic (2007).

stimulation of new business investment in the city, and to obtain advice. When asked which of these responses was closest to their *main* reasons for membership, 37% stated it was to gain direct services, 36% to support local representation, and 26% stated that both services and representation were equally important;[48] i.e. chamber motivation is bundled between services and representation, and the two combined are a *joint* USP for many members.

Other detailed surveys of multiple motivation show the nuances between motives. For example, South-East Hampshire chamber (Portsmouth) in 1990 found the main need was for the chamber to better position its specific offer compared to other organizations. It found that the chamber was viewed 'fundamentally (as) a service organisation', but offered too many practical service benefits that were too similar to other providers, and that there were not enough 'aspirational benefits'— such as professional status that would encourage higher support and solidarity.[49] Central and West Lancashire chamber in 1995 found the four main motives for joining the chamber were, in rank order: to promote my business, to develop business contacts, to support the local business community, and to access the library and information service. Use levels were highest for the services of access to library journals/online databases, information and advice, export and import documents, and telephone enquiry service or helpline. Awareness of representational committees ranged from 20% to 44%.[50] In the mid-1990s Galway chamber found that the two main motives for joining were to be part of an effective agency for local economic development and representation, and to become part of a network through which business opportunities could be grasped, with the latter most significant for SMEs and start-up firms where the chamber offers the potential for new business and contacts.[51]

A North-East chamber survey in 1996 also found the top three reasons for joining the chamber to be 'development of business contacts' (32% key factor), 'to raise our company profile' (15% key), and 'business support and advice' (14% key). Each of these was rated by 75% as at least 'quite important', whilst lobbying was only quite important or greater for 50%, and only key for 6%. Lobbying also had a lower service success rating (46% very good or quite good), compared to 62% success from business support/advice, and 59% for development of business contacts.[52] A more recent survey by Manchester in 2005 confirms a similar pattern, with 'networking opportunities' and access to 'export/international trade services' as the main motive for joining.[53] These accounted for, respectively, 40% and 14% of the most important primary services offered by the chamber, and 22% and 5%, respectively, of the most important secondary services. Lobbying was the fourth

---

[48] Survey of interest representation, in Aberdeen chamber; Jordan (1993); Jordan and Maloney (1997).

[49] S. E. Hants. chamber, *Communication and Marketing Project*, December (1990).

[50] Central and West Lancashire chamber: *Performance Survey Results* (1995).

[51] Goodbody Associates (1996), pp. 43–4.

[52] *Customer Satisfaction Survey*, March (1996), NE chamber of commerce (Market Research UK Ltd.).

[53] Quoted in Mekic (2007, table 13-3); single responses not multiple.

most important primary service (9%) and the third most important secondary motive for joining (12%).

Overall, the evidence of these local surveys confirms that member motivation is certainly complex and multiple. Whilst services may challenge representation for resources (Olson's by-product thesis),[54] representation remains a significant motive for joining, as well as interlinking with other services (in effect contributing to the overall chamber model of 'trust-based' and associational governance). This in turn suggests that members do not regard representation as a pure by-product, but as an underpinning that supports other motives to join: it defines brand and expectations. This nevertheless leaves a major challenge to chamber managers to match expectations, and it is clear that the USP alone is not enough to satisfy the members.

Different motives for different types of business?

We have seen in Chapter 14 that the 'interest' in chambers has varied over time, and membership ranges over all types of businesses. But it is surprising that almost all modern surveys show few systematic differences between firms in joining motives. Sometimes, manufacturing, older, larger, and board-managed companies are a little more likely to be service orientated; and manufacturing and export-focused companies are a little more likely to join, probably reflecting their greater use of document certification services. But few of these sector differences are major or statistically significant.

The only major difference found in almost all studies is for *business size*. The smallest firms are usually significantly more focused on motives to make business contacts, use events for marketing, and to gain specific service benefits; they are a little less interested in representation. They are, like larger businesses, interested in *both* representation and services; but the relative primacy of services over representation is greater.[55] Firm size differences were recognized by chambers from a fairly early stage, and led to differentiated subscription rates between large and small firms for the majority of chambers after 1930. As commented by Leslie Robinson, chief executive of Thames Valley chamber in 1993: 'large companies join chambers because they think they should, not to get services . . . ; SMEs join chambers to further their own business interests: to derive tangible benefit'.[56]

An implication from this is that smaller firms are more likely to join associations that more closely respond to their specific service needs. This opens the way for varied and competing memberships. In comparison to chambers of commerce, the FSB, IoD, FPB, and chambers of trade offer alternative service packages, within which legal help lines and insurance often give a strong competitive edge.[57] Serving

---

[54] Olson (1971); see Chapter 3.

[55] See particularly Mekic (2007). This is similar to other organizations (Knoke 1983).

[56] Quoted in Bennett, Krebs, and Zimmermann (1993), p. 188.

[57] See e.g. Bennett (1996a, 1998b); Bennett and Ramsden (2007); Mekic (2007); see also Salisbury (1984); van Waarden (1991), p. 70 for trade associations; in the CBI small firms are less interested in policy and more concerned to access services (Marsh 1978).

the smaller sized business members, who have become the majority interest in chambers since the 1990s, thus represents major challenges for modern chambers in terms of (i) service emphasis within the bundle, and (ii) how to engage them in broader chamber policy and the community activities.

15.3 RETENTION

Once a business has been recruited, the challenge becomes maintenance, or retention, of membership. Membership renewal (i.e. not lapsing) is a case of repeat buying, or reuse intent (continuance commitment). In marketing literature, explanations for retention draw on: satisfaction and service quality; market share and availability of alternatives; and brand choice and allegiance. These relate to purposive, solidarity, and selective benefits. Retention also depends on scale and frequency of demand, the extent to which services are exclusive to the chamber, whether it is (or is perceived to be) for-profit or non-profit, and the actual service experience.[58] Being not-for-profit may be important not just for joining but also for retention, since this encourages donor commitment and obligation beyond normal market mechanisms.[59] Chambers, like other business associations, as noted in Tables 3.1 and 3.2, offer a number of trusted, exclusive, or semi-exclusive services that may make membership essential (or desirable or lower cost). But completely exclusive markets are rare: NCT and ABCC chambers competed with each other; there are IoD, FSB, and FPB, and for-profit normal market alternatives such as professional service companies, lawyers, accountants, and consultants, as well as local government and government suppliers.

These features all relate to what membership benefits are offered and how paying for membership compares with alternatives. The additional effects of brand choice and allegiance are likely to be a more significant factor the more that a chamber is seen as a non-profit body to which 'affiliation' offers identification, solidarity, communitarian support, social networks, or similar factors. Lapsing behaviour can be reduced for non-excludable goods, because membership is seen as a voluntary contribution even if the benefits can be enjoyed anyway; i.e. membership is not a service decision but one of identification or support to a cause. This is found in a number of analyses of 'membership' of museums, 'friends' of orchestras, and alumni bodies.[60] Lapsing is also significantly reduced where membership involves volunteering, gifting, or other pro-bono inputs. Thus loyalty is stimulated by involvement in chamber committees, sections, and activities.[61] This may have increased modern relevance if 'Big Society' concepts take off.

---

[58] Bhattacharya (1998); Bennett and Robson (2004b); Ramsden and Bennett (2005).
[59] Knoke (1983); Jones (2003, 2004); Bernhagen and Bräuninger (2005).
[60] Bhattacharya (1998).
[61] As also argued more generally by Hirschman (1970); see later below.

Historical aspects

There is no historical source material that allows direct assessment of these retention motives. However, there is commentary that suggests there is a distinction
between *active and passive membership*. The active members are those on the
council and committees, and those that regularly participate in meetings and
other activities; the other members, however, are passive in making little or no
contact with the chamber's committees or events. This is true today as in the past.
This would suggest that problems of retention arise chiefly from those that are least
involved. But the passive are further divided into those that rejoin anyway, and
those that drift away. North Staffordshire in 1957 identified the passive in three
categories: those that might use the chamber but don't, those that join solely from a
sense of duty, and those that 'pay without quite knowing why'. If subscriptions
were increased 'the "silent partners" might well become vocal'.[62]

To encourage attendance and participation at meetings, some early chambers
had fines for non-attendance, or for leaving meetings early, particularly among the
committee or council. In the Belfast chamber in 1783 late attendance at the council
after 15 minutes was fined at 1s. This was clearly insufficient: late attendance fines
in 1787 were increased to 1s. after five minutes, and 2s. 6d. after 20 minutes; but in
1792 this was revised back to 1s. after 15 minutes, and early leaving without the
president's permission was fined at 2s. 8½d.; 'no excuse admitted for non-payment
of fines except sickness and absence from town'.[63] The pattern of fines mirrors
similar fines in New York in the 1768–1790s period.[64] Most early chamber
minutes show that some council members were repeatedly fined and were poor
attendees, whilst a core group of chamber members usually did most of the
business.[65] The London TPS of 1799 used a different pattern of incentives: it
paid members an attendance fee of 3s. to the first nine members attending general
meetings within the first 15 minutes, provided they stayed until the end.[66] No
modern chamber would attempt to enforce or stimulate participation through fines!
But it is indicative of the different social and economic expectations of the early
chambers that this was a typical strategy.

For the wider membership, passiveness remained a major problem. Three
comments in rather different chambers spaced over 100 years sum up the general
problem. The Swansea president in 1876 noted that: 'the subscriber supports the
organisation liberally enough with money, but not sufficiently with personal
attendance.... The chamber had a good list of subscribers, though they did not
often attend meetings... (It is) a little disappointing that when questions of

---

[62] E. James Johnson, secretary of North Staffordshire chamber: quoted in ABCC, GPC minutes,
6 November 1957.

[63] Belfast chamber, Council minutes, 14 November 1783, 25 January 1787, and 7 February 1792.

[64] Bishop (1918). There were fines for late attendance after the first 10–15 people had arrived, and
fines for non-attendance if there were over 20 people present. The fines were a considerable source of
revenue: Stevens (1867).

[65] Belfast chamber, Subcommittee book, contained in envelope of loose papers; D1857/1/AC/1/2.

[66] London Guardians or Society for the Protection of Trade, in 1799 (BL 8246.a.15).

considerable importance came up for discussion, so few gentlemen attended.'[67] In Inverness chamber in 1908 it was observed that whilst the secretary of the chamber 'answers many enquiries every week. It does not appear to be appreciated, however, by the members of the chamber themselves, as they seldom or never institute enquiries'.[68] Whilst in Winchester chamber of trade in 1976 the president mused: 'one wonders why those who "belong" do not partake'.[69]

The Aberdeen chamber undertook a survey in 1970, with the main purpose of finding out 'why a percentage of members never contacted the chamber, never attended any meetings, but nevertheless always paid their subscription!' The main response was that 'all members agreed that it was absolutely essential for the area to have an active chamber of commerce... [but] they did not want to become involved due to pressure of business and other reasons'.[70] Innovations in the chamber that resulted from this survey were the development of a distinctive trades section, diversifying to included more 'lady members', a golf section, and greater frequency of networking events. These were changes that it was thought would increase involvement without increasing burdens on members.

The reasons for the passiveness of many members are easy to understand in chambers that were chiefly focused on political lobbying. Provided someone else was managing the chamber to ensure that sensible statements were being made and the appropriate lobbies mounted, there was no need to attend meetings: this was an insider's response to the free-rider problem. Many members thus relied on the good sense of their council members to look after their interests, and paid their subscriptions as an act of solidarity and to recognize the cost of the exercise. Colchester chamber, for example, acknowledged that it 'was not a fireworks society but it was doing a great deal of quiet and useful work'.[71] For other members, however, chambers of commerce were seen as involving time-consuming committees and being potentially boring, as noted in the Aberdeen survey.

Modern surveys

For the modern period the first large-scale analysis was for the Devlin Report of 1972. This surveyed the services of chambers that were most valued by members. A summary of the results, shown in Table 15.1, demonstrates that export documentation and promotion, together with information on local matters, were the dominant service bundle at this time. In addition contacts, general information, and specific advice were important for many. National representation did figure, but only ranked as third or fifth most valued service. A notable feature is the complexity and variety of the responses. Not only were chambers providing a varied bundle, but different members had quite varied views as to which was their most

[67] Swansea chamber, report of AGM, *The Cambrian*, 28 January 1876.
[68] Inverness chamber, *Annual Report* (1908); quoted in Bristol chamber *Yearbook* (1908–9): Bristol RO 38605/Pu/35.
[69] Winchester chamber, *Bulletin,* December (1976): Hants. RO 65M90W/108.
[70] Aberdeen chamber, *Journal* (1970), p. 589.
[71] *East Anglian Daily Times*, April 1923.

valued part of the bundle. Devlin found strong contrasts between chambers and sector trade associations (where contact with other companies, general market information, and representation to government were dominant first and second ranked services). A survey by London in 1992 found a similar ranking from members: with information and advice (28% most referred), documents at reduced rates (23%), developing exports (15%), to make business contacts (15%), and conferences, seminars, and trade missions below 10%.[72]

Whilst the patterns are similar, there also appear to be important contrasts between retention and joining. The largest and most detailed survey to date of the differences between joining and retention decisions, by Mekic in 2006, shows lobbying and representation to be only a small part of the major motives to join, but they are more important for retention.[73] Mekic found that whilst services were the main motivation for joining, when respondents were asked to select the closest description of why they were members, 33% of members and 27% of lapsers gave 'supporting representation' as their motive.[74] It would thus appear that, as members experience the services of chambers, lobbying activities become more recognized as valuable, although the main motives are still services. This is reflected in other surveys that show that joining and retention is higher for organizations that offer lobbying *and* services.[75]

These interrelationships are made clear in a principal component analysis, which highlights four distinct but overlapping components of the chamber 'bundle': first, revenue generation that facilitates sales and marketing by members to other members (contacts, networking, social events); second, service motivation, which is composed of information, news, with some aspects of insurance that services are available 'just in case'; third, there are ancillary aspects, such as 'trialing' the chamber, 'the thing to do'; and fourth, lobbying/representation. Most importantly the representation factor is *positively* related to the first two factors (marketing and services) indicating the synergies with the bundle, converging on a chamber *USP of representation, marketing benefits, and other services*. Overall, Mekic's analysis explains 58% of the variation, with member service discounts being a significant additional factor in those chambers where they are used.[76]

Another insight is provided by comparison of chambers with rival business associations, shown in Table 15.2. Compared with other associations, chambers are among the least likely to gain retention benefits from representation, but are more strongly influenced by members looking for networking and marketing benefits (because of the local context for business opportunities). In comparison, trade and professional associations have the greatest retention benefits from kudos and accreditation. The FSB and FPB have the sharpest focus of retention on

---

[72] Survey of 400 companies, 1992; R. M. Jacobsen, general manager, London chamber, *Business Needs: The Future Market for Business Services*, quoted in Bennett, Krebs, and Zimmermann (1993), pp. 105–11.

[73] Mekic (2007): stratified random quota sample of members and lapsed members; N = 430.

[74] Mekic (2007), pp. 6.128–6.133.

[75] e.g. Knoke (1983), table 5; Jordan (1993).

[76] Mekic (2007), chapter 6; see also Bennett and Ramsden (2007).

Table 15.1. Assessment of the services most valued by chamber members in 1971: ranked frequencies of the five services valued as the most useful, second most useful, etc.

Rank	1st most useful	2nd most useful	3rd most useful	4th most useful	5th most useful
1	**Export documentation**	**Export promotion**	**Information on local matters**	**Information on local matters**	General information
2	**Export promotion**	**Information on local matters**	**General information**	General information	National representation
3	Information on local matters	Local representation	Local representation	Export documentation	Contact with others
4	Contact with others	General information	Specific advice	Contact with others	Information on local matters
5	General information	Export documentation	National representation	Export documentation	Export documentation

Note: Bold is those receiving over 15% of responses in each column.
Source: Simplified from Devlin Report (1972), table 5, p. 126; N = 870.

Table 15.2. The most important motives for why a member maintains membership: percentage of respondents, multiple responses, stratified random quota sample, telephone interviews in England, Scotland, and Wales 2003

Motive	Chambers	Trade and prof. assoc.	FSB	FPB	IoD	CBI	Business Club	All
Information	52.5	70.9	63.6	75.0	63.0	100	56.3	64.0
Advice	47.4	60.7	72.7	50.0	44.5	66.6	43.8	55.2
Lobbying/ representation	28.8	57.2	72.7	87.5	44.5	66.6	18.8	50.9
Networking	50.8	52.1	27.3	37.5	25.9	33.3	81.2	47.4
Marketing opportunities	33.9	29.9	9.1	25.0	7.4	16.7	37.5	27.2
Social activities	13.5	18.8	4.5	12.5	7.4	16.7	43.8	5.5
For kudos	15.3	32.1	22.7	12.5	29.6	0	6.3	24.1
For accreditation	8.5	32.5	0	12.5	3.7	0	0	18.1
Other	28.8	21.4	13.6	25.0	48.1	0	25.0	23.6

Source: Bennett and Ramsden (2007), table 4 (n = 194).

services *jointly* with representation. Chambers in modern times, in emphasizing services to a greater extent than in the past, may thus have contributed to lowering their retention levels. Whilst networking and services gives them considerable strengths, their link to representation now appears to be less recognized than for most rival bodies: this should be a major concern.

Voice, involvement, loyalty, and commitment

In interpreting joining and retention it is important to remember that membership of chambers in Britain and Ireland is voluntary: thus associations exist because member businesses want them to exist, and are willing to pay and make other voluntary inputs of time and effort. As a process for individual businesses (or more specifically for their owner/manager) the membership joining decision will go through stages of search, awareness, experiment, and exploration. Having joined, a member will then undergo experiential learning during which they will assess the benefits and costs of their membership. As time progresses the assessment of costs and benefits will lead to decisions to maintain membership, lapse, or seek to change the offer received from membership.

Hirschman, in seminal studies, has highlighted the alternative strategies available: exit, voice, loyalty, and involvement.[77] Dissatisfaction with experiences or the cost-benefit trade-offs will result in *exit*: a member lapses. *Exiting* will be influenced by the same motives for joining and retaining membership, strongly affected by elasticity of demand for the chamber services.[78] Members seeking purposive/

[77] Hirschman (1970, 1982).
[78] Bennett (1996a, 2000); Dowding (1994); Mekic (2007).

expressive and solidarity benefits will be less affected by service quality or cost; indeed they may not be users of specific services at all; but members joining for selective service benefits will be more likely to exit as a result of poor service quality or cost.

An alternative to exit is *voice*: a member seeks to change the decisions of the association by expressing dissatisfaction and complaining. However, Hirschman concludes that voice is infrequent because of various limitations: first, it takes effort and is often ineffective; second, it is subject to capture, or at least distortion, by the most active members; and third, if an organization is really failing to reach its constituency, a large number of possible members are likely to have already left or never joined so that the remainder are a self-selective minority: thus exit may drive out voice.

As a result an association has to rely heavily on *loyalty* that, despite possible weaknesses, members feel that they must continue to support it through solidarity or donor commitment. However, loyalty alone is usually insufficient; there also needs to be *involvement* by which the member feels that they have some influence or are valued in some way by the association and do not become detached; e.g. by becoming involved in committees and meetings.

Voice

Voice is a potentially tedious and time-consuming activity. However, in one of the few analyses of this, Mekic has found a surprisingly large proportion of chamber members willing to give voice in various ways. The results, summarized in Table 15.3, show a wide range of methods of voice, most being instant phoning or emailing. Voice is higher among lapsers than members, but the impact they perceived is nearly one-third lower. The leavers seem to be a group who are more willing to voice but have been less satisfied with how their voice has been heard; this is an important factor in their lapsing decision. They become detached. More detailed analysis shows that those who strongly support representation, and volunteer time to their chamber to attend events and meetings, are most likely to be satisfied. This interrelates with a general observation, that many members, and particularly lapsers, are concerned about the time that it takes to be an active chamber member. An important finding is that size of member firm is not a significant influence or propensity to voice or on its perceived impact. Nor are most other possible explanatory factors significant. This contrasts with Useem's expectation that larger firms seek to exert more control over the associations they join, and this creates frustrations for other members.[79]

Involvement

Hirschman identifies involvement as a critical aspect for retaining members. It also interfaces with attempts to move the passive to become more active members.

---

[79] Useem (1983); Mekic (2007).

Table 15.3. Form of voice when dissatisfaction experienced, and its impact among members and lapsers of chambers in 2006 (percentage of respondents)

	Remaining members	Lapsers
Filled in a feedback form	23	6
Attended a General Meeting in order to voice	13	14
Sent a letter about the issue	8	14
Phoned them about the issue	45	50
Emailed them about the issue	25	19
Other	8	33
Total making voice	39	50
Total not making voice	61	50
Impact perceived as positive a little, moderate, or high	64	22

Source: Mekic (2007), tables 17–33 to 17–35; N = 103 members and 72 lapsers.

Marshalling and managing the forces of solidarity and alignment of interests does not happen by chance, and this is where members should be involved. However, this requires input of significant resources of time and effort from chamber managers, members, and elected officers. Initially, chambers, like other societies, relied primarily on the voluntary input of elected officers, especially the president. But as the membership of chambers became larger, professional staff became more significant. This creates barriers, but also opportunities to increase involvement. For example, in the case of London and many of the larger chambers, a membership department was developed with in-house staff that sought members and maintained involvement through contact. A membership canvasser was another way to assist the marketing of membership and follow-up of arrears and potential defection. But the use of staff and canvassers can increase feelings of detachment if the appointees are not close to the chamber and well trained. Hence, there is usually no substitute for effort by the chamber's officers and senior members if involvement is to be maintained. This means that chambers contain the difficult tension of finding active business people who simultaneously have enough time to facilitate all this involvement; this is usually a contradiction and such individuals are rare.

Loyalty

The loyalty of members derives from solidarity and identification with the objectives of the chamber and the amount of effort previously invested in it.[80] However, these are not necessarily well-defined motives. The literature of organizational commitment has been little used in the context of associations,[81] but has been an important part of social network interpretations of partnership/network bodies.[82] In this interpretation,

[80] Barry (1974); Boroff and Lewin (1997); Dowding (1994).
[81] Gruen, Summers, and Acito (2000).
[82] Laumann and Pappi (1976); Knoke (1983); Laumann and Knoke (1987).

commitment is a 'stabilising or obliging force' that 'gives direction to behaviour',[83] or 'the degree of attachment'.[84] There are three dimensions:[85]

- *Affective commitment:* personal ties, the desire to stay, identification with the chamber, status or kudos gained.
- *Normative commitment:* feeling of moral obligation.
- *Continuance commitment:* reuse intent, remaining a member balanced by its costs and the costs of leaving.

Historically, loyalty was stimulated by involvement through large-scale meetings, libraries and coffee rooms, personal networks, and opportunities for discourse. Direct communication and participation was a key feature in increasing commitment (or reducing detachment). In modern bodies other forms of communication and involvement are necessary, which may be possible through different forms of meetings and events (and now through web-based exchange and crowd sourcing). Table 15.2 suggests that for chambers, networking and marketing events will be the prime stimuli. There may also be surrogates of detachment related to association size, as suggested by Olson's argument that increasing size makes it more difficult to achieve agreement or association objectives and strategies.[86] This may explain the persistence of smaller chambers: with higher retention because they have stronger attachment and involvement.

Commitment

Member commitment to chambers seems to come most strongly from reuse intent (continuance commitment), as shown in Table 15.4. This is both relatively narrowly economic and calculative (important to my business), as well as including a level of identification and affective attachment (happy to be a member). However, moral obligation also plays a minor role (normative commitment), but this is less in the form of responsibility to the local community than to the chamber itself. Mekic found some interrelationships between the levels of commitment and the member's orientation towards representation or service benefits, but the main explanatory features were greater commitment by users rather than non-users of services, which rose with duration of membership, and was greater for those who had stronger involvement through attending events or had been in contact. Commitment also increased with service discounts, which created benefits that would be forgone by exit. Smaller chambers also had stronger affective commitment (happy to be a member). Other differences between member firms or chambers were not significant.

Trust-based commitment is also important. Indeed in Ireland, a 2004 branding study of chambers found that 'trust' and 'enabler to business' were key concepts

---

[83] Meyer and Herscovitch (2001).
[84] Gruen, Summers, and Acito (2000).
[85] Mekic (2007); following Allen and Meyer (1990).
[86] Gruen, Summers, and Acito (2000); Knoke (1983); Olson (1971); Mekic (2007).

Table 15.4. Extent of commitment to local chambers among continuing members and lapsers in 2006 (percentage of respondents, multiple responses, agreeing or strongly agreeing with each statement)

	Members	Lapsers
Remaining a member is important to my business	67	13
I would be happy to be a member for a long time	83	50
It would be costly for me to find an alternative	37	16
I am happy to reuse services	92	31
Right now, staying a member is a matter of necessity	26	2
Leaving my chamber would be neglecting my responsibility to the community	29	0
I do not feel any moral obligation to remain a member	58	84

Source: Mekic (2007), tables 17–42 and 17–43; N = 336 members and 105 leavers.

associated with chambers by more than half of respondents.[87] This was relatively higher in chambers than for competing public sector providers, and for more specific market links such as those to customers and suppliers. But chambers did not exceed the trust levels of family and friends, or even lawyers and accountants. Moreover, in the UK levels of trust have been found to be not strongly linked to service impacts or satisfaction. Trust seems to be chiefly interrelated with cost, serving objectives of improving management knowledge and capacity.[88] Similarly, Mekic found trust to be largely independent of the motives for joining, but most important to retention: 64% of members trusted their chambers more than any other association; 62% trusted chambers more than other private sector suppliers; and 59% indicated that they found the chamber more reliable than other suppliers. Compared to these, lapsed members only trusted the chamber more than other associations in 42% of cases, and only 36% thought it was more reliable than alternatives. Thus, trust appears to be a factor in explaining retention for nearly two-thirds of members, with poor service experiences leading to a breakdown of trust encouraging lapsing.[89] Hence, trust is not abstract; it has to deliver.

Detachment

Prior to exit, detachment of members occurs. This seems to have complimentary patterns to those of commitment and trust (Table 15.5). Lapsers become more detached than continuing members, as expected, but the two most frequent aspects of this are the sense that the views of their business are ignored (88%), or that a lapser can rely on others to be active (71%) (i.e. they can free ride). Many continuing members, interestingly, also share these views, so that members may move fairly readily from commitment to detachment and then lapse. Chamber managers need to be

[87] Survey quoted in Chambers Ireland, *Annual Report* (2005), p. 14; survey of 500 member and 500 non-member businesses; however, 82% were not fully aware of what chambers do.
[88] Bennett and Robson (2004b), especially tables II and IV.
[89] Mekic (2007), chapter 6.

Table 15.5. Extent of detachment from local chambers among continuing members and lapsers in 2006 (percentage of respondents agreeing or strongly agreeing with each statement)

	Members	Lapsers
I don't care what my chamber says or does	8	48
I don't care about my chamber's representation and lobbying policy	8	44
I don't agree with my chamber's representation and lobbying policy	7	40
My business does not have much say in what the chamber does	64	88
It doesn't matter whether my business participates as other members are active	33	71
I feel a strong sense of belonging to my chamber	53	8

Source: Mekic (2007), tables 17–40 and 17–41; N = 332 members and 105 leavers.

concerned that 64% of continuing members believe they have no say, and 33% believe they can rely on other members. Indeed only a slim majority have strong affective commitment: a sense of 'belonging' to their chamber. This must be a strong contrast with historic chambers. Factors that reduce detachment are representational activity, volunteering time, use of services, staff competence, and attending events. This is one of the few areas where different types of member firm are significant: non-manufacturing businesses are more detached. This may reflect the historic tensions between manufacturing and retail/commercial members in chambers.

This discussion can be amplified by noting the implications of more complex multivariate analyses of the link between commitment and service indicators such as satisfaction and impact, taking account of the role of service intensity, costs, and distance to supplier. In an analysis of the experience by small firms of a range of suppliers, including chambers, there is a complex range of links and feedbacks on loyalty and membership retention, as shown in Figure 15.1. The experience of service support from chambers leads to a range of impacts and satisfaction levels which have highly significant effects on loyalty and satisfaction from 'hard' impacts (increased profitability to members strongly influences commitment), as well as 'soft' measures (where 'ability to manage' has been increased). The type of firm (its age, size, and sector) influences impacts only for firm size (higher in smaller firms). Intermediate process variables, such as costs, service intensity, and the geographical distance between the chamber and the member have only minor influence.[90] These findings complement other surveys that show that chambers are better at delivering 'hard' impacts on the bottom line than most other suppliers (except direct business customers and suppliers), and they deliver similar levels of 'soft' impacts to those of other suppliers.[91] These features provided the considerably better performance that chambers generally offered to the small firm advisory services through Business Link compared to other franchisees (as noted in Chapter 13).

[90] Stratified quota sample of 210 firms in five contrasted economies with varied chambers: Manchester, Oldham, Derby, Dundee, and Thames Valley; Bennett and Robson (2005).
[91] Bennett and Robson (1999a); Ramsden and Bennett (2005); Bennett and Ramsden (2007).

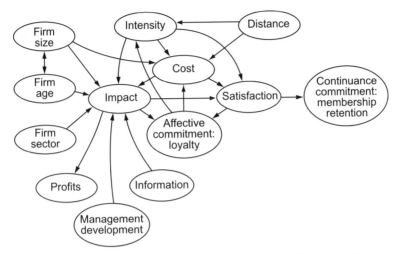

Fig. 15.1. The links between chamber membership retention, loyalty, and the service experience. (*Source*: developed from Bennett and Robson 2005, figure 1.)

This discussion, drawing on modern assessments, suggests strongly that direct voice activities by members are relatively infrequent, and hence loyalty and inertia are dominant aspects of retention, even if members remain dissatisfied (as also concluded by Hirschman). Whilst this may suggest that there is a large passive membership of chambers, modern surveys show high levels of member satisfaction and impact from services. In the modern chamber it appears that individual service experiences are the main motives for reuse intent (retaining membership), with high satisfaction and impact being the strongest positive forces. There is an additional loyalty effect, which comes from trust in the brand of chambers. The 'interest' in the chamber seems to be merged into the general loyalty to the locality and to the chamber itself. There is only one important influence of firm type—firm size. This tends to reduce the concern for voice among small firms to a more minor motive, but increases the positive influence of the service experiences received. This is not new; for example, in London in 1919 'it has constantly been pointed out that the smaller members benefit from membership to a greater extent than the larger and more powerful concerns, which as a general rule, require to make less use of the chamber'.[92] Given the dominance of the small firm in modern chambers, this presents a major challenge.

15.4 LAPSING

Lapsing from membership, unlike joining, was a historical concern for chamber managers and their elected councils, and some of these chambers kept detailed records. London's is the best of these. For the period from 1910 until 1971 its

---

[92] London chamber, Executive Committee, Treasurer's Report, 11 December 1919.

'member books' record for most cases why a member has lapsed. A number of other chambers also maintained historical records for some years. Although the motives for lapsing may differ from those for joining, especially in ranking, with an emphasis on negatives, the records for lapsing are enormously helpful to infer something about historical patterns of joining and retention. Lapsing will be encouraged when purposive/expressive benefits are no longer in congruence with the member's values. Solidarity benefits can turn into disadvantages if the association is found to be a 'closed shop' and if 'patrons' are disliked or seek to accrue too many personal benefits to themselves. Material/selective motives for lapsing will arise from poor services and/or high costs. Lack of use of insurance benefits may eventually lead to lapsing from a sense that these services will never be used.

London's experiences

The available historical information on lapsing from chambers is recorded in different ways. Only London undertook 'exit interviews', usually by telephone.[93] Over the period 1910 to 1931 it recorded a template of ten reasons for lapsing, which were modified and reduced to nine for 1932–71. This allows analysis of 49,649 lapsers over the period. Analysis of the template statistics for all 9–10 categories is shown in Table 15.6. Despite possible inconsistencies over time, three patterns are clear. First, discounting 'other' and 'no reason stated', the main cause of lapsing was being struck off for unpaid subscriptions. Analysis of the 'other' category confirms that some of these were explicit resignations (about 5–10%), but most also just stop paying. It is probably fair to add to this category those with 'no reason stated' since they too certainly did not pay. In this case those members that just gave up paying amount to over 50% of the total up to 1950. The exception to this was during the two world wars, where lapsing rates, with non-payment and no reason significantly reduced to 42% during WW1, and 38% during WW2.

A second pattern evident in Table 15.6 is the relatively wide range of other reasons for lapsing. All are understandable business reasons: death or retirement of the member, bankruptcy or liquidation, movement to another area, or amalgamation. Third, there are some trends in these data: death becomes less important, presumably because of improved life expectancy during working lives, but also because of the shift from individual owner/managers to corporate forms. Moving becomes less important. Financial reasons, either of bankruptcy/liquidation or general 'financial reasons', become more important. The combined category of financial and bankruptcy is around 20% of the total for most of the period after 1931. These patterns suggest an important financial component of the membership decision for many members, possibly of growing significance over time. However,

---

[93] The staff involved in maintaining the 'membership book' changed. Comparing handwriting, the clerks changed in 1916, mid-1921, mid-1951, 1958, and 1961; several clerks handled 1954–7. A new secretary in 1932 modified the recording system. Checks on the recorded pattern against scribbled comments show they are remarkably consistent.

Table 15.6. Analysis of reasons for 49,649 lapsing from London chamber as recorded in template tick list in membership books, 1910–1971

	1910–14	1915–18	1919–30	1931–8	1939–45	1946–50	1951–60	1961–71
Application withdrawn or refused[a]	0.6	1.1	0.1	n/a	n/a	n/a	n/a	n/a
Death	8.7	8.2	5.4	4.9	7.5	3.7	3.0	2.8
Bankruptcy/ Liquidation	6.7	3.4	10.3	10.2	8.4	6.8	5.8	9.1
Subscription unpaid	19.0	16.9	20.3	23.6	24.5	28.4	16.6	21.6
Retired	3.9	1.7	3.4	2.2	2.5	3.4	3.2	2.7
Gone away	7.9	9.6	3.8	2.7	4.3	1.8	0.2	1.7
Chamber no use[b]	4.9	2.3	1.4	n/a	n/a	n/a	n/a	n/a
Financial reasons[b]	n/a	n/a	n/a	9.2	19.7	4.4	19.2	12.0
Amalgamation[b]	n/a	n/a	n/a	3.2	3.2	4.7	3.3	8.2
No reason stated	34.3	25.1	38.9	32.4	13.7	28.6	9.6	5.4
Other	14.0	31.7	16.4	11.6	16.2	18.1	39.1	36.5
N	1841	1892	9808	6976	3480	3879	9881	11892

[a] This category was removed in 1931.
[b] These categories were modified in 1931 when template in member book was changed.
Source: London chamber membership books, MS16456.

the data are frustrating because of the high proportion that just lapse with no reason available.

For most of the period, as well as maintaining the template, London also had scribbled comments for 'other reasons' for lapsing written over the members' payment records; e.g. 'refused to pay', 'says he no longer wants the service'. Samples of these for ten-year periods, shown in Table 15.7, reveal some important trends. Those stating 'no time' to participate overlap with 'seldom in London' in the scribbled comments: they both seem to relate to membership by people whose businesses were relatively distant. London for a long period had a membership that was national as well as local and so this reason for lapsing is quite understandable. It also seems to be bound up with the emergence of other chambers that were more local to the member. 'Joined another chamber' became important after 1920. These were very varied: Bradford, Liverpool, Manchester, Glasgow, Birmingham, and Medway were the most common, but 29 chambers were mentioned in all, some extremely small and minor entities more akin to chambers of trade, e.g. Ealing. The presence of Westminster and Croydon, the other most local major chambers, became of significance for London resignations from the 1950s. It is clear that London was experiencing increasing competition. This is also evident for those leaving to other business associations. Some of these are to the FBI/CBI founded in 1916, but most are to sector trade associations, which emerged as important players from the 1920s.

Cost cutting is the single largest 'other' category in most years, and this could have been included in the template recordings shown in Table 15.6 (for example as 'financial

Table 15.7. Reasons for lapsing from the London chamber as stated in scribbled comments (ascribed to 'other' as listed in Table 15.6); percentage for each year

	1883–1909	1910	1920	1930	1950	1961–2
Struck off	—	5.0	0.3	1.4	1.9	—
No time/seldom in London	50.0	26.7	3.2	2.9	0.6	—
Cost cutting	21.8	11.7	9.4	75.8	40.0	3.6
Liquidation/sale of business	—	13.3	14.0	8.6	—	19.1
Left London	—	15.0	2.8	1.4	3.1	5.6
Sick/ill	—	13.3	0.3	7.1	0.6	1.1
Joined another chamber	—	—	5.7	1.4	11.9	8.0
Joined another association	—	—	3.2	—	5.6	4.1
Another company member belongs to chamber	—	—	6.3	1.4	—	0.9
No use of services	28.2	15.0	2.4	—	36.3	47.6
Subscription increase	—	—	51.0	—	—	9.4
Disagree with chamber policy	—	—	1.4	—	—	—
Dissatisfied	—	—	—	—	—	0.6

Note: Information for 1910–62 from a sample analysis of the members books; for 1883–1909 the information is from council minutes for those cases where comment is noted. After 1962 the scribbled comments cease.
Source: London chamber membership books, MS 16456.

reasons'), but the clerks did not do so. The effect of the slump is particularly prominent, as it is also for liquidation, which is included in both 'other' and the template. Subscription increases are important in the years where they occur (1920 and 1962; especially in 1920), which is discussed further in Chapter 16.

An interesting category is where a negative view is expressed about the chamber's offer. In the template analysis (Table 15.6), a category was included of 'chamber no use' up to 1930. This accounted for a small number of lapsers: ranging from 1.4 to 4.9%. In Table 15.7 those that make 'no use of services' are a similarly titled category which is a large proportion of the 'others' in the early years, and becomes important again after the 1950s. Translated back to proportions of the *total* lapsers, these are a small but important element: 0.5% in 1883–1909, 2.9% in 1910, 0.6% in 1920, then 5.2% in 1950, and 8.6% in 1961–2. This is a generally rising trend. Services not used, although a small element of lapsing, are thus an increasing component of decision to lapse. In addition there is a very small component of the 'dissatisfied' that emerges in the 1960s. A small disaffected group in the 1920 sample arises from specific policy stances by the chamber at that time, where the scribbled comment is 'disagreed with chamber's policies' (this seems to have concerned tariff policy).

Other chambers

Several other chambers have members' information that allows the London data to be assessed for generality. A sample of 11 chambers is reported in Table 15.8, about one-third to one-half of which have information for any one period. In these data the most notable pattern is again the large category of won't pay/resigned. The deceased are a steeply declining group. The retired generally increase. Those leaving

Table 15.8. Main reasons for lapsing from chamber membership 1790–1980 from a sample for 11 chambers (Cardiff, Chesterfield, Edinburgh, Ipswich, Lancaster, Manchester, Middlesbrough, Newcastle-upon-Tyne, North Shields, Sheffield, Worcester)

	1790–1860	1891–1913	1920–1938	1946–1960	1961–1980
Lapsed, resigned, won't pay	42.5	57.6	62.5	53.9	60.9
Deceased	51.6	28.4	19.8	16.4	3.9
Retired	0	0.4	2.5	5.1	4.7
Left area	5.8	5.8	6.0	0.8	6.9
Business sale, closure, amalgamation	0	6.2	5.5	16.4	18.8
Other	0.1	1.6	3.7	7.4	5.1
N of chambers	4	6	7	7	4

the area stay fairly constant, whilst company restructuring through sale, closure, or amalgamation becomes a major factor after WW2. Other comments also show that adverse economic conditions certainly had some influence on joining in periods such as the 1920s and 1930s, and the recessions of the early 1980s and 1990s. For example, Blackburn chamber noted in 1930 that 'the council has made efforts to induce business men to join the chamber, but trade conditions are disheartening, and little progress has been made'.[94] Sheffield chamber in 1929 noted that 'trade depression . . . is perhaps the most direct cause of firms not taking up membership'.[95] Liverpool in 1930 put high lapsing down to 'very bad trade, people going out of business and amalgamations'.[96] Apart from the specific conditions of the slump, one factor in the changing emphases on reasons for lapsing is the progressive shift of industrial structure over this period away from the self-employed entrepreneur and partnership (who lapse through death, retirement, or moving), towards the corporate legal form (who lapse chiefly for economic and internal reasons). Liverpool's chair over the 1970s put down losses to changes in industrial structures and closure of major businesses, as well as the chamber's slowness to adapt.[97] These patterns of lapsing are very similar to the London record, if the categories of 'unpaid' and 'no reason' are aggregated, which suggests that London's generally superior historical data give a valid broad indicator for the chambers as a whole.

A more detailed analysis by the Sheffield chamber in 1953–4 of 41 of its members in arrears classed them into two groups. Of these, 26 were 'unavoidable lapsers' (63.4%) who would not pay or renew. The remaining 15 were discussed as 'not unavoidable lapsers', of which nine were ignoring all reminders to pay or were explicitly refusing. Of the remaining six, almost all gave economic reasons for not paying; e.g. 'two guineas is a lot of money', 'trading is difficult', 'times are bad'.[98] These findings contrast with an earlier Sheffield analysis of 1948–9 lapsers that

[94] Blackburn chamber, *Annual Report* (1930), p. 48.
[95] Sheffield chamber, Council minutes, 28 January 1929, p. H12 (LD 1986/13).
[96] Liverpool, *Annual Report* (1930); quoted in Cherpeau (2010), p. 38.
[97] David Tinsley, comment in September 2010; quoted in Cherpeau (2010), p. 45.
[98] Sheffield chamber, Membership Committee minutes, 1948–9, 1953–4, LD2536/1.

Table 15.9. Reasons for lapsing from individual membership of NCT 1911–1932, analysis of scribbled comments in membership book

	1911	1920	1930
	Cohort of joiners that had resigned by 1915	Cohort of joiners that had resigned by 1925	Cohort of joiners that had resigned by 1935
Removed	0.6	—	—
Dead	20.4	8.4	18.5
Explicitly resigned	29.3	26.2	57.4
Failed to pay/ lapsed	43.1	62.7	22.2
Gone out of business	4.9	0.4	1.9
Retired	0.6	1.3	—
Gone away	1.1	0.9	—

Source: NCT, MS 29342.

emphasized 'lack of common interest' (17%), cost cutting (30%), nationalization (13%), and business closure (13%).

In NCT chambers there was even less attention to member motivation. However, for the *individual* members of the central NCT itself (rather than local chambers), it is possible to gain insight from the scribbled comments in their membership book. This is shown for three cohorts in Table 15.9. As with chambers of commerce, failure to pay with no stated reasons is a major factor, and is larger in the 1920–5 period and 1930–5 slump, than in the earlier periods. For the explicit reasons for lapsing, death is at a similar level to that for chambers of commerce of the same periods (compare Tables 15.7 and 15.8), whilst retirement and gone away are lower. The 'gone out of business' category is smaller, but probably many are hidden in the resigned/lapsed category.

Modern chambers

An increased degree of attention has been directed to assessing reasons for lapsing in recent years. Mekic was able to quote five chamber surveys undertaken in 2006, as shown in Table 15.10. These show that non-payment remains the single largest reason for lapsing in most cases. In Manchester, where all cases of non-payment were followed up (but sample size is very small), the lapsers gave a fuller statement: lack of usefulness of the service was the major reason for leaving, followed by changes in the business member itself. Subscription costs were also a factor, particularly where changes in chamber organization had occurred. At the 2006 survey date, Manchester had merged with many smaller chambers and some of the transferred members clearly felt aggrieved by the resultant large increases in subscription costs. But even in the cases of the other chambers where internal organization was relatively stable (particularly in

Table 15.10. Surveys of six chambers of commerce in 2006: percentage of respondents giving reasons for lapsing in each area

	Total weighted average	Surrey	Portsmouth and SE Hants.	Black Country	Manchester	North-East
Business ceased trading/moved/ takeover	22.2	14	18	19	13	32
Chamber services not used	28.1	25	22	30	54	27
Non-payment/ dormant/lost contact	36.0	51	41	39		25
Subscriptions too high/cost cutting	7.3	4	4	7	21	10
Dissatisfaction/ complaint	1.5	—	—	1	8	3
Change in business policy	1.9	2	5	—	—	3
Other	3.0	4	10	4	4	—
N	1561	410	95	437	24	574

Notes: Categories not always directly comparable, sample sizes vary greatly, methods of data collection vary, and in the case of Manchester and Bradford only respondents giving specific reasons are included in the results quoted.
Source: Recalculated from Mekic (2007), tables 13–4 to 13–8.

the North-East which was last reorganized 15 years earlier), subscription costs were important reasons for lapsing, ranging from 4% to 10%. The cost/benefit trade-off of services and subscriptions is, therefore, a key modern aspect of membership decisions to remain or lapse as it was at many points in the past.

Dissatisfaction with services (other than not using them) is a relatively small feature. Manchester's higher level of dissatisfaction seems to be accounted for, again, mainly by reorganization: half of these respondents had 'bad experiences', but the other half were dissatisfied with their needs not being met, which shows more a mismatch of expectation, marketing, and information availability. An important aspect of these surveys is that only one respondent out of the total of 1561 lapsed because they were 'not happy with the chamber's policy'. Hence, the concern of academic political science/sociology with associations being constrained by the need to align to different members' interests appears to be virtually irrelevant. This may be because the chambers are very good at managing interest alignment, because the policy interests that chambers represent are common effectively to *all* businesses, or because the primary concern of many members (and particularly lapsers) is not representation at all (but services and other benefits).

These individual surveys are complemented by a large-scale national survey by Mekic that found that the largest motive for lapsing was 'not using the service' (68%), followed by 'not finding the services useful' (55%). Subscription costs, 'poor service', 'ineffectiveness of representation', 'can access service anyway', and 'indifference' were all-important secondary factors (each 22–8%) of multiple responses.[99] Businesses ceasing to trade, merger/takeover, and 'changes in corporate policy' together accounted for about 20% of lapsing motives.

It is clear from these various surveys that multiple and overlapping factors influence lapsing, as they do joining. Objective conditions (going out of business, merger, etc.) are important, but the main feature behind lapsing is level of service use, service experiences, and costs. Thus the economic judgement of both costs *and* benefits are clearly important underpinnings to the lapsing decision, whilst for joining and retention the main focus is on a wide range of possible benefits rather than costs.[100]

15.5 'PERSISTENCE' OF MEMBERSHIP

An interesting question is how membership lapsing influences the overall 'age structure' of membership: is there a 'persistent member' that hangs on over many years whose 'loyalty' is the bedrock of the membership, with lapsing occurring mainly from those who have most recently joined, as a result of negative outcomes from the 'trialling' of services. Information on these features relies on detailed collation of historical records of lapsing and joining, which is only possible where these records exist. It has only been attempted in four cases:[101] for Glasgow 1783–1820, Edinburgh 1810–20, Dublin 1925–50, and Middlesbrough 1963 and 1974 (see Tables 15.11 and 15.12). The information gleaned suggests that, in each case, at least 50% of members are persistent in retaining membership for at least ten years, rising to 95% in early Glasgow. But 20–40% of members are relatively

Table 15.11. Proportion of members with years of continuous membership of the Edinburgh and Glasgow chambers at various dates.

Years of membership	Edinburgh		Glasgow	
	1810	1816	1800	1819
0–5	38.5	32.9	2.7	4.8
6–10	11.0	34.2	15.0	43.6
11–15	4.3	5.5	8.8	29.9
16–10	—	—	73.5	2.4
Over 20	46.2	27.4	—	18.3

Note: Chambers founded in 1786 and 1783, respectively, so that long-term membership is not possible in earlier years.
Source: Edinburgh membership roll book ED005/8/3; Glasgow member lists 1783–1847 TD 1670/1/8 and minutes.

[99] Mekic (2007); major motives; stratified quota sample for local economies, regions and chamber types N = 450.
[100] This is similar to sector trade associations, but 'lack of use' is less frequent than in chambers (Bennett 2000).
[101] Note the periods in Glasgow and Edinburgh that used solely a life subscription are excluded.

Table 15.12. Proportion of members with years of continuous membership of the Dublin and Middlesbrough chambers at various dates

Years of membership	Dublin			Middlesbrough	
	1925	1930	1950	1963	1974
0–5 }	28.7	65.0	64.7	24.7	38.6
6–10 }				24.7	13.8
11–15 }	37.1	16.8	17.0	13.6	11.1
16–20 }				14.5	8.5
21–30	12.6	11.7	9.8	8.9	12.9
31–40	8.4	2.9	5.9	6.0	5.1
41–50	8.4	2.2	2.6	4.3	5.3
over 50	4.9	1.5	0	3.4	4.7

Sources: Dublin, published membership lists at each date; Middlesbrough, membership books, U/CC/8/6 and 9.

shorter term. Over this wide span of periods these chambers indicate that a core membership evolves with fairly constant proportions across cohorts for those exceeding 10–15 years of membership; whilst much of the 'churn' is concentrated in the first five or ten years after joining.

Comparison of the chambers also suggests that the speed of lapsing may have increased from the 18th to the 19th, and again into the 20th centuries. Thus membership may have been subject to a declining level of persistence over time, possibly as a result of the shift to greater emphasis on services. Care must be exercised in comparisons, but increase in lapse rates is confirmed by other data presented in Chapter 16.

If these phenomena are general, then they confirm that many businesses take on membership only for a trial period. This contrasts with the stable and committed group that is in continuous membership for many years from which lapsing occurs much more slowly. Once a member has maintained membership for about five years, they are likely to continue until a major change in their circumstances occurs. Indeed, the duration of membership has been found to be a significant negative correlate of lapsing in other studies of memberships.[102] Comparing Tables 15.6–15.10 suggests that reasons for lapsing such as retirement, moving away, or going out of business, are generally those given by long-term members who lapse. This also accords with the expectation that they are the more likely to feel obliged to give an explanation for lapsing. Those who won't pay or are struck off for non-payment are mainly the short-term members who feel little obligation and have been either dissatisfied, make little use, met their needs quickly, or have found an alternative.

---

[102] e.g. Bhattacharya (1998); Mekic (2007).

15.6 COSTS: THE PRICING DECISION

Motives for membership are not based on the benefits alone, but are balanced by the costs. This may be a pure 'rational choice' decision, as argued particularly by Olson, or it may be that cost contains other signals. In a market for general goods high price may signal high quality, often linked to brand; low price may signal lower quality. But in a not-for-profit context low price can also be indicative of trusted benefits, the brand, and the unique value of services that may not be available elsewhere: subscriptions can be treated as a donation or solidarity gift to a good cause.[103]

Chambers finance themselves through subscriptions, fees for services, and other income (of which government contracts have become a major source since the 1980s). The subscription is, however, the key pricing relationship with the members. It is this that is most perceptible on joining. It also provides a baseline against which to evaluate decisions to retain membership when annual payments become due. If fully rational, as each annual invoice arrives, even for solidarity benefits, a member will evaluate the subscription costs against the benefits received, and should be able to factor in the influence of other fees and costs borne over the year.

In fact, historically the subscription rates of chambers have been low, and Grant and Greaves have argued that they are below a 'rationality threshold', too small for a member to be bothered spending the time to consider.[104] This assertion is tested thoroughly in Chapter 17, by comparing joining and lapsing rates over periods of change in subscriptions, where it is shown that subscription costs have significant influences on membership choices and are thus definitely above any rationality threshold.

It is certainly clear that managers and elected committees have seen changes in subscriptions as one of the most sensitive decisions they have to make; and have often made these increases very reluctantly and belatedly. Subscriptions thus seem to embody a critical piece of the relationship between the member and the management of a chamber. Indeed, Dublin in 1820, after first considering a two-guinea subscription modified it to one guinea, recognizing the need to find alternative sources that 'carry into effect some permanent financial project whereby a revenue can be created more certain and less burdensome than that of voluntary individual subscription'.[105] London chamber in 1884 stated 'we must do more and better work for them [members]; and we must, above all aim at giving some palpable return for their money'.[106] Perhaps the issue is best summed up by North Staffordshire chamber in 1957: 'chambers are no different to commercial firms—they must produce the goods for which a demand exists. . . . Alternatively they must be dynamic enough to create

---

[103] Hirschman (1970); Bhattacharya (1998); Jones (2003, 2004); Bernhagen and Bräuninger (2005).
[104] Grant (2000); Greaves (2008).
[105] Dublin chamber, General Meeting minutes, 12 October 1820.
[106] London *CCJ*, 5 February (1884), p. 27.

demand. They cannot reasonably be expected to exist in a kind of vacuum protected from the forces that influence commercial life.'[107]

Subscriptions are important because they represent an exchange encompassing a commitment on both sides: of the member to support the organization, and of the organization to provide something to the member. Moreover, without active continuing payment of subscriptions it becomes highly ambiguous for both sides whether a member is truly a member or not. Subscription costs thus carry the all-important signal of legitimacy to the chamber. The lack of continuing payment has created severe difficulties in the past if arrears are not professionally managed, or if life subscriptions become too large a proportion of the total membership.

Evolution of subscription rates

Average subscription rates since 1790 are shown in Figure 15.2. These are the calculated average subscription income per member; hence, in a chamber with a scale of subscriptions it may not equate to any one member's actual subscription payment. The evolution demonstrates a near constant level of average subscriptions up to about 1914, at nominal prices. By 1917 the ACC was trying to stimulate increases in subscriptions (to a minimum of two guineas) in order to raise additional resources to allow chambers to employ full-time staff and improve their efficiency to meet government 'standards'.[108] After about 1920 a steady growth in subscriptions did indeed occur, with a particularly marked increase in 1970 and in the 1990s. The 1970 increase was partly the result of decimalization, which required many chambers to reset rates that were denominated in guineas. But the 1960s, 1970s, and early 1990s were also periods of high inflation that required the chambers to raise their nominal subscriptions significantly and rapidly. Note that in this figure the scale is logarithmic, allowing contemporary values to be read. Thus the stability of the early chamber subscriptions is at the level of either one guinea or one pound, similar to many comparable bodies of the time.[109] By 2010 the average was £268, remarkably similar to that of £1 guinea in 1780 (which was worth £274 in current prices).[110]

The range of average subscriptions between most chambers was very narrow in the early period, increasing greatly from the mid-19th century as many sought to raise more income and also differentiated their scales. The minimum level also tended to move downwards after 1870 as prices fell and many small chambers of commerce became established. However, the range tended to narrow very considerably over the 1930–60 period, mainly as a result of chambers with very low

---

[107] 'Notes on possible improvements of chamber services': E. James Johnson, secretary of North Staffordshire chamber: quoted in ABCC, GPC minutes, 6 November 1957.

[108] Discussion in ACC *Monthly Proceedings*, 4 October (1917), pp. 16–20.

[109] A guinea was a common subscription for industry bodies in the 18th and 19th centuries; e.g. Ashton (1963), p. 178. Many non-commercial societies used subscriptions of one or two guineas (Clark, 2000a, pp. 194–233), whilst early trade unions and friendly societies most frequently had £1 6s. (based on 6d. per week).

[110] Based on average nominal earnings: <www.Measuringworth.org>.

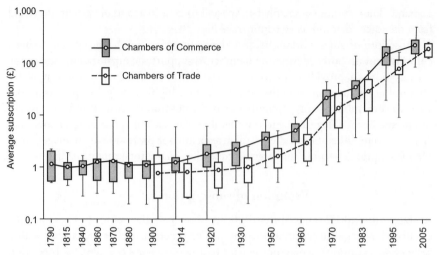

Fig. 15.2. Subscription rates of chambers of commerce and chambers of trade 1790–2005 (log scale): average, range, and 20%/80% box plots of subscription income per member in current prices.

average subscriptions increasing their rates. The range expanded again in the 1970s and 1980s, but has recently tended to contract, becoming very narrow in the 21st century, chiefly as a result of chamber benchmarking activities that have again brought the lowest levels up closer to the average, as discussed in Chapter 8. The chambers of trade, also shown in Figure 15.2, have consistently lower subscriptions, and their maxima rarely reach much above the average of the chambers of commerce. The wide range of different chambers as a whole reflects the variability of a voluntary system, and is similar to that in the USA.[111]

The level of subscriptions for chambers was thus historically modest and stable. A rate of one guinea (£1.05), or in the chambers of trade half a guinea (52.5p), was the most frequent throughout the 19th century, and indeed was used in many chambers up to the 1920s and 1930s. This was particularly true of small chambers; e.g. in 1960 a one-guinea flat rate was still used by a wide range of small chambers, including Dover, Goole, Hereford, Neath, Newark, Newport, North Shields, Plymouth Mercantile Association, Rotherham, Rugby, Spen Valley, Swindon, Trowbridge, Warrington, and Winchester.

Conversely, there were some examples of very high rates for a few early chambers. The highest subscriptions charged by any early chamber were those by Limerick (for markets), and by Jersey (which had a special levy for receipts from privateering, with a top payment of £1440 in the 1813; equivalent to £137,000

---

[111] The USA chambers in 1920 had mean subscriptions of $15.30, and range of $1–$32 (with one exception of $1000). This is significantly higher than the UK mean at the same date (£1.85), and the range is wider than the UK 1:25. Calculated from the listings in US Department of Commerce (1923).

today). These exceptionally high rates, even by modern standards, reflect brief periods of evolution where chambers managed local markets and receipts from privateering. They are excluded from Figure 15.2.

Subscription scales

Many chambers kept a uniform rate of subscriptions well into the 20th century, with no differentiation between the types of business that were members. Thus in 1815, only 18% had differentiated rates, rising slowly to 25–30% over 1860–1920, and then rapidly increasing in numbers to cover the majority of chambers from the 1930s. However, by 1958, 27 chambers of commerce (27%) still had flat rates.[112] This is similar to the differentiation of rates in US chambers, where in 1920 82% had flat rates.[113] Where chambers levied a differentiated rate, the evolution of the range was remarkably stable until the 1840s: from one pound/one guinea to £10 or ten guineas. From the mid-19th century the maximum was slowly reduced, mainly to reflect the influence of declining prices, so that by 1880 the range had narrowed to £1–2 or guineas. By 1920 the maximum was re-established at about £10, but then rose steadily as the chambers introduced wider levels of differentiation by member type. The minimum subscription rates began to lift above about one pound only in 1920, after which increases were slow until 1970. The chambers tried hard to protect the lowest rates for the smallest firms (usually identified as individual subscribers), whilst putting greater demands on the largest firms, but the inflation of the late 1960s and 1970s made this type of protection difficult. Differentials have tended to widen again in the 21st century as the chambers have become more aware of the need to market themselves to the smallest firms, so that in 2010 larger firms generally paid 145 times the rate of the very smallest (usually the individual sole trader), a range from £75 to £11,000.

The larger chambers of trade had a very narrow range between their maximum and minimum up to 1920, after which they sought much larger subscriptions from the largest members. By the 1980s the highest rates in chambers of trade were almost comparable to that in chambers of commerce. Their largest members were frequently the major retail traders who became, from the 1930s, increasingly national multiples and chain stores, as well as banks and insurance companies. Whilst many chamber of trade members were reluctant to recognize the multiples and chain stores as members, they nevertheless started to use them as increasing sources of income!

Pressures for different types of members to be treated differently in subscription demands emerged early, though it was applied in different chambers in highly varied ways. Nine main criteria evolved to differentiate membership subscriptions:

---

[112] Conference of ABCC presidents and secretaries, 21 January 1959; Agenda item 5a; changes in membership and subscriptions; paper held at Croydon chamber.
[113] Calculated from the listings in US Department of Commerce (1923).

1. *Turnover/activity levels.* Several of the earliest chambers had strongly differentiated subscriptions based on the turnover or activity levels of a member business. Thus Jersey at its outset levied 3d. per ton of shipping per annum, and over 1780–2 it also levied 0.5% of the value of the net proceeds from privateering in order to support a seamen's benevolent fund.[114] Several Irish chambers began with a differentiated subscription structure based on Customs dues. At Dublin the merchant committee founded in 1760 was financed by a voluntary payment of 6d. for each entry made in the Customs House book; i.e. for each import/export consignment.[115] As well as an annual subscription, Limerick charged a fee from all members to pay for the chamber's harbour master at a rate according to their tonnage;[116] another subscription was levied for butter marks, hide regulations, etc. The American chamber at Liverpool also scaled its subscriptions to customs book entries over 1811–50.[117] Various other differentiations have been used; e.g. capital value/interest on share capital; asset values; rateable value; or turnover/profit (in Salt: tons of production).[118]

2. *Business Size.* Many chambers evolved subscription structures to differentiate large firms from the rest of their members. One of the earliest methods was to separate 'individuals' and 'firms'. This was the most common distinction until the 1970s. By the 1950s, this was often supplemented by scaling by firm size, usually measured by employees, but also by issued share capital. Birmingham in 1918 developed a complex scaling based on two levels of rateable value for retailers, four levels of nominal capital for firms, and a rate for individuals;[119] Hull used net annual value/rateable value into the 1970s; Rotherham had a scale for companies based on capital value, with a separate subscription for banks and individuals.[120] As time progressed the number of employees of a business became the main criterion in modern chambers to grade subscription levels, with small firms now often favoured by deliberately low rates. London introduced employment size in 1968. The introduction of additional charges for larger firms was seen both as a finance issue and as a means to give greater representation to the larger firms. Often larger firms had additional votes in chamber proceedings at a scaled rate. Liverpool introduced additional fees for additional members in 1851: 'This is not intended to disturb the existing law...but to enable firms consisting of three or four members to acquire membership for all partners, on rather favourable terms'.[121] The large firms were also seen as a way of rescuing some chambers from financial

---

[114] Jersey chamber minutes, *Rules*, 1768; see also Syvret and Stevens (1998).

[115] Although after 1768 amended to one guinea annually, increased to two guineas in 1788, but reverted to fee of 1s. on British customs entries inwards between 1805 and 1820 (Prendeville (1930), pp. 52, 115–16).

[116] Limerick chamber minutes 1807; see also O'Connor (1938), p. 72.

[117] Henderson (1933a, 1933b).

[118] Most sector trade associations used business size as a subscription scale; see e.g. Yarmie (1980), pp. 216–17.

[119] Birmingham chamber Council minutes, 25 March 1918.

[120] *Industrial Sheffield and Rotherham Yearbook* (1919).

[121] Liverpool chamber minutes, *Annual Report* (1851), p. 22.

difficulties. Thus in Sunderland in 1920 'Mr. Wright . . . suggested that many of the larger firms in the Borough, such as the Shipbuilders and Marine Engineers, would be willing to pay an increased subscription but that he thought an all round increase would mean a loss of membership'.[122] An increase to five guineas for larger firms was approved.

3. *'Patrons'*. Large firms have also been sought as providers of subscription income on a special basis giving them some special privilege of publicity or credit, similar to 'friends' or 'corporate sponsors/benefactors' of other institutions. In modern times the term 'patron' is fairly commonly used. In former times the president of the chamber, who was usually a local member of the landed gentry, member of the House of Lords, or industrial magnate, was frequently expected to donate a higher subscription as a goodwill gesture. Little other than local status was conferred by these gestures, but they were significant in many chambers' finances. Donations from major local firms in addition to subscriptions have been fairly common in chambers, but not numerous in any one chamber. General calls, in annual reports, or AGM proceedings such as Preston's in 1921, did not seem to produce much yield: 'A larger subscription from firms who may be voluntarily able, or are disposed, to contribute a donation . . . is strongly advocated.'[123] The Preston chamber was still carrying a similar statement in its publications in the 1930s.[124] In 1944 the Coventry chamber president asked for voluntary increases in subscriptions:[125] 'a letter has been sent to members paying two guineas asking them to increase to a minimum of three guineas. The replies received . . . were all satisfactory.' Gentlemanly support was expected and still provided! The London chamber resolved in 1967 that, 'In addition [to their normal subscriptions] large companies should be invited by the president to make substantial contributions on a voluntary basis above the fixed scale.'[126] The use of patrons has become more common in recent years, covering 80% of chambers by 2010.

4. *Business Type*. An early distinction by many chambers was to differentiate 'firms' from 'individuals'. At face value this separated sole traders or owner-managers from larger partnerships (those with 'works' or 'mills') or from established limited companies. However, detailed analysis of the membership lists of each chamber shows the subscription rates levied and the business type to be used as only approximate guides. Many partners of larger enterprises joined as individual members (at lower cost). Sometimes this is taken to be a membership covering the whole enterprise; in other cases several partners of the same firm might join independently. Similarly, when limited liability companies emerge they might join as companies, or one or more of the directors might join as individuals. It also seems that transfers between the two categories of 'firms' and 'individuals' occurred quite frequently and mostly arbitrarily; for example, about 5% of Manchester's

[122] Sunderland chamber minutes, 6 December 1920.
[123] Preston chamber, *Annual Report* (1921), p. 33.
[124] Preston chamber, *Journal*, August (1936), p. 29.
[125] Coventry chamber, Council minutes, 21 November 1944.
[126] London chamber, GPC minutes, 14 March 1967, pp. 155–6.

membership was transferring to individual membership 1899–1906 for no obvious reason other than cost.[127] Various glaring anomalies between members in the subscription rates charged thus emerged. As a result business type had been largely abolished from subscriptions by most chambers by the end of the 19th century. However, London, which introduced a differentiated fee of one guinea for individuals and two guineas for firms in 1883, maintained the distinction until 1974.

5. *Age.* In general, the age of the individual member or of the firm have never been differentiated by chambers. However, pressure to have a more social, lively, and less formal structure led to the evolution of *junior chambers* especially after WW2; there were 81 in 1964–5. In many cases membership of the junior chamber was an access to the main chamber, or through an associate scheme, at a reduced rate. For example, Newcastle introduced an associate membership scheme in the late 1920s for those less than 40 years old. This was half the lowest rate for individuals (half-guinea compared with one guinea). More recently many chambers have experimented with special rates for start-up and early stage businesses, and this was encouraged by the assimilation of chamber and Business Link payment models in the 1995–2008 period. It is a developing area of subscription management, interlinked with the emphasis on small firms.

6. *Employees rather than employers.* The concept of the chamber has always been based on the assumption that its members are the business owner or decision taker. With the emergence of limited companies the concept had to be stretched to include directors, and then senior managers who were paid employees. With further changes in corporate form, the active member of a chamber might become someone of quite junior managerial level who was tasked with representing the member business in chamber discussions or activities. Some large businesses indeed came to see chamber membership as part of their social responsibility, local networking, or public relations activities. Despite reluctance to accept some of these changes, chambers were forced increasingly to recognize employees as their de facto members as well as directors, owners, and entrepreneurs. In modern times there is usually no obvious differentiation in how they appear in membership lists or how they function as members. But in earlier times some employee members might have no voting rights. For example, Cardiff chamber had a special subscription rate for 'clerks' from 1870 until the 1890s. They paid a half-guinea whilst the normal subscription was one and a half guineas. They were not full members, and could not vote, but had access to chamber facilities, of which the Exchange Newsroom was clearly a key feature. 'Clerks' numbered 43 in 1870 and 33 in 1886, whilst the full members stood at 133 and 255, respectively (24% and 11% of the membership in the respective years). The category was abolished in 1899.[128]

7. *Geographical differences/accessibility.* Several chambers have sought to cover extensive territories where differences in accessibility might mean very different levels of benefits. This has also been linked to chambers such as London and

---

[127] Manchester chamber, register of members, vol. ii, 1899–1906.
[128] Cardiff chamber, *Annual Reports.*

Dublin, which at some stages, and for some members, have acted as de facto national bodies with membership covering the whole country as well as the specific locality. As a result 'town' and 'country' members, with different subscriptions, have been used as different subscription rates; at least in London, Dublin, Llanelli, and Dundee. In London country members had 'no London office and carry on business outside of 20 miles radius from the Bank of England'.[129] In Dundee, the differentiation of membership subscription was chiefly related to accessibility to the chamber's main services in its reading/coffee room and post boxes.

8. *Specific service subscriptions.* Modern chambers have generally sought to keep a standardized subscription schedule, and charge for specific services on a fee basis when the service is used: e.g. for seminars, functions, training services, and consultancy support. However, in earlier times, and in modern chambers for some functions, an additional subscription might be charged that then provided access to specific services. Modern examples are export clubs, telex clubs, productivity associations, and some social functions (such as golf clubs). Important earlier examples were coffee club/reading room subscriptions that provided access to these facilities only for an additional subscription. This was an important feature in Dundee, Cardiff, and Newcastle-upon-Tyne, and some other chambers. It might also be a service that allowed non-members of the chamber to access that specific service, which provided further external earnings to the chamber—again an important aspect of Dundee's coffee room. For chambers operating services such as debt collection or assessments of firms' financial status, and trade protection societies, this could be embodied in subscription differentiation rather than fees. Thus Goole chamber had a complex structure in the 1890s of four subscription bands tied to level of service available:

A: £5 5s.   For 150 status reports; collection of unlimited numbers of accounts of a value of less than £5 at 5%; 2½% for accounts with a value £5–20; and 1¼% for values over £20.
B: £2 2s.   For no more than 50 status reports.
C: £1 1s.   For no more than 25 status reports.
D: 10s.   All status reports prepaid at 6d. each.

However, this subscription structure seems to have run for only a few years before reverting to the previous half-guinea for individuals and one guinea for firms.[130]

9. *Sectors.* Most chambers have been studiously blind to sector differences between their members. However, one sector of members caused continued debate: retailing, as discussed in Chapter 15. In terms of subscriptions, those chambers that actively sought to include retailers, or who acted as merged chambers of commerce and trade, frequently had a separate and lower rate for retailers; e.g. in Plymouth,

[129] London chamber, GPC minutes, 4 January 1906.
[130] Goole chamber, *Annual Reports*, contained in minute book.

Southampton, Portsmouth, Croydon, and Exeter at one-half the normal rate in the 1950s and 1960s. Dudley chamber set up a retail section in the 1940s, which had an entirely different and lower subscription schedule. The retail subscriptions were on a scale of employer size from one to four guineas, whilst the main chamber members paid three to eight guineas (two guineas for individuals).[131] They contributed 174 out of 494 members (35%) in 1960. Sheffield had a special section rate for small retailers, which up to 1961 was two guineas when the rate for other members was seven guineas (the chamber then had about 50 members at this rate out of 1265 (4%)); it was increased to three guineas in 1962. Coventry had a special retail section and subscription rate from the 1920s, which survived into the 1980s. An 'adjustment between the industrial and retails sectors' was recognized as needed in 1964,[132] leading to increases in the retail rate and a rebalancing of membership from over 30% in the 1950s–60s, to about 20% with the rapid growth of other members from the mid-1970s.

A systematic analysis of all the different scales used by chambers is impossible for the whole historical period. However, Table 15.14 shows that the size of firms has become a widespread scaling factor, together with the distinction of individuals and companies. There is some use of sector distinctions.

Another feature of many chambers was, and remains, that local trade associations or other organizations could also be members. This was usually at a special rate, which often exceeded or equalled the highest subscription used for large businesses. This reflected their resources (and in some cases was clearly seen almost as a donation by a large local trade body). It also reflected that a potentially heavier use of a chamber's services might result, since the associations were acting for a large number of other businesses which might lead to higher demand. However, there

Table 15.14. Scales of subscription used by chambers of commerce: percentage of chambers at each year

Subscription scale	1962	1970	2008
Flat rate	29	13	—
Individuals/companies	42	52	50
No. of employees	17	51	50
Capital value	8	4	—
Business turnover; rateable value	3	2	—
Sector	10	16	10
Town/country	2	2	—
Total (no.)	101	89	53

Note: Some chambers used several types of subscription at the same time, hence the percentages do not sum to 100%.
Sources: ABCC MS 17367/1, 3 for 1962 and 1970; BCC *Benchmarking* for 2008.

[131] Dudley chamber, *Annual Report* (1950).
[132] Coventry chamber, *Annual Report* (1964), p. 12.

were always tensions in these relations for both parties. For the chambers there was a continued concern that having an association as a member would undermine their direct membership. As a result unusually special rules were applied to them. Thus, for example, Sheffield chamber allowed membership only 'in light of the extent to which individual members of associations are members of the chamber . . . and it is as representative of Sheffield and district in the trade for which they speak'.[133]

Life subscriptions

A special problem for chamber management was raised by life subscriptions, which were used by many chambers in their early years. Twenty guineas was used by Glasgow in 1783, reduced to ten guineas in 1786, five guineas in 1794, and maintained until 1913. Most common was ten guineas—London in 1882, and Dudley was still offering this in 1912. Bristol used 20 guineas from 1823, only reducing this to ten guineas in 1870. By 1892, 24 chambers out of 54 (44%) allowed 'subscriptions to be commuted' to one payment, which averaged five to ten times the annual fee. Of this sample, 5 (21%) had life fees of five guineas, and 18 (75%) ten guineas. The highest fees were 20 guineas, but this was where it was differentiated between individual members and companies. Five chambers had differentiated life rates: Grimsby, Hull, Wakefield, and Liverpool had 10 and 20 guinea rates; Falmouth had five and 10 guineas.[134]

Difficulties arose when the lifetime subscription was set too low relative to the annual subscription. Edinburgh and Glasgow provide prime cases of these difficulties. These chambers were established by Royal Charter, making it more cumbersome to make subscription changes. The differential between the life and annual fee was sufficient in the early years to keep a balance between the two groups. There was initially a large number of life members, probably because it was judged by many to be a form of a donation to provide working capital to establish the chamber. Thus in 1786 Edinburgh had approximately 72 life members and 53 annual members (58%).[135] By 1790 the ratio was reversed, with 68 life members (46%) out of a total of 147. By 1809 the ratio was 43 life (39%) out of 109 members. However, an incentive was offered to *existing* annual members to become life members in 1809–10, at a reduced rate of five guineas.[136] This had the effect of raising the joining rate: 40 new (mainly life) members joined 1809–11, which was more than any earlier three-year period since its foundation. But this also increased the lapsing rate, presumably because the annual fee payers who could not, or would not, pay the life fee opted out. As a result the net increase in membership was short-

---

[133] Sheffield chamber, Membership Committee minutes, 27 April 1942.

[134] Royal Commission on Labour, *House of Commons Papers*, 1892, xxxiv, Part V, p. xxxiv, and Appendix.

[135] Note that because of the way the records and accounts were kept, all figures quoted are approximate.

[136] From the account books ED5/10, this seems to have been irregular and by independent negotiation with the new members; rates of five, seven, and ten guineas were all used as life fees, sometimes with an additional entry fee if the individual was not already a member.

lived, but the ratio of life to annual members shifted to 72 (59%) out of 123 in 1816, back to almost the same figure as at its foundation. Edinburgh had the low life rate of five guineas from 1809 until 1921. The result was a steadily worsening annual income flow. By 1920 the chamber had *no* subscription income but had increased its other income sources to £391 income. However, this was inadequate to meet its £526 expenditure so a transfer from capital of £135 was required. It was trading in deficit at about 26% of its expenditure. It was living on its past. It reformed its subscriptions in 1921.

In Glasgow, with rapidly decreasing prices in the 1820s and 1830s, the annual subscription was abolished in 1828 so that entrance fees to new members became a life subscription. This was followed by a reduction in the life fee from ten to five guineas from 1836, argued for by the newly elected president (John Macfarlan, a druggist). Again this gave an immediate boost to joining. But lapsing increased of the annual fee payers, and lack of sufficient subscriptions led to reforms in the 1930s.

A more appropriate way to deal with life subscriptions from a financial management perspective is to treat these as a contribution to a reserve or endowment fund. London did this from its outset, in accord with its Articles of Association, investing the £556 from its 117 initial life members (8.4% of its initial membership) into a reserve fund.[137] In 1887 it took £658 from this fund to support current expenditure to start up various services that subsequently proved to be self-supporting.[138] When Birmingham introduced life subscriptions in 1912 it also correctly 'treated them as capital and invested, only drawing the interest received to use as income'.[139]

The experiences of Edinburgh and Glasgow also affected governance and operations. Life members do not have to participate to remain as members. As a result, meetings generally become poorly attended and the chamber has less incentive to understand who its membership is. The main reason for lapsing becomes death of a life member, not withdrawal or resignation. This is bound to have an effect on the closeness to the membership and can encourage complacency by the chamber staff. It also makes it difficult to maintain an accurate membership book, since death records have to be scrutinized to find out whether the members are still extant. Even at the time Edinburgh and Glasgow chambers would have had no clear idea of their real membership base. In practice they operated periodical clean-ups of lists, when efforts were made to track down life members to find out if they were still alive or in the area: hardly the way to keep an engaged membership.

Entrance fees

Entrance fees are a feature in common with many early societies and guilds, and early trade unions. It was understandable that many early chambers, especially

---

[137] London chamber, *Annual Report* (1882), p. 33; (1883), p. 43.
[138] *Annual Report* (1887), pp. 37–8.
[139] Birmingham chamber, GPC minutes, 4 December 1912.

those based on charters, used them. Initially they were sought as a deliberate assertion of status and exclusiveness, and to foster commitment, which was further reinforced by fines for non-attendance. But as chambers evolved a complex set of questions emerged about entrance fees in terms of the incentives they gave to retain membership, and the disincentives to join. They were used by several chambers in their early years. They generally tended to disappear from use, but have made some comeback in modern times with 56% of BCC members charging an entrance fee in 2009 and 61% in 2010, although this is usually relatively nominal (average £47, with a range from £18 to £108 in 2010).

Entrance fees have often been seen as an impediment to recruitment. They raise the threshold for joining, especially if the motivation is trialling the chamber's services: a taster in order to become a more committed member. In London a two-guinea entrance fee was introduced in 1885 three years after its foundation. A vigorous debate immediately began between council members, and from the membership at annual meetings. Eventually, in 1904, the entrance fee was 'temporarily suspended until 500 new members were elected'.[140] There was continued resistance to this, some council members feeling that 'having been imposed … it shall not be abolished … as this was unfair to existing members'.[141] However, it was never reinstated. The London entrance fee was seen chiefly as an income source; for example in 1887 'it would require three times the present annual average of new members to produce the same yearly income without the entrance fee, and there is no reason to believe its abolition would produce anything like such an increase'.[142] In 1887 entrance fees produced an income of £80; this increased to £953 in 1888; but was down to £392 in 1899. The abolition of entrance fees in 1904 responded to the view that it was off-putting to new members and because other sources of income had been secured. By 1907, when the three-year suspension was made permanent, it was recognized that 'The further suspension [of the entrance fee] … would conduce as large a membership as possible'; and that suspension 'had resulted in a steady increase in the number of new members'.[143]

At Newcastle the entrance fee was definitely perceived as a barrier to recruitment. At Newcastle an 'admission' fee of three guineas had been charged (1815). This was reduced later to one guinea plus the annual subscription of one guinea. In 1854 it was abolished. This initially led to a surge in members, an increase from 96 to 143 in 1855 (49%).[144] However, some of this effect was temporary, since by 1860 the membership was back to 107.[145] However, there are also many examples of chambers that successfully maintained entrance fees over long periods of time, and this covers most of the modern chambers still using these fees. For example, Ipswich maintained its 10s. 6d. entrance fee from its inception in 1884 until the 1940s. Croydon had an entrance fee of 10s. 6d. from its inception in 1899. It was

---

[140] London chamber, GPC minutes, 24 October 1904.
[141] Mr Urquhart Fisher at London AGM; *Chamber of Commerce Journal*, May (1905), p. 110.
[142] *Annual Report* (1887), p. 11.
[143] London chamber, *Annual Report* (1907); in *CCJ*, 26 (1907), p. 129.
[144] Newcastle chamber minutes, *Annual Report* (1855).
[145] Newcastle chamber minutes, 1860.

abolished in 1930, but was quickly revived and continued until 2007.[146] When Swindon modernized its subscriptions in about 1980 it introduced an entrance fee of £10 (£11.50 with VAT), which it maintained until 2005 when the chamber became insolvent.[147] Other bodies, such as the IoD also have entrance fees, using them as a means to encourage retention ('You will have to pay a new entrance fee if you allow your membership to lapse').[148] Many modern chambers offer discounts of the entrance fee for those attending events or making their first use of a service as a non-member, so that in practice it is often used more as a promotional waiver than a real financial device.

Donations

The costs of membership of early business bodies included not only the annual subscription. There was also an expectation that members would stand by the chamber in times of need, for example by being willing to pay an additional subscription to relieve a deficit; pay a special donation or subscription to purchase a building, furnish an office, or pay the salaried staff a gratuity or retirement gift. There would also be the costs of attending functions, the most costly usually being an annual dinner. There would also be other periodic social events that often entailed buying drinks or meals. Thus a form of donation, beyond the subscription, became one of time as well as money. This involved obligation and commitment.

The members at large, and particularly major companies and wealthy individuals, were seen as a source of donations. An additional subscription or donation was often raised for a new building, office move, or specific campaign. Also donations were needed to overcome crises. Thus in 1947 Coventry chamber called on members to help with the cost of furnishing its new premises:[149] 'new furnishings for the chamber cost £1445 of which £1198 was donated by 294 members'. The elected officers often bore the disproportionate burden of these costs. Thus, in Hull in 1867 it was noted that 'it may be well to remind the members of the chamber that the deputations to London and other places, have always paid their own expenses, and the cost of furnishing the present room [chamber reading room] was defrayed chiefly by the previous directors'.[150] In Nottingham in 1916, the council members, who were predominantly from larger firms, were asked for more support in order to reduce a deficit; it was unanimously agreed that they should each increase their subscriptions to two guineas a year to give a lead to members. Whilst the chamber subscription remained at one guinea, this was to be treated as a minimum and members were asked to contribute more.[151] Again, when Wolverhampton chamber reported that it was in deficit from about 1883 to 1891, with an accumulated debt in 1891 of £100, the members were asked to subscribe an

---

[146] Until it became part of the London chamber; Croydon chamber, *Annual Accounts*.
[147] Swindon chamber, *Annual Report* and *Directories*.
[148] IoD, standard membership renewal letter, 2006.
[149] Coventry chamber, *Annual Report* (1948), p. 10.
[150] Hull chamber, *Annual Report* (1867), p. 12.
[151] Nottingham chamber, Council minutes, 2 May 1916, p. 26.

additional support to eradicate it.[152] In other cases a significant loss on specific events elicited a call for support: in Hereford in 1923 the members were appealed to for extra subscriptions to make up the loss on an athletic sports event.

Underpricing?

The foregoing discussion all confirms the significance attached to the pricing decision by chamber managers in setting subscription rates. Chapter 17 also confirms that changes in subscriptions had strong influences on lapsing. But have prices been optimal? There is much to suggest that fear of losing members as a result of high subscriptions, and especially fear of raising subscriptions, encouraged chambers to look to other revenues, chiefly for service fees and from government contracts. Yet the increase in subscription rates should not have been seen as a barrier if the chambers were really providing a valuable service worth paying for. Nor should it be a barrier if the costs were effectively viewed as a 'good will donation' to a valuable cause, accounting for up to a third of chamber members.[153] The cost of the modest subscription should be more than offset by the benefits received: such as the additional profits resulting from one minor contract of sale as a result of a chamber contact, or gain in productivity or management efficiency resulting from the acquisition of information or training provided by a chamber. Indeed this is how many modern chambers market membership; e.g. in South-ampton and Fareham in 2006: 'our schemes will save you money . . . all could help you get more out of your business'.[154]

Have the chambers underpriced their services? No historical analysis of the sensitivity of the pricing decision in relation to benefits offered (or taken up) appears to have ever been undertaken. It was claimed in the 1960s by the chamber secretaries, however, that underpricing indeed existed: 'for far too long chambers have undersold themselves . . . . Services and finances have always been thought of as the question of the chicken and the egg'. But the secretaries argued that this was not so: services could be improved and the prices increased: 'if a good service is provided . . . the members will be prepared to pay for it'.[155] As noted in ABCC discussions, higher subscriptions would not limit recruitment if benefits also increased.[156]

However, it has only been in a modern analysis for 1993 that this has been proved. Using a sample of members and non-members in three representative areas (which varied in level of current chamber development), business owners were asked what they 'would be willing to pay for a high quality chamber system and services in their area'. Current members were willing to pay 2.7 times as much as their actual subscriptions, whilst non-members who had no direct experience of the

---

[152] Beaumont, Wolverhampton chamber history, pp. 5–6.
[153] As cited by North Staffordshire chamber in 1957: see above.
[154] Southampton and Fareham chamber, *Directory* (2006), p. 7.
[155] Association of Chamber Secretaries: *Report on the Role of Chambers of Commerce in the Changing Economy;* SA 20-65, September 1965.
[156] ACC, *Monthly Proceedings* (1919), pp. 8–38; Knowles (1949).

services were willing to pay 3.3 times the subscription they would have been charged. The average of all businesses was 2.9 times, with no significant differences between respondents by sector or firm size.[157] But most suggestive was that there were no significant differences between areas, despite the fact that one of the areas (Kent) had much weaker and smaller chambers with very limited services, whilst the other two areas (Manchester and Slough-Thames Valley) were among the largest chambers offering a wide range of services. This tends to suggest that not only were chambers at that time underpricing their subscriptions by a major factor, but they also underestimated the strength of their brand which would have allowed enhanced subscriptions even for relatively weak chambers.

Since the 1993 date of this survey, chamber subscription levels have tended to increase, especially in the smaller chambers. However, despite the fact that sector trade association subscriptions are often 5–10 times higher, chamber managers remain aware of the sensitivity of members to costs. They feel it is essential that subscriptions are kept low and a search made for other income sources. This is perfectly rational, but it does appear to have underpriced subscriptions, which in turn may have led to a perception that chamber membership was too cheap to be worth paying for! Hence, there may have been an inadvertent incentive to free ride, since even 'good will' payments can be viewed as so low that the cause is not valuable. The incentive to free ride may have also increased as chambers have sought greater income from government contracts. This has allowed other income to provide ever greater subsidies to membership, which has suggested that government will support chambers anyway. Thus there was no need to join even for reasons of 'good will' and solidarity as 'the thing to do'. There are also related dangers that an increased focus on government contracts has squeezed out voluntary activity, has encouraged managerial and staff 'sorting' that has undermined chamber links to members, has increased the risk that chamber lobbying becomes a by-product or that voice has to be muted in order not to jeopardize future government contracts, or that the incorporation into the state's agenda has undermined its attractiveness to members. Efforts to increase subscriptions would allow some of these pressures to be reduced.

15.7 CONCLUSION

This chapter has combined historical with modern information to interrogate the motives behind the decisions by business people to join, remain, or lapse as members of chambers, and how they weight the costs and benefits involved. It has sought to establish the balance of weight between purposive (allegiance to a cause), solidarity (sense of obligation), selective services, and insurance benefits. From modern surveys the different roles for voice, involvement, commitment, and

[157] Bennett (1996a), especially table 3.

detachment have been assessed, and an attempt has been made to comment on the 'persistence' of membership.

A key conclusion is that the motives are complex and multiple. For the modern period the different sources of information indicate that *both* lobbying and services are important, particularly as motives for joining chambers, and for remaining a member. Even most businesses that lapse recognize the value of the lobbying function. However, detachment from the activities of the chamber appears to be a critical feature for a lapsing decision. This appears to result both from making little or no use of chamber services, and/or from a feeling that their own business has little say or scope to participate in the lobbying process.

Over time, external influences on members (such as corporate restructuring, business closure, economic pressures, and efforts to cut costs) have generally become more important influences on membership lapsing, whilst selective service use has become a much more significant influence on retention. Virtually no business joins or leaves because it agrees or disagrees with particular policy stances. But commitment to a chamber's policy is mainly a supportive motive for joining and retention along with other parts of the bundle. The policy role may also be a key indicator of the wider purposes that chambers satisfy: it is an indicator of the 'not-for-profit' underpinnings, and a key part of the USP and hence the brand. This also interrelates with how brand, services, and price (as measured through subscriptions), interact. The danger of lobbying becoming peripheralized as a by-product certainly exists; it is a significant danger for chamber managers and is clearly an issue with members. If chambers lose this USP it is not clear that they offer sufficient other benefits to compete successfully with other service organizations.

The shift of chambers to include a large emphasis on specific services in their bundles of offerings has led to a more strongly developed pattern of businesses 'trialling' membership, with those leaving within a few years increasing significantly over time. Since the late 19th century it appears that over 50% of the membership lapse within ten years, and this has increased further since the mid-1990s. These features have also been influenced by the progressive shift of membership from individuals to firms, particularly after WW1. The firm is a more calculative entity than the individual. Purposive and solidarity benefits are of less relevance, and insurance benefits are probably irrelevant since most firms are usually larger entities that can provide for themselves. Hence the national shift in industrial structure towards the corporate form and larger partnership, often accompanied by industrial consolidation, has undermined some of the key offerings of the chambers.

Whilst there are few systematic differences in member motives for different types of firm, the size of a business is often a significant factor. The larger and medium-sized firms have the greatest continuance commitment to chambers. They make less use of services, but have the strongest reuse intent. The joining rate of small firms is lower, retention rate once they join is lower, and their lapsing rate is significantly higher. They are more inveterate 'triallers' of services and look to a package with more networking and marketing opportunities, as well as stronger selective service benefits. But the selective services they seek are often different from the large firm, and the bundle is also often different, with less influence of solidarity and 'good will' motives than for larger firms, with often more concern for purposive causes. This has led to major challenges for chamber management.

The needs of small firms were vacant territory of debate until the Bolton report of 1971. Since then, small firms have grown significantly in number and significance in the economy and hence in national politics; they have become an important fulcrum of business self-identification and allegiance. Being an effective provider of services or supports to small firms is an important marketing tool. The majority of chamber members are now from small firms; but the analysis here suggests there is some way to go to meet their specific needs. Other organizations such as FSB, IoD, FPB, and business clubs offer membership packages that are strongly competitive.

The mix of demands on the chambers to represent the larger corporation, medium-sized firms, partnership, and the smaller firms has tended to drive chamber politics and lobbying towards more generalist policy positions. The value of the larger firm, and its ability to act as a 'patron', to support chamber finances, may also have encouraged chambers to underprice their services, with the result that they become undervalued. This may have been exacerbated by the development of other income streams, particularly from government. The challenge remains one of developing commitment among those who join through satisfactory user experiences leading to strong reuse intents, and nurturing a strong allegiance to the policy objectives of the chambers. In the future there will probably need to be a more complex mix of different bundles, and balances of services within bundles, including more tailored policy positions, that satisfy these different business demands. In general this pressure towards better tailoring is similar to that in the wider professional services market. The future will probably require even better tailoring.

16

Membership Dynamics

16.1 STABILITY OR CHURN?

Most analyses of chambers (and indeed most business associations) treat them as stable entities. Yet they are anything but stable; they are voluntary and their members come and go. This is one of the most fundamental differences between voluntary and public law chambers. It means that to survive, chambers have to recruit a similar number of members just to stand still. This chapter shows that lapsing from chambers was historically low at 4–8%, which may explain why there was little historical concern. But recently lapsing has grown to an average of 10–25%, with some chambers experiencing far higher losses. Thus far from being stable, chambers have become dynamically changing with membership bases that require continuous efforts to maintain.

These changes have been little understood, and chamber assessment of their own situation is sometimes inaccurate. Thus when Derby ascribed its increase in resignations in 1940–2 as 'due to war circumstances',[1] in common with most chambers, it had a decreasing number of resignations in this period (reduced from 2–6 per year in the 1930s to 1–3 per year in 1940–2). Southampton's 1907 Annual Report that 'it is surprising to learn of the insufficient reasons given for these [resignations] in most cases',[2] probably shows more a lack of effort to find out than a lack of reasons among members. Aberdeen's 1970 statement, that it considered its 4.4% lapse rate, as 'not a high figure and many other chambers were experiencing a much greater percentage loss',[3] appears to be based more on guesswork than sound statistical information (although the average at that time was indeed higher, at about 8%).

The turnover, or 'churn', of the membership has important implications for how associations form a view for lobbying, how they are managed, the services that are provided, the breadth of representative weight they can deploy, and perhaps how government views them. The argument that they reflect obligation and represent a stable 'unity' of interests for their area can be challenged when turnover is high. This chapter makes the first large-scale attempt to understand 'churn'. It begins by surveying the trends. It then uses statistical analysis of a sample of chambers to draw out the separate influences on membership dynamics of economic change,

---

[1] Derby chamber minutes.
[2] Southampton chamber, *Annual Report* (1907/8), p. 15.
[3] Aberdeen chamber, Membership Committee minutes, 8 December 1970.

development of different service benefits, varied subscription rates, and the influence of recent changes in government support.

16.2 JOINING AND LAPSING RATES

The general rate of joining and lapsing from chambers can only be meaningfully
assessed by having a standardized representative sample that compares the same
chambers over time. Because of variable record keeping and survival, there are
limits on what can be achieved, and years where chambers have exclusively life
memberships (and hence little lapsing) must be excluded. It has been possible to
develop a long-term sample covering 21 chambers; for modern chambers a national
cross-section is available from BCC *Benchmarking*.

The general pattern is shown in Table 16.1 and Figure 16.1. These demonstrate
a buoyant joining rate for chambers up to 1990 with a slowly moving mean, but a
wide variation between chambers.[4] The main periods of growth were the 1880s,
late 1940s, and since the 1970s. The war years had generally lower rates of joining,
but the slowest periods of growth appear to be the early years 1780–1840, in the
1950s, and in periods since 1990 when lapsing has exceeded joining to give a
decline in overall membership. Lapsing had been highest in the economic slump of
the 1930s, but has reached all-time highs since the 1980s. The lowest rates of
lapsing have been during the two world wars. The war periods also show the
narrowest range of variation between chambers in lapse rates. This is indicative of
the wartime effect of state control of many industries and the heavy use of area and
section planning committees which necessitated local business membership.[5]
When subject to more open market forces the general rates of lapsing have been
higher, but especially in slumps, and periods of rapid economic change, such as the
late 20th and early 21st centuries.

Perhaps the most important feature of these data is the strong long-term continuity of the rate of 'churn' of membership: joining was about 4% until 1840, rising
to about 8% by 1970; lapsing was about 4% in 1780–1880, then 6% up to 1970.
For the first 200 years, therefore, there was a very stable structure of membership,
with high membership retention, and long-term persistence of loyal and committed
members. As indicated in Figure 14.4, market penetration remained very similar,
and net growth of membership was largely organic: an increase of joining rates over
low and stable lapsing rates from a growing population. This was particularly
marked in 1870–1900, the two world wars, and 1960–90.

The modern period, since 1980, is exceptional and suggests that some important
systemic changes have occurred in retention rates—the 'churn' has reached very
high levels on average, and particularly in some chambers. This pattern began in the
1970s and was first marked by increases in joining rates. Over the 1980s there were

[4] Not all chambers have information in all years; up to the 1840s too few chambers have
information to show a valid range in Figure 16.1. The sample sizes are shown in Table 16.1.
[5] See Chapter 13; also Ilersic and Liddle (1960), chapters 15 and 18.

Table 16.1. Mean joining and lapsing rates among 21 chambers 1780–2005, and mean rates 2001–2010 for all BCC chambers

	Joining	Lapsing	N	Net Balance
1780–1810	4.4	3.7	2	+0.7
1811–40	3.8	3.4	3	+0.4
1871–80	5.9	2.7	4	+3.2
1881–90	11.0	5.3	9	+5.7
1891–1900	6.9	5.6	12	+1.3
1901–13	6.2	5.0	10	+0.8
1914–18	7.3	2.4	11	+4.9
1919–30	8.2	7.4	10	+0.8
1931–38	7.6	7.0	10	+0.6
1939–45	7.0	2.6	10	+4.4
1946–50	9.1	6.4	14	+2.7
1951–60	5.5	4.9	11	+0.6
1961–70	8.0	5.6	11	+2.4
1971–80	12.0	7.8	8	+4.2
1981–90	16.6	10.5	9	+6.1
1991–2000	13.8	20.4	17	-6.6
2001–5	18.0	18.4	16	+0.4
2001–5 (all)	18.6	18.2	53	+0.4
2006–10 (all)	21.2	24.0	54	−2.8

Note: The sample of 21 chambers comprises Aberdeen, Burnley, Cardiff, Chesterfield, Croydon, Derby, Edinburgh, Glasgow, Ipswich, Kidderminster, Lancaster, London, Manchester, Middlesbrough, Newcastle-upon-Tyne, North Shields, Nottingham, Portsmouth, Preston, Sheffield, and Southampton.
Sources: Local member books, minutes and reports; 2001–10 from BCC, *Benchmarking*.

even higher joining rates, but lapsing also began to increase markedly. Since the 1990s both joining and lapsing have been at the highest levels ever seen, reaching over 60% in some chambers. The extremes are associated with major crises in individual chambers. But even after taking out the extremes, the box plots in Figure 16.1 show that the main body of chambers had moved to a high level of churn. The modern position is well summed up by the image given by one chamber chief executive's comment that 'maintaining a chamber's membership numbers is now like trying to keep a bath full of water when the plug was not in'.[6] Interestingly a similar analogy was used for early trade unions: 'a sieve, through which a perpetual stream of members was flowing, a small proportion only remaining attached for any length of time'.[7]

A key feature of chambers, as in all comparisons, has been the operation of local context and contingency, producing very wide variance. The variation was particularly high in the 1920s–30s economic downturn, over 1946–50, and to a lesser extent over 1890–1913, but has become a major phenomenon of recent times. The average behaviour thus gives a false sense of local stability. Within individual

[6] Simon Sperryn, chief executive of the London chamber, comments in Bennett (1996a), p. 2.
[7] Webb and Webb (1920), p. 443.

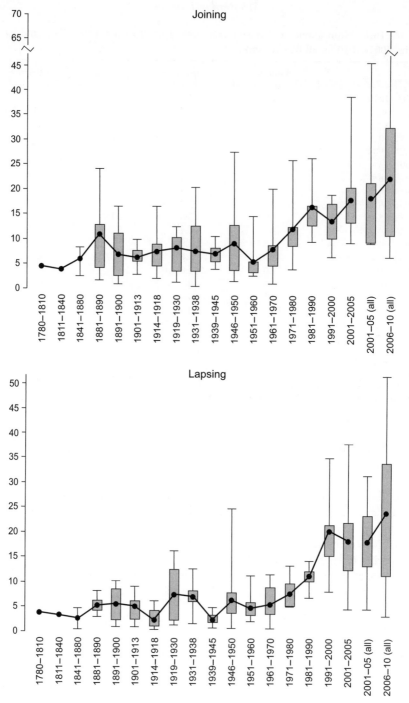

Fig. 16.1. Joining and lapsing rates in a sample of 21 chambers of commerce 1780–2010: new or lapsed members as percentage of membership, mean (shown solid), range, and 20%/80% box plots. The final two plots are for all chambers that are BCC members in 2001–5 and 2006–10.

chambers the rates can fluctuate considerably year on year. Figure 16.2 shows the annual fluctuations in joining and lapsing rates for those chambers with sufficiently long runs of information. For some of the chambers there is very high volatility, particularly notable in Middlesbrough 1910–30, and Croydon 1945–60. For other chambers lapse rates fluctuate only slightly around the general mean over most of the period; e.g. London, Ipswich, Cardiff, Burnley, and Sheffield. Notable visual features are points of instability in Figure 16.2 when subscriptions are raised, analysed further below. Another aspect is the relatively short-lived effect of major economic slumps, such as the early 1930s; joining and lapse rates recovered after 2–3 years.

Other comparisons

These trends can be compared with other organizations. For the early years, Clark quotes lapse rates as high as 30–40% for 18th-century non-commercial societies, which he views as generally having high turnover rates. Compared to these chambers were thus much more stable. In modern times sector trade associations commonly experience a loss of members of 7–11% per year, professional bodies lose an average of 11%, whilst political and activist bodies often lose 20–40% per year. Jordan and Maloney quote lapse rates of up to 42% for membership bodies such as the Green Party, 25% for Amnesty International, down to 5–15% for many other associations. An analysis of net turnover in three American associations shows turnovers of about 10%.[8] Against these comparisons, the higher lapse rates for chambers since 1990 are more akin to activist bodies. However, this comparison is probably less relevant than recognizing that most chamber members are looking for services (as shown in Chapter 15). Hence a better comparison is with reuse of commercial and professional service providers. In that comparison an average of 80% year-on-year loyal customers is judged a very good outcome.

16.3 THE MODERN CHALLENGE

It is clear that something fundamental changed in the 1970–80 period that moved the chamber system from very stable to very unstable membership. The most significant change of this period has been the development of service bundles that provide a significant external income stream funded outside subscriptions. This induced a steady erosion of the cost-benefit links of membership decisions to services received. This became most marked after *c*.1982 with the expansion of government funding streams. If this explains the modern high lapse rates it suggests that members lapse once they realize that they can consume most services anyway, or that the chamber has not needed their obligation in order to survive; this is a special form of government crowding out, as discussed in Chapter 3, a form of the

---

[8] Bennett (2000), table 4 for trade and professional association bodies; Jordan and Maloney (1997), pp. 166–9, and Hansen (1985), for wider membership bodies.

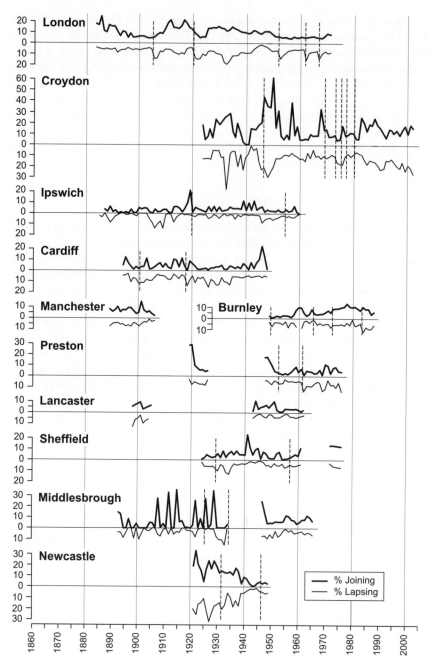

Fig. 16.2. Joining and lapsing rates for a sample of chambers that have continuous membership records for the periods shown. Vertical dashed lines indicate the points at which subscriptions were increased (for Croydon after 1980 there were annual rises which are not shown).

Samaritan's dilemma. There may also be other factors, such as unsatisfied clients after 'taster' sampling of services, or that the services have been largely 'non-preferred'. But the existence of external income as an alternative to member contributions is the most significant feature coincident with increases in lapsing.

For the most recent period, these effects have been convolved with the effects of some chambers becoming CCTEs. This massively increased the external income available, and the extent of 'non-preferred' goods offered. These mergers occurred over 1995–8. With the abolition of TECs, CCTEs had to restructure, with some disappearing altogether when funds ceased in 2003–5 (as discussed in Chapter 13). Figures 16.3 and 16.4 compare joining and lapsing rates between the CCTEs and the rest of the chambers over 1999–2010.[9]

Figure 16.3 shows that the total chamber system experienced a strong decline in joining rates between 1999 and 2001, and then a slow increase. There was, as always, great variety, but between 1999 and 2001 non-CCTEs experienced lower joining. This was, however, cancelled by developments from 2003 when non-CCTE chambers had a more rapid increase in joining rates and CCTEs continued to decline. The differences are statistically significant in 1999, and from 2003.[10] It appears that non-CCTEs initially lost ground, but after the 2001 announcement of the abolition of TECs, the CCTEs slipped against the rest of the chamber system. The differences would be more marked if those CCTE chambers that disappeared were included, since other chambers only slowly took up most of their membership after 2003–5.

For lapsing rates, Figure 16.4 shows an even more marked differentiation between the two types of chamber. Overall, lapsing rates increased, except in 2005. In CCTEs the rise in lapsing was extremely rapid up to 2005, reaching 90% in CCTEs that were under severe stress. Differences between CCTEs and non-CCTEs are not statistically significant over 1999–2003, but become highly significant for 2005. For 2007 and 2009 the comparison set is reduced by the loss of chambers whose members had to be taken over elsewhere. For the surviving chambers that had been CCTEs the lapse rates become similar to the non-CCTE chambers, with no significant differences.

The joining and lapse rate comparisons strongly demonstrate the destabilizing effect of the CCTE episode. Whilst there were immediate benefits of increased membership in the late 1990s, as noted by Taylor, this was mainly from easy situations: many CCTEs were in weaker areas of chamber development, or included an expanded territory where former chambers had been little developed.[11] After this period there was little difference between CCTE and non-CCTE chambers; indeed non-CCTE chambers generally managed to maintain higher joining rates. In 2005, once CCTEs' funding was wound down, lapse rates in the former CCTEs rocketed, but the two types of chamber subsequently converged from 2007.

---

[9] No BCC data on joining or lapsing before 1999; comparison set of CCTEs is reduced from 16 to 10 in 2007, and 9 in 2010.

[10] Two-tailed t-tests; $p = 0.1$.

[11] Taylor (2007), pp. 142–7.

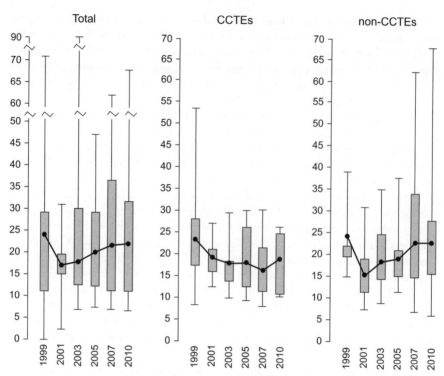

Fig. 16.3. Joining rates for all BCC chambers of commerce 1999–2010, and comparison between CCTE and non-CCTE chambers. (*Source*: BCC *Benchmarking*.)

An analysis by BCC provides further insights into different local dynamics. Over 2000–9, 26 (mostly non-CCTE) chambers merged into nine new bodies, five ceased trading, 15 left BCC though three returned by 2009, with only 35 chambers remaining essentially unchanged (except for name changes). Gross membership change was 25,000 members, with a net loss of 23,000. Within the gross change, net losses contributed (39%) each from merged and non-merged chambers, though the loss per chamber was much higher in the less numerous merged chambers; 14% of losses were contributed by chambers that closed; and there was an offsetting increase of 8% in de-merged chambers (none of which were former CCTEs). BCC concluded that merger was the single most important cause of membership losses, but that some of this was probably spurious since there were duplications in membership lists between merging partners, with some weaker partners having poor quality member databases. Overall the net loss was about 1.8% per year.[12] Given the hiatuses over these years, the recession of 2008–10, and the effects of *Benchmarking* that removed some dubious statistical practices in some chambers, this was perhaps better than might have occurred.

---

[12] *BCC Membership: A Decade 2000–9*: BCC management paper by Sue Deans (April 2010).

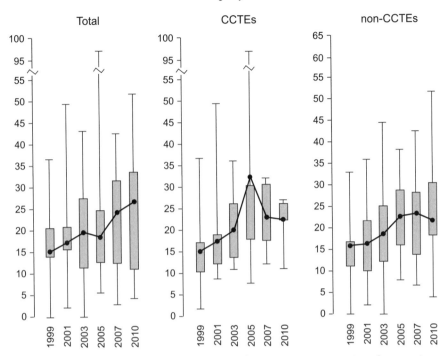

Fig. 16.4. Lapsing rates for all BCC chambers of commerce 1999–2010, and comparison between CCTE and non-CCTE chambers. (*Source*: BCC *Benchmarking*.)

Overall, the experience of this period demonstrates the difficulties of chamber internal dynamics as a result of mergers, and the challenges from external government involvement. Both were destabilizing. Government backing helped chamber development in areas that were historically hard to penetrate, either because of dispersion and rurality, or because they lacked critical mass to support a strong chamber offer. But in other areas, government-backed CCTEs exacerbated the disruptions from the merger process that were occurring anyway as a result of the BCC *Development Strategy*. This suggests that any future government help for chambers should be focused in the most challenging areas. But any such support needs to be based on stronger stability and commitment; otherwise the effect is highly destabilizing when future governments change policy.

16.4. THE INFLUENCE OF SUBSCRIPTION INCREASES AND DECREASES

Subscriptions are a central means by which 'price' is signalled to the membership; they should therefore be a key indicator linking the demand and supply for membership. A change in subscriptions can also be expected to be an important point where that price signal should be particularly noticeable, and thus most likely to be the point at which an influence on joining or lapsing occurs. In modern times we are used to expecting continuous rises in subscriptions year on year. But historically these changes occurred infrequently and often reluctantly. Also, during much of the period up to the 1880s reductions in subscriptions occurred. The discussions around these early decisions give some important insights into later periods when annual increases in subscriptions became the norm.

Reductions in subscriptions

Reductions in subscription rates in the early chambers primarily came from the need to keep subscriptions in line with falling prices. Belfast reduced annual subscriptions from £1 to 10s. in 1822 primarily for this reason. The effect was positive: members in arrears reduced from 28 out of 72 members in early 1822, to 4 out of 71 members in late 1822.[13] A second stimulus was that in several chambers in the early years after foundation, higher initial subscriptions often reflected overestimates of costs and/or likely activity. Thus Nottingham felt able to reduce its subscription in its third year of life in 1863, as the expenditure was only about half the income. The subscription was halved to 10s. 6d. from one guinea, where it remained until 1890.[14] High initial subscriptions may also have been a deliberate policy to help the chamber to build up a cushion of reserves and perhaps purchase office furniture and pay other start-up overheads, after which the expenditure requirements reduced. Thus in Glasgow the reduction in life fee and removal of annual fees in 1828 was justified by the statement that 'the state of capital and income appeared to be such as to render an annual payment unnecessary'.[15] In other cases, a chamber might be involved in a major project that, once completed, allowed it to operate on lower levels of income. For example, North Staffordshire chamber reduced its subscription after 1874 once the high costs associated with publicizing and developing the local Commercial Exchange were covered; subscriptions were halved from one guinea for individuals and two guineas for firms.[16]

Third, a reduced subscription might be linked to reducing services that were no longer required. The early Jersey and Limerick chambers had very high subscriptions, and linkages to specific activities (in Jersey to administering privateering prize money; in Limerick to administering butter, hide, and other local markets). Both chambers later ceased these activities, and as a result reformed their whole subscription structures, significantly reducing rates: in Jersey from an average of over £1000 per member in the 1790s to £1 in 1837; in Limerick from several hundreds pounds per member in the 1810, to £2 10s., and £5 by 1840. In a later case Salt cut its subscription in 1861 when it reduced its offices from two to one. Finding it then had too much income it did not call for one of its half-yearly subscriptions in both

[13] Belfast chamber minutes, 1822.
[14] See R. G. Walton, Nottingham chamber history, pp. 28 and 49.
[15] Glasgow chamber, General Meeting minutes, 2 January 1828.
[16] North Staffordshire chamber minutes, SA/CC/1, 1874–9.

1871 and 1874. Similar causes of reduction in subscriptions occurred in other chambers. Fourth, as noted in Chapter 15, there was pressure on subscription rates from smaller businesses, leading to reduced scales for individuals and the smallest firms, generally from the 1930s.

It is difficult to track all the detailed changes of subscription rates over time as these are less frequently recorded in printed records (such as annual reports); and even in minute books and accounts there is a surprising lack of detail on subscription decisions and rates. However, Table 16.2 shows a sample of chambers that reduced their subscriptions. The changes chiefly occurred in the period 1860–80. As shown in the table, with the exception of Salt, the reductions were entirely in periods of generally declining costs, especially labour costs; e.g. over 1840–80 prices decreased by 25%.[17] The fact that such reductions occurred demonstrates the sensitivity of the early chambers to subscriptions as a price signal and a factor in recruitment/retention.

Subscription increases

In modern times increases in subscriptions have become the norm, usually annually. But up to the late 1960s, before the effects of higher routine inflation, increases in subscriptions were very infrequent. Prices had been falling since the 1870s, rose during WW1, and up to the early 1930s, to fall in the 1940s and 1950s before rising steeply in the 1960s. Hence, the need to increase subscriptions because of inflation was not severe until the 1960s. This allowed chambers to maintain the same subscription rates over long periods.

In the 20th century increases in subscription rates were generally associated with four demands: first, inflation; second, the need to expand the range of services offered; third, crises arising from unforeseen costs (usually of buildings) where the chamber was in debt; and fourth, to contribute towards the costs of the national association. In addition, there might be one-off but substantial income calls required for the establishment of new offices or to finance some specific new initiative. These latter calls were usually supported by a request for donations, a one-off double subscription, lotteries, or some similar means of raising short-term resources.

Contemporary comments show enormous reluctance by chambers to increase subscriptions well into the 1980s. The councils and managers were clearly fearful of the response by their members and daunted by the possible negative effects of increased lapsing. This discouraged or delayed many subscription rises. Many rises were only made when a deficit had occurred, and this could then be used as a *force majeure* to overcome reluctance of members or elected officers to raise the subscription. Even when increases were agreed by chamber councils they were quite frequently turned down or referred back for further consideration at AGMs, leading to further delays in implementation or modifications for certain categories of member. For example, in Dublin in 1892 a proposal from the council to increase the subscription from £1 10s. to £2 had two amendments proposed against it: the

---

[17] Calculated from TNA price test.

Table 16.2. Chambers reducing subscription rates (excludes changes to entrance fees etc.)

Date	Chamber	Change in prices and wage rates over previous decade (+/−)
1795	Glasgow (reduction in annual rate)	−
1819, 1828	Glasgow (commuting of annual to life rate)	−
1820	Dublin	−
1822	Belfast	−
1830s	Limerick	−
1836	Edinburgh (reduction of life rate)	−
1837	Jersey	−
1850s	Bristol	−
1863	Worcester	−
	Bristol	−
1860s	Leeds	−
	Salt	−
1860s	Nottingham	−
1870s	Huddersfield	−
	North Staffordshire	−
1871, 1874	Salt	−
1880s	Belfast	−
1889, 1891	Salt	+
1931	Limerick	−

first to reduce the increase from 10s. to 5s.; and the second to defer the increase for a year. Both were lost, but in many chambers deferral was common. It was also difficult for some chambers to change their by-laws, which discouraged changes; e.g. Glasgow and Edinburgh took many years before redrafting their charter to allow routine subscription changes. In Birmingham in 1917 the by-laws were seen as too cumbersome to change, so a request was made for voluntary increase 'having regard to the size of their firms and the amount of capital and number of workpeople employed'.[18] To overcome reluctance in the Hereford chamber, Mr Gordon Workman offered peer pressure by 'offering to increase his subscription if one third of the members increased theirs'.[19]

But the fears were seldom based on any detailed analysis of what effect increasing subscriptions actually had on membership. Few council minutes comment on the effects that occurred, despite the long and agonized discussions that led to subscription rises. One exception was Liverpool's decision in 1877 to increase the subscription for individuals from one guinea to £1 10s. This precipitated a furore over the chamber being run by a political 'clique',[20] but it was the resignations that led to reform of the chamber: 53 members declined to pay the increase and 36 single members and two firms discontinued subscriptions altogether (15% of the membership).[21] When Burnley raised its subscription from two guineas to three guineas in

---

[18] Birmingham chamber, Council minutes, 29 October 1917.
[19] Hereford chamber minutes, 9 August 1920.
[20] See Chapter 3.
[21] Liverpool chamber, *Annual Report*, January 1878, p. 268; see also Chapter 3.

1949, mainly 'to meet the affiliation fees of ABCC', it expected to lose a few 'luke-warm members' and was pleased to lose only 14 firms who did not renew (6.5% of the membership).[22] In Cheltenham in 1950, on a proposal that subscriptions should be raised to cover income deficiencies, 'the chairman and treasurer said their experience had been that when subscriptions were increased the membership declined.... At this stage the discussion was adjourned without any decision'.[23] When Coventry raised subscriptions in 1957 it experienced a 'reduction in membership accounted for by the increase made in subscriptions', which amounted to a net 4.6% over the next two years. When it again raised subscriptions in 1967 it believed it might lose 7.5% of its members but made no retrospective analysis of its 1957 rise. It was surprised in the following year to have lost only 5%, because of new members added;[24] i.e. almost the same as ten years earlier.

One of the few early systematic analyses of subscription effects appears to be that by London in 1905, and there is evidence in cross-references that other chambers probably used this as some sort of guide. It was certainly quoted by London itself to estimate the likely effect of subsequent subscription rises. For example in 1920 it used an analysis of the 1905 rise to argue that, 'after allowing for an average proportion of resignations arising in the ordinary course, one-fifth of the members resigned during the three or four years following, though new members were secured, so that the total membership was only decreased by less than one seventh'.[25] There was thus a 'shake-out' effect. This is echoed in Norwich's experience in 1962, when its subscription increase raised little new income because 'some members apparently thought they [subscriptions] were too much, although their loss [resignation] was compensated by new members'.[26] These analyses confirm the more general comments in other Chapters, that there was a substantial 'passive' constituency of members. A proportion of these could be precipitated into reconsidering their membership when subscriptions were raised.

These comments also demonstrate some of the difficulties for more detailed analysis. Because of the fear of resignations, when an increase in subscriptions was planned chambers often put greater effort into retaining existing, and recruiting new, members. This was certainly the case in London in 1905 and 1920. When Guernsey raised subscriptions in 1990 it was surprised to experience a 10% dropout and then rapidly launched a membership campaign, streamlined membership elections, more rapidly enacted service expansion, and took public relations advice.[27] Similarly, when Barnstaple increased its subscription in the 1960s, 'The chairman spoke...on the membership fees...it was time to review. Also that it

[22] Burnley chamber, *Annual Report* (1950), p. 5.
[23] Cheltenham chamber, Finance Committee minutes, 12 December 1950.
[24] Coventry chamber, *Annual Report* (1958), p. 9; (1968), p. 23; (1969), p. 28.
[25] London chamber, Executive Committee, minutes, 11 December 1919; the increase in 1905 was a doubling for individuals from one to two guineas; for firms it was an increase from two to three guineas.
[26] Norwich chamber, *Newsletter*, 1963.
[27] Guernsey chamber minutes, Report of Review Committee, 1991, p. 2.

was time that a drive was made to increase membership.'[28] To fully understand membership dynamics, therefore, it is essential to trace joining and lapsing as separate but linked phenomena, not just to look at the total membership count.

Was the contemporary comment by London and Burnley correct, that there were only short-term effects that mainly accelerated the normal shaking out of 'luke-warm' members; and were there changes in this effect over time? Did the immediate effects fade after a few years, or did they have a more permanent effect of modifying the members' relationship with their chamber? Or were there no significant effects of subscription rises on members at all? The cost of chamber subscription has been historically modest, leading Grant and Greaves to argue that they were (and are still) so low as to be too small for members to be bothered working out whether they were value for money or not: below a 'rationality threshold'.[29]

Close inspection of Figure 16.2 indicates that there is certainly some truth in the view that there were only short-term effects. Subscription increases appear to have had short-term effects on increasing lapsing and also joining rates, lasting only for a short time before the general pattern of lower rates of 'churn' are re-established. The analysis is taken further in Figure 16.5, which exhibits the box plot of joining and lapsing rates for 12 chambers for which membership turnover data survive, where there are also occurrences of membership subscription increases that are well documented, and where the subscription rise is isolated by a number of years from the next increase to allow its separate analysis.[30] This need for isolation of changes means that the graphical analysis is not as possible in later years as chambers move to frequent and annual rises. London is included in this sample. To investigate the effect of subscription increases, calculations of lapsing and joining rates are made for two years prior to the change, which may represent the earlier 'steady state'; year zero (0) represents the year when subscriptions were raised; and the effect is then traced for a further three years. Because subscription rises were often under considerable debate for the year or more before implementation, the years (−1) and (−2) may show some early effects of resignation shakeout. Also because many chambers offered some incentive for rapid payment at the old subscription rate in year (0), some effects may be delayed into years (+1) and (+2).

For lapsing, Figure 16.5 shows convincingly that loss of members jumps in year zero (0), the first year of the new rates. The higher lapse rates tend to continue for two or three more years before returning to the previous rates of lapsing. However, in the earlier period shown, the lapse rates are slower to return to their former levels and, within the constraints of the data available, it appears that this earlier period of increase may have left chambers with a permanently higher lapse rate. This applies to each statistic: the maximum, minimum, mean, and the 20% and 80% percentiles. In almost all cases, the increase in subscription for this period was the first

---

[28] Barnstaple chamber minutes, 18 January 1965.
[29] See Grant (2000); Greaves (2008).
[30] These are Aberdeen, Burnley, Cardiff, Croydon, Derby, Ipswich, London, Middlesbrough, Newcastle-upon-Tyne, Preston, Sheffield, and Southampton.

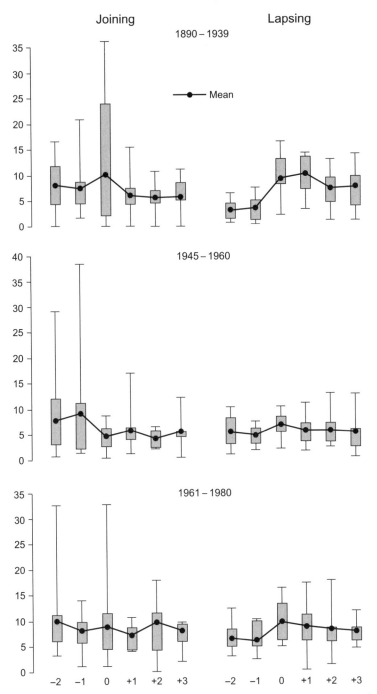

Fig. 16.5. The mean, range, and 20%/80% box plots of joining and lapsing rates (%) over a period of an increase in subscription rate, for the two years prior to, and the three years following, a change.

change the chamber had ever made, after vigorous debate. It most cases it required a doubling of the lowest subscription rate, from one to two guineas and in some cases from one to three guineas, although for three of the sample chambers the increase was lower: from one to one and a half guineas at Southampton; from two to three guineas for London's second increase of 1920; and for Middlesbrough a change only in the higher rate for firms from two to three guineas with the lower rate held at one guinea. Because of the (relative) scale of these increases, and because these changes represented a change in the long-term culture among members which had seen very long periods of price falls and subscription stability, it might be expected that the earlier period would increase lapse rates more significantly. This effect is evident in 1890–1939, not in 1945–60, but increased long-term lapse rates appear again in the 1961–80 period.

Joining rates are expected to be more difficult to interpret. An increased subscription may be off-putting to new members and hence may reduce recruitment in the short and/or long term. But the opposite may also occur: exemplified in London's comment quoted earlier, many chambers made significantly more effort to recruit when they were increasing their subscriptions and so joining rates may rise with subscription increases. Also a subscription rise linked to service initiatives might similarly expand membership.

The data shows both effects to occur. The percentile box ranges for the earlier and later periods show a general reduction in joining rate particularly in the year of change or year +1, but then quickly recover. In the middle period (1945–60), the percentile boxes show little systematic effect of the subscription changes, though the maximum and minimum joining rates reduce. For the earlier and later periods, the year of change generally has a markedly higher maximum rate of recruitment, which brings out the effect of a few chambers making efforts to combat any member losses from subscription rises. Also the mean joining rate, which is strongly influenced by a few very large increases, due to recruitment campaigns, actually rises in two of the three periods analysed. Overall, however, the effect of subscription rises on joining is more confused and variable than that on lapsing.

The London and Burnley comments at the time thus appear to have been correct: resignations accelerated as luke-warm members were shaken out. Both chambers were also broadly correct to be sanguine that lapsing would return to normal fairly quickly, with the evidence here suggesting that after one year lapse rates had generally restabilized. Recruitment efforts could also counteract lapsing effects, though from the sample analysed here it appears that effort to increase numbers was only made for the year of increased subscriptions, or if made in other years was not very successful. Over time it is also fairly clear that the increases in subscription in the period prior to WW2 may have induced a general shift of turnover levels upwards, with lapsing rates moving from a general range of 1–4% to a new level of about 3–8%. These levels continued through to the end of the analysis here in 1980.

The relatively sanguine early view about the effect of subscription rises is also borne out by further analysis of the membership books for London, which are summarized in Table 15.7. Detailed inspection of these books shows that resignations specifically because of subscription rises in 1920 accounted for 51% of 'other' reasons, and 12% of *all* reasons for lapsing; in 1952 the respective figures were 36% and 3%; and in 1962 9% and 3%, respectively. This analysis confirms that subscription increases had mainly short-term effects on lapsing, diminishing over two or three years. It also indicates a trend in declining effects of subscription rises for later periods, as members became more used to the need for them. This again suggests an important culture change in membership loyalty/passiveness induced by the subscription rises compared to earlier periods.

This interpretation challenges the 'threshold of rationality' argument. Greaves suggests that 'in many cases the cost...is too small relative to an individual's income or a firm's turnover that any decision to join (or lapse) will fall below the rationality threshold'. He quotes Grant, who argues that dedicating the resources to making a fully rational decision, and evaluating costs and benefits, exceeds the costs of joining or remaining a member: 'for larger firms, the cost of subscription is such a small proportion of turnover that it is hardly worth the decision costs of considering whether renewal is worthwhile'.[31] It is clear from the analysis here that the Greaves/Grant view does not hold up: increases in subscriptions did precipitate re-evaluation and increased lapsing. On average about 10% of members (above the normal lapse rate) would be lost over a 1–2 year period in the years up to 1939, and in some chambers double that. After 1945 lapsing as a result of subscription rises is smaller, but still leads to an additional 2–5% of members being lost. Hence, firms and business people are not indifferent to what they pay: even at low subscription levels, chamber subscriptions do not fall below a 'rationality threshold'.

16.5 MANAGERIAL DECISIONS

Decisions by chamber managers were critical influences on how joining and lapsing was recorded, and perhaps also on the behaviour of members. If chamber marketing initiatives are poorly targeted, then successful joining is likely to be matched by rapid lapsing. Satisfaction is closely linked with expectations, as shown in the modern analysis in Chapter 15; thus accurate marketing is as critical to achieving high retention rates as ensuring quality services. Similarly, if there are management inefficiencies resulting in lapsing being poorly recorded, then the chamber does not know if its members have actually lapsed or remain committed and active. If poor records of lapsing are accompanied by weak administration of collection of subscriptions, then the effective link between members and management is destroyed; in the most extreme cases it encourages free riding through non-payment.

---

[31] Greaves (2008), p. 1012; Grant (2000), p. 110.

Marketing and recruitment

Until the 1970s membership campaigns by chambers were generally rather generic and relied heavily on existing members to encourage others. As London noted in 1909, 'the members were, after all, the real "recruiting sergeants" for the chamber'.[32] General calls were frequently made at AGMs or in *Annual Reports*, such as that by Plymouth in 1973 that 'increased membership should be the concern of all'.[33] Where specific calls were made, this was usually via mailings to existing members, and in the press or *Annual Reports*.

Membership drives were usually generalized calls for action, repeated in *Annual Reports* in the same words each year, from which it is seldom clear if any major effort was actually made or effect ensued. Newcastle in 1855 had 'regret to observe an absence from the list of a considerable number of merchants, manufacturers, and others connected commercially with the Tyne—a circumstance which . . . most probably arises entirely from inadvertency on the part of the absentees, or want of solicitation on the part of the members',[34] but no systematic action was taken. Oldham in 1888 used the pressure of the council on its members: 'your council would once more urge every member to take a greater interest in the working of the chamber, and assist in increasing the number of members'.[35] Similarly in Bristol in 1903: 'your council again take this opportunity of urging the desirability of increasing the membership by the introduction of new members'.[36] In Kidderminster in 1923: 'it is suggested that every member should endeavour to obtain at least one new member during the year'.[37] A similar call was made in Dublin in 1933, 'the council is of opinion that the membership could be increased if members would take a more active interest in seeking new members';[38] and in Dover in 1956: the 'president says he would like every member to get a new trader to join';[39] or in Cardiff in 1951: 'it is hoped that members individually will use every endeavour to secure an increase in membership'.[40] These general calls did not work very well. Even general letter campaigns received poor responses. For example the membership drive by Exeter chamber of trade in 1930 involved sending 1000 letters to likely local firms. Membership increased from 128 in 1930, to 132 in 1931, but was down to 130 in 1932.[41]

More targeted campaigns, where council members made specific approaches to firms that had been identified as likely to join, seem to have worked better. Indeed it became recognized by ABCC that 'the most satisfactory method was by personal

[32] London chamber, *Annual Report* (1909), in London *CCJ* (1909), p. 127.
[33] Reported in *Western Mail and News*, 17 April 1973.
[34] Newcastle chamber minutes, *Annual Report* (1855).
[35] Oldham chamber, *Annual Report* (1888), p. 10.
[36] Bristol chamber, *Annual Report* (1903), p. 44.
[37] Kidderminster chamber, *Annual Report* (1923), p. 5.
[38] Dublin chamber, *Annual Report* (1933), p. 32.
[39] Dover chamber minutes, 19 April 1956.
[40] Cardiff chamber *Annual Report* (1951), p. 22.
[41] Exeter chamber of trade minutes, 1929–49.

canvas' by existing members.[42] Local experiences confirm this. Leeds established a subscription committee 'to look over the names of parties likely to subscribe'; in 1874–5 it undertook a membership drive by drawing up a list of 'desirable men to join the Chamber', and then each council member volunteered to canvass some of these names. A claimed 60% increase in membership resulted (although the actual increase was from 100 to 141).[43] A more modest increase was achieved in 1952–4 when the Sheffield chamber 'secretary had despatched to each member of the membership committee a lengthy list of names [culled from various sources] of concerns that might be approached for membership'.[44] Cork set up a subscribers' committee to solicit members in 1838, with subcommittees formed for the north, south, and middle of the town. In 1952 it screened lists of non-members and divided them 'among council members who were in touch with the principals of each firm'.[45] Limerick in 1932 appointed a special committee to develop a list of 'desirable members' to approach.[46] In Plymouth in 1951 after 'the Secretary had recently sent out 85 invitations to apply for membership without any success',[47] instead the chamber identified 'possible member firms and circulated to council members with a request for the council member to identify which firms he would approach'.[48] This decision in May produced eight new members by June, 17 by July, and 27 by September.[49] Similarly in Andover chamber of trade in 1923, 'a list of trades people not yet members... was gone through and each member of the Council present agreed to interview a certain number with a view to enrolling them'.[50] In Bury chamber of trade in 1911 'each member of the executive should be supplied with a list of traders who were not members and persuade them to join'.[51]

But even targeted campaigns by council members seem to have had only short-lived success. Thus when Cardiff made a campaign through its council members in 1953, it noted that the 'best results were obtained through a "personal approach" by members of the council' and a 10% increase was achieved. But when this campaign was repeated in 1954 it met 'with limited success', and in 1958 a similar 'new campaign was disappointing'.[52] Similarly, any uplift in membership, as a result of membership drives linked to offsetting possible losses from subscription increases, seems to have lasted only 1–3 years, as shown in Figure 16.5. As a result it was increasingly recognized that marketing must develop on the back of better general awareness of the work of chambers: 'chambers must secure more publicity

[42] ABCC Home Affairs Committee, 4 September 1929.
[43] Leeds chamber minutes, 10 June 1851; also Beresford (1951), Leeds chamber history, p. 35.
[44] Sheffield chamber, Membership Committee minutes, p. M.2, 1952–4; 'concerns' refer to businesses.
[45] Cork chamber, resolutions at General Meeting, 7 January 1838; minutes, 1 October 1838; 3 June 1952.
[46] Limerick chamber minutes, 5 February 1932.
[47] Plymouth chamber, Finance Committee minutes, 10 April 1951.
[48] Plymouth chamber, Membership Committee minutes, 2 May 1951.
[49] Plymouth chamber, Executive Council minutes, 19 June, 10 July, 11 September 1951.
[50] Andover chamber minutes, 4 September 1923.
[51] Bury chamber minutes; 12 July 1911.
[52] Cardiff chamber, *Annual Reports* (1953), p. 22; (1954), p. 22; (1958), p. 24.

for their work . . . and the association must secure greater publicity for the national work'; a chamber must 'be able to show something done for members'.[53]

The form of these marketing campaigns explains a lot about the reasons why chamber joining rates remained stable for so long: most joining decisions were self-selective; where encouraged by active marketing, this was primarily through existing members and councils who could be interrogated by a potential member to assess the value of joining (a reversal of earlier processes where members were assessed by councils). This was all likely to lead to low joining and lapsing rates, since expectations matched the services available, and growth was largely organic, based on the scale of the existing membership and the proportion of self-selecting 'susceptibles' in the local economy. This is a specific form of the 'bureau', where the chamber management was tuned very closely with what was considered to be the market potential that could be achieved.

This 'equilibrium' could be disrupted in several ways. One disruption has been the emergence of external demands for chambers to recruit networks of contacts or client bases to sell services, as a result of government contracts and expectations. As discussed above for CCTEs, this seems to have pushed recruitment to levels that could not be maintained by matching actual use to expectations raised. A second disruption affected earlier chambers, where the secretary, other staff, or canvassers were incentivized to increase membership by receiving additional payments for each new member recruited. This could lead to unrealistic expansions that were not sustained. Such incentives were fairly common in early chambers. For example, Leeds first secretary in the 1850s was paid, in addition to his part time salary of £100 p.a., a 5% commission on the collection of subscriptions and an incentive bonus of 25% of the first subscription payments of all new subscribers.[54] Similarly, in Bristol in the 1850s the secretary's salary is described as a 'salary to collect subscriptions', which in 1859 was £168 5s. 6d., and this was still referred to in a similar way up to 1900.[55] Warrington chamber had a commission fee on subscriptions of 5% paid to the secretary covering the period at least of 1900–30.[56] In Birmingham, the membership secretary was paid 6s. 6d. commission on each new member, and this was extended to all staff who signed a new member in 1924.[57] In general, the incentives used for secretarial salaries do not seem to have had perverse effects, perhaps because secretaries were already very overworked, or because they realized the fruitlessness of achieving short-term joiners that only had to be replaced the following year. However, when canvassers were used, the effects were less predictable.

---

[53] The views of Mr Eyles, Birmingham, and Mr Lloyd-Evans, Portsmouth; quoted in ABCC, Association of Chamber Secretaries, 16 September 1933.
[54] Quoted in Beresford (1951), Leeds chamber history, p. 33.
[55] Bristol chamber minutes.
[56] Warrington chamber, *Annual Reports*.
[57] Birmingham chamber GPC minutes, 14 April 1924.

Canvassing

A 'canvasser' was appointed in many chambers to solicit potential members for whom they received a fee. One reason for this was that personal canvassing by chamber members/councils had limited avenues for contacts and few were prepared to give up the time required; a professional canvasser could fill this gap by travelling to potential members.[58] Canvassing had been used from an early date. For example, Coventry paid a separate 'collector's salary' in the 1870s.[59] In Manchester a canvasser was paid £39 per year in the 1870s and 1880s.[60] This was 5–6% of subscription fees, or about ninepence per member. In London the canvasser's commission cost the chamber £176 in 1898, £200 in 1899, £224 in 1900, and £218 in 1901. In 1902 the canvasser received £1 per week with a one-off 15% commission on each new membership subscription, but a pure commission payment was reverted to in 1903,[61] leading to a reduction on the 40% commission paid to its canvasser in the previous year. In Salisbury a canvasser was used in 1935 and 1936 'because of the difficulties of the depression'.[62] The membership canvasser at Dudley in 1978, Mr Ron Brooks (ex-manager of Woolworths), was paid £5 per day for petrol and half of the first year's subscription fee for each member recruited;[63] he cost about £400 per year.

In Barnstaple chamber of trade a voluntary membership canvasser was sought from the membership in 1959–60, but no one was willing. A Capt. Jones was appointed instead who also became the joint secretary and treasurer after the previous secretary was forced to resign in 1964. Jones was initially paid £11 8s. 2d. in 1961, raised to 12 guineas in 1962, which became an honorarium of 25 guineas over 1964–70.[64] Barnstaple recognized that canvassing 'could not be done by correspondence alone and that the personal approach was the best way to achieve results'. Capt. Jones was, therefore, supported by a new canvasser at a rate of £1 per new member.[65] In 1970, when Jones retired, the secretary's honorarium was increased to £100 per year and that post became responsible for recruitment, with an additional 3s. per member paid to the secretary for each new recruit;[66] this was later increased to 15% of the subscription for new members and 25% for members lapsed more than two years.[67]

Canvassers were not without problems. In Wolverhampton the canvasser used in 1863 to collect subscriptions at 5% commission, was removed due to failure to carry out his duties.[68] Dublin used a canvasser in 1928, gave him up in 1929, appointed a new canvasser in 1930–1, was dissatisfied and appointed another new

[58] ABCC, Association of Chamber Secretaries minutes, 21 October 1927.
[59] Walton (1960), Coventry chamber history.
[60] Manchester chamber, *Annual Reports* and *Accounts*.
[61] London chamber, Finance Committee minutes; MS16465, and *Annual Reports*.
[62] Salisbury chamber history, p. 9.
[63] Report on visit to Dudley chamber, in Worcester chamber minutes, 1978.
[64] Barnstaple chamber Accounts 1961–4; minutes, 28 February 1964.
[65] Barnstaple chamber minutes, 30 December 1968.
[66] Ibid., 8 April 1969.
[67] Ibid., 1 February 1971.
[68] Wolverhampton chamber history, p. 4.

canvasser in 1932. The effects of these changes on membership numbers are difficult to determine; but there was a steady decline in Dublin's membership from 900 in 1928 to 842 (1929), 777 (1930), 733 (1931), 735 (1932) to 714 in 1933.[69] Hereford used a paid canvasser in 1936, but reverted to using their secretary in 1937.[70]

Sheffield in the 1920s found a part-time canvasser not very successful because 'he is not a chamber of commerce man . . . consequently he is unable to discuss any of the matters which arise at the chamber . . . He is not in a position to answer any questions as to the work of the chamber and this is a very severe handicap . . . . There is no doubt that a canvasser who understands the work of a chamber, and who could devote himself entirely to getting new members, would very soon be able to show good results.'[71] However, Sheffield provides a good example of how the tensions were overcome. It moved to a full-time canvasser in 1932, Mr Bridlington, who was very successful. After various other experiments it moved in 1944 to Mr S. J. Barlow, who was also initially very successful. Over seven weeks he made 85 calls and obtained 53 applications. However, he then left for another post, as he was 'not satisfied with the arrangements'. He preferred to identify potential members from his own researches, not the suggestions of the chamber. This modified method was agreed, provided the chamber's membership committee could vet his lists. During mid-1946, Barlow returned to the post and prepared a 'comprehensive list' by industrial sectors. His results in June 1946 were still creditable: he approached 65 firms, received 16 definite applications, 17 definite refusals, 7 more refusals as their parent company was already a member, and 25 replies were awaited.[72]

The Sheffield experience is instructive in several respects. First, it demonstrates the necessity of changing methods of stimulating involvement, increasing commitment, or monitoring loyalty as chamber size increases. Over this period the chamber had grown from 800 to 1400 members. Second, it also indicates the difficulties of in-house staff being effective compared to a canvasser who was dedicated to getting out to the firms: a shift to active marketing from more reactive chasing of arrears. Third, the experience of the chamber goes some way to explaining the enthusiasm of ABCC for canvassers, since the Sheffield secretary from 1935, Arthur Knowles, moved to become secretary of ABCC in late 1945.

The ABCC had proposed in 1923 having its own 'travelling officer' to canvas on behalf of chambers. The idea received little support: Birmingham stated that this should be undertaken by neighbouring chambers, not ABCC; London questioned where the funds were coming from; Hull said it was unnecessary; Northants supported it only for a trial period; most other chambers did not reply.[73] The ABCC renewed the idea of its own membership canvassers under Knowles in 1949.

---

[69] Dublin chamber, *Annual Reports*.
[70] Hereford chamber minutes, 8 February 1937.
[71] Sheffield chamber, Council Minutes and Membership Committee, 28 January 1929 (LD 1986/13).
[72] Sheffield chamber, Membership Committee minutes, 24 October 1932, 12 October 1945, and 20 June 1946.
[73] ABCC, consultation on Improvement Committee recommendations, 1923; MS 14479.

He favoured appointing an ABCC central canvasser, terming this 'field staff' following like use in Canada. This was again dismissed by local chambers, but the use of local canvassers was supported. The Association of Chamber Secretaries prepared a document in 1949 outlining the benefits of canvassers to local chambers.[74] A publicity leaflet, drafted by Knowles, was issued in 1952 to encourage chambers to consider canvassers, with 10,000 copies printed.[75] Thus, Portsmouth in 1950 appointed an official canvasser 'in view of advice received from the ABCC Executive Committee'.[76] Doncaster used a canvasser in the 1950s and 1960s following ABCC suggestions.[77] The ABCC developed a model that canvassing 'must be done by a local man who knows the people and territory'. A 'retired person who was still vigorous was ideal' since the income from canvassing was insufficient as a sole salary. Salaries should be based on a small basic salary and additional payment by results, and not just on enlistment but also renewal for a period of up to five years. A small chamber could find this resource either by working with larger nearby chambers or setting up a cooperative scheme on a regional basis.[78]

The NCT took a different approach to canvassing, using central resources. It employed a central canvasser from 1907 until 1911, and then moved to using the NCT national secretary. Its view on canvassers was that the 'experiment was abandoned when it was found that members recruited under it too often resigned after one year'; hence, 'voluntary recruitment . . . provided the basis for its constant efforts to expand'.[79] When the canvassing agent was considered in 1909, it was commented that: 'Mr Harrison's work has added enormously to the work of your secretaries, and no gain accrues either to them or the chamber for a very large proportion of the existing chambers'.[80] His contact records had to be extracted from him, together with the subscriptions. By late 1910 he had been dismissed, although he subsequently approached other local secretaries and affiliated associates offering his services.[81] For a short period (1910–11) a voluntary approach was used that relied on the local and national associations collecting subscriptions and obtaining new members. However, by late 1911, the central NCT stepped in. The responsibility became part of the NCT secretary's role, for which he was rewarded as support to his salary, '50% of members' subscriptions . . . to cover clerical assistance and cost of collection; and 25% commission on amount paid to the chamber for literature issued from the office'.[82] However, at local level, 83 out of 416 NCT chambers replying to a survey in 1955 still employed a local canvasser (20%).

---

[74] ABCC, Association of Chamber Secretaries, 4 January, 3 March, 24 June 1949; Knowles (1949).

[75] ABCC, Association of Chamber Secretaries, 2 October 1952.

[76] Portsmouth chamber of commerce *Journal* (1950), p. 10.

[77] Doncaster chamber, *Annual Report* (1950, 1960).

[78] ABCC, Development Advisory Committee, second progress report, 8 September 1958; copy at Croydon chamber.

[79] NCT (1957), p. 20, p. 46.

[80] NCT, Finance Committee minutes, 23 November 1909; MS29340/1.

[81] NCT, Joint meeting of Finance Committee and Council, 27 December 1909; MS29340/1.

[82] NCT, Parliament Committee Minutes, 5 December 1911; MS29340/1.

Managing arrears

Non-payment of subscriptions resulting in arrears is a common problem in voluntary bodies. Administration is made complex because continuing membership decisions are often not explicit: lapsing and resignation cannot always be distinguished from failure to pay, and for life subscriptions most lapsing occurs only with death, which makes it difficult to maintain membership lists.[83] Substantial arrears meant a gap between the commitment of members and signals to chamber managers.

Managing the collection of subscriptions was a major challenge from the outset. Where a chamber had premises that were one of the main motives for membership this could be policed on site. Thus Cork in 1821–2 posted a notice in its coffee room 'that gentlemen who have not paid their subscriptions will no longer be admitted', and the waiters were ordered to summon those in the room in arrears to pay.[84] However, even then, problems clearly continued since in 1838 a further decision was made to exclude from the room those who had not paid; and in 1839 to require the waiters to ask for the unpaid subscriptions and 'withhold papers from such as do not pay immediately and that a list of defaulters be posted in the room'.[85]

For the majority of chambers, which used annual subscriptions, many early rules or articles of association were confused in not specifically linking membership to payment of subscriptions. Swansea (founded in 1843 and refounded in 1873), was still debating this in 1876: 'a rule should be added to the existing rules, providing that the non-payment of subscription for a certain time should deprive a person of the rights of membership'.[86] Thus non-payment of subscription did not always result in a member being removed. Indeed, the more common early leverage used was removal of voting power. In an 1892 survey, 46 out of 56 chambers had rules that disallowed the votes of any member in arrears, though even then this was tempered by a period of one to six months before the rule came into effect.[87]

Membership could be considered almost entirely as a 'brand' or 'status' good on both sides, with chambers too gentlemanly to ask for payment. Alternatively members considered subscriptions as a fee that need not be paid if the chamber was not used. Thus in Limerick in 1934, when Mr Hickey agreed to pay his arrears from 1933 and asked to be excused 1934 as he had not used the chamber, the chamber reluctantly accepted.[88] As a result of this sort of attitude, the monitoring of subscriptions arrears was often weak. Guernsey in 1849 set about a review after its secretary failed to call for subscriptions after 1844. It sent out a notice calling a meeting of members, stating that those who did not attend would be judged to have seceded and considered to acquiesce in whatever was decided.[89] The report of the

[83] See Chapter 15; also Clark (2000a), p. 242: 'arrears and mismanagement...was common' in societies.
[84] Cork chamber minutes, 13 April 1821, 20 March and 3 October 1822.
[85] Cork chamber minutes, 16 June 1838, 7 February 1839.
[86] Swansea chamber, Report of AGM, *The Cambrian*, 28 January 1876.
[87] Royal Commission on Labour, *House of Commons Papers* (1892), xxxiv, part V, p. xxxiii.
[88] Limerick chamber minutes, 23 October 1935.
[89] Guernsey chamber minutes; leaflet to members, 1 February 1849.

Kidderminster chamber's exchange on the issue of 1911 arrears is typical: 'Mr. Chadwick: Are there any outstanding subscriptions?—The Secretary: Yes. There are a good many outstanding'.[90] No action is reported in subsequent minutes and arrears continued at the same level.

Many chambers had considered members who had not paid their subscriptions to be debtors; Southampton's 1875 Articles of Association para. 9 states 'any member intending to cease subscribing to the chamber, who has not given a written notice (at lease one month before the year end)...shall be liable for the subscriptions for the following year'. This was also implemented in York in 1920, Hereford in 1921, Cork in 1927, Burnley by 1950, and Barnstaple in 1955.[91] In Limerick the Official Assignee in Bankruptcy accepted arrears as debts and hence a legal claim.[92] This approach led to some highly anomalous accounts: the member lists often included a large number of debtors, who were rarely pursued, with the result that arrears had to be written off in the following year's annual accounts.

The Ipswich chamber articles, amended in 1931, show the weaknesses: a member lapses 'if he shall neglect to pay his annual subscription for 6 months...or if he shall persistently neglect or refuse to pay any other monies which are due... but he may be re-admitted...on paying his subscription or other dues in arrears'.[93] This is fairly typical of the actual policy implemented in most chambers: membership was not policed as an exclusive benefit; readmission was easily possible once subscriptions were paid. Similarly, in Sheffield in 1934, the *Journal* was withheld if arrears were greater than one year; in 1935 a special letter to the member signed by the secretary was introduced to encourage payment of arrears and rejoining the chamber.[94]

Many early chambers explicitly linked subscriptions and membership, and by the late 19th century most chambers had introduced a specific rule or by-law for this. Worcester's statement of 1899 is typical: 'any member intending to leave shall give written notice to the secretary, at least one month before the 23 June, or shall be liable for his subscription for the coming year...[and] the party shall cease to be a member'.[95] Teesside's articles of association of 1929, para. 9, state that 'the secretary shall send a notice requiring payment to all members [who had not paid on time]...and if payment be not made on or before the 30th day of June following by any member to whom such notice shall have been sent, he shall cease to be a member of the chamber'. This gave a six-month grace period and enlarged on the 1873 articles of the predecessor Middlesbrough chamber that had no formal means to strike off a member. Edinburgh built this in from the start, in

---

[90] Kidderminster chamber, report of AGM; in minutes, 27 January 1911.
[91] York chamber of trade minutes. 9 November 1920; Hereford chamber minutes, 7 March 1921; Cork chamber committee book, 3 March 1927; Burnley chamber, *Annual Report* (1950), p. 19; Barnstaple chamber minutes, 29 November 1956.
[92] Limerick chamber minutes, 12 November 1935.
[93] Ipswich chamber minutes, 29 September 1931.
[94] Despite Knowles's stewardship! Sheffield chamber, Membership Committee minutes, 22 June 1934 and 4 March 1935.
[95] Worcester chamber, *Annual Report* (1899), p. 23.

1785: 'every member who fails to pay his annual subscription on or before *Candlemas* shall *ipso facto* be considered to have withdrawn'.[96] Similarly, the businesslike Limerick chamber, which had very high subscription rates (maximum of £62 in 1807), anticipated the problem; it stated 'that should any member refuse or discontinue the payment, . . . he shall be no longer continued a member, and shall not again be [re]admitted without the consent of the committee'.[97]

A six-month grace period became a normal model after 1900, but resulted in major administrative overheads chasing subscriptions and continuing ambiguities about who was a member or had truly lapsed. These difficulties have continued into modern times; e.g. Liverpool only modernized its structures to remove the six-month grace period in the late 1990s.

Reluctance to accept lapsing

Many chambers were reluctant to enforce striking out, hoping a member would return. This is as true in modern chambers as in the past. Even in 2004, the new chief executive of the Edinburgh chamber, coming from a major national company, was amazed by the number of members in arrears. He removed these, reducing the declared membership from 1914 in 2003, to 1459 in 2004 (24%), but this met with criticism from the chamber's executive committee who did not want to see the 'membership' reduced.[98] This reluctance suggests a pervasive effect of the 'bureau' that would have presented a stronger impression of stability than was the case, leading to a systematic under-recording of lapse rates, which may influence Table 16.1 and Figure 16.1.

In the past the discrepancies could be even more extreme. Belfast in 1812 noted that of a listed 74 members, four were dead and 11 would not pay. By 1817, 25 of 76 were not paying. When the first professional secretary was appointed in 1822 (Samuel Bruce), he set about regularizing the membership lists: a count of members in 1822 showed 72, and 28 were not paying. He published new lists showing who were the paying members, asking for subscriptions from the others, which led to 95% paying after two or three reminders.[99] Thus with efficient administration a lapse rate of 5% could be achieved, whilst with lack of reminders and effort there were 39% de facto lapsers (as non-payers). Weak management occurred elsewhere: e.g. a specific question to the secretary by the council of the Newcastle chamber in 1937 received a response that there were 425 members. However, detailed analysis of the roll book of the chamber shows only 248 were paying![100] In Cheltenham in 1959, 43 members (17% of the membership) were in arrears with their

---

[96] Edinburgh chamber, Rules II (1785).
[97] Limerick chamber minutes, initial pages, May 1807.
[98] Comment from Ron Hewitt, Edinburgh chief executive, November 2008; statistics from BCC, *Benchmarking*.
[99] Belfast chamber minutes, 1817, 1822, and inserted papers; see also D1857/1/G3. In fact numbers were only increased in this period in Belfast by reducing subscriptions from £1 to 10s. in 1822: see Chapter 16.
[100] Newcastle chamber minutes, and Membership Book.

subscriptions by September, nine months after they were due, and should have been struck off after three months according to the chamber's rules.[101]

Sheffield provides an interesting case of how membership arrears passed through several periods of different management approaches. It is also valuable as an illustration of the more precise record-keeping that ABCC sought to encourage in local chambers, after the move of Arthur Knowles, Sheffield secretary in 1935–45, to become secretary of the ABCC in 1945. In the 1920s it appears to have become customary in Sheffield to allow some laxity of payment in recognition of difficult trading conditions. By 1927 arrears reached over 8% of subscriptions due. When Knowles arrived in 1935 it proved difficult to tighten up. He was not successful in reducing unpaid arrears until after 1939 with the onset of war conditions.[102] Wars were generally good for increasing membership commitment and reducing arrears.[103] However, the problem of arrears surfaced again in the 1950s, when it was finally admitted that most arrears were really 'unavoidable lapsers'.[104]

Most chambers sought pragmatic solutions by striking off lapsed subscribers after a period (and reinstating when they paid). But even with such rules, the reluctance to strike members off meant that in many cases accounts or minutes record circulation of materials to lapsed members in the hope that they would rejoin, despite increasing recognition that this undermined the incentive to rejoin. As a result, lapsing members were often specifically targeted and cajoled into changing their minds. Derby records several resignations withdrawn 'after the Secretary's solicitations' in the 1930s.[105] Similar efforts in Sunderland are noted: 'An effort had been made to regularise the payment of chambers subscription . . . only six members in arrears for current year.'[106] Galway in the 1920s and 1930s tried to shame those in arrears by posting a list of their names on the notice board in its popular bar and reading rooms.[107]

Only the London chamber made serious early attempts to monitor closely its lapsing and joining rates as a result of establishing a 'membership department' in 1896, reorganized in 1910. As recorded in the chamber's Annual Report for 1909, 'the whole system of recruiting members [has been] revised',[108] and this included a drive to limit resignations by monitoring them, following them up with calls to find the reasons for resignation, and trying to dissuade lapsers. Subsequently joining rates rose rapidly in this period, and lapsing reduced significantly.[109] Similar reforms were undertaken in Birmingham and Manchester, which were looked on

---

[101] Cheltenham chamber, Finance Committee minutes, 7 September 1959.
[102] Derived from a detailed table summarizing membership arrears at 31 December each year, and cleared over year: Sheffield chamber, Registers of Members, LD2536/2/3–5, inside front pages.
[103] Figures 2.2, 16.1, and discussion above.
[104] Sheffield chamber, Membership Committee minutes, 1950, 1953.
[105] Derby chamber minutes, 1930.
[106] Sunderland chamber minutes, 19 August 1913.
[107] Galway chamber history, Woodman (2000), p. 178.
[108] London chamber *Annual Report* 1909; in *CCJ* (1909), p. 127.
[109] See Figure 16.2.

by Liverpool as benchmarks for their own reforms in the 1930s. The Liverpool secretary was sent to Manchester to investigate their processes.[110]

Arrears and free riding

The Goole chamber provides an example of one of the worst subscription management records over 1876–1880s, which is instructive of the effects on member loyalty. Its long-term membership was small: 51 at foundation in 1862 and an average of about 28–9 over the 1870s–90s. But its members who actually paid were far less in number. Due to dilatory administration and a sense of waning support, those paying subscriptions declined from 29 in 1873 to three in 1879, with considerable difficulties of getting their numbers back up. As shown in Table 16.3, the haemorrhaging of subscriptions appears to have been fairly uniform for both the larger firms paying one guinea and the smaller ones at half a guinea. This analysis, which reproduces a table in the chamber's minute book, also demonstrates that whilst there was some real lapsing through one resignation in 1877 and three resignations in 1879, numbers began to increase again when the administration improved. Hence, willingness to free ride was encouraged by inefficiency of collection and monitoring.

Goole was a small chamber of under 30 members at this time. It should have been at a scale where the forces of 'club' solidarity, shame, and social network pressures might be expected to operate with some force. However, it appears that small clubs can produce the opposite effect—because lack of solidarity through non-payment is more obvious to all. Once members start to free ride, most want to free ride, and solidarity can evaporate. In Goole, the free riding, by between one-half, and then two-thirds of members in 1876 and 1877, led to almost all the rest failing to pay over 1879–81, once they realized what was going on. The four who 'resigned' rather just failing to pay, may have done so in disgust since they rejoined by the mid-1880s.[111]

The negative peer effect in small chambers produced by willingness to free ride seems to have been a more general phenomenon: if you could get away without paying and still remain a member, why bother to pay?[112] For example, in Newport (Mon.) chamber in 1876 only 26 of 100 members were paying and this was encouraging other members 'to abstain from paying'.[113] Salt, a small chamber of 23–40 declared members over 1860–90 did not call for subscriptions for a half-year in 1871–2, and for a whole year in 1874–5, because the chamber had large surplus balances. This had the effect of encouraging members to think they did not always need to pay. There was a drop in numbers paying one or two years after the subscriptions were again due: down to 52% in 1873 after the 1871 free period; and

---

[110] See Cherpeau (2010), pp. 39–40.
[111] Deduced by comparing Goole chamber member lists; unfortunately the minute books do not record the full debates about the forces acting on each member.
[112] Clark (2000a), for non-commercial societies; for trade unions, Webb and Webb (1920), p. 443.
[113] Newport chamber minutes, 22 April 1876.

Table 16.3. Goole Chamber of Commerce 1875–1882, records of subscriptions paid and membership

	1875	1876	1877	1878	1879	1880	1881	1882
Subscriptions Paid								
Total	29	14	11	12	3	4	12	16
At 10s. 6d.	23	9	7	8	3	3	9	12
At 21s.	6	5	4	4	0	1	3	4
Number of members declared on lists	29	29	28	28	25	25	25	33
No. of resignations	—	—	1	—	3	—	—	—
Deaths	—	—	—	1	—	—	—	—
New members	—	—	—	1	—	—	—	8
No. of subscriptions unpaid	0	15	17	16	22	21	13	17
Paying members as % of declared	100	48	39	43	12	16	48	48

Source: Chamber minutes, 'list of members and subscriptions paid'.

down to 69% in 1877 after the 1874 free period.[114] By 1880–4 it had only 10–20 paying members (38–56%).

Thus subscription arrears were a persistent problem for chambers (as with most organizations), and were perhaps the main element leading to effects of the 'bureau'. As commented for Belfast, 'it is difficult to understand why the membership of the chamber in the last quarter of the nineteenth century allowed it to be in constant financial difficulty'. The financial problems of the chamber 'verged on the farcical for those "captains of commerce" each handling thousands of pounds daily in his own business . . . to talk gravely each February about such financial balances and deficits; have the plight of the organisation fully revealed in every newspaper the following day; and do nothing about it'.[115] In 1917, the president of ACC, Sir Algernon Firth, commented 'some members have subscriptions of ten shillings per annum. What can a manufacturer expect for ten shillings? They pay more for their golf clubs.'[116]

16.6 OTHER INFLUENCES ON MEMBERSHIP DECISIONS?

It is clear from the discussion in Chapter 15 that a variety of other general economic influences, local chamber service developments, and external factors influenced the dynamics of chamber membership, as well as any subscription effects. But no wide-ranging analysis of these dynamics has ever been attempted. Time series

[114] Comparisons of total declared membership (as published in membership lists) and total paying membership 1859–89: Salt chamber, *Annual Reports and Accounts*.
[115] G. Chambers, Belfast chamber history, pp. 137, 192.
[116] Quoted in Taylor (2007), p. 63.

analysis is used here to assess whether short-term changes in chamber membership are associated with a range of possible external factors, and internal decisions by the chamber (including subscription decisions). The analysis uses information on six of the chambers shown in Figure 16.2 for which membership joining and lapsing are recorded with sufficient accuracy, for a sufficient period, and for which other financial and service information is also available.

The offering: internal chamber characteristics

A range of internal factors influence membership decisions, such as service provision, personnel characteristics, and the effect of the 'bureau' through management decisions on how lapsers and arrears were dealt with. London can be used to some extent as a base case, because it has the longest records of lapsing and joining, from 1882 until 1972 (90 years), and also for this period it properly recorded finances and a range of measures of the service volumes of its main services.[117]

In terms of service provision, London recorded information on numbers of enquiries, employment department activity (the number of employees placed by its employment service and employers satisfied), certificate numbers, education support (the number of examination candidates and centres for its examinations), Arbitration Court cases and value of claims, and 'letters received' (where data exist for 1899–1965). These records offer special opportunities to assess a wide range of possible membership motives. The arbitration service may have acted as an important source of 'brand capital' or insurance. The employment service may have stimulated employer involvement through actively marketed discounts, offering both purposive/expressive and material selective benefits. Enquiries and certificates give measures of direct individual (material/selective) benefits. Letters received offer a crude index of lobbying concerns. The chamber also had a journal and a library, but as these existed fairly uniformly throughout the period, it is not possible to assess their effects. London also gives very useful opportunities for assessing the influence of subscription increases; there were several, well spaced in time, so that short-term effects can be isolated from the next increase, with entrance fees used over 1885–1903.

Other chambers can also be used to assess the generality of the London case. It has been possible to obtain reliable annual series for five other chambers: Croydon 1920–2002 (82 years); Cardiff 1893–1949 (57 years); Burnley 1947–85 (39 years); Sheffield 1924–61 (38 years); and Preston 1948–77 (30 years). In some of these cases service volume information is available, but often provision has to be inferred from the 'other' income of the chamber (after subscription income is deducted from total income). Staff sizes and wages, or total income, are also used as a general measure of service capacity, as no other measures are available. Whilst these five chambers offer less satisfactory information, they are located in different regions, extend the London example, and include chambers with a range of sizes.

---

[117] These records are dispersed (between LMA, the chamber, London *CCJ*, and BCC archives at LMA).

Whilst London was the largest chamber, exceeding 3000 members for almost all the period, Croydon had 230–1400, Preston had between 288 and 520, Sheffield ranged from 732 to 1415, Cardiff from 141 to 538, and Burnley from 168 to 414.

These chambers also offer some contrasted services to London. For example, Croydon had a chequered history of membership of the ABCC; it was a member of ABCC up to 1925, then left to join the NCT in 1926; rejoined in 1934, leaving in 1960–73 because of the high subscription, rejoining in 1974. The Cardiff records offer the opportunity to assess the influence of communication with members, secretarial services, and a library. Expenditure on periodicals and papers printed is used as an indicator of the range of its lobby activity with outsiders, and communication with its members. From 1901 the chamber set up its own library and reading room, which it maintained until 1919, having previously had a joint subscription with the local Exchange buildings. In 1943 it took over the secretarial services of a number of other associations, which may have influenced membership loyalty and recruitment.[118]

Burnley, as a small but growing chamber, allows examination of the influence of starting new services: a reading room/library (introduced in 1969); issuing export certificates (begun in 1958); and staff changes.[119] It had a part-time secretary in its early years (equivalent to about 0.1 full time), supplied by a voluntary input from a local accountancy firm (a quite common arrangement for smaller chambers). Only in 1963 did it appoint a full-time secretary, with its second member of staff appointed in 1977. The Sheffield and Preston chambers collected no consistent or detailed service information, but they provide good financial and member information.[120]

The subscription history of these chambers also gives some useful comparators with London. Over the sample periods, Cardiff increased rates only in 1901 and 1918; Sheffield raised its rates in 1937, 1947, and 1956. However, the other chambers modified rates more frequently, mainly because the sample covers a later period: Croydon raised rates in 1946, 1958, 1968, and then annually from 1970, except in 2000; Burnley raised rates in 1949, 1967, 1974, 1978, 1980, and 1982; and Preston raised rates in 1953, 1963, 1971, 1973, and 1975. The influence of changes in subscriptions is measured in two ways. First, as measures of changes in the real value of the average subscription rate. Second, for the case of London, a categorical variable is used for the period when the chamber charged an entrance fee (the ten years 1885–1904).

---

[118] Membership data reconstructed from membership books; D/D COM/C1/13. Irregular accounting of certificate income of £652 in 1925–9 interpolated from ledger books.

[119] All listed in *Annual Reports*.

[120] Sheffield from Member Books, chamber minutes, and *Annual Reports*. Preston from *Annual Report*.

External factors

As well as internal factors, membership decisions are influenced by a number of external economic factors or other features. If the cost of membership is an influence on lapsing, as suggested in the earlier discussion, then it can be expected that the current financial strength of a business will also influence its choices to join/lapse. In the analysis here, four different measures of general economic conditions are tested: changes in unemployment rates, industrial output, GNP, and wholesale price.[121] However, it may be that it is mainly immediate financial pressure that stimulates joining or lapsing decisions. To gain a grasp of how far immediate conditions of distress may be influential on membership, an economic health index of 'price shocks' is used.[122] In addition, because of the importance of the export support services of chambers, the volume of exports, imports, and re-exports is tested. The role of government is also a critical feature, measured as the total level of government taxation. Three measures of labour organization effects are also examined: trade union membership, the number of unions, and the number of workers involved in stoppages.[123]

The two features examined are the joining rate and the lapsing rate. A first point to observe is that both of these variables are significantly and positively autocorrelated; i.e. the rates each year are very similar to the immediately previous year. This is to be expected behaviourally. As noted earlier, chambers are likely to be strongly influenced by the politics of the 'bureau', so that both internal managerial decisions and membership behaviour are likely to be similar from one year to the next. This is evident in Figure 16.2. Tests of the correlation between the joining and lapsing rates show there to be *no* significant correlation between these two variables either contemporaneously, or for lags between them at $t - 1$ or $t - 2$.

16.6 TIME SERIES ESTIMATES

We can now move to assess the association of internal and external variables with the joining and lapsing rates. Since these data are *rates*, i.e. the numbers that join or lapse divided by the total membership, they are normalized and not dependent on the size of the chamber's membership. But they are also measures of the differential coefficient; i.e. rates of increase or decrease. It is thus appropriate to compare them with the rate of change of each of the other variables. Since all the external variables also have long-term structural as well cyclical components, using rates of change

---

[121] Argued as important by Gayer, Rostow, and Schwarz (1953); Crafts (1985); Bernanke and Gertler (1989).

[122] Bordo, Dueker, and Wheelock (2003) provide a five-way classification over 1790–1999: severe distress, moderate distress, normal, moderate expansion, euphoria; extended on a comparable basis: 2000, moderate expansion; 2001–3, normal; 2004, moderate expansion; 2005, euphoria.

[123] See Appendix 3; because of changes in base, data must be interpreted as *index number series*.

also has the advantage of removing the trend and first order autocorrelation within the other variables.[124]

Many of the economic and other external measures, as well as internal measures, are interrelated with each other (they are multicollinear). For this reason many parts of the analysis can include most of the variables only one at a time (i.e. not in the same statistical equations). Hence, the quoted results are those after assessing the various alternative measures available. It should be borne in mind that the aim here is not final best econometric estimates, but to explore the relative importance of the main potential explanatory factors associated with membership dynamics. Standardized regression coefficients are presented to remove the effects of different scales of measurement of the different variables. In all cases the overall estimates are statistically significant.

Joining rates

For the joining rate, shown in Table 16.4, the influence of the 'bureau' (measured by the previous year's joining rate) is one of the most significant variables in all cases, except Sheffield. The measure of economic conditions used, unemployment, is positive in all cases, indicating that as economic stress rises, joining tends to increase, but it is statistically significant only for London and Cardiff. Unemployment is a superior measure of economic stress to the economic conditions index, which suggests that it is the persistent workforce environment that is the strongest economic pressure on membership decisions.[125]

Government taxation levels have both positive and negative associations with joining. The positive relationships may reflect local economies that depend more on government spending. Higher government activity may reflect greater need for their chambers to be involved in lobbying to maintain benefits; this could explain the positive association for Burnley (as well as Cardiff and Sheffield, although these are not significant). The converse may be represented by the less government-dependent economies of London and Croydon, where members feel government taxation is a pure crowding out pressing their other costs, or despair of the capacity of chambers to influence government.

Trade union membership, where significant, is positively associated with joining, indicating that the chambers may have been seen as some bulwark to help employers in their response to changing levels of union membership. Export volumes, where significant, are positive, and this applies to the two economies of Cardiff and Preston where their strong relation to port trade leads this is to be expected, though surprisingly not to London.

---

[124] First differences rendered each independent variable non-autocorrelated, allowing use of ordinary least squares.

[125] Macgregor (1934, chapter 3) shows unemployment lags behind financial stress and prices by about one year in 1868–1910; thus member decisions may reflect cumulative response to economic pressures; see also Hoppitt (1987).

The Members

Table 16.4. Multiple regression standardized coefficient estimates of joining rate with reduced set of independent variables (all differenced)

Independent variables	London	Burnley	Cardiff	Croydon	Preston	Sheffield
Bureau: joining rate $(t-1)$	0.587**	0.455**	0.179+	0.361**	0.632**	-0.077
Unemployment	0.185+	0.029	0.472**	1.356	0.202	0.090
Government taxation	-0.159+	0.750**	0.174	-0.056	-1.064**	0.238
Trade union membership	0.201*	0.123	-0.029	1.251	-0.065	0.477*
Export volume	-0.024	-0.144	0.539**	0.085	0.996*	-0.294
Other chamber income	-0.136	0.051	-0.039	-0.040	0.711+	0.268*
Chamber wages[a]	0.037	-0.048	-0.185	-0.097	-0.733**	-0.114
Subscription average	–	-0.014	-0.114	-0.020	-0.540**	-0.262+
Subscription increase (0, 1)	-0.168+	-0.133	-0.034	0.102	0.049	0.067
Entrance fee (0, 1)	-0.297*	—	—	—	—	—
Arbitration cases (no.)	0.004	—	—	—	—	—
Employees placed	-0.034	—	—	—	—	—
Examination candidates	0.026	—	—	—	—	—
Enquiries	-0.069	—	—	—	—	—
Meetings	0.014	—	—	—	—	—
Library (0, 1)	—	-0.007	0.077	—	—	—
Library expenditure	—	—	0.300*	—	—	—
Printing costs	—	—	0.017	—	—	—
Letters received	0.067	—	—	—	—	—
BCC (0, 1)	—	—	—	0.115	—	—
Trade association members	—	—	0.177	—	—	—
R^2	0.751	0.795	0.413	0.163	0.652	0.391
F	9.711**	12.035**	3.603**	1.473+	3.963**	1.924*

** $p = 0.01$ or greater;
* $p = 0.05$ or greater; + $p = 0.1$ or greater.
a. replaced by staff numbers for Cardiff and Croydon.

Interestingly, few of the internal chamber features have much association with joining rates. 'Other chamber income' is generally positive, and significant in the case of Sheffield and Preston, indicating that its value is associated by members chiefly with the subsidy from elsewhere: it makes membership look a better deal. But this does not apply more generally. Chamber wages, which were introduced as a means to measure overall chamber human resource capacity, are generally negative related to joining, but only significant in Preston. It appears that the wage budget is seen more as a cost, off-putting to joiners, rather than a positive measure of staff capacity.

Where service volume measures are available, they have no significant association with joining rates (even in London where many more services measures are available), except for changes in library expenditure in Cardiff. This is in contrast to some bivariate relations, and demonstrates the dominant effect of the 'bureau', which already de facto captures much of the internal capacity. For Croydon, there is no significant association with joining rates from the chamber's membership of ABCC. Indeed overall, it appears that there is little relation of the joining decision to the service offer: the Cardiff library is the important exception over the 1901–19 period.

The subscription measures are significantly associated with joining rates in four cases, and in all cases the effect of changes in average subscriptions, and the London entrance fee, are negative (they reduce joining). The effect of the London entrance fee confirms the assessment in 1904, when it was abolished. Subscriptions are associated with increased cost, and hence perceived negatively by potential joiners, with an entrance fee providing a further impediment.

Lapsing rates

For the lapsing rate, shown in Table 16.5, the association with the 'bureau' is again one of the most significant and positive features (with Preston again the exception). This indicates that high lapse rates once established tend to become self-reinforcing; it is a feature of the chamber's retention offer to members and the management response to losses. The economy, as measured by changes in unemployment, generally shows positive associations; i.e. economic stress increases lapsing, but this is significant only in London, where increases in unemployment are one of the most significant associations with lapsing. Government taxation has little or no association with lapsing. Trade union membership is significant only in Burnley, where its negative association (reducing lapsing) is in line with its positive association with joining in the case of Sheffield. Export volumes are not generally significant, but in the case of Preston are associated with reduced lapsing (which is the expected converse of the relationship they have with joining in Preston).

For internal chamber variables, 'other income' is significant in two cases, but in opposite directions. In London is seems to act as a force associated with greater lapsing: there is less need to maintain membership to support the chamber. This interpretation is contrary to the role of the service measures in London, which show, for arbitration cases and employees placed in employment, strong negative relationships. In Cardiff services reduce lapsing: the library, and changes in printing costs, are significantly negatively associated with lapsing and encourage membership retention. For Burnley, however, 'other income' is positively associated with retention probably because its activities were otherwise very small and members may have recognized that the greater the other income, the better the value for money they obtained from their subscription. The same contrary interpretation may account for the two cases where wages are significant.

For other services, it is interesting that meetings have a significant positive association with lapsing: they appear to put members off. This chimes with London's assessment of lapsed members summarized in Table 15.7, that voice and meetings are perceived as burdensome. This view accounts for the largest number of comments from lapsers in 1883–1909 and 1910 (Table 15.7). It is an irony that to get the best value from a chamber, a member has to become involved: the antidote to exit is voice; but this has considerable cost in terms of time and

Table 16.5. Multiple regression standardized coefficient estimates of lapsing rate with reduced set of independent variables (all differenced)

Independent variables	London	Burnley	Cardiff	Croydon	Preston	Sheffield
Lapsing rate $(t-1)$	0.629**	0.321*	0.183+	0.343**	−0.128	0.416*
Unemployment	0.259**	−0.132	0.126	1.449	0.067	0.015
Government taxation	−0.131+	0.042	−0.178*	−0.086	0.399	−0.052
Trade union membership	0.044	−0.386*	0.023	1.421	0.266	−0.089
Export volume	0.077	0.372	−0.099*	0.109	−0.806*	0.117
Other chamber income	0.131*	−0.629*	−0.054	0.027	−0.299	0.030
Chamber wages[a]	−0.126*	0.488	0.077	−0.149	0.491+	−0.189
Subscription average	—	−0.104	0.332*	0.207+	0.702**	0.157
Subscription increase (0, 1)	−0.288**	−0.001	0.054	0.125	−0.392*	−0.218
Entrance fee (0, 1)	−0.089	—	—	—	—	—
Arbitration cases (no.)	−0.322**	—	—	—	—	—
Employees placed	−0.468**	—	—	—	—	—
Examination candidates	0.014	—	—	—	—	—
Enquiry (nos.)	−0.077	—	—	—	—	—
Meetings	0.162*	—	—	—	—	—
Library (0, 1)	—	0.393	−0.269*	—	—	—
Library expenditure	—	—	0.430	—	—	—
Printing costs	—	—	−0.720**	—	—	—
Letters received	0.106	—	—	—	—	—
BCC (0,1)	—	—	—	0.044	—	—
Trade association members	—	—	0.217	—	—	—
R^2	0.850	0.430	0.287	0.242	0.552	0.407
F	18.173**	2.343*	2.057*	2.417*	2.605*	2.062*

** $p = 0.01$ or greater;

* $p = 0.05$ or greater; + $p = 0.1$ or greater).

a. replaced by staff numbers for Cardiff and Croydon.

effort. For the other two chambers where some service measure is available, there is no significant relationship in Burnley (perhaps to be expected as this was a rather limited reading room with only few items available), but in Cardiff there is a significant association with reduced lapsing. This is in line with the positive relation to joining: it does appear that the Cardiff library over 1901–19 was an important membership benefit stimulating joining, encouraging retention, and reducing lapsing. For Croydon's varied membership of ABCC there is no significant association with lapse rates, indicating that ABCC involvement is irrelevant to local members.

Subscription changes have the expected positive relationship with lapsing; an increase in subscriptions is associated with increased lapsing; significant in all cases except Burnley. This also applies to a subscription increase variable, which is highly significant for London. The London entrance fee, though not quite statistically significant, has the expected negative sign, that entrance fees are associated with retention. Again, this vindicates the advocates of its abolition in 1904, who accepted that it had some influence on retention, but argued that its effect was minor.[126]

16.7 CROSS-SECTIONAL ANALYSIS

There have been previous attempts at econometric estimates of membership dynamics for cross-sectional data (for one point of time) by Mekic for 2006. As in the times series analysis, there were more difficulties in finding systematic correlates of the joining rate than for lapsing. The factors that came closest to statistical significance for *joining* were whether or not a chamber offered certificates and document handling (both negative); attendance levels at events (positive); average staff salary levels (positive); and some minor associations with business size and sector (such as an increased joining rate for small chambers that had a high proportion of small firms, but a lower joining rate where chambers had a large manufacturing sector in their catchment).[127] The catchment area was the most significant environmental feature for comparing one chamber with another: this was negative, as in analysis of market penetration.[128] This suggests a similar conclusion: that smaller chambers in smaller areas generally have a stronger loyalty: joining is more an obligation. However, none of these variables has a high level of statistical significance: joining is not well explained in the cross-sectional analysis.

For *lapsing*, Mekic found more consistent and stronger correlates, as in the time series estimates. The main factors were subscription income per member (positive); 'other income' per member, which is mainly fees and government contracts (positive); number of potential members (positive and sometimes significant); and catchment area (negative). The negative sign of catchment area confirms the joining decision: smaller chambers have stronger commitment and retention. The higher rate of lapsing in larger chambers is indicative of the declining role of wider services and broader personnel available as size is increased: material/selective benefits are undermined by loss of geographical 'tightness' leading to reduced solidarity and purposive benefits. This is to some extent confirmed by the positive association of lapsing with both subscription income and other income.

Mekic's cross-sectional study demonstrates considerable challenges to statistical analysis of joining rates, with R^2 generally less than 0.1 for most cases. Lapsing rates were better explained, but still with R^2 of only 0.24. However, in Mekic's best performing models the joining rate achieves an R^2 of 0.55, chiefly by including a categorical variable to distinguish between chambers that have international document services or not. The best lapsing rate models have R^2 of 0.42, mainly from catchment area, subscription income, patron subscriptions, events, and export documentation. Mekic's study, therefore, confirms the role of income/service capacity (especially when events and export documents are included), as well as

[126] See Chapter 15.
[127] Mekic (2007), chapter 5; London is excluded from all Mekic's estimates reported here.
[128] See Chapter 14; Bennett (1998b).

geographical catchment characteristics on modern joining and lapsing, with smaller catchments encouraging higher joining and lower lapsing rates.

16.8 CONCLUSION

This chapter demonstrates that the turnover of membership in chambers through joining and lapsing has been historically low. Average turnover of 4–8% gave them a long-term stability up to the 1960s, even though the variability between chambers at any one time was often high. However, this early stability has been succeeded by a period of rapidly increasing lapsing since the 1980s, reaching all-time highs in the 1990s and into the 21st century.

Generally low rates of 'churn' of members up to WW1 produced stable organizations with high member persistence, commitment, and loyalty. But this was given something of a shock when increased subscriptions were needed. This unsettled the stability of membership, leading to average lapse rates by the 1920s increasing to 6–8%. This introduced more systematic scrutiny of each annual decision to remain as a member in terms of the perceived benefit compared to the (at least nominally) rising costs. Subscription increases shook out the 'lukewarm' members. But after the late 1960s, annual subscription rises became the norm in most chambers, leading to more continuous reassessment by members of their cost and benefits, and this seems to be one factor in increasing lapsing rates. There is no evidence to support the contention that subscription costs, though low, were so low as to be irrelevant to business decision making: below a 'rationality threshold'.

A key challenge has been achieving renewal and payment of subscriptions. Inefficient monitoring of arrears was a major problem for early chambers. Without income, the viability of the chamber was undermined and ultimately it would go bust. Non-payment of subscriptions also undermined the commitment of members: it reduced their de facto involvement and search for value from the chamber; members just melted away; or if they perceived others to be actively involved without paying, it undermined their solidarity, as in Goole. Some of the historical stability of chambers was thus the result of 'bureau' effects on how lapsing was managed.

In the 1990s significant increases in instability resulted from internal changes through mergers, and government initiatives. Comparing the evolution of joining and lapsing across the period 1999–2010, government-supported CCTEs had an important influence in spreading recruitment to a wider range of smaller and more dispersed areas. But after initial increases in joining rates, CCTEs had higher lapsing and lower joining than other chambers. Marketing of their government activity was confused with chamber membership; the distinction, cost-effectiveness, and value for money of each was unclear. Free riding was encouraged by the appearance of government largesse, whilst excessive 'recruitment' was claimed by calling every contact a 'member'. Membership statistics and managerial priorities were dangerously distorted.

When government funding was withdrawn, the demise of CCTEs meant that lapsing rates in some cases became extreme, and destabilizing for the whole system. The episode shows the potential benefits of government support, but also its profound dangers. However, average joining and lapsing rates converged between former CCTEs and other chambers by the late 2000s. The recession over 2009–10 has continued the pressures to lapse; so from the perspective of 2011 it is unclear whether the end of the CCTE era will see lapsing revert to levels seen in the late 1980s, or will remain at permanently higher levels.

From the time series analysis of short-term changes, fluctuations in joining and lapsing rates prove difficult to explain by any systematic statistical analysis; but there is a dominant effect of the member loyalty and stability of the chamber 'bureau' (which includes reluctance to accept lapsing). Second, this also explains why subscription rises can be so disruptive. Even though the effects were usually short-lived, an increase in subscriptions broke an otherwise very stable organizational relationship with members. The shake-ups associated with changes in subscriptions demonstrate that comparison of costs with benefits are critical. The services that are most significantly associated with increased joining and reduced lapsing have been: the London high-volume/high-profile employment service over 1894–1952; London's high brand value/high repute service of arbitration (even though its volumes were low); the introduction of a library over 1901–19 in Cardiff; and Cardiff's printing activity (which measures lobby and communication activity). These conclusions correspond with the surveys of membership motives reviewed in Chapter 15, which suggest that service benefits, costs, and economic factors influence the membership decision. Economic stress influences these decisions, but is best captured in the unemployment measure, which is generally found to be the most significant factor from the external environment associated with lapsing.

The most important aspect of the analysis is to confirm that historically, as in modern times, it is *specific services* that are most important. The continuities of the 'bureau' wrap up a mix of service demands, supply decisions, and member marketing and management practices that led to the core historical stability of most chambers. Specific services stimulate joining but appear chiefly to help to reduce lapsing; and burdensome services such as meetings that involve 'voice' can be negative features which encourage people to leave. In modern chambers voice needs to be replaced by more active and less burdensome methods of involvement, which electronic communications may facilitate. However, the analysis here is certainly not the last word, and further research is needed on the underlying short-term and long-term motives of members in the chamber system.

PART 6
THEN AND NOW

17

Then, Now, and the Future

17.1 THEN AND NOW

Chambers were born from protest and 'reform' zeal. In time they became a highly 'respectable' brand associated with informing and improving legislation, and promoting trade. However, there is nothing in this book to suggest that chambers were or are a privileged interest able excessively to bend the state to their needs; even when 'insiders', chambers have been subject to the whim of government as to how far their voice has had influence. Local business interests have pressed their case, but have succeeded only when the contingency of politics found the case convenient or compelling: policy was and is decided by politicians. This confirms other analyses that have suggested the weakness of business lobbying bodies within a voluntary, private law structure: smallness, fragmentation, and individualism have been endemic. As Trentmann concluded for the period up to 1930, 'business was as atomistic in its associational politics as in its underlying economic structures'.[1] Or as Grant concluded over the whole sweep of the 20th century, 'the economic power of business is not matched by a capacity for developing a coherent political viewpoint and articulating it to government'.[2] Against these forces the chambers have usually been remarkably coherent.

Chambers are one part of a general movement to defend business interests against 'unwarranted' government intrusion. Earlier chapters have quoted 18th-century comments that chambers could help overcome 'imbecility of entire administrations' and the 'ignorance of governments'. In 2010 the BCC business burdens survey stated that 'much of the claimed overall benefit of [government] is no more than "bread and circuses"; . . . In reality, it is . . . damaging for competitiveness and the economy'. The NAO in 2011 found that the 'majority of businesses think that government does not understand them well enough to regulate'. Information asymmetry remains a pervasive constraint on government effectiveness; challenges to its competence seem to have no particular historical bounds. As a result, there is no doubt that, in answer to the question of whether government stimulates business organizations, or business organizations develop autonomously, chambers have always been a response to threats, government 'bads', and the need to make the voice of businesses heard. And when chambers occasionally have had direct supporters in government, as with Joseph Chamberlain in 1880–1905 and Michael

---

[1] Trentmann (1996), p. 1030.   [2] Grant (1993), p. 193.

Heseltine in 1979–97, expensive government alternatives have been favoured rather than using business expertise by delegating responsibility and helping chambers strengthen capacity.

Chambers have been the main business voice of the localities; and they remain so. This was born from the outports and colonies seeking to have their needs understood by a neglectful imperial government, and as a counter to London interests. This engendered a common model for organized lobbying at Westminster that spanned the Atlantic world. This voluntary model remains the common legal basis of the chamber of commerce systems in the UK, Ireland, United States, Canada, and many Commonwealth countries across the world. They have subsequently evolved differently, but retain a fundamental distinction from the public law chambers of many European countries. This book has shown the endemic challenges that these voluntary systems face to make local business needs heard. Their voice can be easily sidelined and ignored by government, and they suffer inherent weaknesses from their voluntary status. Yet this is also their strength: they exist because businesses want them to exist and can provide independence of action. Most of all this gives them a democratic platform to represent the economic interests of each locality; as a counterweight to populism and other countervailing pressure groups.

This book has shown that chamber voice has had an extraordinary continuity over 250 years. The balances struck within its governance structure appear to have provided stability in most cases beyond the personalities themselves. In contrast to those academic commentators that have seen chambers as unstable, divided, and short-lived, this book has shown them to have greater endurance than most government initiatives. This is because they support a basic need. As economic associations chambers have primarily offered strategic and resource support to business through services and improving government actions. The analysis has also shown that judgements about membership and involvement have usually been made primarily on the basis of the marginal utility of the services or voice benefits derived. Subscriptions and other costs have remained important decision criteria; even though they have been relatively low.

But the benefits of chambers have not been just economic. They have also provided status and brand benefits, opportunities for allegiance to a cause, and solidarity with wider local community interests. Member demands for the chambers' 'preferred goods' of services and voice activities have always been jointly sought, as a balanced bundled offer. As a result, there are the same challenges for chamber activity now as in the past: to maintain allegiance, loyalty, and solidarity across diverse and multiple agendas; to balance individual demands for business services with collective issues such as voice; and to encourage involvement between members and chamber managers.

17.2 FROM THE 1980S: CLEAN BREAK WITH THE PAST?

The different themes explored in this book have shown remarkable continuity in most key aspects, until the 1980s. Market penetration, joining and lapsing rates underpinning member loyalty and commitment, were all remarkably stable. Service activities, membership numbers, and resources largely grew organically with the size of the population and economy. Even through the stress of world wars and the slump, disruptions were relatively short term. But from the 1980s this all began to change, with joining and lapsing rates becoming extremely variable, and other aspects of chambers becoming unstable. What has changed so fundamentally over these 30 years? This is a key question to assess for the modern chamber and its future strategy. The earlier chapters have suggested five possible explanations that are examined further here.

1. The product life cycle

Many management theories and extensive marketing case studies demonstrate the existence of product life cycles. Early innovation is succeeded by rapid growth, saturation of the market, market entry and competition by others, consolidation and then decline, when new products displace old.

The chambers show a wave of steady product innovation and adaptation over their history. Starting with a primacy of voice as their USP, this was supplemented from the outset with coffee and reading rooms, libraries, commercial arbitration, information, and advice. From the end of the 19th century technical advice and a range of local service innovations (such as employment bureaus, and commercial examinations) underpinned the rapid expansion of the large chambers such as London, Manchester, Birmingham, Glasgow, and Dublin, as noted in Chapter 12. Further waves of new services emerged with export certification, help in local labour disputes, cooperation with other agencies in debt collection and credit rating, and an increasing business advisory role—especially for exporters. Then came apprenticeships and a growing role as partner and contractor of government in workforce training, local economic development, and school–industry links. By the 1990s chambers had become multi-role business service providers, with a large range of bundled products. These drew on transaction cost advantages, and some elements of 'trust-based goods' deriving from the chamber brand. The service 'bundle', although evolving, seemed to be providing a stable trading offer.

Market competition increased at various points. The rapid development of chambers of trade drew off members in smaller towns, and from the retail and distribution sectors. But this helped chambers of commerce to focus, or allowed local alliances to better serve these other sectors. There was certainly brand confusion between small and large chambers, but for market and service development the main chambers of commerce were never really challenged, in the UK or Ireland.

Within these changes there is little specific about the period since 1980 to suggest why the changes for chambers were so fundamental then. In the UK the frame changes of the Thatcher era should have helped chambers by removing the CBI and sector associations from their privileged role; government emphasis on deregulation, privatization, and the expansion of small firms should have aided chamber services by offering expanded membership. The small firm bodies have certainly been strong competitors in both service markets and voice, but the main competitor (the FSB) expanded mainly after 1992 and so is not the cause of the earlier changes within chambers; in any case the market seems to have been divided between them, with chambers retaining similar or greater memberships from small firms than they had before new SME bodies emerged. In Ireland too, specific service development shows no fundamental reversals in the 1980s; indeed service innovations have expanded rather than contracted since then.

Product bundling provides considerable flexibility for chambers since it allows some services to decline whilst others are developed; it offers an adaptable structure. There is a danger, recognized by David Frost, director general of BCC 'that chambers are "Jack of all trades and masters of none", which may be a real weakness in a sophisticated economy'.[3] Hence, broad bundles may make it more difficult to target different markets appropriately in an economy where clients demand greater tailoring of services. But there is nothing about specific developments over the years since the 1980s to suggest that chamber services are in some terminal stage of product life cycles; rather they are prospering where effectively managed and responsive to new market opportunities.

2. Expansion of chamber territories

A significant change in the size and definition of chamber territories in the UK did occur from the 1980s, and gathered pace during the 1990s. As shown in Chapters 8 and 14, the national association encouraged this: from the 1967 Dixon Report to the 1991 *Development Strategy*. It was also encouraged by reforms of local government to remove County Boroughs in the mid-1970s and emphasize the counties as the largest spending tier with the main 'economic' services. This encouraged chambers to expand to cover whole city regions, counties, or groups of counties. Covering only 13 county areas or larger in 1983, this number grew to 31 by 2010, or from 11% to 57% of the network. By 2011 only St Helens chamber was in a place with less than 100,000 population, compared to 31 chambers (33% of BCC) in 1983. By the early 2000s the whole chamber map had been filled for the first time, but by a smaller number of chambers covering larger areas. Does this mean that they have become too remote from the communities they serve? In Ireland this growth in chamber territory has not occurred; is this why they have been more stable?

The history of chambers was bound up with highly specific networks within the larger cities, which although stretching out to draw in members from whole regions and beyond, were primarily city focused. There is some evidence from the econometric analysis in Chapter 14 that the smaller or most localized chambers achieved greatest density of market penetration. There appears to have been a division in the network, between chamber territories of up to about 1000 sq. km. and those above.

---

[3] Comments to author, June 2008.

This underpins two types of chambers: for large market areas (i.e. generally over 1000 sq. km.—the size of Dublin, Bristol, or Liverpool), penetration is influenced chiefly by the scale *and* range of services offered; but in small chamber areas, service range has little influence on market penetration, but compactness of area does. Tight areas, which facilitate close networking and solidarity, and wide service offers, seem to be substitutes for each other in the different chambers. Whilst long-term comparisons are imperfect, this book shows that either key service developments, or local compactness of territory were (and are) the two most important factors associated with long-term trends in market deepening.

This suggests that there are challenges for achieving intensified market penetration in larger chamber areas. Chapter 14 suggests that a density of about 1.2–2.4 members per thousand local population appears to be a sort of 'equilibrium' for the average of the whole network. Over 1976–2010, where it has been possible to measure market penetration of the *business population* reliably, average density has ranged between 4.5% and 7.9% of established businesses. Densities are considerably higher in some modern and historic chambers (20–30% in 2010): but these are chiefly in more concentrated locations such as larger core cities with tightly focused market settings. For the system as a whole, however, 8–10% market penetration seems to define what is normally realistically possible. The existence of some sort of equilibrium is also indicated by the outcomes of mergers. Generally in the UK the overall membership of the expanded chambers over their larger territories has remained similar to, or less than, the combined membership of their predecessors. Thus the merger process since the 1990s has not increased total membership numbers as much as expected; indeed there has been a hard fight to maintain them, and BCC analysis shows that internal reorganization and mergers was one factor behind the significant instabilities over 2000–9. Hence maintaining stability is itself an important goal.

The modern chamber is thus sometimes remoter from some parts of its catchment, which is likely to affect member retention and market penetration. But increased lapsing should not be inevitable. It should be possible to link larger territories with strong local ties by developing a second stream of chamber activity, focused at the level of localities within larger chamber catchments. There is some evidence that this was appreciated; it led to the development of sub-area sections by chambers from the early 1900s, and geographically based committee structures in the mid-1990s. Also the merger of BCC and NCT in 1992 encouraged local town chambers and chambers of trade to affiliate with the larger BCC chambers. In the UK since the late 1990s there have been about 150–70 affiliated smaller chambers, linking BCC chambers to an additional 24,000–33,000 businesses. This is an important counterpoint to the increasing scale of BCC chambers; but it has still left about 400–50 other town chambers outside the network. In Ireland there is also an affiliation process, but this has been slow to develop, with similar challenges to bind the different chambers, and hence the brand, together.

The precise effect of affiliations on member retention and expansion in the larger chambers is still unfolding, but it would seem possible that a system of town chambers closely linked to larger chamber service providers should be able to maximize market penetration by combining what were otherwise historically deep divisions between two types of member demand. Affiliation should also provide benefits for both types of chamber. This is clearly an area of emerging developments, but would seem a priority for future thinking.

3. Economic change, life cycles of localities, and small firms

Intermeshed with product life cycles and the expansion of territories is the evolution of the economy as a whole. Localities as well as products go through life cycles,[4] and chambers depend on their local economies. Much early chamber development relied on local networks, especially between the manufacturers in industrial districts. Over the last 250 years these have changed radically, but the analysis by Crafts and others suggests that up to the 1980s businesses relied heavily on supply chains and distribution networks that were local and sub-regional rather than national. This produced a bond of obligation to the locality; or at least a mutual interest of local business people to meet and discuss their community or sub-region.

In the traditional industrial areas the recession of 1981–2 was deeper and longer than any since the 1930s slump (including that of 2008–9), and a number of analysts suggest it was fundamental in introducing unavoidable pressures from globalization and national economic integration. This coincided with the effects of the European Single Market initiative, and greater cross-border economic activity. These changes had profound effects on shaking local ties. Many long-established medium-sized private and family firms disappeared overnight and the issue of industrial regeneration became a major government priority. For chambers in the areas most affected the membership suffered the steepest declines ever previously recorded. When David Frost joined the Walsall chamber in 1979 it was one of several boom towns in the West Midlands. It was a 'family town' of second and third generation business owners. Members met every Friday for lunch, they all came from the locality, were all actively involved in everything locally, all also members of the Rotary club, and there was a strong junior chamber. The 1981–2 recession changed all that. Many manufacturing districts had become inherently vulnerable to global changes, and the recession and steel strike tipped many over the brink. Richard Field, president of the Sheffield chamber in 1986,[5] noted the same challenge over the early 1980s; the steel industry 'fell off a cliff' taking much of the Sheffield economy with it.[6] This is a common thread across many chambers in the industrial areas in 1980–2.

However, despite these effects, few chambers disappeared. Except for some mergers, most chambers managed to replace their lost members over the next few years and continued as before. As in the 1930s slump, the changes were relatively short term. But were the new members similar to the old ones? Some of the

---

[4] e.g. Popp and Wilson (2007, 2009).
[5] Subsequently director general of BCC 2002–11; comments to author, June 2009.
[6] Quoted in Bennett, Krebs, and Zimmermann (1993); further comments quoted in Chapter 10.

membership derived from larger geographical areas; as noted above, this may have reduced commitment and retention. But the most critical element of the economic changes was a rapid shift in the structure of the economy, the two main features of which were rapid expansion of service industries and growth of small firms. It was around 1970 that these changes began, and they both suggest important effects on chamber membership.

The national economy in the UK reduced from 34% manufacturing employment to 9% over 1960–2011; and service employment increased from 46% to 80%. Output changes were less marked: over 1950–2000 services grew by 3.5 times, manufacturing by 2.2 times, but manufacturing accounted for only 11% of GNP by 2011.[7] Chambers had always had a large proportion of commercial and service members, but those from the new service economy differed from traditional chamber members in three key respects. First, many service firms were solely concerned with local markets; firms involved in exporting showed little increase in numbers. Hence, key parts of the chamber of commerce service bundle were irrelevant to many of the new service industries. Second, market consolidation and expansion in several services sectors led to a greater preponderance of branches and multi-site businesses for which the community of a locality had little relevance (e.g. banks, building societies, retailers, accountants, logistics, and distribution companies). Although many of these businesses joined a chamber through motives of corporate responsibility, they were less commonly leading players or part of its life-blood. Third, there were also expanded opportunities for market entry by the smallest service businesses and self-employed (e.g. consultants, business advisers, accountants, designers, outsourcing suppliers, and others), which had mixed interest in chambers. Something of a dual market between large multi-site and micro firms has developed, with the medium-sized businesses that traditionally formed the core of chamber members remaining static in numbers.

For small firms, after a steady decline in numbers from the 1930s to under 400,000 businesses employing at least one person in the UK in the 1960s, numbers took off: to 600,000 by 1980, to 1.2 million by 1990, reaching about 1.3 million by 2010. At the same time the number of self-employed people rose from a low of 1.6 million in 1970 to 2.75 million by 1990, and 3.8 million by 2010. This was a fundamental shift in the business structure on which chambers depended, reflected also in Ireland. Members leaving the chambers through recession, death, retirement, or other causes were increasingly replaced by smaller businesses. These are generally less stable (with small firms having 10% average closure rates per year over recent decades), and their owners and managers are interested in a different product mix. As shown in Chapters 14–16, although sector changes have little relationship with different member motivations or service demands, the shift to small firms has had profound effects. This may be partly because free riders can more easily 'hide'

---

[7] ONS, JWT8, JWR7, and other data series.

in a larger population of small firms, but seems to be mainly because they want different things.

The 1980s recession and political frame-change of the Thatcher period coincided with these changes, but were less relevant to chamber stability than the structural shifts to internationalization and to smaller businesses in the economy as a whole. Whilst the medium-sized business remains a key part of the chambers' membership, the increasing weight of the smaller firms is a fundamental cause of changing demand for chamber services, the scope for recruitment, and commitment of members to retention, involvement, and community solidarity.

4. The web and e-communications

There is no doubt that a fundamental change to businesses has occurred as a result of the Internet and other electronic communication media. This has also reinforced the scope for small businesses and expanded their potential international trade in ways that were previously impossible. However, the shifts in chamber membership and stability pre-date the main emergence of the web. This became a major economic medium only from about 1996, and was affecting most businesses only after 2000–2. The instability and shift in chamber stability far pre-dates this. Moreover, chambers have been among some of the early innovators in developing the Internet as a trading medium, as shown in Chapter 12.

There are, and will continue to be, challenges to chambers from the development of communication innovations. This may prove to be the most difficult field for future chamber development. But by 2011 there was nothing to indicate that chambers are particularly disadvantaged by these developments. Indeed, it should be possible for them to turn many changes to advantage. Particularly significant should be the scope to use e-communications to speed up and widen the voices that are sought in chamber surveys, thus reducing costs of participation and involvement for members and chambers, and hence increasing the scope for 'deliberation' and forming stronger lobby platforms. The use of electronic 'crowd sourcing' has been increasingly adopted as a successful technique in marketing, politics, and even in preparing literature. Whilst not without difficulties, it would seem to offer considerable potential for individual chambers and BCC to better connect with members and wider publics and hence strengthen their voice positions.

5. Government contracts, 'non-preferred' goods, and commitment

One of the most fundamental changes noted in the previous chapters has been the increasing role of government and EU finance and partnership with chambers. In the voluntary system of chambers covered in this book, businesses choose to join, or not, and this ensures a direct link between chamber resources, chamber management, and member demands. When a substantial proportion of finance and mission is derived from other sources, this will challenge commitment. If the mission is strongly distorted by what Finer called 'surrogacy', to 'non-preferred' goods and services, then the motive to join or renew membership may altogether disappear.

Chambers became involved in extensive contracting and partnering with government and EU programmes over the 1980s, reaching a peak in 2001 in the UK (2005 in Ireland), but in 2010 government still provided about half of all chamber finance in the UK (about 25% in major Irish chambers), and much higher in some chambers. The scale of this shift is larger and more rapid than any other change in revenues over the whole chamber history. It has allowed a move to a high-cost/high-output structure of services for those chambers that have participated. Given the tensions and perversity of service design and targets for delivering government services (described in Chapter 13), it would seem very unlikely that recent changes in chamber membership behaviour were unrelated to this new role.

Working with government removed some of the tensions of making ends meet, which has been a perennial challenge for the chambers throughout their existence. But it required new managerial structures and different expertise to undertake this work, introducing some 'managerial sorting'; it required new means to maintain independence of voice when working closely with government; it forced the members to accept objectives that were no longer exclusively theirs; and it introduced considerable instability, risk, and uncertainty as government and EU programmes, with tight overheads, have changed, often at short notice.

However, perhaps the greatest danger of the extensive involvement with government has been the perception by members. The analysis here has not be able to give definitive confirmation of all possible effects, but it appears fairly clear that government assistance has tended to undermine voluntarism, commitment, and donor support. This has had some influence on the chairs and councils of chambers, making it more difficult in many cases to obtain effective involvement. It may also have led to a retreat from obligational commitment by members. If government was going to support so much chamber activity, there was less reason to become involved, stay a member, and pay subscriptions—it acted almost as an incentive to free riding. Chapter 16 shows an association between high rates of lapsing and those chambers most involved with government (the CCTEs); after some initial membership growth (some of which was spurious), CCTEs generally had lower joining and higher lapsing.

In 1992 the ABCC director general, Ron Taylor, saw increased government support as essential: 'a sustainable revenue base for business services . . . has to involve the government because some services cannot be sustained commercially and have to be subsidised in one form or another. Hence the ABCC sees *government as a customer* to which a more coordinated and professional service has to be provided. The chambers can, therefore, *sell themselves to government* to replace things which the state presently undertakes.'[8] This has proved to be a precarious strategy. This book has shown the challenges and fragility of support from government or EU in a common law system. Chambers cannot avoid becoming involved in the key government interventions in their areas. But as a consequence, they have been subject to the political pendulum, fluctuations in the extent of civil service

---

[8] Quoted in Bennett, Krebs, and Zimmermann (1993), pp. 179–80; emphases added.

support, and even the whim of ministers and other partners. For the future this remains one of the most severe continuing challenges.

17.3 THE FUTURE

The period since the 1980s has been quite exceptional in chamber history. The discussion above suggests that the most critical changes for chambers have been: expansion of chamber market areas; shifts in the economy that have changed the composition of membership towards a majority of smaller firms; and partnerships with government for some service delivery. These seem to be main elements that can explain the increased membership lapsing, instability, and other changes that have occurred. But there is nothing in these developments that cannot be accommodated. What seems to be required for the future is a rethinking to better focus on a self-sustaining structure, based on a strengthened core chamber offer and USP.

Continuing the development strategies, finding a self-sustaining base

Chamber development in the UK since 1991 has generally followed the BCC *Development Strategy* of that date, and in Ireland has taken forward CI's *Best Practice Manual* of 1993. These instituted inspection and accreditation processes that have moved all BCC chambers, and all the major Irish chambers, to a position of achieving quality control and critical mass—of members and service/staff capacity. These strategies have generally withstood the test of time; they evolved from the system's internal dynamics, building on thinking from earlier periods such as the Dixon Report, as discussed in Chapter 8. In the UK the success of rebuilding the BCC since 2002 has demonstrated the benefits of determined and disciplined focus on the core business, to develop existing strengths.[9] CI has similarly emerged stronger and more independent from its financial difficulties in 2005–7. These approaches will continue to be necessary in the future. The chambers are now in far better shape than 20 years ago, with quality-controlled services generally covering the entire geographical map of the Irish and UK territories. In a period of austerity and curtailed government or EU contracts, the internal development strategies of both British and Irish chambers provide the base for a self-sustaining future based on voice, services, and member contributions.

For services offered, the greater proportion of small firm membership should be a strength, since small firms usually require a higher level of external support. The greater proportion of small firms is not in itself an insuperable challenge for chambers, certainly not compared to their early history; but it needs an adapted mix of services with increasing attention to tailoring. In addition, a core membership of chambers is still medium-sized businesses. For these, chambers remain the main body for voice: there are no local rivals for the medium-sized firm except at

---

[9] See Chapter 8; and discussion of Collins (2009); Baden-Fuller and Stopford (1994).

sector level. This USP should be capable of enhanced development. Networking and social milieus may also offer important opportunities for both the small and medium-sized firm. The scope for increased drop-in facilities and serviced office support seems worth exploring, as successfully begun in St Helens in 2009; and stronger links of service packages to critical stages of business development may be effective ways to recruit members and encourage repeat buying as small firms grow and medium-sized firms explore new fields. Experiences learnt from the chambers' enterprise agency models of the 1980s can be revisited. These voluntary structures were squeezed out by government initiatives and BiTC. They offered examples of close working with banks and other advisers, and developed strong links with incubators, technology parks, research institutions, and through inter-firm networking and mentoring. These and other opportunities are already being explored by chambers; they offer much potential for development.

But the key challenge remains the funding model. Internal income (chiefly subscriptions and service fees), and external income (chiefly sales to non-members, and partner support) seem to have natural limitations rather like the limits on member recruitment. Between the market of business service suppliers and public bodies the chambers offer unique service niches, with complex bundling and 'trust goods' being prominent. But these niches are limited and always under challenge from alternatives. It was natural, therefore, for chambers to grasp at public funding streams when these were readily available. With such funding now in shorter supply chambers have to return to their roots and look for alternatives. This can come from further expansion of services, with many new developments already under way. Secondly, increased funding can also come from increases in subscriptions and fees. This is clearly possible, as underpricing has been historically endemic. However, again the potential is constrained. Subscriptions changes are one of the most persistent influences on lapsing (as shown in Chapters 14 and 16); and if subscriptions were raised (as indicated as possible in Chapter 15), this would simultaneously require expansion of service offers. Also, even a tripling of subscriptions, although useful, can be only a part of the picture, as it would provide only 31% of UK 2010 chamber income, or 50% in Ireland.

A third possibility is to look at encouraging a stronger structure of membership commitment. Subscriptions are a valuable model for member finance and ongoing commitment; but they are not the only one. US chambers have a much wider portfolio of private finance, of which patron schemes and larger scale donor commitment are significant. UK chambers raised about £5 million from patrons in 2010 (about 3% of income); tiny compared to US chambers. Irish chambers have developed this stream further, particularly CI, which derived 15% of its income from large companies in 2010 and has programmes directly tailored for large companies (though this development is very variable within local chambers). The UK chambers have about 30% of all large companies as members, but only 1000 patrons in 2010.[10] Their payments averaged £6030, ranging from £1000 to

---

[10] About 2300 companies with over 250 employees were members in 2010, and 10,000 with over 50 employees.

£10,000. It should be possible to expand the number of large companies as members, and to increase their contributions, even with the different donor culture compared to the USA, and even in a period of austerity. But this shift in financing cannot be achieved without changes in service packages and offers. Currently there are often insufficient benefits for donor commitment, for both small and large firms. Chambers need to learn from the models developed in other fields such as theatres, museums, orchestras, and football clubs, which offer scaled benefits and privileges as 'friends' and 'benefactors' in return for 'privileges'. This has considerable financial potential, but most importantly it offers a way to re-establish the member roots and commitment to chambers that have been damaged by industrial change and by dominance of government funding. It thus attacks the problem of redefining the core values and USP of chambers in a form suitable for the 21st century.

Increased working with rivals and partners

Chamber small business membership increased from about one-third to 50% over 1970–2000, and reached 60% by 2010, for firms of 1–9 employees. This is a fundamental change that brings chambers into different markets with different competitors, where costs of memberships are even more critically assessed. In the UK the main small firm rival is the FSB, which has grown to a membership far exceeding chambers, with a similar network of branches and local presence, that has also increasingly sought to partner local government and other organizations. A less significant development of rivals for SME support has also evolved in Ireland. At the service level this suggests a need to seek some accommodation with FSB to divide the market, as was achieved with chambers of trade. Whilst chambers retain a USP for medium-sized firms that is locally unchallenged, there would appear to be significant scope for market intensification for small firm support by developing alliances and affiliation between chambers and other associations for small firms. Local cooperation in partnering government (as in LEPs, see below), may be useful for this, although this will be challenging for all business organizations.

At national level the chambers have had other rivals over time, most damaging of which was the period when they were placed as second tier organizations contributing to the CBI's input to NEDC from the 1960s until 1979. The CBI remains a working partner of BCC, but it has different purposes and membership. Cooperation could be enhanced further, but merger, as conceived in the Devlin Report, has no obvious relevance to future challenges. In Ireland, excessively close links of government with large corporations were a key aspect leading to the 2007 financial crash. It remains to be seen how the close links of Irish politicians, banks, major companies, and business organizations will evolve in the future. However, in both countries it is inconceivable to think that mergers between the national industry bodies offer significant benefits. Nevertheless, there is potential for closer cooperation.

Localism

Local community commitment is a core USP of chambers. This means that chambers are natural partners with local government and other local organizations. The agenda of the previous 250 years has built brand recognition and technical experience of community support into the chambers in a deeply embedded way. However, the last 10–20 years have inflicted significant damage. First, the experience of the TECs and CCTEs in the 1990s in the UK damaged relations with local government, though mostly these were subsequently repaired. Second, the Blair–Brown years in the UK, and a false sense of financial invulnerability in Ireland, led to largesse being thrown at local government and other publicly financed local bodies, which eroded their spirit to find economical solutions, or to develop durable partnerships with the private sector. There was 'a plethora of public initiatives, all costly, with no coherence, and many with no meaningful role'.[11] Many earlier voluntary partnerships were pushed aside. Chambers turned into bodies seeking to win contracts or funding for localities with rapidly changing, overlapping, and confused objectives, dominated by government micro-targeting. Local government was obliged to create local Community Strategies, but encouraged to view these independently. Without the money for future support these have largely collapsed.

Chambers offer many opportunities for a new localism built on an economically sustainable base, drawing on their entrenched voluntarism, and their democratic interface with the business community. In the 1980s many of the major cities as well as some smaller localities developed strategic partnerships that brought public and private sector leaders together. The earliest and best of these were bottom-up bodies, such as Sheffield's SERC, or London and Birmingham's enterprise agencies, discussed in Chapters 10 and 13. In Ireland, EU programmes offered learning in developing partnerships. The outcome was local capacity building that allowed a locality to take advantage of the different central government, EU, and private initiatives as they emerged, and then shape them towards a long-term *local strategic vision* for its area. Some of this was built into the vision for TECs and RDAs in the UK, and the County Enterprise Boards in Ireland: but both suffered from external top-down targets and vulnerability to the political pendulum. A prudent locality would have retained the bottom-up capacity, but most migrated towards high-cost, public sector-led platforms. Sheffield's SERC languished; chamber-led enterprise agencies have largely disappeared.

Since 2010 the UK Coalition government's objective of seeking greater voluntary involvement under a 'Big Society' narrative has been mainly enunciated for welfare services; but there is also an economic counterpart. In Ireland, continuing financial pressures are forcing similar emphasis on austerity. For such times the chambers offer the obvious leadership at local level. The concept of LEPs launched in the UK in 2010 seems to offer a step towards recognizing business-led and bottom-up leadership from localities, but there are many challenges to the

---

[11] In the words of one Labour Party member and chamber chief executive in northern England.

government's vision as judged from the early experiences. These challenges concern the scope for genuine business involvement; appropriate economic geography; defective 'tick box' design; dangers that ministers accept anything to fill the map; and lack of adequate core funding that recognizes the participation costs for voluntary bodies like chambers. In Ireland, with a more uncertain government situation, and even more extreme financial pressures, the 2011 political narrative has been less clear, but the same potential opportunities exist for chamber roles. In a period of retrenchment in both countries chambers offer better opportunities than ever for government to outsource and develop an assured local business support system at low cost.

Ring-fencing government

The most fundamental change to the chamber system since the 1980s has been overdependence on government: seeing partnership as a means to rescue chambers from the inherent challenges of a voluntary system. Government will always be the elephant in the room. It will inevitably remain important to chambers into the foreseeable future, not least because part of the USP is to work with government to improve legislation and policy, and to bring business involvement to local initiatives. Chambers and BCC/CI have achieved remarkable repositioning since 2002–5 in coping with the changes that have occurred, but the experience should be chastening.

Chambers will always face a dilemma: they have to respond to each new government or EU initiative that is locally relevant to their business communities; but as shown in previous chapters, they must recognize the dangers and serious risks shown by previous history: design will often be imperfect, mis-targeted, costly, and over-bureaucratic; there will be incentives to perverse policy outcomes and moral hazard; and synergies across programmes will be lost as a result of department funding silos. The endemic force that leads to perverse government design is a failure to recognize the information asymmetry that civil servants and ministers face: they are rarely expert in programme design, and even if they were, they would be incapable of designing programme operations in forms that are adapted to each local circumstance. Instead of dictating programmes and targets they should instead truly empower localities to take on design, leadership, and implementation. This is the true meaning of localism. This book has demonstrated that chamber partnering with government is most successful when offered at arm's length: as with 'Form K', document certification, foreign trade missions, or the Enterprise Initiative for small firm support. Government programmes are worst when the design comes ready made and/or competes with existing providers: as with Business Link, Local Strategic Partnerships, Local Community Strategies, or most Irish County Enterprise Boards and the EU-DAWN experience.

However, whatever the aspirations, the next phase of government policies in the UK and Ireland is unlikely to be anything other than a new chapter in an unfolding story. In the UK, LEPs may survive for a few years, but are likely to be superseded by a new government initiative. The chambers have to become strongly involved;

but they need to secure a sustainable local capacity independent of government, to turn each new initiative towards long-term local goals. They need to retain a focus on their core values, using LEPs to develop their USP (not the reverse). The lessons of the period since the 1980s suggest that government programmes should be ring-fenced by chamber managers and leaders. This needs to be at the strategic level, services level, financially, in staff recruitment and management, and in member communications. Government programmes are part of the bundle of chamber services; but should be marketed and managed as no more than one element, whatever their proportion of funding, and boxed in to prevent damage to other parts of the chamber portfolio. The damaging distortions of the CCTE and other funding streams and targets in the UK, or of EU-Dawn and similar programmes in Ireland, should not be repeated. As with the reassertion of the development strategies of UK and Irish chambers, the key need is to focus on the member, not government, as customer.

Repositioning the brand

Much has been achieved in the UK and Ireland since 2002–5 in enhancing core chamber products and USP. But further development and repositioning of the brand is still needed with members. This is where a fundamental weakness has come to lie. The period of government largesse has distorted missions, marketing, and in many cases staff priorities. Many members, especially those who have lapsed, need to be re-engaged with a redirected approach asserting how the chambers have moved on. Many businesses have had profoundly negative experiences of Business Link that they often associate with chambers. To overcome these experiences there needs to be a strong marketing effort to demonstrate chamber commitment to tailored services; but this in turn often needs genuine service redesign. Brand damage can only be repaired by positive new client experiences. This means a bottom-up reform of service delivery processes in many chambers. The 'Big Society' debate provides potential: to encourage support for the local chamber through solidarity and community obligation; and to recognize the opportunities offered by chamber services.

As a longer-term goal there also needs to be a campaign for brand recognition within the wider political and policy classes. Chamber brand has always been under challenge; attacked by lampoon against Josiah Wedgwood and the early Bristol chamber (as shown by the poems quoted in Chapters 5 and 9); appropriated by the chambers of agriculture; emulated by chambers of trade; and subverted by mission distortion through surrogacy to government. For the modern period, surveys of the strength of the chamber brand demonstrate that the distinctions between accredited, affiliated, and other chambers remain unclear to most outsiders, and are little understood by members themselves. Most MPs, ministers, and local councillors cannot distinguish between accredited and non-accredited chambers. The merger of NCT certainly strengthened BCC as a single national chamber voice, but at local level the two chamber networks often remain as confusing and indistinguishable as ever.

There is much work for chambers to do in order to enhance the brand. Some of the comments by civil servants in a recent survey indicate possible directions for change.[12] They state that chambers 'could raise their profile higher', 'provide deeper analytical material to support their policy views', have 'more face-to-face contact', and 'focus on a narrower range of issues' in which they are expert. These are comparative comments relative to other business organizations. One of the most important observations is that BCC could make more use of their local and regional membership: 'their comparative advantage lies in contact at regional and local levels. . . . I would question whether they make the full use they could from these connections.' Other comments suggest the need to 'market the brand', and 'adopt a higher profile locally'. These comments echo assessments made by Algernon Firth in the early 1900s, by Ilersic and Liddle in 1960, by this author in the 1991 *Development Strategy*, and in Ron Taylor's book in 2007. If the observations are correct, they suggest that the modern chambers, and particularly BCC, may be falling into the trap of their predecessors (noted in Chapters 8 and 10) of trying to do too much over too many fields for their resources, with insufficient core focus and link between centre and localities to bring strong enough local and regional expertise and voice to the table of government.

An attack on the challenges to brand could be made in part through extensions to the structure of affiliation of smaller chambers, as outlined above, so that de facto there is one 'system', of different entities with multiple entry points but aiming in the same general direction. However, probably most important is strengthened national and local marketing so that the brand, core service bundle, and USP of chambers is much more widely understood and recognized. Young Chamber has been a useful initiative, but something much more significant in terms of mass recognition is required, perhaps more akin to the Enterprise Initiative launched in 1988, or subsequent populist media efforts that have been used to engage viewers in entrepreneurship and business skilling. 'The Apprentice' and 'Dragon's Den' television programmes, and crowd sourcing, despite some drawbacks, offer important modern examples about how marketing and branding of business issues can be more widely diffused.

Strengthening partnership, reviving contention

The continued repositioning of chambers also needs to include reassessment of government–chamber policy relations. The modern state places partnership of government with business (and other interest groups) as a cornerstone for policy implementation. But this will continue to challenge chambers as voluntary and thinly resourced bodies sensitive to subscription costs. As discussed in Chapter 3, businesses will most actively mobilize to support chambers when there is need, 'strain', and where the legitimacy of central or local government is low; as arose in the local rates campaigns of the 1980s. Yet partnership rhetoric assumes that strain

----

[12] Mekic (2007), pp. 7.236–7.239.

is low and government legitimacy high. Effective and extensive partnerships are thus unlikely to develop far as part of any 'Big Society' narrative unless there is real economic advantage for businesses to participate; the rhetoric of collective commitment and solidarity alone are unlikely to be sufficient. For service delivery this means genuine government contracting out, not piecemeal and half-hearted privatizations like the TECs and Business Link in Britain, or unrealistically low margin programmes such as EU-DAWN that was taken up in Irish chambers.

Conversely, chambers cannot assume that any short-term easy working with government will be sustained, or will provide uniformly supportive policies. Whilst the balances are always difficult, there is much to be said for a much more aggressive campaigning role for the modern chamber. This would enhance the visibility and brand with members and potential members, better tie together small and larger chambers (since voice is their common USP), and would help to prevent reversion to becoming too close to government (and being perceived as such). Historically, chambers have been very concerned to acquire recognition, 'insider' status, and avenues of 'protected consultation'. This has sometimes made them too ready to adopt the government's narrative. But these narratives are invariably short-lived, even within the same government.

Within the common law, voluntary system of British and Irish chambers there are more challenges than for the formal public law chambers of Europe, which enjoy protected public status. Without formal status, British and Irish chambers depend on the receptiveness of the government, and are thus more susceptible to recruitment and inclusion into government agendas, accepting any morsel thrown out. But lack of formal status should be used as an advantage; the debacle over public law status demonstrates the limits of trying to obtain formal recognition in common law systems; and in Europe the protected status of chambers makes them very unpopular with many businesses, especially the smaller ones. Hence, voluntary status should be a strength to allow vigorous attacks on inappropriate government policies. Arguably chambers have become too 'respectable' and too willing to advocate 'polite' reform. The business burdens 'Barometer' used since 2001 is a good example of what can be done. But this raised criticisms from some inside the chamber network which suggests a lack of the 'fire in the belly' that characterized the early chambers: anger, positively focused, is a powerful weapon. In recent years this has meant that there has only been a weak 'chamber narrative'. A stronger narrative and greater campaigning zeal is needed, would help chambers to counter rival bodies, and would be more in line with the views of many members, especially smaller businesses that want more aggressive attacks on government failures. Renewed campaigning zeal need not be 'political', nor always 'noisy' and public; as the history shows, avoiding noise may be more effective, and the threat of open campaigns can often be more effective than actually undertaking them. But whether public or confidential, chambers should be less fearful of being perceived as 'political' by strongly opposing government policies where they clearly impede businesses.

Ongoing history

This book has sought to give an overview of 250 years of history, with major emphasis on origins and current challenges. Although the symmetry between the 1770s and 2010s is not at first obvious, and should not be overstated, the unfolding of the narrative has demonstrated some uncanny resemblances across this vast time period. The problems for business to arrest and engage government remain essentially the same; government efforts to design and implement economic programmes remain as imperfect as ever; effective business–government partnering at national and local level continues as ephemeral episodes, each experiment providing new experiences, but presenting new chapters in an essentiality similar story of government perversity and moral hazard, where government 'bads' are as frequent as 'goods'. It is hoped that this book will help to enlighten current thinking in government about methods of consultation and programme design, and in chambers to look to their long-term core internal strengths and member demands, rather than seeking salvation in the next government initiative.

APPENDIX 1

Archival and Other Sources

The location of all archive materials is quoted in footnotes for individual and scattered items. However, for the major national associations and the main records of individual chambers, the text refers to the documents, but to save space, locations and catalogue numbers are not usually given. The location and cataloguing of these sources are as below.

1. NATIONAL ASSOCIATIONS

Chambers of Commerce in the UK

The records of the ACC, ABCC, and BCC are virtually complete. They are held at the London Guildhall Archives, but are now accessed at the London Metropolitan Archives (LMA). These cover 1860 until about 1980 (most recent date varying by committee). After that date they are still held by the BCC, though mostly in a partially catalogued back store. Some papers derived from ABCC and held only by the author have now been deposited at the LMA. The Catalogue for the LMA records is very good, but has been changed after transfer. The full catalogue reference CLC/B/016 is followed by a MS number; only the MS numbers are quoted in the book text. Some gaps in journals and other publications of the Association are not in the LMA holdings and have been filled from holdings at the LSE (the most complete alternative source), some other libraries, and at the London chamber. Accounts for the Association are also available from the Companies Registry.

Chambers of Commerce in Ireland

There is no complete holding of the Irish Chambers Association formed in 1923. The records quoted in the book text for the early years are all derived from local chamber holdings. The current national body holds all its recent material, but only after about 1990, and only fully from about 2005. Accounts for the Association are available from the Companies Registry.

Chambers of Trade

There are very good archives for the National Chamber of Trade after its foundation in 1897, though the coverage of its membership is only complete for the early years. The records are held at the London Guildhall Archives, and accessed at LMA. A few are held in BCC back store. Only the MS numbers are quoted in the book text. Some accounts for the Association are also available from the Companies Registry, after its incorporation in 1925. These records do not include Ireland, which was never involved in NCT. Irish small chambers either affiliated with the chambers of commerce, or not to any organization.

Appendix 1

Trade Protection Societies

There are good records for the main national association NATPS, formed in 1850 up to its dissolution in 1982, although the information on the later years is less complete. These are held at the Leicester County Record Office under classification DE. Full MS references are quoted in the book text.

Central Chamber of Agriculture

There are relatively poor records of the central chamber of agriculture, and nothing systematic before about 1900. Most available records are held in the British Library, but a few scattered records are held at TNA and in many other libraries. Full catalogue and holding locations are given in the book text.

2. LOCAL BODIES

Table A1.1 summarizes the sources used for the main database and core group of chambers that are tracked throughout the book text. These number about 150 entities, but their names and geographical cover changes. The main source for these is local record offices (ROs). But there is often a complex holding structure locally, with papers split between ROs, libraries, local studies collections, and the continuing chamber; none of which may be complete, and many of which may have no, or only paper, catalogues. The reader is advised to look at these local sources in depth to follow up any specific place. The listing in Table A1.1 can only summarize the main locations. Where an archive item is held in another location as a stray, or relies on a national library, this is recorded in the book text; as are references to chambers with more limited records beyond the core group and database (for more detail see Appendix 2). Undoubtedly many chambers still hold some records that it has not been possible to discover, as they are often maintained imperfectly and not fully catalogued in back stores. Hence, the listing below must be treated as a guide rather than being definitive; however, it is believed to be comprehensive of major collections for the main chambers (not all of which will have been members of their national bodies at any one time). It includes all 'chambers of commerce' and a sample of chambers of trade where significant records exist.

Table A1.1 Chambers which form the main database for this book: foundations dates, dates of reorganization, and main archival sources; where there are gaps these have been filled by national and stray records as described above; BL here refers to contract or franchise for Business Link

Chamber	Archive sources
England	
Barnsley	Founded 1881; merged with Rotherham 2008; minutes and reports 1884–90; Barnsley Archives and Local Studies.
Barnstaple	Founded 1911; minutes, reports, accounts 1939–; at chamber.
Barrow in Furness	Founded 1884; merged into Cumbria 2002; a few records at Whitehaven RO.
Basingstoke and N. Hants.	Founded 1941; removed from BCC 2008 and area taken by Sussex; AGM and accounts 1941–2; Hampshire RO.
Bath	Founded 1902; reports and yearbooks 1902–78; Bath Reference Library.
Batley & Birstal	Batley founded 1856, refounded 1878, merged with Birstal 1888; merged with Huddersfield *c*.1969; minutes 1960–73; Annual Reports 1910–69; Huddersfield Archives.
Bedfordshire	Founded 1991 with TEC; see Luton.
Birkenhead	Founded 1912; limited information in Birkenhead Yearbook 1922–57; Wirral Archives.
Birmingham	Founded 1783, refounded 1813, 1820, 1842; BL 1993–2007; minutes, reports and accounts 1813–1963; Landsdowne-Garbett letters; various stray items separately catalogued; Birmingham Central Library.
Birstal	Founded 1884, merged with Batley 1888.
Black Country	Formed by merger of Walsall and Wolverhampton 2002.
Blackburn	Referred to by SMV/2/4/2/22 (3), 21 January 1779; founded 1887; reports, accounts, minutes 1888–1950; Blackburn Library.
Bolton	Founded 1889; merged with Bury as CCTE 1998; merged into N. Manchester 2004; yearbook 1919; reports 1948–78; journal 1949–59; Bolton City Library.
Boston	Founded by 1930; records at chamber.
Bradford	Founded 1851; merged with Leeds and York *c*.1995, de-merged 2002; BL 1993–2001; minutes, accounts, journals, and reports 1851–1976; accounts, statistics, and other assoc. 1851–1964; W. Yorks. Archives, Bradford City Library.
Bridgwater	Founded 1911; only strays available.
Brighton & Hove	CoT Founded, 1913; 1953 Rules; E. Sussex RO. Federation of Sussex Industries 1945; incomplete records at chamber.
Bristol	Also see SMV; founded 1823; BL 1993–2007; founding papers (Red Lodge papers); minutes, reports, and papers 1823– ; 1875–1892 Journal; Bristol City Archives.
Burnley	Founded 1902; founding papers, reports, and accounts 1913, 1927, 1946–88 at Burnley Central Library.
Burton on Trent	Founded 1936; some records in Derby chamber papers, otherwise strays.

(*continued*)

Table A1.1 Continued

Chamber	Archive sources
Bury	Founded as CoT 1895; merged with Bolton as CCTE 1998; merged into N. Manchester 2004; minutes 1911–38, reports 1929–93; Bury Library.
Camborne	Founded 1928; history (1958) is main source.
Cambridge	Founded 1917; merged with Peterborough 2003; 1917–31 Annual Reports; Cambridgeshire RO; minutes and accounts 1917– at chamber.
Carlisle and Cumbria	Founded 1908; merged with Kendal, Barrow, and Whitehaven 2002; modern records at chamber.
Cheltenham	Founded 1902; Minutes 1902–60; reports and accounts 1925–60; Gloucestershire RO.
Chester & N. Wales	Founded 1921; became W. Cheshire 2008; BCC records.
Chesterfield	Founded 1899; merged with Derby 2004; minutes and papers 1899–1960 at chamber; some archives 1930–6 in Sheffield chamber records.
Chippenham	Founded 1906; minutes and accounts 1917–83; Wiltshire RO.
Cleckheaton	Founded 1877; merged with Heckmondwike 1909; became Spen Valley 1932; minutes and reports 1878–1932 at Huddersfield Archives.
Colchester and Essex	Founded 1907; minutes and accounts 1907–76 including committees; Colchester RO.
Cornwall	Founded as BCC chamber 2007 from various local.
Coventry and Warwickshire	Founded 1856, refounded 1902; BL 1993–2007; CCTE 1997 with Warwicks., reports 1868 at (misc); 1880–32, 1957 (Daffern papers); reports and members 1937/8, 1938/9 (Goate, Bullock papers); Coventry RO and Archives, Warwick RO; journals 1930s and some papers at Stafford RO; minutes, accounts, etc. 1942–, and journals 1961–74 at chamber.
Croydon and S. London	Founded 1891; merged with London 2002, though separate until 2007; minutes, reports, etc. at chamber; records moved to London chamber 2007.
Derby and Derbyshire	Founded 1864; BL 1993–2001; S. Derbyshire CCTE 1996; merged with Chesterfield 2004; merged with Nottingham 2007; some papers & reports (Strutt papers) 1884–1910; Derbyshire RO; minutes 1864–1960 and other papers at chamber.
Devizes	Founded 1905; 1924–86 minutes, members in 1924, 1927, 1986; Wiltshire RO.
Devonport CoT	Devonport Mercantile Association founded 1876; accounts 1879–1957; members 1876–1958; reports 1838–56; Plymouth RO.
Dewsbury	Founded 1861; correspondence and reports 1925–76; W. Yorks. Archives; Bradford City Library.
Doncaster	Founded 1937; directory 1961 and a few records; Doncaster archives (British Coal).
Dover	Founded 1850, refounded 1870; full minutes, reports, and accounts 1850– at chamber.
Dudley	Founded 1884; reports and accounts 1912–50; Worcs. RO.

Exeter	Delegate 1784–1805; founded 1867; liquidated Dec. 1991.
Exeter CoT	Founded *c*.1910; minutes 1914–30 at chamber.
Falmouth	Founded 1866; minutes held at chamber, though *unknown* location; good coverage in history.
Fareham	Founded *c*.1946, merged into Southampton *c*.1995; reports and accounts 1946–63: Hampshire RO.
G. Yarmouth	Founded 1901; BCC records.
Gloucester	Founded 1839; minutes 1883–86; Gloucestershire RO.
Goole	Founded 1862; minutes and accounts 1870–1934; Goole Reference Library; summary minutes 1922–34 at Goole museum (Harold Garside). Reports 1907–10; Waterways Museum.
Grantham	Founded *c*.1920 as CoT; BCC records.
Grimsby	Founded 1883; only strays found.
Guildford and Surrey	Founded 1902 as CoT; administered by Slough/Thames Valley *c*.1996–2002; minutes and reports 1903–2002; also Federation of Surrey Chambers 1914–27; Surrey History Centre, Woking.
Halifax	Delegate 1784–1805; founded 1862, became Calderdale 1984; merged with Huddersfield 1992 to form Mid Yorks.; minutes and reports 1945–61; reports 1938–64 (Horsfall records); W. Yorks Archives, Calderdale.
Hartlepool	Founded 1869, refounded 1875, 1882; a few records at Teesside Archives.
Heckmondwike	Founded *c*.1880; merged with Cleckheaton 1909; became Spen Valley 1932; minutes 1909–32; Huddersfield Archives.
Hereford	Founded 1919; merged as Hereford and Worcs. 1990; BL 1993–2007; CCTE 1996; minutes and reports, letters, 1919–1971; Herefordshire RO.
Hertfordshire	Founded as Welwyn Garden City 1929; BL 1993–2001 and TEC 1993–2001.
Huddersfield	Founded 1853, merged with: Spen Valley 1967, Batley and Birstal *c*.1969, Wakefield 1977, Calderdale (Halifax) 1992; called Kirklees 1975, Kirklees and Wakefield 1977–92, Mid Yorks. 1992; minutes 1853–1977; reports 1893–1953; W. Yorks, Huddersfield RO.
Hull and Humberside	Delegate 1784–1805; founded 1801, refounded 1837; reports and accounts 1889–1985; sector assocs. 1890s–1990s; Hull City Library.
Ipswich and Suffolk	Founded 1884; became Suffolk *c*.1992; minutes, reports, and accounts 1885–; at chamber, some now deposited at Suffolk RO.
Isle of Wight	Founded 1910; reports and membership lists 1935–6; IOW RO; cuttings, reports, and member lists 1910–84 at chamber.
Keighley	Founded 1880, refounded 1895; minutes 1934–74; Keighley Library.
Kendal	Founded 1857; merged into Cumbria 2002; minutes, etc. 1857–1997; Kendal RO.
Kent	Kent Federation founded, 1992, abeyance *c*.1998.
Kent Channel	Founded 2004, previously Shepway, etc.
Kent Invicta	Founded 2005 from Ashford, etc.
Kent Maritime	Founded 2001, closed 2002; attempt to link Folkestone, etc.

(*continued*)

Table A1.1 Continued

Chamber	Archive sources
Kidderminster	Founded 1878; refounded 1982; merged into H & W CCTE 1997; minutes 1898–1990; reports and accounts 1880–1990; at Hereford and Worcs. chamber.
Lancaster	Referred to by SMV/2/4/2/23 (9), 1 January 1781; founded 1897; merged with Preston *c.*1995 to form C. and W. Lancs., renamed N & W Lancs. 2004; minutes and reports at chamber; also holds Merchants Coffee Room records.
Leeds	Founded 1785–93; refounded 1851; merged with Bradford and York *c.*1995, de–merged 2002; merged with York 2009 to form Leeds, York, and N. Yorks.; minutes, journal, reports, and accounts 1785–93; 1851–1964; Leeds University Library.
Leicester	Founded 1848 as Leicester, refounded 1860 as Leicestershire; BL 1993–2001; minutes, journals, reports, and accounts 1860–1969; Leicestershire RO.
Lincoln	Founded 1887; minutes 1919–41; reports and accounts 1899–1987; 1889–1940 register; Lincolnshire Archives.
Liverpool	Founded 1774–96, refounded 1850; included Knowsley and Halton for 2001 only; early records dispersed (see Bennett 2010); minutes, committees, reports, and accounts 1850–1974; Liverpool RO.
Liverpool American	Founded 1801, merged into Liverpool chamber 1908; all records at Liverpool RO.
London	Weskett 1782–1800; delegate 1784–1805; founded 1882; minutes, reports, accounts, 1882–1971; LMA (formerly at Guildhall) MS 16455 ff.; reports 1970– and *CCJ* at LSE and other libraries and the chamber.
Lowestoft	Founded 1923; reports and accounts 1924–33, correspondence 1944–7; Lowestoft RO.
Luton and Beds.	Founded 1877 as Luton & Dunstable; 1934–53; became Bedfordshire with TEC 1991; BL 1993–2007; CCTE 1998; minutes 1877–, reports 1919– at chamber; some reports and section minutes at Bedfordshire and Luton Archives.
Macclesfield	Founded 1865; 1866–70 minutes (Clarke papers); Cheshire & Chester archives; otherwise stray records.
Maidstone	Founded *c.*1915; joined with Ashford to form Kent Gateway 2001; stray records.
Manchester	Founded 1774–1800, refounded 1820; BL 1993–2007; merged with Stockport and Wigan 2004; merged with N. Manchester 2005 called G. Manchester. Minutes of commercial society 1794–1805; chamber minutes and sections 1821–1977; journal and reports 1820–; all at Manchester Central Library.
Medway	Founded 1920; formed Kent, Thameside & Medway 2002; renamed N. Kent 2003; BCC Records.
Mid Yorkshire	Founded 1992; from Huddersfield, Spen Valley, Halifax—Calderdale.
Middlesbrough and Teesside	Founded 1863, merged as Teesside and SW Durham 1971–4; then Teesside; merged into NE Chamber 1995; minutes, reports, and accounts 1893–1974 ; Teesside Archives.

Milton Keynes	Founded 1983; CCTE 1995; BCC records.
Morley	Founded 1868; closed *c.*1920; only strays.
Newark	Founded 1923; BCC records.
Newcastle	Founded 1815; merged with: Gateshead *c.*1917, Sunderland 1969 to form Tyneside; merged with Teesside as North-East 1991; minutes, reports, and accounts 1815–1980; Tyne & Wear Archives.
Newhaven	Founded by 1950; BCC records.
North and West Lancashire	Founded 2004 from Preston and Lancaster.
North-East	Founded 1995 from merger of Newcastle/Tyneside and Teesside.
North Manchester	Founded 2004 from Bolton & Bury, Oldham, and Rochdale; merged with Manchester 2005.
North Shields	Founded 1939 as CoT; minutes 1939–59, reports and other papers 1947–73; Tyne and Wear Archives.
North Staffs.	Potters chamber *c.*1767–90; 1784–90; founded 1813, refounded 1851; early papers in Wedgwood papers at Wedgwood Museum; minutes 1874–1979, reports and accounts 1887–1952; Stoke on Trent City Archive; Staffs. Archive, Lichfield.
Northamptonshire	Founded 1867; refounded 1880, 1916; BL 1993–2007; CCTE 1995; at chamber.
Norwich and Norfolk	Delegate 1784–1805; founded 1847, refounded 1895; early reports and accounts in J. J. Coleman Collection: Norfolk Studies Library; minutes 1963–6; reports and newsletters 1977–8; Norwich Publicity Assoc. papers (committee of chamber) 1924–73; Norfolk RO.
Nottingham	Delegate 1784–1805; 'chamber' 1785–7; founded 1813, refounded 1835; 1860; merged with Derbyshire 2007; accounts and reports 1862–1915, City Local Studies Library; minutes, accounts, and reports 1908–58; Nottingham University Hallwood Library.
Oldham	Founded 1882; BL 1993–2001; CCTE 1995; closed 2001; merged into N. Manchester 2003; minutes, reports, and accounts 1882–1991; Oldham Archives.
Ossett	Founded 1885; minutes and reports for 1890–1910; Huddersfield Archives.
Peterborough	Founded 1926; CCTE 1997; merged with Cambridge 2003; BCC records.
Plymouth	Founded 1813; merged with Plymouth Mercantile Association and Devonport Mercantile Association 1958; founding papers (Monkes of Saltram); minutes 1961–6; (Farley's papers); report 1863 (Woollcombe of Hemendon); reports 1928, 1952 (Viner Carew papers); 1943–50 (Millby Lansby papers): Plymouth RO. Annual reports and papers at Plymouth Library.
Plymouth CoT	Mercantile Association founded 1870; annual reports and some papers 1900–57; Plymouth RO.
Poole and Dorset	Founded 1949; merged into Dorset with TEC *c.*1992; BCC records.
Portsmouth	Referred to for 1798 by Taylor (2007), but unconfirmed; founded 1879; 1879–1949 minutes; 1917–50 subcommittees; 1947–58 journals; Portsmouth RO; annual reports and journal 1920–70 at Portsmouth Library; other records at chamber.

(continued)

Table A1.1 Continued

Chamber	Archive sources
Preston	Founded 1916; 1990; included Skelmersdale 1990 to form C. and W. Lancs., merged with Lancaster, named N & W Lancs., 2004; some reports 1920–30 and journal 1937–73 at Harris Library Preston; full reports and accounts at chamber.
Reading	Founded 1903; reports and accounts 1903–23; Berkshire RO.
Redditch	Founded by 1978; BCC records.
Rochdale	Delegate 1784–1805; founded 1868, refounded 1948; CCTE 1998; merged into N. Manchester 2004; closed 2001; reports 1869–85; minutes 1939–47; 1961–83; Rochdale Local Studies Library.
Rotherham	Founded 1909; with TEC 1991; CCTE 1996; merged with Barnsley 2008; only strays found.
Rugby	Founded 1908; BCC records.
Runcorn	Founded 1925; became Halton with TEC 1993; BCC records.
Salisbury	Founded 1912; 1912–82 reports; Wiltshire RO.
Salt, Northwich	Founded 1858, closed 1930; annual reports 1858–92, at Manchester University Library; constitutions 1860–; reports and accounts 1889–1929, also other Salt assocs., at Cheshire & Chester Archives (ICI archive); strays at British Library.
Scunthorpe	Founded by 1978; BCC records.
Sheffield	Delegate 1784–1805; founded 1857; BL 1993–2001; minutes, reports, subcommittees 1864–1994 (contain some Chesterfield material); Sheffield Archives.
Shropshire	Shrewsbury founded 1902; Shropshire 1992 as TEC; BL 1993–2007; CCTE 1996; BCC records.
Slough and Thames Valley	Founded 1911 as CoT, refounded 1949; became Thames Chiltern, Thames Valley, etc.; administered Surrey and Oxford *c.*1996–2002; records at chamber (also holds Windsor CoT records).
South Staffs.	Formed 2002, from Tamworth, etc.; BCC records.
Southampton	Founded 1851; minutes and reports 1851–1992; Southampton City Archive; articles of association, reports, and journals 1890–, and stray items in Local Studies Library.
Southend	Founded by 1913; BCC records.
Spen Valley	Founded 1878 from Cleckheaton; merged with Heckmondwike 1909; merged with Huddersfield 1967; minutes 1878–1967; 1930s reports at Huddersfield Archives.
St Helens	Founded 1914 as CoT; called chamber 1993; CCTE 1996; minutes and records 1914–18 at chamber. Some reports in St Helens Library.
Stockport	Founded 1928; merged into Manchester 2004; reports and accounts 1929–2005; journal; directory 1978–, other papers; Stockport Local Heritage Library.
Sunderland	Founded 1879; merged with Newcastle 1969; minutes and reports 1879–1939; Tyne & Wear archives.

Sussex	Founded as Federation of Sussex Industries 1945; TEC 1992; BL 1993–2007; CCTE 1996; see Brighton.
Swindon	Founded 1894; minutes 1912–74; Annual Reports 1912–75; Wiltshire RO. Reports and directories 1958–2002: Swindon Library.
Thames Valley	Also termed Thames Chiltern; see Slough.
Trowbridge	Founded 1901; minutes 1901–94; reports and accounts; 1910–94; Wiltshire RO.
Wakefield	Delegate 1784–1805; founded 1864, merged with Huddersfield 1977; minutes 1953–89; reports 1866–99; Calderdale Archives.
Walsall	Founded 1881; merged with Wolverhampton as Black Country 2002; BL 1993–2007; minutes and accounts 1881–1951; journals, directories; Walsall Local History Centre.
Warrington	Founded 1876; minutes, reports, and accounts 1876–1915; reports and yearbooks 1900–60; Warrington Central Library.
Welwyn Garden City	Founded 1929; some reports, members lists, and correspondence; Welwyn GC Library.
Westminster	Founded 1947; merged with London *c*.1996; reports 1950–87, yearbook 1949–51, Westminster RO; journal 1954–5 at Cambridge University Library.
Whitehaven	Referred to for 1783 in Glasgow letters TD 1670/4/15; founded 1956; merged into Cumbria 2002; minutes and accounts 1976–77 Whitehaven RO.
Widnes	Founded 1922; BCC records.
Wigan	Founded 1884, refounded 1926 as CoT; with TEC 1991; CCTE 1996; merged into Manchester 2004. BCC records.
Winchester	Founded 1919; articles 1918; accounts 1932; minutes, reports, and accounts 1946–7; carnival papers 1922; report 1962, 64; journal 1970–86; Hants. RO.
Woking CoT	Founded 1898; Tradesmen's Alliance 1898–2003; minutes and reports 1898–2000; Surrey History Centre, Woking.
Wolverhampton	'Delegate chamber' 1785–7; founded 1819, refounded 1856; CCTE 1996; merged with Walsall as Black Country 2002; minutes 1856–1983; accounts 1915–87; Wolverhampton Archives.
Worcester	Founded 1839; merged as Hereford and Worcs. 1990; BL 1993–2007; CCTE 1996; reports and some papers 1839–90; Worcester RO; minutes and accounts 1853–60, reports 1970– ; at Hereford and Worcs. chamber.
York & N. Yorks.	Founded 1895; CoT 1912; merged with Bradford and Leeds *c*.1995, de-merged 2002; merged with Leeds 2009 to form Leeds, York, and N. Yorks.; annual reports 1896–1912 and some papers at Merchant Adventurers Archive; York CoT minutes, reports, and papers 1912–92 at chamber.
Wales	
Cardiff	Founded 1866; insolvent 2006; area taken by Newport 2007, became part of S. Wales; minutes, reports, accounts, papers 1866–1970; other association records; Glamorgan RO.

(*continued*)

Table A1.1 Continued

Chamber	Archive sources
Llanelli	Founded 1890, refounded 1914; BCC records.
Neath	Founded 1876; BCC records.
Newport	Founded 1870; became Newport and Gwent *c*.1990; becomes S. Wales 2007 and took Cardiff area; merged with W. Wales to form S. Wales 2010; minutes, reports, accounts, directories 1870–1972, newsletter to 1998–2005; Newport Library.
Port Talbot	Founded 1907; BCC records.
Swansea	Founded 1846, refounded 1873; became W. Wales *c*.1995; merged with Newport and Cardiff to form S. Wales 2010; minutes 1884–8, Yearbook 1915 minutes, W. Glamorgan Archives; reports 1930–2, Swansea Library.
Scotland	
Aberdeen	Founded 1853; minutes, accounts, journals, and reports 1853–1954; Aberdeen City archives. Other reports and journals: Aberdeen City Library.
Arbroath	Founded 1902; BCC records.
Ayr	Founded 1949; BCC records.
C. Scotland	Founded *c*.1950; became 'group' with Fife 2001; insolvent 2002, Fife reconstituted; BCC records.
Dundee	Forfarshire founded 1814, refounded as Dundee 1835; minutes 1819–1823; letterbook 1819–31; minutes, reports, and accounts 1844–1972; Dundee City Archive.
Edinburgh	Founded 1785; minutes, reports, and accounts 1786–1971; Edinburgh City Archives.
Fife	Founded 1825, merged with Kirkcaldy 1925; became 'group' with C. Scotland 2001, independent 2002; BCC records.
Glasgow	Founded 1783; minutes, journals, and reports 1783–1960; Colquhoun papers; Glasgow Central Library.
Greenock	Founded 1813; minutes and reports 1813–1960; Greenock Archives.
Inverness	Founded 1893; BCC records.
Kirkcaldy	Founded *c*.1913, merged Fife 1925.
Leith	Founded 1840; BCC records.
Paisley	Founded *c*.1950; became Renfrewshire 2001; BCC records.
Perthshire	Founded 1871; BCC records.
Shetland	Founded *c*.1945; a few records at Shetland Library.
South of Scotland	Founded 1860; later termed Borders *c*.1995. Stray records; some at British Library.
Crown Territories	
Jersey	Founded 1767; minutes, reports, and journals 1768–1979; Jersey Archives.
Guernsey	Founded *c*.1769, refounded 1808; stray records of first chamber; minutes and accounts 1805–1980, reports to 1992; Guernsey Island Archives.
Isle of Man	Founded 1956; at chamber.

N. Ireland

Belfast   Founded 1783; minutes, reports, and accounts 1783–1950; PRONI. Journals and some reports at Belfast City Library.

Londonderry   Founded 1790–*c.*1850, refounded 1885; early records all strays; 1885– at Londonderry Library and chamber.

Irish Republic

Cork   Founded 1814 informally, 1819 formally; split 1882, merged back 1952; full documents at chamber.

Cork Incorporated   Founded 1882, merged into Cork 1952; full documents at Cork chamber.

Dublin   Founded 1783, refounded 1805, 1820; minutes, reports, and accounts 1820–1951 at Irish National Archives; 1783–1800 minutes and reports still held at chamber, but unable to provide them. Some reports and stray documents at Dublin City Library.

Galway   Founded 1923; records at chamber.

Limerick   Founded 1807; minutes, reports, and accounts 1807–1973; Limerick Archives; later material at chamber.

Waterford   Founded 1787, re-established 1804, 1833; minutes, reports, and accounts 1787–1997; Waterford Archives.

APPENDIX 2

Historical Benchmarking: Data
Compilation and Alignment

This book attempts to construct an aligned historical database that is consistent with
modern benchmarking. This can be consulted and downloaded from the UK Data Archive.
This compliments the qualitative and narrative materials used in the text to allow statistical
analysis, and consistent presentation in the graphs and tables. Consistent data cross sections
have been produced for the following series:

1. Number of members.

2. Joining and lapsing rates of members.

3. Number of staff (full-time equivalent).

4. Subscription level(s) by type of member.

5. Total income.

6. Subscription income.

7. Non-subscription income.

8. Services provided (by type and number).

9. Committees (by name).

10. Publications (by type).

11. Members by industry sector (four categories).

12. Members by legal form of their business (four categories).

13. Geographical area covered (derived from statements and analysis of member lists).

14. Debates, lobbies mounted, and activities discussed.

The information has been constructed for 16 cross sections, every 10–20 years, 1790–
2005. All significant chambers of commerce are included, and a sample of the chambers of
trade where a reasonably complete record survives (as listed in Appendix 1). Which
chambers fall into the chamber of trade or commerce category changes over time; this is
controlled by coding in the database. Similarly, those chambers that became merged CCTEs
or operated closely with Business Link are identified by specific codes. Significant research
potential exists to widen the study of smaller chambers. In total, the resulting database
contains records on 150 chambers of commerce and trade. These cover the UK, Channel
Islands, Isle of Man, and Ireland. The general test for inclusion has been that a chamber has
surviving records for at least 75% of its existence. Other chambers with more partial records
are included in the text of the book, but only in a few cases in the database. The data have
been constructed from local and national sources.

LOCAL SOURCES

At the outset it was recognized that most systematic and accurate information for the database was likely to be available from national sources only from the late 1980s. Hence, a major effort was mounted to gather information from local Record Offices, Libraries, and the chambers themselves. The annual financial accounts of local chambers have been used as definitive sources, as these were normally independently audited. Once incorporated, annual returns were also made to the Companies Registrar. Minutes are usually the main source on subscription rates. In addition, many chambers published annual reports, journals, and other publications that provide more piecemeal sources. Information can also be found in local newspaper reports, which often contain full reports of chamber AGMs, and sometimes contain summaries of financial accounts and other information. In several cases newspapers provide the only surviving records. Newspapers have been used mainly to fill gaps, but in-depth trawls have been made for the 18th century for all areas where there was some suggestion that a chamber existed.

An important further source is Companies Registration records, for those bodies that were incorporated. From the 1950s, and occasionally for some earlier dates, this provides an invaluable source that preserves unique local records. The reports mainly cover financial accounts, but some are more extensive and cover some chambers that were not ABCC/BCC members (for Exeter and other chambers with lost records this is invaluable). In the case of Ireland, the Companies Registries in Belfast and Dublin have been used.

In some cases local trade directories can also be used to fill gaps of information. Some of these records may be unique. Occasionally directories report the total number of members, in a very few cases they report income levels and subscriptions rates (e.g. *Wrights*, Nottingham 1860–70), but often they have a full list of the elected officers and council. With councils numbering 20–30, which turn over by 25% or 30% per year, and where directories are printed and updated frequently, this provides the opportunity for quite large samples of members. Checks against full member lists show only a 5% margin of error for calculations of sector and company composition, which is well within the tolerances of the classifications possible. Local histories, university theses, British Association annual meeting reports, and the diary of one secretary (Raymond Street for Manchester, 1931–9) are also useful. The LSE has many chamber journals and reports; whilst the BL, Cambridge University Library, Bodleian, TNA, PRONI, and Irish National Archives, and many other libraries are important sources for stray records. A search of major American sources yielded some critical material.

Some difficulties have resulted from the loss or destruction of information. The archival records of the Exeter and Coventry chambers were lost in WW2, and the liquidators destroyed Exeter's later records when the chamber went into administration in 1992. Many records of the Norwich Chamber were lost in a fire at the local library in 1994. The Barnsley archival records were stolen from the chamber in about 1990. One of the early Goole minute books has gone missing from the local reference library. When some chambers were merged with TECs in the 1990s, thoughtless disposal of many records occurred. Despite these difficulties, in general, a good coverage has been achieved for most chambers through local sources, especially when supplemented with national and other information.

NATIONAL SOURCES

Nevertheless, national statistics provide some invaluable information that is otherwise unavailable. Unfortunately, not all national records have survived or been deposited. The following national listings of chamber statistics for individual chambers in the early years (for the UK and Ireland until 1922) have been discovered and are believed to be all that now exist (all held at the LMA unless otherwise stated) (Table A2.1).

Regular systematic information began to be collected by ABCC only from 1976, when the chamber secretaries compiled *Some Basic Statistics*. Copies of early years seem to no longer exist in the ABCC or BCC archives, but personal copies obtained from ABCC in earlier years by the author have now been deposited at the LMA. These cover 1979 and 1982, with retrospective data for 1976. These reports are better in quality and wider in coverage, but are still quite limited in content. They include statistics on members, staff, total income, subscription income, and membership by type (retail, non-retail). These data have been checked with available local sources and are reasonably accurate.

Table A2.1 Sources of national archival records for chambers 1882–1972

Date	Information
*c.*1882/3	Number of members (*Chamber of Commerce Journal*, 5 March 1884, p. 65).
*c.*1885	Income and expenditure (ACC MS 14477/2).
*c.*1914	Number of members (ACC MS 14477/5).
1920	Number of members (ABCC MS 14476/10).
1923	Number of members of Scottish Chambers (ABCC MS 14479).
1914–60	Number of members annually; foundation year, date of incorporation; in ABCC *Proceedings* (also ABCC MS 14477/1–7; LMA Store 734; note, although reprinted each year, many numbers were clearly not regularly updated).
1941	Number of retail members (ABCC 4 June 1941, MS 14482/3).
1958	Number of members 1948, 1953, 1958; subscription rates 21 January 1958 (ABCC paper 21 January 1959; held at Croydon chamber).
1962	Subscription rates (minimum, maximum, and classification criteria) (ABCC MS 17367/1).
1968	Annual income and staff (ABCC MS 17367/2).
1970	Subscription rates (minimum, maximum and classification criteria) (ABCC MS 17367/3).
1970	Classification of members by sector, no. of exporters and certificates issued, including inspection reports (MS 17556).
1970	Classification of members by sector and whether a journal is published (ABCC MS 17367/3).
1971	Number of enquiries per chamber, and number of small firm members less than 250 employees (ABCC MS 17548/3).
1972	Staff and members (ABCC MS 17556 and 17557).
1979 & 1982	ABCC *Some Basic Statistics* (members, members by type, staff, finance) (now at LMA).

Wider and more systematic data over a wider range of fields of information were collected for the first time from 1988 in what was termed a *Census*. The *Census* lists members by number, type (manufacturing, non-manufacturing; less than 20 employees, 20–199 employees, over 200 employees), total income, staff numbers and further data on number of meetings, overseas missions, seminars, size of council, etc. Further surveys of members to record their sector type began in the early 1990s (manufacturing, non-manufacturing, retail) and committee structure. Subscription rates were monitored on a systematic annual basis from about 1991. The size categories of member types were extended from 1994 to cover businesses in five categories: no employees, 1–5, 6–19, 20–199, and over 200 employees. The whole data-gathering exercise was combined with the process of accrediting chambers from 1991 and the *Census* was re-termed *Benchmarking* from 1998, with an increasingly wide set of information collected, including joining and lapsing. The information for the period since 1988 is held by BCC and has been made available for this study. Unfortunately no historic CI data has been found for Irish chambers prior to the 1990s, so that local and other sources have had to be used.

Fragmentary coverage of local chambers also occurs in the various national journals that the chamber system has produced. These are mostly given as news items or reports on 'Deliberations of Chambers' and 'The Work of the Chambers' for the 1870s and 1880s, especially in London's *CCJ*, and later in Dublin's. In addition, material is frequently reported on specific local chambers in the ACC/ABCC/BCC papers and minute books. Some local records also include useful statistics of other chambers for comparative purposes. Chamber *Handbooks* and directories published by Bemrose of Derby in the period 1915–30 are a valuable addition. Thirty-one smaller chambers are covered by a *Chambers Register* in three regional groups (compiled by Thomas Keens, Luton chamber secretary, and published by Bemrose in 1920–2), although, unfortunately, copies of only volumes i and ii have been found.[1]

For some periods other national surveys are available. A survey of chambers and other organizations undertaken by the Royal Commission on Labour in 1892 provides information on formal rules and voting structures, subscriptions, entrance fees, involvement with labour Conciliation Boards, and in about 12 cases gives information on membership and employees of member firms. In several cases this is the only information on these chambers for this period (some of the original responses are at the TNA). A second survey was compiled for the US Department of Commerce in 1913 (Woolf 1915a),[2] although checks show the data to have numerous omissions as well as errors. Almost contemporaneous with Woolf's survey, the Bristol chamber surveyed all ACC members of the time, gathering their annual reports for *c*.1908 and other information, which it summarized in a *Yearbook* of 1908–9. This provides a small amount of useful unique information and comment.

The reliability and consistency of the national data is sometimes doubtful, with local chambers tending to exaggerate their size. Also, the statistics may refer to different local financial or reporting years. In some later years, when the subscription to ABCC was based on local membership numbers, there becomes a tendency to underestimate by excluding some members (e.g. retailers who might be NCT members, or in a few cases manufacturers who were affiliated to the CBI), or overestimate to meet recognition criteria. Hence, audited

---

[1] The effect of economic slump and Bemrose's efforts to publish individual *Yearbooks* may mean that vol. iii was never published. All efforts to find it have failed, including contacting the modern chambers and local libraries; it was compiled, since correspondence at Portsmouth chamber shows that 'publication was imminent'. Vols. i and ii are at the Bodleian, and vol. i also at Lancaster chamber.

[2] This survey must have been conducted with help from ACC, since the coverage is of the ACC-affiliated chambers of that time; but there appears to be no record of it in ACC minutes.

local accounts and listings must be preferred over national data, when available. After 1998 it is believed that BCC *Benchmarking* statistics become fully reliable.

MEMBER CHARACTERISTICS

Information on two main characteristics of members has been gathered systematically: their sector and legal status. It was hoped to gather some measures of firm size, but this proved impossible except through surveys that already exist, as reported in the text. The sector and legal status information was gathered either from the chamber's own lists or from local directories and trade directories. The member lists usually contain no information on the type of business of the member until about 1900. A classified member directory is not common until the 1930s. In order to identify the character of the members' business, reference has been made to other local directories. To gain the best possible coverage, the extensive collections of directories at the London Guildhall Library, Society of Genealogists, local libraries/record offices, and other e-sources have been used.

There are a number of problems to be overcome in using membership lists. First there is a problem of reading between chamber lists and directories with common names, particularly in large cities. Similarly, misspelling and alternative spellings have to be traced. If no specific identifiers can be found, these members are excluded and the statistics quoted rely on using the remaining members as a sample. Second, not all directories are inclusive, accurate, and up-to-date. A third problem is the match between date of publication of directories and the available lists of members. Where considerable gaps occur, directories for the preceding and following periods are both used. Usually sectors of business stay the same. However, legal status can change quite rapidly, particularly in the period following 1900. These difficulties can usually be mitigated by checking across more than one directory source. Also, for the foundation members, and often for the key early years, the membership has been analysed in detail using wider local historical and genealogical sources in some local chamber histories. It is estimated that there is at most 2–3% mis-attribution of business sector or status in any one year.

A fourth difficulty is how to ascribe members who had multiple business operations. The description 'merchant and manufacturer', 'merchant and retailer', 'manufacturer and trader' are quite common so that even the simple split between major sectors is not always possible. But wider ranges of different businesses are also possible; e.g. 'sail maker and insurance agent'; 'salt manufacturer and ship builder'; 'ship-owner and brewer'; 'consul and merchant'. In these cases the business is allocated either to what appears to be its main sector (if that is obvious) or its activities are split equally between its different sectors in the categorization analysis.

As a result, all analyses of business characteristics have to be treated as approximate. In addition, where chamber membership is very large and where information had to be checked with directories, samples had to be taken: this was done on a random basis to avoid systematic error. Chamber memberships of 100 or fewer were fully analysed, but for larger chambers a sample of 100–200 was used. However, where a full listing of members by type was available this was used, even in the largest chambers such as London.

As a result of these approximations, all business characteristics have to be treated with care and used as estimates not definitive numbers. The accuracy, in general, is believed to be within ±3%, and even in the few extreme cases (which occur where there are both poor local directories and badly recorded member lists, e.g. as a result of poor handwriting) it is believed that an accuracy of ±5% has been achieved. No doubt, further research on each locality will improve the precision of these estimates, but for the purposes of this study, this level of accuracy is adequate.

COMPLETENESS

As a result of the limitations of the data there are a number of gaps. The main gaps, ironically, are for relatively recent periods. Whilst many early records have found their way into archives and record offices, and current records are in chambers or libraries, there is often a gap of preservation of materials for the 1960s–1980s. For the 1980s cross-section, only *average* subscription rates derived from an ABCC survey are available for many chambers. Because of this, to make the cross-sections as complete as possible, some data have been used for adjacent years, where no alternative is available. In general, no data are substituted in this way if they are further than ± 3 years from the cross-section date. The Data Archive deposit gives full details of the completeness of the information that it has been possible to collect, compared with the chambers in existence at each time period. Coverage of at least 90% has been achieved across the years, the data for most chambers being almost 100% complete.

Population and Economic Data

URBAN POPULATION DATA

Population data for 1801–1911 has been derived primarily from the research of Chris Law (1967) who originally prepared it; and Brian Robson (1973) who developed the data further and transcribed and preserved it. Robson also added information on some smaller settlements for years before they became 'urban' under Law's criteria. There are uncertainties in some of these estimates, but these have little effect for chamber comparisons where only the larger towns and cities are normally required. Robson (1973, p. 52) comments that 'Law's figures provide as sensitive and accurate a set of estimates of urban populations as one could hope to derive'. The data have been keyed for this study and are contained in the UK Data Archive deposit for chambers.

The Law–Robson data cover all settlements of 2500 and above with a density of at least one person per acre up to 1911. They only cover England and Wales so that they have been supplemented here by adding Scotland, Ireland, Isle of Man, and Channel Isles information using Census tables. After 1911 these data have been run forward for the same settlements using extrapolation, normed to match the national population totals. In effect this provides comparisons over the same centres as if they had evolved without merging with each other. For 1790 they have been extrapolated back in the same way for the system as a whole, but any population statistics available has been used from other sources (this covers all the larger centres). These methods provide only rough estimates, but allow consistent results for rank size plots used in Chapter 5 for 1790–1951.

A second basis of comparison after 1911 is based on the city-system of the twentieth century. This employs a second set of population data derived from Champion (2003). These data are for aggregations of local government districts 1901–91. This takes the information forwards and includes Scotland; Ireland, Isle of Man and Channel Islands have again had to be added, and 2001 information has been added from the Census. The information given by Champion does not extend far down the size spectrum, and only 282 places are included compared to 934 in Law–Robson, but for comparisons of chambers of commerce in the later period this includes all relevant centres. The two data sources overlap for 1901–11 so that comparisons are possible on the two bases, as used in the text.

ECONOMIC DATA

The economic statistics used in the book are taken from specialist sources that have sought to align long-term time series. These are B. R. Mitchell (1988), *British Historical Statistics*; B. R. Mitchell (1975), *European Historical Statistics 1750–1970*; Department of Employment and Productivity (1971), *British Labour Statistics: Historical Abstracts 1886–1968*.

These are supplemented with modern sources and linked to align new and old series: J. Denman and P. McDonald, 'Unemployment statistics from 1881 to the present day', *Labour Market Trends*, Jan. (1996), pp. 5–18; A. Sneade, 'Trade Union membership 1999–2000', *Labour Market Trends*, Sept. (2001), pp. 433–44 (and earlier issues). Modern series used are ABMX, RP02/CHAW, CKYW/IKBH, IKBI, ABMI, BLUU, BLUT, PLLU, CMH/ANBY and other sources from the Offices of National Statistics.

In all cases there are changes in definitions over time and various inconsistencies. Different series have been aligned with each other by re-scaling backwards or forwards to a common base, but this does not entirely overcome changes in how series were collected. Full explanations of the changes and difficulties of interpretation are given in the sources cited. The implication is that time series data must be interpreted as a broad *index number series*, and not as precise figures for comparisons. This approach, with its recognized deficiencies, is the same as that used in all other similar historical econometric studies.

Bibliography of Chamber Histories

Note that these histories vary considerably in size, quality, and detail. Where they contain conflicting information compared to archival records, the latter have been used. The archive location of these sources is noted after each entry. American chamber histories are cited in the main text and references.

Aberdeen	'History of the Chamber', *The Journal of the Aberdeen Chamber of Commerce*, 1 (1) (October 1919), 1–4 (Aberdeen Central Library). 'History of the Aberdeen Chamber', *The Journal of the Aberdeen Chamber of Commerce*, 15 (2) (January 1934), 50–4 (Aberdeen Central Library).
Belfast	George Chambers (1983), *Faces of Change: The Belfast and Northern Ireland Chambers of Commerce and Industry, 1783–1983* (Belfast: Northern Ireland Chamber of Commerce and Industry) (various libraries).
Birkenhead	'Birkenhead Chamber of Commerce', in *Birkenhead Official Yearbook, 1957* (Wirral Archives).
Birmingham	G. H. Wright (1913), *Chronicles of the Birmingham Chamber of Commerce 1813–1913* (Birmingham: Chamber of Commerce) (Birmingham Local Studies Library).
Bradford	W. H. Sawyer (ed.) (*c.*1951), *Bradford Chamber of Commerce Centenary 1851–1951* (Derby: Bemrose), 67 pp. (various libraries).
Brighton and Sussex	*A History of the Chamber 1945–1995, Sussex Enterprise (1945)* (*c.*2000) (typescript) (held at chamber).
Bristol	*Strictures on the Late Reports and Proceedings of the Bristol Chamber of Commerce*, by 'A. Burgess'; reprinted from *Bristol Mercury* (1836), covering 1833–6 (BL 8247.a.38).
Cambourne	J. F. Odgers (1958), *Cambourne Chamber of Commerce 1908–1958* (Cambourne: Chamber of Commerce) (Exeter, West Country Studies Library).
Cardiff	Peter Acton (2006), *A History of the Chamber of Commerce* (Cardiff Chamber of Commerce, website, 5pages: accessed 23/4/2006), (<www.cardiffchamber.co.uk/content/public/dynamic/default.asp?id=291>).

Chesterfield (North Derbyshire)	'Our first 100 years', pp. 11–12, in North Derbyshire Chamber of Commerce (1999), *Members Diary and Directory* (Derby: Chamber of Commerce) (City Local Studies Library).
Cork	*Handbook of the Cork Incorporated Chamber of Commerce and Shipping (1919)* (Cork: Greg & Co.) (London Guildhall Library).
	Sean Beecher (*c.*2007), *History of Cork Chamber of Commerce* (typescript), 8 pp. (held at chamber).
Coventry	F. Andrew (1978), *The History of Coventry Chamber of Commerce and Industry 1903–1978*, 21 pp. (typescript) (held at chamber).
Croydon	Paula McInnes, Bill Sparks, and Peter Broderick (1991), *One Hundred Years of Croydon at Work: Celebrating the Century of the Croydon Chamber of Commerce and Industry* (Croydon Society and Croydon Chamber) (Croydon Local Studies Library).
Derby	'History of the Chamber', pp. 37–41 in *Commercial Yearbook of the Derby Chamber of Commerce,* compiled by the Secretary L. W. Wilshire (1916) (Derby: Bemrose) (Derby Local Studies Library).
	'The story of Derby and Derbyshire Chamber of Commerce', Centenary issue of *Derby Enterprise, Journal of the Derby and Derbyshire Chamber of Commerce* (1964), 23–9.
Dover	Ruth Weinberg (*c.*1999), *Dover and District Chamber of Commerce and Industry* (draft typescript), 12 pp. (Dover Library).
Dublin	L. M. Cullen (1983), *Princes and Pirates: The Dublin Chamber of Commerce 1783–1983* (Dublin: Chamber of Commerce), 126 pp. (British Library).
Dundee	*Dundee Chamber of Commerce Centenary Souvenir, 1936* (Dundee: Chamber of Commerce) (Dundee City Archives and Record Office).
	Harry Terrell (2006), *Business in Action: A History of Dundee and Tayside Chamber of Commerce and Industry* (typescript), 16 pp.
Edinburgh	*A Brief Account of the Rise, Progress and Present Position of the Chamber of Commerce and Manufacturers in the City of Edinburgh* (1861) (Edinburgh: Chamber) (National Library of Scotland, Edinburgh).
	Edinburgh Chamber of Commerce and Manufacturers 160th Anniversary 1785–1945 (1945) (Edinburgh: Chamber) (mainly a history of family companies and the charter) (BL 8231.f.88).
Falmouth	A. V. Baker (1966), *The First Hundred Years: A Brief Account of the History of the Port of Falmouth Chamber of Commerce* (Falmouth: Chamber of Commerce), 75 pp. (Falmouth Library).
Galway	Kieran Woodman (2000), *Tribes and Tigers: A History of the Galway Chamber of Commerce and Industry* (Galway: Chamber of Commerce), 383 pp.

Glasgow

George Stewart (1883), *Progress of Glasgow: A Sketch of the Commercial and Industrial Increase of the City during the Last Century, as Shown in the Records of Glasgow Chamber of Commerce and Other Authentic Documents*, 178 pp. (Glasgow: Chamber) (various libraries).

C. A. Oakley (1983), *Our Illustrious Forbears: The Glasgow Chamber of Commerce 1783–1983* (Glasgow: Blackie and Sons), 357 pp. (Glasgow: Chamber) (various libraries).

Glasgow Chamber of Commerce Journal, Bicentenary issue, January (1983), 144 pp. (contains useful supplement to Oakley; various libraries).

Grimsby

'100 Years: A look back over a century of the Grimsby and Immingham Incorporated Chamber of Commerce and Shipping', special publication by *Grimsby Gazette* (1985) (Grimsby Library).

Guernsey

Gregory Stevens Cox (1983), *The Guernsey Chamber of Commerce 1808–1983: A Celebration of 175 Years of Activity* (Guernsey: Chamber of Commerce) (Guernsey, Islands Archives).

Guildford

'Guildford chamber of commerce', *Guildford City Outlook*, July (1932).

Guildford and District Chamber of Commerce Official Yearbook, 1980–1 (Chamber of Commerce) (both at Surrey History Centre).

Huddersfield

Huddersfield Chamber Yearbook (Derby: Bemrose) for 1914, 1920, 1925 (LSE).

MYCCCI: Celebrating 150 Years Supporting Business (2003) (Huddersfield: Mid-Yorkshire Chamber of Commerce and Industry) (held at chamber).

Hull

In the Beginning was an Orchard: A Commentary on the Origins of the Hull Incorporated Chamber of Commerce and Shipping (c.1987) compiled by W. J. Hope (held at chamber).

Isle of Wight

R. Reynolds (ed.) (1990), *Isle of Wight Chamber of Commerce: The First 80 Years 1910–1990* (Isle of Wight: Chamber), 20 pp. (typescript) (held at chamber).

Jersey

'The Jersey chamber of commerce—the early years', *Bulletin Societé Jersiaise*, 19 (1968), 299–306 (no author stated).

Stuart Nicolle (2008), 'Jersey Chamber of Commerce Archive', *Heritage*, pp. 11–19 (Magazine of Jersey Heritage Archives).

Lancaster

J. Paull (1996), *Subscribers and Strangers: A History of Lancaster District Chambers of Commerce, Trade and Industry* (Lancaster: Chamber) (Lancaster Central Library).

Leeds

'History of the Chamber', *Leeds Commercial Yearbook 1920* (Leeds: Chamber of Commerce), pp. 43–4 (Leeds University Library).

M. W. Beresford (1951), *The Leeds Chamber of Commerce* (Leeds: Chamber of Commerce) (various libraries).

Leicester — *Leicester and County Chamber of Commerce, Centenary 1860–1960* (1960) (Leicester: Leicestershire Chamber of Commerce) (Leicestershire County Record Office).

Harry Purt (1961), *The History of Leicester and County Chamber of Commerce and Industry (Inc.)* (Leicester: Chamber of Commerce) (held at chamber).

Liverpool — W. A. Gilson Martin (1950), *A Century of Liverpool's Commerce: Centenary History of Liverpool Chamber of Commerce (1850–1950)* (Liverpool: Charles Birchall and Sons) (BL, Liverpool and Warrington Libraries).

A Short History of the Liverpool Chamber of Commerce (1997) (Liverpool: Chamber of Commerce) (Liverpool City Records Office).

R. J. Bennett (2010), *The Voice of Liverpool Business: The First Chamber of Commerce and the Atlantic Economy, 1774–c.1796* (Liverpool: Liverpool Chamber of Commerce).

London — E. Musgrave (1914), *The London Chamber of Commerce from 1881 to 1914: A Retrospective Appreciation* (London: London Chamber of Commerce) (London Guildhall Library).

S. R. B. Smith (1982), 'The centenary of the London Chamber of Commerce: its origins and early policy', *The London Journal*, 8 (2), 156–70.

Kenneth Lysons (1988), *A Passport to Employment: A History of the London Chamber of Commerce and Industry Education Scheme 1887–1987* (London: Chamber of Commerce and Industry: Pitman) (London Guildhall Library).

Macclesfield — 'The Chamber of Commerce', pp. 198–204 in C. Stella Davies (1976), *A History of Macclesfield* (Didsbury: E. J. Manton) (various libraries).

Keith Austin (2000), 'The Macclesfield Board of Trade', chapter 13 in *Troubled Times: Macclesfield 1790–1870* (Macclesfield: Churnet Valley Books) (Macclesfield Silk Museum).

Manchester — E. Helm (1897), *Chapters in the History of the Manchester Chamber of Commerce* (London: Simpkin, Marshall, Hamilton, Kent & Co.) (various libraries).

A. Redford (1934), *Manchester Merchants and Foreign Trade 1794–1858* (Manchester: Manchester University Press) (various libraries).

A. Redford and B. W. Clapp (1956), *Manchester Merchants and Foreign Trade*, vol. ii: *1850–1939* (Manchester: Manchester University Press) (various libraries).

Mansfield — 'Mansfield chamber of commerce', in *Industrial Nottinghamshire* (1920), p. 114 ff. (Derby: Bemrose) (LSE).

Middlesbrough and Teesside — 'Centenary 1863–1963', *Teesside Journal of Commerce*, 28 (7) (July 1963), 118–24 (Teesside Archive).

Newcastle	*175 Years 1815–1990* (1990) (Newcastle: Tyne and Wear Chamber of Commerce) (Tyne and Wear Archives).
North Staffordshire	*North Staffordshire Chamber Yearbook*, for 1912, 1921, 1928 (Derby: Bemrose) (LSE).
Northwich (Salt)	W. H. Chaloner (1961), 'William Furnival, H. E. Falk and the Salt Chamber of Commerce, 1815–1889: some chapters in the economic history of Cheshire', *Transactions of the Historic Society of Lancashire and Cheshire*, 112, 121–45 (various libraries).
Norwich	B. M. Doyle (1997), 'The development of the Norwich Chamber of Commerce, 1896–1930', *Norwich Archaeology*, 42, 468–80 (Norwich City Library, etc.). This has some of the only surviving comments on *Annual Reports* of the 1920s, now lost by fire.
Nottingham	'History of the Nottingham Chamber of Commerce', pp. 47–52 in *Nottingham Chamber of Commerce Yearbook* (1914) (Derby: Bemrose) (Nottingham City Library*)*.
	'Nottingham chamber of commerce', pp. 65–6 in *Industrial Nottinghamshire* (1920) (Derby: Bemrose) (LSE).
	Ronald Walton (1960), *The History of the Nottingham Chamber of Commerce 1860–1960* (Nottingham: Chamber of Commerce) (Nottingham City Library).
Oldham	'History of the Oldham Chamber of Commerce', *Commercial Oldham*, 23 (3) (1949), 13–15 (Oldham Local Studies Library and Archive).
Portsmouth	'South East Hampshire Chamber of Commerce and Industry', p. 25 in *South and East Hampshire Chamber of Commerce and Industry 1879–1979 Centenary Exhibition Catalogue* (Portsmouth Record Office; and City Library).
Preston	C. Heywood (1966), *Golden Jubilee: A History of the First Fifty Years of the Preston and District Chamber of Commerce* (Preston: Chamber of Commerce) (Preston Central Library).
Reading	'21st Commemoration Issue and survey for 21 years', *Annual Report and Accounts* (1923) (Reading: Chamber of Commerce) (Berkshire County Record Office, Reading).
Rotherham	'History of Rotherham and District Chamber of Commerce', pp. 132–7 in R. T. Wilson and E. J. Thigg (1919), *Industrial Sheffield and Rotherham* (Derby: Bemrose) (Rotherham Archives; LSE).
Salisbury	History of Salisbury Chamber (1987), *Salisbury Chamber of Commerce* (typescript) (Wiltshire County Record Office).
Sheffield	'History of Sheffield Chamber of Commerce', pp. 94–101, in R. T. Wilson and E. J. Thigg (1919), *Industrial Sheffield and Rotherham* (Derby: Bemrose) (Rotherham Archives; LSE).
	Harry Townsend (1956), 'The Sheffield Chamber of Commerce and Manufacturing (Incorporated)', pp. 188–90 in D. L. Linton

(ed.), *Sheffield and its Region: A Scientific and Historical Survey* (Sheffield: British Association Local Executive Committee) (various libraries).

Paul Dennison–Edson (1977), *The Golden Years: A Commemorative Booklet Illustrating the First 50 Years of the Sheffield Chamber of Commerce 1927–1977* (Sheffield: Chamber of Commerce) (Sheffield Central Library).

'One day in 1857', *Quality* (Journal of Sheffield Chamber of Commerce), 29 (2) (March/April 1989), 20–3 (Sheffield Archives).

Southampton
Gordon Sewell (1918), *Southampton Chamber of Commerce 1851–1951: A Brief History* (Southampton: Chamber of Commerce) (Southampton Local Studies Library).

Norman Kemish (2001), *Southampton Chamber of Commerce and Industry: 150 Years on, or Southampton and its Chamber* (Southampton: Chamber of Commerce) (Southampton Local Studies Library).

Stockport
Stockport Chamber of Commerce and Industry: Draft History (c.1990) (typescript) (Stockport Chamber) (BCC Store L39).

Swansea
'Swansea Chamber of Commerce', pp. 47–8 in *Yearbook 1915* (Derby: Bemrose) (Swansea Central Library, LSE).

Truro
City of Truro Chamber of Commerce Centenary: 1887–1987 (1987) 4 pp. (Truro: Chamber of Commerce) (Truro Library).

Walsall
'Walsall Chamber of Commerce', *Commercial Yearbook 1916* (Bemrose: Derby) (Walsall Library, LSE).

Warrington
Continuing to Serve: Warrington and District Chamber of Commerce and Industry 1876–2001 (2001) (Warrington: Chamber) (Warrington Library).

Waterford
Des Cowman (1988), *Perceptions and Promotions: The Role of the Waterford Chamber of Commerce, 1787–1987* (Waterford: Chamber), 77 pp. (Waterford Library, etc.).

Wolverhampton
V. B. Beaumont (1956), *The Wolverhampton Chamber of Commerce 1856–1956* (Wolverhampton: Chamber of Commerce), 151 pp. (various libraries).

Worcester
Alistair Clarke (1990), *1839–1989: A Short History of the Worcester and Hereford Area Chamber of Commerce* (Worcester and Hereford Chamber) (Worcester Local History Centre).

References

ABCC (1991), *Effective Business Support: A UK Strategy* (London: Association of British Chambers of Commence).

——(1992), *Effective Business Support: A UK Strategy: Phase 2* (London: Association of British Chambers of Commence).

Acemoglu, D., Johnson, S., and Robinson, J. A. (2001), 'Reversal of fortune: geography and institutions in the making of the modern world income distribution', *NBER* Working Papers, 8460, Cambridge, Mass.

ACFCI (1987, 1990), *Les Chambres de commerce dans l'Europe des Douze*, 2 vols. (Paris: Assemblée des Chambres Françaises de Commerce et d'Industrie).

Adams, E. D. (1904), *The Influence of Grenville on Pitt's Foreign Policy 1784–1798* (Washington: Carnegie Institution of Washington).

Akins, B. (1895), *History of Halifax City* (Halifax: Nova Scotia Historical Society).

Alderman, G. (1973), *The Railway Interest* (Leicester: Leicester University Press).

Aldrich, H. E. (1976), 'Resource dependence and interorganizational relations: relations between local employment service offices and social service sector organizations', *Administration and Society*, 7, 419–54.

Allan, D. G. C. (1968), *William Shipley: Founder of the Royal Society of Arts* (London: Hutchinson).

Allen, N. J., and Meyer, J. P. (1990), 'The measurement of antecedents of affective, continuance and normative commitment to the organisation', *Journal of Occupational Psychology*, 63, 1–18.

Ambler, T., Chittenden, F., and Miccini, A. (2010), *Is Regulation really Good for us?* (London: British Chambers of Commerce).

Amery, J. (1969), *Joseph Chamberlain and the Tariff Reform Campaign: The Life of Joseph Chamberlain* (London: Macmillan).

Andrews, C. M. (1916), 'The Boston merchants and the non-importation movement', *Transactions of the Colonial Society of Massachusetts*, 19, 159–259.

——(1929), 'The Acts of Trade', chapter IX in J. Holland Rose, A. P. Newton, and E. A. Benjions (eds.), *Cambridge History of the British Empire*, vol. i. (Cambridge: Cambridge University Press).

Armitage, D. (2003), 'Parliament and international law in the eighteenth century', in Hoppit (2003: 169–86).

Armytage, F. (1953), *The Free Port System in the British West Indies: A Study in Commercial Policy, 1766–1822* (London: Longmans).

Ashton, T. S. (1963), *Iron and Steel in the Industrial Revolution*, 3rd edn. (London: Methuen).

Ashworth, H. (1876), *Recollections of Richard Cobden MP and the Anti-Corn-Law League* (London: Routledge; reprinted 1993).

Aspinall, A. (1973), *Politics and the Press, c.1750–1850* (Brighton: Harvester Press).

Auckland, Lord (1861–2), *The Journal and Correspondence of William, Lord Auckland*, 4 vols. (London: Richard Bentley).

Audit Commission (1989), *Urban Regeneration and Economic Development: The Local Government Dimension* (London: Audit Commission).

——(1990), *Urban Regeneration and Economic Development: Audit Guide* (London: Audit Commission).

——(1999), *A Life's Work: Local Authorities, Economic Development and Economic Regeneration* (London: Audit Commission).

Baden-Fuller, C., and Stopford, J. M. (1994), *Rejuvenating the Mature Business: The Competitive Challenge*, 2nd edn. (London: Routledge).

Baines, T. (1852), *History of the Commerce and Town of Liverpool* (London: Longman Brown).

Bairoch, P., Batou, J., and Chèvre, P. (1988), *La Population des villes européennes: Banque de données et analyse sommaire des résultats* (Geneva: Libraire Droz).

Ball, S. (1988), *Baldwin and the Conservative Party: The Crisis of 1929–1931* (New Haven: Yale University Press).

Bannock, G. (1981), *The Economics of Small Firms* (Oxford: Basil Blackwell).

——(1989), *Government and Small Business* (London: Paul Chapman).

Bargar, B. D. (1956), 'Matthew Boulton and the Birmingham Petition of 1775', *William and Mary Quarterly*, 13 (3), 26–39.

Barker, H. (2004), ' "Smoke cities": northern industrial towns in later Georgian England', *Urban History*, 31 (2), 175–90.

Barry, B. (1974), 'Review article: "Exit voice and loyalty" ', *British Journal of Political Science*, 4, 79–107.

Barty-King, H. (1977), *The Baltic Exchange* (London: Hutchinson Benham).

Basye, A. H. (1925), *The Lords Commissions of Trade and Plantations: Commonly Known as the Board of Trade, 1748–1782* (New Haven: Yale University Press).

Beaumont, J. T. B. (1844), *Free Trade, with Reference to its Effects upon the Operative Classes, Briefly Considered* (London: Painter).

Becattini, G., Bellandi, M., and de Propis, L. (eds.) (2009), *A Handbook of Industrial Districts* (London: Edward Elgar).

Becker, G. S. (1983), 'A theory of competition among pressure groups', *Quarterly Journal of Economics*, 98, 372–99.

Beer, S. (1965), *Modern British Politics* (London: Faber).

Bemis, S. F. (1924), *Jay's Treaty: A Study in Commerce and Diplomacy* (New York: Macmillan).

Ben-Ner, A., and Van Hoomissen, T. (1991), 'Nonprofit organisations in the mixed economy: a demand and supply analysis', *Annals of Public and Cooperative Economics*, 62 (4), 519–50.

Bennett, R. J. (1982), *Central Grants to Local Government: The Political and Economic Impact of the Rate Support Grant in England and Wales* (Cambridge: Cambridge University Press).

——(1991), *Developing the National Chamber Network* (London: Association of British Chambers of Commence).

——(1995), *Meeting the Needs of Business: Engaging the Business Community through New-Style Chambers* (London: British Chambers of Commerce).

——(1996a), 'The logic of local business associations: an analysis of voluntary chambers of commerce', *Journal of Public Policy*, 15, 251–79.

——(1996b), 'Can transaction cost economics explain voluntary Chambers of Commerce?', *Journal of Institutional and Theoretical Economics*, 152, 654–80.

——(1997), 'The relation between government and business associations in Britain: an evaluation of recent developments', *Journal of Policy Studies*, 18 (1), 5–33.

——(1998a), 'Business associations and their potential to contribute to economic development: re-exploring an interface between the state and market', *Environment and Planning A*, 30, 1367–87.

——(1998b), 'Explaining the membership of voluntary local business associations: the example of British Chambers of Commerce', *Regional Studies*, 32, 503–14.

——(2000), 'The logic of membership of sectoral business associations', *Review of Social Economy*, 58 (1), 19–20.

——(2006), 'Government and small business', chapter 4, pp. 49–75, in S. Carter and D. Jones-Evans (eds.), *Enterprise and Small Business* (London: Financial Times, Prentice Hall).

——(2007), 'Expectations-based evaluation of SME advice and consultancy: an example of Business Link service', *Journal of Small Business and Enterprise Development*, 14 (3), 435–57.

——(2008), 'Government SME policy since the 1990s: what have we learnt?', *Environment and Planning C: Government and Policy*, 26, 375–97.

——(2010), *The Voice of Liverpool Business: The First Chamber of Commerce and the Atlantic Economy, 1774–c.1796* (Liverpool: Chamber of Commerce).

——(2011a), 'Malachy Postlethwayt 1707–67: discovering his genealogy and influence', *Genealogists' Magazine*, 30(6), 187–94.

——(2011b), 'Network interlocks: the connected emergence of chambers of commerce and country banking 1768–1819', forthcoming.

——Fuller, C., and Ramsden, M. (2004), 'Local government and local economic development in Britain: an evaluation of developments under Labour', *Progress in Planning*, 62, 209–74.

——and Krebs, G. (1991), *Local Economic Development: Public–Private Partnerships Initiatives in Britain and Germany* (London: Belhaven).

————(1993a), *Costs and Organisation of Chamber of Commerce Business Services: A Detailed Accounting Study*, Department of Geography Research Papers, London School of Economics.

————(1993b), *Chambers of Commerce in Britain: Survey of Organisation and Services*, Department of Geography Research Papers, London School of Economics.

————and Zimmermann, H. (eds.) (1993), *Chambers of Commerce in Britain and Germany and the Single European Market* (London: Anglo-German Foundation).

——————(eds.) (1997), *Trade Associations in Britain and Germany: Responding to Internationalisation and the EU* (London: Anglo-German Foundation).

——and McCoshan, A. (1993), *Enterprise and Human Resource Development: Local Capacity Building* (London: Paul Chapman).

————and Sellgren, J. (1990), *Local Employer Networks (LENs): Their Experience and Lessons for TECs*, Department of Geography Research Papers, London School of Economics.

——and Payne, D. (2000), *Local and Regional Economic Development: Renegotiating Power under Labour* (Aldershot: Ashgate).

——and Ramsden, M. (2007), 'The contribution of business associations to SMEs: strategy, bundling or reassurance?', *International Small Business Journal*, 25 (1), 49–76.

——and Robson, P. J. A. (1999a), 'Intensity of interaction in supply of business advice: a comparison of consultancy, business associations and government support initiatives for SMEs', *British Journal of Management*, 10, 351–69.

————(1999b), 'Business Link: use, satisfaction and comparison with Business Shop and Business Connect', *Policy Studies*, 20 (2), 107–31.

————(2001), 'Exploring the market potential and bundling of business association services', *Journal of Services Marketing*, 15 (3), 222–39.

————(2003), 'Business Link: use, satisfaction and the influence of local governance regime', *Policy Studies*, 24 (4), 163–86.

————(2004a), 'Support services for SMEs: does the 'franchisee' make a difference to Business Link offer?', *Environment and Planning C: Government & Policy*, 22, 859–80.

————(2004b), 'The role of trust and contract in the supply of business advice', *Cambridge Journal of Economics*, 28, 471–88.

————(2005), 'The advisor–SME client relationship: impact, satisfaction and commitment', Small Business Economics, 25, 255–71.

————Wicks, P., and McCoshan, A. (1994). *Local Empowerment and Business Services* (London: UCL Press).

Berg, H. D. (1943), 'The organization of business in colonial Philadelphia', *Pennsylvania History*, 10 (3), 157–77.

Berg, M. (1985), *The Age of Manufactures: Industry, Innovation and Work in Britain, 1700–1820* (Oxford: Basil Blackwell).

————(1991), 'Commerce and creativity in eighteenth century Birmingham', pp. 173–201 in M. Berg (ed.), *Markets and Manufactures in Early Industrial Europe* (London: Routledge).

Bernanke, B. S., and Gertler, N. (1989), 'Agency costs, net worth, and business fluctuations', *American Economic Review*, 79, 14–31.

Bernhagen, P., and Bräuninger, Y. (2005), 'Structural power and public policy: a signalling model of business lobbying in democratic capitalism', *Political Studies Journal*, 53 (1), 43–64.

Berry, B. J. L. (1967), *Geography of Market Centres and Retail Distribution* (Englewood Cliffs, NJ: Prentice Hall).

Berry, H. (2004), 'Creating polite space: the organisation and social function of the Newcastle Assembly Rooms', chapter 8 in H. Berry and J. Gregory (eds.), *Creating and Consuming Culture in North-East England, 1660–1830* (Aldershot: Ashgate).

Berry, J. (1977), *Lobbying for the People: The Political Behaviour of Public Interest Groups* (Princeton: Princeton University Press).

Bettsworth, M. (1999), *Federation of Small Businesses, 1974–1999: 25th Anniversary Commemorative History* (Lytham St Annes: National Federation of Self-Employed and Small Business).

Bhattacharya, C. B. (1998), 'When customers are members: customer retention in paid membership contexts', *Journal of the Academy of Sciences*, 26 (1), 31–44.

Bird, J. H. (1963), *Major Seaports of the United Kingdom* (London: Hutchinson).

Bishop, J. B. (1918), *A Chronicle of One Hundred and Fifty Years: The Chamber of Commerce of the State of New York* (New York: Charles Scribner) (BL mic.A.1677a).

Black, E. C. (1963), *Association: British Extraparliamentary Political Organisation, 1769–1793* (Oxford: Oxford University Press).

Black, J. (1994), *British Foreign Policy in an Age of Revolution, 1783–1793* (Cambridge: Cambridge University Press).

Blank, S. (1973), *Industry and Government in Britain: The Federation of British Industries in Politics, 1945–65* (Farnborough: Saxon House).

Boadle, D. G. (1977), 'The formation of the Foreign Office Economic Relations Section, 1930–1937', *Historical Journal*, 20 (4), 919–36.

Bois, F. de L. (1970), *A Constitutional History of Jersey* (Jersey: States' Greffe).

Boleat, M. (2000), *Models of Trade Association Co-operation* (London: Trade Association Forum).

——(2003), *Managing Trade Associations* (London: Trade Association Forum).

Bolton Report (1971), *Small Firms: Report of the Committee of Inquiry*, Cmnd. 4811 (London: HMSO).

Boney, K. (1957), *Liverpool Porcelain of the Eighteenth Century and its Makers* (London: Portman Press).

Bordo, M. D., Dueker, M. J., and Wheelock, D. C. (2003), 'Aggregate price shocks and financial stability: the United Kingdom 1796–1999', *Explorations in Economic History*, 40, 143–69.

Boroff, K. E., and Lewin, D. (1997), 'Exit, voice and intent to exit a union firm: a conceptual and empirical analysis', *Industrial and Labor Relations Review*, 51, 50–62.

Borsay, P. (1989), *The English Urban Renaissance: Culture and Society in the Provincial Town 1660–1770* (Oxford: Clarendon Press).

Boschma, R. A. (2009), *Evolutionary Economic Geography and its Implications for Regional Innovation Policy* (Paris: OECD).

Boswell, J. S. (1980), 'Social cooperation in economic systems: a business history approach', *Review of Social Economy*, 38, 155–78.

Bowden, W. (1919–20), 'The English manufacturers and the commercial Treaty of 1786 with France', *American Historical Review*, 25, 18–35.

——(1930), *The Industrial History of the United States* (New York: Adelphi).

——(1965), *Industrial Society in England towards the End of the Eighteenth Century* (London: Frank Cass).

Bowen, H. V. (1996), *Elites, Enterprise and the Making of the British Overseas Empire 1688–1775* (London: Macmillan).

——(2006), *The Business of Empire: The East India Company and Imperial Britain 1756–1833* (Cambridge: Cambridge University Press).

Bowman, J. R. (1989), *Capitalist Collective Action: Competition, Cooperation and Conflict in the Coal Industry* (Cambridge: Cambridge University Press).

Bradley, J. E. (1986), *Popular Politics and the American Revolution in England: Petitions, the Crown, and Public Opinion* (Macon, Ga.: Mercer University Press).

——(1990), *Religion, Revolution, and English Radicalism: Nonconformity in Eighteenth Century Politics and Society* (Cambridge: Cambridge University Press).

Bratton, W. (2000), 'The geography of local business support organisations in Britain', unpublished PhD thesis, Cambridge University.

——Bennett, R. J., and Robson, P. J. A. (2003), 'Critical mass and economies of scale in the supply of business support organisations', *Journal of Services Marketing*, 17 (7), 730–50.

Braudel, F. (1983), *Civilisation and Capitalism Fifteenth–Eighteenth Century*, ii: *The Wheels of Commerce* (London: Harper & Row).

Brenner, R. (1993), *Merchants and Revolution: Commercial Change, Political Conflict and London's Overseas Traders, 1550–1653* (Cambridge: Cambridge University Press).

Brewer, J. (1976), *Party, Ideology and Popular Politics at the Accession of George III* (Cambridge: Cambridge University Press).

——(1982), 'Commercialization and politics', pp. 197–262, in McKendrick, Brewer, and Plumb (1982).

——(1989), *Sinews of Power: War and the English State, 1688–1783* (London: Unwin Hyman).

——(1997), *The Pleasures of the Imagination: English Culture in the Eighteenth Century* (London: Harper Collins).

Bridenbaugh, C. (1955), *Cities in Revolt: Urban Life in America 1743–1766* (New York: Knopf).

——(1962), *Mitre and Sceptre: Transatlantic Faiths, Ideas, Personalities and Politics, 1689–1775* (New York: Oxford University Press).

Bristow, E. (1975), 'The Liberty and Property Defence League and individualism', *Historical Journal*, 18, 761–89.

Brooke, R. (1853), *Liverpool as it was during the Last Quarter of the Eighteenth Century 1775–1780* (Liverpool: J. Mawdsley; reprinted City of Liverpool, 2003).

Brown. B. J. H. (1943), *The Tariff Reform Movement in Great Britain, 1881–1895* (New York: Columbia University Press).

Brown, L. (1958), *The Board of Trade and the Free Trade Movement 1830–42* (Oxford: Clarendon Press).

Buchanan, J. M. (1975), 'The Samaritan's dilemma', in E. S. Phelps (ed.), *Altruism, Morality and Economic Theory* (New York: Russell Sage Foundation).

Bueno de Mesquita, B. (1994), 'Political forecasting: an expected utility method', pp. 71–104 in B. Bueno de Mesquita and F. N. N. Stokman (eds.), *European Community Decision Making: Models, Applications, and Comparisons* (New Haven: Yale University Press).

Burns, E. (1926), *The General Strike May 1926: Trades Councils in Action* (London: Labour Research Department).

Burt, R. S. (1980), 'On the functional form of corporate cooption', *Social Science Research*, 9, 146–77.

Butler, G. F. (1942), 'The early organisation and influence of Halifax merchants', *Collections of the Nova Scotia Historical Society*, 25, 1–16.

Butterfield, H. (1949), *George III, Lord North and the People, 1779–80* (London: Bell).

——(1957), *George III and the Historians* (London: Collins).

Cain, P. J., and Hopkins, A. G. (1980), 'The political economy of British expansion overseas, 1750–1914', *Economic History Review*, 33, 463–90.

————(1986), 'Gentlemanly capitalism and British expansion overseas I: the all-colonial system, 1688–1850', *Economic History Review*, 34, 501–25.

————(2002), *British Imperialism 1688–2000*, 2nd edn. (London: Longmans).

Calvert, A. F. (1913), *A History of the Salt Union: A Record of 25 years of Disunion and Depreciation* (London: Effingham Wilson).

Cambers, A., and Wolfe, M. (2004), 'Reading, family religion, and evangelical identity in late Stuart England', *Historical Journal*, 47 (4), 875–96.

Campbell, R. H. (1961), *The Carron Company* (London: Oliver and Boyd).

Cannan, E. (1919), *The Paper Pound of 1797–1821: A Reprint of the Bullion Report* (London: P. S. King).

Casson, M. (1991), *The Economics of Business Culture: Game Theory, Transaction Costs and Economic Performance* (Oxford: Oxford University Press).

——(1997), 'Institutional economics and business history: a way forward', *Business History*, 39 (4), 151–71.

——and Cox, H. (1993) 'International business networks: theory and history', *Business and Economic History*, 22, 42–53.

——and Rose, M. B. (1997), 'Institutions and the evolution of modern business: introduction', *Business History*, 39 (4), 1–8.

Castles, F. G. (1969), 'Business and government: a typology of pressure group activity', *Political Studies*, 17 (2), 160–76.

Caunce, S. A. (1997), 'Complexity, community structure and competitive advantage within the Yorkshire woollen industry, *c.*1700–1850', *Business History*, 39 (4), 26–43.

CCA/ECU (1931), *Report of a Joint Committee on Agricultural Policy, with Special Reference to British Manufacturing Industry and Imperial Cooperation* (London: Central Chamber of Agriculture, and Empire Economic Union).

Chalmers, K. (1811), *Considerations on Commerce, Bullion and Coin ... etc.* (London: J. J. Stockdale).

Chamberlain, J. (1974), 'Provision of public goods as a function of group size', *American Political Science Review*, 68, 707–16.

Champion, T. (2003), 'Testing the differential urbanisation model in Great Britain, 1901–91', *Tijschrift voor economische en sociale Geografie*, 94, 11–22.

Chandler, G. (1964), *Four Centuries of Banking*, 2 vols. (London: Batsford).

Chang, C. F., and Tuckmann, H. P. (1991), 'Financial vulnerability and attrition as measures of nonprofit performance', *Annals of Public and Cooperative Economics*, 62 (4), 655–72.

Chapman, S. (1984), *The Rise of Merchant Banking* (London: George Allen and Unwin).

——(1992), *Merchant Enterprise in Britain: From the Industrial Revolution to World War I* (Cambridge: Cambridge University Press).

Checkland, S. G. (1952), 'Economic attitudes in Liverpool 1793–1807', *Economic History Review*, 5, 58–75.

——(1958), 'American versus West Indian traders in Liverpool 1793–1815', *Journal of Economic History*, 18, 141–60.

——(1964), *The Rise of Industrial Society in England 1815–1885* (London: Longmans).

——(1975), *Scottish Banking: A History 1695–1973* (Glasgow: Collins).

——(1983), *British Public Policy 1776–1939: An Economic, Social and Political Perspective* (Cambridge: Cambridge University Press).

Cherpeau, P. (2010), 'The evolution of Liverpool's Chamber of Commerce and its business community: continuity and change 1850–2010', unpublished MBA thesis, University of Liverpool.

Child, J. (1698), *A New Discourse on Trade* (London: A. Sowle).

Christie, I. R. (1962), *Wilkes, Wyvill and Reform: The Parliamentary Reform Movement in British Politics 1760–1785* (London: Macmillan).

——(1982), *War and Revolutions: Britain 1760–1815* (Cambridge, Mass.: Harvard University Press).

——and Labaree, B. W. (1976), *Empire or Independence 1760–1776: A British–American Dialogue on the Coming of the American Revolution* (New York: W. W. Norton).

Church, R. A., and Chapman, S. D. (1967), 'Gravener Henson and the making of the English working class', pp. 131–61 in E. L. Jones and J. D. Chambers (eds.), *Land, Labour and Population in the Industrial Revolution* (London: Edward Arnold).

Clapham, J. H. (1926), *An Economic History of Modern Britain*, i: *The Early Railway Age 1820–1850* (Cambridge: Cambridge University Press).

——(1932), *An Economic History of Modern Britain*, ii: *Free Trade and Steel 1850–1886* (Cambridge: Cambridge University Press).

——(1944), *The Bank of England: A History*, 2 vols. (Cambridge: Cambridge University Press).

Clark, P. (2000a), *British Clubs and Societies 1580–1800* (Oxford: Clarendon Press).

——(2000b), 'Small towns 1700–1840', pp. 733–73 in P. Clark (ed.), *The Cambridge Urban History of Britain*, ii: *1540–1840* (Cambridge: Cambridge University Press).

Clark, T. (1995), *Managing Consultants: Consultancy as the Management of Impressions* (Buckingham: Open University Press).

Clarke, P. F. (1971), *Lancashire and the New Liberalism* (Cambridge: Cambridge University Press).

——(1972), 'The end of laissez faire and the politics of cotton', *Historical Journal*, 15 (3), 493–512.

Clayton, T. R. (1986), 'Sophistry, security, and socio-political structures in the American Revolution; or why Jamaica did not rebel', *The Historical Journal*, 29 (2), 319–44.

Clinton, A. (1977), *The Trade Union Rank and File: Trades Councils in Britain 1900–1940* (Manchester: Manchester University Press).

Cohen, J., and Rogers, J. (1992), 'Secondary associations and democratic governance', *Politics and Society*, 20, 393–472.

Coleman, J. (1990), *Foundations of Social Theory* (Cambridge, Mass. Belknap and Harvard University Press).

Coleman, W. D. (1988), *Business and Politics: A Study of Collective Action* (Kingston: McGill-Queen's University Press).

Colley, L. (1982), *In Defiance of Oligarchy: The Tory Party 1714–60* (Cambridge: Cambridge University Press).

Collins, J. (2009), *How the Mighty Fail: And Why Some Companies Never Give in* (New York: Harper Collins).

Colquhoun, P. (1802) 'An account of the public services of Patrick Colquhuon Esq., with appendix of testimonies of public service', National Archives HO 42/66 fos. 105–29, 1 September 1802.

Commission on Municipal Corporations (England and Wales) (1835–9), *House of Commons Papers*, xxiii, xxiv, xxv, xxvi (1835); xxv, xxvi, xxvii, xxviii (1837); xxxv (1837–8); xxviii (1839).

Commission on Municipal Corporations (Ireland) (1835), *House of Commons Papers*, xxiv, xxvii, xxviii.

Commission on Municipal Corporations (Scotland) (1835), *House of Commons Papers*, xxii, xxix, xlviii.

Committee on Trusts (1918), *Report*, Parliamentary Papers Cd. 9236 (London: HMSO).

Conquet, A. (1976), *Si les Chambres de Commerce m'étaient contées* (Lyon: Audin-Tixier).

Corfield, P. J. (1982), *The Impact of English Towns, 1700–1800* (Oxford: Oxford University Press).

——(1995), *Power and the Professions in Britain 1700–1850* (London: Routledge).

Countryman, E. (1981), *A People in Revolution: The American Revolution and Political Society in New York 1760–1790* (Baltimore: Johns Hopkins University Press).

Cox, A., and Cox, A. (1983), *Rockingham Pottery and Porcelain 1745–1842* (London: Faber).

Crafts, N. F. R. (1984), 'Patterns of development in nineteenth century Europe', *Oxford Economic Papers*, 36, 438–58.

——(1985), *British Economic Growth during the Industrial Revolution* (Oxford: Oxford University Press).

——(1997), 'Economic history and endogenous growth', pp. 43–78 in D. M. Kreps and K. F. Wallis (eds.), *Advances in Economics and Econometrics: Theory and Applications*, vol. ii (Cambridge: Cambridge University Press).

——(2005), 'Market potential in British regions 1871–1931', *Regional Studies*, 39, 1159–66.

——and Mulatu, A. (2005), 'What explains the location of industry in Britain, 1871–1931?', *Journal of Economic Geography*, 5, 499–518.

Cranfield, G. A. (1962), *The Development of the Provincial Newspaper, 1700–1760* (Oxford: Clarendon Press).

Creighton, D. (1937), *The Empire of the St. Lawrence: A Study in Commerce and Politics* (Toronto: University of Toronto Press).

Crossick, G. (1984), 'Shopkeepers and the state in Britain, 1870–1914', chapter 11, pp. 239–69, in G. Crossick and H. Heinz-Gerhard (eds.), *Shopkeepers and Master Artisans in Nineteenth-Century Europe* (London: Methuen).

Crouch, C. (1983), 'Corporative industrial relations and the welfare state', pp. 139–66, in R. J. Barry-Jones (ed.), *Perspectives on Political Economy* (London: Frances Pinter).

Crowhurst, P. (1977), *The Defence of British Trade, 1689–1815* (Folkestone: Dawson).

Crump, H. J. (1931), *Colonial Admiralty Jurisdiction in the Seventeenth Century*, for the Royal Empire Society (London: Longman Green).

Cullen, L. M. (1968), *Anglo-Irish Trade, 1660–1800* (Manchester: Manchester University Press).

——(1977), 'Merchant communities overseas, the Navigation Acts and Irish and Scottish responses', in Cullen and Smout (1977: 165–76).

——(1983), *Princes and Pirates: The Dublin Chamber of Commerce 1783–1983* (Dublin: Chamber of Commerce).

——and Smout, T. C. (eds.) (1977), *Comparative Aspects of Scottish and Irish Economic and Social History* (Edinburgh: John Donald).

Cunningham, W. (1919), *The Growth of English Industry and Commerce in Modern Times: The Mercantile System* (Cambridge: Cambridge University Press).

Curl, J. S. (2000), *The Honourable The Irish Society and the Plantation of Ulster, 1608–2000* (Chichester: Phillimore).

Curran, J., and Blackburn, R. A. (1994), *Small Firms and Local Networks: The Death of the Local Economy?* (London: Paul Chapman).

Cuthbertson, B. (2000), *Voices of Business: A History of Commerce in Halifax, 1750–2000* (Halifax, Nova Scotia: Metropolitan Halifax Chamber of Commerce).

Dahl, R. (1956), *A Preface to Democratic Theory* (Chicago: Chicago University Press).

Dahrendorf, R. (1995), *LSE: A History of the London School of Economics and Political Science, 1895–1995* (Oxford: Oxford University Press).

Dannreuther, C. (2005), *Collective Memory and the Establishment of the British State: Or how a Nation of Shopkeepers Learnt to Live without a Small Business Sector*, Department of Politics, University of Leeds.

Danson, J. T. (1860), *Chambers of Commerce and the Government*, address to Liverpool Chamber of Commerce, circulated to all chambers, (Liverpool: Geo. M'Corquodale & Co.) (Bodleian; Vet.A7 d.75).

Daunton, M. J. (1977), *Coal Metropolis: Cardiff 1870–1914* (Leicester: Leicester University Press).

——(1995), *Progress and Poverty: An Economic and Social History of Britain 1700–1850* (Oxford: Oxford University Press).

——(1996), 'Middle-Class Voluntarism and the City in Britain and America: Review Essay', *Journal of Urban History*, 22 (2), 253–63.

——(2001), *Trusting Leviathan: The Politics of Taxation in Britain, 1799–1914* (Cambridge: Cambridge University Press).

——(2008), *State and Market in Victorian Britain: War, Welfare and Capitalism* (Wood-bridge: Boydell Press).

Davenport-Hines, R. P. T. (1984), *Dudley Docker: The Life and Times of a Trade Warrior* (Cambridge: Cambridge University Press).

Davies, W. T. (1946), *Trade Associations and Industrial Coordination*, 3rd edn., London Machinery Users' Association (London: Pitman).

Davis, L. E., and Huttenback, R. A. (1984), *Mammon and the Pursuit of Empire: The Political Economy of British Imperialism, 1860–1912* (Cambridge: Cambridge University Press).

Davis, R. (1962), *The Rise of the English Shipping Industry in the Seventeenth and Eighteenth Centuries* (London: National Maritime Museum).

DE (1988), *Employment in the 1990s*, Cm 540 (London: Department of Employment).

de Courcey Ireland, J. (1986), *Ireland and the Irish Maritime History* (Dublin: Glendale Press).

Della Porta, D., and Tarrow, S. (2005), *Transnational Protest and Global Activism* (Lanham, Md.: Rowman and Littlefield).

Dent, R. K. (1973), *Old and New Birmingham: A History of the Town and its People*, reprint (Birmingham: EP Publishing).

De Propris, L. (2005), 'Mapping local production systems in the UK: methodology and application', *Regional Studies*, 39, 197–211.

——and Lazzeretti, L. (2009), 'Measuring the decline of a Marshallian industrial district: the Birmingham jewellery quarter', *Regional Studies*, 43, 1135–54.

Devine, T. M. (1971), 'Transport problems of Glasgow–West Indian merchants during the American War of Independence 1775–83', *Transport History*, 4, 266–304.

——(1975), *The Tobacco Lords: A Study of the Tobacco Merchants of Glasgow and their Trading Activities, c.1740–1790* (Edinburgh: Donald).

——(1977), 'Colonial commerce and the Scottish economy, c.1730–1815', in Cullen and Smout (1977: 177–90).

——(1978), 'An eighteenth century business elite: Glasgow–West India merchants, c.1750–1815', *Scottish Historical Review*, 57, 40–67.

——(2003), *Scotland's Empire, 1600–1815* (London: Penguin Allen Lane).

——(2004), *Scotland's Empire and the Shaping of the Americas 1700–1815* (Washington: Smithsonian Institution).

——and Jackson, G. (eds.) (1995), *Glasgow*, i: *Beginnings to 1830* (Manchester: Manchester University Press).

Devlin Commission (1972), *Report of the Commission of Inquiry into Industrial and Commercial Representation*, ABCC / CBI (London: Confederation of British Industry).

De Vries, J. (1984), *European Urbanisation 1500–1800* (London: Methuen).

Dickson, T. (ed.) (1980), *Scottish Capitalism: Class, State and Nation from before the Union to the Present* (London: Lawrence and Wishart).

Dietz, V. E. (1991), 'Before the age of capital: manufacturing interests and the British state 1780–1800', unpublished PhD thesis, Princeton University.

DiMaggio, P. J., and Powell, W. W. (1990), *The New Institutionalism in Organizational Analysis* (Chicago: University of Chicago Press).

Ditchfield, G. M. (1988), 'The subscription issue in British parliamentary politics, 1772–79', *Parliamentary History*, 7 (1), 45–80.

Dixit, A. K., and Stiglitz, J. E. (1977), 'Monopolistic competition and optimum product diversity', *American Economic Review*, 67, 297–308.

Doerflinger, T. M. (1986), *A Vigorous Spirit: Merchants and Economic Development in Revolutionary Philadelphia* (Chapel Hill, NC: North Carolina University Press).

Dolman, F. (1895), 'Mr. Chamberlain's municipal career', *Fortnightly Review*, 57 (342), 904–12.

Dowding, K. (1994), 'Rational mobilisation', in P. Dunleavy and J. Stanyer (eds.), *Contemporary Political Studies*, vol. i (Belfast: Political Studies Association).

Downer, M. (2004), *Nelson's Purse* (London: Bantam Press).

Dunleavy, P. (1991), *Democracy, Bureaucracy and Public Choice: Economic Expectations in Political Science* (London: Harvester-Wheatsheaf).

Dunwoody, R. B. (1935), *Chambers of Commerce: A Brief History* (London: ABCC) (LMA, MS 17585).

Dupree, M. (1987), *Lancashire and Whitehall: The Diary of Raymond Streat*, 2 vols. (Manchester: Manchester University Press).

Eckstein, H. (1960), *Pressure Group Politics: The Case of the British Medical Association* (London: Allen and Unwin).

Edwards, P., Gilman, M., Ram, M., and Arrowsmith, J. (2002), 'Public policy, the performance of firms and the missing "middle way"', *Policy Studies*, 23, 5–20.

Ehrman, J. (1962), *The British Government and Commercial Negotiation with Europe 1783–1793* (Cambridge: Cambridge University Press).

——(1969), *The Younger Pitt: The Years of Acclaim* (London: Constable).

Ellis, M. (2004), *The Coffee House: A Cultural History* (London: Weidenfeld and Nicolson).

Ernle, Lord (1936), *English Farming, Past and Present*, 5th edn. (London: Frank Cass).

Evans, P. (1996), *Farming for Ever* (Whitbourne: Sapley Press).

Everard, R. (1850), *The Effect of Free Trade on the Various Classes of Society: A Letter to the Members of the Spalding Protection Society* (Spalding: Simpkin and Marshall) (BL 8245. b.29).

Falkus, M. (1977), 'The development of municipal trading in the nineteenth century', *Business History*, 19 (2), 134–61.

Fallon, G., and Brown, R. B. (2000), 'Does Britain Need Public Law Chambers of Commerce?', *European Business Review*, 12 (1), 19–27.

Farrer, K. E. (ed.) (1906), *Correspondence of Josiah Wedgwood, 1781–94* (London: Women's Printing Society).

Feldstein, M. (1980), 'A contribution to the theory of tax expenditures: the case of charitable giving', pp. 99–122 in H. J. Aaron and M. Boskin (eds.), *The Economics of Taxation* (Washington: Brookings Institution).

Field, R. (1991), 'The business role in local economic regeneration: the Sheffield story', pp. 49–64 in R. J. Bennett, G. Krebs, and H. Zimmermann (eds.), *Local Economic Development in Britain and Germany* (London: Anglo-German Foundation).

Finer, S. E. (1955), 'The political power of private capital, Parts 1 and 2', *Sociological Review*, NS 3, 279–94; NS 4, 5–29.

——(1966), *Anonymous Empire: A Study of the Lobby in Great Britain*, 2nd edn. (London: Pall Mall Press).

Finlayson, G. B. A. M. (1963), 'The Municipal Corporation Commission and Reports, 1833–35', *Historical Research*, 36, 36–52.

Fischer, F. (2003), *Reframing Public Policy: Discursive Politics and Deliberative Practices* (Oxford: Oxford University Press).

Flick, A. C. (1901), *Loyalism in New York during the American Revolution* (New York: Columbia University Press).

Forster, N. (1983), *Chambers of Commerce: A Comparative Study of their Role in the UK and in Other EEC Countries* (London: IAL Publications).

Fowler, H. (1900), 'Municipal finance and municipal enterprise', *Journal of the Royal Statistical Society*, 63 (3), 383–407.

Fox-Bourne, H. R. (1886), *English Merchants* (London: Chatto and Windus).

Fraser, P. (1956), *The Intelligence of the Secretaries of State and their Monopoly of Licensed News 1660–1688* (Cambridge: Cambridge University Press).

Fraser, T. C. (1967), 'Economic Development Committees: a new dimension in government industry relations', *Journal of Management Studies*, 4, 154–67.

French, C. J. (1992), ' "Crowded with traders and a great commerce": London's dominance of English overseas trade 1700–1775', *London Journal*, 17, 27–35.

Friedman, L. M. (1947), 'The first chamber of commerce in the United States', *Bulletin of the Business History Society*, 21 (5), 137–43.

Fujita, M., and Krugman, P. (2004), 'The new economic geography: past, present and future', *Papers in Regional Science*, 83, 139–64.

Galaskiewicz, J. (1979), *Exchange Networks and Community Politics* (London: Sage).

Gamble, A. (2002), 'Policy agendas in a multi-level polity', in P. Dunleavy et al. (eds.), *Developments in British Politics* (Basingstoke: Palgrave).

Garrard, J. (1983), *Leadership and Power in Victorian Industrial Cities 1830–80* (Manchester: Manchester University Press).

Gash, N. (1977), *Politics in the Age of Peel: A Study in the Technique of Parliamentary Representation 1830–1850* (Aldershot: Harvester Press).

Gatty, C. T. (1882), *The Mayer Collection: The Liverpool Potteries* (Liverpool: Liverpool Art Club).

Gayer, A. D., Rostow, W. W., and Schwartz, A. J. (1953), *The Growth and Fluctuation of the British Economy, 1790–1850* (Oxford: Clarendon Press).

Gibbons, H. J. (1901), 'The opposition to municipal socialism in England', *Journal of Political Economy*, 9 (2), 243–59.

Gilbart, J. W. (1836), *The History of Banking in Ireland* (London: Longmans).

Glaeser, E. L., Scheinkman, J. A., and Schleifer, A. (1995), 'Economic growth in a cross section of cities', *Journal of Monetary Economics*, 36, 117–43.

Godwin, R. K. (1988), *One Billion Dollars of Influence* (Chatham, NJ: Chatham House).

Gollin, A. (1965), *Balfour's Burden: Arthur Balfour and Imperial Preference* (London: Anthony Blond).

Goodbody Associates (1996), *Study of Business Representative Associations in Ireland* (Dublin: Goodbody Economic Consultants Ltd.).

Goodwin, A. (1979), *The Friends of Liberty: The English Democratic Movement in the Age of the French Revolution* (London: Hutchinson).

Goodwin, H. J. (1982), 'The politics of the Manchester Chamber of Commerce: 1921–51', unpublished PhD thesis, University of Manchester.

Grant, W. (1983), *Chambers of Commerce in the UK System of Business Interest Representation*, Working Paper 32, Department of Politics, University of Warwick.

——(ed.) (1987), 'Introduction', in *Business Interests, Organizational Development and Private Interest Government* (Berlin: Walter de Gruyter).

——(1991), 'Continuity and change in British business associations', pp. 23–46 in W. Grant, J. Nekkers, and F. van Waarden (eds.), *Organising Business for War: Corporatist Economic Organisation during the Second World War* (Oxford: Berg).

——(1993), *Business and Politics in Britain*, 2nd edn. (London: Macmillan).

——(2000), *Pressure Groups and British Politics* (London: Macmillan).

——(2001), 'From "insider" politics to direct action', *Parliamentary Affairs*, 54 (2), 337–48.

——and Marsh, D. (1973), 'Government and industry: a new pattern of representation?', *Public Administration Bulletin*, 13, 10–19.

———(1977), *The Confederation of British Industry* (London: Hodder and Stoughton).

Greaves, J. M. (2008), 'Continuity or change in business representation? An assessment of the Heseltine initiatives of the 1990s in Britain', *Environment and Planning: Government and Policy C*, 26, 998–1015.

Greenwood, J. (1997), *Representing Interests in the European Union* (London: Macmillan).

——Grote, J., and Ronit, K. (eds.) (1992), *Organised Interests and the European Community* (London: Sage).

Grindon, L. H. (1877), *Manchester Banks and Bankers* (Manchester: Palmer and How).

Gross, C. (1890), *Gild Merchant: A Contribution to Municipal History* (Oxford: Clarendon Press).

Grove, J. W. (1962), *Government and Industry in Britain* (London: Longmans).

Gruen, T. W., Summers, J. O., and Acito, F. (2000), 'Relationship marketing activities, commitment and membership behaviours in professional associations', *Journal of Marketing*, 64, 34–49.

Gulvin, C. (1973), *Tweedmakers: A History of the Scottish Fancy Woollen Industry* (Newton Abbot: David and Charles).

Gurney, J. (1791), *The Whole Proceedings on the Trial of an Action Brought by a Merchant Thomas Walker against William Roberts, Barrister for Libel* (Manchester: Charles Wheeler) (Cambridge University Library Ddd.25.217/1).

Guttridge, G. H. (ed.) (1934), *The American Correspondence of a Bristol Merchant 1766–1776: Letters of Richard Champion* (Berkeley and Los Angeles: California University Press).

Gyford, J. (1985), *The Politics of Local Socialism* (London: Allen and Unwin).

Haggerty, J., and Haggerty, S. (2010), 'Visual analytics of an eighteenth-century business network', *Enterprise and Society*, 11 (1), 1–25.

Haggerty, S. (2002), 'The structure of the trading community in Liverpool 1760–1810', *Transactions of the Historic Society of Lancashire and Cheshire*, 151, 97–125.

——(2006), *The British Atlantic Trading Community 1760–1810: Men, Women, and the Distribution of Goods* (Boston: Brill).

Hajer, M., and Wagenaar, H. (2003), *Deliberative Policy Analysis: Understanding Governance in the Network Society* (Cambridge: Cambridge University Press).

Hall, F. G. (1949), *History of the Bank of Ireland* (Dublin: Hodges, Figgis).

Hall, P. (1998), *Cities in Civilisation: Culture, Innovation and Urban Order* (London: Weidenfeld and Nicolson).

Hamilton, D. J. (2005), *Scotland, the Caribbean and the Atlantic world, 1750–1820* (Manchester: Manchester University Press).

Hamilton, H. (1967), *The English Brass and Copper Industries to 1800*, 2nd edn. (London: Frank Cass).

Hannah, L. (1983), *The Rise of the Corporate Economy*, 2nd edn. (London: Methuen).

Hansen, J. M. (1985), 'The political economy of group membership', *American Political Science Review*, 79, 79–96.

Hansmann, H. B. (1980), 'The role of the nonprofit enterprise', *Yale Law Journal*, 89 (5), 835–98.

Hardin, R. (1981), *Collective Action* (London: Johns Hopkins University Press).

Harlow, V. T. (1952), *The Founding of the Second British Empire 1763–1793* (London: Longmans).

Harrington, V. D. (1935), *The New York Merchant on the Eve of the Revolution* (New York: Columbia University Studies in History and Economics, No. 404, Faculty of Political Science).

Harris, B. (1998), *Politics and the Rise of the Press: Britain and France, 1620–1800* (London: Routledge).

Harris, J. R. (1997), *Industrial Espionage and Technology Transfer: Britain and France in the Eighteenth Century* (Aldershot: Ashgate).

Harris, M. (1987), *London Newspapers in the Age of Walpole: A Study of the Origins of the Modern English Press* (London: Associated University Presses).

——and Lee, A. (eds.) (1986), *The Press in English Society from the Seventeenth to Nineteenth Centuries* (London: Associated University Presses).

Harris, R. (1997), 'Political economy, interest groups, legal institutions, and the repeal of the Bubble Act in 1825', *Economic History Review*, 50, 675–96.

Hay, R. (1977), 'Employers and social policy in Britain: the evolution of welfare legislation, 1905–14', *Social History*, 4, 435–55.

Heaton, H. (1965), *The Yorkshire Woollen and Worsted Industries: From the Earliest Times up to the Industrial Revolution* (Oxford: Clarendon Press).

Helm, E. (1897) *Chapters in the History of the Manchester Chamber of Commerce* (London: Simpkin, Marshall, Hamilton, Kent & Co.).

Henderson, W. O. (1933a), 'The American Chamber of Commerce for the Port of Liverpool, 1801–1908', *Transactions of the Historic Society of Lancashire and Cheshire*, 85, 1–61.

——(1933b), 'The Liverpool Office in London', *Economica*, 18, 473–9.

Hennock, E. P. (1963), 'Finance and politics in urban local government in England, 1825–1900', *Historical Journal*, 6, 212–25.

——(1973), *Fit and Proper Persons: Ideal and Reality in Nineteenth Century Urban Government* (London: Edward Arnold).

——(1982), 'Central/local government relations in England: an outline 1800–1950', *Urban History Yearbook*, 38–49.

Heron, A. (1903), *The Rise and Progress of the Company of Merchants of the City of Edinburgh, 1681–1902* (Edinburgh: T. & T. Clark).

Herring, E. P. (1928), 'Chambres de Commerce: their legal status and political significance', *American Political Science Review*, 25 (3), 689–99.

Heseltine, M. (1987), *Where There's a Will* (London: Hutchinson).

——(1989), *The Challenge of Europe: Can Britain Win?* (London: Weidenfeld and Nicolson).

——(1992a), 'Forging partnerships for World Class Support', *TEC Director*, 15 Sept./Oct., 8–9.

——(1992b), *Text of Speech to TECs Annual Conference*, 10 July 1992 (London: DTI).

——(1993), *Speech on Trade Associations*, at CBI, 17 June 1993 (London: DTI).

——(2000), *Life in the Jungle: My Autobiography* (London: Hodder and Stoughton).

Hilton, A. J. B. (1977), *Corn, Cash and Commerce: The Economic Policies of the Tory Government 1815–1830* (Oxford: Oxford University Press).

Hilton, B. (1988), *The Age of Atonement: The Influence of Evangelicalism on Social and Economic Thought 1785–1865* (Oxford: Oxford University Press).

——(2006), *A Mad, Bad and Dangerous People? England 1783–1846* (Oxford: Clarendon Press).

Hilton, J. (1917), *Report to Committee on Trusts*, Cd. 9236 (London: HMSO).

Hirschman, A. O. (1970), *Exit, Voice and Loyalty* (Cambridge, Mass.: Harvard University Press).

——(1982), *Shifting Involvements* (Oxford: Martin Robertson).

HM Government (1995), *Competitiveness: Forging Ahead*, Cm. 2867 (London: HMSO).

Hohenberg, P., and Lees, L. (1985), *The Making of Urban Europe 1000–1950* (Cambridge, Mass.: Harvard University Press).

Homer, F. X. (1971), 'Foreign trade and foreign policy: the British Department of Overseas Trade, 1916–1922', unpublished PhD thesis, University of Virginia.

Hoppit, J. (1987), *Risk and Failure in English Business, 1700–1800* (Cambridge: Cambridge University Press).

——(ed.) (2003), *Parliaments, Nations and Identities in Britain and Ireland, 1660–1850* (Manchester: Manchester University Press).

Horn, D. B. (1961), *The British Diplomatic Service 1689–1789* (Oxford: Clarendon Press).

Horn, N., and Kocka, J. (1979), *Law and the Formation of the Big Enterprises in the Nineteenth and Early Twentieth Centuries* (Göttingen: Vandenhoeck and Ruprecht).

Howe, A. (1997), *Free Trade and Liberal England 1846–1946* (Oxford: Clarendon Press).

Hudson, P. (1986), *The Genesis of Industrial Capital: A Study of the West Riding Wool Textile Industry, c.1750–1850* (Cambridge: Cambridge University Press).

——(ed.) (1989), *Regions and Industries: A Perspective on the Industrial Revolution in Britain* (Cambridge: Cambridge University Press).

Huggins, R. (2000), *The Business of Networks: Inter-firm Interactions, Institutional Policy and the TEC Experiment* (Aldershot: Ashgate).

Hughes, J. (1906), *Liverpool Banks and Bankers 1760–1837* (Liverpool: Henry Young).

Ilersic, A. R., and Liddle, P. F. B. (1960), *Parliament of Commerce: The Story of the Association of British Chambers of Commerce 1860–1960* (London: ABCC).

Innes, J. (1998), 'The Local Acts of a National Parliament: Parliament's Role in Sanctioning Local Action in Eighteenth-Century Britain', *Parliamentary History*, 17, 23–47.

——(2003), '"Reform" in English public life: the fortunes of a word', pp. 71–97 in A. Burns and J. Innes (eds.), *Rethinking the Age of Reform: Britain 1780–1850* (Cambridge: Cambridge University Press).

——and Burns, A. (2003), 'Introduction', pp. 1–70 in A. Burns and J. Innes (eds.), *Rethinking the Age of Reform: Britain 1780–1850* (Cambridge: Cambridge University Press).

——and Rogers, N. (2000), 'Politics and government 1700–1840', pp. 529–74 in P. Clark (ed.), *The Cambridge Urban History of Britain*, ii: *1540–1840* (Cambridge: Cambridge University Press).

Irish Society (1842), *A Concise View of the Origin, Constitution and Procedures of the . . . Irish Society* (London: Bleadon for Irish Society) (LMA: PD/154/22: CLA/049/AD/14/008).

Jackson, G. (2000), 'Ports 1700–1840', pp. 705–31 in P. Clark (ed.), *The Cambridge Urban History of Britain*, ii: *1540–1840* (Cambridge: Cambridge University Press).

Jackson, I. (1971), *The Provincial Press and the Community* (Manchester: Manchester University Press).

Jackson, J. N. (1950), 'Regional functions', pp. 331–4 in M. J. Wise (ed.), *Birmingham in its Regional Setting: A Scientific Survey* (Birmingham: British Association).

Jacobs, J. (1969), *The Economy of Cities* (New York: Random House).

——(1984), *Cities and the Wealth of Nations* (New York: Random House).

——(1992), *Systems of Survival* (New York: Random House).

James, E. (1998), 'Commercialism among nonprofits: objectives, opportunities, and constraints', pp. 271–85 in B. Weisbrod (ed.), *To Profit or Not to Profit: The Commercial Transformation of the Nonprofit Sector* (Cambridge: Cambridge University Press).

James, F. G. (1973), *Ireland in the Empire 1688–1770* (Cambridge, Mass.: Harvard University Press).

Jameson, J. F. (1926), *The American Revolution Considered as a Social Movement* (Princeton: Princeton University Press).

Jamieson, A. G. (ed.) (1986), *A People of the Sea: The Maritime History of the Channel Islands* (London: Methuen).

Jeffcock, W. P. (1937), *Agricultural Politics 1915–1935: Being a History of the Central Chamber of Agriculture during that Period* (Ipswich: Harrison).

Jennings, I. (1962), *Party Politics*, iii: *The Stuff of Politics* (Cambridge: Cambridge University Press).

Jensen, A. (1963), *The Maritime Commerce of Colonial Philadelphia* (Madison: State Historical Society of Wisconsin).

Jerrold, B. (1874), Biographical sketch of Thomas Walker, *The Original Magazine*, preface.

Johnson, E. A. J. (1937), *Predecessors of Adam Smith: The Growth of British Economic Thought* (London: P. S. King).

Johnson, P. B. (1968), *Land Fit for Heroes: The Planning of British Reconstruction, 1916–1919* (Chicago: University of Chicago Press).

Jones, C. A. (1987), *International Business in the Nineteenth Century* (Brighton: Wheatsheaf).

Jones, D. W. (1988), *War and Economy in the Age of William III and Marlborough* (Oxford: Basil Blackwell).

Jones, G. (2000), *Merchants to Multinationals: British Trading Companies in the Nineteenth and Twentieth Centuries* (Oxford: Oxford University Press).

Jones, G. M. (1916), *Ports of the United States: Report on Terminal Facilities, Commerce, Port Charges and Administration at 68 Selected Ports* (Washington: US Department of Commerce, Bureau of Foreign and Domestic Commerce).

Jones, L. J. (1983), 'Public pursuit of private profit? Liberal businessmen and municipal politics in Birmingham, 1865–1900', *Business History*, 25 (3), 240–59.

Jones, P. (2003), 'Public choice in political markets: the absence of quid pro quo', *European Journal of Political Research*, 42 (1), 77–93.

——(2004), 'All for one and one for all: transactions cost and collective action', *Political Studies Journal*, 52 (3), 450–68.

Jones, S. R. H. (1997), 'Transactions costs and the theory of the firm: the scope and limitations of the new institutional approach', *Business History*, 39 (4), 9–25.

Jordan, G. (1993), *Interest Group Activity and Membership: Survey Instrument*, SN3207, <www.data-archive.ac.uk>.

——and Halpin, D. (2003), 'Cultivating small business influence in the UK: the Federation of Small Business: journey from outsider to insider', *Journal of Public Affairs*, 3 (4), 313–25.

————(2004), 'Olson triumphant? Recruitment strategies and the growth of a small business organisation', *Political Studies*, 52 (2), 431–49.

——and Maloney, W. (1997), *The Protest Business* (Manchester: Manchester University Press).

——and Richardson. J. (1987), *Government and Pressure Groups in Britain* (Oxford: Clarendon Press).

Kahnemann, D., and Tversky, A. (1979), 'Prospect theory: an analysis of decisions under risk', *Econometrica*, 47, 263–91.

Kammen, M. G. (1968), *A Rope of Sand: The Colonial Agents, British Politics, and the American Revolution* (Ithaca, NY: Cornell University Press).

——(1970), *Empire and Interest: The American Colonies and the Politics of Mercantilism* (Philadelphia: Lippincott).

Kay, J., and King, M. A. (2006), *The British Tax System*, 5th edn. (London: Allen and Unwin).

Keens, T. (1919–20), *Chambers of Commerce Register*, vols. i and ii (Derby: Bemrose Publicity Co.) (Bodleian, Dir., 232318 d.55).

Keith-Lucas B. (1977), *English Local Government in the Nineteenth and Twentieth Centuries* (London: Historical Association).

Kellett, J. R. (1968), *The Impact of the Railways on Victorian Cities* (London: Routledge).

——(1978), 'Municipal socialism, enterprise and trading in the Victorian city', *Urban History Yearbook*, 36–45.

Kellock, K. A. (1974), 'London merchants and the pre-1776 American debts', *Guildhall Studies in London History*, 1 (3), 109–49.

Kelly, I. (1995), 'Leeds Chamber of Commerce: roles, strategy and influence 1990–95', unpublished PhD thesis, University of Leeds.

Kemp, B. (1953), 'Crewe's Act, 1782', *English Historical Review*, 68, 258–63.

Kerr, W. B. (1932), 'The merchants of Nova Scotia and the American Revolution', *Canadian Historical Review*, 13, 20–36.

King, D. C., and Walker, J. L. (1992), 'The provision of benefits by interest groups in the United States', *Journal of Politics*, 54, 394–426.

King, R., and Nugent, N. (eds.) (1979), *Respectable Rebels* (London: Hodder & Stoughton).

Klinge, D. S. (1979) 'Edmund Burke, economical reform, and the Board of Trade, 1777–1780', *Journal of Modern History*, 51, D1185–D1200.

Knight, F. (1957), *The Strange Case of Thomas Walker: Ten Years in the Life of a Manchester Radical* (London: Lawrence and Wishart).

Knoke, D. (1983), 'Organisation, sponsorship and influence representation of social influence associations', *Social Forces*, 61, 1065–87.

Knowles, A. R. (1949), *Memorandum on the Chamber of Commerce Organisation* (London: ABCC, Association of Chamber Secretaries) (LMA, MS 17586/1).

——(1952), *Structure, Role and Importance of Chambers of Commerce: The Chamber of Commerce under Private Law, Chambers of Commerce in the UK* (London: ABCC, Association of Chamber Secretaries) (LMA, MS 17586/2).

Kreps, D. (1999), 'Corporate culture and economic theory', in J. Alt and L. Schepsle (eds.), *Perspectives in Positive Economic Theory* (Cambridge: Cambridge University Press).

Labaree, B. (1963), *Patriots and Partisans: The Merchants of Newberryport, 1764–1826* (Cambridge, Mass.: Harvard University Press).

Lambert, R. S. (1988), *South Carolina Loyalists in the American Revolution* (Charleston, SC: South Carolina University Press).

Lammey, D. (1988), 'The growth of the "patriot opposition" in Ireland during the 1790s', *Parliamentary History*, 7 (2), 257–81.

Lamoreaux, N. R. (1985), *The Great Merger Movement in American Business, 1895–1904* (Cambridge: Cambridge University Press).

Lane, C. (1997), 'Trade associations and inter-firm relations in Britain and Germany', in Bennett, Krebs, and Zimmermann (1997: 23–32).

Langford, P. (1973), *The First Rockingham Administration 1765–66* (Oxford: Oxford University Press).

——(1975), *The Excise Tax Crisis: Society and Politics in the Age of Walpole* (Oxford: Clarendon Press).

——(1980), 'Old Whigs, Old Tories, and the American Revolution', *Journal of Imperial and Commonwealth History*, 8 (2), 106–30.

——(1986a), 'The role of the commercial lobby and economic pressures', pp. 89–118 in W. H. Conser, R. M. McCarthy, D. Toscano, and G. Sharp (eds.), *Resistance, Political Conflict and the American Struggle for Independence 1765–1775* (Boulder, Colo.: Reinner).

——(1986b), 'The British business community and the later non-importation movements 1768–1776', pp. 278–324, in W. H. Conser, R. M. McCarthy, D. Toscano, and G. Sharp (eds.), *Resistance, Political Conflict and the American Struggle for Independence 1765–1775* (Boulder, Colo.: Reinner).

——(1989), *A Polite and Commercial People: England 1727–1783* (Oxford: Clarendon Press).

——(1991), *Public Life and the Propertied Englishman 1689–1798* (Oxford: Clarendon Press).

——(2002), 'The uses of eighteenth-century politeness', *Transactions, Royal Historical Society*, 12, 311–31.

Langlois, R. N., and Robertson, P. L. (1995), *Firms, Markets and Economic Change: A Dynamic Theory of Business Institutions* (London: Routledge).

Langton, J. (1983), 'Liverpool and its hinterland in the late eighteenth century', pp. 1–25 in B. L. Anderson and P. J. M. Stoney (eds.), *Commerce, Industry and Transport: Studies in Economic Change on Merseyside* (Liverpool: Liverpool University Press).

——(1984), 'The industrial revolution and the regional geography of England', *Transactions, Institute of British Geographers*, 9, 145–67.

——(2000), 'Urban growth and economic change: from the late seventeenth century to 1841', pp. 453–90 in P. Clark (ed.), *The Cambridge Urban History of Britain*, ii: *1540–1840* (Cambridge: Cambridge University Press).

Lanzalaco, L. (1992), 'Coping with heterogeneity: peak organisations of business within and across Western European nations', in Greenwood, Grote, and Ronit (1992: 173–92).

Laprade, W. T. (1930), 'The Stamp Act in British politics', *American Historical Review*, 35, 735–57.

Latimer, J. (1903), *The History of the Society of Merchant Venturers of the City of Bristol* (Bristol: J. W. Arrowsmith).

Laumann, E. O., and Knoke, D. (1987), *The Organizational State: Social Change in National Policy Domains* (Madison: Wisconsin University Press).

——and Pappi, F. U. (1976), *Networks of Collective Action: A Perspective on Community Influence Systems* (New York: Academic Press).

Law, C. M. (1967), 'The growth of urban population in England and Wales, 1801–1911', *Transactions, Institute of British Geographers*, 41, 125–43.

Lawson-Tancred, M. (1960), 'The Anti-League and the Corn Law crisis of 1846', *The Historical Journal*, 3, 162–83.

Lee, C. H. (1971), *Regional Economic Growth in the United Kingdom since the 1880s* (London: McGraw-Hill).

——(1981), 'Regional growth and structural change in Victorian Britain', *Economic History Review*, 34, 438–52.

Lees, R. M. (1939), 'Parliament and the proposal for a Council of Trade, 1695–6', *English Historical Review*, 54, 38–66.

Lefevre, C. (1977), *Les Chambres de Commerce en France* (Paris: Éditions Sirey).

Le Grand, J. (1991), 'The theory of government failure', *British Journal of Political Science*, 21, 423–42.

Leicester TPS (1950), *Leicester Trade Protection Society 1850–1950: Centenary History* (Leicester: Leicester Record Office, L381).

Lemisch, J. (1968), 'Jack tar in the streets: merchant seamen in the politics of revolutionary America', *William and Mary Quarterly*, 25, 371–407.

Levi, L. (1849), *Chambers and Tribunal of Commerce and Proposed General Chamber of Commerce in Liverpool* (London: Simpkin, Marshall).

——(1855), *The Law of Nature and Nations as Affected by Divine Law* (London: private).

——(1870), 'On joint stock companies', *Journal of the Royal Statistical Society*, 33, 1–41.

——(1872), *History of British Commerce: And of the Economic Progress of the British Nation, 1763–1870* (London: John Murray).

——(1888), *The Story of my Life: The First Ten Years of my Residence in England, 1845–1855* (London: private).

Lillywhite, B. (1963), *London Coffee Houses: A Reference Book of Coffee Houses of the Seventeenth, Eighteenth and Nineteenth Centuries* (London: George Allen and Unwin).

Lindberg, L. N., Campbell, J. L., and Hollingsworth, J. R. (1991), 'Economic governance and the analysis of structural change in the American economy', in J. L. Campbell, J. R. Hollingsworth, and L. N. Lindberg (eds.), *Governance of the American Economy* (Cambridge: Cambridge University Press).

Lingelbach, A. L. (1938), 'William Huskisson as President of the Board of Trade', *American Historical Review*, 43 (4), 759–74.

Lipman, V. D. (1949), *Local Government Areas 1834–1945* (Oxford: Basil Blackwell).

Little, B. D. G. (1954), *The City and County of Bristol: A Study of Atlantic Civilisation* (Birmingham: T. Werner Laurie).

Liverpool Chamber of Commerce (1852), *Report of Special Committee on Mercantile Law Reform and Tribunals of Commerce*, read and adopted at Special Council Meeting, 6 Sept. 1852 (London: Effingham Wilson) (Cambridge UL Bbb.23.16).

Llewellyn-Smith, H. (1928), *The Board of Trade* (London: Putnam).

Lloyd-Jones, R., and Lewis, M. J. (1988), *Manchester and the Age of the Factory: The Business Structure of Cottonopolis in the Industrial Revolution* (London: Croom Helm).

Lurie, J. (1972), 'Private associations, internal regulation and progressivism: the Chicago Board of Trade, 1880–1923, as a case study', *American Journal of Legal History*, 16, 215–38.

Lyne, F. (1876), *Tribunals of Commerce and Reconcilement Courts: A Letter to the Rt. Hon. the Lord Mayor of London* (London: Edward Stanford).

——(1882), *The New City of London Chamber of Commerce: Qui Bono?* (London: private).

Lyons, B., and Mehta, J. (1997), 'Contracts, opportunism, and trust', *Cambridge Journal of Economics*, 21, 239–57.

Lyssons, K. (1988), *A Passport to Employment: A History of the London Chamber of Commerce and Industry Education Scheme 1887–1987* (London: Pitman).

McAdam, D., Tarrow, S., and Tilly, C. (2001), *Dynamics of Contention* (Cambridge: Cambridge University Press).

McCarthy, R. M. (1986), 'Resistance politics and the growth of parallel governance in America, 1765–1775', pp. 472–532 in W. H. Conser, R. M. McCarthy, D. Toscano, and G. Sharp (eds.), *Resistance, Political Conflict and the American Struggle for Independence 1765–1775* (Boulder, Colo.: Reinner).

McCord, N. (1958), *The Anti-Corn Law League* (London: George Allen and Unwin).

McCrady, E. (1899), *The History of South Carolina under the Royal Government 1719–1776* (London: Macmillan).

——(1901), *The History of South Carolina in the Revolution 1775–1780* (London: Macmillan).

McCusker, J. J. (ed.) (1997), *Essays in the Economic History of the Atlantic World* (London: Routledge).

——and Gravesteijn, C. (1991), *The Beginnings of Commercial and Financial Journalism: The Commodity Price Current, Exchange Rate Currents, and Modern Currents in Early Modern Europe* (Amsterdam: Neha).

——and Menard, R. R. (1985), *The Economy of British America, 1607–1789* (Chapel Hill, NC: North Carolina University Press).

——and Morgan, K. (2000), *The Early Modern Atlantic Economy* (Cambridge: Cambridge University Press).

MacDonald, A. (2001), *The Business of Representation* (London: Trade Association Forum).

McDonald, G. (1973), 'The Report of the Commission of Inquiry into industrial and commercial representation: the Devlin Report of 1972. An historical background', *Business Archives*, 38, 29–37.

McDowell, R. B. (1944), *Irish Public Opinion 1750–1800* (London: Faber and Faber).

McGrath, P. (1975), *The Merchant Adventurers of Bristol: A History* (Bristol: Society of Merchant Venturers).

Macgregor, D. H. (1906), *Industrial Combination* (London: George Bell).

——(1934), *Enterprise, Purpose and Profit* (Oxford: Clarendon Press).

McHugh, J. (1979), 'The self employed and the small independent entrepreneur', in King and Nugent (1979: 46–75).

McKendrick, N. (1982), 'Josiah Wedgwood and the commercialisation of the potteries', chapter 3 in McKendrick, Brewer, and Plumb (1982).

——J. Brewer, and J. H. Plumb (1982), *The Birth of Consumer Society: The Commercialization of Eighteenth Century England* (London: Europa).

Mackenzie, W. J. M. (1955), 'Pressure groups in British government', *British Journal of Sociology*, 6.

McKeown, T. J. (1989), 'The politics of Corn Law repeal and theories of commercial policy', *British Journal of Political Science*, 19, 353–80.

McLaughlin, J., Jordan, A. G., and Maloney, W. (1993), 'Corporate lobbying in the European Community', *Journal of Common Market Studies*, 31 (2), 192–211.

Macrosty, H. W. (1907), *The Trust Movement in British Industry: A Study of Business Organisation* (London: Longmans Green).

Magens, N. (1755), *An Essay on Insurances*, 2 vols. (London: Haberkorn).

Magliulo, B. (1980), *Les Chambres de commerce et d'industrie* (Paris: Presses Universitaires de France).

Maier, P. (1973), *From Resistance to Revolution: Colonial Radicals and the Development of American Opposition in Britain, 1765–1776* (London: Routledge and Kegan Paul).

Maloney, W. A., Jordan, G., and McLaughlin, A. M. (1994), 'Interest groups and public policy: the insider/outsider model revisited', *Journal of Public Policy*, 14 (1), 17–38.

Mannion, J. (1980), 'The Waterford merchants and the Irish Newfoundland provisions trade, 1770–1820', pp. 27–43 in P. Butel and L. M. Cullen (eds.), *Trade and Industry in France and Ireland in the Seventeenth and Eighteenth Centuries* (Paris: CNRS).

Markussen, A. (1985), *Profit Cycles, Oligopoly and Regional Development* (Cambridge, Mass.: MIT Press).

——(1996), 'Sticky places in slippery space: a typology of industrial districts', *Economic Geography*, 72 (3), 293–313.

Marmion, A. (1855), *The Ancient and Modern History of the Maritime Ports of Ireland* (London: J. H. Banks).

Marrison, A. J. (1983), 'Businessmen, industries and tariff reform in Great Britain, 1903–1930', *Business History*, 25, 148–76.

——(1996), *British Business and Protection 1903–1932* (Oxford: Clarendon Press).

——(ed.) (1998), *Free Trade and its Reception 1815–1960* (London: Routledge).

Marsh, D. (1978), 'On joining interest groups: an empirical consideration of the work of Mancur Olson jnr.', *British Journal of Political Science*, 6 (3), 257–71.

Marshall, A. (1919), *Industry and Trade: A Story of Industrial Technique and Business Organisation, and of their Influences on the Conditions of Various Classes and Nations* (London: Macmillan).

Marshall, P. (1971), 'The incorporation of Quebec in the British Empire, 1973–1774', pp. 43–62 in V. B. Platt and D. C. Skaggs (eds.), *Of Mother Country and Plantations: Proceedings of the 27th Conference on Early American History* (Bowling Green, OH.: Bowling Green State University Press).

Martin, F. (1876), *The History of Lloyds and of Marine Insurance in Great Britain* (London: Macmillan).

Martin, Rachel (2002), 'The Manchester business community and anti-slavery 1787–1833', unpublished PhD thesis, University of Cambridge.

Martin, Ron, and Sunley, P. (2003), 'Deconstructing clusters: chaotic concept of policy panacea?', *Journal of Economic Geography*, 3, 353–79.

Mathias, P. (1983), *The First Industrial Nation: Economic History of Britain 1700–1914*, 2nd edn. (London: Methuen).

——(2000), 'Risk, credit and kinship in early modern enterprise', in McCusker and Morgan (2000: 15–35).

Matthew, H. C. G. (1973), *The Liberal Imperialists: The Ideas and Politics of a Post-Gladstonian Elite* (Oxford: Oxford University Press).

Matthews, A. H. H. (1915), *Fifty Years of Agricultural Politics Being the History of the Central Chamber of Agriculture 1865–1915* (London: P. S. King).

Maydwell, I. (1845), *The Origin and Progress of the Central Society for the Protection of Agriculture: Is it a Plot or is it Not?* (London: W. Lake) (BL 7074.cc.35).

Meister, A. (1984), *Participation, Associations, Development, and Change* (New Brunswick, NJ: Transaction Books).

Mekic, D. (2007), 'Understanding local business associations: the case of chambers of commerce', unpublished PhD thesis, University of Cambridge.

Metcalf, G. (1965), *Royal Government and Political Conflict in Jamaica, 1729–1783* (London: Longmans).

Meteyard, E. (1866), *The Life of Josiah Wedgwood*, 2 vols. (London: Hurst and Blackett).

Meyer, J. P., and Herscovitch, L. (2001), *Commitment in the Workplace: Theory, Research and Application* (Newbury Park, Calif.: Sage).

Middlemas, K. (1979), *Politics in Industrial Society: The Experience of the British System since 1911* (London: Andre Deutsch).

——(1983), *Industry, Unions and Government: Twenty One Years of NEDC* (London: Macmillan).

——(1986), *Power, Competition and the State*, i: *Britain in Search of Balance 1940–6* (London: Macmillan).

——(1990), *Power, Competition and the State*, ii: *Threats to the Post War Settlement: Britain 1961–74* (London: Macmillan).

Middleton, C. R. (1977), *The Administration of British Foreign Policy 1782–1846* (Durham, NC: Duke University Press).

Miliband, R. (1969), *The State in Capitalist Society* (London: Weidenfeld and Nicolson).

Millar, J. (1787), *Elements of the Law Relating to Insurance* (London: J. Bell).

Millin, S. S. (1927), 'Belfast trading and banking in the eighteenth century', *Belfast Chamber of Commerce Journal*, March, 184–7; April, 11–17.

Minchinton, W. E. (1957), 'The merchants in England in the eighteenth century', *Explorations in Entrepreneurial History*, 10 (2), 62–71.

——(1965), 'The Stamp Act crisis: Bristol and Virginia', *Virginia Magazine of History and Biography*, 73, 145–55.

——(1971), 'The political activities of Bristol merchants with respect to the Southern Colonies before the revolution', *Virginia Magazine of History and Biography*, 79, 167–89.

Mitchell, N. J. (1990), 'The decentralization of business in Britain', *Journal of Politics*, 52 (2), 622–37.

Mizruchi, M. S. (1982), *The American Corporate Network, 1904–1974* (London: Sage).

——and Galaskiewicz, J. (1994), 'Networks of interorganisational relations', in S. Wasserman and J. Galaskiewicz (eds.), *Advances in Social Network Analysis* (London: Sage).

Moe, T. M. (1980), *The Organization of Interests: Incentives and Internal Dynamics of Political Interest Groups* (Chicago: Chicago University Press).

Moellering, G. (2003), 'Perceived trustworthiness and inter-firm governance: empirical evidence from the UK printing industry', *Cambridge Journal of Economics*, 26, 139–60.

Mole, K., Hart, M., Roper, S., and Saal, D. (2008), 'Differential gains from Business Link support and advice: a treatment effect approach', *Environment and Planning C: Government and Policy*, 26, 315–34.

Money, J. (1977), *Experience and Identity: Birmingham and the West Midlands, 1760–1800* (Manchester: Manchester University Press).

Moore, J. B. (ed.) (1931), *International Jurisdictions, Arbitration of Claims . . . Mixed Commission under Article VI of Treaty of 1794*, vol. iii (Oxford: Oxford University Press).

Morgan, E. S., and Morgan, H. M. (1962), *The Stamp Act Crisis: Prologue to Revolution*, 3rd edn. (Chapel Hill, NC: North Carolina University Press).

Morgan, K. (1993), *Bristol and the Atlantic Trade in the Eighteenth Century* (Cambridge: Cambridge University Press).

——(1997), 'Atlantic trade and British economic growth in the eighteenth century', pp. 14–46 in P. Mathias and J. A. Davis (eds.), *International Trade and British Economic Growth: From the Eighteenth Century to the Present Day* (Oxford: Basil Blackwell).

——(2000), 'Business networks in British export trade to North America, 1750–1780', in McCusker and Morgan (2000: 36–63).

——(ed.) (2007), *The Bright–Meyer Papers: A Bristol–West India Connection, 1732–1837* (Oxford: Oxford University Press).

Morris, R. (2004), *Naval Power and British Culture: Public Trust and Government Ideology* (Aldershot: Ashgate).

Morris, R. B. (1967), *John Jay: The Nation and the Court* (Boston: Boston University Press).

Morris, R. J. (1983), 'Voluntary societies and British urban elites, 1780–1850: an analysis', *Historical Journal*, 26 (1), 95–118.

——(1986), *Class, Power and Social Structure of British Nineteenth Century Towns* (Leicester: Leicester University Press).

——(1990), *Class, Sect and Party: The Making of the British Middle Classes, Leeds, 1820–1850* (Manchester: Manchester University Press).

——(1992), 'The state, the elite and the market: the visible land in the British industrial city system', pp. 177–99 in H. Diederiks, P. Hohenberg, and M. Wagenaar (eds.), *Economic Policy in Europe since the Late Middle Ages: The Visible Land and the Fortune of Cities* (Leicester: Leicester University Press).

Mortimer, T. (1772), *The Elements of Commerce, Politics and Finances, in Three Treatises* (London: R. Baldwin).

Moses, R. (1914), *The Civil Service of Great Britain* (New York: Columbia University Studies in History of Economics).

Mosse, G. L. (1947), 'The Anti-League: 1844–1846', *Economic History Review*, 17, 132–42.

Mowatt, C. L. (1969), *The General Strike of 1926* (London: private).

Murphy, D. (1981), *Derry, Donegal and Modern Ulster, 1790–1921* (Londonderry: Aileach).

Musgrave, C. E. (1914), *The London Chamber of Commerce from 1881 to 1914: A Retrospective Appreciation* (London: Effingham Wilson).

Namier, L. B. (1961), *England in the Age of the American Revolution* (London: Macmillan).

——and Brooke, J. (eds.) (1964), *The House of Commons 1754–1790*, 3 vols. (London: HMSO).

NCT (1957), *National Chamber of Trade Diamond Jubilee 1897–1957* (London: NCT) (LMA, MS 29348).

Nenadic, S. (1991), 'Businessmen, the urban middle class and the "dominance" of manufacturers in nineteenth century Britain', *Economic History Review*, 44, 66–85.

Nettl, J. P. (1965) 'Consensus or elite domination: the case of business', *Political Studies*, 13 (1), 22–44.

——(1968), 'The state as a conceptual variable', *World Politics*, 559–92.

Norris, J. M. (1957), 'Samuel Garbett and the early development of industrial lobbying in Britain', *Economic History Review*, 10, 450–60.

North, D. C. (1985), 'Transaction costs in history', *Journal of European Economic History*, 14, 557–76.

——(1990), *Institutions, Institutional Change and Economic Performance* (Cambridge: Cambridge University Press).

Oaks, R. F. (1973), 'Philadelphia merchants and the first Continental Congress', *Pennsylvania History*, 40, 149–66.

——(1977), 'Philadelphia merchants and the origins of American independence', *Proceedings of the American Philosophical Society*, 121 (6), 407–36.

O'Brian, P. K. (1988), 'The political economy of British taxation 1660–1815', *Economic History Review*, 2nd series, 41, 1–32.

O'Brien, P. (2000), *Provincialising the First Industrial Revolution*, Working Paper 17/06 (London: London School of Economics, Global Economic History Network).

——and Engerman, S. (1991) 'Exports and the growth of the British economy from the Glorious Revolution to the Peace of Amiens', pp. 117–210 in B. Solow (ed.), *Slavery and the Rise of the Atlantic System* (Cambridge: Cambridge University Press).

O'Connell, M. R. (1965), *Irish Politics and Social Conflict in the Age of the American Revolution* (Philadelphia: Philadelphia University Press).

O'Connor, D. P. (1938), 'The history and functions of the Limerick chamber of commerce 1807–1902', unpublished MSc thesis, University College Dublin.

Offee, C., and Wissenthal, H. (1985), 'Two logics of collective action', in C. Offee (ed.), *Disorganized Capitalism* (Cambridge: Polity).

O'Gorman, F. (1982), *The Emergence of the British Two-Party System 1760–1832* (London: Edward Arnold).

——(1989), *Voters, Patrons and Parties: The Unreformed Electoral System of Hanoverian England 1734–1832* (Oxford: Clarendon Press).

Olson, A. G. (1973), *Anglo-American Politics 1660–1775* (Oxford: Oxford University Press).

——(1979), 'Parliament, the London lobbies, and provincial interests in England and America', *Historical Reflections*, 6, 367–86.

——(1980), 'The Board of Trade and London–American interest groups in the eighteenth century', *Journal of Imperial and Commonwealth History*, 8, 33–50.

——(1982), 'The London mercantile Lobby and the coming of the American Revolution', *Journal of American History*, 69 (1), 21–41.

——(1991), 'Coffee house lobbying', *History Today*, 41 (January), 36–41.

Olson, M. (1971), *The Logic of Collective Action: Public Goods and the Theory of Groups*, 2nd edn. (Cambridge, Mass.: Harvard University Press).

Opp, K.-D. (1986), 'Soft incentives and collective action participation in the Anti-Nuclear movement', *British Journal of Political Science*, 16, 87–112.

Orr, A. E. (1895), 'Commercial organizations', chapter IX, pp. 50–4, in C. M. Depew (ed.), *One Hundred Years of American Commerce, 1795–1895* (New York: Greenwood Press, reprinted 1968).

O'Shaughnessy, A. J. (1994), 'The Stamp Act crisis in the British Caribbean', *William and Mary Quarterly*, 51 (2), 71–95.

——(2000), *An Empire Divided: The American Revolution and the British Caribbean* (Philadelphia: University of Pennsylvania Press).

Ouchi, W. G. (1980), 'Markets, bureaucracies and clans', *Administrative Science Quarterly*, 25, 129–41.

Palmer, S. (1990), *Politics, Shipping and the Repeal of the Navigation Laws* (Manchester: Manchester University Press).

Papenfuse, E. (1975), *In Pursuit of Profit: The Annapolis Merchants in the Era of the American Revolution: 1703–1805* (Baltimore: Johns Hopkins University Press).

Peacock, A. T., and Wiseman, J. (1961), *The Growth of Public Expenditure in the United Kingdom* (Princeton: Princeton University Press).

Pearson, R. (2004), *Insuring the Industrial Revolution: Fire Insurance in Great Britain, 1700–1850* (Aldershot: Ashgate).

——and Richardson, D. (2001), 'Business networking in the industrial revolution', *Economic History Review*, 54, 657–79.

Penson, L. M. (1924), *The Colonial Agents of the British West Indies: A Study of Colonial Administration in the Eighteenth Century* (London: London University Press).

PEP (1952), *Government and Industry: A Survey of the Relations between the Government and Privately Owned Industry* (London: Political and Economic Planning).

——(1957), *Industrial Trade Associations: Activities and Organisation* (London: Political and Economic Planning).

Pfeffer, J., and Salancik, G. R. (1978), *The External Control of Organizations: A Resource Dependence Perspective* (London: Harper and Row).

Phelps, N. A. (2004), 'Clusters, dispersion and the spaces in between: for an economic geography of the banal', *Urban Studies*, 41, 971–89.

——and Ozawa, T. (2003), 'Contrasts in agglomeration: proto-industrial, industrial and post-industrial forms compared', *Progress in Human Geography*, 27, 583–604.

Phelps Brown, E. H. (1959), *The Growth of British Industrial Relations: A Study from the Standpoint of 1906–14* (London: Macmillan).

Philips, C. H. (1961), *The East India Company, 1784–1834*, 2nd edn. (London: Routledge).

Phillips, J. A. (1992), *The Great Reform Bill in the Boroughs: English Electoral Behaviour 1818–1841* (Oxford: Clarendon Press).

Pickering, P. A., and Tyrrell, A. (2000), *The People's Bread: A History of the Anti-Corn Law League* (Leicester: Leicester University Press).

Pigou, A. C. (1947), *A Study of Public Finance*, 3rd edn. (London: Macmillan).

Pitman, F. W. (1917), *Development of the British West Indies, 1700–1763* (New Haven: Yale University Press).

Platt, D. C. M. (1963), 'The role of the British consular service in overseas trade, 1825–1914', *Economic History Review*, 15, 494–512.

——(1968), *Finance, Trade, and Politics in British Foreign Policy, 1815–1914* (Oxford: Clarendon Press).

——(1971), *The Cinderella Service: British Consuls since 1825* (London: Longmans).

Plumb, J. H. (1960), *Sir Robert Walpole*, ii: *The King's Minister* (London: Allen Lane).

Pocock, J. G. A. (1986), '1776: the revolution against parliament', pp. 265–88 in J. G. A. Pocock (ed.), *Three British Revolutions: 1641, 1688, 1776* (Princeton: Princeton University Press).

Pope, D. J. (1970), 'Shipping and trade in the port of Liverpool 1783–1793', 3 vols., PhD thesis, University of Liverpool.

Popp, A. (2003), '"The true potter": identity and entrepreneurism in the north Staffordshire potteries in the later nineteenth century', *Journal of Historical Geography*, 29 (3), 317–35.

——(2005), '"An indissoluble mutual destiny": the north Staffordshire potteries and the limits of regional trade associationalism', *Organisation Studies*, 26 (12), 1831–49.

——and Wilson, J. F. (eds.) (2003), *Industrial Districts and Regional Business Networks in England 1750–1970* (Aldershot: Ashgate).

————(2007), 'Life cycles, contingency, and agency: growth, development and change in English industrial districts and clusters', *Environment and Planning A*, 39, 2975–92.

————(2009), 'Business in the regions: from "old districts" to "new clusters"?', pp. 65–81 in R. Coopey and P. Lyth (eds.), *Business in Britain in the Twentieth Century: Decline and Renaissance?* (Oxford: Oxford University Press).

Porritt, E., and Porritt, A. G. (1903), *The Unreformed House of Commons: Parliamentary Representation before 1832*, 2 vols. (Cambridge: Cambridge University Press).

Porter, G. R. (1851), *The Progress of the Nation in its Various Social and Economical Relations from the Beginning of the Nineteenth Century* (London: John Murray).

Porter, R. P. (1907), *The Dangers of Municipal Trading* (London: Routledge).

Postlethwayt, M. (1744), *The African Trade: The Great Pillar and Support of the British Plantation Trade in America* (London: Robinson).

——(1749), *A Dissertation on the Plan, Use, and Importance, of the Universal Dictionary of Trade and Commerce* (London: Knapton).

——(1750), *The Merchant's Public Counting House or New Mercantile Institution . . . and Practicable Plan*, 1st edition; 2nd edn. with additional supplement, 1751 (London: Knapton).

——(1751), *Universal Dictionary of Trade and Commerce: Translated from the French of . . . Monsieur Savary . . . with Large Additions and Improvements* (London: Knapton).

——(1757), *Great Britain's True System* (London: Millar).

——(1759), *The merchants advocate, or an enquiry whether the merchants are not intitled to a discount of 5 percent . . . addressed to the merchants of Great Britain. To be continued upon all occasions wherein the interests of that respectable body is concerned; A blot is no blot, till it is bit* (London: M. Cooper).

Powell, E. T. (1966), *The Evolution of the Money Market, 1385–1915: An Historical and Analytical Study of the Rise and Development of Finance as a Centralised, Co-ordinated Force* (Cass: London).

Powell, M. J. (2003), *Britain and Ireland in the Eighteenth-Century Crises of Empire* (London: Palgrave).

Pred, A. R. (1973), *Urban Growth and the Circulation of Information: The United States System of Cities 1790–1840* (Cambridge, Mass.: Harvard University Press).

——(1977), *City Systems in Advanced Economics, Past Growth, Present Processes and Future Development Options* (London: Hutchinson).

Prendeville, P. L. (1930), 'History of the Dublin Chamber of Commerce 1760–1860, with an introduction on the chamber of commerce movement', unpublished M.Comm. thesis, University College Dublin. (Prendeville was assistant secretary of the chamber.)

Prentice, A. (1851), *Historical Sketches and Personal Recollections of Manchester: Intended to Illustrate the Progress of Public Opinion 1792–1832* (London: Charles Gilpin).

——(1853), *History of the Anti-Corn Law League* (London: W. & F. G. Cash).

Pressnell, L. S. (1956), *Country Banking in the Industrial Revolution* (Oxford: Oxford University Press).

Price, J. M. (1974), 'Economic function and the growth of American port towns in the eighteenth century', *Perspective in American History*, 8, 123–88.

——(1978), 'Colonial trade and British economic development, 1660–1775', *Lex et Scientia*, 14, 106–26.

——(1980), *Capital and Credit in British Overseas Trade: The View from the Chesapeake, 1700–1776* (Cambridge, Mass.: Harvard University Press).

——(1983), 'The excise affair: the administrative and colonial dimensions of a parliamentary crisis', pp. 257–321 in S. B. Baxter (ed.), *England's Rise to Greatness, 1660–1763* (Berkeley and Los Angeles: University of California Press).

——(1986), 'Who cared about the colonies? The impact of the thirteen colonies on British society and politics, circa 1714–1775', pp. 395–436 in Institute of Early American History and Culture, *Strangers within the Realm: Cultural Margins of the First British Empire* (Chapel Hill, NC: University of North Carolina Press).

——(1989), 'What did merchants do? Reflections on British overseas trade, 1660–1790', *Journal of Economic History*, 49, 267–84.

——(1991), 'Transaction costs: a note on merchant credit and the organisation of private trade', pp. 276–97 in J. D. Tracy (ed.), *The Political Economy of Merchant Empires* (Cambridge: Cambridge University Press).

——(1992), 'The Bank of England's discount activity and the merchants of London, 1694–1773', pp. 92–114 in I. Blanchard, A. Goodman, and J. Newman (eds.), *Industry and Finance in Early Modern History: Essays Presented to George Hammersley* (Stuttgart: Franz Steiner).

Priem, R., and Butler, J. (2001), 'Is the resource-based view a useful perspective for strategic management research?', *Academy of Management Review*, 26, 57–67.

Priest, S. P. (1998), 'Stimulating the performance of SMEs through Business Link: an assessment of customer satisfaction, dissatisfaction and complaining behaviour', unpublished PhD thesis, University of Cambridge.

——(1999), 'Business Link SME services: targeting, innovation and charging', *Environment and Planning C: Government and Policy*, 17, 177–94.

Ramsden, M., and Bennett, R. J. (2005), 'The benefits of external support to SMEs: "hard" versus "soft" outcomes and satisfaction levels', *Journal of Small Business and Enterprise Development*, 12 (2), 227–43.

————(2007), 'Local economic development initiatives and the transition from Training and Enterprise Councils to new institutional structures in England: partnership, discretion and local flexibility', *Policy Studies*, 28 (3), 225–45.

Randall, A. (2006), *Riotous Assemblies: Popular Protest in Hanoverian England* (Oxford: Oxford University Press).

Raynes, H. E. (1964), *A History of British Insurance* (London: Pitman).

Read, D. (1964), *The English Provinces, c.1760–1960: A Study in Influence* (London: Edward Arnold).

Redford, A. (1934), *Manchester Merchants and Foreign Trade 1794–1858* (Manchester: Manchester University Press).

——and Clapp, B. W. (1956), *Manchester Merchants and Foreign Trade*, ii: *1850–1939* (Manchester: Manchester University Press).

Rees, J. M. (1922), *Trusts in British Industry 1914–21: A Story of Recent Developments in Business Organisation* (London: George Allen and Unwin).

Reid, J. G. (2004), '*Pax Britannica* or *Pax Indigena*? Planter Nova Scotia (1760–1782) and competing strategies of pacification', *Canadian Historical Review*, 85, 687–92.

Reilly, R. (1992), *Josiah Wedgwood 1730–1795* (London: Macmillan).

Rempel, R. A. (1972), *Unionists Divided: Arthur Balfour, Joseph Chamberlain and the Unionist Free Traders* (Newton Abbot: David and Charles).

Rhodes, R. A. W. (1992), *Beyond Westminster and Whitehall*, 2nd edn. (London: Routledge).

Richardson, J., and Jordon, G. (1979), *Governing under Pressure* (Oxford: Martin Robertson).

Richmond, L., and Stockford, B. (1986), *Company Archives: The Survey of the Records of 1000 of the First Registered Companies in England and Wales* (Aldershot: Gower).

Ridden, J. (2003), 'Irish reform between the 1798 Rebellion and Great Famine', pp. 271–94 in *Rethinking the Age of Reform: Britain 1780–1850* (Cambridge: Cambridge University Press).

Ridgeway, G. L. (1938), *Merchants of Peace: Twenty Years of Business Diplomacy through the International Chamber of Commerce, 1919–1938* (New York: Columbia University Press).

Roberts, R. (1984), 'Business, politics, and municipal socialism', in Turner (1984: 20–32).

Robson, B. T. (1973), *Urban Growth: An Approach* (London: Methuen).

Rodger, N. A. M. (2004), *The Command of the Ocean: A Naval History of Britain, 1649–1815* (London: Allen Lane).

Rogers, G. C. (1974), 'The Charleston tea party: the significance of December 3, 1773', *South Carolina Historical Magazine*, 75, 153–68.

Rogers, N. (1989), *Whigs and Cities: Popular Politics in the Age of Walpole and Pitt* (Oxford: Clarendon Press).

Rooth, T. (1992), *British Protectionism and the International Economy: Overseas Commercial Policy in the 1930s* (Cambridge: Cambridge University Press).

Rose, M. B. (2000), *Firms, Networks and Business Values: The British and American Cotton Industries since 1750* (Cambridge: Cambridge University Press).

Rose, R. (1989), *Politics in England: Change and Persistence*, 5th edn. (London: Macmillan).

Rose, R. B. (1958), 'A Liverpool seaman's strike in the eighteenth century', *Transactions of the Historic Society of Lancashire and Cheshire*, 68, 85–92.

Rose-Ackerman, S. (1987), 'Ideals vs. dollars: donors, charity managers, and government grants', *Journal of Political Economy*, 95, 810–23.

Rothenberg, L. S. (1988), 'Organisational maintenance and the retention decision in groups', *American Political Science Review*, 82 (4), 1129–52.

——(1992), *Linking Citizens to Government* (Cambridge: Cambridge University Press).

Rubin, G. R., and Sugarman, D. (1984), *Law, Economy and Society: Essays in the History of English Law* (London: Butterworths).

Rudé, G. (1962), *Wilkes and Liberty* (Oxford: Oxford University Press).

Rydz, D. L. (1979), *The Parliamentary Agents: A History* (London: Royal Historical Society).

Sabine, L. (1859), 'The origins of Board of Trade', *Bankers Magazine New York and Baltimore*, 13 March, 678–92.

Sadowski, D., and Jacobi, O. (eds.) (1991), *Employers' Associations in Europe: Policy and Organisation* (Baden-Baden: Nomos).

Salisbury, R. H. (1984), 'Interest representation: the dominance of institutions', *American Political Science Review*, 78, 64–76.

Sandbrook, D. (2010), *State of Emergency: The Way we Were. Britain 1970–1974* (London: Allen Lane).

Sanderson, F. E. (1977), 'The structure of politics in Liverpool 1780–1807', *Transactions of the Historic Society of Lancashire and Cheshire*, 127, 65–88.

——(1989), 'The Liverpool abolitionists', pp. 196–233 in R. Anstey and P. E. Hair (eds.), *Liverpool, the African Slave Trade, and Abolition* (Liverpool: Historic Society of Lancashire and Cheshire).

Saul, S. B. (1960), *Studies in British Overseas Trade 1870–1914* (Liverpool: Liverpool University Press).

Schlesinger, A. M. (1917), *The Colonial Merchants and the American Revolution, 1763–1776* (New York: Columbia University Studies in History No. 78).

Schmitter, P. C., and Lehmbruch, G. (eds.) (1979), *Trends towards Corporatist Intermediation* (New York: Sage).

Schneiberg, M., and Hollingsworth, J. R. (1991), 'Can transaction cost economics explain trade associations?', pp. 199–256 in R. M. Czada and A. Windhoff-Héritier (eds.), *Political Choice: Institutions, Rules, and the Limits of Rationality* (Frankfurt: Campus).

Schofield, R. E. (1963), *The Lunar Society of Birmingham: A Social History of Provincial Science and Industry in Eighteenth Century England* (Oxford: Clarendon Press).

Scott, A. J. (1998), *Regions and the World Economy; The Coming Shape of Global Production, Competition and Political Order* (Oxford: Oxford University Press).

Scott, B. (1867a), *Statistical Vindication of the City of London* (London: Longmans).

——(1867b), *Suggestions for a Chamber of Commerce for the City of London* (London: Effingham Wilson, Royal Exchange) (LMA: COL/SJ/27/055/1).

Scott, J. (2003), 'Transformations in the British economic elite', *Comparative Sociology*, 2, 155–73.

Scott, J. P. (1987), 'Intercorporate structures in Western Europe: a comparative historical analysis', pp. 208–232 in M. S. Mizruchi and M. Schwartz (eds.), *Intercorporate Relations* (Cambridge: Cambridge University Press).

Searle, G. R. (1971), *The Quest for National Efficiency: A Study of British Politics and Political Thought, 1899–1914* (Berkeley: University of California Press).

——(1993), *Entrepreneurial Politics in Mid-Victorian Britain* (Oxford: Oxford University Press).

——(2001), *The Liberal Party, Triumph and Disintegration, 1886–1929*, 2nd edn. (London: Palgrave).

Sée, H. (1930), 'The Normandy chamber of commerce and the commercial treaty of 1786', *Economic History Review*, 2, 308–13.

Self, P., and Storing, H. J. (1962), *The State and the Farmer* (London: George Allen and Unwin).

Sellers, L. (1934), *Charleston Business on the Eve of the American Revolution* (Chapel Hill, NC: North Carolina University Press).

Sellgren, J. (1987), 'Local economic development and local initiatives in the mid-1980s: an analysis of the Local Economic Development Information Service', *Local Government Studies*, 13 (6), 51–68.

——(1989), 'Local economic development in Great Britain: an evolving local government role', unpublished PhD thesis, London School of Economics.

Selznick, P. (1949), *TVA and the Grass Roots* (New York: Harper and Row).

Seyd, P. (1993), 'The political management of decline', pp. 151–86 in *The History of the City of Sheffield, 1843–1993* (Sheffield: Sheffield Academic Press).

Sheppard, E. (2005), 'Constructing free trade: from Manchester boosterism to global management', *Transactions of the Institute of British Geographers*, 30 (2), 151–72.

Sheridan, R. B. (1960), 'The British credit crisis of 1772 and the American colonies', *Journal of Economic History*, 20, 161–86.

Shortt, A., and Doughty, A. G. (eds.) (1914), *Canada and its Provinces: A History of the Canadian People and their Institutions, by One Hundred Associates*, 23 vols. (Toronto: General Book Co.).

Sigsworth, E. M. (1958), *Black Dyke Mills: A History* (Liverpool: Liverpool University Press).

Smail, J. (1994), *The Origins of Middle-Class Culture: Halifax, Yorkshire, 1660–1780* (New York: Cornell University Press).

——(1999), *Merchants, Markets and Manufacture: The English Wool Textile Industry in the Eighteenth Century* (London: Macmillan).

Smith, A. (1776), *An Inquiry into the Nature and Causes of the Wealth of Nations*, 3 vols. (London: A. Strahan).

Smith, B. C. (1995), 'Social visions of the American resistance movement', pp. 27–57 in R. Hoffman and P. J. Albert (eds.), *The Transforming Hand of Revolution: Reconsidering the American Revolution as a Social Movement* (Charlottesville, VA.: US Capitol Historical Society, University of Virginia Press).

Smith, B. R. (1956), 'The Committee of the Whole House to consider the American papers (January and February 1766)', unpublished MA thesis, University of Sheffield.

Smith, R. (1955), 'The Manchester chamber of commerce and the increasing foreign competition to Lancashire cotton textiles, 1873–1896', *Bulletin of the John Rylands Library*, 28.

Soldon, N. (1974), 'Laissez-faire as dogma: the Liberty and Property Defence League', pp. 208–33 in K. D. Brown (ed.), *Essays in Anti-Labour History* (London: Macmillan).

Sosin, J. M. (1965), *Agents and Merchants: British Colonial Policy and the Origins of the American Revolution, 1763–1775* (Lincoln, Nebr.: University of Nebraska Press).

Spall, R. F. (1988), 'Free trade, foreign relations, and the Anti-Corn-Law League', *International History Review*, 10 (3), 405–31.

Steffan, C. G. (1984), *The Mechanics of Baltimore: Members and Politics in the Age of Revolution 1763–1812* (Urbana, Ill.: University of Illinois Press).

Steinberg, R. (1991), 'Does government spending crowd out donations? Interpreting the evidence', *Annals of Public and Cooperative Economics*, 62 (4), 591–612.

Stevens, J. A. (1867), *Colonial Records of the New York Chamber of Commerce 1768–1784*, 2 vols. (New York: John Trow) (BL 8246.g.31).

Stewart, J. D. (1958), *British Pressure Groups: Their Role in Relation to the House of Commons* (Oxford: Oxford University Press).

Stewart, M. (1984), *Talking to Local Business: The Involvement of Chambers of Commerce in Local Affairs*, Working Paper No. 38, School for Advanced Urban Studies, University of Bristol.

Stewart, R. (1985), *Henry Brougham: His Public Career 1778–1868* (London: Bodley Head).

Stokman, F. N. N., and Stokman, J. (1995), 'Strategic Control and Interests, its effects on decision outcomes', *Journal of Mathematical Sociology*, 20 (4), 289–317.

Storey, D. (1994), *Understanding the Small Business Sector* (London: Routledge).

——(2003), 'Entrepreneurship, small and medium sized enterprises and public policies', pp. 473–511 in Z. J. Acs and D. B. Audretsch (eds.), *Handbook of Entrepreneurship Research: An Interdisciplinary Survey and Introduction* (Dordrecht: Kluwer).

Storper, M. (1997), *The Regional World: Territorial Development in a Global Economy* (London: Guilford).

Streeck, W., and Schmitter, P. C. (eds.) (1985), *Private Interest Government: Beyond Market and State* (London: Sage).

————(1991), 'From national corporatism to transnational pluralism: organised interests in the single European market', *Politics and Society*, 19 (2), 133–64.

Sturges, K. (1915), *American Chambers of Commerce*, Department of Political Science Papers No. 4, Williams College, Williamstown (BL 08245.h.2.).

Sunley, P. (1992), 'Marshallian industrial districts: the case of the Lancashire cotton industry in the inter-war years', *Transactions of the Institute of British Geographers*, 17, 306–20.

Surtees Society (1895, 1899), *Extracts from the Records of the Merchant Adventurers of Newcastle-on-Tyne*, 2 vols. (York: Surtees Society Vols. 93, 101).

——(1918), *The York Mercers and Merchant Adventurers, 1356–1917* (York: Surtees Society Vol. 129).

Sutherland, L. S. (1933), *A London Merchant 1695–1774* (Oxford: Oxford University Press).

——(1952), *The East India Company in Eighteenth Century Politics* (Oxford: Clarendon Press).

——(1956), 'The City of London in eighteenth-century politics', pp. 49–74 in R. Pares and A. J. Taylor (eds.), *Essays Presented to Lewis Namier* (London: Macmillan).

Swann, D. (1960), 'The pace and progress of port investment in England, 1660–1830', *Yorkshire Bulletin of Economic and Social Research*, 12 (1), 32–44.

Sweet, R. H. (2002), 'Topographies of politeness', *Transactions Royal Historical Society*, 12, 355–74.

——(2003), 'Local identities and a national parliament, *c.*1688–1835', in Hoppit (2003: 48–63).

Syvret, M., and Stevens, J. (1998), *Balleine's History of Jersey* (Chichester: Phillimore).

Taine, H. (1865), *Philosophie de l'art* (Paris: Hachette).

Tann, J. (1993), *Birmingham Assay Office, 1773–1993* (Birmingham: The Assay Office).

Taraschio, V. J. (1981), 'Cantillon's theory of population size and distribution', *Atlantic Economic Journal*, 9 (2), 12–18.

Tarrow, S. G. (1994), *Power in Movement* (Cambridge: Cambridge University Press).

Taylor, J. S. (1985), *Jonas Henway, Founder of the Marine Society: Charity and Policy in Eighteenth Century England* (London: Scholar Press).

Taylor, M., and Singleton, S. (1993), 'The communal resource: transaction costs and the solution of collective action problems', *Politics and Society*, 21 (2), 195–214.

Taylor, R. (2007), *A History of Chambers of Commerce in the United Kingdom: 1768–2007* (London: BCC).

Tenison, C. M. (1894), 'The old Dublin bankers', *Cork Historical and Archaeological Society*, 1st series, 3, 143–6, 168–71, 221–4, 242–7.

Thomas, J. (1934), 'The development of the North Staffordshire potteries since 1730, with special reference to the industrial revolution', unpublished PhD thesis, London School of Economics.

——(1935), 'The potters of Staffordshire and their relations with the Manchester Committee of Commerce, 1784 to 1790', *Manchester Statistical Society*, Papers 1934–5.

Thomas, J. H. (2002), 'East India Company agency work in the British Isles, 1700–1800', pp. 33–47 in H. V. Bowen, M. Lincoln, and N. Rigby (eds.), *The World of the East India Company* (London: Boydell Press and National Maritime Museum).

Thomas, P. G. (1975), *British Politics and the Stamp Act Crisis: The First Phase of the American Revolution, 1763–1767* (Oxford: Clarendon Press).

——(1987), *The Townshend Duties Crisis: The Second Phase of the American Revolution, 1767–1773* (Oxford: Clarendon Press).

——(1991), *Tea Party to Independence: The Third Phase of the American Revolution, 1773–1776* (Oxford: Clarendon Press).

Thompson, E. P. (1963), *The Making of the English Working Class* (London: Gollancz).

Tilly, C. (1978), *From Mobilisation to Revolution* (Reading, Mass.: Addison-Wesley).

——(1994), 'Entanglements of European cities and states', pp. 1–27 in C. Tilly and W. P. Blackman (eds.), *Cities and the Rise of States in Europe, AD 1000 to 1800* (Oxford: Westview Press).

——(2004), *Contention and Democracy in Europe, 1650–2000* (Cambridge: Cambridge University Press).

——(2005), *Trust and Rule* (Cambridge: Cambridge University Press).

Tooke, T., and Newmarch, W. (1838–57), *A History of Prices*, 6 vols. (London).

Towler, W. G. (1909), *Socialism in Local Government* (London: Allen and Unwin).

Trainor, R. H. (1993), *Black Country Elites: The Exercise of Authority in an Industrialized Area, 1830–1900* (Oxford: Clarendon Press).

——(1996), 'The elite', chapter 7, pp. 227–64, in *Glasgow*, ii: *1830 to 1912* (Manchester: Manchester University Press).

Trentmann, F. (1996), 'The transformation of fiscal reform: reciprocity, modernisation, and the fiscal debate within the business community in early twentieth-century Britain', *Historical Journal*, 39 (4), 1005–48.

——(2008), *Free Trade Nation: Commerce, Consumption and Civil Society in Modern Britain* (Oxford: Oxford University Press).

Tribunals of Commerce Association (1854a), *Report of the Executive Committee at a Public Meeting 15 March 1854* (London: Effingham Wilson) (BL 8220.aa.6 (6)(1)).

——(1854b), *A Letter to the Bankers of London by Francis Lyne, Chair of the Executive Committee* (London: Effingham Wilson) (BL 8220.aa.6 (6)(2)).

——(1856), *Fourth Report* (London: Effingham Wilson) (BL 8220.aa.6. (5)).

Trinder, B. (1981), *The Industrial Revolution in Shropshire* (London: Phillimore).

——(2000), 'Industrialising towns 1700–1840', pp. 805–20 in P. Clark (ed.), *The Cambridge Urban History of Britain*, ii: *1540–1840* (Cambridge: Cambridge University Press).

Trumbull, J. (1841), *Autobiography of John Trumbull, Patriot and Artist 1756–1843*, ed. T. Sizer (New Haven: Yale University Press).

Truxes, T. M. (1988), *Irish–American Trade 1660–1783* (Cambridge: Cambridge University Press).

——(ed.) (2001), *Letterbook of Greg & Cunningham: Merchants of New York and Belfast* (Oxford: Oxford University Press).

Turner, J. A. (1978), 'The British Commonwealth Union and the general election of 1918', *English Historical Review*, 93, 528–59.

——(ed.) (1984), *Businessmen and Politics: Studies of Business Activity in British Politics, 1945–65* (London: Heinemann).

——(1988), 'Servants of two masters: British trade associations in the first half of the twentieth century', pp. 173–203 in H. Yamozaki and M. Miyamoto (eds.), *Trade Associations in Business History* (Tokyo: University of Tokyo Press).

Turner, M. J. (1994), 'Before the Manchester School: economic theory in early nineteenth-century Manchester', *History*, 79, 216–41.

Tyler, J. W. (1986), *Smugglers and Patriots: Boston Merchants and the Advent of the American Revolution* (Boston: North Eastern University Press).

Uglow, J. (2002), *The Lunar Men: The Friends Who Made the Future, 1730–1810* (London: Faber and Faber).

Urwick, Orr, and Partners Ltd. (1968), *Economic Development Committee for Newspaper, Printing and Publishing Industry, Printing Survey* (London: National Economic Development Office).

US Department of Commerce (1923), *Industrial and Commercial Organizations of the United States* (Washington: Bureau of Foreign and Domestic Commerce, GPO).

Useem, M. (1984), *The Inner Circle: Large Corporations and the Rise of Business Political Activity in the U.S. and U.K.* (Oxford: Oxford University Press).

——(1993), *Executive Defence: Shareholder Power and Corporate Reorganisation* (Cambridge, Mass.: Harvard University Press).

Vale, E. (1967), *The Mail-Coach Men of the Late Eighteenth Century* (Newton Abbot: David and Charles).

Valentine, A. (1967), *Lord North*, 2 vols. (Norman, Okla.: University of Oklahoma Press).

Van Waarden, F. (1991), 'Two logics of collective action? Business associations as distinct from trade unions: the problems of associations of organisations', in Sadowski and Jacobi (1991: 51–84).

Ville, S. P. (1987), *English Shipowning during the Industrial Revolution: Michael Henley and Son, London Shipowners, 1770–1830* (Manchester: Manchester University Press).

Wagner, A. (1890), *Finanzwissenschaft* (Leipzig: C. F. Winter).

Wakeford, E. (1812), *An Account of Ireland, Statistical and Political* (London: Longman Hurst).

Walker, J. L. (1983), 'The origins and maintenance of interest groups in America', *American Journal of Political Science*, 77, 390–406.

Walker, T. (1784), *The Original*, ed. B. Jerrold, 2 vols. (London: Grant and Co.) (BL P.P5841b).

——(1794), *A Review of Some of the Political Events which have Occurred in Manchester during the Last Five Years* (London: J. Johnson) (Cambridge University Library, Bbb.25.25/1).

Walsh, R., and Fox, W. L. (1974) *Maryland: A History 1632–1974* (Baltimore: Maryland Historical Society).

Walsh, R. W. (1959), *Charleston's Sons of Liberty: A Study of the Artisans 1763–1789* (Columbia, SC: South Carolina University Press).

Waters, S. (1995), 'The Chamber of Commerce and local development in France and Italy', unpublished PhD thesis, University of Limerick.

Watson, D. H. (1957), 'Barlow Trecothick and other associates of Lord Rockingham during the Stamp Act crisis', unpublished MA thesis, Sheffield University.

——(1968), 'The Duke of Newcastle, the Marquis of Rockingham, and mercantile interest in London and the provinces, 1761–1768', unpublished PhD thesis, Sheffield University.

Weatherill, L. (1996), *Consumer Behaviour and Material Culture in Britain 1660–1760*, 2nd edn. (London: Routledge).

Webb, S., and Webb, B. (1920), *The History of Trade Unionism*, 2nd edn. (London: Longmans).

Weber, A. F. (1899), *The Growth of Cities in the Nineteenth Century: A Study in Statistics* (New York: Cornell University Press).

Wedgwood, J. (1915), *The Personal Life of Josiah Wedgwood, the Potter* (London: Macmillan).

Weir, R. M. (1983), *Colonial South Carolina: A History* (New York: KTO Press).

Weisbrod, B. A. (1988), *The Nonprofit Economy* (Cambridge, Mass.: Harvard University Press).

——(ed.) (1998), *To Profit or Not to Profit: The Commercial Transformation of the Nonprofit Sector* (Cambridge: Cambridge University Press).

Wells, C. (1909), *A Short History of the Port of Bristol* (Bristol: J. W. Arrowsmith).

Werking, R. H. (1978), 'Bureaucrats, businessmen, and foreign trade: the origins of the United States chamber of commerce', *Business History Review*, 52 (3), 321–41.

Weskett, J. (1782), *Plan of the Chamber of Commerce* (London: Richardson and Urquart).

——(1783), *A Complete Digest of the Theory, Laws and Practice of Insurance* (London: Frys, Couchman and Collier).

Westerfield, R. B. (1915), *Middlemen in English Business: Particularly between 1660 and 1760* (New Haven: Yale University Press: Transactions of the Connecticut Academy of Arts and Sciences, 19, 111–445).

Whitley, P. (1996), *Lord North: The Prime Minister who Lost America* (London: Hambledon Press).

Wicks, P. J. (1990), 'Bureaucratic change in further education', unpublished PhD thesis, London School of Economics.

Williamson, O. E. (1985), *The Economic Institutions of Capitalism* (New York: Free Press).

——(1993), *The Economic Analysis of Institutions and Organisations: In General and with Respect to Country Studies*, OECD Working Paper 133 (Paris: OECD).

Williamson, P. (1992), *National Crisis and National Government: British Politics, the Economy and Empire, 1926–1932* (Cambridge: Cambridge University Press).

Wilson, A. (1997), 'The cultural identity of Liverpool 1790–1850: the early learned societies', *Transactions of the Historic Society of Lancashire and Cheshire*, 147, 55–80.

Wilson, J. F., and Popp, A. (eds.) (2003a), *Industrial Clusters and Regional Business Networks in England, 1750–1970* (Aldershot: Ashgate).

————(2003b), 'Business networking in the industrial revolution: some comments', *Economic History Review*, 54 (2), 355–61.

Wolf, C. (1988) *Markets or Governments: Choosing between Imperfect Alternatives* (Cambridge, Mass.: MIT Press).

Wolfe, A. J. (1915a), *Commercial Organisations in the United Kingdom*, US Department of Commerce, Bureau of Foreign and Domestic Commerce, Special Agent Series No. 102, (Washington: GPO).

————(1915b), *Commercial Organisations in France*, US Department of Commerce, Bureau of Foreign and Domestic Commerce, Special Agent Series No. 98 (Washington: GPO).

————(1919), *Theory and Practice of International Commerce* (New York: International Book Publishing).

Wolfe, D. A., and Gertler, M. S. (2004), 'Clusters from the inside and out: local dynamics and global linkage', *Urban Studies*, 41, 1071–93.

Wood, H. T. (1913), *A History of the Royal Society of Arts* (London: John Murray).

Wood, N. (1999), 'Debt, credit and business strategy: the law and the local economy, 1850–1900', unpublished PhD thesis, University of Leicester.

Wootton, G. (1970), *Interest-Groups* (Hemel Hempstead: Prentice Hall).

————(1975), *Pressure Groups in Britain 1720–1970: An Essay in Interpretation with Original Documents* (London: Allen Lane).

Wright, G. H. (1913), *Chronicles of the Birmingham Chamber of Commerce 1813–1913* (Birmingham: Chamber of Commerce).

Wrigley, E. A. (1987), *People, Cities and Wealth: The Transformation of Traditional Society* (Oxford: Basil Blackwell).

Yarmie, A. H. (1980), 'Employer organisations in mid-Victorian England', *International Review of Social History*, 25, 209–35.

Yeats, G. D. (1818), *A Biographical Sketch of the Life and Writings of Patrick Colquhoun, Esq.* (London: G. Smeeton) (Cambridge University Library VI.12.69).

York, N. L. (1998), 'The impact of the American Revolution on Ireland', pp. 205–32 in H. T. Dickinson (ed.), *Britain and the American Revolution* (London: Longman).

Young, A. E. (1995), 'The transforming hand of revolution', pp. 246–492 in R. Hoffman and P. J. Albert (eds.), *The Transforming Hand of Revolution: Reconsidering the American Revolution as a Social Movement* (Charlottesville, VA: US Capitol Historical Society, University of Virginia Press).

Young, D. (Lord) (1990), *The Enterprise Years: A Businessman in Government* (London: Headline).

Zald, M. N., and McCarthy, J. D. (1987), *Social Movements in an Organizational Society* (New Brunswick, NJ: Transaction Press).

Index

* Indicates that this chamber has further material in the UK Data Archive deposit

reading rooms *see* libraries, and accommodation
recession 812
reciprocal trade 382, 439
reciprocity 65, 374, 396–8
Reciprocity Duties Act (1823) 429
Reciprocity Free Trade Association 449
Recognition of chambers 251–90
'reconstruction' 318–27, 359–61
recruitment 595, 782–4
red tape 493–6
Redditch chamber* 832
Reeve, William 106, 120, 122
Reform Acts (1835–6) 75, 111, 193, 256, 425,
    428, 596–7
regalia 89
regeneration initiatives 624–7
regional chambers 343, 436, 651
regional development 436
    lobbying on 434
Regional Development Agencies 357, 436, 651
regional differences 189–90
Regional Economic Planning Councils 496, 601
Regional Growth Fund 655
regional identity 190–2
Regional and Small Firms Directorate (CBI) 41
regions 183–4
Register of Assignments (1850s) 31
regulatory issues 493–6
Regulatory Policy Committee 495
Reilly, Patrick 268
religious dissenters 683–5
Renfrewshire chamber 834
repertoires 69, 71–2
Reports
    Bennett Report (1991) 352, 353, 355
    Benson-Brown report (1963) 497, 498
    Bolton Report (1971) 41, 243, 362, 637, 709
    Booth-Luxton Report (1973) 348
    Commons Select Committee on Tribunals
        (1872) 287
    Danson Report (1860) 263–5
    Devlin Report (1972) 20, 41, 267, 268, 334,
        347, 362, 496–9, 818
    Dixon Report (1967) 341–5, 355, 810, 816
    Forster Report (1983) 268–9, 273–4, 348–9
    Luxton Report (1967) 341–5
    Millichap Report (1976) 267, 348–9
    Urwick Orr Report (1968) 267, 341–5
representation 3
Restart 622
Restrictive Practices Act (1956) 582
retail sector 230, 703–4, 705
retention of membership 728–39
    commitment 736–7
    detachment 737–9
    historical aspects 729–30
    involvement 734–5
    loyalty 735–6
    modern surveys 730–3

and service experience 739
    voice 733–4
Rhode Island chamber 701
Richardson, David 643, 646
Richardson, Thomas 399, 401–2
Richardson, William 285
Riddoch, Alexander 211
Ridley, Matthew White 445–6
Ridley, Nicholas 351, 352, 637, 639, 659
Rings for pricing 582
Rintoul, Alan 565
Ritchie, James 392
rivals, working with 818
river navigation routes 186
Roberts, Albert 398
Roberts, W. 465
Robertson, George 123
Robinson, Frederick 198, 429, 439
Robinson, Leslie 352, 727
Rochdale chamber* 15, 93, 190, 395–9, 570,
        634, 649, 667, 832
    debt collection 557
Roche, James 298, 299
Rockingham, Marquis of 102–3, 104, 109, 116,
        118–19, 128, 158, 159, 170, 399
Rogers, Hallewell 465, 478
Rolle, John 382
Rollitt, Albert 473
Rosebery, Lord 483
Rotherham chamber* 326, 360, 473, 634, 695,
        750, 752, 832, 848
    Conciliation Board 573
Royal Bank of Scotland 675
Royal Commission on the Depression of Trade
    and Industry (1886) 449–50, 576
Royal Commission on Labour (1892) 257,
    570–1
Royal Commission Technical Education
    (1881) 17, 576
Royal Exchange 239, 507
Royal Society 103–4
Rugby chamber* 332, 346, 750, 832
Rugeley chamber 332
Runciman, Lord 479
Runcorn chamber* 532, 628, 832
Rural Project Grants 628
Russell, Thomas 394
Russian Trade Treaty (1816) 388
Ryan, Thomas 513
Ryland, Arthur 309

safeguarding 38, 432, 463
Safeguarding of Industries Act (1921) 463–4
St Austell chamber 181
St Helens canal 186
St Helens chamber* 360, 533, 645, 810, 832
    debt collection 558
    drop-in facilities 538, 817
    TEC merger 634